Useful Websites

General business and finance information
www.dowjones.com
www.economist.com   *The Economist*
www.wsj.com   *The Wall Street Journal*
www.ft.com   *The Financial Times*
www.businessweek.com
www.euromoney.com
www.forbes.com
www.fortune.com

Sources of data on individual companies and industries
www.mhhe.com/edumarketinsight   Available to users of this text, a source of extensive financial statement data as well as stock price histories

www.bloomberg.com
http://finance.yahoo.com   Stock price and company information
http://money.cnn.com
www.hoovers.com
www.reportgallery.com   Annual reports
www.sec.gov   Annual reports and other financial statements from the EDGAR database

Macroeconomic data
www.bea.doc.gov   Bureau of Economic Analysis, Department of Commerce
www.federalreserve.gov   Board of Governors of the Federal Reserve System
www.fms.treas.gov   Links to publications of the Treasury Department
http://stats.bls.gov   Bureau of Labor Statistics

Sites with links to other resources
www.financewise.com
www.investorlinks.com
www.finpipe.com
www.corpfinet.com
www.ceoexpress.com
www.cob.ohio-state.edu/fin/journal/jofsites.htm (site maintained by Ohio State University College of Business)

With the purchase of a New Book*

You Can Access the Real Financial Data that the Experts Use!

*If you purchased a used book, see other side for access information.

This card entitles the purchaser of a new textbook to a semester of access to the Educational Version of Standard & Poor's Market Insight®, a rich online resource featuring hundreds of the most often researched companies in the Market Insight database.

For hundreds of companies, this website provides you:

- Access to six years' worth of fundamental financial data from the renowned Standard & Poor's COMPUSTAT® database
- 14 Excel Analytics Reports, including balance sheets, income statements, ratio reports and cash flow statements; adjusted prices reports, and profitability; forecasted values and monthly valuation data reports
- Access to Financial Highlights Reports including key ratios
- Business Descriptions discussing a company's business operations
- Company Profile
- Corporate Actions Report including acquisition activity and other recent corporate actions
- Industry Profile Report and Industry Constituents Listing
- News feeds (updated hourly) for companies and industries.

STANDARD &POOR'S
Setting the Standard

See other side for your unique site ID access code.

Welcome to the Educational Version of Market Insight!

www.mhhe.com/edumarketinsight

Check out your textbook's website for details on how this special offer enhances the value of your purchase!

1. To get started, use your web browser to go to **www.mhhe.com/edumarketinsight**

2. Enter your site ID exactly as it appears below.

3. You may be prompted to enter the site ID for future use— please keep this card.

*If you purchased a used book, this site ID may have expired. For new password purchase, please go to www.mhhe.com/edumarketinsight. Password activation is good for a 6 month duration.

Your site ID is:

ap187875

ISBN # 0072867280

STANDARD
&POOR'S
Setting the Standard

ESSENTIALS *of* INVESTMENTS

The McGraw-Hill/Irwin Series in Finance, Insurance, and Real Estate

Stephen A. Ross
Franco Modigliani Professor of Finance and Economics
Sloan School of Management
Massachusetts Institute of Technology
Consulting Editor

FINANCIAL MANAGEMENT

Benninga and Sarig
Corporate Finance: A Valuation Approach

Block and Hirt
Foundations of Financial Management
Tenth Edition

Brealey and Myers
Principles of Corporate Finance
Seventh Edition

Brealey, Myers, and Marcus
Fundamentals of Corporate Finance
Fourth Edition

Brooks
FinGame Online 4.0

Bruner
Case Studies in Finance: Managing for Corporate Value Creation
Fourth Edition

Chew
The New Corporate Finance: Where Theory Meets Practice
Fourth Edition

Crabb
Finance and Investments Using *The Wall Street Journal*

DeMello
Cases in Finance

Grinblatt and Titman
Financial Markets and Corporate Strategy
Second Edition

Helfert
Techniques of Financial Analysis: A Guide to Value Creation
Eleventh Edition

Higgins
Analysis for Financial Management
Seventh Edition

Kester, Fruhan, Piper, and Ruback
Case Problems in Finance
Eleventh Edition

Nunnally and Plath
Cases in Finance
Second Edition

Ross, Westerfield, and Jaffe
Corporate Finance
Sixth Edition

Ross, Westerfield, and Jordan
Essentials of Corporate Finance
Fourth Edition

Ross, Westerfield, and Jordan
Fundamentals of Corporate Finance
Sixth Edition

Smith
The Modern Theory of Corporate Finance
Second Edition

White
Financial Analysis with an Electronic Calculator
Fourth Edition

INVESTMENTS

Bodie, Kane, and Marcus
Essentials of Investments
Fifth Edition

Bodie, Kane, and Marcus
Investments
Fifth Edition

Cohen, Zinbarg, and Zeikel
Investment Analysis and Portfolio Management
Fifth Edition

Corrado and Jordan
Fundamentals of Investments: Valuation and Management
Second Edition

Crabb
Finance and Investments Using *The Wall Street Journal*

Farrell
Portfolio Management: Theory and Applications
Second Edition

Hirt and Block
Fundamentals of Investment Management
Seventh Edition

FINANCIAL INSTITUTIONS AND MARKETS

Cornett and Saunders
Fundamentals of Financial Institutions Management

Rose
Commercial Bank Management
Fifth Edition

Rose
Money and Capital Markets: Financial Institutions and Instruments in a Global Marketplace
Eighth Edition

Santomero and Babbel
Financial Markets, Instruments, and Institutions
Second Edition

Saunders and Cornett
Financial Institutions Management: A Modern Perspective
Fourth Edition

Saunders and Cornett
Financial Markets and Institutions: A Modern Perspective
Second Edition

INTERNATIONAL FINANCE

Beim and Calomiris
Emerging Financial Markets

Eun and Resnick
International Financial Management
Third Edition

Levich
International Financial Markets: Prices and Policies
Second Edition

REAL ESTATE

Brueggeman and Fisher
Real Estate Finance and Investments
Eleventh Edition

Corgel, Ling, and Smith
Real Estate Perspectives: An Introduction to Real Estate
Fourth Edition

**FINANCIAL PLANNING
AND INSURANCE**

Allen, Melone, Rosenbloom, and VanDerhei
**Pension Planning: Pension, Profit-
Sharing, and Other Deferred
Compensation Plans**
Eighth Edition

Crawford
Life and Health Insurance Law
Eighth Edition (LOMA)

Harrington and Niehaus
Risk Management and Insurance

Hirsch
Casualty Claim Practice
Sixth Edition

Kapoor, Dlabay, and Hughes
Personal Finance
Seventh Edition

Skipper
**International Risk and Insurance: An
Environmental-Managerial Approach**

Williams, Smith, and Young
Risk Management and Insurance
Eighth Edition

ESSENTIALS *of* INVESTMENTS

Fifth Edition

ZVI BODIE
Boston University

ALEX KANE
University of California, San Diego

ALAN J. MARCUS
Boston College

 Irwin

Boston   Burr Ridge, IL   Dubuque, IA   Madison, WI   New York
San Francisco   St. Louis   Bangkok   Bogotá   Caracas   Kuala Lumpur
Lisbon   London   Madrid   Mexico City   Milan   Montreal   New Delhi
Santiago   Seoul   Singapore   Sydney   Taipei   Toronto

The McGraw·Hill Companies

ESSENTIALS OF INVESTMENTS

Published by McGraw-Hill/Irwin, a business unit of The McGraw-Hill Companies, Inc., 1221 Avenue of the Americas, New York, NY, 10020. Copyright © 2004, 2001, 1998, 1995, 1992 by The McGraw-Hill Companies, Inc. All rights reserved. No part of this publication may be reproduced or distributed in any form or by any means, or stored in a database or retrieval system, without the prior written consent of The McGraw-Hill Companies, Inc., including, but not limited to, in any network or other electronic storage or transmission, or broadcast for distance learning. Some ancillaries, including electronic and print components, may not be available to customers outside the United States.

This book is printed on acid-free paper.

domestic   2 3 4 5 6 7 8 9 0 DOW/DOW 0 9 8 7 6 5 4 3
international   1 2 3 4 5 6 7 8 9 0 DOW/DOW 0 9 8 7 6 5 4 3

ISBN 0-07-251077-3

Publisher: *Stephen M. Patterson*
Senior developmental editor: *Sarah Ebel*
Executive marketing manager: *Rhonda Seelinger*
Senior producer, Media technology: *Melissa Kansa*
Senior project manager: *Jean Lou Hess*
Senior production supervisor: *Rose Hepburn*
Director of design BR: *Keith J. McPherson*
Supplement producer: *Joyce J. Chappetto*
Senior digital content specialist: *Brian Nacik*
Cover design: *Keith J. McPherson*
Interior design: *Kay Fulton*
Cover image: *Traneburg Bridge, © Photonica*
Typeface: *10/12 Times Roman*
Compositor: *GAC Indianapolis*
Printer: *R. R. Donnelley, Willard*

Library of Congress Cataloging-in-Publication Data

Bodie, Zvi.
    Essentials of investments / Zvi Bodie, Alex Kane, Alan J. Marcus. — 5th ed.
        p. cm. — (McGraw-Hill/Irwin series in finance, insurance, and real estate)
    Includes bibliographical references and indexes.
    ISBN 0-07-251077-3 (alk. paper)
    1. Investments.   I. Kane, Alex.   II. Marcus, Alan J.   III. Title. IV. Series
HG4521.B563   2004
    332.6—dc21   2002033771

www.mhhe.com

To our families with love and gratitude

Zvi Bodie

Boston University

Zvi Bodie is professor of finance at Boston University School of Management. He holds a PhD from the Massachusetts Institute of Technology and has served as visiting professor at Harvard University and MIT. He currently serves as a member of the Pension Research Council at the University of Pennsylvania. He has published widely on pension finance, the management of financial guarantees in both the private and public sector, and investment strategy in an inflationary environment. His edited volumes include *The Foundations of Pension Finance; Pensions and the Economy: Sources, Uses and Limitations of Data; Pensions in the U.S. Economy; Issues in Pension Economics;* and *Financial Aspects of the U.S. Pension System.* His research on pensions has focused on the funding and investment policies of private pension plans and on public policies such as the provision of government pension insurance. He has consulted on pension policy for the U.S. Department of Labor, the State of Israel, Bankers Trust Co., and J.P. Morgan.

Alex Kane

University of California, San Diego

Alex Kane is professor of finance and economics at the Graduate School of International Relations and Pacific Studies at the University of California, San Diego. He has been visiting professor at the Faculty of Economics, University of Tokyo; Graduate School of Business, Harvard; Kennedy School of Government, Harvard; and research associate, National Bureau of Economic Research. An author of many articles in finance and management journals, Professor Kane's research is mainly in corporate finance, portfolio management, and capital markets, most recently in the measurement of market volatility and pricing of options.

Alan J. Marcus

Boston College

Alan Marcus is professor of finance in the Wallace E. Carroll School of Management at Boston College. He received his PhD in economics from MIT. Professor Marcus has been a visiting professor at the Athens Laboratory of Business Administration and at MIT's Sloan School of Management and has served as a research associate at the National Bureau of Economic Research. Professor Marcus has published widely in the fields of capital markets and portfolio management, with an emphasis on applications of futures and options pricing models. His consulting work has ranged from new product development to provision of expert testimony in utility rate proceedings. He also spent two years at the Federal Home Loan Mortgage Corporation (Freddie Mac), where he developed models of mortgage pricing and credit risk. He currently serves on the Research Foundation Advisory Board of the Association for Investment Management and the Research (AIMR) and the Advisory Council for the Currency Risk Management Alliance of State Street Bank and Windham Capital Management, Boston.

Brief Contents

Part ONE
Elements of Investments 1

1 Investments: Background and Issues 2

2 Global Financial Instruments 24

3 How Securities Are Traded 58

4 Mutual Funds and Other Investment Companies 98

Part TWO
Portfolio Theory 129

5 Risk and Return: Past and Prologue 130

6 Efficient Diversification 168

7 Capital Asset Pricing and Arbitrage Pricing Theory 214

8 The Efficient Market Hypothesis 260

Part THREE
Debt Securities 293

9 Bond Prices and Yields 294

10 Managing Bond Portfolios 338

Part FOUR
Security Analysis 379

11 Macroeconomic and Industry Analysis 380

12 Equity Valuation 412

13 Financial Statement Analysis 450

Part FIVE
Derivative Markets 489

14 Options Markets 490

15 Option Valuation 530

16 Futures Markets 564

Part SIX
Active Investment Management 597

17 Investors and the Investment Process 598

18 Taxes, Inflation, and Investment Strategy 624

19 Behavioral Finance and Technical Analysis 650

20 Performance Evaluation and Active Portfolio Management 682

21 International Investing 720

Appendixes

A References 756

B References to CFA Questions 763

Index I-1

Contents

Part ONE
Elements of Investments   1

1   Investments: Background and Issues   2
1.1   Real Assets versus Financial Assets   4
1.2   A Taxonomy of Financial Assets   5
1.3   Financial Markets and the Economy   7
Consumption Timing   7
Allocation of Risk   7
Separation of Ownership and Management   7
1.4   The Investment Process   8
1.5   Markets Are Competitive   9
The Risk-Return Trade-Off   9
Efficient Markets   10
1.6   The Players   11
Financial Intermediaries   11
Investment Bankers   13
1.7   Markets and Market Structure   14
Direct Search Markets   14
Brokered Markets   14
Dealer Markets   14
Auction Markets   15
1.8   Recent Trends   15
Globalization   15
Securitization   16
Financial Engineering   18
Computer Networks   19
1.9   Outline of the Text   20
Summary   20

2   Global Financial Instruments   24
2.1   The Money Market   26
Treasury Bills   27
Certificates of Deposit   27
Commercial Paper   28
Bankers' Acceptances   28
Eurodollars   28
Repos and Reverses   29
Brokers' Calls   29
Federal Funds   29
The LIBOR Market   29
Yields on Money Market Instruments   30
2.2   The Bond Market   30
Treasury Notes and Bonds   31
Federal Agency Debt   32
International Bonds   33
Municipal Bonds   33
Corporate Bonds   35
Mortgages and Mortgage-Backed Securities   37
2.3   Equity Securities   39
Common Stock as Ownership Shares   39
Characteristics of Common Stock   40
Stock Market Listings   40
Preferred Stock   41
2.4   Stock and Bond Market Indexes   42
Stock Market Indexes   42
Dow Jones Averages   42
Standard & Poor's Indexes   45
Other U.S. Market Value Indexes   46

Equally Weighted Indexes 46

*Foreign and International Stock
Market Indexes* 46

Bond Market Indicators 47

2.5 Derivative Markets 47

Options 48

Futures Contracts 51

Summary 53

3 **How Securities Are Traded 58**

3.1 How Firms Issue Securities 60

Investment Banking 60

Shelf Registration 61

Private Placements 61

Initial Public Offerings 61

3.2 Where Securities Are Traded 65

The Secondary Markets 65

The Over-the-Counter Market 67

The Third and Fourth Markets 68

The National Market System 69

Bond Trading 70

3.3 Trading on Exchanges 71

The Participants 71

Types of Orders 72

*Specialists and the Execution
of Trades* 74

Block Sales 75

The SuperDot System 76

Settlement 76

3.4 Trading on the OTC Market 76

*Market Structure in Other
Countries* 77

Globalization of Stock Markets 79

3.5 Trading Costs 80

3.6 Buying on Margin 82

3.7 Short Sales 86

3.8 Regulation of Securities Markets 89

*Self-Regulation and Circuit
Breakers* 89

Insider Trading 91

Summary 92

4 **Mutual Funds and Other Investment
Companies 98**

4.1 Investment Companies 100

4.2 Types of Investment Companies 100

Unit Investment Trusts 101

Managed Investment Companies 101

Other Investment Organizations 103

4.3 Mutual Funds 104

Investment Policies 104

How Funds Are Sold 107

4.4 Costs of Investing in Mutual Funds 107

Fee Structure 107

Fees and Mutual Fund Returns 109

4.5 Taxation of Mutual Fund Income 111

4.6 Exchange-Traded Funds 112

4.7 Mutual Fund Investment Performance:
A First Look 114

4.8 Information on Mutual Funds 118

Summary 123

**Part TWO
Portfolio Theory 129**

5 **Risk and Return: Past and
Prologue 130**

5.1 Rates of Return 132

*Measuring Investment Returns over
Multiple Periods* 132

*Conventions for Quoting Rates of
Return* 134

5.2 Risk and Risk Premiums 135

*Scenario Analysis and Probability
Distributions* 135

*Risk Premiums and Risk
Aversion* 137

5.3 The Historical Record 139

*Bills, Bonds, and Stocks,
1926–2001* 139

5.4 Inflation and Real Rates of Return 146

*The Equilibrium Nominal Rate of
Interest* 147

5.5   Asset Allocation across Risky and Risk-Free Portfolios   148

     The Risky Asset   *149*

     The Risk-Free Asset   *150*

     Portfolio Expected Return and Risk   *151*

     The Capital Allocation Line   *152*

     Risk Tolerance and Asset Allocation   *154*

5.6   Passive Strategies and the Capital Market Line   155

     Historical Evidence on the Capital Market Line   *156*

     Costs and Benefits of Passive Investing   *158*

     Summary   158

6   **Efficient Diversification**   **168**

6.1   Diversification and Portfolio Risk   170

6.2   Asset Allocation with Two Risky Assets   171

     Covariance and Correlation   *171*

     Using Historical Data   *175*

     The Three Rules of Two-Risky-Assets Portfolios   *177*

     The Risk-Return Trade-Off with Two-Risky-Assets Portfolios   *177*

     The Mean-Variance Criterion   *178*

6.3   The Optimal Risky Portfolio with a Risk-Free Asset   184

6.4   Efficient Diversification with Many Risky Assets   187

     The Efficient Frontier of Risky Assets   *188*

     Choosing the Optimal Risk Portfolio   *191*

     The Preferred Complete Portfolio and the Separation Property   *192*

6.5   A Single-Factor Asset Market   192

     Specification of a Single-Index Model of Security Returns   *193*

     Statistical and Graphical Representation of the Single-Index Model   *194*

     Diversification in a Single-Factor Security Market   *199*

     Summary   199

Appendix: The Fallacy of Time Diversification   **211**

7   **Capital Asset Pricing and Arbitrage Pricing Theory**   **214**

7.1   Demand for Stocks and Equilibrium Prices   216

     Sigma's Demand for Shares   *216*

     Index Funds' Demands for Stock   *219*

     Equilibrium Prices and the Capital Asset Pricing Model   *220*

7.2   The Capital Asset Pricing Model   221

     Why All Investors Would Hold the Market Portfolio   *222*

     The Passive Strategy Is Efficient   *223*

     The Risk Premium of the Market Portfolio   *223*

     Expected Returns on Individual Securities   *224*

     The Security Market Line   *226*

     Applications of the CAPM   *227*

7.3   The CAPM and Index Models   228

     The Index Model, Realized Returns, and the Expected Return—Beta Relationship   *229*

     Estimating the Index Model   *230*

     The CAPM and the Index Model   *232*

     Predicting Betas   *238*

7.4   The CAPM and the Real World   239

7.5   Arbitrage Pricing Theory   241

     Arbitrage Opportunities and Profits   *242*

     Well-Diversified Portfolios and the Arbitrage Pricing Theory   *244*

     The APT and the CAPM   *247*

     Multifactor Generalization of the APT and CAPM   *247*

     Summary   250

8   **The Efficient Market Hypothesis**   **260**

8.1   Random Walks and the Efficient Market Hypothesis   262

     Competition as the Source of Efficiency   *263*

     Versions of the Efficient Market Hypothesis   *265*

8.2   Implications of the EMH   265

     Technical Analysis   *265*

Fundamental Analysis   266

Active versus Passive Portfolio Management   267

The Role of Portfolio Management in an Efficient Market   268

Resource Allocation   268

8.3   Are Markets Efficient?   269

The Issues   269

Weak-Form Tests: Predictability in Stock Returns   270

Predictors of Broad Market Movements   273

Semistrong-Form Tests: Market Anomalies   273

Strong-Form Tests: Inside Information   278

Interpreting the Evidence   278

Mutual Fund Performance   281

So, Are Markets Efficient?   285

Summary   287

Part THREE
Debt Securities   293

9   Bond Prices and Yields   294

9.1   Bond Characteristics   296

Treasury Bonds and Notes   296

Corporate Bonds   298

Preferred Stock   300

Other Domestic Issuers   301

International Bonds   301

Innovation in the Bond Market   301

9.2   Bond Pricing   303

9.3   Bond Yields   306

Yield to Maturity   306

Yield to Call   309

Realized Compound Yield versus Yield to Maturity   310

9.4   Bond Prices over Time   312

Yield to Maturity versus Holding-Period Return   313

Zero-Coupon Bonds   314

After-Tax Returns   315

9.5   Default Risk and Bond Pricing   316

Junk Bonds   317

Determinants of Bond Safety   318

Bond Indentures   318

Yield to Maturity and Default Risk   320

9.6   The Yield Curve   322

The Expectations Theory   323

The Liquidity Preference Theory   325

A Synthesis   327

Summary   328

10   Managing Bond Portfolios   338

10.1   Interest Rate Risk   340

Interest Rate Sensitivity   340

Duration   342

What Determines Duration?   346

10.2   Passive Bond Management   350

Immunization   350

Cash Flow Matching and Dedication   357

10.3   Convexity   358

Why Do Investors Like Convexity?   361

10.4   Active Bond Management   361

Sources of Potential Profit   361

Horizon Analysis   363

Contingent Immunization   364

An Example of a Fixed-Income Investment Strategy   364

10.5   Interest Rate Swaps   366

Summary   368

Part FOUR
Security Analysis   379

11   Macroeconomic and Industry Analysis   380

11.1   The Global Economy   382

11.2   The Domestic Macroeconomy   384

Gross Domestic Product   384

Employment   385

Inflation   385

Interest Rates   385

Budget Deficit   385

Sentiment   385

11.3 Interest Rates   386

11.4 Demand and Supply Shocks   387

11.5 Federal Government Policy   388

    Fiscal Policy   388

    Monetary Policy   389

    Supply-Side Policies   390

11.6 Business Cycles   391

    The Business Cycle   391

    Economic Indicators   393

11.7 Industry Analysis   396

    Defining an Industry   396

    Sensitivity to the Business Cycle   398

    Sector Rotation   400

    Industry Life Cycles   401

    Industry Structure and Performance   404

    Summary   405

12 Equity Valuation   412

12.1 Balance Sheet Valuation Methods   414

12.2 Intrinsic Value versus Market Price   415

12.3 Dividend Discount Methods   416

    The Constant Growth DDM   417

    Stock Prices and Investment Opportunities   420

    Life Cycles and Multistage Growth Models   423

    Multistage Growth Models   427

12.4 Price–Earnings Ratios   428

    The Price–Earnings Ratio and Growth Opportunities   428

    P/E Ratios and Stock Risk   432

    Pitfalls in P/E Analysis   434

    Combining P/E Analysis and the DDM   438

    Other Comparative Valuation Ratios   438

    Free Cash Flow Valuation Approaches   438

12.5 The Aggregate Stock Market   439

    Summary   441

13 Financial Statement Analysis   450

13.1 The Major Financial Statements   452

    The Income Statement   452

    The Balance Sheet   452

    The Statement of Cash Flows   454

13.2 Accounting versus Economic Earnings   456

13.3 Return on Equity   456

    Past versus Future ROE   456

    Financial Leverage and ROE   456

13.4 Ratio Analysis   458

    Decomposition of ROE   458

    Turnover and Other Asset Utilization Ratios   461

    Liquidity and Coverage Ratios   462

    Market Price Ratios   463

    Choosing a Benchmark   465

13.5 Economic Value Added   466

13.6 An Illustration of Financial Statement Analysis   468

13.7 Comparability Problems   470

    Inventory Valuation   470

    Depreciation   471

    Inflation and Interest Expense   471

    Quality of Earnings and Accounting Practices   472

    International Accounting Conventions   474

13.8 Value Investing: The Graham Technique   477

    Summary   478

Part FIVE
Derivative Markets   489

14 Options Markets   490

14.1 The Option Contract   492

    Options Trading   493

    American and European Options   495

    The Option Clearing Corporation   495

    Other Listed Options   496

14.2 Values of Options at Expiration   498

    Call Options   498

    Put Options   499

    Options versus Stock Investments   500

    Option Strategies   504

    Collars   511

14.3 Optionlike Securities 512
   Callable Bonds 512
   Convertible Securities 514
   Warrants 516
   Collateralized Loans 517
   Levered Equity and Risky Debt 517
14.4 Exotic Options 519
   Asian Options 519
   Barrier Options 519
   Lookback Options 519
   Currency-Translated Options 519
   Binary Options 520
   Summary 520

15 Option Valuation 530
15.1 Option Valuation: Introduction 532
   Intrinsic and Time Values 532
   Determinants of Option Values 533
15.2 Binomial Option Pricing 534
   Two-State Option Pricing 534
   Generalizing the Two-State Approach 537
15.3 Black-Scholes Option Valuation 540
   The Black-Scholes Formula 540
   The Put-Call Parity Relationship 546
   Put Option Valuation 549
15.4 Using the Black-Scholes Formula 550
   Hedge Ratios and the Black-Scholes Formula 550
   Portfolio Insurance 552
15.5 Empirical Evidence 556
   Summary 557

16 Futures Markets 564
16.1 The Futures Contract 566
   The Basics of Futures Contracts 567
   Existing Contracts 570
16.2 Mechanics of Trading in Futures Markets 571
   The Clearinghouse and Open Interest 571
   Marking to Market and the Margin Account 573

   Cash versus Actual Delivery 576
   Regulations 576
   Taxation 576
16.3 Futures Market Strategies 577
   Hedging and Speculation 577
   Basic Risk and Hedging 579
16.4 The Determination of Futures Prices 580
   Spot-Futures Parity 580
   Spreads 583
16.5 Financial Futures 584
   Stock Index Futures 584
   Creating Synthetic Stock Positions 585
   Index Arbitrage and the Triple-Witching Hour 587
   Foreign Exchange Futures 587
   Interest Rate Futures 589
   Summary 590

**Part SIX
Active Investment
Management 597**

17 Investors and the Investment Process 598
17.1 Investors and Objectives 600
   Individual Investors 601
   Professional Investors 602
   Life Insurance Companies 604
   Non-Life-Insurance Companies 605
   Banks 605
   Endowment Funds 606
17.2 Investor Constraints 606
   Liquidity 606
   Investment Horizon 607
   Regulations 607
   Tax Considerations 607
   Unique Needs 607
17.3 Objectives and Constraints of Various Investors 609
   Objectives 609
   Constraints 610

17.4 Investment Policies 611

    Top-Down Policies for Institutional Investors 612

    Active versus Passive Policies 614

17.5 Monitoring and Revising Investment Portfolios 615

    Summary 616

18 Taxes, Inflation, and Investment Strategy 624

18.1 Saving for the Long Run 626

    A Hypothetical Household 626

    The Retirement Annuity 626

18.2 Accounting for Inflation 628

    A Real Savings Plan 628

    An Alternate Savings Plan 629

18.3 Accounting for Taxes 630

18.4 The Economics of Tax Shelters 632

    A Benchmark Tax Shelter 632

    The Effect of the Progressive Nature of the Tax Code 632

18.5 A Menu of Tax Shelters 634

    Individual Retirement Accounts 634

    Roth IRA with the Progressive Tax Code 635

    401k and 403b Plans 637

    Risky Investments and Capital Gains as Tax Shelters 637

    Sheltered versus Unsheltered Savings 638

18.6 Social Security 639

    The Indexing Factor Series 640

    The Average Indexed Monthly Income 641

    The Primary Insurance Amount 641

18.7 Children's Education and Large Purchases 643

18.8 Home Ownership: The Rent-versus-Buy Decision 644

18.9 Uncertain Longevity and Other Contingencies 645

18.10 Matrimony, Bequest, and Intergenerational Transfers 646

    Summary 647

19 Behavioral Finance and Technical Analysis 650

19.1 What Is Behavioral Finance? 652

19.2 Individual Behavior 652

    Cooperation and Altruism 652

    Bidding and the Winner's Curse 653

    The Endowment Effect, the Status Quo Bias, and Loss Aversion 653

    Mental Accounts 654

19.3 Asset Returns and Behavioral Explanations 656

    Calendar Effects 656

    Cash Dividends 656

    Overreaction and Mean Reversion 656

19.4 Controversial Explanations from Behavioral Finance 657

    Publicly Traded (Closed-End) Funds 657

    Excessive Volatility of Stock Market Prices 658

19.5 Technical Analysis 659

19.6 Charting 660

    The Dow Theory 661

    Other Charting Techniques 663

    A Warning 665

19.7 Technical Indicators 667

    Sentiment Indicators 668

    Flow of Funds 669

    Market Structure 670

19.8 The Value Line System 674

19.9 Can Technical Analysis Work in Efficient Markets? 675

    Self-Destructing Patterns 675

    Summary 676

20 Performance Evaluation and Active Portfolio Management 682

20.1 Risk-Adjusted Returns 684

    Comparison Groups 684

    Risk Adjustments 685

    The M2 Measure of Performance 686

    Choosing the Right Measure of Risk 688

    Risk Adjustments with Changing Portfolio Composition 691

20.2   Performance Attribution Procedures   693
   Asset Allocation Decisions   697
   *Sector and Security Selection
   Decisions   697*
   *Summing Up Component
   Contributions   698*

20.3   The Lure of Active Management   699
   Objectives of Active Portfolios   701

20.4   Market Timing   702
   Valuing Market Timing as an Option   703
   The Value of Imperfect Forecasting   704
   *Measurement of Market Timing
   Performance   705*

20.5   Style Analysis   706

20.6   Morningstar's Risk-Adjusted Rating   708

20.7   Security Selection: the Treynor-
   Black Model   709
   *Overview of the Treynor-
   Black Model   709*
   Portfolio Construction   710
   Summary   712

21   International Investing   720

21.1   Global Markets for Equity   722
   Developed Countries   722
   Emerging Markets   722
   Market Capitalization and GDP   725
   Home-Country Bias   726

21.2   Risk Factors in International Investing   726
   Exchange Rate Risk   726
   Country-Specific Risk   731

21.3   International Investing: Risk, Return, and
   Benefits from Diversification   734
   Risk and Return: Summary Statistics   735
   *Are Investments in Emerging Markets
   Riskier?   735*
   *Are Average Returns in Emerging Markets
   Greater?   738*
   *Is Exchange Risk Important in
   International Portfolios?   738*
   *Benefits from International
   Diversification   738*
   *Misleading Representation of
   Diversification Benefits   739*
   *Realistic Benefits from International
   Diversification   742*
   *Are Benefits from International
   Diversification Preserved in Bear
   Markets?   743*

21.4   International Investing and Performance
   Attribution   745
   *Constructing a Benchmark Portfolio of
   Foreign Assets   745*
   Performance Attribution   746
   Summary   749

Appendixes

A   References   756

B   References to CFA Questions   763

Index   I-1

The last decade has been one of rapid, profound, and ongoing change in the investments industry. This is due in part to an abundance of newly designed securities, in part to the creation of new trading strategies that would have been impossible without concurrent advances in computer and communications technology, and in part to continuing advances in the theory of investments. Of necessity, our text has evolved along with the financial markets. In this edition, we address many of the changes in the investment environment.

At the same time, many basic *principles* remain important. We continue to organize our book around one basic theme—that *security markets are nearly efficient,* meaning that most securities are usually priced appropriately given their risk and return attributes. There are few free lunches found in markets as competitive as the financial market. This simple observation is, nevertheless, remarkably powerful in its implications for the design of investment strategies, and our discussions of strategy are always guided by the implications of the efficient markets hypothesis. While the degree of market efficiency is, and will always be, a matter of debate, we hope our discussions throughout the book convey a good dose of healthy criticism concerning much conventional wisdom.

This text also continues to emphasize *asset allocation* more than most other books. We prefer this emphasis for two important reasons. First, it corresponds to the procedure that most individuals actually follow when building an investment portfolio. Typically, you start with all of your money in a bank account, only then considering how much to invest in something riskier that might offer a higher expected return. The logical step at this point is to consider other risky asset classes, such as stock, bonds, or real estate. This is an asset allocation decision. Second, in most cases the asset allocation choice is far more important

than specific security-selection decisions in determining overall investment performance. Asset allocation is the primary determinant of the risk-return profile of the investment portfolio, and so it deserves primary attention in a study of investment policy.

Our book also focuses on investment analysis, which allows us to present the practical applications of investment theory, and to convey insights of practical value. In this edition of the text, we have continued to expand a systematic collection of Excel spreadsheets that give you tools to explore concepts more deeply than was previously possible. These spreadsheets are available through the World Wide Web, and provide a taste of the sophisticated analytic tools available to professional investors.

In our efforts to link theory to practice, we also have attempted to make our approach consistent with that of the Institute of Chartered Financial Analysts (ICFA). The ICFA administers an education and certification program to candidates for the title of Chartered Financial Analyst (CFA). The CFA curriculum represents the consensus of a committee of distinguished scholars and practitioners regarding the core of knowledge required by the investment professional.

This text will introduce you to the major issues currently of concern to all investors. It can give you the skills to conduct a sophisticated assessment of current issues and debates covered by both the popular media as well as more specialized finance journals. Whether you plan to become an investment professional, or simply a sophisticated individual investor, you will find these skills essential.

Zvi Bodie
Alex Kane
Alan J. Marcus

Organization of the Fifth Edition

Essentials of Investments, Fifth Edition, is intended as a textbook on investment analysis most applicable for the undergraduate student's first course in investments. The chapters are written in a modular format to give instructors the flexibility to either omit certain chapters or rearrange their order. The highlights in the margins describe updates for this edition.

This part lays out the general framework for the investment process in a nontechnical manner. We discuss the major players in the financial markets, and provide an overview of security types and trading mechanisms. The organization of these chapters makes it possible for instructors to assign term projects analyzing securities early in the course.

Thoroughly updated to reflect changes in financial markets such as electronic communication networks (ECNs), on-line and Internet trading, and Internet IPOs—the most current textbook available!

Includes excerpts from the "Code of Ethics and Standards of Professional Conduct" of the ICFA

Contains the core of modern portfolio theory. For courses emphasizing security analysis, this part may be skipped without loss of continuity.

All data is updated in this edition

This chapter introduces simple in-chapter spreadsheets that can be used to compute covariance matrixes, investment opportunity sets, and the index model. The spreadsheet material is modular; it can be integrated with class material, but also may be skipped without problem.

This chapter contains a unique section showing the links among the determination of optimal portfolios, security analysis, investors' buy/sell decisions, and equilibrium prices and expected rates of return.

Discusses the rationales of the EMH, as well as evidence for and against it.

First of three parts on security valuation

Contains spreadsheet material on duration and convexity

Part ONE
Elements of Investments   1
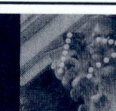

1 Investments: Background and Issues   2

2 Global Financial Instruments   24

3 How Securities Are Traded   58

4 Mutual Funds and Other Investment Companies   98

Part TWO
Portfolio Theory   129

5 Risk and Return: Past and Prologue   130

6 Efficient Diversification   168

7 Capital Asset Pricing and Arbitrage Pricing Theory   214

8 The Efficient Market Hypothesis   260

Part THREE
Debt Securities   293

9 Bond Prices and Yields   294

10 Managing Bond Portfolios   338

Part FOUR
Security Analysis 379

11 Macroeconomic and Industry Analysis 380

12 Equity Valuation 412

13 Financial Statement Analysis 450

Part FIVE
Derivative Markets 489

14 Options Markets 490

15 Option Valuation 530

16 Futures Markets 564

Part SIX
Active Investment Management 597

17 Investors and the Investment Process 598

18 Taxes, Inflation, and Investment Strategy 624

19 Behavioral Finance and Technical Analysis 650

20 Performance Evaluation and Active Portfolio Management 682

21 International Investing 720

Presented in a "top-down" manner, starting with the broad macroeconomic environment before moving to more specific analysis.

Current coverage of how international political developments have had major impacts on economic prospects.

Now contains free cash flow approach to valuation as well as a discussion of how corporate earnings management strategies can affect valuation measures.

Contains new section on quality of earnings and the veracity of financial reports. Also contains new section on economic value added.

These markets have become crucial and integral to the financial universe and are major sources of innovation.

Put-call parity discussion has been removed from this chapter and added to Chapter 15 because it is more naturally related to option pricing.

In-chapter spreadsheet material on the Black-Scholes model and estimation of implied volatility.

Material on active management has been unified in one part. Ideal for closing-semester unit on applying theory to actual portfolio management.

Modeled after the ICFA curriculum, this chapter also includes guidelines on "How to Become a Chartered Financial Analyst"

Extensive spreadsheet analysis of the interaction of taxes and inflation on long-term financial strategies.

Extensive new material on behavioral finance. This new material also provides a foundation for the study of technical analysis.

New evidence on international correlation and the benefit of diversification.

Pedagogical
Features

Chapter Objectives

Each chapter begins with a summary of the objectives of the chapter and describes the material to be covered, providing students with an overview of the concepts they should understand after reading the chapter.

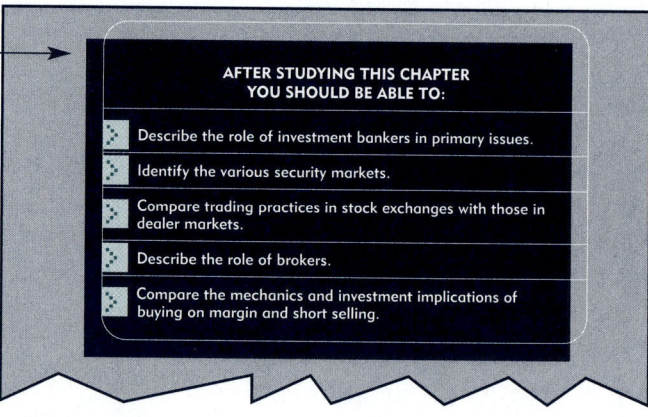

AFTER STUDYING THIS CHAPTER YOU SHOULD BE ABLE TO:

- Describe the role of investment bankers in primary issues.
- Identify the various security markets.
- Compare trading practices in stock exchanges with those in dealer markets.
- Describe the role of brokers.
- Compare the mechanics and investment implications of buying on margin and short selling.

Boxed Readings

Current articles from financial publications such as *The Wall Street Journal* are featured as boxed readings. Each box is discussed in the narrative of the text, and, therefore, its real-world relevance to the chapter material is clearly defined for the students.

Shorter, Clearer Mutual-Fund Disclosure May Omit Vital Investment Information

Mutual-fund investors will receive shorter and clearer disclosure documents, under new rules adopted by the Securities and Exchange Commission.

But despite all the hoopla surrounding the improvements—including a new "profile" prospectus and an easier-to-read full prospectus—there's still a slew of vital information fund investors don't get from any disclosure documents, long or short.

Of course, more information isn't necessarily better. As it is, investors rarely read fund disclosure docu-ments such as the prospectus [...] funds must

What's in the fund: If you're about to put your retirement nest egg in a fund, shouldn't you get to see what's in it first? The zippy new profile prospectus describes a fund's investment strategy, as did the old-style prospectus. But neither gives investors a look at what the fund actually owns. To get the fund's holdings, you have to have its latest semiannual or annual report. Most people don't get those documents until after they invest, and even then it can be as much as six months old. Many investment advisers think funds should begin reporting their holdings monthly [...] far funds [...]

Related Websites

Websites are now listed on the chapter opening page so students are able to easily reference the most current and relevant information on the Web.

Related Websites

http://www.nasdaq.com
www.nyse.com
http://www.amex.com
These sites contain information and listing requirements for each of the markets. They also provide substantial data on equities.

http://www.spglobal.com
This site contains information on construction of Standard & Poor's Indexes and has links to most major exchanges.

http://www.ipo.com
http://www.unlockdates.com
http://www.123jump.com/ipomaven.htm
http://moneycentral.msn.com/investor/market/ipomain.asp
These sites contain information on initial public offerings.

http://www.sec.gov/index.htm
http://www.nasdr.com
These sites provide information on market regulation and trading.

Key Terms in Margin

Key terms are indicated in color and defined in the margin the first time the term is used.

When firms need to raise capital they may choose to sell or *float* securities. These new i[ssues] of stocks, bonds, or other securities typically are marketed to the public by investment ba[nkers] in what is called the **primary market.** Trading of already-issued securities among inve[stors] occurs in the **secondary market.**

There are two types of primary market issues of common stock. **Initial public offer[ings,]** or **IPOs,** are stocks issued by a formerly privately owned company that is going public [that] is, selling stock to the public for the first time. *Seasoned* new issues are offered by comp[anies] that already ha[ve] [...] IBM [...]

primary market
Market for new issues of securities.

secondary market

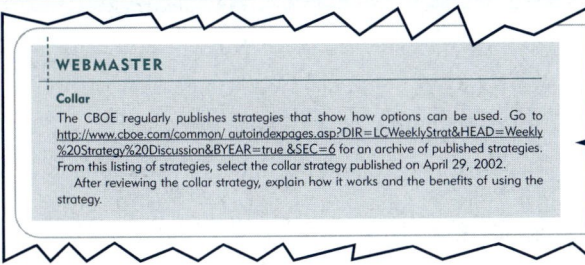

WEBMASTER

Collar

The CBOE regularly publishes strategies that show how options can be used. Go to http://www.cboe.com/common/ autoindexpages.asp?DIR=LCWeeklyStrat&HEAD=Weekly %20Strategy%20Discussion&BYEAR=true &SEC=6 for an archive of published strategies. From this listing of strategies, select the collar strategy published on April 29, 2002.

After reviewing the collar strategy, explain how it works and the benefits of using the strategy.

WebMaster Exercises

New to this edition, WebMaster exercises are found in each chapter allowing students to test their skills on the Internet. Each exercise provides the student with an activity related to practical problems and real-world scenarios.

Concept Checks

These self-test questions and problems in the body of the chapter enable the student to determine whether he or she has understood the preceding material and to reinforce that understanding before reading further. Detailed solutions to these questions are found at the end of each chapter.

2. A share of stock of A-Star Inc. is now selling for $23.50. A financial analyst summarizes the uncertainty about the rate of return on the stock by specifying three possible scenarios:

Concept CHECK

Business Conditions	Scenario, s	Probability, p	End-of-Year Price	Annual Dividend
High growth	1	0.35	$35	$4.40
Normal growth	2	0.30	27	4.00
No growth	3	0.35	15	4.00

What are the holding-period returns for a one-year investment in the stock of A-Star Inc. for each of the three scenarios? Calculate the expected HPR and standard deviation of the HPR.

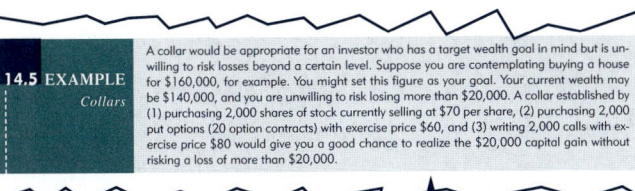

14.5 EXAMPLE

Collars

A collar would be appropriate for an investor who has a target wealth goal in mind but is unwilling to risk losses beyond a certain level. Suppose you are contemplating buying a house for $160,000, for example. You might set this figure as your goal. Your current wealth may be $140,000, and you are unwilling to risk losing more than $20,000. A collar established by (1) purchasing 2,000 shares of stock currently selling at $70 per share, (2) purchasing 2,000 put options (20 option contracts) with exercise price $60, and (3) writing 2,000 calls with exercise price $80 would give you a good chance to realize the $20,000 capital gain without risking a loss of more than $20,000.

Numbered Examples

Separate numbered and titled examples are integrated in the chapters and indicated by a colored sidebar. Using the worked-out solutions to these examples as models, students can learn how to solve specific problems in a step-by-step manner as well as gain insight into general principles by seeing how they are applied to answer concrete questions.

Numbered Equations

Key equations are called out in the text and identified by equation numbers. Equations that are frequently used are also featured on the text's back end sheets for convenient reference.

$$\text{Var}(r) \equiv \sigma^2 = \sum_{s=1}^{S} p(s)[r(s) - E(r)]^2 \qquad (5.4)$$

We square the deviations because if we did not, negative deviations would offset positive deviations, with the result that the expected deviation from the mean return would necessarily be

Pedagogical
Features (cont.)

Excel Applications

Since many courses now require students to perform analyses in spreadsheet format, Excel has been integrated throughout the book once again. It is used in examples as well as in this chapter feature which shows students how to create and manipulate spreadsheets to solve specific problems. This feature starts with an example presented in the chapter, briefly discusses how a spreadsheet can be valuable for investigating the topic, shows a sample spreadsheet, and then directs the student to the Web to work with an interactive version of the spreadsheet. The student can obtain the actual spreadsheet from the book's website (www.mhhe.com/bkm). At this site, there is a more detailed discussion on how the spreadsheet is built, and how it can be used to solve problems. As extra guidance, the spreadsheets include a comment feature that documents both inputs and outputs. Solutions for these exercises are located on the password-protected instructor site only, so instructors can assign these exercises either for homework or just for practice.

Spreadsheets available:

Chapter 3: Buying on Margin, Short Sales

Chapter 6: Two Security Portfolio, Efficient Frontier for Many Stocks

Chapter 7: Betas

Chapter 10: Duration, Holding Period Immunization

Chapter 12: Two- and Three-Stage Growth Models

Chapter 14: Spreads and Straddles, Options, Stocks, and Lending

Chapter 15: Black-Scholes Pricing Model

Chapter 20: Performance Attribution, Performance Measures

Chapter 21: International Diversification

End-of-Chapter

Features

SUMMARY

- The expected rate of return of a portfolio is the weighted average of the component asset expected returns with the investment proportions as weights.
- The variance of a portfolio is a sum of the contributions of the component-security variances *plus* terms involving the correlation among assets.
- Even if correlations are positive, the portfolio standard deviation will be less than the weighted average of the component standard deviations, as long as the assets are not *perfectly* positively correlated. Thus, portfolio diversification is of value as long as assets are less than perfectly correlated.

www.mhhe.com/bkm

Summary

This bulleted feature helps the student review key points and provides closure to the chapter.

Key Terms

The list of key terms includes page references, facilitating student review of the chapter's key concepts.

KEY TERMS

bankers' acceptance, 28
call option, 48
capital markets, 26
certificate of deposit, 27
commercial paper, 28
common stocks, 39
corporate bonds, 35
derivative asset/contingent

equally weighted index, 46
Eurodollars, 28
Federal funds, 29
futures contract, 51
LIBOR, 29
market value-weighted index, 45
money markets, 26

preferred stock, 41
price-weighted average, 42
put option, 49
repurchase agreements, 29
Treasury bills, 27
Treasury bonds, 31
Treasury notes, 31

PROBLEM SETS

1. A portfolio of nondividend-paying stocks earned a geometric mean return of 5.0% between January 1, 1996, and December 31, 2002. The arithmetic mean return for the same period was 6.0 %. If the market value of the portfolio at the beginning of 1996 was $100,000, what was the market value of the portfolio at the end of 2002?
2. Which of the following statements about the standard deviation is/are **true**? A standard deviation:
   i. Is the square root of the variance.
   ii. Is denominated in the same units as the original data.
   iii. Can be a positive or a negative number.
3. Which of the following statements reflects the importance of the asset allocation decision to the investment process? The asset allocation decision:

CFA
CFA

Problem Sets

The end-of-chapter problems progress from the simple to the complex. We strongly believe that practice in solving problems is a critical part of learning investments, so we provide a good variety of problems. Many of the problems are new or revised from the previous edition.

CFA Questions

We provide several questions from recent CFA exams in applicable chapters. These questions represent the kinds of questions that professionals in the field believe are relevant to the practicing money manager. These problems are identified by an icon in the text margin. Appendix B lists each CFA question and the level and year of the CFA Exam it was included in, for easy reference when studying for the exam.

S&P Problems

Relevant chapters contain several new problems directly related to Standard & Poor's Educational Version of Market Insight. Because of our unique relationship with S&P, students have free access to this remarkable database. Problems are based on market data provided by real companies to gain better understanding of practical business situations. The site is updated daily to ensure the most current information is available.

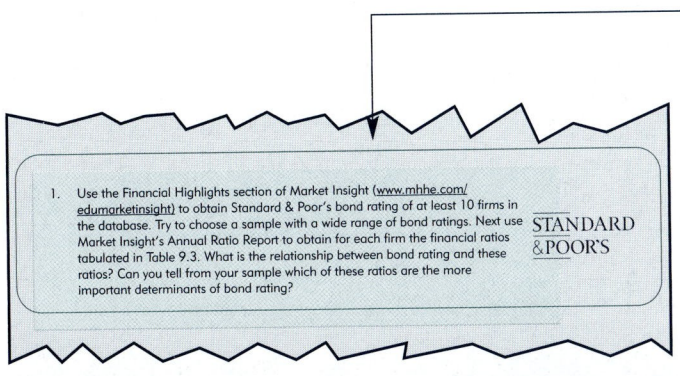

1. Use the Financial Highlights section of Market Insight (www.mhhe.com/edumarketinsight) to obtain Standard & Poor's bond rating of at least 10 firms in the database. Try to choose a sample with a wide range of bond ratings. Next use Market Insight's Annual Ratio Report to obtain for each firm the financial ratios tabulated in Table 9.3. What is the relationship between bond rating and these ratios? Can you tell from your sample which of these ratios are the more important determinants of bond rating?

STANDARD &POOR'S

For the Instructor

INSTRUCTOR'S RESOURCE CD   0-07-285533-9

This comprehensive CD contains all of the following instructor supplements. We put them in one place for easier access and convenience. Print copies are available through your publisher's representative.

Instructor's Resource Manual

Prepared by Richard D. Johnson, Colorado State University, this instructional tool provides an integrated learning approach revised for this edition. Each chapter includes a Chapter Overview, Learning Objectives, and Presentation of Chapter Material, which outlines the material and organizes it around the Transparency Masters/PowerPoint Presentation Software. Transparency Masters are located at the end of each chapter.

PowerPoint Presentation Software

These presentation slides, also developed by Richard D. Johnson, provide the instructor with an electronic format of the Transparency Masters. These slides, revised for this edition, follow the order of the chapters, but if you have PowerPoint software, you may customize the program to fit your lecture presentation.

Test Bank

Prepared by Douglas Kahl, University of Akron, the Test Bank has again been expanded to more than 1,200 questions. Each question is ranked by level of difficulty (easy, medium, hard), which allows greater flexibility in creating a test. The Test Bank is also available in a computerized format for Windows.

THE WALL STREET JOURNAL EDITION   0-07-422390-9

Your students can subscribe to *The Wall Street Journal* for 15 weeks at a specially priced rate of $20.00 in addition to the price of the text. Students will receive a "How to Use the WSJ" handbook plus a pass code card shrink-wrapped with the text. This special offer also gives students access to Dow Jones Interactive online for the span of the 15-week period.

VIDEOS   0-07-287272-1

There are seven video segments covering careers, financial markets, bonds, going public, derivatives, portfolio management, and foreign exchange.

For the Student

SOLUTIONS MANUAL   0-07-283739-X

The Solutions Manual, prepared by Bruce Swensen, Adelphi University, provides detailed solutions to the end-of-chapter problems. The authors' involvement in the Solutions Manual ensures consistency between the solution approaches in the examples in the text and those presented in the manual.

READY NOTES   0-07-283742-X

This note-taking supplement contains a reduced copy of every image from the Transparency Masters/PowerPoint Presentation Software package. There is room to take notes next to each image, allowing students a more complete and organized method for recording lecture notes.

STUDENT PROBLEM MANUAL   0-07-28374-89

New to this edition! To give students a better resource for working through problems, we have created a comprehensive problem manual. This useful supplement contains problems created to specifically relate to the concepts discussed in each chapter. Solutions are provided at the end of each chapter in the manual.

Online Support

BKM *ESSENTIALS* WEBSITE

Find a wealth of information online! At www.mhhe.com/bkm, instructors will have access to teaching support such as electronic files for the ancillary material and students will have access to study materials created specifically for this text. The Excel Applications spreadsheets are located at this site. Also available is additional information on the text and authors; links to our powerful support materials described below.

POWERWEB

With PowerWeb, getting information has never been easier. This McGraw-Hill website is a reservoir of course-specific articles and current events. Simply type in a discipline-specific topic for instant access to articles, essays, and news for your class.

All the articles have been recommended to PowerWeb by professors, which means you won't get all the clutter that seems to pop up with typical search engines. However, PowerWeb is much more than a search engine. Students can visit PowerWeb to take a self-grading quiz, work through interactive exercises, click through an interactive glossary, and even check the daily news. In fact, an expert for each discipline analyzes the day's news to show students how it is relevant to their field of study.

INVESTMENTS ONLINE

Introducing Investments Online! For each of 18 different topics, the student completes challenging exercises and discussion questions that draw on recent articles, company reports, government data, and other Web-based resources. The "Finance Tutor Series" provides questions and problems that not only assess and improve students' understanding of the subject but also help students to apply it in real-world contexts.

STANDARD & POOR'S EDUCATIONAL VERSION OF MARKET INSIGHT

McGraw-Hill/Irwin and the Institutional Market Services division of Standard & Poor's is pleased to announce an exclusive partnership that offers instructors and students access to the educational version of Standard & Poor's Market Insight. The Educational Version of Market Insight is a rich online resource that provides six years of fundamental financial data for over 370 companies in the renowned COMPUSTAT® database. S&P and McGraw-Hill/Irwin have selected the best, most-often researched companies in the database. S&P-specific problems can be found at the end of relevant chapters in this text.

Acknowledgments

We received help from many people as we prepared this book. An insightful group of reviewers commented on this and previous editions of this text. Their comments and suggestions improved the exposition of the material considerably. These reviewers all deserve special thanks for their contributions.

Bala Arshanapalli
Indiana University Northwest

Randall S. Billingsley
Virginia Polytechnic Institute and State University

Howard Bohnen
St. Cloud State University

Paul Bolster
Northeastern University

Lyle Bowlin
University of Northern Iowa

Alyce R. Campbell
University of Oregon

Greg Chaudoin
Loyola University

Ji Chen
University of Colorado, Denver

Mustafa Chowdhury
Louisiana State University

Shane Corwin
University of Notre Dame

Diane Del Guercio
University of Oregon

David C. Distad
University of California at Berkeley

Gary R. Dokes
University of San Diego

Peter D. Ekman
Kansas State University

James F. Feller
Middle Tennessee State University

Ken Froewiss
New York University

Deborah Gunthorpe
University of Tennessee

Weiyu Guo
University of Nebraska, Omaha

Pamela Hall
Western Washington University

Thomas Hamilton
St. Mary's University

Gay Hatfield
University of Mississippi

Larry C. Holland
Oklahoma State University

Ron E. Hutchins
Eastern Michigan University

Richard Johnson
Colorado State University

Douglas Kahl
University of Akron

Donald Kummer
University of Missouri, St. Louis

Angeline Lavin
University of South Dakota

John Loughlin
St. Louis University

David Louton
Bryant College

David Loy
Illinois State University

Laurian Casson Lytle
University of Wisconsin, Whitewater

Leo Mahoney
Bryant College

Herman Manakyan
Salisbury State University

Steven V. Mann
University of South Carolina

Jeffrey A. Manzi
Ohio University

James Marchand
Westminster College

Robert J. Martel
Bentley College

Linda J. Martin
Arizona State University

Edward Miller
University of New Orleans

Walter Morales
Louisiana State University

Majed Muhtaseb
California State Polytechnic University

Deborah Murphy
University of Tennessee, Knoxville

Mike Murray
Winona State University

C. R. Narayanaswamy
Georgia Institute of Technology

Raj Padmaraj
Bowling Green University

John C. Park
Frostburg State University

Percy Poon
University of Nevada, Las Vegas

Rose Prasad
Central Michigan University

Elias A. Raad
Ithaca College

Murli Rajan
University of Scranton

Cecilia Ricci
Montclair University

Craig Ruff
Georgia State University

David Schirm
John Carroll University

Ravi Shukla
Syracuse University

Edwin Stuart
Southeastern Oklahoma State University

George S. Swales
Southwest Missouri State University

Paul Swanson
University of Cincinnati

Bruce Swensen
Adelphi University

Glenn Tanner
University of Hawaii

Donald J. Thompson
Georgia State University

Steven Thorley
Brigham Young University

Steven Todd
DePaul University

Joseph Vu
DePaul University

Jessica Wachter
New York University

Joe Walker
University of Alabama at Birmingham

William Welch
Florida International University

Andrew L. Whitaker
North Central College

Howard Whitney
Franklin University

Michael E. Williams
University of Texas at Austin

Tony Wingler
University of North Carolina

Annie Wong
Western Connecticut State University

Richard H. Yanow
North Adams State College

Thomas J. Zwirlein
University of Colorado, Colorado Springs

Zhong-guo Zhou
California State University, Northridge

For granting us permission to include many of their examination questions in the text, we are grateful to the Institute of Chartered Financial Analysts.

Much credit is also due to the development and production team: Steve Patterson, Publisher; Sarah Ebel, Senior Development Editor; Jean Lou Hess, Senior Project Manager; and Keith McPherson, Director of Design.

Finally, once again, our most important debts are to Judy, Hava, and Sheryl for their unflagging support.

Zvi Bodie
Alex Kane
Alan J. Marcus

PART ONE

ELEMENTS OF INVESTMENTS

Even a cursory glance at *The Wall Street Journal* reveals a bewildering collection of securities, markets, and financial institutions. Although it may appear so, the financial environment is not chaotic: There is a rhyme or reason behind the vast array of financial instruments and the markets in which they trade.

These introductory chapters provide a bird's-eye view of the investing environment. We will give you a tour of the major types of markets in which securities trade, the trading process, and the major players in these arenas. You will see that both markets and securities have evolved to meet the changing and complex needs of different participants in the financial system.

Markets innovate and compete with each other for traders' business just as vigorously as competitors in other industries. The competi-

tion between the National Association of Securities Dealers Automatic Quotation System (Nasdaq), the New York Stock Exchange (NYSE), and a number of non-U.S. exchanges is fierce and public.

Trading practices can mean big money to investors. The explosive growth of online trading has saved them many millions of dollars in trading costs. Even more dramatically, new electronic communication networks will allow investors to trade directly without a broker. These advances promise to change the face of the investments industry, and Wall Street firms are scrambling to formulate strategies that respond to these changes.

These chapters will give you a good foundation with which to understand the basic types of securities and financial markets as well as how trading in those markets is conducted.

1	Investments: Background and Issues
2	Global Financial Instruments
3	How Securities Are Traded
4	Mutual Funds and Other Investment Companies

www.mhhe.com/bkm

McGraw-Hill / Irwin presents
Investments online

INVESTMENTS: BACKGROUND AND ISSUES

> **AFTER STUDYING THIS CHAPTER YOU SHOULD BE ABLE TO:**
>
> > Define an investment.
>
> > Distinguish between real assets and financial assets.
>
> > Describe the major steps in the construction of an investment portfolio.
>
> > Identify major participants in financial markets.
>
> > Identify types of financial markets and recent trends in those markets.

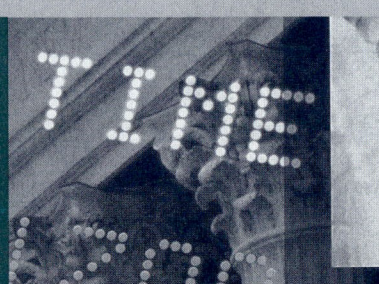

Related Websites

http://www.ceoexpress.com

This site provides a list of links related to all aspects of business, including extensive sites related to finance and investment.

http://www.corpgov.net

Dedicated to corporate governance issues, this site has extensive coverage and numerous links to other sites related to corporate governance.

http://www.finpipe.com

This is an excellent general site that is dedicated to finance education. It contains information on debt securities, equities, and derivative instruments.

http://www.financewise.com

This is a thorough finance search engine for other financial sites.

http://www.federalreserve.gov/otherfrb.htm

This site contains a map that allows you to access all of the Federal Reserve Bank sites. Most of the economic research from the various banks is available online. The Federal Reserve Economic Database, or FRED, is available through the St. Louis Federal Reserve Bank. A search engine for all of the Bank's research articles is available at the San Francisco Federal Reserve Bank.

http://www.cob.ohio-state.edu/fin/journal/jofsites.htm

This site contains a directory of finance journals and associations related to education in the financial area.

http://finance.yahoo.com

This investment site contains information on financial markets. Portfolios can be constructed and monitored at no charge. Limited historical return data is available for actively traded securities.

http://moneycentral.msn.com/home.asp

Similar to Yahoo! Finance, this investment site contains comprehensive information on financial markets.

An **investment** is the *current* commitment of money or other resources in the expectation of reaping *future* benefits. For example, an individual might purchase shares of stock anticipating that the future proceeds from the shares will justify both the time that her money is tied up as well as the risk of the investment. The time you will spend studying this text (not to mention its cost) also is an investment. You are forgoing either current leisure or the income you could be earning at a job in the expectation that your future career will be sufficiently enhanced to justify this commitment of time and effort. While these two investments differ in many ways, they share one key attribute that is central to all investments: You sacrifice something of value now, expecting to benefit from that sacrifice later.

This text can help you become an informed practitioner of investments. We will focus on investments in securities such as stocks, bonds, or options and futures contracts, but much of what we discuss will be useful in the analysis of any type of investment. The text will provide you with background in the organization of various securities markets, will survey the valuation and risk-management principles useful in particular markets, such as those for bonds or stocks, and will introduce you to the principles of portfolio construction.

Broadly speaking, this chapter addresses three topics that will provide a useful perspective for the material that is to come later. First, before delving into the topic of "investments," we consider the role of financial assets in the economy. We discuss the relationship between securities and the "real" assets that actually produce goods and services for consumers, and we consider why financial assets are important to the functioning of a developed economy. Given this background, we then take a first look at the types of decisions that confront investors as they assemble a portfolio of

investment

Commitment of current resources in the expectation of deriving greater resources in the future.

assets. These investment decisions are made in an environment where higher returns usually can be obtained only at the price of greater risk, and in which it is rare to find assets that are so mispriced as to be obvious bargains. These themes—the risk-return trade-off and the efficient pricing of financial assets—are central to the investment process, so it is worth pausing for a brief discussion of their implications as we begin the text. These implications will be fleshed out in much greater detail in later chapters.

Finally, we conclude the chapter with an introduction to the organization of security markets, the various players that participate in those markets, and a brief overview of some of the more important changes in those markets in recent years. Together, these various topics should give you a feel for who the major participants are in the securities markets as well as the setting in which they act. We close the chapter with an overview of the remainder of the text.

1.1 REAL ASSETS VERSUS FINANCIAL ASSETS

real assets

Assets used to produce goods and services.

financial assets

Claims on real assets or the income generated by them.

The material wealth of a society is ultimately determined by the productive capacity of its economy, that is, the goods and services its members can create. This capacity is a function of the **real assets** of the economy: the land, buildings, machines, and knowledge that can be used to produce goods and services.

In contrast to such real assets are **financial assets,** such as stocks and bonds. Such securities are no more than sheets of paper or, more likely, computer entries and do not contribute directly to the productive capacity of the economy. Instead, these assets are the means by which individuals in well-developed economies hold their claims on real assets. Financial assets are claims to the income generated by real assets (or claims on income from the government). If we cannot own our own auto plant (a real asset), we can still buy shares in General Motors or Toyota (financial assets) and, thereby, share in the income derived from the production of automobiles.

While real assets generate net income to the economy, financial assets simply define the allocation of income or wealth among investors. Individuals can choose between consuming their wealth today or investing for the future. If they choose to invest, they may place their wealth in financial assets by purchasing various securities. When investors buy these securities from companies, the firms use the money so raised to pay for real assets, such as plant, equipment, technology, or inventory. So investors' returns on securities ultimately come from the income produced by the real assets that were financed by the issuance of those securities.

The distinction between real and financial assets is apparent when we compare the balance sheet of U.S. households, shown in Table 1.1, with the composition of national wealth in the United States, shown in Table 1.2. Household wealth includes financial assets such as bank accounts, corporate stock, or bonds. However, these securities, which are financial assets of households, are *liabilities* of the issuers of the securities. For example, a bond that you treat as an asset because it gives you a claim on interest income and repayment of principal from General Motors is a liability of General Motors, which is obligated to make these payments to you. Your asset is GM's liability. Therefore, when we aggregate over all balance sheets, these claims cancel out, leaving only real assets as the net wealth of the economy. National wealth consists of structures, equipment, inventories of goods, and land.

We will focus almost exclusively on financial assets. But you shouldn't lose sight of the fact that the successes or failures of the financial assets we choose to purchase ultimately depend on the performance of the underlying real assets.

TABLE 1.1
Balance sheet of U.S. households

Assets	$ Billion	% Total	Liabilities and Net Worth	$ Billion	% Total
Real assets					
Real estate	$12,567	26.7%	Mortgages	$ 5,210	11.1%
Durables	2,820	6.0	Consumer credit	1,558	3.3
Other	117	0.2	Bank & other loans	316	0.7
			Other	498	1.1
Total real assets	$15,504	32.9%			
			Total liabilities	$ 7,582	16.1%
Financial assets					
Deposits	$ 4,698	10.0%			
Live insurance reserves	817	1.7			
Pension reserves	8,590	18.2			
Corporate equity	5,917	12.6			
Equity in noncorp. business	5,056	10.7			
Mutual funds shares	2,780	5.9			
Personal trusts	949	2.0			
Debt securities	2,075	4.4			
Other	746	1.6			
Total financial assets	31,628	67.1	Net worth	39,550	83.9
Total	$47,132	100.0%		$47,132	100.0%

Note: Column sums may differ from total because of rounding error.

Source: *Flow of Funds Accounts of the United States,* Board of Governors of the Federal Reserve System, June 2001.

TABLE 1.2
Domestic net worth

Assets	$ Billion
Real estate	$17,438
Plant and equipment	18,643
Inventories	1,350
Total	$37,431

Note: Column sums may differ from total because of rounding error.

Sources: *Flow of Funds Accounts of the United States,* Board of Governors of the Federal Reserve System, June 2001; *Statistical Abstract of the United States: 2000,* US Census Bureau.

1. Are the following assets real or financial?
   a. Patents
   b. Lease obligations
   c. Customer goodwill
   d. A college education
   e. A $5 bill

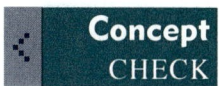

Concept CHECK

1.2 A TAXONOMY OF FINANCIAL ASSETS

It is common to distinguish among three broad types of financial assets: fixed income, equity, and derivatives. **Fixed-income securities** promise either a fixed stream of income or a stream

fixed-income securities

Pay a specified cash flow over a specific period.

of income that is determined according to a specified formula. For example, a corporate bond typically would promise that the bondholder will receive a fixed amount of interest each year. Other so-called floating-rate bonds promise payments that depend on current interest rates. For example, a bond may pay an interest rate that is fixed at two percentage points above the rate paid on U.S. Treasury bills. Unless the borrower is declared bankrupt, the payments on these securities are either fixed or determined by formula. For this reason, the investment performance of fixed-income securities typically is least closely tied to the financial condition of the issuer.

Nevertheless, fixed-income securities come in a tremendous variety of maturities and payment provisions. At one extreme, the *money market* refers to fixed-income securities that are short term, highly marketable, and generally of very low risk. Examples of money market securities are U.S. Treasury bills or bank certificates of deposit (CDs). In contrast, the fixed-income *capital market* includes long-term securities such as Treasury bonds, as well as bonds issued by federal agencies, state and local municipalities, and corporations. These bonds range from very safe in terms of default risk (for example, Treasury securities) to relatively risky (for example, high yield or "junk" bonds). They also are designed with extremely diverse provisions regarding payments provided to the investor and protection against the bankruptcy of the issuer. We will take a first look at these securities in Chapter 2 and undertake a more detailed analysis of the fixed-income market in Part Three.

equity

An ownership share in a corporation.

Unlike fixed-income securities, common stock, or **equity,** in a firm represents an ownership share in the corporation. Equity holders are not promised any particular payment. They receive any dividends the firm may pay and have prorated ownership in the real assets of the firm. If the firm is successful, the value of equity will increase; if not, it will decrease. The performance of equity investments, therefore, is tied directly to the success of the firm and its real assets. For this reason, equity investments tend to be riskier than investments in fixed-income securities. Equity markets and equity valuation are the topics of Part Four.

derivative securities

Securities providing payoffs that depend on the values of other assets.

Finally, **derivative securities** such as options and futures contracts provide payoffs that are determined by the prices of *other* assets such as bond or stock prices. For example, a call option on a share of Intel stock might turn out to be worthless if Intel's share price remains below a threshold or "exercise" price such as $30 a share, but it can be quite valuable if the stock price rises above that level.[1] Derivative securities are so named because their values derive from the prices of other assets. For example, the value of the call option will depend on the price of Intel stock. Other important derivative securities are futures and swap contracts. We will treat these in Part Five.

Derivatives have become an integral part of the investment environment. One use of derivatives, perhaps the primary use, is to hedge risks or transfer them to other parties. This is done successfully every day, and the use of these securities for risk management is so commonplace that the multitrillion-dollar market in derivative assets is routinely taken for granted. Derivatives also can be used to take highly speculative positions, however. Every so often, one of these positions blows up, resulting in well-publicized losses of hundreds of millions of dollars. While these losses attract considerable attention, they are in fact the exception to the more common use of such securities as risk management tools. Derivatives will continue to play an important role in portfolio construction and the financial system. We will return to this topic later in the text.

In addition to these financial assets, individuals might invest directly in some real assets. For example, real estate or commodities such as precious metals or agricultural products are real assets that might form part of an investment portfolio.

---

[1]A call option is the right to buy a share of stock at a given exercise price on or before the option's maturity date. If the market price of Intel remains below $30 a share, the right to buy for $30 will turn out to be valueless. If the share price rises above $30 before the option matures, however, the option can be exercised to obtain the share for only $30.

1.3 FINANCIAL MARKETS AND THE ECONOMY

We stated earlier that real assets determine the wealth of an economy, while financial assets merely represent claims on real assets. Nevertheless, financial assets and the markets in which they are traded play several crucial roles in developed economies. Financial assets allow us to make the most of the economy's real assets.

Consumption Timing

Some individuals in an economy are earning more than they currently wish to spend. Others, for example, retirees, spend more than they currently earn. How can you shift your purchasing power from high-earnings periods to low-earnings periods of life? One way is to "store" your wealth in financial assets. In high-earnings periods, you can invest your savings in financial assets such as stocks and bonds. In low-earnings periods, you can sell these assets to provide funds for your consumption needs. By so doing, you can "shift" your consumption over the course of your lifetime, thereby allocating your consumption to periods that provide the greatest satisfaction. Thus, financial markets allow individuals to separate decisions concerning current consumption from constraints that otherwise would be imposed by current earnings.

Allocation of Risk

Virtually all real assets involve some risk. When GM builds its auto plants, for example, it cannot know for sure what cash flows those plants will generate. Financial markets and the diverse financial instruments traded in those markets allow investors with the greatest taste for risk to bear that risk, while other, less risk-tolerant individuals can, to a greater extent, stay on the sidelines. For example, if GM raises the funds to build its auto plant by selling both stocks and bonds to the public, the more optimistic or risk-tolerant investors can buy shares of stock in GM, while the more conservative ones can buy GM bonds. Because the bonds promise to provide a fixed payment, the stockholders bear most of the business risk. Thus, capital markets allow the risk that is inherent to all investments to be borne by the investors most willing to bear that risk.

This allocation of risk also benefits the firms that need to raise capital to finance their investments. When investors are able to select security types with the risk-return characteristics that best suit their preferences, each security can be sold for the best possible price. This facilitates the process of building the economy's stock of real assets.

Separation of Ownership and Management

Many businesses are owned and managed by the same individual. This simple organization is well-suited to small businesses and, in fact, was the most common form of business organization before the Industrial Revolution. Today, however, with global markets and large-scale production, the size and capital requirements of firms have skyrocketed. For example, General Electric has property, plant, and equipment worth over $40 billion, and total assets in excess of $400 billion. Corporations of such size simply cannot exist as owner-operated firms. GE actually has over one-half million stockholders with an ownership stake in the firm proportional to their holdings of shares.

Such a large group of individuals obviously cannot actively participate in the day-to-day management of the firm. Instead, they elect a board of directors which in turn hires and supervises the management of the firm. This structure means that the owners and managers of the firm are different parties. This gives the firm a stability that the owner-managed firm cannot achieve. For example, if some stockholders decide they no longer wish to hold shares in the firm, they can sell their shares to another investor, with no impact on the management of the firm. Thus, financial assets and the ability to buy and sell those assets in the financial markets allow for easy separation of ownership and management.

How can all of the disparate owners of the firm, ranging from large pension funds holding hundreds of thousands of shares to small investors who may hold only a single share, agree on the objectives of the firm? Again, the financial markets provide some guidance. All may agree that the firm's management should pursue strategies that enhance the value of their shares. Such policies will make all shareholders wealthier and allow them all to better pursue their personal goals, whatever those goals might be.

Do managers really attempt to maximize firm value? It is easy to see how they might be tempted to engage in activities not in the best interest of shareholders. For example, they might engage in empire building or avoid risky projects to protect their own jobs or overconsume luxuries such as corporate jets, reasoning that the cost of such perquisites is largely borne by the shareholders. These potential conflicts of interest are called **agency problems** because managers, who are hired as agents of the shareholders, may pursue their own interests instead.

Several mechanisms have evolved to mitigate potential agency problems. First, compensation plans tie the income of managers to the success of the firm. A major part of the total compensation of top executives is typically in the form of stock options, which means that the managers will not do well unless the stock price increases, benefiting shareholders. (Of course, we've learned more recently that overuse of options can create its own agency problem. Options can create an incentive for managers to manipulate information to prop up a stock price temporarily, giving them a chance to cash out before the price returns to a level reflective of the firm's true prospects.) Second, while boards of directors are sometimes portrayed as defenders of top management, they can, and in recent years increasingly do, force out management teams that are underperforming. Third, outsiders such as security analysts and large institutional investors such as pension funds monitor the firm closely and make the life of poor performers at the least uncomfortable.

Finally, bad performers are subject to the threat of takeover. If the board of directors is lax in monitoring management, unhappy shareholders in principle can elect a different board. They can do this by launching a *proxy contest* in which they seek to obtain enough proxies (i.e., rights to vote the shares of other shareholders) to take control of the firm and vote in another board. However, this threat is usually minimal. Shareholders who attempt such a fight have to use their own funds, while management can defend itself using corporate coffers. Most proxy fights fail. The real takeover threat is from other firms. If one firm observes another underperforming, it can acquire the underperforming business and replace management with its own team.

agency problem

Conflicts of interest between managers and stockholders.

1.4 THE INVESTMENT PROCESS

asset allocation

Allocation of an investment portfolio across broad asset classes.

security selection

Choice of specific securities within each asset class.

An investor's *portfolio* is simply his collection of investment assets. Once the portfolio is established, it is updated or "rebalanced" by selling existing securities and using the proceeds to buy new securities, by investing additional funds to increase the overall size of the portfolio, or by selling securities to decrease the size of the portfolio.

Investment assets can be categorized into broad asset classes, such as stocks, bonds, real estate, commodities, and so on. Investors make two types of decisions in constructing their portfolios. The **asset allocation** decision is the choice among these broad asset classes, while the **security selection** decision is the choice of which particular securities to hold *within* each asset class.

"Top-down" portfolio construction starts with asset allocation. For example, an individual who currently holds all of his money in a bank account would first decide what proportion of the overall portfolio ought to be moved into stocks, bonds, and so on. In this way, the broad features of the portfolio are established. For example, while the average annual return on the common stock of large firms since 1926 has been about 12% per year, the average return on U.S. Treasury bills has been only 3.8%. On the other hand, stocks are far riskier, with annual returns that have ranged as low as −46% and as high as 55%. In contrast, T-bill returns are effectively risk-free: you know what interest rate you will earn when you buy the bills. Therefore, the decision to allocate your investments to the stock market or to the money market where Treasury bills are traded will have great ramifications for both the risk and the return of your portfolio. A top-down investor first makes this and other crucial asset allocation decisions before turning to the decision of the particular securities to be held in each asset class.

Security analysis involves the valuation of particular securities that might be included in the portfolio. For example, an investor might ask whether Merck or Pfizer is more attractively priced. Both bonds and stocks must be evaluated for investment attractiveness, but valuation is far more difficult for stocks because a stock's performance usually is far more sensitive to the condition of the issuing firm.

security analysis

Analysis of the value of securities.

In contrast to top-down portfolio management is the "bottom-up" strategy. In this process, the portfolio is constructed from the securities that seem attractively priced without as much concern for the resultant asset allocation. Such a technique can result in unintended bets on one or another sector of the economy. For example, it might turn out that the portfolio ends up with a very heavy representation of firms in one industry, from one part of the country, or with exposure to one source of uncertainty. However, a bottom-up strategy does focus the portfolio on the assets that seem to offer the most attractive investment opportunities.

1.5 | MARKETS ARE COMPETITIVE

Financial markets are highly competitive. Thousands of intelligent and well-backed analysts constantly scour the securities markets searching for the best buys. This competition means that we should expect to find few, if any, "free lunches," securities that are so underpriced that they represent obvious bargains. There are several implications of this no-free-lunch proposition. Let's examine two.

The Risk-Return Trade-Off

Investors invest for anticipated future returns, but those returns rarely can be predicted precisely. There will almost always be risk associated with investments. Actual or realized returns will almost always deviate from the expected return anticipated at the start of the investment period. For example, in 1931 (the worst calendar year for the market since 1926), the stock market lost 43% of its value. In 1933 (the best year), the stock market gained 54%. You can be sure that investors did not anticipate such extreme performance at the start of either of these years.

Naturally, if all else could be held equal, investors would prefer investments with the highest expected return.[2] However, the no-free-lunch rule tells us that all else cannot be held equal. If you want higher expected returns, you will have to pay a price in terms of accepting higher investment risk. If higher expected return can be achieved without bearing extra risk, there will be

---

[2] The "expected" return is not the return investors believe they necessarily will earn, or even their most likely return. It is instead the result of averaging across all possible outcomes, recognizing that some outcomes are more likely than others. It is the average rate of return across possible economic scenarios.

a rush to buy the high-return assets, with the result that their prices will be driven up. Individuals considering investing in the asset at the now-higher price will find the investment less attractive: If you buy at a higher price, your expected rate of return (that is, profit per dollar invested) is lower. The asset will be considered attractive and its price will continue to rise until its expected return is no more than commensurate with risk. At this point, investors can anticipate a "fair" return relative to the asset's risk, but no more. Similarly, if returns are independent of risk, there will be a rush to sell high-risk assets. Their prices will fall (and their expected future rates of return will rise) until they eventually become attractive enough to be included again in investor portfolios. We conclude that there should be a **risk-return trade-off** in the securities markets, with higher-risk assets priced to offer higher expected returns than lower-risk assets.

risk-return trade-off

Assets with higher expected returns have greater risk.

Of course, this discussion leaves several important questions unanswered. How should one measure the risk of an asset? What should be the quantitative trade-off between risk (properly measured) and expected return? One would think that risk would have something to do with the volatility of an asset's returns, but this guess turns out to be only partly correct. When we mix assets into diversified portfolios, we need to consider the interplay among assets and the effect of diversification on the risk of the entire portfolio. *Diversification* means that many assets are held in the portfolio so that the exposure to any particular asset is limited. The effect of diversification on portfolio risk, the implications for the proper measurement of risk, and the risk-return relationship are the topics of Part Two. These topics are the subject of what has come to be known as *modern portfolio theory*. The development of this theory brought two of its pioneers, Harry Markowitz and William Sharpe, Nobel Prizes.

Efficient Markets

Another implication of the no-free-lunch proposition is that we should rarely expect to find bargains in the security markets. We will spend all of Chapter 8 examining the theory and evidence concerning the hypothesis that financial markets process all relevant information about securities quickly and efficiently, that is, that the security price usually reflects all the information available to investors concerning the value of the security. According to this hypothesis, as new information about a security becomes available, the price of the security quickly adjusts so that at any time, the security price equals the market consensus estimate of the value of the security. If this were so, there would be neither underpriced nor overpriced securities.

passive management

Buying and holding a diversified portfolio without attempting to identify mispriced securities.

One interesting implication of this "efficient market hypothesis" concerns the choice between active and passive investment-management strategies. **Passive management** calls for holding highly diversified portfolios without spending effort or other resources attempting to improve investment performance through security analysis. **Active management** is the attempt to improve performance either by identifying mispriced securities or by timing the performance of broad asset classes—for example, increasing one's commitment to stocks when one is bullish on the stock market. If markets are efficient and prices reflect all relevant information, perhaps it is better to follow passive strategies instead of spending resources in a futile attempt to outguess your competitors in the financial markets.

active management

Attempting to identify mispriced securities or to forecast broad market trends.

If the efficient market hypothesis were taken to the extreme, there would be no point in active security analysis; only fools would commit resources to actively analyze securities. Without ongoing security analysis, however, prices eventually would depart from "correct" values, creating new incentives for experts to move in. Therefore, even in environments as competitive as the financial markets, we may observe only *near*-efficiency, and profit opportunities may exist for especially diligent and creative investors. This motivates our discussion of active portfolio management in Part Six. More importantly, our discussions of security analysis and portfolio construction generally must account for the likelihood of nearly efficient markets.

1.6 | THE PLAYERS

From a bird's-eye view, there would appear to be three major players in the financial markets:

1. Firms are net borrowers. They raise capital now to pay for investments in plant and equipment. The income generated by those real assets provides the returns to investors who purchase the securities issued by the firm.

2. Households typically are net savers. They purchase the securities issued by firms that need to raise funds.

3. Governments can be borrowers or lenders, depending on the relationship between tax revenue and government expenditures. Since World War II, the U.S. government typically has run budget deficits, meaning that its tax receipts have been less than its expenditures. The government, therefore, has had to borrow funds to cover its budget deficit. Issuance of Treasury bills, notes, and bonds is the major way that the government borrows funds from the public. In contrast, in the latter part of the 1990s, the government enjoyed a budget surplus and was able to retire some outstanding debt.

Corporations and governments do not sell all or even most of their securities directly to individuals. For example, about half of all stock is held by large financial institutions such as pension funds, mutual funds, insurance companies, and banks. These financial institutions stand between the security issuer (the firm) and the ultimate owner of the security (the individual investor). For this reason, they are called *financial intermediaries*. Similarly, corporations do not market their own securities to the public. Instead, they hire agents, called investment bankers, to represent them to the investing public. Let's examine the roles of these intermediaries.

Financial Intermediaries

Households want desirable investments for their savings, yet the small (financial) size of most households makes direct investment difficult. A small investor seeking to lend money to businesses that need to finance investments doesn't advertise in the local newspaper to find a willing and desirable borrower. Moreover, an individual lender would not be able to diversify across borrowers to reduce risk. Finally, an individual lender is not equipped to assess and monitor the credit risk of borrowers.

For these reasons, **financial intermediaries** have evolved to bring lenders and borrowers together. These financial intermediaries include banks, investment companies, insurance companies, and credit unions. Financial intermediaries issue their own securities to raise funds to purchase the securities of other corporations.

For example, a bank raises funds by borrowing (taking deposits) and lending that money to other borrowers. The spread between the interest rates paid to depositors and the rates charged to borrowers is the source of the bank's profit. In this way, lenders and borrowers do not need to contact each other directly. Instead, each goes to the bank, which acts as an intermediary between the two. The problem of matching lenders with borrowers is solved when each comes independently to the common intermediary.

Financial intermediaries are distinguished from other businesses in that both their assets and their liabilities are overwhelmingly financial. Table 1.3 shows that the balance sheets of financial institutions include very small amounts of tangible assets. Compare Table 1.3 to the aggregated balance sheet of the nonfinancial corporate sector in Table 1.4. The contrast arises because intermediaries simply move funds from one sector to another. In fact, the primary social function of such intermediaries is to channel household savings to the business sector.

financial intermediaries

Institutions that "connect" borrowers and lenders by accepting funds from lenders and loaning funds to borrowers.

TABLE 1.3
Balance sheet of financial institutions

Assets	$ Billion	% Total	Liabilities and Net Worth	$ Billion	% Total
Tangible assets			Liabilities		
Equipment and structures	$ 528	3.1%	Deposits	$ 3,462	20.1%
Land	99	0.6	Mutual fund shares	1,564	9.1
Total tangibles	$ 628	3.6%	Life insurance reserves	478	2.8
			Pension reserves	4,651	27.0
			Money market securities	1,150	6.7
			Bonds and mortgages	1,589	9.2
Financial assets			Other	3,078	17.8
Deposits and cash	$ 364	2.1%	Total liabilities	$15,971	92.6%
Government securities	3,548	20.6			
Corporate bonds	1,924	11.2			
Mortgages	2,311	13.4			
Consumer credit	894	5.2			
Other loans	1,803	10.4			
Corporate equity	3,310	19.2			
Other	2,471	14.3			
Total financial assets	16,625	96.4	Net worth	1,281	7.4
Total	$17,252	100.0%	Total	$17,252	100.0%

Note: Column sums subject to rounding error.

Source: *Balance Sheets for the U.S. Economy, 1945–94*, Board of Governors of the Federal Reserve System, June 1995.

TABLE 1.4
Balance sheet of nonfinancial U.S. business

Assets	$ Billion	% Total	Liabilities and Net Worth	$ Billion	% Total
Real assets			Liabilities		
Equipment and software	$ 3,346	18.9%	Bonds & mortgages	$ 2,754	15.6%
Real estate	4,872	27.6	Bank loans	929	5.3
Inventories	1,350	7.6	Other loans	934	5.3
Total real assets	$ 9,568	54.2%	Trade debt	1,266	7.2
			Other	2,804	15.9
Financial assets			Total liabilities	$ 8,687	49.2%
Deposits and cash	$ 532	3.0%			
Marketable securities	509	2.9			
Consumer credit	72	0.4			
Trade credit	1,705	9.7			
Other	5,275	29.9			
Total financial assets	8,093	45.8	Net worth	8,974	50.8
Total	$17,661	100.0%		$17,661	100.0%

Note: Column sums may differ from total because of rounding error.

Source: *Flow of Funds Accounts of the United States*, Board of Governors of the Federal Reserve System, June 2001.

Other examples of financial intermediaries are investment companies, insurance companies, and credit unions. All these firms offer similar advantages in their intermediary role. First, by pooling the resources of many small investors, they are able to lend considerable sums to large borrowers. Second, by lending to many borrowers, intermediaries achieve significant diversification, so they can accept loans that individually might be too risky. Third, intermediaries build expertise through the volume of business they do and can use economies of scale and scope to assess and monitor risk.

Investment companies, which pool and manage the money of many investors, also arise out of economies of scale. Here, the problem is that most household portfolios are not large enough to be spread among a wide variety of securities. It is very expensive in terms of brokerage fees and research costs to purchase one or two shares of many different firms. Mutual funds have the advantage of large-scale trading and portfolio management, while participating investors are assigned a prorated share of the total funds according to the size of their investment. This system gives small investors advantages they are willing to pay for via a management fee to the mutual fund operator.

Investment companies also can design portfolios specifically for large investors with particular goals. In contrast, mutual funds are sold in the retail market, and their investment philosophies are differentiated mainly by strategies that are likely to attract a large number of clients.

Economies of scale also explain the proliferation of analytic services available to investors. Newsletters, databases, and brokerage house research services all engage in research to be sold to a large client base. This setup arises naturally. Investors clearly want information, but with small portfolios to manage, they do not find it economical to personally gather all of it. Hence, a profit opportunity emerges: A firm can perform this service for many clients and charge for it.

> **investment companies**
>
> Firms managing funds for investors. An investment company may manage several mutual funds.

2. Computer networks have made it much cheaper and easier for small investors to trade for their own accounts and perform their own security analysis. What will be the likely effect on financial intermediation?

Concept CHECK

Investment Bankers

Just as economies of scale and specialization create profit opportunities for financial intermediaries, so too do these economies create niches for firms that perform specialized services for businesses. Firms raise much of their capital by selling securities such as stocks and bonds to the public. Because these firms do not do so frequently, however, investment banking firms that specialize in such activities can offer their services at a cost below that of maintaining an in-house security issuance division.

Investment bankers such as Goldman, Sachs, or Merrill Lynch, or Salomon Smith Barney advise the issuing corporation on the prices it can charge for the securities issued, appropriate interest rates, and so forth. Ultimately, the investment banking firm handles the marketing of the security issue to the public.

Investment bankers can provide more than just expertise to security issuers. Because investment bankers are constantly in the market, assisting one firm or another in issuing securities, the public knows that it is in the banker's own interest to protect and maintain its reputation for honesty. The investment banker will suffer along with investors if the securities it underwrites are marketed to the public with overly optimistic or exaggerated claims; the public will not be so trusting the next time that investment banker participates in a security sale. The investment banker's effectiveness and ability to command future business thus depend on the reputation it has established over time. Obviously, the economic incentives to maintain a trustworthy reputation are not nearly as strong for firms that plan to go to the securities markets only once or very infrequently. Therefore, investment bankers can provide a certification role—a

> **investment bankers**
>
> Firms specializing in the sale of new securities to the public, typically by underwriting the issue.

"seal of approval"—to security issuers. Their investment in reputation is another type of scale economy that arises from frequent participation in the capital markets.

1.7 | MARKETS AND MARKET STRUCTURE

Just as securities and financial institutions are born and evolve in response to investor demands, financial markets also develop to meet the needs of particular traders. Consider what would happen if organized markets did not exist. Any household wishing to invest in some type of financial asset would have to find others wishing to sell.

This is how financial markets evolved. Meeting places established for buyers and sellers of financial assets became a financial market. A pub in old London called Lloyd's launched the maritime insurance industry. A Manhattan curb on Wall Street became synonymous with the financial world.

We can differentiate four types of markets: direct search markets, brokered markets, dealer markets, and auction markets.

Direct Search Markets

A *direct search market* is the least organized market. Buyers and sellers must seek each other out directly. An example of a transaction in such a market is the sale of a used refrigerator where the seller advertises for buyers in a local newspaper. Such markets are characterized by sporadic participation and low-priced and nonstandard goods. It does not pay most people or firms to seek profits by specializing in such an environment.

Brokered Markets

The next level of organization is a *brokered market*. In markets where trading in a good is active, brokers find it profitable to offer search services to buyers and sellers. A good example is the real estate market, where economies of scale in searches for available homes and for prospective buyers make it worthwhile for participants to pay brokers to conduct the searches. Brokers in particular markets develop specialized knowledge on valuing assets traded in that market.

primary market

A market in which new issues of securities are offered to the public.

An important brokered investment market is the so-called **primary market,** where new issues of securities are offered to the public. In the primary market, investment bankers who market a firm's securities to the public act as brokers; they seek investors to purchase securities directly from the issuing corporation.

Another brokered market is that for large block transactions, in which very large blocks of stock are bought or sold. These blocks are so large (technically more than 10,000 shares but usually much larger) that brokers or "block houses" often are engaged to search directly for other large traders, rather than bring the trade directly to the stock exchange where relatively smaller investors trade.

Dealer Markets

dealer markets

Markets in which traders specializing in particular assets buy and sell for their own accounts.

When trading activity in a particular type of asset increases, **dealer markets** arise. Dealers specialize in various assets, purchase these assets for their own accounts, and later sell them for a profit from their inventory. The spreads between dealers' buy (or "bid") prices and sell (or "ask") prices are a source of profit. Dealer markets save traders on search costs because market participants can easily look up the prices at which they can buy from or sell to dealers. A fair amount of market activity is required before dealing in a market is an attractive source of income. The over-the-counter (OTC) market is one example of a dealer market.

Trading among investors of already-issued securities is said to take place in **secondary markets.** Therefore, the over-the-counter market is also an example of a secondary market. Trading in secondary markets does not affect the outstanding amount of securities; ownership is simply transferred from one investor to another.

Auction Markets

The most integrated market is an **auction market,** in which all traders converge at one place to buy or sell an asset. The New York Stock Exchange (NYSE) is an example of an auction market. An advantage of auction markets over dealer markets is that one need not search across dealers to find the best price for a good. If all participants converge, they can arrive at mutually agreeable prices and save the bid-ask spread.

Continuous auction markets (as opposed to periodic auctions, such as in the art world) require very heavy and frequent trading to cover the expense of maintaining the market. For this reason, the NYSE and other exchanges set up listing requirements, which limit the stocks traded on the exchange to those of firms in which sufficient trading interest is likely to exist.

The organized stock exchanges are also secondary markets. They are organized for investors to trade existing securities among themselves.

3. Many assets trade in more than one type of market. What types of markets do the following trade in?
    a. Used cars
    b. Paintings
    c. Rare coins

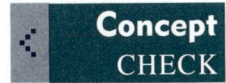

Concept
CHECK

1.8 | RECENT TRENDS

Four important trends have changed the contemporary investment environment: (1) globalization, (2) securitization, (3) financial engineering, and (4) information and computer networks.

Globalization

If a wider range of investment choices can benefit investors, why should we limit ourselves to purely domestic assets? Increasingly efficient communication technology and the dismantling of regulatory constraints have encouraged **globalization** in recent years.

U.S. investors commonly can participate in foreign investment opportunities in several ways: (1) purchase foreign securities using American Depository Receipts (ADRs), which are domestically traded securities that represent claims to shares of foreign stocks; (2) purchase foreign securities that are offered in dollars; (3) buy mutual funds that invest internationally; and (4) buy derivative securities with payoffs that depend on prices in foreign security markets.

Brokers who act as intermediaries for American Depository Receipts purchase an inventory of stock from some foreign issuer. The broker then issues an American Depository Receipt that represents a claim to some number of those foreign shares held in inventory. The ADR is denominated in dollars and can be traded on U.S. stock exchanges but is in essence no more than a claim on a foreign stock. Thus, from the investor's point of view, there is no more difference between buying a British versus a U.S. stock than there is in holding a Massachusetts-based company compared with a California-based one. Of course, the investment implication may differ: ADRs still expose investors to exchange-rate risk.

World Equity Benchmark Shares (WEBS) are a variation on ADRs. WEBS use the same depository structure to allow investors to trade *portfolios* of foreign stocks in a selected country. Each WEBS security tracks the performance of an index of share returns for a particular country. WEBS can be traded by investors just like any other security (they trade on the Amer-

---

secondary markets

Already existing securities are bought and sold on the exchanges or in the OTC market.

auction market

A market where all traders meet at one place to buy or sell an asset.

globalization

Tendency toward a worldwide investment environment, and the integration of national capital markets.

ican Stock Exchange) and thus enable U.S. investors to obtain diversified portfolios of foreign stocks in one fell swoop.

A giant step toward globalization took place recently when 11 European countries replaced their existing currencies with a new currency called the *euro*. The idea behind the euro is that a common currency will facilitate global trade and encourage integration of markets across national boundaries. Figure 1.1 is an announcement of a debt offering in the amount of 500 million euros. (Each euro is currently worth just about $1; the symbol for the euro is €.)

pass-through securities

Pools of loans (such as home mortgage loans) sold in one package. Owners of pass-throughs receive all of the principal and interest payments made by the borrowers.

Securitization

In 1970, mortgage **pass-through securities** were introduced by the Government National Mortgage Association (GNMA, or Ginnie Mae). These securities aggregate individual home mortgages into relatively homogeneous pools. Each pool acts as backing for a GNMA pass-through security. Investors who buy GNMA securities receive prorated shares of all the principal and interest payments made on the underlying mortgage pool.

For example, the pool might total $100 million of 8%, 30-year conventional mortgages. The rights to the cash flows could then be sold as 5,000 units, each worth $20,000. Each unit

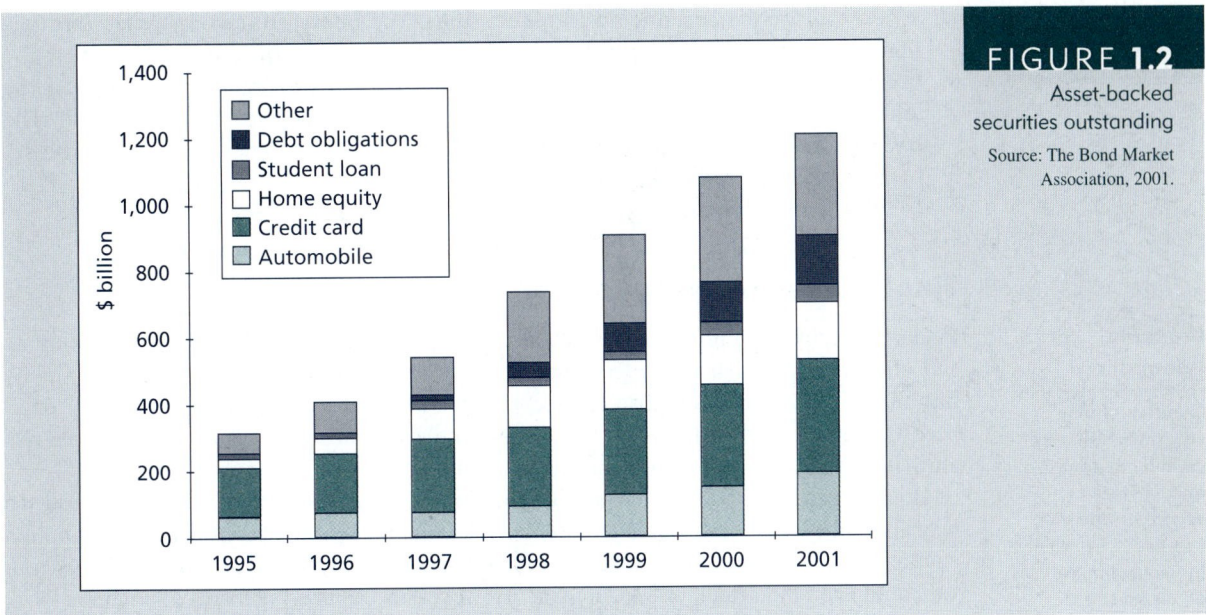

FIGURE **1.2**

Asset-backed
securities outstanding

Source: The Bond Market
Association, 2001.

holder would then receive 1/5,000 of all monthly interest and principal payments made on the pool. The banks that originated the mortgages continue to service them (receiving fee-for-service), but they no longer own the mortgage investment; the investment has been passed through to the GNMA security holders.

Pass-through securities represent a tremendous innovation in mortgage markets. The **securitization** of mortgages means mortgages can be traded just like other securities. Availability of funds to homebuyers no longer depends on local credit conditions and is no longer subject to local banks' potential monopoly powers; with mortgage pass-throughs trading in national markets, mortgage funds can flow from any region (literally worldwide) to wherever demand is greatest.

Securitization also expands the menu of choices for the investor. Whereas it would have been impossible before 1970 for investors to invest in mortgages directly, they now can purchase mortgage pass-through securities or invest in mutual funds that offer portfolios of such securities.

Today, the majority of home mortgages are pooled into mortgage-backed securities. The two biggest players in the market are the Federal National Mortgage Association (FNMA, or Fannie Mae) and the Federal Home Loan Mortgage Corporation (FHLMC, or Freddie Mac). Over $2.5 trillion of mortgage-backed securities are outstanding, making this market larger than the market for corporate bonds.

Other loans that have been securitized into pass-through arrangements include car loans, student loans, home equity loans, credit card loans, and debts of firms. Figure 1.2 documents the rapid growth of nonmortgage asset-backed securities since 1995.

Securitization also has been used to allow U.S. banks to unload their portfolios of shaky loans to developing nations. So-called *Brady bonds* (named after former Secretary of Treasury Nicholas Brady) were formed by securitizing bank loans to several countries in shaky fiscal condition. The U.S. banks exchange their loans to developing nations for bonds backed by those loans. The payments that the borrowing nation would otherwise make to the lending bank are directed instead to the holder of the bond. These bonds are traded in capital markets. Therefore, if they choose, banks can remove these loans from their portfolios simply by selling the bonds. In addition, the U.S. in many cases has enhanced the credit quality of these bonds by designating a quantity of Treasury bonds to serve as partial collateral for the loans. In the event of a foreign default, the holders of the Brady bonds have claim to the collateral.

securitization

Pooling loans into standardized securities backed by those loans, which can then be traded like any other security.

4. When mortgages are pooled into securities, the pass-through agencies (Freddie Mac and Fannie Mae) typically guarantee the underlying mortgage loans. If the homeowner defaults on the loan, the pass-through agency makes good on the loan; the investor in the mortgage-backed security does not bear the credit risk.
   a. Why does the allocation of risk to the pass-through agency rather than the security holder make economic sense?
   b. Why is the allocation of credit risk less of an issue for Brady bonds?

Financial Engineering

bundling, unbundling

Creation of new securities either by combining primitive and derivative securities into one composite hybrid or by separating returns on an asset into classes.

Financial engineering refers to the creation of new securities by **unbundling**—breaking up and allocating the cash flows from one security to create several new securities—or by **bundling**—combining more than one security into a composite security. Such creative engineering of new investment products allows one to design securities with custom-tailored risk attributes. An example of bundling appears in Figure 1.3.

Boise Cascade, with the assistance of Goldman, Sachs and other underwriters, has issued a hybrid security with features of preferred stock combined with various call and put option contracts. The security is structured as preferred stock for four years, at which time it is converted into common stock of the company. However, the number of shares of common stock into which the security can be converted depends on the price of the stock in four years, which means that the security holders are exposed to risk similar to the risk they would bear if they held option positions on the firm.

FIGURE **1.3**

Bundling creates a complex security

Source: *The Wall Street Journal,* December 19, 2001.

$172,500,000

Boise Cascade Corporation

7.50% Adjustable Conversion-rate Equity Security Unit

Price $50 Per Unit

Upon request, a copy of the Prospectus Supplement and the related Prospectus describing these securities and the business of the Company may be obtained within any State from any Underwriter who may legally distribute it within such State. The securities are offered only by means of the Prospectus Supplement and the related Prospectus and this announcement is neither an offer to sell nor a solicitation of any offer to buy.

Goldman, Sachs & Co.
ABN AMRO Rothschild LLC
Banc of America Securities LLC
JPMorgan
Wachovia Securities

December 19, 2001

Often, creating a security that appears to be attractive requires the unbundling of an asset. An example is given in Figure 1.4. There, a mortgage pass-through certificate is unbundled into classes. Class 1 receives only principal payments from the mortgage pool, whereas Class 2 receives only interest payments.

The process of bundling and unbundling is called **financial engineering,** which refers to the creation and design of securities with custom-tailored characteristics, often regarding exposures to various sources of risk. Financial engineers view securities as bundles of (possible risky) cash flows that may be carved up and rearranged according to the needs or desires of traders in the security markets.

> **financial engineering**
>
> The process of creating and designing securities with custom-tailored characteristics.

Computer Networks

The Internet and other advances in computer networking are transforming many sectors of the economy, and few more so than the financial sector. These advances will be treated in greater detail in Chapter 3, but for now we can mention a few important innovations: online trading, online information dissemination, and automated trade crossing.

Online trading connects a customer directly to a brokerage firm. Online brokerage firms can process trades more cheaply and therefore can charge lower commissions. The average commission for an online trade is now below $20, compared to perhaps $100–$300 at full-service brokers.

FIGURE 1.4

Unbundling of mortgages into principal- and interest-only securities

Source: Goldman, Sachs & Co., March 1985.

This announcement appears as a matter of record only.

$200,000,000*

Federal National Mortgage Association

FannieMae

Stripped Mortgage-Backed Securities

Principal and Interest payable on the 25th day of
each month, commencing August 25, 1987

SMBS Trust 20-CL—Fixed-Rate Residential Mortgage Loans

SMBS Class 1: 100% of Principal Payments on Underlying
$9^{1}/_{2}$% Fannie Mae Guaranteed Mortgage Pass-Through Certificates
SMBS Class 2: 100% of Interest Payments on Underlying
$9^{1}/_{2}$% Fannie Mae Guaranteed Mortgage Pass-Through Certificates

The obligations of Fannie Mae under its guaranty of the SMBS Certificates are obligations of Fannie Mae and are not backed by the full faith and credit of the United States. The SMBS Certificates are exempt from the registration requirements of the Securities Act of 1933 and are "Exempted Securities" within the meaning of the Securities Exchange Act of 1934.

Class 1 $200,000,000 Principal Amount*
Class 2 $200,000,000 Notional Principal Amount*

Goldman, Sachs & Co.

July 9, 1987   *Approximate

The Internet has also allowed vast amounts of information to be made cheaply and widely available to the public. Individual investors today can obtain data, investment tools, and even analyst reports that just a decade ago would have been available only to professionals.

Electronic communication networks that allow direct trading among investors have exploded in recent years. These networks allow members to post buy or sell orders and to have those orders automatically matched up or "crossed" with orders of other traders in the system without benefit of an intermediary such as a securities dealer.

1.9 | OUTLINE OF THE TEXT

The text has six parts, which are fairly independent and may be studied in a variety of sequences. Part One is an introduction to financial markets, instruments, and trading of securities. This part also describes the mutual fund industry.

Part Two is a fairly detailed presentation of "modern portfolio theory." This part of the text treats the effect of diversification on portfolio risk, the efficient diversification of investor portfolios, the choice of portfolios that strike an attractive balance between risk and return, and the trade-off between risk and expected return.

Parts Three through Five cover security analysis and valuation. Part Three is devoted to debt markets and Part Four to equity markets. Part Five covers derivative assets, such as options and futures contracts.

Part Six is an introduction to active investment management. It shows how different investors' objectives and constraints can lead to a variety of investment policies. This part discusses the role of active management in nearly efficient markets and considers how one should evaluate the performance of managers who pursue active strategies. It also shows how the principles of portfolio construction can be extended to the international setting.

SUMMARY

- Real assets create wealth. Financial assets represent claims to parts or all of that wealth. Financial assets determine how the ownership of real assets is distributed among investors.
- Financial assets can be categorized as fixed income, equity, or derivative instruments. Top-down portfolio construction techniques start with the asset allocation decision—the allocation of funds across broad asset classes—and then progress to more specific security-selection decisions.
- Competition in financial markets leads to a risk-return trade-off, in which securities that offer higher expected rates of return also impose greater risks on investors. The presence of risk, however, implies that actual returns can differ considerably from expected returns at the beginning of the investment period. Competition among security analysts also results in financial markets that are nearly informationally efficient, meaning that prices reflect all available information concerning the value of the security. Passive investment strategies may make sense in nearly efficient markets.
- Financial intermediaries pool investor funds and invest them. Their services are in demand because small investors cannot efficiently gather information, diversify, and monitor portfolios. The financial intermediary sells its own securities to the small investors. The intermediary invests the funds thus raised, uses the proceeds to pay back the small investors, and profits from the difference (the spread).
- Investment banking brings efficiency to corporate fund-raising. Investment bankers develop expertise in pricing new issues and in marketing them to investors.
- There are four types of financial markets. Direct search markets are the least efficient and sophisticated, where each transactor must find a counterpart. In brokered markets, brokers

specialize in advising and finding counterparts for fee-paying traders. Dealers provide a step up in convenience. They keep an inventory of the asset and stand ready to buy or sell on demand, profiting from the bid-ask spread. Auction markets allow a trader to benefit from direct competition. All interested parties bid for the goods or services.
- Recent trends in financial markets include globalization, securitization, financial engineering of assets, and growth of information and computer networks.

active management, 10
agency problem, 8
asset allocation, 8
auction market, 15
bundling, 18
dealer markets, 14
derivative securities, 6
equity, 6
financial assets, 4

financial engineering, 19
financial intermediaries, 11
fixed-income securities, 5
globalization, 15
investment, 3
investment bankers, 13
investment companies, 13
passive management, 10
pass-through securities, 16

primary market, 14
real assets, 4
risk-return trade-off, 10
secondary markets, 15
securitization, 17
security analysis, 9
security selection, 8
unbundling, 18

PROBLEM SETS

1. Suppose you discover a treasure chest of $10 billion in cash.
   a. Is this a real or financial asset?
   b. Is society any richer for the discovery?
   c. Are you wealthier?
   d. Can you reconcile your answers to (b) and (c)? Is anyone worse off as a result of the discovery?

2. Lanni Products is a start-up computer software development firm. It currently owns computer equipment worth $30,000 and has cash on hand of $20,000 contributed by Lanni's owners. For each of the following transactions, identify the real and/or financial assets that trade hands. Are any financial assets created or destroyed in the transaction?
   a. Lanni takes out a bank loan. It receives $50,000 in cash and signs a note promising to pay back the loan over three years.
   b. Lanni uses the cash from the bank plus $20,000 of its own funds to finance the development of new financial planning software.
   c. Lanni sells the software product to Microsoft, which will market it to the public under the Microsoft name. Lanni accepts payment in the form of 1,500 shares of Microsoft stock.
   d. Lanni sells the shares of stock for $80 per share and uses part of the proceeds to pay off the bank loan.

3. Reconsider Lanni Products from problem 2.
   a. Prepare its balance sheet just after it gets the bank loan. What is the ratio of real assets to total assets?
   b. Prepare the balance sheet after Lanni spends the $70,000 to develop its software product. What is the ratio of real assets to total assets?
   c. Prepare the balance sheet after Lanni accepts the payment of shares from Microsoft. What is the ratio of real assets to total assets?

4. Financial engineering has been disparaged as nothing more than paper shuffling. Critics argue that resources used for *rearranging* wealth (that is, bundling and unbundling financial assets) might be better spent on *creating* wealth (that is, creating real assets). Evaluate this criticism. Are any benefits realized by creating an array of derivative securities from various primary securities?

5. Examine the balance sheet of the financial sector in Table 1.3. What is the ratio of tangible assets to total assets? What is that ratio for nonfinancial firms (Table 1.4)? Why should this difference be expected?

6. Consider Figure 1.5, below, which describes an issue of American gold certificates.
   a. Is this issue a primary or secondary market transaction?
   b. Are the certificates primitive or derivative assets?
   c. What market niche is filled by this offering?

7. Discuss the advantages and disadvantages of the following forms of managerial compensation in terms of mitigating agency problems, that is, potential conflicts of interest between managers and shareholders.
   a. A fixed salary.
   b. Stock in the firm.
   c. Call options on shares of the firm.

8. We noted that oversight by large institutional investors or creditors is one mechanism to reduce agency problems. Why don't individual investors in the firm have the same incentive to keep an eye on management?

9. Why would you expect securitization to take place only in highly developed capital markets?

10. What is the relationship between securitization and the role of financial intermediaries in the economy? What happens to financial intermediaries as securitization progresses?

11. Although we stated that real assets comprise the true productive capacity of an economy, it is hard to conceive of a modern economy without well-developed financial markets and security types. How would the productive capacity of the U.S. economy be affected if there were no markets in which one could trade financial assets?

12. Give an example of three financial intermediaries and explain how they act as a bridge between small investors and large capital markets or corporations.

13. Firms raise capital from investors by issuing shares in the primary markets. Does this imply that corporate financial managers can ignore trading of previously issued shares in the secondary market?

FIGURE 1.5

A gold-backed security

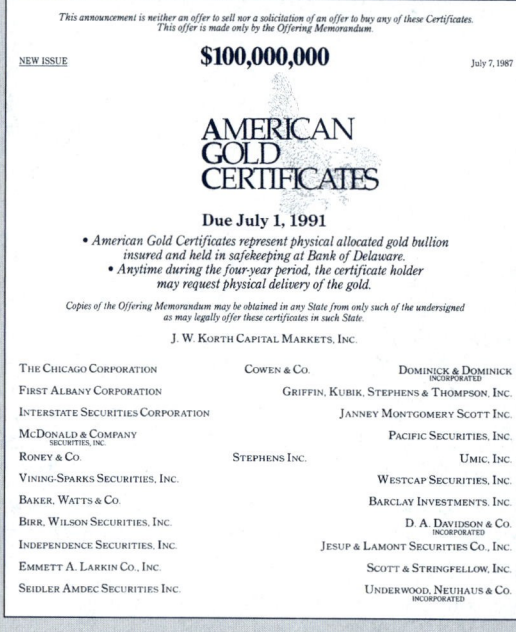

This announcement is neither an offer to sell nor a solicitation of an offer to buy any of these Certificates. This offer is made only by the Offering Memorandum.

NEW ISSUE   **$100,000,000**   July 7, 1987

AMERICAN GOLD CERTIFICATES

Due July 1, 1991

• American Gold Certificates represent physical allocated gold bullion insured and held in safekeeping at Bank of Delaware.
• Anytime during the four-year period, the certificate holder may request physical delivery of the gold.

Copies of the Offering Memorandum may be obtained in any State from only such of the undersigned as may legally offer these certificates in such State.

J. W. KORTH CAPITAL MARKETS, INC.

THE CHICAGO CORPORATION	COWEN & CO.	DOMINICK & DOMINICK INCORPORATED
FIRST ALBANY CORPORATION		GRIFFIN, KUBIK, STEPHENS & THOMPSON, INC.
INTERSTATE SECURITIES CORPORATION		JANNEY MONTGOMERY SCOTT INC.
MCDONALD & COMPANY SECURITIES, INC.		PACIFIC SECURITIES, INC.
RONEY & CO.	STEPHENS INC.	UMIC, INC.
VINING-SPARKS SECURITIES, INC.		WESTCAP SECURITIES, INC.
BAKER, WATTS & CO.		BARCLAY INVESTMENTS, INC.
BIRR, WILSON SECURITIES, INC.		D. A. DAVIDSON & CO. INCORPORATED
INDEPENDENCE SECURITIES, INC.		JESUP & LAMONT SECURITIES CO., INC.
EMMETT A. LARKIN CO., INC.		SCOTT & STRINGFELLOW, INC.
SEIDLER AMDEC SECURITIES INC.		UNDERWOOD, NEUHAUS & CO. INCORPORATED

14. The rate of return on investments in large stocks has outpaced that on investments in Treasury bills by over 8% since 1926. Why, then, does anyone invest in Treasury bills?

15. What are some advantages and disadvantages of top-down versus bottom-up investing styles?

16. You see an advertisement for a book that claims to show how you can make $1 million with no risk and with no money down. Will you buy the book?

WEBMASTER

Stock Options

Go to http://www.businessweek.com/magazine/content/ 02_09/b3772049.htm to view the article "Too Much of a Good Incentive." This article discusses current issues related to stock option compensation.

After reading this article, answer the following questions:

1. What factors did the author suggest caused problems with options being granted to companies in the late 1990s?

2. What is the controversy related to having companies expense options when they are given rather than the current method of not recording an expense?

3. What does the author suggest is the real cost associated with options that is not recognized when the options are granted?

SOLUTIONS TO

Concept CHECKS

1. *a.* Real
   b. Financial
   c. Real
   d. Real
   e. Financial

2. If the new technology enables investors to trade and perform research for themselves, the need for financial intermediaries will decline. Part of the service intermediaries now offer is a lower-cost method for individuals to participate in securities markets. This part of the intermediaries' service would be less sought after.

3. *a.* Used cars trade in dealer markets (used-car lots or auto dealerships) and in direct search markets when individuals advertise in local newspapers.
   b. Paintings trade in broker markets when clients commission brokers to buy or sell art for them, in dealer markets at art galleries, and in auction markets.
   c. Rare coins trade mostly in dealer markets in coin shops, but they also trade in auctions and in direct search markets when individuals advertise they want to buy or sell coins.

4. *a.* The pass-through agencies are far better equipped to evaluate the credit risk associated with the pool of mortgages. They are constantly in the market, have ongoing relationships with the originators of the loans, and find it economical to set up "quality control" departments to monitor the credit risk of the mortgage pools. Therefore, the pass-through agencies are better able to incur the risk; they charge for this "service" via a "guarantee fee." Investors might not find it worthwhile to purchase these securities if they must assess the credit risk of these loans for themselves. It is far cheaper for them to allow the agencies to collect the guarantee fee.
   b. In contrast to mortgage-backed securities, which are backed by large numbers of mortgages, Brady bonds are backed by large government loans. It is more feasible for the investor to evaluate the credit quality of a few governments than it is to evaluate dozens or hundreds of individual mortgages.

www.mhhe.com/bkm

2

GLOBAL FINANCIAL INSTRUMENTS

AFTER STUDYING THIS CHAPTER YOU SHOULD BE ABLE TO:

> Distinguish among the major assets that trade in money markets and in capital markets.

> Describe the construction of stock market indexes.

> Calculate the profit or loss on investments in options and futures contracts.

This chapter covers a range of financial securities and the markets in which they trade. Our goal is to introduce you to the features of various security types. This foundation will be necessary to understand the more analytic material that follows in later chapters.

We first describe money market instruments. We then move on to debt and equity securities. We explain the structure of various stock market indexes in this chapter because market benchmark portfolios play an important role in portfolio construction and evaluation. Finally, we survey the derivative security markets for options and futures contracts. A summary of the markets, instruments, and indexes covered in this chapter appears in Table 2.1.

TABLE **2.1** Financial markets and indexes	The money market	The bond market
	Treasury bills	Treasury bonds and notes
	Certificates of deposit	Federal agency debt
	Commercial paper	Municipal bonds
	Bankers' acceptances	Corporate bonds
	Eurodollars	Mortgage-backed securities
	Repos and reverses	**Equity markets**
	Federal funds	Common stocks
	Brokers' calls	Preferred stocks
	Indexes	**Derivative markets**
	Dow Jones averages	Options
	Standard & Poor's indexes	Futures and forwards
	Bond market indicators	
	International indexes	

2.1 | THE MONEY MARKET

money markets

Include short-term, highly liquid, and relatively low-risk debt instruments.

capital markets

Include longer-term, relatively riskier securities.

Financial markets are traditionally segmented into **money markets** and **capital markets.** Money market instruments include short-term, marketable, liquid, low-risk debt securities. Money market instruments sometimes are called *cash equivalents,* or just *cash* for short. Capital markets, in contrast, include longer-term and riskier securities. Securities in the capital market are much more diverse than those found within the money market. For this reason, we will subdivide the capital market into four segments: longer-term debt markets, equity markets, and the derivative markets for options and futures.

The money market is a subsector of the debt market. It consists of very short-term debt securities that are highly marketable. Many of these securities trade in large denominations and so are out of the reach of individual investors. Money market mutual funds, however, are easily accessible to small investors. These mutual funds pool the resources of many investors and purchase a wide variety of money market securities on their behalf.

Figure 2.1 is a reprint of a money rates listing from *The Wall Street Journal.* It includes the various instruments of the money market that we describe in detail below. Table 2.2 lists outstanding volume in 2000 of the major instruments of the money market.

FIGURE 2.1

Rates on money market securities

Source: From *The Wall Street Journal,* October 19, 2001. Reprinted by permission of Dow Jones & Company, Inc. via Copyright Clearance Center, Inc. © 2001 Dow Jones & Company, Inc. All Rights Reserved Worldwide.

MONEY RATES

Thursday, October 18, 2001

The key U. S. and foreign annual interest rates below are a guide to general levels but don't always represent actual transactions.

PRIME RATE: 5.50% (effective 10/03/01). The base rate on corporate loans posted by at least 75% of the nation's 30 largest banks.

DISCOUNT RATE: 2.00% (effective 10/02/01). The charge on loans to depository institutions by the Federal Reserve Banks.

FEDERAL FUNDS: 2 9/16% high, 2 7/16% low, 2 7/16% near closing bid, 2 1/2 % offered. Reserves traded among commercial banks for overnight use in amounts of $1 million or more. Source: Prebon Yamane(U.S.A) Inc. FOMC fed funds target rate 2.50% effective 10/02/01.

CALL MONEY: 4.25% (effective 10/03/01). The charge on loans to brokers on stock exchange collateral. Source: Reuters.

COMMERCIAL PAPER: Placed directly by General Electric Capital Corp.: 2.41% 30 to 33 days; 2.35% 34 to 41 days; 2.28% 42 to 59 days; 2.26% 60 to 77 days; 2.28% 78 to 98 days; 2.22% 99 to 179 days; 2.23% 180 to 270 days.

EURO COMMERCIAL PAPER: Placed directly by General Electric Capital Corp.: 3.73% 30 days; 3.63% two months; 3.59% three months; 3.53% four months; 3.48% five months; 3.44% six months.

DEALER COMMERCIAL PAPER: High-grade unsecured notes sold through dealers by major corporations: 2.40% 30 days; 2.30% 60 days; 2.27% 90 days.

CERTIFICATES OF DEPOSIT: Typical rates in the secondary market. 2.42% one month; 2.29% three months; 2.26% six months.

BANKERS ACCEPTANCES: 2.46% 30 days; 2.36% 60 days; 2.35% 90 days; 2.33% 120 days; 2.32% 150 days; 2.31% 180 days. Offered rates of negotiable, bank-backed business credit instruments typically financing an import order. Source: Reuters

LONDON LATE EURODOLLARS: 2.44% - 2.31% one month; 2.44% - 2.31% two months; 2.38% - 2.25% three months; 2.38% - 2.25% four months; 2.38% - 2.25% five months; 2.38% - 2.25% six months.

LONDON INTERBANK OFFERED RATES (LIBOR): 2.4625% one month; 2.3900% three months; 2.3525% six months;

2.53625% one year. British Banker's Association average of interbank offered rates for dollar deposits in the London market based on quotations at 16 major banks. Effective rate for contracts entered into two days from date appearing at top of this column.

EURO LIBOR: 3.77775% one month; 3.63038% three months; 3.48038% six months; 3.39550% one year. British Banker's Association average of interbank offered rates for euro deposits in the London market based on quotations at 16 major banks. Effective rate for contracts entered into two days from date appearing at top of this column.

EURO INTERBANK OFFERED RATES (EURIBOR): 3.782% one month; 3.633% three months; 3.483% six months; 3.399% one year. European Banking Federation-sponsored rate among 57 Euro zone banks.

FOREIGN PRIME RATES: Canada 5.25%; Germany 3.75%; Japan 1.375%; Switzerland 4.25%; Britain 4.50%. These rate indications aren't directly comparable; lending practices vary widely by location.

TREASURY BILLS: Results of the Monday, October 15, 2001, auction of short-term U.S. government bills, sold at a discount from face value in units of $1,000 to $1 million: 2.200% 13 weeks; 2.160% 26 weeks. Tuesday, October 16, 2001 auction: 2.280% 4 weeks.

OVERNIGHT REPURCHASE RATE: 2.54%. Dealer financing rate for overnight sale and repurchase of Treasury securities. Source: Reuters.

FREDDIE MAC: Posted yields on 30-year mortgage commitments. Delivery within 30 days 6.26%, 60 days 6.35%, standard conventional fixed-rate mortgages: 3.375%, 2% rate capped one-year adjustable rate mortgages. Source: Reuters.

FANNIE MAE: Posted yields on 30 year mortgage commitments (priced at par) for delivery within 30 days 6.37%, 60 days 6.48%, standard conventional fixed-rate mortgages; 4.25%, 6/2 rate capped one-year adjustable rate mortgages. Source: Reuters.

MERRILL LYNCH READY ASSETS TRUST: 2.82%. Annualized average rate of return after expenses for the past 30 days; not a forecast of future returns.

CONSUMER PRICE INDEX: August, 177.5, up 2.7% from a year ago (10/17 corrected to up 2.7%). Bureau of Labor Statistics.

Treasury Bills

U.S. **Treasury bills** (T-bills, or just bills, for short) are the most marketable of all money market instruments. T-bills represent the simplest form of borrowing. The government raises money by selling bills to the public. Investors buy the bills at a discount from the stated maturity value. At the bill's maturity, the holder receives from the government a payment equal to the face value of the bill. The difference between the purchase price and the ultimate maturity value represents the investor's earnings.

T-bills with initial maturities of 28, 91, and 182 days are issued weekly. Sales are conducted by an auction where investors can submit competitive or noncompetitive bids.

A competitive bid is an order for a given quantity of bills at a specific offered price. The order is filled only if the bid is high enough relative to other bids to be accepted. If the bid is high enough to be accepted, the bidder gets the order at the bid price. Thus, the bidder risks paying one of the highest prices for the same bill (bidding at the top), against the hope of bidding "at the tail," that is, making the cutoff at the lowest price.

A noncompetitive bid is an unconditional offer to purchase bills at the average price of the successful competitive bids. The Treasury ranks bids by offering price and accepts bids in order of descending price until the entire issue is absorbed by the competitive plus noncompetitive bids. Competitive bidders face two dangers: They may bid too high and overpay for the bills or bid too low and be shut out of the auction. Noncompetitive bidders, by contrast, pay the average price for the issue, and all noncompetitive bids are accepted up to a maximum of $1 million per bid.

Individuals can purchase T-bills directly at the auction or on the secondary market from a government securities dealer. T-bills are highly liquid; that is, they are easily converted to cash and sold at low transaction cost and with little price risk. Unlike most other money market instruments, which sell in minimum denominations of $100,000, T-bills sell in minimum denominations of only $10,000. While the income earned on T-bills is taxable at the Federal level, it is exempt from all state and local taxes, another characteristic distinguishing T-bills from other money market instruments.

> **Treasury bills**
>
> Short-term government securities issued at a discount from face value and returning the face amount at maturity.

Certificates of Deposit

A **certificate of deposit** (CD) is a time deposit with a bank. Time deposits may not be withdrawn on demand. The bank pays interest and principal to the depositor only at the end of the

> **certificate of deposit**
>
> A bank time deposit.

TABLE **2.2**		$ Billion
Components of the money market	Repurchase agreements	354.3
	Small-denomination time deposits*	1,037.8
	Large-denomination time deposits†	766.0
	Bankers' acceptances	7.8
	Eurodollars	196.1
	Treasury bills	682.1
	Commercial paper	1,539.0
	Savings deposits	1,852.6
	Money market mutual funds	1,657.1

*Small denominations are less than $100,000.

†Large denominations are greater than or equal to $100,000.

Source: *Economic Report of the President,* U.S. Government Printing Office, 2001; and *Flow of Funds Accounts: Flows and Outstandings,* Board of Governors of the Federal Reserve System, June 2000.

fixed term of the CD. CDs issued in denominations larger than $100,000 are usually negotiable, however; that is, they can be sold to another investor if the owner needs to cash in the certificate before its maturity date. Short-term CDs are highly marketable, although the market significantly thins out for maturities of three months or more. CDs are treated as bank deposits by the Federal Deposit Insurance Corporation, so they are insured for up to $100,000 in the event of a bank insolvency.

Commercial Paper

commercial paper

Short-term unsecured debt issued by large corporations.

The typical corporation is a net borrower of both long-term funds (for capital investments) and short-term funds (for working capital). Large, well-known companies often issue their own short-term unsecured debt notes directly to the public, rather than borrowing from banks. These notes are called **commercial paper** (CP). Sometimes, CP is backed by a bank line of credit, which gives the borrower access to cash that can be used if needed to pay off the paper at maturity.

CP maturities range up to 270 days; longer maturities require registration with the Securities and Exchange Commission and so are almost never issued. CP most commonly is issued with maturities of less than one or two months in denominations of multiples of $100,000. Therefore, small investors can invest in commercial paper only indirectly, through money market mutual funds.

CP is considered to be a fairly safe asset, given that a firm's condition presumably can be monitored and predicted over a term as short as one month. It is worth noting, though, that many firms issue commercial paper intending to roll it over at maturity, that is, issue new paper to obtain the funds necessary to retire the old paper. If lenders become complacent about monitoring a firm's prospects and grant rollovers willy-nilly, they can suffer big losses. When Penn Central defaulted in 1970, it had $82 million of commercial paper outstanding—the only major default on commercial paper in the past 40 years.

CP trades in secondary markets and so is quite liquid. Most issues are rated by at least one agency such as Standard & Poor's. The yield on CP depends on the time to maturity and the credit rating.

Bankers' Acceptances

bankers' acceptance

An order to a bank by a customer to pay a sum of money at a future date.

A **bankers' acceptance** starts as an order to a bank by a bank's customer to pay a sum of money at a future date, typically within six months. At this stage, it is like a postdated check. When the bank endorses the order for payment as "accepted," it assumes responsibility for ultimate payment to the holder of the acceptance. At this point, the acceptance may be traded in secondary markets much like any other claim on the bank. Bankers' acceptances are considered very safe assets, as they allow traders to substitute the bank's credit standing for their own. They are used widely in foreign trade where the creditworthiness of one trader is unknown to the trading partner. Acceptances sell at a discount from the face value of the payment order, just as T-bills sell at a discount from par value.

Eurodollars

Eurodollars

Dollar-denominated deposits at foreign banks or foreign branches of American banks.

Eurodollars are dollar-denominated deposits at foreign banks or foreign branches of American banks. By locating outside the United States, these banks escape regulation by the Federal Reserve Board. Despite the tag "Euro," these accounts need not be in European banks, although that is where the practice of accepting dollar-denominated deposits outside the United States began.

Most Eurodollar deposits are for large sums, and most are time deposits of less than six months' maturity. A variation on the Eurodollar time deposit is the Eurodollar certificate of deposit. A Eurodollar CD resembles a domestic bank CD except it is the liability of a non-U.S. branch of a bank, typically a London branch. The advantage of Eurodollar CDs over Eurodollar time deposits is that the holder can sell the asset to realize its cash value before maturity. Eurodollar CDs are considered less liquid and riskier than domestic CDs, however, and so offer higher yields. Firms also issue Eurodollar bonds, that is, dollar-denominated bonds outside the U.S., although such bonds are not a money market investment by virtue of their long maturities.

Repos and Reverses

Dealers in government securities use **repurchase agreements,** also called repos, or RPs, as a form of short-term, usually overnight, borrowing. The dealer sells securities to an investor on an overnight basis, with an agreement to buy back those securities the next day at a slightly higher price. The increase in the price is the overnight interest. The dealer thus takes out a one-day loan from the investor. The securities serve as collateral for the loan.

A *term repo* is essentially an identical transaction, except the term of the implicit loan can be 30 days or more. Repos are considered very safe in terms of credit risk because the loans are backed by the government securities. A *reverse repo* is the mirror image of a repo. Here, the dealer finds an investor holding government securities and buys them with an agreement to resell them at a specified higher price on a future date.

> **repurchase agreements (repos)**
>
> Short-term sales of government securities with an agreement to repurchase the securities at a higher price.

Brokers' Calls

Individuals who buy stocks on margin borrow part of the funds to pay for the stocks from their broker. The broker in turn may borrow the funds from a bank, agreeing to repay the bank immediately (on call) if the bank requests it. The rate paid on such loans is usually about one percentage point higher than the rate on short-term T-bills.

Federal Funds

Just as most of us maintain deposits at banks, banks maintain deposits of their own at the Federal Reserve Bank, or the Fed. Each member bank of the Federal Reserve System is required to maintain a minimum balance in a reserve account with the Fed. The required balance depends on the total deposits of the bank's customers. Funds in the bank's reserve account are called **Federal funds** or *Fed funds.* At any time, some banks have more funds than required at the Fed. Other banks, primarily big New York and other financial center banks, tend to have a shortage of Federal funds. In the Federal funds market, banks with excess funds lend to those with a shortage. These loans, which are usually overnight transactions, are arranged at a rate of interest called the Federal funds rate.

While the Fed funds rate is not directly relevant to investors, it is used as one of the barometers of the money market and so is widely watched by them.

> **Federal funds**
>
> Funds in the accounts of commercial banks at the Federal Reserve Bank.

The LIBOR Market

The **London Interbank Offer Rate (LIBOR)** is the rate at which large banks in London are willing to lend money among themselves. This rate has become the premier short-term interest rate quoted in the European money market and serves as a reference rate for a wide range of transactions. A corporation might borrow at a rate equal to LIBOR plus two percentage points, for example. Like the Fed funds rate, LIBOR is a statistic widely followed by investors.

> **LIBOR**
>
> Lending rate among banks in the London market.

Spread between three-month CD and T-bill rates

Yields on Money Market Instruments

Although most money market securities are of low risk, they are not risk-free. As we noted earlier, the commercial paper market was rocked by the Penn Central bankruptcy, which precipitated a default on $82 million of commercial paper. Money market investments became more sensitive to creditworthiness after this episode, and the yield spread between low- and high-quality paper widened.

The securities of the money market do promise yields greater than those on default-free T-bills, at least in part because of greater relative riskiness. Investors who require more liquidity also will accept lower yields on securities, such as T-bills, that can be more quickly and cheaply sold for cash. Figure 2.2 shows that bank CDs, for example, consistently have paid a risk premium over T-bills. Moreover, that risk premium increases with economic crises such as the energy price shocks associated with the Organization of Petroleum Exporting Countries (OPEC) disturbances, the failure of Penn Square Bank, the stock market crash in 1987, or the collapse of Long Term Capital Management in 1998.

2.2 | THE BOND MARKET

The bond market is composed of longer-term borrowing or debt instruments than those that trade in the money market. This market includes Treasury notes and bonds, corporate bonds, municipal bonds, mortgage securities, and federal agency debt.

These instruments are sometimes said to comprise the *fixed-income capital market,* because most of them promise either a fixed stream of income or stream of income that is determined according to a specified formula. In practice, these formulas can result in a flow of

TREASURY BONDS, NOTES & BILLS

Thursday, October 18, 2001

Representative Over-the-Counter quotation based on transactions of $1 million or more.

Treasury bond, note and bill quotes are as of mid-afternoon. Colons in bid-and-asked quotes represent 32nds; 101:01 means 101 1/32. Net changes in 32nds. n-Treasury note. i-Inflation-Indexed issue. Treasury bill quotes in hundredths, quoted on terms of a rate of discount. Days to maturity calculated from settlement date. All yields are to maturity and based on the asked quote. Latest 13-week and 26-week bills are boldfaced. For bonds callable prior to maturity, yields are computed to the earliest call date for issues quoted above par and to the maturity date for issues below par. *-When issued.
Source: Telerate/Cantor Fitzgerald

U.S. Treasury strips as of 3 p.m. Eastern time, also based on transactions of $1 million or more. Colons in bid-and-asked quotes represent 32nds; 99:01 means 99 1/32. Net changes in 32nds. Yields calculated on the asked quotation. ci-stripped coupon interest. bp-Treasury bond, stripped principal. np-Treasury note, stripped principal. For bonds callable prior to maturity, yields are computed to the earliest call date for issues quoted above par and to the maturity date for issues below par.
Source: Bear, Stearns & Co. via Street Software Technology Inc.

GOVT. BOND & NOTES

RATE	MATURITY MO/YR	BID	ASKED	CHG.	ASKED YLD.	RATE	MATURITY MO/YR	BID	ASKED	CHG.	ASKED YLD.
5⅞	Oct 01n	100:01	100:04	....	1.98	5⅝	May 08n	107:24	107:27	− 2	4.24
6¼	Oct 01n	100:01	100:04	....	2.35	8⅜	Aug 08	109:17	109:20	+ 1	n.a.
7½	Nov 01n	100:09	100:12	− 1	2.31	4¾	Nov 08n	102:17	102:20	− 1	4.31
15¾	Nov 01	101:00	101:00	− 1	1.97	8¾	Nov 08	111:14	111:17	+ 2	n.a.
5⅞	Nov 01n	100:10	100:13	− 1	2.27	3⅞	Jan 09i	105:13	105:16	+ 1	3.02
6⅛	Dec 01n	100:22	100:25	....	2.13	5½	May 09n	107:02	107:05	− 2	4.38
6¼	Jan 02n	101:01	101:04	....	2.21	9⅛	May 09	113:20	113:23	....	n.a.
6⅜	Jan 02n	101:03	101:06	+ 1	2.12	6	Aug 09n	110:06	110:09	− 3	4.43
14¼	Feb 02	103:25	103:28	− 1	2.13	10⅜	Nov 09	119:26	119:29	....	n.a.
6¼	Feb 02n	101:12	101:15	....	2.17	4¼	Jan 10i	108:05	108:08	+ 1	3.11
6½	Feb 02n	101:16	101:19	+ 1	2.08	6½	Feb 10n	113:26	113:29	....	4.48
6½	Mar 02n	101:27	101:30	+ 1	2.12	11¾	Feb 10	125:09	125:12	+ 1	n.a.
6⅜	Mar 02n	102:00	102:00	+ 1	2.11	10	May 10	120:23	120:26	+ 1	n.a.
6⅜	Apr 02n	102:04	102:07	....	2.16	5¾	Aug 10n	108:21	108:24	− 2	4.53
						12¾	Nov 10	133:16	133:19	+ 1	n.a.

FIGURE 2.3

Listing of Treasury issues

Source: From *The Wall Street Journal*, October 19, 2001. Reprinted by permission of Dow Jones & Company, Inc. via Copyright Clearance Center, Inc. © 2001 Dow Jones & Company, Inc. All Rights Reserved Worldwide.

income that is far from fixed. Therefore, the term "fixed income" is probably not fully appropriate. It is simpler and more straightforward to call these securities either debt instruments or bonds.

Treasury Notes and Bonds

The U.S. government borrows funds in large part by selling **Treasury notes** and **bonds.** T-note maturities range up to 10 years, while T-bonds are issued with maturities ranging from 10 to 30 years. The Treasury announced in late 2001 that it would no longer issue bonds with maturities beyond 10 years. Nevertheless, investors often refer to all of these securities collectively as Treasury or T-bonds. They are issued in denominations of $1,000 or more. Both bonds and notes make semiannual interest payments called *coupon payments,* so named because in precomputer days, investors would literally clip a coupon attached to the bond and present it to an agent of the issuing firm to receive the interest payment. Aside from their differing maturities at issuance, the only major distinction between T-notes and T-bonds is that T-bonds may be callable during a given period, usually the last five years of the bond's life. The call provision gives the Treasury the right to repurchase the bond at par value. While callable T-bonds still are outstanding, the Treasury no longer issues callable bonds.

Figure 2.3 is an excerpt from a listing of Treasury issues in *The Wall Street Journal.* The highlighted bond matures in August 2009. The coupon income or interest paid by the bond is 6% of par value, meaning that for a $1,000 face value bond, $60 in annual interest payments will be made in two semiannual installments of $30 each. The numbers to the right of the colon in the bid and ask prices represent units of 1/32 of a point.

Treasury notes or bonds

Debt obligations of the federal government with original maturities of one year or more.

The bid price of the highlighted bond is 110$\frac{6}{32}$, or 110.1875. The ask price is 110$\frac{9}{32}$, or 110.28125. Although bonds are sold in denominations of $1,000 par value, the prices are quoted as a percentage of par value. Thus, the ask price of 110.28125 should be interpreted as 110.28125% of par or $1,102.8125 for the $1,000 par value bond. Similarly, the bond could be sold to a dealer for $1,101.875. The −3 change means the closing price on this day fell $\frac{3}{32}$ (as a percentage of par value) from the previous day's closing price. Finally, the yield to maturity on the bond based on the ask price is 4.43%.

The yield to maturity reported in the last column is a measure of the annualized rate of return to an investor who buys the bond and holds it until maturity. It is calculated by determining the semiannual yield and then doubling it, rather than compounding it for two half-year periods. This use of a simple interest technique to annualize means that the yield is quoted on an annual percentage rate (APR) basis rather than as an effective annual yield. The APR method in this context is also called the bond equivalent yield. We discuss the yield to maturity in detail in Chapter 9.

Federal Agency Debt

Some government agencies issue their own securities to finance their activities. These agencies usually are formed for public policy reasons to channel credit to a particular sector of the economy that Congress believes is not receiving adequate credit through normal private sources. Figure 2.4 reproduces listings of some of these securities from *The Wall Street Journal.*

The major mortgage-related agencies are the Federal Home Loan Bank (FHLB), the Federal National Mortgage Association (FNMA, or Fannie Mae), the Government National Mortgage Association (GNMA, or Ginnie Mae), and the Federal Home Loan Mortgage Corporation (FHLMC, or Freddie Mac).

Freddie Mac, Fannie Mae, and Ginnie Mae were organized to provide liquidity to the mortgage market. Until establishment of the pass-through securities sponsored by these government agencies, the lack of a secondary market in mortgages hampered the flow of investment

---

FIGURE 2.4

Listing of government agency securities

Source: From *The Wall Street Journal,* October 19, 2001. Reprinted by permission of Dow Jones & Company, Inc. via Copyright Clearance Center, Inc. © 2001 Dow Jones & Company, Inc. All Rights Reserved Worldwide.

GOVERNMENT AGENCY & SIMILAR ISSUES

Thursday, October 18, 2001

Over-the-Counter mid-afternoon quotations based on large transactions, usually $1 million or more. Colons in-bid-and asked quotes represent 32nds; 101:01 means 101 1/32. All yields are calculated to maturity, and based on the asked quote. *-callable issue, maturity date shown. For issues callable prior to maturity, yields are computed to the earliest call date for issues quoted above par, or 100, and to the maturity date for issues below par.

Source: Bear, Stearns & Co. via Street Software Technology Inc.

Fannie Mae Issues

RATE	MAT.	BID	ASKED	YLD.	RATE	MAT.	BID	ASKED	YLD.
6.75	8-02	103:23	103:25	2.04	7.00	7-05	110:12	110:15	3.95
6.38	10-02	103:28	103:30	2.27	6.00	12-05	107:03	107:06	4.09
6.25	11-02	103:31	104:02	2.35	5.50	2-06	105:05	105:08	4.16
5.25	1-03	103:09	103:12	2.46	5.50	5-06	104:08	104:11	4.43
5.00	2-03	103:02	103:05	2.54	5.25	6-06	104:03	104:06	4.25
5.75	4-03	104:11	104:14	2.67	5.50	7-06*	102:24	102:27	3.80
4.63	5-03	102:25	102:28	2.72	5.25	8-06*	101:02	101:05	4.57
4.00	8-03	101:26	101:29	2.91	4.50	10-06*	100:00	100:03	4.48
4.75	11-03	103:09	103:12	3.05	7.13	3-07	112:27	112:30	4.40
5.13	2-04	104:04	104:07	3.22	6.63	10-07	110:27	110:30	4.52
4.75	3-04	103:10	103:13	3.26	5.75	2-08	105:24	105:28	4.66
5.63	5-04	105:13	105:16	3.36	6.00	5-08	106:30	107:02	4.73
6.50	8-04	107:30	108:01	3.48	5.25	1-09	102:01	102:05	4.89
3.50	9-04	99:25	99:28	3.55	6.50	4-09*	101:17	101:21	3.24
7.13	2-05	110:11	110:14	3.74	7.63	5-09*	103:29	104:01	4.71
5.75	6-05	105:29	106:00	3.97	6.38	6-09	108:24	108:28	4.97
					6.63	9-09	110:06	110:10	5.02
					7.25	1-10	114:12	114:16	5.07

RATE	MAT.	BID	ASKED	YLD.	RATE	MAT.	BID	ASKED	YLD.
7.13	6-10	113:20	113:24	5.13	5.63	3-11	102:28	103:00	5.22
6.63	11-10	110:10	110:14	5.17	5.88	3-11	102:23	102:27	5.49
6.25	2-11	105:14	105:18	5.47	6.75	3-31	110:03	110:07	6.01
5.50	3-11	101:30	102:02	5.22	**Federal Farm Credit Bank**				
6.00	5-11	105:21	105:25	5.22	6.75	9-02	103:28	103:30	2.11
6.25	7-11*	103:01	103:05	5.00	6.25	12-02	103:29	104:00	2.58
5.50	10-11*	99:08	99:12	5.58	**Federal Home Loan Bank**				
6.25	5-29	103:03	103:07	6.01	6.75	8-02	103:23	103:25	2.04
7.25	5-30	116:24	116:28	6.01	6.38	11-02	104:12	104:15	2.10
6.63	11-30	108:13	108:17	6.00	6.38	11-02	104:01	104:04	2.41

Freddie Mac

RATE	MAT.	BID	ASKED	YLD.	RATE	MAT.	BID	ASKED	YLD.
6.63	8-02	103:19	103:21	2.04	5.13	1-03	103:03	103:06	2.46
6.25	10-02	103:23	103:25	2.31	5.00	2-03	103:03	103:06	2.59
4.75	3-03	102:27	102:30	2.59	6.88	8-03	105:25	106:28	2.96
5.75	7-03	104:25	104:28	2.83	5.13	9-03	103:28	103:31	2.95
6.38	11-03	106:15	106:18	3.06	5.38	1-04	104:18	104:21	3.16
5.00	1-04	103:23	103:26	3.22	6.88	8-05	109:17	109:20	4.12
6.88	1-05	109:14	109:17	3.71	5.13	3-06	103:17	103:20	4.21
7.00	7-05	110:12	110:15	3.95	5.80	9-08	105:19	105:23	4.81
5.25	1-06	104:07	104:10	4.13	**GNMA Mtge. Issues**				
5.75	4-08	105:18	105:22	4.72	5.50	30Yr	98:12	98:14	5.83
5.13	10-08	101:19	101:23	4.83	6.00	30Yr	100:26	100:28	5.88
5.75	3-09	104:31	105:03	4.92	6.50	30Yr	102:17	102:19	6.02
6.45	4-09*	101:16	101:20	3.24	7.00	30Yr	104:00	104:02	5.93
7.63	9-09	103:30	104:02	6.94	7.50	30Yr	104:25	104:27	5.34
6.63	9-09	110:06	110:10	5.03	8.00	30Yr	105:14	105:16	5.32
7.00	3-10	112:23	112:27	5.10	8.50	30Yr	106:02	106:04	5.56
6.88	9-10	112:01	112:05	5.15	9.00	30Yr	106:01	106:03	6.25
					9.50	30Yr	106:06	106:08	6.74

funds into mortgages and made mortgage markets dependent on local, rather than national, credit availability. The pass-through financing initiated by these agencies represents one of the most important financial innovations of the 1980s.

Although the debt of federal agencies is not explicitly insured by the federal government, it is assumed the government will assist an agency nearing default. Thus, these securities are considered extremely safe assets, and their yield spread over Treasury securities is usually small.

1. Using Figures 2.3 and 2.4, compare the yield to maturity on one of the agency bonds with that of the T-bond with the nearest maturity date.

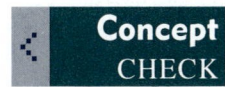

Concept
CHECK

International Bonds

Many firms borrow abroad and many investors buy bonds from foreign issuers. In addition to national capital markets, there is a thriving international capital market, largely centered in London, where banks of over 70 countries have offices.

A *Eurobond* is a bond denominated in a currency other than that of the country in which it is issued. For example, a dollar-denominated bond sold in Britain would be called a Euro-dollar bond. Similarly, investors might speak of Euroyen bonds, yen-denominated bonds sold outside Japan. Since the new European currency is called the euro, the term Eurobond may be confusing. It is best to think of them simply as international bonds.

In contrast to bonds that are issued in foreign currencies, many firms issue bonds in foreign countries but in the currency of the investor. For example, a Yankee bond is a dollar-denominated bond sold in the U.S. by a non-U.S. issuer. Similarly, Samurai bonds are yen-denominated bonds sold in Japan by non-Japanese issuers.

Municipal Bonds

Municipal bonds ("munis") are issued by state and local governments. They are similar to Treasury and corporate bonds, except their interest income is exempt from federal income taxation. The interest income also is exempt from state and local taxation in the issuing state. Capital gains taxes, however, must be paid on munis if the bonds mature or are sold for more than the investor's purchase price.

municipal bonds

Tax-exempt bonds issued by state and local governments.

There are basically two types of municipal bonds. These are *general obligation bonds,* which are backed by the "full faith and credit" (i.e., the taxing power) of the issuer, and *revenue bonds,* which are issued to finance particular projects and are backed either by the revenues from that project or by the municipal agency operating the project. Typical issuers of revenue bonds are airports, hospitals, and turnpike or port authorities. Revenue bonds are riskier in terms of default than general obligation bonds.

A particular type of revenue bond is the industrial development bond, which is issued to finance commercial enterprises, such as the construction of a factory that can be operated by a private firm. In effect, this device gives the firm access to the municipality's ability to borrow at tax-exempt rates.

Like Treasury bonds, municipal bonds vary widely in maturity. A good deal of the debt issued is in the form of short-term tax anticipation notes that raise funds to pay for expenses before actual collection of taxes. Other municipal debt may be long term and used to fund large capital investments. Maturities range up to 30 years.

The key feature of municipal bonds is their tax-exempt status. Because investors pay neither federal nor state taxes on the interest proceeds, they are willing to accept lower yields on these securities. This represents a huge savings to state and local governments. Correspondingly,

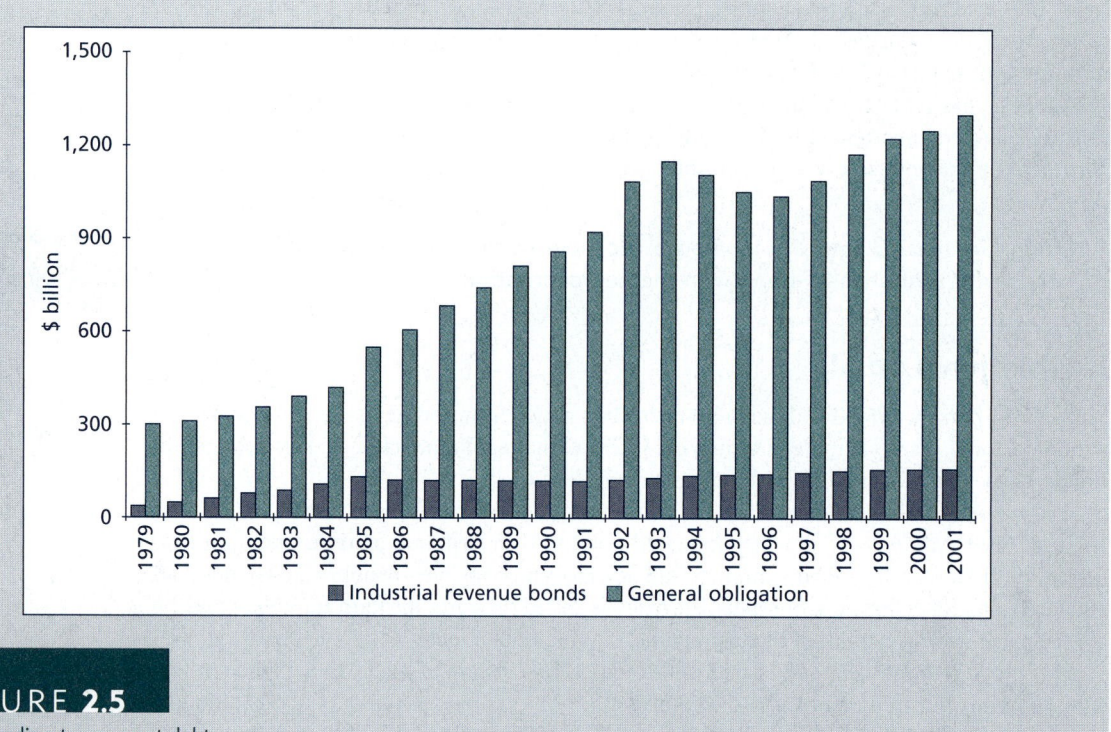

FIGURE **2.5**

Outstanding tax-exempt debt

Source: *Flow of Funds Accounts of the U.S.,* Board of Governors of the Federal Reserve System, 2001.

exempting interest earned on these bonds from taxes results in a huge drain of potential tax revenue from the federal government, which has shown some dismay over the explosive increase in the use of industrial development bonds.

Because of concern that these bonds were being used to take advantage of the tax-exempt feature of municipal bonds rather than as a source of funds for publicly desirable investments, the Tax Reform Act of 1986 restricted their use. A state is now allowed to issue mortgage revenue and private purpose tax-exempt bonds only up to a limit of $50 per capita or $150 million, whichever is larger. In fact, the outstanding amount of industrial revenue bonds stopped growing after 1986, as evidenced in Figure 2.5.

An investor choosing between taxable and tax-exempt bonds needs to compare after-tax returns on each bond. An exact comparison requires the computation of after-tax rates of return with explicit recognition of taxes on income and realized capital gains. In practice, there is a simpler rule of thumb. If we let t denote the investor's federal plus local marginal tax rate and r denote the total before-tax rate of return available on taxable bonds, then $r(1 - t)$ is the after-tax rate available on those securities. If this value exceeds the rate on municipal bonds, r_m, the investor does better holding the taxable bonds. Otherwise, the tax-exempt municipals provide higher after-tax returns.

One way of comparing bonds is to determine the interest rate on taxable bonds that would be necessary to provide an after-tax return equal to that of municipals. To derive this value, we set after-tax yields equal and solve for the *equivalent taxable yield* of the tax-exempt bond. This is the rate a taxable bond would need to offer in order to match the after-tax yield on the tax-free municipal.

TABLE **2.3**		Tax-Exempt Yield				
Equivalent taxable yields corresponding to various tax-exempt yields	**Marginal Tax Rate**	**2%**	**4%**	**6%**	**8%**	**10%**
	20%	2.5	5.0	7.5	10.0	12.5
	30	2.9	5.7	8.6	11.4	14.3
	40	3.3	6.7	10.0	13.3	16.7
	50	4.0	8.0	12.0	16.0	20.0

$$r(1 - t) = r_m \qquad \text{(2.1)}$$

or

$$r = \frac{r_m}{1 - t} \qquad \text{(2.2)}$$

Thus, the equivalent taxable yield is simply the tax-free rate divided by $1 - t$. Table 2.3 presents equivalent taxable yields for several municipal yields and tax rates.

This table frequently appears in the marketing literature for tax-exempt mutual bond funds because it demonstrates to high tax-bracket investors that municipal bonds offer highly attractive equivalent taxable yields. Each entry is calculated from Equation 2.2. If the equivalent taxable yield exceeds the actual yields offered on taxable bonds, after taxes the investor is better off holding municipal bonds. The equivalent taxable interest rate increases with the investor's tax bracket; the higher the bracket, the more valuable the tax-exempt feature of municipals. Thus, high-bracket individuals tend to hold municipals.

We also can use Equation 2.1 or 2.2 to find the tax bracket at which investors are indifferent between taxable and tax-exempt bonds. The cutoff tax bracket is given by solving Equation 2.1 for the tax bracket at which after-tax yields are equal. Doing so, we find

$$t = 1 - \frac{r_m}{r} \qquad \text{(2.3)}$$

Thus, the yield ratio r_m/r is a key determinant of the attractiveness of municipal bonds. The higher the yield ratio, the lower the cutoff tax bracket, and the more individuals will prefer to hold municipal debt. Figure 2.6 graphs the yield ratio since 1955.

In recent years, the ratio of tax-exempt to taxable yields has hovered around .75. What does this imply about the cutoff tax bracket above which tax-exempt bonds provide higher after-tax yields? Equation 2.3 shows that an investor whose tax bracket (federal plus local) exceeds $1 - .75 = .25$, or 25%, will derive a greater after-tax yield from municipals. Note, however, that it is difficult to control precisely for differences in the risks of these bonds, so the cutoff tax bracket must be taken as approximate.

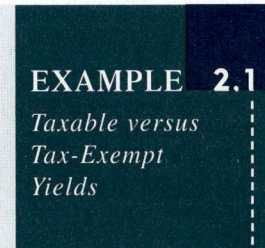

EXAMPLE 2.1
Taxable versus Tax-Exempt Yields

2. Suppose your tax bracket is 28%. Would you prefer to earn a 6% taxable return or a 4% tax-free yield? What is the equivalent taxable yield of the 4% tax-free yield?

Concept CHECK

Corporate Bonds

Corporate bonds are the means by which private firms borrow money directly from the public. These bonds are structured much like Treasury issues in that they typically pay semiannual

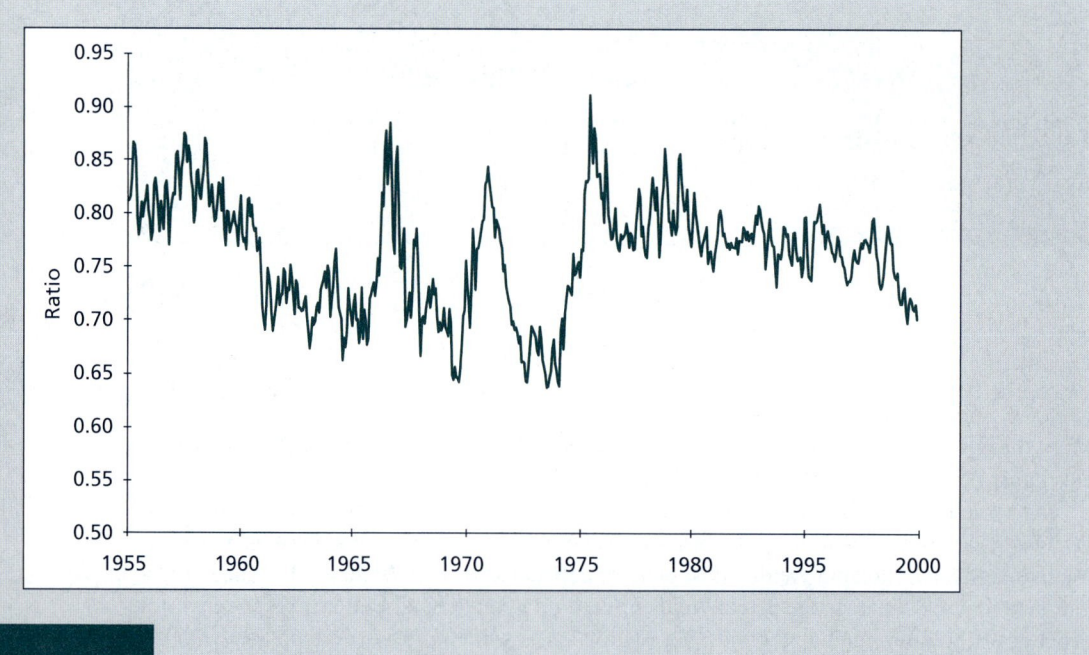

FIGURE **2.6**

Ratio of yields on tax-exempt to taxable bonds

corporate bonds

Long-term debt issued by private corporations typically paying semiannual coupons and returning the face value of the bond at maturity.

coupons over their lives and return the face value to the bondholder at maturity. Where they differ most importantly from Treasury bonds is in risk.

Default risk is a real consideration in the purchase of corporate bonds. We treat this issue in considerable detail in Chapter 9. For now, we distinguish only among secured bonds, which have specific collateral backing them in the event of firm bankruptcy; unsecured bonds, called *debentures*, which have no collateral; and subordinated debentures, which have a lower priority claim to the firm's assets in the event of bankruptcy.

Corporate bonds sometimes come with options attached. Callable bonds give the firm the option to repurchase the bond from the holder at a stipulated call price. Convertible bonds give the bondholder the option to convert each bond into a stipulated number of shares of stock. These options are treated in more detail in Part Three.

Figure 2.7 is a partial listing of corporate bond prices from *The Wall Street Journal.* The listings are similar to those for Treasury bonds. The highlighted AT&T bond has a coupon rate of 6½% and a maturity date of 2029. Only 37 AT&T bonds traded on this day. The closing price of the bond was 90½% of par, or $905, which was up ¼ of a point from the previous day's close. In contrast to Treasury bonds, price quotes on corporate bonds use explicit fractions.

The current yield on a bond is annual coupon income per dollar invested in the bond. For this bond, the current yield is calculated as

$$\text{Current yield} = \frac{\text{Annual coupon income}}{\text{Price}} = \frac{65}{905} = .072, \text{ or } 7.2\%$$

U.S. EXCHANGE BONDS

NEW YORK BONDS
Corporation Bonds

BONDS	CUR YLD.	VOL.	CLOSE	NET CHG.
AES Cp 4½05	cv	124	84½	+ ½
AES Cp 8s8	8.8	15	90⅝	...
AMR 9s16	9.4	5	95½	+ 2¼
ATT 6¾04	6.5	19	104½	...
ATT 5⅝04	5.5	15	102⅞	+ ½
ATT 7½06	7.0	25	107⅛	...
ATT 7¾407	7.2	45	107¼	− ¼
ATT 6s09	6.1	265	98¾	...
ATT 8½22	8.0	180	102	− ⅜
ATT 8⅛24	7.9	25	103¾	+ ⅛
ATT 8.35s25	8.0	80	104⅝	...
ATT 6⅛29	7.2	37	90½	− ¼
ATT 8⅝31	8.2	80	104⅞	+ ⅛
AmFnGp 7⅛09	7.9	30	90	− 7

BONDS	CUR YLD.	VOL.	CLOSE	NET CHG.
BPAmer 7⅞02	7.8	5	101¹¹⁄₃₂	− ⁵⁄₃₂
Coeur 13⅜03	cv	1	84	− 1
Consec 8⅛03	9.7	255	83¾	− ¼
Conseco 10½04	11.6	25	90½	...
Conseco 10¼02	11.1	120	91³¹⁄₃₂	− ¹⁷⁄₃₂
ConPort 10½04	13.9	2	75½	+ ⅜
CrownC 7⅛02	9.9	307	72	− 4
CrwnCk 7⅞26	16.8	60	44	− 2
DR Hrtn 10s06	9.7	30	103	+ ½
DVI 9⅞04	10.0	35	98½	+ ½
DevonE 4.9s08	cv	64	102	...
DevonE 4.95s08	cv	130	101	...
Dole 7⅞13	8.1	35	97½	+ ⅜
DukeEn 6¾25	6.8	12	99⅝	− ⅜
DukeEn 7½25	7.3	15	103	− 1⅝
DukeEn 7s33	6.9	50	101½	+ 1⅜

FIGURE 2.7

Listing of corporate bond prices

Source: From *The Wall Street Journal*, October 19, 2001. Reprinted by permission of Dow Jones & Company, Inc. via Copyright Clearance Center, Inc. © 2001 Dow Jones & Company, Inc. All Rights Reserved Worldwide.

Note that current yield ignores the difference between the price of a bond and its eventual value at maturity, and is a different measure than yield to maturity. The differences are explored in Part Three.

Mortgages and Mortgage-Backed Securities

Thirty years ago, your investments text probably would not have included a section on mortgage loans, for investors could not invest in these loans. Now, because of the explosion in mortgage-backed securities, almost anyone can invest in a portfolio of mortgage loans, and these securities have become a major component of the fixed-income market.

Until the 1970s, almost all home mortgages were written for a long term (15- to 30-year maturity), with a fixed interest rate over the life of the loan, and with equal, fixed monthly payments. These so-called conventional mortgages are still the most popular, but a diverse set of alternative mortgage designs have appeared.

Fixed-rate mortgages can create considerable difficulties for banks in years of increasing interest rates. Because banks commonly issue short-term liabilities (the deposits of their customers) and hold long-term assets, such as fixed-rate mortgages, they suffer losses when interest rates increase. The rates they pay on deposits increase, while their mortgage income remains fixed.

A response to this problem is the adjustable-rate mortgage. These mortgages require the borrower to pay an interest rate that varies with some measure of the current market interest rate. The interest rate, for example, might be set at two points above the current rate on one-year Treasury bills and might be adjusted once a year. Often, the maximum interest rate change within a year and over the life of the loan is limited. The adjustable-rate contract shifts the risk of fluctuations in interest rates from the bank to the borrower.

Because of the shifting of interest rate risk to their customers, lenders are willing to offer lower rates on adjustable-rate mortgages than on conventional fixed-rate mortgages. This has encouraged borrowers during periods of high interest rates, such as in the early 1980s. But as interest rates fall, conventional mortgages tend to regain popularity.

A *mortgage-backed security* is either an ownership claim in a pool of mortgages or an obligation that is secured by such a pool. These claims represent securitization of mortgage loans. Mortgage lenders originate loans and then sell packages of these loans in the secondary market. Specifically, they sell their claim to the cash inflows from the mortgages as those loans are paid off. The mortgage originator continues to service the loan, collecting principal and interest payments, and passes these payments along to the purchaser of the mortgage. For this reason, these mortgage-backed securities are called *pass-throughs.*

Mortgage-backed pass-through securities were introduced by the Government National Mortgage Association (GNMA, or Ginnie Mae) in 1970. GNMA pass-throughs carry a guarantee from the U.S. government that ensures timely payment of principal and interest, even if

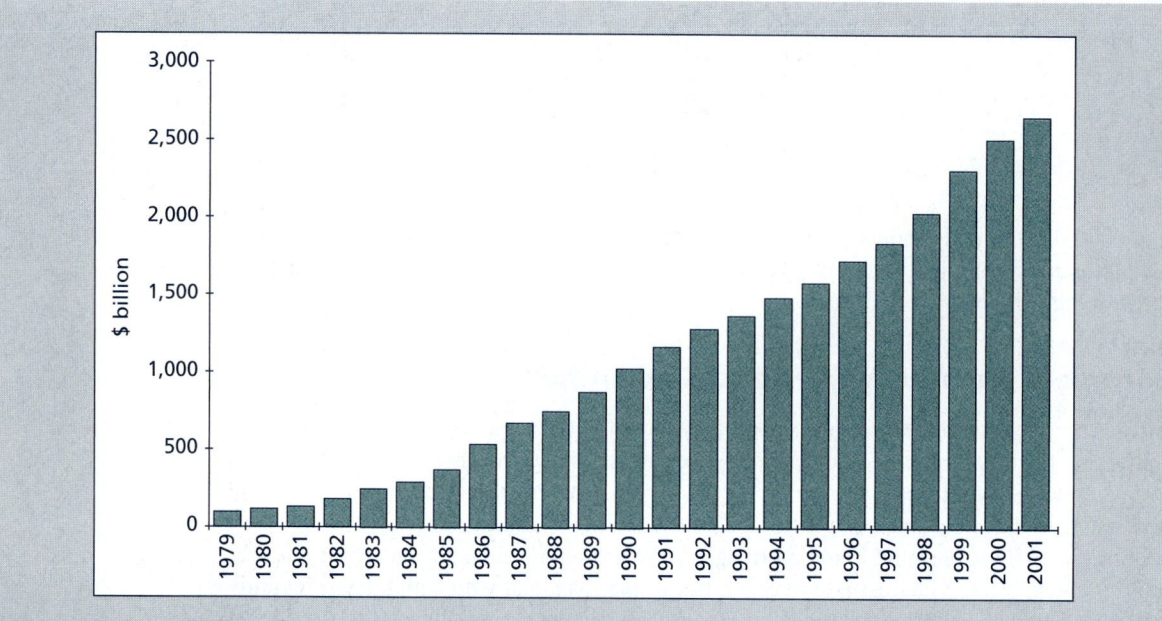

FIGURE **2.8**
Mortgage-backed securities outstanding

Source: *Flow of Funds Accounts of the U.S.,* Board of Governors of the Federal Reserve System, June 2001.

WEBMASTER

Subprime Mortgage Lending

Go to the Federal Reserve Bank of San Francisco's website, http://www.frbsf.org/ publications/economics/letter/2001/el2001-38.pdf, to access Elizabeth Laderman's article "Subprime Mortgage Lending and the Capital Markets."

After reading this article, answer the following questions:

1. What is subprime lending?

2. Describe the growth characteristics of this market. What role has securitization played in development of subprime lending?

the borrower defaults on the mortgage. This guarantee increases the marketability of the pass-through. Thus, investors can buy and sell GNMA securities like any other bond.

Other mortgage pass-throughs have since become popular. These are sponsored by FNMA (Fannie Mae) and FHLMC (Freddie Mac). By 2001, more than $2.5 trillion of outstanding mortgages were securitized into mortgage-backed securities, making the mortgage-backed securities market larger than the $2.4 trillion corporate bond market and nearly the size of the $3 trillion market in Treasury securities. Figure 2.8 illustrates the explosive growth of these securities since 1979.

The success of mortgage-backed pass-throughs has encouraged the introduction of pass-through securities backed by other assets. These "asset-backed" securities have grown rapidly, from a level of about $316 billion in 1995 to $1,202 billion in 2001.

2.3 EQUITY SECURITIES

Common Stock as Ownership Shares

Common stocks, also known as equity securities, or equities, represent ownership shares in a corporation. Each share of common stock entitles its owners to one vote on any matters of corporate governance put to a vote at the corporation's annual meeting and to a share in the financial benefits of ownership[1] (e.g., the right to any dividends that the corporation may choose to distribute).

> **common stocks**
>
> Ownership shares in a publicly held corporation. Shareholders have voting rights and may receive dividends.

A corporation is controlled by a board of directors elected by the shareholders.[2] The board, which meets only a few times each year, selects managers who run the corporation on a day-to-day basis. Managers have the authority to make most business decisions without the board's approval. The board's mandate is to oversee management to ensure that it acts in the best interests of shareholders.

The members of the board are elected at the annual meeting. Shareholders who do not attend the annual meeting can vote by proxy, empowering another party to vote in their name. Management usually solicits the proxies of shareholders and normally gets a vast majority of these proxy votes. Thus, management usually has considerable discretion to run the firm as it sees fit, without daily oversight from the equityholders who actually own the firm.

We noted in Chapter 1 that there are several mechanisms to alleviate the potential agency problems that might arise from this arrangement. Among these are compensation schemes that link the success of the manager to that of the firm; oversight by the board of directors as well as outsiders such as security analysts, creditors, or large institutional investors; the threat of a proxy contest in which unhappy shareholders attempt to replace the current management team; or the threat of a takeover by another firm.

The common stock of most large corporations can be bought or sold freely on one or more of the stock exchanges. A corporation whose stock is not publicly traded is said to be *closely held.* In most closely held corporations, the owners of the firm also take an active role in its management. Takeovers generally are not an issue.

---

[1]Sometimes a corporation issues two classes of common stock, one bearing the right to vote, the other not. Because of their restricted rights, the nonvoting stocks sell for a lower price, reflecting the value of control.

[2]The voting system specified in the corporate articles determines the chances of affecting the elections to specific directorship seats. In a majority voting system, each shareholder can cast one vote per share for each seat. A cumulative voting system allows shareholders to concentrate all their votes in one seat, enabling minority shareholders to gain representation.

Characteristics of Common Stock

The two most important characteristics of common stock as an investment are its residual claim and its limited liability features.

Residual claim means stockholders are the last in line of all those who have a claim on the assets and income of the corporation. In a liquidation of the firm's assets, the shareholders have claim to what is left after paying all other claimants, such as the tax authorities, employees, suppliers, bondholders, and other creditors. In a going concern, shareholders have claim to the part of operating income left after interest and income taxes have been paid. Management either can pay this residual as cash dividends to shareholders or reinvest it in the business to increase the value of the shares.

Limited liability means that the most shareholders can lose in event of the failure of the corporation is their original investment. Shareholders are not like owners of unincorporated businesses, whose creditors can lay claim to the personal assets of the owner—such as houses, cars, and furniture. In the event of the firm's bankruptcy, corporate stockholders at worst have worthless stock. They are not personally liable for the firm's obligations: Their liability is limited.

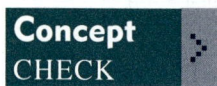

Concept
CHECK

3. *a.* If you buy 100 shares of IBM common stock, to what are you entitled?
   b. What is the most money you can make over the next year?
   c. If you pay $95 per share, what is the most money you could lose over the year?

Stock Market Listings

Figure 2.9 is a partial listing from *The Wall Street Journal* of stocks traded on the New York Stock Exchange. The NYSE is one of several markets in which investors may buy or sell shares of stock. We will examine issues of trading in these markets in the next chapter.

To interpret the information provided for each stock, consider the highlighted listing for General Electric. The first column is the percentage change in the stock price from the start of the year. GE shares have fallen 22.3% this year. The next two columns give the highest and lowest prices at which the stock has traded during the previous 52 weeks, $57.88 and $28.50, respectively. Until 1997, the minimum "tick size" on the New York Stock Exchange was $⅛, which meant that prices could be quoted only as dollars and eighths of dollars. In 1997, all U.S. exchanges began allowing price quotes in increments of $1⁄16. By 2001, U.S. markets

---

FIGURE 2.9

Listing of stocks traded on the New York Stock Exchange

Source: From *The Wall Street Journal*, October 19, 2001. Reprinted by permission of Dow Jones & Company, Inc. via Copyright Clearance Center, Inc. © 2001 Dow Jones & Company, Inc. All Rights Reserved Worldwide.

NEW YORK STOCK EXCHANGE COMPOSITE TRANSACTIONS

YTD %CHG	52 WEEKS HI	52 WEEKS LO	STOCK (SYM)	DIV	YLD %	PE	VOL 100S	LAST	NET CHG
+ 36.6	10.60	4.95	Gartner B ITB	...	...	...	2362	8.66	+ 0.21
− 70.0	57.28	4.24	Gateway GTW	...	...	dd	11758	5.39	− 0.16
− 3.0	29.15	18.49	GaylEnt GET	j	...	dd	441	20.25	− 0.70
+ 28.8	14.25	7.38	GenCorp GY	.12	1.0	17	483	12.40	− 0.24
− 45.7	92	37.99	Genentech DNA s	...	...	cc	20361	44.25	+ 0.01
+ 137.5	19.24	4.19	GenICbl BGC	.20	1.9	25	719	10.54	+ 0.36
+ 3.0	96	60.50	GenDynam GD	1.12	1.4	18	58144	80.36	− 3.39
− 22.3	57.88	28.50	GenElec GE	.64	1.7	27	151392	37.25	+ 0.10
+ 2.7	39.51	28.69♣	GenGrthProp GGP	2.60f	7.0	28	4952	37.18	− 0.33
− 42.7	18.04	8.50	GenMaritime GMR n	...	...	...	104	9.60	− 0.41
− 3.6	46.59	36.50	GenMills GIS	1.10	2.6	18	15922	42.98	− 0.02
− 34.3	33.50	11.50	GenMotor H GMH	e	...	...	52852	15.10	+ 0.75
− 17.5	67.80	39.17	GenMotor GM	2.00	4.8	22	27372	42.02	− 0.75
− 0.8	26	24.10	LehCBTCS 2001-8 n	.50p	...	...	10	24.90	− 0.05
+ 81.6	13.65	6.13	GenSemi SEM	...	...	24	814	11.35	− 0.34
− 28.6	35	15.53	Genesco GCO	...	...	12	5449	17.45	− 0.35
− 0.4	26.75	24.57	IBM CorTS n	.29p	...	...	30	25.11	− 0.01
+ 33.7	31.60	14.69	IntFlavor IFF	.60	2.2	32	2236	27.16	+ 0.24
+ 4.4	66.04	33.31♠	IntGameTch IGT	.12	.2	18	10759	50.10	− 0.61
− 14.6	23.31	15.89	IntMultfood IMC	.80	4.6	20	960	17.35	+ 0.65
− 11.2	43.31	26.31	IntPaper IP	1.00	2.8	dd	23439	36.26	− 0.06
− 9.3	46.74	28.25	IntlPwr ADS IPR	...	...	...	19	31.75	− 0.57
+ 2.0	69.50	24.05	IntRectifr IRF	...	...	24	6936	30.60	− 0.08
+ 13.6	10	5.94	IntShiphld ISH	.25	3.5	dd	14	7.10	+ 0.20
+ 20.5	11.25	5.19	IntSpcPdt ISP	...	...	...	175	8.06	+ 0.01
− 17.4	19.50	11.63♠	Interpool IPX	.20	1.4	9	15	14.10	− 0.18
− 51.4	47.44	18.25	Interpublic IPG	.38	1.8	cc	11769	20.70	− 0.57
+ 64.6	25.95	10.50	IntstBaker IBC	.28a	1.2	27	1251	23.14	+ 0.09
− 30.3	14.49	6.01	IntertanInc ITN	...	...	10	1852	8.10	− 0.06
+ 20.3	15.60	7	♠IntrtapPly g ITP	16g	...	...	149	8.80	+ 0.20
− 27.9	24.31	8.50	IntimtBrnd A IBI	.28	2.6	14	2813	10.81	− 0.19
− 27.5	20.01	12	Intrawest IDR	16g	1.1	10	48	14.45	+ 0.04

moved to decimal pricing, which means that stock prices can be quoted in terms of dollars and cents, as in Figure 2.9.

The .64 figure in the listing for GE means that the last quarter's dividend was $.16 a share, which is consistent with annual dividend payments of $.16 × 4 = $.64. This value corresponds to a dividend yield of 1.7%: Since GE stock is selling at 37.25 (the last recorded, or "close," price in the next-to-last column), the dividend yield is .64/37.25 = .017, or 1.7%.

The stock listings show that dividend yields vary widely among firms. High dividend-yield stocks are not necessarily better investments than low-yield stocks. Total return to an investor comes from both dividends and capital gains, or appreciation in the value of the stock. Low dividend-yield firms presumably offer greater prospects for capital gains, or else investors would not be willing to hold the low-yield firms in their portfolios.

The P/E ratio, or price-to-earnings ratio, is the ratio of the current stock price to last year's earnings. The P/E ratio tells us how much stock purchasers must pay per dollar of earnings the firm generates for each share. For GE, the ratio of price to earnings is 27. The P/E ratio also varies widely across firms. Where the dividend yield and P/E ratio are not reported in Figure 2.9, the firms have zero dividends, or zero or negative earnings. We shall have much to say about P/E ratios in Part Four.

The sales column ("Vol") shows that 151,392 hundred shares of GE were traded on this day. Shares commonly are traded in round lots of 100 shares each. Investors who wish to trade in smaller "odd lots" generally must pay higher commissions to their stockbrokers. The last, or closing, price of $37.25 was up $.10 from the closing price of the previous day.

Preferred Stock

Preferred stock has features similar to both equity and debt. Like a bond, it promises to pay to its holder a fixed stream of income each year. In this sense, preferred stock is similar to an infinite-maturity bond, that is, a perpetuity. It also resembles a bond in that it does not give the holder voting power regarding the firm's management.

preferred stock

Nonvoting shares in a corporation, usually paying a fixed stream of dividends.

Preferred stock is an equity investment, however. The firm retains discretion to make the dividend payments to the preferred stockholders: It has no contractual obligation to pay those dividends. Instead, preferred dividends are usually *cumulative;* that is, unpaid dividends cumulate and must be paid in full before any dividends may be paid to holders of common stock. In contrast, the firm does have a contractual obligation to make the interest payments on the debt. Failure to make these payments sets off corporate bankruptcy proceedings.

Preferred stock also differs from bonds in terms of its tax treatment for the firm. Because preferred stock payments are treated as dividends rather than as interest on debt, they are not tax-deductible expenses for the firm. This disadvantage is largely offset by the fact that corporations may exclude 70% of dividends received from domestic corporations in the computation of their taxable income. Preferred stocks, therefore, make desirable fixed-income investments for some corporations.

Even though preferred stock ranks after bonds in terms of the priority of its claim to the assets of the firm in the event of corporate bankruptcy, preferred stock often sells at lower yields than corporate bonds. Presumably this reflects the value of the dividend exclusion, for risk considerations alone indicate that preferred stock ought to offer higher yields than bonds. Individual investors, who cannot use the 70% exclusion, generally will find preferred stock yields unattractive relative to those on other available assets.

Corporations issue preferred stock in variations similar to those of corporate bonds. Preferred stock can be callable by the issuing firm, in which case it is said to be *redeemable.* It also can be convertible into common stock at some specified conversion ratio. A relatively recent innovation in the market is adjustable-rate preferred stock, which, like adjustable-rate mortgages, ties the dividend rate to current market interest rates.

2.4 STOCK AND BOND MARKET INDEXES

Stock Market Indexes

The daily performance of the Dow Jones Industrial Average is a staple portion of the evening news report. While the Dow is the best-known measure of the performance of the stock market, it is only one of several indicators. Other more broadly based indexes are computed and published daily. In addition, several indexes of bond market performance are widely available.

The ever-increasing role of international trade and investments has made indexes of foreign financial markets part of the general news. Thus, foreign stock exchange indexes such as the Nikkei Average of Tokyo and the *Financial Times* index of London have become household names.

Dow Jones Averages

The Dow Jones Industrial Average (DJIA) of 30 large, "blue-chip" corporations has been computed since 1896. Its long history probably accounts for its preeminence in the public mind. (The average covered only 20 stocks until 1928.)

Originally, the DJIA was calculated as the simple average of the stocks included in the index. So, if there were 30 stocks in the index, one would add up the value of the 30 stocks and divide by 30. The percentage change in the DJIA would then be the percentage change in the average price of the 30 shares.

This procedure means that the percentage change in the DJIA measures the return (excluding any dividends paid) on a portfolio that invests one share in each of the 30 stocks in the index. The value of such a portfolio (holding one share of each stock in the index) is the sum of the 30 prices. Because the percentage change in the *average* of the 30 prices is the same as the percentage change in the *sum* of the 30 prices, the index and the portfolio have the same percentage change each day.

price-weighted average

An average computed by adding the prices of the stocks and dividing by a "divisor."

The Dow measures the return (excluding dividends) on a portfolio that holds one share of each stock, so it is called a **price-weighted average.** The amount of money invested in each company represented in the portfolio is proportional to that company's share price.

2.2 EXAMPLE

Price-Weighted Average

Consider the data in Table 2.4 for a hypothetical two-stock version of the Dow Jones Average. Stock ABC sells initially at $25 a share, while XYZ sells for $100. Therefore, the initial value of the index would be (25 + 100)/2 = 62.5. The final share prices are $30 for stock ABC and $90 for XYZ, so the average falls by 2.5 to (30 + 90)/2 = 60. The 2.5 point drop in the index is a 4% decrease: 2.5/62.5 = .04. Similarly, a portfolio holding one share of each stock would have an initial value of $25 + $100 = $125 and a final value of $30 + $90 = $120, for an identical 4% decrease.

Notice that price-weighted averages give higher-priced shares more weight in determining the performance of the index. For example, although ABC increased by 20% while XYZ fell by only 10%, the index dropped in value. This is because the 20% increase in ABC represented a smaller price gain ($5 per share) than the 10% decrease in XYZ ($10 per share). The "Dow portfolio" has four times as much invested in XYZ as in ABC because XYZ's price is four times that of ABC. Therefore, XYZ dominates the average.

You might wonder why the DJIA is now (in mid-2002) at a level of about 8,500 if it is supposed to be the average price of the 30 stocks in the index. The DJIA no longer equals the average price of the 30 stocks because the averaging procedure is adjusted whenever a stock

TABLE **2.4** Data to construct stock price indexes	Stock	Initial Price	Final Price	Shares (millions)	Initial Value of Outstanding Stock ($ million)	Final Value of Outstanding Stock ($ million)
	ABC	$25	$30	20	$500	$600
	XYZ	100	90	1	100	90
	Total				$600	$690

TABLE **2.5** Data to construct stock price indexes after a stock split	Stock	Initial Price	Final Price	Shares (millions)	Initial Value of Outstanding Stock ($ million)	Final Value of Outstanding Stock ($ million)
	ABC	$25	$30	20	$500	$600
	XYZ	50	45	2	100	90
	Total				$600	$690

splits, pays a stock dividend of more than 10%, or when one company in the group of 30 industrial firms is replaced by another. When these events occur, the divisor used to compute the "average price" is adjusted so as to leave the index unaffected by the event.

For example, if XYZ were to split two for one and its share price to fall to $50, we would not want the average to fall, as that would incorrectly indicate a fall in the general level of market prices. Following a split, the divisor must be reduced to a value that leaves the average unaffected by the split. Table 2.5 illustrates this point. The initial share price of XYZ, which was $100 in Table 2.4, falls to $50 if the stock splits at the beginning of the period. Notice that the number of shares outstanding doubles, leaving the market value of the total shares unaffected. The divisor, d, which originally was 2.0 when the two-stock average was initiated, must be reset to a value that leaves the "average" unchanged. Because the sum of the postsplit stock prices is 75, while the presplit average price was 62.5, we calculate the new value of d by solving $75/d = 62.5$. The value of d, therefore, falls from its original value of 2.0 to $75/62.5$ = 1.20, and the initial value of the average is unaffected by the split: $75/1.20 = 62.5$.

At period-end, ABC will sell for $30, while XYZ will sell for $45, representing the same negative 10% return it was assumed to earn in Table 2.4. The new value of the price-weighted average is $(30 + 45)/1.20 = 62.5$. The index is unchanged, so the rate of return is zero, greater than the -4% return that would be calculated in the absence of a split. The relative weight of XYZ, which is the poorer-performing stock, is reduced by a split because its price is lower; so the performance of the average is higher. This example illustrates that the implicit weighting scheme of a price-weighted average is somewhat arbitrary, being determined by the prices rather than by the outstanding market values (price per share times number of shares) of the shares in the average.

Because the Dow Jones averages are based on small numbers of firms, care must be taken to ensure that they are representative of the broad market. As a result, the composition of the average is changed every so often to reflect changes in the economy. The last change took place on November 1, 1999, when Microsoft, Intel, Home Depot, and SBC Communications were added to the index, and Chevron, Goodyear Tire & Rubber, Sears, Roebuck, and Union Carbide were dropped. The nearby box presents the history of the firms in the index since 1928. The fate of many companies once considered "the bluest of the blue chips" is striking evidence of the changes in the U.S. economy in the last 75 years.

In the same way that the divisor is updated for stock splits, if one firm is dropped from the average and another firm with a different price is added, the divisor has to be updated to leave

Oct. 1, 1928	1929	1930s	1940s	1950s	1960s	1970s	1980s	1990s	Nov. 1, 1999
Wright Aeronautical	Curtiss-Wright ('29)	Hudson Motor ('30) Coca-Cola ('32) National Steel ('35)	Aluminum Co. of America ('59)						Alcoa* ('99)
Allied Chemical & Dye							Allied Signal* ('85)		Honeywell*
North American		Johns-Manville ('30)					Amer. Express ('82)		American Express
Victor Talking Machine	Natl Cash Register ('29)	IBM ('32) AT&T ('39)							AT&T
International Nickel						Inco Ltd.* ('76)	Boeing ('87)		Boeing
International Harvester							Navistar* ('86)	Caterpillar ('91)	Caterpillar
Westinghouse Electric								Travelers Group ('97)	Citigroup* ('98)
Texas Gulf Sulphur		Intl. Shoe ('32) United Aircraft ('33) National Distillers ('34)		Owens-Illinois ('59)			Coca-Cola ('87)		Coca-Cola
American Sugar		Borden ('30) DuPont ('35)							DuPont
American Tobacco (B)		Eastman Kodak ('30)							Eastman Kodak
Standard Oil (N.J.)						Exxon* ('72)			ExxonMobil*
General Electric									General Electric
General Motors									General Motors
Texas Corp.				Texaco* ('59)				Hewlett-Packard ('97)	Hewlett-Packard
Sears Roebuck									Home Depot†
Chrysler						IBM ('79)			IBM
Atlantic Refining		Goodyear ('30)							Intel†
Paramount Publix		Loew's ('32)		Intl. Paper ('56)					International Paper
Bethlehem Steel								Johnson & Johnson ('97)	Johnson & Johnson
General Railway Signal		Liggett & Myers ('30) Amer. Tobacco ('32)					McDonald's ('85)		McDonald's
Mack Trucks		Drug Inc. ('32) Corn Products ('33)		Swift & Co. ('59)		Esmark* ('73) Merck ('79)			Merck
Union Carbide									Microsoft†
American Smelting				Anaconda ('59)		Minn. Mining ('76)			Minn. Mining (3M)
American Can							Primerica* ('87)	J.P. Morgan ('91)	J.P. Morgan
Postum Inc.	General Foods* ('29)						Philip Morris ('85)		Philip Morris
Nash Motors		United Air Trans. ('30) Procter & Gamble ('32)							Procter & Gamble
Goodrich		Standard Oil (Calif) ('30)					Chevron* ('84)		SBC Communications
Radio Corp.		Nash Motors ('32) United Aircraft ('39)				United Tech.* ('75)			United Technologies
Woolworth								Wal-Mart Stores ('97)	Wal-Mart Stores
U.S. Steel							USX Corp.* ('86)	Walt Disney ('91)	Walt Disney

Note: Year of change shown in (); * denotes name change, in some cases following a takeover or merger. To track changes in the components, begin in the column for 1928 and work across. For instance, American Sugar was replaced by Borden in 1930, which in turn was replaced by Du Pont in 1935. Unlike past changes, each of the four new stocks being added doesn't specifically replace any of the departing stocks; it's simply a four-for-four switch. Home Depot has been grouped as replacing Sears because of their shared industry, but the other three incoming stocks are designated alphabetically next to a departing stock.

SOURCE: From **The Wall Street Journal**, October 27, 1999. Reprinted by permission of Dow Jones & Company, Inc. via Copyright Clearance Center, Inc. © 1999. Dow Jones & Company, Inc. All Rights Reserved Worldwide.

the average unchanged by the substitution. By now, the divisor for the Dow Jones Industrial Average has fallen to a value of about .145.

4. Suppose XYZ's final price in Table 2.4 increases in price to $110, while ABC falls to $20. Find the percentage change in the price-weighted average of these two stocks. Compare that to the percentage return of a portfolio that holds one share in each company.

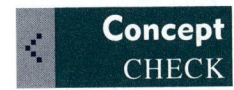

Concept
CHECK

Dow Jones & Company also computes a Transportation Average of 20 airline, trucking, and railroad stocks; a Public Utility Average of 15 electric and natural gas utilities; and a Composite Average combining the 65 firms of the three separate averages. Each is a price-weighted average and thus overweights the performance of high-priced stocks.

Standard & Poor's Indexes

The Standard & Poor's Composite 500 (S&P 500) stock index represents an improvement over the Dow Jones averages in two ways. First, it is a more broadly based index of 500 firms. Second, it is a **market value-weighted index.** In the case of the firms XYZ and ABC in Example 2.2, the S&P 500 would give ABC five times the weight given to XYZ because the market value of its outstanding equity is five times larger, $500 million versus $100 million.

The S&P 500 is computed by calculating the total market value of the 500 firms in the index and the total market value of those firms on the previous day of trading. The percentage increase in the total market value from one day to the next represents the increase in the index. The rate of return of the index equals the rate of return that would be earned by an investor holding a portfolio of all 500 firms in the index in proportion to their market value, except that the index does not reflect cash dividends paid by those firms.

market value-weighted index

Computed by calculating a weighted average of the returns of each security in the index, with weights proportional to outstanding market value.

To illustrate how value-weighted indexes are computed, look again at Table 2.4. The final value of all outstanding stock in our two-stock universe is $690 million. The initial value was $600 million. Therefore, if the initial level of a market value-weighted index of stocks ABC and XYZ were set equal to an arbitrarily chosen starting value such as 100, the index value at year-end would be 100 × (690/600) = 115. The increase in the index would reflect the 15% return earned on a portfolio consisting of those two stocks held in proportion to outstanding market values.

Unlike the price-weighted index, the value-weighted index gives more weight to ABC. Whereas the price-weighted index fell because it was dominated by higher-price XYZ, the value-weighted index rose because it gave more weight to ABC, the stock with the higher total market value.

Note also from Tables 2.4 and 2.5 that market value-weighted indexes are unaffected by stock splits. The total market value of the outstanding XYZ stock increases from $100 million to $110 million regardless of the stock split, thereby rendering the split irrelevant to the performance of the index.

EXAMPLE 2.3
Value-Weighted Indexes

A nice feature of both market value-weighted and price-weighted indexes is that they reflect the returns to straightforward portfolio strategies. If one were to buy each share in the index in proportion to its outstanding market value, the value-weighted index would perfectly track capital gains on the underlying portfolio. Similarly, a price-weighted index tracks the returns on a portfolio comprised of equal shares of each firm.

Investors today can purchase shares in mutual funds that hold shares in proportion to their representation in the S&P 500 as well as other stock indexes. These *index funds* yield a return equal to that of the particular index and so provide a low-cost passive investment strategy for equity investors.

Standard & Poor's also publishes a 400-stock Industrial Index, a 20-stock Transportation Index, a 40-stock Utility Index, and a 40-stock Financial Index.

> **Concept**
> CHECK

> 5. Reconsider companies XYZ and ABC from Concept Check Question 4. Calculate the percentage change in the market value-weighted index. Compare that to the rate of return of a portfolio that holds $500 of ABC stock for every $100 of XYZ stock (i.e., an index portfolio).

Other U.S. Market Value Indexes

The New York Stock Exchange publishes a market value-weighted composite index of all NYSE-listed stocks, in addition to subindexes for industrial, utility, transportation, and financial stocks. These indexes are even more broadly based than the S&P 500. The National Association of Securities Dealers publishes an index of 4,000 over-the-counter firms using the National Association of Securities Dealers Automatic Quotations (Nasdaq) service.

The ultimate U.S. equity index so far computed is the Wilshire 5000 Index of the market value of all NYSE and American Stock Exchange (Amex) stocks plus actively traded Nasdaq stocks. Despite its name, the index actually includes about 7,000 stocks. Figure 2.10 reproduces a listing of stock index performance that appears daily in *The Wall Street Journal*. Vanguard offers mutual funds to small investors, which enables them to match the performance of the Wilshire 5000 Index, the S&P 500, or the Russell 2000 index of small firms.

Equally Weighted Indexes

Market performance is sometimes measured by an equally weighted average of the returns of each stock in an index. Such an averaging technique, by placing equal weight on each return, corresponds to a portfolio strategy that places equal dollar values in each stock. This is in contrast to both price weighting, which requires equal numbers of shares of each stock, and market value weighting, which requires investments in proportion to outstanding value.

equally weighted index

An index computed from a simple average of returns.

Unlike price- or market value-weighted indexes, **equally weighted indexes** do not correspond to buy-and-hold portfolio strategies. Suppose you start with equal dollar investments in the two stocks of Table 2.4, ABC and XYZ. Because ABC increases in value by 20% over the year, while XYZ decreases by 10%, your portfolio is no longer equally weighted but is now more heavily invested in ABC. To reset the portfolio to equal weights, you would need to rebalance: Either sell some ABC stock and/or purchase more XYZ stock. Such rebalancing would be necessary to align the return on your portfolio with that on the equally weighted index.

Foreign and International Stock Market Indexes

Development in financial markets worldwide includes the construction of indexes for these markets. The most important are the Nikkei, FTSE (pronounced "footsie"), and DAX. The Nikkei 225 is a price-weighted average of the largest Tokyo Stock Exchange (TSE) stocks. The Nikkei 300 is a value-weighted index. FTSE is published by the *Financial Times* of London and is a value-weighted index of 100 of the largest London Stock Exchange corporations. The DAX index is the premier German stock index.

More recently, market value-weighted indexes of other non-U.S. stock markets have proliferated. A leader in this field has been MSCI (Morgan Stanley Capital International), which

STOCK MARKET DATA BANK   **10/18/01**

MAJOR INDEXES

†12-MO HIGH	LOW		DAILY HIGH	LOW	CLOSE	NET CHG	% CHG	†12-MO CHG	% CHG	FROM 12/31	% CHG
DOW JONES AVERAGES											
11337.92	8235.81	30 Industrials	9233.94	9134.30	x9163.22	− 69.75	− 0.76	− 979.76	− 9.66	−1623.63	− 15.05
3145.65	2033.86	20 Transportation	2229.04	2194.19	2204.70	− 23.80	− 1.07	− 255.11	− 10.37	− 741.90	− 25.18
416.11	293.91	15 Utilities	315.06	306.61	307.14	− 7.83	− 2.49	− 81.54	− 20.98	− 105.02	− 25.48
3392.23	2489.27	65 Composite	2698.37	2660.65	x2665.79	− 32.32	− 1.20	− 387.66	− 12.70	− 651.62	− 19.64
336.59	222.35	DJ US Total Mkt	248.06	245.05	245.97	− 1.92	− 0.77	− 78.83	− 24.27	− 60.91	− 19.85
STANDARD & POOR'S INDEXES											
1432.19	965.80	500 Index	1077.94	1064.54	1068.61	− 8.48	− 0.79	− 320.15	− 23.05	− 251.67	− 19.06
1706.71	1113.25	Industrials	1243.27	1228.88	1234.34	− 7.99	− 0.64	− 432.20	− 25.93	− 293.52	− 19.21
353.03	237.27	Utilities	266.10	257.60	257.89	− 8.21	− 3.09	− 63.76	− 19.82	− 92.72	− 26.45
547.06	404.34	400 MidCap	447.98	442.32	443.27	− 3.98	− 0.89	− 64.83	− 12.76	− 73.49	− 14.22
236.76	181.09	600 SmallCap	201.30	199.21	199.44	− 1.84	− 0.91	− 6.84	− 3.32	− 20.15	− 9.18
306.28	209.52	1500 Index	233.64	230.82	231.64	− 1.86	− 0.80	− 64.92	− 21.89	− 52.46	− 18.47
NASDAQ STOCK MARKET											
3483.14	1423.19	Composite	1668.00	1634.72	1652.72	+ 6.38	+ 0.39	−1765.88	− 51.66	− 817.80	− 33.10
3456.61	1126.95	Nasdaq 100	1344.43	1302.75	1330.33	+ 15.53	+ 1.18	−2072.62	− 60.91	−1011.37	− 43.19
1878.56	1027.69	Industrials	1177.99	1160.36	1166.36	− 9.98	− 0.85	− 660.49	− 36.15	− 316.63	− 21.35
2367.59	1846.50	Insurance	2270.88	2241.68	2245.30	− 26.77	− 1.18	+ 398.80	+ 21.60	+ 51.93	+ 2.37
2240.86	1658.03	Banks	1953.13	1939.94	1941.74	− 5.42	− 0.28	+ 264.05	+ 15.74	+ 2.29	+ 0.12
2079.62	653.13	Computer	811.35	785.80	804.16	+ 11.15	+ 1.41	−1233.75	− 60.54	− 490.81	− 37.90
656.22	192.87	Telecommunications	214.11	209.36	210.53	− 0.61	− 0.29	− 432.06	− 67.24	− 252.91	− 54.57
NEW YORK STOCK EXCHANGE											
666.57	504.21	Composite	557.92	550.81	552.23	− 5.69	− 1.02	− 86.43	− 13.53	− 104.64	− 15.93
826.70	620.11	Industrials	689.21	680.93	682.94	− 6.27	− 0.91	− 111.98	− 14.09	− 120.35	− 14.98
476.75	331.96	Utilities	346.50	338.80	339.63	− 6.75	− 1.95	− 108.23	− 24.17	− 100.91	− 22.91
494.71	332.91	Transportation	369.15	364.94	367.94	− 0.12	− 0.03	− 24.79	− 6.31	− 94.82	− 20.49
657.52	494.41	Finance	557.49	549.91	550.87	− 5.44	− 0.98	− 36.87	− 6.27	− 96.08	− 14.85
OTHERS											
958.75	780.46	Amex Composite	824.88	812.07	812.29	− 10.72	− 1.30	− 91.35	− 10.11	− 85.46	− 9.52
767.15	507.98	Russell 1000	566.18	559.23	561.36	− 4.44	− 0.78	− 179.37	− 24.22	− 138.73	− 19.82
517.23	378.90	Russell 2000	424.86	420.55	421.06	− 3.43	− 0.81	− 60.24	− 12.52	− 62.47	− 12.92
792.61	529.66	Russell 3000	590.50	583.43	585.53	− 4.64	− 0.79	− 179.25	− 23.44	− 140.22	− 19.32
422.43	294.60	Value-Line	328.56	324.41	325.01	− 3.55	− 1.08	− 68.88	− 17.49	− 68.46	− 17.40
13404.68	8900.45	Wilshire 5000	9921.97	9806.88	9841.65	− 74.69	− 0.75	−3101.15	− 23.96	−2334.23	− 19.17

†-Based on comparable trading day in preceding year.

FIGURE 2.10

Listing of stock index performance

Source: From *The Wall Street Journal*, October 19, 2001. Reprinted by permission of Dow Jones & Company, Inc. via Copyright Clearance Center, Inc. © 2001 Dow Jones & Company, Inc. All Rights Reserved Worldwide.

computes over 50 country indexes and several regional indexes. Table 2.6 presents many of the indexes computed by MCSI.

Bond Market Indicators

Just as stock market indexes provide guidance concerning the performance of the overall stock market, several bond market indicators measure the performance of various categories of bonds. The three most well-known groups of indexes are those of Merrill Lynch, Lehman Brothers, and Salomon Smith Barney.

Table 2.7, Panel A, lists the components of the bond market in mid-2001. Panel B presents a profile of the characteristics of the three major bond indexes.

The major problem with these indexes is that true rates of return on many bonds are difficult to compute because bonds trade infrequently, which makes it hard to get reliable, up-to-date prices. In practice, some prices must be estimated from bond valuation models. These so-called matrix prices may differ from true market values.

2.5 | DERIVATIVE MARKETS

A significant development in financial markets in recent years has been the growth of futures and options markets. Futures and options provide payoffs that depend on the values of other assets, such as commodity prices, bond and stock prices, or market index values. For this reason,

TABLE 2.6
Sample of MSCI stock indexes

Regional Indexes		Countries	
Developed Markets	**Emerging Markets**	**Developed Markets**	**Emerging Markets**
EAFE (Europe, Australia, Far East)	Emerging Markets (EM)	Australia	Argentina
EASEA (EAFE ex Japan)	EM Asia	Austria	Brazil
Europe	EM Far East	Belgium	Chile
EMU	EM Latin America	Canada	China
Far East	Emerging Markets Free (EMF)	Denmark	Colombia
Kokusai (World ex Japan)	EMF Asia	Finland	Czech Republic
Nordic Countries	EMF Eastern Europe	France	Egypt
North America	EMF Europe	Germany	Greece
Pacific	EMF Europe & Middle East	Hong Kong	Hungary
The World Index	EMF Far East	Ireland	India
	EMF Latin America	Italy	Indonesia
		Japan	Israel
		Netherlands	Jordan
		New Zealand	Korea
		Norway	Malaysia
		Portugal	Mexico
		Singapore	Morocco
		Spain	Pakistan
		Sweden	Peru
		Switzerland	Philippines
		UK	Poland
		US	Russia
			South Africa
			Sri Lanka
			Taiwan
			Thailand
			Turkey
			Venezuela

Source: www.msci.com.

derivative asset or contingent claim

A security with a payoff that depends on the prices of other securities.

call option

The right to buy an asset at a specified price on or before a specified expiration date.

these instruments sometimes are called **derivative assets** or **contingent claims.** Their values derive from or are contingent on the values of other assets. We discuss derivative assets in detail in Part Five, but the nearby box serves as a brief primer.

Options

A **call option** gives its holder the right to purchase an asset for a specified price, called the *exercise* or *strike price,* on or before some specified expiration date. An October call option on IBM stock with exercise price $100, for example, entitles its owner to purchase IBM stock for a price of $100 at any time up to and including the option's expiration date in October. Each option contract is for the purchase of 100 shares, with quotations made on a per share basis. The holder of the call need not exercise the option; it will make sense to exercise only if the market value of the asset that may be purchased exceeds the exercise price.

TABLE 2.7
The U.S. bond market and its indexes

A. The Bond Market		
Sector	**Size ($ billions)**	**Percentage of Market**
Treasury	$ 3,048.4	23.6%
Gov't sponsored enterprise	1,957.6	15.2
Corporate	2,441.3	18.9
Tax-exempt*	1,629.3	12.6
Mortgage-backed	2,635.8	20.4
Asset-backed	1,201.8	9.3
Total	$12,914.2	100.0%

*Includes private purpose tax-exempt debt.

B. Profile of Bond Indexes			
	Lehman Brothers	**Merrill Lynch**	**Salomon Smith Barney**
Number of issues	Over 6,500	Over 5,000	Over 5,000
Maturity of included bonds	≥ 1 year	≥ 1 year	≥ 1 year
Excluded issues	Junk bonds Convertibles Floating rate	Junk bonds Convertibles	Junk bonds Convertibles Floating-rate bonds
Weighting	Market value	Market value	Market value
Reinvestment of intramonth cash flows	No	Yes (in specific bond)	Yes (at one-month T-bill rate)
Daily availability	Yes	Yes	Yes

Sources: Panel A: *Flow of Funds Accounts, Flows and Outstandings,* Board of Governors of the Federal Reserve System, June 2001 and The Bond Market Association. Panel B: Frank K. Reilly, G. Wenchi Kao, and David J. Wright, "Alternative Bond Market Indexes," *Financial Analysts Journal* (May–June 1992), pp. 44–58.

When the market price exceeds the exercise price, the option holder may "call away" the asset for the exercise price and reap a benefit equal to the difference between the stock price and the exercise price. Otherwise, the option will be left unexercised. If not exercised before the expiration date, the option expires and no longer has value. Calls, therefore, provide greater profits when stock prices increase and so represent bullish investment vehicles.

A **put option** gives its holder the right to sell an asset for a specified exercise price on or before a specified expiration date. An October put on IBM with exercise price $100 entitles its owner to sell IBM stock to the put writer at a price of $100 at any time before expiration in October even if the market price of IBM is lower than $100. While profits on call options increase when the asset increases in value, profits on put options increase when the asset value falls. The put is exercised only if its holder can deliver an asset worth less than the exercise price in return for the exercise price.

Figure 2.11 presents stock option quotations from *The Wall Street Journal.* The highlighted options are for IBM. The repeated number below the name of the firm is the current price of IBM shares, $101.26. The two columns to the right of the firm name give the exercise price and expiration month of each option. Thus, we see listings for call and put options on IBM with exercise prices ranging from $90 to $110, and with expiration dates in October, November, and January.

put option

The right to sell an asset at a specified exercise price on or before a specified expiration date.

Understanding the World of Derivatives

What are derivatives anyway, and why are people saying such terrible things about them?

Some critics see the derivatives market as a multi-trillion-dollar house of cards composed of interlocking, highly leveraged transactions. They fear that the default of a single large player could stun the world financial system.

But others, including Federal Reserve Chairman Alan Greenspan, say the risk of such a meltdown is negligible. Proponents stress that the market's hazards are more than outweighed by the benefits derivatives provide in helping banks, corporations, and investors manage their risks.

Because the science of derivatives is relatively new, there's no easy way to gauge the ultimate impact these instruments will have. There are now more than 1,200 different kinds of derivatives on the market, most of which require a computer program to figure out. Surveying this complex subject, dozens of derivatives experts offered these insights:

Q: What is the broadest definition of derivatives?

A: Derivatives are financial arrangements between two parties whose payments are based on, or "derived" from, the performance of some agreed-upon benchmark. Derivatives can be issued based on currencies, commodities, government or corporate debt, home mortgages, stocks, interest rates, or any combination of these.

Company stock options, for instance, allow employees and executives to profit from changes in a company's stock price without actually owning shares. Without knowing it, homeowners frequently use a type of privately traded "forward" contract when they apply for a mortgage and lock in a borrowing rate for their house closing, typically for as many as 60 days in the future.

Q: What are the most common forms of derivatives?

A: Derivatives come in two basic categories—option-type contracts and forward-type contracts. These may be exchange-listed, such as futures and stock options, or they may be privately traded.

Options give buyers the right, but not the obligation, to buy or sell an asset at a preset price over a specific period. The option's price is usually a small percentage of the underlying asset's value.

Forward-type contracts, which include forwards, futures, and swaps, commit the buyer and the seller to trade a given asset at a set price on a future date. These are "price-fixing" agreements that saddle the buyer with the same price risks as actually owning the asset. But normally, no money changes hands until the delivery date, when the contract is often settled in cash rather than by exchanging the asset.

Q: In business, what are they used for?

A: While derivatives can be powerful speculative instruments, businesses most often use them to hedge. For instance, companies often use forwards and exchange-listed futures to protect against fluctuations in currency or commodity prices, thereby helping to manage import and raw-materials costs. Options can serve a similar purpose; interest-rate options such as caps and floors help companies control financing costs in much the same way that caps on adjustable-rate mortgages do for homeowners.

Q: Why are derivatives potentially dangerous?

A: Because these contracts expose the two parties to market moves with little or no money actually changing hands, they involve leverage. And that leverage may be vastly increased by the terms of a particular contract. In the derivatives that hurt P&G, for instance, a given move in U.S. or German interest rates was multiplied 10 times or more.

When things go well, that leverage provides a big return, compared with the amount of capital at risk. But it also causes equally big losses when markets move the wrong way. Even companies that use derivatives to hedge, rather than speculate, may be at risk, since their operation would rarely produce perfectly offsetting gains.

Q: If they are so dangerous, why are so many businesses using derivatives?

A: They are among the cheapest and most readily available means at companies' disposal to buffer themselves against shocks in currency values, commodity prices, and interest rates. Donald Nicoliasen, a Price Waterhouse expert on derivatives, says derivatives "are a new tool in everybody's bag to better manage business returns and risks."

SOURCE: Lee Berton, "Understanding the Complex World of Derivatives," *The Wall Street Journal*, June 14, 1994. Excerpted by permission of Dow Jones & Company, Inc. via Copyright Clearance Center, Inc. © 1994 Dow Jones & Company, Inc. All Rights Reserved Worldwide.

LISTED OPTIONS QUOTATIONS

OPTION/STRIKE	EXP.	-CALL- VOL.	LAST	-PUT- VOL.	LAST	OPTION/STRIKE	EXP.	-CALL- VOL.	LAST	-PUT- VOL.	LAST
I B M 90	Nov	14	12^{20}	2296	1^{10}	18^{78} 20	Jan	1738	1^{95}	34	3^{20}
10126 90	Jan	7	14^{90}	2106	3^{30}	NortelNwk 5	Mar	8	1^{65}	3776	0^{75}
10126 95	Oct	2327	6^{50}	20347	0^{15}	5^{92} 750	Nov	1694	0^{20}	90	1^{75}
10126 95	Nov	1887	8^{40}	1031	2^{20}	Nthrop 100	Oct	2003	3^{10}	35	0^{25}
10126 100	Oct	16292	1^{80}	47726	0^{80}	104 100	Nov	2000	5^{90}	30	3
10126 100	Nov	1165	5^{20}	4832	4^{10}	Novartis 40	Apr	1000	3	2000	3^{10}
10126 100	Jan	542	8^{50}	2306	6^{50}	OpenwvSys 750	Jan	...	...	1565	1^{60}
10126 105	Oct	14610	0^{20}	14350	4	767 10	Jan	1523	1^{15}	3	3^{10}
10126 105	Nov	1240	2^{60}	1709	6^{30}	Oracle 1250	Oct	1583	1^{85}	240	0^{05}
10126 110	Oct	3204	0^{05}	·56	8^{30}	14^{26} 1250	Nov	372	2^{35}	5368	0^{50}
10126 110	Nov	2408	1^{15}	53	9^{90}	14^{26} 15	Oct	1852	0^{05}	532	0^{75}
10126 110	Jan	6912	3^{70}	109	12	14^{26} 1750	Mar	1819	3	40	4^{30}
10126 110	Apr	6818	6^{80}	28	14^{50}	PMC Srra 1750	Oct	3797	0^{65}	569	1^{80}

FIGURE 2.11

Listing of stock option quotations

The next four columns provide the trading volume and closing prices of each option. For example, 16,292 contracts traded on the October expiration call with an exercise price of $100. The last trade was at $1.80, meaning that an option to purchase one share of IBM at an exercise price of $100 sold for $1.80. Each option *contract* (on 100 shares of stock), therefore, costs $1.80 × 100 = $180.

Notice that the prices of call options decrease as the exercise price increases. For example, the October 2001 maturity call with exercise price $105 costs only $.20. This makes sense, as the right to purchase a share at a higher exercise price is less valuable. Conversely, put prices increase with the exercise price. The right to sell a share of IBM in October at a price of $100 costs $0.80 while the right to sell at $105 costs $4.

Option prices also increase with time until expiration. Clearly, one would rather have the right to buy IBM for $100 at any time until November than at any time until October. Not surprisingly, this shows up in a higher price for the November expiration options. For example, the call with exercise price $100 expiring in November sells for $5.20, compared to only $1.80 for the October call.

6. **What would be the profit or loss per share of stock to an investor who bought the October maturity IBM call option with exercise price $100, if the stock price at the expiration of the option is $104? What about a purchaser of the put option with the same exercise price and maturity?**

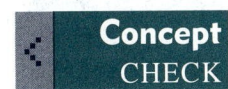

Concept
CHECK

Futures Contracts

A **futures contract** calls for delivery of an asset (or in some cases, its cash value) at a specified delivery or maturity date, for an agreed-upon price, called the *futures price,* to be paid at contract maturity. The long position is held by the trader who commits to purchasing the commodity on the delivery date. The trader who takes the short position commits to delivering the commodity at contract maturity.

Figure 2.12 illustrates the listing of several futures contracts for trading on October 26, 2001, as they appeared in *The Wall Street Journal.* The top line in boldface type gives the contract name, the exchange on which the futures contract is traded (in parentheses), and the contract size. Thus, the first contract listed is for corn traded on the Chicago Board of Trade (CBT). Each contract calls for delivery of 5,000 bushels of corn.

futures contract

Obliges traders to purchase or sell an asset at an agreed-upon price at a specified future date.

FIGURE **2.12**

Listing of commodity futures contracts

Source: From *The Wall Street Journal*, October 29, 2001. Reprinted by permission of Dow Jones & Company, Inc. via Copyright Clearance Center, Inc. © 2001 Dow Jones & Company, Inc. All Rights Reserved Worldwide.

FUTURES PRICES

Friday, October 26, 2001
Open Interest Reflects Previous Trading Day.

GRAINS AND OILSEEDS

Corn (CBT) 5,000 bu.; cents per bu.

	OPEN	HIGH	LOW	SETTLE	CHANGE	LIFETIME HIGH	LIFETIME LOW	OPEN INT.
Nov	201¾	201¾	200¼	200¾	− 1¼	242½	198¾	2,209
Dec	206½	206¾	204¾	205½	− 1	275	202¼	211,394
Ja02	211¼	211¼	209½	209¾	− 1¼	243	208¼	687
Mar	219	219¼	217½	218	− 1	270	205	115,318
May	226¾	227	225¼	225¾	− 1	266½	221	38,955
July	232¾	232¾	231¼	231¾	− 1	279½	210	35,977
Sept	238¼	238¼	237¼	237½	− ¼	262	233	4,917
Dec	246¼	247½	246	246¼	− ½	272	239¾	20,722
Dc03	259¾	259¾	259½	259¾	− ¼	269	253½	1,134

Est vol 42,000; vol Thu 38,372; open int 431,670, +2,440.

METALS AND PETROLEUM

Copper-High (Cmx.Div.NYM)-25,000 lbs.; cents per lb.

	OPEN	HIGH	LOW	SETTLE	CHANGE	LIFETIME HIGH	LIFETIME LOW	OPEN INT.
Oct	63.30	63.30	62.30	63.05	+ 0.95	92.40	61.80	925
Nov	63.25	63.55	63.10	63.20	+ 0.90	91.75	62.00	3,548
Dec	62.60	63.90	62.45	63.50	+ 0.90	92.00	62.00	52,147
Ja02	63.95	63.95	63.80	63.80	+ 0.90	90.80	62.55	2,487
Mar	64.25	64.70	64.25	64.30	+ 0.90	91.00	63.00	11,251
Apr	64.65	64.65	64.55	64.55	+ 0.90	89.70	63.80	1,094
May	65.20	65.20	64.85	64.85	+ 0.90	89.60	63.50	4,320
June	65.20	65.20	65.15	65.15	+ 0.90	89.50	64.00	1,075
July	65.85	65.85	65.40	65.40	+ 0.90	88.90	64.00	2,899
Sept	66.15	66.30	65.90	65.90	+ 0.90	88.00	64.70	2,893
Dec	66.70	66.70	66.40	66.40	+ 0.90	83.00	65.10	4,948
Mr03	67.50	67.50	67.00	67.00	+ 0.90	80.40	65.80	215

Est vol 8,000; vol Thu 6,760; open int 92,567, +194.

Gold (Cmx.Div.NYM)-100 troy oz.; $ per troy oz.

	OPEN	HIGH	LOW	SETTLE	CHANGE	LIFETIME HIGH	LIFETIME LOW	OPEN INT.
Oct	....	....	....	277.90	+ 0.10	300.00	260.00	12
Dec	277.70	279.00	277.50	278.30	+ 0.10	429.50	260.00	77,991
Fb02	278.60	279.50	278.00	278.80	+ 0.10	297.50	262.90	12,680
Apr	280.00	280.00	278.90	279.30	+ 0.10	297.50	267.50	3,762
Dec	281.50	281.50	280.50	281.10	+ 0.10	358.00	268.10	3,926
Dc03	286.00	286.10	286.00	286.10	- 0.10	359.30	280.00	1,398

Est vol 13,000; vol Thu 20,658; open int 116,280, −1,463.

Platinum (NYM)-50 troy oz.; $ per troy oz.

	OPEN	HIGH	LOW	SETTLE	CHANGE	LIFETIME HIGH	LIFETIME LOW	OPEN INT.
Oct	....	....	....	430.40	− 0.50	627.00	406.00	2
Ja02	413.00	423.50	412.00	423.40	+ 9.50	605.00	401.00	5,617

Est vol 491; vol Thu 292; open int 5,735, +12.

Silver (Cmx.Div.NYM)-5,000 troy oz.; cnts per troy oz.

	OPEN	HIGH	LOW	SETTLE	CHANGE	LIFETIME HIGH	LIFETIME LOW	OPEN INT.
Oct	....	....	....	420.3	− 0.5	467.0	412.0	3
Dec	422.5	424.0	421.0	421.5	− 0.5	680.0	415.0	35,083
Mr02	424.0	426.5	424.0	424.1	− 0.6	508.0	421.0	19,652
July	428.0	428.5	427.0	427.0	− 0.7	559.0	425.0	1,939
Dec	433.0	433.0	429.0	430.0	− 1.0	613.0	429.0	4,341

Est vol 8,500; vol Thu 8,276; open int 65,282, +826.

Crude Oil, Light Sweet (NYM) 1,000 bbls.; $ per bbl.

	OPEN	HIGH	LOW	SETTLE	CHANGE	LIFETIME HIGH	LIFETIME LOW	OPEN INT.
Dec	21.98	22.25	21.83	22.03	+ 0.02	30.50	14.70	146,897
Ja02	22.11	22.45	22.05	22.20	+ 0.01	29.40	18.90	47,604
Feb	22.42	22.47	22.25	22.31	+ 0.02	29.00	19.94	22,608

INTEREST RATE

Treasury Bonds (CBT)-$100,000; pts 32nds of 100%

	OPEN	HIGH	LOW	SETTLE	CHANGE	LIFETIME HIGH	LIFETIME LOW	OPEN INT.
Dec	107-13	107-25	107-00	107-22	+ 4	107-26	97-25	543,948
Mr02	106-12	106-23	105-31	106-21	+ 4	106-25	101-19	32,859

Est vol 186,000; vol Thu 260,065; open int 577,366, −680.

Treasury Notes (CBT)-$100,000; pts 32nds of 100%

	OPEN	HIGH	LOW	SETTLE	CHANGE	LIFETIME HIGH	LIFETIME LOW	OPEN INT.
Dec	09-175	109-26	09-115	09-235	+ 3.0	09-275	100-26	581,495
Mr02	108-17	08-225	08-095	08-205	+ 3	08-235	101-23	26,167

Est vol 143,000; vol Thu 227,784; open int 607,663, +2,028.

10 Yr Agency Notes (CBT)-$100,000; pts 32nds of 100%

	OPEN	HIGH	LOW	SETTLE	CHANGE	LIFETIME HIGH	LIFETIME LOW	OPEN INT.
Dec	105-08	05-135	104-31	105-11	+ 1.0	105-16	100-10	39,289

Est vol 600; vol Thu 1,105; open int 39,289, +97.

5 Yr Treasury Notes (CBT)-$100,000; pts 32nds of 100%

	OPEN	HIGH	LOW	SETTLE	CHANGE	LIFETIME HIGH	LIFETIME LOW	OPEN INT.
Dec	108-23	108-27	108-19	08-255	+ 1.5	108-27	103-17	461,264

Est vol 74,000; vol Thu 113,543; open int 478,939, +1,440.

CURRENCY

Japan Yen (CME)-12.5 million yen; $ per yen (.00)

	OPEN	HIGH	LOW	SETTLE	CHANGE	LIFETIME HIGH	LIFETIME LOW	OPEN INT.
Dec	.8160	.8192	.8137	.8170	+ .0010	.9880	.8060	79,815
Mr02	....	.8214	+ .0010	.8760	.8165			233

Est vol 8,292; vol Thu 14,519; open int 80,421, +3,979.

Deutschemark (CME)-125,000 marks; $ per mark

	OPEN	HIGH	LOW	SETTLE	CHANGE	LIFETIME HIGH	LIFETIME LOW	OPEN INT.
Dec	....	....	.4552	− .0009	.4742	.4400		204

Est vol 0; vol Thu 1, open int 204, unch.

INDEX

DJ Industrial Average (CBOT)-$10 times average

	OPEN	HIGH	LOW	SETTLE	CHANGE	LIFETIME HIGH	LIFETIME LOW	OPEN INT.
Dec	9475	9600	9415	9510	+ 23	11950	7800	32,696
Mr02	9540	9605	9435	9517	+ 25	11150	7900	710

Est vol 24,000; vol Thu 31,674; open int 33,548, +557.
Idx prl: Hi 9598.17; Lo 9423.32; Close 9545.17, +82.27.

S&P 500 Index (CME)-$250 times index

	OPEN	HIGH	LOW	SETTLE	CHANGE	LIFETIME HIGH	LIFETIME LOW	OPEN INT.
Dec	110210	111250	109500	110200	− 70	171460	93900	517,644
Mr02	109950	111430	109850	110390	− 80	134960	94100	16,476

Est vol 66,064; vol Thu 85,746; open int 535,839, +2,284.
Idx prl: Hi 1110.61; Lo 1094.24; Close 1104.61, +4.52.

The next several rows detail prices for contracts expiring on various dates. The December 2001 maturity contract opened during the day at a futures price of $2.065 per bushel. The highest futures price during the day was $2.0675, the lowest was $2.0475, and the settlement price (a representative trading price during the last few minutes of trading) was $2.055. The settlement price decreased by $.01 from the previous trading day. The highest and lowest futures prices over the contract's life to date have been $2.75 and $2.0225, respectively. Finally, open interest, or the number of outstanding contracts, was 211,394. Corresponding information is given for each maturity date.

The trader holding the long position profits from price increases. Suppose that at expiration, corn is selling for $2.255 per bushel. The long position trader who entered the contract at the futures price of $2.055 on October 26 would pay the previously agreed-upon $2.055 for each unit of the index, which at contract maturity would be worth $2.255.

Because each contract calls for delivery of 5,000 bushels, the profit to the long position, ignoring brokerage fees, would equal $5,000 \times ($2.255 − $2.055) = $1,000$. Conversely, the short position must deliver 5,000 bushels for the previously agreed-upon futures price. The short position's loss equals the long position's profit.

The distinction between the *right* to purchase and the *obligation* to purchase the asset is the difference between a call option and a long position in a futures contract. A futures contract *obliges* the long position to purchase the asset at the futures price; the call option merely *conveys the right* to purchase the asset at the exercise price. The purchase will be made only if it yields a profit.

Clearly, the holder of a call has a better position than the holder of a long position on a futures contract with a futures price equal to the option's exercise price. This advantage, of course, comes only at a price. Call options must be purchased; futures investments are contracts only. The purchase price of an option is called the *premium*. It represents the compensation the purchaser of the call must pay for the ability to exercise the option only when it is profitable to do so. Similarly, the difference between a put option and a short futures position is the right, as opposed to the obligation, to sell an asset at an agreed-upon price.

SUMMARY

- Money market securities are very short-term debt obligations. They are usually highly marketable and have relatively low credit risk. Their low maturities and low credit risk ensure minimal capital gains or losses. These securities trade in large denominations, but they may be purchased indirectly through money market funds.
- Much of U.S. government borrowing is in the form of Treasury bonds and notes. These are coupon-paying bonds usually issued at or near par value. Treasury bonds are similar in design to coupon-paying corporate bonds.
- Municipal bonds are distinguished largely by their tax-exempt status. Interest payments (but not capital gains) on these securities are exempt from income taxes.
- Mortgage pass-through securities are pools of mortgages sold in one package. Owners of pass-throughs receive all principal and interest payments made by the borrower. The firm that originally issued the mortgage merely services the mortgage, simply "passing through" the payments to the purchasers of the mortgage. The pass-through agency usually guarantees the payment of interest and principal on mortgages pooled into these pass-through securities.
- Common stock is an ownership share in a corporation. Each share entitles its owner to one vote on matters of corporate governance and to a prorated share of the dividends paid to shareholders. Stock, or equity, owners are the residual claimants on the income earned by the firm.
- Preferred stock usually pays a fixed stream of dividends for the life of the firm: It is a perpetuity. A firm's failure to pay the dividend due on preferred stock, however, does not set off corporate bankruptcy. Instead, unpaid dividends simply cumulate. New varieties of preferred stock include convertible and adjustable-rate issues.
- Many stock market indexes measure the performance of the overall market. The Dow Jones averages, the oldest and best-known indicators, are price-weighted indexes. Today, many broad-based, market value-weighted indexes are computed daily. These include the Standard & Poor's composite 500 stock index, the NYSE, the Nasdaq index, the Wilshire 5000 Index, and several international indexes, including the Nikkei, FTSE, and Dax.
- A call option is a right to purchase an asset at a stipulated exercise price on or before an expiration date. A put option is the right to sell an asset at some exercise price. Calls increase in value, while puts decrease in value as the value of the underlying asset increases.
- A futures contract is an obligation to buy or sell an asset at a stipulated futures price on a maturity date. The long position, which commits to purchasing, gains if the asset value increases, while the short position, which commits to delivering the asset, loses.

www.mhhe.com/bkm

**KEY
TERMS**

bankers' acceptance, 28
call option, 48
capital markets, 26
certificate of deposit, 27
commercial paper, 28
common stocks, 39
corporate bonds, 35
derivative asset/contingent
    claim, 48

equally weighted index, 46
Eurodollars, 28
Federal funds, 29
futures contract, 51
LIBOR, 29
market value-weighted
    index, 45
money markets, 26
municipal bonds, 33

preferred stock, 41
price-weighted average, 42
put option, 49
repurchase agreements, 29
Treasury bills, 27
Treasury bonds, 31
Treasury notes, 31

**PROBLEM
SETS**

1. Preferred stock
   a. Is actually a form of equity.
   b. Pays dividends not fully taxable to U.S. corporations.
   c. Is normally considered a fixed-income security.
   d. All of the above.

2. Straight preferred stock yields often are lower than yields on straight bonds of the same quality because of
   a. Marketability
   b. Risk
   c. Taxation
   d. Call protection

3. Turn back to Figure 2.3 and look at the Treasury bond maturing in May 2008.
   a. How much would you have to pay to purchase one of these bonds?
   b. What is its coupon rate?
   c. What is the current yield of the bond?

4. In what ways is preferred stock like long-term debt? In what ways is it like equity?

5. Why are money market securities sometimes referred to as "cash equivalents?"

6. Find the after-tax return to a corporation that buys a share of preferred stock at $40, sells it at year-end at $40, and receives a $4 year-end dividend. The firm is in the 30% tax bracket.

7. Turn to Figure 2.9 and look at the listing for General Dynamics (GenDynam).
   a. What was the firm's closing price *yesterday?*
   b. How many shares could you buy for $5,000?
   c. What would be your annual dividend income from those shares?
   d. What must be its earnings per share?

8. Consider the three stocks in the following table. P_t represents price at time t, and Q_t represents shares outstanding at time t. Stock C splits two-for-one in the last period.

	P_0	Q_0	P_1	Q_1	P_2	Q_2
A	90	100	95	100	95	100
B	50	200	45	200	45	200
C	100	200	110	200	55	400

   a. Calculate the rate of return on a price-weighted index of the three stocks for the first period ($t = 0$ to $t = 1$).
   b. What must happen to the divisor for the price-weighted index in year 2?
   c. Calculate the rate of return of the price-weighted index for the second period ($t = 1$ to $t = 2$).

9. Using the data in problem 8, calculate the first period rates of return on the following indexes of the three stocks:
   a. a market value-weighted index.
   b. an equally weighted index.

10. An investor is in a 28% tax bracket. If corporate bonds offer 9% yields, what must municipals offer for the investor to prefer them to corporate bonds?

11. Suppose that short-term municipal bonds currently offer yields of 4%, while comparable taxable bonds pay 5%. Which gives you the higher after-tax yield if your tax bracket is:
    a. Zero
    b. 10%
    c. 20%
    d. 30%

12. Find the equivalent taxable yield of the municipal bond in the previous question for tax brackets of zero, 10%, 20%, and 30%.

13. Which security should sell at a greater price?
    a. A 10-year Treasury bond with a 9% coupon rate or a 10-year T-bond with a 10% coupon.
    b. A three-month maturity call option with an exercise price of $40 or a three-month call on the same stock with an exercise price of $35.
    c. A put option on a stock selling at $50 or a put option on another stock selling at $60. (All other relevant features of the stocks and options are assumed to be identical.)

14. Look at the futures listings for gold in Figure 2.12.
    a. Suppose you buy one gold contract for December 2001 delivery. If the contract closes in December at a price of $283 per ounce, what will your profit be?
    b. How many December 2001 maturity contracts are outstanding? How many ounces of gold do they represent?

15. Turn back to Figure 2.11 and look at the IBM options. Suppose you buy a November maturity call option with exercise price 105.
    a. If the stock price in November is 107, will you exercise your call? What are the profit and rate of return on your position?
    b. What if you had bought the call with exercise price 100?
    c. What if you had bought a put with exercise price 105?

16. Why do call options with exercise prices higher than the price of the underlying stock sell for positive prices?

17. Both a call and a put currently are traded on stock XYZ; both have strike prices of $50 and maturities of six months. What will be the profit to an investor who buys the call for $4 in the following scenarios for stock prices in six months? (a) $40; (b) $45; (c) $50; (d) $55; (e) $60. What will be the profit in each scenario to an investor who buys the put for $6?

18. Explain the difference between a put option and a short position in a futures contract.

19. Explain the difference between a call option and a long position in a futures contract.

20. What would you expect to happen to the spread between yields on commercial paper and Treasury bills if the economy were to enter a steep recession?

21. Examine the first 25 stocks listed in Figure 2.9. For how many of these stocks is the 52-week high price at least 50% greater than the 52-week low price? What do you conclude about the volatility of prices on individual stocks?

WEBMASTER

Interest Rates

Go to http://www.bloomberg.com/markets/index.html. In the markets section under Rates & Bonds, find the rates in the Key Rates and Municipal Bond Rates sections.

1. Describe the trend over the last six months in

    a. Municipal bond yields

    b. AAA-rated industrial bonds

    c. 30-year mortgage rates

SOLUTIONS TO

Concept
CHECK

1. Compare the 4.81% yield on the Federal Home Loan Bank bond maturing in 9-08 (September 2008) with the 4.31% yield on the November 2008 T-bond. The differential can be attributed largely to the difference in default risk.

2. A 6% taxable return is equivalent to an after-tax return of $6(1 - .28) = 4.32\%$. Therefore, you would be better off in the taxable bond. The equivalent taxable yield of the tax-free bond is $4/(1 - .28) = 5.55\%$. So a taxable bond would have to pay a 5.55% yield to provide the same after-tax return as a tax-free bond offering a 4% yield.

3. *a.* You are entitled to a prorated share of IBM's dividend payments and to vote in any of IBM's stockholder meetings.
   b. Your potential gain is unlimited because IBM's stock price has no upper bound.
   c. Your outlay was $\$95 \times 100 = \$9,500$. Because of limited liability, this is the most you can lose.

4. The price-weighted index increases from 62.50 [$= (100 + 25)/2$] to 65 [$= (110 + 20)/2$)], a gain of 4%. An investment of one share in each company requires an outlay of $125 that would increase in value to $130, for a return of 4% (5/125), which equals the return to the price-weighted index.

5. The market value-weighted index return is calculated by computing the increase in value of the stock portfolio. The portfolio of the two stocks starts with an initial value of $100 million + $500 million = $600 million and falls in value to $110 million + $400 million = $510 million, a loss of 90/600 = .15, or 15%. The index portfolio return is a weighted average of the returns on each stock with weights of ⅙ on XYZ and ⅚ on ABC (weights proportional to relative investments). Because the return on XYZ is 10%, while that on ABC is −20%, the index portfolio return is (⅙)10 + (⅚)(−20) = −15%, equal to the return on the market value-weighted index.

6. The payoff to the call option is $104 - 100 = \$4$. The call cost $1.80. The profit is $2.20 per share. The put will pay off zero—it expires worthless since the stock price exceeds the exercise price. The loss is the cost of the put, $0.80.

HOW SECURITIES ARE TRADED

AFTER STUDYING THIS CHAPTER YOU SHOULD BE ABLE TO:

> Describe the role of investment bankers in primary issues.

> Identify the various security markets.

> Compare trading practices in stock exchanges with those in dealer markets.

> Describe the role of brokers.

> Compare the mechanics and investment implications of buying on margin and short selling.

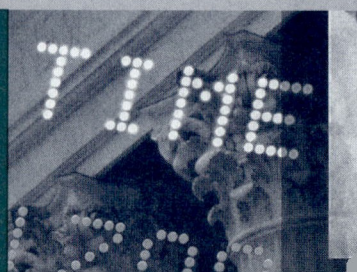

The first time a security trades is when it is issued. Therefore, we begin our examination of trading with a look at how securities are first marketed to the public by investment bankers, the midwives of securities. Then, we turn to the various exchanges where already-issued securities can be traded among investors. We examine the competition among the New York Stock Exchange, regional exchanges, Nasdaq, and several foreign markets for the patronage of security traders.

Next, we turn to the mechanics of trading in these various markets. We describe the role of the specialist in exchange markets and the dealer in over-the-counter markets. We also touch briefly on block trading and the SuperDot system of the NYSE for electronically routing orders to the floor of the exchange. We discuss the costs of trading and consider the ongoing debate between the NYSE and its competitors over which market provides the lowest-cost trading arena.

Finally, we describe the essentials of specific transactions, such as buying on margin and selling stock short and discuss relevant regulations governing security trading. In the process, we will see that some regulations, such as those governing insider trading, can be difficult to interpret in practice.

3.1 HOW FIRMS ISSUE SECURITIES

When firms need to raise capital they may choose to sell or *float* securities. These new issues of stocks, bonds, or other securities typically are marketed to the public by investment bankers in what is called the **primary market.** Trading of already-issued securities among investors occurs in the **secondary market.**

There are two types of primary market issues of common stock. **Initial public offerings, or IPOs,** are stocks issued by a formerly privately owned company that is going public, that is, selling stock to the public for the first time. *Seasoned* new issues are offered by companies that already have floated equity. For example, a sale by IBM of new shares of stock would constitute a seasoned new issue.

In the case of bonds, we also distinguish between two types of primary market issues, a *public offering* and a *private placement.* The former refers to an issue of bonds sold to the general investing public that can then be traded on the secondary market. The latter refers to an issue that usually is sold to one or a few institutional investors and is generally held to maturity.

Investment Banking

Public offerings of both stocks and bonds typically are marketed by investment bankers who in this role are called **underwriters.** More than one investment banker usually markets the securities. A lead firm forms an underwriting syndicate of other investment bankers to share the responsibility for the stock issue.

Investment bankers advise the firm regarding the terms on which it should attempt to sell the securities. A preliminary registration statement must be filed with the Securities and Exchange Commission (SEC), describing the issue and the prospects of the company. This preliminary prospectus is known as a *red herring* because it includes a statement printed in red, stating that the company is not attempting to sell the security before the registration is approved. When the statement is in final form, and approved by the SEC, it is called the **prospectus.** At this point, the price at which the securities will be offered to the public is announced.

In a typical underwriting arrangement, the investment bankers purchase the securities from the issuing company and then resell them to the public. The issuing firm sells the securities to the underwriting syndicate for the public offering price less a spread that serves as compensation to the underwriters. This procedure is called a *firm commitment;* the underwriters receive the issue and assume the risk that the shares cannot be sold to the public at the stipulated offering price. Figure 3.1 depicts the relationships among the firm issuing the security, the lead underwriter, the underwriting syndicate, and the public.

An alternative to the firm commitment is the *best-efforts* agreement. In this case, the investment banker does not actually purchase the securities but agrees to help the firm sell the issue to the public. The banker simply acts as an intermediary between the public and the firm and does not bear the risk of not being able to resell purchased securities at the offering price. The best-efforts procedure is more common for initial public offerings of common stock, where the appropriate share price is less certain.

Corporations engage investment bankers either by negotiation or competitive bidding, although negotiation is far more common. In addition to the compensation resulting from the spread between the purchase price and the public offering price, an investment banker may receive shares of common stock or other securities of the firm.

As part of its marketing of the firm's securities, the underwriting syndicate typically takes out advertisements in the financial press to announce the prospective sale. An example of

primary market

Market for new issues of securities.

secondary market

Market for already-existing securities.

initial public offering (IPO)

First sale of stock by a formerly private company.

underwriters

Underwriters purchase securities from the issuing company and resell them.

prospectus

A description of the firm and the security it is issuing.

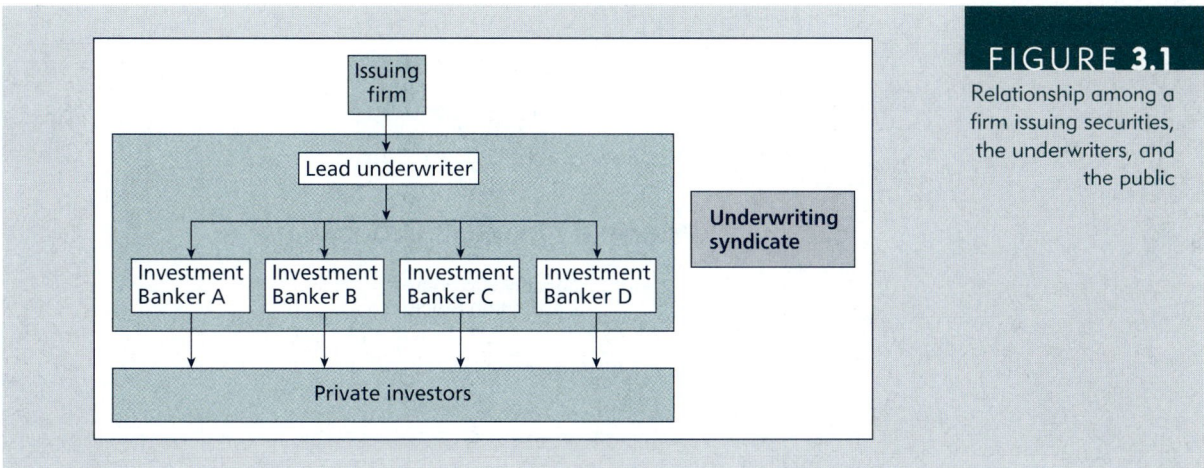

FIGURE **3.1**

Relationship among a
firm issuing securities,
the underwriters, and
the public

these so-called *tombstone* advertisements is given in Figure 3.2. The underwriters plan to sell 115 million shares of stock at a price of $18.50 each, to raise $2,127.5 million for the Principal Financial Group. The four lead underwriters are presented in larger type; the firms taking a smaller role in marketing the securities are presented below in smaller type. Most of the shares will be sold in the U.S., but 15% of the issue will be sold abroad. Notice that the underwriters for the non-U.S. portion of the issue have far greater international representation.

Shelf Registration

An important innovation in the issuing of securities was introduced in 1982 when the SEC approved Rule 415, which allows firms to register securities and gradually sell them to the public for two years following the initial registration. Because the securities are already registered, they can be sold on short notice, with little additional paperwork. Moreover, they can be sold in small amounts without incurring substantial flotation costs. The securities are "on the shelf," ready to be issued, which has given rise to the term *shelf registration.*

1. Why does it make sense for shelf registration to be limited in time?

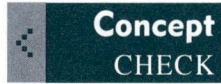

Concept
CHECK

Private Placements

Primary offerings also can be sold in a **private placement** rather than a public offering. In this case, the firm (using an investment banker) sells shares directly to a small group of institutional or wealthy investors. Private placements can be far cheaper than public offerings. This is because Rule 144A of the SEC allows corporations to make these placements without preparing the extensive and costly registration statements required of a public offering. On the other hand, because private placements are not made available to the general public, they generally will be less suited for very large offerings. Moreover, private placements do not trade in secondary markets like stock exchanges. This greatly reduces their liquidity and presumably reduces the prices that investors will pay for the issue.

**private
placement**

**Primary offerings in
which shares are sold
directly to a small
group of institutional
or wealthy investors.**

Initial Public Offerings

Investment bankers manage the issuance of new securities to the public. Once the SEC has commented on the registration statement and a preliminary prospectus has been distributed to interested investors, the investment bankers organize *road shows* in which they travel around the country to publicize the imminent offering. These road shows serve two purposes. First, they generate interest among potential investors and provide information about the offering. Second, they provide information to the issuing firm and its underwriters about the price at which they will be able to market the securities. Large investors communicate their interest in purchasing shares of the IPO to the underwriters; these indications of interest are called a *book* and the process of polling potential investors is called *bookbuilding*. These indications of interest provide valuable information to the issuing firm because institutional investors often will have useful insights about both the market demand for the security as well as the prospects of the firm and its competitors. It is common for investment bankers to revise both their initial estimates of the offering price of a security and the number of shares offered based on feedback from the investing community.

Why do investors truthfully reveal their interest in an offering to the investment banker? Might they be better off expressing little interest, in the hope that this will drive down the offering price? Truth is the better policy in this case because truth telling is rewarded. Shares of

IPOs are allocated across investors in part based on the strength of each investor's expressed interest in the offering. If a firm wishes to get a large allocation when it is optimistic about the security, it needs to reveal its optimism. In turn, the underwriter needs to offer the security at a bargain price to these investors to induce them to participate in bookbuilding and share their information. Thus, IPOs commonly are underpriced compared to the price at which they could be marketed. Such underpricing is reflected in price jumps that occur on the date when the shares are first traded in public security markets. The most dramatic case of underpricing occurred in December 1999 when shares in VA Linux were sold in a IPO at $30 a share and closed on the first day of trading at $239.25, a 698% one-day return. Similarly, in November 1998, 3.1 million shares in theglobe.com were sold in an IPO at a price of $9 a share. In the first day of trading the price reached $97 before closing at $63.50 a share.[1]

While the explicit costs of an IPO tend to be around 7% of the funds raised, such underpricing should be viewed as another cost of the issue. For example, if theglobe.com had sold its 3.1 million shares for the $63.50 that investors obviously were willing to pay for them, its IPO would have raised $197 million instead of only $27.9 million. The money "left on the table" in this case far exceeded the explicit cost of the stock issue. This degree of underpricing is far more dramatic than is common, but underpricing seems to be a universal phenomenon.

Figure 3.3 presents average first-day returns on IPOs of stocks across the world. The results consistently indicate that IPOs are marketed to investors at attractive prices. Underpricing of IPOs makes them appealing to all investors, yet institutional investors are allocated the bulk of a typical new issue. Some view this as unfair discrimination against small investors. However, this analysis suggests that the apparent discounts on IPOs may be in part payments for a valuable service, specifically, the information contributed by the institutional investors. The right to allocate shares in this way may contribute to efficiency by promoting the collection and dissemination of such information.[2]

Pricing of IPOs is not trivial and not all IPOs turn out to be underpriced. Some do poorly after issue and others cannot even be fully sold to the market. Underwriters left with unmarketable securities are forced to sell them at a loss on the secondary market. Therefore, the investment banker bears the price risk of an underwritten issue.

Interestingly, despite their dramatic initial investment performance, IPOs have been poor long-term investments. Figure 3.4 compares the stock price performance of IPOs with shares of other firms of the same size for each of the five years after issue of the IPO. The year-by-year underperformance of the IPOs is dramatic, suggesting that, on average, the investing public may be too optimistic about the prospects of these firms. (Theglobe.com, which enjoyed one of the greatest first-day price gains in history, is a case in point. Within the year after its IPO, its stock was selling at less than one-third of its first-day peak and in November 2001 was at about 5 cents a share.)

IPOs can be expensive, especially for small firms. However, the landscape changed in 1995, when Spring Street Brewing Company, which produces Wit beer, came out with an Internet IPO. It posted a page on the World Wide Web to let investors know of the stock offering, and distributed the prospectus along with a subscription agreement as word processing documents

---

[1] It is worth noting, however, that by December 2000, shares in VA Linux were selling for less than $9 a share, and by December 2001, less than $2 a share; similarly, by December 2000 theglobe.com was selling below $1 and in December 2001, below $.05. These examples are extreme, but as we will see, the long-term investment performance of IPOs has actually been below average.

[2] An elaboration of this point and a more complete discussion of the bookbuilding process is provided in "Going by the Book," by Lawrence Benveniste and William Wilhelm. See the References appendix at the end of the text for a complete citation.

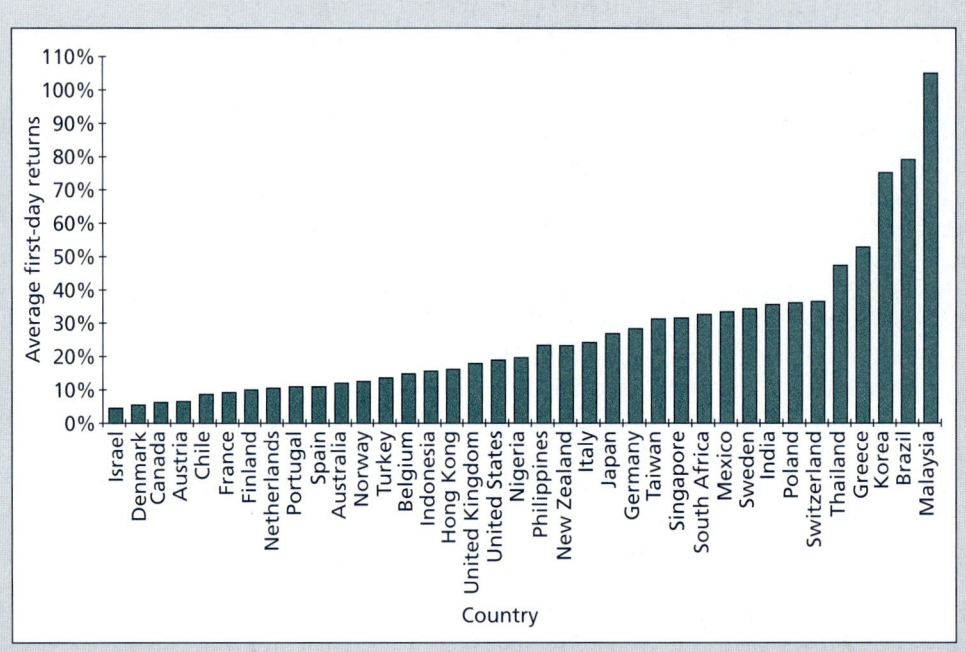

FIGURE **3.3**

Average initial returns for IPOs in various countries

Source: Provided by Professor J. Ritter of the University of Florida, 2001. This is an updated version of the information contained in T. Loughran, J. Ritter, and K. Rydqvist, "Initial Public Offerings," *Pacific-Basin Finance Journal* 2 (1994), pp. 165–199.

FIGURE **3.4**

Long-term relative performance of initial public offerings

Source: Prof. Jay R. Ritter, University of Florida, 2001.

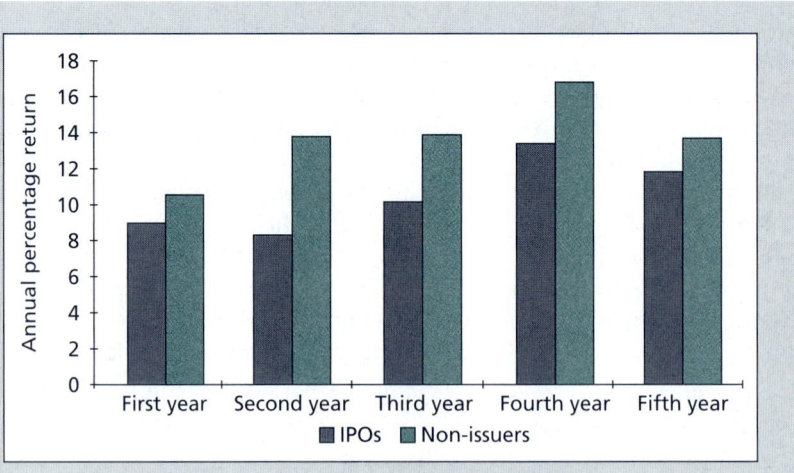

over the Web. By the end of the year, the firm had sold 860,000 shares to 3,500 investors, and had raised $1.6 million, all without an investment banker. This was admittedly a small IPO, but a low-cost one that was well-suited to such a small firm. Based on this success, a new company named Wit Capital was formed, with the goal of arranging low-cost Web-based IPOs for other firms. Wit also participates in the underwriting syndicates of more conventional IPOs; unlike conventional investment bankers, it allocates shares on a first-come, first-served basis.

Another new entry to the underwriting field is W. R. Hambrecht & Co., which also conducts IPOs on the Internet geared toward smaller, retail investors. Unlike typical investment bankers that tend to favor institutional investors in the allocation of shares and determine an offer price through the bookbuilding process, Hambrecht conducts a "Dutch auction." In this procedure, which Hambrecht has dubbed OpenIPO, investors submit a price for a given number of shares. The bids are ranked in order of bid price, and shares are allocated to the highest bidders until the entire issue is absorbed. All shares are sold at an offer price equal to the highest price at which all the issued shares will be absorbed by investors. Those investors who bid below that cutoff price get no shares. This procedure minimizes underpricing, by allocating shares based on bids.

To date, upstarts like Wit Capital and Hambrecht have captured only a tiny share of the underwriting market. But the threat to traditional practices that they and similar firms may pose in the future has already caused a stir on Wall Street.

3.2 | WHERE SECURITIES ARE TRADED

Once securities are issued to the public, investors may trade them among themselves. Purchase and sale of already-issued securities occur in the secondary markets, which include (1) national and local securities exchanges, (2) the over-the-counter market, and (3) direct trading between two parties.

The Secondary Markets

There are several **stock exchanges** in the United States. Two of these, the New York Stock Exchange (NYSE, or the Big Board) and the American Stock Exchange (Amex), are national in scope and are located in New York City. The others, such as the Boston or Pacific stock exchanges, are to a considerable extent regional exchanges, which tend to list firms located in a particular geographic area. There also are several exchanges for the trading of options and futures contracts, which we will discuss later in the options and futures chapters.

An exchange provides a facility for its members to trade securities, and only members of the exchange may trade there. Therefore, memberships or *seats* on the exchange are valuable assets. The majority of seats are *commission broker* seats, most of which are owned by the large full-service brokerage firms. The seat entitles the firm to place one of its brokers on the floor of the exchange where he or she can execute trades. The exchange member charges investors for executing trades on their behalf. The commissions that members can earn through this activity determine the market value of a seat. A seat on the NYSE has sold over the years for as little as $4,000 (in 1878) and as much as $2,650,000 (in 1999). See Table 3.1 for a history of seat prices since 1875.

The NYSE is by far the largest single exchange. The shares of nearly 3,000 firms trade there, and more than 3,000 stock issues (common plus preferred stock) are listed. Daily trading volume on the NYSE averaged 1.04 billion shares in 2000. The NYSE accounts for about 85–90% of the trading that takes place on U.S. stock exchanges.

The American Stock Exchange also is national in scope, but it focuses on listing smaller and younger firms than the NYSE.[3] The national exchanges are willing to *list* a stock (i.e., allow trading in that stock on the exchange) only if the firm meets certain criteria of size and stability.

stock exchanges

Secondary markets where already-issued securities are bought and sold by members.

---

[3]Amex merged with the Nasdaq market in 1998 but still operates as an independent exchange. Amex is home as well to considerable trading in exchange-traded funds, which are securities that represent claims to entire portfolios of stock and which today account for a large share of total trading on the exchange. These products are described in greater detail in the following chapter.

TABLE **3.1** Seat prices on the NYSE	Year	High	Low
	1875	$ 6,800	$ 4,300
	1905	85,000	72,000
	1935	140,000	65,000
	1965	250,000	190,000
	1975	138,000	55,000
	1980	275,000	175,000
	1985	480,000	310,000
	1990	430,000	250,000
	1995	1,050,000	785,000
	1996	1,450,000	1,225,000
	1997	1,750,000	1,175,000
	1998	2,000,000	1,225,000
	1999	2,650,000	2,000,000
	2000	2,000,000	1,650,000

Source: From the New York Stock Exchange *Fact Book*, 2001.

TABLE **3.2** Some initial listing requirements for the NYSE	
Pretax income in last year	$ 2,500,000
Average annual pretax income in previous two years	$ 2,000,000
Revenue	$100,000,000
Market value of publicly held stock	$ 60,000,000
Shares publicly held	1,100,000
Number of holders of 100 shares or more	2,000

Source: Data from the New York Stock Exchange *Fact Book*, 2001.

Regional exchanges provide a market for the trading of shares of local firms that do not meet the more stringent listing requirements of the national exchanges.

Table 3.2 gives some of the initial listing requirements for the NYSE. These requirements ensure that a firm is of significant trading interest before the NYSE will allocate facilities for it to be traded on the floor of the exchange. If a listed company suffers a decline and fails to meet the criteria in Table 3.2, it may be delisted.

Regional exchanges also sponsor trading of some firms that are traded on national exchanges. This dual listing enables local brokerage firms to trade in shares of large firms without purchasing a membership on the NYSE.

The NYSE recently has lost market share to the regional exchanges and, more dramatically, to the over-the-counter market. Today, approximately 75% of the trades in stocks listed on the NYSE are actually executed on the NYSE. In contrast, more than 80% of the trades in NYSE-listed shares were executed on the exchange in the early 1980s. The loss is attributed to lower commissions charged on other exchanges, although, as we will see below, the NYSE believes that a more comprehensive treatment of trading costs would show that it is the most cost-effective trading arena. In any case, many of these non-NYSE trades were for relatively small transactions. The NYSE is still by far the preferred exchange for large traders, and its market share of exchange-listed companies—when measured in share volume rather than number of trades—has been stable since 1990, between 82% and 84%.

The over-the-counter Nasdaq market (described in detail shortly) has posed a bigger competitive challenge to the NYSE. Its share of trading volume in NYSE-listed firms increased from 2.5% in 1983 to about 8% in 2000. Moreover, many large firms that would be eligible to list their shares on the NYSE now choose instead to list on Nasdaq. Some of the well-known firms

TABLE **3.3** Trading in national stock markets, 2000	Market	Trading Volume (billions of shares)	Dollar Volume of Trading ($ billion)
	New York	262.5	$11,060.0
	American	13.3	945.4
	Nasdaq	442.8	19,798.8

Source: International Federation of Stock Exchanges.

currently trading on Nasdaq are Microsoft, Intel, Apple Computer, and Sun Microsystems. Total trading volume in over-the-counter stocks on the computerized Nasdaq system has increased rapidly, rising from about 50 million shares per day in 1984 to 1.8 billion shares per day in 2000. Share volume on Nasdaq actually surpasses that on the NYSE. Table 3.3 shows the trading activity in securities listed on the national exchanges in 2000.

Other new sources of competition to the NYSE have come from abroad. For example, the London Stock Exchange is preferred by some traders because it offers greater anonymity. In addition, new restrictions introduced by the NYSE to limit price volatility in the wake of the market crash of 1987 are viewed by some traders as another reason to trade abroad. These so-called circuit breakers are discussed below.

The Over-the-Counter Market

Roughly 35,000 issues are traded on the **over-the-counter (OTC) market,** which allows any security to be traded there, but the OTC market is not a formal exchange. There are no membership requirements for trading or listing requirements for securities (although there are requirements to be listed on Nasdaq, the computer-linked network for trading securities of larger OTC firms). Thousands of brokers register with the SEC as dealers in OTC securities. Security dealers quote prices at which they are willing to buy or sell securities. A broker then executes a trade by contacting the dealer listing an attractive quote.

Before 1971, all OTC quotations of stock were recorded manually and published daily. The so-called pink sheets were the means by which dealers communicated their interest in trading at various prices. This was a cumbersome and inefficient technique, and published quotes were a day out of date. In 1971, the National Association of Securities Dealers Automatic Quotation System, or **NASDAQ,** was developed to offer via a computer-linked system immediate information on bid and ask prices for stocks offered by various dealers. The **bid price** is the price at which a dealer is willing to purchase a security; the **ask price** is the one at which the dealer will sell a security. Hence, the ask price is always higher than the bid price, and the difference, the *bid–ask spread,* makes up the dealer's profit. The system allows a broker who receives a buy or sell order from an investor to examine all current quotes, call the dealer with the best quote, and execute a trade. The system, now called the Nasdaq Stock Market, is divided into two sectors, the Nasdaq National Market System (comprising almost 4,000 companies), and the Nasdaq SmallCap Market (comprising over 1,000 smaller companies). The National Market System securities must meet more stringent listing requirements and trade in a more liquid market. Some of the more important initial listing requirements for each of these markets are presented in Table 3.4. For even smaller firms, Nasdaq maintains an electronic "OTC Bulletin Board," which is not part of the Nasdaq market, but is simply a means for brokers and dealers to get and post current price quotes over a computer network. Finally, the smallest stocks continue to be listed on the pink sheets distributed through the National Association of Securities Dealers.

over-the-counter (OTC) market

An informal network of brokers and dealers who negotiate sales of securities.

Nasdaq stock market

The computer-linked price quotation system for the OTC market.

bid price

The price at which a dealer is willing to purchase a security.

ask price

The price at which a dealer will sell a security.

TABLE **3.4** Partial requirements for initial listing on Nasdaq markets	Nasdaq National Market	Nasdaq SmallCap Market
Shareholders' equity	$15 million	$5 million
Shares in public hands	1.1 million	1 million
Market value of publicly traded shares	$8 million	$5 million
Minimum price of stock	$5	$4
Pretax income	$1 million	$750,000
Shareholders	400	300

Source: The Nasdaq Stock Market.

Nasdaq has three levels of subscribers. The highest, level 3 subscribers, are for firms dealing, or "making markets," in OTC securities. These market makers maintain inventories of a security and constantly stand ready to buy or sell these shares from or to the public at the quoted bid and ask prices. They earn profits from the spread between the bid and ask prices.

Level 3 subscribers may enter the bid and ask prices at which they are willing to buy or sell stocks into the computer network and may update these quotes as desired.

Level 2 subscribers receive all bid and ask quotes, but they cannot enter their own quotes. These subscribers tend to be brokerage firms that execute trades for clients but do not actively deal in the stocks on their own account. Brokers attempting to buy or sell shares call the market maker (a level 3 subscriber) with the best quote in order to execute a trade. Notice that Nasdaq is a price quotation, rather than a trading, system. While bid and ask prices can be obtained from the Nasdaq computer network, the actual trade still requires direct negotiation (often over the phone) between the broker and the dealer in the security.

Level 1 subscribers receive only the *inside quotes* (i.e., the highest bid and lowest ask prices on each stock). Level 1 subscribers are investors who are not actively buying and selling securities but want information on current prices.

The Third and Fourth Markets

third market

Trading of exchange-listed securities on the OTC market.

The **third market** refers to trading of exchange-listed securities on the over-the-counter market. In the past, members of an exchange were required to execute all their trades of exchange-listed securities on the exchange and to charge commissions according to a fixed schedule. This procedure was disadvantageous to large traders when it prevented them from realizing economies of scale on large trades. Because of this restriction, brokerage firms that were not members of the NYSE and so not bound by its rules, established trading in the OTC market of large NYSE-listed stocks. These trades could be accomplished at lower commissions than would have been charged on the NYSE, and the third market grew dramatically until 1972, when the NYSE allowed negotiated commissions on orders exceeding $300,000. On May 1, 1975, frequently referred to as "May Day," commissions on all NYSE orders became negotiable, and they have been ever since.

Concept CHECK

2. Look again at Table 3.1, which gives the history of seat prices on the NYSE. Interpret the data for 1975 in light of the changes instituted on May Day.

The **fourth market** refers to direct trading between investors in exchange-listed securities without the benefit of a broker. The direct trading among investors that characterizes the fourth market has exploded in recent years due to the advent of **electronic communication networks,** or **ECNs.** ECNs are an alternative to either formal stock exchanges like the NYSE or dealer markets like Nasdaq for trading securities. These ECNs allow members to post buy or sell orders and to have those orders matched up or "crossed" with orders of other traders in

TABLE **3.5** Registered Electronic Communication Networks (ECNs)	Archipelago Attain B-Trade Services The BRASS Utility Instinet Corporation The Island ECN Market XT NexTrade REDIbook

Source: *Nasdaq in Black & White,* Nasdaq, 2001.

the system. Both sides of the trade benefit because direct crossing eliminates the bid–ask spread that otherwise would be incurred. Early versions of ECNs were available exclusively to large institutional traders. In addition to cost savings, systems such as Instinet and Posit allowed these large traders greater anonymity than they could otherwise achieve. This was important to the traders since they did not want to publicly signal their desire to buy or sell large quantities of shares for fear of moving prices in advance of their trades. Posit also enabled trading in portfolios as well as individual stocks.

ECNs have captured about 30% of the trading volume in Nasdaq-listed stocks. They must be certified by the SEC and registered with the National Association of Security Dealers to participate in the Nasdaq market. Table 3.5 is a list of registered ECNs at the start of 2001.

While small investors today typically do not access an ECN directly, they can send orders through their brokers, including online brokers, who can then have the order executed on the ECN. Eventually, individuals will likely have direct access to most ECNs through the Internet. In fact, several financial firms (Goldman, Sachs; Merrill Lynch; Salomon Smith Barney; Morgan Stanley; and Bernard Madoff) have combined to build an electronic trading network called Primex, which is open to NASD broker/dealers, who in turn have the ability to offer public access to the market. Other ECNs, such as Instinet, which have traditionally served institutional investors, are considering opening up their services to retail brokerages.

The advent of ECNs is putting increasing pressure on the NYSE to respond. In particular, big brokerage firms such as Goldman, Sachs and Merrill Lynch are calling for the NYSE to beef up its capabilities to automate orders without human intervention. Moreover, as they push the NYSE to change, these firms are hedging their bets by investing in ECNs on their own.

The NYSE also has announced its intention to go public. In its current organization as a member-owned cooperative, it needs the approval of members to institute major changes. However, many of these members are precisely the floor brokers who will be most hurt by electronic trading. This has made it difficult for the NYSE to respond flexibly to the challenge of electronic trading. By converting to a publicly held for-profit corporate organization, it hopes to be able to compete more vigorously in the marketplace of stock markets.

> **fourth market**
>
> Direct trading in exchange-listed securities between one investor and another without the benefit of a broker.

> **electronic communication networks (ECNs)**
>
> Computer networks that allow direct trading without the need for market makers.

The National Market System

The Securities Act Amendments of 1975 directed the Securities and Exchange Commission to implement a national competitive securities market. Such a market would entail centralized reporting of transactions and a centralized quotation system, with the aim of enhanced competition among market makers.

In 1975, Consolidated Tape began reporting trades on the NYSE, Amex, and major regional exchanges, as well as trades of Nasdaq-listed stocks. In 1977, the Consolidated Quotations Service began providing online bid and ask quotes for NYSE securities also traded on various other exchanges. This has enhanced competition by allowing market participants, including brokers or dealers who are at different locations, to interact and for orders to be directed to the market in which the best price can be obtained.

In 1978, the Intermarket Trading System (ITS) was implemented. ITS currently links nine exchanges by computer (NYSE, Amex, Boston, Cincinnati, Pacific, Philadelphia, Chicago, Nasdaq, and the Chicago Board Options Exchange). Nearly 5,000 issues are eligible for trading on the ITS; these account for most of the securities that are traded on more than one exchange. The system allows brokers and market makers to display and view quotes for all markets and to execute cross-market trades when the Consolidated Quotation System shows better prices in other markets. For example, suppose a specialist firm on the Boston Exchange is currently offering to buy a security for $20, but a broker in Boston who is attempting to sell shares for a client observes a superior bid price on the NYSE, say $20.12. The broker should route the order to the specialist's post on the NYSE, where it can be executed at the higher price. The transaction is then reported on the Consolidated Tape. Moreover, a specialist who observes a better price on another exchange is also expected either to match that price or route the trade to that market.

While the ITS does much to unify markets, it has some important shortcomings. First, it does not provide for automatic execution in the market with the best price. The trade must be directed there by a market participant, who might find it inconvenient (or unprofitable) to do so. Moreover, some feel that the ITS is too slow to integrate prices off the NYSE.

A logical extension of the ITS as a means to integrate securities markets would be the establishment of a central *limit order* book. Such an electronic "book" would contain all orders conditional on both prices and dates. All markets would be linked and all traders could compete for all orders.

While market integration seems like a desirable goal, the recent growth of ECNs has led to some concern that markets are in fact becoming more fragmented. This is because participants in one ECN do not necessarily know what prices are being quoted on other networks. ECNs do display their best-priced offers on the Nasdaq system, but other limit orders are not available. Only stock exchanges may participate in the Intermarket Trading System, which means that ECNs are excluded. Moreover, during the after-hours trading enabled by ECNs, trades take place on these private networks while other larger markets are closed, and current prices for securities are harder to access. In the wake of growing concern about market fragmentation, some big Wall Street brokerage houses have called for an electronically driven central limit order book. But full market integration has proven to be elusive.

Bond Trading

The New York Stock Exchange also operates a bond exchange where U.S. government, corporate, municipal, and foreign bonds may be traded. The centerpiece of the NYSE bond market is the Automated Bond System (ABS), which is an automated trading system that allows trading firms to obtain market information, to enter and execute trades over a computer network, and to receive immediate confirmations of trade execution.

However, the vast majority of bond trading occurs in the OTC market among bond dealers, even for bonds that are actually listed on the NYSE. This market is a network of bond dealers such as Merrill Lynch, Salomon Smith Barney, or Goldman, Sachs that is linked by a computer quotation system. However, because these dealers do not carry extensive inventories of the wide range of bonds that have been issued to the public, they cannot necessarily offer to sell bonds from their inventory to clients or even buy bonds for their own inventory. They may instead work to locate an investor who wishes to take the opposite side of a trade. In practice, however, the corporate bond market often is quite "thin," in that there may be few investors interested in trading a bond at any particular time. As a result, the bond market is subject to a type of liquidity risk, for it can be difficult to sell one's holdings quickly if the need arises.

WEBMASTER

Electronic Communication Networks

Go to the New York Federal Reserve's website, http://www.ny.frb.org/rmaghome/curr_iss/ci6-12.html, to read "The Emergence of Electronic Communication Networks (ECNs) in the U.S. Equity Markets," by James McAndrews and Chris Stefanadis, researchers at the Federal Reserve Bank of New York.

   After reading this article, answer the following questions:

1.   What is an ECN and how does it differ from a traditional market such as the NYSE?

2.   List and briefly describe the four potential advantages of an ECN as identified by the authors.

3.   What risk is related to the fragmentation that may accompany the development of the ECNs?

Listing Requirements

Go to http://www.nasdaq.com/about/listing_information.stm. On the sitemap there is an item labeled listing information. Select that item and identify the following items in Initial Listing Standards for the National Market System 1, 2, and 3 and the Nasdaq SmallCap Market for domestic companies:

1.   Public float in millions of shares.

2.   Market value of public float.

3.   Shareholders of round lots.

Go to www.nyse.com and select the listed company item or information bullet. Under the bullet select the listing standards tab. Identify the same items for NYSE (U.S. Standards) initial listing requirements.

4.   In what two categories are the listing requirements most significantly different?

3.3 TRADING ON EXCHANGES

Most of the information in this section applies to all securities traded on exchanges. Some of it, however, applies just to stocks, and in such cases we use the specific words, *stocks* or *shares*.

The Participants

We begin our discussion of the mechanics of exchange trading with a brief description of the potential parties to a trade. When an investor instructs a broker to buy or sell securities, a number of players must act to consummate the deal.

   The investor places an order with a broker. The brokerage firm for which the broker works, and which owns a seat on the exchange, contacts its *commission broker,* who is on the floor of the exchange, to execute the order. When the firm's commission brokers are overloaded and have too many orders to handle, they will use the services of *floor brokers,* who are independent members of the exchange (and own seats), to execute orders.

   The *specialist* is central to the trading process. All trading in a given stock takes place at one location on the floor of the exchange called the specialist's post. At the specialist's post is a monitor called the Display Book that presents all the current offers from interested traders to buy or sell shares at various prices as well as the number of shares these quotes are good for.

The specialist manages the trading in the stock. The market making responsibility for each stock is assigned by the NYSE to one specialist firm. There is only one specialist firm per stock but most firms will have responsibility for trading in several stocks. The specialist firm also may act as a dealer in the stock, trading for its own account. We will examine the role of the specialist in more detail shortly.

Types of Orders

Market orders   Market orders are simply buy or sell orders that are to be executed immediately at current market prices. For example, an investor might call his broker and ask for the market price of IBM. The retail broker will wire this request to the commission broker on the floor of the exchange, who will approach the specialist's post and ask the specialist for best current quotes. Finding that the current quotes are $98 per share bid, and $98.10 asked, the investor might direct the broker to buy 100 shares "at market," meaning that he is willing to pay $98.10 per share for an immediate transaction. Similarly, an order to "sell at market" will result in stock sales at $98 per share. (Until 2001, when U.S. markets adopted decimal pricing, the minimum possible bid–ask spread was "one tick," which on the NYSE was $⅛ until 1997 and $1⁄16 thereafter. With decimal pricing, the spread can be far lower.) When a trade is executed, the specialist's clerk will fill out an order card that reports the time, price, and quantity of shares traded and the transaction will be reported on the exchange's ticker tape.

There are two potential complications to this simple scenario, however. First, as noted earlier, the posted quotes of $98 and $98.10 actually represent commitments to trade up to a specified number of shares. If the market order is for more than this number of shares, the order may be filled at multiple prices. For example, if the asked price is good for orders up to 600 shares and the investor wishes to purchase 1,000 shares, it may be necessary to pay a slightly higher price for the last 400 shares than the quoted asked price.

The second complication arises from the possibility of trading "inside the quoted spread." If the broker who has received a market buy order for IBM meets another broker who has received a market sell order for IBM, they can agree to trade with each other at a price of $98.05 per share. By meeting in the middle of the quoted spread, both the buyer and the seller obtain "price improvements," that is, transaction prices better than the best quoted prices. Such "meetings" of brokers are more than accidental. Because all trading takes place at the specialist's post, floor brokers know where to look for counterparties to take the other side of a trade.

Limit orders   Investors also may choose to place a *limit order,* where they specify prices at which they are willing to buy or sell a security. If IBM is selling at $98 bid, $98.10 asked, for example, a limit buy order may instruct the broker to buy the stock if and when the share price falls *below* $97. Correspondingly, a limit sell order instructs the broker to sell as soon as the stock price goes *above* the specified limit.

Figure 3.5 is a portion of the limit order book for shares in Intel on the Island exchange on one day in 2001. Notice that the best orders are at the top of the list: the offers to buy at the highest price and to sell at the lowest price. The buy and sell orders at the top of the list— $27.88 and $27.93—are called the *inside quotes;* they are the buy and sell orders with the closest prices. For Intel, the inside spread is only 5 cents per share.

What happens if a limit order is placed in between the quoted bid and ask prices? For example, suppose you have instructed your broker to buy IBM at a price of $98.05 or better. The order may not be executed immediately, since the quoted asked price for the shares is $98.10, which is more than you are willing to pay. However, your willingness to buy at $98.05 is better than the quoted bid price of $98 per share. Therefore, you may find that there are traders who were unwilling to sell their shares at the currently quoted $98 bid price but are happy to sell shares to you at your higher bid price of $98.05.

FIGURE **3.5**

The limit order book for Intel on the Island exchange, November 9, 2001.

refresh | island home | disclamer | help

∂INTC

GET STOCK
INTC go

LAST MATCH		TODAY'S ACTIVITY	
Price	27.8900	Orders	16,774
Time	14:24:45	Volume	4,631,778

BUY ORDERS		SELL ORDERS	
Shares	Price	Shares	Price
100	27.8800	1,000	27.9300
500	27.8500	1,000	27.9690
200	27.8500	1,000	27.9800
1,000	27.8200	1,000	27.9900
3,300	27.8100	1,000	28.0000
300	27.8000	1,800	28.0600
75	27.7500	1,000	28.0800
101	27.7300	1,000	28.1000
5,000	27.7200	2,000	28.1100
1,000	27.72	1,000	28.1800
(416 more)		(395 more)	

FIGURE **3.6**

Limit orders

		Condition	
		Price below the limit	**Price above the limit**
Action	**Buy**	Limit buy order	Stop-buy order
	Sell	Stop-loss order	Limit sell order

Stop-loss orders are similar to limit orders in that the trade is not to be executed unless the stock hits a price limit. Here, however, the stock is to be *sold* if its price falls *below* a stipulated level. As the name suggests, the order lets the stock be sold to stop further losses from accumulating. Similarly, stop-buy orders specify that a stock should be bought when its price rises above a limit. These trades often accompany *short sales* (sales of securities you don't own but have borrowed from your broker) and are used to limit potential losses from the short position. Short sales are discussed in greater detail later in this chapter. Figure 3.6 organizes these types of trades in a convenient matrix.

Orders also can be limited by a time period. Day orders, for example, expire at the close of the trading day. If it is not executed on that day, the order is canceled. Open or good-till-canceled orders, in contrast, remain in force for up to six months, unless canceled by the customer.

Specialists and the Execution of Trades

specialist

A trader who makes a
market in the shares
of one or more firms
and who maintains a
"fair and orderly
market" by dealing
personally in the
market.

A **specialist** "makes a market" in the shares of one or more firms. This task may require the specialist to act as either a broker or a dealer. The specialist's role as a broker is simply to execute the orders of other brokers. Specialists also may buy or sell shares of stock for their own portfolios. When no other broker can be found to take the other side of a trade, specialists will do so even if it means they must buy for or sell from their own accounts. The NYSE commissions these companies to perform this service and monitors their performance.

Part of the specialist's job as a broker is simply clerical. The specialist maintains a "book" listing all outstanding unexecuted limit orders entered by brokers on behalf of clients. Actually, the book is now a computer console. When limit orders can be executed at market prices, the specialist executes, or "crosses," the trade.

The specialist is required to use the highest outstanding offered purchase price and the lowest outstanding offered selling price when matching trades. Therefore, the specialist system results in an auction market, meaning all buy and all sell orders come to one location, and the best orders "win" the trades. In this role, the specialist acts merely as a facilitator.

The more interesting function of the specialist is to maintain a "fair and orderly market" by acting as a dealer in the stock. In return for the exclusive right to make the market in a specific stock on the exchange, the specialist is required by the exchange to maintain an orderly market by buying and selling shares from inventory. Specialists maintain their own portfolios of stock and quoted bid and ask prices at which they are obligated to meet at least a limited amount of market orders. If market buy orders come in, specialists must sell shares from their own accounts at the ask price; if sell orders come in, they must stand willing to buy at the listed bid price.[4]

Ordinarily, however, in an active market, specialists can match buy and sell orders without using their own accounts. That is, the specialist's own inventory of securities need not be the primary means of order execution. Sometimes, the specialist's bid and ask prices are better than those offered by any other market participant. Therefore, at any point, the effective ask price in the market is the lower of either the specialist's ask price or the lowest of the unfilled limit-sell orders. Similarly, the effective bid price is the highest of the unfilled limit buy orders or the specialist's bid. These procedures ensure that the specialist provides liquidity to the market. In practice, specialists participate in approximately one-quarter of the transactions on the NYSE.

By standing ready to trade at quoted bid and ask prices, the specialist is exposed to exploitation by other traders. Larger traders with ready access to superior information will trade with specialists when the specialist's quotes are temporarily out of line with assessments of value based on that information. Specialists who cannot match the information resources of large traders will be at a disadvantage when their quoted prices offer profit opportunities to more advantaged traders.

You might wonder why specialists do not protect their interests by setting a low bid price and a high ask price. Specialists using that strategy would protect themselves from losses in a period of dramatic movements in the stock price. In contrast, specialists who offer a narrow spread between the bid and ask price have little leeway for error and must constantly monitor market conditions to avoid offering other investors advantageous terms.

Large bid–ask spreads are not viable options for the specialist for two reasons. First, one source of the specialist's income is frequent trading at the bid and ask prices, with the spread as a trading profit. A too-large spread would make the specialist's quotes uncompetitive with the limit orders placed by other traders. If the specialist's bid and asked quotes are consistently

---

[4]The specialist's published quotes are valid only for a given number of shares. If a buy or sell order is placed for more shares than the quotation size, the specialist has the right to revise the quote.

worse than those of public traders, the specialist will not participate in any trades and will lose the ability to profit from the bid–ask spread. An equally important reason that specialists cannot use large bid–ask spreads to protect their interests is that they are obligated to provide *price continuity* to the market. To illustrate the principle of price continuity, suppose the highest limit buy order for a stock is $30, while the lowest limit sell order is $32. When a market buy order comes in, it is matched to the best limit sell at $32. A market sell order would be matched to the best limit buy at $30. As market buys and sells come to the floor randomly, the stock price would fluctuate between $30 and $32. The exchange authorities would consider this excessive volatility, and the specialist would be expected to step in with bid and/or ask prices between these values to reduce the bid–ask spread to an acceptable level, typically less than $.15 for large firms. When a firm is newly listed on an exchange, specialist firms vigorously compete to be awarded the rights by the exchange to maintain the market in those shares. Since specialists are evaluated on their past performance in maintaining price continuity, they have considerable incentive to maintain tight spreads.

Specialists earn income both from commissions for acting as brokers for orders and from the spreads at which they buy and sell securities. Some believe specialists' access to their "books" of limit orders gives them unique knowledge about the probable direction of price movement over short periods of time. However, these days, interested floor traders also have access to the Display Books of outstanding limit orders.

For example, suppose the specialist sees that a stock now selling for $45 has limit buy orders for over 100,000 shares at prices ranging from $44.50 to $44.75. This latent buying demand provides a cushion of support, in that it is unlikely that enough sell pressure will come in during the next few hours to cause the price to drop below $44.50. If there are very few limit sell orders above $45, in contrast, some transient buying demand could raise the price substantially.

The specialist in such circumstances realizes that a position in the stock offers little downside risk and substantial upside potential. Such access to the trading intentions of other market participants seems to allow a specialist and agile floor traders to earn profits on personal transactions and for selected clients. One can easily overestimate such advantages, however, because ever more of the large orders are negotiated "upstairs," that is, as fourth-market deals.

Block Sales

Institutional investors frequently trade blocks of tens of thousands of shares of stock. Table 3.6 shows that **block transactions** of over 10,000 shares now account for about half of all trading. The larger block transactions are often too large for specialists to handle, as they do not wish to hold such large blocks of stock in their inventory. For example, the largest block transaction in the first half of 2001 was for 34 million shares of USX-Marathon stock.

block transactions

Large transactions in which at least 10,000 shares of stock are bought or sold.

TABLE **3.6** Block transactions on the New York Stock Exchange	Year	Shares (millions)	% Reported Volume	Average Number of Block Transactions per Day
	1965	48	3.1%	9
	1970	451	15.4	68
	1975	779	16.6	136
	1980	3,311	29.2	528
	1985	14,222	51.7	2,139
	1990	19,682	49.6	3,333
	1995	49,737	57.0	7,793
	2000	135,772	51.7	21,941

Source: Data from the New York Stock Exchange *Fact Book,* 2001.

"Block houses" have evolved to aid in the placement of larger block trades. Block houses are brokerage firms that specialize in matching block buyers and sellers. Once a buyer and a seller have been matched, the block is sent to the exchange floor where specialists execute the trade. If a buyer cannot be found, the block house might purchase all or part of a block sale for its own account. The block house then can resell the shares to the public.

The SuperDot System

SuperDot enables exchange members to send orders directly to the specialist's Display Book over computer lines. The largest market order that can be handled is 30,099 shares. In 2000, SuperDot processed an average of 1.5 million orders per day; the average time to execute market orders submitted through SuperDot was 15 seconds.

program trade

Coordinated sale or purchase of a portfolio of stocks.

SuperDot is especially useful to program traders. A **program trade** is a coordinated purchase or sale of an entire portfolio of stocks. Many trading strategies (such as index arbitrage, a topic we will study in Chapter 16) require that an entire portfolio of stocks be purchased or sold simultaneously in a coordinated program. SuperDot is the tool that enables many trading orders to be sent out at once and executed almost simultaneously.

The vast majority of all orders are submitted through SuperDot. However, these tend to be smaller orders and account for only a bit more than half of total share volume.

Settlement

Since June 1995, an order executed on the exchange must be settled within three working days. This requirement is often called T + 3, for trade date plus three days. The purchaser must deliver the cash, and the seller must deliver the stock to the broker, who in turn delivers it to the buyer's broker. Frequently, a firm's clients keep their securities in *street name,* which means the broker holds the shares registered in the firm's own name on behalf of the client. This convention can speed security transfer. T + 3 settlement has made such arrangements more important: It can be quite difficult for a seller of a security to complete delivery to the purchaser within the three-day period if the stock is kept in a safe deposit box.

Settlement is simplified further by the existence of a clearinghouse. The trades of all exchange members are recorded each day, with members' transactions netted out, so that each member need transfer or receive only the net number of shares sold or bought that day. An exchange member then settles with the clearinghouse instead of individually with every firm with which it made trades.

3.4 TRADING ON THE OTC MARKET

On the exchanges, all trading occurs through a specialist. On the over-the-counter (OTC) market, however, trades are negotiated directly through dealers who maintain an inventory of selected securities. Dealers sell from their inventories at ask prices and buy for them at bid prices.

An investor who wishes to purchase or sell shares engages a broker who tries to locate the dealer offering the best deal on the security. This is in contrast to exchange trading, where all buy or sell orders are negotiated through the specialist, who arranges for the best bids to get the trade. In the OTC market, brokers must search the offers of dealers directly to find the best trading opportunity. In this sense, Nasdaq is a price quotation system, not a trading system. While bid and ask prices can be obtained from the Nasdaq computer network, the actual trade still requires direct negotiation (often over the phone) between the broker and the dealer in the security.

However, in the wake of the stock market crash of 1987, Nasdaq instituted a Small Order Execution System (SOES), which is in effect a trading system. Under SOES, market makers in a security who post bid or ask prices on the Nasdaq network may be contacted over the network by other traders and are required to trade at the prices they currently quote. Dealers must accept SOES orders at their posted prices up to a limit which may be 1,000 shares, but usually is smaller, depending on factors such as trading volume in the stock.

Because the Nasdaq system does not use a specialist, OTC trades do not require a centralized trading floor as do exchange-listed stocks. Dealers can be located anywhere they can communicate effectively with other buyers and sellers.

One disadvantage of the decentralized dealer market is that the investing public is vulnerable to *trading through,* which refers to the possibility that dealers can trade with the public at their quoted bid or asked prices even if other customers have offered to trade at better prices. A dealer who posts $20 bid and $20.15 asked prices for a stock may continue to fill market buy orders at the ask price and fill market sell orders at the bid price—even if there are limit orders by public customers "inside the spread," for example, limit orders to buy at $20.05 or limit orders to sell at $20.10. This practice harms the investor whose limit order is not filled (is "traded through") as well as the investor whose market buy or sell order is not filled at the best available price.

Trading through on Nasdaq sometimes results from imperfect coordination among dealers. A limit order placed with one broker may not be seen by brokers for other traders because computer systems are not linked and only the broker's own bid and asked prices are posted on the Nasdaq system. In contrast, trading through is strictly forbidden on the NYSE or Amex, where "price priority" requires that the specialist fill the best-priced order first. Moreover, because all traders in an exchange market must trade through the specialist, the exchange provides true *price discovery,* meaning that market prices reflect the prices at which *all* participants at that moment are willing to trade. This is the advantage of a centralized auction market.

In October 1994, the Justice Department announced an investigation of the Nasdaq Stock Market regarding possible collusion among market makers to maintain spreads at artificially high levels. In 1996, the Justice Department settled with the Nasdaq dealers. The dealers agreed to refrain from pressuring any other market maker to maintain wide spreads and from refusing to deal with other traders who try to undercut an existing spread.

Also in 1996, the SEC settled with the National Association of Securities Dealers (NASD) as well as with the Nasdaq stock market. The settlement called for NASD to take steps to prohibit market makers from colluding on spreads. In addition, the SEC mandated the following three rules on Nasdaq dealers:

1. *Publicly display all limit orders.* Limit orders from all investors that exceed 100 shares must now be displayed. Therefore, the quoted bid or ask price for a stock must now be the best price quoted by any investor, not simply the best dealer quote. This shrinks the effective spread on the stock.

2. *Make best dealer quotes public.* Nasdaq dealers must now disclose whether they have posted better quotes in private trading systems or ECNs such as Instinet than they are quoting in the Nasdaq market.

3. *Reveal the size of best customer limit orders.* For example, if a dealer quotes an offer to buy 1,000 shares of stock at a quoted bid price and a customer places a limit buy order for 500 shares at the same price, the dealer must advertise the bid price as good for 1,500 shares.

Market Structure in Other Countries

The structure of security markets varies considerably from one country to another. A full cross-country comparison is far beyond the scope of this text. Therefore, we will instead briefly review three of the biggest non-U.S. stock markets: the London, Euronext, and Tokyo exchanges. Figure 3.7 shows the volume of trading in major world markets.

London   Until 1997, trading arrangements in London were similar to those on Nasdaq. Competing dealers who wished to make a market in a stock would enter bid and ask prices into the Stock Exchange Automated Quotations (SEAQ) system. As in the U.S., London security firms acted as both dealers and as brokerage firms, that is, both making a market in securities and executing trades for their clients.

In 1997, the London Stock Exchange introduced an electronic trading system dubbed SETS (Stock Exchange Electronic Trading Service). This is an electronic clearing system similar to ECNs in which buy and sell orders are submitted via computer networks and any buy and sell orders that can be crossed are executed automatically.

Most trading in London equities is now conducted using SETS, particularly for shares in larger firms. However, SEAQ continues to operate and may be more likely to be used for the "upstairs market" in large block transactions or other less liquid transactions.

Euronext   Euronext was formed in 2000 by a merger of the Paris, Amsterdam, and Brussels exchanges. Euronext, like most European exchanges, uses an electronic trading system. Its system, called NSC (for Nouveau Système de Cotation, or New Quotation System), has fully automated order routing and execution. In fact, investors can enter their orders directly without contacting their brokers. An order submitted to the system is executed immediately if it can be crossed against an order in the public limit order book; if it cannot be executed, it is entered into the limit order book.

Euronext is in the process of establishing cross-trading agreements with several other European exchanges such as Helsinki or Luxembourg. In 2001, it also purchased LIFFE, the London International Financial Futures and Options Exchange.

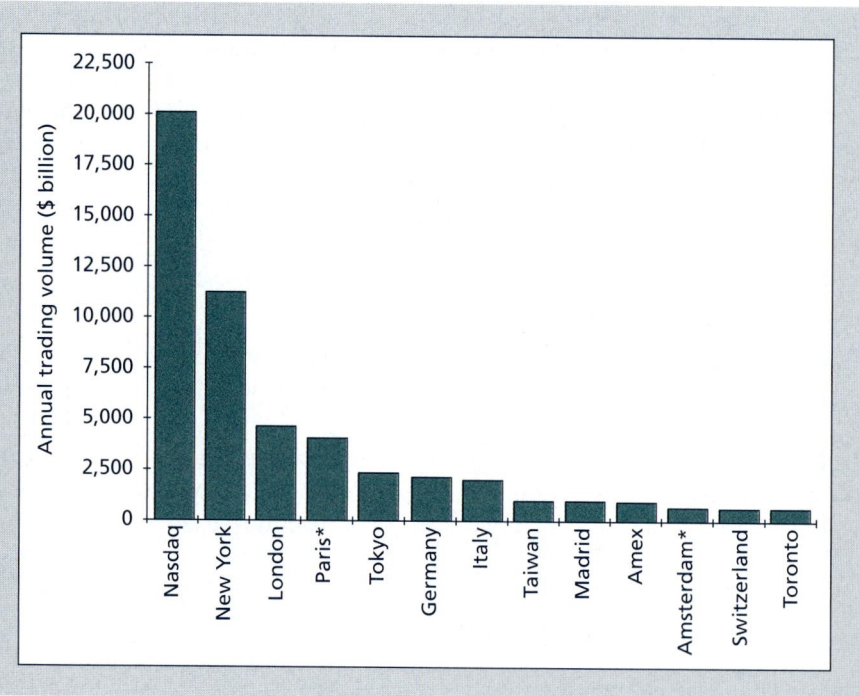

FIGURE 3.7

Dollar volume of equity trading in major world markets, 2000

Source: International Federation of Stock Exchanges, www.fibv.com.

*The Paris and Amsterdam exchanges have (together with the Brussels exchange) merged to form the Euronext exchange. Although the exchanges have been integrated, trading continues to be conducted in each of these cities.

Tokyo The Tokyo Stock Exchange (TSE) is the largest stock exchange in Japan, accounting for about 80% of total trading. There is no specialist system on the TSE. Instead, a *saitori* maintains a public limit order book, matches market and limit orders, and is obliged to follow certain actions to slow down price movements when simple matching of orders would result in price changes greater than exchange-prescribed minimums. In their clerical role of matching orders, *saitoris* are somewhat similar to specialists on the NYSE. However, *saitoris* do not trade for their own accounts, and therefore they are quite different from either dealers or specialists in the United States.

Because the *saitori* performs an essentially clerical role, there are no market making services or liquidity provided to the market by dealers or specialists. The limit order book is the primary provider of liquidity. In this regard, the TSE bears some resemblance to the fourth market in the United States, in which buyers and sellers trade directly via networks such as Instinet or Posit. On the TSE, however, if order imbalances result in price movements across sequential trades that are considered too extreme by the exchange, the *saitori* may temporarily halt trading and advertise the imbalance in the hope of attracting additional trading interest to the "weak" side of the market.

The TSE organizes stocks into two categories. The First Section consists of about 1,200 of the most actively traded stocks. The Second Section is for about 400 of the less actively traded stocks. Trading in the larger First Section stocks occurs on the floor of the exchange. The remaining securities in the First Section and the Second Section trade electronically.

Globalization of Stock Markets

All stock markets have come under increasing pressure in recent years to make international alliances or mergers. Much of this pressure is due to the impact of electronic trading. To a growing extent, traders view stock markets as computer networks that link them to other traders, and there are increasingly fewer limits on the securities around the world that they can trade. Against this background, it becomes more important for exchanges to provide the cheapest and most efficient mechanism by which trades can be executed and cleared. This argues for global alliances that can facilitate the nuts and bolts of cross-border trading and can benefit from economies of scale. Moreover, in the face of competition from electronic networks, established exchanges feel that they eventually need to offer 24-hour global markets. Finally, companies want to be able to go beyond national borders when they wish to raise capital.

Merger talks and international strategic alliances blossomed in the late 1990s. We have noted the Euronext merger as well as its alliance with other European exchanges. The Stockholm, Copenhagen, and Oslo exchanges formed a "Nordic Country Alliance" in 1999. In the last few years, Nasdaq has instituted a pilot program to co-list shares on the Stock Exchange of Hong Kong; has launched Nasdaq Europe, Nasdaq Japan, and Nasdaq Canada markets; and has entered negotiations on joint ventures with both the London and Frankfurt exchanges. The NYSE and Tokyo Stock Exchange are exploring the possibility of common listing standards. The NYSE also is exploring the possibility of an alliance with Euronext, in which the shares of commonly listed large multinational firms could be traded on both exchanges. In the wake of the stock market decline of 2001–2002, however, globalization initiatives have faltered. With less investor interest in markets and a dearth of initial public offerings, both Nasdaq Europe and Nasdaq Japan have been less successful, and Nasdaq reportedly was considering pulling out of its Japanese venture.

Meanwhile, many markets are increasing their international focus. For example, Nasdaq and the NYSE each list over 400 non-U.S. firms, and foreign firms account for about 10% of trading volume on the NYSE.

3.5 | TRADING COSTS

Part of the cost of trading a security is obvious and explicit. Your broker must be paid a commission. Individuals may choose from two kinds of brokers: full-service or discount brokers. Full-service brokers who provide a variety of services often are referred to as account executives or financial consultants.

Besides carrying out the basic services of executing orders, holding securities for safekeeping, extending margin loans, and facilitating short sales, brokers routinely provide information and advice relating to investment alternatives.

Full-service brokers usually depend on a research staff that prepares analyses and forecasts of general economic as well as industry and company conditions and often makes specific buy or sell recommendations. Some customers take the ultimate leap of faith and allow a full-service broker to make buy and sell decisions for them by establishing a *discretionary account.* In this account, the broker can buy and sell prespecified securities whenever deemed fit. (The broker cannot withdraw any funds, though.) This action requires an unusual degree of trust on the part of the customer, for an unscrupulous broker can "churn" an account, that is, trade securities excessively with the sole purpose of generating commissions.

Discount brokers, on the other hand, provide "no-frills" services. They buy and sell securities, hold them for safekeeping, offer margin loans, and facilitate short sales, and that is all. The only information they provide about the securities they handle is price quotations. Discount brokerage services have become increasingly available in recent years. Many banks, thrift institutions, and mutual fund management companies now offer such services to the investing public as part of a general trend toward the creation of one-stop "financial supermarkets."

The commission schedule for trades in common stocks for one prominent discount broker is as follows:

Transaction Method	Commission
Online trading	$20 or $0.02 per share, whichever is greater
Automated telephone trading	$40 or $0.02 per share, whichever is greater
Orders desk (through an associate)	$45 + $0.03 per share

Notice that there is a minimum charge regardless of trade size and cost as a fraction of the value of traded shares falls as trade size increases. Note also that these prices (and most advertised prices) are for the cheapest market orders. Limit orders are more expensive.

In addition to the explicit part of trading costs—the broker's commission—there is an implicit part—the dealer's **bid–ask spread.** Sometimes the broker is a dealer in the security being traded and charges no commission but instead collects the fee entirely in the form of the bid–ask spread.

bid–ask spread

The difference between a dealer's bid and asked price.

Another implicit cost of trading that some observers would distinguish is the price concession an investor may be forced to make for trading in any quantity that exceeds the quantity the dealer is willing to trade at the posted bid or asked price.

One continuing trend is toward online trading either through the Internet or through software that connects a customer directly to a brokerage firm. In 1994, there were no online brokerage accounts; only five years later, there were around 7 million such accounts at "e brokers" such as Ameritrade, Charles Schwab, Fidelity, and E*Trade, and roughly one in five trades was initiated over the Internet.

While there is little conceptual difference between placing your order using a phone call versus through a computer link, online brokerage firms can process trades more cheaply since they do not have to pay as many brokers. The average commission for an online trade is now less than $20, compared to perhaps $100–$300 at full-service brokers.

SEC Prepares for a New World of Stock Trading

What should our securities markets look like to serve today's investor best? Congress addressed this very question a generation ago, when markets were threatened with fragmentation from an increasing number of competing dealers and exchanges. This led the SEC to establish the national market system, which enabled investors to obtain the best quotes on stocks from any of the major exchanges.

Today it is the proliferation of electronic exchanges and after-hours trading venues that threatens to fragment the market. But the solution is simple, and would take the intermarket trading system devised by the SEC a quarter century ago to its next logical step. The highest bid and the lowest offer for every stock, no matter where they originate, should be displayed on a screen that would be available to all investors, 24 hours a day, seven days a week.

If the SEC mandated this centralization of order flow, competition would significantly enhance investor choice and the quality of the trading environment.

Would brokerage houses or even exchanges exist, as we now know them? I believe so, but electronic communication networks would provide the crucial links between buyers and sellers. ECNs would compete by providing far more sophisticated services to the investor than are currently available—not only the entering and execution of standard limit and market orders, but the execution of contingent orders, buys and sells dependent on the levels of other stocks, bonds, commodities, even indexes.

The services of brokerage houses would still be in much demand, but their transformation from commission-based to flat-fee or asset-based pricing would be accelerated. Although ECNs will offer almost costless processing of the basic investor transactions, brokerages would aid investors in placing more sophisticated orders. More importantly, brokers would provide investment advice. Although today's investor has access to more and more information, this does not mean that he has more understanding of the forces that rule the market or the principles of constructing the best portfolio.

As the spread between the best bid and offer price has collapsed, some traditional concerns of regulators are less pressing than they once were. Whether to allow dealers to step in front of customers to buy or sell, or allow brokerages to cross their orders internally at the best price, regardless of other orders at the price on the book, have traditionally been burning regulatory issues. But with spreads so small and getting smaller, these issues are of virtually no consequence to the average investor as long as the integrity of the order flow information is maintained.

None of this means that the SEC can disappear once it establishes the central order-flow system. A regulatory authority is needed to monitor the functioning of the new systems and ensure that participants live up to their promises. The rise of technology threatens many established power centers and has prompted some to call for more controls and a go-slow approach. By making clear that the commission's role is to encourage competition to best serve investors, not to impose or dictate the ultimate structure of the markets, the SEC is poised to take stock trading into the new millennium.

SOURCE: Abridged from Jeremy J. Siegel, "The SEC Prepares for a New World of Stock Trading," *The Wall Street Journal*, September 27, 1999. Reprinted by permission of Dow Jones & Company, Inc. via Copyright Clearance Center, Inc. © 1999 Dow Jones & Company, Inc. All Rights Reserved Worldwide.

Moreover, these e-brokers are beginning to provide some of the same services offered by full-service brokers such as online company research and, to a lesser extent, the opportunity to participate in IPOs. The traditional full-service brokerage firms have responded to this competitive challenge by introducing online trading for their own customers. Some of these firms are charging by the trade; others charge for such trading through fee-based accounts, in which the customer pays a percentage of assets in the account for the right to trade online.

An ongoing controversy between the NYSE and its competitors is the extent to which better execution on the NYSE offsets the generally lower explicit costs of trading in other markets. Execution refers to the size of the effective bid–ask spread and the amount of price impact in a market. The NYSE believes that many investors focus too intently on the costs they can see, despite the fact that quality of execution can be a far more important determinant of total costs. Many NYSE trades are executed at a price inside the quoted spread. This can happen because floor brokers at the specialist's post can bid above or sell below the specialist's quote. In this way, two public orders can cross without incurring the specialist's spread.

In contrast, in a dealer market, all trades go through the dealer, and all trades, therefore, are subject to a bid–ask spread. The client never sees the spread as an explicit cost, however. The price at which the trade is executed incorporates the dealer's spread, but this part of the price is never reported to the investor. Similarly, regional markets are disadvantaged in terms of execution because their lower trading volume means that fewer brokers congregate at a specialist's post, resulting in a lower probability of two public orders crossing.

A controversial practice related to the bid–ask spread and the quality of trade execution is "paying for order flow." This entails paying a broker a rebate for directing the trade to a particular dealer rather than to the NYSE. By bringing the trade to a dealer instead of to the exchange, however, the broker eliminates the possibility that the trade could have been executed without incurring a spread. In fact, the opportunity to profit from the bid–ask spread is the major reason that the dealer is willing to pay the broker for the order flow. Moreover, a broker that is paid for order flow might direct a trade to a dealer that does not even offer the most competitive price. (Indeed, the fact that dealers can afford to pay for order flow suggests that they are able to lay off the trade at better prices elsewhere and, possibly, that the broker also could have found a better price with some additional effort.) Many of the online brokerage firms rely heavily on payment for order flow, since their explicit commissions are so minimal. They typically do not actually execute orders, instead sending an order either to a market maker or to a stock exchange for listed stocks.

Such practices raise serious ethical questions, because the broker's primary obligation is to obtain the best deal for the client. Payment for order flow might be justified if the rebate is passed along to the client either directly or through lower commissions, but it is not clear that such rebates are passed through.

Online trading and electronic communications networks have already changed the landscape of the financial markets, and this trend can only be expected to continue. The nearby box considers some of the implications of these new technologies for the future structure of financial markets.

3.6 | BUYING ON MARGIN

When purchasing securities, investors have easy access to a source of debt financing called *broker's call loans*. The act of taking advantage of broker's call loans is called *buying on margin*.

Purchasing stocks on margin means the investor borrows part of the purchase price of the stock from a broker. The **margin** in the account is the portion of the purchase price contributed by the investor; the remainder is borrowed from the broker. The brokers in turn borrow money from banks at the call money rate to finance these purchases; they then charge their clients that rate (defined in Chapter 2), plus a service charge for the loan. All securities purchased on margin must be maintained with the brokerage firm in street name, for the securities are collateral for the loan.

margin

Describes securities purchased with money borrowed in part from a broker. The margin is the net worth of the investor's account.

The Board of Governors of the Federal Reserve System limits the extent to which stock purchases can be financed using margin loans. The current initial margin requirement is 50%, meaning that at least 50% of the purchase price must be paid for in cash, with the rest borrowed.

The percentage margin is defined as the ratio of the net worth, or the "equity value," of the account to the market value of the securities. To demonstrate, suppose an investor initially pays $6,000 toward the purchase of $10,000 worth of stock (100 shares at $100 per share), borrowing the remaining $4,000 from a broker. The initial balance sheet looks like this:

Assets		Liabilities and Owners' Equity	
Value of stock	$10,000	Loan from broker	$4,000
		Equity	$6,000

The initial percentage margin is

$$\text{Margin} = \frac{\text{Equity in account}}{\text{Value of stock}} = \frac{\$6,000}{\$10,000} = .60, \text{ or } 60\%$$

If the stock's price declines to $70 per share, the account balance becomes:

Assets		Liabilities and Owners' Equity	
Value of stock	$7,000	Loan from broker	$4,000
		Equity	$3,000

The assets in the account fall by the full decrease in the stock value, as does the equity. The percentage margin is now

$$\text{Margin} = \frac{\text{Equity in account}}{\text{Value of stock}} = \frac{\$3,000}{\$7,000} = .43, \text{ or } 43\%$$

If the stock value were to fall below $4,000, owners' equity would become negative, meaning the value of the stock is no longer sufficient collateral to cover the loan from the broker. To guard against this possibility, the broker sets a *maintenance margin.* If the percentage margin falls below the maintenance level, the broker will issue a *margin call,* which requires the investor to add new cash or securities to the margin account. If the investor does not act, the broker may sell securities from the account to pay off enough of the loan to restore the percentage margin to an acceptable level.

Margin calls can occur with little warning. For example, on April 14, 2000, when the Nasdaq index fell by a record 355 points, or 9.7%, the accounts of many investors who had purchased stock with borrowed funds ran afoul of their maintenance margin requirements. Some brokerage houses, concerned about the incredible volatility in the market and the possibility that stock prices would fall below the point that remaining shares could cover the amount of the loan, gave their customers only a few hours or less to meet a margin call rather than the more typical notice of a few days. If customers could not come up with the cash, or were not at a phone to receive the notification of the margin call until later in the day, their accounts were sold out. In other cases, brokerage houses sold out accounts without notifying their customers. The nearby box discussed this episode.

An example will show how maintenance margin works. Suppose the maintenance margin is 30%. How far could the stock price fall before the investor would get a margin call? Answering this question requires some algebra.

Let P be the price of the stock. The value of the investor's 100 shares is then $100P$, and the equity in the account is $100P - \$4,000$. The percentage margin is $(100P - \$4,000)/100P$. The price at which the percentage margin equals the maintenance margin of .3 is found by solving the equation

$$\frac{100P - 4,000}{100P} = .3$$

which implies that $P = \$57.14$. If the price of the stock were to fall below $57.14 per share, the investor would get a margin call.

3. Suppose the maintenance margin is 40%. How far can the stock price fall before the investor gets a margin call?

Concept
CHECK

Margin Investors Learn the Hard Way That Brokers Can Get Tough on Loans

For many investors, Friday, April 14, was a frightening day, as the Nasdaq Composite Index plunged a record 355.49 points, or 9.7%. For Mehrdad Bradaran, who had been trading on margin—with borrowed funds—it was a disaster.

The value of the California engineer's technology-laden portfolio plummeted, forcing him to sell $18,000 of stock and to deposit an additional $2,000 in cash in his account to meet a margin call from his broker, TD Waterhouse Group, to reduce his $52,000 in borrowings.

At least the worst was over, Mr. Bradaran figured, as tech stocks soared the following Monday—only to learn Monday evening that Waterhouse's Santa Monica, Calif., branch had sold an additional $20,000 of stock "without even notifying me," he says. His account, which had been worth $28,000 not including his borrowed funds, is now worth just $8,000, he says. "If they had given me a call, and I had deposited the money, I would have gained back at least half" of the $20,000 in losses when the market rebounded, he claims.

Mr. Bradaran is one of many investors who have discovered that buying stocks with borrowed funds—always a risky strategy—can be riskier than they ever imagined when the market is going wild. That's because some brokerage firms exercised their right to change margin-loan practices without notice during the market's recent nose dive.

The result: Customers were given only a few hours or less to meet a margin call, rather than the several days they typically are given to deposit additional cash or stock in their brokerage account, or to decide which securities they want to sell to cover their debts. And some firms, such as Waterhouse, also sold out some customers' accounts without any prior notice, as they are allowed to under margin-loan agreements signed by customers.

Investors generally can borrow as much as 50% of the value of their stocks. Once the purchase is completed, an investor's equity—the current value of the stocks less the amount of the loan—must be equal to at least 25% of the current market value of the shares. Many brokerage firms set stricter requirements. If falling stock prices reduce equity below the minimum, an investor may receive a margin call.

The actual amount an investor must fork over to meet a margin call can be a multiple of the amount of the call. That is because the value of the loan stays constant even when the market value of the securities falls.

Many investors were stunned by their firms' actions, either because they didn't understand the margin rules or ignored the potential risks. There aren't any public statistics on the number of investors affected, but the margin calls accompanying April's market roller coaster have clearly hit a nerve.

Some clients of other brokerage firms were affected as well. Larry Marshall, the owner of an executive-search firm who lives in Malibu, Calif., says Merrill Lynch & Co. told him the Monday after the market's drop that he would have to meet an $850,000 margin call immediately. Normally, he says, the firm gives him three to five days to come up with additional funds.

A Merrill Lynch spokeswoman says "as a matter of good business practice in periods of extreme volatility, offices may be asked to exercise the most prudent measures—clearly outlined in our margin policy—to responsibly manage the risk associated with leveraged accounts."

Clearly, a lot of investors would have benefited from additional time because of the market's sharp rebound. But they, and the brokerage firms on the hook for their loans, could have been in even worse shape if stock prices had continued to plummet.

SOURCE: Abridged from Ruth Smith, "Margin Investors Learn the Hard Way That Brokers Can Get Tough on Loans," *The Wall Street Journal*, April 27, 2000.

Why do investors buy securities on margin? They do so when they wish to invest an amount greater than their own money allows. Thus, they can achieve greater upside potential, but they also expose themselves to greater downside risk.

To see how, let's suppose an investor is bullish on IBM stock, which is selling for $100 per share. An investor with $10,000 to invest expects IBM to go up in price by 30% during the next year. Ignoring any dividends, the expected rate of return would be 30% if the investor invested $10,000 to buy 100 shares.

But now assume the investor borrows another $10,000 from the broker and invests it in IBM, too. The total investment in IBM would be $20,000 (for 200 shares). Assuming an interest rate on the margin loan of 9% per year, what will the investor's rate of return be now (again ignoring dividends) if IBM stock goes up 30% by year's end?

Buying on Margin

The Excel spreadsheet model below is built using the text example for IBM. The model makes it easy to analyze the impacts of different margin levels and the volatility of stock prices. It also allows you to compare return on investment for a margin trade with a trade using no borrowed funds. The original price ranges for the text example are highlighted for your reference.

You can learn more about this spreadsheet model using the interactive version available on our website at www.mhhe.com/bkm.

	A	B	C	D	E	F	G	H
1								
2	**Buying on Margin**			Ending	Return on		Ending	Return with
3				St Price	Investment		St Price	No Margin
4	Initial Equity Investment	10,000.00			51.00%			30.00%
5	Amount Borrowed	10,000.00		30	-149.00%		30	-70.00%
6	Initial Stock Price	100.00		40	-129.00%		40	-60.00%
7	Shares Purchased	200		50	-109.00%		50	-50.00%
8	Ending Stock Price	130.00		60	-89.00%		60	-40.00%
9	Cash Dividends During Hold Per.	0.00		70	-69.00%		70	-30.00%
10	Initial Margin Percentage	50.00%		80	-49.00%		80	-20.00%
11	Maintenance Margin Percentage	30.00%		90	-29.00%		90	-10.00%
12				100	-9.00%		100	0.00%
13	Rate on Margin Loan	9.00%		110	11.00%		110	10.00%
14	Holding Period in Months	12		120	31.00%		120	20.00%
15				130	51.00%		130	30.00%
16	**Return on Investment**			140	71.00%		140	40.00%
17	Capital Gain on Stock	6000.00		150	91.00%		150	50.00%
18	Dividends	0.00						
19	Interest on Margin Loan	900.00						
20	Net Income	5100.00						
21	Initial Investment	10000.00						
22	Return on Investment	51.00%						
23								
24	**Margin Call:**							
25	Margin Based on Ending Price	61.54%						
26	Price When Margin Call Occurs	$71.43						
27								
28								
29	Return on Stock without Margin	30.00%						

The 200 shares will be worth $26,000. Paying off $10,900 of principal and interest on the margin loan leaves $15,100 (i.e., $26,000 − $10,900). The rate of return in this case will be

$$\frac{\$15,100 - \$10,000}{\$10,000} = 51\%$$

The investor has parlayed a 30% rise in the stock's price into a 51% rate of return on the $10,000 investment.

Doing so, however, magnifies the downside risk. Suppose that, instead of going up by 30%, the price of IBM stock goes down by 30% to $70 per share. In that case, the 200 shares will be worth $14,000, and the investor is left with $3,100 after paying off the $10,900 of principal and interest on the loan. The result is a disastrous return of

$$\frac{3,100 - 10,000}{10,000} = -69\%$$

Table 3.7 summarizes the possible results of these hypothetical transactions. If there is no change in IBM's stock price, the investor loses 9%, the cost of the loan.

Concept CHECK ⠆⠆>

4. Suppose that in the previous example, the investor borrows only $5,000 at the same interest rate of 9% per year. What will the rate of return be if the price of IBM goes up by 30%? If it goes down by 30%? If it remains unchanged?

3.7 | SHORT SALES

Normally, an investor would first buy a stock and later sell it. With a short sale, the order is reversed. First, you sell and then you buy the shares. In both cases, you begin and end with no shares.

A **short sale** allows investors to profit from a decline in a security's price. An investor borrows a share of stock from a broker and sells it. Later, the short-seller must purchase a share of the same stock in the market in order to replace the share that was borrowed. This is called *covering the short position*. Table 3.8 compares stock purchases to short sales.

The short-seller anticipates the stock price will fall, so that the share can be purchased later at a lower price than it initially sold for; if so, the short-seller will reap a profit. Short-sellers must not only replace the shares but also pay the lender of the security any dividends paid during the short sale.

In practice, the shares loaned out for a short sale are typically provided by the short-seller's brokerage firm, which holds a wide variety of securities of its other investors in street name.

short sale

The sale of shares not owned by the investor but borrowed through a broker and later purchased to replace the loan.

TABLE **3.7**	Change in Stock Price	End-of-Year Value of Shares	Repayment of Principal and Interest*	Investor's Rate of Return
Illustration of buying stock on margin	30% increase	$26,000	$10,900	51%
	No change	20,000	10,900	−9
	30% decrease	14,000	10,900	−69

*Assuming the investor buys $20,000 worth of stock by borrowing $10,000 as an interest rate of 9% per year.

TABLE **3.8**	Purchase of Stock		
Cash flows from purchasing versus short-selling shares of stock	**Time**	**Action**	**Cash Flow***
	0	Buy share	− Initial price
	1	Receive dividend, sell share	Ending price + Dividend
	Profit = (Ending price + Dividend) − Initial price		

	Short Sale of Stock		
	Time	**Action**	**Cash Flow**
	0	Borrow share: sell it	+ Initial price
	1	Repay dividend and buy share to replace the share originally borrowed	− (Ending price + Dividend)
	Profit = Initial price − (Ending price + Dividend)		

*Note: A negative cash flow implies a cash *outflow*.

The owner of the shares need not know that the shares have been lent to the short-seller. If the owner wishes to sell the shares, the brokerage firm will simply borrow shares from another investor. Therefore, the short sale may have an indefinite term. However, if the brokerage firm cannot locate new shares to replace the ones sold, the short-seller will need to repay the loan immediately by purchasing shares in the market and turning them over to the brokerage house to close out the loan.

Exchange rules permit short sales only when the last recorded change in the stock price is positive. This rule apparently is meant to prevent waves of speculation against the stock. In essence, the votes of "no confidence" in the stock that short sales represent may be entered only after a price increase.

Finally, exchange rules require that proceeds from a short sale must be kept on account with the broker. The short-seller cannot invest these funds to generate income, although large or institutional investors typically will receive some income from the proceeds of a short sale being held with the broker. Short-sellers also are required to post margin (cash or collateral) with the broker to cover losses should the stock price rise during the short sale.

To illustrate the mechanics of short-selling, suppose you are bearish (pessimistic) on Dot Bomb stock, and its market price is $100 per share. You tell your broker to sell short 1,000 shares. The broker borrows 1,000 shares either from another customer's account or from another broker.

The $100,000 cash proceeds from the short sale are credited to your account. Suppose the broker has a 50% margin requirement on short sales. This means you must have other cash or securities in your account worth at least $50,000 that can serve as margin on the short sale. Let's say that you have $50,000 in Treasury bills. Your account with the broker after the short sale will then be:

Assets		Liabilities and Owners' Equity	
Cash	$100,000	Short position in Dot Bomb stock (1,000 shares owed)	$100,000
T-bills	50,000	Equity	50,000

Your initial percentage margin is the ratio of the equity in the account, $50,000, to the current value of the shares you have borrowed and eventually must return, $100,000:

$$\text{Percentage margin} = \frac{\text{Equity}}{\text{Value of stock owed}} = \frac{\$50,000}{\$100,000} = .50$$

Suppose you are right and Dot Bomb falls to $70 per share. You can now close out your position at a profit. To cover the short sale, you buy 1,000 shares to replace the ones you borrowed. Because the shares now sell for $70, the purchase costs only $70,000.[5] Because your account was credited for $100,000 when the shares were borrowed and sold, your profit is $30,000: The profit equals the decline in the share price times the number of shares sold short. On the other hand, if the price of Dot Bomb goes up unexpectedly while you are short, you may get a margin call from your broker.

Suppose the broker has a maintenance margin of 30% on short sales. This means the equity in your account must be at least 30% of the value of your short position at all times. How much can the price of Dot Bomb stock rise before you get a margin call?

---

[5]Notice that when buying on margin, you borrow a given amount of dollars from your broker, so the amount of the loan is independent of the share price. In contrast, when short-selling you borrow a given number of *shares*, which must be returned. Therefore, when the price of the shares changes, the value of the loan also changes.

Short Sale

This Excel spreadsheet model was built using the text example for Dot Bomb. The model allows you to analyze the effects of returns, margin calls, and different levels of initial and maintenance margins. The model also includes a sensitivity analysis for ending stock price and return on investment. The original price for the text example is highlighted for your reference.

You can learn more about this spreadsheet model using the interactive version available on our website at www.mhhe.com/bkm.

	A	B	C	D	E	F
1	Chapter 3					
2	Short Sale					
3	Dot Bomb Short Sale					
4					Ending	Return on
5	Initial Investment	50000.00			St Price	Investment
6	Beginning Share Price	100.00				60.00%
7	Number of Shares Sold Short	1000.00			40	120.00%
8	Ending Share Price	70.00			50	100.00%
9	Dividends Per Share	0.00			60	80.00%
10	Initial Margin Percentage	50.00%			70	60.00%
11	Maintenance Margin Percentage	30.00%			80	40.00%
12					90	20.00%
13	Return on Short Sale				100	0.00%
14	Gain or Loss on Price	30000.00			110	-20.00%
15	Dividends Paid	0.00			120	-40.00%
16	Net Income	30000.00			130	-60.00%
17	Return on Investment	60.00%				
18						
19						
20	Margin Positions					
21	Margin Based on Ending Price	114.29%				
22						
23	Price for Margin Call	115.38				

Let P be the price of Dot Bomb stock. Then the value of the shares you must pay back is 1,000P, and the equity in your account is $150,000 − 1,000$P$. Your short position margin ratio is equity/value of stock = (150,000 − 1,000P)/1,000P. The critical value of P is thus

$$\frac{\text{Equity}}{\text{Value of shares owed}} = \frac{150,000 - 1,000P}{1,000P} = .3$$

which implies that P = $115.38 per share. If Dot Bomb stock should *rise* above $115.38 per share, you will get a margin call, and you will either have to put up additional cash or cover your short position by buying shares to replace the ones borrowed.

Concept
CHECK

5. a. Construct the balance sheet if Dot Bomb goes up to $110.
   b. If the short position maintenance margin in the Dot Bomb example is 40%, how far can the stock price rise before the investor gets a margin call?

You can see now why stop-buy orders often accompany short sales. Imagine that you short sell Dot Bomb when it is selling at $100 per share. If the share price falls, you will profit from the short sale. On the other hand, if the share price rises, let's say to $130, you will lose $30 per share. But suppose that when you initiate the short sale, you also enter a stop-buy order at $120. The stop-buy will be executed if the share price surpasses $120, thereby limiting your losses to $20 per share. (If the stock price drops, the stop-buy will never be executed.) The stop-buy order thus provides protection to the short-seller if the share price moves up.

3.8 REGULATION OF SECURITIES MARKETS

Trading in securities markets in the United States is regulated by a myriad of laws. The major governing legislation includes the Securities Act of 1933 and the Securities Exchange Act of 1934. The 1933 Act requires full disclosure of relevant information relating to the issue of new securities. This is the act that requires registration of new securities and issuance of a prospectus that details the financial prospects of the firm. SEC approval of a prospectus or financial report is not an endorsement of the security as a good investment. The SEC cares only that the relevant facts are disclosed; investors must make their own evaluation of the security's value.

The 1934 Act established the Securities and Exchange Commission to administer the provisions of the 1933 Act. It also extended the disclosure principle of the 1933 Act by requiring periodic disclosure of relevant financial information by firms with already-issued securities on secondary exchanges. Of course, disclosure is valuable only if the information disclosed faithfully represents the condition of the firm; in the wake of the corporate reporting scandals of 2001 and 2002, confidence in such reports justifiably waned. Under legislation passed in 2002, CEOs and chief financial officers of public firms will be required to swear to the accuracy and completeness of the major financial statements filed by their firms.

The 1934 Act also empowers the SEC to register and regulate securities exchanges, OTC trading, brokers, and dealers. While the SEC is the administrative agency responsible for broad oversight of the securities markets, it shares responsibility with other regulatory agencies. The Commodity Futures Trading Commission (CFTC) regulates trading in futures markets, while the Federal Reserve has broad responsibility for the health of the U.S. financial system. In this role, the Fed sets margin requirements on stocks and stock options and regulates bank lending to securities markets participants.

The Securities Investor Protection Act of 1970 established the Securities Investor Protection Corporation (SIPC) to protect investors from losses if their brokerage firms fail. Just as the Federal Deposit Insurance Corporation provides depositors with federal protection against bank failure, the SIPC ensures that investors will receive securities held for their account in street name by a failed brokerage firm up to a limit of $500,000 per customer. The SIPC is financed by levying an "insurance premium" on its participating, or member, brokerage firms. It also may borrow money from the SEC if its own funds are insufficient to meet its obligations.

In addition to federal regulations, security trading is subject to state laws, known generally as *blue sky laws* because they are intended to give investors a clearer view of investment prospects. State laws to outlaw fraud in security sales existed before the Securities Act of 1933. Varying state laws were somewhat unified when many states adopted portions of the Uniform Securities Act, which was enacted in 1956.

Self-Regulation and Circuit Breakers

Much of the securities industry relies on self-regulation. The SEC delegates to secondary exchanges such as the NYSE much of the responsibility for day-to-day oversight of trading. Similarly, the National Association of Securities Dealers oversees trading of OTC securities. The Institute of Chartered Financial Analysts' Code of Ethics and Professional Conduct sets out principles that govern the behavior of CFAs. The nearby box presents a brief outline of those principles.

The market collapse of October 19, 1987, prompted several suggestions for regulatory change. Among these was a call for "circuit breakers" to slow or stop trading during periods of extreme volatility. Some of the current circuit breakers being used are as follows:

- *Trading halts.* If the Dow Jones Industrial Average falls by 10%, trading will be halted for one hour if the drop occurs before 2:00 P.M. (Eastern Standard Time), for one-half hour if

AIMR Standards of Professional Conduct

STANDARD I: FUNDAMENTAL RESPONSIBILITIES

Members shall maintain knowledge of and comply with all applicable laws, rules, and regulations including AIMR's Code of Ethics and Standards of Professional Conduct.

STANDARD II: RESPONSIBILITIES TO THE PROFESSION

- *Professional misconduct.* Members shall not engage in any professional conduct involving dishonesty, fraud, deceit, or misrepresentation,
- *Prohibition against plagiarism.*

STANDARD III: RESPONSIBILITIES TO THE EMPLOYER

- *Obligation to inform employer of code and standards.* Members shall inform their employer that they are obligated to comply with these Code and Standards.
- *Disclosure of additional compensation arrangements.* Members shall disclose to their employer all benefits that they receive in addition to compensation from that employer.

STANDARD IV: RESPONSIBILITIES TO CLIENTS AND PROSPECTS

- *Investment process and research reports.* Members shall exercise diligence and thoroughness in making investment recommendations . . . distinguish between facts and opinions in research reports . . . and use reasonable care to maintain objectivity.
- *Interactions with clients and prospects.* Members must place their clients' interests before their own.
- *Portfolio investment recommendations.* Members shall make a reasonable inquiry into a client's financial situation, investment experience, and investment objectives prior to making appropriate investment recommendations . . .
- *Priority of transactions.* Transactions for clients and employers shall have priority over transactions for the benefit of a member.
- *Disclosure of conflicts to clients and prospects.* Members shall disclose to their clients and prospects all matters, including ownership of securities or other investments, that reasonably could be expected to impair the member's ability to make objective recommendations.

STANDARD V: RESPONSIBILITIES TO THE PUBLIC

- *Prohibition against use of material nonpublic [inside] information.* Members who possess material nonpublic information related to the value of a security shall not trade in that security.
- *Performance presentation.* Members shall not make any statements that misrepresent the investment performance that they have accomplished or can reasonably be expected to achieve.

SOURCE: Abridged from *The Standards of Professional Conduct* of the AIMR.

---

the drop occurs between 2:00 and 2:30, but not at all if the drop occurs after 2:30. If the Dow falls by 20%, trading will be halted for two hours if the drop occurs before 1:00 P.M., for one hour if the drop occurs between 1:00 and 2:00, and for the rest of the day if the drop occurs after 2:00. A 30% drop in the Dow would close the market for the rest of the day, regardless of the time.

- *Collars.* When the Dow moves about two percentage points[6] in either direction from the previous day's close, Rule 80A of the NYSE requires that index arbitrage orders pass a "tick test." In a falling market, sell orders may be executed only at a plus tick or zero-plus tick, meaning that the trade may be done at a higher price than the last trade (a plus tick) or at the last price if the last recorded change in the stock price is positive (a zero-plus tick). The rule remains in effect for the rest of the day unless the Dow returns to within one percentage point of the previous day's close.

[6]The exact threshold is computed as 2% of the value of the Dow, updated quarterly, rounded to the nearest 10 points.

The idea behind circuit breakers is that a temporary halt in trading during periods of very high volatility can help mitigate informational problems that might contribute to excessive price swings. For example, even if a trader is unaware of any specific adverse economic news, if he sees the market plummeting, he will suspect that there might be a good reason for the price drop and will become unwilling to buy shares. In fact, he might decide to sell shares to avoid losses. Thus, feedback from price swings to trading behavior can exacerbate market movements. Circuit breakers give participants a chance to assess market fundamentals while prices are temporarily frozen. In this way, they have a chance to decide whether price movements are warranted while the market is closed.

Of course, circuit breakers have no bearing on trading in non-U.S. markets. It is quite possible that they simply have induced those who engage in program trading to move their operations into foreign exchanges.

Insider Trading

Regulations also prohibit insider trading. It is illegal for anyone to transact in securities to profit from **inside information,** that is, private information held by officers, directors, or major stockholders that has not yet been divulged to the public. But the definition of insiders can be ambiguous. While it is obvious that the chief financial officer of a firm is an insider, it is less clear whether the firm's biggest supplier can be considered an insider. Yet a supplier may deduce the firm's near-term prospects from significant changes in orders. This gives the supplier a unique form of private information, yet the supplier is not technically an insider. These ambiguities plague security analysts, whose job is to uncover as much information as possible concerning the firm's expected prospects. The distinction between legal private information and illegal inside information can be fuzzy.

An important Supreme Court decision in 1997, however, ruled on the side of an expansive view of what constitutes illegal insider trading. The decision upheld the so-called misappropriation theory of insider trading, which holds that traders may not trade on nonpublic information even if they are not company insiders.

The SEC requires officers, directors, and major stockholders to report all transactions in their firm's stock. A compendium of insider trades is published monthly in the SEC's *Official Summary of Securities Transactions and Holdings.* The idea is to inform the public of any implicit vote of confidence or no confidence made by insiders.

Insiders *do* exploit their knowledge. Three forms of evidence support this conclusion. First, there have been well-publicized convictions of principals in insider trading schemes.

Second, there is considerable evidence of "leakage" of useful information to some traders before any public announcement of that information. For example, share prices of firms announcing dividend increases (which the market interprets as good news concerning the firm's prospects) commonly increase in value a few days *before* the public announcement of the increase. Clearly, some investors are acting on the good news before it is released to the public. Similarly, share prices tend to increase a few days before the public announcement of above-trend earnings growth. Share prices still rise substantially on the day of the public release of good news, however, indicating that insiders, or their associates, have not fully bid up the price of the stock to the level commensurate with the news.

A third form of evidence on insider trading has to do with returns earned on trades by insiders. Researchers have examined the SEC's summary of insider trading to measure the performance of insiders. In one of the best known of these studies, Jaffee (1974) examined the abnormal return of stocks over the months following purchases or sales by insiders. For months in which insider purchasers of a stock exceeded insider sellers of the stock by three or more, the stock had an abnormal return in the following eight months of about 5%. Moreover, when insider sellers exceeded insider buyers, the stock tended to perform poorly.

inside information

Nonpublic knowledge about a corporation possessed by corporate officers, major owners, or other individuals with privileged access to information about the firm.

Restriction of the use of inside information is not universal. Japan has no such prohibition. An argument in favor of free use of inside information is that investors are not misled to believe that the financial market is a level playing field for all. At the same time, free use of inside information means that such information will more quickly be reflected in stock prices.

Most Americans believe, however, that it is valuable as well as virtuous to outlaw such advantage, even if less-than-perfect enforcement may leave the door open for some profitable violations of the law.

SUMMARY

- Firms issue securities to raise the capital necessary to finance their investments. Investment bankers market these securities to the public on the primary market. Investment bankers generally act as underwriters who purchase the securities from the firm and resell them to the public at a markup. Before the securities may be sold to the public, the firm must publish an SEC-approved prospectus that provides information on the firm's prospects.

- Already-issued securities are traded on the secondary market, that is, on organized stock exchanges; the over-the-counter market; and for large trades, through direct negotiation. Only members of exchanges may trade on the exchange. Brokerage firms holding seats on the exchange sell their services to individuals, charging commissions for executing trades on their behalf. The NYSE maintains strict listing requirements. Regional exchanges provide listing opportunities for local firms that do not meet the requirements of the national exchanges.

- Trading of common stocks on exchanges occurs through specialists. The specialist acts to maintain an orderly market in the shares of one or more firms. The specialist maintains "books" of limit buy and sell orders and matches trades at mutually acceptable prices. Specialists also accept market orders by selling from or buying for their own inventory of stocks when there is an imbalance of buy and sell orders.

- The over-the-counter market is not a formal exchange but a network of brokers and dealers who negotiate sales of securities. The Nasdaq system provides online computer quotes offered by dealers in the stock. When an individual wishes to purchase or sell a share, the broker can search the listing of bid and ask prices, contact the dealer with the best quote, and execute the trade.

- Block transactions are a fast-growing segment of the securities market that currently accounts for about half of trading volume. These trades often are too large to be handled readily by specialists and so have given rise to block houses that specialize in identifying potential trading partners for their clients.

- Buying on margin means borrowing money from a broker in order to buy more securities than can be purchased with one's own money alone. By buying securities on a margin, an investor magnifies both the upside potential and the downside risk. If the equity in a margin account falls below the required maintenance level, the investor will get a margin call from the broker.

- Short-selling is the practice of selling securities that the seller does not own. The short-seller borrows the securities sold through a broker and may be required to cover the short position at any time on demand. The cash proceeds of a short sale are kept in escrow by the broker, and the broker usually requires that the short-seller deposit additional cash or securities to serve as margin (collateral) for the short sale.

- Securities trading is regulated by the Securities and Exchange Commission, other government agencies, and self-regulation of the exchanges. Many of the important regulations have to do with full disclosure of relevant information concerning the securities in question. Insider trading rules also prohibit traders from attempting to profit from inside information.

- In addition to providing the basic services of executing buy and sell orders, holding securities for safekeeping, making margin loans, and facilitating short sales, full-service brokers offer investors information, advice, and even investment decisions. Discount brokers offer only the basic brokerage services but usually charge less. Total trading costs consist of commissions, the dealer's bid–ask spread, and price concessions.

KEY TERMS

ask price, 67
bid–ask spread 80
bid price, 67
block transactions, 75
electronic communication
    networks (ECNs), 68
fourth market, 68
initial public offerings
    (IPOs), 60

inside information, 91
margin, 82
Nasdaq, 67
over-the-counter (OTC)
    market, 67
primary market, 60
private placement, 61
program trade, 76
prospectus, 60

secondary market, 60
short sale, 86
specialist, 74
stock exchanges, 65
third market, 68
underwriters, 60

PROBLEM SETS

1. FBN, Inc., has just sold 100,000 shares in an initial public offering. The underwriter's explicit fees were $70,000. The offering price for the shares was $50, but immediately upon issue, the share price jumped to $53.
   a. What is your best guess as to the total cost to FBN of the equity issue?
   b. Is the entire cost of the underwriting a source of profit to the underwriters?

2. Suppose you short sell 100 shares of IBM, now selling at $120 per share.
   a. What is your maximum possible loss?
   b. What happens to the maximum loss if you simultaneously place a stop-buy order at $128?

3. Dée Trader opens a brokerage account, and purchases 300 shares of Internet Dreams at $40 per share. She borrows $4,000 from her broker to help pay for the purchase. The interest rate on the loan is 8%.
   a. What is the margin in Dée's account when she first purchases the stock?
   b. If the share price falls to $30 per share by the end of the year, what is the remaining margin in her account? If the maintenance margin requirement is 30%, will she receive a margin call?
   c. What is the rate of return on her investment?

4. Old Economy Traders opened an account to short sell 1,000 shares of Internet Dreams from the previous question. The initial margin requirement was 50%. (The margin account pays no interest.) A year later, the price of Internet Dreams has risen from $40 to $50, and the stock has paid a dividend of $2 per share.
   a. What is the remaining margin in the account?
   b. If the maintenance margin requirement is 30%, will Old Economy receive a margin call?
   c. What is the rate of return on the investment?

5. Do you think it is possible to replace market-making specialists with a fully automated, computerized trade-matching system?

6. Consider the following limit order book of a specialist. The last trade in the stock occurred at a price of $50.

Limit Buy Orders		Limit Sell Orders	
Price	Shares	Price	Shares
$49.75	500	$50.25	100
49.50	800	51.50	100
49.25	500	54.75	300
49.00	200	58.25	100
48.50	600		

- -

a. If a market buy order for 100 shares comes in, at what price will it be filled?

b. At what price would the next market buy order be filled?

c. If you were the specialist, would you want to increase or decrease your inventory of this stock?

7. You are bullish on Telecom stock. The current market price is $50 per share, and you have $5,000 of your own to invest. You borrow an additional $5,000 from your broker at an interest rate of 8% per year and invest $10,000 in the stock.

a. What will be your rate of return if the price of Telecom stock goes up by 10% during the next year? (Ignore the expected dividend.)

b. How far does the price of Telecom stock have to fall for you to get a margin call if the maintenance margin is 30%? Assume the price fall happens immediately.

8. You are bearish on Telecom and decide to sell short 100 shares at the current market price of $50 per share.

a. How much in cash or securities must you put into your brokerage account if the broker's initial margin requirement is 50% of the value of the short position?

b. How high can the price of the stock go before you get a margin call if the maintenance margin is 30% of the value of the short position?

9. Suppose that Intel currently is selling at $40 per share. You buy 500 shares using $15,000 of your own money and borrowing the remainder of the purchase price from your broker. The rate on the margin loan is 8%.

a. What is the percentage increase in the net worth of your brokerage account if the price of Intel *immediately* changes to: (i) $44; (ii) $40; (iii) $36? What is the relationship between your percentage return and the percentage change in the price of Intel?

b. If the maintenance margin is 25%, how low can Intel's price fall before you get a margin call?

c. How would your answer to (b) change if you had financed the initial purchase with only $10,000 of your own money?

d. What is the rate of return on your margined position (assuming again that you invest $15,000 of your own money) if Intel is selling *after one year* at: (i) $44; (ii) $40; (iii) $36? What is the relationship between your percentage return and the percentage change in the price of Intel? Assume that Intel pays no dividends.

e. Continue to assume that a year has passed. How low can Intel's price fall before you get a margin call?

10. Suppose that you sell short 500 shares of Intel, currently selling for $40 per share, and give your broker $15,000 to establish your margin account.

a. If you earn no interest on the funds in your margin account, what will be your rate of return after one year if Intel stock is selling at: (i) $44; (ii) $40; (iii) $36? Assume that Intel pays no dividends.

b. If the maintenance margin is 25%, how high can Intel's price rise before you get a margin call?

c. Redo parts (*a*) and (*b*), but now assume that Intel also has paid a year-end dividend of $1 per share. The prices in part (*a*) should be interpreted as ex-dividend, that is, prices after the dividend has been paid.

11. Call one full-service broker and one discount broker and find out the transaction costs of implementing the following strategies:
    a. Buying 100 shares of IBM now and selling them six months from now.
    b. Investing an equivalent amount in six-month at-the-money call options on IBM stock now and selling them six months from now.

12. Here is some price information on Marriott:

	Bid	Asked
Marriott	37.25	38.12

You have placed a stop-loss order to sell at $38. What are you telling your broker? Given market prices, will your order be executed?

13. Here is some price information on Fincorp stock. Suppose first that Fincorp trades in a dealer market such as Nasdaq.

Bid	Asked
55.25	55.50

   a. Suppose you have submitted an order to your broker to buy at market. At what price will your trade be executed?
   b. Suppose you have submitted an order to sell at market. At what price will your trade be executed?
   c. Suppose you have submitted a limit order to sell at $55.62. What will happen?
   d. Suppose you have submitted a limit order to buy at $55.37. What will happen?

14. Now reconsider problem 13 assuming that Fincorp sells in an exchange market like the NYSE.
   a. Is there any chance for price improvement in the market orders considered in parts (*a*) and (*b*)?
   b. Is there any chance of an immediate trade at $55.37 for the limit buy order in part (*d*)?

15. What purpose does the SuperDot system serve on the New York Stock Exchange?

16. Who sets the bid and asked price for a stock traded over the counter? Would you expect the spread to be higher on actively or inactively traded stocks?

17. Consider the following data concerning the NYSE:

Year	Average Daily Trading Volume (thousands of shares)	Annual High Price of an Exchange Membership
1985	109,169	$ 480,000
1987	188,938	1,150,000
1989	165,470	675,000
1991	178,917	440,000
1993	264,519	775,000
1995	346,101	1,050,000
1997	526,925	1,750,000

   a. What do you conclude about the short-run relationship between trading activity and the value of a seat?

b. Based on these data, what do you think has happened to the average commission charged to traders in the last decade?

18. On January 1, you sold short one round lot (that is, 100 shares) of Zenith stock at $14 per share. On March 1, a dividend of $2 per share was paid. On April 1, you covered the short sale by buying the stock at a price of $9 per share. You paid 50 cents per share in commissions for each transaction. What is the value of your account on April 1?

The following questions are from past CFA examinations.

19. If you place a stop-loss order to sell 100 shares of stock at $55 when the current price is $62, how much will you receive for each share if the price drops to $50?
    a. $50.
    b. $55.
    c. $54.87.
    d. Cannot tell from the information given.

20. You wish to sell short 100 shares of XYZ Corporation stock. If the last two transactions were at $34.12 followed by $34.25, you can sell short on the next transaction only at a price of
    a. 34.12 or higher
    b. 34.25 or higher
    c. 34.25 or lower
    d. 34.12 or lower

21. Specialists on the New York Stock Exchange do all of the following *except:*
    a. Act as dealers for their own accounts.
    b. Execute limit orders.
    c. Help provide liquidity to the marketplace.
    d. Act as odd-lot dealers.

WEBMASTER

Short Sales

Go to the website for Nasdaq at http://www.nasdaq.com. When you enter the site, a dialog box appears that allows you to get quotes for up to 10 stocks. Request quotes for the following companies as identified by their ticker: Noble Drilling (NE), Diamond Offshore (DO), and Haliburton (HAL). Once you have entered the tickers for each company, click the item called info quotes that appears directly below the dialog box for quotes.

1. On which market or exchange do these stocks trade? Identify the high and low price based on the current day's trading.

    Below each of the info quotes another dialog box is present. Click the item labeled fundamentals for the first stock. Some basic information on the company will appear along with an additional submenu. One of the items is labeled short interest. When you select that item a 12-month history of short interest will appear. You will need to complete the above process for each of the stocks.

2. Describe the trend, if any, for short sales over the last year.

3. What is meant by the term Days to Cover that appears on the history for each company?

4. Which of the companies has the largest relative number of shares that have been sold short?

SOLUTIONS TO

Concept
CHECKS

1. Limited time shelf registration was introduced because of its favorable trade-off of saving issue cost against mandated disclosure. Allowing unlimited shelf registration would circumvent "blue sky" laws that ensure proper disclosure as the financial circumstances of the firm change over time.

2. The advent of negotiated commissions reduced the prices that brokers charged to execute trades on the NYSE. This reduced the profitability of a seat on the exchange, which in turn resulted in the lower seat prices in 1975 that is evident in Table 3.1. Eventually, however, trading volume increased dramatically, which more than made up for lower commissions per trade, and the value of a seat on the exchange rapidly increased after 1975.

3. Solving

$$\frac{100P - \$4,000}{100P} = .4$$

yields $P = \$66.67$ per share.

4. The investor will purchase 150 shares, with a rate of return as follows:

Year-End Change in Price	Year-End Value of Shares	Repayment of Principal and Interest	Investor's Rate of Return
30%	$19,500	$5,450	40.5%
No change	15,000	5,450	−4.5
−30%	10,500	5,450	−49.5

5. *a.* Once Dot Bomb stock goes up to $110, your balance sheet will be:

Assets		Liabilities and Owner's Equity	
Cash	$100,000	Short position in Dot Bomb	$110,000
T-bills	50,000	Equity	40,000

b. Solving

$$\frac{\$150,000 - 1,000P}{1,000P} = .4$$

yields $P = \$107.14$ per share.

www.mhhe.com/bkm

4

MUTUAL FUNDS AND OTHER INVESTMENT COMPANIES

AFTER STUDYING THIS CHAPTER YOU SHOULD BE ABLE TO:

> Cite advantages and disadvantages of investing with an investment company rather than buying securities directly.

> Contrast open-end mutual funds with closed-end funds and unit investment trusts.

> Define net asset value and measure the rate of return on a mutual fund.

> Classify mutual funds according to investment style.

> Demonstrate the impact of expenses and turnover on mutual fund investment performance.

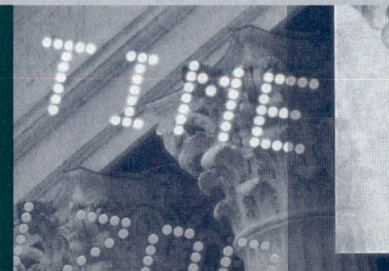

The previous chapter provided an introduction to the mechanics of trading securities and the structure of the markets in which securities trade. Increasingly, however, individual investors are choosing not to trade securities directly for their own accounts. Instead, they direct their funds to investment companies that purchase securities on their behalf. The most important of these financial intermediaries are mutual funds, which are currently owned by about one-half of U.S. households. Other types of investment companies, such as unit investment trusts and closed-end funds, also merit distinctions.

We begin the chapter by describing and comparing the various types of investment companies available to investors—unit investment trusts, closed-end investment companies, and open-end investment companies, more commonly known as mutual funds. We devote most of our attention to mutual funds, examining the functions of such funds, their investment styles and policies, and the costs of investing in these funds.

Next, we take a first look at the investment performance of these funds. We consider the impact of expenses and turnover on net performance and examine the extent to which performance is consistent from one period to the next. In other words, will the mutual funds that were the best past performers be the best *future* performers? Finally, we discuss sources of information on mutual funds and consider in detail the information provided in the most comprehensive guide, Morningstar's *Mutual Fund Sourcebook*.

4.1 INVESTMENT COMPANIES

investment companies

Financial intermediaries that invest the funds of individual investors in securities or other assets.

Investment companies are financial intermediaries that collect funds from individual investors and invest those funds in a potentially wide range of securities or other assets. Pooling of assets is the key idea behind investment companies. Each investor has a claim to the portfolio established by the investment company in proportion to the amount invested. These companies thus provide a mechanism for small investors to "team up" to obtain the benefits of large-scale investing.

Investment companies perform several important functions for their investors:

1. *Record keeping and administration.* Investment companies issue periodic status reports, keeping track of capital gains distributions, dividends, investments, and redemptions, and they may reinvest dividend and interest income for shareholders.

2. *Diversification and divisibility.* By pooling their money, investment companies enable investors to hold fractional shares of many different securities. They can act as large investors even if any individual shareholder cannot.

3. *Professional management.* Most, but not all, investment companies have full-time staffs of security analysts and portfolio managers who attempt to achieve superior investment results for their investors.

4. *Lower transaction costs.* Because they trade large blocks of securities, investment companies can achieve substantial savings on brokerage fees and commissions.

While all investment companies pool the assets of individual investors, they also need to divide claims to those assets among those investors. Investors buy shares in investment companies, and ownership is proportional to the number of shares purchased. The value of each share is called the **net asset value,** or **NAV.** Net asset value equals assets minus liabilities expressed on a per-share basis:

net asset value (NAV)

Assets minus liabilities expressed on a per-share basis.

$$\text{Net asset value} = \frac{\text{Market value of assets minus liabilities}}{\text{Shares outstanding}}$$

Consider a mutual fund that manages a portfolio of securities worth $120 million. Suppose the fund owes $4 million to its investment advisers and owes another $1 million for rent, wages due, and miscellaneous expenses. The fund has 5 million shareholders. Then

$$\text{Net asset value} = \frac{\$120 \text{ million} - \$5 \text{ million}}{5 \text{ million shares}} = \$23 \text{ per share}$$

 Concept CHECK

1. Consider these data from the December 2000 balance sheet of the Growth Index mutual fund sponsored by the Vanguard Group. (All values are in millions.) What was the net asset value of the portfolio?

Assets:	$14,754
Liabilities:	$ 1,934
Shares:	419.4

4.2 TYPES OF INVESTMENT COMPANIES

In the United States, investment companies are classified by the Investment Company Act of 1940 as either unit investment trusts or managed investment companies. The portfolios of unit investment trusts are essentially fixed and thus are called "unmanaged." In contrast, managed companies are so named because securities in their investment portfolios continually are bought and sold: The portfolios are managed. Managed companies are further classified as either closed-end or open-end. Open-end companies are what we commonly call mutual funds.

Unit Investment Trusts

Unit investment trusts are pools of money invested in a portfolio that is fixed for the life of the fund. To form a unit investment trust, a sponsor, typically a brokerage firm, buys a portfolio of securities which are deposited into a trust. It then sells to the public shares, or "units," in the trust, called *redeemable trust certificates*. All income and payments of principal from the portfolio are paid out by the fund's trustees (a bank or trust company) to the shareholders.

There is little active management of a unit investment trust because once established, the portfolio composition is fixed; hence these trusts are referred to as *unmanaged*. Trusts tend to invest in relatively uniform types of assets; for example, one trust may invest in municipal bonds, another in corporate bonds. The uniformity of the portfolio is consistent with the lack of active management. The trusts provide investors a vehicle to purchase a pool of one particular type of asset, which can be included in an overall portfolio as desired. The lack of active management of the portfolio implies that management fees can be lower than those of managed funds.

Sponsors of unit investment trusts earn their profit by selling shares in the trust at a premium to the cost of acquiring the underlying assets. For example, a trust that has purchased $5 million of assets may sell 5,000 shares to the public at a price of $1,030 per share, which (assuming the trust has no liabilities) represents a 3% premium over the net asset value of the securities held by the trust. The 3% premium is the trustee's fee for establishing the trust.

Investors who wish to liquidate their holdings of a unit investment trust may sell the shares back to the trustee for net asset value. The trustees can either sell enough securities from the asset portfolio to obtain the cash necessary to pay the investor, or they may instead sell the shares to a new investor (again at a slight premium to net asset value).

Managed Investment Companies

There are two types of managed companies: closed-end and open-end. In both cases, the fund's board of directors, which is elected by shareholders, hires a management company to manage the portfolio for an annual fee that typically ranges from .2% to 1.5% of assets. In many cases the management company is the firm that organized the fund. For example, Fidelity Management and Research Corporation sponsors many Fidelity mutual funds and is responsible for managing the portfolios. It assesses a management fee on each Fidelity fund. In other cases, a mutual fund will hire an outside portfolio manager. For example, Vanguard has hired Wellington Management as the investment adviser for its Wellington Fund. Most management companies have contracts to manage several funds.

Open-end funds stand ready to redeem or issue shares at their net asset value (although both purchases and redemptions may involve sales charges). When investors in open-end funds wish to "cash out" their shares, they sell them back to the fund at NAV. In contrast, **closed-end funds** do not redeem or issue shares. Investors in closed-end funds who wish to cash out must sell their shares to other investors. Shares of closed-end funds are traded on organized exchanges and can be purchased through brokers just like other common stock; their prices therefore can differ from NAV.

Figure 4.1 is a listing of closed-end funds from *The Wall Street Journal*. The first column after the name of the fund indicates the exchange on which the shares trade (A: Amex; C: Chicago; N: NYSE; O: Nasdaq; T: Toronto; z: does not trade on an exchange). The next four

unit investment trusts

Money pooled from many investors that is invested in a portfolio fixed for the life of the fund.

open-end funds

A fund that issues or redeems its shares at net asset value.

closed-end funds

A fund whose shares are traded at prices that can differ from net asset value. Shares may not be redeemed at NAV.

FIGURE 4.1

Closed-end
mutual funds

Source: *The Wall Street Journal*, November 19, 2001. Reprinted by permission of Dow Jones & Company, Inc., via Copyright Clearance Center, Inc. © 2001 Dow Jones & Company, Inc. All Rights Reserved Worldwide.

CLOSED-END FUNDS

Closed-end funds sell a limited number of shares and invest the proceeds in securities. Unlike open-end funds, closed-ends generally do not buy their shares back from investors who wish to cash in their holdings. Instead, fund shares trade on a stock exchange.

Friday, November 16, 2001

STOCK (SYM)	EXCH	NAV	CLOSE	NET CHG	VOL 100s	PREM /DISC	DIV	52 WK MKT RET
General Equity Funds								
♦AdamsExp **ADX** a	N	16.18	14.39	− 0.08	869	− 11.1	1.65e	− 28.3
AllncAll **AMO**	N	22.13	21.94	0.14	85	− 0.9	7.12e	− 24.3
Avalon Capital **MIST**	O	15.80	15.00	NA	NA	− 5.1	NA	15.4
BergstrmCap **BEM**	A	165.14	149.00	− 2.00	10	− 9.8	11.25e	− 29.6
♦BlueChipVal **BLU**	N	6.97	7.56	0.02	333	8.5	.81e	8.3
BouldrTotR **BTF**	N	17.02	15.21	− 0.28	31	− 10.6	.20	30.6
BrntlyCap **BBDC**	O	NA	8.75	− 0.30	78	NA	.62	6.8
CntlSec **CET** a	A	27.52	23.75	1.45	124	− 13.7	1.80e	− 14.0
Specialized Equity Funds								
♦ASA **ASA** c	N	22.87	18.80	0.05	786	− 17.8	.60a	33.2
♦CntlFdCan g **CEF** cl	A	3.33	3.32	0.02	132	− 0.3	.01g	13.2
CohnStrsAdvtg **RLF** a	N	13.60	14.56	0.21	375	7.1	1.26	NS
♦CohenStrsTR **RFI** a	N	13.17	13.65	0.11	117	3.6	.96a	30.7
Dundee Prec Mtls **DPM.A** cy	T	13.10	9.30	NA	NA	− 29.0	NA	26.1
FstFnlFd **FF**	N	14.36	12.15	0.05	349	− 15.4	e	30.0
GabelliMlti **GGT**	N	10.16	8.60	0.05	103	− 15.4	1.56e	− 18.0
GabelliUt **GUT**	N	7.34	9.04	− 0.05	73	23.2	.72	26.4

STOCK (SYM)	EXCH	NAV	CLOSE	NET CHG	VOL 100s	PREM /DISC	DIV	12 MO YIELD
U.S. Govt. Bond Funds								
ACM OppFd **AOF**	N	8.05	8.89	0.01	50	10.4	.72a	8.7
ACM IncFd **ACG**	N	8.38	8.13	− 0.13	7100	− 3.0	.84	10.2
♦EIS Fund **EIS** c	N	18.41	16.70	− 0.02	1	− 9.3	1.05e	6.2
MFS GvMkTr **MGF** a	N	7.27	6.67	0.05	526	− 8.3	.38	6.5
MSDW Gvtln **GVT**	N	9.65	8.96	− 0.07	785	− 7.2	.54	5.9
♦ScudderGvt **KGT** a	N	7.39	7.07	− 0.01	641	− 4.3	.48	6.9
Convertible Sec's. Funds								
♦BancroftFd **BCV**	A	21.03	19.35	0.05	78	− 8.0	.69e	1.2
CastleFd **CVF**	A	26.10	24.41	− 0.19	17	− 6.5	1.32a	18.3
♦ElsworthFd **ECF**	A	8.80	8.62	− 0.18	279	− 2.0	.48e	11.2
GabelliConv **GCV**	N	9.95	10.75	0.04	34	8.0	.80a	24.5
♦LncInNtlSec **LNV** c	N	16.08	14.14	− 0.06	57	− 12.1	.72m	− 12.4
PutnmCvOpp **PCV** a	N	17.82	17.20	0.15	34	− 3.5	1.22	1.8
PutnmHilnco **PCF** a	N	7.03	7.00	0.00	48	− 0.4	.65	6.4
RensncCap **RENN**	O	12.11	10.78	0.07	4	− 11.0	.54e	8.0
♦TCW Fd **CVT**	N	6.80	8.75	0.08	643	28.7	.84a	4.6
World Equity Funds								
AbrdnAusEq **IAF**	A	6.41	5.52	− 0.03	103	− 13.9	.68e	5.7
ArgntnaFd **AF**	N	8.41	8.16	0.01	135	− 3.0	.50	− 18.8
AsiaPacFd **APB**	N	9.53	7.70	0.08	649	− 19.2	e	− 12.3
AsiaTigers **GRR**	N	7.67	6.51	− 0.06	173	− 15.1	.29e	− 6.4
AustriaFd **OST**	N	6.63	6.30	0.05	172	− 5.0	.16e	− 16.2
BrazilFd **BZF**	N	17.46	14.30	− 0.05	6	− 18.1	.92	− 1.2
♦BrazilEqty **BZL**	N	4.95	4.00	− 0.10	31	− 19.2	.42	− 20.9

columns give the fund's most recent net asset value, the closing share price, the change in the closing price from the previous day, and trading volume in round lots of 100 shares. The premium or discount is the percentage difference between price and NAV: (Price − NAV)/NAV. Notice that there are more funds selling at discounts to NAV (indicated by negative differences) than premiums. Finally, the annual dividend and the 52-week return based on the percentage change in share price plus dividend income is presented in the last two columns.

The common divergence of price from net asset value, often by wide margins, is a puzzle that has yet to be fully explained. To see why this is a puzzle, consider a closed-end fund that is selling at a discount from net asset value. If the fund were to sell all the assets in the portfolio, it would realize proceeds equal to net asset value. The difference between the market price of the fund and the fund's NAV would represent the per-share increase in the wealth of the fund's investors. Despite this apparent profit opportunity, sizable discounts seem to persist for long periods of time.

Interestingly, while many closed-end funds sell at a discount from net asset value, the prices of these funds when originally issued are often above NAV. This is a further puzzle, as it is hard to explain why investors would purchase these newly issued funds at a premium to NAV when the shares tend to fall to a discount shortly after issue.

Many investors consider closed-end funds selling at a discount to NAV to be a bargain. Even if the market price never rises to the level of NAV, the dividend yield on an investment in the fund at this price would exceed the dividend yield on the same securities held outside the fund. To see this, imagine a fund with an NAV of $10 per share holding a portfolio that pays an annual dividend of $1 per share; that is, the dividend yield to investors that hold this portfolio directly is 10%. Now suppose that the market price of a share of this closed-end fund is $9. If management pays out dividends received from the shares as they come in, then the dividend yield to those that hold the same portfolio through the closed-end fund will be $1/$9, or 11.1%.

Variations on closed-end funds are *interval closed-end funds* and *discretionary closed-end funds*. Interval closed-end funds may purchase from 5 to 25% of outstanding shares from investors at intervals of 3, 6, or 12 months. Discretionary closed-end funds may purchase any or all of outstanding shares from investors, but no more frequently than once every two years. The repurchase of shares for either of these funds takes place at net asset value plus a repurchase fee that may not exceed 2%.

In contrast to closed-end funds, the price of open-end funds cannot fall below NAV, because these funds stand ready to redeem shares at NAV. The offering price will exceed NAV, however, if the fund carries a **load.** A load is, in effect, a sales charge, which is paid to the seller. Load funds are sold by securities brokers and directly by mutual fund groups.

Unlike closed-end funds, open-end mutual funds do not trade on organized exchanges. Instead, investors simply buy shares from and liquidate through the investment company at net asset value. Thus, the number of outstanding shares of these funds changes daily.

> **load**
>
> A sales commission charged on a mutual fund.

Other Investment Organizations

There are intermediaries not formally organized or regulated as investment companies that nevertheless serve functions similar to investment companies. Among the more important are commingled funds, real estate investment trusts, and hedge funds.

Commingled funds   Commingled funds are partnerships of investors that pool their funds. The management firm that organizes the partnership, for example, a bank or insurance company, manages the funds for a fee. Typical partners in a commingled fund might be trust or retirement accounts which have portfolios that are much larger than those of most individual investors but are still too small to warrant managing on a separate basis.

Commingled funds are similar in form to open-end mutual funds. Instead of shares, though, the fund offers units, which are bought and sold at net asset value. A bank or insurance company may offer an array of different commingled funds from which trust or retirement accounts can choose. Examples are a money market fund, a bond fund, and a common stock fund.

Real Estate Investment Trusts (REITs)   A REIT is similar to a closed-end fund. REITs invest in real estate or loans secured by real estate. Besides issuing shares, they raise capital by borrowing from banks and issuing bonds or mortgages. Most of them are highly leveraged, with a typical debt ratio of 70%.

There are two principal kinds of REITs. *Equity trusts* invest in real estate directly, whereas *mortgage trusts* invest primarily in mortgage and construction loans. REITs generally are established by banks, insurance companies, or mortgage companies, which then serve as investment managers to earn a fee.

REITs are exempt from taxes as long as at least 95% of their taxable income is distributed to shareholders. For shareholders, however, the dividends are taxable as personal income.

Hedge funds   Like mutual funds, **hedge funds** are vehicles that allow private investors to pool assets to be invested by a fund manager. However, hedge funds are not registered as mutual funds and are not subject to SEC regulation. They typically are open only to wealthy or institutional investors. As hedge funds are only lightly regulated, their managers can pursue investment strategies that are not open to mutual fund managers, for example, heavy use of derivatives, short sales, and leverage.

Hedge funds typically attempt to exploit temporary misalignments in security valuations. For example, if the yield on mortgage-backed securities seems abnormally high compared to that on Treasury bonds, the hedge fund would buy mortgage-backed and short sell Treasury securities. Notice that the fund is *not* betting on broad movement in the entire bond market; it

> **hedge fund**
>
> A private investment pool, open to wealthy or institutional investors, that is exempt from SEC regulation and can therefore pursue more speculative policies than mutual funds.

buys one type of bond and sells another. By taking a long mortgage/short Treasury position, the fund "hedges" its interest rate exposure, while making a bet on the *relative* valuation across the two sectors. The idea is that when yield spreads converge back to their "normal" relationship, the fund will profit from the realignment regardless of the general trend in the level of interest rates. In this respect, it strives to be "market neutral," which gives rise to the term "hedge fund."

Of course even if the fund's position is market neutral, this does not mean that it is low risk. The fund still is speculating on valuation differences across the two sectors, often taking a very large position, and this decision can turn out to be right or wrong. Because the funds often operate with considerable leverage, returns can be quite volatile.

One of the major financial stories of 1998 was the collapse of Long-Term Capital Management (LTCM), probably the best-known hedge fund at the time. Among its many investments were several "convergence bets," such as the mortgage-backed/Treasury spread we have described. When Russia defaulted on some of its debts in August 1998, risk and liquidity premiums increased, so that instead of converging, the yield spread between safe Treasuries and almost all other bonds widened. LTCM lost billions of dollars in August and September of 1998; the fear was that given its extreme leverage, continued losses might more than wipe out the firm's capital and force it to default on its positions. Eventually, several Wall Street firms contributed a total of about $3.5 billion to bail out the fund, in return receiving a 90% ownership stake in the firm.

4.3 | MUTUAL FUNDS

Mutual fund is the common name for an open-end investment company. This is the dominant investment company today, accounting for roughly 90% of investment company assets. Assets under management in the mutual fund industry reached $7 trillion by year-end 2001.

Investment Policies

Each mutual fund has a specified investment policy, which is described in the fund's prospectus. For example, money market mutual funds hold the short-term, low-risk instruments of the money market (see Chapter 2 for a review of these securities), while bond funds hold fixed-income securities. Some funds have even more narrowly defined mandates. For example, some bond funds will hold primarily Treasury bonds, others primarily mortgage-backed securities.

Management companies manage a family, or "complex," of mutual funds. They organize an entire collection of funds and then collect a management fee for operating them. By managing a collection of funds under one umbrella, these companies make it easy for investors to allocate assets across market sectors and to switch assets across funds while still benefiting from centralized record keeping. Some of the most well-known management companies are Fidelity, Vanguard, Putnam, and Dreyfus. Each offers an array of open-end mutual funds with different investment policies. There were over 8,000 mutual funds at the end of 2000, which were offered by fewer than 500 fund complexes.

Some of the more important fund types, classified by investment policy, are discussed next.

Money market funds   These funds invest in money market securities. They usually offer check-writing features, and net asset value is fixed at $1 per share, so that there are no tax implications such as capital gains or losses associated with redemption of shares.

Equity funds   Equity funds invest primarily in stock, although they may, at the portfolio manager's discretion, also hold fixed-income or other types of securities. Funds commonly will hold about 5% of total assets in money market securities to provide the liquidity necessary to meet potential redemption of shares.

It is traditional to classify stock funds according to their emphasis on capital appreciation versus current income. Thus *income funds* tend to hold shares of firms with high dividend yields that provide high current income. *Growth funds* are willing to forgo current income, focusing instead on prospects for capital gains. While the classification of these funds is couched in terms of income versus capital gains, it is worth noting that in practice the more relevant distinction concerns the level of risk these funds assume. Growth stocks—and therefore growth funds—are typically riskier and respond far more dramatically to changes in economic conditions than do income funds.

Bond funds   As the name suggests, these funds specialize in the fixed-income sector. Within that sector, however, there is considerable room for specialization. For example, various funds will concentrate on corporate bonds, Treasury bonds, mortgage-backed securities, or municipal (tax-free) bonds. Indeed, some of the municipal bond funds will invest only in bonds of a particular state (or even city!) in order to satisfy the investment desires of residents of that state who wish to avoid local as well as federal taxes on the interest paid on the bonds. Many funds also will specialize by the maturity of the securities, ranging from short-term to intermediate to long-term, or by the credit risk of the issuer, ranging from very safe to high-yield or "junk" bonds.

Balanced and income funds   Some funds are designed to be candidates for an individual's entire investment portfolio. Therefore, they hold both equities and fixed-income securities in relatively stable proportions. According to Wiesenberger, such funds are classified as income or balanced funds. *Income funds* strive to maintain safety of principal consistent with "as liberal a current income from investments as possible," while *balanced funds* "minimize investment risks so far as this is possible without unduly sacrificing possibilities for long-term growth and current income."

Asset allocation funds   These funds are similar to balanced funds in that they hold both stocks and bonds. However, asset allocation funds may dramatically vary the proportions allocated to each market in accord with the portfolio manager's forecast of the relative performance of each sector. Hence, these funds are engaged in market timing and are not designed to be low-risk investment vehicles.

Index funds   An index fund tries to match the performance of a broad market index. The fund buys shares in securities included in a particular index in proportion to the security's representation in that index. For example, the Vanguard 500 Index Fund is a mutual fund that replicates the composition of the Standard & Poor's 500 stock price index. Because the S&P 500 is a value-weighted index, the fund buys shares in each S&P 500 company in proportion to the market value of that company's outstanding equity. Investment in an index fund is a low-cost way for small investors to pursue a passive investment strategy—that is, to invest without engaging in security analysis. Of course, index funds can be tied to nonequity indexes as well. For example, Vanguard offers a bond index fund and a real estate index fund.

Specialized sector funds   Some funds concentrate on a particular industry. For example, Fidelity markets dozens of "select funds," each of which invests in specific industry such as biotechnology, utilities, precious metals, or telecommunications. Other funds specialize in securities of particular countries.

Table 4.1 breaks down the number of mutual funds by investment orientation as of the end of 2001. Figure 4.2 is part of the listings for mutual funds from *The Wall Street Journal.*

TABLE **4.1** Classification of mutual funds, December 2001		Assets ($ billion)	% of Total
	Common Stock		
	Aggressive growth	$ 576.2	8.3%
	Growth	1,047.5	15.0
	Growth & income	1,066.6	15.3
	Equity income	125.4	1.8
	International	415.1	6.0
	Emerging markets	13.7	0.2
	Sector funds	173.6	2.5
	Total equity funds	$3,418.1	49.0%
	Bond Funds		
	Corporate, investment grade	$ 161.0	2.3%
	Corporate, high yield	94.3	1.4
	Government & agency	90.9	1.3
	Mortgage-backed	73.4	1.1
	Global bond funds	19.0	0.3
	Strategic income	191.6	2.7
	Municipal single state	141.0	2.0
	Municipal general	154.0	2.2
	Total bond funds	$ 925.2	13.3%
	Mixed (hybrid) Asset Classes		
	Balanced	$ 231.1	3.3%
	Asset allocation & flexible	115.3	1.7
	Total hybrid funds	$ 346.3	5.0%
	Money Market		
	Taxable	$2,012.9	28.9%
	Tax-free	272.4	3.9
	Total money market funds	$2,285.3	32.8%
	Total	$6,974.9	100.0%

Note: Column sums subject to rounding error.

Source: *Mutual Fund Fact Book,* Investment Company Institute, 2002.

Notice that the funds are organized by the fund family. For example, funds sponsored by the Vanguard Group comprise most of the figure. The first two columns after the name of each fund present the net asset value of the fund and the change in NAV from the previous day. The last column is the year-to-date return on the fund.

Often the fund name describes its investment policy. For example, Vanguard's GNMA fund invests in mortgage-backed securities, the municipal intermediate fund (MuInt) invests in intermediate-term municipal bonds, and the high-yield corporate bond fund (HYCor) invests in large part in speculative grade, or "junk," bonds with high yields. You can see that Vanguard offers about 20 index funds, including portfolios indexed to the bond market (TotBd), the Wilshire 5000 Index (TotSt), the Russell 2000 Index of small firms (SmCap), as well as European- and Pacific Basin-indexed portfolios (Europe and Pacific). However, names of common stock funds frequently reflect little or nothing about their investment policies. Examples are Vanguard's Windsor and Wellington funds.

MUTUAL FUND QUOTATIONS

NAME	NAV	NET CHG	YTD %RET
Touchstone Family Fd			
EmgGro p	17.81	+0.13	− 0.7
EquityA	12.24	+0.05	− 25.5
GroValA p	19.08	...	− 29.5
OhlnsA	12.13	−0.03	+ 5.6
Value A p	10.30	+0.06	− 3.9
Transamerica Premier			
AggGwthl p	14.67	+0.12	− 23.8
Balncel p	19.31	−0.03	− 3.9
Equity p	16.72	+0.22	− 19.5
HiYdInst	8.02	+0.03	+ 4.5
SmCompl p	15.11	+0.10	− 27.4
Turner Funds			
MicroCap	35.76	+0.20	+ 6.1
Midcap	20.83	+0.06	− 31.9
SelGrEq	5.53	+0.05	− 22.2
ShDrFxdl l	10.16	−0.03	+ 7.0
SmallCap	18.63	+0.14	− 24.7
SmCpVal	17.94	+0.15	+ 16.9
Top20	7.35	+0.02	− 40.9
UltShDrFl l	10.23	−0.01	+ 5.7
TweedyAmerVal	23.64	+0.10	− 3.2
TweedyGlVal	18.34	+0.16	− 8.2
VANGUARD FDS			
AssetA	22.26	−0.02	− 4.7
CAInsIT	11.33	−0.02	+ 7.1

NAME	NAV	NET CHG	YTD %RET
CAInsLT	11.95	−0.03	+ 6.7
CapOp r	22.32	+0.10	− 14.9
Convrt	12.00	−0.01	− 4.4
Energy r	25.63	−1.27	− 8.7
EqInc	22.97	−0.09	− 4.4
Explr	55.51	+0.42	− 7.6
FLInsLT	11.75	−0.02	+ 7.4
GlbEq	11.75	+0.06	− 6.9
GNMA	10.54	−0.02	+ 8.7
GroInc	28.08	+0.04	− 12.0
GrowthEq	9.64	+0.05	− 27.4
HlthCare r	118.96	−0.64	− 9.1
HYCor r	6.35	+0.01	+ 2.7
InflaPro	11.10	−0.05	+ 11.2
IntlGr	14.62	+0.08	− 22.5
IntlVal	21.44	−0.02	− 17.6
ITCorp	9.97	−0.06	+ 11.2
ITTsry	11.41	−0.09	+ 10.4
LifeCon	14.28	−0.02	+ 0.2
LifeGro	17.47	+0.01	− 9.7
LifeInc	13.17	−0.04	+ 5.0
LifeMod	16.16	−0.01	− 4.7
LTCorp	9.02	−0.09	+ 12.9
LTTsry	11.43	−0.15	+ 10.0
MATxEx	10.16	−0.02	+ 7.3
Morg	14.31	+0.05	− 15.9

NAME	NAV	NET CHG	YTD %RET
MuHY	10.76	−0.01	+ 7.4
MuInlg	12.89	−0.02	+ 7.3
MuInt	13.66	−0.01	+ 7.2
MuLong	11.43	−0.02	+ 7.8
MuLtd	11.01	...	+ 6.5
MuSht	15.75	−0.01	+ 4.7
NJInsLT	12.12	−0.02	+ 7.0
NYInsLT	11.42	−0.02	+ 7.0
OHLTte	12.19	−0.01	+ 7.3
PAInsLT	11.58	−0.02	+ 7.5
PrecMtls r	8.40	+0.02	+ 12.4
Primcp r	49.56	+0.12	− 17.3
REIT r	11.91	+0.07	+ 7.7
SelValu r	12.43	−0.02	+ 8.7
STAR	16.47	−0.03	− 1.2
STCor	10.97	−0.03	+ 8.8
STFed	10.61	−0.02	+ 9.3
StratgcEq	14.61	+0.05	+ 0.2
STTsry	10.67	−0.04	+ 8.5
TxMBal r	17.37	+0.01	− 3.3
TxMCap r	25.41	+0.06	− 16.9
TxMGI r	24.84	+0.05	− 12.6
TxMIn r	7.83	−0.02	− 22.8
TxMSC r	13.84	+0.12	− 2.7
USGro	19.08	+0.12	− 31.0
USValue	11.06	+0.08	− 1.6

NAME	NAV	NET CHG	YTD %RET
Utility	11.95	−0.15	− 19.6
Wellsl	20.99	−0.13	+ 7.7
Welltn	28.19	−0.06	+ 2.5
Wndsr	15.19	+0.04	0.0
Wndsrll	25.48	−0.10	− 5.4
VANGUARD INDEX FDS			
500	105.48	+0.22	− 12.7
Balanced	17.93	...	− 3.6
CalSoc	7.76	+0.04	− 14.6
DevMkt	7.00	−0.02	− 22.8
EmerMkt r	7.87	+0.09	− 10.9
Europe	20.26	+0.01	− 22.0
Extnd	21.72	+0.14	− 15.3
Growth	26.33	+0.11	− 13.5
ITBond	10.54	−0.07	+ 11.1
LTBond	11.30	−0.13	+ 11.9
MidCp	11.24	+0.01	− 6.1
Pacific	6.73	−0.08	− 24.8
SmCap	18.56	+0.18	− 4.5
SmGth	10.12	+0.09	− 7.7
SmVal	9.56	+0.09	+ 3.9
STBond	10.39	−0.04	+ 9.6
TotBd	10.37	−0.05	+ 9.9
TotIntl	9.27	−0.02	− 21.6
TotSt	25.33	+0.09	− 12.7
Value	18.96	−0.01	− 12.5

FIGURE 4.2

Listing of mutual fund quotations

Source: *The Wall Street Journal*, November 15, 2001. Reprinted by permission of Dow Jones & Company, Inc., via Copyright Clearance Center, Inc. © 2001 Dow Jones & Company, Inc. All Rights Reserved Worldwide.

How Funds Are Sold

Most mutual funds have an underwriter that has exclusive rights to distribute shares to investors. Mutual funds are generally marketed to the public either directly by the fund underwriter or indirectly through brokers acting on behalf of the underwriter. Direct-marketed funds are sold through the mail, various offices of the fund, over the phone, and increasingly, over the Internet. Investors contact the fund directly to purchase shares. For example, if you look at the financial pages of your local newspaper, you will see several advertisements for funds, along with toll-free phone numbers that you can call to receive a fund's prospectus and an application to open an account with the fund.

A bit less than half of fund sales today are distributed through a sales force. Brokers or financial advisers receive a commission for selling shares to investors. (Ultimately, the commission is paid by the investor. More on this shortly.) In some cases, funds use a "captive" sales force that sells only shares in funds of the mutual fund group they represent.

The trend today, however, is toward "financial supermarkets" that can sell shares in funds of many complexes. This approach was made popular by the OneSource program of Charles Schwab & Co. Schwab allows customers of the OneSource program to buy funds from many different fund groups. Instead of charging customers a sales commission, Schwab splits management fees with the mutual fund company. The supermarket approach has proven to be popular. For example, Fidelity now sells non-Fidelity mutual funds through its FundsNetwork even though many of those funds compete with Fidelity products. Like Schwab, Fidelity shares a portion of the management fee from the non-Fidelity funds it sells.

4.4 COSTS OF INVESTING IN MUTUAL FUNDS

Fee Structure

An individual investor choosing a mutual fund should consider not only the fund's stated investment policy and past performance, but also its management fees and other expenses.

Comparative data on virtually all important aspects of mutual funds are available in the annual reports prepared by Wiesenberger Investment Companies Services or in Morningstar's *Mutual Fund Sourcebook,* which can be found in many academic and public libraries. You should be aware of four general classes of fees.

Front-end load

A front-end load is a commission or sales charge paid when you purchase the shares. These charges, which are used primarily to pay the brokers who sell the funds, may not exceed 8.5%, but in practice they are rarely higher than 6%. *Low-load funds* have loads that range up to 3% of invested funds. *No-load funds* have no front-end sales charges. Loads effectively reduce the amount of money invested. For example, each $1,000 paid for a fund with an 8.5% load results in a sales charge of $85 and fund investment of only $915. You need cumulative returns of 9.3% of your net investment (85/915 = .093) just to break even.

Back-end load

A back-end load is a redemption, or "exit," fee incurred when you sell your shares. Typically, funds that impose back-end loads start them at 5% or 6% and reduce them by one percentage point for every year the funds are left invested. Thus, an exit fee that starts at 6% would fall to 4% by the start of your third year. These charges are known more formally as "contingent deferred sales charges."

Operating expenses

Operating expenses are the costs incurred by the mutual fund in operating the portfolio, including administrative expenses and advisory fees paid to the investment manager. These expenses, usually expressed as a percentage of total assets under management, may range from 0.2% to 2%. Shareholders do not receive an explicit bill for these operating expenses; however, the expenses periodically are deducted from the assets of the fund. Shareholders pay for these expenses through the reduced value of the portfolio.

12b-1 charges

12b-1 fees

Annual fees charged by a mutual fund to pay for marketing and distribution costs.

The Securities and Exchange Commission allows the managers of so-called 12b-1 funds to use fund assets to pay for distribution costs such as advertising, promotional literature including annual reports and prospectuses, and, most important, commissions paid to brokers who sell the fund to investors. These **12b-1 fees** are named after the SEC rule that permits use of these plans. Funds may use 12b-1 charges instead of, or in addition to, front-end loads to generate the fees with which to pay brokers. As with operating expenses, investors are not explicitly billed for 12b-1 charges. Instead, the fees are deducted from the assets of the fund. Therefore, 12b-1 fees (if any) must be added to operating expenses to obtain the true annual expense ratio of the fund. The SEC now requires that all funds include in the prospectus a consolidated expense table that summarizes all relevant fees. The 12b-1 fees are limited to 1% of a fund's average net assets per year.[1]

A relatively recent innovation in the fee structure of mutual funds is the creation of different "classes"; they represent ownership in the same portfolio of securities but impose different combinations of fees. For example, Class A shares typically are sold with front-end loads of between 4% to 5%. Class B shares impose 12b-1 charges and back-end loads. Because Class B shares pay 12b-1 fees while Class A shares do not, the reported rate of return on the B

---

[1]The maximum 12b-1 charge for the sale of the fund is .75%. However, an additional service fee of .25% of the fund's assets also is allowed for personal service and/or maintenance of shareholder accounts.

shares will be less than that of the A shares despite the fact that they represent holdings in the same portfolio. (The reported return on the shares does not reflect the impact of loads paid by the investor.) Class C shares do not impose back-end redemption fees, but they impose 12b-1 fees higher than those in Class B, often as high as 1% annually. Other classes and combinations of fees are also marketed by mutual fund companies. For example, Merrill Lynch has introduced Class D shares of some of its funds, which include front-end loads and 12b-1 charges of .25%.

Each investor must choose the best combination of fees. Obviously, pure no-load no-fee funds distributed directly by the mutual fund group are the cheapest alternative, and these will often make the most sense for knowledgeable investors. However, many investors are willing to pay for financial advice, and the commissions paid to advisers who sell these funds are the most common form of payment. Alternatively, investors may choose to hire a fee-only financial manager who charges directly for services and does not accept commissions. These advisers can help investors select portfolios of low- or no-load funds (as well as provide other financial advice). Independent financial planners have become increasingly important distribution channels for funds in recent years.

If you do buy a fund through a broker, the choice between paying a load and paying 12b-1 fees will depend primarily on your expected time horizon. Loads are paid only once for each purchase, whereas 12b-1 fees are paid annually. Thus, if you plan to hold your fund for a long time, a one-time load may be preferable to recurring 12b-1 charges.

You can identify funds with various charges by the following letters placed after the fund name in the listing of mutual funds in the financial pages: r denotes redemption or exit fees; p denotes 12b-1 fees; and t denotes both redemption and 12b-1 fees. The listings do not allow you to identify funds that involve front-end loads, however; while NAV for each fund is presented, the offering price at which the fund can be purchased, which may include a load, is not.

Fees and Mutual Fund Returns

The rate of return on an investment in a mutual fund is measured as the increase or decrease in net asset value plus income distributions such as dividends or distributions of capital gains expressed as a fraction of net asset value at the beginning of the investment period. If we denote the net asset value at the start and end of the period as NAV_0 and NAV_1, respectively, then

$$\text{Rate of return} = \frac{NAV_1 - NAV_0 + \text{Income and capital gain distributions}}{NAV_0}$$

For example, if a fund has an initial NAV of $20 at the start of the month, makes income distributions of $.15 and capital gain distributions of $.05, and ends the month with NAV of $20.10, the monthly rate of return is computed as

$$\text{Rate of return} = \frac{\$20.10 - \$20.00 + \$.15 + \$.05}{\$20.00} = .015, \text{ or } 1.5\%$$

Notice that this measure of the rate of return ignores any commissions such as front-end loads paid to purchase the fund.

On the other hand, the rate of return is affected by the fund's expenses and 12b-1 fees. This is because such charges are periodically deducted from the portfolio, which reduces net asset value. Thus the rate of return on the fund equals the gross return on the underlying portfolio minus the total expense ratio.

TABLE **4.2**	Cumulative Proceeds (all dividends reinvested)		
Impact of costs on investment performance	Fund A	Fund B	Fund C
Initial investment*	$10,000	$10,000	$ 9,200
5 years	17,234	16,474	15,502
10 years	29,699	27,141	26,123
15 years	51,183	44,713	44,018
20 years	88,206	73,662	74,173

*After front-end load, if any.

Notes:

1. Fund A is no-load with .5% expense ratio.

2. Fund B is no-load with 1.5% expense ratio.

3. Fund C has an 8% load on purchases and a 1% expense ratio.

4. Gross return on all funds is 12% per year before expenses.

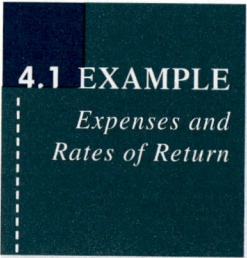

4.1 EXAMPLE

Expenses and Rates of Return

To see how expenses can affect rate of return, consider a fund with $100 million in assets at the start of the year and with 10 million shares outstanding. The fund invests in a portfolio of stocks that provides no income but increases in value by 10%. The expense ratio, including 12b-1 fees, is 1%. What is the rate of return for an investor in the fund?

The initial NAV equals $100 million/10 million shares = $10 per share. In the absence of expenses, fund assets would grow to $110 million and NAV would grow to $11 per share, for a 10% rate of return. However, the expense ratio of the fund is 1%. Therefore, $1 million will be deducted from the fund to pay these fees, leaving the portfolio worth only $109 million, and NAV equal to $10.90. The rate of return on the fund is only 9%, which equals the gross return on the underlying portfolio minus the total expense ratio.

Fees can have a big effect on performance. Table 4.2 considers an investor who starts with $10,000 and can choose between three funds that all earn an annual 12% return on investment before fees but have different fee structures. The table shows the cumulative amount in each fund after several investment horizons. Fund A has total operating expenses of .5%, no load, and no 12b-1 charges. This might represent a low-cost producer like Vanguard. Fund B has no load but has 1% management expenses and .5% in 12b-1 fees. This level of charges is fairly typical of actively managed equity funds. Finally, Fund C has 1% in management expenses, no 12b-1 charges, but assesses an 8% front-end load on purchases.

Note the substantial return advantage of low-cost Fund A. Moreover, that differential is greater for longer investment horizons.

Although expenses can have a big impact on net investment performance, it is sometimes difficult for the investor in a mutual fund to measure true expenses accurately. This is because of the common practice of paying for some expenses in **soft dollars.** A portfolio manager earns soft-dollar credits with a stockbroker by directing the fund's trades to that broker. Based on those credits, the broker will pay for some of the mutual fund's expenses, such as databases, computer hardware, or stock-quotation systems. The soft-dollar arrangement means that the stockbroker effectively returns part of the trading commission to the fund. The advantage to the mutual fund is that purchases made with soft dollars are not included in the fund's expenses, so the fund can advertise an unrealistically low expense ratio to the public.

soft dollars

The value of research services brokerage houses provide "free of charge" in exchange for the investment manager's business.

Although the fund may have paid the broker needlessly high commissions to obtain the soft-dollar "rebate," trading costs are not included in the fund's expenses. The impact of the higher trading commission shows up instead in net investment performance. Soft-dollar arrangements make it difficult for investors to compare fund expenses, and periodically these arrangements come under attack.

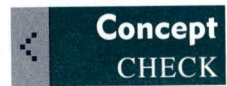

Concept
CHECK

2. The Equity Fund sells Class A shares with a front-end load of 4% and Class B shares with 12b-1 fees of .5% annually as well as back-end load fees that start at 5% and fall by 1% for each full year the investor holds the portfolio (until the fifth year). Assume the rate of return on the fund portfolio net of operating expenses is 10% annually. What will be the value of a $10,000 investment in Class A and Class B shares if the shares are sold after (a) 1 year, (b) 4 years, (c) 10 years? Which fee structure provides higher net proceeds at the end of each investment horizon?

4.5 TAXATION OF MUTUAL FUND INCOME

Investment returns of mutual funds are granted "pass-through status" under the U.S. tax code, meaning that taxes are paid only by the investor in the mutual fund, not by the fund itself. The income is treated as passed through to the investor as long as the fund meets several requirements, most notably that at least 90% of all income is distributed to shareholders. In addition, the fund must receive less than 30% of its gross income from the sale of securities held for less than three months, and the fund must satisfy some diversification criteria. Actually, the earnings pass-through requirements can be even more stringent than 90%, since to avoid a separate excise tax, a fund must distribute at least 98% of income in the calendar year that it is earned.

A fund's short-term capital gains, long-term capital gains, and dividends are passed through to investors as though the investor earned the income directly. The investor will pay taxes at the appropriate rate depending upon the type of income as well as the investor's own tax bracket.[2]

The pass through of investment income has one important disadvantage for individual investors. If you manage your own portfolio, you decide when to realize capital gains and losses on any security; therefore, you can time those realizations to efficiently manage your tax liabilities. When you invest through a mutual fund, however, the timing of the sale of securities from the portfolio is out of your control, which reduces your ability to engage in tax management. Of course, if the mutual fund is held in a tax-deferred retirement account such as an IRA or 401(k) account, these tax management issues are irrelevant.

A fund with a high portfolio turnover rate can be particularly "tax inefficient." **Turnover** is the ratio of the trading activity of a portfolio to the assets of the portfolio. It measures the fraction of the portfolio that is "replaced" each year. For example, a $100 million portfolio with $50 million in sales of some securities with purchases of other securities would have a turnover rate of 50%. High turnover means that capital gains or losses are being realized constantly, and therefore that the investor cannot time the realizations to manage his or her overall tax obligation.

turnover

The ratio of the trading activity of a portfolio to the assets of the portfolio.

---

[2]An interesting problem that an investor needs to be aware of derives from the fact that capital gains and dividends on mutual funds are typically paid out to shareholders once or twice a year. This means that an investor who has just purchased shares in a mutual fund can receive a capital gain distribution (and be taxed on that distribution) on transactions that occurred long before he or she purchased shares in the fund. This is particularly a concern late in the year when such distributions typically are made.

In 2000, the SEC instituted new rules that require funds to disclose the tax impact of portfolio turnover. Funds must include in their prospectus after-tax returns for the past 1-, 5-, and 10-year periods. Marketing literature that includes performance data also must include after-tax results. The after-tax returns are computed accounting for the impact of the taxable distributions of income and capital gains passed through to the investor, assuming the investor is in the maximum tax bracket.

3. An investor's portfolio currently is worth $1 million. During the year, the investor sells 1,000 shares of Microsoft at a price of $80 per share and 2,000 shares of Ford at a price of $40 per share. The proceeds are used to buy 1,600 shares of IBM at $100 per share.
   a. What was the portfolio turnover rate?
   b. If the shares in Microsoft originally were purchased for $70 each and those in Ford were purchased for $35, and if the investor's tax rate on capital gains income is 20%, how much extra will the investor owe on this year's taxes as a result of these transactions?

4.6 EXCHANGE-TRADED FUNDS

exchange-traded funds

Offshoots of mutual funds that allow investors to trade index portfolios.

Exchange-traded funds (ETFs) are offshoots of mutual funds that allow investors to trade index portfolios just as they do shares of stock. The first ETF was the "Spider," a nickname for SPDR or Standard & Poor's Depository Receipt, which is a unit investment trust holding a portfolio matching the S&P 500 index. Unlike mutual funds, which can be bought or sold only at the end of the day when NAV is calculated, investors could trade Spiders throughout the day, just like any other share of stock. Spiders gave rise to many similar products such as "Diamonds" (based on the Dow Jones Industrial Average, ticker DIA), Cubes (based on the Nasdaq 100 Index, ticker QQQ), and WEBS (World Equity Benchmark Shares, which are shares in portfolios of foreign stock market indexes). By 2000, there were dozens of ETFs in three general classes: broad U.S. market indexes, narrow industry or "sector" portfolios, and international indexes, marketed as WEBS. Table 4.3, Panel A, presents some of the sponsors of ETFs; Panel B is a sample of ETFs.

ETFs offer several advantages over conventional mutual funds. First, as we just noted, a mutual fund's net asset value is quoted—and therefore, investors can buy or sell their shares in the fund—only once a day. In contrast, ETFs trade continuously. Moreover, like other shares, but unlike mutual funds, ETFs can be sold short or purchased on margin.

ETFs also offer a potential tax advantage over mutual funds. When large numbers of mutual fund investors redeem their shares, the fund must sell securities to meet the redemptions. This can trigger capital gains taxes, which are passed through to and must be paid by the remaining shareholders. In contrast, when small investors wish to redeem their position in an ETF they simply sell their shares to other traders, with no need for the fund to sell any of the underlying portfolio. Moreover, when large traders wish to redeem their position in the ETF, redemptions are satisfied with shares of stock in the underlying portfolio. Again, a redemption does not trigger a stock sale by the fund sponsor.

The ability of large investors to redeem ETFs for a portfolio of stocks comprising the index, or to exchange a portfolio of stocks for shares in the corresponding ETF, ensures that the price of an ETF cannot depart significantly from the NAV of that portfolio. Any meaningful discrepancy would offer arbitrage trading opportunities for these large traders, which would quickly eliminate the disparity.

ETFs are also cheaper than mutual funds. Investors who buy ETFs do so through brokers, rather than buying directly from the fund. Therefore, the fund saves the cost of marketing

TABLE **4.3**	A. ETF Sponsors	
ETF sponsors and products	**Sponsor**	**Product Name**
	Barclays Global Investors	i-Shares
	Merrill Lynch	HOLDRS (Holding Company Depository Receipts: "Holders")
	StateStreet/Merrill Lynch	Select Sector SPDRs (S&P Depository Receipts: "Spiders")
	Vanguard	VIPER (Vanguard Index Participation Equity Receipts: "VIPERS")

B. Sample of ETF Products		
Name	**Ticker**	**Index Tracked**
Broad U.S. Indexes		
Spiders	SPY	S&P 500
Diamonds	DIA	Dow Jones Industrials
Cubes	QQQ	Nasdaq 100
iShares Russell 2000	IWM	Russell 2000
VIPER	VTI	Wilshire 5000
Industry Indexes		
Energy Select Spider	XLE	S&P 500 energy companies
iShares Energy Sector	IYE	Dow Jones energy companies
Financial Sector Spider	XLF	S&P 500 financial companies
iShares Financial Sector	IYF	Dow Jones financial companies
International Indexes		
WEBS United Kingdom	EWU	MCSI U.K. Index
WEBS France	EWQ	MCSI France Index
WEBS Japan	EWJ	MCSI Japan Index

itself directly to small investors. This reduction in expenses translates into lower management fees. For example, Barclays charges annual expenses of just over 9 basis points (i.e., .09%) of NAV per year on its S&P 500 ETF, whereas Vanguard charges 18 basis points on its S&P 500 index mutual fund.

There are some disadvantages to ETFs, however. Because they trade as securities, there is the possibility that their prices can depart by small amounts from NAV. As noted, this discrepancy cannot be too large without giving rise to arbitrage opportunities for large traders, but even small discrepancies can easily swamp the cost advantage of ETFs over mutual funds. Second, while mutual funds can be bought for NAV with no expense from no-load funds, ETFs must be purchased from brokers for a fee. Investors also incur a bid–ask spread when purchasing an ETF.

ETFs have to date been a huge success. Most trade on the Amex and currently account for about half of Amex trading volume. So far, ETFs have been limited to index portfolios.

A variant on large exchange-traded funds in a "built-to-order" fund, marketed by sponsors to retail investors as *folios, e-baskets,* or *personal funds.* The sponsor establishes several model portfolios that investors can purchase as a basket. These baskets may be sector or broader-based portfolios. Alternatively, investors can custom-design their own portfolios. In either case, investors can trade these portfolios with the sponsor just as though it were a personalized mutual fund. The advantage of this arrangement is that, as is true of ETFs, the individual investor is fully in charge of the timing of purchases and sales of securities. In contrast to mutual funds, the investor's tax liability is unaffected by the redemption activity of other investors. (Remember that in the case of mutual funds, redemptions can trigger the realization of capital gains that are passed through to all shareholders.) Of course, investors would similarly control their tax position using a typical brokerage account, but these basket accounts allow one to trade ready-made diversified portfolios. Investors typically pay an annual fee to participate in these plans.

WEBMASTER

Exchange Traded Funds

Go to William J. Bernstein's website, http://www.efficientfrontier.com/ef/901/shootout.htm, for a discussion of potential advantages and disadvantages of ETFs versus index mutual funds.

After reading the discussion, address the following questions:

1. What did Mr. Bernstein conclude about tracking error on ETFs compared to index funds?

2. What four reasons did he give for possibly favoring ETFs over index funds?

3. What did the author mean by the statement that the ETF is only as good as its underlying index?

4.7 MUTUAL FUND INVESTMENT PERFORMANCE: A FIRST LOOK

We noted earlier that one of the benefits of mutual funds for the individual investor is the ability to delegate management of the portfolio to investment professionals. The investor retains control over the broad features of the overall portfolio through the asset allocation decision: Each individual chooses the percentages of the portfolio to invest in bond funds versus equity funds versus money market funds, and so forth, but can leave the specific security selection decisions within each investment class to the managers of each fund. Shareholders hope that these portfolio managers can achieve better investment performance than they could obtain on their own.

What is the investment record of the mutual fund industry? This seemingly straightforward question is deceptively difficult to answer because we need a standard against which to evaluate performance. For example, we clearly would not want to compare the investment performance of an equity fund to the rate of return available in the money market. The vast differences in the risk of these two markets dictate that year-by-year as well as average performance will differ considerably. We would expect to find that equity funds outperform money market funds (on average) as compensation to investors for the extra risk incurred in equity markets. How can we determine whether mutual fund portfolio managers are performing up to par *given* the level of risk they incur? In other words, what is the proper benchmark against which investment performance ought to be evaluated?

Measuring portfolio risk properly and using such measures to choose an appropriate benchmark is an extremely difficult task. We devote all of Parts II and III of the text to issues surrounding the proper measurement of portfolio risk and the trade-off between risk and return. In this chapter, therefore, we will satisfy ourselves with a first look at the question of fund performance by using only very simple performance benchmarks and ignoring the more subtle issues of risk differences across funds. However, we will return to this topic in Chapter 11, where we take a closer look at mutual fund performance after adjusting for differences in the exposure of portfolios to various sources of risk.

Here, we will use as a benchmark for the performance of equity fund managers the rate of return on the Wilshire 5000 Index. Recall from Chapter 2 that this is a value-weighted index of about 7,000 stocks that trade on the NYSE, Nasdaq, and Amex stock markets. It is the most inclusive index of the performance of U.S. equities. The performance of the Wilshire 5000 is a useful benchmark with which to evaluate professional managers because it corresponds to a simple passive investment strategy: Buy all the shares in the index in proportion to their outstanding market value. Moreover, this is a feasible strategy for even small investors, because the Vanguard Group offers an index fund (its Total Stock Market Portfolio) designed to replicate the performance of the Wilshire 5000 Index. The expense ratio of the fund is extremely small by the standards of other equity funds, only .20% per year. Using the Wilshire 5000 Index as a benchmark, we may pose the problem of evaluating the performance of mutual fund portfolio managers this way: How does the typical performance of actively managed equity mutual funds compare to the performance of a passively managed portfolio that simply replicates the composition of a broad index of the stock market?

By using the Wilshire 5000 as a benchmark, we use a well-diversified equity index to evaluate the performance of managers of diversified equity funds. Nevertheless, as noted earlier, this is only an imperfect comparison, as the risk of the Wilshire 5000 portfolio may not be comparable to that of any particular fund.

Casual comparisons of the performance of the Wilshire 5000 Index versus that of professionally managed mutual fund portfolios show disappointing results for most fund managers. Figure 4.3 shows the percent of mutual fund managers whose performance was inferior in each year to the Wilshire 5000. In more years than not, the Index has outperformed the median manager. Figure 4.4 shows the cumulative return since 1970 of the Wilshire 5000 compared to the Lipper General Equity Fund Average. The annualized compound return of the Wilshire 5000 was 12.20% versus 11.11% for the average fund. The 1.09% margin is substantial.

To some extent, however, this comparison is unfair. Real funds incur expenses that reduce the rate of return of the portfolio, as well as trading costs such as commissions and bid–ask

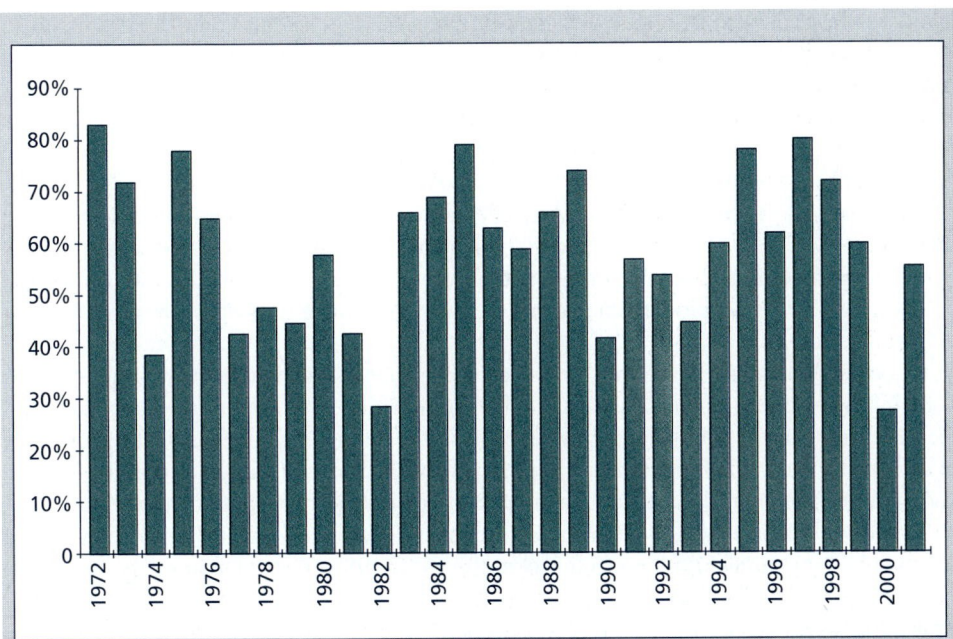

FIGURE 4.3

Percent of equity mutual funds outperformed by Wilshire 5000 Index, 1972–2001

Source: The Vanguard Group.

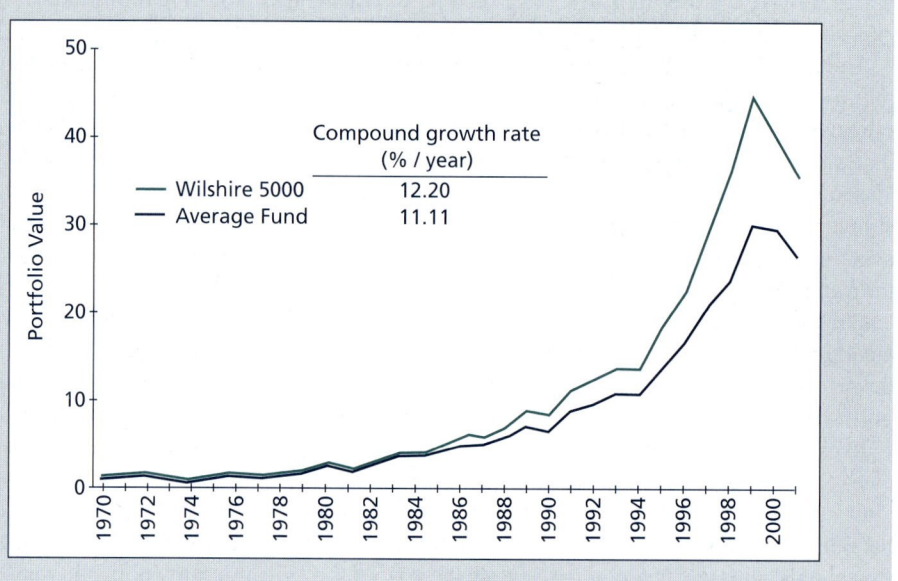

FIGURE **4.4**

Growth of $1 invested in Wilshire 5000 Index versus average general equity fund

Source: The Vanguard Group.

spreads that also reduce returns. John Bogle, former chairman of the Vanguard Group, has estimated that operating expenses reduce the return of typical managed portfolios by about 1% and that transaction fees associated with trading reduce returns by an additional .7%. In contrast, the return to the Wilshire index is calculated as though investors can buy or sell the index with reinvested dividends without incurring any expenses.

These considerations suggest that a better benchmark for the performance of actively managed funds is the performance of index funds, rather than the performance of the indexes themselves. Vanguard's Wilshire 5000 fund was established in 1992, and so has a relatively short track record. However, because it is passively managed, its expense ratio is only about 0.20%; moreover because index funds need to engage in very little trading, its turnover rate is about 3% per year, also extremely low. If we reduce the rate of return on the index by about 0.30%, we ought to obtain a good estimate of the rate of return achievable by a low-cost indexed portfolio. This procedure reduces the average margin of superiority of the index strategy over the average mutual fund from 1.09% to 0.79%, still suggesting that over the past two decades, passively managed (indexed) equity funds would have outperformed the typical actively managed fund.

This result may seem surprising to you. After all, it would not seem unreasonable to expect that professional money managers should be able to outperform a very simple rule such as "hold an indexed portfolio." As it turns out, however, there may be good reasons to expect such a result. We will explore them in detail in Chapter 8, where we discuss the efficient market hypothesis.

Of course, one might argue that there are good managers and bad managers, and that the good managers can, in fact, consistently outperform the index. To test this notion, we examine whether managers with good performance in one year are likely to repeat that performance in a following year. In other words, is superior performance in any particular year due to luck, and therefore random, or due to skill, and therefore consistent from year to year?

To answer this question, Goetzmann and Ibbotson[3] examined the performance of a large sample of equity mutual fund portfolios over the 1976–1985 period. Dividing the funds into

[3]William N. Goetzmann and Roger G. Ibbotson, "Do Winners Repeat?" *Journal of Portfolio Management* (Winter 1994), pp. 9–18.

TABLE **4.4**		Successive Period Performance	
Consistency of investment results	**Initial Period Performance**	**Top Half**	**Bottom Half**
	A. Goetzmann and Ibbotson study		
	Top half	62.0%	38.0%
	Bottom half	36.6%	63.4%
	B. Malkiel study, 1970s		
	Top half	65.1%	34.9%
	Bottom half	35.5%	64.5%
	C. Malkiel study, 1980s		
	Top half	51.7%	48.3%
	Bottom half	47.5%	52.5%

Sources: Panel A: From "Do Winners Repeat?" by William N. Goetzmann and Roger G. Ibbotson, *Journal of Portfolio Management,* Winter 1994, pp. 9–18. Reprinted by permission of Institutional Investor. Panels B and C: From "Returns from Investing in Equity Mutual Funds 1971–1991," by Burton G. Malkiel, *Journal of Finance* 50 (June 1995), pp. 549–572. Reprinted by permission of Blackwell Science, UK.

two groups based on total investment return for different subperiods, they posed the question: "Do funds with investment returns in the top half of the sample in one two-year period continue to perform well in the subsequent two-year period?"

Panel A of Table 4.4 presents a summary of their results. The table shows the fraction of "winners" (i.e., top-half performers) in the initial period that turn out to be winners or losers in the following two-year period. If performance were purely random from one period to the next, there would be entries of 50% in each cell of the table, as top- or bottom-half performers would be equally likely to perform in either the top or bottom half of the sample in the following period. On the other hand, if performance were due entirely to skill, with no randomness, we would expect to see entries of 100% on the diagonals and entries of 0% on the off-diagonals: Top-half performers would all remain in the top half while all bottom-half performers similarly would all remain in the bottom half. In fact, the table shows that 62.0% of initial top-half performers fall in the top half of the sample in the following period, while 63.4% of initial bottom-half performers fall in the bottom half in the following period. This evidence is consistent with the notion that at least part of a fund's performance is a function of skill as opposed to luck, so that relative performance tends to persist from one period to the next.[4]

On the other hand, this relationship does not seem stable across different sample periods. Malkiel[5] uses a larger sample, but a similar methodology (except that he uses one-year instead of two-year investment returns) to examine performance consistency. He finds that while initial-year performance predicts subsequent-year performance in the 1970s (see Table 4.4, Panel B), the pattern of persistence in performance virtually disappears in the 1980s (Panel C).

To summarize, the evidence that performance is consistent from one period to the next is suggestive, but it is inconclusive. In the 1970s, top-half funds in one year were twice as likely in the following year to be in the top half rather as the bottom half of funds. In the 1980s, the odds that a top-half fund would fall in the top half in the following year were essentially equivalent to those of a coin flip.

Other studies suggest that bad performance is more likely to persist than good performance. This makes some sense: It is easy to identify fund characteristics that will predictably lead to consistently poor investment performance, notably high expense ratios, and high turnover

[4]Another possibility is that performance consistency is due to variation in fee structure across funds. We return to this possibility in Chapter 11.

[5]Burton G. Malkiel, "Returns from Investing in Equity Mutual Funds 1971–1991," *Journal of Finance* 50 (June 1995), pp. 549–72.

ratios with associated trading costs. It is far harder to identify the secrets of successful stock picking. (If it were easy, we would all be rich!) Thus the consistency we do observe in fund performance may be due in large part to the poor performers. This suggests that the real value of past performance data is to avoid truly poor funds, even if identifying the future top performers is still a daunting task.

4. Suppose you observe the investment performance of 400 portfolio managers and rank them by investment returns during the year. Twenty percent of all managers are truly skilled, and therefore always fall in the top half, but the others fall in the top half purely because of good luck. What fraction of these top-half managers would you expect to be top-half performers next year? Assume skilled managers always are top-half performers.

4.8 | INFORMATION ON MUTUAL FUNDS

The first place to find information on a mutual fund is in its prospectus. The Securities and Exchange Commission requires that the prospectus describe the fund's investment objectives and policies in a concise "Statement of Investment Objectives" as well as in lengthy discussions of investment policies and risks. The fund's investment adviser and its portfolio manager also are described. The prospectus also presents the costs associated with purchasing shares in the fund in a fee table. Sales charges such as front-end and back-end loads as well as annual operating expenses such as management fees and 12b-1 fees are detailed in the fee table.

Despite this useful information, there is widespread agreement that until recently most prospectuses were difficult to read and laden with legalese. In 1999, however, the SEC required firms to prepare more easily understood prospectuses using less jargon, simpler sentences, and more charts. The nearby box contains some illustrative changes from two prospectuses that illustrate the scope of the problem the SEC was attempting to address. Still, even with these improvements, there remains a question as to whether these plain-English prospectuses contain the information an investor should know when selecting a fund. The answer, unfortunately, is that they still do not. The box also contains a discussion of the information one should look for, as well as what tends to be missing, from the usual prospectus.

Funds provide information about themselves in two other sources. The Statement of Additional Information, also known as Part B of the prospectus, includes a list of the securities in the portfolio at the end of the fiscal year, audited financial statements, and a list of the directors and officers of the fund. The fund's annual report, which generally is issued semiannually, also includes portfolio composition and financial statements, as well as a discussion of the factors that influenced fund performance over the last reporting period.

With more than 8,000 mutual funds to choose from, it can be difficult to find and select the fund that is best suited for a particular need. Several publications now offer "encyclopedias" of mutual fund information to help in the search process. Two prominent sources are Wiesenberger's *Investment Companies* and Morningstar's *Mutual Fund Sourcebook.* The Investment Company Institute—the national association of mutual funds, closed-end funds, and unit investment trusts—publishes an annual *Directory of Mutual Funds* that includes information on fees as well as phone numbers to contact funds. To illustrate the range of information available about funds, we consider Morningstar's report on Fidelity's Magellan fund, reproduced in Figure 4.5.

Some of Morningstar's analysis is qualitative. The top box on the left-hand side of the page provides a short description of fund strategy, in particular the types of securities in which the fund manager tends to invest. The bottom box on the left ("Analysis") is a more detailed discussion of the fund's income strategy. The short statement of the fund's investment policy is in the top right-hand corner: Magellan is a "large blend" fund, meaning that it tends to

FIGURE 4.5

Morningstar report

Source: Morningstar Mutual Funds. © 2002 Morningstar, Inc. All rights reserved. 225 W. Wacker Dr., Chicago, IL . Although data are gathered from reliable sources, Morningstar cannot guarantee completeness and accuracy.

Shorter, Clearer Mutual-Fund Disclosure May Omit Vital Investment Information

Mutual-fund investors will receive shorter and clearer disclosure documents, under new rules adopted by the Securities and Exchange Commission.

But despite all the hoopla surrounding the improvements—including a new "profile" prospectus and an easier-to-read full prospectus—there's still a slew of vital information fund investors don't get from any disclosure documents, long or short.

Of course, more information.isn't necessarily better. As it is, investors rarely read fund disclosure documents, such as the prospectus (which funds must provide to prospective investors), the semiannual reports (provided to all fund investors) or the statement of additional information (made available upon request). Buried in each are a few nuggets of useful data; but for the most part, they're full of legalese and technical terms.

So what should funds be required to disclose that they currently don't—and won't have to even under the SEC's new rules? Here's a partial list:

Tax-adjusted returns: Under the new rules, both the full prospectus and the fund profile must contain a bar chart of annual returns over the past 10 years, and the fund's best and worst quarterly returns during that period. That's a huge improvement over not long ago when a fund's raw returns were sometimes nowhere to be found in the prospectus.

But that doesn't go far enough, according to some investment advisers. Many would like to see funds report returns after taxes—using assumptions about an investor's tax bracket that would be disclosed in footnotes. The reason: Many funds make big payouts of dividends and capital gains, forcing investors to fork over a big chunk of their gains to the Internal Revenue Service.

What's in the fund: If you're about to put your retirement nest egg in a fund, shouldn't you get to see what's in it first? The zippy new profile prospectus describes a fund's investment strategy, as did the old-style prospectus. But neither gives investors a look at what the fund actually owns. To get the fund's holdings, you have to have its latest semiannual or annual report. Most people don't get those documents until after they invest, and even then it can be as much as six months old. Many investment advisers think funds should begin reporting their holdings monthly, but so far funds have resisted doing so.

A manager's stake in a fund: Funds should be required to tell investors whether the fund manager owns any of its shares so investors can see just how confident a manager is in his or her own ability to pick stocks, some investment advisers say. As it stands now, many fund groups don't even disclose the names and backgrounds of the men and women calling the shots, and instead report that their funds are managed by a "team" of individuals whose identities they don't disclose.

A breakdown of fees: Investors will see in the profile prospectus a clearer outline of the expenses incurred by the fund company that manages the portfolio. But there's no way to tell whether you are picking up the tab for another guy's lunch.

The problem is, some no-load funds impose a so-called 12b-1 marketing fee on all shareholders. But they use the money gathered from the fee to cover the cost of participating in mutual-fund supermarket distribution programs. Only some fund shareholders buy the fund shares through these programs, but all shareholders bear the expense—including those who purchased shares directly from the fund.

---

invest in large firms, and not to specialize in either value versus growth stocks—it holds a blend of these.

The table on the left labeled "Performance" reports on the fund's returns over the last few years and over longer periods up to 15 years. Comparisons of returns to relevant indexes, in this case, the S&P 500 and the Wilshire top 750 indexes, are provided to serve as benchmarks in evaluating the performance of the fund. The values under these columns give the performance of the fund relative to the index. For example, Magellan's return was 1.87% below the S&P 500 over the last three months, but 0.55% per year above the S&P over the past 5 years. The returns reported for the fund are calculated net of expenses, 12b-1 fees, and any other fees automatically deducted from fund assets, but they do not account for any sales charges such as front-end loads or back-end charges. Next appear the percentile ranks of the fund compared to all other funds (see column headed by All) and to all funds with the same investment objective (see column headed by Cat). A rank of 1 means the fund is a top performer. A rank of 80 would mean that it was beaten by 80% of funds in the comparison group. You can see

Nice, Light Read: the Prospectus

	Old Language	**Plain English**
Dreyfus example	The Transfer Agent has adopted standards and procedures pursuant to which signature-guarantees in proper form generally will be accepted from domestic banks, brokers, dealers, credit unions, national securities exchanges, registered securities associations, clearing agencies and savings associations, as well as from participants in the New York Stock Exchange Medallion Signature Program, the Securities Transfer Agents Medallion Program ("STAMP") and the Stock Exchange Medallion Program.	A signature guarantee helps protect against fraud. You can obtain one from most banks or securities dealers, but not from a notary public.
T. Rowe Price example	Total Return. The Fund may advertise total return figures on both a cumulative and compound average annual basis. Cumulative total return compares the amount invested at the beginning of a period with the amount redeemed at the end of the period, assuming the reinvestment of all dividends and capital gain distributions. The compound average annual total return, derived from the cumulative total return figure, indicates a yearly average of the Fund's performance. The annual compound rate of return for the Fund may vary from any average.	Total Return. This tells you how much an investment in a fund has changed in value over a given time period. It reflects any net increase or decrease in the share price and assumes that all dividends and capital gains (if any) paid during the period were reinvested in additional shares. Therefore, total return numbers include the effect of compounding. Advertisements for a fund may include cumulative or average annual total return figures, which may be compared with various indices, other performance measures, or other mutual funds.

Sources: Adapted from Vanessa O'Connell, "Shorter, Clearer, Mutual-Fund Disclosure May Omit Vital Investment Information," *The Wall Street Journal*, March 12, 1999. Reprinted by permission of Dow Jones & Company, Inc., via Copyright Clearance Center, Inc. © 1999 Dow Jones & Company, Inc. All Rights Reserved Worldwide. "A Little Light Reading? Try a Fund Prospectus," *The Wall Street Journal*, May 3, 1999. p. R1. Reprinted by permission of Dow Jones & Company, Inc., via Copyright Clearance Center, Inc. © 1999 Dow Jones & Company, Inc. All Rights Reserved Worldwide.

from the table that Magellan has had below-par recent (three month to three year) performance compared to other growth and income funds, but excellent longer-term performance. For example, over the past 15 years, its average return was higher than all but 13% of the funds in its category. Finally, growth of $10,000 invested in the fund over various periods ranging from the past three months to the past 15 years is given in the last column.

More data on the performance of the fund are provided in the graph at the top right of the figure. The bar charts give the fund's rate of return for each quarter of the last 10 years. Below the graph is a box for each year that depicts the relative performance of the fund for that year. The shaded area on the box shows the quartile in which the fund's performance falls relative to other funds with the same objective. If the shaded band is at the top of the box, the firm was a top quartile performer in that period, and so on.

The table below the bar charts presents historical data on characteristics of the fund. These data include return, return relative to appropriate benchmark indexes such as the S&P 500, the component of returns due to income (dividends) or capital gains, the percentile rank of the fund compared to all funds and funds in its objective class (where, again, 1% is the best performer and 99% would mean that the fund was outperformed by 99% of its comparison group), the expense ratio, and the turnover rate of the portfolio.

The table on the right entitled Portfolio Analysis presents the 25 largest holdings of the portfolio, showing the price–earnings ratio and year-to-date return of each of those securities. Investors can thus get a quick look at the manager's biggest bets.

Below the portfolio analysis table is a box labeled Current Investment Style. In this box, Morningstar evaluates style along two dimensions: One dimension is the size of the firms held in the portfolio as measured by the market value of outstanding equity; the other dimension is a value/growth continuum. Morningstar defines *value stocks* as those with low ratios of market price per share to various measures of value. It puts stocks on a growth-value continuum based on the ratios of stock price to the firm's earnings, book value, sales, cash flow, and dividends. Value stocks are those with a low price relative to these measures of value. In contrast, *growth stocks* have high ratios, suggesting that investors in these firms must believe that the firm will experience rapid growth to justify the prices at which the stocks sell. The shaded box for Magellan shows that the portfolio tends to hold larger firms (top row) and blend stocks (middle column). A year-by-year history of Magellan's investment style is presented in the sequence of such boxes at the top of the figure.

The center of the figure, labeled Risk Analysis, is one of the more complicated but interesting facets of Morningstar's analysis. The column labeled Load-Adj Return rates a fund's return compared to other funds with the same investment policy. Returns for periods ranging from 1 to 10 years are calculated with all loads and back-end fees applicable to that investment period subtracted from total income. The return is then divided by the average return for the comparison group of funds to obtain the Morningstar Return; therefore, a value of 1.0 in the Return column would indicate average performance while a value of 1.10 would indicate returns 10% above the average for the comparison group (e.g., 11% return for the fund versus 10% for the comparison group).

The risk measure indicates the portfolio's exposure to poor performance, that is, the "downside risk" of the fund. Morningstar bases its risk measure in part on the overall volatility of returns. However, it focuses more intently on episodes of underperformance relative to Treasury bills. The total underperformance compared to T-bills in those months with poor portfolio performance divided by total months sampled is part of the measure of downside risk. The risk measure also is scaled by dividing by the average risk measure for all firms with the same investment objective. Therefore, the average value in the Risk column is 1.0.

The two columns to the left of the Morningstar Risk and Return columns are the percentile scores of risk and return for each fund. The risk-adjusted rating, ranging from one to five stars, is based on the Morningstar return score minus the risk score. The stars each fund earns are based on risk-adjusted performance relative to other funds in the same style group. To allow funds to be compared to other funds with similar investment styles, Morningstar recently increased the number of categories; there are now 18 separate stock fund groups and 20 fixed income categories.

The tax analysis box on the left provides some evidence on the tax efficiency of the fund by comparing pretax and after-tax returns. The after-tax return, given in the first column, is computed based on the dividends paid to the portfolio as well as realized capital gains, assuming the investor is in the maximum tax bracket at the time of the distribution. State and local taxes are ignored. The "tax efficiency" of the fund is defined as the ratio of after-tax to pretax returns; it is presented in the second column, labeled % Pretax Return. Tax efficiency will be lower when turnover is higher because capital gains are taxed as they are realized.

The bottom of the page provides information on the expenses and loads associated with investments in the fund, as well as information on the fund's investment adviser. Thus, Morningstar provides a considerable amount of the information you would need to decide among several competing funds.

- Unit investment trusts, closed-end management companies, and open-end management companies are all classified and regulated as investment companies. Unit investment trusts are essentially unmanaged in the sense that the portfolio, once established, is fixed. Managed investment companies, in contrast, may change the composition of the portfolio as deemed fit by the portfolio manager. Closed-end funds are traded like other securities; they do not redeem shares for their investors. Open-end funds will redeem shares for net asset value at the request of the investor.
- Net asset value equals the market value of assets held by a fund minus the liabilities of the fund divided by the shares outstanding.
- Mutual funds free the individual from many of the administrative burdens of owning individual securities and offer professional management of the portfolio. They also offer advantages that are available only to large-scale investors, such as lower trading costs. On the other hand, funds are assessed management fees and incur other expenses, which reduce the investor's rate of return. Funds also eliminate some of the individual's control over the timing of capital gains realizations.
- Mutual funds often are categorized by investment policy. Major policy groups include money market funds; equity funds, which are further grouped according to emphasis on income versus growth; fixed-income funds; balanced and income funds; asset allocation funds; index funds; and specialized sector funds.
- Costs of investing in mutual funds include front-end loads, which are sales charges; back-end loads, which are redemption fees or, more formally, contingent-deferred sales charges; fund operating expenses; and 12b-1 charges, which are recurring fees used to pay for the expenses of marketing the fund to the public.
- Income earned on mutual fund portfolios is not taxed at the level of the fund. Instead, as long as the fund meets certain requirements for pass-through status, the income is treated as being earned by the investors in the fund.
- The average rate of return of the average equity mutual fund in the last 25 years has been below that of a passive index fund holding a portfolio to replicate a broad-based index like the S&P 500 or Wilshire 5000. Some of the reasons for this disappointing record are the costs incurred by actively managed funds, such as the expense of conducting the research to guide stock-picking activities, and trading costs due to higher portfolio turnover. The record on the consistency of fund performance is mixed. In some sample periods, the better-performing funds continue to perform well in the following periods; in other sample periods they do not.

closed-end fund, 101	investment company, 100	soft dollars, 110
exchange-traded funds, 112	load, 103	12b-1 fees, 108
	net asset value (NAV), 100	turnover, 111
hedge fund, 103	open-end fund, 101	unit investment trust, 101

PROBLEM SETS

1. Would you expect a typical open-end fixed-income mutual fund to have higher or lower operating expenses than a fixed-income unit investment trust? Why?

2. An open-end fund has a net asset value of $10.70 per share. It is sold with a front-end load of 6%. What is the offering price?

3. If the offering price of an open-end fund is $12.30 per share and the fund is sold with a front-end load of 5%, what is its net asset value?

4. The composition of the Fingroup Fund portfolio is as follows:

Stock	Shares	Price
A	200,000	$35
B	300,000	40
C	400,000	20
D	600,000	25

The fund has not borrowed any funds, but its accrued management fee with the portfolio manager currently totals $30,000. There are 4 million shares outstanding. What is the net asset value of the fund?

5. Reconsider the Fingroup Fund in the previous problem. If during the year the portfolio manager sells all of the holdings of stock D and replaces it with 200,000 shares of stock E at $50 per share and 200,000 shares of stock F at $25 per share, what is the portfolio turnover rate?

6. The Closed Fund is a closed-end investment company with a portfolio currently worth $200 million. It has liabilities of $3 million and 5 million shares outstanding.
   a. What is the NAV of the fund?
   b. If the fund sells for $36 per share, what is its premium or discount as a percent of NAV?

7. Corporate Fund started the year with a net asset value of $12.50. By year-end, its NAV equaled $12.10. The fund paid year-end distributions of income and capital gains of $1.50. What was the rate of return to an investor in the fund?

8. A closed-end fund starts the year with a net asset value of $12.00. By year-end, NAV equals $12.10. At the beginning of the year, the fund is selling at a 2% premium to NAV. By the end of the year, the fund is selling at a 7% discount to NAV. The fund paid year-end distributions of income and capital gains of $1.50.
   a. What is the rate of return to an investor in the fund during the year?
   b. What would have been the rate of return to an investor who held the same securities as the fund manager during the year?

9. What are some comparative advantages of investing your assets in the following:
   a. Unit investment trusts.
   b. Open-end mutual funds.
   c. Individual stocks and bonds that you choose for yourself.

10. Open-end equity mutual funds find it necessary to keep a significant percentage of total investments, typically around 5% of the portfolio, in very liquid money market assets. Closed-end funds do not have to maintain such a position in "cash-equivalent" securities. What difference between open-end and closed-end funds might account for their differing policies?

11. Balanced funds and asset allocation funds invest in both the stock and bond markets. What is the difference between these types of funds?

12. *a.* Impressive Fund had excellent investment performance last year, with portfolio returns that placed it in the top 10% of all funds with the same investment policy. Do you expect it to be a top performer next year? Why or why not?

    b. Suppose instead that the fund was among the poorest performers in its comparison group. Would you be more or less likely to believe its relative performance will persist into the following year? Why?

13. Consider a mutual fund with $200 million in assets at the start of the year and with 10 million shares outstanding. The fund invests in a portfolio of stocks that provides dividend income at the end of the year of $2 million. The stocks included in the fund's portfolio increase in price by 8%, but no securities are sold, and there are no capital gains distributions. The fund charges 12b-1 fees of 1%, which are deducted from portfolio assets at year-end. What is net asset value at the start and end of the year? What is the rate of return for an investor in the fund?

14. The New Fund had average daily assets of $2.2 billion in the past year. The fund sold $400 million and purchased $500 million worth of stock during the year. What was its turnover ratio?

15. If New Fund's expense ratio was 1.1% and the management fee was .7%, what were the total fees paid to the fund's investment managers during the year? What were the other administrative expenses?

16. You purchased 1,000 shares of the New Fund at a price of $20 per share at the beginning of the year. You paid a front-end load of 4%. The securities in which the fund invests increase in value by 12% during the year. The fund's expense ratio is 1.2%. What is your rate of return on the fund if you sell your shares at the end of the year?

17. The Investments Fund sells Class A shares with a front-end load of 6% and Class B shares with 12b-1 fees of .5% annually as well as back-end load fees that start at 5% and fall by 1% for each full year the investor holds the portfolio (until the fifth year). Assume the portfolio rate of return net of operating expenses is 10% annually. If you plan to sell the fund after four years, are Class A or Class B shares the better choice for you? What if you plan to sell after 15 years?

18. Suppose you observe the investment performance of 350 portfolio managers for five years, and rank them by investment returns during each year. After five years, you find that 11 of the funds have investment returns that place the fund in the top half of the sample in each and every year of your sample. Such consistency of performance indicates to you that these must be the funds whose managers are in fact skilled, and you invest your money in these funds. Is your conclusion warranted?

19. You are considering an investment in a mutual fund with a 4% load and an expense ratio of .5%. You can invest instead in a bank CD paying 6% interest.

    a. If you plan to invest for two years, what annual rate of return must the fund portfolio earn for you to be better off in the fund than in the CD? Assume annual compounding of returns.

    b. How does your answer change if you plan to invest for six years? Why does your answer change?

    c. Now suppose that instead of a front-end load the fund assesses a 12b-1 fee of .75% per year. What annual rate of return must the fund portfolio earn for you to be better off in the fund than in the CD? Does your answer in this case depend on your time horizon?

20. Suppose that every time a fund manager trades stock, transaction costs such as commissions and bid–ask spreads amount to .4% of the value of the trade. If the portfolio turnover rate is 50%, by how much is the total return of the portfolio reduced by trading costs?

21. You expect a tax-free municipal bond portfolio to provide a rate of return of 4%. Management fees of the fund are .6%. What fraction of portfolio income is given up to fees? If the management fees for an equity fund also are .6%, but you expect a portfolio return of 12%, what fraction of portfolio income is given up to fees? Why might management fees be a bigger factor in your investment decision for bond funds than for stock funds? Can your conclusion help explain why unmanaged unit investment trusts tend to focus on the fixed-income market?

WEBMASTER

Mutual Fund Report

Go to http://www.morningstar.com. From the home page select the Funds tab. From this location you can request information on an individual fund. In the dialog box enter the ticker JANSX, for the Janus Fund, and enter Go. This contains the report information on the fund. On the left-hand side of the screen are tabs that allow you to view the various components of the report.

Using the components specified, answer the following questions on the Janus Fund:

1. Morningstar analysis: What is the Morningstar rating? What has been the fund's year-to-date return?

2. Total returns: What are the 5- and 10-year returns and how do they compare with the return of the S&P?

3. Ratings and risk: What is the beta of the fund? What are the mean and standard deviation of returns? What is the 10-year rating on the fund?

4. Portfolio: What two sectors' weightings are the largest? What percent of the portfolio assets are in cash?

5. Nuts and bolts: What is the fund's total expense ratio? Who is the current manager of the fund and what was his/her start date? How long has the fund been in operation?

SOLUTIONS TO

Concept
CHECK

1. NAV = ($14,754 − $1,934)/419.4 = $30.57

2. The net investment in the Class A shares after the 4% commission is $9,600. If the fund earns a 10% return, the investment will grow after n years to $9,600 × $(1.10)^n$. The Class B shares have no front-end load. However, the net return to the investor after 12b-1 fees will be only 9.5%. In addition, there is a back-end load that reduces the sales proceeds by a percentage equal to (5 − years until sale) until the fifth year, when the back-end load expires.

Horizon	Class A Shares $9,600 × $(1.10)^n$	Class B Shares $10,000 × $(1.095)^n$ × (1 − percentage exit fee)	
1 year	$10,560.00	$10,000 × (1.095) × (1 − .04)	= $10,512.00
4 years	14,055.36	$10,000 × (1.095)^4 × (1 − .01)	= $14,232.89
10 years	$24,899.93	$10,000 × (1.095)^{10}	= $24,782.28

For a very short horizon such as one year, the Class A shares are the better choice. The front-end and back-end loads are equal, but the Class A shares don't have to pay the 12b-1 fees. For moderate horizons such as four years, the Class B shares dominate because the front-end load of the Class A shares is more costly than the 12b-1 fees and the now smaller exit fee. For long horizons of 10 years or more, Class A again dominates. In this case, the one-time front-end load is less expensive than the continuing 12b-1 fees.

3. *a.* Turnover = $160,000 in trades per $1 million of portfolio value = 16%.

   b. Realized capital gains are $10 × 1,000 = $10,000 on Microsoft and $5 × 2,000 = $10,000 on Ford. The tax owed on the capital gains is therefore .20 × $20,000 = $4,000.

4. Twenty percent of the managers are skilled, which accounts for .2 × 400 = 80 of those managers who appear in the top half. There are 120 slots left in the top half, and 320 other managers, so the probability of an unskilled manager "lucking into" the top half in any year is 120/320, or .375. Therefore, of the 120 lucky managers in the first year, we would expect .375 × 120 = 45 to repeat as top-half performers next year. Thus, we should expect a total of 80 + 45 = 125, or 62.5%, of the better initial performers to repeat their top-half performance.

PART TWO

PORTFOLIO THEORY

Suppose you believe that investments in stocks offer an expected rate of return of 10% while the expected rate of return on bonds is only 6%. Would you invest all of your money in stocks? Probably not: putting all of your eggs in one basket in such a manner would violate even the most basic notion of diversification. But what is the optimal combination of these two asset classes? And how will the opportunity to invest in other asset classes—for example, real estate, foreign stocks, precious metals, and so on—affect your decision? In short, is there a "best" solution to your asset allocation problem?

These questions are the focus of the first chapters of Part II, which address what has come to be known as Modern Portfolio Theory, or MPT. In large part, MPT addresses the question of "efficient diversification," how to achieve the best trade-off between portfolio risk and reward.

This analysis quickly leads to other questions. For example, how should one measure the risk of an individual asset held as part of a diversified portfolio? You will probably be surprised at the answer. Once we have an acceptable measure of risk, what precisely should be the relation between risk and return? And what is the minimally acceptable rate of return for an investment to be considered attractive? These questions also are addressed in this Part of the text.

Finally, we come to one of the most controversial topics in investment management, the question of whether portfolio managers—amateur or professional—can outperform simple investment strategies such as "buy a market index fund." The evidence will at least make you pause before pursuing active strategies.

You will come to appreciate how good active managers must be to outperform their passive counterparts.

5   Risk and Return: Past and Prologue

6   Efficient Diversification

7   Capital Asset Pricing and Arbitrage Pricing Theory

8   The Efficient Market Hypothesis

www.mhhe.com/bkm

McGraw-Hill / Irwin presents
Investments online

5

RISK AND RETURN: PAST AND PROLOGUE

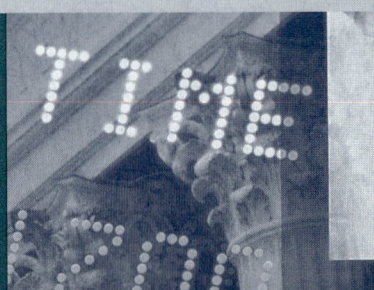

**AFTER STUDYING THIS CHAPTER
YOU SHOULD BE ABLE TO:**

> Use data on the past performance of stocks and bonds to characterize the risk and return features of these investments.

> Determine the expected return and risk of portfolios that are constructed by combining risky assets with risk-free investments in Treasury bills.

> Evaluate the performance of a passive strategy.

What constitutes a satisfactory investment portfolio? Until the early 1970s, a reasonable answer would have been a bank savings account (a risk-free asset) plus a risky portfolio of U.S. stocks. Nowadays, investors have access to a vastly wider array of assets and may contemplate complex portfolio strategies that may include foreign stocks and bonds, real estate, precious metals, and collectibles. Even more complex strategies may include futures and options to insure portfolios against unacceptable losses. How might such portfolios be constructed?

Clearly every individual security must be judged on its contributions to both the expected return and the risk of the entire portfolio. These contributions must be evaluated in the context of the expected performance of the overall portfolio. To guide us in forming reasonable expectations for portfolio performance, we will start this chapter with an examination of various conventions for measuring and reporting rates of return. Given these measures, we turn to the historical performance of several broadly diversified investment portfolios. In doing so, we use a risk-free portfolio of Treasury bills as a benchmark to evaluate the historical performance of diversified stock and bond portfolios.

We then proceed to consider the trade-offs investors face when they practice the simplest form of risk control: choosing the fraction of the portfolio invested in virtually risk-free money market securities versus risky securities such as stocks. We show how to calculate the performance one may reasonably expect from various allocations between a risk-free asset and a risky portfolio and discuss the considerations that determine the mix that would best suit different investors. With this background, we can evaluate a passive strategy that will serve as a benchmark for the active strategies considered in the next chapter.

holding-period return

Rate of return over a given investment period.

A key measure of investors' success is the rate at which their funds have grown during the investment period. The total **holding-period return (HPR)** of a share of stock depends on the increase (or decrease) in the price of the share over the investment period as well as on any dividend income the share has provided. The rate of return is defined as dollars earned over the investment period (price appreciation as well as dividends) per dollar invested

$$HPR = \frac{\text{Ending price} - \text{Beginning price} + \text{Cash dividend}}{\text{Beginning price}}$$

This definition of the HPR assumes that the dividend is paid at the end of the holding period. To the extent that dividends are received earlier, the definition ignores reinvestment income between the receipt of the dividend and the end of the holding period. Recall also that the percentage return from dividends is called the dividend yield, and so the dividend yield plus the capital gains yield equals the HPR.

This definition of holding return is easy to modify for other types of investments. For example, the HPR on a bond would be calculated using the same formula, except that the bond's interest or coupon payments would take the place of the stock's dividend payments.

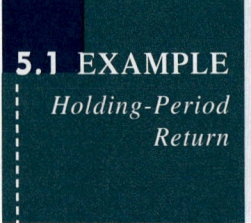

5.1 EXAMPLE
Holding-Period Return

Suppose you are considering investing some of your money, now all invested in a bank account, in a stock market index fund. The price of a share in the fund is currently $100, and your time horizon is one year. You expect the cash dividend during the year to be $4, so your expected dividend yield is 4%.

Your HPR will depend on the price one year from now. Suppose your best guess is that it will be $110 per share. Then your *capital gain* will be $10, so your capital gains yield is $10/$100 = .10, or 10%. The total holding period rate of return is the sum of the dividend yield plus the capital gain yield, 4% + 10% = 14%.

$$HPR = \frac{\$110 - \$100 + \$4}{\$100} = .14, \text{ or } 14\%$$

Measuring Investment Returns over Multiple Periods

The holding period return is a simple and unambiguous measure of investment return over a single period. But often you will be interested in average returns over longer periods of time. For example, you might want to measure how well a mutual fund has performed over the preceding five-year period. In this case, return measurement is more ambiguous.

Consider, for example, a fund that starts with $1 million under management at the beginning of the year. The fund receives additional funds to invest from new and existing shareholders, and also receives requests for redemptions from existing shareholders. Its net cash inflow can be positive or negative. Suppose its quarterly results are as given in Table 5.1 with negative numbers reported in parentheses.

The story behind these numbers is that when the firm does well (i.e., reports a good HPR), it attracts new funds; otherwise it may suffer a net outflow. For example, the 10% return in the first quarter by itself increased assets under management by 0.10 × $1 million = $100,000; it also elicited new investments of $100,000, thus bringing assets under management to $1.2 million by the end of the quarter. An even better HPR in the second quarter elicited a larger net inflow, and the second quarter ended with $2 million under management. However, HPR in the third quarter was negative, and net inflows were negative.

TABLE **5.1** Quarterly cash flows and rates of return of a mutual fund		1st Quarter	2nd Quarter	3rd Quarter	4th Quarter
	Assets under management at start of quarter ($ million)	1.0	1.2	2.0	0.8
	Holding-period return (%)	10.0	25.0	(20.0)	25.0
	Total assets before net inflows	1.1	1.5	1.6	1.0
	Net inflow ($ million)*	0.1	0.5	(0.8)	0.0
	Assets under management at end of quarter ($ million)	1.2	2.0	0.8	1.0

*New investment less redemptions and distributions, all assumed to occur at the end of each quarter.

How would we characterize fund performance over the year, given that the fund experienced both cash inflows and outflows? There are several candidate measures of performance, each with its own advantages and shortcomings. These are the *arithmetic average,* the *geometric average,* and the *dollar-weighted return.* These measures may vary considerably, so it is important to understand their differences.

Arithmetic average   The **arithmetic average** of the quarterly returns is just the sum of the quarterly returns divided by the number of quarters; in the above example: $(10 + 25 - 20 + 25)/4 = 10\%$. Since this statistic ignores compounding, it does not represent an equivalent, single quarterly rate for the year. The arithmetic average is useful, though, because it is the best forecast of performance in future quarters, using this particular sample of historic returns. (Whether the sample is large enough or representative enough to make accurate forecasts is, of course, another question.)

> **arithmetic average**
>
> The sum of returns in each period divided by the number of periods.

Geometric average   The **geometric average** of the quarterly returns is equal to the single per-period return that would give the same cumulative performance as the sequence of actual returns. We calculate the geometric average by compounding the actual period-by-period returns and then finding the equivalent single per-period return. In this case, the geometric average quarterly return, r_G, is defined by:

$$(1 + 0.10) \times (1 + 0.25) \times (1 - 0.20) \times (1 + 0.25) = (1 + r_G)^4$$

so that

$$r_G = [(1 + 0.10) \times (1 + 0.25) \times (1 - 0.20) \times (1 + 0.25)]^{1/4} - 1 = .0829, \text{ or } 8.29\%$$

> **geometric average**
>
> The single per-period return that gives the same cumulative performance as the sequence of actual returns.

The geometric return also is called a *time-weighted average return* because it ignores the quarter-to-quarter variation in funds under management. In fact, an investor will obtain a larger cumulative return if high returns are earned in those periods when additional sums have been invested, while the lower returns are realized when less money is at risk. Here, the highest returns (25%) were achieved in quarters 2 and 4, when the fund managed $1,200,000 and $800,000, respectively. The worst returns (-20% and 10%) occurred when the fund managed $2,000,000 and $1,000,000, respectively. In this case, better returns were earned when *less* money was under management—an unfavorable combination.

The appeal of the time-weighted return is that in some cases we *wish* to ignore variation in money under management. For example, published data on past returns earned by mutual funds actually are *required* to be time-weighted returns. The rationale for this practice is that since the fund manager does not have full control over the amount of assets under management, we should not weight returns in one period more heavily than those in other periods when assessing "typical" past performance.

Dollar-weighted return When we wish to account for the varying amounts under management, we treat the fund cash flows to investors as we would a capital budgeting problem in corporate finance. The initial value of $1 million and the net cash inflows are treated as the cash flows associated with an investment "project." The final "liquidation value" of the project is the ending value of the portfolio. In this case, therefore, investor net cash flows are as follows:

	Time				
	0	**1**	**2**	**3**	**4**
Net cash flow ($ million)	−1.0	−0.1	−0.5	0.8	1.0

The entry for time 0 reflects the starting contribution of $1 million, while the entries for times 1, 2, and 3 represent net inflows at the end of the first three quarters. Finally, the entry for time 4 represents the value of the portfolio at the end of the fourth quarter. This is the value for which the portfolio could have been liquidated by year-end based on the initial investment and net additional investments earlier in the year.

dollar-weighted average return

The internal rate of return on an investment.

The **dollar-weighted average return** is the internal rate of return (IRR) of the project, which is 4.17%. The IRR is the interest rate that sets the present value of the cash flows realized on the portfolio (including the $1 million for which the portfolio can be liquidated at the end of the year) equal to the initial cost of establishing the portfolio. It therefore is the interest rate that satisfies the following equation:

$$1.0 = \frac{-0.1}{1 + IRR} + \frac{-0.5}{(1 + IRR)^2} + \frac{0.8}{(1 + IRR)^3} + \frac{1.0}{(1 + IRR)^4}$$

The dollar-weighted return in this example is less than the time-weighted return of 8.29% because, as we noted, the portfolio returns were higher when less money was under management. The difference between the dollar- and time-weighted average return in this case is quite large.

Concept CHECK

1. A fund begins with $10 million and reports the following three-month results (with negative figures in parentheses):

	Month		
	1	**2**	**3**
Net inflows (end of month, $ million)	3	5	0
HPR (%)	2	8	(4)

Compute the arithmetic, time-weighted, and dollar-weighted average returns.

Conventions for Quoting Rates of Return

We've seen that there are several ways to compute average rates of return. There also is some variation in how the mutual fund in our example might annualize its quarterly returns.

Returns on assets with regular cash flows, such as mortgages (with monthly payments) and bonds (with semiannual coupons), usually are quoted as annual percentage rates, or APRs, which annualize per-period rates using a simple interest approach, ignoring compound interest. The APR can be translated to an effective annual rate (EAR) by remembering that

$$APR = \text{Per-period rate} \times \text{Periods per year}$$

Therefore, to obtain the EAR if there are n compounding periods in the year, we first recover the rate per period as APR/n and then compound that rate for the number of periods in a year. (For example, $n = 12$ for mortgages and $n = 2$ for bonds making payments semiannually).

$$1 + \text{EAR} = (1 + \text{Rate per period})^n = \left(1 + \frac{\text{APR}}{n}\right)^n$$

Rearranging,

$$\text{APR} = [(1 + \text{EAR})^{1/n} - 1] \times n \tag{5.1}$$

The formula assumes that you can earn the APR each period. Therefore, after one year (when n periods have passed), your cumulative return would be $(1 + \text{APR}/n)^n$. Note that one needs to know the holding period when given an APR in order to convert it to an effective rate.

The EAR diverges from the APR as n becomes larger (that is, as we compound cash flows more frequently). In the limit, we can envision continuous compounding when n becomes extremely large in Equation 5.1. With continuous compounding, the relationship between the APR and EAR becomes

$$\text{EAR} = e^{\text{APR}} - 1$$

or equivalently,

$$\text{APR} = \ln(1 + \text{EAR}) \tag{5.2}$$

EXAMPLE 5.2

Annualizing Treasury-Bill Returns

Suppose you buy a Treasury bill maturing in one month for $9,900. On the bill's maturity date, you collect the face value of $10,000. Since there are no other interest payments, the holding period return for this one-month investment is:

$$\text{HPR} = \frac{\text{Cash income} + \text{Price change}}{\text{Initial price}} = \frac{\$100}{\$9,900} = 0.0101 = 1.01\%$$

The APR on this investment is therefore $1.01\% \times 12 = 12.12\%$. The effective annual rate is higher:

$$1 + \text{EAR} = (1.0101)^{12} = 1.1282$$

which implies that $\text{EAR} = .1282 = 12.82\%$

The difficulties in interpreting rates of return over time do not end here. Two thorny issues remain: the uncertainty surrounding the investment in question and the effect of inflation.

5.2 RISK AND RISK PREMIUMS

Any investment involves some degree of uncertainty about future holding period returns, and in most cases that uncertainty is considerable. Sources of investment risk range from macroeconomic fluctuations, to the changing fortunes of various industries, to asset-specific unexpected developments. Analysis of these multiple sources of risk is presented in Part Four on Security Analysis.

Scenario Analysis and Probability Distributions

When we attempt to quantify risk, we begin with the question: What HPRs are possible, and how likely are they? A good way to approach this question is to devise a list of possible economic

TABLE **5.2**	State of the Economy	Scenario, s	Probability, p(s)	HPR
Probability distribution of HPR on the stock market	Boom	1	0.25	44%
	Normal growth	2	0.50	14
	Recession	3	0.25	−16

scenario analysis

Process of devising a list of possible economic scenarios and specifying the likelihood of each one, as well as the HPR that will be realized in each case.

probability distribution

List of possible outcomes with associated probabilities.

expected return

The mean value of the distribution of holding period returns.

variance

The expected value of the squared deviation from the mean.

standard deviation

The square root of the variance.

outcomes, or *scenarios,* and specify both the likelihood (i.e., the probability) of each scenario and the HPR the asset will realize in that scenario. Therefore, this approach is called **scenario analysis.** The list of possible HPRs with associated probabilities is called the **probability distribution** of HPRs. Consider an investment in a broad portfolio of stocks, say an index fund, which we will refer to as the "stock market." A very simple scenario analysis for the stock market (assuming only three possible scenarios) is illustrated in Table 5.2.

The probability distribution lets us derive measurements for both the reward and the risk of the investment. The reward from the investment is its **expected return,** which you can think of as the average HPR you would earn if you were to repeat an investment in the asset many times. The expected return also is called the mean of the distribution of HPRs and often is referred to as the *mean return.*

To compute the expected return from the data provided, we label scenarios by s and denote the HPR in each scenario as $r(s)$, with probability $p(s)$. The expected return, denoted $E(r)$, is then the weighted average of returns in all possible scenarios, $s = 1, \ldots, S$, with weights equal to the probability of that particular scenario.

$$E(r) = \sum_{s=1}^{S} p(s)r(s) \tag{5.3}$$

We show in Example 5.3, which follows shortly, that the data in Table 5.2 imply $E(r) = 14\%$.

Of course, there is risk to the investment, and the actual return may be more or less than 14%. If a "boom" materializes, the return will be better, 44%, but in a recession, the return will be only −16%. How can we quantify the uncertainty of the investment?

The "surprise" return on the investment in any scenario is the difference between the actual return and the expected return. For example, in a boom (scenario 1) the surprise is 30%: $r(1) - E(r) = 44\% - 14\% = 30\%$. In a recession (scenario 3), the surprise is −30%: $r(3) - E(r) = -16\% - 14\% = -30\%$.

Uncertainty surrounding the investment is a function of the magnitudes of the possible surprises. To summarize risk with a single number we first define the **variance** as the expected value of the *squared* deviation from the mean (i.e., the expected value of the squared "surprise" across scenarios).

$$\text{Var}(r) \equiv \sigma^2 = \sum_{s=1}^{S} p(s)[r(s) - E(r)]^2 \tag{5.4}$$

We square the deviations because if we did not, negative deviations would offset positive deviations, with the result that the expected deviation from the mean return would necessarily be zero. Squared deviations are necessarily positive. Of course, squaring (a nonlinear transformation) exaggerates large (positive or negative) deviations and relatively deemphasizes small deviations.

Another result of squaring deviations is that the variance has a dimension of percent squared. To give the measure of risk the same dimension as expected return (%), we use the **standard deviation,** defined as the square root of the variance:

$$SD(r) \equiv \sigma = \sqrt{\text{Var}(r)} \tag{5.5}$$

A potential drawback to the use of variance and standard deviation as measures of risk is that they treat positive deviations and negative deviations from the expected return symmetrically. In practice, of course, investors welcome positive surprises, and a natural measure of risk would focus only on bad outcomes. However, if the distribution of returns is symmetric (meaning that the likelihood of negative surprises is roughly equal to the probability of positive surprises of the same magnitude), then standard deviation will approximate risk measures that concentrate solely on negative deviations. In the special case that the distribution of returns is approximately normal—represented by the well-known bell-shaped curve—the standard deviation will be perfectly adequate to measure risk. The evidence shows that for fairly short holding periods, the returns of most diversified portfolios are well described by a normal distribution.

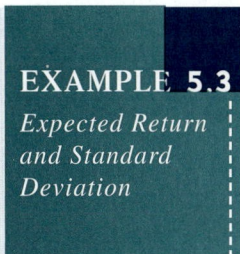

EXAMPLE 5.3

Expected Return and Standard Deviation

Applying Equation 5.3 to the data in Table 5.2, we find that the expected rate of return on the stock index fund is

$$E(r) = 0.25 \times 44\% + 0.50 \times 14\% + 0.25 \times (-16\%) = 14\%$$

We use Equation 5.4 to find the variance. First we take the difference between the holding period return in each scenario and the mean return, then we square that difference, and finally we multiply by the probability of each scenario to find the average of the squared deviations. The result is

$$\sigma^2 = 0.25(44 - 14)^2 + 0.50(14 - 14)^2 + 0.25(-16 - 14)^2 = 450$$

and so the standard deviation is

$$\sigma = \sqrt{450} = 21.21\%$$

> **Concept**
> CHECK

2. A share of stock of A-Star Inc. is now selling for $23.50. A financial analyst summarizes the uncertainty about the rate of return on the stock by specifying three possible scenarios:

Business Conditions	Scenario, s	Probability, p	End-of-Year Price	Annual Dividend
High growth	1	0.35	$35	$4.40
Normal growth	2	0.30	27	4.00
No growth	3	0.35	15	4.00

What are the holding-period returns for a one-year investment in the stock of A-Star Inc. for each of the three scenarios? Calculate the expected HPR and standard deviation of the HPR.

Risk Premiums and Risk Aversion

How much, if anything, should you invest in an index stock fund such as the one described in Table 5.2? First, you must ask how much of an expected reward is offered to compensate for the risk involved in investing money in stocks.

We measure the "reward" as the difference between the expected HPR on the index stock fund and the **risk-free rate,** that is, the rate you can earn by leaving money in risk-free assets such as Treasury bills, money market funds, or the bank. We call this difference the **risk premium** on common stocks. For example, if the risk-free rate in the example is 6% per year, and the expected index fund return is 14%, then the risk premium on stocks is 8% per year.

> **risk-free rate**
>
> The rate of return that can be earned with certainty.

> **risk premium**
>
> An expected return in excess of that on risk-free securities.

The rate of return on Treasury bills also varies over time. However, we know the rate of return we will earn on T-bills *at the beginning* of the holding period, while we can't know the return we will earn on risky assets until the end of the holding period. Therefore, to study the risk premium available on risky assets we compile a series of **excess returns,** that is, returns in excess of the T-bill rate in each period. One possible estimate of the risk premium of any asset is the average of its historical excess returns.

excess return

Rate of return in excess of the Treasury-bill rate.

The degree to which investors are willing to commit funds to stocks depends on **risk aversion.** It seems obvious that investors are risk averse in the sense that, if the risk premium were zero, people would not be willing to invest any money in stocks. In theory then, there must always be a positive risk premium on stocks in order to induce risk-averse investors to hold the existing supply of stocks instead of placing all their money in risk-free assets.

risk aversion

Reluctance to accept risk.

In fact, the risk premium is what distinguishes gambling from speculation. Investors who are willing to take on risk because they expect to earn a risk premium are speculating. Speculation is undertaken *despite* the risk because the speculator sees a favorable risk-return trade-off. In contrast, gambling is the assumption of risk for no purpose beyond the enjoyment of the risk itself. Gamblers take on risk even without the prospect of a risk premium.[1]

It occasionally will be useful to quantify an investor's degree of risk aversion. To do so, suppose that investors choose portfolios based on both expected return, $E(r_P)$, and the volatility of returns as measured by the variance, σ_P^2. If we denote the risk-free rate on Treasury bills as r_f, then the risk premium of a portfolio is $E(r_P) - r_f$. Risk-averse investors will demand higher expected returns to place their wealth in portfolios with higher volatility; that risk premium will be greater the greater their risk aversion. Therefore, if we quantify the degree of risk aversion with the parameter A, it makes sense to assert that the risk premium an investor demands of a portfolio will be dependent on both risk aversion A and the risk of the portfolio, σ_P^2.

We will write the risk premium that an investor demands of a portfolio as a function of its risk as

$$E(r_P) - r_f = \tfrac{1}{2}A\sigma_P^2 \tag{5.6}$$

Equation 5.6 describes how investors are willing to trade off risk against expected return. (The equation requires that we put rates of return in decimal form.) As a benchmark, we note that risk-free portfolios have zero variance, so the investor does not require a risk premium—the return must be equal only to the risk-free rate. A risk premium of $\tfrac{1}{2}A\sigma_P^2$ is required to induce the investor to establish an overall portfolio that has positive volatility. The term $\tfrac{1}{2}$ is merely a scale factor chosen for convenience and has no real bearing on the analysis.

It turns out that if investors trade off risk against return in the manner specified by Equation 5.6, then we would be able to infer their risk aversion if we could observe risk premiums and volatilities of their actual portfolios. We can solve Equation 5.6 for A as

$$A = \frac{E(r_P) - r_f}{\tfrac{1}{2}\sigma_P^2} \tag{5.7}$$

For example, if an investor believes the risk premium on her portfolio is 8%, and the standard deviation is 20%, then we could infer risk aversion as $A = .08/(.5 \times .20^2) = 4$.

In practice, we cannot observe the risk premium investors *expect* to earn. We can observe only actual returns after the fact. Moreover, different investors may have different expectations about the risk and return of various assets. Finally, Equations 5.6 and 5.7 apply only to the variance of an investor's overall portfolio, not to individual assets held in that portfolio. We cannot observe an investor's total portfolio of assets. While the exact relationship between risk and

---

[1]Sometimes a gamble might *seem* like speculation to the participants. If two investors have different views about the future, they might take opposite positions on a security, and both may have an expectation of earning a positive risk premium. In such cases, only one party can, in fact, be correct.

return in capital markets cannot be known exactly, many studies conclude that investors' risk aversion is likely in the range of 2–4.

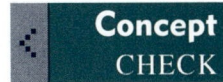

3. A respected analyst forecasts that the return of the S&P 500 index portfolio over the coming year will be 10%. The one-year T-bill rate is 5%. Examination of recent returns of the S&P 500 Index suggest that the standard deviation of returns will be 18%. What does this information suggest about the degree of risk aversion of the average investor, assuming that the average portfolio resembles the S&P 500?

WEBMASTER

Estimating the Equity Risk Premium

A research report by Stern Stewart & Company, the consulting firm that specializes in Economic Value Added, presents some analysis on this subject. Go to http://www.eva.com/content/evaluation/info/032001.pdf to read the report entitled "The Equity Risk Measurement Handbook."

After reading pages 1–8 of this report, answer the following questions:

1. What range of estimates does this report indicate are being used in the market?

2. What factors does the report indicate should lead toward using a shorter estimation period over which to estimate the market risk premium?

3. What did the report show with respect to the convergence of stock and bonds with respect to volatility and returns?

4. Does the estimate of market risk premium appear to be sensitive to the measurement period?

5.3 THE HISTORICAL RECORD

Bills, Bonds, and Stocks, 1926–2001

The record of past rates of return is one possible source of information about risk premiums and standard deviations. We can estimate the historical risk premium by taking an average of the past differences between the HPRs on an asset class and the risk-free rate. Table 5.3 presents the annual HPRs on five asset classes for the period 1926–2001.

"Large Stocks" in Table 5.3 refer to Standard & Poor's market-value-weighted portfolio of 500 U.S. common stocks selected from the largest market capitalization stocks. "Small Company Stocks" are represented by the Russell 2000 Index as of 1996. Stocks in this portfolio rank below the 1,000 U.S. largest-capitalization stocks. Prior to 1996, "Small Stocks" were represented by the smallest 20% of the stocks trading on the NYSE.

Until 1996, "Long-Term T-Bonds" were represented by government bonds with at least a 20-year maturity and approximately current-level coupon rate,[2] and "Intermediate-Term T-Bonds" were represented by government bonds with a seven-year maturity and a current-level coupon rate. Since 1996, these two bond series have been measured by the Lehman Brothers Long-Term or Intermediate-Term Bond Indexes, respectively.

"T-Bills" in Table 5.3 are of approximately 30-day maturity, and the one-year HPR represents a policy of "rolling over" the bills as they mature. Because T-bill rates can change from

---

[2]The importance of the coupon rate when comparing returns on bonds is discussed in Part Three.

TABLE **5.3**
Rates of return 1926–2001

Year	Small Stocks	Large Stocks	Long-Term T-Bonds	Intermediate-Term T-Bonds	T-Bills	Inflation
1926	−8.91	12.21	4.54	4.96	3.19	−1.12
1927	32.23	35.99	8.11	3.34	3.12	−2.26
1928	45.02	39.29	−0.93	0.96	3.21	−1.16
1929	−50.81	−7.66	4.41	5.89	4.74	0.58
1930	−45.69	−25.90	6.22	5.51	2.35	−6.40
1931	−49.17	−45.56	−5.31	−5.81	0.96	−9.32
1932	10.95	−9.14	11.89	8.44	1.16	−10.27
1933	187.82	54.56	1.03	0.35	0.07	0.76
1934	25.13	−2.32	10.15	9.00	0.60	1.52
1935	68.44	45.67	4.98	7.01	−1.59	2.99
1936	84.47	33.55	6.52	3.77	−0.95	1.45
1937	−52.71	−36.03	0.43	1.56	0.35	2.86
1938	24.69	29.42	5.25	5.64	0.09	−2.78
1939	−0.10	−1.06	5.90	4.52	0.02	0.00
1940	−11.81	−9.65	6.54	2.03	0.00	0.71
1941	−13.08	−11.20	0.99	−0.59	0.06	9.93
1942	51.01	20.80	5.39	1.81	0.26	9.03
1943	99.79	26.54	4.87	2.78	0.35	2.96
1944	60.53	20.96	3.59	1.98	−0.07	2.30
1945	82.24	36.11	6.84	3.60	0.33	2.25
1946	−12.80	−9.26	0.15	0.69	0.57	18.13
1947	−3.09	4.88	−1.19	0.32	0.50	8.84
1948	−6.15	5.29	3.07	2.21	0.81	2.99
1949	21.56	18.24	6.03	2.22	1.10	−2.07
1950	45.48	32.68	−0.96	0.25	1.20	5.93
1951	9.41	23.47	−1.95	0.36	1.49	6.00
1952	6.36	18.91	1.93	1.63	1.66	0.75
1953	−5.68	−1.74	3.83	3.63	1.82	0.75
1954	65.13	52.55	4.88	1.73	0.86	−0.74
1955	21.84	31.44	−1.34	−0.52	1.57	0.37
1956	3.82	6.45	−5.12	−0.90	2.46	2.99
1957	−15.03	−11.14	9.46	7.84	3.14	2.90
1958	70.63	43.78	−3.71	−1.29	1.54	1.76
1959	17.82	12.95	−3.55	−1.26	2.95	1.73
1960	−5.16	0.19	13.78	11.98	2.66	1.36
1961	30.48	27.63	0.19	2.23	2.13	0.67
1962	−16.41	−8.79	6.81	7.38	2.72	1.33
1963	12.20	22.63	−0.49	1.79	3.12	1.64
1964	18.75	16.67	4.51	4.45	3.54	0.97
1965	37.67	12.50	−0.27	1.27	3.94	1.92
1966	−8.08	−10.25	3.70	5.14	4.77	3.46
1967	103.39	24.11	−7.41	0.16	4.24	3.04
1968	50.61	11.00	−1.20	2.48	5.24	4.72
1969	−32.27	−8.33	−6.52	−2.10	6.59	6.20
1970	−16.54	4.10	12.69	13.93	6.50	5.57
1971	18.44	14.17	17.47	8.71	4.34	3.27

TABLE **5.3**
(Concluded)

Year	Small Stocks	Large Stocks	Long-Term T-Bonds	Intermediate-Term T-Bonds	T-Bills	Inflation
1972	−0.62	19.14	5.55	3.80	3.81	3.41
1973	−40.54	−14.75	1.40	2.90	6.91	8.71
1974	−29.74	−26.40	5.53	6.03	7.93	12.34
1975	69.54	37.26	8.50	6.79	5.80	6.94
1976	54.81	23.98	11.07	14.20	5.06	4.86
1977	22.02	−7.26	0.90	1.12	5.10	6.70
1978	22.29	6.50	−4.16	0.32	7.15	9.02
1979	43.99	18.77	9.02	4.29	10.45	13.29
1980	35.34	32.48	13.17	0.83	11.57	12.52
1981	7.79	−4.98	3.61	6.09	14.95	8.92
1982	27.44	22.09	6.52	33.39	10.71	3.83
1983	34.49	22.37	−0.53	5.44	8.85	3.79
1984	−14.02	6.46	15.29	14.46	10.02	3.95
1985	28.21	32.00	32.68	23.65	7.83	3.80
1986	3.40	18.40	23.96	17.22	6.18	1.10
1987	−13.95	5.34	−2.65	1.68	5.50	4.43
1988	21.72	16.86	8.40	6.63	6.44	4.42
1989	8.37	31.34	19.49	14.82	8.32	4.65
1990	−27.08	−3.20	7.13	9.05	7.86	6.11
1991	50.24	30.66	18.39	16.67	5.65	3.06
1992	27.84	7.71	7.79	7.25	3.54	2.90
1993	20.30	9.87	15.48	12.02	2.97	2.75
1994	−3.34	1.29	−7.18	−4.42	3.91	2.67
1995	33.21	37.71	31.67	18.07	5.58	2.54
1996	16.50	23.07	−0.81	3.99	5.50	3.32
1997	22.40	33.17	15.08	7.69	5.32	1.70
1998	−2.50	28.53	13.02	8.62	5.11	1.61
1999	21.26	21.04	−8.74	0.41	4.80	2.68
2000	−3.02	−9.10	20.27	10.26	5.85	3.39
2001	1.03	−11.89	4.21	8.16	4.09	1.67
Rate of Return Statistics						
Geometric average	12.19	10.51	5.23	5.12	3.80	3.06
Arithmetic average	18.29	12.49	5.53	5.30	3.85	3.15
Standard deviation	39.28	20.30	8.18	6.33	3.25	4.40
Minimum	−52.71	−45.56	−8.74	−5.81	−1.59	−10.27
Maximum	187.82	54.56	32.68	33.39	14.95	18.13
Excess Return Statistics						
Average	14.44	8.64	1.68	1.45		
Standard deviation	39.98	20.70	7.94	5.73		
Minimum	−55.55	−46.52	−13.54	−10.74		
Maximum	187.75	54.49	26.09	22.68		

Sources: Inflation data: Bureau of Labor Statistics; security return data for 1926–1995: Center for Research in Security Prices; security return data for 1996–2001: returns on appropriate index portfolios (large stocks, S&P 500; small stocks, Russell 2000; long-term/intermediate T-bonds, Lehman Bros.; T-bills, Salomon Smith Barney).

month to month, the total rate of return on these T-bills is riskless only for 30-day holding periods.[3] The last column gives the annual inflation rate as measured by the rate of change in the Consumer Price Index.

Figure 5.1 summarizes some of the data in Table 5.3. The first column gives the geometric averages of the historical rates of return on each asset class; this figure thus represents the compound rate of growth in the value of an investment in these assets. The second column shows the arithmetic averages. The last column is the variability of asset returns, as measured by standard deviation. The historical results are consistent with the risk-return trade-off: Riskier assets have provided higher average returns, and historical risk premiums are considerable, commensurate with their greater risk.

5.4 EXAMPLE
The Risk Premium and Growth of Wealth

The dollar import of the risk premiums suggested by Table 5.3 can be illustrated with a simple example. Consider two investors with $1,000 as of December 31, 1991. One invests in the small-stock portfolio, and the other in T-bills. Both investors reinvest all income from their portfolios and liquidate their investments on December 31, 2001. Using the rates from Table 5.3 we have:

	Small Stocks	T-Bills
December 31, 1991	$1,000	$1,000
December 31, 2001	$3,271	$1,577

The value of the portfolio in 2001 is obtained by multiplying the initial $1,000 investment in 1991 by 1 plus the rate of return (expressed as a decimal) for each year. The results show an increase of 227.1% in the value of the small-stock portfolio and an increase of 57.7% for T-bills.

We also can calculate the geometric average return over this period. For small stocks, the geometric average, r_G, over this 10-year period is defined by:

$$(1 + r_G)^{10} = 3.271$$
$$1 + r_G = (3.271)^{1/10} = 1.1258$$
$$r_G = .1258 = 12.58\%$$

You can confirm that the geometric average return of T-bills was 4.66%. Therefore, the 10-year period 1991–2001 was more favorable to both small stocks and T-bills than the 1926–2001 period. The geometric average return on small stocks in the most recent 10-year period was 12.58% versus an average of 12.19% in the longer period; the average return on bills was 4.66% in the recent period versus 3.80% in the longer period. In both periods, there was a considerable risk premium to be earned from the risky investment.

The third statistic reported in Figure 5.1 is the standard deviation. The higher the standard deviation, the more volatile the HPR. The standard deviation reported in Figure 5.1, however, is based on historical data rather than forecasts of future scenarios, as in Equation 5.5. To calculate standard deviation from historical data, we treat each year's outcome as one possible scenario in a scenario analysis. Each historical outcome is taken as equally likely and given a "probability" of $1/n$.

The formula for historical variance is thus similar to Equation 5.5, but instead of using deviations of returns around *mean* returns based on the scenario analysis, we use deviations from

---

[3]The few negative returns in this column, all dating from before World War II, reflect periods where, in the absence of T-bills, returns on government securities with about 30-day maturity were used. However, these securities included options to be exchanged for other securities, thus increasing their price and lowering their yield relative to what a simple T-bill would have offered.

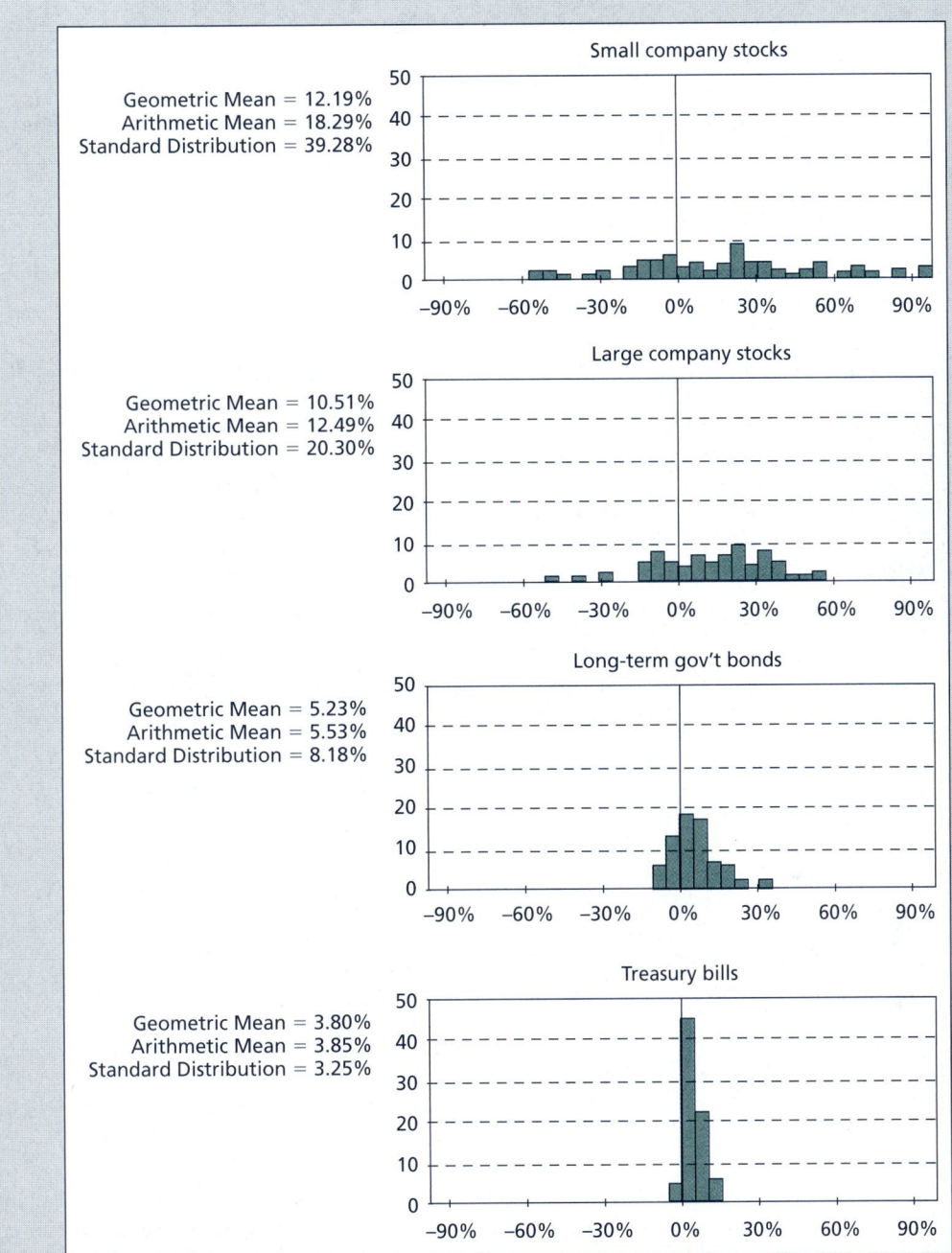

FIGURE **5.1**

Frequency distribution of annual HPRs, 1926–2001. Each bar shows the number of years that the rate of return of the particular market fell within a specified range.

average returns during the sample period. This procedure results in one minor complication. When we use the sample average return $\bar{r}$ in place of the mean return, $E(r)$, we must modify the average of the squared deviations for what statisticians call a "lost degree of freedom." The modification is easy: Multiply the average value of the squared deviations by $\frac{n}{n-1}$. The formula for variance based on historical data is thus:

$$\sigma^2 = \frac{n}{n-1} \times \text{Sample average of squared deviations from average return}$$

$$= \frac{n}{n-1} \times \sum_{i=1}^{n} \frac{(r_i - \bar{r})^2}{n} = \frac{1}{n-1} \sum_{i=1}^{n} (r_i - \bar{r})^2 \tag{5.8}$$

When you are using large samples and n is large, the modification is unimportant, since $n/(n-1)$ is close to 1.0 and $1/(n-1)$ is close to $1/n$.

5.5 EXAMPLE

Historical Means and Standard Deviations

To illustrate how to calculate average returns and standard deviations from historical data, let's compute these statistics for the returns on the S&P 500 portfolio using the five years of data in Table 5.3 from 1988–1992. The average return is 16.7%, computed by dividing the sum of column (1) below, by the number of observations. In column (2), we take the deviation of each year's return from the 16.7% average return. In column (3), we calculate the squared deviation. The variance is, from equation 5.8, the sum of the five squared deviations divided by (5 − 1). The standard deviation is the square root of the variance. If you input the column of rates into a spreadsheet, the "Average" and "StdDev" functions will give you the statistics directly.

Year	(1) Rate of Return	(2) Deviation from Average Return	(3) Squared Deviation
1988	16.9%	0.2%	0.0
1989	31.3	14.6	213.2
1990	−3.2	−19.9	396.0
1991	30.7	14.0	196.0
1992	7.7	−9.0	81.0
Total	83.4%		886.2

Average rate of return = 83.4/5 = 16.7

$$\text{Variance} = \frac{1}{5-1} \times 886.2 = 221.6$$

$$\text{Standard deviation} = \sqrt{221.6} = 14.9\%$$

Figure 5.2 presents a graphic representation of the relative variabilities of the annual HPR for three different asset classes: large stocks, long-term T-bonds, and T-bills. We have plotted the three time series on the same set of axes to demonstrate clearly that the annual HPR on stocks is the most variable series. The standard deviation of large-stock returns has been 20.30% compared to 8.18% for long-term government bonds and 3.25% for bills. Here is evidence of the risk-return trade-off that characterizes security markets: The markets with the highest average returns are also the most volatile.

An all-stock portfolio with a standard deviation of 20.3% would represent a very volatile investment. For example, if stock returns are normally distributed with a standard deviation of 20.3% and an expected rate of return of 12.5% (the historical average), then in roughly one year out of three, returns will be less than 12.5 − 20.3 = −7.8%, or greater than 12.5 + 20.3 = 32.8%.

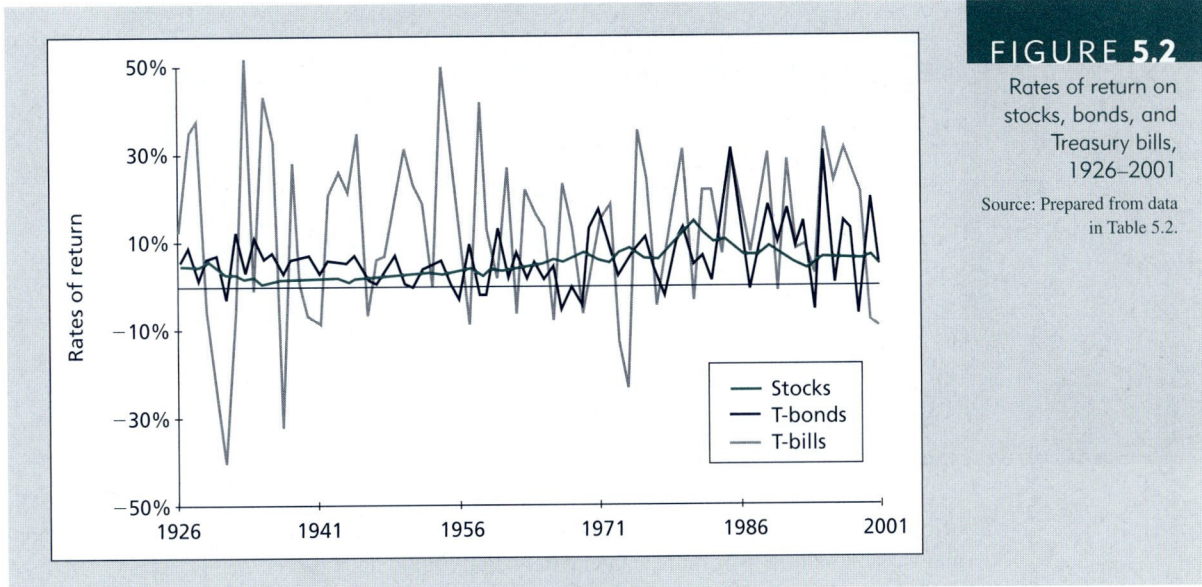

FIGURE **5.2**

Rates of return on stocks, bonds, and Treasury bills, 1926–2001

Source: Prepared from data in Table 5.2.

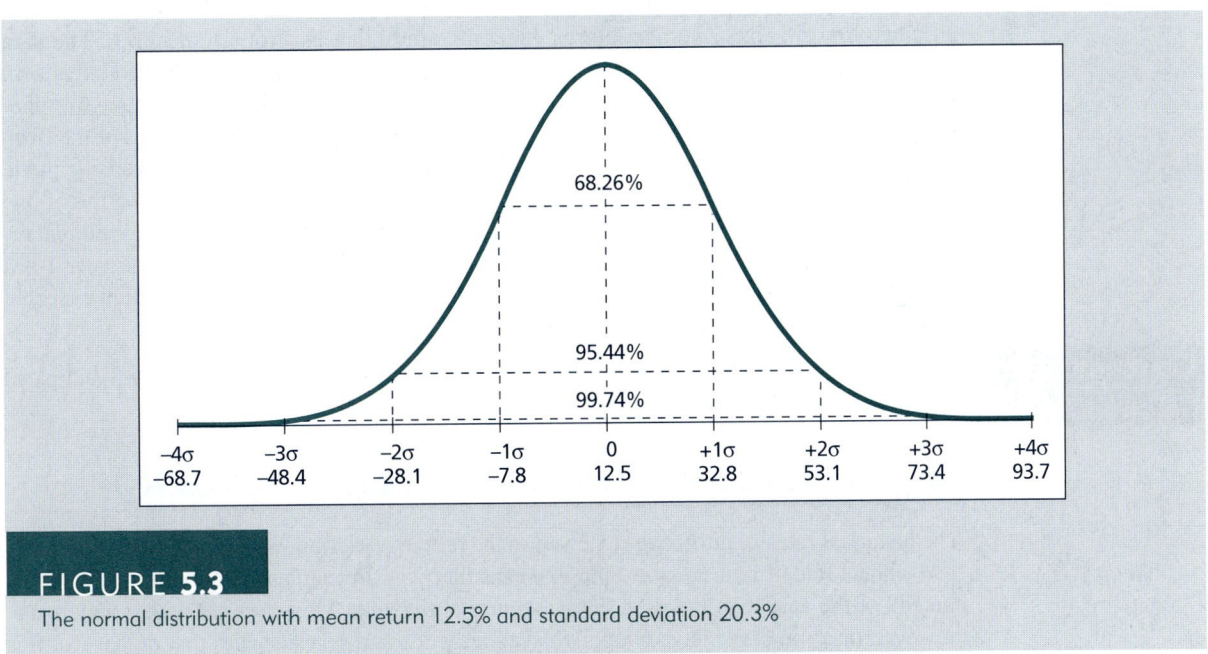

FIGURE **5.3**

The normal distribution with mean return 12.5% and standard deviation 20.3%

Figure 5.3 is a graph of the normal curve with mean 12.5% and standard deviation 20.3%. The graph shows the theoretical probability of rates of return within various ranges given these parameters. Now observe the frequency distributions in Figure 5.1. The resemblance to the normal distribution is clear, and the variation in the dispersion of the frequency distributions across the different asset classes vividly illustrates the difference in standard deviation and its implication for risk.

The similarity to a normal distribution allows us to use the historical average and standard deviation to estimate probabilities for various scenarios. For example, we estimate the probability that the return on the large-stock portfolio will fall below zero in the next year at .27. This is so because a rate of zero is 12.5 percentage points, or .6 standard deviations (= 12.5/20.3)

TABLE **5.4** Size-Decile Portfolios of the NYSE/ AMEX/NASDAQ *Summary Statistics of Annual Returns, 1926–2000*	Decile	Geometric Mean	Arithmetic Mean	Standard Deviation
	1-Largest	10.3%	12.1%	19.05%
	2	11.3	13.6	22.00
	3	11.6	14.2	23.94
	4	11.5	14.6	26.25
	5	11.8	15.2	27.07
	6	11.8	15.5	28.15
	7	11.6	15.7	30.43
	8	11.7	16.6	34.21
	9	11.8	17.4	37.13
	10-Smallest	13.1	20.9	45.82
	NYSE/AMEX/NASDAQ Total Value Weighted Index	10.6%	12.6%	20.20%

below the mean. Using a table of the normal distribution, we find that the probability of a normal variable falling .6 or more standard deviations below its mean is .27.

The performance of the small-stock portfolio documented in the preceding figures and tables is striking. Table 5.4 shows average returns and standard deviations for NYSE portfolios arranged by firm size. Average returns generally are higher as firm size declines. The data clearly suggest that small firms have earned a substantial risk premium and therefore that firm size seems to be an important proxy for risk. In later chapters we will further explore this phenomenon and will see that the size effect can be further related to other attributes of the firm.

We should stress that variability of HPR in the past sometimes can be an unreliable guide to risk, at least in the case of the risk-free asset. For an investor with a holding period of one year, for example, a one-year T-bill is a riskless investment, at least in terms of its nominal return, which is known with certainty. However, the standard deviation of the one-year T-bill rate estimated from historical data is not zero: This reflects year-by-year variation in expected returns rather than fluctuations of actual returns around prior expectations.

> **Concept CHECK** >
>
> 4. Compute the average excess return on large company stocks (over the T-bill rate) and the standard deviation for the years 1926–1934.

5.4 INFLATION AND REAL RATES OF RETURN

The historical rates of return we reviewed in the previous section were measured in dollars. A 10% annual rate of return, for example, means that your investment was worth 10% more at the end of the year than it was at the beginning of the year. This does not necessarily mean, however, that you could have bought 10% more goods and services with that money, for it is possible that in the course of the year prices of goods also increased. If prices have changed, the increase in your purchasing power will not equal the increase in your dollar wealth.

At any time, the prices of some goods may rise while the prices of other goods may fall; the *general* trend in prices is measured by examining changes in the consumer price index, or CPI. The CPI measures the cost of purchasing a bundle of goods that is considered representative of the "consumption basket" of a typical urban family of four. Increases in the cost of this standardized consumption basket are indicative of a general trend toward higher prices. The **inflation rate,** or the rate at which prices are rising, is measured as the rate of increase of the CPI.

inflation rate

The rate at which prices are rising, measured as the rate of increase of the CPI.

Suppose the rate of inflation (the percentage change in the CPI, denoted by i) for the last year amounted to $i = 6\%$. This tells you the purchasing power of money is reduced by 6% a year. The value of each dollar depreciates by 6% a year in terms of the goods it can buy. Therefore, part of your interest earnings are offset by the reduction in the purchasing power of the dollars you will receive at the end of the year. With a 10% interest rate, after you net out the 6% reduction in the purchasing power of money, you are left with a net increase in purchasing power of about 4%. Thus, we need to distinguish between a **nominal interest rate**— the growth rate of your money—and a **real interest rate**—the growth rate of your purchasing power. If we call R the nominal rate, r the real rate, and i the inflation rate, then we conclude

$$r \approx R - i$$

nominal interest rate

The interest rate in terms of nominal (not adjusted for purchasing power) dollars.

In words, the real rate of interest is the nominal rate reduced by the loss of purchasing power resulting from inflation.

In fact, the exact relationship between the real and nominal interest rate is given by

$$1 + r = \frac{1 + R}{1 + i}$$

real interest rate

The excess of the interest rate over the inflation rate. The growth rate of purchasing power derived from an investment.

In words, the growth factor of your purchasing power, $1 + r$, equals the growth factor of your money, $1 + R$, divided by the new price level that is $1 + i$ times its value in the previous period. The exact relationship can be rearranged to

$$r = \frac{R - i}{1 + i}$$

which shows that the approximate rule overstates the real rate by the factor $1 + i$.

For example, if the interest rate on a one-year CD is 8%, and you expect inflation to be 5% over the coming year, then using the approximation formula, you expect the real rate to be $r = 8\% - 5\% = 3\%$. Using the exact formula, the real rate is $r = \dfrac{.08 - .05}{1 + .05} = .0286$, or 2.86%. Therefore, the approximation rule overstates the expected real rate by only 0.14 percentage points. The approximation rule is more accurate for small inflation rates and is perfectly exact for continuously compounded rates.

To summarize, in interpreting the historical returns on various asset classes presented in Table 5.3, we must recognize that to obtain the real returns on these assets, we must reduce the nominal returns by the inflation rate presented in the last column of the table. In fact, while the return on a U.S. Treasury bill usually is considered to be riskless, this is true only with regard to its nominal return. To infer the expected real rate of return on a Treasury bill, you must subtract your estimate of the inflation rate over the coming period.

It is always possible to calculate the real rate after the fact. The inflation rate is published by the Bureau of Labor Statistics. The *future* real rate, however, is unknown, and one has to rely on expectations. In other words, because future inflation is risky, the real rate of return is risky even if the nominal rate is risk-free.

The Equilibrium Nominal Rate of Interest

We've seen that the real rate of return on an asset is approximately equal to the nominal rate minus the inflation rate. Because investors should be concerned with their real returns—the increase in their purchasing power—we would expect that as inflation increases, investors will demand higher nominal rates of return on their investments. This higher rate is necessary to maintain the expected real return offered by an investment.

Irving Fisher (1930) argued that the nominal rate ought to increase one-for-one with increases in the expected inflation rate. If we use the notation $E(i)$ to denote the current expectation of the inflation rate that will prevail over the coming period, then we can state the so-called Fisher equation formally as

$$R = r + E(i)$$

FIGURE **5.4**

Inflation and interest
rates, 1953–2001

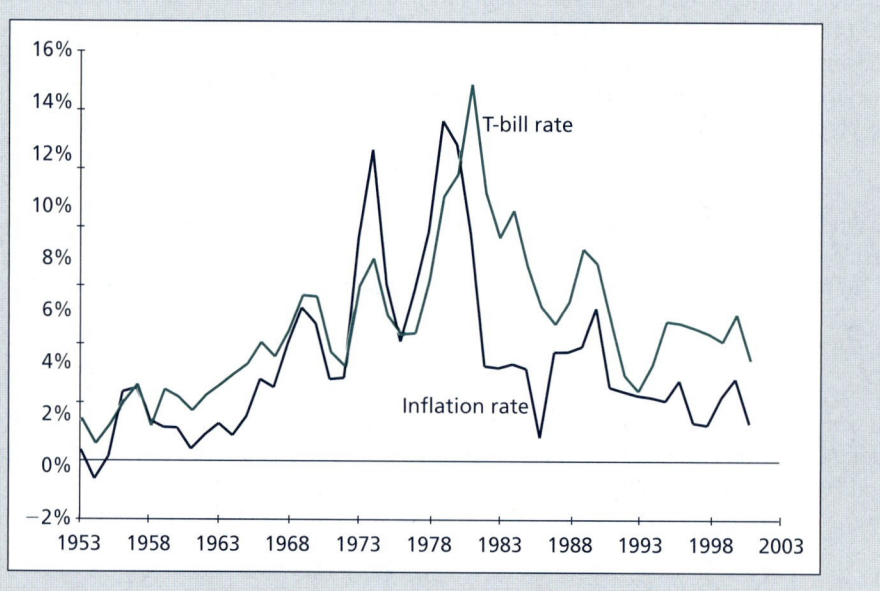

FIGURE **5.4**

Inflation and interest
rates, 1953–2001

Suppose the real rate of interest is 2%, and the inflation rate is 4%, so that the nominal interest rate is about 6%. If the rate of inflation increases to 5%, the nominal rate should climb
to roughly 7%. The increase in the nominal rate offsets the increase in the inflation rate, giving investors an unchanged growth of purchasing power at a 2% real rate. The evidence for the
Fisher equation is that periods of high inflation and high nominal rates generally coincide.
Figure 5.4 illustrates this fact.

Concept
CHECK

5. *a.* Suppose the real interest rate is 3% per year, and the expected inflation rate is
8%. What is the nominal interest rate?
b. Suppose the expected inflation rate rises to 10%, but the real rate is unchanged. What happens to the nominal interest rate?

5.5 | ASSET ALLOCATION ACROSS RISKY AND RISK-FREE PORTFOLIOS

History shows us that long-term bonds have been riskier investments than investments in
Treasury bills and that stock investments have been riskier still. On the other hand, the riskier
investments have offered higher average returns. Investors, of course, do not make all-or-
nothing choices from these investment classes. They can and do construct their portfolios
using securities from all asset classes. Some of the portfolio may be in risk-free Treasury bills
and some in high-risk stocks.

The most straightforward way to control the risk of the portfolio is through the fraction of
the portfolio invested in Treasury bills and other safe money market securities versus risky as-

asset allocation

Portfolio choice
among broad
investment classes.

sets. This is an example of an **asset allocation** choice—a choice among broad investment
classes, rather than among the specific securities within each asset class. Most investment professionals consider asset allocation the most important part of portfolio construction. Consider
this statement by John Bogle, made when he was the chairman of the Vanguard Group of
Investment Companies:

The most fundamental decision of investing is the allocation of your assets: How much should
you own in stock? How much should you own in bonds? How much should you own in cash reserves? . . . That decision [has been shown to account] for an astonishing 94% of the differences

in total returns achieved by institutionally managed pension funds. . . . There is no reason to believe that the same relationship does not also hold true for individual investors.[4]

Therefore, we start our discussion of the risk-return trade-off available to investors by examining the most basic asset allocation choice: the choice of how much of the portfolio to place in risk-free money market securities versus other risky asset classes.

We will denote the investor's portfolio of risky assets as P, and the risk-free asset as F. We will assume for the sake of illustration that the risky component of the investor's overall portfolio comprises two mutual funds: one invested in stocks and the other invested in long-term bonds. For now, we take the composition of the risky portfolio as given and focus only on the allocation between it and risk-free securities. In the next chapter, we turn to asset allocation and security selection across risky assets.

The Risky Asset

When we shift wealth from the risky portfolio (P) to the risk-free asset, we do not change the relative proportions of the various risky assets within the risky portfolio. Rather, we reduce the relative weight of the risky portfolio as a whole in favor of risk-free assets.

A simple example demonstrates the procedure. Assume the total market value of an investor's portfolio is $300,000. Of that, $90,000 is invested in the Ready Assets money market fund, a risk-free asset. The remaining $210,000 is in risky securities, say $113,400 in the Vanguard S&P 500 index fund (called the Vanguard 500 Index Fund) and $96,600 in Fidelity's Investment Grade Bond Fund.

The Vanguard fund (V) is a passive equity fund that replicates the S&P 500 portfolio. The Fidelity Investment Grade Bond Fund (IG) invests primarily in corporate bonds with high safety ratings and also in Treasury bonds. We choose these two funds for the risky portfolio in the spirit of a low-cost, well-diversified portfolio. While in the next chapter we discuss portfolio optimization, here we simply assume the investor considers the given weighting of V and IG to be optimal.

The holdings in Vanguard and Fidelity make up the risky portfolio, with 54% in V and 46% in IG.

$$w_V = 113{,}400/210{,}000 = 0.54 \text{ (Vanguard)}$$

$$w_{IG} = 96{,}600/210{,}000 = 0.46 \text{ (Fidelity)}$$

The weight of the risky portfolio, P, in the **complete portfolio,** *including* risk-free as well as risky investments, is denoted by y, and so the weight of the money market fund is $1 - y$.

$$y = 210{,}000/300{,}000 = 0.7 \text{ (risky assets, portfolio } P)$$

$$1 - y = 90{,}000/300{,}000 = 0.3 \text{ (risk-free assets)}$$

complete portfolio

The entire portfolio including risky and risk-free assets.

The weights of the individual assets in the *complete* portfolio (C) are:

Vanguard	113,400/300,000 = 0.378
Fidelity	96,600/300,000 = 0.322
Portfolio P	210,000/300,000 = 0.700
Ready Assets F	90,000/300,000 = 0.300
Portfolio C	300,000/300,000 = 1.000

Suppose the investor decides to decrease risk by reducing the exposure to the risky portfolio from $y = 0.7$ to $y = 0.56$. The risky portfolio would total only $0.56 \times 300{,}000 = \$168{,}000$, requiring the sale of $42,000 of the original $210,000 risky holdings, with the proceeds used to

---

[4]John C. Bogle, *Bogle on Mutual Funds* (Burr Ridge, IL: Irwin Professional Publishing, 1994), p. 235.

purchase more shares in Ready Assets. Total holdings in the risk-free asset will increase to 300,000 (1 − 0.56) = $132,000 (the original holdings plus the new contribution to the money market fund: 90,000 + 42,000 = $132,000).

The key point is that we leave the proportion of each asset in the risky portfolio unchanged. Because the weights of Vanguard and Fidelity in the risky portfolio are 0.54 and 0.46 respectively, we sell 0.54 × 42,000 = $22,680 of Vanguard and 0.46 × 42,000 = $19,320 of Fidelity. After the sale, the proportions of each fund in the risky portfolio are unchanged.

$$w_V = \frac{113,400 - 22,680}{210,000 - 42,000} = 0.54 \text{ (Vanguard)}$$

$$w_{IG} = \frac{96,600 - 19,320}{210,000 - 42,000} = 0.46 \text{ (Fidelity)}$$

This procedure shows that rather than thinking of our risky holdings as Vanguard and Fidelity separately, we may view our holdings as if they are in a single fund holding Vanguard and Fidelity in fixed proportions. In this sense, we may treat the risky fund as a single risky asset, that asset being a particular bundle of securities. As we shift in and out of safe assets, we simply alter our holdings of that bundle of securities commensurately.

Given this simplification, we now can turn to the desirability of reducing risk by changing the risky/risk-free asset mix, that is, reducing risk by decreasing the proportion y. Because we do not alter the weights of each asset within the risky portfolio, the probability distribution of the rate of return on the *risky portfolio* remains unchanged by the asset reallocation. What will change is the probability distribution of the rate of return on the *complete portfolio* that is made up of the risky and risk-free assets.

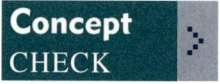

6. **What will be the dollar value of your position in Vanguard and its proportion in your complete portfolio if you decide to hold 50% of your investment budget in Ready Assets?**

The Risk-Free Asset

The power to tax and to control the money supply lets the government, and only government, issue default-free bonds. The default-free guarantee by itself is not sufficient to make the bonds risk-free in real terms, since inflation affects the purchasing power of the proceeds from an investment in T-bills. The only risk-free asset in real terms would be a price-indexed government bond. Even then, a default-free, perfectly indexed bond offers a guaranteed real rate to an investor only if the maturity of the bond is identical to the investor's desired holding period.

These qualifications notwithstanding, it is common to view Treasury bills as *the* risk-free asset. Because they are short-term investments, their prices are relatively insensitive to interest rate fluctuations. An investor can lock in a short-term nominal return by buying a bill and holding it to maturity. Any inflation uncertainty over the course of a few weeks, or even months, is negligible compared to the uncertainty of stock market returns.

In practice, most investors treat a broader range of money market instruments as effectively risk-free assets. All the money market instruments are virtually immune to interest rate risk (unexpected fluctuations in the price of a bond due to changes in market interest rates) because of their short maturities, and all are fairly safe in terms of default or credit risk.

Money market mutual funds hold, for the most part, three types of securities: Treasury bills, bank certificates of deposit (CDs), and commercial paper. The instruments differ slightly in their default risk. The yields to maturity on CDs and commercial paper, for identical maturities, are always slightly higher than those of T-bills. A history of this yield spread for 90-day CDs is shown in Figure 2.3 in Chapter 2.

Money market funds have changed their relative holdings of these securities over time, but by and large, T-bills make up only about 15% of their portfolios. Nevertheless, the risk of such blue-chip, short-term investments as CDs and commercial paper is minuscule compared to that of most other assets, such as long-term corporate bonds, common stocks, or real estate. Hence, we treat money market funds as representing the most easily accessible risk-free asset for most investors.

Portfolio Expected Return and Risk

Now that we have specified the risky portfolio and the risk-free asset, we can examine the risk-return combinations that result from various investment allocations between these two assets. Finding the available combinations of risk and return is the "technical" part of asset allocation; it deals only with the opportunities available to investors given the features of the asset markets in which they can invest. In the next section, we address the "personal" part of the problem, the specific individual's choice of the best risk-return combination from the set of feasible combinations, given his or her level of risk aversion.

Since we assume the composition of the optimal risky portfolio (P) already has been determined, the concern here is with the proportion of the investment budget (y) to be allocated to the risky portfolio. The remaining proportion ($1 - y$) is to be invested in the risk-free asset (F).

We denote the *actual* risky rate of return by r_P, the *expected* rate of return on P by $E(r_P)$, and its standard deviation by σ_P. The rate of return on the risk-free asset is denoted as r_f. In the numerical example, we assume $E(r_P) = 15\%$, $\sigma_P = 22\%$, and $r_f = 7\%$. Thus, the risk premium on the risky asset is $E(r_P) - r_f = 8\%$.

Let's start with two extreme cases. If you invest all of your funds in the risky asset, that is, if you choose $y = 1.0$, the expected return on your complete portfolio will be 15% and the standard deviation will be 22%. This combination of risk and return is plotted as point P in Figure 5.5. At the other extreme, you might put all of your funds into the risk-free asset, that

FIGURE 5.5
The investment opportunity set with a risky asset and a risk-free asset

is, you choose $y = 0$. In this case, your portfolio would behave just as the risk-free asset, and you would earn a riskless return of 7%. (This choice is plotted as point F in Figure 5.5.)

Now consider more moderate choices. For example, if you allocate equal amounts of your overall or *complete portfolio, C,* to the risky and risk-free assets, that is, if you choose $y = 0.5$, the expected return on the complete portfolio will be an average of the expected return on portfolios F and P. Therefore, $E(r_C) = 0.5 \times 7\% + 0.5 \times 15\% = 11\%$. The risk premium of the complete portfolio is therefore $11\% - 7\% = 4\%$, which is half of the risk premium of P. The standard deviation of the portfolio also is one-half of P's, that is, 11%. When you reduce the fraction of the complete portfolio allocated to the risky asset by half, you reduce both the risk and risk premium by half.

To generalize, the risk premium of the complete portfolio, C, will equal the risk premium of the risky asset times the fraction of the portfolio invested in the risky asset.

$$E(r_C) - r_f = y[E(r_P) - r_f] \tag{5.9}$$

The standard deviation of the complete portfolio will equal the standard deviation of the risky asset times the fraction of the portfolio invested in the risky asset.

$$\sigma_C = y\sigma_P \tag{5.10}$$

In sum, both the risk premium and the standard deviation of the complete portfolio increase in proportion to the investment in the risky portfolio. Therefore, the points that describe the risk and return of the complete portfolio for various asset allocations, that is, for various choices of y, all plot on the straight line connecting F and P, as shown in Figure 5.5, with an intercept of r_f and slope (rise/run) of

$$S = \frac{E(r_P) - r_f}{\sigma_P} = \frac{15 - 7}{22} = 0.36 \tag{5.11}$$

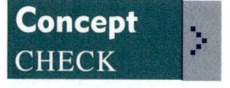

7. What are the expected return, risk premium, standard deviation, and ratio of risk premium to standard deviation for a complete portfolio with $y = 0.75$?

The Capital Allocation Line

capital allocation line

Plot of risk-return combinations available by varying portfolio allocation between a risk-free asset and a risky portfolio.

The line plotted in Figure 5.5 depicts the risk-return combinations available by varying asset allocation, that is, by choosing different values of y. For this reason, it is called the **capital allocation line,** or **CAL.** The slope, S, of the CAL equals the increase in expected return that an investor can obtain per unit of additional standard deviation. In other words, it shows extra return per extra risk. For this reason, the slope also is called the **reward-to-variability ratio.**

Notice that the reward-to-variability ratio is the same for risky portfolio P and the complete portfolio that was formed by mixing P and the risk-free asset in equal proportions.

reward-to-variability ratio

Ratio of risk premium to standard deviation.

	Expected Return	Risk Premium	Standard Deviation	Reward-to-Variability Ratio
Portfolio P:	15%	8%	22%	$\frac{8}{22} = 0.36$
Portfolio C:	11%	4%	11%	$\frac{4}{11} = 0.36$

In fact, the reward-to-variability ratio is the same for all complete portfolios that plot on the capital allocation line. While the risk-return combinations differ, the *ratio* of reward to risk is constant.

What about points on the line to the right of portfolio *P* in the investment opportunity set? If investors can borrow at the (risk-free) rate of $r_f = 7\%$, they can construct complete portfolios that plot on the CAL to the right of *P*. They simply choose values of *y* greater than 1.0.

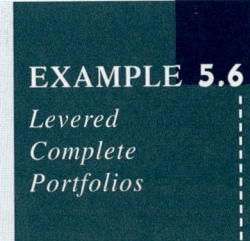

EXAMPLE 5.6

Levered Complete Portfolios

Suppose the investment budget is $300,000, and our investor borrows an additional $120,000, investing the $420,000 in the risky asset. This is a levered position in the risky asset, which is financed in part by borrowing. In that case

$$y = \frac{420,000}{300,000} = 1.4$$

and $1 - y = 1 - 1.4 = -0.4$, reflecting a short position in the risk-free asset, or a borrowing position. Rather than lending at a 7% interest rate, the investor borrows at 7%. The portfolio rate of return is

$$E(r_C) = 7 + (1.4 \times 8) = 18.2$$

Another way to find this portfolio rate of return is as follows. Your income statement will show that you expect to earn $63,000 (15% of $420,000) and pay $8,400 (7% of $120,000) in interest on the loan. Simple subtraction yields an expected profit of $54,000, which is 18.2% of your investment budget of $300,000.

Your portfolio still exhibits the same reward-to-variability ratio:

$$\sigma_C = 1.4 \times 22 = 30.8$$

$$S = \frac{E(r_C) - r_f}{\sigma_C} = \frac{11.2}{30.8} = 0.36$$

As you might have expected, the levered portfolio has both a higher expected return and a higher standard deviation than an unlevered position in the risky asset.

Of course, nongovernment investors cannot borrow at the risk-free rate. The risk of a borrower's default leads lenders to demand higher interest rates on loans. Therefore, the nongovernment investor's borrowing cost will exceed the lending rate of $r_f = 7\%$.

Suppose the borrowing rate is $r_B = 9\%$. Then, for *y* greater than 1.0 (the borrowing range), the reward-to-variability ratio (the slope of the CAL) will be: $[E(r_P) - r_B]/\sigma_P = 6/22 = 0.27$. Here, the borrowing rate (r_B) replaces the lending rate (r_f), reducing the "reward" (numerator) in the reward-to-variability ratio. The CAL will be "kinked" at point *P* as in Figure 5.6. To the left of *P*, where $y < 1$, the investor is lending at 7% and the slope of the CAL is 0.36. To the right of *P*, where $y > 1$, the investor is borrowing (at a higher than risk-free rate) to finance extra investments in the risky asset, and the slope is 0.27.

In practice, borrowing to invest in the risky portfolio is easy and straightforward if you have a margin account with a broker. All you have to do is tell your broker you want to buy "on margin." Margin purchases may not exceed 50% of the purchase value. For example, if your net worth in the account is $300,000, the broker is allowed to lend you up to $300,000 to purchase additional stock. You would then have $600,000 on the asset side of your account and $300,000 on the liability side, resulting in $y = 2.0$.

8. **Suppose there is a shift upward in the expected rate of return on the risky asset, from 15% to 17%. If all other parameters remain unchanged, what will be the slope of the CAL for $y \le 1$ and $y > 1$?**

Concept CHECK

FIGURE 5.6

The opportunity set with differential borrowing and lending rates

Risk Tolerance and Asset Allocation

We have developed the CAL, the graph of all feasible risk-return combinations available from allocating the complete portfolio between a risky portfolio and a risk-free asset. The investor confronting the CAL now must choose one optimal combination from the set of feasible choices. This choice entails a trade-off between risk and return. Individual investors with different levels of risk aversion, given an identical capital allocation line, will choose different positions in the risky asset. Specifically, the more risk-averse investors will choose to hold *less* of the risky asset and *more* of the risk-free asset.

Graphically, more risk-averse investors will choose portfolios near point F on the capital allocation line plotted in Figure 5.5. More risk-tolerant investors will choose points closer to P, with higher expected return and higher risk. The most risk-tolerant investors will choose portfolios to the right of point P. These levered portfolios provide even higher expected returns, but even greater risk.

The nearby box contains a further discussion of this risk-return trade-off, which sometimes is characterized as a decision to "eat well," versus "sleep well." You will eat well if you earn a high expected rate of return on your portfolio. However, this requires that you accept a large risk premium and, therefore, a large amount of risk. Unfortunately, this risk may make it difficult to sleep well.

The investor's asset allocation choice also will depend on the trade-off between risk and return. If the reward-to-variability ratio increases, then investors might well decide to take on riskier positions. For example, suppose an investor reevaluates the probability distribution of the risky portfolio and now perceives a greater expected return without an accompanying increase in the standard deviation. This amounts to an increase in the reward-to-variability ratio

The Right Mix: Make Money vs. Sleep Soundly

Plunged into doubt?

Amid the recent market turmoil, maybe you are wondering whether you really have the right mix of investments. Here are a few thoughts to keep in mind:

TAKING STOCK

If you are a bond investor who is petrified of stocks, the wild price swings of the past few weeks have probably confirmed all of your worst suspicions. But the truth is, adding stocks to your bond portfolio could bolster your returns, without boosting your portfolio's overall gyrations.

How can that be? While stocks and bonds often move up and down in tandem, this isn't always the case, and sometimes stocks rise when bonds are tumbling.

Indeed, Chicago researchers Ibbotson Associates figure a portfolio that's 100% in longer-term government bonds has the same risk profile as a mix that includes 83% in longer-term government bonds and 17% in the blue-chip stocks that constitute Standard & Poor's 500 stock index.

The bottom line? Everybody should own some stocks. Even cowards.

PADDING THE MATTRESS

On the other hand, maybe you're a committed stock market investor, but you would like to add a calming influence to your portfolio. What's your best bet?

When investors look to mellow their stock portfolios, they usually turn to bonds. Indeed, the traditional balanced portfolio, which typically includes 60% stocks and 40% bonds, remains a firm favorite with many investment experts.

A balanced portfolio isn't a bad bet. But if you want to calm your stock portfolio, I would skip bonds and instead add cash investments such as Treasury bills and money market funds. Ibbotson calculates that, over the past 25 years, a mix of 75% stocks and 25% Treasury bills would have performed about as well as a mix of 60% stocks and 40% longer-term government bonds, and with a similar level of portfolio price gyrations.

Moreover, the stock–cash mix offers more certainty, because you know that even if your stocks fall in value, your cash never will. By contrast, both the stocks and bonds in a balanced portfolio can get hammered at the same time.

PATIENCE HAS ITS REWARDS, SOMETIMES

Stocks are capable of generating miserable short-run results. During the past 50 years, the worst five-calendar-year stretch for stocks left investors with an annualized loss of 2.4%.

But while any investment can disappoint in the short run, stocks do at least sparkle over the long haul. As a long-term investor, your goal is to fend off the dual threats of inflation and taxes and make your money grow. And on that score, stocks have been supreme.

SOURCE: Abridged from Jonathan Clements, "The Right Mix: Fine-Tuning a Portfolio to Make Money and Still Sleep Soundly," *The Wall Street Journal*, July 23, 1996. Reprinted by permission of Dow Jones & Company, Inc. via Copyright Clearance Center, Inc. © 1996 Dow Jones & Company, Inc. All rights reserved Worldwide.

or, equivalently, an increase in the slope of the CAL. As a result, this investor will choose a higher y, that is, a greater position in the risky portfolio.

One role of a professional financial adviser is to present investment opportunity alternatives to clients, obtain an assessment of the client's risk tolerance, and help determine the appropriate complete portfolio.[5]

5.6 PASSIVE STRATEGIES AND THE CAPITAL MARKET LINE

The capital allocation line shows the risk-return trade-offs available by mixing risk-free assets with the investor's risky portfolio. Investors can choose the assets included in the risky

---

[5]"Risk tolerance" is simply the flip side of "risk aversion." Either term is a reasonable way to describe attitudes toward risk. We generally find it easier to talk about risk aversion, but practitioners often use the term risk tolerance.

TABLE **5.5**		Risk Premium (%)		
Average rates of return, standard deviations, and the reward-to-variability ratio of the risk premiums of large common stocks over one-month bills over 1926–2001 and various subperiods.		Mean	Standard Deviation	Reward-to-Variability Ratio
	1926–1944	8.03	28.69	0.2798
	1945–1963	14.41	18.83	0.7655
	1964–1982	2.22	17.56	0.1265
	1983–2001	9.91	14.77	0.6709
	1926–2001	8.64	20.70	0.4176

Source: Prepared from data in Table 5.3.

passive strategy

Investment policy that avoids security analysis.

portfolio using either passive or active strategies. A **passive strategy** is based on the premise that securities are fairly priced and it avoids the costs involved in undertaking security analysis. Such a strategy might at first blush appear to be naive. However, we will see in Chapter 8 that intense competition among professional money managers might indeed force security prices to levels at which further security analysis is unlikely to turn up significant profit opportunities. Passive investment strategies may make sense for many investors.

To avoid the costs of acquiring information on any individual stock or group of stocks, we may follow a "neutral" diversification approach. A natural strategy is to select a diversified portfolio of common stocks that mirrors the corporate sector of the broad economy. This results in a value-weighted portfolio, which, for example, invests a proportion in GM stock that equals the ratio of GM's market value to the market value of all listed stocks.

Such strategies are called *indexing*. The investor chooses a portfolio with all the stocks in a broad market index such as the Standard & Poor's 500 index. The rate of return on the portfolio then replicates the return on the index. Indexing has become an extremely popular strategy for passive investors. We call the capital allocation line provided by one-month T-bills and a broad index of common stocks the **capital market line** (CML). That is, a passive strategy based on stocks and bills generates an investment opportunity set that is represented by the CML.

capital market line

The capital allocation line using the market index portfolio as the risky asset.

Historical Evidence on the Capital Market Line

Can we use past data to help forecast the risk-return trade-off offered by the CML? The notion that one can use historical returns to forecast the future seems straightforward but actually is somewhat problematic. On one hand, you wish to use all available data to obtain a large sample. But when using long time series, old data may no longer be representative of future circumstances. Another reason for weeding out subperiods is that some past events simply may be too improbable to be given equal weight with results from other periods. Do the data we have pose this problem?

Table 5.5 breaks the 76-year period, 1926–2001 into four subperiods and shows the risk premium, standard deviation, and reward-to-variability ratio for each subperiod. That ratio is

Triumph of the Optimists

As a whole, the last 7 decades have been very kind to U.S. equity investors. Stock investments have outperformed investments in safe Treasury bills by more than 8% per year. The real rate of return averaged more than 9%, implying an expected doubling of the real value of the investment portfolio about every 8 years!

Is this experience representative? A new book by three professors at the London Business School, Elroy Dimson, Paul Marsh, and Mike Staunton, extends the U.S. evidence to other countries and to longer time periods. Their conclusion is given in the book's title, *Triumph of the Optimists**: in every country in their study (which included markets in North America, Europe, Asia, and Africa), the investment optimists—those who bet on the economy by investing in stocks rather than bonds or bills—were vindicated. Over the long haul, stocks beat bonds everywhere.

On the other hand, the equity risk premium is probably not as large as the post-1926 evidence from Table 5.1 would seem to indicate. First, results from the first 25 years of the last century (which included the first World War) were less favorable to stocks. Second, U.S. returns have been better than that of most other countries, and so a more representative value for the historical risk premium may be lower than the U.S. experience. Finally, the sample that is amenable to historical analysis suffers from a self-selection problem. Only those markets that have survived to be studied can be included in the analysis. This leaves out countries such as Russia or China, whose markets were shut down during communist rule, and whose results if included would surely bring down the average performance of equity investments. Nevertheless, there is powerful evidence of a risk premium that shows its force everywhere the authors looked.

*Elroy Dimson, Paul Marsh, Mike Staunton, *Triumph of the Optimists: 101 Years of Global Investment Returns*. Princeton University Press, Princeton, N.J.: 2002.

the slope of the CML based on the subperiod data. Indeed, the differences across subperiods are quite striking.

The most plausible explanation for the variation in subperiod returns is based on the observation that the standard deviation of returns is quite large in all subperiods. If we take the 76-year standard deviation of 20.3% as representative and assume that returns in one year are nearly uncorrelated with those in other years (the evidence suggests that any correlation across years is small), then the standard deviation of our estimate of the mean return in any of our 19-year subperiods will be $20.3/\sqrt{19} = 4.7\%$, which is fairly large. This means that in approximately one out of three cases, a 19-year average will deviate by 4.7% or more from the true mean. Applying this insight to the data in Table 5.5 tells us that we cannot reject with any confidence the possibility that the true mean is similar in all subperiods! In other words, the "noise" in the data is so large that we simply cannot make reliable inferences from average returns in any subperiod. The variation in returns across subperiods may simply reflect statistical variation, and we have to reconcile ourselves to the fact that the market return and the reward-to-variability ratio for passive (as well as active!) strategies is simply very hard to predict.

The instability of average excess return on stocks over the 19-year subperiods in Table 5.5 also calls into question the precision of the 76-year average excess return (8.64%) as an estimate of the risk premium on stocks looking into the future. In fact, there has been considerable recent debate among financial economists about the "true" equity risk premium, with an emerging consensus that the historical average is an unrealistically high estimate of the future risk premium. This argument is based on several factors: the use of longer time periods in which equity returns are examined; a broad range of countries rather than just the U.S. in which excess returns are computed (Dimson, Marsh, and Staunton, 2001); direct surveys of financial executives about their expectations for stock market returns (Graham and Harvey, 2001); and inferences from stock market data about investor expectations (Jagannathan, McGrattan, and Scherbina, 2000; Fama and French, 2002). The nearby box discusses some of this evidence.

Costs and Benefits of Passive Investing

How reasonable is it for an investor to pursue a passive strategy? We cannot answer such a question definitively without comparing passive strategy results to the costs and benefits accruing to an active portfolio strategy. Some issues are worth considering, however.

First, the alternative active strategy entails costs. Whether you choose to invest your own valuable time to acquire the information needed to generate an optimal active portfolio of risky assets or whether you delegate the task to a professional who will charge a fee, constructing an active portfolio is more expensive than constructing a passive one. The passive portfolio requires only small commissions on purchases of U.S. T-bills (or zero commissions if you purchase bills directly from the government) and management fees to a mutual fund company that offers a market index fund to the public. An index fund has the lowest operating expenses of all mutual stock funds because it requires minimal effort.

A second argument supporting a passive strategy is the free-rider benefit. If you assume there are many active, knowledgeable investors who quickly bid up prices of undervalued assets and offer down overvalued assets (by selling), you have to conclude that most of the time most assets will be fairly priced. Therefore, a well-diversified portfolio of common stock will be a reasonably fair buy, and the passive strategy may not be inferior to that of the average active investor. We will expand on this insight and provide a more comprehensive analysis of the relative success of passive strategies in Chapter 8.

To summarize, a passive strategy involves investment in two passive portfolios: virtually risk-free short-term T-bills (or a money market fund) and a fund of common stocks that mimics a broad market index. Recall that the capital allocation line representing such a strategy is called the *capital market line*. Using Table 5.5, we see that using 1926 to 2001 data, the passive risky portfolio has offered an average excess return of 8.6% with a standard deviation of 20.7%, resulting in a reward-to-variability ratio of 0.42.

SUMMARY

- Investors face a trade-off between risk and expected return. Historical data confirm our intuition that assets with low degrees of risk provide lower returns on average than do those of higher risk.
- Shifting funds from the risky portfolio to the risk-free asset is the simplest way to reduce risk. Another method involves diversification of the risky portfolio. We take up diversification in later chapters.
- U.S. T-bills provide a perfectly risk-free asset in nominal terms only. Nevertheless, the standard deviation of real rates on short-term T-bills is small compared to that of assets such as long-term bonds and common stocks, so for the purpose of our analysis, we consider T-bills the risk-free asset. Besides T-bills, money market funds hold short-term, safe obligations such as commercial paper and CDs. These entail some default risk but relatively little compared to most other risky assets. For convenience, we often refer to money market funds as risk-free assets.
- A risky investment portfolio (referred to here as the risky asset) can be characterized by its reward-to-variability ratio. This ratio is the slope of the capital allocation line (CAL), the

line connecting the risk-free asset to the risky asset. All combinations of the risky and risk-free asset lie on this line. Investors would prefer a steeper sloping CAL, because that means higher expected returns for any level of risk. If the borrowing rate is greater than the lending rate, the CAL will be "kinked" at the point corresponding to an investment of 100% of the complete portfolio in the risky asset.

- An investor's preferred choice among the portfolios on the capital allocation line will depend on risk aversion. Risk-averse investors will weight their complete portfolios more heavily toward Treasury bills. Risk-tolerant investors will hold higher proportions of their complete portfolios in the risky asset.

- The capital market line is the capital allocation line that results from using a passive investment strategy that treats a market index portfolio, such as the Standard & Poor's 500, as the risky asset. Passive strategies are low-cost ways of obtaining well-diversified portfolios with performance that will reflect that of the broad stock market.

KEY TERMS

arithmetic average, 133
asset allocation, 148
capital allocation line, 152
capital market line, 156
complete portfolio, 149
dollar-weighted average
    return, 134
excess return, 138

expected return, 136
geometric average, 133
holding-period return, 132
inflation rate, 147
nominal interest rate, 147
passive strategy, 156
probability distribution, 136
real interest rate, 147

reward-to-variability
    ratio, 152
risk aversion, 138
risk-free rate, 137
risk premium, 137
scenario analysis, 136
standard deviation, 136
variance, 136

PROBLEM SETS

1. A portfolio of nondividend-paying stocks earned a geometric mean return of 5.0% between January 1, 1996, and December 31, 2002. The arithmetic mean return for the same period was 6.0 %. If the market value of the portfolio at the beginning of 1996 was $100,000, what was the market value of the portfolio at the end of 2002?

2. Which of the following statements about the standard deviation is/are **true**? A standard deviation:
   i. Is the square root of the variance.
   ii. Is denominated in the same units as the original data.
   iii. Can be a positive or a negative number.

3. Which of the following statements reflects the importance of the asset allocation decision to the investment process? The asset allocation decision:
   a. Helps the investor decide on realistic investment goals.
   b. Identifies the specific securities to include in a portfolio.
   c. Determines most of the portfolio's returns and volatility over time.
   d. Creates a standard by which to establish an appropriate investment time horizon.

4. Look at Table 5.2 in the text. Suppose you now revise your expectations regarding the stock market as follows:

State of the Economy	Probability	HPR
Boom	0.3	44%
Normal growth	0.4	14
Recession	0.3	−16

Use Equations 5.3–5.5 to compute the mean and standard deviation of the HPR on stocks. Compare your revised parameters with the ones in the text.

5. The stock of Business Adventures sells for $40 a share. Its likely dividend payout and end-of-year price depend on the state of the economy by the end of the year as follows:

	Dividend	Stock Price
Boom	$2.00	$50
Normal economy	1.00	43
Recession	.50	34

a. Calculate the expected holding-period return and standard deviation of the holding-period return. All three scenarios are equally likely.
b. Calculate the expected return and standard deviation of a portfolio invested half in Business Adventures and half in Treasury bills. The return on bills is 4%.

Use the following data in answering questions 6, 7, and 8.

			Standard
Utility Formula Data			
Investment	Expected Return $E(r)$		Deviation σ
1	.12		.30
2	.15		.50
3	.21		.16
4	.24		.21

$$U = E(r) - \tfrac{1}{2}A\sigma^2 \qquad \text{where } A = 4$$

6. Based on the utility formula above, which investment would you select if you were risk averse with $A = 4$?
   a. 1
   b. 2
   c. 3
   d. 4

7. Based on the utility formula above, which investment would you select if you were risk neutral?
   a. 1
   b. 2
   c. 3
   d. 4

8. The variable (A) in the utility formula represents the:
   a. investor's return requirement.
   b. investor's aversion to risk.
   c. certainty equivalent rate of the portfolio.
   d. preference for one unit of return per four units of risk.

Use the following expectations on Stocks X and Y to answer questions 9 through 12 (round to the nearest percent).

	Bear Market	Normal Market	Bull Market
Probability	0.2	0.5	0.3
Stock X	−20%	18%	50%
Stock Y	−15%	20%	10%

9. What are the expected returns for Stocks X and Y?

	Stock X	Stock Y
a.	18%	5%
b.	18%	12%
c.	20%	11%
d.	20%	10%

10. What are the standard deviations of returns on Stocks X and Y?

	Stock X	Stock Y
a.	15%	26%
b.	20%	4%
c.	24%	13%
d.	28%	8%

11. Assume that of your $10,000 portfolio, you invest $9,000 in Stock X and $1,000 in Stock Y. What is the expected return on your portfolio?
   a. 18%
   b. 19%
   c. 20%
   d. 23%

12. Probabilities for three states of the economy, and probabilities for the returns on a particular stock in each state are shown in the table below.

State of Economy	Probability of Economic State	Stock Performance	Probability of Stock Performance in Given Economic State
Good	.3	Good	.6
		Neutral	.3
		Poor	.1
Neutral	.5	Good	.4
		Neutral	.3
		Poor	.3
Poor	.2	Good	.2
		Neutral	.3
		Poor	.5

The probability that the economy will be neutral *and* the stock will experience poor performance is

a. .06   c. .50
b. .15   d. .80

13. An analyst estimates that a stock has the following probabilities of return depending on the state of the economy:

State of Economy	Probability	Return
Good	.1	15%
Normal	.6	13
Poor	.3	7

The expected return of the stock is:

a. 7.8%

b. 11.4%

c. 11.7%

d. 13.0%

14. XYZ stock price and dividend history are as follows:

Year	Beginning-of-Year Price	Dividend Paid at Year-End
1999	$100	$4
2000	$110	$4
2001	$ 90	$4
2002	$ 95	$4

An investor buys three shares of XYZ at the beginning of 1999 buys another two shares at the beginning of 2000, sells one share at the beginning of 2001, and sells all four remaining shares at the beginning of 2002.

a. What are the arithmetic and geometric average time-weighted rates of return for the investor?

b. What is the dollar-weighted rate of return. Hint: Carefully prepare a chart of cash flows for the *four* dates corresponding to the turns of the year for January 1, 1999, to January 1, 2002. If your calculator cannot calculate internal rate of return, you will have to use trial and error.

15. a. Suppose you forecast that the standard deviation of the market return will be 20% in the coming year. If the measure of risk aversion in equation 5.6 is $A = 4$, what would be a reasonable guess for the expected market risk premium?

b. What value of A is consistent with a risk premium of 9%?

c. What will happen to the risk premium if investors become more risk tolerant?

16. Using the historical risk premiums as your guide, what is your estimate of the expected annual HPR on the S&P 500 stock portfolio if the current risk-free interest rate is 5%?

17. What has been the historical average *real* rate of return on stocks, Treasury bonds, and Treasury notes?

18. Consider a risky portfolio. The end-of-year cash flow derived from the portfolio will be either $50,000 or $150,000, with equal probabilities of 0.5. The alternative riskless investment in T-bills pays 5%.

a. If you require a risk premium of 10%, how much will you be willing to pay for the portfolio?

b. Suppose the portfolio can be purchased for the amount you found in (*a*). What will the expected rate of return on the portfolio be?

c. Now suppose you require a risk premium of 15%. What is the price you will be willing to pay now?

d. Comparing your answers to (*a*) and (*c*), what do you conclude about the relationship between the required risk premium on a portfolio and the price at which the portfolio will sell?

For problems 19–23, assume that you manage a risky portfolio with an expected rate of return of 17% and a standard deviation of 27%. The T-bill rate is 7%.

19. *a.* Your client chooses to invest 70% of a portfolio in your fund and 30% in a T-bill money market fund. What is the expected return and standard deviation of your client's portfolio?

b. Suppose your risky portfolio includes the following investments in the given proportions:

Stock A	27%
Stock B	33%
Stock C	40%

What are the investment proportions of your client's overall portfolio, including the position in T-bills?

c. What is the reward-to-variability ratio (*S*) of your risky portfolio and your client's overall portfolio?

d. Draw the CAL of your portfolio on an expected return/standard deviation diagram. What is the slope of the CAL? Show the position of your client on your fund's CAL.

20. Suppose the same client in problem 19 decides to invest in your risky portfolio a proportion (*y*) of his total investment budget so that his overall portfolio will have an expected rate of return of 15%.

a. What is the proportion *y*?

b. What are your client's investment proportions in your three stocks and the T-bill fund?

c. What is the standard deviation of the rate of return on your client's portfolio?

21. Suppose the same client in problem 19 prefers to invest in your portfolio a proportion (*y*) that maximizes the expected return on the overall portfolio subject to the constraint that the overall portfolio's standard deviation will not exceed 20%.

a. What is the investment proportion, *y*?

b. What is the expected rate of return on the overall portfolio?

22. You estimate that a passive portfolio invested to mimic the S&P 500 stock index yields an expected rate of return of 13% with a standard deviation of 25%. Draw the CML and your fund's CAL on an expected return/standard deviation diagram.

a. What is the slope of the CML?

b. Characterize in one short paragraph the advantage of your fund over the passive fund.

23. Your client (see problem 19) wonders whether to switch the 70% that is invested in your fund to the passive portfolio.

a. Explain to your client the disadvantage of the switch.

b. Show your client the maximum fee you could charge (as a percent of the investment in your fund deducted at the end of the year) that would still leave him at least as well off investing in your fund as in the passive one. (Hint: The fee will lower the slope of your client's CAL by reducing the expected return net of the fee.)

24. What do you think would happen to the expected return on stocks if investors perceived an increase in the volatility of stocks?

25. The change from a straight to a kinked capital allocation line is a result of the:
    a. Reward-to-variability ratio increasing.
    b. Borrowing rate exceeding the lending rate.
    c. Investor's risk tolerance decreasing.
    d. Increase in the portfolio proportion of the risk-free asset.

26. You manage an equity fund with an expected risk premium of 10% and an expected standard deviation of 14%. The rate on Treasury bills is 6%. Your client chooses to invest $60,000 of her portfolio in your equity fund and $40,000 in a T-bill money market fund. What is the expected return and standard deviation of return on your client's portfolio?

	Expected Return	Standard Deviation of Return
a.	8.4%	8.4%
b.	8.4	14.0
c.	12.0	8.4
d.	12.0	14.0

27. What is the reward-to-variability ratio for the *equity fund* in problem 26?
    a. .71
    b. 1.00
    c. 1.19
    d. 1.91

For problems 28–30, download Table 5.3: Rates of return, 1926–2001, from www.mhhe.com/blkm.

28. Calculate the same subperiod means and standard deviations for small stocks as Table 5.5 of the text provides for large stocks.
    a. Do small stocks provide better reward-to-variability ratios than large stocks?
    b. Do small stocks show a similar declining trend in standard deviation as Table 5.5 documents for large stocks?

29. Convert the nominal returns on both large and small stocks to real rates. Reproduce Table 5.5 using real rates instead of excess returns. Compare the results to those of Table 5.5.

30. Repeat problem 29 for small stocks and compare with the results for nominal rates.

WEBMASTER

Inflation and Interest Rates

The Federal Reserve Bank of St. Louis has several sources of information available on interest rates and economic conditions. One publication called *Monetary Trends* contains graphs and tabular information relevant to assess conditions in the capital markets. Go to the most recent edition of *Monetary Trends* at http://research. stlouisfed.org/publications/mt/mt.pdf and answer the following questions:

1. What is the current level of three-month and long-term Treasury yields?

2. Have nominal interest rates increased, decreased, or remained the same over the last three months?

3. Have real interest rates increased, decreased, or remained the same over the last two years?

4. Examine the information comparing recent U.S. inflation and long-term interest rates with the inflation and long-term interest rate experience of Japan. Are the results consistent with theory?

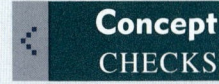

SOLUTIONS TO

Concept
CHECKS

1. *a.* The arithmetic average is $(2 + 8 - 4)/3 = 2\%$ per month.

  b. The time-weighted (geometric) average is
    $[(1 + .02) \times (1 + .08) \times (1 - .04)]^{1/3} = .0188 = 1.88\%$ per month

  c. We compute the dollar-weighted average (IRR) from the cash flow sequence (in $ millions):

	Month		
	1	**2**	**3**
Assets under management at beginning of month	10.0	13.2	19.256
Investment profits during month (HPR × Assets)	0.2	1.056	(0.77)
Net inflows during month	3.0	5.0	0.0
Assets under management at end of month	13.2	19.256	18.486

	Time			
	0	**1**	**2**	**3**
Net cash flow*	−10	−3.0	−5.0	+18.486

*Time 0 is today. Time 1 is the end of the first month. Time 3 is the end of the third month, when net cash flow equals the ending value (potential liquidation value) of the portfolio.

The IRR of the sequence of net cash flows is 1.17% per month.
The dollar-weighted average is less than the time-weighted average because the negative return was realized when the fund had the most money under management.

www.mhhe.com/bkm

2. Computing the HPR for each scenario we convert the price and dividend data to rate of return data:

Business Conditions	Probability	HPR
High growth	0.35	67.66% = (4.40 + 35 − 23.50)/23.50
Normal growth	0.30	31.91% = (4.00 + 27 − 23.50)/23.50
No growth	0.35	−19.15% = (4.00 + 15 − 23.50)/23.50

Using Equations 5.1 and 5.2 we obtain

$$E(r) = 0.35 \times 67.66 + 0.30 \times 31.91 + 0.35 \times (-19.15) = 26.55\%$$

$$\sigma^2 = 0.35 \times (67.66 - 26.55)^2 + 0.30 \times (31.91 - 26.55)^2 + 0.35 \times (-19.15 - 26.55)^2 = 1331$$

and

$$\sigma = \sqrt{1331} = 36.5\%$$

3. If the average investor chooses the S&P 500 portfolio, then the implied degree of risk aversion is given by Equation 5.7:

$$A = \frac{.10 - .05}{\frac{1}{2} \times .18^2} = 3.09$$

4. The mean excess return for the period 1926–1934 is 3.56% (below the historical average), and the standard deviation (using $n - 1$ degrees of freedom) is 32.69% (above the historical average). These results reflect the severe downturn of the great crash and the unusually high volatility of stock returns in this period.

5. *a.* Solving

$$1 + R = (1 + r)(1 + i) = (1.03)(1.08) = 1.1124$$

$$R = 11.24\%$$

   b. Solving

$$1 + R = (1.03)(1.10) = 1.133$$

$$R = 13.3\%$$

6. Holding 50% of your invested capital in Ready Assets means your investment proportion in the risky portfolio is reduced from 70% to 50%.

   Your risky portfolio is constructed to invest 54% in Vanguard and 46% in Fidelity. Thus, the proportion of Vanguard in your overall portfolio is 0.5 × 54% = 27%, and the dollar value of your position in Vanguard is 300,000 × 0.27 = $81,000.

7.
$$E(r) = 7 + 0.75 \times 8\% = 13\%$$

$$\sigma = 0.75 \times 22\% = 16.5\%$$

$$\text{Risk premium} = 13 - 7 = 6\%$$

$$\frac{\text{Risk premium}}{\text{Standard deviation}} = \frac{13 - 7}{16.5} = .36$$

8. The lending and borrowing rates are unchanged at $r_f = 7\%$ and $r_B = 9\%$. The standard deviation of the risky portfolio is still 22%, but its expected rate of return shifts from 15% to 17%. The slope of the kinked CAL is

$$\frac{E(r_P) - r_f}{\sigma_P} \text{ for the lending range}$$

$$\frac{E(r_P) - r_B}{\sigma_P} \text{ for the borrowing range}$$

Thus, in both cases, the slope increases: from 8/22 to 10/22 for the lending range, and from 6/22 to 8/22 for the borrowing range.

6

EFFICIENT DIVERSIFICATION

AFTER STUDYING THIS CHAPTER YOU SHOULD BE ABLE TO:

> Show how covariance and correlation affect the power of diversification to reduce portfolio risk.

> Construct efficient portfolios.

> Calculate the composition of the optimal risky portfolio.

> Use factor models to analyze the risk characteristics of securities and portfolios.

In this chapter we describe how investors can construct the best possible risky portfolio. The key concept is efficient diversification.

The notion of diversification is age-old. The adage "don't put all your eggs in one basket" obviously predates economic theory. However, a formal model showing how to make the most of the power of diversification was not devised until 1952, a feat for which Harry Markowitz eventually won the Nobel Prize in economics. This chapter is largely developed from his work, as well as from later insights that built on his work.

We start with a bird's-eye view of how diversification reduces the variability of portfolio returns. We then turn to the construction of optimal risky portfolios. We follow a top-down approach, starting with asset allocation across a small set of broad asset classes, such as stocks, bonds, and money market securities. Then we show how the principles of optimal asset allocation can easily be generalized to solve the problem of security selection among many risky assets. We discuss the efficient set of risky portfolios and show how it leads us to the best attainable capital allocation. Finally, we show how factor models of security returns can simplify the search for efficient portfolios and the interpretation of the risk characteristics of individual securities.

An appendix examines the common fallacy that long-term investment horizons mitigate the impact of asset risk. We argue that the common belief in "time diversification" is in fact an illusion and is not real diversification.

6.1 DIVERSIFICATION AND PORTFOLIO RISK

Suppose you have in your risky portfolio only one stock, say, Dell Computer Corporation. What are the sources of risk affecting this "portfolio"?

We can identify two broad sources of uncertainty. The first is the risk that has to do with general economic conditions, such as the business cycle, the inflation rate, interest rates, exchange rates, and so forth. None of these macroeconomic factors can be predicted with certainty, and all affect the rate of return Dell stock eventually will provide. Then you must add to these macro factors firm-specific influences, such as Dell's success in research and development, its management style and philosophy, and so on. Firm-specific factors are those that affect Dell without noticeably affecting other firms.

Now consider a naive diversification strategy, adding another security to the risky portfolio. If you invest half of your risky portfolio in ExxonMobil, leaving the other half in Dell, what happens to portfolio risk? Because the firm-specific influences on the two stocks differ (statistically speaking, the influences are independent), this strategy should reduce portfolio risk. For example, when oil prices fall, hurting ExxonMobil, computer prices might rise, helping Dell. The two effects are offsetting, which stabilizes portfolio return.

But why stop at only two stocks? Diversifying into many more securities continues to reduce exposure to firm-specific factors, so portfolio volatility should continue to fall. Ultimately, however, even with a large number of risky securities in a portfolio, there is no way to avoid all risk. To the extent that virtually all securities are affected by common (risky) macroeconomic factors, we cannot eliminate our exposure to general economic risk, no matter how many stocks we hold.

Figure 6.1 illustrates these concepts. When all risk is firm-specific, as in Figure 6.1A, diversification can reduce risk to low levels. With all risk sources independent, and with investment spread across many securities, exposure to any particular source of risk is negligible. This is just an application of the law of averages. The reduction of risk to very low levels because of independent risk sources is sometimes called the *insurance principle*.

When common sources of risk affect all firms, however, even extensive diversification cannot eliminate risk. In Figure 6.1B, portfolio standard deviation falls as the number of securities increases, but it is not reduced to zero. The risk that remains even after diversification is called **market risk,** risk that is attributable to marketwide risk sources. Other names are **systematic**

> **market risk, systematic risk, nondiversifiable risk**
>
> Risk factors common to the whole economy.

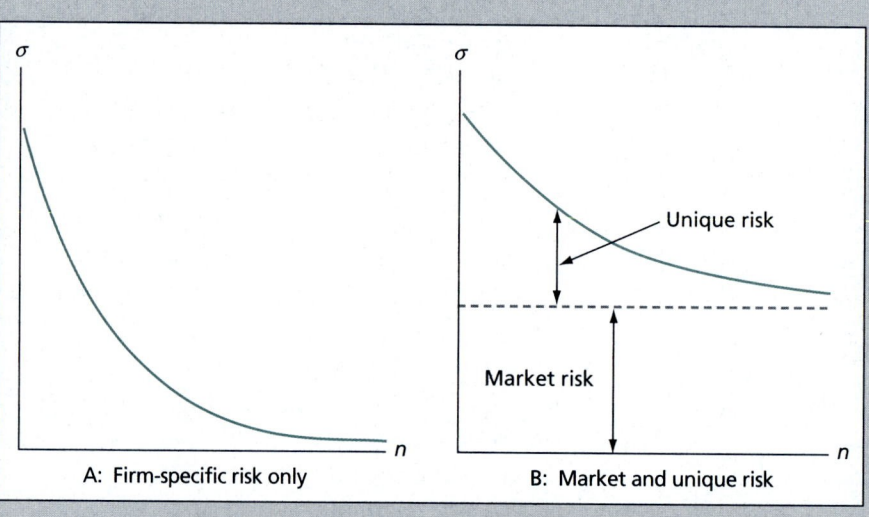

FIGURE 6.1

Portfolio risk as a function of the number of stocks in the portfolio

A: Firm-specific risk only

B: Market and unique risk

risk or **nondiversifiable risk.** The risk that *can* be eliminated by diversification is called **unique risk, firm-specific risk, nonsystematic risk,** or **diversifiable risk.**

This analysis is borne out by empirical studies. Figure 6.2 shows the effect of portfolio diversification, using data on NYSE stocks. The figure shows the average standard deviations of equally weighted portfolios constructed by selecting stocks at random as a function of the number of stocks in the portfolio. On average, portfolio risk does fall with diversification, but the power of diversification to reduce risk is limited by common sources of risk. The box on the following page highlights the dangers of neglecting diversification and points out that such neglect is widespread.

unique risk, firm-specific risk, nonsystematic risk, diversifiable risk

Risk that can be eliminated by diversification.

6.2 | ASSET ALLOCATION WITH TWO RISKY ASSETS

In the last chapter we examined the simplest asset allocation decision, that involving the choice of how much of the portfolio to place in risk-free money market securities versus in a risky portfolio. We simply assumed that the risky portfolio comprised a stock and a bond fund in given proportions. Of course, investors need to decide on the proportion of their portfolios to allocate to the stock versus the bond market. This, too, is an asset allocation decision. As the box on page 173 emphasizes, most investment professionals recognize that the asset allocation decision must take precedence over the choice of particular stocks or mutual funds.

We examined capital allocation between risky and risk-free assets in the last chapter. We turn now to asset allocation between two risky assets, which we will continue to assume are two mutual funds, one a bond fund and the other a stock fund. After we understand the properties of portfolios formed by mixing two risky assets, we will reintroduce the choice of the third, risk-free portfolio. This will allow us to complete the basic problem of asset allocation across the three key asset classes: stocks, bonds, and risk-free money market securities. Once you understand this case, it will be easy to see how portfolios of many risky securities might best be constructed.

Covariance and Correlation

Because we now envision forming a risky portfolio from two risky assets, we need to understand how the uncertainties of asset returns interact. It turns out that the key determinant of portfolio risk is the extent to which the returns on the two assets tend to vary either in tandem

FIGURE 6.2

Portfolio risk decreases as diversification increases

Source: Meir Statman, "How Many Stocks Make a Diversified Portfolio?" *Journal of Financial and Quantitative Analysis* 22, September 1987.

Enron, Tech Bubble Are Wake-Up Calls

Mutual-fund firms and financial planners have droned on about the topic for years. But suddenly, it's at the epicenter of lawsuits, congressional hearings and presidential reform proposals.

Diversification—that most basic of investing principles—has returned with a vengeance. During the late 1990s, many people scoffed at being diversified, because the idea of investing in a mix of stocks, bonds and other financial assets meant missing out on some of the soaring gains of tech stocks.

But with the collapse of the tech bubble and now the fall of Enron Corp. wiping out the 401(k) holdings of many current and retired Enron employees, the dangers of overloading a portfolio with one stock—or even with a group of similar stocks—has hit home for many investors.

The pitfalls of holding too much of one company's stock aren't limited to Enron. Since the beginning of 2000, nearly one of every five U.S. stocks has fallen by two-thirds or more, while only 1% of diversified stock mutual funds have swooned as much, according to research firm Morningstar Inc.

While not immune from losses, mutual funds tend to weather storms better, because they spread their bets over dozens or hundreds of companies. "Most people think their company is safer than a stock mutual fund, when the data show that the opposite is true," says John Rekenthaler, president of Morningstar's on-line-advice unit.

While some companies will match employees' 401(k) contributions exclusively in company stock, investors can almost always diversify a large portion of their 401(k)—namely, the part they contribute themselves. Half or more of the assets in a typical 401(k) portfolio are contributed by employees themselves, so diversifying this portion of their portfolio can make a significant difference in reducing overall investing risk.

But in picking an investing alternative to buying your employer's stock, some choices are more useful than others. For example, investors should take into account the type of company they work for when diversifying. Workers at small technology companies—the type of stock often held by growth funds—might find better diversification with a fund focusing on large undervalued companies. Conversely, an auto-company worker might want to put more money in funds that specialize in smaller companies that are less tied to economic cycles.

SOURCE: Abridged from Aaron Luccheth and Theo Francis, "Dangers of Not Diversifying Hit Investors," *The Wall Street Journal*, February 15, 2002.

---

or in opposition. Portfolio risk depends on the *correlation* between the returns of the assets in the portfolio. We can see why using a simple scenario analysis.

Suppose there are three possible scenarios for the economy: a recession, normal growth, and a boom. The performance of stock funds tends to follow the performance of the broad economy. So suppose that in a recession, the stock fund will have a rate of return of −11%, in a normal period it will have a rate of return of 13%, and in a boom period it will have a rate of return of 27%. In contrast, bond funds often do better when the economy is weak. This is because interest rates fall in a recession, which means that bond prices rise. Suppose that a bond fund will provide a rate of return of 16% in a recession, 6% in a normal period, and −4% in a boom. These assumptions and the probabilities of each scenario are summarized in Spreadsheet 6.1.

The expected return on each fund equals the probability-weighted average of the outcomes in the three scenarios. The last row of Spreadsheet 6.1 shows that the expected return of the stock fund is 10%, and that of the bond fund is 6%. As we discussed in the last chapter, the variance is the probability-weighted average across all scenarios of the squared deviation between the actual return of the fund and its expected return; the standard deviation is the square root of the variance. These values are computed in Spreadsheet 6.2.

What about the risk and return characteristics of a portfolio made up from the stock and bond funds? The portfolio return is the weighted average of the returns on each fund with weights equal to the proportion of the portfolio invested in each fund. Suppose we form a portfolio with 60% invested in the stock fund and 40% in the bond fund. Then the portfolio return in each scenario is the weighted average of the returns on the two funds. For example

$$\text{Portfolio return in recession} = 0.60 \times (-11\%) + 0.40 \times 16\% = -0.20\%$$

which appears in cell C5 of Spreadsheet 6.3.

Spreadsheet 6.3 shows the rate of return of the portfolio in each scenario, as well as the portfolio's expected return, variance, and standard deviation. Notice that while the portfolio's expected return is just the average of the expected return of the two assets, the standard deviation is actually less than that of *either* asset.

SPREADSHEET 6.1

Capital market expectations for the stock and bond funds

	A	B	C	D	E	F
1			Stock Fund		Bond Fund	
2	Scenario	Probability	Rate of Return	Col. B × Col. C	Rate of Return	Col. B × Col. E
3	Recession	0.3	−11	−3.3	16	4.8
4	Normal	0.4	13	5.2	6	2.4
5	Boom	0.3	27	8.1	−4	−1.2
6	Expected or Mean Return:		SUM:	10.0	SUM:	6.0

SPREADSHEET 6.2
Variance of returns

	A	B	C	D	E	F	G	H	I	J
1					Stock Fund				Bond Fund	
2				Deviation				Deviation		
3			Rate	from		Column B	Rate	from		Column B
4			of	Expected	Squared	x	of	Expected	Squared	x
5	Scenario	Prob.	Return	Return	Deviation	Column E	Return	Return	Deviation	Column I
6	Recession	0.3	-11	-21	441	132.3	16	10	100	30
7	Normal	0.4	13	3	9	3.6	6	0	0	0
8	Boom	0.3	27	17	289	86.7	-4	-10	100	30
9					Variance = SUM	222.6			Sum:	60
10				Standard deviation = SQRT(Variance)		14.92			Sum:	7.75

SPREADSHEET 6.3
Performance of the portfolio of stock and bond funds

	A	B	C	D	E	F	G
1			Portfolio of 60% in stocks and 40% in bonds				
2			Rate	Column B	Deviation from		Column B
3			of	x	Expected	Squared	x
4	Scenario	Probability	Return	Column C	Return	Deviation	Column F
5	Recession	0.3	-0.2	-0.06	-8.60	73.96	22.188
6	Normal	0.4	10.2	4.08	1.80	3.24	1.296
7	Boom	0.3	14.6	4.38	6.20	38.44	11.532
8			Expected return:	8.40		Variance:	35.016
9						Standard deviation:	5.92

The low risk of the portfolio is due to the inverse relationship between the performance of the two funds. In a recession, stocks fare poorly, but this is offset by the good performance of the bond fund. Conversely, in a boom scenario, bonds fall, but stocks do well. Therefore, the portfolio of the two risky assets is less risky than either asset individually. Portfolio risk is reduced most when the returns of the two assets most reliably offset each other.

The natural question investors should ask, therefore, is how one can measure the tendency of the returns on two assets to vary either in tandem or in opposition to each other. The statistics that provide this measure are the covariance and the correlation coefficient.

The covariance is calculated in a manner similar to the variance. Instead of measuring the typical difference of an asset return from its expected value, however, we wish to measure the extent to which the variation in the returns on the two assets tend to reinforce or offset each other.

We start in Spreadsheet 6.4 with the deviation of the return on each fund from its expected or mean value. For each scenario, we multiply the deviation of the stock fund return from its mean by the deviation of the bond fund return from its mean. The product will be positive if both asset returns exceed their respective means in that scenario or if both fall short of their respective means. The product will be negative if one asset exceeds its mean return, while the other falls short of its mean return. For example, Spreadsheet 6.4 shows that the stock fund return in the recession falls short of its expected value by 21%, while the bond fund return exceeds its mean by 10%. Therefore, the product of the two deviations in the recession is $-21 \times 10 = -210$, as reported in column E. The product of deviations is negative if one asset performs well when the other is performing poorly. It is positive if both assets perform well or poorly in the same scenarios.

SPREADSHEET 6.4
Covariance between the returns of the stock and bond funds

	A	B	C	D	E	F
1			Deviation from Mean Return		Covariance	
2	Scenario	Probability	Stock Fund	Bond Fund	Product of Dev	Col. B × Col. E
3	Recession	0.3	−21	10	−210	−63
4	Normal	0.4	3	0	0	0
5	Boom	0.3	17	−10	−170	−51
6				Covariance:	SUM:	−114
7	Correlation coefficient = Covariance/(StdDev(stocks)*StdDev(bonds)):					−0.99

If we compute the probability-weighted average of the products across all scenarios, we obtain a measure of the *average* tendency of the asset returns to vary in tandem. Since this is a measure of the extent to which the returns tend to vary with each other, that is, to co-vary, it is called the *covariance*. The covariance of the stock and bond funds is computed in the next-to-last line of Spreadsheet 6.4. The negative value for the covariance indicates that the two assets vary inversely, that is, when one asset performs well, the other tends to perform poorly.

Unfortunately, it is difficult to interpret the magnitude of the covariance. For instance, does the covariance of −114 indicate that the inverse relationship between the returns on stock and bond funds is strong or weak? It's hard to say. An easier statistic to interpret is the *correlation coefficient,* which is simply the covariance divided by the product of the standard deviations of the returns on each fund. We denote the correlation coefficient by the Greek letter rho, ρ.

$$\text{Correlation coefficient} = \rho = \frac{\text{Covariance}}{\sigma_{\text{stock}} \times \sigma_{\text{bond}}} = \frac{-114}{14.92 \times 7.75} = -.99$$

Correlations can range from values of −1 to +1. Values of −1 indicate perfect negative correlation, that is, the strongest possible tendency for two returns to vary inversely. Values of +1 indicate perfect positive correlation. Correlations of zero indicate that the returns on the two assets are unrelated to each other. The correlation coefficient of −0.99 confirms the overwhelming tendency of the returns on the stock and bond funds to vary inversely in this scenario analysis.

We are now in a position to derive the risk and return features of portfolios of risky assets.

1. Suppose the rates of return of the bond portfolio in the three scenarios of Spreadsheet 6.4 are 10% in a recession, 7% in a normal period, and +2% in a boom. The stock returns in the three scenarios are −12% (recession), 10% (normal), and 28% (boom). What are the covariance and correlation coefficient between the rates of return on the two portfolios?

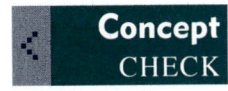

Concept
CHECK

Using Historical Data

We've seen that portfolio risk and return depend on the means and variances of the component securities, as well as on the covariance between their returns. One way to obtain these inputs is a scenario analysis as in Spreadsheets 6.1–6.4. As we noted in Chapter 5, however, a common alternative approach to produce these inputs is to make use of historical data.

In this approach, we use realized returns to estimate mean returns and volatility as well as the tendency for security returns to co-vary. The estimate of the mean return for each security is its average value in the sample period; the estimate of variance is the average value of the squared deviations around the sample average; the estimate of the covariance is the average value of the cross-product of deviations. As we noted in Chapter 5, Example 5.5, the averages used to compute variance and covariance are adjusted by the ratio $n/(n-1)$ to account for the "lost degree of freedom" when using the sample average in place of the true mean return, $E(r)$.

Notice that, as in scenario analysis, the focus for risk and return analysis is on average returns and the deviations of returns from their average value. Here, however, instead of using mean returns based on the scenario analysis, we use average returns during the sample period.

We can illustrate this approach with a simple example.

6.1 EXAMPLE

Using Historical Data to Estimate Means, Variances, and Covariances

More often than not, variances, covariances, and correlation coefficients are estimated from past data. The idea is that variability and covariability change slowly over time. Thus, if we estimate these statistics from a recent data sample, our estimates will provide useful predictions for the near future—perhaps next month or next quarter.

The computation of sample variances, covariances, and correlation coefficients is quite easy using a spreadsheet. Suppose you input 10 weekly, annualized returns for two NYSE stocks, ABC and XYZ, into columns B and C of the Excel spreadsheet below. The column averages in cells B15 and C15 provide estimates of the means, which are used in columns D and E to compute deviations of each return from the average return. These deviations are used in columns F and G to compute the squared deviations from means that are necessary to calculate variance and the cross-product of deviations to calculate covariance (column H). Row 15 of columns F, G, and H shows the averages of squared deviations and cross-product of deviations from the means.

As we noted above, to eliminate the bias in the estimate of the variance and covariance we need to multiply the average squared deviation by $n/(n-1)$, in this case, by 10/9, as we see in row 16.

Observe that the Excel commands from the Data Analysis menu provide a simple shortcut to this procedure. This feature of Excel can calculate a matrix of variances and covariances directly. The results from this procedure appear at the bottom of the spreadsheet.

	A	B	C	D	E	F	G	H
1		Rate of return		Deviations from		Squared Deviations		Product of
2		(annualized, %)		Average Return (%)		from Average Return		Deviations
3	Week	ABC	XYZ	ABC	XYZ	ABC	XYZ	ABC x XYZ
4	1	65.13	-22.55	45.51	-34.52	2071.34	1191.56	-1571.03
5	2	51.84	31.44	32.22	19.47	1038.26	379.12	627.39
6	3	-30.82	-6.45	-50.44	-18.42	2543.99	339.26	929.02
7	4	-15.13	-51.14	-34.75	-63.11	1207.42	3982.75	2192.91
8	5	70.63	33.78	51.01	21.81	2602.22	475.72	1112.62
9	6	107.82	32.95	88.20	20.98	7779.59	440.20	1850.57
10	7	-25.16	70.19	-44.78	58.22	2005.07	3389.68	-2607.02
11	8	50.48	27.63	30.86	15.66	952.46	245.27	483.33
12	9	-36.41	-48.79	-56.03	-60.76	3139.14	3691.66	3404.21
13	10	-42.20	52.63	-61.82	40.66	3821.47	1653.32	-2513.58
14								
15	Average	19.62	11.97			2716.10	1578.85	390.84
16	Average x 10/9					3017.89	1754.28	434.27
17								
18	Std. Deviation	54.94	41 88			Variances		Covariance
19								
20	AVERAGE(B4:B13)		STDEV(C4:C13)					0.19
21								
22						Correlation Coefficient =H16/(B18*C18)		
23		ABC return	XYZ return					
24	ABC return	3017.8851				Variances and Covariance		
25	XYZ return	434.26858	1754.2815			using "Covariance" from Data		
26						Analysis menu		
27		ABC return	XYZ return					
28	ABC return	1				"Correlation" from Data Analysis menu		
29	XYZ return	0.1887372	1					
30								

The Three Rules of Two-Risky-Assets Portfolios

Suppose a proportion denoted by w_B is invested in the bond fund, and the remainder $1 - w_B$, denoted by w_S, is invested in the stock fund. The properties of the portfolio are determined by the following three rules, which apply the rules of statistics governing combinations of random variables:

Rule 1: The rate of return on the portfolio is a weighted average of the returns on the component securities, with the investment proportions as weights.

$$r_P = w_B r_B + w_S r_S \qquad \text{(6.1)}$$

Rule 2: The expected rate of return on the portfolio is a weighted average of the expected returns on the component securities, with the same portfolio proportions as weights. In symbols, the expectation of Equation 6.1 is

$$E(r_P) = w_B E(r_B) + w_S E(r_S) \qquad \text{(6.2)}$$

The first two rules are simple linear expressions. This is not so in the case of the portfolio variance, as the third rule shows.

Rule 3: The variance of the rate of return on the two-risky-asset portfolio is

$$\sigma_P^2 = (w_B \sigma_B)^2 + (w_S \sigma_S)^2 + 2(w_B \sigma_B)(w_S \sigma_S)\rho_{BS} \qquad \text{(6.3)}$$

where ρ_{BS} is the correlation coefficient between the returns on the stock and bond funds.

The variance of the portfolio is a *sum* of the contributions of the component security variances *plus* a term that involves the correlation coefficient between the returns on the component securities. We know from the last section why this last term arises. If the correlation between the component securities is small or negative, then there will be a greater tendency for the variability in the returns on the two assets to offset each other. This will reduce portfolio risk. Notice in Equation 6.3 that portfolio variance is lower when the correlation coefficient is lower.

The formula describing portfolio variance is more complicated than that describing portfolio return. This complication has a virtue, however: namely, the tremendous potential for gains from diversification.

The Risk-Return Trade-Off with Two-Risky-Assets Portfolios

Suppose now that the standard deviation of bonds is 12% and that of stocks is 25%, and assume that there is zero correlation between the return on the bond fund and the return on the stock fund. A correlation coefficient of zero means that stock and bond returns vary independently of each other.

Say we start out with a position of 100% in bonds, and we now consider a shift: Invest 50% in bonds and 50% in stocks. We can compute the portfolio variance from Equation 6.3.

Input data:

$$E(r_B) = 6\%; \; E(r_S) = 10\%; \; \sigma_B = 12\%; \; \sigma_S = 25\%; \; \rho_{BS} = 0; \; w_B = 0.5; \; w_S = 0.5$$

Portfolio variance:

$$\sigma_P^2 = (0.5 \times 12)^2 + (0.5 \times 25)^2 + 2(0.5 \times 12) \times (0.5 \times 25) \times 0 = 192.25$$

The standard deviation of the portfolio (the square root of the variance) is 13.87%. Had we mistakenly calculated portfolio risk by averaging the two standard deviations [(25 + 12)/2], we would have incorrectly predicted an increase in the portfolio standard deviation by a full 6.50 percentage points, to 18.5%. Instead, the portfolio variance equation shows that the addition of stocks to the formerly all-bond portfolio actually increases the portfolio standard deviation by only 1.87 percentage points. So the gain from diversification can be seen as a full 4.63%.

This gain is cost-free in the sense that diversification allows us to experience the full contribution of the stock's higher expected return, while keeping the portfolio standard deviation below the average of the component standard deviations. As Equation 6.2 shows, the portfolio's expected return is the weighted average of expected returns of the component securities. If the expected return on bonds is 6% and the expected return on stocks is 10%, then shifting from 0% to 50% investment in stocks will increase our expected return from 6% to 8%.

6.2 EXAMPLE

Benefits from Diversification

Suppose we invest 75% in bonds and only 25% in stocks. We can construct a portfolio with an expected return higher than bonds (0.75 × 6) + (0.25 × 10) = 7% and, at the same time, a standard deviation that is less than bonds. Using Equation 6.3 again, we find that the portfolio variance is

$$(0.75 \times 12)^2 + (0.25 \times 25)^2 + 2(0.75 \times 12)(0.25 \times 25) \times 0 = 120$$

and, accordingly, the portfolio standard deviation is $\sqrt{120} = 10.96\%$, which is less than the standard deviation of either bonds or stocks alone. Taking on a more volatile asset (stocks) actually reduces portfolio risk! Such is the power of diversification.

We can find investment proportions that will reduce portfolio risk even further. The risk-minimizing proportions will be 81.27% in bonds and 18.73% in stocks.[1] With these proportions, the portfolio standard deviation will be 10.82%, and the portfolio's expected return will be 6.75%.

investment opportunity set

Set of available portfolio risk-return combinations.

Is this portfolio preferable to the one with 25% in the stock fund? That depends on investor preferences, because the portfolio with the lower variance also has a lower expected return.

What the analyst can and must do, however, is to show investors the entire **investment opportunity set** as we do in Figure 6.3. This is the set of all attainable combinations of risk and return offered by portfolios formed using the available assets in differing proportions.

Points on the investment opportunity set of Figure 6.3 can be found by varying the investment proportions and computing the resulting expected returns and standard deviations from Equations 6.2 and 6.3. We can feed the input data and the two equations into a personal computer and let it draw the graph. With the aid of the computer, we can easily find the portfolio composition corresponding to any point on the opportunity set. Spreadsheet 6.5 shows the investment proportions and the mean and standard deviation for a few portfolios.

The Mean-Variance Criterion

Investors desire portfolios that lie to the "northwest" in Figure 6.3. These are portfolios with high expected returns (toward the "north" of the figure) and low volatility (to the "west"). These preferences mean that we can compare portfolios using a *mean-variance criterion* in the following way. Portfolio A is said to dominate portfolio B if all investors prefer A over B. This will be the case if it has higher mean return and lower variance:

$$E(r_A) \geq E(r_B) \qquad \text{and} \qquad \sigma_A \leq \sigma_B$$

---

[1]With a zero correlation coefficient, the variance-minimizing proportion in the bond fund is given by the expression: $\sigma_S^2/(\sigma_B^2 + \sigma_S^2)$.

FIGURE **6.3**

Investment
opportunity set for
bond and stock funds

SPREADSHEET **6.5**

Investment opportunity set for bond and stock funds

	A	B	C	D	E
1			**Data**		
2	$E(r_S)$	$E(r_B)$	σ_S	σ_B	ρ_{SB}
3	10%	6%	25%	12%	0%
4	**Portfolio Weights**		**Expected Return**		
5	w_S	$w_B = 1 - w_S$	$E(r_P)$=Col A×A3+Col B×B3		Std. Deviation*
6	0	1	6.00%		12.00%
7	0.1	0.9	6.40%		11.09%
8	0.1873	0.8127	6.75%		10.8183%
9	0.2	0.8	6.80%		10.8240%
10	0.3	0.7	7.20%		11.26%
11	0.4	0.6	7.60%		12.32%
12	0.5	0.5	8.00%		13.87%
13	0.6	0.4	8.40%		15.75%
14	0.7	0.3	8.80%		17.87%
15	0.8	0.2	9.20%		20.14%
16	0.9	0.1	9.60%		22.53%
17	1	0	10.00%		25.00%
18	**Note: The minimum variance portfolio weight in stocks is**				
19	$w_S=(\sigma_B{}^2-\sigma_B\sigma_S\rho)/(\sigma_S{}^2+\sigma_B{}^2-2*\sigma_B\sigma_S\rho)$=.1873				
20	* The formula for portfolio standard deviation is:				
21	σ_P=[(Col A*C3)^2+(Col B*D3)^2+2*Col A*C3*Col B*D3*E3]^.5				

Graphically, if the expected return and standard deviation combination of each portfolio were plotted in Figure 6.3, portfolio *A* would lie to the northwest of *B*. Given a choice between portfolios *A* and *B, all* investors would choose *A*. For example, the stock fund in Figure 6.3 dominates portfolio *Z*; the stock fund has higher expected return and lower volatility.

Portfolios that lie below the minimum-variance portfolio in the figure can therefore be re-jected out of hand as inefficient. Any portfolio on the downward sloping portion of the curve is "dominated" by the portfolio that lies directly above it on the upward sloping portion of the curve since that portfolio has higher expected return and equal standard deviation. The best choice among the portfolios on the upward sloping portion of the curve is not as obvious, because in this region higher expected return is accompanied by higher risk. The best choice will depend on the investor's willingness to trade off risk against expected return.

So far we have assumed a correlation of zero between stock and bond returns. We know that low correlations aid diversification and that a higher correlation coefficient between stocks and bonds results in a reduced effect of diversification. What are the implications of perfect positive correlation between bonds and stocks?

Assuming the correlation coefficient is 1.0 simplifies Equation 6.3 for portfolio variance. Looking at it again, you will see that substitution of $\rho_{BS} = 1$ in Equation 6.3 means we can "complete the square" of the quantities $w_B\sigma_B$ and $w_S\sigma_S$ to obtain

$$\sigma_P^2 = (w_B\sigma_B + w_S\sigma_S)^2$$

and, therefore,

$$\sigma_P = w_B\sigma_B + w_S\sigma_S$$

The portfolio standard deviation is a weighted average of the component security standard deviations only in the special case of perfect positive correlation. In this circumstance, there are no gains to be had from diversification. Whatever the proportions of stocks and bonds, both the portfolio mean and the standard deviation are simple weighted averages. Figure 6.4 shows the opportunity set with perfect positive correlation—a straight line through the component securities. No portfolio can be discarded as inefficient in this case, and the choice among portfolios depends only on risk preference. Diversification in the case of perfect positive correlation is not effective.

Perfect positive correlation is the *only* case in which there is no benefit from diversification. Whenever $\rho < 1$, the portfolio standard deviation is less than the weighted average of the standard deviations of the component securities. Therefore, *there are benefits to diversification whenever asset returns are less than perfectly correlated.*

Our analysis has ranged from very attractive diversification benefits ($\rho_{BS} < 0$) to no benefits at all ($\rho_{BS} = 1.0$). For ρ_{BS} within this range, the benefits will be somewhere in between. As Figure 6.4 illustrates, $\rho_{BS} = 0.5$ is a lot better for diversification than perfect positive correlation and quite a bit worse than zero correlation.

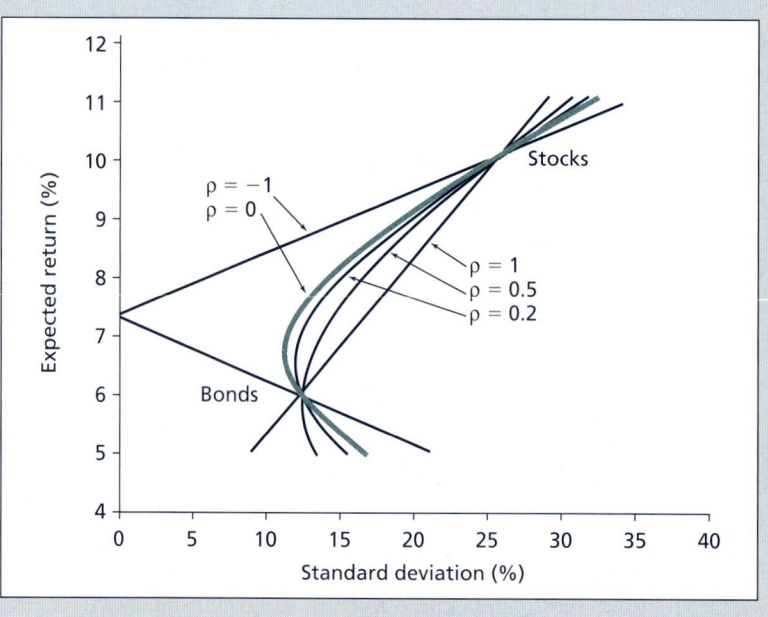

FIGURE 6.4

Investment opportunity sets for bonds and stocks with various correlation coefficients

A realistic correlation coefficient between stocks and bonds based on historical experience is actually around 0.20. The expected returns and standard deviations that we have so far assumed also reflect historical experience, which is why we include a graph for $\rho_{BS} = 0.2$ in Figure 6.4. Spreadsheet 6.6 enumerates some of the points on the various opportunity sets in Figure 6.4.

Negative correlation between a pair of assets is also possible. Where negative correlation is present, there will be even greater diversification benefits. Again, let us start with an extreme. With perfect negative correlation, we substitute $\rho_{BS} = -1.0$ in Equation 6.3 and simplify it in the same way as with positive perfect correlation. Here, too, we can complete the square, this time, however, with different results

$$\sigma_P^2 = (w_B\sigma_B - w_S\sigma_S)^2$$

and, therefore,

$$\sigma_P = ABS[w_B\sigma_B - w_S\sigma_S] \tag{6.4}$$

The right-hand side of Equation 6.4 denotes the absolute value of $w_B\sigma_B - w_S\sigma_S$. The solution involves the absolute value because standard deviation is never negative.

With perfect negative correlation, the benefits from diversification stretch to the limit. Equation 6.4 points to the proportions that will reduce the portfolio standard deviation all the

SPREADSHEET 6.6

Investment opportunity set for bonds and stocks with various correlation coefficients

	A	B	C	D	E	F	G
1			**Data**				
2	E(r$_S$)	E(r$_B$)	σ_S	σ_B			
3	10	6	25	12			
4	**Weight in**	**Portfolio**	**Portfolio Standard Deviation for Given Correlation (ρ)**				
5	**Stocks**	**Expected Return**	$\sigma_P=[(A*C3)^2+((1-A)*D3)^2+2*A*C3*(1-A)*D3*\rho]^.5$				
6	w$_S$	E(r$_P$)=A*A3+(1-A)*B3	-1	0	0.2	0.5	1
7	0	6	12	12	12	12	12
8	0.2	6.8	4.6	10.8	11.7	12.9	14.6
9	0.4	7.6	2.8	12.3	13.4	15.0	17.2
10	0.6	8.4	10.2	15.7	16.6	17.9	19.8
11	0.8	9.2	17.6	20.1	20.6	21.3	22.4
12	1	10	25	25	25	25	25
13	**Minimum Variance Portfolio:**		w$_S$(min) = (σ_B^2-$\sigma_B\sigma_S\rho$)/(σ_S^2+σ_B^2-2*$\sigma_B\sigma_S\rho$)				
14	w$_S$(min)		0.3243	0.1873	0.1294	-0.0128	-0.9231
15	E(r$_P$) = w$_S$(min)*A3+(1-w$_S$(min))*B3		7.30	6.75	6.52	5.95	2.31
16	σ_P		0.00	10.82	11.54	11.997	0.00
17	Notes: (1) The standard deviation is calculated from equation 6.3 with the weights of the						
18	minimum-variance portfolio:						
19			$\sigma_P=((w_S(min)*C3)^2+((1-w_S(min))*D3)^2+2*w_S(min)*C3*(1-w_S(min))*D3*\rho]^.5$				
20	(2) As the correlation coefficient grows, the minimum variance portfolio requires a smaller						
21	position in stocks (even a negative position for higher correlations), and the performance						
22	of this portfolio becomes less attractive.						
23	(3) With correlation of .5, minimum variance is achieved with a short position in stocks.						
24	The standard deviation is slightly lower than that of bonds, but with a slightly lower mean as well.						
25	(4) With perfectly positive correlation you can get the standard deviation to zero by taking						
26	a large, short position in stocks. The mean return is then as low as 2.31%.						

way to zero.[2] With our data, this will happen when $w_B = 67.57\%$. While exposing us to zero risk, investing 32.43% in stocks (rather than placing all funds in bonds) will still increase the portfolio expected return from 6% to 7.30%. Of course, we can hardly expect results this attractive in reality.

2. Suppose that for some reason you are *required* to invest 50% of your portfolio in bonds and 50% in stocks.
   a. If the standard deviation of your portfolio is 15%, what must be the correlation coefficient between stock and bond returns?
   b. What is the expected rate of return on your portfolio?
   c. Now suppose that the correlation between stock and bond returns is 0.22 but that you are free to choose whatever portfolio proportions you desire. Are you likely to be better or worse off than you were in part (a)?

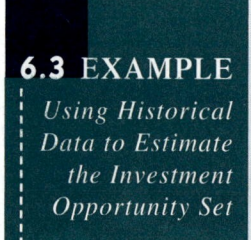

Let's return to the data for ABC and XYZ in Example 6.1. Using the spreadsheet estimates of the means and standard deviations obtained from the AVERAGE and STDEV functions, and the estimate of the correlation coefficient we obtained in that example, we can compute the risk-return trade-off for various portfolios formed from ABC and XYZ.

Columns E and F in the lower half of the spreadsheet on the following page are calculated from Equations 6.2 and 6.3 respectively, and show the risk-return opportunities. These calculations use the estimates of the stocks' means in cells B16 and C16, the standard deviations in cells B17 and C17, and the correlation coefficient in cell F10.

Examination of column E shows that the portfolio mean starts at XYZ's mean of 11.97% and moves toward ABC's mean as we increase the weight of ABC and correspondingly reduce that of XYZ. Examination of the standard deviation in column F shows that diversification reduces the standard deviation until the proportion in ABC increases above 30%; thereafter, standard deviation increases. Hence, the minimum-variance portfolio uses weights of approximately 30% in ABC and 70% in XYZ.

The exact proportion in ABC in the minimum-variance portfolio can be computed from the formula shown in Spreadsheet 6.6. Note, however, that achieving a minimum-variance portfolio is not a compelling goal. Investors may well be willing to take on more risk in order to increase expected return. The investment opportunity set offered by stocks ABC and XYZ may be found by graphing the expected return–standard deviation pairs in columns E and F.

3. The following tables present returns on various pairs of stocks in several periods. In part A, we show you a scatter diagram of the returns on the first pair of stocks. Draw (or prepare in Excel) similar scatter diagrams for cases B through E. Match up the diagrams (A–E) to the following list of correlation coefficients by choosing the correlation that best describes the relationship between the returns on the two stocks: $\rho = -1, 0, 0.2, 0.5, 1.0$.

(continued)

[2]The proportion in bonds that will drive the standard deviation to zero when $\rho = -1$ is:

$$w_B = \frac{\sigma_S}{\sigma_B + \sigma_S}$$

Compare this formula to the formula in footnote 1 for the variance-minimizing proportions when $\rho = 0$.

Spreadsheet for Example 6.3

	A	B	C	D	E	F	G	H
1		Here are the data on ABC and XYZ from Example 6.1, shown below with the computed						
2		statistics of average, standard deviation and correlation.						
3								
4	Week	Anualized	%					
5		ABC return	XYZ return					
6	1	65.13	-22.55					
7	2	51.84	31.44					
8	3	-30.82	-6.45			*ABC return*	*XYZ return*	
9	4	-15.13	-51.14		ABC return	1		
10	5	70.63	33.78		XYZ return	0.18873716	1	
11	6	107.82	32.95					
12	7	-25.16	70.19					
13	8	50.48	27.63					
14	9	-36.41	-48.79	AVERAGE(C6:C15)			Correlation from	
15	10	-42.20	52.63				Data Analysis menu	
16	Average:	19.62	11.97	STDEV(C6:C15)				
17	Std deviation:	54.94	41.88					
18								
19								
20	CALCULATION OF INVESTMENT OPPORTUNITY SET:							
21								
22			Portfolio	Proportions		Portfolio		
23			ABC	XYZ	Mean	Std. Dev.		
24	=C27*$B$16+D27*$C$16		0.00	1.00	11.97	41.88		
25			0.10	0.90	12.73	39.11		
26			0.20	0.80	13.50	37.18		
27			0.30	0.70	14.26	36.24		
28			0.40	0.60	15.03	36.37		
29			0.50	0.50	15.79	37.55		
30			0.60	0.40	16.56	39.69		
31			0.70	0.30	17.32	42.65		
32			0.80	0.20	18.09	46.27		
33			0.90	0.10	18.85	50.40		
34			1.00	0.00	19.62	54.94		
35	Minimum Variance Portfolio		0.3382	0.6618	14.56	36.17		
36								
37								
38	(C17^2-B17*C17*F10)/				=(C32^2*$B$17^2+D32^2*$C$17^2			
39	(B17^2+C17^2-2*B17*C17*F10)				+2*C32*D32*$B$17*$C$17*$F$10)^.5			
40								
41								
42								

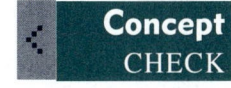

A. **% Return**

Stock 1	Stock 2
5	1
1	1
4	3
2	3
3	5

(continued)

(concluded)

B.	% Return		C.	% Return		D.	% Return		E.	% Return	
	Stock 1	Stock 2		Stock 1	Stock 2		Stock 1	Stock 2		Stock 1	Stock 2
	1	1		1	5		5	5		5	4
	2	2		2	4		1	3		1	3
	3	3		3	3		4	3		4	1
	4	4		4	2		2	0		2	0
	5	5		5	1		3	5		3	5

6.3 THE OPTIMAL RISKY PORTFOLIO WITH A RISK-FREE ASSET

Now we can expand the asset allocation problem to include a risk-free asset. Let us continue to use the input data from the bottom of Spreadsheet 6.5, but now assume a realistic correlation coefficient between stocks and bonds of 0.20. Suppose then that we are still confined to the risky bond and stock funds, but now can also invest in risk-free T-bills yielding 5%. Figure 6.5 shows the opportunity set generated from the bond and stock funds. This is the same opportunity set as graphed in Figure 6.4 with $\rho_{BS} = 0.20$.

Two possible capital allocation lines (CALs) are drawn from the risk-free rate ($r_f = 5\%$) to two feasible portfolios. The first possible CAL is drawn through the variance-minimizing portfolio (A), which invests 87.06% in bonds and 12.94% in stocks. Portfolio A's expected return is 6.52% and its standard deviation is 11.54%. With a T-bill rate (r_f) of 5%, the reward-to-variability ratio of portfolio A (which is also the slope of the CAL that combines T-bills with portfolio A) is

$$S_A = \frac{E(r_A) - r_f}{\sigma_A} = \frac{6.52 - 5}{11.54} = 0.13$$

FIGURE 6.5

The opportunity set using bonds and stocks and two capital allocation lines

Now consider the CAL that uses portfolio B instead of A. Portfolio B invests 80% in bonds and 20% in stocks, providing an expected return of 6.80% with a standard deviation of 11.68%. Thus, the reward-to-variability ratio of any portfolio on the CAL of B is

$$S_B = \frac{6.80 - 5}{11.68} = .15$$

This is higher than the reward-to-variability ratio of the CAL of the variance-minimizing portfolio A.

The difference in the reward-to-variability ratios is $S_B - S_A = 0.02$. This implies that portfolio B provides 2 extra basis points (0.02%) of expected return for every percentage point increase in standard deviation.

The higher reward-to-variability ratio of portfolio B means that its capital allocation line is steeper than that of A. Therefore, CAL_B plots above CAL_A in Figure 6.5. In other words, combinations of portfolio B and the risk-free asset provide a higher expected return for any level of risk (standard deviation) than combinations of portfolio A and the risk-free asset. Therefore, all risk-averse investors would prefer to form their complete portfolio using the risk-free asset with portfolio B rather than with portfolio A. In this sense, portfolio B dominates A.

But why stop at portfolio B? We can continue to ratchet the CAL upward until it reaches the ultimate point of tangency with the investment opportunity set. This must yield the CAL with the highest feasible reward-to-variability ratio. Therefore, the tangency portfolio (O) in Figure 6.6 is the **optimal risky portfolio** to mix with T-bills, which may be defined as the risky portfolio resulting in the highest possible CAL. We can read the expected return and standard deviation of portfolio O (for "optimal") off the graph in Figure 6.6 as

$$E(r_O) = 8.68\%$$

$$\sigma_O = 17.97\%$$

which can be identified as the portfolio that invests 32.99% in bonds and 67.01% in stocks.[3] We can obtain a numerical solution to this problem using a computer program.

optimal risky portfolio

The best combination of risky assets to be mixed with safe assets to form the complete portfolio.

---

[3]The proportion of portfolio O invested in bonds is:

$$w_B = \frac{[E(r_B) - r_f]\sigma_S^2 - [E(r_S) - r_f]\sigma_B\sigma_S\rho_{BS}}{[E(r_B) - r_f]\sigma_S^2 + [E(r_S) - r_f]\sigma_B^2 - [E(r_B) - r_f + E(r_S) - r_f]\sigma_B\sigma_S\rho_{BS}}$$

FIGURE 6.7

The complete portfolio

The CAL with our optimal portfolio has a slope of

$$S_O = \frac{8.68 - 5}{17.97} = .20$$

which is the reward-to-variability ratio of portfolio O. This slope exceeds the slope of any other feasible portfolio, as it must if it is to be the slope of the best feasible CAL.

In the last chapter we saw that the preferred *complete* portfolio formed from a risky portfolio and a risk-free asset depends on the investor's risk aversion. More risk-averse investors will prefer low-risk portfolios despite the lower expected return, while more risk-tolerant investors will choose higher-risk, higher-return portfolios. Both investors, however, will choose portfolio O as their risky portfolio since that portfolio results in the highest return per unit of risk, that is, the steepest capital allocation line. Investors will differ only in their allocation of investment funds between portfolio O and the risk-free asset.

Figure 6.7 shows one possible choice for the preferred complete portfolio, C. The investor places 55% of wealth in portfolio O and 45% in Treasury bills. The rate of return and volatility of the portfolio are

$$E(r_C) = 5 + 0.55 \times (8.68 - 5) = 7.02\%$$

$$\sigma_C = 0.55 \times 17.97 = 9.88\%$$

In turn, we found above that portfolio O is formed by mixing the bond fund and stock fund with weights of 32.99% and 67.01%. Therefore, the overall asset allocation of the complete portfolio is as follows:

Weight in risk-free asset		45.00%
Weight in bond fund	$0.3299 \times 55\% =$	18.14
Weight in stock fund	$0.6701 \times 55\% =$	36.86
Total		100.00%

Figure 6.8 depicts the overall asset allocation. The allocation reflects considerations of both efficient diversification (the construction of the optimal risky portfolio, O) and risk aversion (the allocation of funds between the risk-free asset and the risky portfolio O to form the complete portfolio, C).

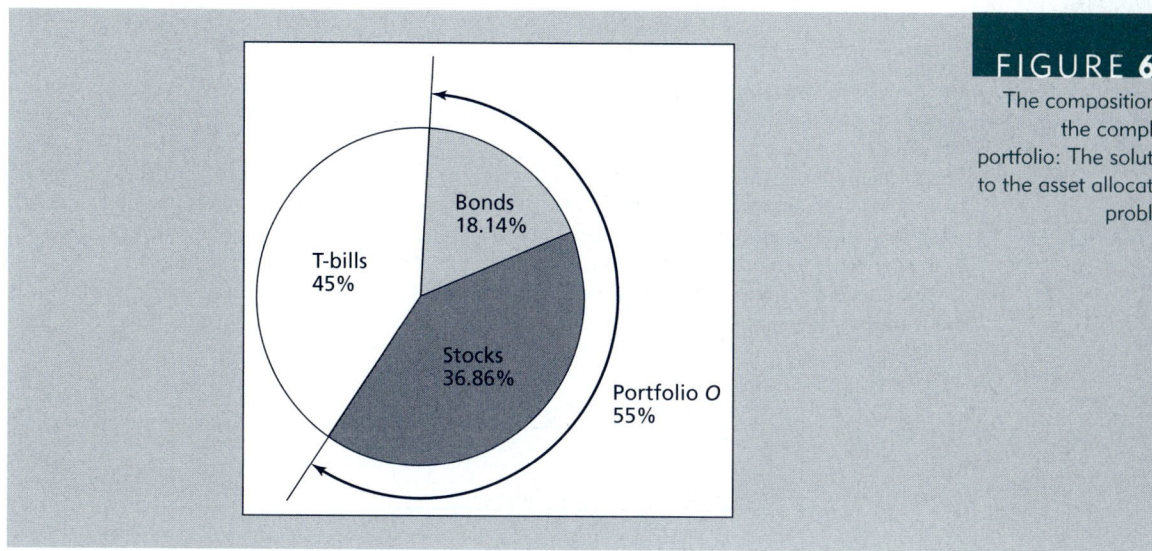

FIGURE **6.8**

The composition of
the complete
portfolio: The solution
to the asset allocation
problem

4. A universe of securities includes a risky stock (X), a stock index fund (M), and T-bills. The data for the universe are:

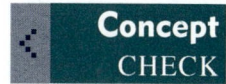

Concept
CHECK

	Expected Return	Standard Deviation
X	15%	50%
M	10	20
T-bills	5	0

The correlation coefficient between X and M is −0.2.
a. Draw the opportunity set of securities X and M.
b. Find the optimal risky portfolio (O) and its expected return and standard deviation.
c. Find the slope of the CAL generated by T-bills and portfolio O.
d. Suppose an investor places 2/9 (i.e., 22.22%) of the complete portfolio in the risky portfolio O and the remainder in T-bills. Calculate the composition of the complete portfolio.

6.4 EFFICIENT DIVERSIFICATION WITH MANY RISKY ASSETS

We can extend the two-risky-assets portfolio construction methodology to cover the case of many risky assets and a risk-free asset. First, we offer an overview. As in the two-risky-assets example, the problem has three separate steps. To begin, we identify the best possible or most *efficient* risk-return combinations available from the universe of risky assets. Next we determine the optimal portfolio of risky assets by finding the portfolio that supports the steepest CAL. Finally, we choose an appropriate complete portfolio based on the investor's risk aversion by mixing the risk-free asset with the optimal risky portfolio.

Two-Security Portfolio

The Excel model "Two-Security Portfolio" is based on the asset allocation problem between stocks and bonds that appears in this chapter. You can change correlations, mean returns, and standard deviation of return for any two securities or, as it is used in the text example, any two portfolios. All of the concepts that are covered in this section can be explored using the model.

You can learn more about this spreadsheet model by using the interactive version available on our website at www.mhhe.com/bkm.

	A	B	C	D	E	F
1						
2						
3						
4	Asset Allocation Analysis: Risk and Return					
5		Expected	Standard		Corr.		
6		Return	Deviation	Coeff s,b	Covariance	
7	Bonds	6.00%	12.00%	0	0	
8	Stocks	10.00%	25.00%			
9	T-Bill	5.00%	0.00%			
10						
11						
12	Weight	Weight		Expected	Standard	Reward to
13	Bonds	Stocks		Return	Deviation	Variability
14	1	0		6.0000%	12.0000%	0.08333
15	0.9	0.1		6.4000%	11.0856%	0.12629
16	0.8	0.2		6.8000%	10.8240%	0.16630
17	0.7	0.3		7.2000%	11.2610%	0.19536
18	0.6	0.4		7.6000%	12.3223%	0.21100
19	0.5	0.5		8.0000%	13.8654%	0.21637
20	0.4	0.6		8.4000%	15.7493%	0.21588
21	0.3	0.7		8.8000%	17.8664%	0.21269
22	0.2	0.8		9.2000%	20.1435%	0.20850
23	0.1	0.9		9.6000%	22.5320%	0.20415
24	0	1		10.0000%	25.0000%	0.20000
25						
26	Minimum Variance Portfolio		Short Sales	No Short		
27			Allowed	Sales		
28		Weight Bonds	0.81274	0.81274		
29		Weight Stocks	0.18726	0.18726		
30		Return	6.7490%	6.7490%		
31		Risk	10.8183%	10.8183%		
32		CAL$_{(MV)}$				
33						

The Efficient Frontier of Risky Assets

To get a sense of how additional risky assets can improve the investor's investment opportunities, look at Figure 6.9. Points *A*, *B*, and *C* represent the expected returns and standard deviations of three stocks. The curve passing through *A* and *B* shows the risk-return combinations of all the portfolios that can be formed by combining those two stocks. Similarly, the curve passing through *B* and *C* shows all the portfolios that can be formed from those two stocks. Now observe point *E* on the *AB* curve and point *F* on the *BC* curve. These points represent two

FIGURE 6.9
Portfolios constructed with three stocks (A, B, and C)

portfolios chosen from the set of *AB* combinations and *BC* combinations. The curve that passes through *E* and *F* in turn represents all the portfolios that can be constructed from portfolios *E* and *F*. Since *E* and *F* are themselves constructed from *A, B,* and *C,* this curve also may be viewed as depicting some of the portfolios that can be constructed from these *three* securities. Notice that curve *EF* extends the investment opportunity set to the northwest, which is the desired direction.

Now we can continue to take other points (each representing portfolios) from these three curves and further combine them into new portfolios, thus shifting the opportunity set even farther to the northwest. You can see that this process would work even better with more stocks. Moreover, the efficient frontier, the boundary or "envelope" of all the curves thus developed, will lie quite away from the individual stocks in the northwesterly direction, as shown in Figure 6.10.

The analytical technique to derive the efficient frontier of risky assets was developed by Harry Markowitz at the University of Chicago in 1951 and ultimately earned him the Nobel Prize in economics. We will sketch his approach here.

First, we determine the risk-return opportunity set. The aim is to construct the northwestern-most portfolios in terms of expected return and standard deviation from the universe of securities. The inputs are the expected returns and standard deviations of each asset in the universe, along with the correlation coefficients between each pair of assets. These data come from security analysis, to be discussed in Part Four. The graph that connects all the northwestern-most portfolios is called the **efficient frontier** of risky assets. It represents

efficient frontier

Graph representing a set of portfolios that maximizes expected return at each level of portfolio risk.

FIGURE 6.10

The efficient frontier of risky assets and individual assets

the set of portfolios that offers the highest possible expected rate of return for each level of portfolio standard deviation. These portfolios may be viewed as efficiently diversified. One such frontier is shown in Figure 6.10.

Expected return-standard deviation combinations for any *individual* asset end up inside the efficient frontier, because single-asset portfolios are inefficient—they are not efficiently diversified.

When we choose among portfolios on the efficient frontier, we can immediately discard portfolios below the minimum-variance portfolio. These are dominated by portfolios on the upper half of the frontier with equal risk but higher expected returns. Therefore, the real choice is among portfolios on the efficient frontier above the minimum-variance portfolio.

Various constraints may preclude a particular investor from choosing portfolios on the efficient frontier, however. If an institution is prohibited by law from taking short positions in any asset, for example, the portfolio manager must add constraints to the computer-optimization program that rule out negative (short) positions.

Short sale restrictions are only one possible constraint. Some clients may want to assure a minimum level of expected dividend yield. In this case, data input must include a set of expected dividend yields. The optimization program is made to include a constraint to ensure that the expected *portfolio* dividend yield will equal or exceed the desired level. Another common constraint forbids investments in companies engaged in "undesirable social activity."

In principle, portfolio managers can tailor an efficient frontier to meet any particular objective. Of course, satisfying constraints carries a price tag. An efficient frontier subject to a number of constraints will offer a lower reward-to-variability ratio than a less constrained one. Clients should be aware of this cost and may want to think twice about constraints that are not mandated by law.

Deriving the efficient frontier may be quite difficult conceptually, but computing and graphing it with any number of assets and any set of constraints is quite straightforward. For a small number of assets, and in the absence of constraints beyond the obvious one that

EXCEL Applications

Efficient Frontier for Many Stocks

Excel spreadsheets can be used to construct an efficient frontier for a group of individual securities or a group of portfolios of securities. The Excel model "Efficient Portfolio" is built using a sample of actual returns on stocks that make up a part of the Dow Jones Industrial Average Index. The efficient frontier is graphed, similar to Figure 6.10, using various possible target returns. The model is built for eight securities and can be easily modified for any group of eight assets.

You can learn more about this spreadsheet model by using the interactive version available on our website at www.mhhe.com/bkm.

	A	B	C	D	E	F	G	H	I
1									
2									
3	TKR SYM	Return	S.D.						
4	C	46.6	34.8						
5	GE	37.3	25.0						
6	HD	41.8	31.4						
7	INTC	46.0	45.9						
8	JNJ	24.6	26.2						
9	MRK	32.6	31.0						
10	SBC	19.0	28.1						
11	WMT	41.2	31.4						
12									
13				Correlation Matrix					
14									
15		C	GE	HD	INTC	JNJ	MRK	SBC	WMT
16	C	1.00	0.54	0.26	0.26	0.35	0.29	0.25	0.40
17	GE	0.54	1.00	0.58	0.26	0.29	0.20	0.34	0.52
18	HD	0.26	0.58	1.00	-0.09	-0.02	-0.12	0.15	0.58
19	INTC	0.26	0.26	-0.09	1.00	0.09	0.11	-0.05	-0.02
20	JNJ	0.35	0.29	-0.02	0.09	1.00	0.58	0.28	0.28
21	MRK	0.29	0.20	-0.12	0.11	0.58	1.00	0.37	0.12
22	SBC	0.25	0.34	0.15	-0.05	0.28	0.37	1.00	0.16
23	WMT	0.40	0.52	0.58	-0.02	0.28	0.12	0.16	1.00
24									
25				Covariance Matrix					
26		C	GE	HD	INTC	JNJ	MRK	SBC	WMT
27	C	1211.55	468.81	282.30	419.81	320.52	308.52	239.86	440.95
28	GE	468.81	627.47	451.99	299.86	189.64	158.28	240.96	409.29
29	HD	282.30	451.99	983.39	-133.54	-17.19	-117.25	133.28	566.72
30	INTC	419.81	299.86	-133.54	2106.34	113.73	151.78	-63.77	-34.46
31	JNJ	320.52	189.64	-17.19	113.73	686.88	473.15	203.37	229.77
32	MRK	308.52	158.28	-117.25	151.78	473.15	961.63	324.53	119.16
33	SBC	239.86	240.96	133.28	-63.77	203.37	324.53	790.22	140.90
34	WMT	440.95	409.29	566.72	-34.46	229.77	119.16	140.90	987.13

portfolio proportions must sum to 1.0, the efficient frontier can be computed and graphed with a spreadsheet program.

Choosing the Optimal Risky Portfolio

The second step of the optimization plan involves the risk-free asset. Using the current risk-free rate, we search for the capital allocation line with the highest reward-to-variability ratio (the steepest slope), as shown in Figures 6.5 and 6.6.

The CAL formed from the optimal risky portfolio (O) will be tangent to the efficient frontier of risky assets discussed above. This CAL dominates all alternative feasible lines (the dashed lines that are drawn through the frontier). Portfolio O, therefore, is the optimal risky portfolio.

The Preferred Complete Portfolio and the Separation Property

Finally, in the third step, the investor chooses the appropriate mix between the optimal risky portfolio (O) and T-bills, exactly as in Figure 6.7.

A portfolio manager will offer the same risky portfolio (O) to all clients, no matter what their degrees of risk aversion. Risk aversion comes into play only when clients select their desired point on the CAL. More risk-averse clients will invest more in the risk-free asset and less in the optimal risky portfolio O than less risk-averse clients, but both will use portfolio O as the optimal risky investment vehicle.

This result is called a **separation property,** introduced by James Tobin (1958), the 1983 Nobel Laureate for economics: It implies that portfolio choice can be separated into two independent tasks. The first task, which includes steps one and two, determination of the optimal risky portfolio (O), is purely technical. Given the particular input data, the best risky portfolio is the same for all clients regardless of risk aversion. The second task, construction of the complete portfolio from bills and portfolio O, however, depends on personal preference. Here the client is the decision maker.

Of course, the optimal risky portfolio for different clients may vary because of portfolio constraints such as dividend yield requirements, tax considerations, or other client preferences. Our analysis, though, suggests that a few portfolios may be sufficient to serve the demands of a wide range of investors. We see here the theoretical basis of the mutual fund industry.

If the optimal portfolio is the same for all clients, professional management is more efficient and less costly. One management firm can serve a number of clients with relatively small incremental administrative costs.

The (computerized) optimization technique is the easiest part of portfolio construction. If different managers use different input data to develop different efficient frontiers, they will offer different "optimal" portfolios. Therefore, the real arena of the competition among portfolio managers is in the sophisticated security analysis that underlies their choices. The rule of GIGO (garbage in–garbage out) applies fully to portfolio selection. If the quality of the security analysis is poor, a passive portfolio such as a market index fund can yield better results than an active portfolio tilted toward *seemingly* favorable securities.

> **Concept CHECK** ►
>
> 5. Two portfolio managers work for competing investment management houses. Each employs security analysts to prepare input data for the construction of the optimal portfolio. When all is completed, the efficient frontier obtained by manager A dominates that of manager B in that A's optimal risky portfolio lies northwest of B's. Is the more attractive efficient frontier asserted by manager A evidence that she really employs better security analysts?

6.5   A SINGLE-FACTOR ASSET MARKET

We started this chapter with the distinction between systematic and firm-specific risk. Systematic risk is largely macroeconomic, affecting all securities, while firm-specific risk factors affect only one particular firm or, perhaps, its industry. **Factor models** are statistical models designed to estimate these two components of risk for a particular security or portfolio. The first to use a factor model to explain the benefits of diversification was another Nobel Prize winner, William S. Sharpe (1963). We will introduce his major work (the capital asset pricing model) in the next chapter.

The popularity of factor models is due to their practicality. To construct the efficient frontier from a universe of 100 securities, we would need to estimate 100 expected returns, 100 variances, and $100 \times 99/2 = 4{,}950$ covariances. And a universe of 100 securities is actually quite small. A universe of 1,000 securities would require estimates of $1{,}000 \times 999/2 = 499{,}500$ covariances, as well as 1,000 expected returns and variances. We will see shortly that the assumption that one common factor is responsible for all the covariability of stock returns, with all other variability due to firm-specific factors, dramatically simplifies the analysis.

Let us use R_i to denote the **excess return** on a security, that is, the rate of return in excess of the risk-free rate: $R_i = r_i - r_f$. Then we can express the distinction between macroeconomic and firm-specific factors by decomposing this excess return in some holding period into three components

$$R_i = E(R_i) + \beta_i M + e_i \qquad (6.5)$$

In Equation 6.5, $E(R_i)$ is the *expected* excess holding-period return (HPR) at the start of the holding period. The next two terms reflect the impact of two sources of uncertainty. M quantifies the market or macroeconomic surprises (with zero meaning that there is "no surprise") during the holding period. β_i is the sensitivity of the security to the macroeconomic factor. Finally, e_i is the impact of unanticipated firm-specific events.

Both M and e_i have zero expected values because each represents the impact of unanticipated events, which by definition must average out to zero. The **beta** (β_i) denotes the responsiveness of security i to macroeconomic events; this sensitivity will be different for different securities.

As an example of a factor model, suppose that the excess return on Dell stock is *expected* to be 9% in the coming holding period. However, on average, for every unanticipated increase of 1% in the vitality of the general economy, which we take as the macroeconomic factor M, Dell's stock return will be enhanced by 1.2%. Dell's β is therefore 1.2. Finally, Dell is affected by firm-specific surprises as well. Therefore, we can write the realized excess return on Dell stock as follows

$$R_D = 9\% + 1.2M + e_i$$

If the economy outperforms expectations by 2%, then we would revise upward our expectations of Dell's excess return by $1.2 \times 2\%$, or 2.4%, resulting in a new expected excess return of 11.4%. Finally, the effects of Dell's firm-specific news during the holding period must be added to arrive at the actual holding-period return on Dell stock.

Equation 6.5 describes a factor model for stock returns. This is a simplification of reality; a more realistic decomposition of security returns would require more than one factor in Equation 6.5. We treat this issue in the next chapter, but for now, let us examine the single-factor case.

Specification of a Single-Index Model of Security Returns

A factor model description of security returns is of little use if we cannot specify a way to measure the factor that we say affects security returns. One reasonable approach is to use the rate of return on a broad index of securities, such as the S&P 500, as a proxy for the common macro factor. With this assumption, we can use the excess return on the market index, R_M, to measure the direction of macro shocks in any period.

index model

A model of stock returns using a market index such as the S&P 500 to represent common or systematic risk factors.

The **index model** separates the realized rate of return on a security into macro (systematic) and micro (firm-specific) components much like Equation 6.5. The excess rate of return on each security is the sum of three components:

	Symbol
1. The stock's excess return if the market factor is neutral, that is, if the market's excess return is zero.	α_i
2. The component of return due to movements in the overall market (as represented by the index R_M); β_i is the security's responsiveness to the market.	$\beta_i R_M$
3. The component attributable to unexpected events that are relevant only to this security (firm-specific).	e_i

The excess return on the stock now can be stated as

$$R_i = \alpha_i + \beta_i R_M + e_i \tag{6.6}$$

Equation 6.6 specifies two sources of security risk: market or systematic risk ($\beta_i R_M$), attributable to the security's sensitivity (as measured by beta) to movements in the overall market, and firm-specific risk (e_i), which is the part of uncertainty independent of the market factor. Because the firm-specific component of the firm's return is uncorrelated with the market return, we can write the variance of the excess return of the stock as[4]

$$\text{Variance } (R_i) = \text{Variance } (\alpha_i + \beta_i R_M + e_i)$$

$$= \text{Variance } (\beta_i R_M) + \text{Variance } (e_i)$$

$$= \beta_i^2 \sigma_M^2 \qquad\qquad + \sigma^2(e_i)$$

$$= \text{Systematic risk } + \text{Firm-specific risk} \tag{6.7}$$

Therefore, the total variability of the rate of return of each security depends on two components:

1. The variance attributable to the uncertainty common to the entire market. This systematic risk is attributable to the uncertainty in R_M. Notice that the systematic risk of each stock depends on both the volatility in R_M (that is, σ_M^2) *and* the sensitivity of the stock to fluctuations in R_M. That sensitivity is measured by β_i.

2. The variance attributable to firm-specific risk factors, the effects of which are measured by e_i. This is the variance in the part of the stock's return that is independent of market performance.

This single-index model is convenient. It relates security returns to a market index that investors follow. Moreover, as we soon shall see, its usefulness goes beyond mere convenience.

Statistical and Graphical Representation of the Single-Index Model

Equation 6.6, $R_i = \alpha_i + \beta_i R_M + e_i$, may be interpreted as a single-variable *regression equation* of R_i on the market excess return R_M. The excess return on the security (R_i) is the dependent variable that is to be explained by the regression. On the right-hand side of the equation are the intercept α_i; the regression (or slope) coefficient beta, β_i, multiplying the independent (or explanatory) variable R_M; and the security residual (unexplained) return, e_i.

---

[4]Notice that because α_i is a constant, it has no bearing on the variance of R_i.

We can plot this regression relationship as in Figure 6.11, which shows a possible scatter diagram for Dell Computer Corporation's excess return against the excess return of the market index.

The horizontal axis of the scatter diagram measures the explanatory variable, here the market excess return, R_M. The vertical axis measures the dependent variable, here Dell's excess return, R_D. Each point on the scatter diagram represents a sample pair of returns (R_M, R_D) that might be observed for a particular holding period. Point T, for instance, describes a holding period when the excess return was 17% on the market index and 27% on Dell.

Regression analysis lets us use the sample of historical returns to estimate a relationship between the dependent variable and the explanatory variable. The regression line in Figure 6.11 is drawn so as to minimize the sum of all the squared deviations around it. Hence, we say the regression line "best fits" the data in the scatter diagram. The line is called the **security characteristic line,** or SCL.

The regression intercept (α_D) is measured from the origin to the intersection of the regression line with the vertical axis. Any point on the vertical axis represents zero market excess return, so the intercept gives us the *expected* excess return on Dell during the sample period when market performance was neutral. The intercept in Figure 6.11 is about 4.5%.

The slope of the regression line can be measured by dividing the rise of the line by its run. It also is expressed by the number multiplying the explanatory variable, which is called the regression coefficient or the slope coefficient or simply the beta. The regression beta is a natural measure of systematic risk since it measures the typical response of the security return to market fluctuations.

The regression line does not represent the *actual* returns: that is, the points on the scatter diagram almost never lie on the regression line, although the actual returns are used to calculate the regression coefficients. Rather, the line represents average tendencies; it shows the effect of the index return on our *expectation* of R_D. The algebraic representation of the regression line is

$$E(R_D \mid R_M) = \alpha_D + \beta_D R_M \qquad \text{(6.8)}$$

which reads: The expectation of R_D *given* a value of R_M equals the intercept plus the slope coefficient times the given value of R_M.

security characteristic line

Plot of a security's excess return as a function of the excess return of the market.

FIGURE **6.11**

Scatter diagram for Dell

Because the regression line represents expectations, and because these expectations may not be realized in any or all of the actual returns (as the scatter diagram shows), the *actual* security returns also include a residual, the firm-specific surprise, e_i. This surprise (at point T, for example) is measured by the vertical distance between the point of the scatter diagram and the regression line. For example, the expected return on Dell, given a market return of 17%, would have been $4.5\% + 1.4 \times 17\% = 28.3\%$. The actual return was only 27%, so point T falls below the regression line by 1.3%.

Equation 6.7 shows that the greater the beta of the security, that is, the greater the slope of the regression, the greater the security's systematic risk ($\beta_D^2 \sigma_M^2$), as well as its total variance (σ_D^2). The *average security* has a slope coefficient (beta) of 1.0: Because the market is composed of all securities, the typical response to a market movement must be one for one. An "aggressive" investment will have a beta higher than 1.0; that is, the security has above-average market risk.[5] In Figure 6.11, Dell's beta is 1.4. Conversely, securities with betas lower than 1.0 are called defensive.

A security may have a negative beta. Its regression line will then slope downward, meaning that, for more favorable macro events (higher R_M), we would expect a *lower* return, and vice versa. The latter means that when the macro economy goes bad (negative R_M) and securities with positive beta are expected to have negative excess returns, the negative-beta security will shine. The result is that a negative-beta security has *negative* systematic risk, that is, it provides a hedge against systematic risk.

The dispersion of the scatter of actual returns about the regression line is determined by the residual variance $\sigma^2(e_D)$, which measures the effects of firm-specific events. The magnitude of firm-specific risk varies across securities. One way to measure the relative importance of systematic risk is to measure the ratio of systematic variance to total variance.

$$\rho^2 = \frac{\text{Systematic (or explained) variance}}{\text{Total variance}}$$

$$= \frac{\beta_D^2 \sigma_M^2}{\sigma_D^2} = \frac{\beta_D^2 \sigma_M^2}{\beta_D^2 \sigma_M^2 + \sigma^2(e_D)} \tag{6.9}$$

where ρ is the correlation coefficient between R_D and R_M. Its square measures the ratio of explained variance to total variance, that is, the proportion of total variance that can be attributed to market fluctuations. But if beta is negative, so is the correlation coefficient, an indication that the explanatory and dependent variables are expected to move in opposite directions.

At the extreme, when the correlation coefficient is either 1.0 or -1.0, the security return is fully explained by the market return, that is, there are no firm-specific effects. All the points of the scatter diagram will lie exactly on the line. This is called perfect correlation (either positive or negative); the return on the security is perfectly predictable from the market return. A large correlation coefficient (in absolute value terms) means systematic variance dominates the total variance; that is, firm-specific variance is relatively unimportant. When the correlation coefficient is small (in absolute value terms), the market factor plays a relatively unimportant part in explaining the variance of the asset, and firm-specific factors predominate.

---

[5]Note that the average beta of all securities will be 1.0 only when we compute a *weighted* average of betas (using market values as weights), since the stock market index is value weighted. We know from Chapter 5 that the distribution of securities by market value is not symmetric: There are relatively few large corporations and many more smaller ones. Thus, if you were to take a randomly selected sample of stocks, you should expect smaller companies to dominate. As a result, the simple average of the betas of individual securities, when computed against a value-weighted index such as the S&P 500, will be greater than 1.0, pushed up by the tendency for stocks of low-capitalization companies to have betas greater than 1.0.

6. Interpret the eight scatter diagrams of Figure 6.12 in terms of systematic risk, diversifiable risk, and the intercept.

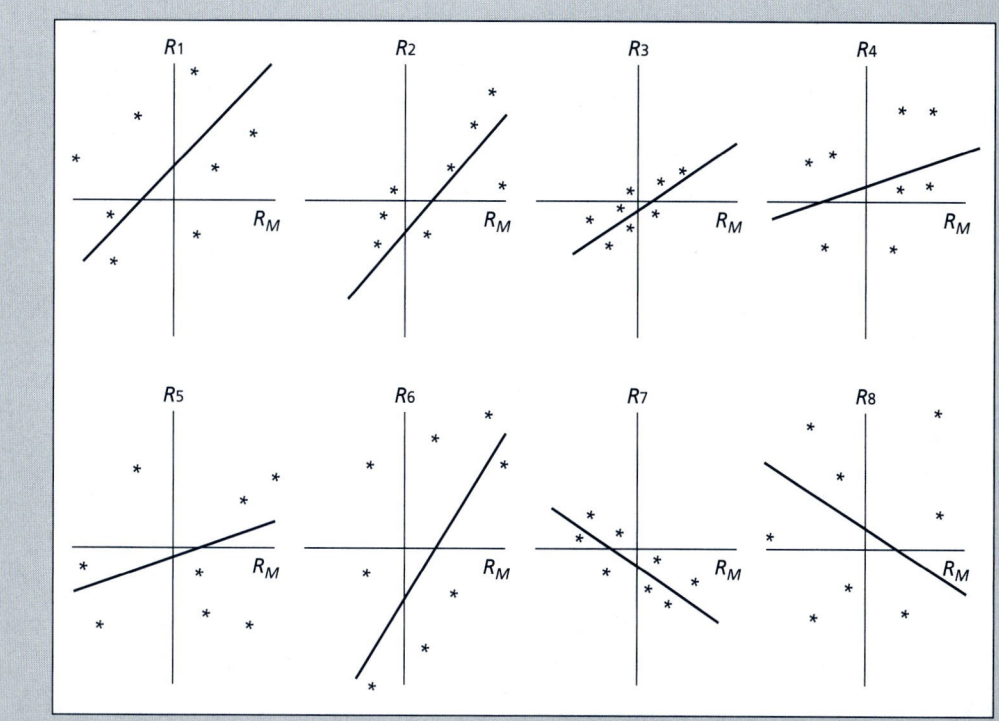

FIGURE **6.12**
Various scatter diagrams

The direct way to calculate the slope and intercept of the characteristic lines for ABC and XYZ is from the variances and covariances. Here, we use the Data Analysis menu of Excel to obtain the covariance matrix in the following spreadsheet.

The slope coefficient for ABC is given by the formula

$$\beta_{ABC} = \frac{Cov(R_{ABC}, R_{Market})}{Var(R_{Market})} = \frac{773.31}{684.01} = 1.156$$

The intercept for ABC is

$$\alpha_{ABC} = Average(R_{ABC}) - \beta_{ABC} \times Average(R_{Market})$$
$$= 15.20 - 1.156 \times 9.40 = 4.33$$

Therefore, the security characteristic line of ABC is given by

$$R_{ABC} = 4.33 + 1.156\, R_{Market}$$

This result also can be obtained by using the "Regression" command from Excel's Data Analysis menu, as we show at the bottom of the spreadsheet. The minor differences between the direct regression output and our calculations above are due to rounding error.

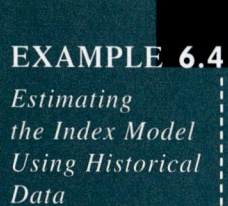

EXAMPLE 6.4

Estimating the Index Model Using Historical Data

	A	B	C	D	E	F	G	H	I
2			Annualized rates of return					Excess Returns	
3	Week	ABC	XYZ	Mkt. Index	Risk free		ABC	XYZ	Market
4	1	65.13	-22.55	64.40	5.23		59.90	-27.78	59.17
5	2	51.84	31.44	24.00	4.76		47.08	26.68	19.24
6	3	-30.82	-6.45	9.15	6.22		-37.04	-12.67	2.93
7	4	-15.13	-51.14	-35.57	3.78		-18.91	-54.92	-39.35
8	5	70.63	33.78	11.59	4.43		66.20	29.35	7.16
9	6	107.82	32.95	23.13	3.78		104.04	29.17	19.35
10	7	-25.16	70.19	8.54	3.87		-29.03	66.32	4.67
11	8	50.48	27.63	25.87	4.15		46.33	23.48	21.72
12	9	-36.41	-48.79	-13.15	3.99		-40.40	-52.78	-17.14
13	10	-42.20	52.63	20.21	4.01		-46.21	48.62	16.20
14	Average:						15.20	7.55	9.40
15									
16	COVARIANCE MATRIX:								
17		ABC	XYZ	Market					
18	ABC	3020.933							
19	XYZ	442.114	1766.923						
20	Market	773.306	396.789	669.010					
21									
22	SUMMARY OUTPUT OF EXCEL REGRESSION:								
23									
24	Regression Statistics								
25	Multiple R	0.544							
26	R Square	0.296							
27	Adj. R Square	0.208							
28	Standard Error	48.918							
29	Observations	10.000							
30									
31									
32		Coefficients	Std. Error	t Stat	P-value				
33	Intercept	4.336	16.564	0.262	0.800				
34	Market return	1.156	0.630	1.834	0.104				
35									

Diversification in a Single-Factor Security Market

Imagine a portfolio that is divided equally among securities whose returns are given by the single-index model in Equation 6.6. What are the systematic and nonsystematic (firm-specific) variances of this portfolio?

The beta of the portfolio is the simple average of the individual security betas, which we denote β. Hence, the systematic variance equals $\beta_P^2 \sigma_M^2$. This is the level of market risk in Figure 6.1B. The market variance (σ_M^2) and the market sensitivity of the portfolio (β_P) determine the market risk of the portfolio.

The systematic component of each security return, $\beta_i R_M$, is fully determined by the market factor and therefore is perfectly correlated with the systematic part of any other security's return. Hence, there are no diversification effects on systematic risk no matter how many securities are involved. As far as *market risk* goes, a single-security portfolio with a small beta will result in a low market-risk portfolio. The number of securities makes no difference.

It is quite different with firm-specific or unique risk. If you choose securities with small residual variances for a portfolio, it, too, will have low unique risk. But you can do even better simply by holding more securities, even if each has a large residual variance. Because the firm-specific effects are independent of each other, their risk effects are offsetting. This is the insurance principle applied to the firm-specific component of risk. The portfolio ends up with a negligible level of nonsystematic risk.

In sum, when we control the systematic risk of the portfolio by manipulating the average beta of the component securities, the number of securities is of no consequence. But in the case of *nonsystematic* risk, the number of securities involved is more important than the firm-specific variance of the securities. Sufficient diversification can virtually eliminate firm-specific risk. Understanding this distinction is essential to understanding the role of diversification in portfolio construction.

We have just seen that when forming highly diversified portfolios, firm-specific risk becomes *irrelevant*. Only systematic risk remains. We conclude that in measuring security risk for diversified investors, we should focus our attention on the security's systematic risk. This means that for diversified investors, the relevant risk measure for a security will be the security's beta, β, since firms with higher β have greater sensitivity to broad market disturbances. As Equation 6.7 makes clear, systematic risk will be determined both by market volatility, σ_M^2, and the firm's sensitivity to the market, β.

7. *a.*   What is the characteristic line of XYZ in Example 6.4?
    b.   Does ABC or XYZ have greater systematic risk?
    c.   What percent of the variance of XYZ is firm-specific risk?

Concept
CHECK

SUMMARY

- The expected rate of return of a portfolio is the weighted average of the component asset expected returns with the investment proportions as weights.
- The variance of a portfolio is a sum of the contributions of the component-security variances *plus* terms involving the correlation among assets.
- Even if correlations are positive, the portfolio standard deviation will be less than the weighted average of the component standard deviations, as long as the assets are not *perfectly* positively correlated. Thus, portfolio diversification is of value as long as assets are less than perfectly correlated.

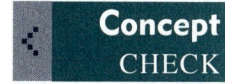
www.mhhe.com/bkm

- The contribution of an asset to portfolio variance depends on its correlation with the other assets in the portfolio, as well as on its own variance. An asset that is perfectly negatively correlated with a portfolio can be used to reduce the portfolio variance to zero. Thus, it can serve as a perfect hedge.
- The efficient frontier of risky assets is the graphical representation of the set of portfolios that maximizes portfolio expected return for a given level of portfolio standard deviation. Rational investors will choose a portfolio on the efficient frontier.
- A portfolio manager identifies the efficient frontier by first establishing estimates for the expected returns and standard deviations and determining the correlations among them. The input data are then fed into an optimization program that produces the investment proportions, expected returns, and standard deviations of the portfolios on the efficient frontier.
- In general, portfolio managers will identify different efficient portfolios because of differences in the methods and quality of security analysis. Managers compete on the quality of their security analysis relative to their management fees.
- If a risk-free asset is available and input data are identical, all investors will choose the same portfolio on the efficient frontier, the one that is tangent to the CAL. All investors with identical input data will hold the identical risky portfolio, differing only in how much each allocates to this optimal portfolio and to the risk-free asset. This result is characterized as the separation principle of portfolio selection.
- The single-index representation of a single-factor security market expresses the excess rate of return on a security as a function of the market excess return: $R_i = \alpha_i + \beta_i R_M + e_i$. This equation also can be interpreted as a regression of the security excess return on the market-index excess return. The regression line has intercept α_i and slope β_i and is called the security characteristic line.
- In a single-index model, the variance of the rate of return on a security or portfolio can be decomposed into systematic and firm-specific risk. The systematic component of variance equals β^2 times the variance of the market excess return. The firm-specific component is the variance of the residual term in the index model equation.
- The beta of a portfolio is the weighted average of the betas of the component securities. A security with negative beta reduces the portfolio beta, thereby reducing exposure to market volatility. The unique risk of a portfolio approaches zero as the portfolio becomes more highly diversified.

KEY TERMS

beta, 193	investment opportunity set, 178	security characteristic line, 195
diversifiable risk, 171	market risk, 170	separation property, 192
efficient frontier, 189	nondiversifiable risk, 170	systematic risk, 170
excess return, 193	nonsystematic risk, 171	unique risk, 171
factor model, 192	optimal risky portfolio, 185	
firm-specific risk, 171		
index model, 194		

PROBLEM SETS

1. A three-asset portfolio has the following characteristics:

Asset	Expected Return	Standard Deviation	Weight
X	15%	22%	0.50
Y	10	8	0.40
Z	6	3	0.10

What is the expected return on this three-asset portfolio?

2. An investor is considering adding another investment to a portfolio. To achieve the maximum diversification benefits, the investor should add, if possible, an investment that has which of the following correlation coefficients with the other investments in the portfolio?
   a. −1.0
   b. −0.5
   c. 0.0
   d. +1.0

3. Consistent with capital market theory, systematic risk:
   i. Refers to the variability in all risky assets caused by macroeconomic and other aggregate market-related variables.
   ii. Is measured by the coefficient of variation of returns on the market portfolio.
   iii. Refers to nondiversifiable risk.
   a. i only
   b. ii only
   c. i and iii only
   d. ii and iii only

4. Suppose that the returns on the stock fund presented in Spreadsheet 6.1 were −14%, 13%, and +30% in the three scenarios.
   a. Would you expect the mean return and variance of the stock fund to be more than, less than, or equal to the values computed in Spreadsheet 6.2? Why?
   b. Calculate the new values of mean return and variance for the stock fund using a format similar to Spreadsheet 6.2. Confirm your intuition from part (a).
   c. Calculate the new value of the covariance between the stock and bond funds using a format similar to Spreadsheet 6.4. Explain intuitively why covariance has increased.

5. Use the rate of return data for the stock and bond funds presented in Spreadsheet 6.1, but now assume that the probability of each scenario is: Recession: 0.4; Normal: 0.2; Boom: 0.4.
   a. Would you expect the mean return and variance of the stock fund to be more than, less than, or equal to the values computed in Spreadsheet 6.2? Why?
   b. Calculate the new values of mean return and variance for the stock fund using a format similar to Spreadsheet 6.2. Confirm your intuition from part (a).
   c. Calculate the new value of the covariance between the stock and bond funds using a format similar to Spreadsheet 6.4. Explain intuitively why the absolute value of the covariance has increased.

The following data apply to problems 6–10.

A pension fund manager is considering three mutual funds. The first is a stock fund, the second is a long-term government and corporate bond fund, and the third is a T-bill money market fund that yields a sure rate of 5.5%. The probability distributions of the risky funds are:

	Expected Return	Standard Deviation
Stock fund (S)	15%	32%
Bond fund (B)	9	23

The correlation between the fund returns is 0.15.

6. Tabulate and draw the investment opportunity set of the two risky funds. Use investment proportions for the stock fund of 0 to 100% in increments of 20%. What expected return and standard deviation does your graph show for the minimum variance portfolio?

7. Draw a tangent from the risk-free rate to the opportunity set. What does your graph show for the expected return and standard deviation of the optimal risky portfolio?

8. What is the reward-to-variability ratio of the best feasible CAL?

9. Suppose now that your portfolio must yield an expected return of 12% and be efficient, that is, on the best feasible CAL.
   a. What is the standard deviation of your portfolio?
   b. What is the proportion invested in the T-bill fund and each of the two risky funds?

10. If you were to use only the two risky funds and still require an expected return of 12%, what would be the investment proportions of your portfolio? Compare its standard deviation to that of the optimal portfolio in the previous problem. What do you conclude?

11. Stocks offer an expected rate of return of 10% with a standard deviation of 20% and gold offers an expected return of 5% with a standard deviation of 25%.
   a. In light of the apparent inferiority of gold to stocks with respect to both mean return and volatility, would anyone hold gold? If so, demonstrate graphically why one would do so.
   b. How would you answer (*a*) if the correlation coefficient between gold and stocks were 1.0? Draw a graph illustrating why one would or would not hold gold. Could these expected returns, standard deviations, and correlation represent an equilibrium for the security market?

12. Suppose that many stocks are traded in the market and that it is possible to borrow at the risk-free rate, r_f. The characteristics of two of the stocks are as follows:

Stock	Expected Return	Standard Deviation
A	8%	40%
B	13	60
Correlation = -1		

Could the equilibrium r_f be greater than 10%? (Hint: Can a particular stock portfolio be substituted for the risk-free asset?)

13. Assume expected returns and standard deviations for all securities, as well as the risk-free rate for lending and borrowing, are known. Will investors arrive at the same optimal risky portfolio? Explain.

14. Your assistant gives you the following diagram as the efficient frontier of the group of stocks you asked him to analyze. The diagram looks a bit odd, but your assistant insists he got the diagram from his analysis. Would you trust him? Is it possible to get such a diagram?

15. What is the relationship of the portfolio standard deviation to the weighted average of the standard deviations of the component assets?

16. A project has a 0.7 chance of doubling your investment in a year and a 0.3 chance of halving your investment in a year. What is the standard deviation of the rate of return on this investment?

17. Investors expect the market rate of return this year to be 10%. The expected rate of return on a stock with a beta of 1.2 is currently 12%. If the market return this year turns out to be 8%, how would you revise your expectation of the rate of return on the stock?

18. The following figure shows plots of monthly rates of return and the stock market for two stocks.
    a. Which stock is riskiest to an investor currently holding her portfolio in a diversified portfolio of common stock?
    b. Which stock is riskiest to an undiversified investor who puts all of his funds in only one of these stocks?

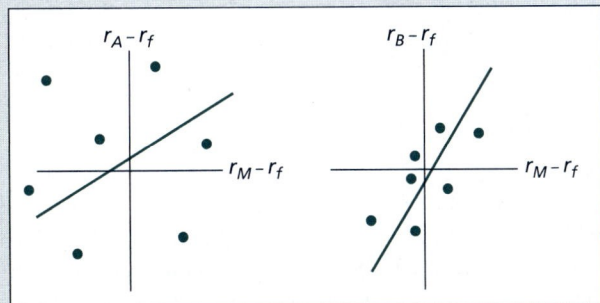

19. Here are rates of return for six months for Generic Risk, Inc. What is Generic's beta?
    (Hint: Find the answer by plotting the scatter diagram.)

Month	Market Return	Generic Return
1	0%	+2%
2	0	0
3	−1	0
4	−1	−2
5	+1	+4
6	+1	+2

The following data apply to problems 20–22:

Hennessy & Associates manages a $30 million equity portfolio for the multimanager Wilstead Pension Fund. Jason Jones, financial vice president of Wilstead, noted that Hennessy had rather consistently achieved the best record among the Wilstead's six equity managers. Performance of the Hennessy portfolio had been clearly superior to that of the S&P 500 in four of the past five years. In the one less favorable year, the shortfall was trivial.

Hennessy is a "bottom-up" manager. The firm largely avoids any attempt to "time the market." It also focuses on selection of individual stocks, rather than the weighting of favored industries.

There is no apparent conformity of style among the six equity managers. The five managers, other than Hennessy, manage portfolios aggregating $250 million, made up of more than 150 individual issues.

Jones is convinced that Hennessy is able to apply superior skill to stock selection, but the favorable results are limited by the high degree of diversification in the portfolio. Over the years, the portfolio generally held 40–50 stocks, with about 2% to 3% of total funds committed to each issue. The reason Hennessy seemed to do well most years was because the firm was able to identify each year 10 or 12 issues that registered particularly large gains.

Based on this overview, Jones outlined the following plan to the Wilstead pension committee:

> Let's tell Hennessy to limit the portfolio to no more than 20 stocks. Hennessy will double the commitments to the stocks that it really favors and eliminate the remainder. Except for this one new restriction, Hennessy should be free to manage the portfolio exactly as before.

All the members of the pension committee generally supported Jones's proposal, because all agreed that Hennessy had seemed to demonstrate superior skill in selecting stocks. Yet, the proposal was a considerable departure from previous practice, and several committee members raised questions.

20. Answer the following:
    a. Will the limitation of 20 stocks likely increase or decrease the risk of the portfolio? Explain.
    b. Is there any way Hennessy could reduce the number of issues from 40 to 20 without significantly affecting risk? Explain.

21. One committee member was particularly enthusiastic concerning Jones's proposal. He suggested that Hennessy's performance might benefit further from reduction in the number of issues to 10. If the reduction to 20 could be expected to be advantageous, explain why reduction to 10 might be less likely to be advantageous. (Assume that

Wilstead will evaluate the Hennessy portfolio independently of the other portfolios in the fund.)

22. Another committee member suggested that, rather than evaluate each managed portfolio independently of other portfolios, it might be better to consider the effects of a change in the Hennessy portfolio on the total fund. Explain how this broader point of view could affect the committee decision to limit the holdings in the Hennessy portfolio to either 10 or 20 issues.

23. What percent of the variance of stock ABC in Example 6.4 is systematic (market) risk?

STANDARD & POOR'S

1. Go to www.mhhe.com/edumarketinsight. Use data from Market Insight to calculate the beta of Apple Computer (AAPL). Start by copying the daily price changes of Apple and the S&P 500 (Daily Adjusted Prices Report) into Excel, calculating the daily rate of return for each of the series, and then calculating a regression with Apple's return as the dependent variable and the S&P 500 return as the explanatory variable. Calculate beta using daily beta over a period of one month and repeat for several months. How stable is the beta estimate?

2. You can also calculate betas using monthly data from the *Monthly Valuation Data* report in Market Insight. Calculate beta using 2 years of monthly data, and repeat for different periods. Are the 2-year betas more stable than the one month betas computed in question 1? What are the trade-offs that an analyst might consider in using beta computed from long-term versus short-term data sets?

STANDARD
&POOR'S

WEBMASTER

Returns, Risk, and Correlations

Go to www.mhhe.com/edumarketinsight. Pull the monthly returns for General Electric, The Home Depot, Johnson & Johnson, Honeywell, and H.J. Heinz. Merge the returns for these five firms into a single Excel workbook, with the returns for each company properly aligned.

Then,

1. Using the Excel functions for average and standard deviation (sample), calculate the average and standard deviation for each of the firms.

2. Using the correlation function, construct the correlation matrix for the five funds based on their monthly returns for the entire period. What are the lowest and highest individual pair of correlation coefficients?

1. Recalculation of Spreadsheets 6.1, 6.2, and 6.4 shows that the correlation coefficient with the new rates of return is $-.98$.

	A	B	C	D	E	F
1			Stock Fund		Bond Fund	
2	Scenario	Probability	Rate of Return	Col. B × Col. C	Rate of Return	Col. B × Col. E
3	Recession	0.3	-12	-3.6	10	3
4	Normal	0.4	10	4	7	2.8
5	Boom	0.3	28	8.4	2	0.6
6	Expected or Mean Return		SUM:	8.8	SUM:	6.4
7						
8						
9			Stock Fund		Bond Fund	
10			Squared Deviations from Mean	Col. B × Col. C	Squared Deviations from Mean	Col. B × Col. E
11	Scenario	Probability				
12	Recession	0.3	432.64	129.792	12.96	3.888
13	Normal	0.4	1.44	0.576	0.36	0.144
14	Boom	0.3	368.64	110.592	19.36	5.808
15			Variance = SUM:	240.96	SUM:	9.84
16			Std Dev = √Variance	15.52		3.14
17						
18			Deviation from Mean Return		Covariance	
19	Scenario	Probability	Stock Fund	Bond Fund	Product of Dev	Col. B × Col. E
20	Recession	0.3	-20.8	3.6	-74.88	-22.464
21	Normal	0.4	1.2	0.6	0.72	0.288
22	Boom	0.3	19.2	-4.4	-84.48	-25.344
23				Covariance:	SUM:	-47.52
24	Correlation coefficient = Covariance/(StdDev(stocks)*StdDev(bonds)):					-0.98

2. *a.* Using Equation 6.3 with the data: $\sigma_B = 12$; $\sigma_S = 25$; $w_B = 0.5$; and $w_S = 1 - w_B = 0.5$, we obtain the equation

$$\sigma_P^2 = 15^2 = (w_B\sigma_B)^2 + (w_S\sigma_S)^2 + 2(w_B\sigma_B)(w_S\sigma_S)\rho_{BS}$$

$$= (0.5 \times 12)^2 + (0.5 \times 25)^2 + 2(0.5 \times 12)(0.5 \times 25)\rho_{BS}$$

which yields $\rho = 0.2183$.

b. Using Equation 6.2 and the additional data: $E(r_B) = 6$; $E(r_S) = 10$, we obtain

$$E(r_P) = w_BE(r_B) + w_SE(r_S) = (0.5 \times 6) + (0.5 \times 10) = 8\%$$

c. On the one hand, you should be happier with a correlation of 0.2183 than with 0.22 since the lower correlation implies greater benefits from diversification and means that, for any level of expected return, there will be lower risk. On the other hand, the constraint that you must hold 50% of the portfolio in bonds represents a cost to you since it prevents you from choosing the risk-return trade-off most suited to your tastes. Unless you would choose to hold about 50% of the portfolio in bonds anyway, you are better off with the slightly higher correlation but with the ability to choose your own portfolio weights.

3. The scatter diagrams for pairs B–E are shown below. Scatter diagram A shows an exact conflict between the pattern of points 1,2,3 versus 3,4,5. Therefore the correlation coefficient is zero. Scatter diagram B shows perfect positive correlation (1.0). Similarly, C shows perfect negative correlation (-1.0). Now compare the scatters of D and E. Both show a general positive correlation, but scatter D is tighter. Therefore D is associated with a correlation of about .5 (use a spreadsheet to show that the exact correlation is .54) and E is associated with a correlation of about .2 (show that the exact correlation coefficient is .23).

	A	B	C	D	E	F	G
5		Data	X	M	T-Bills		
6		Mean (%)	15	10	5		
7		Std. Dev. (%)	50	20	0		
8		Corr. Coeff. X and S		-0.20			
9		Portfolio Opportunity set					
10		Weight in X	Weight in S	Pf Mean (%)	Pf Std Dev (%)		
11		-1.00	2.00	5.00	70.00		
12		-0.90	1.90	5.50	64.44		
13		-0.80	1.80	6.00	58.92		
14		-0.70	1.70	6.50	53.45	=B13*$C$6+C13*$D$6	
15		-0.60	1.60	7.00	48.04		
16		-0.50	1.50	7.50	42.72		
17		-0.40	1.40	8.00	37.52		
18		-0.30	1.30	8.50	32.51	=(B15^2*$C$7^2	
19		-0.20	1.20	9.00	27.78	+C15^2*$D$7^2	
20		-0.10	1.10	9.50	23.52	+2*B15*C15	
21		0.00	1.00	10.00	20.00	*$C$7*$D$7*$D$8)^0.5	
22		0.10	0.90	10.50	17.69		
23		0.20	0.80	11.00	17.09		
24		0.30	0.70	11.50	18.36		
25		0.40	0.60	12.00	21.17		
26		0.50	0.50	12.50	25.00		
27		0.60	0.40	13.00	29.46		
28		0.70	0.30	13.50	34.31		
29		0.80	0.20	14.00	39.40		
30		0.90	0.10	14.50	44.64		
31		1.00	0.00	15.00	50.00		
32		1.10	-0.10	15.50	55.43		
33		1.20	-0.20	16.00	60.93		
34		1.30	-0.30	16.50	66.46		
35		1.40	-0.40	17.00	72.03		
36		1.50	-0.50	17.50	77.62		
37		1.60	-0.60	18.00	83.23		
38		1.70	-0.70	18.50	88.87		
39		1.80	-0.80	19.00	94.51		
40		1.90	-0.90	19.50	100.16		
41		2.00	-1.00	20.00	105.83		
42	Min. Var Pf	0.18	0.82	10.91	17.06		
43	Optimal Pf	0.26	0.74	11.28	17.59		
44							
45				Formula in fn3 Chapter 7			
46		=((C6-E6)*D7^2-(D6-E6)*C7*D7*D8)/					
47		((C6-E6)*D7^2+(D6-E6)*C7^2-(C6-E6+D6-E6)*C7*D7*D8)					
48							
49							

4. *a.* Implementing Equations 6.2 and 6.3 we generate data for the graph. See the spreadsheet above.
   b. Implementing the formulas indicated in the following spreadsheet we generate the optimal risky portfolio (*O*) and the minimum variance portfolio.
   c. The slope of the CAL is equal to the risk premium of the optimal risky portfolio divided by its standard deviation, $(11.28 - 5)/17.59 = .357$.
   d. The mean of the complete portfolio $.2222 \times 11.28 + .7778 \times 5 = 6.40\%$ and its standard deviation is $.2222 \times 17.58 = 3.91\%$.
   The composition of the complete portfolio is
   $.2222 \times .26 = .06$ (i.e., 6%) in X
   $.2222 \times .74 = .16$ (i.e., 16%) in M
   and 78% in T-bills.

5. Efficient frontiers derived by portfolio managers depend on forecasts of the rates of return on various securities and estimates of risk, that is, standard deviations and correlation coefficients. The forecasts themselves do not control outcomes. Thus, to prefer a manager with a rosier forecast (northwesterly frontier) is tantamount to rewarding the bearers of good news and punishing the

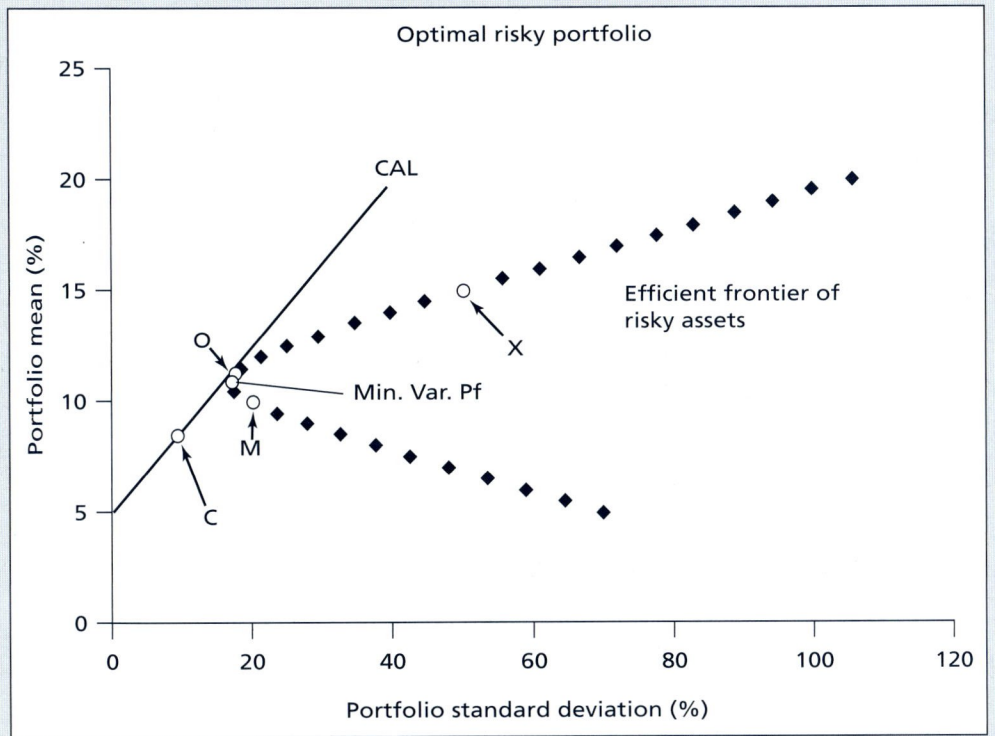

bearers of bad news. What the investor wants is to reward bearers of *accurate* news. Investors should monitor forecasts of portfolio managers on a regular basis to develop a track record of their forecasting accuracy. Portfolio choices of the more accurate forecasters will, in the long run, outperform the field.

6. *a.* Beta, the slope coefficient of the security on the factor: Securities R_1–R_6 have a positive beta. These securities move, on average, in the same direction as the market (R_M). R_1, R_2, R_6 have large betas, so they are "aggressive" in that they carry more systematic risk than R_3, R_4, R_5, which are "defensive." R_7 and R_8 have a negative beta. These are hedge assets that carry negative systematic risk.

   b. Intercept, the expected return when the market is neutral: The estimates show that R_1, R_4, R_8 have a positive intercept, while R_2, R_3, R_5, R_6, R_7 have negative intercepts. To the extent that one believes these intercepts will persist, a positive value is preferred.

   c. Residual variance, the nonsystematic risk: R_2, R_3, R_7 have a relatively low residual variance. With sufficient diversification, residual risk eventually will be eliminated, and hence, the difference in the residual variance is of little economic significance.

   d. Total variance, the sum of systematic and nonsystematic risk: R_3 has a low beta and low residual variance, so its total variance will be low. R_1, R_6 have high betas and high residual variance, so their total variance will be high. But R_4 has a low beta and high residual variance, while R_2 has a high beta with a low residual variance. In sum, total variance often will misrepresent systematic risk, which is the part that matters.

7. *a.* To obtain the characteristic line of XYZ we continue the spreadsheet of Example 6.4 and run a regression of the excess return of XYZ on the excess return of the market index fund.

www.mhhe.com/bkm

	Summary Output

Regression Statistics	
Multiple R	0.363
R Square	0.132
Adjusted R Square	0.023
Standard Error	41.839
Observations	10

	Coefficients	Standard Error	t Stat	P-value	Lower 95%	Upper 95%
Intercept	3.930	14.98	0.262	0.800	−30.62	38.48
Market	0.582	0.528	1.103	0.302	−0.635	1.798

The regression output shows that the slope coefficient of XYZ is .58 and the intercept is 3.93%, hence the characteristic line is: $R_{XYZ} = 3.93 + .582R_{Market}$.

b. The beta coefficient of ABC is 1.15, greater than XYZ's .58, implying that ABC has greater systematic risk.

c. The regression of XYZ on the market index shows an R-Square of .132. Hence the percent of unexplained variance (nonsystematic risk) is .868, or 86.8%.

Appendix

THE FALLACY OF TIME DIVERSIFICATION

RISK POOLING VERSUS RISK SHARING

Suppose the probability of death within a year of a healthy 35-year-old is 5%. If we treat the event of death as a zero-one random variable, the standard deviation is 21.79%. In a group of 1,000 healthy 35-year-olds, we expect 50 deaths within a year (5% of the sample), with a standard deviation of 6.89 deaths (.689%). Measured by the mean-standard deviation criterion, the life insurance business apparently becomes less risky the more policies an insurer can write. This is the concept of **risk pooling.**

However, the apparent risk reduction from pooling many policies is really a fallacy; risk is not always appropriately measured by standard deviation. The complication in this case is that insuring more people puts more capital at risk. The owners of a small insurance company may be unwilling to take the increasing risk of ruin that would be incurred by insuring very large groups of clients.

What really makes the insurance industry tick is *risk sharing*. When an insurer sells more policies, it can also bring in more partners. Each partner then takes a smaller share of the growing pie, thus obtaining the benefits of diversification without scaling up the amount of capital put at risk.

To reiterate, the reason that risk pooling alone does not improve the welfare of an investor (insurer) is that the size of the capital at risk, that is, total risk, is increasing. Risk-averse investors will shy away from a large degree of risk pooling unless they can share the risk of a growing pool with other investors, thereby keeping the size of their investment relatively stable.

Risk sharing is analogous to portfolio investment. You take a *fixed* budget and by investing it in many risky assets, that is, investing small proportions in various assets, you lower the risk without giving up expected returns.

> **risk pooling**
> Lowering the variance of returns by combining risky projects.

> **risk sharing**
> Lowering the risk per invested dollar by selling shares to investors.

TIME DIVERSIFICATION

A related version of the risk pooling versus sharing misconception is "time diversification." Consider the case of Mr. Frier. Planning to retire in five years, he has a five-year horizon. Confronted with the fact that the standard deviation of stock returns exceeds 20% per year,

Mr. Frier has become aware of his acute risk aversion and is keeping most of his retirement portfolio in money market assets.

Recently, Mr. Frier has learned of the large potential gains from diversification. He wonders whether investing for as long as five years might not take the standard deviation sting out of stocks without giving up expected return.

Mr. Mavin, a highly recommended financial adviser, argues that the time factor is all-important. He cites academic research showing that asset rates of return over successive holding periods are nearly independent. Therefore, he argues that over a five-year period, returns in good years and bad years will cancel out, making the average rate of return on the portfolio over the investment period less risky than would appear from an analysis of single-year volatility. Because returns in each year are nearly independent, Mr. Mavin tells Mr. Frier that a five-year investment is equivalent to a portfolio of five equally weighted, independent assets.

Mr. Frier is convinced and intends to transfer his funds to a stock mutual fund right away. Is his conviction warranted? Does Mr. Mavin's time diversification really reduce risk?

It is true that the standard deviation of the *average* annual rate of return over the five years will be smaller than the one-year standard deviations, as Mr. Mavin claims. But what about the volatility of Mr. Frier's total retirement fund?

Mr. Mavin is wrong: Time diversification does not reduce risk. While it is true that the per-year *average* rate of return has a smaller standard deviation for a longer time horizon, it is also true that the uncertainty compounds over a greater number of years. Unfortunately, this latter effect dominates; that is, the total T-year return becomes more uncertain the longer the investment horizon (T years).

Investing for more than one holding period means total risk is growing. This is analogous to an insurer taking on more insurance policies. The fact that these policies are independent does not offset the effect of placing more funds at risk. Focus on the standard deviation of the *average* rate of return should never obscure the more proper emphasis on the ultimate dollar value of a portfolio strategy. Indeed, insuring a portfolio to guarantee a minimum T-year return equal to a money market fund rate will cost you more as T grows longer. This is an empirically verifiable fact that is well anchored in economic theory.

There may in fact be good reasons for the commonly accepted belief that younger investors with longer investment horizons should invest higher fractions of their portfolios in risky assets with higher expected returns, such as stocks. For example, if things go wrong, there is more time to spread out the burden and recover from the loss. But the rationale for these investors to direct their funds to the stock market should not be that the stock market is less risky if one's investment horizon is longer.

7

CAPITAL ASSET PRICING AND ARBITRAGE PRICING THEORY

AFTER STUDYING THIS CHAPTER YOU SHOULD BE ABLE TO:

> Use the implications of capital market theory to compute security risk premiums.

> Construct and use the security market line.

> Take advantage of an arbitrage opportunity with a portfolio that includes mispriced securities.

> Use arbitrage pricing theory with more than one factor to identify mispriced securities.

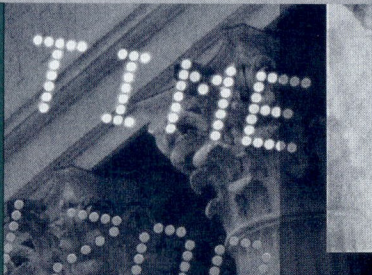

The capital asset pricing model, almost always referred to as the CAPM, is a centerpiece of modern financial economics. It was first proposed by William F. Sharpe, who was awarded the 1990 Nobel Prize for economics.

The CAPM provides a precise prediction of the relationship we should observe between the risk of an asset and its expected return. This relationship serves two vital functions.

First, it provides a benchmark rate of return for evaluating possible investments. For example, a security analyst might want to know whether the expected return she forecasts for a stock is more or less than its "fair" return given its risk. Second, the model helps us make an educated guess as to the expected return on assets that have not yet been traded in the marketplace. For example, how do we price an initial public offering of stock? How will a major new investment project affect the return investors require on a company's stock? Although the CAPM does not fully withstand empirical tests, it is widely used because of the insight it offers and because its accuracy suffices for many important applications.

The exploitation of security mispricing to earn risk-free economic profits is called *arbitrage*. It typically involves the simultaneous purchase and sale of equivalent securities (often in different markets) in order to profit from discrepancies in their price relationship.

The most basic principle of capital market theory is that equilibrium market prices should rule out arbitrage opportunities. If actual security prices allow for arbitrage, the resulting opportunities for profitable trading will lead to strong pressure on security prices that will persist until equilibrium is restored. Only a few investors need be aware of arbitrage opportunities to bring about a large volume of trades, and these trades will bring prices back into alignment. Therefore, no-arbitrage restrictions on security prices are extremely powerful. The implications of no-arbitrage principles for financial economics were first explored by Modigliani and Miller, both Nobel Laureates (1985 and 1990).

TABLE **7.1**		BU	TD
Share prices and market values of Bottom Up (BU) and Top Down (TD)	Price per share ($)	39.00	39.00
	Shares outstanding	5,000,000	4,000,000
	Market value ($ millions)	195	156

The Arbitrage Pricing Theory (APT) developed by Stephen Ross uses a no-arbitrage argument to derive the same relationship between expected return and risk as the CAPM. We explore the risk-return relationship using well-diversified portfolios and discuss the similarities and differences between the APT and the CAPM.

7.1 DEMAND FOR STOCKS AND EQUILIBRIUM PRICES

So far we have been concerned with efficient diversification, the optimal risky portfolio, and its risk-return profile. We haven't had much to say about how expected returns are determined in a competitive securities market. To understand how market equilibrium is formed we must connect the determination of optimal portfolios with security analysis and actual buy/sell transactions of investors. We will show in this section how the quest for efficient diversification leads to a demand schedule for shares. In turn, the supply and demand for shares determine equilibrium prices and expected rates of return.

Imagine a simple world with only two corporations: Bottom Up Inc. (BU) and Top Down Inc. (TD). Stock prices and market values are shown in Table 7.1. Investors can also invest in a money market fund (MMF) that yields a risk-free interest rate of 5%.

Sigma Fund is a new actively managed mutual fund that has raised $220 million to invest in the stock market. The security analysis staff of Sigma believes that neither BU nor TD will grow in the future and, therefore, each firm will pay level annual dividends for the foreseeable future. This is a useful simplifying assumption because, if a stock is expected to pay a stream of level dividends, the income derived from each share is a perpetuity. The present value of each share—often called the *intrinsic value* of the share—equals the dividend divided by the appropriate discount rate. A summary of the report of the security analysts appears in Table 7.2.

The expected returns in Table 7.2 are based on the assumption that next year's dividends will conform to Sigma's forecasts, and share prices will be equal to intrinsic values at year-end. The standard deviations and the correlation coefficient between the two stocks were estimated by Sigma's security analysts from past returns and assumed to remain at these levels for the coming year.

Using these data and assumptions Sigma easily generates the efficient frontier shown in Figure 7.1 and computes the optimal portfolio proportions corresponding to the tangency portfolio. These proportions, combined with the total investment budget, yield the Fund's buy orders. With a budget of $220 million, Sigma wants a position in BU of $220,000,000 × .8070 = $177,540,000, or $177,540,000/39 = 4,552,308 shares, and a position in TD of $220,000,000 × .1930 = $42,460,000, which corresponds to 1,088,718 shares.

Sigma's Demand for Shares

The expected rates of return that Sigma used to derive its demand for shares of BU and TD were computed from the forecast of year-end stock prices and the current prices. If, say, a share of BU could be purchased at a lower price, Sigma's forecast of the rate of return on BU would be higher. Conversely, if BU shares were selling at a higher price, expected returns would be lower. A new expected return would result in a different optimal portfolio and a different demand for shares.

TABLE **7.2**

Capital market expectations of Sigma's portfolio manager and optimal portfolio weights

	BU	TD
Expected annual dividend ($/share)	6.40	3.80
Discount rate = Required return* (%)	16	10
Expected end-of-year price† ($/share)	40	38
Current price	39	39
Expected return (%): Dividend yield (div/price)	16.41	9.74
Capital gain $(P_1 - P_0)/P_0$	2.56	−2.56
Total rate of return	18.97	7.18
Standard deviation of rate of return (%)	40	20
Correlation coefficient between BU and TD (ρ)	.20	
Risk-free rate (%)	5	
Optimal portfolio weight‡	.8070	.1930

*Based on assessment of risk.

†Obtained by discounting the dividend perpetuity at the required rate of return.

‡Using footnote 3 of Chapter 6, we obtain the weight in BU as

$$w_{BU} = \frac{[E(r_{BU}) - r_f]\sigma_{TD}^2 - [E(r_{TD}) - r_f]\sigma_{BU}\sigma_{TD}\rho}{[E(r_{BU}) - r_f]\sigma_{TD}^2 + [E(r_{TD}) - r_f]\sigma_{BU}^2 - [E(r_{BU}) - r_f + E(r_{TD}) - r_f]\sigma_{BU}\sigma_{TD}\rho}$$

The weight in TD equals $1.0 - w_{BU}$.

FIGURE **7.1**

Sigma's efficient frontier and optimal portfolio

We can think of Sigma's demand schedule for a stock as the number of shares Sigma would want to hold at different share prices. In our simplified world, producing the demand for BU

TABLE **7.3**
Calculation of Sigma's demand for BU shares

Current Price ($)	Capital Gain (%)	Dividend Yield (%)	Expected Return (%)	BU Optimal Proportion	Desired BU Shares
45.0	−11.11	14.22	3.11	−.4113	−2,010,582
42.5	−5.88	15.06	9.18	.3192	1,652,482
40.0	0	16.00	16.00	.7011	3,856,053
37.5	6.67	17.07	23.73	.9358	5,490,247
35.0	14.29	18.29	32.57	1.0947	6,881,225

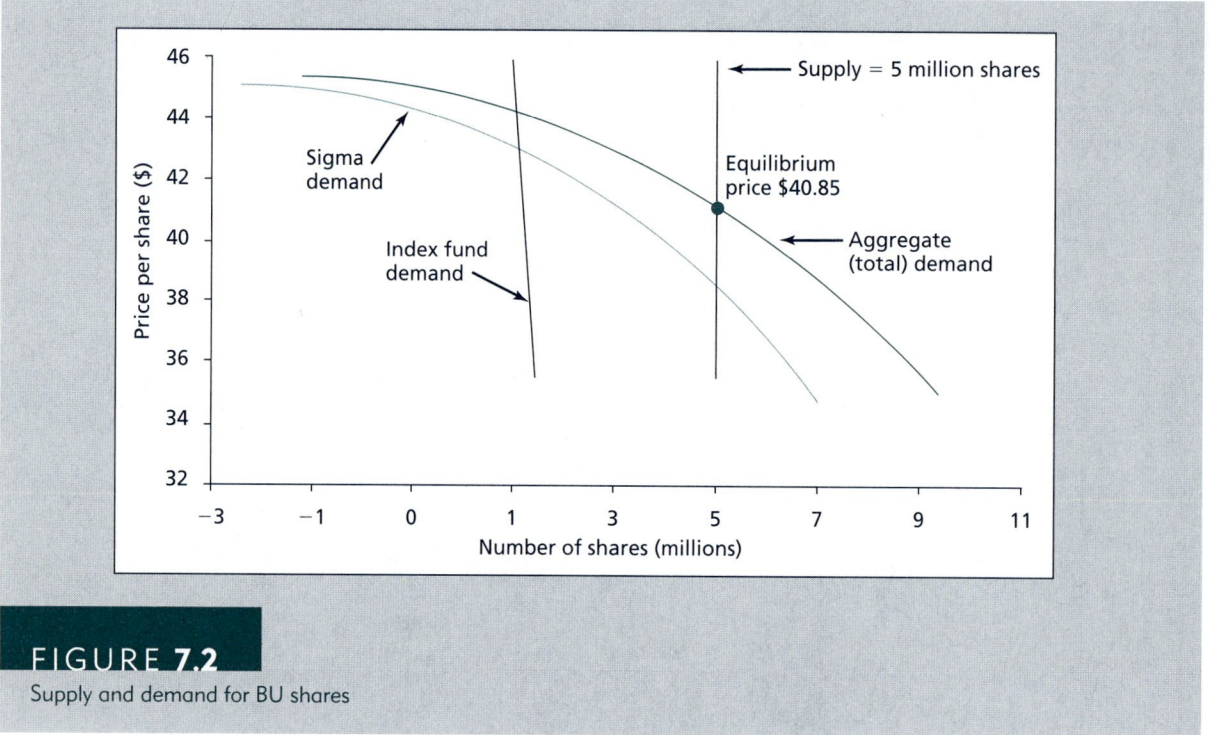

FIGURE **7.2**
Supply and demand for BU shares

shares is not difficult. First, we revise Table 7.2 to recompute the expected return on BU at different current prices given the forecasted year-end price. Then, for each price and associated expected return, we construct the optimal portfolio and find the implied position in BU. A few samples of these calculations are shown in Table 7.3. The first four columns in Table 7.3 show the expected returns on BU shares given their current price. The optimal proportion (column 5) is calculated using these expected returns. Finally, Sigma's investment budget, the optimal proportion in BU, and the current price of a BU share determine the desired number of shares. Note that we compute the demand for BU shares given the price and expected return for TD. This means that the entire demand schedule must be revised whenever the price and expected return on TD are changed.

FIGURE 7.3

Supply and demand for TD shares

Sigma's demand curve for BU stock is given by the Desired Shares column in Table 7.3 and is plotted in Figure 7.2. Notice that the demand curve for the stock slopes downward. When BU's stock price falls, Sigma will desire more shares for two reasons: (1) an income effect—at a lower price Sigma can purchase more shares with the same budget—and (2) a substitution effect—the increased expected return at the lower price will make BU shares more attractive relative to TD shares. Notice that one can desire a negative number of shares, that is, a short position. If the stock price is high enough, its expected return will be so low that the desire to sell will overwhelm diversification motives and investors will want to take a short position. Figure 7.2 shows that when the price exceeds $44, Sigma wants a short position in BU.

The demand curve for BU shares assumes that the price of TD remains constant. A similar demand curve can be constructed for TD shares given a price for BU shares. As before, we would generate the demand for TD shares by revising Table 7.2 for various current prices of TD, leaving the price of BU unchanged. We use the revised expected returns to calculate the optimal portfolio for each possible price of TD, ultimately obtaining the demand curve shown in Figure 7.3.

Index Funds' Demands for Stock

We will see shortly that index funds play an important role in portfolio selection, so let's see how an index fund would derive its demand for shares. Suppose that $130 million of investor funds in our hypothesized economy are given to an index fund—named Index—to manage. What will it do?

Index is looking for a portfolio that will mimic the market. Suppose current prices and market values are as in Table 7.1. Then the required proportions to mimic the market portfolio are:

$$w_{BU} = 195/(195 + 156) = .5556 \, (55.56\%); \quad w_{TD} = 1 - .5556 = .4444 \, (44.44\%)$$

With $130 million to invest, Index will place .5556 × $130 million = $72.22 million in BU shares. Table 7.4 shows a few other points on Index's demand curve for BU shares. The second column of the table shows the proportion of BU in total stock market value at each assumed price. In our two-stock example, this is BU's value as a fraction of the combined value of BU and TD. The third column is Index's desired dollar investment in BU and the last column shows shares demanded. The bold row corresponds to the case we analyzed in Table 7.1, for which BU is selling at $39.

Index's demand curve for BU shares is plotted in Figure 7.2 next to Sigma's demand, and in Figure 7.3 for TD shares. Index's demand is smaller than Sigma's because its budget is smaller. Moreover, the demand curve of the index fund is very steep, or "inelastic," that is, demand hardly responds to price changes. This is because an index fund's demand for shares does not respond to expected returns. Index funds seek only to replicate market proportions. As the stock price goes up, so does its proportion in the market. This leads the index fund to invest more in the stock. Nevertheless, because each share costs more, the fund will desire fewer shares.

Equilibrium Prices and the Capital Asset Pricing Model

Market prices are determined by supply and demand. At any one time, the supply of shares of a stock is fixed, so supply is vertical at 5,000,000 shares of BU in Figure 7.2 and 4,000,000 shares of TD in Figure 7.3. Market demand is obtained by "horizontal aggregation," that is, for each price we add up the quantity demanded by all investors. You can examine the horizontal aggregation of the demand curves of Sigma and Index in Figures 7.2 and 7.3. The equilibrium prices are at the intersection of supply and demand.

However, the prices shown in Figures 7.2 and 7.3 will likely not persist for more than an instant. The reason is that the equilibrium price of BU ($40.85) was generated by demand curves derived by assuming that the price of TD was $39. Similarly, the equilibrium price of TD ($38.41) is an equilibrium price only when BU is at $39, which also is not the case. A full equilibrium would require that the demand curves derived for each stock be consistent with the actual prices of all other stocks. Thus, our model is only a beginning. But it does illustrate the important link between security analysis and the process by which portfolio demands, market prices, and expected returns are jointly determined.

In the next section we will introduce the capital asset pricing model, which treats the problem of finding a set of mutually consistent equilibrium prices and expected rates of return across all stocks. When we argue there that market expected returns adjust to demand pressures, you will understand the process that underlies this adjustment.

TABLE **7.4** Calculation of index demand for BU shares	Current Price	BU Market-Value Proportion	Dollar Investment* ($ million)	Shares Desired
	$45.00	.5906	76.772	1,706,037
	42.50	.5767	74.966	1,763,908
	40.00	.5618	73.034	1,825,843
	39.00	**.5556**	**72.222**	**1,851,852**
	37.50	.5459	70.961	1,892,285
	35.00	.5287	68.731	1,963,746

*Dollar investment = BU proportion × $130 million.

7.2 THE CAPITAL ASSET PRICING MODEL

The **capital asset pricing model,** or **CAPM,** was developed by Treynor, Sharpe, Lintner, and Mossin in the early 1960s, and further refined later. The model predicts the relationship between the risk and equilibrium expected returns on risky assets. We will approach the CAPM in a simplified setting. Thinking about an admittedly unrealistic world allows a relatively easy leap to the solution. With this accomplished, we can add complexity to the environment, one step at a time, and see how the theory must be amended. This process allows us to develop a reasonably realistic and comprehensible model.

> **capital asset pricing model (CAPM)**
>
> A model that relates the required rate of return for a security to its risk as measured by beta.

A number of simplifying assumptions lead to the basic version of the CAPM. The fundamental idea is that individuals are as alike as possible, with the notable exceptions of initial wealth and risk aversion. The list of assumptions that describes the necessary conformity of investors follows:

1. Investors cannot affect prices by their individual trades. This means that there are many investors, each with an endowment of wealth that is small compared with the total endowment of all investors. This assumption is analogous to the perfect competition assumption of microeconomics.

2. All investors plan for one identical holding period.

3. Investors form portfolios from a universe of publicly traded financial assets, such as stocks and bonds, and have access to unlimited risk-free borrowing or lending opportunities.

4. Investors pay neither taxes on returns nor transaction costs (commissions and service charges) on trades in securities. In such a simple world, investors will not care about the difference between returns from capital gains and those from dividends.

5. All investors attempt to construct efficient frontier portfolios; that is, they are rational mean-variance optimizers.

6. All investors analyze securities in the same way and share the same economic view of the world. Hence, they all end with identical estimates of the probability distribution of future cash flows from investing in the available securities. This means that, given a set of security prices and the risk-free interest rate, all investors use the same expected returns, standard deviations, and correlations to generate the efficient frontier and the unique optimal risky portfolio. This assumption is called *homogeneous expectations*.

Obviously, these assumptions ignore many real-world complexities. However, they lead to some powerful insights into the nature of equilibrium in security markets.

Given these assumptions, we summarize the equilibrium that will prevail in this hypothetical world of securities and investors. We elaborate on these implications in the following sections.

1. All investors will choose to hold the **market portfolio (M),** which includes all assets of the security universe. For simplicity, we shall refer to all assets as stocks. The proportion of each stock in the market portfolio equals the market value of the stock (price per share times the number of shares outstanding) divided by the total market value of all stocks.

> **market portfolio**
>
> The portfolio for which each security is held in proportion to its market value.

2. The market portfolio will be on the efficient frontier. Moreover, it will be the optimal risky portfolio, the tangency point of the capital allocation line (CAL) to the efficient frontier. As a result, the capital market line (CML), the line from the risk-free rate through the market portfolio, *M,* is also the best attainable capital allocation line. All investors hold *M* as their optimal risky portfolio, differing only in the amount invested in it as compared to investment in the risk-free asset.

3. The risk premium on the market portfolio will be proportional to the variance of the market portfolio and investors' typical degree of risk aversion. Mathematically

$$E(r_M) - r_f = A^* \sigma_M^2 \tag{7.1}$$

where σ_M is the standard deviation of the return on the market portfolio and A^* is a scale factor representing the degree of risk aversion of the average investor.

4. The risk premium on individual assets will be proportional to the risk premium on the market portfolio (M) and to the *beta coefficient* of the security on the market portfolio. This implies that the rate of return on the market portfolio is the single factor of the security market. The beta measures the extent to which returns on the stock respond to the returns of the market portfolio. Formally, beta is the regression (slope) coefficient of the security return on the market portfolio return, representing the sensitivity of the stock return to fluctuations in the overall security market.

Why All Investors Would Hold the Market Portfolio

Given all our assumptions, it is easy to see why all investors hold identical risky portfolios. If all investors use identical mean-variance analysis (assumption 5), apply it to the same universe of securities (assumption 3), with an identical time horizon (assumption 2), use the same security analysis (assumption 6), and experience identical tax consequences (assumption 4), they all must arrive at the same determination of the optimal risky portfolio. That is, they all derive identical efficient frontiers and find the same tangency portfolio for the capital allocation line (CAL) from T-bills (the risk-free rate, with zero standard deviation) to that frontier, as in Figure 7.4.

With everyone choosing to hold the same risky portfolio, stocks will be represented in the aggregate risky portfolio in the same proportion as they are in each investor's (common) risky portfolio. If GM represents 1% in each common risky portfolio, GM will be 1% of the aggregate risky portfolio. This in fact is the market portfolio since the market is no more than the aggregate of all individual portfolios. Because each investor uses the market portfolio for the optimal risky portfolio, the CAL in this case is called the capital market line, or CML, as in Figure 7.4.

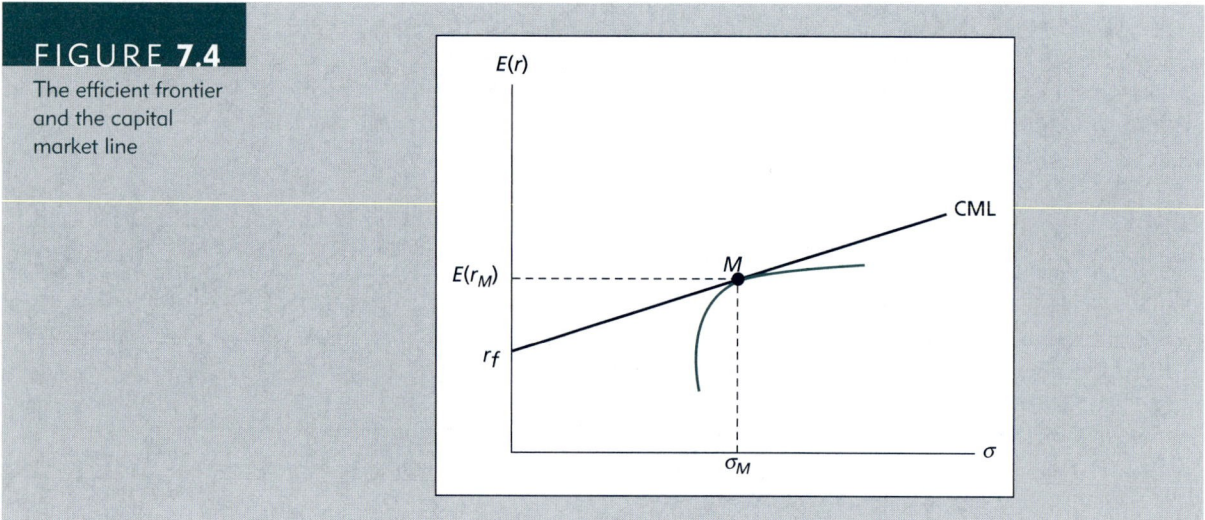

FIGURE 7.4

The efficient frontier and the capital market line

Suppose the optimal portfolio of our investors does not include the stock of some company, say, Delta Air Lines. When no investor is willing to hold Delta stock, the demand is zero, and the stock price will take a free fall. As Delta stock gets progressively cheaper, it begins to look more attractive, while all other stocks look (relatively) less attractive. Ultimately, Delta will reach a price at which it is desirable to include it in the optimal stock portfolio, and investors will buy.

This price adjustment process guarantees that all stocks will be included in the optimal portfolio. The only issue is the price. At a given price level, investors will be willing to buy a stock; at another price, they will not. The bottom line is this: If all investors hold an *identical* risky portfolio, this portfolio must be the *market* portfolio.

The Passive Strategy Is Efficient

A passive strategy, using the CML as the optimal CAL, is a powerful alternative to an active strategy. The market portfolio proportions are a result of profit-oriented "buy" and "sell" orders that cease only when there is no more profit to be made. And in the simple world of the CAPM, all investors use precious resources in security analysis. A passive investor who takes a free ride by simply investing in the market portfolio benefits from the efficiency of that portfolio. In fact, an active investor who chooses any other portfolio will end on a CAL that is less efficient than the CML used by passive investors.

We sometimes call this result a **mutual fund theorem** because it implies that only one mutual fund of risky assets—the market portfolio—is sufficient to satisfy the investment demands of all investors. The mutual fund theorem is another incarnation of the separation property discussed in Chapter 6. Assuming all investors choose to hold a market index mutual fund, we can separate portfolio selection into two components: (1) a technical side, in which an efficient mutual fund is created by professional management; and (2) a personal side, in which an investor's risk aversion determines the allocation of the complete portfolio between the mutual fund and the risk-free asset. Here, all investors agree that the mutual fund they would like to hold is the market portfolio.

While different investment managers do create risky portfolios that differ from the market index, we attribute this in part to the use of different estimates of risk and expected return. Still, a passive investor may view the market index as a reasonable first approximation to an efficient risky portfolio.

The logical inconsistency of the CAPM is this: If a passive strategy is costless *and* efficient, why would anyone follow an active strategy? But if no one does any security analysis, what brings about the efficiency of the market portfolio?

We have acknowledged from the outset that the CAPM simplifies the real world in its search for a tractable solution. Its applicability to the real world depends on whether its predictions are accurate enough. The model's use is some indication that its predictions are reasonable. We discuss this issue in Section 7.4 and in greater depth in Chapter 8.

> **mutual fund theorem**
>
> States that all investors desire the same portfolio of risky assets and can be satisfied by a single mutual fund composed of that portfolio.

1. If only some investors perform security analysis while all others hold the market portfolio (M), would the CML still be the efficient CAL for investors who do not engage in security analysis? Explain.

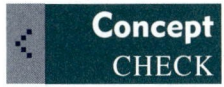

Concept
CHECK

The Risk Premium of the Market Portfolio

In Chapters 5 and 6 we showed how individual investors decide how much to invest in the risky portfolio when they can include a risk-free asset in the investment budget. Returning now to the decision of how much to invest in the market portfolio M and how much in the risk-free asset, what can we deduce about the equilibrium risk premium of portfolio M?

We asserted earlier that the equilibrium risk premium of the market portfolio, $E(r_M) - r_f$, will be proportional to the degree of risk aversion of the average investor and to the risk of the market portfolio, σ_M^2. Now we can explain this result.

When investors purchase stocks, their demand drives up prices, thereby lowering expected rates of return and risk premiums. But if risk premiums fall, then relatively more risk-averse investors will pull their funds out of the risky market portfolio, placing them instead in the risk-free asset. In equilibrium, of course, the risk premium on the market portfolio must be just high enough to induce investors to hold the available supply of stocks. If the risk premium is too high compared to the average degree of risk aversion, there will be excess demand for securities, and prices will rise; if it is too low, investors will not hold enough stock to absorb the supply, and prices will fall. The *equilibrium* risk premium of the market portfolio is therefore proportional to both the risk of the market, as measured by the variance of its returns, and to the degree of risk aversion of the average investor, denoted by A^* in Equation 7.1.

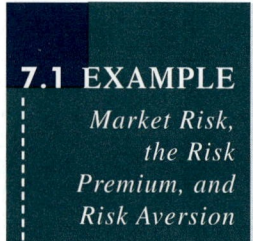
7.1 EXAMPLE

*Market Risk,
the Risk
Premium, and
Risk Aversion*

Suppose the risk-free rate is 5%, the average investor has a risk-aversion coefficient of $A^* = 2$, and the standard deviation of the market portfolio is 20%. Then, from Equation 7.1, we estimate the equilibrium value of the market risk premium[1] as $2 \times 0.20^2 = 0.08$. So the expected rate of return on the market must be

$$E(r_M) = r_f + \text{Equilibrium risk premium}$$
$$= 0.05 + 0.08 = 0.13 = 13\%$$

If investors were more risk averse, it would take a higher risk premium to induce them to hold shares. For example, if the average degree of risk aversion were 3, the market risk premium would be $3 \times 0.20^2 = 0.12$, or 12%, and the expected return would be 17%.

**Concept
CHECK**

2. Historical data for the S&P 500 index show an average excess return over Treasury bills of about 8.5% with standard deviation of about 20%. To the extent that these averages approximate investor expectations for the sample period, what must have been the coefficient of risk aversion of the average investor? If the coefficient of risk aversion were 3.5, what risk premium would have been consistent with the market's historical standard deviation?

Expected Returns on Individual Securities

The CAPM is built on the insight that the appropriate risk premium on an asset will be determined by its contribution to the risk of investors' overall portfolios. Portfolio risk is what matters to investors, and portfolio risk is what governs the risk premiums they demand.

We know that nonsystematic risk can be reduced to an arbitrarily low level through diversification (Chapter 6); therefore, investors do not require a risk premium as compensation for bearing nonsystematic risk. They need to be compensated only for bearing systematic risk, which cannot be diversified. We know also that the contribution of a single security to the risk of a large diversified portfolio depends only on the systematic risk of the security as measured by its beta.[2] Therefore, it should not be surprising that the risk premium of an asset is proportional to its beta; for example, if you double a security's systematic risk, you must double its risk premium for investors still to be willing to hold the security. Thus, the ratio of risk premium to beta should be the same for any two securities or portfolios.

[1]To use Equation 7.1, we must express returns in decimal form rather than as percentages.

[2]See Section 6.5. This is literally true with a sufficient number of securities so that all nonsystematic risk is diversified away. In a market as diversified as the U.S. stock market, this would be true for all practical purposes.

For example, if we were to compare the ratio of risk premium to systematic risk for the market portfolio, which has a beta of 1.0, with the corresponding ratio for Dell stock, we would conclude that

$$\frac{E(r_M) - r_f}{1} = \frac{E(r_D) - r_f}{\beta_D}$$

Rearranging this relationship results in the CAPM's **expected return–beta relationship**

$$E(r_D) = r_f + \beta_D\,[E(r_M) - r_f] \tag{7.2}$$

In words, the rate of return on any asset exceeds the risk-free rate by a risk premium equal to the asset's systematic risk measure (its beta) times the risk premium of the (benchmark) market portfolio. This expected return–beta relationship is the most familiar expression of the CAPM.

The expected return–beta relationship of the CAPM makes a powerful economic statement. It implies, for example, that a security with a high variance but a relatively low beta of 0.5 will carry one-third the risk premium of a low-variance security with a beta of 1.5. Thus, Equation 7.2 quantifies the conclusion we reached in Chapter 6 that only systematic risk matters to investors who can diversify and that systematic risk is measured by the beta of the security.

> **expected return–beta relationship**
>
> Implication of the CAPM that security risk premiums (expected excess returns) will be proportional to beta.

Suppose the risk premium of the market portfolio is 9%, and we estimate the beta of Dell as $\beta_D = 1.3$. The risk premium predicted for the stock is therefore 1.3 times the market risk premium, or $1.3 \times 9\% = 11.7\%$. The expected rate of return on Dell is the risk-free rate plus the risk premium. For example, if the T-bill rate were 5%, the expected rate of return would be $5\% + 11.7\% = 16.7\%$, or using Equation 7.2 directly,

$$E(r_D) = r_f + \beta_D[\text{Market risk premium}]$$
$$= 5\% + 1.3 \times 9\% = 16.7\%$$

If the estimate of the beta of Dell were only 1.2, the required risk premium for Dell would fall to 10.8%. Similarly, if the market risk premium were only 8% and $\beta_D = 1.3$, Dell's risk premium would be only 10.4%.

EXAMPLE 7.2

Expected Returns and Risk Premiums

The fact that few real-life investors actually hold the market portfolio does not necessarily invalidate the CAPM. Recall from Chapter 6 that reasonably well-diversified portfolios shed (for practical purposes) firm-specific risk and are subject only to systematic or market risk. Even if one does not hold the precise market portfolio, a well-diversified portfolio will be so highly correlated with the market that a stock's beta relative to the market still will be a useful risk measure.

In fact, several researchers have shown that modified versions of the CAPM will hold despite differences among individuals that may cause them to hold different portfolios. A study by Brennan (1970) examines the impact of differences in investors' personal tax rates on market equilibrium. Another study by Mayers (1972) looks at the impact of nontraded assets such as human capital (earning power). Both find that while the market portfolio is no longer each investor's optimal risky portfolio, a modified version of the expected return–beta relationship still holds.

If the expected return–beta relationship holds for any individual asset, it must hold for any combination of assets. The beta of a portfolio is simply the weighted average of the betas of the stocks in the portfolio, using as weights the portfolio proportions. Thus, beta also predicts the portfolio's risk premium in accordance with Equation 7.2.

7.3 EXAMPLE

Portfolio Beta and Risk Premium

Consider the following portfolio:

Asset	Beta	Risk Premium	Portfolio Weight
Microsoft	1.2	9.0%	0.5
Con Edison	0.8	6.0	0.3
Gold	0.0	0.0	0.2
Portfolio	0.84	?	1.0

If the market risk premium is 7.5%, the CAPM predicts that the risk premium on each stock is its beta times 7.5%, and the risk premium on the portfolio is $0.84 \times 7.5\% = 6.3\%$. This is the same result that is obtained by taking the weighted average of the risk premiums of the individual stocks. (Verify this for yourself.)

A word of caution: We often hear that well-managed firms will provide high rates of return. We agree this is true if one measures the *firm's* return on investments in plant and equipment. The CAPM, however, predicts returns on investments in the *securities* of the firm.

Say that everyone knows a firm is well run. Its stock price should, therefore, be bid up, and returns to stockholders who buy at those high prices will not be extreme. Security *prices* reflect public information about a firm's prospects, but only the risk of the company (as measured by beta in the context of the CAPM) should affect *expected returns.* In a rational market, investors receive high expected returns only if they are willing to bear risk.

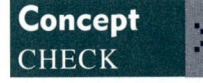

Concept CHECK

3. Suppose the risk premium on the market portfolio is estimated at 8% with a standard deviation of 22%. What is the risk premium on a portfolio invested 25% in GM with a beta of 1.15 and 75% in Ford with a beta of 1.25?

The Security Market Line

We can view the expected return–beta relationship as a reward-risk equation. The beta of a security is the appropriate measure of its risk because beta is proportional to the risk the security contributes to the optimal risky portfolio.

Risk-averse investors measure the risk of the optimal risky portfolio by its standard deviation. In this world, we would expect the reward, or the risk premium on individual assets, to depend on the risk an individual asset contributes to the overall portfolio. Because the beta of a stock measures the stock's contribution to the standard deviation of the market portfolio, we expect the required risk premium to be a function of beta. The CAPM confirms this intuition, stating further that the security's risk premium is directly proportional to both the beta and the risk premium of the market portfolio; that is, the risk premium equals $\beta[E(r_M) - r_f]$.

The expected return–beta relationship is graphed as the **security market line (SML)** in Figure 7.5. Its slope is the risk premium of the market portfolio. At the point where $\beta = 1.0$ (which is the beta of the market portfolio) on the horizontal axis, we can read off the vertical axis the expected return on the market portfolio.

It is useful to compare the security market line to the capital market line. The CML graphs the risk premiums of efficient portfolios (that is, complete portfolios made up of the risky market portfolio and the risk-free asset) as a function of portfolio standard deviation. This is appropriate because standard deviation is a valid measure of risk for portfolios that are candidates for an investor's complete (overall) portfolio.

security market line (SML)

Graphical representation of the expected return–beta relationship of the CAPM.

FIGURE **7.5**

The security market
line and a positive-
alpha stock

The SML, in contrast, graphs *individual asset* risk premiums as a function of asset risk. The relevant measure of risk for individual assets (which are held as parts of a well-diversified portfolio) is not the asset's standard deviation; it is, instead, the contribution of the asset to the portfolio standard deviation as measured by the asset's beta. The SML is valid both for portfolios and individual assets.

The security market line provides a benchmark for evaluation of investment performance. Given the risk of an investment as measured by its beta, the SML provides the required rate of return that will compensate investors for the risk of that investment, as well as for the time value of money.

Because the security market line is the graphical representation of the expected return–beta relationship, "fairly priced" assets plot exactly on the SML. The expected returns of such assets are commensurate with their risk. Whenever the CAPM holds, all securities must lie on the SML in market equilibrium. Underpriced stocks plot above the SML: Given their betas, their expected returns are greater than is indicated by the CAPM. Overpriced stocks plot below the SML. The difference between the fair and actually expected rate of return on a stock is called the stock's **alpha,** denoted α.

alpha

The abnormal rate of
return on a security in
excess of what would
be predicted by an
equilibrium model
such as the CAPM.

Suppose the return on the market is expected to be 14%, a stock has a beta of 1.2, and the T-bill rate is 6%. The SML would predict an expected return on the stock of

$$E(r) = r_f + \beta[E(r_M) - r_f]$$
$$= 6 + 1.2\,(14 - 6) = 15.6\%$$

If one believes the stock will provide instead a return of 17%, its implied alpha would be 1.4%, as shown in Figure 7.5.

EXAMPLE 7.4

*The Alpha of
a Security*

Applications of the CAPM

One place the CAPM may be used is in the investment management industry. Suppose the SML is taken as a benchmark to assess the *fair* expected return on a risky asset. Then an analyst calculates the return he or she actually expects. Notice that we depart here from the simple CAPM world in that some investors apply their own analysis to derive an "input list" that may differ from their competitors'. If a stock is perceived to be a good buy, or underpriced, it will provide a positive alpha, that is, an expected return in excess of the fair return stipulated by the SML.

The CAPM also is useful in capital budgeting decisions. If a firm is considering a new project, the CAPM can provide the return the project needs to yield to be acceptable to investors. Managers can use the CAPM to obtain this cutoff internal rate of return (IRR) or "hurdle rate" for the project.

7.5 EXAMPLE

The CAPM and Capital Budgeting

Suppose Silverado Springs Inc. is considering a new spring-water bottling plant. The business plan forecasts an internal rate of return of 14% on the investment. Research shows the beta of similar products is 1.3. Thus, if the risk-free rate is 4%, and the market risk premium is estimated at 8%, the hurdle rate for the project should be $4 + 1.3 \times 8 = 14.4\%$. Because the IRR is less than the risk-adjusted discount or hurdle rate, the project has a negative net present value and ought to be rejected.

Yet another use of the CAPM is in utility rate-making cases. Here the issue is the rate of return a regulated utility should be allowed to earn on its investment in plant and equipment.

7.6 EXAMPLE

The CAPM and Regulation

Suppose equityholders' investment in the firm is $100 million, and the beta of the equity is 0.6. If the T-bill rate is 6%, and the market risk premium is 8%, then a fair annual profit will be $6 + (0.6 \times 8) = 10.8\%$ of $100 million, or $10.8 million. Since regulators accept the CAPM, they will allow the utility to set prices at a level expected to generate these profits.

Concept CHECK

4. *a.* Stock XYZ has an expected return of 12% and risk of $\beta = 1.0$. Stock ABC is expected to return 13% with a beta of 1.5. The market's expected return is 11% and $r_f = 5\%$. According to the CAPM, which stock is a better buy? What is the alpha of each stock? Plot the SML and the two stocks and show the alphas of each on the graph.

   b. The risk-free rate is 8% and the expected return on the market portfolio is 16%. A firm considers a project with an estimated beta of 1.3. What is the required rate of return on the project? If the IRR of the project is 19%, what is the project alpha?

7.3 | THE CAPM AND INDEX MODELS

The CAPM has two limitations: It relies on the theoretical market portfolio, which includes *all* assets (such as real estate, foreign stocks, etc.), and it deals with *expected* as opposed to actual returns. To implement the CAPM, we cast it in the form of an *index model* and use realized, not expected, returns.

An index model uses actual portfolios, such as the S&P 500, rather than the theoretical market portfolio to represent the relevant systematic factors in the economy. The important advantage of index models is that the composition and rate of return of the index is easily measured and unambiguous.

In contrast to an index model, the CAPM revolves around the "market portfolio." However, because many assets are not traded, investors would not have full access to the market portfolio even if they could exactly identify it. Thus, the theory behind the CAPM rests on a shaky real-world foundation. But, as in all science, a theory may be viewed as legitimate if its predictions approximate real-world outcomes with a sufficient degree of accuracy. In particular, the reliance on the market portfolio shouldn't faze us if we can verify that the predictions of the CAPM are sufficiently accurate when the index portfolio is substituted for the market.

We can start with one central prediction of the CAPM: The market portfolio is mean-variance efficient. An index model can be used to test this hypothesis by verifying that an index chosen to be representative of the full market is a mean-variance efficient portfolio.

Another aspect of the CAPM is that it predicts relationships among *expected* returns, while all we can observe are realized (historical) holding-period returns; actual returns in a particular holding period seldom, if ever, match our initial expectations. To test the mean-variance efficiency of an index portfolio, we would have to show that the reward-to-variability ratio of the index is not surpassed by any other portfolio. The reward-to-variability ratio, however, is set in terms of expectations, and we can measure it only in terms of realizations.

The Index Model, Realized Returns, and the Expected Return–Beta Relationship

To move from a model cast in expectations to a realized-return framework, we start with a form of the single-index regression equation in realized excess returns, similar to that of Equation 6.6 in Chapter 6:

$$r_i - r_f = \alpha_i + \beta_i(r_M - r_f) + e_i \tag{7.3}$$

where r_i is the holding-period return (HPR) on asset i, and α_i and β_i are the intercept and slope of the line that relates asset i's realized excess return to the realized excess return of the index. We denote the index return by r_M to emphasize that the index portfolio is proxying for the market. The e_i measures firm-specific effects during the holding period; it is the deviation of security i's realized HPR from the regression line, that is, the deviation from the forecast that accounts for the index's HPR. We set the relationship in terms of *excess* returns (over the risk-free rate, r_f), for consistency with the CAPM's logic of risk premiums.

Given that the CAPM is a statement about the expectation of asset returns, we look at the expected return of security i predicted by Equation 7.3. Recall that the expectation of e_i is zero (the firm-specific surprise is expected to average zero over time), so the relationship expressed in terms of expectations is

$$E(r_i) - r_f = \alpha_i + \beta_i[E(r_M) - r_f] \tag{7.4}$$

Comparing this relationship to the expected return–beta relationship (Equation 7.2) of the CAPM reveals that the CAPM predicts $\alpha_i = 0$. Thus, we have converted the CAPM prediction about unobserved expectations of security returns relative to an unobserved market portfolio into a prediction about the intercept in a regression of observed variables: realized excess returns of a security relative to those of a specified index.

Operationalizing the CAPM in the form of an index model has a drawback, however. If intercepts of regressions of returns on an index differ substantially from zero, you will not be able to tell whether it is because you chose a bad index to proxy for the market or because the theory is not useful.

In actuality, few instances of persistent, positive significant alpha values have been identified; these will be discussed in Chapter 8. Among these are: (1) small versus large stocks; (2) stocks of companies that have recently announced unexpectedly good earnings; (3) stocks with high ratios of book value to market value; and (4) stocks that have experienced recent sharp price declines. In general, however, future alphas are practically impossible to predict from past values. The result is that index models are widely used to operationalize capital asset pricing theory.

Estimating the Index Model

Equation 7.3 also suggests how we might go about actually measuring market and firm-specific risk. Suppose that we observe the excess return on the market index and a specific asset over a number of holding periods. We use as an example monthly excess returns on the S&P 500 index and GM stock for a particular year. We can summarize the results for a sample period in a scatter diagram, as illustrated in Figure 7.6.

The horizontal axis in Figure 7.6 measures the excess return (over the risk-free rate) on the market index; the vertical axis measures the excess return on the asset in question (GM stock in our example). A pair of excess returns (one for the market index, one for GM stock) over a holding period constitutes one point on this scatter diagram. The points are numbered 1 through 12, representing excess returns for the S&P 500 and GM for each month from January through December. The single-index model states that the relationship between the excess returns on GM and the S&P 500 is given by

$$R_{GMt} = \alpha_{GM} + \beta_{GM}R_{Mt} + e_{GMt}$$

We have noted the resemblance of this relationship to a regression equation.

In a single-variable linear regression equation, the dependent variable plots around a straight line with an intercept α and a slope β. The deviations from the line, e_i, are assumed to

FIGURE 7.6

Characteristic line for GM

be mutually independent and independent of the right-hand side variable. Because these assumptions are identical to those of the index model, we can look at the index model as a regression model. The sensitivity of GM to the market, measured by β_{GM}, is the slope of the regression line. The intercept of the regression line is α (which represents the average firm-specific return), and deviations of particular observations from the regression line are denoted e. These *residuals* are the differences between the actual stock return and the return that would be predicted from the regression equation describing the usual relationship between the stock and the market; therefore, they measure the impact of firm-specific events during the particular month. The parameters of interest, α, β, and Var(e), can be estimated using standard regression techniques.

Estimating the regression equation of the single-index model gives us the **security characteristic line (SCL),** which is plotted in Figure 7.6. (The regression results and raw data appear in Table 7.5.) The SCL is a plot of the typical excess return on a security over the risk-free rate as a function of the excess return on the market.

This sample of 12 monthly holding-period returns is, of course, too small to yield reliable statistics. We use it only for demonstration. For this sample period, we find that the beta coefficient of GM stock, as estimated by the slope of the regression line, is 1.136, and that the intercept for this SCL is −2.59% per month.

For each month, our estimate of the residual, e, which is the deviation of GM's excess return from the prediction of the SCL, equals

$$\text{Residual} = \text{Actual} - \text{Predicted return}$$

$$e_{GMt} = R_{GMt} - (\beta_{GM}R_{Mt} + \alpha_{GM})$$

> **security characteristic line (SCL)**
>
> A plot of a security's expected excess return over the risk-free rate as a function of the excess return on the market.

TABLE **7.5** Characteristic line for GM stock	Month	GM Return	Market Return	Monthly T-Bill Rate	Excess GM Return	Excess Market Return
	January	6.06	7.89	0.65	5.41	7.24
	February	−2.86	1.51	0.58	−3.44	0.93
	March	−8.17	0.23	0.62	−8.79	−0.39
	April	−7.36	−0.29	0.72	−8.08	−1.01
	May	7.76	5.58	0.66	7.10	4.92
	June	0.52	1.73	0.55	−0.03	1.18
	July	−1.74	−0.21	0.62	−2.36	−0.83
	August	−3.00	−0.36	0.55	−3.55	−0.91
	September	−0.56	−3.58	0.60	−1.16	−4.18
	October	−0.37	4.62	0.65	−1.02	3.97
	November	6.93	6.85	0.61	6.32	6.24
	December	3.08	4.55	0.65	2.43	3.90
	Mean	0.02	2.38	0.62	−0.60	1.76
	Standard deviation	5.19	3.48	0.05	5.19	3.46

Regression results

$$r_{GM} - r_f = \alpha + \beta(r_M - r_f)$$

	α	β
Estimated coefficient	−2.591	1.136
Standard error of estimate	(1.59)	(0.309)

Variance of residuals = 12.585
Standard deviation of residuals = 3.548
R-SQR = 0.575

TABLE 7.6

True parameters of securities

A. Market index
Expected excess return over T-bill rate, $E(R_M) = 8\%$
Standard deviation of excess return, $\sigma(R_M) = 20\%$

B. Individual stocks

	Beta	Standard Deviation of Residual, $\sigma(e)$	Total Standard Deviation of Returns*
Stock A	1.30	54.07%	60%
Stock B	0.70	37.47	40

*Standard deviation $= [\beta^2 \sigma_M^2 + \sigma^2(e)]^{1/2}$
     Stock A: $[1.3^2 \times 20^2 + 54.07^2]^{1/2} = 60\%$
     Stock B: $[0.7^2 \times 20^2 + 37.47^2]^{1/2} = 40\%$

C. T-bills
Average value in sample period $= 5\%$
Month-to-month variation results in a standard deviation across months of 1.5%

These residuals are estimates of the monthly unexpected *firm-specific* component of the rate of return on GM stock. Hence we can estimate the firm-specific variance by[3]

$$\sigma^2(e_{GM}) = \frac{1}{10} \sum_{t=1}^{12} e_t^2 = 12.60$$

Therefore, the standard deviation of the firm-specific component of GM's return, $\sigma(e_{GM})$, equals 3.55% per month.

The CAPM and the Index Model

We have introduced the CAPM and shown how the model can be made operational and how beta can be estimated with the additional simplification of the index model of security returns. Of course, when we estimate the statistical properties of security returns (e.g., betas or variances) using historical data, we are subject to sampling error. Regression parameters are only estimates and necessarily are subject to some imprecision.

In this section, we put together much of the preceding material in an extended example. We show how historical data can be used in conjunction with the CAPM, but we also highlight some pitfalls to be avoided.

Suppose that the *true* parameters for two stocks, A and B, and the market index portfolio are given in Table 7.6. However, investors cannot observe this information directly. They must estimate these parameters using historical returns.

To illustrate the investor's problem, we first produce 24 possible observations for the risk-free rate and the market index. Using the random number generator from a spreadsheet package (e.g., you can use "data analysis tools" in Microsoft Excel), we draw 24 observations from a normal distribution. These random numbers capture the phenomenon that actual returns will differ from expected returns: This is the "statistical noise" that accompanies all real-world return data. For the risk-free rate we set a mean of 5% and a standard deviation of 1.5% and

---

[3]Because the mean of e_t is zero, e_t^2 is the squared deviation from its mean. The average value of e_t^2 is therefore the estimate of the variance of the firm-specific component. We divide the sum of squared residuals by the degrees of freedom of the regression, $n - 2 = 12 - 2 = 10$, to obtain an unbiased estimate of $\sigma^2(e)$.

TABLE 7.7

Simulated data for estimation of security characteristic line (raw data from random number generator)

T-Bill Rate	Excess Return on Index	Residuals for Each Stock		Excess Returns	
		Stock A	Stock B	Stock A	Stock B
5.97	−3.75	7.52	44.13	2.64	41.50
4.45	−9.46	26.14	−38.79	13.85	−45.41
3.24	26.33	18.09	−65.43	52.32	−46.99
5.70	6.06	−0.88	69.24	7.00	73.49
3.89	38.97	48.37	61.51	99.03	88.78
5.56	−1.35	−30.80	26.25	−32.56	25.30
5.03	−24.18	−10.74	0.93	−42.18	−16.00
2.70	15.20	68.91	−18.53	88.66	−7.89
5.57	39.52	−14.09	16.80	37.29	44.46
5.94	−2.84	0.43	−36.15	−3.26	−38.14
4.41	−0.97	73.75	−20.33	72.48	−21.01
4.43	29.82	25.31	68.88	64.08	89.76
2.88	0.73	−83.07	−10.82	−82.13	−10.31
5.77	16.54	−33.45	43.85	−11.95	55.43
2.85	−39.43	60.21	−11.82	8.95	−39.42
5.11	−4.94	3.84	2.95	−2.59	−0.51
5.89	3.01	47.37	12.80	51.29	14.91
7.96	36.98	−32.91	−30.88	15.16	−4.99
7.13	42.22	−58.15	−58.68	−3.26	−29.12
3.46	24.67	77.05	3.89	109.11	21.15
4.72	−11.64	−51.49	−16.87	−66.62	−25.02
4.21	19.15	14.06	−18.79	38.95	−5.39
5.27	−19.13	−80.44	59.07	−105.31	45.69
6.05	5.05	−91.90	−67.83	−85.33	−64.29
True mean	5.00	8.00	0.00	0.00	10.40	5.60
True standard deviation	1.50	20.00	54.07	37.47	60.00	40.00
Sample average	4.93	7.77	−0.70	0.64	9.40	6.08
Sample standard deviation	1.34	21.56	50.02	41.48	58.31	43.95

record the results in the first column of Table 7.7. We then generate 24 observations for excess returns of the market index, using a mean of 8% and a standard deviation of 20%. We record these observations in the second column of Table 7.7.

The bottom four rows in Table 7.7 show the true values for the means and standard deviations as well as the actual sample averages and standard deviations. As you would expect, the sample averages and standard deviations are close but not precisely equal to the true parameters of the probability distribution. This is a reflection of the statistical variation that gives rise to sampling error.

In the next step we wish to generate excess returns for stocks A and B that are consistent with the CAPM. According to the CAPM, the rate of return on any security is given by

$$r - r_f = \beta(r_M - r_f) + e$$

or using capital letters to denote excess returns,

$$R = \beta R_M + e$$

TABLE **7.8**		Coefficients	Standard Error	t Stat
Regression analysis for stock A	Alpha—Stock A	−0.46	11.12	−0.04
	Beta—Stock A	1.27	0.50	2.52

Residual Output—Stock A			
Observation	Predicted A	Residuals	Actual Returns
1	−5.22	7.86	2.64
2	−12.45	26.29	13.85
3	32.93	19.40	52.32
4	7.23	−0.23	7.00
5	48.94	50.08	99.03
6	−2.17	−30.38	−32.56
7	−31.12	−11.05	−42.18
8	4.86	69.50	74.36
9	49.65	−12.36	37.29
10	−4.06	0.80	−3.26
11	−1.69	74.17	72.48
12	37.35	26.73	64.08
13	0.46	−82.59	−82.13
14	20.51	−32.46	−11.95
15	−50.45	59.40	8.95
16	−6.73	4.14	−2.59
17	3.36	47.92	51.29
18	46.43	−31.27	15.16
19	53.08	−56.33	−3.26
20	30.82	78.30	109.11
21	−15.22	−51.40	−66.62
22	23.81	15.13	38.95
23	−15.83	−80.38	−96.21
24	5.95	−91.28	−85.33

Therefore, the CAPM hypothesizes an alpha of zero in Equation 7.3. Given the values of β and R_M, we need only random residuals, e, to generate a simulated sample of returns on each stock. Using the random number generator once again, we generate 24 observations for the residuals of stock A from a normal distribution with a mean of zero and a standard deviation of 54.07%. These observations are recorded in the third column of Table 7.7. Similarly, the randomly generated residuals for stock B use a standard deviation of 37.47% and are recorded in the fourth column of Table 7.7.

The excess rates of return of stocks A and B are computed by multiplying the excess return on the market index by beta and adding the residual. The results appear in the last two columns of Table 7.7. Thus, the first two and last two columns of Table 7.7 correspond to the type of historical data that we might observe if the CAPM adequately describes capital market equilibrium. The numbers come from probability distributions consistent with the CAPM, but, because of the residuals, the CAPM's expected return–beta relationship will not hold exactly due to sampling error.

We now use a regression program (again, from the "data analysis" menu of our spreadsheet) to regress the excess return of each stock against the excess return of the index. The regression routine allows us to save the predicted return for each stock, based on the market return in that period, as well as the regression residuals. These values, and the regression statistics, are presented in Table 7.8 for stock A and Table 7.9 for stock B.

TABLE **7.9**		Coefficients	Standard Error	t Stat
Regression analysis for stock B	Alpha—Stock B	0.39	9.22	0.04
	Beta—Stock B	0.73	0.42	1.76

Residual Output—Stock B			
Observation	Predicted B	Residuals	Actual Returns
1	−2.36	43.87	41.50
2	−6.55	−38.86	−45.41
3	19.70	−66.69	−46.99
4	4.83	68.65	73.49
5	28.96	59.82	88.78
6	−0.60	25.91	25.30
7	−17.35	1.35	−16.00
8	3.46	−19.05	−15.59
9	29.37	15.09	44.46
10	−1.70	−36.45	−38.14
11	−0.33	−20.68	−21.01
12	22.25	67.50	89.76
13	0.92	−11.23	−10.31
14	12.52	42.91	55.43
15	−28.52	−10.90	−39.42
16	−3.24	2.72	−0.51
17	2.60	12.31	14.91
18	27.51	−32.50	−4.99
19	31.35	−60.47	−29.12
20	18.48	2.68	21.15
21	−8.15	−16.87	−25.02
22	14.43	−19.82	−5.39
23	−8.50	59.09	50.59
24	4.09	−68.38	−64.29

Observe from the regression statistics in Tables 7.8 and 7.9 that the beta of stock A is estimated at 1.27 (versus the true value of 1.3) and the beta of stock B is estimated at 0.73 (versus the true value of 0.7). The regression also shows estimates of alpha as −0.46% for A and 0.39% for B (versus a true value of zero for both stocks), but the standard error of these estimates is large and their t-values are low, indicating that these are not statistically significant. The regression estimates allow us to plot the security characteristic line (SCL) for both stocks, shown in Figure 7.7 for stock A and Figure 7.8 for stock B.

The CAPM representation of the securities is shown in Figures 7.9 and 7.10. Figure 7.9 shows the security market line (SML) supported by the risk-free rate and the market index. Stock A has a negative estimated alpha and is therefore below the line. This suggests that stock A is overpriced, that is, its expected return is below that which can be obtained with efficient portfolios and the risk-free rate. The negative estimated alpha is due to the effect of the firm-specific residuals. Similarly, stock B plots above the SML. Here, it appears that stock B is underpriced and has an expected return above that which can be obtained with the market index and the risk-free asset (given by the SML).

Figure 7.10 shows the capital market line (CML) that is supported by the risk-free rate and the market index. The efficient frontier is generated by the Markowitz algorithm applied to the

FIGURE **7.7**
Security characteristic line for stock A

FIGURE **7.8**
Security characteristic line for stock B

means, standard deviations, and correlation coefficients of the full set of risky assets in the universe of securities. (This additional information is not shown here.) Stocks *A* and *B* plot far

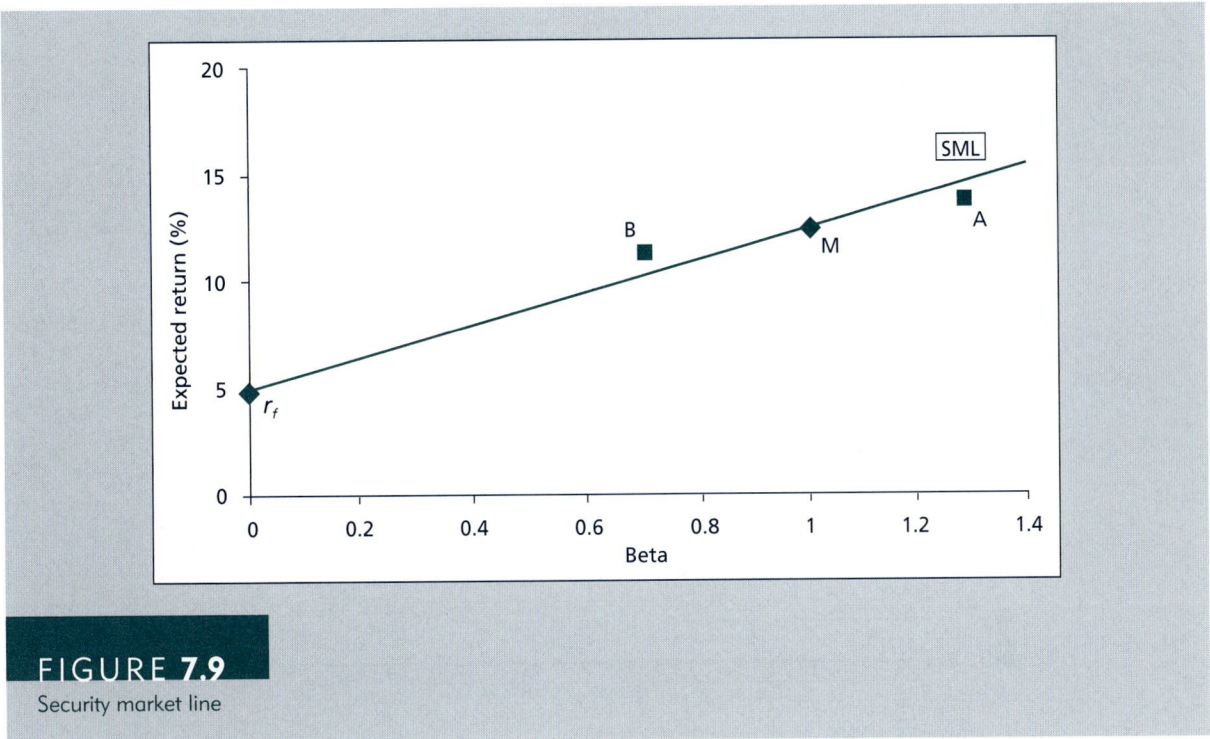

FIGURE **7.9**

Security market line

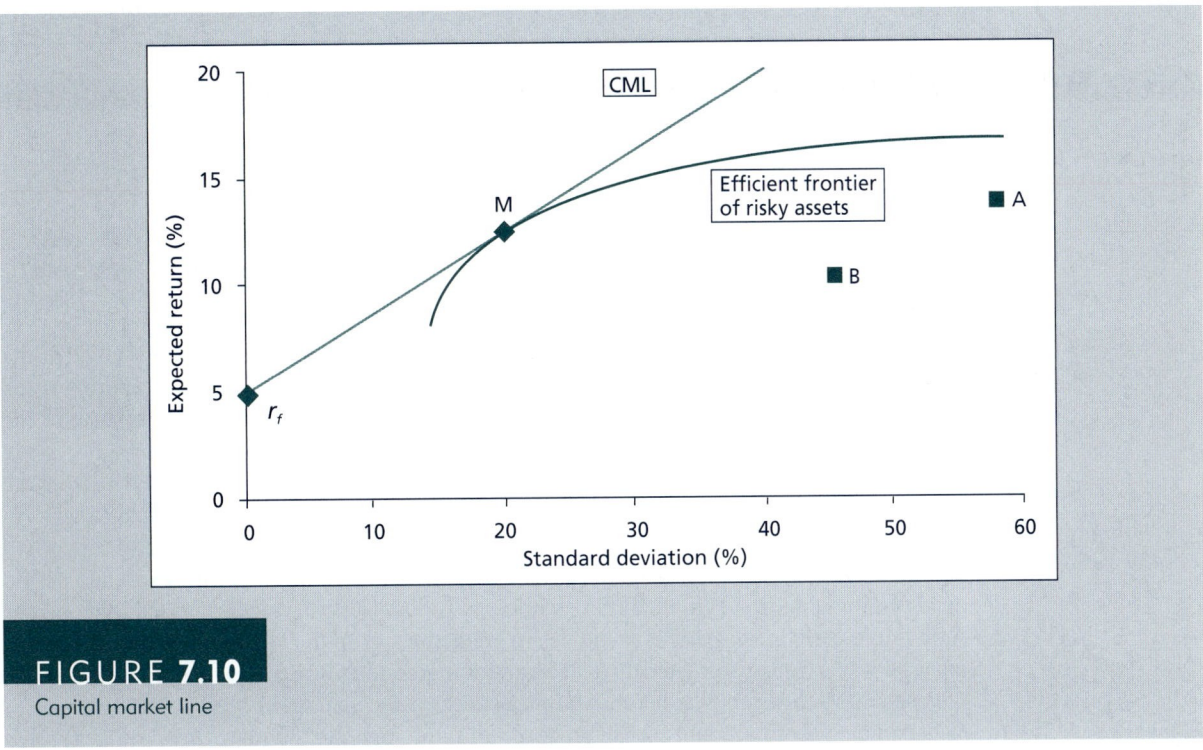

FIGURE **7.10**

Capital market line

below the CML and below the efficient frontier, demonstrating that undiversified individual
securities are dominated by efficiently diversified portfolios.

Beta

This Excel model contains a data set that can be used to estimate beta coefficients for a number of stocks. The data contain individual stock and index returns and returns on Treasury bills. These were obtained from the Standard & Poor's Educational Version of Market Insight, available at www.mhhe.com/edumarketinsight.com, and are analyzed using the regression function in Excel that was discussed in section 6.5, "A Single-Factor Asset Market."

You can learn more about this spreadsheet model by using the interactive version available on our website at www.mhhe.com/bkm.

	A	B	C	D	E	F	G	H	I
1	SUMMARY OUTPUT	AXP							
2									
3	*Regression Statistics*								
4	Multiple R	0.69288601							
5	R Square	0.48009103							
6	Adjusted R Square	0.47112708							
7	Standard Error	0.05887426							
8	Observations	60							
9									
10	ANOVA								
11		*df*	*SS*	*MS*	*F*	*Significance F*			
12	Regression	1	0.185641557	0.1856416	53.55799	8.55186E-10			
13	Residual	58	0.201038358	0.0034662					
14	Total	59	0.386679915						
15									
16		*Coefficients*	*Standard Error*	*t Stat*	*P-value*	*Lower 95%*	*Upper 95%*	*Lower 95.0%*	*Upper 95.0%*
17	Intercept	0.01181687	0.00776211	1.522379	0.133348	−0.003720666	0.027354414	−0.0037207	0.02735441
18	X Variable 1	1.20877413	0.165170705	7.3183324	8.55E-10	0.878149288	1.539398969	0.87814929	1.53939897

Predicting Betas

Even if a single-index model representation is not fully consistent with the CAPM, the concept of systematic versus diversifiable risk is still useful. Systematic risk is approximated well by the regression equation beta and nonsystematic risk by the residual variance of the regression.

Often, we estimate betas in order to forecast the rate of return of an asset. The beta from the regression equation is an estimate based on past history; it will not reveal possible changes in future beta. As an empirical rule, it appears that betas exhibit a statistical property called "regression toward the mean." This means that high β (that is, $\beta > 1$) securities in one period tend to exhibit a lower β in the future, while low β (that is, $\beta < 1$) securities exhibit a higher β in future periods. Researchers who desire predictions of future betas often adjust beta estimates derived from historical data to account for regression toward the mean. For this reason, it is necessary to verify whether the estimates are already "adjusted betas."

A simple way to account for the tendency of future betas to "regress" toward the average value of 1.0 is to use as your forecast of beta a weighted average of the sample estimate with the value 1.0.

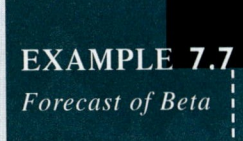

Suppose that past data yield a beta estimate of 0.65. A common weighting scheme is ⅔ on the sample estimate and ⅓ on the value 1.0. Thus, the final forecast of beta will be

$$\text{Adjusted beta} = \tfrac{2}{3} \times 0.65 + \tfrac{1}{3} \times 1.0 = 0.77$$

The final forecast of beta is in fact closer to 1.0 than the sample estimate.

EXAMPLE 7.7

Forecast of Beta

A more sophisticated technique would base the weight assigned to the sample estimate of beta on its statistical reliability. That is, if we have a more precise estimate of beta from historical data, we increase the weight placed on the sample estimate.

However, obtaining a precise statistical estimate of beta from past data on individual stocks is a formidable task, because the volatility of rates of return is so large. In other words, there is a lot of "noise" in the data due to the impact of firm-specific events. The problem is less severe with diversified portfolios because diversification reduces the effect of firm-specific events.

One might hope that more precise estimates of beta could be obtained by using more data, that is, by using a long time series of the returns on the stock. Unfortunately, this is not a solution, because regression analysis presumes that the regression coefficient (the beta) is constant over the sample period. If betas change over time, old data could provide a misleading guide to current betas. More complicated regression techniques that allow for time-varying coefficients also have not proved to be very successful.

One promising avenue is an application of a technique that goes by the name of ARCH models.[4] An ARCH model posits that changes in stock volatility, and covariance with other stocks, are partially predictable and analyzes recent levels and trends in volatility and covariance. This technique has penetrated the industry only recently and so has not yet produced truly reliable betas. Thus, the problem of estimating the critical parameters of the CAPM and index models has been a stick in the wheels of testing and applying the theory.

7.4 THE CAPM AND THE REAL WORLD

In limited ways, portfolio theory and the CAPM have become accepted tools in the practitioner community. Many investment professionals think about the distinction between firm-specific and systematic risk and are comfortable with the use of beta to measure systematic

WEBMASTER

Beta Comparisons

Go to http://moneycentral.msn.com/investor/research/welcome.asp and http:nasdaq.com. Obtain the beta coefficients for IMB, PG, HWP, AEIS, and INTC. (Betas on the Nasdaq site can be found by using the info quotes and fundamental locations.)

Compare the betas reported by these two sites. Then, answer the following questions:

1. Are there any significant differences in the reported beta coefficients?

2. What factors could lead to such differences?

[4]ARCH stands for autoregressive conditional heteroskedasticity. This is a fancy way of saying that the volatility (and covariance) of stocks changes over time in ways that can be at least partially predicted from their past levels.

Beta Beaten

A battle between some of the top names in financial economics is attracting attention on Wall Street. Under attack is the famous capital asset pricing model (CAPM), widely used to assess risk and return. A new paper by two Chicago economists, Eugene Fama and Kenneth French, explodes that model by showing that its key analytical tool does not explain why returns on shares differ.

According to the CAPM, returns reflect risk. The model uses a measure called beta—shorthand for relative volatility—to compare the riskiness of one share with that of the whole market, on the basis of past price changes. A share with a beta of one is just as risky as the market; one with a beta of 0.5 is less risky. Because investors need to earn more on riskier investments, share prices will reflect the requirement for higher-than-average returns on shares with higher betas.

Whether beta does predict returns has long been debated. Studies have found that market capitalization, price/earnings ratios, leverage and book-to-market ratios do just as well. Messrs Fama and French are clear: Beta is not a good guide.

The two economists look at all nonfinancial shares traded on the NYSE, Amex and Nasdaq between 1963 and 1990. The shares were grouped into portfolios. When grouped solely on the basis of size (that is, market capitalization), the CAPM worked—but each portfolio contained a wide range of betas. So the authors grouped shares of similar beta and size. Betas now were a bad guide to returns.

Instead of beta, say Messrs Fama and French, differences in firm size and in the ratio of book value to market value explain differences in returns—especially the latter. When shares were grouped by book-to-market ratios, the gap in returns between the portfolio with the lowest ratio and that with the highest was far wider than when shares were grouped by size.

So should analysts stop using the CAPM? Probably not. Although Mr. Fama and Mr. French have produced intriguing results, they lack a theory to explain them. Their best hope is that size and book-to-market ratios are proxies for other fundamentals. For instance, a high book-to-market ratio may indicate a firm in trouble; its earnings prospects might thus be especially sensitive to economic conditions, so its shares would need to earn a higher return than its beta suggested.

Advocates of CAPM—including Fischer Black, of Goldman Sachs, an investment bank, and William Sharpe of Stanford University, who won the Nobel Prize for economics in 1990—reckon the results of the new study can be explained without discarding beta. Investors may irrationally favor big firms. Or they may lack the cash to buy enough shares to spread risk completely, so that risk and return are not perfectly matched in the market.

Those looking for a theoretical alternative to CAPM will find little satisfaction, however. Voguish rivals, such as the "arbitrage pricing theory," are no better than CAPM and betas at explaining actual share returns. Which leaves Wall Street with an awkward choice: Believe the Fama–French evidence, despite its theoretical vacuum, and use size and the book-to-market ratios as a guide to returns; or stick with a theory that, despite the data, is built on impeccable logic.

SOURCE: "Beta Beaten," *The Economist*, March 7, 1992, p. 87, based on Eugene Fama and Kenneth French, "The Cross-Section of Expected Stock Returns," University of Chicago Center for Research in Security Prices, 1991.

risk. Still, the nuances of the CAPM are not nearly as well established in the community. For example, the compensation of portfolio managers is not based on appropriate performance measures (see Chapter 20). What can we make of this?

New ways of thinking about the world (that is, new models or theories) displace old ones when the old models become either intolerably inconsistent with data or when the new model is demonstrably more consistent with available data. For example, when Copernicus overthrew the age-old belief that the Earth is fixed in the center of the Universe and that the stars orbit about it in circular motions, it took many years before astronomers and navigators replaced old astronomical tables with superior ones based on his theory. The old tools fit the data available from astronomical observation with sufficient precision to suffice for the needs of the time. To some extent, the slowness with which the CAPM has permeated daily practice in the money management industry also has to do with its precision in fitting data, that is, in precisely explaining variation in rates of return across assets. Let's review some of the evidence on this score.

The CAPM was first published by Sharpe in the *Journal of Finance* (the journal of the American Finance Association) in 1964 and took the world of finance by storm. Early tests by Black, Jensen, and Scholes (1972) and Fama and MacBeth (1973) were only partially supportive of the CAPM: average returns were higher for higher-beta portfolios, but the reward for beta risk was less than the predictions of the simple theory.

While all this accumulating evidence against the CAPM remained largely within the ivory towers of academia, Roll's (1977) paper "A Critique of Capital Asset Pricing Tests" shook the practitioner world as well. Roll argued that since the true market portfolio can never be observed, the CAPM is *necessarily* untestable.

The publicity given the now classic "Roll's critique" resulted in popular articles such as "Is Beta Dead?" that effectively slowed the permeation of portfolio theory through the world of finance.[5] This is quite ironic since, although Roll is absolutely correct on theoretical grounds, some tests suggest that the error introduced by using a broad market index as proxy for the true, unobserved market portfolio is perhaps the lesser of the problems involved in testing the CAPM.

Fama and French (1992) published a study that dealt the CAPM an even harsher blow. They claimed that once you control for a set of widely followed characteristics of the firm, such as the size of the firm and its ratio of market value to book value, the firm's beta (that is, its systematic risk) does not contribute anything to the prediction of future returns. This time, the piece was picked up by *The Economist* and the *New York Times* (see the nearby box) even before it was published in the *Journal of Finance*.

Fama and French and several others have published many follow-up studies of this topic. We will review some of this literature in the next chapter. However, it seems clear from these studies that beta does not tell the whole story of risk. There seem to be risk factors that affect security returns beyond beta's one-dimensional measurement of market sensitivity. In fact, in the next section of this chapter, we will introduce a theory of risk premiums that explicitly allows for multiple risk factors.

Liquidity, a different kind of risk factor, has been ignored for a long time. Although first analyzed by Amihud and Mendelson as early as 1986, it is yet to be accurately measured and incorporated in portfolio management. Measuring liquidity and the premium commensurate with illiquidity is part of a larger field in financial economics, namely, market structure. We now know that trading mechanisms on stock exchanges affect the liquidity of assets traded on these exchanges and thus significantly affect their market value.

Despite all these issues, beta is not dead. Other research shows that when we use a more inclusive proxy for the market portfolio than the S&P 500 (specifically, an index that includes human capital) and allow for the fact that beta changes over time, the performance of beta in explaining security returns is considerably enhanced (Jagannathan and Wang, 1996). We know that the CAPM is not a perfect model and that ultimately it will be far from the last word on security pricing. Still, the logic of the model is compelling, and more sophisticated models of security pricing all rely on the key distinction between systematic versus diversifiable risk. The CAPM therefore provides a useful framework for thinking rigorously about the relationship between security risk and return. This is as much as Copernicus had when he was shown the prepublication version of his book just before he passed away.

7.5 ARBITRAGE PRICING THEORY

In the 1970s, as researchers were working on test methodologies for variants of the CAPM, Stephen Ross (1976) stunned the world of finance with the arbitrage pricing theory (APT).

---

[5]A. Wallace, "Is Beta Dead?" *Institutional Investor* 14 (July 1980), pp. 22–30.

Moving away from construction of mean-variance efficient portfolios, Ross instead calculated relations among expected rates of return that would rule out riskless profits by any investor in well-functioning capital markets. This generated a theory of risk and return similar to the CAPM.

Arbitrage Opportunities and Profits

arbitrage

Creation of riskless profits made possible by relative mispricing among securities.

zero-investment portfolio

A portfolio of zero net value, established by buying and shorting component securities, usually in the context of an arbitrage strategy.

To explain the APT, we begin with the concept of **arbitrage,** which is the exploitation of relative mispricing among two or more securities to earn risk-free economic profits.

A riskless arbitrage opportunity arises when an investor can construct a **zero-investment portfolio** that will yield a sure profit. Zero investment means investors need not use any of their own money. To construct a zero-investment portfolio, one has to be able to sell short at least one asset and use the proceeds to purchase (go long) one or more assets. Even a small investor, using borrowed money in this fashion, can take a large position in such a portfolio.

An obvious case of an arbitrage opportunity arises in the violation of the law of one price: When an asset is trading at different prices in two markets (and the price differential exceeds transaction costs), a simultaneous trade in the two markets will produce a sure profit (the net price differential) without any net investment. One simply sells short the asset in the high-priced market and buys it in the low-priced market. The net proceeds are positive, and there is no risk because the long and short positions offset each other.

In modern markets with electronic communications and instantaneous execution, such opportunities have become rare but not extinct. The same technology that enables the market to absorb new information quickly also enables fast operators to make large profits by trading huge volumes at the instant an arbitrage opportunity opens. This is the essence of program trading and index arbitrage, to be discussed in Part Five.

From the simple case of a violation of the law of one price, let us proceed to a less obvious (yet just as profitable) arbitrage opportunity. Imagine that four stocks are traded in an economy with only four possible scenarios. The rates of return on the four stocks for each inflation-interest rate scenario appear in Table 7.10. The current prices of the stocks and rate of return statistics are shown in Table 7.11.

The rate of return data give no immediate clue to any arbitrage opportunity lurking in this set of investments. The expected returns, standard deviations, and correlations do not reveal any abnormality to the naked eye.

Consider, however, an equally weighted portfolio of the first three stocks (Apex, Bull, and Crush), and contrast its possible future rates of return with those of the fourth stock, Dreck. We do this in Table 7.12.

Table 7.12 reveals that in all four scenarios, the equally weighted portfolio will outperform Dreck. The rate of return statistics of the two alternatives are

	Mean	Standard Deviation	Correlation
Three-stock portfolio	25.83	6.40	
			0.94
Dreck	22.25	8.58	

The two investments are not perfectly correlated and are not perfect substitutes. Nevertheless, the equally weighted portfolio will fare better under *any* circumstances. Any investor, no matter how risk averse, can take advantage of this dominance by taking a short position in Dreck and using the proceeds to purchase the equally weighted portfolio. Let us see how it would work.

TABLE **7.10** Rate of return projections		High Real Interest Rates		Low Real Interest Rates	
		High Inflation	**Low Inflation**	**High Inflation**	**Low Inflation**
	Probability:	0.25	0.25	0.25	0.25
	Stock				
	Apex (A)	−20	20	40	60
	Bull (B)	0	70	30	−20
	Crush (C)	90	−20	−10	70
	Dreck (D)	15	23	15	36

TABLE **7.11** Rate of return statistics	Stock	Current Price	Expected Return (%)	Standard Deviation (%)	Correlation Matrix			
					A	**B**	**C**	**D**
	A	$10	25.0%	29.58%	1.00	−0.15	−0.29	0.68
	B	10	20.0	33.91	−0.15	1.00	−0.87	−0.38
	C	10	32.5	48.15	−0.29	−0.87	1.00	0.22
	D	10	22.25	8.58	0.68	−0.38	0.22	1.00

TABLE **7.12** Rate of return projections		High Real Interest Rates		Low Real Interest Rates	
		Rate of Inflation		Rate of Inflation	
		High	**Low**	**High**	**Low**
	Equally weighted portfolio:				
	A, B, and C	23.33	23.33	20.00	36.67
	Dreck (D)	15.00	23.00	15.00	36.00

Suppose we sell short 300,000 shares of Dreck and use the $3 million proceeds to buy 100,000 shares each of Apex, Bull, and Crush. The dollar profits in each of the four scenarios will be as follows.

Stock	Dollar Investment	High Real Interest Rates		Low Real Interest Rates	
		Inflation Rate		Inflation Rate	
		High	**Low**	**High**	**Low**
Apex	$ 1,000,000	$−200,000	$ 200,000	$ 400,000	$ 600,000
Bull	1,000,000	0	700,000	300,000	−200,000
Crush	1,000,000	900,000	−200,000	−100,000	700,000
Dreck	−3,000,000	−450,000	−690,000	−450,000	−1,080,000
Portfolio	$ 0	$ 250,000	$ 10,000	$ 150,000	$ 20,000

The first column verifies that the net investment in our portfolio is zero. Yet this portfolio yields a positive profit in all scenarios. It is therefore a money machine. Investors will want to take an infinite position in such a portfolio, for larger positions entail no risk of losses yet yield ever-growing profits.[6] In principle, even a single investor would take such large positions that the market would react to the buying and selling pressure: The price of Dreck would come down, and/or the prices of Apex, Bull, and Crush would go up. The pressure would persist until the arbitrage opportunity was eliminated.

> **Concept CHECK** ›
>
> 5. Suppose Dreck's price starts falling without any change in its per-share dollar payoffs. How far must the price fall before arbitrage between Dreck and the equally weighted portfolio is no longer possible? (Hint: Account for the amount of the equally weighted portfolio that can be purchased with the proceeds of the short sale as Dreck's price falls.)

The critical property of an arbitrage portfolio is that any investor, regardless of risk aversion or wealth, will want to take an infinite position in it so that profits will be driven to an infinite level. Because those large positions will force some prices up and/or some down until the opportunity vanishes, we can derive restrictions on security prices that satisfy the condition that no arbitrage opportunities are left in the marketplace.

The idea that equilibrium market prices ought to be rational in the sense that they rule out arbitrage opportunities is perhaps the most fundamental concept in capital market theory. Violation of this principle would indicate the grossest form of market irrationality.

There is an important distinction between arbitrage and CAPM risk-versus-return dominance arguments in support of equilibrium price relationships. A dominance argument, as in the CAPM, holds that when an equilibrium price relationship is violated, many investors will make portfolio changes. Each individual investor will make a limited change, though, depending on wealth and degree of risk aversion. Aggregation of these limited portfolio changes over many investors is required to create a large volume of buying and selling, which restores equilibrium prices.

When arbitrage opportunities exist, by contrast, each investor wants to take as large a position as possible; in this case, it will not take many investors to bring about the price pressures necessary to restore equilibrium. Implications derived from the no-arbitrage argument, therefore, are stronger than implications derived from a risk-versus-return dominance argument, because they do not depend on a large, well-educated population of investors.

The CAPM argues that all investors hold mean-variance efficient portfolios. When a security (or a bundle of securities) is mispriced, investors will tilt their portfolios toward the underpriced and away from the overpriced securities. The resulting pressure on prices comes from many investors shifting their portfolios, each by a relatively small dollar amount. The assumption that a large number of investors are mean-variance optimizers, is critical; in contrast, even few arbitrageurs will mobilize large dollar amounts to take advantage of an arbitrage opportunity.

Well-Diversified Portfolios and the Arbitrage Pricing Theory

> **arbitrage pricing theory (APT)**
>
> A theory of risk-return relationships derived from no-arbitrage considerations in large capital markets

The arbitrage opportunity described in the previous section is further obscured by the fact that it is almost always impossible to construct a precise scenario analysis for individual stocks that would uncover an event of such straightforward mispricing.

Using the concept of well-diversified portfolios, the **arbitrage pricing theory,** or **APT,** resorts to statistical modeling to attack the problem more systematically. By showing that

---

[6]We have described pure arbitrage: the search for a costless sure profit. Practitioners often use the terms *arbitrage* and *arbitrageurs* more loosely. An arbitrageur may be a professional searching for mispriced securities in specific areas such as merger-target stocks, rather than one looking for strict (risk-free) arbitrage opportunities in the sense that no loss is possible. The search for mispriced securities is called risk arbitrage to distinguish it from pure arbitrage.

mispriced portfolios would give rise to arbitrage opportunities, the APT arrives at an expected return–beta relationship for portfolios identical to that of the CAPM. In the next section, we will compare and contrast the two theories.

In its simple form, just like the CAPM, the APT posits a single-factor security market. Thus, the excess rate of return on each security, $R_i = r_i - r_f$, can be represented by

$$R_i = \alpha_i + \beta_i R_M + e \qquad (7.5)$$

where alpha, α_i, and beta, β_i, are known, and where we treat R_M as the single factor.

Suppose now that we construct a highly diversified portfolio with a given beta. If we use enough securities to form the portfolio, the resulting diversification will strip the portfolio of nonsystematic risk. Because such a **well-diversified portfolio** has for all practical purposes zero firm-specific risk, we can write its returns as

$$R_P = \alpha_P + \beta_P R_M \qquad (7.6)$$

(This portfolio is risky, however, because the excess return on the index, R_M, is random.)

Figure 7.11 illustrates the difference between a single security with a beta of 1.0 and a well-diversified portfolio with the same beta. For the portfolio (Panel A), all the returns plot exactly on the security characteristic line. There is no dispersion around the line, as in Panel B, because the effects of firm-specific events are eliminated by diversification. Therefore, in Equation 7.6, there is no residual term, e.

Notice that Equation 7.6 implies that if the portfolio beta is zero, then $R_P = \alpha_P$. This implies a riskless rate of return: There is no firm-specific risk because of diversification and no factor risk because beta is zero. Remember, however, that R denotes excess returns. So the equation implies that a portfolio with a beta of zero has a riskless *excess* return of α_P, that is, a return higher than the risk-free rate by the amount α_P. But this implies that α_P must equal zero, or else an immediate arbitrage opportunity opens up. For example, if α_P is greater than zero, you can borrow at the risk-free rate and use the proceeds to buy the well-diversified zero-beta portfolio. You borrow risklessly at rate r_f and invest risklessly at rate $r_f + \alpha_P$, clearing the riskless differential of α_P.

well-diversified portfolio

A portfolio sufficiently diversified that nonsystematic risk is negligible.

FIGURE 7.11
Security characteristic lines

Suppose that the risk-free rate is 6%, and a well-diversified zero-beta portfolio earns (a sure) rate of return of 7%, that is, an excess return of 1%. Then borrow at 6% and invest in the zero-beta portfolio to earn 7%. You will earn a sure profit of 1% of the invested funds without putting up any of your own money. If the zero-beta portfolio earns 5%, then you can sell it short and lend at 6% with the same result.

In fact, we can go further and show that the alpha of *any* well-diversified portfolio in Equation 7.6 must be zero, even if the beta is not zero. The proof is similar to the easy zero-beta case. If the alphas were not zero, then we could combine two of these portfolios into a zero-beta riskless portfolio with a rate of return not equal to the risk-free rate. But this, as we have just seen, would be an arbitrage opportunity.

To see how the arbitrage strategy would work, suppose that portfolio V has a beta of β_v and an alpha of α_v. Similarly, suppose portfolio U has a beta of β_u and an alpha of α_u.

Taking advantage of any arbitrage opportunity involves buying and selling assets in proportions that create a risk-free profit on a costless position. To eliminate risk, we buy portfolio V and sell portfolio U in proportions chosen so that the combination portfolio $(V + U)$ will have a beta of zero. The portfolio weights that satisfy this condition are

$$w_v = \frac{-\beta_u}{\beta_v - \beta_u} \qquad w_u = \frac{\beta_v}{\beta_v - \beta_u}$$

Note that w_v plus w_u add up to 1.0 and that the beta of the combination is in fact zero:

$$\text{Beta}(V + U) = \beta_v \frac{-\beta_u}{\beta_v - \beta_u} + \beta_u \frac{\beta_v}{\beta_v - \beta_u} = 0$$

Therefore, the portfolio is riskless: It has no sensitivity to the factor. But the excess return of the portfolio is not zero unless α_v and α_u equal zero.

$$R(V + U) = \alpha_v \frac{-\beta_u}{\beta_v - \beta_u} + \alpha_u \frac{\beta_v}{\beta_v - \beta_u} \neq 0$$

Therefore, unless α_v and α_u equal zero, the zero-beta portfolio has a certain rate of return that differs from the risk-free rate (its excess return is different from zero). We have seen that this gives rise to an arbitrage opportunity.

Suppose that the risk-free rate is 7% and a well-diversified portfolio, *V*, with beta of 1.3 has an alpha of 2% and another well-diversified portfolio, *U*, with beta of 0.8 has an alpha of 1%. We go long on *V* and short on *U* with proportions

$$w_v = \frac{-0.8}{1.3 - 0.8} = -1.6 \qquad w_u = \frac{1.3}{1.3 - 0.8} = 2.6$$

These proportions add up to 1.0 and result in a portfolio with beta = $-1.6 \times 1.3 + 2.6 \times 0.8 = 0$. The alpha of the portfolio is: $-1.6 \times 2\% + 2.6 \times 1\% = -0.6\%$. This means that the riskless portfolio will earn a rate of return that is less than the risk-free rate by .6%. We now complete the arbitrage by selling (or going short on) the combination portfolio and investing the proceeds at 7%, risklessly profiting by the 60 basis point differential in returns.

We conclude that the only value for alpha that rules out arbitrage opportunities is zero. Therefore, rewrite Equation 7.6 setting alpha equal to zero

$$R_P = \beta_P R_M$$

$$r_P - r_f = \beta_P(r_M - r_f)$$

$$E(r_P) = r_f + \beta_P[E(r_M) - r_f]$$

Hence, we arrive at the same expected return–beta relationship as the CAPM without any assumption about either investor preferences or access to the all-inclusive (and elusive) market portfolio.

The APT and the CAPM

Why did we need so many restrictive assumptions to derive the CAPM when the APT seems to arrive at the expected return–beta relationship with seemingly fewer and less objectionable assumptions? The answer is simple: The APT applies only to well-diversified portfolios. Absence of riskless arbitrage alone cannot guarantee that, in equilibrium, the expected return–beta relationship will hold for any and all assets.

With additional effort, however, one can use the APT to show that the relationship must hold approximately even for individual assets. The essence of the proof is that if the expected return–beta relationship were violated by many individual securities, it would be virtually impossible for all well-diversified portfolios to satisfy the relationship. So the relationship must *almost* surely hold true for individual securities.

We say "almost" because, according to the APT, there is no guarantee that all individual assets will lie on the SML. If only a few securities violated the SML, their effect on well-diversified portfolios could conceivably be offsetting. In this sense, it is possible that the SML relationship is violated for single securities. If many securities violate the expected return–beta relationship, however, the relationship will no longer hold for well-diversified portfolios comprising these securities, and arbitrage opportunities will be available.

The APT serves many of the same functions as the CAPM. It gives us a benchmark for fair rates of return that can be used for capital budgeting, security evaluation, or investment performance evaluation. Moreover, the APT highlights the crucial distinction between nondiversifiable risk (systematic or factor risk) that requires a reward in the form of a risk premium and diversifiable risk that does not.

The bottom line is that neither of these theories dominates the other. The APT is more general in that it gets us to the expected return–beta relationship without requiring many of the unrealistic assumptions of the CAPM, particularly the reliance on the market portfolio. The latter improves the prospects for testing the APT. But the CAPM is more general in that it applies to all assets without reservation. The good news is that both theories agree on the expected return–beta relationship.

It is worth noting that because past tests of the expected return–beta relationship examined the rates of return on highly diversified portfolios, they actually came closer to testing the APT than the CAPM. Thus, it appears that econometric concerns, too, favor the APT.

Multifactor Generalization of the APT and CAPM

We've assumed all along that there is only one systematic factor affecting stock returns. This assumption may be too simplistic. It is easy to think of several factors that might affect stock returns: business cycles, interest rate fluctuations, inflation rates, oil prices, and so on. Presumably, exposure to any of these factors singly or together will affect a stock's perceived riskiness and appropriate expected rate of return. We can use a multifactor version of the APT to accommodate these multiple sources of risk.

Suppose we generalize the single-factor model expressed in Equation 7.5 to a two-factor model:

$$R_i = \alpha_i + \beta_{i1}R_{M1} + \beta_{i2}R_{M2} + e_i \tag{7.7}$$

where R_{M1} and R_{M2} are the excess returns on portfolios that represent the two systematic factors. Factor 1 might be, for example, unanticipated changes in industrial production, while factor 2 might represent unanticipated changes in short-term interest rates. We assume again that there are many securities available with any combination of betas. This implies that we can form well-diversified **factor portfolios,** that is, portfolios that have a beta of 1.0 on one factor and a beta of zero on all others. Thus, a factor portfolio with a beta of 1.0 on the first factor will have a rate of return of R_{M1}; a factor portfolio with a beta of 1.0 on the second factor will have a rate of return of R_{M2}; and so on. Factor portfolios can serve as the benchmark portfolios for a multifactor generalization of the security market line relationship.

factor portfolio

A well-diversified portfolio constructed to have a beta of 1.0 on one factor and a beta of zero on any other factor.

Suppose the two-factor portfolios, here called portfolios 1 and 2, have expected returns $E(r_1) = 10\%$ and $E(r_2) = 12\%$. Suppose further that the risk-free rate is 4%. The risk premium on the first factor portfolio is therefore 6%, while that on the second factor portfolio is 8%.

Now consider an arbitrary well-diversified portfolio (A), with beta on the first factor, $\beta_{A1} = 0.5$, and on the second factor, $\beta_{A2} = 0.75$. The multifactor APT states that the portfolio risk premium must equal the sum of the risk premiums required as compensation to investors for each source of systematic risk. The risk premium attributable to risk factor 1 is the portfolio's exposure to factor 1, β_{A1}, times the risk premium earned on the first factor portfolio, $E(r_1) - r_f$. Therefore, the portion of portfolio A's risk premium that is compensation for its exposure to the first risk factor is $\beta_{A1}[E(r_1) - r_f] = 0.5(10\% - 4\%) = 3\%$, while the risk premium attributable to risk factor 2 is $\beta_{A2}[E(r_2) - r_f] = 0.75(12\% - 4\%) = 6\%$. The total risk premium on the portfolio, therefore, should be $3 + 6 = 9\%$, and the total return on the portfolio should be 13%.

4%	Risk-free rate
+ 3%	Risk premium for exposure to factor 1
+ 6%	Risk premium for exposure to factor 2
13%	Total expected return

To generalize this argument, note that the factor exposure of any portfolio P is given by its betas, β_{P1} and β_{P2}. A competing portfolio, Q, can be formed from factor portfolios with the following weights: β_{P1} in the first factor portfolio; β_{P2} in the second factor portfolio; and $1 - \beta_{P2} - \beta_{P2}$ in T-bills. By construction, Q will have betas equal to those of portfolio P and an expected return of

$$E(r_Q) = \beta_{P1}E(r_1) + \beta_{P2}E(r_2) + (1 - \beta_{P1} - \beta_{P2})r_f$$
$$= r_f + \beta_{P1}[E(r_1) - r_f] + \beta_{P2}[E(r_2) - r_f] \tag{7.8}$$

Using our numbers,

$$E(r_Q) = 4 + .5 \times (10 - 4) + .75 \times (12 - 4) = 13\%$$

Because portfolio Q has precisely the same exposures as portfolio A to the two sources of risk, their expected returns also ought to be equal. So portfolio A also ought to have an expected return of 13%.

Estimating the Index Model

The spreadsheet below (available at www.mhhe.com/bkm) also contains monthly returns for the stocks that comprise the Dow Jones Industrial Average. The spreadsheet contains workbooks that show raw returns, risk premiums, correlation coefficients, and beta coefficients for the stocks that are in the DJIA. The security characteristic lines are estimated with five years of monthly returns.

	A	B	C	D	E	F	G	H	I
1	SUMMARY OUTPUT	AXP							
2									
3	Regression Statistics								
4	Multiple R	0.69288601							
5	R Square	0.48009103							
6	Adjusted R Square	0.47112708							
7	Standard Error	0.05887426							
8	Observations	60							
9									
10	ANOVA								
11		df	SS	MS	F	Significance F			
12	Regression	1	0.185641557	0.1856416	53.55799	8.55186E-10			
13	Residual	58	0.201038358	0.0034662					
14	Total	59	0.386679915						
15									
16		Coefficients	Standard Error	t Stat	P-value	Lower 95%	Upper 95%	Lower 95.0%	Upper 95.0%
17	Intercept	0.01181687	0.00776211	1.522379	0.133348	−0.003720666	0.027354414	−0.0037207	0.02735441
18	X Variable 1	1.20877413	0.165170705	7.3183324	8.55E-10	0.878149288	1.539398969	0.87814929	1.53939897

Suppose, however, that the expected return on portfolio A is 12% rather than 13%. This return would give rise to an arbitrage opportunity. Form a portfolio from the factor portfolios with the same betas as portfolio A. This requires weights of 0.5 on the first factor portfolio, 0.75 on the second portfolio, and − 0.25 on the risk-free asset. This portfolio has exactly the same factor betas as portfolio A: a beta of 0.5 on the first factor because of its 0.5 weight on the first factor portfolio and a beta of 0.75 on the second factor.

Now invest \$1 in portfolio Q and sell (short) \$1 in portfolio A. Your net investment is zero, but your expected dollar profit is positive and equal to

$$\$1 \times E(r_Q) - \$1 \times E(r_A) = \$1 \times .13 - \$1 \times .12 = \$.01.$$

Moreover, your net position is riskless. Your exposure to each risk factor cancels out because you are long \$1 in portfolio Q and short \$1 in portfolio $A,$ and both of these well-diversified portfolios have exactly the same factor betas. Thus, if portfolio A's expected return differs from that of portfolio Q's, you can earn positive risk-free profits on a zero net investment position. This is an arbitrage opportunity.

Hence, any well-diversified portfolio with betas β_{P1} and β_{P2} must have the return given in Equation 7.8 if arbitrage opportunities are to be ruled out. A comparison of Equations 7.2 and 7.8 shows that 7.8 is simply a generalization of the one-factor SML.

Finally, extension of the multifactor SML of Equation 7.8 to individual assets is precisely the same as for the one-factor APT. Equation 7.8 cannot be satisfied by every well-diversified portfolio unless it is satisfied by virtually every security taken individually. Equation 7.8 thus represents the multifactor SML for an economy with multiple sources of risk.

The generalized APT must be qualified with respect to individual assets just as in the single-factor case. A multifactor CAPM would, at the cost of additional assumptions, apply to any and all individual assets. As we have seen, the result will be a security market equation (a multidimensional SML) that is identical to that of the multifactor APT.

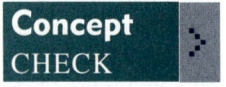

Concept
CHECK

6. **Using the factor portfolios just considered, find the fair rate of return on a security with $\beta_1 = 0.2$ and $\beta_2 = 1.4$.**

SUMMARY

- The CAPM assumes investors are rational, single-period planners who agree on a common input list from security analysis and seek mean-variance optimal portfolios.
- The CAPM assumes ideal security markets in the sense that: (*a*) markets are large and investors are price takers, (*b*) there are no taxes or transaction costs, (*c*) all risky assets are publicly traded, and (*d*) any amount can be borrowed and lent at a fixed, risk-free rate.
- These assumptions mean that all investors will hold identical risky portfolios. The CAPM implies that, in equilibrium, the market portfolio is the unique mean-variance efficient tangency portfolio, which indicates that a passive strategy is efficient.
- The market portfolio is a value-weighted portfolio. Each security is held in a proportion equal to its market value divided by the total market value of all securities. The risk premium on the market portfolio is proportional to its variance, σ_M^2, and to the risk aversion of the average investor.
- The CAPM implies that the risk premium on any individual asset or portfolio is the product of the risk premium of the market portfolio and the asset's beta. The security market line shows the return demanded by investors as a function of the beta of their investment. This expected return is a benchmark for evaluating investment performance.
- In a single-index security market, once an index is specified, a security beta can be estimated from a regression of the security's excess return on the index's excess return. This regression line is called the security characteristic line (SCL). The intercept of the SCL, called alpha, represents the average excess return on the security when the index excess return is zero. The CAPM implies that alphas should be zero.
- An arbitrage opportunity arises when the disparity between two or more security prices enables investors to construct a zero net investment portfolio that will yield a sure profit. Rational investors will want to take infinitely large positions in arbitrage portfolios regardless of their degree of risk aversion.
- The presence of arbitrage opportunities and the resulting volume of trades will create pressure on security prices that will persist until prices reach levels that preclude arbitrage. Only a few investors need to become aware of arbitrage opportunities to trigger this process because of the large volume of trades in which they will engage.
- When securities are priced so that there are no arbitrage opportunities, the market satisfies the no-arbitrage condition. Price relationships that satisfy the no-arbitrage condition are important because we expect them to hold in real-world markets.
- Portfolios are called *well diversified* if they include a large number of securities in such proportions that the residual or diversifiable risk of the portfolio is negligible.
- In a single-factor security market, all well-diversified portfolios must satisfy the expected return–beta relationship of the SML in order to satisfy the no-arbitrage condition.
- If all well-diversified portfolios satisfy the expected return–beta relationship, then all but a small number of securities also must satisfy this relationship.

- The APT implies the same expected return–beta relationship as the CAPM, yet does not require that all investors be mean-variance optimizers. The price of this generality is that the APT does not guarantee this relationship for all securities at all times.
- A multifactor APT generalizes the single-factor model to accommodate several sources of systematic risk.

alpha, 227
arbitrage, 242
arbitrage pricing theory
  (APT), 244
capital asset pricing model
  (CAPM), 221

expected return–beta
  relationship, 225
factor portfolio, 248
market portfolio, 221
mutual fund theorem, 223
security characteristic
  line (SCL), 231

security market line
  (SML), 226
well-diversified
  portfolio, 245
zero-investment
  portfolio, 242

1. Which of the following statements about the security market line (SML) are **true**?
   a. The SML provides a benchmark for evaluating expected investment performance.
   b. The SML leads all investors to invest in the same portfolio of risky assets.
   c. The SML is a graphic representation of the relationship between expected return and beta.
   d. Properly valued assets plot exactly on the SML.

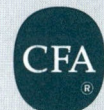

2. Risk aversion has *all* of the following implications for the investment process *except:*
   a. The security market line is upward sloping.
   b. The promised yield on AAA-rated bonds is higher than on A-rated bonds.
   c. Investors expect a positive relationship between expected return and risk.
   d. Investors prefer portfolios that lie on the efficient frontier to other portfolios with equal expected rates of return.

3. What is the beta of a portfolio with $E(r_P) = 20\%$, if $r_f = 5\%$ and $E(r_M) = 15\%$?

4. The market price of a security is $40. Its expected rate of return is 13%. The risk-free rate is 7%, and the market risk premium is 8%. What will the market price of the security be if its beta doubles (and all other variables remain unchanged)? Assume the stock is expected to pay a constant dividend in perpetuity.

5. You are a consultant to a large manufacturing corporation considering a project with the following net after-tax cash flows (in millions of dollars)

Years from Now	After-Tax CF
0	−20
1–9	10
10	20

  The project's beta is 1.7. Assuming $r_f = 9\%$ and $E(r_M) = 19\%$, what is the net present value of the project? What is the highest possible beta estimate for the project before its NPV becomes negative?

6. Are the following statements true or false? Explain.
   a. Stocks with a beta of zero offer an expected rate of return of zero.
   b. The CAPM implies that investors require a higher return to hold highly volatile securities.
   c. You can construct a portfolio with a beta of 0.75 by investing 0.75 of the budget in T-bills and the remainder in the market portfolio.

7. Consider the following table, which gives a security analyst's expected return on two stocks for two particular market returns:

Market Return	Aggressive Stock	Defensive Stock
5%	2%	3.5%
20	32	14

    a. What are the betas of the two stocks?

    b. What is the expected rate of return on each stock if the market return is equally likely to be 5% or 20%?

    c. If the T-bill rate is 8%, and the market return is equally likely to be 5% or 20%, draw the SML for this economy.

    d. Plot the two securities on the SML graph. What are the alphas of each?

    e. What hurdle rate should be used by the management of the aggressive firm for a project with the risk characteristics of the defensive firm's stock?

If the simple CAPM is valid, which of the situations in problems 8–14 below are possible? Explain. Consider each situation independently.

8.

Portfolio	Expected Return	Beta
A	20%	1.4
B	25	1.2

9.

Portfolio	Expected Return	Standard Deviation
A	30%	35%
B	40	25

10.

Portfolio	Expected Return	Standard Deviation
Risk-free	10%	0%
Market	18	24
A	16	12

11.

Portfolio	Expected Return	Standard Deviation
Risk-free	10%	0%
Market	18	24
A	20	22

12.

Portfolio	Expected Return	Beta
Risk-free	10%	0
Market	18	1.0
A	16	1.5

13.

Portfolio	Expected Return	Beta
Risk-free	10%	0
Market	18	1.0
A	16	.9

14.

Portfolio	Expected Return	Standard Deviation
Risk-free	10%	0%
Market	18	24
A	16	22

In problems 15–17 below, assume the risk-free rate is 8% and the expected rate of return on the market is 18%.

15. A share of stock is now selling for $100. It will pay a dividend of $9 per share at the end of the year. Its beta is 1.0. What do investors expect the stock to sell for at the end of the year?

16. I am buying a firm with an expected perpetual cash flow of $1,000 but am unsure of its risk. If I think the beta of the firm is zero, when the beta is really 1.0, how much *more* will I offer for the firm than it is truly worth?

17. A stock has an expected return of 6%. What is its beta?

18. Two investment advisers are comparing performance. One averaged a 19% return and the other a 16% return. However, the beta of the first adviser was 1.5, while that of the second was 1.0.
    a. Can you tell which adviser was a better selector of individual stocks (aside from the issue of general movements in the market)?
    b. If the T-bill rate were 6%, and the market return during the period were 14%, which adviser would be the superior stock selector?
    c. What if the T-bill rate were 3% and the market return 15%?

19. In 2002, the yield on short-term government securities (perceived to be risk-free) was about 4%. Suppose the expected return required by the market for a portfolio with a beta of 1.0 is 12%. According to the capital asset pricing model:
    a. What is the expected return on the market portfolio?
    b. What would be the expected return on a zero-beta stock?
    c. Suppose you consider buying a share of stock at a price of $40. The stock is expected to pay a dividend of $3 next year and to sell then for $41. The stock risk has been evaluated at $\beta = -0.5$. Is the stock overpriced or underpriced?

www.mhhe.com/bkm

20. Based on current dividend yields and expected capital gains, the expected rates of return on portfolio A and B are 11% and 14%, respectively. The beta of A is 0.8 while that of B is 1.5. The T-bill rate is currently 6%, while the expected rate of return of the S&P 500 Index is 12%. The standard deviation of portfolio A is 10% annually, while that of B is 31%, and that of the index is 20%.

    a. If you currently hold a market index portfolio, would you choose to add either of these portfolios to your holdings? Explain.

    b. If instead you could invest *only* in bills and one of these portfolios, which would you choose?

21. Consider the following data for a one-factor economy. All portfolios are well diversified.

Portfolio	E(r)	Beta
A	10%	1.0
F	4	0

    Suppose another portfolio E is well diversified with a beta of 2/3 and expected return of 9%. Would an arbitrage opportunity exist? If so, what would the arbitrage strategy be?

22. Following is a scenario for three stocks constructed by the security analysts of PF Inc.

Stock	Price ($)	Scenario Rate of Return (%)		
		Recession	Average	Boom
A	10	−15	20	30
B	15	25	10	−10
C	50	12	15	12

    a. Construct an arbitrage portfolio using these stocks.

    b. How might these prices change when equilibrium is restored? Give an example where a change in stock C's price is sufficient to restore equilibrium, assuming the dollar payoffs to stock C remain the same.

23. Assume both portfolios A and B are well diversified, that $E(r_A) = 14\%$ and $E(r_B) = 14.8\%$. If the economy has only one factor, and $\beta_A = 1.0$ while $\beta_B = 1.1$, what must be the risk-free rate?

24. Assume a market index represents the common factor, and all stocks in the economy have a beta of 1.0. Firm-specific returns all have a standard deviation of 30%.

    Suppose an analyst studies 20 stocks and finds that one-half have an alpha of 3%, and one-half have an alpha of −3%. The analyst then buys $1 million of an equally weighted portfolio of the positive alpha stocks and sells short $1 million of an equally weighted portfolio of the negative alpha stocks.

    a. What is the expected profit (in dollars), and what is the standard deviation of the analyst's profit?

    b. How does your answer change if the analyst examines 50 stocks instead of 20? 100 stocks?

25. If the APT is to be a useful theory, the number of systematic factors in the economy must be small. Why?

26. The APT itself does not provide information on the factors that one might expect to determine risk premiums. How should researchers decide which factors to investigate? Is industrial production a reasonable factor to test for a risk premium? Why or why not?

27. Suppose two factors are identified for the U.S. economy: the growth rate of industrial production, IP, and the inflation rate, IR. IP is expected to be 4% and IR 6%. A stock with a beta of 1.0 on IP and 0.4 on IR currently is expected to provide a rate of return of 14%. If industrial production actually grows by 5%, while the inflation rate turns out to be 7%, what is your best guess for the rate of return on the stock?

28. Suppose there are two independent economic factors, M_1 and M_2. The risk-free rate is 7%, and all stocks have independent firm-specific components with a standard deviation of 50%. Portfolios A and B are both well diversified.

Portfolio	Beta on M_1	Beta on M_2	Expected Return (%)
A	1.8	2.1	40
B	2.0	−0.5	10

What is the expected return–beta relationship in this economy?

29. The security market line depicts:
    a. A security's expected return as a function of its systematic risk.
    b. The market portfolio as the optimal portfolio of risky securities.
    c. The relationship between a security's return and the return on an index.
    d. The complete portfolio as a combination of the market portfolio and the risk-free asset.

30. Within the context of the capital asset pricing model (CAPM), assume:
    - Expected return on the market = 15%.
    - Risk-free rate = 8%.
    - Expected rate of return on XYZ security = 17%.
    - Beta of XYZ security = 1.25.

    Which one of the following is correct?
    a. XYZ is overpriced.
    b. XYZ is fairly priced.
    c. XYZ's alpha is −.25%.
    d. XYZ's alpha is .25%.

31. What is the expected return of a zero-beta security?
    a. Market rate of return.
    b. Zero rate of return.
    d. Negative rate of return.
    d. Risk-free rate of return.

32. Capital asset pricing theory asserts that expected returns are best explained by:
    a. Economic factors
    b. Specific risk
    c. Systematic risk
    d. Diversification

33. According to CAPM, the expected rate of return of a portfolio with a beta of 1.0 and an alpha of 0 is:
    a. Between r_M and r_f.
    b. The risk-free rate, r_f.

    c. $\beta(r_M - r_f)$.

    d. The expected return on the market, r_M.

The following table shows risk and return measures for two portfolios.

Portfolio	Average Annual Rate of Return	Standard Deviation	Beta
R	11%	10%	0.5
S&P 500	14%	12%	1.0

34. When plotting portfolio R on the preceding table relative to the SML, portfolio R lies:
    a. On the SML.
    b. Below the SML.
    c. Above the SML.
    d. Insufficient data given.

35. When plotting portfolio R relative to the capital market line, portfolio R lies:
    a. On the CML.
    b. Below the CML.
    c. Above the CML.
    d. Insufficient data given.

36. Briefly explain whether investors should expect a higher return from holding portfolio A versus portfolio B under capital asset pricing theory (CAPM). Assume that both portfolios are fully diversified.

	Portfolio A	Portfolio B
Systematic risk (beta)	1.0	1.0
Specific risk for each individual security	High	Low

37. Assume that both X and Y are well-diversified portfolios and the risk-free rate is 8%.

Portfolio	Expected Return	Beta
X	16%	1.00
Y	12%	0.25

In this situation you could conclude that portfolios X and Y:
    a. Are in equilibrium.
    b. Offer an arbitrage opportunity.
    c. Are both underpriced.
    d. Are both fairly priced.

38. According to the theory of arbitrage:
    a. High-beta stocks are consistently overpriced.
    b. Low-beta stocks are consistently overpriced.
    c. Positive alpha investment opportunities will quickly disappear.
    d. Rational investors will pursue arbitrage consistent with their risk tolerance.

39. A zero-investment portfolio with a positive alpha could arise if:
    a. The expected return of the portfolio equals zero.
    b. The capital market line is tangent to the opportunity set.
    c. The law of one price remains unviolated.
    d. A risk-free arbitrage opportunity exists.

40. The APT differs from the single-factor CAPM because the APT:
    a. Places more emphasis on market risk.
    b. Minimizes the importance of diversification.
    c. Recognizes multiple unsystematic risk factors.
    d. Recognizes multiple systematic risk factors.

41. An investor takes as large a position as possible when an equilibrium price relationship is violated. This is an example of:
    a. A dominance argument.
    b. The mean-variance efficient frontier.
    c. Arbitrage activity.
    d. The capital asset pricing model.

42. The feature of APT that offers the greatest potential advantage over the simple CAPM is the:
    a. Identification of anticipated changes in production, inflation, and term structure of interest rates as key factors explaining the risk-return relationship.
    b. Superior measurement of the risk-free rate of return over historical time periods.
    c. Variability of coefficients of sensitivity to the APT factors for a given asset over time.
    d. Use of several factors instead of a single market index to explain the risk-return relationship.

43. In contrast to the capital asset pricing model, arbitrage pricing theory:
    a. Requires that markets be in equilibrium.
    b. Uses risk premiums based on micro variables.
    c. Specifies the number and identifies specific factors that determine expected returns.
    d. Does not require the restrictive assumptions concerning the market portfolio.

STANDARD & POOR'S

1. In the previous chapter, you used data from Market Insight to calculate the beta of Apple Computer (AAPL). Now let's compute the alpha of the stock in two consecutive periods. Estimate the index model regression using the first two years of monthly data. (You can get monthly T-bill rates to calculate excess returns from the Federal Reserve website at http://www.federalreserve.gov/releases/h15/data.htm.) The intercept of the regression is Apple's alpha over that 2-year period. Now repeat this exercise using the next two years of monthly data. This will give you alpha and beta estimates for two consecutive time periods. Finally, repeat this regression exercise for several (e.g., a dozen) other firms.

2. Given your results for question 1, we can now investigate the extent to which beta in one period predicts beta in future periods and whether alpha in one period predicts alpha in future periods. Regress the beta of each firm in the second period against the beta in the first period. (If you estimated regressions for a dozen firms in question 1, you will have 12 observations in this regression.) Do the same for the alphas of each firm.

3. We would expect that beta in the first period predicts beta in the next period, but that alpha in the first period has no power to predict alpha in the next period. (The regression coefficient on first-period beta will be statistically significant, but the coefficient on alpha will not be.) Why does this expectation make sense? Is it borne out by the data?

STANDARD
&POOR'S

WEBMASTER

Beta Coefficients

Go to www.mhhe.com/edumarketinsight. Click on Monthly Valuation Data. The report summarizes seven months of data related to stock market activity and contains several comparison reports to the market indexes. Pull the monthly valuation data for General Electric, The Home Depot, Johnson and Johnson, Honeywell, and H.J. Heinz.

After reviewing the reports, answer the following questions:

1. Which of the firms are low-beta firms?

2. Does the beta coefficient for these low-beta firms make sense given what type of firms they are? Briefly explain.

3. Describe the variation in the reported beta coefficients over the seven months of data.

SOLUTIONS TO

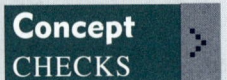

1. The CML would still represent efficient investments. We can characterize the entire population by two representative investors. One is the "uninformed" investor, who does not engage in security analysis and holds the market portfolio, while the other optimizes using the Markowitz algorithm with input from security analysis. The uninformed investor does not know what input the informed investor uses to make portfolio purchases. The uninformed investor knows, however, that if the other investor is informed, the market portfolio proportions will be optimal. Therefore, to depart from these proportions would constitute an uninformed bet, which will, on average, reduce the efficiency of diversification with no compensating improvement in expected returns.

2. Substituting the historical mean and standard deviation in Equation 7.1 yields a coefficient of risk aversion of

$$A^* = \frac{E(r_M) - r_f}{\sigma_M^2} = \frac{.085}{0.20^2} = 2.1$$

This relationship also tells us that for the historical standard deviation and a coefficient of risk aversion of 3.5, the risk premium would be

$$E(r_M) - r_f = A^*\sigma_M^2 = 3.5 \times 0.20^2 = 0.14 = 14\%$$

3. $\beta_{Ford} = 1.25$, $\beta_{GM} = 1.15$. Therefore, given the investment proportions, the portfolio beta is

$$\beta_P = w_{Ford}\beta_{Ford} + w_{GM}\beta_{GM} = (0.75 \times 1.25) + (0.25 \times 1.15) = 1.225$$

and the risk premium of the portfolio will be

$$E(r_P) - r_f = \beta_P[E(r_M) - r_f] = 1.225 \times 8\% = 9.8\%$$

4. *a.* The alpha of a stock is its expected return in excess of that required by the CAPM.

$$\alpha = E(r) - \{r_f + \beta[E(r_M) - r_f]\}$$

$$\alpha_{XYZ} = 12 - [5 + 1.0(11 - 5)] = 1$$

$$\alpha_{ABC} = 13 - [5 + 1.5(11 - 5)] = -1\%$$

b. The project-specific required rate of return is determined by the project beta coupled with the market risk premium and the risk-free rate. The CAPM tells us that an acceptable expected rate of return for the project is

$$r_f + \beta[E(r_M) - r_f] = 8 + 1.3(16 - 8) = 18.4\%$$

which becomes the project's hurdle rate. If the IRR of the project is 19%, then it is desirable. Any project (of similar beta) with an IRR less than 18.4% should be rejected.

5. The least profitable scenario currently yields a profit of $10,000 and gross proceeds from the equally weighted portfolio of $700,000. As the price of Dreck falls, less of the equally weighted portfolio can be purchased from the proceeds of the short sale. When Dreck's price falls by more than a factor of 10,000/700,000, arbitrage no longer will be feasible, because the profits in the worst state will be driven below zero.

To see this, suppose Dreck's price falls to $10 \times (1 - 1/70)$. The short sale of 300,000 shares now yields $2,957,142, which allows dollar investments of only $985,714 in each of the other shares. In the high real interest rate, low inflation scenario, profits will be driven to zero.

Stock	Dollar Investment	Rate of Return (%)	Dollar Return
Apex	$ 985,714	20	$ 197,143
Bull	985,714	70	690,000
Crush	985,714	-20	-197,143
Dreck	-2,957,142	NA*	-690,000
Total	$ 0		$ 0

*The dollar return on Dreck is assumed to be held fixed as its price falls. Therefore, Dreck's rate of return will depend on the price to which its stock price falls, but in any case the rate of return is not necessary to answer the question.

At any price for Dreck stock below $10 \times (1 - 1/70) = \$9.857$, profits will be negative, which means the arbitrage opportunity is eliminated. Note: $9.857 is not the equilibrium price of Dreck. It is simply the upper bound on Dreck's price that rules out the simple arbitrage opportunity.

6. Using Equation 7.8, the expected return is

$$4 + (0.2 \times 6) + (1.4 \times 8) = 16.4\%$$

8

THE EFFICIENT MARKET HYPOTHESIS

AFTER STUDYING THIS CHAPTER YOU SHOULD BE ABLE TO:

> Demonstrate why security price movements should be essentially unpredictable.

> Cite evidence that supports and contradicts the efficient market hypothesis.

> Formulate investment strategies that make sense in informationally efficient markets.

One of the early applications of computers in economics in the 1950s was to analyze economic time series. Business cycle theorists believed tracing the evolution of several economic variables over time would clarify and predict the progress of the economy through boom and bust periods. A natural candidate for analysis was the behavior of stock market prices over time. Assuming stock prices reflect the prospects of the firm, recurring patterns of peaks and troughs in economic performance ought to show up in those prices.

Maurice Kendall (1953) was one of the first to examine this proposition. He found to his great surprise that he could identify *no* predictable patterns in stock prices. Prices seemed to evolve randomly. They were as likely to go up as they were to go down on any particular day regardless of past performance. The data provided no way to predict price movements.

At first blush, Kendall's results disturbed some financial economists. They seemed to imply that the stock market is dominated by erratic market psychology, or "animal spirits," and that it follows no logical rules. In short, the results appeared to confirm the irrationality of the market. On further reflection, however, economists reversed their interpretation of Kendall's study.

It soon became apparent that random price movements indicated a well-functioning or efficient market, not an irrational one. In this chapter, we will explore the reasoning behind what may seem to be a surprising conclusion. We show how competition among analysts leads naturally to market efficiency, and we examine the implications of the efficient market hypothesis for investment policy. We also consider empirical evidence that supports and contradicts the notion of market efficiency.

8.1 RANDOM WALKS AND THE EFFICIENT MARKET HYPOTHESIS

Suppose Kendall had discovered that stock prices are predictable. Imagine the gold mine for investors! If they could use Kendall's equations to predict stock prices, investors would reap unending profits simply by purchasing stocks the computer model implied were about to increase in price and selling those stocks about to fall in price.

A moment's reflection should be enough to convince you that this situation could not persist for long. For example, suppose the model predicts with great confidence that XYZ's stock price, currently at $100 per share, will rise dramatically in three days to $110. All investors with access to the model's prediction would place a great wave of immediate buy orders to cash in on the prospective increase in stock price. No one in the know holding XYZ, however, would be willing to sell, and the net effect would be an *immediate* jump in the stock price to $110. The forecast of a future price increase leads instead to an immediate price increase. Another way of putting this is that the stock price will immediately reflect the "good news" implicit in the model's forecast.

This simple example illustrates why Kendall's attempts to find recurring patterns in stock price movements were in vain. A forecast about favorable *future* performance leads instead to favorable *current* performance, as market participants all try to get in on the action before the price jump.

More generally, one could say that any publicly available information that might be used to predict stock performance, including information on the macroeconomy, the firm's industry, and its operations, plans, and management, should already be reflected in stock prices. As soon as there is any information indicating a stock is underpriced and offers a profit opportunity, investors flock to buy the stock and immediately bid up its price to a fair level, where again only ordinary rates of return can be expected. These "ordinary rates" are simply rates of return commensurate with the risk of the stock.

But if prices are bid immediately to fair levels, given all available information, it must be that prices increase or decrease only in response to new information. New information, by definition, must be unpredictable; if it could be predicted, then that prediction would be part of today's information! Thus, stock prices that change in response to new (unpredictable) information also must move unpredictably.

random walk

The notion that stock price changes are random and unpredictable.

This is the essence of the argument that stock prices should follow a **random walk,** that is, that price changes should be random and unpredictable. Far from being a proof of market irrationality, randomly evolving stock prices are the necessary consequence of intelligent investors competing to discover relevant information before the rest of the market becomes aware of that information.

Don't confuse randomness in price *changes* with irrationality in the *level* of prices. If prices are determined rationally, then only new information will cause them to change. Therefore, a random walk would be the natural consequence of prices that always reflect all current knowledge.

efficient market hypothesis

The hypothesis that prices of securities fully reflect available information about securities.

Indeed, if stock price movements were predictable, that would be damning evidence of stock market *inefficiency,* because the ability to predict prices would indicate that all available information was not already impounded in stock prices. Therefore, the notion that stocks already reflect all available information is referred to as the **efficient market hypothesis** (EMH).

Figure 8.1 illustrates the response of stock prices to new information in an efficient market. The graph plots the price response of a sample of 194 firms that were targets of takeover attempts. In most takeovers, the acquiring firm pays a substantial premium over current market prices. Therefore, announcement of a takeover attempt should cause the stock price to jump.

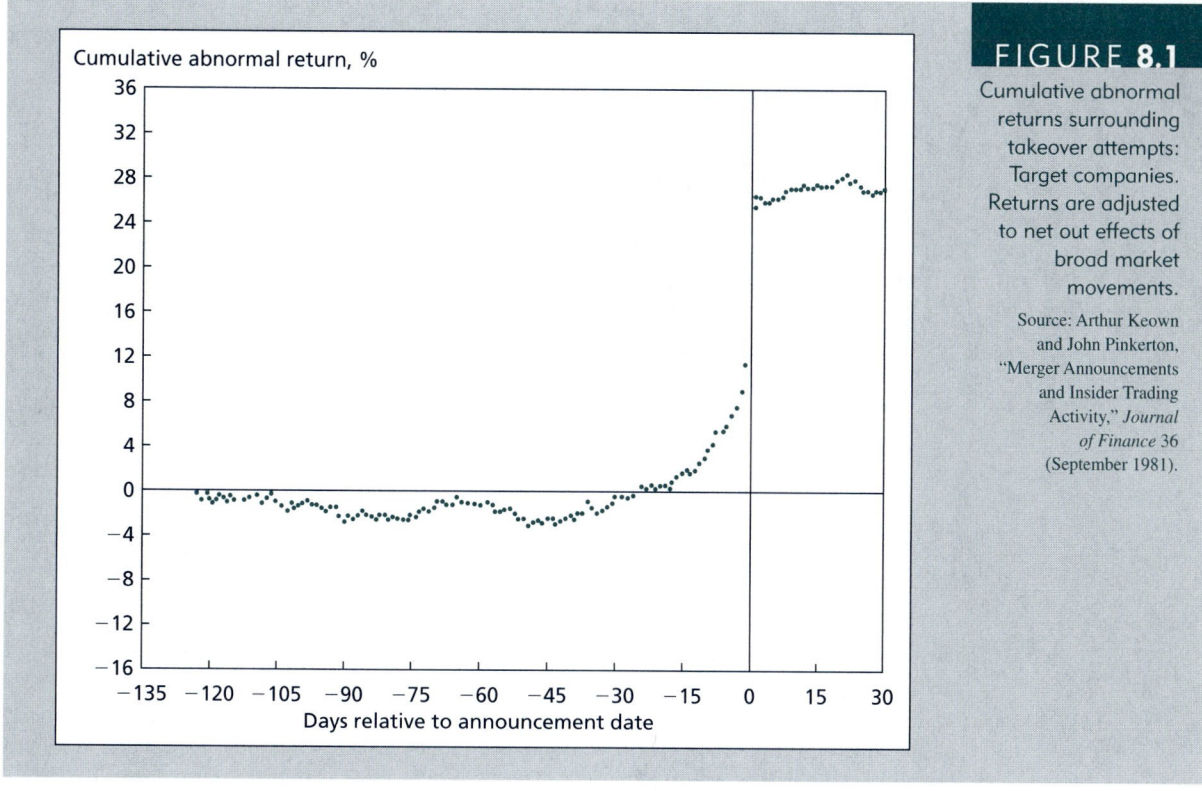

FIGURE **8.1**

Cumulative abnormal
returns surrounding
takeover attempts:
Target companies.
Returns are adjusted
to net out effects of
broad market
movements.

Source: Arthur Keown
and John Pinkerton,
"Merger Announcements
and Insider Trading
Activity," *Journal
of Finance* 36
(September 1981).

The figure shows that stock prices jump dramatically on the day the news becomes public. However, there is no further drift in prices *after* the announcement date, suggesting that prices reflect the new information, including the likely magnitude of the takeover premium, by the end of the trading day.

An even more dramatic demonstration of the speed of price response appears in Figure 8.2. Suppose that you bought shares of firms announcing positive earnings surprises and sold short shares of firms with negative earnings surprises. (A positive surprise is defined as earnings that exceed the prior forecast published by the Value Line Investment Survey.) The figure tracks the average profits to this strategy for each half-hour period following the public announcement. The figure demonstrates that the vast majority of the profits to this strategy would be realized in the first half-hour following the announcement. Only 30 minutes after the public announcement, it is virtually too late to profitably trade on the information, suggesting that the market responds to the news within that short time period.

Competition as the Source of Efficiency

Why should we expect stock prices to reflect all available information? After all, if you were to spend time and money gathering information, you would hope to turn up something that had been overlooked by the rest of the investment community. When information costs you money to uncover and analyze, you expect your investment analysis to result in an increased expected return.

Investors will have an incentive to spend time and resources to analyze and uncover new information only if such activity is likely to generate higher investment returns. Therefore, in

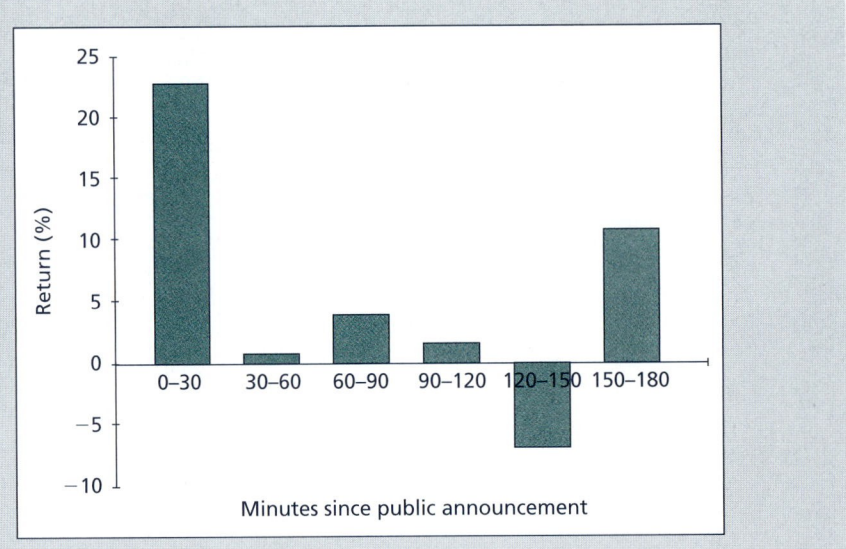

FIGURE **8.2**

Returns following earnings announcements

Note: Only the return in the first 30 minutes was statistically significantly different from that of a control sample at 5 or 10% confidence levels.
Source: James M. Patell and Mark A. Wolfson, "The Intraday Speed of Stock Prices to Earnings and Dividend Announcements," *Journal of Financial Economics,* June 1984, pp. 223–52.

market equilibrium, efficient informational gathering activity should be fruitful.[1] Moreover, it would not be surprising to find that the degree of efficiency across various markets may differ. For example, emerging markets, which are less intensively analyzed than U.S. markets and in which information is harder to come by, may be less efficient than U.S. markets. Small stocks, which receive less coverage by Wall Street analysts, may be less efficiently priced than large ones. Still, while we would not go so far as to say you absolutely cannot come up with new information, it makes sense to consider and respect your competition.

Assume an investment management firm is managing a $5 billion portfolio. Suppose the fund manager can devise a research program that could increase the portfolio rate of return by one-tenth of 1% per year, a seemingly modest amount. This program would increase the dollar return to the portfolio by $5 billion $\times$ .001, or $5 million. Therefore, the fund is presumably willing to spend up to $5 million per year on research to increase stock returns by a mere one-tenth of 1% per year.

With such large rewards for such small increases in investment performance, is it any surprise that professional portfolio managers are willing to spend large sums on industry analysts, computer support, and research effort? With so many well-backed analysts willing to spend considerable resources on research, there cannot be many easy pickings in the market. Moreover, the incremental rates of return on research activity are likely to be so small that only managers of the largest portfolios will find them worth pursuing.

While it may not literally be true that *all* relevant information will be uncovered, it is virtually certain there are many investigators hot on the trail of any leads that seem likely to improve investment performance. Competition among these many well-backed, highly paid, aggressive analysts ensures that, as a general rule, stock prices ought to reflect available information regarding their proper levels.

---

[1]A challenging and insightful discussion of this point may be found in Sanford J. Grossman and Joseph E. Stiglitz, "On the Impossibility of Informationally Efficient Markets," *American Economic Review* 70 (June 1980).

Versions of the Efficient Market Hypothesis

It is common to distinguish among three versions of the EMH: the weak, the semistrong, and the strong forms of the hypothesis. These versions differ according to their notions of what is meant by the term *all available information.*

The **weak-form EMH** asserts that stock prices already reflect all information that can be derived by examining market trading data such as the history of past prices, trading volume, or short interest. This version of the hypothesis implies that trend analysis is fruitless. Past stock price data are publicly available and virtually costless to obtain. The weak-form hypothesis holds that if such data ever conveyed reliable signals about future performance, all investors would have learned long since to exploit the signals. Ultimately, the signals lose their value as they become widely known, because a buy signal, for instance, would result in an immediate price increase.

The **semistrong-form EMH** states that all publicly available information regarding the prospects of a firm must be already reflected in the stock price. Such information includes, in addition to past prices, fundamental data on the firm's product line, quality of management, balance sheet composition, patents held, earnings forecasts, and accounting practices, and so forth. Again, if any investor has access to such information from publicly available sources, one would expect it to be reflected in stock prices.

Finally, the **strong-form EMH** states that stock prices reflect all information relevant to the firm, even including information available only to company insiders. This version of the hypothesis is quite extreme. Few would argue with the proposition that corporate officers have access to pertinent information long enough before public release to enable them to profit from trading on that information. Indeed, much of the activity of the Securities and Exchange Commission (SEC) is directed toward preventing insiders from profiting by exploiting their privileged situation. Rule 10b-5 of the Security Exchange Act of 1934 limits trading by corporate officers, directors, and substantial owners, requiring them to report trades to the SEC. Anyone trading on information supplied by insiders is considered in violation of the law.

Defining insider trading is not always easy, however. After all, stock analysts are in the business of uncovering information not already widely known to market participants. As we saw in Chapter 3, the distinction between private and inside information is sometimes murky.

weak-form EMH	The assertion that stock prices already reflect all information contained in the history of past trading.
semistrong-form EMH	The assertion that stock prices already reflect all publicly available information.
strong-form EMH	The assertion that stock prices reflect all relevant information, including inside information.

1. *a.* Suppose you observed that high-level managers were making superior returns on investments in their company's stock. Would this be a violation of weak-form market efficiency? Would it be a violation of strong-form market efficiency?
   b. If the weak form of the efficient market hypothesis is valid, must the strong form also hold? Conversely, does strong-form efficiency imply weak-form efficiency?

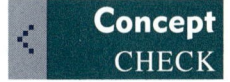

Concept
CHECK

8.2 IMPLICATIONS OF THE EMH

Technical Analysis

Technical analysis is essentially the search for recurring and predictable patterns in stock prices. Although technicians recognize the value of information that has to do with future economic prospects of the firm, they believe such information is not necessary for a successful trading

technical analysis

Research on recurrent and predictable stock price patterns and on proxies for buy or sell pressure in the market.

strategy. Whatever the fundamental reason for a change in stock price, if the stock price responds slowly enough, the analyst will be able to identify a trend that can be exploited during the adjustment period. Technical analysis assumes a sluggish response of stock prices to fundamental supply and demand factors. This assumption is diametrically opposed to the notion of an efficient market.

Technical analysts sometimes are called *chartists* because they study records or charts of past stock prices, hoping to find patterns they can exploit to make a profit. As an example of technical analysis, consider the *relative strength* approach. The chartist compares stock performance over a recent period to performance of the market or other stocks in the same industry. A simple version of relative strength takes the ratio of the stock price to a market indicator such as the S&P 500 index. If the ratio increases over time, the stock is said to exhibit relative strength, because its price performance is better than that of the broad market. Such strength presumably may continue for a long enough period to offer profit opportunities.

The efficient market hypothesis predicts that technical analysis is without merit. The past history of prices and trading volume is publicly available at minimal cost. Therefore, any information that was ever available from analyzing past prices has already been reflected in stock prices. As investors compete to exploit their common knowledge of a stock's price history, they necessarily drive stock prices to levels where expected rates of return are commensurate with risk. At those levels, stocks are neither bad nor good buys. They are just fairly priced, meaning one should not expect abnormal returns.

Despite these theoretical considerations, some technically oriented trading strategies would have generated abnormal profits in the past. We will consider these strategies, and technical analysis more generally in Chapter 19.

Fundamental Analysis

fundamental analysis

Research on determinants of stock value, such as earnings and dividends prospects, expectations for future interest rates, and risk of the firm.

Fundamental analysis uses earnings and dividend prospects of the firm, expectations of future interest rates, and risk evaluation of the firm to determine proper stock prices. Ultimately, it represents an attempt to determine the present discounted value of all the payments a stockholder will receive from each share of stock. If that value exceeds the stock price, the fundamental analyst would recommend purchasing the stock.

Fundamental analysts usually start with a study of past earnings and an examination of company financial statements. They supplement this analysis with further detailed economic analysis, ordinarily including an evaluation of the quality of the firm's management, the firm's standing within its industry, and the prospects for the industry as a whole. The hope is to attain some insight into the future performance of the firm that is not yet recognized by the rest of the market. Chapters 11 to 13 provide a detailed discussion of the types of analyses that underlie fundamental analysis.

Once again, the efficient market hypothesis predicts that *most* fundamental analysis will add little value. If analysts rely on publicly available earnings and industry information, one analyst's evaluation of the firm's prospects is not likely to be significantly more accurate than another's. There are many well-informed, well-financed firms conducting such market research, and in the face of such competition, it will be difficult to uncover data not also available to other analysts. Only analysts with a unique insight will be rewarded.

Fundamental analysis is much more difficult than merely identifying well-run firms with good prospects. Discovery of good firms does an investor no good in and of itself if the rest of the market also knows those firms are good. If the knowledge is already public, the investor will be forced to pay a high price for those firms and will not realize a superior rate of return.

The trick is not to identify firms that are good, but to find firms that are *better* than everyone else's estimate. Similarly, poorly run firms can be great bargains if they are not quite as bad as their stock prices suggest.

This is why fundamental analysis is difficult. It is not enough to do a good analysis of a firm; you can make money only if your analysis is better than that of your competitors because the market price is expected to already reflect all commonly available information.

Active versus Passive Portfolio Management

Casual efforts to pick stocks are not likely to pay off. Competition among investors ensures that any easily implemented stock evaluation technique will be used widely enough so that any insights derived will be reflected in stock prices. Only serious analyses and uncommon techniques are likely to generate the *differential* insight necessary to generate trading profits.

Moreover, these techniques are economically feasible only for managers of large portfolios. If you have only $100,000 to invest, even a 1% per year improvement in performance generates only $1,000 per year, hardly enough to justify herculean efforts. The billion-dollar manager, however, would reap extra income of $10 million annually for the same 1% increment.

If small investors are not in a favored position to conduct active portfolio management, what are their choices? The small investor probably is better off placing funds in a mutual fund. By pooling resources in this way, small investors can obtain the advantages of large size.

More difficult decisions remain, though. Can investors be sure that even large mutual funds have the ability or resources to uncover mispriced stocks? Further, will any mispricing uncovered be sufficiently large to repay the costs entailed in active portfolio management?

Proponents of the efficient market hypothesis believe active management is largely wasted effort and unlikely to justify the expenses incurred. Therefore, they advocate a **passive investment strategy** that makes no attempt to outsmart the market. A passive strategy aims only at establishing a well-diversified portfolio of securities without attempting to find under- or overvalued stocks. Passive management usually is characterized by a buy-and-hold strategy. Because the efficient market theory indicates stock prices are at fair levels, given all available information, it makes no sense to buy and sell securities frequently, as transactions generate large trading costs without increasing expected performance.

One common strategy for passive management is to create an **index fund,** which is a fund designed to replicate the performance of a broad-based index of stocks. For example, in 1976, the Vanguard Group of mutual funds introduced a mutual fund called the Index 500 Portfolio that holds stocks in direct proportion to their weight in the Standard & Poor's 500 stock price index. The performance of the Index 500 fund replicates the performance of the S&P 500. Investors in this fund obtain broad diversification with relatively low management fees. The fees can be kept to a minimum because Vanguard does not need to pay analysts to assess stock prospects and does not incur transaction costs from high portfolio turnover. While the typical annual expense ratio for an actively managed fund is over 1% of assets, Vanguard charges less than 0.2% for the Index 500 Portfolio.

Indexing has grown in appeal considerably since 1976. Vanguard's Index 500 Portfolio was the largest mutual fund in August 2002, with $86 billion in assets. Several other firms have introduced S&P 500 index funds but Vanguard still dominates the retail market for indexing. Including pension funds and mutual funds, more than $1 trillion was indexed to the S&P 500 by early 2001. Many institutional investors now hold indexed bond portfolios as well as indexed stock portfolios.

Mutual funds now offer indexed portfolios that match a wide variety of market indexes. For example, some of the funds offered by the Vanguard Group track the S&P 500 Index, the Wilshire 5000 Index, the Lehman Brothers Aggregate Bond Index, the Russell 2000

passive investment strategy

Buying a well-diversified portfolio without attempting to search out mispriced securities.

index fund

A mutual fund holding shares in proportion to their representation in a market index such as the S&P 500.

index of small capitalization companies, the European equity market, and the Pacific Basin equity market.

2. **What would happen to market efficiency if *all* investors attempted to follow a passive strategy?**

The Role of Portfolio Management in an Efficient Market

If the market is efficient, why not throw darts at *The Wall Street Journal* instead of trying to choose a stock portfolio rationally? It's tempting to draw this sort of conclusion from the notion that security prices are fairly set, but it's a far too simple one. There is a role for rational portfolio management, even in perfectly efficient markets.

A basic principle in portfolio selection is diversification. Even if all stocks are priced fairly, each still poses firm-specific risk that can be eliminated through diversification. Therefore, rational security selection, even in an efficient market, calls for the selection of a carefully diversified portfolio. Moreover, that portfolio should provide the systematic risk level the investor wants. Even in an efficient market, investors must choose the risk-return profiles they deem appropriate.

Rational investment policy also requires that investors take tax considerations into account in security choice. If you are in a high tax bracket, you generally will not want the same securities that low-bracket investors find favorable. At an obvious level, high-bracket investors find it advantageous to buy tax-exempt municipal bonds despite their relatively low pretax yields, while those same bonds are unattractive to low-bracket investors. At a more subtle level, high-bracket investors might want to tilt or specialize their portfolios toward securities that provide capital gains as opposed to dividend or interest income, because capital gains are taxed less heavily, and the option to defer the realization of capital gains income is more valuable, the higher the investor's current tax bracket. High tax bracket investors also will be more attracted to investment opportunities where returns are sensitive to tax benefits, such as real estate ventures.

A third argument for rational portfolio management relates to the particular risk profile of the investor. For example, a General Motors executive whose annual bonus depends on GM's profits generally should not invest additional amounts in auto stocks. To the extent that his or her compensation already depends on GM's well-being, the executive is overinvested in GM now and should not exacerbate the lack of diversification.

Investors of varying ages also might warrant different portfolio policies with regard to risk bearing. For example, older investors who are essentially living off savings might avoid long-term bonds, whose market values fluctuate dramatically with changes in interest rates. Because these investors rely on accumulated savings, they require conservation of principal. In contrast, younger investors might be more inclined toward long-term inflation-indexed bonds. The steady flow of real income over long periods that is locked in with these bonds can be more important than preservation of principal to those with long life expectancies.

In short, there is a role for portfolio management even in an efficient market. Investors' optimal positions will vary according to factors such as age, tax bracket, risk aversion, and employment. The role of the portfolio manager in an efficient market is to tailor the portfolio to these needs, rather than to attempt to beat the market.

Resource Allocation

We've focused so far on the investment implications of the efficient market hypothesis. Deviations from efficiency may offer profit opportunities to better-informed traders at the expense of less-informed traders.

However, deviations from informational efficiency would also result in a large cost that will be borne by all citizens, namely, inefficient resource allocation. Recall that in a capitalist economy, investments in *real* assets such as plant, equipment, and know-how are guided in large part by the prices of financial assets. For example, if the values of biotech assets as reflected in the stock market prices of biotech firms exceed the cost of acquiring those assets, the managers of such firms have a strong signal that further investments in the firm will be regarded by the market as a positive net present value venture. In this manner, capital market prices guide resource allocation. Security mispricing thus could entail severe social costs by fostering inappropriate investments on the real side of the economy.

Section 7.1 demonstrates how security analysis impounds information into security prices. To the extend that only part of this information is reflected in prices, corporations with overpriced securities will be able to obtain capital too cheaply and corporations with undervalued securities might forego investment opportunities because the cost of raising capital will be too high. Therefore, inefficient capital markets will diminish one of the most potent benefits of a market economy.

8.3 ARE MARKETS EFFICIENT?

The Issues

Not surprisingly, the efficient market hypothesis is not enthusiastically hailed by professional portfolio managers. It implies that a great deal of the activity of portfolio managers—the search for undervalued securities—is at best wasted effort and possibly harmful to clients because it costs money and leads to imperfectly diversified portfolios. Consequently, the EMH has never been widely accepted on Wall Street, and debate continues today on the degree to which security analysis can improve investment performance. Before discussing empirical tests of the hypothesis, we want to note three factors that together imply the debate probably never will be settled: the *magnitude issue,* the *selection bias issue,* and the *lucky event issue.*

The magnitude issue   We noted that an investment manager overseeing a $5 billion portfolio who can improve performance by only one-tenth of 1% per year will increase investment earnings by .001 × $5 billion = $5 million annually. This manager clearly would be worth her salary! Yet we, as observers, probably cannot statistically measure her contribution. A one-tenth of 1% contribution would be swamped by the yearly volatility of the market. Remember, the annual standard deviation of the well-diversified S&P 500 index has been approximately 20% per year. Against these fluctuations, a small increase in performance would be hard to detect. Nevertheless, $5 million remains an extremely valuable improvement in performance.

All might agree that stock prices are very close to fair values, and that only managers of large portfolios can earn enough trading profits to make the exploitation of minor mispricing worth the effort. According to this view, the actions of intelligent investment managers are the driving force behind the constant evolution of market prices to fair levels. Rather than ask the qualitative question, Are markets efficient? we ought instead to ask the quantitative question, How efficient are markets?

The selection bias issue   Suppose you discover an investment scheme that could really make money. You have two choices: Either publish your technique in *The Wall Street Journal* to win fleeting fame or keep your technique secret and use it to earn millions of dollars. Most investors would choose the latter option, which presents us with a conundrum. Only investors who find that an investment scheme cannot generate abnormal returns will be willing to report their findings to the whole world. Hence, opponents of the efficient market's view of the world always can use evidence that various techniques do not provide investment rewards as proof that the techniques that do work simply are not being reported to the public. This is a problem in *selection bias*; the outcomes we are able to observe have been preselected in favor of failed attempts. Therefore, we cannot fairly evaluate the true ability of portfolio managers to generate winning stock market strategies.

The lucky event issue   In virtually any month, it seems we read an article in *The Wall Street Journal* about some investor or investment company with a fantastic investment performance over the recent past. Surely the superior records of such investors disprove the efficient market hypothesis.

This conclusion is far from obvious, however. As an analogy to the "contest" among portfolio managers, consider a contest to flip the most heads out of 50 trials using a fair coin. The expected outcome for any person is 50% heads and 50% tails. If 10,000 people, however, compete in this contest, it would not be surprising if at least one or two contestants flipped more than 75% heads. In fact, elementary statistics tells us that the expected number of contestants flipping 75% or more heads would be two. It would be silly, though, to crown these people the head-flipping champions of the world. They are simply the contestants who happened to get lucky on the day of the event (see the nearby box).

The analogy to efficient markets is clear. Under the hypothesis that any stock is fairly priced given all available information, any bet on a stock is simply a coin toss. There is equal likelihood of winning or losing the bet. Yet, if many investors using a variety of schemes make fair bets, statistically speaking, *some* of those investors will be lucky and win a great majority of bets. For every big winner, there may be many big losers, but we never hear of these managers. The winners, though, turn up in *The Wall Street Journal* as the latest stock market gurus; then they can make a fortune publishing market newsletters.

Our point is that after the fact there will have been at least one successful investment scheme. A doubter will call the results luck; the successful investor will call it skill. The proper test would be to see whether the successful investors can repeat their performance in another period, yet this approach is rarely taken.

With these caveats in mind, we now turn to some of the empirical tests of the efficient market hypothesis.

Concept CHECK

3. Fidelity's Magellan Fund outperformed the S&P 500 in 11 of the 13 years that Peter Lynch managed the fund, resulting in an average annual return for this period more than 10% better than that of the index. Is Lynch's performance sufficient to cause you to doubt the efficient markets theory? If not, would *any* performance record be sufficient to dissuade you?

Weak-Form Tests: Predictability in Stock Returns

Returns over short horizons   Early tests of efficient markets were tests of the weak form. Could speculators find trends in past prices that would enable them to earn abnormal profits? This is essentially a test of the efficacy of technical analysis. The already-cited work of Kendall and of Roberts (1959), both of whom analyzed the possible existence of patterns in stock prices, suggests that such patterns are not to be found.

One way of discerning trends in stock prices is by measuring the *serial correlation* of stock market returns. Serial correlation refers to the tendency for stock returns to be related to past returns. Positive serial correlation means that positive returns tend to follow positive returns (a momentum type of property). Negative serial correlation means that positive returns tend to be followed by negative returns (a reversal or "correction" property).

Both Conrad and Kaul (1988) and Lo and MacKinlay (1988) examine weekly returns of NYSE stocks and find positive serial correlation over short horizons. However, the correlation

How to Guarantee Successful Market Timing

Suppose you want to make your fortune publishing a market newsletter. You need first to convince potential subscribers that you have talent worth paying for. But what if you have no market prediction talent? The solution is simple: Start eight market newsletters.

In year one, let four of your newsletters predict an up market and four a down market. In year two, let half of the originally optimistic group of newsletters continue to predict an up market and the other half a down market. Do the same for the originally pessimistic group. Continue in this manner to obtain the following pattern of predictions (U = prediction of an up market, D = prediction of a down market).

After three years, no matter what has happened to the market, one of the newsletters would have had a perfect prediction record. This is because after three years, there are $2^3 = 8$ outcomes for the market, and we've covered all eight possibilities with the eight letters. Now, we simply slough off the seven unsuccessful newsletters and market the eighth letter based on its perfect track record. If we want to establish a letter with a perfect track record over a four-year period, we need $2^4 = 16$ newsletters. A five-year period requires 32 newsletters, and so on.

After the fact, the one newsletter that was always right will attract attention for your uncanny foresight and investors will rush to pay large fees for its advice. Your fortune is made, and you never even researched the market!

WARNING: This scheme is illegal! The point, however, is that with hundreds of market newsletters, you can find one that has stumbled onto an apparently remarkable string of successful predictions without any real degree of skill. After the fact, someone's prediction history can seem to imply great forecasting skill. This person is the one we will read about in The Wall Street Journal; the others will be forgotten.

	Newsletter Predictions							
Year	1	2	3	4	5	6	7	8
1	U	U	U	U	D	D	D	D
2	U	U	D	D	U	U	D	D
3	U	D	U	D	U	D	U	D

---

coefficients of weekly returns tend to be fairly small, at least for large stocks for which price data are the most reliably up-to-date. Thus, while these studies demonstrate price trends over short periods, the evidence does not clearly suggest the existence of trading opportunities.

A more sophisticated version of trend analysis is a **filter rule.** A filter technique gives a rule for buying or selling a stock depending on past price movements. One rule, for example, might be: "Buy if the last two trades each resulted in a stock price increase." A more conventional one might be: "Buy a security if its price increased by 1%, and hold it until its price falls by more than 1% from the subsequent high." Alexander (1964) and Fama and Blume (1966) found that such filter rules generally could not generate trading profits.

> **filter rule**
>
> A rule for buying or selling stock according to recent price movements.

These very short-horizon studies offer the suggestion of momentum in stock market prices, albeit of a magnitude that may be too small to exploit. However, in an investigation of intermediate horizon stock price behavior (using 3- to 12-month holding periods), Jegadeesh and Titman (1993) found that stocks exhibit a momentum property in which good or bad recent performance continues. They conclude that while the performance of individual stocks is highly unpredictable, *portfolios* of the best-performing stocks in the recent past appear to outperform other stocks with enough reliability to offer profit opportunities.

Returns over long horizons
While studies of short-horizon returns have detected minor positive serial correlation in stock market prices, tests[2] of long-horizon returns (that is, returns over multiyear periods) have found suggestions of pronounced negative long-term serial

---

[2] Eugene F. Fama and Kenneth R. French, "Permanent and Temporary Components of Stock Prices," *Journal of Political Economy* 96 (April 1988), pp. 246–73; James Poterba and Lawrence Summers, "Mean Reversion in Stock Prices: Evidence and Implications," *Journal of Financial Economics* 22 (October 1988), pp. 27–59.

correlation. The latter result has given rise to a "fads hypothesis," which asserts that stock prices might overreact to relevant news. Such overreaction leads to positive serial correlation (momentum) over short time horizons. Subsequent correction of the overreaction leads to poor performance following good performance and vice versa. The corrections mean that a run of positive returns eventually will tend to be followed by negative returns, leading to negative serial correlation over longer horizons. These episodes of apparent overshooting followed by correction give stock prices the appearance of fluctuating around their fair values and suggest that market prices exhibit excessive volatility compared to intrinsic value.[3]

These long-horizon results are dramatic, but the studies offer far from conclusive evidence regarding efficient markets. First, the study results need not be interpreted as evidence for stock market fads. An alternative interpretation of these results holds that they indicate only that market risk premiums vary over time: The response of market prices to variation in the risk premium can lead one to incorrectly infer the presence of mean reversion and excess volatility in prices. For example, when the risk premium and the required return on the market rises, stock prices will fall. When the market then rises (on average) at this higher rate of return, the data convey the impression of a stock price recovery. The impression of overshooting and correction is in fact no more than a rational response of market prices to changes in discount rates.

Second, these studies suffer from statistical problems. Because they rely on returns measured over long time periods, these tests of necessity are based on few observations of long-horizon returns.

Reversals   While some of the studies just cited suggest momentum in stock market prices over short horizons (of less than one year), other studies suggest that over longer horizons, extreme stock market performance tends to reverse itself: The stocks that have performed best in the recent past seem to underperform the rest of the market in the following periods, while the worst past performers tend to offer above-average future performance. DeBondt and Thaler (1985) and Chopra, Lakonishok, and Ritter (1992) find strong tendencies for poorly performing stocks in one period to experience sizable reversals over the subsequent period, while the best-performing stocks in a given period tend to follow with poor performance in the following period.

For example, the DeBondt and Thaler study found that if one were to rank order the performance of stocks over a five-year period and then group stocks into portfolios based on investment performance, the base-period "loser" portfolio (defined as the 35 stocks with the worst investment performance) would outperform the "winner" portfolio (the top 35 stocks) by an average of 25% (cumulative return) in the following three-year period. This **reversal effect,** in which losers rebound and winners fade back, seems to suggest that the stock market overreacts to relevant news. After the overreaction is recognized, extreme investment performance is reversed. This phenomenon would imply that a *contrarian* investment strategy—investing in recent losers and avoiding recent winners—should be profitable. Moreover, these returns seem pronounced enough to be exploited profitably.

The reversal effect also seems to depend on the time horizon of the investment. While DeBondt and Thaler (1992) found reversals over long (multiyear) horizons, and studies by Jegadeesh (1990) and Lehmann (1990) documented reversals over short horizons of a month

reversal effect

The tendency of poorly performing stocks and well-performing stocks in one period to experience reversals in the following period.

[3]The fads debate started as a controversy over whether stock prices exhibit excess volatility. See Robert J. Shiller, "Do Stock Prices Move Too Much to Be Justified by Subsequent Changes in Dividends?" *American Economic Review* 71 (June 1971), pp. 421–36. However, it is now apparent that excess volatility and fads are essentially different ways of describing the same phenomenon.

or less, we note above that an investigation of intermediate-term stock price behavior (using 3- to 12-month holding periods) by Jegadeesh and Titman (1993) found that stocks exhibit a momentum property in which good or bad recent performance continues. This of course is the opposite of a reversal phenomenon.

Thus it appears that there may be short-run momentum but long-run reversal patterns in price behavior. One interpretation of these patterns is that short-run overreaction (which causes momentum in prices) may lead to long-term reversals (when the market recognizes and corrects its past errors). This interpretation is emphasized by Haugen (1995).

Predictors of Broad Market Movements

Several studies have documented the ability of easily observed variables to predict market returns. For example, Fama and French (1988) show that the return on the aggregate stock market tends to be higher when the dividend/price ratio, or the dividend yield, is high. Campbell and Shiller (1988) find that the earnings yield can predict market returns. Keim and Stambaugh (1986) show that bond market data such as the spread between yields on high- and low-grade corporate bonds also help predict broad market returns.

Again, the interpretation of these results is difficult. On the one hand, they may imply that stock returns can be predicted, in violation of the efficient market hypothesis. More probably, however, these variables are proxying for variation in the market risk premium. For example, given a level of dividends or earnings, stock prices will be lower and dividend and earnings yields will be higher when the risk premium (and therefore the expected market return) is larger. Thus, a high dividend or earnings yield will be associated with higher market returns. This does not indicate a violation of market efficiency. The predictability of market returns is due to predictability in the risk premium, not in risk-adjusted abnormal returns.

Fama and French (1989) show that the yield spread between high- and low-grade bonds has greater predictive power for returns on low-grade bonds than for returns on high-grade bonds, and greater predictive power for stock returns than for bond returns, suggesting that the predictability in returns is in fact a risk premium rather than evidence of market inefficiency. Similarly, the fact that the dividend yield on stocks helps to predict bond market returns suggests that the yield captures a risk premium common to both markets rather than mispricing in the equity market.

Semistrong-Form Tests: Market Anomalies

Fundamental analysis uses a much wider range of information to create portfolios than does technical analysis. Investigations of the efficacy of fundamental analysis ask whether publicly available information beyond the trading history of a security can be used to improve investment performance and, therefore, are tests of semistrong-form market efficiency. Surprisingly, several easily accessible statistics, for example a stock's price–earnings ratio or its market capitalization, seem to predict abnormal risk-adjusted returns. Findings such as these, which we will review in the following pages, are inconsistent with the efficient market hypothesis and, therefore, are often referred to as market anomalies.

A difficulty in interpreting these tests is that we usually need to adjust for portfolio risk before evaluating the success of an investment strategy. For example, many tests use the CAPM to adjust for risk. However, we know that even if beta is a relevant descriptor of stock risk, the empirically measured quantitative trade-off between risk as measured by beta and expected return differs from the predictions of the CAPM. If we use the CAPM to adjust portfolio returns for risk, inappropriate adjustments might lead to the incorrect conclusion that various portfolio strategies can generate superior returns.

Tests of risk-adjusted returns are *joint tests* of the efficient market hypothesis *and* the risk adjustment procedure. If it appears that a portfolio strategy can generate superior returns, we then must choose between rejecting the EMH or rejecting the risk adjustment technique. Usually, the risk adjustment technique is based on more questionable assumptions than the EMH; if we reject the procedure, we are left with no conclusion about market efficiency.

An example of this problem is the discovery by Basu (1977, 1983) that portfolios of low price/earnings ratio stocks have higher average returns than high P/E portfolios. The **P/E effect** holds up even if returns are adjusted for portfolio beta. Is this a confirmation that the market systematically misprices stocks according to the P/E ratio?

This would be a surprising and, to us, disturbing conclusion, because analysis of P/E ratios is such a simple procedure. While it may be possible to earn superior returns using hard work and much insight, it hardly seems likely that following such a basic technique is enough to generate abnormal returns.

One possible interpretation of these results is that the model of capital market equilibrium is at fault in that the returns are not properly adjusted for risk. This makes sense, since if two firms have the same expected earnings, then the riskier stock will sell at a lower price and lower P/E ratio. Because of its higher risk, the low P/E stock also will have higher expected returns. Therefore, unless the CAPM beta fully adjusts for risk, P/E will act as a useful additional descriptor of risk and will be associated with abnormal returns if the CAPM is used to establish benchmark performance.

The small-firm-in-January effect   One of the most frequently cited anomalies with respect to the efficient market hypothesis is the so-called size or **small-firm effect,** originally documented by Banz (1981). Figure 8.3 illustrates the size effect. It shows the historical performance of portfolios formed by dividing the NYSE stocks into 10 portfolios each year according to firm size (i.e., the total value of outstanding equity). Average annual returns are consistently higher on the small-firm portfolios. The difference in average annual return between portfolio 10 (with the largest firms) and portfolio 1 (with the smallest firms) is 8.59%. Of course, the smaller-firm portfolios tend to be riskier. But even when returns are adjusted for risk by using the CAPM, there is still a consistent premium for the smaller-sized portfolios. Even on a risk-adjusted basis, the smallest-size portfolio outperforms the largest-firm portfolio by an average of 4.3% annually.

This is a huge premium; imagine earning an extra return of this amount on a billion-dollar portfolio. Yet it is remarkable that following a simple (even simplistic) rule such as "invest in

P/E effect

Portfolios of low P/E stocks have exhibited higher average risk-adjusted returns than high P/E stocks.

small-firm effect

Stocks of small firms have earned abnormal returns, primarily in the month of January.

FIGURE 8.3

Returns in excess of risk-free rate and in excess of the Security Market Line for 10 size-based portfolios

Source: *Stocks, Bonds, Bills, and Inflation 2000 Yearbook,* Ibbotson Associates, 2000.

low capitalization stocks" should enable an investor to earn excess returns. After all, any investor can measure firm size costlessly. One would not expect such minimal effort to yield such large rewards.

Later studies (Keim, 1983; Reinganum, 1983; and Blume and Stambaugh, 1983) showed that the small-firm effect occurs virtually entirely in the first two weeks of January. The size effect is in fact a small-firm-in-January effect.

Some researchers believe the January effect is tied to tax-loss selling at the end of the year. The hypothesis is that many people sell stocks that have declined in price during the previous months to realize their capital losses before the end of the tax year. Such investors do not put the proceeds from these sales back into the stock market until after the turn of the year. At that point, the rush of demand for stock places an upward pressure on prices that results in the January effect. Finally, the January effect is said to show up most dramatically for the smallest firms because the small-firm group includes, as an empirical matter, stocks with the greatest variability of prices during the year. The group, therefore, includes a relatively large number of firms that have declined sufficiently to induce tax-loss selling.

Some empirical evidence supports the belief that the January effect is connected to tax-loss selling. For example, Ritter (1988) shows that the ratio of stock purchases to sales by individual investors is below normal in late December and above normal in early January. This is consistent with tax-loss rebalancing.

The fundamental question is why market participants do not exploit the January effect and thereby ultimately eliminate it by bidding stock prices to appropriate levels. One possible explanation lies in segmentation of the market into two groups: institutional investors who invest primarily in large firms and individual investors who invest disproportionately in smaller firms. According to this view, managers of large institutional portfolios are the moving force behind efficient markets. It is professionals who seek out profit opportunities and bid prices to their appropriate levels. Institutional investors do not seem to buy at the small-size end of the market, perhaps because of limits on allowed portfolio positions, so the small-firm anomaly persists without the force of their participation.

4. **Does this market segmentation theory get the efficient market hypothesis off the hook, or are there still market mechanisms that, in theory, ought to eliminate the small-firm anomaly?**

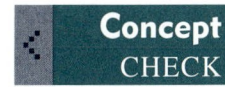

Concept
CHECK

The neglected-firm effect and liquidity effects

Arbel and Strebel (1983) give another interpretation of the small-firm effect. Because small firms tend to be neglected by large institutional traders, information about such firms is less available. This information deficiency makes smaller firms riskier investments that command higher returns. "Brand-name" firms, after all, are subject to considerable monitoring from institutional investors that assures high-quality information, and presumably investors do not purchase "generic" stocks without the prospect of greater returns. An article by Merton (1987) shows that neglected firms might be expected to earn higher equilibrium returns as compensation for the risk associated with limited information. In this sense the neglected firm premium is not strictly a market inefficiency, but is a type of risk premium.

As evidence for the **neglected-firm effect,** Arbel (1985) divided firms into highly researched, moderately researched, and neglected groups based on the number of institutions holding their stock. The January effect was largest for the neglected firms.

Research by Amihud and Mendelson (1991) on the effect of liquidity on stock returns might be related to both the small-firm and neglected-firm effects. They argue that investors will demand a rate-of-return premium to invest in less liquid stocks that entail higher trading costs. Indeed, spreads for the least liquid stocks easily can be more than 5% of stock value. In

**neglected-
firm effect**

The tendency of
investments in stock
of less well-known
firms to generate
abnormal returns.

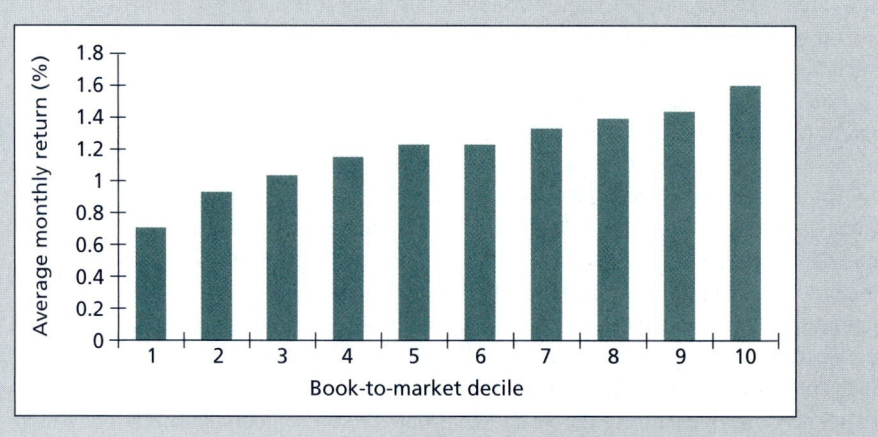

FIGURE 8.4

Average rate of return as a function of the book-to-market ratio

Source: Eugene Fama and Kenneth R. French, "The Cross Section of Expected Stock Returns," *Journal of Finance* 47 (1992), pp. 427–65.

accord with their hypothesis, Amihud and Mendelson show that these stocks show a strong tendency to exhibit abnormally high risk-adjusted rates of return. Because small and less-analyzed stocks as a rule are less liquid, the liquidity effect might be a partial explanation of their abnormal returns. However, this theory does not explain why the abnormal returns of small firms should be concentrated in January. In any case, exploiting these effects can be more difficult than it would appear. The effect of trading costs on small stocks can easily wipe out any apparent abnormal profit opportunity.

Book-to-market ratios Fama and French (1992) and Reinganum (1988) show that a seemingly powerful predictor of returns across securities is the ratio of the book value of the firm's equity to the market value of equity. Fama and French stratify firms into 10 groups according to book-to-market ratios and examine the average monthly rate of return of each of the 10 groups during the period July 1963 through December 1990. The decile with the highest book-to-market ratio had an average monthly return of 1.65%, while the lowest-ratio decile averaged only 0.72% per month. Figure 8.4 shows the pattern of returns across deciles. The dramatic dependence of returns on book-to-market ratio is independent of beta, suggesting either that high book-to-market ratio firms are relatively underpriced or that the book-to-market ratio is serving as a proxy for a risk factor that affects equilibrium expected returns.

book-to-market effect

The tendency for investments in shares of firms with high ratios of book value to market value to generate abnormal returns.

In fact, Fama and French found that after controlling for the size effect and **book-to-market effect,** beta seemed to have no power to explain average security returns.[4] This finding is an important challenge to the notion of rational markets, since it seems to imply that a factor that *should* affect returns—systematic risk—seems not to matter, while a factor that should *not* matter—the book-to-market ratio—seems capable of predicting future returns. We will return to the interpretation of this anomaly.

Postearnings announcement price drift A fundamental principle of efficient markets is that any new information ought to be reflected in stock prices very rapidly. When good news is made public, for example, the stock price should jump immediately. A puzzling

[4]However, Kothari, Shanken, and Sloan (1995) found that when betas are estimated using annual rather than monthly returns, securities with high beta values do in fact have higher average returns. Moreover, they found a book-to-market effect that is attenuated compared to the results in Fama and French and furthermore is inconsistent across different samples of securities. They conclude that the empirical case for the importance of the book-to-market ratio may be somewhat weaker than the Fama–French study would suggest.

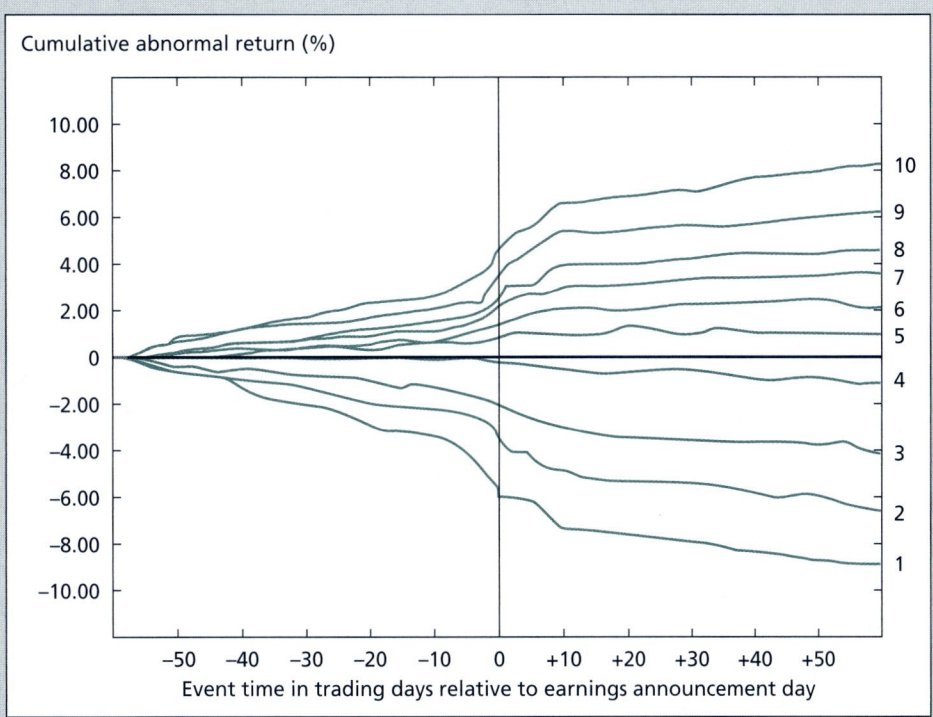

Cumulative abnormal return (%)

Event time in trading days relative to earnings announcement day

FIGURE 8.5

Cumulative abnormal returns in response to earnings announcements

Source: George Foster, Chris Olsen, and Terry Shevlin. "Earnings Releases, Anomalies, and the Behavior of Security Returns," *The Accounting Review* 59 (October 1984).

anomaly, therefore, is the apparently sluggish response of stock prices to firms' earnings announcements.

The "news content" of an earnings announcement can be evaluated by comparing the announcement of actual earnings to the value previously expected by market participants. The difference is the "earnings surprise." (Market expectations of earnings can be roughly measured by averaging the published earnings forecasts of Wall Street analysts or by applying trend analysis to past earnings.) Foster, Olsen, and Shevlin (1984) have examined the impact of earnings announcements on stock returns.

Each earnings announcement for a large sample of firms was placed in 1 of 10 deciles ranked by the magnitude of the earnings surprise, and the abnormal returns of the stock in each decile were calculated. The abnormal return in a period is the return of a portfolio of all stocks in a given decile after adjusting for both the market return in that period and the portfolio beta. It measures return over and above what would be expected given market conditions in that period. Figure 8.5 is a graph of the cumulative abnormal returns for each decile.

The results of this study are dramatic. The correlation between ranking by earnings surprise and abnormal returns across deciles is as predicted. There is a large abnormal return (a large increase in cumulative abnormal return) on the earnings announcement day (time 0). The abnormal return is positive for positive-surprise firms and negative for negative-surprise firms.

The more remarkable, and interesting, result of the study concerns stock price movements *after* the announcement date. The cumulative abnormal returns of positive-surprise stocks continue to grow even after the earnings information becomes public, while the negative-surprise firms continue to suffer negative abnormal returns. The market appears to adjust to the earnings information only gradually, resulting in a sustained period of abnormal returns.

Evidently, one could have earned abnormal profits simply by waiting for earnings announcements and purchasing a stock portfolio of positive earnings-surprise companies. These are precisely the types of predictable continuing trends that ought to be impossible in an efficient market.

Some research suggests that the postannouncement drift in security prices might be related in part to trading costs. Bernard and Thomas (1989) find that postannouncement abnormal returns increase with the magnitude of the earnings surprise until it becomes fairly large. Beyond this point, they speculate, the change in the perceived value of the firm due to the earnings announcement is so large that transaction costs no longer impede trading and prices change more rapidly. They also point out that postannouncement abnormal returns are larger for smaller firms, for which trading costs are higher. Still, these results do not fully explain the postannouncement drift anomaly. First, while trading costs may explain the existence of postannouncement drift, they do not explain why the total *postannouncement* abnormal return is higher for firms with higher earnings surprises. Second, Bernard and Thomas show that firms with positive earnings surprises in one quarter exhibit positive abnormal returns at the earnings announcement in the *following* quarter, suggesting that the market does not fully account for the implications of current earnings announcements when it revises its expectations for future earnings. This suggests informational inefficiency, leaving this phenomenon a topic for future research.

Strong-Form Tests: Inside Information

It would not be surprising if insiders were able to make superior profits trading in their firms' stock. In other words, we do not expect markets to be strong-form efficient. The ability of insiders to trade profitability in their own stock has been documented in studies by Jaffee (1974), Seyhun (1986), Givoly and Palmon (1985), and others. Jaffee's was one of the earliest studies to show the tendency for stock prices to rise after insiders intensively bought shares and to fall after intensive insider sales.

To level the playing field, the Securities and Exchange Commission requires all insiders to register all their trading activity, and it publishes these trades in an *Official Summary of Insider Trading*. Once the *Official Summary* is published, the trades become public information. At that point, if markets are efficient, fully and immediately processing the information released, an investor should no longer be able to profit from following the pattern of those trades. Seyhun, who carefully tracked the public release dates of the *Official Summary,* found that following insider transactions would be to no avail. While there is some tendency for stock prices to increase even after the *Official Summary* reports insider buying, the abnormal returns are not of sufficient magnitude to overcome transaction costs.

Interpreting the Evidence

How should we interpret the ever-growing anomalies literature? Does it imply that markets are grossly inefficient, allowing for simplistic trading rules to offer large profit opportunities? Or are there other, more subtle interpretations?

Risk premiums or inefficiencies?   The price–earnings, small-firm, book-to-market, and reversal effects are currently among the most puzzling phenomena in empirical finance.

There are several interpretations of these effects. First note that, to some extent, these three phenomena may be related. The feature that low-price, low capitalization, high book-to-market firms, and recent stock market "losers" seem to have in common is a stock price that has fallen considerably in recent months or years. Indeed, a firm can become a small firm, or can become a high book-to-market firm, by suffering a sharp drop in its stock price. These groups therefore may contain a relatively high proportion of distressed firms that have suffered recent difficulties.

Fama and French (1993) argue that these anomalies can be explained as manifestations of risk premiums. Using an arbitrage pricing approach,[5] they show that stocks with greater sensitivity to size or book-to-market factors have higher average returns and interpret these returns as evidence of a risk premium associated with these factors. Fama and French argue that a so-called *three-factor model,* in which risk is determined by the sensitivity of a stock to (1) the market portfolio, (2) a portfolio that reflects the relative returns of small versus large firms, and (3) a portfolio that reflects the relative returns of firms with high versus low ratios of book value to market value, does a good job in explaining security returns. While size or book-to-market ratios per se are obviously not risk factors, they perhaps might act as proxies for more fundamental determinants of risk. Fama and French argue that these patterns of returns may therefore be consistent with an efficient market in which expected returns are consistent with risk.

The opposite interpretation is offered by Lakonishok, Shleifer, and Vishney (1995), who argue that these phenomena are evidence of inefficient markets—more specifically, of systematic errors in the forecasts of stock market analysts. They present evidence that analysts extrapolate past performance too far into the future and therefore overprice firms with recent good performance and underprice firms with recent poor performance.

Anomalies or data mining? We have covered many of the so-called anomalies cited in the literature, but our list could go on and on. Some wonder whether these anomalies are really unexplained puzzles in financial markets, or whether they instead are artifacts of data mining. After all, if one spins the computer tape of past returns over and over and examines stock returns along enough dimensions, some criteria will *appear* to predict returns simply by chance.

In this regard, it is noteworthy that some anomalies have not shown much staying power after being reported in the academic literature. For example, after the small-firm effect was published in the early 1980s, it promptly disappeared for much of the rest of the decade. Similarly, the book-to-market strategy, which commanded considerable attention in the early 1990s, was ineffective for the rest of that decade.

Still, even acknowledging the potential for data mining, there seems to be a common thread to many of the anomalies we have considered that lends support to the notion that there is a real puzzle to explain. It seems that value stocks—defined either by low P/E ratio, high book-to-market ratio, or depressed prices relative to historic levels—seem to have provided higher average returns than "glamour" or growth stocks.

One way to address the problem of data mining is to find a data set that has not already been researched, and see whether the relationship in question shows up in that new data. Such studies have revealed size, momentum, and book-to-market effects in other security markets around the world. Thus, while these phenomena may be a manifestation of a systematic risk premium, the precise nature of that risk is not fully understood.

A behavioral interpretation Those who believe that the anomalies literature is in fact an indication of investor irrationality sometimes refer to evidence from research in the

---

[5]We discussed arbitrage pricing models in Chapter 7, Section 7.5.

psychology of decision making. Psychologists have identified several "irrationalities" that seem to characterize individuals making complicated decisions. Here is a sample of some of these irrationalities and some anomalies with which they might be consistent.[6]

1. *Forecasting errors.* A series of experiments by Kahneman and Tversky (1972, 1973) indicate that people give too much weight to recent experience compared with prior beliefs when making forecasts, and tend to make forecasts that are too extreme given the uncertainty inherent in their information. DeBondt and Thaler (1990) argue that the P/E effect can be explained by earnings expectations that are too extreme. In this view, when forecasts of a firm's future earnings are high, they tend to be *too* high relative to the objective prospects of the firm. This results in a high initial P/E (due to the optimism built into the stock price) and poor subsequent performance when investors recognize their error. Thus, high P/E firms tend to be poor investments in general.

2. *Overconfidence.* People tend to underestimate the imprecision of their beliefs or forecasts, and they tend to overestimate their abilities. In one famous survey, 90% of drivers in Sweden ranked themselves as better-than-average drivers. Such overconfidence may be responsible for the prevalence of active versus passive investment management—itself an anomaly to an adherent of the efficient market hypothesis. Despite the recent growth in indexing, less than 10% of the equity in the mutual fund industry is held in indexed accounts. The dominance of active management in the face of the typical underperformance of such strategies (consider the disappointing performance of actively managed mutual funds documented in Chapter 4 as well as in the following pages) is consistent with a tendency to overestimate ability.

An interesting example of overconfidence in financial markets is provided by Barber and Odean (2000, 2001), who compare trading activity and average returns in brokerage accounts of men and women. They find that men (in particular single men) trade far more actively than women, consistent with the greater overconfidence among men

---

[6]This discussion is based on W.F.M. De Bondt and R. H. Thaler, "Financial Decision Making in Markets and Firms," in *Handbooks in Operations Research and Management Science, Volume 9: Finance,* eds. R. A. Jarrow, V. Maksimovic, W. T. Ziemba (Amsterdam: Elsevier, 1995).

well-documented in the psychology literature. They also find that high trading activity is highly predictive of poor investment performance. The top 20% of accounts ranked by portfolio turnover had average returns seven percentage points lower than the 20% of the accounts with the lowest turnover rates. As they conclude, "Trading [and by implication, overconfidence] is hazardous to your wealth."

3. *Regret avoidance.* Psychologists have found that individuals who make decisions that turn out badly have more regret (blame themselves more) when that decision was more unconventional. For example, buying a blue-chip portfolio that turns down is not as painful as experiencing the same losses on an unknown start-up firm. Any losses on the blue-chip stocks can be more easily attributed to bad luck rather than bad decision making and cause less regret. De Bondt and Thaler (1987) argue that such regret theory is consistent with both the size and book-to-market effect. Higher book-to-market firms tend to have lower stock prices. These firms are "out of favor" and more likely to be in a financially precarious position. Similarly, smaller less-well-known firms are also less conventional investments. Such firms require more "courage" on the part of the investor, which increases the required rate of return.

4. *Framing and mental accounting.* Decisions seem to be affected by how choices are framed. For example, an individual may reject a bet when it is posed in terms of possible losses but may accept that same bet when described in terms of potential gains. Mental accounting is another form of framing in which people segregate certain decisions. For example, an investor may take a lot of risk with one investment account but establish a very conservative position with another account that is dedicated to her child's education. But it might be better to view both accounts as part of the investor's overall portfolio with the risk-return profiles of each integrated into a unified framework. Statman (1997) argues that mental accounting is consistent with some investors' irrational preference for stocks with high cash dividends (they feel free to spend dividend income, but will not "dip into capital" by selling a few shares of another stock with the same total rate of return) and with a tendency to ride losing stock positions for too long (since "behavioral investors" are reluctant to realize losses).

The nearby box offers good examples of several of these psychological tendencies in an investment setting.

Mutual Fund Performance

We have documented some of the apparent chinks in the armor of efficient market proponents. Ultimately, however, from the perspective of portfolio management, the issue of market efficiency boils down to whether skilled investors can make consistent abnormal trading profits. The best test is simply to look at the performance of market professionals and see if their performance is superior to that of a passive index fund that buys and holds the market.

As we pointed out in Chapter 4, casual evidence does not support the claim that professionally managed portfolios can consistently beat the market. Figures 4.3 and 4.4 in that chapter demonstrated that between 1972 and 2000, a passive portfolio indexed to the Wilshire 5000 typically would have better returns than the average equity fund. On the other hand, there was some (admittedly inconsistent) evidence (see Table 4.3) of persistence in performance, meaning that the better managers in one period tended to be better managers in following periods. Such a pattern would suggest that the better managers can with some consistency outperform their competitors and would be inconsistent with the notion that market prices already reflect all relevant information.

Don't Ignore Luck's Role in Stock Picks

When stock-market investors take a hit, they rail at their stupidity and question their investment strategy. But when lottery ticket buyers lose, they shrug off their bad luck and pony up for another ticket.

Maybe those lottery players have the right idea.

Sure, if you lose a bundle in the stock market, it could be your fault. But there is a fair chance that the real culprits are bad luck and skewed expectations.

Examples? Consider these three:

Picking on Yourself

If one of your stocks craters, that doesn't necessarily mean you are a fool and that your investment research was inadequate. By the same token, a soaring stock doesn't make you a genius. The fact is, the stock market is pretty darn efficient.

"When people buy stocks, they think they are playing a game of skill," says Meir Statman, a finance professor at Santa Clara University in California. "When the stock goes down rather than up, they think they have lost their knack. But they should take heart. All they have lost is luck. And next time, when the stock goes up, they should remember that that was luck, too."

All Over the Map

Just as your portfolio likely will include a fair number of losing stocks, so you may have exposure to stock-market sectors that post lackluster returns for long periods. Were you wrong to invest in those sectors? Probably not.

"In the 1990s, U.S. stocks beat international stocks," notes William Retchenstein, an investments professor at Baylor University in Waco, Texas. "That doesn't mean international diversification isn't needed or doesn't work. International diversification is about reducing risk before the fact. In 1990, no one knew that the U.S. would be the hottest market for the decade. Similarly, today no one knows which region will be the hottest market. That's why we diversify.

"People say, 'My investment adviser didn't get me out of tech stocks in time, so I'm going to fire him.'" Mr. Reichenstein says, "The assumption is that you can successfully pick sectors. But nobody can do that."

Timing Patterns

Did you load up on stocks, only to see the market tank? Don't feel bad. Short-run market activity is utterly unpredictable. That is why investors who buy stocks need a long time horizon.

"When people buy and the market goes down, that is when regret hits the most, because they can easily imagine postponing the purchase," Mr. Statman says. "People feel that the market is picking on them personally." But in truth, buying stocks ahead of a market decline is just bad luck.

Similarly, folks can also draw the wrong lesson from their successes. For instance, if you made a brilliantly timed switch between stocks and cash, that may bolster your self-confidence and make you think you are smarter than you really are.

Once you accept that investment gains and losses are often the result of luck rather than brains, you may find it easier to cope with market turmoil. But what if you still kick yourself with every investment loss? A financial adviser could come in handy. Sure, the cost involved will hurt your investment returns. But there is a little-mentioned benefit.

"Investors use advisers as scapegoats, blaming them for all the stocks that went down while claiming credit themselves for all the stocks that went up," Mr. Statman says. "In an odd way, when people hire advisers, they get their money's worth."

SOURCE: Jonathan Clements, "Don't Ignore Luck's Role in Stock Picks," *The Wall Street Journal*, September 26, 2000. Reprinted by permission of *The Wall Street Journal*, © 2000 Dow Jones & Company, Inc. All Rights Reserved Worldwide.

On the other hand, the analyses in Chapter 4 were based on total returns unadjusted for exposure to systematic risk factors. In this section, we will revisit the question of mutual fund performance, paying more attention to the benchmark against which performance ought to be evaluated.

As a first pass, we can examine the risk-adjusted returns (i.e., the alpha, or return in excess of required return based on beta and the market return in each period) of a large sample of mutual funds. Malkiel (1995) computes these abnormal returns for a large sample of mutual funds between 1972 and 1991. The results, which appear in Figure 8.6, show that the distribution of alphas is roughly bell shaped, with a mean that is slightly negative but statistically indistinguishable from zero. On average, it does not appear that these funds outperformed the market index (the S&P 500) on a risk-adjusted basis.

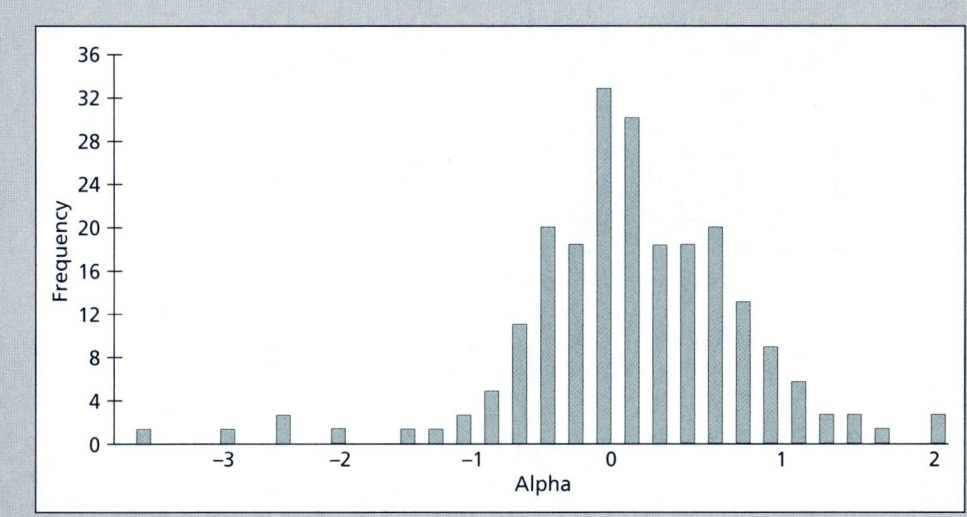

FIGURE **8.6**

Estimates of individual mutual fund alphas, 1972 to 1991

Note: The frequency distribution of estimated alphas for all equity mutual funds with 10-year continuous records.
Source: Burton G. Malkiel, "Returns from Investing in Equity Mutual Funds 1971–1991," *Journal of Finance* 50 (June 1995), pp. 549–72.

One problem in interpreting these alphas is that the S&P 500 may not be an adequate benchmark against which to evaluate mutual fund returns. Because mutual funds tend to maintain considerable holdings in the equity of small firms, while the S&P 500 exclusively comprises large firms, mutual funds as a whole will tend to outperform the index when small firms outperform large ones, and underperform when small firms fare worse. Thus, a better benchmark for the performance of funds would be an index that incorporates the stock market performance of smaller firms.

The importance of the benchmark can be illustrated by examining the returns on small stocks in various subperiods.[7] In the 20-year period between 1945 and 1964, a small stock index underperformed the S&P 500 by about 4% per year on a risk-adjusted basis. In the following 20-year period between 1965 and 1984, small stocks outperformed the S&P index by 10%. Thus, if one were to examine mutual fund returns in the earlier period, they would tend to look poor, not necessarily because small-fund managers were poor stock pickers, but simply because mutual funds as a group tend to hold more small stocks than are represented in the S&P 500. In the later period, funds would look better on a risk-adjusted basis relative to the S&P 500 because small funds performed better. The "style choice" (i.e., the exposure to small stocks, which is an asset allocation decision) would dominate the evaluation of performance even though it has little to do with managers' stock-picking ability.[8]

Elton, Gruber, Das, and Hlavka (1993) attempt to control for the impact of non-S&P assets on mutual fund performance. They calculate mutual fund alphas controlling for both the effects

---

[7]This illustration and the statistics cited are based on a paper by Elton, Gruber, Das, and Hlavka (1993).

[8]Remember from Chapter 1 that the asset allocation decision is usually in the hands of the individual investor. Investors allocate their investment portfolios to mutual funds with holdings in asset classes they desire and can reasonably expect only that portfolio managers will choose stocks advantageously *within* those asset classes.

TABLE **8.1** Performance of mutual funds based on the three-index model	Type of Fund (Wiesenberger classification)	Number of Funds	Alpha	t-Statistic for Alpha
	Equity funds			
	Maximum capital gain	12	−4.59	−1.87
	Growth	33	−1.55	−1.23
	Growth and income	40	−0.68	−1.65
	Balanced funds	**31**	**−1.27**	**−2.73**

Note: The three-index model calculates the alpha of each fund as the intercept of the following regression:

$$r - r_f = \alpha + \beta_M(r_M - r_f) + \beta_S(r_S - r_f) + \beta_D(r_D - r_f) + e$$

where r is the return on the fund, r_f is the risk-free rate, r_M is the return on the S&P 500 index, r_S is the return on a non-S&P small-stock index, r_D is the return on a bond index, e is the fund's residual return, and the betas measure the sensitivity of fund returns to the various indexes.

Source: E. J. Elton, M. J. Gruber, S. Das, and M. Hlavka, "Efficiency with Costly Information: A Reinterpretation of Evidence from Managed Portfolios," *Review of Financial Studies* 6 (1993), pp. 1–22.

of firm size and interest rate movements. Some of their results are presented in Table 8.1, which shows that average alphas are negative for each type of equity fund, although generally not of statistically significant magnitude. They conclude that after controlling for the relative performance of these three asset classes—large stocks, small stocks, and bonds—mutual fund managers as a group do not demonstrate an ability to beat passive strategies that would simply mix index funds from among these asset classes. They also find that mutual fund performance is worse for firms that have higher expense ratios and higher turnover ratios. Thus, it appears that funds with higher fees do not increase gross returns by enough to justify those fees.

Carhart (1997) reexamines the issue of consistency in mutual fund performance controlling for non-S&P factors in a manner similar to Elton, Gruber, Das, and Hlavka. He finds that there is persistence in relative performance across managers but that much of the persistence seems due to expenses and transaction costs rather than gross investment returns. This last point is important: While there can be no consistently superior performers in a fully efficient market, there *can* be consistently inferior performers. Repeated weak performance would not be due to a tendency to pick bad stocks consistently (that would be impossible in an efficient market!), but it could result from a consistently high expense ratio, high portfolio turnover or higher-than-average transaction costs per trade. Carhart also finds that the evidence of persistence is concentrated at the two extremes of the best and worst performers. Figure 8.7 from Carhart's study documents performance persistence. Equity funds are ranked into one of 10 groups by performance in the formation year, and the performance of each group in the following years is plotted. It is clear that except for the best-performing top-decile group and the worst-performing tenth-decile group, performance in future periods is almost independent of earlier-year returns. Carhart's results suggest that there may be a small group of exceptional managers who can with some consistency outperform a passive strategy, but that for the majority of managers, over- or underperformance in any period is largely a matter of chance.

Thus, the evidence on the risk-adjusted performance of professional managers is mixed at best. We conclude that the performance of professional managers is broadly consistent with market efficiency. The amounts by which professional managers as a group beat or are beaten by the market fall within the margin of statistical uncertainty. In any event, it is quite clear that performance superior to passive strategies is far from routine. Studies show either that most managers cannot outperform passive strategies or that if there is a margin of superiority, it is small.

On the other hand, a small number of investment superstars—Peter Lynch (formerly of Fidelity's Magellan Fund), Warren Buffet (of Berkshire Hathaway), John Templeton (of

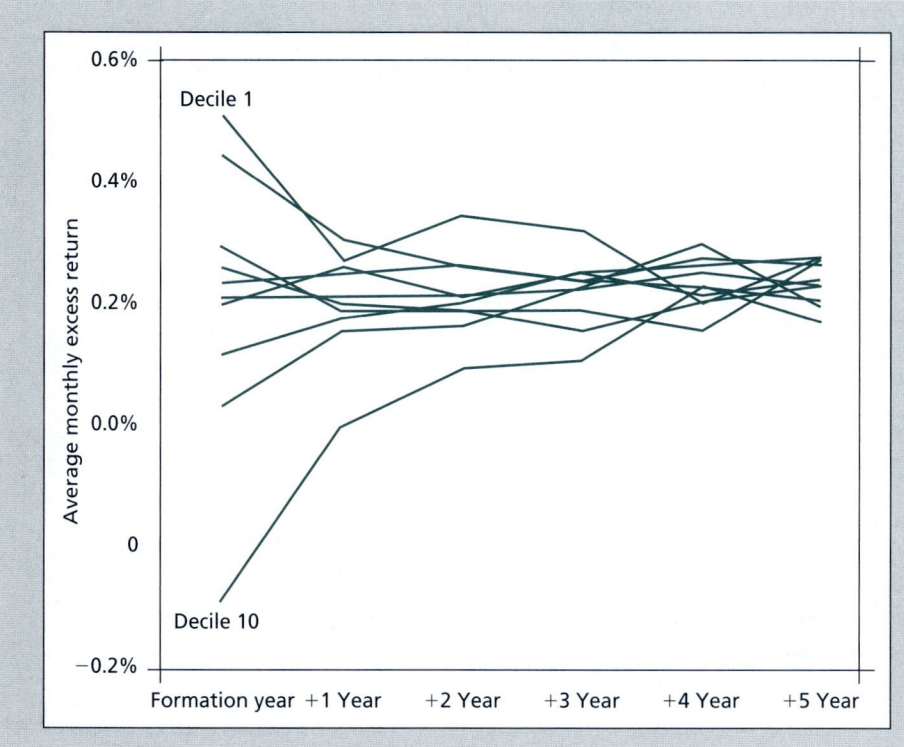

FIGURE 8.7

Persistence of mutual fund performance. Performance over time of mutual funds groups ranked by initial year performance.

Source: Marc M. Carhart, "On Persistence in Mutual Fund Performance," *Journal of Finance* 52 (March 1997), pp. 57–82.

Templeton Funds), and George Soros (of the Quantum Fund), among them—have compiled career records that show a consistency of superior performance hard to reconcile with absolutely efficient markets. Nobel Prize winner Paul Samuelson (1989) reviews this investment hall of fame but concludes that the records of the vast majority of professional money managers offer convincing evidence that there are no easy strategies to guarantee success in the securities markets. The nearby box points out the perils of trying to identify the next superstar manager.

So, Are Markets Efficient?

There is a telling joke about two economists walking down the street. They spot a $20 bill on the sidewalk. One starts to pick it up, but the other one says, "Don't bother; if the bill were real someone would have picked it up already."

The lesson here is clear. An overly doctrinaire belief in efficient markets can paralyze the investor and make it appear that no research effort can be justified. This extreme view is probably unwarranted. There are enough anomalies in the empirical evidence to justify the search for underpriced securities that clearly goes on.

The bulk of the evidence suggests that any supposedly superior investment strategy should be taken with many grains of salt. The market is competitive *enough* that only differentially superior information or insight will earn money; the easy pickings have been picked. In the end, it is likely that the margin of superiority that any professional manager can add is so slight that the statistician will not be able to detect it.

We conclude that markets are very efficient, but rewards to the especially diligent, intelligent, or creative may be waiting.

TRY LUCK—AND ASK THE RIGHT QUESTIONS

As manager of Fidelity Magellan Fund from 1977 to 1990, Peter Lynch made a lot of money for shareholders. But he did a big disservice to everybody else.

How so? Mr. Lynch had an astonishing 13-year run, beating the market in every calendar year but two. He . . . gave hope to amateur investors, who had tried picking stocks themselves and failed. Now they had a new strategy. Instead of picking stocks, they would pick the managers who picked the stocks.

That was the theory. The reality? Every day, thousands of amateur investors, fund analysts, investment advisers and financial journalists pore over the country's 4,000-plus stock funds all looking for the next Peter Lynch.

They are still looking.

Falling Stars

The 44 Wall Street Fund was also a dazzling performer in the 1970s. In the 1970s, 44 Wall Street generated even higher returns than Magellan and it ranked as the third-best-performing stock fund.

But the 1980s weren't quite so kind. It ranked as the worst fund in the 1980s, losing 73.1%. Past performance may be a guide to future results. But it's a mighty tough guide to read.

Fortunately, most stock funds don't self-destruct with quite the vigor of 44 Wall Street. Instead, "superstar" funds follow a rather predictable life cycle. A new fund, or an old fund with a new manager, puts together a decent three-year or five-year record. A great feat? Hardly.

If a manager specializes in, say, blue-chip growth stocks, eventually these shares will catch the market's fancy and—providing the manager doesn't do anything too silly—three or four years of market-beating performance might follow. This strong performance catches the media's attention and the inevitable profile follows, possibly in *Forbes* or *Money* or *SmartMoney*. By the time the story reaches print, our manager comes across as opinionated and insightful. The money starts rolling in. That's when the blue-chip growth stocks go out of favor. You can guess the rest.

Five Questions

I think it is possible to identify winning managers. But the odds are stacked against you. Over a 10-year period, maybe only a quarter of diversified U.S. stock funds will beat Standard & Poor's 500 stock index, which is why market-tracking index funds make so much sense.

So if you are going to try to identify star managers, what should you do? First, stack the odds in your favor by avoiding funds with high annual expenses and sales commissions. Then kick the tires on those funds that remain. Here are five questions to ask:

- Does the fund make sense for your portfolio?

  Start by deciding what sort of stock funds you want. You might opt to buy a large-company fund, a small-company fund, an international fund, and an emerging-markets fund. Having settled on your target mix, then buy the best funds to fill each slot in your portfolio.

- How has the manager performed?

  Funds don't pick stocks. Fund managers do. If a fund has a great record but a new, untested manager, the record is meaningless. By contrast, a spanking new fund with a veteran manager can be a great investment.

- What explains the manager's good performance?

  You want to invest with managers who regularly beat the market by diligently picking one good stock after another. Meanwhile, avoid those who have scored big by switching between stocks and cash or by making hefty bets on one market sector after another.

  Why? If a manager performs well by picking stocks, he or she has made the right stock-picking decision on hundreds of occasions, thus suggesting a real skill. By contrast, managers who score big with market timing or sector rotating may have built their record on just half-a-dozen good calls. With such managers, it's much more difficult to say whether they are truly skillful or just unusually lucky.

- Has the manager performed consistently well?

  Look at a manager's record on a year-by-year basis. By doing so, you can see whether the manager has performed consistently well or whether the record is built on just one or two years of sizzling returns.

- Has the fund grown absurdly large?

  As investors pile into a top-ranked fund, its stellar returns inevitably dull because the manager can no longer stick with his or her favorite stocks but instead must spread the fund's ballooning assets among a growing group of companies.

- Statistical research has shown that stock prices seem to follow a random walk with no discernible predictable patterns that investors can exploit. Such findings now are taken to be evidence of market efficiency, that is, of evidence that market prices reflect all currently available information. Only new information will move stock prices, and this information is equally likely to be good news or bad news.

- Market participants distinguish among three forms of the efficient market hypothesis. The weak form asserts that all information to be derived from past stock prices already is reflected in stock prices. The semistrong form claims that all publicly available information is already reflected. The strong form, usually taken only as a straw man, asserts that all information, including inside information, is reflected in prices.

- Technical analysis focuses on stock price patterns and on proxies for buy or sell pressure in the market. Fundamental analysis focuses on the determinants of the underlying value of the firm, such as current profitability and growth prospects. As both types of analysis are based on public information, neither should generate excess profits if markets are operating efficiently.

- Proponents of the efficient market hypothesis often advocate passive as opposed to active investment strategies. The policy of passive investors is to buy and hold a broad-based market index. They expend resources neither on market research nor on frequent purchase and sale of stocks. Passive strategies may be tailored to meet individual investor requirements.

- Empirical studies of technical analysis generally do not support the hypothesis that such analysis can generate trading profits. Some patterns are suggestive, but these would be either expensive in terms of trading costs or can be due to time-varying risk premiums.

- Several anomalies regarding fundamental analysis have been uncovered. These include the P/E effect, the small-firm effect, the neglected-firm effect, and the book-to-market effect.

- By and large, the performance record of professionally managed funds lends little credence to claims that professionals can consistently beat the market.

SUMMARY

KEY TERMS

book-to-market effects, 276
efficient market
    hypothesis, 262
filter rule, 271
fundamental analysis, 266
index fund, 267

neglected-firm effect, 275
passive investment
    strategy, 267
P/E effect, 274
random walk, 262
reversal effect, 272

semistrong-form EMH, 265
small-firm effect, 274
strong-form EMH, 265
technical analysis, 265
weak-form EMH, 265

PROBLEM SETS

1. Which of the following assumptions imply(ies) an informationally efficient market?
   a. Many profit-maximizing participants, each acting independently of the others, analyze and value securities.
   b. The timing of one news announcement is generally dependent on other news announcements.
   c. Security prices adjust rapidly to reflect new information.
   d. A risk-free asset exists, and investors can borrow and lend unlimited amounts at the risk-free rate.

2. If markets are efficient, what should be the correlation coefficient between stock returns for two nonoverlapping time periods?

3. Which of the following most appears to contradict the proposition that the stock market is *weakly* efficient? Explain.
   a. Over 25% of mutual funds outperform the market on average.
   b. Insiders earn abnormal trading profits.
   c. Every January, the stock market earns above normal returns.

4. Suppose, after conducting an analysis of past stock prices, you come up with the following observations. Which would appear to *contradict* the *weak* form of the efficient market hypothesis? Explain.
   a. The average rate of return is significantly greater than zero.
   b. The correlation between the market return one week and the return the following week is zero.
   c. One could have made superior returns by buying stock after a 10% rise in price and selling after a 10% fall.
   d. One could have made higher than average capital gains by holding stock with low dividend yields.

5. Which of the following statements are true if the efficient market hypothesis holds?
   a. It implies perfect forecasting ability.
   b. It implies that prices reflect all available information.
   c. It implies that the market is irrational.
   d. It implies that prices do not fluctuate.

6. A market anomaly refers to:
   a. An exogenous shock to the market that is sharp but not persistent.
   b. A price or volume event that is inconsistent with historical price or volume trends.
   c. A trading or pricing structure that interferes with efficient buying and selling of securities.
   d. Price behavior that differs from the behavior predicted by the efficient market hypothesis.

7. Which of the following observations would provide evidence *against* the *semistrong form* of the efficient market theory? Explain.
   a. Mutual fund managers do not on average make superior returns.
   b. You cannot make superior profits by buying (or selling) stocks after the announcement of an abnormal rise in earnings.
   c. Low P/E stocks tend to provide abnormal risk-adjusted returns.
   d. In any year, approximately 50% of pension funds outperform the market.

8. A successful firm like Intel has consistently generated large profits for years. Is this a violation of the EMH?

9. Prices of stocks before stock splits show on average consistently positive abnormal returns. Is this a violation of the EMH?

10. "If the business cycle is predictable, and a stock has a positive beta, the stock's returns also must be predictable." Respond.

11. "The expected return on all securities must be equal if markets are efficient." Comment.

12. We know the market should respond positively to good news, and good news events such as the coming end of a recession can be predicted with at least some accuracy. Why, then, can we not predict that the market will go up as the economy recovers?

13. If prices are as likely to increase or decrease, why do investors earn positive returns from the market on average?

14. You know that firm XYZ is very poorly run. On a management scale of 1 (worst) to 10 (best), you would give it a score of 3. The market consensus evaluation is that the management score is only 2. Should you buy or sell the stock?

15. Some scholars contend that professional managers are incapable of outperforming the market. Others come to an opposite conclusion. Compare and contrast the assumptions about the stock market that support (a) passive portfolio management and (b) active portfolio management.

16. You are a portfolio manager meeting a client. During the conversation that followed your formal review of her account, your client asked the following question:

    > My grandson, who is studying investments, tells me that one of the best ways to make money in the stock market is to buy the stocks of small-capitalization firms late in December and to sell the stocks one month later. What is he talking about?

    a. Identify the apparent market anomalies that would justify the proposed strategy.

    b. Explain why you believe such a strategy might or might not work in the future.

17. Which of the following phenomena would be either consistent with or in violation of the efficient market hypothesis? Explain briefly.

    a. Nearly half of all professionally managed mutual funds are able to outperform the S&P 500 in a typical year.

    b. Money managers that outperform the market (on a risk-adjusted basis) in one year are likely to outperform the market in the following year.

    c. Stock prices tend to be predictably more volatile in January than in other months.

    d. Stock prices of companies that announce increased earnings in January tend to outperform the market in February.

    e. Stocks that perform well in one week perform poorly in the following week.

18. Dollar-cost averaging means that you buy equal dollar amounts of a stock every period, for example, $500 per month. The strategy is based on the idea that when the stock price is low, your fixed monthly purchase will buy more shares, and when the price is high, fewer shares. Averaging over time, you will end up buying more shares when the stock is cheaper and fewer when it is relatively expensive. Therefore, by design, you will exhibit good market timing. Evaluate this strategy.

19. Steady Growth Industries has never missed a dividend payment in its 94-year history. Does this make it more attractive to you as a possible purchase for your stock portfolio?

20. Good News, Inc., just announced an increase in its annual earnings, yet its stock price fell. Is there a rational explanation for this phenomenon?

Use the following information to solve problems 21 and 22:

As director of research for a medium-sized investment firm, Jeff Cheney was concerned about the mediocre investment results experienced by the firm in recent years. He met with his two senior equity analysts to consider alternatives to the stock selection techniques employed in the past.

One of the analysts suggested that the current literature has examined the relationship between price–earnings (P/E) ratios and securities returns. A number of studies had concluded that high P/E stocks tended to have higher betas and lower risk-adjusted returns than stocks with low P/E ratios.

The analyst also referred to recent studies analyzing the relationship between security returns and company size as measured by equity capitalization. The studies concluded that when compared to the S&P 500 index, small-capitalization stocks tended to provide above-average risk-adjusted returns, while large-capitalization stocks tended to provide below-average risk-adjusted returns. It was further noted that little correlation was found to exist between a company's P/E ratio and the size of its equity capitalization.

Jeff's firm has employed a strategy of complete diversification and the use of beta as a measure of portfolio risk. He and his analysts were intrigued as to how these recent studies might be applied to their stock selection techniques and thereby improve their performance. Given the results of the studies indicated above:

21. Explain how the results of these studies might be used in the stock selection and portfolio management process. Briefly discuss the effects on the objectives of diversification and on the measurement of portfolio risk.

22. List the reasons and briefly discuss why this firm might *not* want to adopt a new strategy based on these studies in place of its current strategy of complete diversification and the use of beta as a measure of portfolio risk.

23. "Growth" and "Value" can be defined in several ways, but "growth" usually conveys the idea of a portfolio emphasizing or including only issues believed to possess above-average future rates of per-share earnings growth. Low current yield, high price-to-book ratios, and high price-to-earnings ratios are typical characteristics of such portfolios.

"Value" usually conveys the idea of portfolios emphasizing or including only issues currently showing low price-to-book ratios, low price-to-earnings ratios, above-average levels of dividend yield, and market prices believed to be below the issues' intrinsic values.

   a. Identify and explain *three* reasons why, over an extended period of time, *value stock investing* might outperform *growth stock investing*.

   b. Explain why the outcome suggested in (*a*) above should *not* be possible in a market widely regarded as being highly efficient.

STANDARD
&POOR'S

1. Use data from Market Insight (www.mhhe.com/edumarketinsight) to rank firms based on one of these criteria:

    a. Market-to-book ratio.
    b. Price–earnings ratio.
    c. Market capitalization (size).
    d. Another criterion that interest you.

    Divide the firms into five groups based on their ranking for the criterion that you choose, and calculate the average rate of return of the firms in each group. Do you confirm or reject any of the anomalies cited in this chapter? Can you uncover a new anomaly? Note: For your test to be valid, you must form your portfolios based on criteria observed at the *beginning* of the period when you form the stock groups. Why?

2. Use the price history supplied by Market Insight (www.mhhe.com/edumarket insight) to calculate the beta of each of the firms in the previous question. Use this beta, the T-bill rate, and the return on the S&P 500 to calculate the risk-adjusted abnormal return of each stock group. Does any anomaly uncovered in the previous question persist after controlling for risk?

3. Now form stock groups that use more than one criterion simultaneously. For example, form a portfolio of stocks that are both in the lowest quintile of price–earnings ratios and in the lowest quintile of market-to-book ratio. Does selecting stocks based on more than one characteristic improve your ability to devise portfolios with abnormal returns?

SOLUTIONS TO

Concept

CHECKS

1. *a.* A high-level manager might well have private information about the firm. Her ability to trade profitably on that information is not surprising. This ability does not violate weak-form efficiency: The abnormal profits are not derived from an analysis of past price and trading data. If they were, this would indicate that there is valuable information that can be gleaned from such analysis. But this ability does violate strong-form efficiency. Apparently, there is some private information that is not already reflected in stock prices.

   b. The information sets that pertain to the weak, semistrong, and strong form of the EMH can be described by:

The weak-form information set includes only the history of prices and trading. The semistrong-form set includes the weak-form set *plus* all other publicly available information. In turn, the strong-form set includes the semistrong set *plus* inside information. The direction of *valid* implication is

   Strong-form efficiency ⇒ semistrong-form efficiency ⇒ weak-form efficiency

The reverse direction implication is *not* valid. For example, stock prices may reflect all past price data (weak-form efficiency) but may not reflect relevant fundamental data (semistrong-form inefficiency).

2. If *everyone* follows a passive strategy, sooner or later prices will fail to reflect new information. At this point, there are profit opportunities for active investors who uncover mispriced securities. As they buy and sell these assets, prices again will be driven to fair levels.

3. The answer depends on your prior beliefs about market efficiency. Magellan's record was incredibly strong. On the other hand, with so many funds in existence, it is less surprising that *some*

www.mhhe.com/bkm

fund would appear to be consistently superior after the fact. In fact, Magellan's record was so good that even accounting for its selection after the fact as the "winner" of an investment "contest," it still appears to be too good to be attributed to chance. For further analysis and discussion of Magellan's performance, refer to the articles by Marcus and Samuelson in Appendix A.

4. If profit opportunities can be made, one would expect mutual funds specializing in small stocks to spring into existence. Moreover, one wonders why buyers of small stocks don't compete for those stocks in December and bid up their prices before the January rise.

PART THREE

DEBT SECURITIES

Bond markets used to be a sedate arena for risk-averse investors who wanted worry-free investments with modest but stable returns. They are no longer so quiet. Annual trading in U.S. government bonds alone is about 10 times the total amount of national debt. The market in mortgage-backed securities alone is now about $2.6 trillion.

Higher trading activity is not the only reason these markets are more interesting than they once were. These markets are no longer free of risk. Interest rates in the last decade or so have become more volatile than anyone in 1965 would have dreamed possible. Volatility means that investors have great opportunities for gain, but also for losses, and we have seen dramatic examples of both in recent years. A single trader at Merrill Lynch lost $250 hundred million in less than a month trading mortgage-backed securities in 1987. Procter & Gamble lost about $100 million in interest rate swaps in 1994. Long-Term Capital Management lost more than $1 billion on its interest-rate positions in 1998. Of course, there were traders on the other side of these transactions who did quite well in these instances.

The chapters in Part Three provide an introduction to debt markets and securities. We will show you how to value such securities and why their values change with interest rates. We will see what features determine the sensitivity of bond prices to interest rates, and how investors measure and manage interest rate risk.

9	Bond Prices and Yields
10	Managing Bond Investments

9

BOND PRICES AND YIELDS

AFTER STUDYING THIS CHAPTER YOU SHOULD BE ABLE TO:

> Compute a bond's price given its yield to maturity, and compute its yield to maturity given its price.

> Calculate how bond prices will change over time for a given interest rate projection.

> Identify the determinants of bond safety and rating.

> Analyze how call, convertibility, and sinking fund provisions will affect a bond's equilibrium yield to maturity.

> Analyze the factors likely to affect the shape of the yield curve at any time.

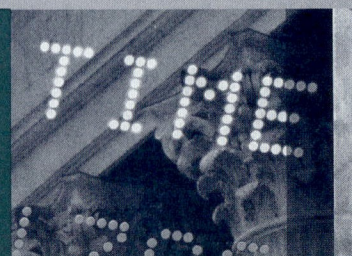

In the previous chapters on risk and return relationships, we have treated securities at a high level of abstraction. We have assumed implicitly that a prior, detailed analysis of each security already has been performed, and that its risk and return features have been assessed.

We turn now to specific analyses of particular security markets. We examine valuation principles, determinants of risk and return, and portfolio strategies commonly used within and across the various markets.

We begin by analyzing debt securities. A debt security is a claim on a specified periodic stream of income. Debt securities are often called *fixed-income securities*, because they promise either a fixed stream of income or a stream of income that is determined according to a specified formula. These securities have the advantage of being relatively easy to understand because the payment formulas are specified in advance. Uncertainty surrounding cash flows paid to the security holder is minimal as long as the issuer of the security is sufficiently creditworthy. That makes these securities a convenient starting point for our analysis of the universe of potential investment vehicles.

The bond is the basic debt security, and this chapter starts with an overview of bond markets, including Treasury, corporate, and international bonds. We turn next to bond pricing, showing how bond prices are set in accordance with market interest rates and why bond prices change with those rates. Given this background, we can compare the myriad measures of bond returns such as yield to maturity, yield to call, holding-period return, or realized compound yield to maturity. We show how bond prices evolve over time, discuss certain tax rules that apply to debt securities, and show how to calculate after-tax returns. Next, we consider the impact of default or

debt security

A security such as a bond that pays a specified cash flow over a specific period.

bond

A security that obligates the issuer to make specified payments to the holder over a period of time.

face value, par value

The payment to the bondholder at the maturity of the bond.

coupon rate

A bond's annual interest payment per dollar of par value.

zero-coupon bond

A bond paying no coupons that sells at a discount and provides only a payment of par value at maturity.

callable bonds

Bonds that may be repurchased by the issuer at a specified call price during the call period.

credit risk on bond pricing and look at the determinants of credit risk and the default premium built into bond yields. Finally, we turn to the term structure of interest rates, the relationship between yield to maturity and time to maturity.

9.1 BOND CHARACTERISTICS

A **bond** is a security that is issued in connection with a borrowing arrangement. The borrower issues (i.e., sells) a bond to the lender for some amount of cash; the bond is in essence the "IOU" of the borrower. The arrangement obligates the issuer to make specified payments to the bondholder on specified dates. A typical coupon bond obligates the issuer to make semi-annual payments of interest, called *coupon payments,* to the bondholder for the life of the bond. These are called coupon payments because, in precomputer days, most bonds had coupons that investors would clip off and mail to the issuer of the bond to claim the interest payment. When the bond matures, the issuer repays the debt by paying the bondholder the bond's **par value** (or equivalently, its **face value**). The **coupon rate** of the bond serves to determine the interest payment: The annual payment equals the coupon rate times the bond's par value. The coupon rate, maturity date, and par value of the bond are part of the *bond indenture,* which is the contract between the issuer and the bondholder.

To illustrate, a bond with a par value of $1,000 and a coupon rate of 8% might be sold to a buyer for $1,000. The issuer then pays the bondholder 8% of $1,000, or $80 per year, for the stated life of the bond, say 30 years. The $80 payment typically comes in two semiannual installments of $40 each. At the end of the 30-year life of the bond, the issuer also pays the $1,000 par value to the bondholder.

Bonds usually are issued with coupon rates set high enough to induce investors to pay par value to buy the bond. Sometimes, however, **zero-coupon bonds** are issued that make no coupon payments. In this case, investors receive par value at the maturity date, but receive no interest payments until then: The bond has a coupon rate of zero. These bonds are issued at prices considerably below par value, and the investor's return comes solely from the difference between issue price and the payment of par value at maturity. We will return to these bonds below.

Treasury Bonds and Notes

Figure 9.1 is an excerpt from the listing of Treasury issues in *The Wall Street Journal.* Treasury note maturities range up to 10 years, while Treasury bonds with maturities ranging from 10 to 30 years appear in the figure. In 2001, the Treasury suspended new issues of 30-year bonds, making the 10-year note the longest currently issued Treasury. As of 2002, there have been no announcements of any plans to resume issuing the 30-year bond. Both bonds and notes are issued in denominations of $1,000 or more. Both make semiannual coupon payments. Aside from their differing maturities at issue date, the only major distinction between T-notes and T-bonds is that in the past, some T-bonds were **callable** for a given period, usually during the last five years of the bond's life. The call provision gives the Treasury the right to repurchase the bond at par value during the call period.

The highlighted bond in Figure 9.1 matures in October 2006. Its coupon rate is 6½%. Par value is $1,000; thus, the bond pays interest of $65 per year in two semiannual payments of $32.50. Payments are made in April and October of each year. The bid and ask prices[1] are quoted

---

[1]Recall that the bid price is the price at which you can sell the bond to a dealer. The ask price, which is slightly higher, is the price at which you can buy the bond from a dealer.

TREASURY BONDS, NOTES & BILLS

Wednesday, November 28, 2001

Representative Over-the-Counter quotation based on transactions of $1 million or more.

Treasury bond, note and bill quotes are as of mid-afternoon. Colons in bid-and-asked quotes represent 32nds; 101:01 means 101 1/32. Net changes in 32nds. n-Treasury note. i-Inflation-Indexed issue. Treasury bill quotes in hundredths, quoted on terms of a rate of discount. Days to maturity calculated from settlement date. All yields are to maturity and based on the asked quote. Latest 13-week and 26-week bills are boldfaced. For bonds callable prior to maturity, yields are computed to the earliest call date for issues quoted above par and to the maturity date for issues below par. *-When issued.
Source: eSpeed/Cantor Fitzgerald

U.S. Treasury strips as of 3 p.m. Eastern time, also based on transactions of $1 million or more. Colons in bid-and-asked quotes represent 32nds; 99:01 means 99 1/32. Net changes in 32nds. Yields calculated on the asked quotation. ci-stripped coupon interest. bp-Treasury bond, stripped principal. np-Treasury note, stripped principal. For bonds callable prior to maturity, yields are computed to the earliest call date for issues quoted above par and to the maturity date for issues below par.
Source: Bear, Stearns & Co. via Street Software Technology Inc.

GOVT. BOND & NOTES

RATE	MATURITY MO/YR	BID	ASKED	CHG.	ASKED YLD.
5⅞	Nov 01n	100:00	100:01	....	0.15
6⅛	Dec 01n	100:09	100:12	....	1.76
6¼	Jan 02n	100:21	100:24	− 1	1.82
2¾	Oct 03n	99:13	99:16	+ 1	3.02
4¼	Nov 03n	102:06	102:09	....	3.03
11⅞	Nov 03	116:17	116:20	....	3.07
4¾	Nov 03n	103:07	103:10	− 1	3.18
5⅞	Feb 04n	105:18	105:21	− 1	3.20
5¼	May 04n	104:13	104:16	....	3.33
7¼	May 04n	109:00	109:03	− 1	3.37
12⅜	May 04	121:00	121:02	....	3.38
6	Aug 04n	106:11	106:14	....	3.49
7¼	Aug 04n	109:17	109:20	+ 1	3.50
13¾	Aug 04	126:04	126:07	− 2	3.52
5⅞	Nov 04n	106:03	106:06	− 1	3.65
7⅞	Nov 04n	111:19	111:22	− 1	3.67
11⅝	Nov 04	122:00	122:01	− 1	3.70
7½	Feb 05n	111:06	111:09	+ 1	3.74
6½	May 05n	108:12	108:15	+ 1	3.86
6¾	May 05n	109:00	109:03	....	3.91
12	May 05	126:00	126:02	....	n.a.
6½	Aug 05n	108:18	108:21	+ 1	3.96
10¾	Aug 05	123:00	123:00	+ 1	4.01
5¾	Nov 05n	105:28	105:31	....	4.10
5⅞	Nov 05n	106:15	106:18	+ 1	4.06
5⅝	Feb 06n	105:18	105:21	+ 1	4.14

RATE	MATURITY MO/YR	BID	ASKED	CHG.	ASKED YLD.
9⅜	Feb 06	119:27	119:30	....	4.16
4⅝	May 06n	101:19	101:22	....	4.21
6⅞	May 06n	110:18	110:21	+ 2	4.23
7	Jul 06n	111:05	111:08	+ 1	4.29
6½	Oct 06n	109:08	109:11	+ 1	4.35
3½	Nov 06n	96:13	96:16	+ 1	4.29
3⅜	Jan 07i	100:28	100:31	+ 1	3.17
6¼	Feb 07n	108:13	108:16	....	4.40
7⅝	Feb 07	101:02	101:05	− 1	n.a.
6⅝	May 07n	110:09	110:12	....	4.46
6⅛	Aug 07n	108:00	108:01	− 1	4.51
6½	Nov 26	111:05	111:08	− 17	5.65
6⅝	Feb 27	113:00	113:03	− 18	5.64
6⅜	Aug 27	109:27	109:30	− 18	5.64
6⅛	Nov 27	106:27	106:30	− 15	5.61
3⅝	Apr 28i	102:07	102:10	− 19	3.49
5½	Aug 28	98:15	98:18	− 14	5.60
5¼	Nov 28	95:09	95:12	− 13	5.58
5¼	Feb 29	95:16	95:19	− 15	5.57
3⅞	Apr 29i	107:00	107:01	− 16	3.47
6⅛	Aug 29	107:28	107:31	− 18	5.56
6¼	May 30	110:19	110:22	− 20	5.50
5⅜	Feb 31	100:05	100:08	− 12	5.36
3⅜	Apr 32i	98:26	98:29	− 19	3.43

U.S. TREASURY STRIPS

MATURITY	TYPE	BID	ASKED	CHG.	ASKED YLD.
Jan 02	ci	99:27	99:27	....	1.28
Feb 02	ci	99:23	99:24	....	1.26

MAT.	TYPE	BID	ASKED	CHG.	ASKED YLD.
May 02	ci	99:05	99:05	+ 1	1.82
May 02	np	99:04	99:05	+ 1	1.87
Aug 02	ci	98:21	98:21	+ 1	1.91
Aug 02	np	98:19	98:19	....	1.99
Nov 02	ci	98:06	98:06	+ 2	1.91
Feb 03	ci	97:00	97:00	+ 4	2.53
Feb 03	np	97:02	97:03	+ 5	2.46
May 03	ci	96:07	96:08	+ 1	2.64
Jul 03	ci	95:20	95:21	+ 1	2.75
Aug 03	ci	95:11	95:12	+ 1	2.79
Aug 03	np	95:04	95:05	+ 3	2.92
Nov 03	ci	94:22	94:24	+ 1	2.78
Nov 03	np	94:05	94:06	+ 1	3.09
Jan 04	ci	93:16	93:17	+ 1	3.17
Feb 04	ci	93:06	93:07	+ 1	3.20
Feb 04	np	93:04	93:05	+ 1	3.23
May 04	ci	92:04	92:06	+ 1	3.34
May 04	np	91:30	91:31	+ 1	3.43
Jul 04	ci	91:08	91:09	....	3.50
Aug 04	ci	90:29	90:30	....	3.53
Aug 04	np	90:26	90:27	+ 2	3.57
Nov 04	ci	89:17	89:19	....	3.75
Nov 04	bp	89:11	89:12	+ 2	3.83
Nov 04	np	89:14	89:16	....	3.78
Jan 05	ci	88:25	88:27	....	3.82
Feb 05	ci	88:14	88:16	....	3.84
Feb 05	np	88:16	88:17	+ 2	3.83
May 05	ci	87:09	87:10	....	3.96
May 05	bp	87:03	87:05	....	4.01
May 05	np	87:04	87:05	− 1	4.01
May 05	np	87:10	87:11	....	3.95
Jul 05	ci	86:21	86:23	....	3.97
Aug 05	ci	86:10	86:12	....	3.99
Aug 05	bp	85:22	85:24	− 1	4.19
Aug 05	np	86:03	86:05	....	4.06
Nov 05	ci	85:21	85:23	....	3.93
Nov 05	np	84:25	84:27	....	4.20
Nov 05	np	84:29	84:31	....	4.16
Jan 06	ci	84:09	84:11	− 1	4.17
Nov 09	bp	65:21	65:24	....	5.34
Feb 10	ci	65:14	65:17	....	5.22
Feb 10	np	66:09	66:12	+ 6	5.05
May 10	ci	64:11	64:14	....	5.26
Aug 10	ci	63:18	63:22	....	5.25
Aug 10	np	64:21	64:25	+ 7	5.05
Nov 10	ci	62:27	62:31	....	5.23
Feb 11	ci	61:14	61:17	....	5.34
Feb 11	np	63:04	63:08	+ 4	5.04
May 11	ci	60:13	60:15	....	5.39
Aug 11	ci	59:18	59:19	....	5.40
Nov 11	ci	58:23	58:24	....	5.41

FIGURE 9.1

Listing of Treasury issues

Source: *The Wall Street Journal*, November 29, 2001. Reprinted by permission of Dow Jones & Company, Inc. via Copyright Clearance Center, Inc. © 2001 Dow Jones & Company. All Rights Reserved Worldwide.

in points plus fractions of $\frac{1}{32}$ of a point (the numbers after the colons are the fractions of a point). Although bonds are sold in denominations of $1,000 par value, the prices are quoted as a percentage of par value. Therefore, the bid price of the bond is 109:08 = $109\frac{8}{32}$ = 109.25% of par value or $1,092.50, while the ask price is $109\frac{11}{32}$ percent of par, or $1,093.44.

The last column, labeled Ask Yld, is the bond's yield to maturity based on the ask price. The yield to maturity is often interpreted as a measure of the average rate of return to an investor who purchases the bond for the ask price and holds it until its maturity date. We will have much to say about yield to maturity below.

Accrued interest and quoted bond prices The bond prices that you see quoted in the financial pages are not actually the prices that investors pay for the bond. This is because the quoted price does not include the interest that accrues between coupon payment dates.

If a bond is purchased between coupon payments, the buyer must pay the seller for accrued interest, the prorated share of the upcoming semiannual coupon. For example, if 40 days have passed since the last coupon payment, and there are 182 days in the semiannual coupon period, the seller is entitled to a payment of accrued interest of 40/182 of the semiannual coupon. The sale, or *invoice price* of the bond, which is the amount the buyer actually pays, would equal the stated price plus the accrued interest.

In general, the formula for the amount of accrued interest between two dates is

$$\text{Accrued interest} = \frac{\text{Annual coupon payment}}{2} \times \frac{\text{Days since last coupon payment}}{\text{Days separating coupon payments}}$$

9.1 EXAMPLE
Accrued Interest

Suppose that the coupon rate is 8%. Then the semiannual coupon payment is $40. Because 40 days have passed since the last coupon payment, the accrued interest on the bond is $40 × (40/182) = $8.79. If the quoted price of the bond is $990, then the invoice price will be $990 + $8.79 = $998.79.

The practice of quoting bond prices net of accrued interest explains why the price of a maturing bond is listed at $1,000 rather than $1,000 plus one coupon payment. A purchaser of an 8% coupon bond one day before the bond's maturity would receive $1,040 on the following day and so should be willing to pay a total price of $1,040 for the bond. In fact, $40 of that total payment constitutes the accrued interest for the preceding half-year period. The bond price is quoted net of accrued interest in the financial pages and thus appears as $1,000.

Corporate Bonds

Like the government, corporations borrow money by issuing bonds. Figure 9.2 is a sample of corporate bond listings in *The Wall Street Journal*. The data presented here differ only slightly from U.S. Treasury bond listings. For example, the highlighted AT&T bond pays a coupon rate of 8⅛% and matures in 2022. Like Treasury bonds, corporate bonds trade in increments of ½₂ point. AT&T's *current yield* is 8.1%, which is simply the annual coupon payment divided by the bond price ($81.25/$997.50). Note that current yield measures only the annual interest income the bondholder receives as a percentage of the price paid for the bond. It ignores the fact that an investor who buys the bond for $997.50 will be able to redeem it for $1,000 on the maturity date. Prospective price appreciation or depreciation does not enter the computation of the current yield. The trading volume column shows that 300 bonds traded on that day. The change from yesterday's closing price is given in the last column. Like government bonds, corporate bonds sell in units of $1,000 par value but are quoted as a percentage of par value.

Although the bonds listed in Figure 9.2 trade on a formal exchange operated by the New York Stock Exchange, most bonds are traded over-the-counter in a loosely organized network of bond dealers linked by a computer quotation system. (See Chapter 3 for a comparison of exchange versus OTC trading.) In practice, the bond market can be quite "thin," in that there are few investors interested in trading a particular bond at any particular time. Figure 9.2 shows that trading volume of many bonds on the New York exchange is quite low.

Bonds issued in the United States today are *registered,* meaning that the issuing firm keeps records of the owner of the bond and can mail interest checks to the owner. Registration of

U.S. EXCHANGE BONDS

NEW YORK BONDS

Corporation Bonds

BONDS	CUR YLD.	VOL.	CLOSE	NET CHG.
AES Cp 8s8	8.5	45	94	+ ⅞
ATT 7⅛02	7.1	20	100⅜	...
ATT 6½02	6.6	10	98¾	− ⅝
ATT 6¾04	6.9	25	98¼	− ⅝
ATT 5⅞04	5.9	40	94⅞	+ ⅜
ATT 7s05	7.0	65	99½	− ½
ATT 7⅛06	7.5	30	100½	− 1
ATT 7¾07	7.6	23	102	+ ¼
ATT 6s09	6.7	75	89	− ½
ATT 8½22	8.1	300	99¾	+ ⅛
ATT 8⅛24	8.1	59	99¾	...
ATT 8.35s25	8.2	35	102¼	+ ¾
ATT 6½29	7.9	130	82⅛	+ ⅜
ATT 8⅝31	8.5	132	102	− ⅛
Alza zr14	...	2	97	+ 3
Amresco 10s03	27.8	121	36	− 3
Amresco 10s04	28.7	35	34⅞	+ 1¾
ArmWld 9¾08	10.0	60	97	− 1
ARch 10⅞05	9.5	25	115⅛	+ ¼
BayView 9s07	11.9	116	75⅜	+ ⅜
BellsoT 6¼03	6.4	8	98	+ ⅜

BONDS	CUR YLD.	VOL.	CLOSE	NET CHG.
IBM 7¼02	7.2	150	101⅛	+ ¼
IBM 6.45s07	6.7	10	96⅛	− 1
IBM 7½13	7.3	20	102⅝	− 1
IntShip 9s03	9.0	15	99⅝	+ ⅜
vjKCS En 8⅞08f	...	35	78	− 1
KaufB 9⅜03	9.5	85	99¼	− ⅝
KaufB 7¾04	8.1	5	96	+ 2½
KaufB 9⅝06	9.5	170	101	+ ⅜
KentE 4½04	cv	210	90⅛	+ ⅞
KerrM 7½14	cv	20	99	− ⅜
LTC Pr 8¼01	cv	50	81	− 11
LehmnBr 8¾02	8.5	15	102⅝	− ⅜
Leucadia 8¼05	8.4	32	98	
Leucadia 7¾13	8.5	235	91	+ 1¼
Loews 3⅛07	cv	402	92¾	+ 2¼
LglsLt 8.2s23	8.3	70	98⅞	...
MBNA 8.28s26	9.1	5	91¼	+ ¼
MSC Sf 7⅞04	cv	25	93	− 1¾
Malan 9½04	cv	35	91⅜	+ ⅛
MarO 7s02	7.0	86	99¼	+ ⅛
Mascotch 03	cv	40	70	...
McDnl 6⅝05	6.9	5	96¼	...
Medtrst 9s02	cv	33	86	...
MKT 5½33f	...	1	88	− ½
MPac 5s45f	...	1	52⅛	...

FIGURE 9.2

Listing of corporate bonds

Source: *The Wall Street Journal*, September 7, 2000. Reprinted by permission of Dow Jones & Company, Inc. via Copyright Clearance Center, Inc. © 2000 Dow Jones & Company, Inc. All Rights Reserved Worldwide.

bonds is helpful to tax authorities in the enforcement of tax collection. *Bearer bonds* are those traded without any record of ownership. The investor's physical possession of the bond certificate is the only evidence of ownership. These are now rare in the United States, but less rare in Europe.

Call provisions on corporate bonds

While the Treasury no longer issues callable bonds, some corporate bonds are issued with call provisions. The call provision allows the issuer to repurchase the bond at a specified *call price* before the maturity date. For example, if a company issues a bond with a high coupon rate when market interest rates are high, and interest rates later fall, the firm might like to retire the high-coupon debt and issue new bonds at a lower coupon rate to reduce interest payments. The proceeds from the new bond issue are used to pay for the repurchase of the existing higher coupon bonds at the call price. This is called *refunding*.

Callable bonds typically come with a period of call protection, an initial time during which the bonds are not callable. Such bonds are referred to as *deferred* callable bonds.

The option to call the bond is valuable to the firm, allowing it to buy back the bonds and refinance at lower interest rates when market rates fall. Of course, the firm's benefit is the bondholder's burden. Holders of called bonds forfeit their bonds for the call price, thereby giving up the prospect of an attractive rate of interest on their original investment. To compensate investors for this risk, callable bonds are issued with higher coupons and promised yields to maturity than noncallable bonds.

1. Suppose that General Motors issues two bonds with identical coupon rates and maturity dates. One bond is callable, however, while the other is not. Which bond will sell at a higher price?

Concept
CHECK

Convertible bonds

Convertible bonds give bondholders an option to exchange each bond for a specified number of shares of common stock of the firm. The *conversion ratio* gives the number of shares for which each bond may be exchanged. To see the value of this

convertible bond

A bond with an option allowing the bondholder to exchange the bond for a specified number of shares of common stock in the firm.

right, suppose a convertible bond that is issued at par value of $1,000 is convertible into 40 shares of a firm's stock. The current stock price is $20 per share, so the option to convert is not profitable now. Should the stock price later rise to $30, however, each bond may be converted profitably into $1,200 worth of stock. The *market conversion value* is the current value of the shares for which the bonds may be exchanged. At the $20 stock price, for example, the bond's conversion value is $800. The *conversion premium* is the excess of the bond value over its conversion value. If the bond were selling currently for $950, its premium would be $150.

Convertible bonds give their holders the ability to share in price appreciation of the company's stock. Again, this benefit comes at a price; convertible bonds offer lower coupon rates and stated or promised yields to maturity than nonconvertible bonds. At the same time, the actual return on the convertible bond may exceed the stated yield to maturity if the option to convert becomes profitable.

We discuss convertible and callable bonds further in Chapter 16.

Puttable bonds   While the callable bond gives the issuer the option to extend or retire the bond at the call date, the extendable or **put bond** gives this option to the bondholder. If the bond's coupon rate exceeds current market yields, for instance, the bondholder will choose to extend the bond's life. If the bond's coupon rate is too low, it will be optimal not to extend; the bondholder instead reclaims principal, which can be invested at current yields.

put bond

A bond that the holder may choose either to exchange for par value at some date or to extend for a given number of years.

Floating-rate bonds   Floating-rate bonds make interest payments that are tied to some measure of current market rates. For example, the rate might be adjusted annually to the current T-bill rate plus 2%. If the one-year T-bill rate at the adjustment date is 4%, the bond's coupon rate over the next year would then be 6%. This arrangement means that the bond always pays approximately current market rates.

floating-rate bonds

Bonds with coupon rates periodically reset according to a specified market rate.

The major risk involved in floaters has to do with changing credit conditions. The yield spread is fixed over the life of the security, which may be many years. If the financial health of the firm deteriorates, then a greater yield premium would be required than is offered by the security. In this case, the price of the bond would fall. While the coupon rate on floaters adjusts to changes in the general level of market interest rates, it does not adjust to changes in the financial condition of the firm.

Preferred Stock

Although preferred stock strictly speaking is considered to be equity, it often is included in the fixed-income universe. This is because, like bonds, preferred stock promises to pay a specified stream of dividends. However, unlike bonds, the failure to pay the promised dividend does not result in corporate bankruptcy. Instead, the dividends owed simply cumulate, and the common stockholders may not receive any dividends until the preferred stockholders have been paid in full. In the event of bankruptcy, the claim of preferred stockholders to the firm's assets has lower priority than that of bondholders, but higher priority than that of common stockholders.

Most preferred stock pays a fixed dividend. Therefore, it is in effect a perpetuity, providing a level cash flow indefinitely. More recently, however, adjustable or floating-rate preferred stock has become popular. Floating-rate preferred stock is much like floating-rate bonds. The dividend rate is linked to a measure of current market interest rates and is adjusted at regular intervals.

Unlike interest payments on bonds, dividends on preferred stock are not considered tax-deductible expenses to the firm. This reduces their attractiveness as a source of capital to issuing firms. On the other hand, there is an offsetting tax advantage to preferred stock. When one corporation buys the preferred stock of another corporation, it pays taxes on only 30% of the dividends received. For example, if the firm's tax bracket is 35%, and it receives $10,000 in preferred dividend payments, it will pay taxes on only $3,000 of that income: Total taxes owed on the income will be $0.35 \times \$3,000 = \$1,050$. The firm's effective tax rate on preferred dividends is therefore only $0.30 \times 35\% = 10.5\%$. Given this tax rule, it is not surprising that most preferred stock is held by corporations.

Preferred stock rarely gives its holders full voting privileges in the firm. However, if the preferred dividend is skipped, the preferred stockholders will then be provided some voting power.

Other Domestic Issuers

There are, of course, several issuers of bonds in addition to the Treasury and private corporations. For example, state and local governments issue municipal bonds. The outstanding feature of these is that interest payments are tax-free. We examined municipal bonds and the value of the tax exemption in Chapter 2.

Government agencies, such as the Federal Home Loan Bank Board, the Farm Credit agencies, and the mortgage pass-through agencies Ginnie Mae, Fannie Mae, and Freddie Mac also issue considerable amounts of bonds. These too were reviewed in Chapter 2.

As the Federal government ran large budgetary surpluses in the late 1990s, it was able to retire part of its debt. If this trend were to continue, the stock of outstanding Treasury bonds would fall dramatically; with fewer such bonds traded, the depth and liquidity of the Treasury market would be reduced. Some observers predict that in this event, Federal agency debt, particularly that of Fannie Mae and perhaps Freddie Mac, would replace Treasury bonds as the "benchmark" assets of the debt market.

International Bonds

International bonds are commonly divided into two categories: *foreign bonds* and *Eurobonds*. Foreign bonds are issued by a borrower from a country other than the one in which the bond is sold. The bond is denominated in the currency of the country in which it is marketed. For example, if a German firm sells a dollar-denominated bond in the U.S., the bond is considered a foreign bond. These bonds are given colorful names based on the countries in which they are marketed. For example, foreign bonds sold in the U.S. are called *Yankee bonds*. Like other bonds sold in the U.S., they are registered with the Securities and Exchange Commission. Yen-denominated bonds sold in Japan by non-Japanese issuers are called *Samurai bonds*. British pound-denominated foreign bonds sold in the U.K. are called *bulldog bonds*.

In contrast to foreign bonds, Eurobonds are bonds issued in the currency of one country but sold in other national markets. For example, the Eurodollar market refers to dollar-denominated bonds sold outside the U.S. (not just in Europe), although London is the largest market for Eurodollar bonds. Because the Eurodollar market falls outside of U.S. jurisdiction, these bonds are not regulated by U.S. federal agencies. Similarly, Euroyen bonds are yen-denominated bonds selling outside Japan, Eurosterling bonds are pound-denominated Eurobonds selling outside the U.K., and so on.

Innovation in the Bond Market

Issuers constantly develop innovative bonds with unusual features; these issues illustrate that bond design can be extremely flexible. Here are examples of some novel bonds. They should give you a sense of the potential variety in security design.

Reverse floaters These are similar to the floating-rate bonds we described earlier, except that the coupon rate on these bonds *falls* when the general level of interest rates rises. Investors in these bonds suffer doubly when rates rise. Not only does the present value of each dollar of cash flow from the bond fall as the discount rate rises but the level of those cash flows falls as well. (Of course investors in these bonds benefit doubly when rates fall.)

Asset-backed bonds Walt Disney has issued bonds with coupon rates tied to the financial performance of several of its films. Similarly, "David Bowie bonds" have been issued with payments that will be tied to royalties on some of his albums. These are examples of asset-backed securities. The income from a specified group of assets is used to service the debt. More conventional asset-backed securities are mortgage-backed securities or securities backed by auto or credit card loans, as we discussed in Chapter 2.

Pay-in-kind bonds Issuers of pay-in-kind bonds may choose to pay interest either in cash or in additional bonds. If the issuer is short on cash, it will likely choose to pay with new bonds rather than scarce cash.

Catastrophe bonds Electrolux once issued a bond with a final payment that depended on whether there had been an earthquake in Japan. Winterthur has issued a bond whose payments depend on whether there has been a severe hailstorm in Switzerland. These bonds are a way to transfer "catastrophe risk" from the firm to the capital markets. They represent a novel way of obtaining insurance from the capital markets against specified disasters. Investors in these bonds receive compensation in the form of higher coupon rates for taking on the risk.

Indexed bonds Indexed bonds make payments that are tied to a general price index or the price of a particular commodity. For example, Mexico has issued 20-year bonds with payments that depend on the price of oil. Some bonds are indexed to the general price level. The United States Treasury started issuing such inflation-indexed bonds in January 1997. They are called Treasury Inflation Protected Securities (TIPS). By tying the par value of the bond to the general level of prices, coupon payments, as well as the final repayment of par value, on these bonds will increase in direct proportion to the consumer price index. Therefore, the interest rate on these bonds is a risk-free real rate.

To illustrate how TIPS work, consider a newly issued bond with a three-year maturity, par value of $1,000, and a coupon rate of 4%. For simplicity, we will assume the bond makes annual coupon payments. Assume that inflation turns out to be 2%, 3%, and 1% in the next three years. Table 9.1 shows how the bond cash flows will be calculated. The first payment comes at the end of the first year, at $t = 1$. Because inflation over the year was 2%, the par value of the bond is increased from $1,000 to $1,020; since the coupon rate is 4%, the coupon payment is 4% of this amount, or $40.80. Notice that principal value increases in tandem with inflation, and because the coupon payments are 4% of principal, they too increase in proportion to the general price level. Therefore, the cash flows paid by the bond are fixed in *real* terms. When the bond matures, the investor receives a final coupon payment of $42.44 plus the (price-level-indexed) repayment of principal, $1,061.11.[2]

The *nominal* rate of return on the bond in the first year is

$$\text{Nominal return} = \frac{\text{Interest} + \text{Price appreciation}}{\text{Initial price}} = \frac{40.80 + 20}{1000} = 6.08\%$$

---

[2]By the way, total nominal income (i.e., coupon plus that year's increase in principal) is treated as taxable income in each year.

TABLE **9.1**	Time	Inflation in Year Just Ended	Par Value	Coupon Payment	+	Principal Repayment	=	Total Payment
Principal and interest payments for a Treasury Inflation Protected Security	0		$1,000.00					
	1	2%	1,020.00	$40.80		0		$ 40.80
	2	3	1,050.60	42.02		0		42.02
	3	1	1,061.11	42.44		$1,061.11		1,103.55

The real rate of return is precisely the 4% real yield on the bond:

$$\text{Real return} = \frac{1 + \text{Nominal return}}{1 + \text{Inflation}} - 1 = \frac{1.0608}{1.02} = .04, \text{ or } 4\%$$

One can show in a similar manner (see problem 12 in the end-of-chapter questions) that the rate of return in each of the three years is 4% as long as the real yield on the bond remains constant. If real yields do change, then there will be capital gains or losses on the bond. In mid-2002, the real yield on TIPS bonds was about 2.5%.

9.2 BOND PRICING

Because a bond's coupon and principal repayments all occur months or years in the future, the price an investor would be willing to pay for a claim to those payments depends on the value of dollars to be received in the future compared to dollars in hand today. This "present value" calculation depends in turn on market interest rates. As we saw in Chapter 5, the nominal risk-free interest rate equals the sum of (1) a real risk-free rate of return and (2) a premium above the real rate to compensate for expected inflation. In addition, because most bonds are not riskless, the discount rate will embody an additional premium that reflects bond-specific characteristics such as default risk, liquidity, tax attributes, call risk, and so on.

We simplify for now by assuming there is one interest rate that is appropriate for discounting cash flows of any maturity, but we can relax this assumption easily. In practice, there may be different discount rates for cash flows accruing in different periods. For the time being, however, we ignore this refinement.

To value a security, we discount its expected cash flows by the appropriate discount rate. The cash flows from a bond consist of coupon payments until the maturity date plus the final payment of par value. Therefore

Bond value = Present value of coupons + Present value of par value

If we call the maturity date T and call the discount rate r, the bond value can be written as

$$\text{Bond value} = \sum_{t=1}^{T} \frac{\text{Coupon}}{(1 + r)^t} + \frac{\text{Par value}}{(1 + r)^T} \tag{9.1}$$

The summation sign in Equation 9.1 directs us to add the present value of each coupon payment; each coupon is discounted based on the time until it will be paid. The first term on the right-hand side of Equation 9.1 is the present value of an annuity. The second term is the present value of a single amount, the final payment of the bond's par value.

You may recall from an introductory finance class that the present value of a $1 annuity that lasts for T periods when the interest rate equals r is $\frac{1}{r}\left(1 - \frac{1}{(1 + r)^T}\right)$. We call this expression the *T*-period *annuity factor* for an interest rate of *r*.[3] Similarly, we call $\frac{1}{(1 + r)^T}$ the *PV factor*, i.e., the present value of a single payment of $1 to be received in *T* periods. Therefore, we can write the price of the bond as

$$\text{Price} = \text{Coupon} \times \frac{1}{r}\left(1 - \frac{1}{(1 + r)^T}\right) + \text{Par value} \times \frac{1}{(1 + r)^T} \tag{9.2}$$

$$= \text{Coupon} \times \text{Annuity factor}(r, T) + \text{Par value} \times \text{PV factor}(r, T)$$

9.2 EXAMPLE

Bond Pricing

We discussed earlier an 8% coupon, 30-year maturity bond with par value of $1,000 paying 60 semiannual coupon payments of $40 each. Suppose that the interest rate is 8% annually, or *r* = 4% per six-month period. Then the value of the bond can be written as

$$\text{Price} = \sum_{t=1}^{60} \frac{\$40}{(1.04)^t} + \frac{\$1,000}{(1.04)^{60}}$$

$$= \$40 \times \text{Annuity factor}(4\%, 60) + \$1,000 \times \text{PV factor}(4\%, 60)$$

It is easy to confirm that the present value of the bond's 60 semiannual coupon payments of $40 each is $904.94, and that the $1,000 final payment of par value has a present value of $95.06, for a total bond value of $1,000. You can calculate the value directly from Equation 9.2, perform these calculations on any financial calculator,[4] or use a set of present value tables.

In this example, the coupon rate equals the market interest rate, and the bond price equals par value. If the interest rate were not equal to the bond's coupon rate, the bond would not sell at par value. For example, if the interest rate were to rise to 10% (5% per six months), the bond's price would fall by $189.29, to $810.71, as follows

$$\$40 \times \text{Annuity factor (5\%, 60)} + \$1,000 \times \text{PV factor}(5\%, 60)$$

$$= \$757.17 + \$53.54 = \$810.71$$

At a higher interest rate, the present value of the payments to be received by the bondholder is lower. Therefore, the bond price will fall as market interest rates rise. This illustrates a crucial general rule in bond valuation. When interest rates rise, bond prices must fall because the present value of the bond's payments is obtained by discounting at a higher interest rate.

Figure 9.3 shows the price of the 30-year, 8% coupon bond for a range of interest rates including 8%, at which the bond sells at par, and 10%, at which it sells for $810.71. The negative slope illustrates the inverse relationship between prices and yields. Note also from the figure (and from Table 9.2) that the shape of the curve implies that an increase in the interest

---

[3]Here is a quick derivation of the formula for the present value of an annuity. An annuity lasting *T* periods can be viewed as an equivalent to a perpetuity whose first payment comes at the end of the current period *less* another perpetuity whose first payment doesn't come until the end of period *T* + 1. The immediate perpetuity net of the delayed perpetuity provides exactly *T* payments. We know that the value of a $1 per period perpetuity is $1/*r*. Therefore, the present value of the delayed perpetuity is $1/*r* discounted for *T* additional periods, or $\frac{1}{r} \times \frac{1}{(1 + r)^T}$. The present value of the annuity is the presentvalue of the first perpetuity minus the present value of the delayed perpetuity, or $\frac{1}{r}\left(1 - \frac{1}{(1 + r)^T}\right)$.

[4]On your financial calculator, you would enter the following inputs: *n* (number of periods) = 60; FV (face or future value) = 1000; PMT (payment each period) = 40; *i* (per period interest rate) = 4%; then you would compute the price of the bond (COMP PV or CPT PV). You should find that the price is $1,000. Actually, most calculators will display the result as *minus* $1,000. This is because most (but not all) calculators treat the initial purchase price of the bond as a cash *outflow*. We will discuss financial calculators more fully in a few pages.

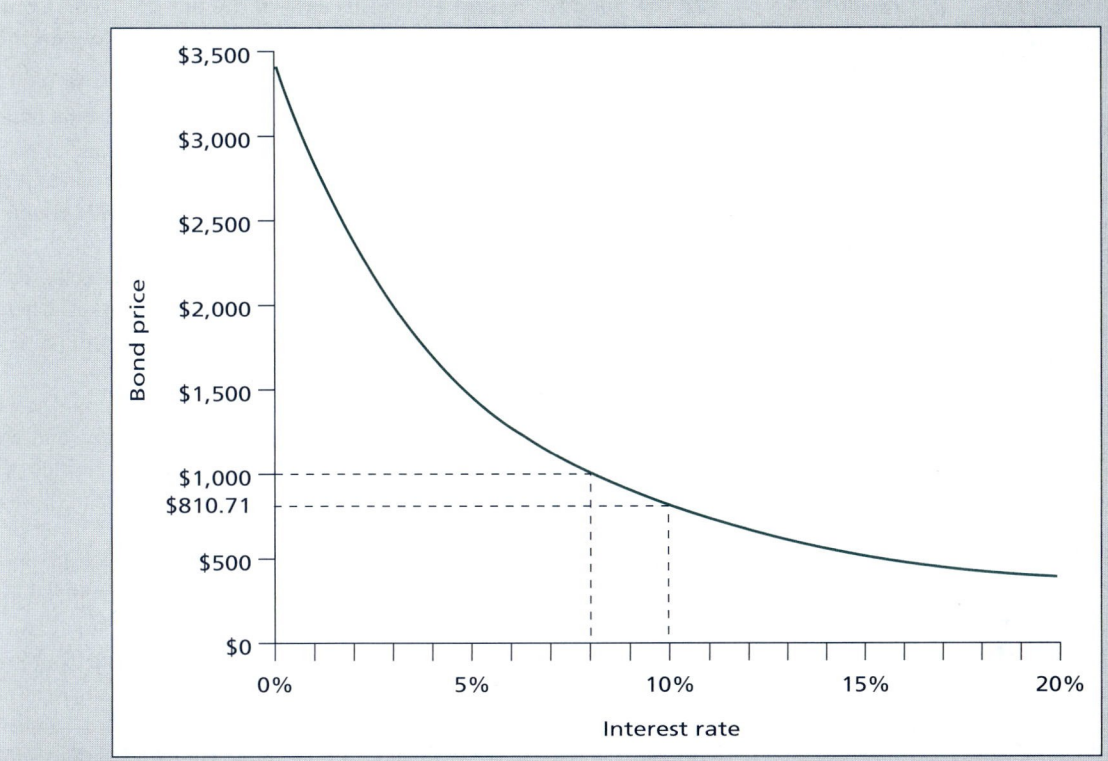

FIGURE **9.3**

The inverse relationship between bond prices and yields. Price of an 8% coupon bond with 30-year maturity making semiannual coupon payments.

TABLE **9.2**	Bond Price at Given Market Interest Rate				
Bond prices at different interest rates (8% coupon bond, coupons paid semiannually)	Time to Maturity	4%	6%	8%	10%	12%
	1 year	$1,038.83	$1,019.13	$1,000.00	$981.41	$963.33
	10 years	1,327.03	1,148.77	1,000.00	875.38	770.60
	20 years	1,547.11	1,231.15	1,000.00	828.41	699.07
	30 years	1,695.22	1,276.76	1,000.00	810.71	676.77

rate results in a price decline that is smaller than the price gain resulting from a decrease of equal magnitude in the interest rate. This property of bond prices is called *convexity* because of the convex shape of the bond price curve. This curvature reflects the fact that progressive increases in the interest rate result in progressively smaller reductions in the bond price.[5] Therefore, the price curve becomes flatter at higher interest rates. We will return to the issue of convexity in the next chapter.

[5]The progressively smaller impact of interest rate increases results from the fact that at higher rates the bond is worth less. Therefore, an additional increase in rates operates on a smaller initial base, resulting in a smaller price reduction.

Concept
CHECK

2. Calculate the price of the bond for a market interest rate of 3% per half year. Compare the capital gains for the interest rate decline to the losses incurred when the rate increases to 5%.

Corporate bonds typically are issued at par value. This means the underwriters of the bond issue (the firms that market the bonds to the public for the issuing corporation) must choose a coupon rate that very closely approximates market yields. In a primary issue of bonds, the underwriters attempt to sell the newly issued bonds directly to their customers. If the coupon rate is inadequate, investors will not pay par value for the bonds.

After the bonds are issued, bondholders may buy or sell bonds in secondary markets, such as the one operated by the New York Stock Exchange or the over-the-counter market, where most bonds trade. In these secondary markets, bond prices move in accordance with market forces. The bond prices fluctuate inversely with the market interest rate.

The inverse relationship between price and yield is a central feature of fixed-income securities. Interest rate fluctuations represent the main source of risk in the bond market, and we devote considerable attention in the next chapter to assessing the sensitivity of bond prices to market yields. For now, however, it is sufficient to highlight one key factor that determines that sensitivity, namely, the maturity of the bond.

A general rule in evaluating bond price risk is that, keeping all other factors the same, the longer the maturity of the bond, the greater the sensitivity of its price to fluctuations in the interest rate. For example, consider Table 9.2, which presents the price of an 8% coupon bond at different market yields and times to maturity. For any departure of the interest rate from 8% (the rate at which the bond sells at par value), the change in the bond price is smaller for shorter times to maturity.

This makes sense. If you buy the bond at par with an 8% coupon rate, and market rates subsequently rise, then you suffer a loss: You have tied up your money earning 8% when alternative investments offer higher returns. This is reflected in a capital loss on the bond—a fall in its market price. The longer the period for which your money is tied up, the greater the loss and, correspondingly, the greater the drop in the bond price. In Table 9.2, the row for one-year maturity bonds shows little price sensitivity—that is, with only one year's earnings at stake, changes in interest rates are not too threatening. But for 30-year maturity bonds, interest rate swings have a large impact on bond prices.

This is why short-term Treasury securities such as T-bills are considered to be the safest. They are free not only of default risk but also largely of price risk attributable to interest rate volatility.

9.3 | BOND YIELDS

We have noted that the current yield of a bond measures only the cash income provided by the bond as a percentage of bond price and ignores any prospective capital gains or losses. We would like a measure of rate of return that accounts for both current income as well as the price increase or decrease over the bond's life. The yield to maturity is the standard measure of the total rate of return of the bond over its life. However, it is far from perfect, and we will explore several variations of this measure.

yield to maturity (YTM)

The discount rate that makes the present value of a bond's payments equal to its price.

Yield to Maturity

In practice, an investor considering the purchase of a bond is not quoted a promised rate of return. Instead, the investor must use the bond price, maturity date, and coupon payments to infer the return offered by the bond over its life. The **yield to maturity** (YTM) is defined as the discount rate that makes the present value of a bond's payments equal to its price. This rate is often viewed as a measure of the average rate of return that will be earned on a bond if it is bought now and held until maturity. To calculate the yield to maturity, we solve the bond price equation for the interest rate given the bond's price.

For example, suppose an 8% coupon, 30-year bond is selling at $1,276.76. What average rate of return would be earned by an investor purchasing the bond at this price? To answer this question, we find the interest rate at which the present value of the remaining 60 semiannual bond payments equals the bond price. This is the rate that is consistent with the observed price of the bond. Therefore, we solve for r in the following equation

$$\$1{,}276.76 = \sum_{t=1}^{60} \frac{\$40}{(1+r)^t} + \frac{\$1{,}000}{(1+r)^{60}}$$

or, equivalently,

$$1{,}276.76 = 40 \times \text{Annuity factor}(r, 60) + 1{,}000 \times \text{PV factor}(r, 60)$$

These equations have only one unknown variable, the interest rate, r. You can use a financial calculator to confirm that the solution to the equation is $r = .03$, or 3% per half-year.[6] This is considered the bond's yield to maturity, as the bond would be fairly priced at $1,276.76 if the fair market rate of return on the bond over its entire life were 3% per half-year.

The financial press reports yields on an annualized basis, however, and annualizes the bond's semiannual yield using simple interest techniques, resulting in an annual percentage rate or APR. Yields annualized using simple interest are also called *bond equivalent yields*. Therefore, the semiannual yield would be doubled and reported in the newspaper as a bond equivalent yield of 6%. The *effective* annual yield of the bond, however, accounts for compound interest. If one earns 3% interest every six months, then after one year, each dollar invested grows with interest to $1 \times (1.03)^2 = 1.0609$, and the effective annual interest rate on the bond is 6.09%.

The bond's yield to maturity is the internal rate of return on an investment in the bond. The yield to maturity can be interpreted as the compound rate of return over the life of the bond under the assumption that all bond coupons can be reinvested at an interest rate equal to the bond's yield to maturity.[7] Yield to maturity therefore is widely accepted as a proxy for average return.

Yield to maturity can be difficult to calculate without a financial calculator. However, it is easy to calculate with one. Financial calculators are designed with present value and future value formulas already programmed. The basic financial calculator uses five keys that correspond to the inputs for time value of money problems such as bond pricing:

- n is the number of time periods. In the case of a bond, n equals the number of periods until the bond matures. If the bond makes semiannual payments, n is the number of half-year periods or, equivalently, the number of semiannual coupon payments. For example, if the bond has 10 years until maturity, you would enter 20 for n, since each payment period is one-half year.

[6]Without a financial calculator, you still could solve the equation, but you would need to use a trial-and-error approach.

[7]If the reinvestment rate does not equal the bond's yield to maturity, the compound rate of return will differ from YTM. This is demonstrated in Examples 9.5 and 9.6.

- i is the interest rate per period, expressed as a percentage (not a decimal). For example, if the interest rate is 6%, you would enter 6, not 0.06.
- *PV* is the present value. Many calculators will require that PV be entered as a negative number, in recognition of the fact that purchase of the bond is a cash *outflow,* while the receipt of coupon payments and face value are cash *inflows.*
- *FV* is the future value or face value of the bond. In general, FV is interpreted as a one-time future payment of a cash flow, which, for bonds, is the face (i.e., par) value.
- *PMT* is the amount of any recurring payment. For coupon bonds, PMT is the coupon payment; for zero-coupon bonds, PMT will be zero.

Given any four of these inputs, the calculator will solve for the fifth. We can illustrate with some examples.

9.3 EXAMPLE

Bond Valuation Using a Financial Calculator

Consider the yield to maturity problem that we just solved. We would enter the following inputs (in any order):

n	60	The bond has a maturity of 30 years, so it makes 60 semiannual payments.
PMT	40	Each semiannual coupon payment is $40.
PV	(−)1,276.76	The bond can be purchased for $1,276.76, which on some calculators must be entered as a negative number as it is a cash outflow.
FV	1,000	The bond will provide a one-time cash flow of $1,000 when it matures.

Given these inputs, you now use the calculator to find the interest rate at which $1,276.76 actually equals the present value of the 60 payments of $40 each plus the one-time payment of $1,000 at maturity. On most calculators, you first punch the "compute" key (labeled *COMP* or *CPT*) and then enter *i* to have the interest rate computed. If you do so, you will find that *i* = 3, or 3% semiannually, as we claimed. (Notice that just as the cash flows are paid semiannually, the computed interest rate is a rate per semiannual time period.)

You can also find bond prices given a yield to maturity. For example, we saw in Example 9.2 that if the yield to maturity is 5% semiannually, the bond price will be $810.71. You can confirm this with the following inputs on your calculator:

$$n = 60; i = 5; FV = 1,000; PMT = 40$$

and then computing PV to find that PV = 810.71. Once again, your calculator may report the result as −810.71.

---

current yield

Annual coupon divided by bond price.

Yield to maturity is different from the **current yield** of a bond, which is the bond's annual coupon payment divided by the bond price. For example, for the 8%, 30-year bond currently selling at $1,276.76, the current yield would be $80/$1,276.76 = 0.0627, or 6.27% per year. In contrast, recall that the effective annual yield to maturity is 6.09%. For this bond, which is selling at a premium over par value ($1,276 rather than $1,000), the coupon rate (8%) exceeds the current yield (6.27%), which exceeds the yield to maturity (6.09%). The coupon rate exceeds current yield because the coupon rate divides the coupon payments by par value ($1,000) rather than by the bond price ($1,276). In turn, the current yield exceeds yield to maturity because the yield to maturity accounts for the built-in capital loss on the bond; the bond bought today for $1,276 will eventually fall in value to $1,000 at maturity.

premium bonds

Bonds selling above par value.

This example illustrates a general role: for **premium bonds** (bonds selling above par value), coupon rate is greater than current yield, which in turn is greater than yield to maturity.

For **discount bonds** (bonds selling below par value), these relationships are reversed (see Concept Check 3).

discount bonds

Bonds selling below par value.

It is common to hear people talking loosely about the yield on a bond. In these cases, they almost always are referring to the yield to maturity.

3. **What will be the relationship among coupon rate, current yield, and yield to maturity for bonds selling at discounts from par? Illustrate using the 8% (semiannual payment) coupon bond assuming it is selling at a yield to maturity of 10%.**

Concept
CHECK

Yield to Call

Yield to maturity is calculated on the assumption that the bond will be held until maturity. What if the bond is callable, however, and may be retired prior to the maturity date? How should we measure average rate of return for bonds subject to a call provision?

Figure 9.4 illustrates the risk of call to the bondholder. The colored line is the value at various market interest rates of a "straight" (that is, noncallable) bond with par value of $1,000, an 8% coupon rate, and a 30-year time to maturity. If interest rates fall, the bond price, which equals the present value of the promised payments, can rise substantially. Now consider a bond that has the same coupon rate and maturity date but is callable at 110% of par value, or $1,100. When interest rates fall, the present value of the bond's *scheduled* payments rises, but the call provision allows the issuer to repurchase the bond at the call price. If the call price is less than the present value of the scheduled payments, the issuer can call the bond at the expense of the bondholder.

The dark line in Figure 9.4 is the value of the callable bond. At high interest rates, the risk of call is negligible, and the values of the straight and callable bonds converge. At lower rates, however, the values of the bonds begin to diverge, with the difference reflecting the value of the firm's option to reclaim the callable bond at the call price. At very low rates, the bond is called, and its value is simply the call price, $1,100.

This analysis suggests that bond market analysts might be more interested in a bond's yield to call rather than its yield to maturity if the bond is especially vulnerable to being called. The yield to call is calculated just like the yield to maturity, except that the time until call replaces time until maturity and the call price replaces the par value. This computation is sometimes called "yield to first call," as it assumes the bond will be called as soon as it is first callable.

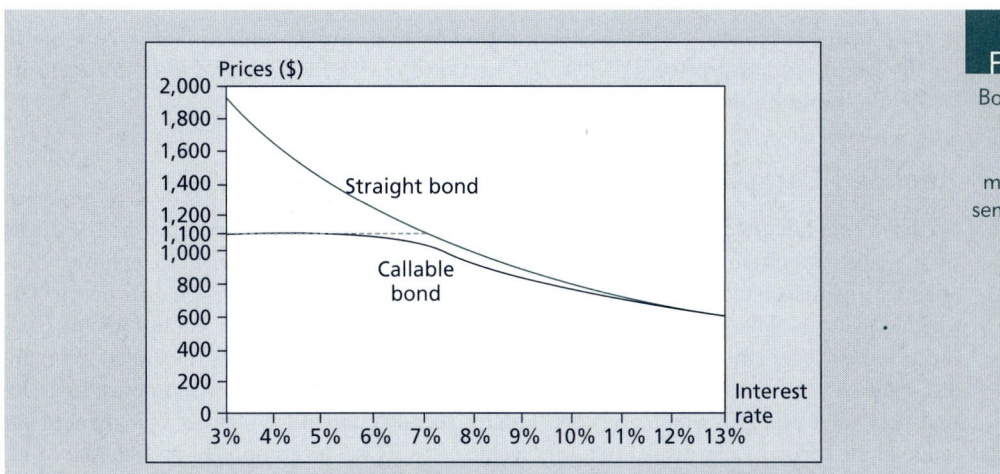

FIGURE **9.4**

Bond prices: Callable and straight debt. Coupon = 8%; maturity = 30 years; semiannual payments

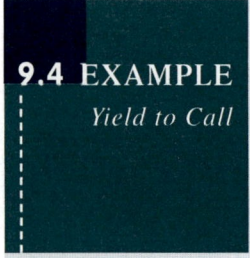

9.4 EXAMPLE

Yield to Call

Suppose the 8% coupon, 30-year maturity bond sells for $1,150 and is callable in 10 years at a call price of $1,100. Its yield to maturity and yield to call would be calculated using the following inputs:

	Yield to Call	Yield to Maturity
Coupon payment	$40	$40
Number of semiannual periods	20 periods	60 periods
Final payment	$1,100	$1,000
Price	$1,150	$1,150

Yield to call is then 6.64% [to confirm this on your calculator, input **n** = 20; **PV** = (−)1,150; **FV** = 1,100; **PMT** = 40; compute **i** as 3.32%, or 6.64% bond equivalent yield], while yield to maturity is 6.82% [to confirm, input **n** = 60; **PV** = (−)1,150; **FV** = 1,000; **PMT** = 40; compute **i** as 3.41%, or 6.82% bond equivalent yield].

We have noted that most callable bonds are issued with an initial period of call protection. In addition, an implicit form of call protection operates for bonds selling at deep discounts from their call prices. Even if interest rates fall a bit, deep-discount bonds still will sell below the call price and thus will not be subject to a call.

Premium bonds that might be selling near their call prices, however, are especially apt to be called if rates fall further. If interest rates fall, a callable premium bond is likely to provide a lower return than could be earned on a discount bond whose potential price appreciation is not limited by the likelihood of a call. Investors in premium bonds often are more interested in the bond's yield to call rather than yield to maturity as a consequence, because it may appear to them that the bond will be retired at the call date.

In fact, the yield reported for callable Treasury bonds in the financial pages of the newspaper (see Figure 9.1) is the yield to *call* for premium bonds and the yield to *maturity* for discount bonds. This is because the call price on Treasury issues is simply par value. If the bond is selling at a premium, it is more likely that the Treasury will find it advantageous to call the bond when it enters the call period. If the bond is selling at a discount from par, the Treasury will not find it advantageous to exercise its option to call.

Concept
CHECK

4. A 20-year maturity 9% coupon bond paying coupons semiannually is callable in five years at a call price of $1,050. The bond currently sells at a yield to maturity of 8% (bond equivalent yield). What is the yield to call?

Realized Compound Yield versus Yield to Maturity

We have noted that yield to maturity will equal the rate of return realized over the life of the bond if all coupons are reinvested at an interest rate equal to the bond's yield to maturity. Consider for example, a two-year bond selling at par value paying a 10% coupon once a year. The yield to maturity is 10%. If the $100 coupon payment is reinvested at an interest rate of 10%, the $1,000 investment in the bond will grow after two years to $1,210, as illustrated in Figure 9.5, Panel A. The coupon paid in the first year is reinvested and grows with interest to a second-year value of $110, which, together with the second coupon payment and payment of par value in the second year, results in a total value of $1,210. The compound growth rate of invested funds, therefore, is calculated from

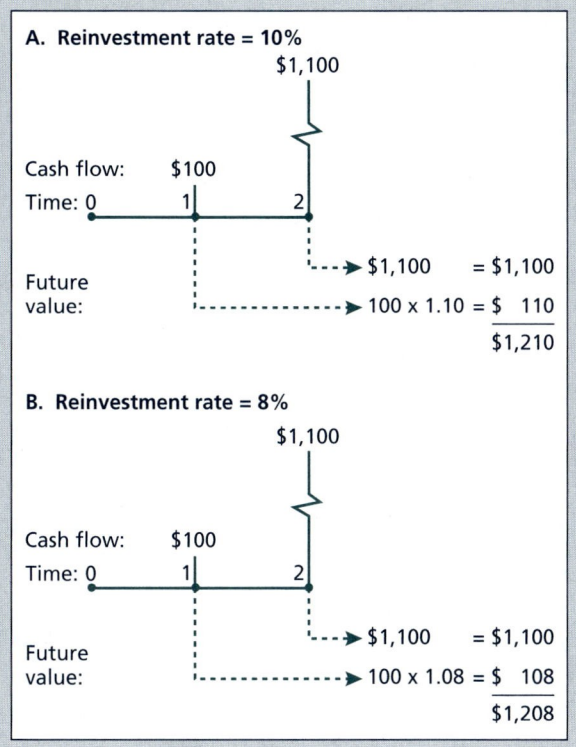

FIGURE **9.5**

Growth of
invested funds

$$\$1,000 \, (1 + y_{\text{realized}})^2 = \$1,210$$

$$y_{\text{realized}} = 0.10 = 10\%$$

With a reinvestment rate equal to the 10% yield to maturity, the *realized* compound yield equals yield to maturity.

But what if the reinvestment rate is not 10%? If the coupon can be invested at more than 10%, funds will grow to more than $1,210, and the realized compound return will exceed 10%. If the reinvestment rate is less than 10%, so will be the realized compound return. Consider the following example.

If the interest rate earned on the first coupon is less than 10%, the final value of the investment will be less than $1,210, and the realized compound yield will be less than 10%. Suppose the interest rate at which the coupon can be invested equals 8%. The following calculations are illustrated in Panel B of Figure 9.5.

EXAMPLE **9.5**

*Realized
Compound Yield*

Future value of first coupon payment with interest earnings	$100 $\times$ 1.08 = $ 108
Cash payment in second year (final coupon plus par value)	1,100
Total value of investment with reinvested coupons	$1,208

The realized compound yield is computed by calculating the compound rate of growth of invested funds, assuming that all coupon payments are reinvested. The investor purchased the bond for par at $1,000, and this investment grew to $1,208.

$$\$1,000(1 + y_{\text{realized}})^2 = \$1,208$$

$$y_{\text{realized}} = 0.0991 = 9.91\%$$

$$RCY = \left[\frac{\text{Total Ending Wealth}}{\text{Purchase price of Bond}} \right]^{\frac{1}{n}} - 1$$

Example 9.5 highlights the problem with conventional yield to maturity when reinvestment rates can change over time. However, in an economy with future interest rate uncertainty, the rates at which interim coupons will be reinvested are not yet known. Therefore, while realized compound yield can be computed *after* the investment period ends, it cannot be computed in advance without a forecast of future reinvestment rates. This reduces much of the attraction of the realized yield measure.

horizon analysis

Analysis of bond returns over multiyear horizon, based on forecasts of bond's yield to maturity and reinvestment rate of coupons.

We also can calculate realized compound yield over holding periods greater than one period. This is called **horizon analysis** and is similar to the procedure in Example 9.5. The forecast of total return will depend on your forecasts of *both* the yield to maturity of the bond when you sell it *and* the rate at which you are able to reinvest coupon income. With a longer investment horizon, however, reinvested coupons will be a larger component of your final proceeds.

9.6 EXAMPLE

Horizon Analysis

Suppose you buy a 30-year, 7.5% (annual payment) coupon bond for $980 (when its yield to maturity is 7.67%) and plan to hold it for 20 years. Your forecast is that the bond's yield to maturity will be 8% when it is sold and that the reinvestment rate on the coupons will be 6%. At the end of your investment horizon, the bond will have 10 years remaining until expiration, so the forecast sales price (using a yield to maturity of 8%) will be $966.45. The 20 coupon payments will grow with compound interest to $2,758.92. (This is the future value of a 20-year $75 annuity with an interest rate of 6%.

Based on these forecasts, your $980 investment will grow in 20 years to $966.45 + $2,758.92 = $3,725.37. This corresponds to an annualized compound return of 6.90%, calculated by solving for r in the equation $980 (1 + r)^{20} = \$3,725.37$.

9.4 BOND PRICES OVER TIME

As we noted earlier, a bond will sell at par value when its coupon rate equals the market interest rate. In these circumstances, the investor receives fair compensation for the time value of money in the form of the recurring interest payments. No further capital gain is necessary to provide fair compensation.

When the coupon rate is lower than the market interest rate, the coupon payments alone will not provide investors as high a return as they could earn elsewhere in the market. To receive a fair return on such an investment, investors also need to earn price appreciation on their bonds. The bonds, therefore, would have to sell below par value to provide a "built-in" capital gain on the investment.

To illustrate this point, suppose a bond was issued several years ago when the interest rate was 7%. The bond's annual coupon rate was thus set at 7%. (We will suppose for simplicity that the bond pays its coupon annually.) Now, with three years left in the bond's life, the interest rate is 8% per year. The bond's fair market price is the present value of the remaining annual coupons plus payment of par value. That present value is

$$\$70 \times \text{Annuity factor(8\%, 3)} + \$1,000 \times \text{PV factor(8\%, 3)} = \$974.23$$

which is less than par value.

In another year, after the next coupon is paid, the bond would sell at

$$\$70 \times \text{Annuity factor(8\%, 2)} + \$1,000 \times \text{PV factor(8\%, 2)} = \$982.17$$

thereby yielding a capital gain over the year of $7.94. If an investor had purchased the bond at $974.23, the total return over the year would equal the coupon payment plus capital gain, or $70 + $7.94 = $77.94. This represents a rate of return of $77.94/$974.23, or 8%, exactly the current rate of return available elsewhere in the market.

FIGURE **9.6**

Price paths of coupon bonds in the case of constant market interest rates

5. **What will the bond price be in yet another year, when only one year remains until maturity? What is the rate of return to an investor who purchases the bond at $982.17 and sells it one year hence?**

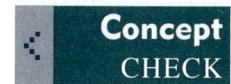

Concept
CHECK

When bond prices are set according to the present value formula, any discount from par value provides an anticipated capital gain that will augment a below-market coupon rate just sufficiently to provide a fair total rate of return. Conversely, if the coupon rate exceeds the market interest rate, the interest income by itself is greater than that available elsewhere in the market. Investors will bid up the price of these bonds above their par values. As the bonds approach maturity, they will fall in value because fewer of these above-market coupon payments remain. The resulting capital losses offset the large coupon payments so that the bondholder again receives only a fair rate of return.

Problem 9 at the end of the chapter asks you to work through the case of the high coupon bond. Figure 9.6 traces out the price paths of high and low coupon bonds (net of accrued interest) as time to maturity approaches, at least for the case in which the market interest rate is constant. The low coupon bond enjoys capital gains, while the high coupon bond suffers capital losses.[8]

We use these examples to show that each bond offers investors the same total rate of return. Although the capital gain versus income components differ, the price of each bond is set to provide competitive rates, as we should expect in well-functioning capital markets. Security returns all should be comparable on an after-tax risk-adjusted basis. If they are not, investors will try to sell low-return securities, thereby driving down the prices until the total return at the now lower price is competitive with other securities. Prices should continue to adjust until all securities are fairly priced in that expected returns are appropriate (given necessary risk and tax adjustments).

Yield to Maturity versus Holding-Period Return

We just considered an example in which the holding-period return and the yield to maturity were equal: in our example, the bond yield started and ended the year at 8%, and the bond's holding-period return also equaled 8%. This turns out to be a general result. When the yield to

[8]If interest rates are volatile, the price path will be "jumpy," vibrating around the price path in Figure 9.6, and reflecting capital gains or losses as interest rates fall or rise. Ultimately, however, the price must reach par value at the maturity date, so on average, the price of the premium bond will fall over time while that of the discount bond will rise.

maturity is unchanged over the period, the rate of return on the bond will equal that yield. As we noted, this should not be a surprising result: the bond must offer a rate of return competitive with those available on other securities.

However, when yields fluctuate, so will a bond's rate of return. Unanticipated changes in market rates will result in unanticipated changes in bond returns, and after the fact, a bond's holding-period return can be better or worse than the yield at which it initially sells. An increase in the bond's yield to maturity acts to reduce its price, which means that the holding-period return will be less than the initial yield. Conversely, a decline in yield to maturity results in a holding-period return greater than the initial yield.

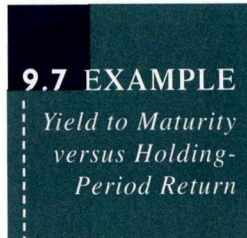

9.7 EXAMPLE

*Yield to Maturity
versus Holding-
Period Return*

Consider a 30-year bond paying an annual coupon of $80 and selling at par value of $1,000. The bond's initial yield to maturity is 8%. If the yield remains at 8% over the year, the bond price will remain at par, so the holding-period return also will be 8%. But if the yield falls below 8%, the bond price will increase. Suppose the price increases to $1,050. Then the holding-period return is greater than 8%:

$$\text{Holding-period return} = \frac{\$80 + (\$1,050 - \$1,000)}{\$1,000} = .13, \text{ or } 13\%$$

Concept
CHECK

6. Show that if yield to maturity increases, then holding-period return is *less* than initial yield. For example, suppose that by the end of the first year, the bond's yield to maturity is 8.5%. Find the one-year holding-period return and compare it to the bond's initial 8% yield to maturity.

Here is another way to think about the difference between yield to maturity and holding-period return. Yield to maturity depends only on the bond's coupon, *current* price, and par value at maturity. All of these values are observable today, so yield to maturity can be easily calculated. Yield to maturity can be interpreted as a measure of the *average* rate of return if the investment in the bond is held until the bond matures. In contrast, holding-period return is the rate of return over a particular investment period and depends on the market price of the bond at the end of that holding period; of course this price is *not* known today. Since bond prices over the holding period will respond to unanticipated changes in interest rates, holding-period return can at most be forecast.

Zero-Coupon Bonds

Original issue discount bonds are less common than coupon bonds issued at par. These are bonds that are issued intentionally with low coupon rates that cause the bond to sell at a discount from par value. An extreme example of this type of bond is the *zero-coupon bond,* which carries no coupons and must provide all its return in the form of price appreciation. Zeros provide only one cash flow to their owners, and that is on the maturity date of the bond.

U.S. Treasury bills are examples of short-term zero-coupon instruments. The Treasury issues or sells a bill for some amount less than $10,000, agreeing to repay $10,000 at the bill's maturity. All of the investor's return comes in the form of price appreciation over time.

Longer term zero-coupon bonds are commonly created from coupon-bearing notes and bonds with the help of the U.S. Treasury. A broker that purchases a Treasury coupon bond may ask the Treasury to break down the cash flows to be paid by the bond into a series of independent securities, where each security is a claim to one of the payments of the original bond. For example, a 10-year coupon bond would be "stripped" of its 20 semiannual coupons and

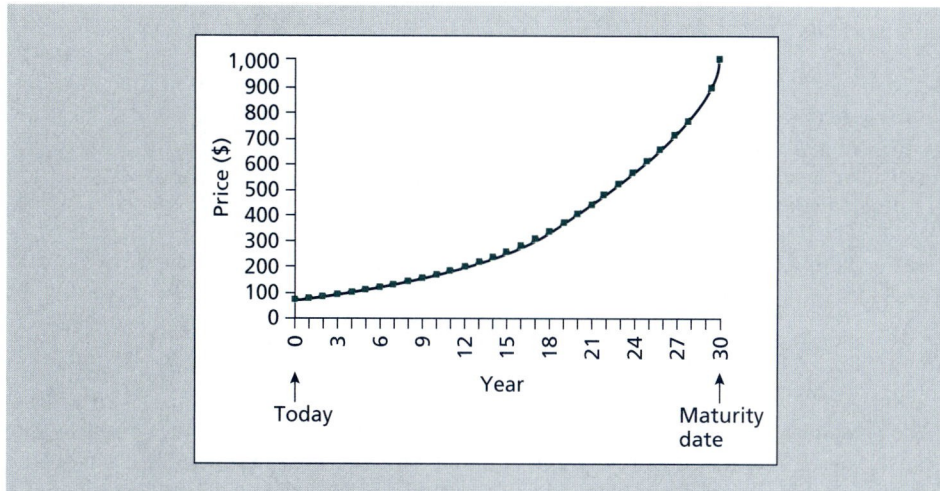

FIGURE **9.7**
The price of a 30-year zero-coupon bond over time at a yield to maturity of 10%. Price equals $1000/(1.10)^T$ where T is time until maturity.

each coupon payment would be treated as a stand-alone zero-coupon bond. The maturities of these bonds would thus range from six months to 10 years. The final payment of principal would be treated as another stand-alone zero-coupon security. Each of the payments would then be treated as an independent security and assigned its own CUSIP number, the security identifier that allows for electronic trading over the Fedwire system. The payments are still considered obligations of the U.S. Treasury. The Treasury program under which coupon stripping is performed is called STRIPS (Separate Trading of Registered Interest and Principal of Securities), and these zero-coupon securities are called *Treasury strips.* Turn back to Figure 9.1 for a listing of these bonds appearing in *The Wall Street Journal.*

What should happen to prices of zeros as time passes? On their maturity dates, zeros must sell for par value. Before maturity, however, they should sell at discounts from par, because of the time value of money. As time passes, price should approach par value. In fact, if the interest rate is constant, a zero's price will increase at exactly the rate of interest.

To illustrate this property, consider a zero with 30 years until maturity, and suppose the market interest rate is 10% per year. The price of the bond today will be $\$1,000/(1.10)^{30} = \$57.31$. Next year, with only 29 years until maturity, if the yield to maturity is still 10%, the price will be $\$1,000/(1.10)^{29} = \$63.04$, a 10% increase over its previous-year value. Because the par value of the bond is now discounted for one fewer year, its price has increased by the one-year discount factor.

Figure 9.7 presents the price path of a 30-year zero-coupon bond until its maturity date for an annual market interest rate of 10%. The bond's price rises exponentially, not linearly, until its maturity.

After-Tax Returns

The tax authorities recognize that the "built-in" price appreciation on original-issue discount (OID) bonds such as zero-coupon bonds represents an implicit interest payment to the holder of the security. The Internal Revenue Service (IRS), therefore, calculates a price appreciation schedule to impute taxable interest income for the built-in appreciation during a tax year, even if the asset is not sold or does not mature until a future year. Any additional gains or losses that arise from changes in market interest rates are treated as capital gains or losses if the OID bond is sold during the tax year.

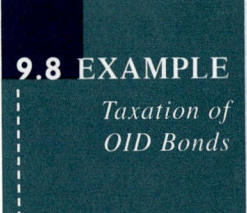

9.8 EXAMPLE

Taxation of OID Bonds

If the interest rate originally is 10%, the 30-year zero would be issued at a price of $1,000/(1.10)^{30} = $57.31. The following year, the IRS calculates what the bond price would be if the yield remains at 10%. This is $1,000/(1.10)^{29} = $63.04. Therefore, the IRS imputes interest income of $63.04 − $57.31 = $5.73. This amount is subject to tax. Notice that the imputed interest income is based on a "constant yield method" that ignores any changes in market interest rates.

If interest rates actually fall, let's say to 9.9%, the bond price actually will be $1,000/(1.099)^{29} = $64.72. If the bond is sold, then the difference between $64.72 and $63.04 will be treated as capital gains income and taxed at the capital gains tax rate. If the bond is not sold, then the price difference is an unrealized capital gain and does not result in taxes in that year. In either case, the investor must pay taxes on the $5.73 of imputed interest at the ordinary income tax rate.

The procedure illustrated in Example 9.8 is applied to the taxation of other original issue discount bonds, even if they are not zero-coupon bonds. Consider, as another example, a 30-year maturity bond that is issued with a coupon rate of 4% and a yield to maturity of 8%. For simplicity, we will assume that the bond pays coupons once annually. Because of the low coupon rate, the bond will be issued at a price far below par value, specifically at a price of $549.69. (Confirm this for yourself.) If the bond's yield to maturity remains at 8%, then its price in one year will rise to $553.66. (Confirm this also.) This provides a pretax holding-period return of exactly 8%:

$$\text{HPR} = \frac{\$40 + (\$553.66 - \$549.69)}{\$549.69} = 0.08$$

The increase in the bond price based on a constant yield, however, is treated as interest income, so the investor is required to pay taxes on imputed interest income of $553.66 − $549.69 = $3.97, as well as on the explicit coupon income of $40. If the bond's yield actually changes during the year, the difference between the bond's price and the "constant yield value" of $553.66 would be treated as capital gains income if the bond were sold at year-end.

Concept CHECK

7. Suppose that the yield to maturity of the 4% coupon, 30-year maturity bond actually falls to 7% by the end of the first year, and that the investor sells the bond after the first year. If the investor's tax rate on interest income is 36% and the tax rate on capital gains is 28%, what is the investor's after-tax rate of return?

9.5 DEFAULT RISK AND BOND PRICING

Although bonds generally *promise* a fixed flow of income, that income stream is not riskless unless the investor can be sure the issuer will not default on the obligation. While U.S. government bonds may be treated as free of default risk, this is not true of corporate bonds. If the company goes bankrupt, the bondholders will not receive all the payments they have been promised. Therefore, the actual payments on these bonds are uncertain, for they depend to some degree on the ultimate financial status of the firm.

Bond default risk is measured by Moody's Investor Services, Standard & Poor's Corporation, Duff and Phelps, and Fitch Investors Service, all of which provide financial information on firms as well as quality ratings of large corporate and municipal bond issues. Each firm assigns letter grades to the bonds of corporations and municipalities to reflect their assessment of the safety of the bond issue. The top rating is AAA or Aaa. Moody's modifies each rating class with a 1, 2, or 3 suffix (e.g., Aaa1, Aaa2, Aaa3) to provide a finer gradation of ratings. The other agencies use a + or − modification.

Those rated BBB or above (S&P, Duff and Phelps, Fitch) or Baa and above (Moody's) are considered **investment grade bonds,** while lower-rated bonds are classified as **speculative**

investment grade bond

A bond rated BBB and above by Standard & Poor's, or Baa and above by Moody's.

speculative grade or junk bond

A bond rated BB or lower by Standard & Poor's, Ba or lower by Moody's, or an unrated bond.

	Bond Ratings			
	Very High Quality	**High Quality**	**Speculative**	**Very Poor**
Standard & Poor's	AAA AA	A BBB	BB B	CCC D
Moody's	Aaa Aa	A Baa	Ba B	Caa C

At times both Moody's and Standard & Poor's use adjustments to these ratings. S&P uses plus and minus signs: A+ is the strongest A rating and A− the weakest. Moody's uses a 1, 2, or 3 designation—with 1 indicating the strongest.

Moody's	S&P	
Aaa	AAA	Debt rated Aaa and AAA has the highest rating. Capacity to pay interest and principal is extremely strong.
Aa	AA	Debt rated Aa and AA has a very strong capacity to pay interest and repay principal. Together with the highest rating, this group comprises the high-grade bond class.
A	A	Debt rated A has a strong capacity to pay interest and repay principal, although it is somewhat more susceptible to the adverse effects of changes in circumstances and economic conditions than debt in higher-rated categories.
Baa	BBB	Debt rated Baa and BBB is regarded as having an adequate capacity to pay interest and repay principal. Whereas it normally exhibits adequate protection parameters, adverse economic conditions or changing circumstances are more likely to lead to a weakened capacity to pay interest and repay principal for debt in this category than in higher-rated categories. These bonds are medium grade obligations.
Ba	BB	Debt rated in these categories is regarded, on balance, as predomi-
B	B	antly speculative with respect to capacity to pay interest and repay
Caa	CCC	principal in accordance with the terms of the obligation. BB and Ba
Ca	CC	indicate the lowest degree of speculation, and CC and Ca the highest degree of speculation. Although such debt will likely have some quality and protective characteristics, these are outweighed by large uncertainties or major risk exposures to adverse conditions. Some issues may be in default.
C	C	This rating is reserved for income bonds on which no interest is being paid.
D	D	Debt rated D is in default, and payment of interest and/or repayment of principal is in arrears.

FIGURE 9.8

Definitions of each bond rating class

Sources: From Stephen A. Ross, Randolph W. Westerfield, and Jeffrey A. Jaffe, *Corporate Finance*, McGraw-Hill Publishing. Data from various editions of *Standard & Poor's Bond Guide* and *Moody's Bond Guide*.

grade or **junk bonds.** Certain regulated institutional investors such as insurance companies have not always been allowed to invest in speculative grade bonds.

Figure 9.8 provides the definitions of each bond rating classification.

Junk Bonds

Junk bonds, also known as *high-yield bonds,* are nothing more than speculative grade (low-rated or unrated) bonds. Before 1977, almost all junk bonds were "fallen angels," that is, bonds issued by firms that originally had investment grade ratings but that had since been downgraded. In 1977, however, firms began to issue "original-issue junk."

Much of the credit for this innovation is given to Drexel Burnham Lambert, and especially its trader, Michael Milken. Drexel had long enjoyed a niche as a junk bond trader and had established a network of potential investors in junk bonds. Firms not able to muster an investment grade rating were happy to have Drexel (and other investment bankers) market their bonds directly to the public, as this opened up a new source of financing. Junk issues were a lower-cost financing alternative than borrowing from banks.

High-yield bonds gained considerable notoriety in the 1980s when they were used as financing vehicles in leveraged buyouts and hostile takeover attempts. Shortly thereafter, however, the legal difficulties of Drexel and Michael Milken in connection with Wall Street's insider trading scandals of the late 1980s tainted the junk bond market.

At the height of Drexel's difficulties, the high-yield bond market nearly dried up. Since then, the market has rebounded dramatically. However, it is worth noting that the average credit quality of high-yield debt issued today is higher than the average quality in the boom years of the 1980s.

Determinants of Bond Safety

Bond rating agencies base their quality ratings largely on an analysis of the level and trend of some of the issuer's financial ratios. The key ratios used to evaluate safety are:

1. *Coverage ratios.* Ratios of company earnings to fixed costs. For example, the *times-interest-earned ratio* is the ratio of earnings before interest payments and taxes to interest obligations. The *fixed-charge coverage ratio* adds lease payments and sinking fund payments to interest obligations to arrive at the ratio of earnings to all fixed cash obligations. Low or falling coverage ratios signal possible cash flow difficulties.

2. *Leverage ratio.* Debt-to-equity ratio. A too-high leverage ratio indicates excessive indebtedness, signaling the possibility the firm will be unable to earn enough to satisfy the obligations on its bonds.

3. *Liquidity ratios.* The two common liquidity ratios are the *current ratio* (current assets/current liabilities) and the *quick ratio* (current assets excluding inventories/current liabilities). These ratios measure the firm's ability to pay bills coming due with cash currently being collected.

4. *Profitability ratios.* Measures of rates of return on assets or equity. Profitability ratios are indicators of a firm's overall financial health. The *return on assets* (earnings before interest and taxes divided by total assets) is the most popular of these measures. Firms with higher return on assets should be better able to raise money in security markets because they offer prospects for better returns on the firm's investments.

5. *Cash flow-to-debt ratio.* This is the ratio of total cash flow to outstanding debt.

Standard & Poor's periodically computes median values of selected ratios for firms in several rating classes, which we present in Table 9.3. Of course, ratios must be evaluated in the context of industry standards, and analysts differ in the weights they place on particular ratios. Nevertheless, Table 9.3 demonstrates the tendency of ratios to improve along with the firm's rating class.

Bond Indentures

indenture

The document defining the contract between the bond issuer and the bondholder.

In addition to specifying a payment schedule, the bond **indenture,** which is the contract between the issuer and the bondholder, also specifies a set of restrictions on the issuer to protect the rights of the bondholders. Such restrictions include provisions relating to collateral, sinking funds, dividend policy, and further borrowing. The issuing firm agrees to these so-called

TABLE **9.3** Financial ratios by rating class	U.S. Industrial Long-Term Debt, Three-Year (1997 to 1999) Medians	AAA	AA	A	BBB	BB	B
	EBIT interest coverage ratio	17.5	10.8	6.8	3.9	2.3	1.0
	EBITDA interest coverage ratio	21.8	14.6	9.6	6.1	3.8	2.0
	Funds flow/total debt (%)	105.8	55.8	46.1	30.5	19.2	9.4
	Free operating cash flow/total debt (%)	55.4	24.6	15.6	6.6	1.9	(4.6)
	Return on capital (%)	28.2	22.9	19.9	14.0	11.7	7.2
	Operating income/sales (%)	29.2	21.3	18.3	15.3	15.4	11.2
	Long-term debt/capital (incl. STD) (%)	15.2	26.4	32.5	41.0	55.8	70.7
	Total debt/capital (incl. STD) (%)	26.9	35.6	40.1	47.4	61.3	74.6

EBIT—Earnings before interest and taxes.

EBITDA—Earnings before interest, taxes, depreciation, and amortization.

STD—Short-term debt

Source: www.standardandpoors.com/ResourceCenter/CorporateFinance, December 2000.

protective covenants in order to market its bonds to investors concerned about the safety of the bond issue.

Sinking funds Bonds call for the payment of par value at the end of the bond's life. This payment constitutes a large cash commitment for the issuer. To help ensure that the commitment does not create a cash flow crisis, the firm agrees to establish a **sinking fund** to spread the payment burden over several years. The fund may operate in one of two ways:

1. The firm may repurchase a fraction of the outstanding bonds in the open market each year.
2. The firm may purchase a fraction of outstanding bonds at a special call price associated with the sinking fund provision. The firm has an option to purchase the bonds at either the market price or the sinking fund price, whichever is lower. To allocate the burden of the sinking fund call fairly among bondholders, the bonds chosen for the call are selected at random based on serial number.[9]

sinking fund

A bond indenture that calls for the issuer to periodically repurchase some proportion of the outstanding bonds prior to maturity.

The sinking fund call differs from a conventional call provision in two important ways. First, the firm can repurchase only a limited fraction of the bond issue at the sinking fund call price. At best, some indentures allow firms to use a *doubling option,* which allows repurchase of double the required number of bonds at the sinking fund call price. Second, the sinking fund call price generally is lower than the call price established by other call provisions in the indenture. The sinking fund call price usually is set at the bond's par value.

Although sinking funds ostensibly protect bondholders by making principal repayment more likely, they can hurt the investor. The firm will choose to buy back discount bonds (selling below par) at their market price, while exercising its option to buy back premium bonds (selling above par) at par. Therefore, if interest rates fall and bond prices rise, firms will benefit from the sinking fund provision that enables them to repurchase their bonds at below-market prices. In these circumstances, the firm's gain is the bondholder's loss.

One bond issue that does not require a sinking fund is a *serial bond* issue. In a serial bond issue, the firm sells bonds with staggered maturity dates. As bonds mature sequentially, the principal repayment burden for the firm is spread over time just as it is with a sinking fund.

[9]While it is uncommon, the sinking fund provision also may call for periodic payments to a trustee, with the payments invested so that the accumulated sum can be used for retirement of the entire issue at maturity.

Serial bonds do not include call provisions. Unlike sinking fund bonds, serial bonds do not confront security holders with the risk that a particular bond may be called for the sinking fund. The disadvantage of serial bonds, however, is that the bonds of each maturity date are different bonds, which reduces the liquidity of the issue. Trading these bonds, therefore, is more expensive.

Subordination of further debt

subordination clauses

Restrictions on additional borrowing that stipulate that senior bondholders will be paid first in the event of bankruptcy.

One of the factors determining bond safety is the total outstanding debt of the issuer. If you bought a bond today, you would be understandably distressed to see the firm tripling its outstanding debt tomorrow. Your bond would be of lower quality than it appeared when you bought it. To prevent firms from harming bondholders in this manner, **subordination clauses** restrict the amount of their additional borrowing. Additional debt might be required to be subordinated in priority to existing debt; that is, in the event of bankruptcy, *subordinated* or *junior* debtholders will not be paid unless and until the prior senior debt is fully paid off. For this reason, subordination is sometimes called a "me-first rule," meaning the senior (earlier) bondholders are to be paid first in the event of bankruptcy.

Dividend restrictions

Covenants also limit firms in the amount of dividends they are allowed to pay. These limitations protect the bondholders because they force the firm to retain assets rather than paying them out to stockholders. A typical restriction disallows payments of dividends if cumulative dividends paid since the firm's inception exceed cumulative net income plus proceeds from sales of stock.

Collateral

collateral

A specific asset pledged against possible default on a bond.

Some bonds are issued with specific collateral behind them. **Collateral** can take several forms, but it represents a particular asset of the firm that the bondholders receive if the firm defaults on the bond. If the collateral is property, the bond is called a *mortgage bond*. If the collateral takes the form of other securities held by the firm, the bond is a *collateral trust bond*. In the case of equipment, the bond is known as an *equipment obligation bond*. This last form of collateral is used most commonly by firms such as railroads, where the equipment is fairly standard and can be easily sold to another firm should the firm default and the bondholders acquire the collateral.

debenture

A bond not backed by specific collateral.

Because of the specific collateral that backs them, collateralized bonds generally are considered the safest variety of corporate bonds. General **debenture** bonds by contrast do not provide for specific collateral; they are *unsecured* bonds. The bondholder relies solely on the general earning power of the firm for the bond's safety. If the firm defaults, debenture owners become general creditors of the firm. Because they are safer, collateralized bonds generally offer lower yields than general debentures.

Figure 9.9 shows the terms of a bond issued by Mobil as described in *Moody's Industrial Manual*. The terms of the bond are typical and illustrate many of the indenture provisions we have mentioned. The bond is registered and listed on the NYSE. Although it was issued in 1991, it was not callable until 2002. Although the call price started at 105.007% of par value, it falls gradually until it reaches par after 2020.

Yield to Maturity and Default Risk

Because corporate bonds are subject to default risk, we must distinguish between the bond's promised yield to maturity and its expected yield. The promised or stated yield will be realized only if the firm meets the obligations of the bond issue. Therefore, the stated yield is the *maximum possible* yield to maturity of the bond. The expected yield to maturity must take into account the possibility of a default.

For example, in November 2001, as Enron Corp. approached bankruptcy, its 6.4% coupon bonds due in 2006 were selling at about 20% of par value, resulting in a yield to maturity of

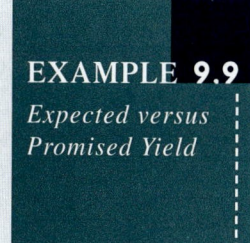

& **Mobil Corp. debenture 8s, due 2032:**
Rating — Aa2
AUTH — $250,000,000.
OUTSTG — Dec. 31, 1993, $250,000,000.
DATED — Oct. 30, 1991.
INTEREST — F&A 12.
TRUSTEE — Chemical Bank.
DENOMINATION — Fully registered, $1,000 and integral multiples thereof. Transferable and exchangeable without service charge.
CALLABLE — As a whole or in part, at any time, on or after Aug. 12, 2002, at the option of Co. on at least 30 but not more than 60 days' notice to each Aug. 11 as follows:

2003..........105.007 2004 ....104.756 2005 ....104.506
2006..........104.256 2007 ....104.005 2008 ....103.755
2009..........103.505 2010 ....103.254 2011 ....103.004
2012..........102.754 2013 ....102.503 2014 ....102.253
2015..........102.003 2016 ....101.752 2017 ....101.502
2018..........101.252 2019 ....101.001 2020 ....100.751
2021..........100.501 2022 ....100.250

and thereafter at 100 plus accrued interest.
SECURITY — Not secured. Ranks equally with all other unsecured and unsubordinated indebtedness of Co. Co. nor any Affiliate will not incurr any indebtedness; provided that Co. will not create as security for any indebtedness for borrowed money, any mortgage, pledge, security interest or lien on any stock or indebtedness is directly owned by Co., without effectively providing that the debt securities shall be secured equally and ratably with such indebtedness, so long as such indebtedness shall be so secured.
INDENTURE   MODIFICATION — Indenture may be modified, except as provided with, consent of 66⅔% of debs. outstg.
RIGHTS ON DEFAULT — Trustee, or 25% of debs. outstg., may declare principal dua nad payable (30 days' grace for payment of interest).
LISTED — On New York Stock Exchange.
PURPOSE — Proceeds used for general corporate purposes.
OFFERED — ($250,000,000) at 99.51 plus accrued interest (proceeds to Co., 99.11) on Aug. 5, 1992 thru Merrill Lynch & Co., Donaldson, Lufkin & Jenerette Securities Corp., PaineWebber Inc., Prudential Securities Inc., Smith Barney, Harris Upham & Co. Inc. and associates.

FIGURE 9.9

Callable bond issued by Mobil

Source: *Moody's Industrial Manual*, Moody's Investor Services, 1997.

about 57%. Investors did not really expect these bonds to provide a 57% rate of return. They recognized that bondholders were very unlikely to receive all the payments promised in the bond contract and that the yield based on *expected* cash flows was far less than the yield based on *promised* cash flows.

Suppose a firm issued a 9% coupon bond 20 years ago. The bond now has 10 years left until its maturity date but the firm is having financial difficulties. Investors believe that the firm will be able to make good on the remaining interest payments but that at the maturity date, the firm will be forced into bankruptcy, and bondholders will receive only 70% of par value. The bond is selling at $750.

Yield to maturity (YTM) would then be calculated using the following inputs:

	Expected YTM	Stated YTM
Coupon payment	$45	$45
Number of semiannual periods	20 periods	20 periods
Final payment	$700	$1,000
Price	$750	$750

EXAMPLE 9.9

Expected versus Promised Yield

The yield to maturity based on promised payments is 13.7%. Based on the expected payment of $700 at maturity, however, the yield would be only 11.6%. The stated yield to maturity is greater than the yield investors actually expect to receive.

8. What is the expected yield to maturity if the firm in Example 9.9 is in even worse condition and investors expect a final payment of only $600?

To compensate for the possibility of default, corporate bonds must offer a **default premium.** The default premium is the difference between the promised yield on a corporate bond and the yield of an otherwise identical government bond that is riskless in terms of default. If the firm remains solvent and actually pays the investor all of the promised cash flows, the investor will realize a higher yield to maturity than would be realized from the government bond. If, however, the firm goes bankrupt, the corporate bond is likely to provide a lower return than the government bond. The corporate bond has the potential for both better and worse performance than the default-free Treasury bond. In other words, it is riskier.

The pattern of default premiums offered on risky bonds is sometimes called the *risk structure of interest rates.* The greater the default risk, the higher the default premium. Figure 9.10 shows the yield to maturity of bonds of different risk classes since 1954 and the yields on junk bonds since 1984. You can see here clear evidence of default-risk premiums on promised yields.

9.6   THE YIELD CURVE

Return to Figure 9.1 again, and you will see that while yields to maturity on bonds of various maturities are reasonably similar, yields do differ. Bonds with shorter maturities generally offer lower yields to maturity than longer term bonds. The graphical relationship between the yield to maturity and the term to maturity is called the **yield curve.** The relationship also is called the **term structure of interest rates** because it relates yields to maturity to the term (maturity) of each bond. The yield curve is published regularly in *The Wall Street Journal*; four such sets of curves are reproduced in Figure 9.11. Figure 9.11 illustrates that a wide range of yield curves may be observed in practice. Panel A is a downward sloping, or "inverted" yield curve. Panel B is an upward sloping curve, and Panel C is a hump-shaped curve, first rising and then falling. Finally the yield curve in Panel D is essentially flat. Rising yield curves are most commonly observed. We will see why momentarily.

Why should bonds of differing maturity offer different yields? The two most plausible possibilities have to do with expectations of future rates and risk premiums. We will consider each of these arguments in turn.

FIGURE 9.11

Treasury yield curves

Source: Various editions of *The Wall Street Journal*. Reprinted by permission of *The Wall Street Journal*, © 1989, 1997, 2000 Dow Jones & Company, Inc. All Rights Reserved Worldwide.

The Expectations Theory

Suppose everyone in the market believes firmly that while the current one-year interest rate is 8%, the interest rate on one-year bonds next year will rise to 10%. What would this belief imply about the proper yield to maturity on two-year bonds issued today?

It is easy to see that an investor who buys the one-year bond and rolls the proceeds into another one-year bond in the following year will earn, on average, about 9% per year. This value

---

WEBMASTER

Term Structure of Interest Rates

The bond section of the Smart Money website has a section called the Living Yield Curve. It has a graph that allows you to compare the shape of the yield curve at different points in time. Go to Smart Money's website at http://www.smartmoney.com/onebond/index.cfm?story=yieldcurve. Then, use the site to answer the following questions:

1. What is considered a normal yield curve?

2. Compare the yield curve for December 2001 with the average yield curve. According to their explanations what would the market be expecting with a steep upward sloping yield curve?

3. What type of yield curve was present in March 1980? How does that curve compare with the typical yield curve?

is just the average of the 8% earned this year and the 10% expected for next year. More precisely, the investment will grow by a factor of 1.08 in the first year and 1.10 in the second year, for a total two-year growth factor of $1.08 \times 1.10 = 1.188$. This corresponds to an annual growth rate of 8.995% (because $1.08995^2 = 1.188$).

For investments in two-year bonds to be competitive with the strategy of rolling over one-year bonds, these two-year bonds also must offer an average annual return of 8.995% over the two-year holding period. This is illustrated in Figure 9.12. The current short-term rate of 8% and the expected value of next year's short-term rate are depicted above the time line. The two-year rate that provides the same expected two-year total return is below the time line. In this example, therefore, the yield curve will be upward sloping; while one-year bonds offer an 8% yield to maturity, two-year bonds offer an 8.995% yield.

expectations hypothesis

The theory that yields to maturity are determined solely by expectations of future short-term interest rates.

This notion is the essence of the **expectations hypothesis** of the yield curve, which asserts that the slope of the yield curve is attributable to expectations of changes in short-term rates. Relatively high yields on long-term bonds are attributed to expectations of future increases in rates, while relatively low yields on long-term bonds (a downward-sloping or inverted yield curve) are attributed to expectations of falling short-term rates.

One of the implications of the expectations hypothesis is that expected holding-period returns on bonds of all maturities ought to be about equal. Even if the yield curve is upward sloping (so that two-year bonds offer higher yields to maturity than one-year bonds), this does not necessarily mean investors expect higher rates of return on the two-year bonds. As we've seen, the higher initial yield to maturity on the two-year bond is necessary to compensate investors for the fact that interest rates the next year will be even higher. Over the two-year period, and indeed over any holding period, this theory predicts that holding-period returns will be equalized across bonds of all maturities.

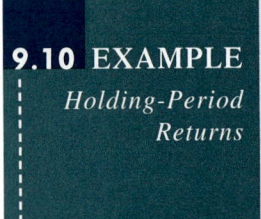

9.10 EXAMPLE

Holding-Period Returns

Suppose we buy the one-year zero-coupon bond with a current yield to maturity of 8%. If its face value is $1,000, its price will be $925.93, providing an 8% rate of return over the coming year. Suppose instead that we buy the two-year zero-coupon bond at its yield of 8.995%. Its price today is $1,000/(1.08995)^2 = 841.76. After a year passes, the zero will have a remaining maturity of only one year; based on the forecast that the one-year yield next year will be 10%, it then will sell for $1,000/1.10 = $909.09. The expected rate of return over the year is thus ($909.09 − $841.76)/$841.76 = .08, or 8%, precisely the same return provided by the one-year bond. This makes sense: If risk considerations are ignored when pricing the two bonds, they ought to provide equal expected rates of return.

In fact, advocates of the expectations hypothesis commonly invert this analysis to *infer* the market's expectation of future short-term rates. They note that we do not directly observe the expectation of next year's rate, but we *can* observe yields on bonds of different maturities.

FIGURE 9.12

Returns to two 2-year investment strategies

Suppose, as in this example, we see that one-year bonds offer yields of 8% and two-year bonds offer yields of 8.995%. Each dollar invested in the two-year zero would grow after two years to $\$1 \times 1.08995^2 = \$1.188$. A dollar invested in the one-year zero would grow by a factor of 1.08 in the first year and, then, if reinvested or "rolled over" into another one-year zero in the second year, would grow by an additional factor of $1 + r_2$. Final proceeds would be $\$1 \times 1.08 \times (1 + r_2)$.

The final proceeds of the rollover strategy depend on the interest rate that actually transpires in year 2. However, we can solve for the second-year interest rate that makes the expected payoff of these two strategies equal. This "breakeven" value is called the **forward rate** for the second year, f_2, and is derived as follows:

$$1.08995^2 = 1.08 \times (1 + f_2)$$

which implies that $f_2 = .10$, or 10%. Notice that the forward rate equals the market's expectation of the year 2 short rate. Hence, we conclude that when the expected total return of a long-term bond equals that of a rolling over a short-term bond, the forward rate equals the expected short-term interest rate. This is why the theory is called the expectations hypothesis.

More generally, we obtain the forward rate by equating the return on an n-period zero-coupon bond with that of an $(n - 1)$-period zero-coupon bond rolled over into a one-year bond in year n:

$$(1 + y_n)^n = (1 + y_{n-1})^{n-1} (1 + f_n)$$

The actual total returns on the two n-year strategies will be equal if the short-term interest rate in year n turns out to equal f_n.

> **forward rate**
>
> The inferred short-term rate of interest for a future period that makes the expected total return of a long-term bond equal to that of rolling over short-term bonds.

Suppose that two-year maturity bonds offer yields to maturity of 6%, and three-year bonds have yields of 7%. What is the forward rate for the third year? We could compare these two strategies as follows:

1. Buy a three-year bond. Total proceeds per dollar invested will be

    $$\$1 \times (1.07)^3 = \$1.2250$$

2. Buy a two-year bond. Reinvest all proceeds in a one-year bond in the third year, which will provide a return in that year of r_3. Total proceeds per dollar invested will be the result of two years' growth of invested funds at 6% plus the final year's growth at rate r_3:

    $$\$1 \times (1.06)^2 \times (1 + r_3) = \$1.1236 \times (1 + r_3)$$

The forward rate is the rate in year 3 that makes the total return on these strategies equal:

$$1.2250 = 1.1236 \times (1 + f_3)$$

We conclude that the forward rate for the third year satisfies $(1 + f_3) = 1.0902$, so that f_3 is 9.02%.

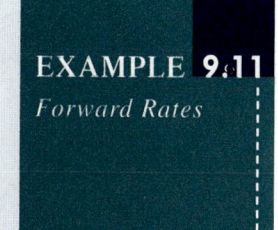

EXAMPLE 9.11

Forward Rates

The Liquidity Preference Theory

The expectations hypothesis starts from the assertion that bonds are priced so that "buy and hold" investments in long-term bonds provide the same returns as rolling over a series of short-term bonds. However, the risks of long- and short-term bonds are not equivalent.

We have seen that longer term bonds are subject to greater interest rate risk than short-term bonds. As a result, investors in long-term bonds might require a risk premium to compensate them for this risk. In this case, the yield curve will be upward sloping even in the absence of any expectations of future increases in rates. The source of the upward slope in the yield curve is investor demand for higher expected returns on assets that are perceived as riskier.

**liquidity
preference theory**

The theory that
investors demand
a risk premium on
long-term bonds.

This viewpoint is called the **liquidity preference theory** of the term structure. Its name derives from the fact that shorter term bonds have more "liquidity" than longer term bonds, in the sense that they offer greater price certainty and trade in more active markets with lower bid–ask spreads. The preference of investors for greater liquidity makes them willing to hold these shorter term bonds even if they do not offer expected returns as high as those of longer term bonds.

liquidity premium

The extra expected
return demanded
by investors as
compensation for
the greater risk of
longer term bonds.

We can think of a **liquidity premium** as resulting from the extra compensation investors demand for holding longer term bonds with lower liquidity. We measure it as the spread between the forward rate of interest and the expected short rate:

$$f_n = E(r_n) + \text{Liquidity premium}$$

In the absence of a liquidity premium, the forward rate would equal the expectation of the future short rate. But generally, we expect the forward rate to exceed that expectation to compensate investors for the lower liquidity of longer term bonds.

Advocates of the liquidity preference theory also note that issuers of bonds seem to prefer to issue long-term bonds. This allows them to lock in an interest rate on their borrowing for long periods. If issuers do prefer to issue long-term bonds, they will be willing to pay higher yields on these issues as a way of eliminating interest rate risk. In sum, borrowers demand higher rates on longer term bonds, and issuers are willing to pay higher rates on longer term bonds. The conjunction of these two preferences means longer term bonds typically should offer higher expected rates of return to investors than shorter term bonds. These expectations will show up in an upward-sloping yield curve.

If the liquidity preference theory is valid, the forward rate of interest is not a good estimate of market expectations of future interest rates. Even if rates are expected to remain unchanged, for example, the yield curve will slope upward because of the liquidity premium. That upward slope would be mistakenly attributed to expectations of rising rates if one were to use the pure expectations hypothesis to interpret the yield curve.

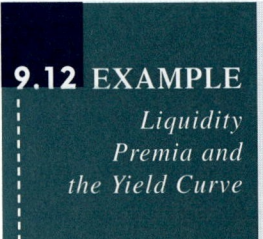

9.12 EXAMPLE

*Liquidity
Premia and
the Yield Curve*

Suppose that the short-term rate of interest is currently 8% and that investors expect it to remain at 8% next year. In the absence of a liquidity premium, with no expectation of a change in yields, the yield to maturity on two-year bonds also would be 8%, the yield curve would be flat, and the forward rate would be 8%. But what if investors demand a risk premium to invest in two-year rather than one-year bonds? If the liquidity premium is 1%, then the forward rate would be 8% + 1% = 9%, and the yield to maturity on the two-year bond would be determined by

$$(1 + y_2)^2 = 1.08 \times 1.09 = 1.1772$$

implying that $y_2 = .085 = 8.5\%$. Here, the yield curve is upward sloping due solely to the liquidity premium embedded in the price of the longer term bond.

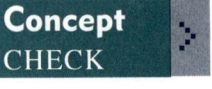

Concept
CHECK

9. Suppose that the expected value of the interest rate for year 3 remains at 8% but that the liquidity premium for that year is also 1%. What would be the yield to maturity on three-year zeros? What would this imply about the slope of the yield curve?

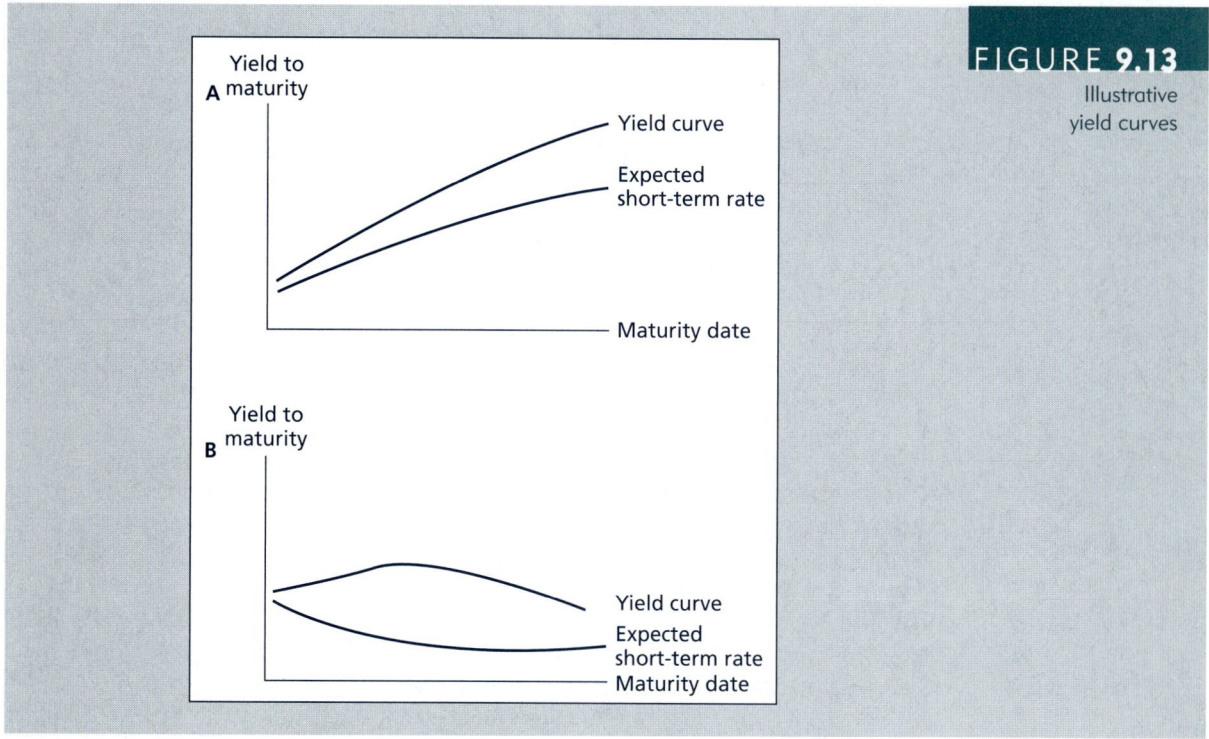

FIGURE **9.13**

Illustrative
yield curves

A Synthesis

Of course, we do not need to make an either/or choice between expectations and risk premiums. Both of these factors influence the yield curve, and both should be considered in interpreting the curve.

Figure 9.13 shows two possible yield curves. In Figure 9.13A, rates are expected to rise over time. This fact, together with a liquidity premium, makes the yield curve steeply upward sloping. In Figure 9.13B, rates are expected to fall, which tends to make the yield curve slope downward, even though the liquidity premium lends something of an upward slope. The net effect of these two opposing factors is a "hump-shaped" curve.

These two examples make it clear that the combination of varying expectations and liquidity premiums can result in a wide array of yield-curve profiles. For example, an upward-sloping curve does not in and of itself imply expectations of higher future interest rates, because the slope can result either from expectations or from risk premiums. A curve that is more steeply sloped than usual might signal expectations of higher rates, but even this inference is perilous.

Figure 9.14 presents yield spreads between 90-day T-bills and 10-year T-bonds since 1970. The figure shows that the yield curve is generally upward sloping in that the longer-term bonds usually offer higher yields to maturity, despite the fact that rates could not have been expected to increase throughout the entire period. This tendency is the empirical basis for the liquidity premium doctrine that at least part of the upward slope in the yield curve must be because of a risk premium.

FIGURE 9.14

Term spread. Yields to maturity on 90-day T-bills and 10-year T-bonds

SUMMARY

- Debt securities are distinguished by their promise to pay a fixed or specified stream of income to their holders. The coupon bond is a typical debt security.

- Treasury notes and bonds have original maturities greater than one year. They are issued at or near par value, with their prices quoted net of accrued interest. T-bonds may be callable during their last five years of life.

- Callable bonds should offer higher promised yields to maturity to compensate investors for the fact that they will not realize full capital gains should the interest rate fall and the bonds be called away from them at the stipulated call price. Bonds often are issued with a period of call protection. In addition, discount bonds selling significantly below their call price offer implicit call protection.

- Put bonds give the bondholder rather than the issuer the option to terminate or extend the life of the bond.

- Convertible bonds may be exchanged, at the bondholder's discretion, for a specified number of shares of stock. Convertible bondholders "pay" for this option by accepting a lower coupon rate on the security.

- Floating-rate bonds pay a fixed premium over a referenced short-term interest rate. Risk is limited because the rate paid is tied to current market conditions.

- The yield to maturity is the single interest rate that equates the present value of a security's cash flows to its price. Bond prices and yields are inversely related. For premium bonds, the coupon rate is greater than the current yield, which is greater than the yield to maturity. The order of these inequalities is reversed for discount bonds.

- The yield to maturity often is interpreted as an estimate of the average rate of return to an investor who purchases a bond and holds it until maturity. This interpretation is subject to error, however. Related measures are yield to call, realized compound yield, and expected (versus promised) yield to maturity.

- Treasury bills are U.S. government-issued zero-coupon bonds with original maturities of up to one year. Prices of zero-coupon bonds rise exponentially over time, providing a rate of appreciation equal to the interest rate. The IRS treats this price appreciation as imputed taxable interest income to the investor.

- When bonds are subject to potential default, the stated yield to maturity is the maximum possible yield to maturity that can be realized by the bondholder. In the event of default, however, that promised yield will not be realized. To compensate bond investors for default risk, bonds must offer default premiums, that is, promised yields in excess of those offered by default-free government securities. If the firm remains healthy, its bonds will provide higher returns than government bonds. Otherwise, the returns may be lower.
- Bond safety often is measured using financial ratio analysis. Bond indentures are another safeguard to protect the claims of bondholders. Common indentures specify sinking fund requirements, collateralization of the loan, dividend restrictions, and subordination of future debt.

KEY TERMS

bond, 296
callable bonds, 296
collateral, 320
convertible bonds, 299
coupon rate, 296
current yield, 308
debenture, 320
debt securities, 295
default premium, 322
discount bonds, 309
expectations hypothesis, 324

face value, 296
floating-rate bonds, 300
forward rate, 325
horizon analysis, 312
indenture, 318
investment grade bonds, 316
liquidity preference
   theory, 326
liquidity premium, 326
par value, 296
premium bonds, 308

put bond, 300
sinking fund, 319
speculative grade or junk
   bonds, 316
subordination clauses, 320
term structure of interest
   rates, 322
yield curve, 322
yield to maturity, 306
zero-coupon bond, 296

PROBLEM SETS

1. Which security has a higher *effective* annual interest rate?
   a. A three-month T-bill selling at $97,645.
   b. A coupon bond selling at par and paying a 10% coupon semiannually.

2. Treasury bonds paying an 8% coupon rate with *semiannual* payments currently sell at par value. What coupon rate would they have to pay in order to sell at par if they paid their coupons *annually*?

3. Two bonds have identical times to maturity and coupon rates. One is callable at 105, the other at 110. Which should have the higher yield to maturity? Why?

4. Consider a bond with a 10% coupon and with yield to maturity = 8%. If the bond's YTM remains constant, then in one year, will the bond price be higher, lower, or unchanged? Why?

5. Under the expectations hypothesis, if the yield curve is upward sloping, the market must expect an increase in short-term interest rates. True/false/uncertain? Why?

6. A "fallen angel" bond is *best* defined as a bond issued:
   a. Below investment grade.
   b. At an original issue discount.
   c. As investment grade, but declined to speculative grade.
   d. As a secured bond, but the collateral value declined below par value.

7. Under the liquidity preference theory, if inflation is expected to be falling over the next few years, long-term interest rates will be higher than short-term rates. True/false/uncertain? Why?

8. The yield curve is upward sloping. Can you conclude that investors expect short-term interest rates to rise? Why or why not?

9. Consider a bond paying a coupon rate of 10% per year semiannually when the market interest rate is only 4% per half year. The bond has three years until maturity.

a. Find the bond's price today and six months from now after the next coupon is paid.

b. What is the total rate of return on the bond?

10. A 20-year maturity bond with par value $1,000 makes semiannual coupon payments at a coupon rate of 8%. Find the bond equivalent and effective annual yield to maturity of the bond if the bond price is:

  a. $950

  b. $1,000

  c. $1,050

11. Redo problem 10 using the same data, but assume that the bond makes its coupon payments annually. Why are the yields you compute lower in this case?

12. Return to Table 9.1 and calculate both the real and nominal rates of return on the TIPS bond in the second and third years.

13. Fill in the table below for the following zero-coupon bonds, all of which have par values of $1,000.

Price	Maturity (years)	Bond-Equivalent Yield to Maturity
$400	20	?
$500	20	?
$500	10	?
?	10	10%
?	10	8%
$400	?	8%

14. Assume you have a one-year investment horizon and are trying to choose among three bonds. All have the same degree of default risk and mature in 10 years. The first is a zero-coupon bond that pays $1,000 at maturity. The second has an 8% coupon rate and pays the $80 coupon once per year. The third has a 10% coupon rate and pays the $100 coupon once per year.

  a. If all three bonds are now priced to yield 8% to maturity, what are their prices?

  b. If you expect their yields to maturity to be 8% at the beginning of next year, what will their prices be then? What is your rate of return on each bond during the one-year holding period?

15. A bond with a coupon rate of 7% makes semiannual coupon payments on January 15 and July 15 of each year. *The Wall Street Journal* reports the ask price for the bond on January 30 at 100:02. What is the invoice price of the bond? The coupon period has 182 days.

16. A bond has a current yield of 9% and a yield to maturity of 10%. Is the bond selling above or below par value? Explain.

17. Is the coupon rate of the bond in the previous problem more or less than 9%?

18. On May 30, 1999, Janice Kerr is considering the newly issued 10-year AAA corporate bonds shown in the following exhibit:

Description	Coupon	Price	Callable	Call Price
Sentinal, due May 30, 2009	6.00%	100	Noncallable	NA
Colina, due May 30, 2009	6.20%	100	Currently callable	102

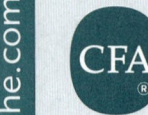

a. Suppose that market interest rates decline by 100 basis points (i.e., 1%). Contrast the effect of this decline on the price of each bond.

b. Should Kerr prefer the Colina over the Sentinal bond when rates are expected to rise or to fall?

c. What would be the effect, if any, of an increase in the *volatility* of interest rates on the prices of each bond?

19. A newly issued 20-year maturity, zero-coupon bond is issued with a yield to maturity of 8% and face value $1,000. Find the imputed interest income in the first, second, and last year of the bond's life.

20. A newly issued 10-year maturity, 4% coupon bond making *annual* coupon payments is sold to the public at a price of $800. What will be an investor's taxable income from the bond over the coming year? The bond will not be sold at the end of the year. The bond is treated as an original-issue discount bond.

21. A newly issued bond pays its coupons once annually. Its coupon rate is 5%, its maturity is 20 years, and its yield to maturity is 8%.

a. Find the holding-period return for a one-year investment period if the bond is selling at a yield to maturity of 7% by the end of the year.

b. If you sell the bond after one year when its yield is 7%, what taxes will you owe if the tax rate on interest income is 40% and the tax rate on capital gains income is 30%? The bond is subject to original-issue discount (OID) tax treatment.

c. What is the after-tax holding-period return on the bond?

d. Find the realized compound yield *before taxes* for a two-year holding period, assuming that (*i*) you sell the bond after two years, (*ii*) the bond yield is 7% at the end of the second year, and (*iii*) the coupon can be reinvested for one year at a 3% interest rate.

e. Use the tax rates in part (*b*) to compute the *after-tax* two-year realized compound yield. Remember to take account of OID tax rules.

22. A 30-year maturity, 8% coupon bond paying coupons semiannually is callable in five years at a call price of $1,100. The bond currently sells at a yield to maturity of 7% (3.5% per half year).

a. What is the yield to call?

b. What is the yield to call if the call price is only $1,050?

c. What is the yield to call if the call price is $1,100, but the bond can be called in two years instead of five years?

23. A 10-year bond of a firm in severe financial distress has a coupon rate of 14% and sells for $900. The firm is currently renegotiating the debt, and it appears that the lenders will allow the firm to reduce coupon payments on the bond to one-half the originally contracted amount. The firm can handle these lower payments. What are the stated and expected yields to maturity of the bonds? The bond makes its coupon payments annually.

24. A two-year bond with par value $1,000 making annual coupon payments of $100 is priced at $1,000. What is the yield to maturity of the bond? What will be the realized compound yield to maturity if the one-year interest rate next year turns out to be (*a*) 8%, (*b*) 10%, (*c*) 12%?

25. The stated yield to maturity and realized compound yield to maturity of a (default-free) zero-coupon bond will always be equal. Why?

26. Suppose that today's date is April 15. A bond with a 10% coupon paid semiannually every January 15 and July 15 is listed in *The Wall Street Journal* as selling at an ask price of 101:04. If you buy the bond from a dealer today, what price will you pay for it?

27. Assume that two firms issue bonds with the following characteristics. Both bonds are issued at par.

	ABC Bonds	XYZ Bonds
Issue size	$1.2 billion	$150 million
Maturity	10 years*	20 years
Coupon	9%	10%
Collateral	First mortgage	General debenture
Callable	Not callable	In 10 years
Call price	None	110
Sinking fund	None	Starting in 5 years

*Bond is extendible at the discretion of the bondholder for an additional 10 years.

Ignoring credit quality, identify four features of these issues that might account for the lower coupon on the ABC debt. Explain.

28. A large corporation issued both fixed and floating-rate notes five years ago, with terms given in the following table:

	9% Coupon Notes	Floating-Rate Note
Issue size	$250 million	$280 million
Maturity	20 years	15 years
Current price (% of par)	93	98
Current coupon	9%	8%
Coupon adjusts	Fixed coupon	Every year
Coupon reset rule	—	1-year T-bill rate + 2%
Callable	10 years after issue	10 years after issue
Call price	106	102
Sinking fund	None	None
Yield to maturity	9.9%	—
Price range since issued	$85–$112	$97–$102

    a. Why is the price range greater for the 9% coupon bond than the floating-rate note?

    b. What factors could explain why the floating-rate note is not always sold at par value?

    c. Why is the call price for the floating-rate note not of great importance to investors?

    d. Is the probability of call for the fixed-rate note high or low?

    e. If the firm were to issue a fixed-rate note with a 15-year maturity, what coupon rate would it need to offer to issue the bond at par value?

    f. Why is an entry for yield to maturity for the floating-rate note not appropriate?

29. Bonds of Zello Corporation with a par value of $1,000 sell for $960, mature in five years, and have a 7% annual coupon rate paid semiannually.

    a. Calculate the:

        (1) Current yield.

        (2) Yield-to-maturity.

        (3) Horizon yield (also called realized compound yield) for an investor with a three-year holding period and a reinvestment rate of 6% over the period. At the end of three years the 7% coupon bonds with two years remaining will sell to yield 7%.

b. Cite *one* major shortcoming for *each* of the following fixed-income yield measures:
   (1) Current yield.
   (2) Yield to maturity.
   (3) Horizon yield (also called realized compound yield).

30. Masters Corp. issues two bonds with 20-year maturities. Both bonds are callable at $1,050. The first bond is issued at a deep discount with a coupon rate of 4% and a price of $580 to yield 8.4%. The second bond is issued at par value with a coupon rate of 8¾%.
   a. What is the yield to maturity of the par bond? Why is it higher than the yield of the discount bond?
   b. If you expect rates to fall substantially in the next two years, which bond would you prefer to hold?
   c. In what sense does the discount bond offer "implicit call protection"?

31. A convertible bond has the following features:

Coupon	5.25%
Maturity	June 15, 2017
Market price of bond	$77.50
Market price of underlying common stock	$28.00
Annual dividend	$ 1.20
Conversion ratio	20.83 shares

Calculate the conversion premium for this bond.

32. *a.* Explain the impact on the offering yield of adding a call feature to a proposed bond issue.
   b. Explain the impact on the bond's expected life of adding a call feature to a proposed bond issue.
   c. Describe one advantage and one disadvantage of including callable bonds in a portfolio.

33. The yield to maturity on one-year zero-coupon bonds is 8%. The yield to maturity on two-year zero-coupon bonds is 9%.
   a. What is the forward rate of interest for the second year?
   b. If you believe in the expectations hypothesis, what is your best guess as to the expected value of the short-term interest rate next year?
   c. If you believe in the liquidity preference theory, is your best guess as to next year's short-term interest rate higher or lower than in (*b*)?

34. Following are the spot rates and forward rates for three years. However, the labels got mixed up. Can you identify which row of the interest rates represents spot rates and which one the forward rates?

Year:	1	2	3
Spot rates or Forward rates?	10%	12%	14%
Spot rates or Forward rates?	10%	14.0364%	18.1078%

35. The current yield curve for default-free zero-coupon bonds is as follows:

Maturity (Years)	YTM
1	10%
2	11
3	12

 a. What are the implied one-year forward rates?
 b. Assume that the pure expectations hypothesis of the term structure is correct. If market expectations are accurate, what will the pure yield curve (that is, the yields to maturity on one- and two-year zero coupon bonds) be next year?
 c. If you purchase a two-year zero-coupon bond now, what is the expected total rate of return over the next year? What if you purchase a three-year zero-coupon bond? (Hint: Compute the current and expected future prices.) Ignore taxes.

36. The term structure for zero-coupon bonds is currently:

Maturity (Years)	YTM
1	4%
2	5
3	6

Next year at this time, *you* expect it to be:

Maturity (Years)	YTM
1	5%
2	6
3	7

 a. What do *you* expect the rate of return to be over the coming year on a three-year zero-coupon bond?
 b. Under the expectations theory, what yields to maturity does *the market* expect to observe on one- and two-year zeros next year? Is the market's expectation of the return on the three-year bond greater or less than yours?

37. The following multiple-choice problems are based on questions that appeared in past CFA examinations.
 a. Which bond probably has the highest credit quality?
    (1) Sumter, South Carolina, Water and Sewer Revenue Bond.
    (2) Riley County, Kansas, General Obligation Bond.
    (3) University of Kansas Medical Center Refunding Revenue Bonds (insured by American Municipal Bond Assurance Corporation).
    (4) Euless, Texas, General Obligation Bond (refunded and secured by U.S. government securities held in escrow).
 b. The market risk of an AAA-rated preferred stock relative to an AAA-rated bond is:
    (1) Lower
    (2) Higher
    (3) Equal
    (4) Unknown

c. A bond with a call feature:
   (1) Is attractive because the immediate receipt of principal plus premium produces a high return.
   (2) Is more apt to be called when interest rates are high because the interest saving will be greater.
   (3) Will usually have a higher yield than a similar noncallable bond.
   (4) None of the above.

d. The yield to maturity on a bond is:
   (1) Below the coupon rate when the bond sells at a discount, and above the coupon rate when the bond sells at a premium.
   (2) The discount rate that will set the present value of the payments equal to the bond price.
   (3) The current yield plus the average annual capital gains rate.
   (4) Based on the assumption that any payments received are reinvested at the coupon rate.

e. In which *one* of the following cases is the bond selling at a discount?
   (1) Coupon rate is greater than current yield, which is greater than yield to maturity.
   (2) Coupon rate, current yield, and yield to maturity are all the same.
   (3) Coupon rate is less than current yield, which is less than yield to maturity.
   (4) Coupon rate is less than current yield, which is greater than yield to maturity.

f. Consider a five-year bond with a 10% coupon selling at a yield to maturity of 8%. If interest rates remain constant, one year from now the price of this bond will be:
   (1) Higher
   (2) Lower
   (3) The same
   (4) Par

g. Which of the following statements is *true*?
   (1) The expectations hypothesis indicates a flat yield curve if anticipated future short-term rates exceed current short-term rates.
   (2) The basic conclusion of the expectations hypothesis is that the long-term rate is equal to the anticipated short-term rate.
   (3) The liquidity hypothesis indicates that, all other things being equal, longer maturities will have higher yields.
   (4) The liquidity preference theory states that a rising yield curve implies that the market anticipates increases in interest rates.

1. Use the Financial Highlights section of Market Insight (www.mhhe.com/edumarketinsight) to obtain Standard & Poor's bond rating of at least 10 firms in the database. Try to choose a sample with a wide range of bond ratings. Next use Market Insight's Annual Ratio Report to obtain for each firm the financial ratios tabulated in Table 9.3. What is the relationship between bond rating and these ratios? Can you tell from your sample which of these ratios are the more important determinants of bond rating?

STANDARD &POOR'S

www.mhhe.com/bkm

WEBMASTER

Bond Ratings and Yields

The Federal Reserve Bank of St. Louis publishes a monthly report on monetary trends. The report provides a wealth of information on money supply, interest rates and levels of outstanding borrowing. The current report can be found at the following location: http://research.stlouisfed.org/publications/mt/mt.pdf. After securing the most current report and examining its graphs and data answer the following questions.

1. How does the current yield curve compare to the yield curve one year ago?

2. What has been the trend in short-term and long-term interest rates over the last 3 years?

3. What is the spread of Corporate AAAs over the 10 year Treasury? Has that spread widened or narrowed over the last three years?

4. What is the spread of Corporate BBBs over the 10 year Treasury? Has that spread widened or narrowed over the last three years?

5. What is the current real rate of interest on Treasuries? Does the real rate show any discernable trends over the last three years?

SOLUTIONS TO

Concept
CHECKS

1. The callable bond will sell at the *lower* price. Investors will not be willing to pay as much if they know that the firm retains a valuable option to reclaim the bond for the call price if interest rates fall.

2. At a semiannual interest rate of 3%, the bond is worth $40 × Annuity factor (3%, 60) + $1,000 × PV factor (3%, 60) = $1,276.76, which results in a capital gain of $276.76. This exceeds the capital loss of $189.29 ($1,000 − $810.71) when the interest rate increased to 5%.

3. Yield to maturity exceeds current yield, which exceeds coupon rate. Take as an example the 8% coupon bond with a yield to maturity of 10% per year (5% per half year). Its price is $810.71, and therefore its current yield is 80/810.77 = 0.0987, or 9.87%, which is higher than the coupon rate but lower than the yield to maturity.

4. The current price of the bond can be derived from the yield to maturity. Using your calculator, set: $n = 40$ (semiannual periods); PMT = $45 per period; FV = $1,000; $i = 4\%$ per semiannual period. Calculate present value as $1,098.96. Now we can calculate yield to call. The time to call is five years, or 10 semiannual periods. The price at which the bond will be called is $1,050. To find yield to call, we set: $n = 10$ (semiannual periods); PMT = $45 per period; FV = $1,050; PV = $1,098.96. Calculate the semiannual yield to call as 3.72%.

5. Price = $70 × Annuity factor (8%, 1) + $1,000 × PV factor (8%, 1) = $990.74

$$\text{Rate of return to investor} = \frac{\$70 + (\$990.74 - \$982.17)}{\$982.17} = 0.080 = 8\%$$

6. By year-end, remaining maturity is 29 years. If the yield to maturity were still 8%, the bond would still sell at par and the holding-period return would be 8%. At a higher yield, price and return will be lower. The yield to maturity is 8.5%. With annual payments of $80 and a face value of $1,000,

the price of the bond is $946.70 ($n = 29$; $i = 8.5\%$; PMT = 80; FV = 1000). The bond initially sold at $1,000 when issued at the start of the year. The holding-period return is

$$\text{HPR} = \frac{80 + (946.70 - 1,000)}{1,000} = .0267 = 2.67\%$$

which is less than the initial yield to maturity of 8%.

7. At the lower yield, the bond price will be $631.67 [$n = 29$, $i = 7\%$, FV = $1,000$, PMT = 40]. Therefore, total after-tax income is

Coupon	$40 \times (1 - 0.36) = $25.60
Imputed interest ($553.66 - $549.69) \times (1 - 0.36) =	2.54
Capital gains ($631.67 - $553.66) \times (1 - 0.28) =	56.17
Total income after taxes:	$84.31

Rate of return = 84.31/549.69 = .153 = 15.3%

8. The coupon payment is $45. There are 20 semiannual periods. The final payment is assumed to be $600. The present value of expected cash flows is $750. The yield to maturity is 5.42% semiannually, or 10.8% as an annualized bond equivalent yield.

9. The yield to maturity on two-year bonds is 8.5%. The forward rate for the third year is $f_3 = 8\% + 1\% = 9\%$. We obtain the yield to maturity on three-year zeros from:

$$(1 + y_3)^3 = (1 + y_2)^2 (1 + f_3) = 1.085^2 \times 1.09 = 1.2832$$

Therefore, $y_3 = .0866 = 8.67\%$. We note that the yield on one-year bonds is 8%, on two-year bonds is 8.5%, and on three-year bonds is 8.67%. The yield curve is upward sloping due solely to the liquidity premium.

10

MANAGING BOND PORTFOLIOS

**AFTER STUDYING THIS CHAPTER
YOU SHOULD BE ABLE TO:**

Analyze the features of a bond that affect the sensitivity of its price to interest rates.

Compute the duration of bonds.

Formulate fixed-income immunization strategies for various investment horizons.

Analyze the choices to be made in an actively managed bond portfolio.

Determine how swaps can be used to mitigate interest rate risk.

In this chapter, we turn to various strategies that bond managers can pursue, making a distinction between passive and active strategies. A *passive investment strategy* takes market prices of securities as fairly set. Rather than attempting to beat the market by exploiting superior information or insight, passive managers act to maintain an appropriate risk-return balance given market opportunities. One special case of passive management is an immunization strategy that attempts to insulate the portfolio from interest rate risk.

An *active investment strategy* attempts to achieve returns that are more than commensurate with the risk borne. In the context of bond portfolios, this style of management can take two forms. Active managers either use interest rate forecasts to predict movements in the entire bond market, or they employ some form of intramarket analysis to identify particular sectors of the market (or particular securities) that are relatively mispriced.

Because interest rate risk is crucial to formulating both active and passive strategies, we begin our discussion with an analysis of the sensitivity of bond prices to interest rate fluctuations. This sensitivity is measured by the duration of the bond, and we devote considerable attention to what determines bond duration. We discuss several passive investment strategies, and show how duration-matching techniques can be used to immunize the holding-period return of a portfolio from interest rate risk. After examining the broad range of applications of the duration measure, we consider refinements in the way that interest rate sensitivity is measured, focusing on the concept of bond convexity. Duration is important in formulating active investment strategies as well, and we next explore several of these strategies. We consider strategies based on intramarket analysis as well as on interest rate forecasting. We also show how interest rate swaps may be used in bond portfolio management.

10.1 INTEREST RATE RISK

You know already that there is an inverse relationship between bond prices and yields and that interest rates can fluctuate substantially. As interest rates rise and fall, bondholders experience capital losses and gains. It is these gains or losses that make fixed-income investments risky, even if the coupon and principal payments are guaranteed, as in the case of Treasury obligations.

Why do bond prices respond to interest rate fluctuations? In a competitive market, all securities must offer investors fair expected rates of return. If a bond is issued with an 8% coupon when competitive yields are 8%, then it will sell at par value. If the market rate rises to 9%, however, who would purchase an 8% coupon bond at par value? The bond price must fall until its expected return increases to the competitive level of 9%. Conversely, if the market rate falls to 7%, the 8% coupon on the bond is attractive compared to yields on alternative investments. Investors eager for that return will respond by bidding the bond price above its par value until the total rate of return falls to the market rate.

Interest Rate Sensitivity

The sensitivity of bond prices to changes in market interest rates is obviously of great concern to investors. To gain some insight into the determinants of interest rate risk, turn to Figure 10.1, which presents the percentage changes in price corresponding to changes in yield to maturity for four bonds that differ according to coupon rate, initial yield to maturity, and time

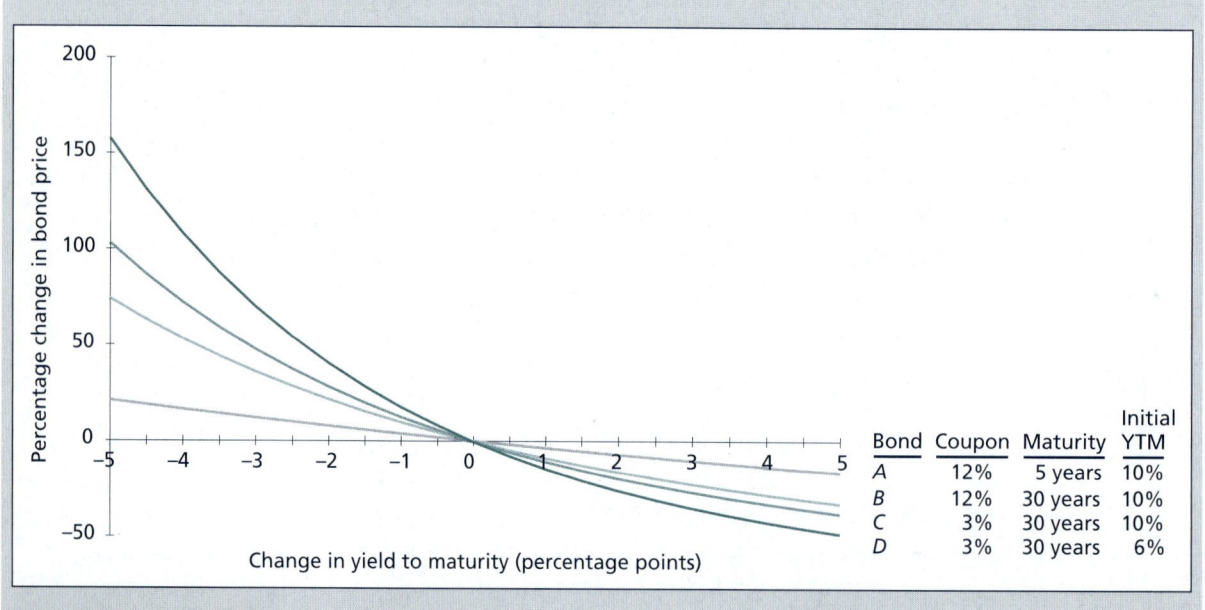

Bond	Coupon	Maturity	Initial YTM
A	12%	5 years	10%
B	12%	30 years	10%
C	3%	30 years	10%
D	3%	30 years	6%

FIGURE 10.1
Change in bond price as a function of change in yield to maturity

to maturity. All four bonds illustrate that bond prices decrease when yields rise, and that the price curve is convex, meaning that decreases in yields have bigger impacts on price than increases in yields of equal magnitude. We summarize these observations in the following two propositions:

1. Bond prices and yields are inversely related: as yields increase, bond prices fall; as yields fall, bond prices rise.
2. An increase in a bond's yield to maturity results in a smaller price change than a decrease in yield of equal magnitude.

Now compare the interest rate sensitivity of bonds *A* and *B*, which are identical except for maturity. Figure 10.1 shows that bond *B*, which has a longer maturity than bond *A*, exhibits greater sensitivity to interest rate changes. This illustrates another general property:

3. Prices of long-term bonds tend to be more sensitive to interest rate changes than prices of short-term bonds.

Although bond *B* has six times the maturity of bond *A*, it has less than six times the interest rate sensitivity. Although interest rate sensitivity seems to increase with maturity, it does so less than proportionally as bond maturity increases. Therefore, our fourth property is that:

4. The sensitivity of bond prices to changes in yields increases at a decreasing rate as maturity increases. In other words, interest rate risk is less than proportional to bond maturity.

Bonds *B* and *C*, which are alike in all respects except for coupon rate, illustrate another point. The lower-coupon bond exhibits greater sensitivity to changes in interest rates. This turns out to be a general property of bond prices:

5. Interest rate risk is inversely related to the bond's coupon rate. Prices of high-coupon bonds are less sensitive to changes in interest rates than prices of low-coupon bonds.

Finally, bonds *C* and *D* are identical except for the yield to maturity at which the bonds currently sell. Yet bond *C*, with a higher yield to maturity, is less sensitive to changes in yields. This illustrates our final property:

6. The sensitivity of a bond's price to a change in its yield is inversely related to the yield to maturity at which the bond currently is selling.

The first five of these general properties were described by Malkiel (1962) and are sometimes known as Malkiel's bond-pricing relationships. The last property was demonstrated by Homer and Liebowitz (1972).

These six propositions confirm that maturity is a major determinant of interest rate risk. However, they also show that maturity alone is not sufficient to measure interest rate sensitivity. For example, bonds *B* and *C* in Figure 10.1 have the same maturity, but the higher coupon bond has less price sensitivity to interest rate changes. Obviously, we need to know more than a bond's maturity to quantify its interest rate risk.

To see why bond characteristics such as coupon rate or yield to maturity affect interest rate sensitivity, let's start with a simple numerical example.

Table 10.1 gives bond prices for 8% annual coupon bonds at different yields to maturity and times to maturity. (For simplicity, we assume coupons are paid once a year rather than semiannually.) The shortest term bond falls in value by less than 1% when the interest rate increases from 8% to 9%. The 10-year bond falls by 6.4% and the 20-year bond by more than 9%.

TABLE **10.1**	Bond's Yield to Maturity	*T* = 1 Year	*T* = 10 Years	*T* = 20 Years
Prices of 8% annual coupon bonds	8%	1,000	1,000	1,000
	9%	990.83	935.82	908.71
	Percent change in price*	−0.92%	−6.42%	−9.13%

*Equals value of bond at a 9% yield to maturity minus value of bond at (the original) 8% yield, divided by the value at 8% yield.

TABLE **10.2**	Bond's Yield to Maturity	*T* = 1 Year	*T* = 10 Years	*T* = 20 Years
Prices of zero-coupon bonds	8%	925.93	463.19	214.55
	9%	917.43	422.41	178.43
	Percent change in price*	−0.92%	−8.80%	−16.84%

*Equals value of bond at a 9% yield to maturity minus value of bond at (the original) 8% yield, divided by the value at 8% yield.

Let us now look at a similar computation using a zero-coupon bond rather than the 8% coupon bond. The results are shown in Table 10.2.

For both maturities beyond one year, the price of the zero-coupon bond falls by a greater proportional amount than the price of the 8% coupon bond. The observation that long-term bonds are more sensitive to interest rate movements than short-term bonds suggests that in some sense a zero-coupon bond represents a longer term investment than an equal-time-to-maturity coupon bond. In fact, this insight about effective maturity is a useful one that we can make mathematically precise.

To start, note that the times to maturity of the two bonds in this example are not perfect measures of the long- or short-term nature of the bonds. The 8% bond makes many coupon payments, most of which come years before the bond's maturity date. Each payment may be considered to have its own "maturity date," which suggests that the *effective* maturity of the bond should be measured as some sort of average of the maturities of *all* the cash flows paid out by the bond. The zero-coupon bond, by contrast, makes only one payment at maturity. Its time to maturity is a well-defined concept.

Duration

To deal with the concept of the "maturity" of a bond that makes many payments, we need a measure of the average maturity of the bond's promised cash flows to serve as a summary statistic of the effective maturity of the bond. This measure also should give us some information on the sensitivity of a bond to interest rate changes because we have noted that price sensitivity tends to increase with time to maturity.

Macaulay's duration

A measure of the effective maturity of a bond, defined as the weighted average of the times until each payment, with weights proportional to the present value of the payment.

Frederick Macaulay (1938) called the effective maturity concept the duration of the bond. **Macaulay's duration** is computed as the weighted average of the times to each coupon or principal payment made by the bond. The weight applied to each time to payment clearly should be related to the "importance" of that payment to the value of the bond. Therefore, the weight for each payment time is the proportion of the total value of the bond accounted for by that payment. This proportion is just the present value of the payment divided by the bond price.

Figure 10.2 can help us interpret Macaulay's duration by showing the cash flows made by an eight-year maturity bond with a coupon of 9%, selling at a yield to maturity of 10%. In the

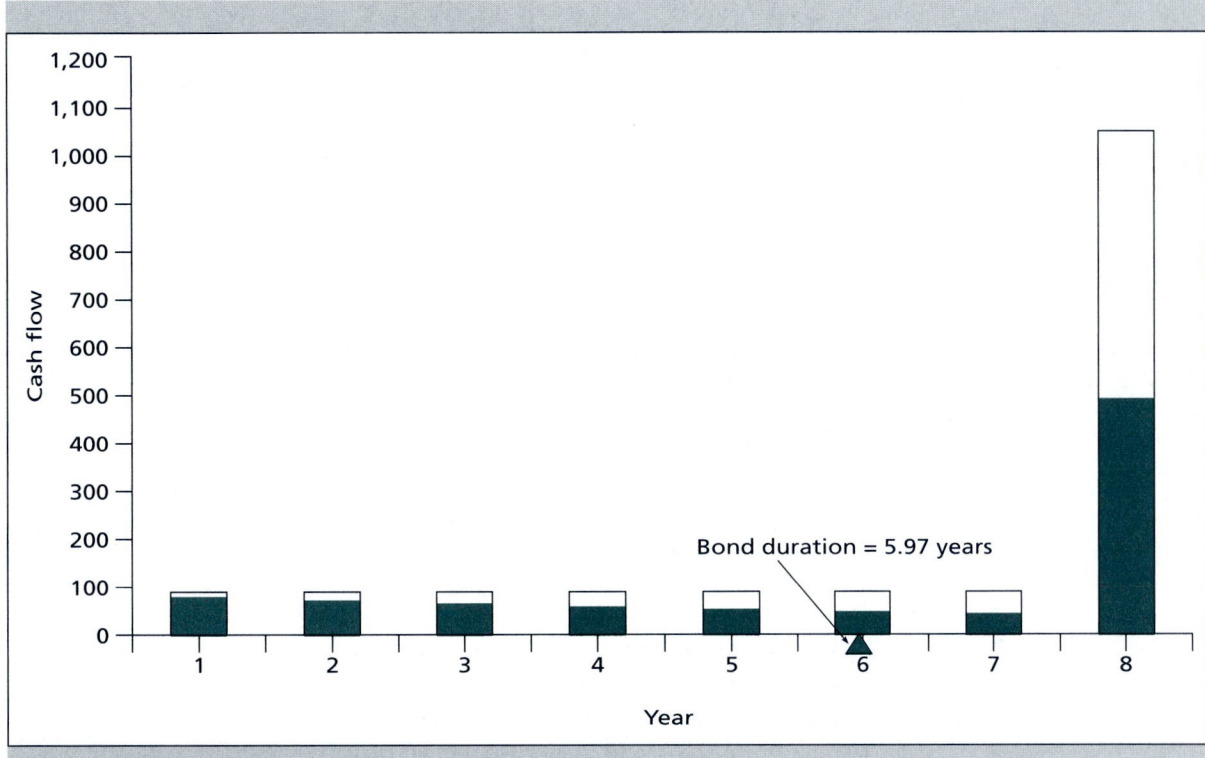

Bond duration = 5.97 years

FIGURE 10.2

Cash flows paid by 9% coupon, annual payment bond with 8-year maturity. The height of each bar is the total of interest and principal. The shaded portion of each bar is the present value of that cash flow. The fulcrum point is Macaulay's duration, the weighted average of the time until each payment.

first seven years, cash flow is simply the $90 coupon payment; in the last year, cash flow is the sum of the coupon plus par value, or $1,090. The height of each bar is the size of the cash flow; the shaded part of each bar is the *present value* of that cash flow using a discount rate of 10%. If you view the cash flow diagram as a balancing scale, like a child's seesaw, the duration of the bond is the fulcrum point where the scale would be balanced using the present values of each cash flow as weights. The balancing point in Figure 10.2 is at 5.97 years, which is the weighted average of the times until each payment, with weights proportional to the present value of each cash flow. The coupon payments made prior to maturity make the effective (i.e., weighted average) maturity of the bond less than its actual time to maturity.

To calculate the weighted average directly, we define the weight, w_t, associated with the cash flow made at time t (denoted CF_t) as:

$$w_t = \frac{CF_t/(1 + y)^t}{\text{Bond price}}$$

where y is the bond's yield to maturity. The numerator on the right-hand side of this equation is the present value of the cash flow occurring at time t, while the denominator is the value of all the payments forthcoming from the bond. These weights sum to 1.0 because the sum of the cash flows discounted at the yield to maturity equals the bond price.

Using these values to calculate the weighted average of the times until the receipt of each of the bond's payments, we obtain Macaulay's formula for duration, denoted D.

$$D = \sum_{t=1}^{T} t \times w_t \qquad\qquad (10.1)$$

If we write out each term in the summation sign, we can express duration in the following equivalent equation

$$D = w_1 + \qquad 2w_2 + \qquad 3w_3 + \qquad 4w_4 + \qquad \cdots + \qquad Tw_T$$

$$\nearrow \uparrow \qquad\qquad \nearrow \uparrow$$

time until   weight   time until weight of
2nd cash   of 2nd   4th CF   4th CF
flow   CF

An example of how to apply Equation 10.1 appears in Table 10.3, where we derive the durations of an 8% coupon and zero-coupon bond each with three years to maturity. We assume that the yield to maturity on each bond is 10%. The present value of each payment is discounted at 10% for the number of years shown in column B. The weight associated with each payment time (column E) equals the present value of the payment (column D) divided by the bond price (the sum of the present values in column D).

The numbers in column F are the products of time to payment and payment weight. Each of these products corresponds to one of the terms in Equation 10.1. According to that equation, we can calculate the duration of each bond by adding the numbers in column F.

The duration of the zero-coupon bond is exactly equal to its time to maturity, three years. This makes sense for, with only one payment, the average time until payment must be the bond's maturity. The three-year coupon bond, in contrast, has a shorter duration of 2.7774 years.

While the top panel of the spreadsheet in Spreadsheet 10.1 presents numbers for our particular example, the bottom panel presents the formulas we actually entered in each cell. The inputs in the spreadsheet—specifying the cash flows the bond will pay—are given in columns B and C. In column D we calculate the present value of each cash flow using a discount rate of 10%, in column E we calculate the weights for Equation 10.1, and in column F we compute the product of time until payment and payment weight. Each of these terms corresponds to one of the terms in Equation 10.1. The sum of these terms, reported in cells F9 and F14, is therefore the duration of each bond. Using the spreadsheet, you can easily answer several "what if " questions such as the one in Concept Check 1.

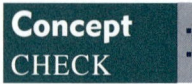

Concept CHECK

1. Suppose the interest rate decreases to 9%. What will happen to the price and duration of each bond in Spreadsheet 10.1?

Duration is a key concept in bond portfolio management for at least three reasons. First, it is a simple summary measure of the effective average maturity of the portfolio. Second, it turns out to be an essential tool in immunizing portfolios from interest rate risk. We will explore this application in the next section. Third, duration is a measure of the interest rate sensitivity of a bond portfolio, which we explore here.

We have already noted that long-term bonds are more sensitive to interest rate movements than short-term bonds. The duration measure enables us to quantify this relationship. It turns out that, when interest rates change, the percentage change in a bond's price is proportional to its duration. Specifically, the proportional change in a bond's price can be related to the change in its yield to maturity, y, according to the rule

SPREADSHEET 10.1

Calculation of the duration of two bonds using Excel spreadsheet

	A	B	C	D	E	F
1	Interest rate:	0.10				
2						
3		Time until		Payment		Column B
4		Payment		Discounted		×
5		(Years)	Payment	at 10%	Weight*	Column E
6	A. 8% coupon bond	1	80	72.727	0.0765	0.0765
7		2	80	66.116	0.0696	0.1392
8		3	1080	811.420	0.8539	2.5617
9	Sum:			950.263	1.0000	2.7774
10						
11	B. Zero-coupon bond	1	0	0.000	0.0000	0.0000
12		2	0	0.000	0.0000	0.0000
13		3	1000	751.315	1.0000	3.0000
14	Sum:			751.315	1.0000	3.0000
15						
16	*Weight = Present value of each payment (column D) divided by bond price					

	A	B	C	D	E	F
1	Interest rate:	0.10				
2						
3		Time until		Payment		Column B
4		Payment		Discounted		×
5		(Years)	Payment	at 10%	Weight	Column E
6	A. 8% coupon bond	1	80	=C6/(1+$B$1)^B6	=D6/D$9	=E6*B6
7		2	80	=C7/(1+$B$1)^B7	=D7/D$9	=E7*B7
8		3	1080	=C8/(1+$B$1)^B8	=D8/D$9	=E8*B8
9	Sum:			=SUM(D6:D8)	=D9/D$9	=SUM(F6:F8)
10						
11	B. Zero-coupon	1	0	=C11/(1+$B$1)^B11	=D11/D$14	=E11*B11
12		2	0	=C12/(1+$B$1)^B12	=D12/D$14	=E12*B12
13		3	1000	=C13/(1+$B$1)^B13	=D13/D$14	=E13*B13
14	Sum:			=SUM(D11:D13)	=D14/D$14	=SUM(F11:F13)

$$\frac{\Delta P}{P} = -D \times \left[\frac{\Delta(1 + y)}{1 + y}\right] \qquad (10.2)$$

The proportional price change equals the proportional change in (1 plus the bond's yield) times the bond's duration. Therefore, bond price volatility is proportional to the bond's duration, and duration becomes a natural measure of interest rate exposure.[1] This relationship is key to interest rate risk management.

Practitioners commonly use Equation 10.2 in a slightly different form. They define **modified duration** as $D^* = D/(1 + y)$ and rewrite Equation 10.2 as

$$\frac{\Delta P}{P} = -D^* \Delta y \qquad (10.3)$$

The percentage change in bond price is just the product of modified duration and the change in the bond's yield to maturity. Because the percentage change in the bond price is proportional

modified duration

Macaulay's duration divided by 1 + yield to maturity. Measures interest rate sensitivity of bond.

[1]Actually, as we will see later, Equation 10.3 is only approximately valid for large changes in the bond's yield. The approximation becomes exact as one considers smaller, or localized, changes in yields.

to modified duration, modified duration is a natural measure of the bond's exposure to interest rate volatility.

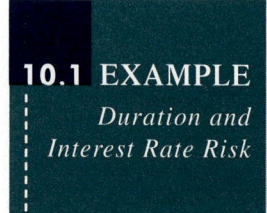

10.1 EXAMPLE

Duration and Interest Rate Risk

A bond with maturity of 30 years has a coupon rate of 8% (paid annually) and a yield to maturity of 9%. Its price is $897.26, and its duration is 11.37 years. What will happen to the bond price if the bond's yield to maturity increases to 9.1%?

Equation 10.3 tells us that an increase of 0.1% in the bond's yield to maturity ($\Delta y = .001$ in decimal terms) will result in a price change of

$$\Delta P = -(D^* \, \Delta y) \times P$$

$$= -\frac{11.37}{1.09} \times 0.001 \times \$897.26 = -\$9.36$$

To confirm the relationship between duration and the sensitivity of bond price to interest rate changes, let's compare the price sensitivity of the three-year coupon bond in Spreadsheet 10.1, which has a duration of 2.7774 years, to the sensitivity of a zero-coupon bond with maturity and duration of 2.7774 years. Both should have equal interest rate exposure if duration is a useful measure of price sensitivity.

The three-year bond sells for $950.263 at the initial interest rate of 10%. If the bond's yield increases by 1 basis point (1/100 of a percent) to 10.01%, its price will fall to $950.0231, a percentage decline of 0.0252%. The zero-coupon bond has a maturity of 2.7774 years. At the initial interest rate of 10%, it sells at a price of $1,000/1.10^{2.7774} = $767.425. When the interest rate increases, its price falls to $1,000/1.1001^{2.7774} = $767.2313, for an identical 0.0252% capital loss. We conclude, therefore, that equal-duration assets are equally sensitive to interest rate movements.

Incidentally, this example confirms the validity of Equation 10.2. The equation predicts that the proportional price change of the two bonds should have been $-2.7774 \times 0.0001/1.10 = 0.000252$, or 0.0252%, just as we found from direct computation.

Concept
CHECK

2. *a.* In Concept Check 1, you calculated the price and duration of a three-year maturity, 8% coupon bond for an interest rate of 9%. Now suppose the interest rate increases to 9.05%. What is the new value of the bond and the percentage change in the bond's price?

   b. Calculate the percentage change in the bond's price predicted by the duration formula in Equation 10.2 or 10.3. Compare this value to your answer for (a).

What Determines Duration?

Malkiel's bond price relations, which we laid out in the previous section, characterize the determinants of interest rate sensitivity. Duration allows us to quantify that sensitivity, which greatly enhances our ability to formulate investment strategies. For example, if we wish to speculate on interest rates, duration tells us how strong a bet we are making. Conversely, if we wish to remain "neutral" on rates, and simply match the interest rate sensitivity of a chosen bond market index, duration allows us to measure that sensitivity and mimic it in our own portfolio. For these reasons, it is crucial to understand the determinants of duration and convenient to have formulas to calculate the duration of some commonly encountered securities. Therefore, in this section, we present several "rules" that summarize most of the important properties of duration. These rules are also illustrated in Figure 10.3, which contains plots of durations of bonds of various coupon rates, yields to maturity, and times to maturity.

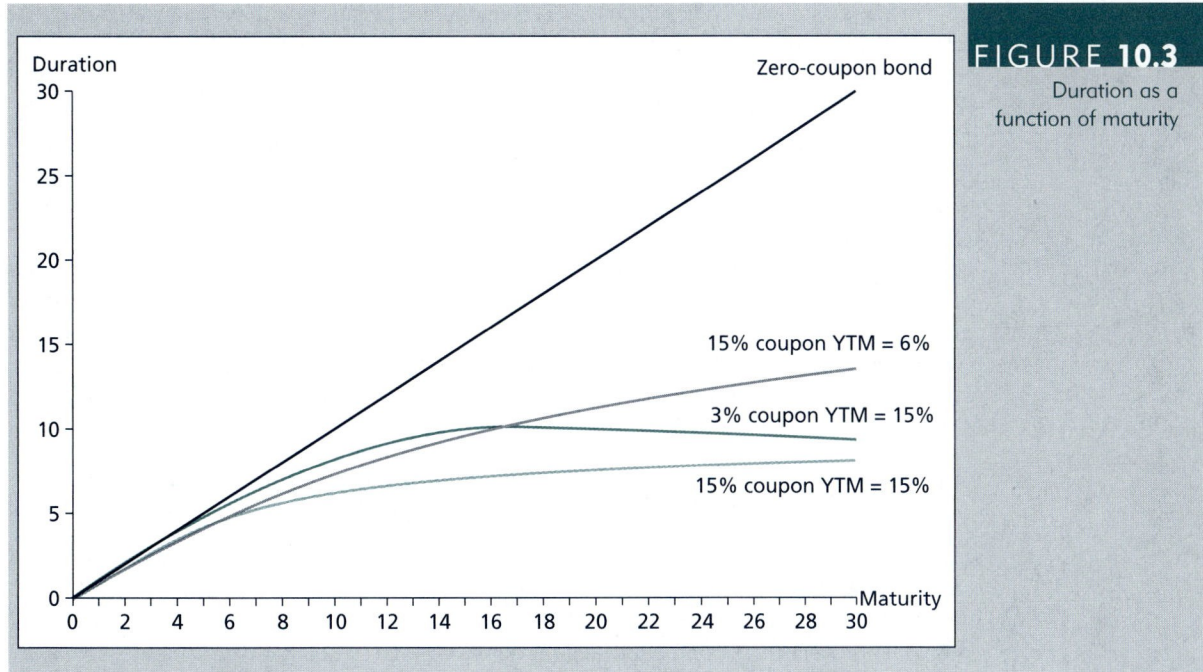

FIGURE **10.3**

Duration as a
function of maturity

We have already established:

Rule 1: The duration of a zero-coupon bond equals its time to maturity.

We also have seen that the three-year coupon bond has a lower duration than the three-year zero because coupons early in the bond's life reduce the bond's weighted average time until payments. This illustrates another general property:

Rule 2: Holding time to maturity and yield to maturity constant, a bond's duration and interest rate sensitivity are higher when the coupon rate is lower.

This property corresponds to Malkiel's fifth bond-pricing relationship, and is attributable to the impact of early coupons on the average maturity of a bond's payments. The lower these coupons, the less weight these early payments have on the weighted average maturity of all the bond's payments. Compare the plots in Figure 10.3 of the durations of the 3% coupon and 15% coupon bonds, each with identical yields of 15%. The plot of the duration of the 15% coupon bond lies below the corresponding plot for the 3% coupon bond.

Rule 3: Holding the coupon rate constant, a bond's duration and interest rate sensitivity generally increase with time to maturity. Duration always increases with maturity for bonds selling at par or at a premium to par.

This property of duration corresponds to Malkiel's third relationship and is fairly intuitive. What is surprising is that duration need not always increase with time to maturity. For some deep discount bonds, such as the 3% coupon bond selling to yield 15% in Figure 10.3, duration may eventually fall with increases in maturity. For virtually all traded bonds, however, it is safe to assume that duration increases with maturity.

Notice in Figure 10.3 that for the zero-coupon bond, maturity and duration are equal. For all the coupon bonds, however, duration increases by less than a year for each year's increase in maturity. The slope of the duration graph is less than 1.0, and duration is always less than maturity for positive-coupon bonds.

While long-maturity bonds generally will be high-duration bonds, duration is a better measure of the long-term nature of the bond because it also accounts for coupon payments. Only when the bond pays no coupons is time to maturity an adequate measure; then maturity and duration are equal.

Notice also in Figure 10.3 that the two 15% coupon bonds have different durations when they sell at different yields to maturity. The lower yield bond has longer duration. This makes sense, because at lower yields the more distant payments have relatively greater present values and thereby account for a greater share of the bond's total value. Thus, in the weighted-average calculation of duration, the distant payments receive greater weights, which results in a higher duration measure. This establishes

Rule 4: Holding other factors constant, the duration and interest rate sensitivity of a coupon bond are higher when the bond's yield to maturity is lower.

Rule 4, which is the sixth bond-pricing relationship noted above, applies to coupon bonds. For zeros, duration equals time to maturity, regardless of the yield to maturity.

Finally, we present an algebraic rule for the duration of a perpetuity. This rule is derived from and is consistent with the formula for duration given in Equation 10.1, but it is far easier to use for infinitely lived bonds.

Rule 5: The duration of a level perpetuity is $(1 + y)/y$. For example, at a 15% yield, the duration of a perpetuity that pays $100 once a year forever will equal $1.15/.15 = 7.67$ years, while at an 8% yield, it will equal $1.08/.08 = 13.5$ years.

Rule 5 makes it obvious that maturity and duration can differ substantially. The maturity of the perpetuity is infinite, while the duration of the instrument at a 15% yield is only 7.67 years. The present-value-weighted cash flows early on in the life of the perpetuity dominate the computation of duration. Notice from Figure 10.3 that as their maturities become ever longer, the durations of the two coupon bonds with yields of 15% both converge to the duration of the perpetuity with the same yield, 7.67 years.

3. **Show that the duration of a perpetuity increases as the interest rate decreases, in accordance with Rule 4.**

Durations can vary widely among traded bonds. Table 10.3 presents durations for several bonds all assumed to pay annual coupons and to yield 8% per year. Duration decreases as

TABLE **10.3**		Coupon Rates (% per year)			
Durations of annual coupon bonds (initial bond yield = 8%)	Years to Maturity	6	8	10	12
	1	1.000	1.000	1.000	1.000
	5	4.439	4.312	4.204	4.110
	10	7.615	7.247	6.996	6.744
	20	11.231	10.604	10.182	9.880
	Infinite (perpetuity)	13.500	13.500	13.500	13.500

Duration

The Excel duration model analyzes the duration of bonds using the same methodology employed in Spreadsheet 10.1. The model allows you to analyze durations of bonds for varying coupon rates and yields. It contains a sensitivity analysis for price and duration of bonds relative to coupon rate and yield to maturities. The concepts discussed in Section 10.1 can be investigated using the spreadsheet.

You can learn more about this spreadsheet model by using the interactive version available on our website at www.mhhe.com/bkm.

	A	B	C	D	E	F
1	**Duration of Bonds**					
2						
3	Bond					
4	Coupon Rate	0.08				
5	Par Value	1000				
6	Years Mat	10				
7	YTM	0.06		Present		
8				Value of		
9	Bond Price	Years	Cashflow	Cashflow	PVCF(t)	
10		1	80	75.4717	75.4717	
11		2	80	71.1997	142.3994	
12		3	80	67.1695	201.5086	
13		4	80	63.3675	253.4700	
14		5	80	59.7807	298.9033	
15		6	80	56.3968	338.3811	
16		7	80	53.2046	372.4320	
17		8	80	50.1930	401.5439	
18		9	80	47.3519	426.1669	
19		10	1080	603.0664	6030.6636	
20						
21	Sum			1147.2017	8540.9404	
22						
23	Price	1147.20				
24	Duration	7.4450				
25						
26						
27		YTM	Price		YTM	Duration
28	One-Way Table		1147.20			7.4450
29		0.04	1324.44		0.04	7.6372
30		0.045	1276.95		0.045	7.5898
31		0.05	1231.65		0.05	7.5419

coupon rates increase and increases with time to maturity. According to Table 10.3 and Equation 10.2, if the interest rate were to increase from 8% to 8.1%, the 6% coupon, 20-year bond would fall in value by about 1.04% ($= -11.231 \times 0.1\%/1.08$) while the 10% coupon, one-year bond would fall by only 0.093% ($= -1 \times 0.1\%/1.08$). Notice also from Table 10.3 that duration is independent of coupon rate only for perpetuities.

10.2 | PASSIVE BOND MANAGEMENT

Passive managers take bond prices as fairly set and seek to control only the risk of their fixed-income portfolios. Generally, there are two ways of viewing this risk, depending on the investor's circumstances. Some institutions, such as banks, are concerned with protecting the portfolio's current net worth or net market value against interest rate fluctuations. Risk-based capital guidelines for commercial banks and thrift institutions require the setting aside of additional capital as a buffer against potential losses in market value incurred from interest rate fluctuations. The amount of capital required is directly related to the losses that may be incurred under various changes in market interest rates. Other investors, such as pension funds, may have an investment goal to be reached after a given number of years. These investors are more concerned with protecting the future values of their portfolios.

What is common to the bank and pension fund, however, is interest rate risk. The net worth of the firm and its ability to meet future obligations fluctuate with interest rates. If they adjust the maturity structure of their portfolios, these institutions can shed their interest rate risk. **Immunization** and dedication techniques refer to strategies that investors use to shield their net worth from exposure to interest rate fluctuations.

immunization

A strategy to shield
net worth from
interest rate
movements.

Immunization

Many banks and thrift institutions have a natural mismatch between the maturities of assets and liabilities. For example, bank liabilities are primarily the deposits owed to customers; these liabilities are short-term in nature and consequently of low duration. Assets largely comprise commercial and consumer loans or mortgages. These assets are of longer duration than deposits, which means their values are correspondingly more sensitive than deposits to interest rate fluctuations. When interest rates increase unexpectedly, banks can suffer serious decreases in net worth—their assets fall in value by more than their liabilities.

Similarly, a pension fund may have a mismatch between the interest rate sensitivity of the assets held in the fund and the present value of its liabilities—the promise to make payments to retirees. The nearby box illustrates the dangers that pension funds face when they neglect the interest rate exposure of *both* assets and liabilities. The article points out that when interest rates change, the present value of the fund's liabilities change. For example, in some recent years pension funds lost ground despite the fact that they enjoyed excellent investment returns. As interest rates fell, the value of their liabilities grew even faster than the value of their assets. The article concludes that funds should match the interest rate exposure of assets and liabilities so that the value of assets will track the value of liabilities whether rates rise or fall. In other words, the financial manager might want to *immunize* the fund against interest rate volatility.

Pension funds are not alone in this concern. Any institution with a future fixed obligation might consider immunization a reasonable risk management policy. Insurance companies, for example, also pursue immunization strategies. The notion of immunization was introduced by F. M. Redington (1952), an actuary for a life insurance company. The idea behind immunization is that duration-matched assets and liabilities let the asset portfolio meet the firm's obligations despite interest rate movements.

Consider, for example, an insurance company that issues a guaranteed investment contract, or GIC, for $10,000. (GICs are essentially zero-coupon bonds issued by the insurance company to its customers. They are popular products for individuals' retirement-savings accounts.) If the GIC has a five-year maturity and a guaranteed interest rate of 8%, the insurance company is obligated to pay $10,000 \times (1.08)^5 = $14,693.28$ in five years.

In one of the happiest reports to come out of Detroit lately, General Motors proclaimed Tuesday that its U.S. pension funds are now "fully funded on an economic basis." Less noticed was GM's admission that, in accounting terms, it is still a few cents—well, $3 billion—shy of the mark.

Wait a minute. If GM's pension plans were $9.3 billion in the hole when the year began, and if the company, to its credit, shoveled in $10.4 billion more during the year, how come its pension deficit wasn't wiped out in full?

We'll get to that, but the real news here is broader than GM. According to experts, most pension funds actually *lost* ground, even though, as you may recall, it was a rather good year for stocks and bonds.

True, pension-fund assets did have a banner year. But as is sometimes overlooked, pension funds also have liabilities (their obligations to retirees). And at most funds, liabilities grew at a rate that put asset growth to shame. At the margin, that means more companies' pension plans will be "underfunded." And down the road, assuming no reversal in the trend, more companies will have to pony up more cash.

What's to blame? The decline in interest rates that brought joy to everyone else. As rates fall, pension funds have to set aside more money today to pay off a fixed obligation tomorrow. In accounting-speak, this "discounted present value" of their liabilities rises.

By now, maybe you sense that pension liabilities swing more, in either direction, than assets. How come? In a phrase, most funds are "mismatched," meaning their liabilities are longer-lived than their investments. The longer an obligation, the more its current value reacts to changes in rates. And at a typical pension fund, even though the average obligation is 15 years away, the average duration of its bond portfolio is roughly five years.

If this seems to defy common sense, it does. No sensible family puts its grocery money (a short-term obligation) into common stocks (a long-term asset). Ordinary Joes and Janes grasp the principle of "matching" without even thinking about it.

But fund managers—the pros—insist on shorter, unmatching bond portfolios for a simple, stupefying reason. They are graded—usually by consultants—according to how they perform against standard (and shorter term) bond indexes. Thus, rather than invest to keep up with liabilities, managers are investing so as to avoid lagging behind the popular index in any year.

SOURCE: Roger Lowenstein, "How Pension Funds Lost in Market Boom," *The Wall Street Journal*, February 1, 1996. Reprinted by permission of Dow Jones & Company, Inc. via Copyright Clearance Center, Inc. © 1996 Dow Jones & Company, Inc. All Rights Reserved Worldwide.

Suppose that the insurance company chooses to fund its obligation with $10,000 of 8% *annual* coupon bonds, selling at par value, with six years to maturity. As long as the market interest rate stays at 8%, the company has fully funded the obligation, as the present value of the obligation exactly equals the value of the bonds.

Table 10.4A shows that if interest rates remain at 8%, the accumulated funds from the bond will grow to exactly the $14,693.28 obligation. Over the five-year period, the year-end coupon income of $800 is reinvested at the prevailing 8% market interest rate. At the end of the period, the bonds can be sold for $10,000; they still will sell at par value because the coupon rate still equals the market interest rate. Total income after five years from reinvested coupons and the sale of the bond is precisely $14,693.28.

If interest rates change, however, two offsetting influences will affect the ability of the fund to grow to the targeted value of $14,693.28. If interest rates rise, the fund will suffer a capital loss, impairing its ability to satisfy the obligation. The bonds will be worth less in five years than if interest rates had remained at 8%. However, at a higher interest rate, reinvested coupons will grow at a faster rate, offsetting the capital loss. In other words, fixed-income investors face two offsetting types of interest rate risk: *price risk* and *reinvestment rate risk.* Increases in interest rates cause capital losses but at the same time increase the rate at which reinvested income will grow. If the portfolio duration is chosen appropriately, these two effects will cancel out exactly. When the portfolio duration is set equal to the investor's horizon date, the accumulated value of the investment fund at the horizon date will be unaffected by

TABLE 10.4	Payment Number	Years Remaining until Obligation	Accumulated Value of Invested Payment
Terminal value of a bond portfolio after five years (all proceeds reinvested)	**A. Rates remain at 8%**		
	1	4	$800 \times (1.08)^4 =$ 1,088.39
	2	3	$800 \times (1.08)^3 =$ 1,007.77
	3	2	$800 \times (1.08)^2 =$ 933.12
	4	1	$800 \times (1.08)^1 =$ 864.00
	5	0	$800 \times (1.08)^0 =$ 800.00
	Sale of bond	0	$10,800/1.08 =$ 10,000.00
			14,693.28
	B. Rates fall to 7%		
	1	4	$800 \times (1.07)^4 =$ 1,048.64
	2	3	$800 \times (1.07)^3 =$ 980.03
	3	2	$800 \times (1.07)^2 =$ 915.92
	4	1	$800 \times (1.07)^1 =$ 856.00
	5	0	$800 \times (1.07)^0 =$ 800.00
	Sale of bond	0	$10,800/1.07 =$ 10,093.46
			14,694.05
	C. Rates increase to 9%		
	1	4	$800 \times (1.09)^4 =$ 1,129.27
	2	3	$800 \times (1.09)^3 =$ 1,036.02
	3	2	$800 \times (1.09)^2 =$ 950.48
	4	1	$800 \times (1.09)^1 =$ 872.00
	5	0	$800 \times (1.09)^0 =$ 800.00
	Sale of bond	0	$10,800/1.09 =$ 9,908.26
			14,696.02

Note: The sale price of the bond portfolio equals the portfolio's final payment ($10,800) divided by $1 + r$, because the time to maturity of the bonds will be one year at the time of sale.

interest rate fluctuations. *For a horizon equal to the portfolio's duration, price risk and reinvestment risk exactly cancel out.* The obligation is immunized.

In the example we are discussing, the duration of the six-year maturity bonds used to fund the GIC is five years. You can confirm this following the procedure in Spreadsheet 10.1. The duration of the (zero-coupon) GIC is also five years. Because the fully funded plan has equal duration for its assets and liabilities, the insurance company should be immunized against interest rate fluctuations. To confirm that this is the case, let us now investigate whether the bond can generate enough income to pay off the obligation five years from now regardless of interest rate movements.

Tables 10.4B and C consider two possible interest rate scenarios: Rates either fall to 7% or increase to 9%. In both cases, the annual coupon payments from the bond are reinvested at the new interest rate, which is assumed to change before the first coupon payment, and the bond is sold in year 5 to help satisfy the obligation of the GIC.

Table 10.4B shows that if interest rates fall to 7%, the total funds will accumulate to $14,694.05, providing a small surplus of $0.77. If rates increase to 9% as in Table 10.4C, the fund accumulates to $14,696.02, providing a small surplus of $2.74.

Several points are worth highlighting. First, duration matching balances the difference between the accumulated value of the coupon payments (reinvestment rate risk) and the sale value of the bond (price risk). That is, when interest rates fall, the coupons grow less than in

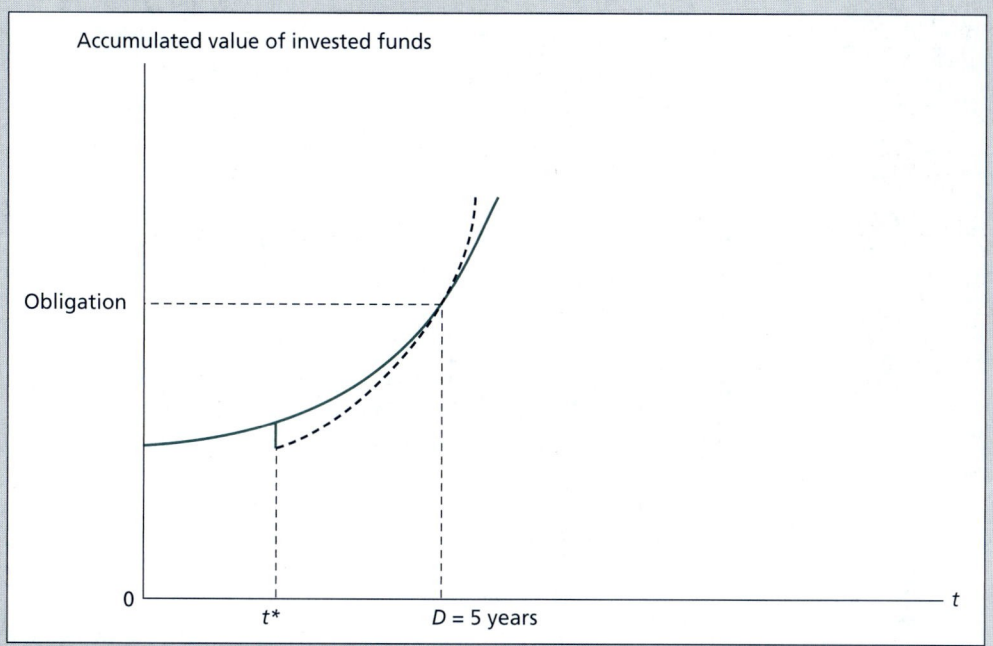

FIGURE 10.4
Growth of invested funds

Note: The solid curve represents the growth of portfolio value at the original interest rate. If interest rates increase at time t^* the portfolio value falls but increases thereafter at the faster rate represented by the broken curve. At time D (duration) the curves cross.

the base case, but the gain on the sale of the bond offsets this. When interest rates rise, the re-sale value of the bond falls, but the coupons more than make up for this loss because they are reinvested at the higher rate. Figure 10.4 illustrates this case. The solid curve traces out the ac-cumulated value of the bonds if interest rates remain at 8%. The dashed curve shows that value if interest rates happen to increase. The initial impact is a capital loss, but this loss even-tually is offset by the now-faster growth rate of reinvested funds. At the five-year horizon date, the two effects just cancel, leaving the company able to satisfy its obligation with the accu-mulated proceeds from the bond. The nearby box discusses this trade-off between price and reinvestment rate risk, suggesting how duration can be used to tailor a bond portfolio to the horizon of the investor.

We can also analyze immunization in terms of present as opposed to future values. Table 10.5A shows the initial balance sheet for the insurance company's GIC account. Both assets and the obligation have market values of $10,000, so that the plan is just fully funded. Table 10.5B and C show that whether the interest rate increases or decreases, the value of the bonds funding the GIC and the present value of the company's obligation change by virtually iden-tical amounts. Regardless of the interest rate change, the plan remains fully funded, with the surplus in Table 10.5B and C just about zero. The duration-matching strategy has ensured that both assets and liabilities react equally to interest rate fluctuations.

Figure 10.5 is a graph of the present values of the bond and the single-payment obligation as a function of the interest rate. At the current rate of 8%, the values are equal, and the ob-ligation is fully funded by the bond. Moreover, the two present value curves are tangent at

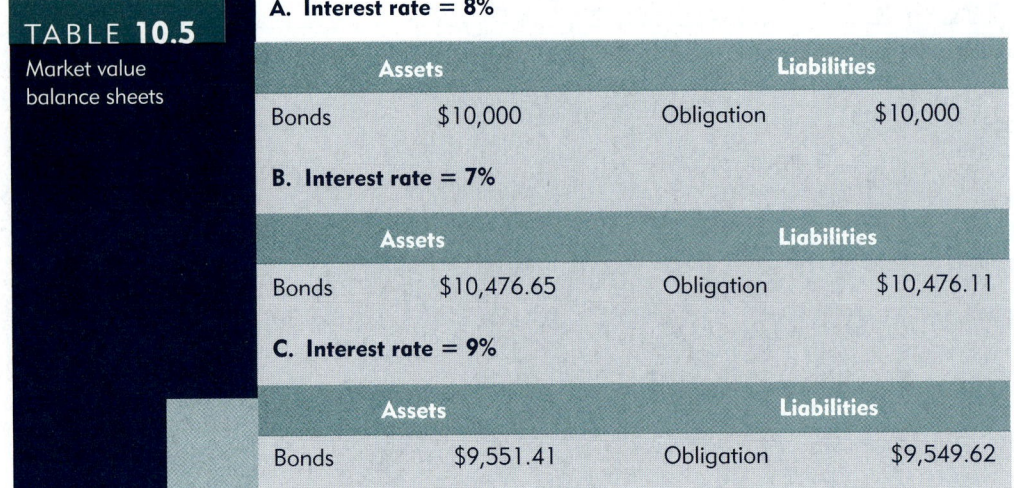

TABLE 10.5
Market value balance sheets

A. Interest rate = 8%

Assets		Liabilities	
Bonds	$10,000	Obligation	$10,000

B. Interest rate = 7%

Assets		Liabilities	
Bonds	$10,476.65	Obligation	$10,476.11

C. Interest rate = 9%

Assets		Liabilities	
Bonds	$9,551.41	Obligation	$9,549.62

Notes:

Value of bonds = 800 × Annuity factor(r, 6) + 10,000 × PV factor(r, 6)

$$\text{Value of obligation} = \frac{14{,}693.28}{(1 + r)^5} = 14{,}693.28 \times \text{PV factor}(r, 5)$$

FIGURE 10.5
Immunization. The coupon bond fully funds the obligation at an interest rate of 8%. Moreover, the present value curves are tangent at 8%, so the obligation will remain fully funded even if rates change.

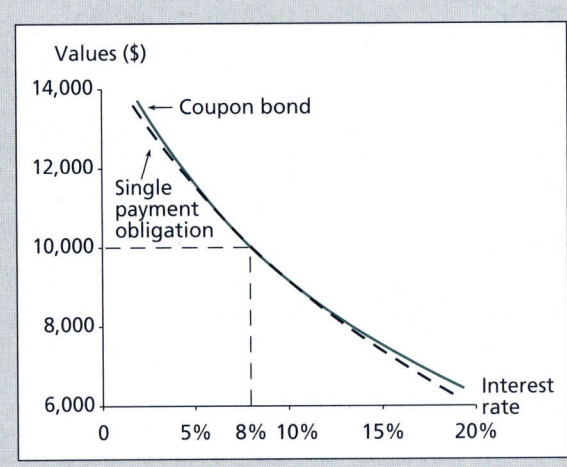

$y = 8\%$. As interest rates change, the change in value of both the asset and the obligation are equal, so the obligation remains fully funded. For greater changes in the interest rate, however, the present value curves diverge. This reflects the fact that the fund actually shows a small surplus at market interest rates other than 8%.

Why is there any surplus in the fund? After all, we claimed that a duration-matched asset and liability mix would make the investor indifferent to interest rate shifts. Actually, such a claim is valid only for *small* changes in the interest rate, because as bond yields change, so too does duration. (Recall Rule 4 for duration.) In fact, while the duration of the bond in this example is equal to five years at a yield to maturity of 8%, the duration rises to 5.02 years when the bond yield falls to 7% and drops to 4.97 years at $y = 9\%$. That is, the bond and the

Bond's Duration Is Handy Guide on Rates

Suppose you buy a 10-year Treasury note today at a yield to maturity of 6% and interest rates shoot up to 8%. What happens to your investment?

A. You lose money.

B. You make money.

C. Nothing happens.

D. All of the above.

The answer: D. All of the above.

How is that possible? The trick is how long you hold the investment.

In the short run, you lose money. Since interest rates and bond prices move inversely to one another, higher rates mean the value of your bond investment withers when rates go up. For a 10-year Treasury yielding 6%, a two percentage-point rise in rates would cause the value of your principal to sink by roughly 14%.

However, if you hold the note, rather than selling it, you'll get to reinvest the interest received from it at the new, higher 8% rate. Over time, this higher "interest on interest" adds up, allowing you not only to offset your initial loss of principal but also to profit more than if rates had never moved at all.

Perhaps the best way to judge a bond's interest-rate sensitivity is to get a handle on its "duration." Duration is one measure of a bond's life. It's that sweet spot, somewhere between the short term and the long term, where a bond's return remains practically unchanged, no matter what happens to interest rates.

BOND'S DURATION

The duration of a 10-year Treasury note yielding 6% in today's market is between seven and 7½ years. By that time in that note's life, potential price changes as rates go down or up would be about equally offset by consequent changes in the amount of interest-on-interest that would be received.

As a result, the bond's total return will about equal its initial yield to maturity, even if rates change.

Duration is a reassuring feature for investors who have expenses coming due in the future—for retirement or tuition payments, for instance—that they need to cover with the proceeds of their bond investments. By making sure the duration of their investments roughly matches the due date of their expenses, they can avoid being caught off guard by adverse rises in interest rates.

GAUGE OF RISK

But the best thing about duration may be that it provides an extremely handy gauge of interest-rate risk in a given bond or bond fund. To figure out how much prices will move in response to rate changes, simply multiply the percentage change in rates by the duration of the bond or bond fund and, voila, you have a pretty good estimate of what to expect.

For instance, if rates go from 6% to 8%, a 10-year Treasury note with a duration of 7.4 will take a price hit of about 13.5%, or a bit less than two percentage points times the duration.

Source: Barbara Donnelly Granito, "Bond's Duration Is Handy Guide on Rates," *The Wall Street Journal*, April 19, 1993. Reprinted by permission of Dow Jones & Company, Inc. via Copyright Clearance Center, Inc. © 1993 Dow Jones & Company, Inc. All Rights Reserved Worldwide.

---

obligation were not duration-matched *across* the interest rate shift, so the position was not fully immunized.

This example demonstrates the need for **rebalancing** immunized portfolios. As interest rates and asset durations continually change, managers must rebalance, that is, change the composition of, the portfolio of fixed-income assets to realign its duration with the duration of the obligation. Moreover, even if interest rates do not change, asset durations *will* change solely because of the passage of time. Recall from Figure 10.3 that duration generally decreases less rapidly than maturity as time passes, so even if an obligation is immunized at the outset, the durations of the asset and liability will fall at different rates. Without portfolio rebalancing, durations will become unmatched and the goals of immunization will not be realized. Therefore, immunization is a passive strategy only in the sense that it does not involve attempts to identify undervalued securities. Immunization managers still actively update and monitor their positions.

> **rebalancing**
>
> Realigning the proportions of assets in a portfolio as needed.

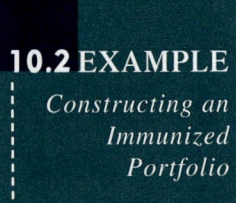

10.2 EXAMPLE

Constructing an Immunized Portfolio

An insurance company must make a payment of $19,487 in seven years. The market interest rate is 10%, so the present value of the obligation is $10,000. The company's portfolio manager wishes to fund the obligation using three-year zero-coupon bonds and perpetuities paying annual coupons. (We focus on zeros and perpetuities to keep the algebra simple.) How can the manager immunize the obligation?

Immunization requires that the duration of the portfolio of assets equal the duration of the liability. We can proceed in four steps:

Step 1. Calculate the duration of the liability. In this case, the liability duration is simple to compute. It is a single-payment obligation with duration of seven years.

Step 2. Calculate the duration of the asset portfolio. The portfolio duration is the weighted average of duration of each component asset, with weights proportional to the funds placed in each asset. The duration of the zero-coupon bond is simply its maturity, three years. The duration of the perpetuity is $1.10/.10 = 11$ years. Therefore, if the fraction of the portfolio invested in the zero is called w, and the fraction invested in the perpetuity is $(1 - w)$, the portfolio duration will be

$$\text{Asset duration} = w \times 3 \text{ years} + (1 - w) \times 11 \text{ years}$$

Step 3. Find the asset mix that sets the duration of assets equal to the seven-year duration of liabilities. This requires us to solve for w in the following equation

$$w \times 3 \text{ years} + (1 - w) \times 11 \text{ years} = 7 \text{ years}$$

This implies that $w = 1/2$. The manager should invest half the portfolio in the zero and half in the perpetuity. This will result in an asset duration of seven years.

Step 4. Fully fund the obligation. Since the obligation has a present value of $10,000, and the fund will be invested equally in the zero and the perpetuity, the manager must purchase $5,000 of the zero-coupon bond and $5,000 of the perpetuity. (Note that the *face value* of the zero will be $5,000 \times (1.10)^3 = $6,655.)

Even if a position is immunized, however, the portfolio manager still cannot rest. This is because of the need for rebalancing in response to changes in interest rates. Moreover, even if rates do not change, the passage of time also will affect duration and require rebalancing. Let us continue Example 10.2 and see how the portfolio manager can maintain an immunized position.

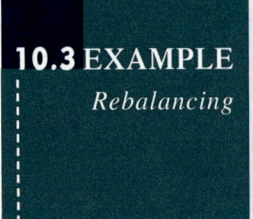

10.3 EXAMPLE

Rebalancing

Suppose that one year has passed, and the interest rate remains at 10%. The portfolio manager of Example 10.2 needs to reexamine her position. Is the position still fully funded? Is it still immunized? If not, what actions are required?

First, examine funding. The present value of the obligation will have grown to $11,000, as it is one year closer to maturity. The manager's funds also have grown to $11,000: The zero-coupon bonds have increased in value from $5,000 to $5,500 with the passage of time, while the perpetuity has paid its annual $500 coupons and remains worth $5,000. Therefore, the obligation is still fully funded.

The portfolio weights must be changed, however. The zero-coupon bond now will have a duration of two years, while the perpetuity duration remains at 11 years. The obligation is now due in six years. The weights must now satisfy the equation

$$w \times 2 + (1 - w) \times 11 = 6$$

which implies that $w = 5/9$. To rebalance the portfolio and maintain the duration match, the manager now must invest a total of $11,000 \times 5/9 = $6,111.11 in the zero-coupon bond. This requires that the entire $500 coupon payment be invested in the zero, with an additional $111.11 of the perpetuity sold and invested in the zero-coupon bond.

Immunization

The Excel immunization model allows you to analyze any number of time-period or holding-period immunization examples. The model is built using formulas for bond duration, which allow the investigation of any maturity bond without building a table of cash flows. (This model contains sample relationships similar to those displayed in Table 10.4.)

You can learn more about this spreadsheet model by using the interactive version available on our website at www.mhhe.com/bkm.

	A	B	C	D	E	F	G	H
1	**Holding Peiod Immunization**							
2								
3	YTM	0.0800	Mar Price	1000.00				
4	Coupon R	0.0800						
5	Maturity	6						
6	Par Value	1000.00						
7	Holding P	5						
8	Duration	4.9927						
9								
10								
11	If Rates Increase by 200 basis points				If Rates Increase by 100 basis points			
12	Rate	0.1000			Rate	0.0900		
13	FV of CPS	488.41			FV of CPS	478.78		
14	SalesP	981.82			SalesP	990.83		
15	Total	1470.23			Total	1469.60		
16	IRR	0.0801			IRR	0.0800		
17								
18								
19								
20	If Rates Decrease by 200 basis points				If Rates Decrease by 100 basis points			
21	Rate	0.0600			Rate	0.0700		
22	FV of CPS	450.97			FV of CPS	460.06		
23	SalesP	1018.87			SalesP	1009.35		
24	Total	1469.84			Total	1469.40		
25	IRR	0.0801			IRR	0.0800		

Of course, rebalancing of the portfolio entails transaction costs as assets are bought or sold, so continuous rebalancing is not feasible. In practice, managers strike some compromise between the desire for perfect immunization, which requires continual rebalancing, and the need to control trading costs, which dictates less frequent rebalancing.

4. **What would be the immunizing weights in the second year if the interest rate were to fall to 8%?**

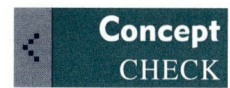

Concept
CHECK

Cash Flow Matching and Dedication

The problems associated with immunization seem to have a simple solution. Why not simply buy a zero-coupon bond that provides a payment in an amount exactly sufficient to cover the

cash flow matching

Matching cash flows from a fixed-income portfolio with those of an obligation.

dedication strategy

Refers to multiperiod cash flow matching.

projected cash outlay? This is **cash flow matching,** which automatically immunizes a portfolio from interest rate movements because the cash flow from the bond and the obligation exactly offset each other.

Cash flow matching on a multiperiod basis is referred to as a **dedication strategy.** In this case, the manager selects either zero-coupon or coupon bonds that provide total cash flows that match a series of obligations in each period. The advantage of dedication is that it is a once-and-for-all approach to eliminating interest rate risk. Once the cash flows are matched, there is no need for rebalancing. The dedicated portfolio provides the cash necessary to pay the firm's liabilities regardless of the eventual path of interest rates.

Cash flow matching is not widely pursued, however, probably because of the constraints it imposes on bond selection. Immunization/dedication strategies are appealing to firms that do not wish to bet on general movements in interest rates, yet these firms may want to immunize using bonds they believe are undervalued. Cash flow matching places enough constraints on bond selection that it can make it impossible to pursue a dedication strategy using only "underpriced" bonds. Firms looking for underpriced bonds exchange exact and easy dedication for the possibility of achieving superior returns from their bond portfolios.

Sometimes, cash flow matching is not even possible. To cash flow match for a pension fund that is obligated to pay out a perpetual flow of income to current and future retirees, the pension fund would need to purchase fixed-income securities with maturities ranging up to hundreds of years. Such securities do not exist, making exact dedication infeasible. Immunization is easy, however. If the interest rate is 8%, for example, the duration of the pension fund obligation is $1.08/.08 = 13.5$ years (see Rule 5 above). Therefore, the fund can immunize its obligation by purchasing zero-coupon bonds with maturity of 13.5 years and a market value equal to that of the pension liabilities.

Concept CHECK

5. *a.* Suppose that this pension fund is obligated to pay out $800,000 per year in perpetuity. What should be the maturity and face value of the zero-coupon bond it purchases to immunize its obligation?

   b. Now suppose the interest rate immediately increases to 8.1%. How should the fund rebalance in order to remain immunized against further interest rate shocks? Ignore transaction costs.

6. How would an increase in trading costs affect the attractiveness of dedication versus immunization?

10.3 CONVEXITY

Duration clearly is a key tool in bond portfolio management. Yet, the duration rule for the impact of interest rates on bond prices is only an approximation. Equation 10.3, which we repeat here, states that the percentage change in the value of a bond approximately equals the product of modified duration times the change in the bond's yield:

$$\frac{\Delta P}{P} = -D^* \, \Delta y \qquad \text{(10.3)}$$

This rule asserts that the percentage price change is directly proportional to the change in the bond's yield. If this were *exactly* so, however, a graph of the percentage change in bond price as a function of the change in its yield would plot as a straight line, with slope equal to $-D^*$. Yet we know from Figure 10.1, and more generally from Malkiel's five bond-pricing relationships (specifically relationship 2), that the relationship between bond prices and yields is *not* linear. The duration rule is a good approximation for small changes in bond yield, but it is less accurate for larger changes.

FIGURE **10.6**
Bond price convexity. The percentage change in bond price is a convex function of the change in yield to maturity.

Figure 10.6 illustrates this point. Like Figure 10.1, this figure presents the percentage change in bond price in response to a change in the bond's yield to maturity. The curved line is the percentage price change for a 30-year maturity, 8% coupon bond, selling at an initial yield to maturity of 8%. The straight line is the percentage price change predicted by the duration rule: The modified duration of the bond at its initial yield is 11.26 years, so the straight line is a plot of $-D^* \, \Delta y = -11.26 \times \Delta y$. Notice that the two plots are tangent at the initial yield. Thus, for small changes in the bond's yield to maturity, the duration rule is quite accurate. However, for larger changes in yield, there is progressively more "daylight" between the two plots, demonstrating that the duration rule becomes progressively less accurate.

Notice from Figure 10.6 that the duration approximation (the straight line) always understates the value of the bond; it underestimates the increase in bond price when the yield falls, and it overestimates the decline in price when the yield rises. This is due to the curvature of the true price-yield relationship. Curves with shapes such as that of the price-yield relationship are said to be convex, and the curvature of the price-yield curve is called the **convexity** of the bond.

We can quantify convexity as the rate of change of the slope of the price-yield curve, expressed as a fraction of the bond price.[2] As a practical rule, you can view bonds with higher convexity as exhibiting higher curvature in the price-yield relationship. The convexity of noncallable bonds, such as that in Figure 10.6, is positive: The slope increases (i.e., becomes less negative) at higher yields.

convexity

The curvature of the price-yield relationship of a bond.

[2]If you have taken a calculus class, you will recognize that Equation 10.3 for modified duration can be written as $dP/P = -D^* \, dy$. Thus, $-D^* = 1/P \times dP/dy$ is the slope of the price-yield curve expressed as a fraction of the bond price. Similarly, the convexity of a bond equals the second derivative (the rate of change of the slope) of the price-yield curve divided by bond price: $1/P \times d^2P/dy^2$. The formula for the convexity of a bond with a maturity of n years making annual coupon payments is:

$$\text{Convexity} = \frac{1}{P \times (1 + y)^2} \sum_{t=1}^{n} \left[\frac{CF_t}{(1 + y)^t} (t^2 + t) \right]$$

where CF_t is the cash flow paid to the bondholder at date t; CF_t represents either a coupon payment before maturity or final coupon plus par value at the maturity date.

Convexity allows us to improve the duration approximation for bond price changes. Accounting for convexity, Equation 10.3 can be modified as follows:[3]

$$\frac{\Delta P}{P} = -D^* \, \Delta y + \frac{1}{2} \times \text{Convexity} \times (\Delta y)^2 \qquad \textbf{(10.4)}$$

The first term on the right-hand side is the same as the duration rule, Equation 10.3. The second term is the modification for convexity. Notice that for a bond with positive convexity, the second term is positive, regardless of whether the yield rises or falls. This insight corresponds to the fact noted just above that the duration rule always underestimates the new value of a bond following a change in its yield. The more accurate Equation 10.4, which accounts for convexity, always predicts a higher bond price than Equation 10.3. Of course, if the change in yield is small, the convexity term, which is multiplied by $(\Delta y)^2$ in Equation 10.4, will be extremely small and will add little to the approximation. In this case, the linear approximation given by the duration rule will be sufficiently accurate. Thus, convexity is more important as a practical matter when potential interest rate changes are large.

Convexity is the reason that the immunization examples we considered above resulted in small errors. For example, if you turn back to Table 10.5 and Figure 10.5, you will see that the single payment obligation that was funded with a coupon bond of the same duration was well immunized for small changes in yields. However, for larger yield changes, the two pricing curves diverged a bit, implying that such changes in yields would result in small surpluses. This is due to the greater convexity of the coupon bond.

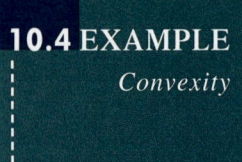

10.4 EXAMPLE

Convexity

The bond in Figure 10.6 has a 30-year maturity, an 8% coupon, and sells at an initial yield to maturity of 8%. Because the coupon rate equals yield to maturity, the bond sells at par value, or $1,000. The modified duration of the bond at its initial yield is 11.26 years, and its convexity is 212.4. (Convexity can be calculated using the formula in footnote 2.) If the bond's yield increases from 8% to 10%, the bond price will fall to $811.46, a decline of 18.85%. The duration rule, Equation 10.3, would predict a price decline of

$$\frac{\Delta P}{P} = -D^* \, \Delta y = -11.26 \times 0.02 = -0.2252 = -22.52\%$$

which is considerably more than the bond price actually falls. The duration-with-convexity rule, Equation 10.4, is more accurate:

$$\frac{\Delta P}{P} = -D^* \, \Delta y + \frac{1}{2} \times \text{Convexity} \times (\Delta y)^2$$

$$= -11.26 \times 0.02 + \frac{1}{2} \times 212.4 \times (0.02)^2 = -0.1827 = -18.27\%$$

which is far closer to the exact change in bond price.

Notice that if the change in yield were smaller, say 0.1%, convexity would matter less. The price of the bond actually would fall to $988.85, a decline of 1.115%. Without accounting for convexity, we would predict a price decline of

$$\frac{\Delta P}{P} = -D^* \, \Delta y = -11.26 \times 0.001 = 0.01126 = 1.126\%$$

Accounting for convexity, we get almost the precisely correct answer:

$$\frac{\Delta P}{P} = -11.26 \times 0.001 + \frac{1}{2} \times 212.4 \times (0.001)^2 = 0.01115 = 1.115\%$$

Nevertheless, the duration rule is quite accurate in this case, even without accounting for convexity.

---

[3]To use the convexity rule, you must express interest rates as decimals rather than percentages.

Why Do Investors Like Convexity?

Convexity is generally considered a desirable trait. Bonds with greater curvature gain more in price when yields fall than they lose when yields rise. For example, in Figure 10.7 bonds *A* and *B* have the same duration at the initial yield. The plots of their proportional price changes as a function of interest rate changes are tangent, meaning that their sensitivities to changes in yields at that point are equal. However, bond *A* is more convex than bond *B*. It enjoys greater price increases and smaller price decreases when interest rates fluctuate by larger amounts. If interest rates are volatile, this is an attractive asymmetry that increases the expected return on the bond, since bond *A* will benefit more from rate decreases and suffer less from rate increases. Of course, if convexity is desirable, it will not be available for free: Investors will have to pay more and accept lower yields on bonds with greater convexity.

10.4 ACTIVE BOND MANAGEMENT

Sources of Potential Profit

Broadly speaking, there are two sources of potential value in active bond management. The first is interest rate forecasting; that is, anticipating movements across the entire spectrum of the fixed-income market. If interest rate declines are forecast, managers will increase portfolio duration; if increases seem likely, they will shorten duration. The second source of potential profit is identification of relative mispricing within the fixed-income market. An analyst might believe, for example, that the default premium on one bond is unnecessarily large and the bond is underpriced.

These techniques will generate abnormal returns only if the analyst's information or insight is superior to that of the market. There is no way of profiting from knowledge that rates are about to fall if everyone else in the market is onto this. In that case, the anticipated lower future rates are built into bond prices in the sense that long-duration bonds are already selling

FIGURE 10.7

Convexity of two bonds. Bond A has greater convexity than bond B.

at higher prices that reflect the anticipated fall in future short rates. If the analyst does not have information before the market does, it will be too late to act on that information—prices will have responded already to the news. You know this from our discussion of market efficiency.

For now we simply repeat that valuable information is differential information. And it is worth noting that interest rate forecasters have a notoriously poor track record.

Homer and Leibowitz have developed a popular taxonomy of active bond portfolio strategies. They characterize portfolio rebalancing activities as one of four types of *bond swaps*. In the first two swaps, the investor typically believes the yield relationship between bonds or sectors is only temporarily out of alignment. Until the aberration is eliminated, gains can be realized on the underpriced bond during a period of realignment called the *workout period*.

substitution swap

Exchange of one bond for a bond with similar attributes but more attractively priced.

1. The **substitution swap** is an exchange of one bond for a nearly identical substitute. The substituted bonds should be of essentially equal coupon, maturity, quality, call features, sinking fund provisions, and so on. A substitution swap would be motivated by a belief that the market has temporarily mispriced the two bonds, with a discrepancy representing a profit opportunity.

    An example of a substitution swap would be a sale of a 20-year maturity, 9% coupon Ford bond callable after five years at $1,050 that is priced to provide a yield to maturity of 9.05% coupled with a purchase of a 9% coupon General Motors bond with the same call provisions and time to maturity that yields 9.15%. If the bonds have about the same credit rating, there is no apparent reason for the GM bonds to provide a higher yield. Therefore, the higher yield actually available in the market makes the GM bond seem relatively attractive. Of course, the equality of credit risk is an important condition. If the GM bond is in fact riskier, then its higher yield does not represent a bargain.

intermarket spread swap

Switching from one segment of the bond market to another.

2. The **intermarket spread swap** is an exchange of two bonds from different sectors of the bond market. It is pursued when an investor believes the yield spread between two sectors of the bond market is temporarily out of line.

    For example, if the yield spread between 10-year Treasury bonds and 10-year Baa-rated corporate bonds is now 3%, and the historical spread has been only 2%, an investor might consider selling holdings of Treasury bonds and replacing them with corporates. If the yield spread eventually narrows, the Baa-rated corporate bonds will outperform the Treasury bonds.

    Of course, the investor must consider carefully whether there is a good reason that the yield spread seems out of alignment. For example, the default premium on corporate bonds might have increased because the market is expecting a severe recession. In this case, the wider spread would not represent attractive pricing of corporates relative to Treasuries, but would simply be an adjustment for a perceived increase in credit risk.

rate anticipation swap

A switch made in response to forecasts of interest rate changes.

3. The **rate anticipation swap** is an exchange of bonds with different maturities. It is pegged to interest rate forecasting. Investors who believe rates will fall will swap into bonds of longer duration. For example, the investor might sell a five-year maturity Treasury bond, replacing it with a 25-year maturity Treasury bond. The new bond has the same lack of credit risk as the old one, but it has longer duration.

pure yield pickup swap

Moving to higher yield bonds, usually with longer maturities.

4. The **pure yield pickup swap** is an exchange of a shorter duration bond for a longer duration bond. This swap is pursued not in response to perceived mispricing but as a means of increasing return by holding higher yielding, longer maturity bonds. The investor is willing to bear the interest rate risk this strategy entails.

    A yield pickup swap can be illustrated using the Treasury bond listings in Figure 9.1 from the last chapter. You can see from that table that a Treasury note maturing in October 2006 yields 4.35%, while one maturing in February 2031 yields 5.36%. The investor who swaps the shorter term bond for the longer one will earn a higher rate of return as long as the yield curve does not shift upward during the holding period. Of course, if it does, the longer duration bond will suffer a greater capital loss.

We can add a fifth swap, called a **tax swap** to this list. This simply refers to a swap to exploit some tax advantage. For example, an investor may swap from one bond that has decreased in price to another similar bond if realization of capital losses is advantageous for tax purposes.

> **tax swap**
>
> Swapping two similar bonds to receive a tax benefit.

Horizon Analysis

One form of interest rate forecasting is called **horizon analysis.** The analyst selects a particular investment period and predicts bond yields at the end of that period. Given the predicted yield to maturity at the end of the investment period, the bond price can be calculated. The coupon income earned over the period is then added to the predicted capital gain or loss to obtain a forecast of the total return on the bond over the holding period.

> **horizon analysis**
>
> Forecast of bond returns based largely on a prediction of the yield curve at the end of the investment horizon.

EXAMPLE 10.5
Horizon Analysis

A 20-year maturity bond with a 10% coupon rate (paid annually) currently sells at a yield to maturity of 9%. A portfolio manager with a two-year horizon needs to forecast the total return on the bond over the coming two years. In two years, the bond will have an 18-year maturity. The analyst forecasts that two years from now, 18-year bonds will sell at yields to maturity of 8%, and that coupon payments can be reinvested in short-term securities over the coming two years at a rate of 7%.

To calculate the two-year return on the bond, the analyst would perform the following calculations:

1. Current price = $100 × Annuity factor(9%, 20 years) + $1,000 × PV factor(9%, 20 years)
   = $1,091.29
2. Forecast price = $100 × Annuity factor(8%, 18 years) + $1,000 × PV factor(8%, 18 years)
   = $1,187.44
3. The future value of reinvested coupons will be ($100 × 1.07) + $100 = $207
4. The two-year return is $\dfrac{\$207 + (\$1,187.44 - \$1,091.29)}{\$1,091.29} = 0.278$, or 27.8%

The annualized rate of return over the two-year period would then be $(1.278)^{1/2} - 1 = 0.13$, or 13%.

WEBMASTER

Bond Swapping Strategies

Go to http://www.investinginbonds.com. This site has several publications that are designed for the individual investor.

After you have read the short pamphlet on swapping strategies, answer the following questions:

1. What potential benefits may be found from swapping?
2. What strategy would you employ if you believed that interest rates were going to fall?
3. What is a wash sale, and how can you avoid wash sales?

7. What will be the rate of return in the example above if the manager forecasts that in two years the yield to maturity on 18-year maturity bonds will be 10% and that the reinvestment rate for coupons will be 8%?

Contingent Immunization

contingent immunization

A strategy that immunizes a portfolio if necessary to guarantee a minimum acceptable return but otherwise allows active management.

Some investment styles fall within the spectrum of active versus passive strategies. An example is a technique called **contingent immunization,** first suggested by Liebowitz and Weinberger (1982). The idea is to allow the fixed-income manager to manage the portfolio actively unless and until poor performance endangers the prospect of achieving a minimum acceptable portfolio return. At that point, the portfolio is immunized, providing a guaranteed rate of return over the remaining portion of the investment period.

To illustrate, suppose a manager with a two-year horizon is responsible for a $10 million portfolio. The manager wishes to provide a two-year cumulative return of at least 10%, that is, the minimum acceptable final value of the portfolio is $11 million. If the interest rate currently is 10%, only $9.09 million would be necessary to guarantee a terminal value of $11 million, because $9.09 million invested in an immunized portfolio would grow after two years to $9.09 \times (1.10)^2 = $11 million. Since the manager starts with $10 million, she can afford to risk some losses at the outset and might therefore start out with an active strategy rather than immediately immunizing.

How much can the manager risk losing? If the interest rate at any time is r, and T is the time left until the horizon date, the amount needed to achieve a terminal value of $11 million is simply the present value of $11 million, or $11 million$/(1 + r)^T$. A portfolio of this size, if immunized, will grow risk-free to $11 million by the horizon date. This value becomes a trigger point: If and when the actual portfolio value dips to the trigger point, active management will cease. *Contingent* upon reaching the trigger point, an immunization strategy is initiated.

Figure 10.8 illustrates two possible outcomes in a contingent immunization strategy. In Figure 10.8A, the portfolio falls in value and hits the trigger at time t^*. At that point, immunization is pursued, and the portfolio rises smoothly to the $11 million value. In Figure 10.8B, the portfolio does well, never reaches the trigger point, and is worth more than $11 million at the horizon date.

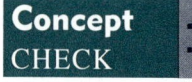

8. What is the trigger point if the manager has a three-year horizon, the interest rate is 8%, and the minimum acceptable terminal value is $10 million?

An Example of a Fixed-Income Investment Strategy

To demonstrate a reasonable, active fixed-income portfolio strategy, we discuss here the policies of Sanford Bernstein & Co., as explained in a speech by its manager of fixed-income investments, Francis Trainer. The company believes big bets on general marketwide interest movements are unwise. Instead, it concentrates on exploiting numerous instances of perceived *relative* minor pricing misalignments *within* the fixed-income sector. The firm takes as a risk benchmark the Lehman [Aggregate] Bond Index, which includes the vast majority of publicly traded bonds with maturities greater than one year. Any deviation from this passive or neutral position must be justified by active analysis. Bernstein considers a neutral portfolio duration to be equal to that of the index.

The firm is willing to make only limited bets on interest rate movements. As Francis Trainer puts it in his speech:

> If we set duration of our portfolios at a level equal to the index and never allow them to vary, this would imply that we are perpetually neutral on the direction of interest rates. However, we believe

FIGURE **10.8**
Contingent
immunization

the utilization of these forecasts will add value and, therefore, we incorporate our economic fore-cast into the bond management process by altering the durations of our portfolios.

However, in order to prevent fixed-income performance from being dominated by the ac-curacy of just a single aspect of our research effort, we limit the degree to which we are willing to alter our interest rate exposure. Under the vast majority of circumstances, we will not permit the duration of our portfolios to differ from that of the [Lehman Brothers] Index by more than one year.

The company expends most of its effort in exploiting numerous but minor inefficiencies in bond prices that result from lack of attention by its competitors. Its analysts follow about 1,000 securities, attempting to "identify specific securities that are attractive or unattractive as well as identify trends in the richness or cheapness of industries and sectors." These two ac-tivities would be characterized as substitution swaps and intermarket spread swaps in the Homer–Leibowitz scheme.

Sanford Bernstein & Co. realizes that market opportunities will arise, if at all, only in sec-tors of the bond market that present the least competition from other analysts. For this reason, it tends to focus on relatively more complicated bond issues in the belief that extensive research efforts give the firm a comparative advantage in that sector. Finally, the company does not take unnecessary risks. If there do not appear to be enough seemingly attractive bonds, funds are placed in Treasury securities as a "neutral" parking space until new opportunities are identified.

To summarize the key features of this sort of strategy, we can make the following observations:

1. A firm like Bernstein has a respect for market prices. It believes that only minor mispricing usually can be detected. It works toward meaningful abnormal returns by combining numerous *small* profit opportunities, not by hoping for the success of one big bet.

2. To have value, information cannot be reflected already in market prices. A large research staff must focus on market niches that appear to be neglected by others.

3. Interest rate movements are extremely hard to predict, and attempts to time the market can wipe out all the profits of intramarket analysis.

10.5   INTEREST RATE SWAPS

interest rate swaps

Contracts between two parties to trade the cash flows corresponding to different securities without actually exchanging the securities directly.

An **interest rate swap** is a contract between two parties to exchange a series of cash flows similar to those that would result if the parties instead were to exchange equal dollar values of different types of bonds. Swaps arose originally as a means of managing interest rate risk. The volume of swaps has increased from virtually zero in 1980 to about $60 trillion today. (Interest rate swaps do not have anything to do with the Homer–Leibowitz bond swap taxonomy set out earlier.)

To illustrate how swaps work, consider the manager of a large portfolio that currently includes $100 million par value of long-term bonds paying an average coupon rate of 7%. The manager believes that interest rates are about to rise. As a result, he would like to sell the bonds and replace them with either short-term or floating-rate issues. However, it would be exceedingly expensive in terms of transaction costs to replace the portfolio every time the forecast for interest rates is updated. A cheaper and more flexible way to modify the portfolio is for the manager to "swap" the $7 million a year in interest income the portfolio currently generates for an amount of money that is tied to the short-term interest rate. That way, if rates do rise, so will the portfolio's interest income.

A swap dealer might advertise its willingness to exchange or "swap" a cash flow based on the six-month LIBOR rate for one based on a fixed rate of 7%. (The LIBOR, or London InterBank Offer Rate, is the interest rate at which banks borrow from each other in the Eurodollar market. It is the most commonly used short-term interest rate in the swap market.) The portfolio manager would then enter into a swap agreement with the dealer to *pay* 7% on **notional principal** of $100 million and *receive* payment of the LIBOR rate on that amount of notional principal.[4] In other words, the manager swaps a payment of 0.07 × $100 million for a payment of LIBOR × $100 million. The manager's *net* cash flow from the swap agreement is therefore (LIBOR − 0.07) × $100 million.

notional principal

Principal amount used to calculate swap payments.

[4]The participants to the swap do not loan each other money. They agree only to exchange a fixed cash flow for a variable cash flow that depends on the short-term interest rate. This is why the principal is described as *notional*. The notional principal is simply a way to describe the size of the swap agreement. In this example, the parties to the swap exchange a 7% fixed rate for the LIBOR rate; the difference between LIBOR and 7% is multiplied by notional principal to determine the cash flow exchanged by the parties.

Now consider the net cash flow to the manager's portfolio in three interest rate scenarios:

	LIBOR Rate		
	6.5%	**7.0%**	**7.5%**
Interest income from bond portfolio (= 7% of $100 million bond portfolio)	$7,000,000	$7,000,000	$7,000,000
Cash flow from swap [= (LIBOR − 7%) × notional principal of $100 million]	(500,000)	0	500,000
Total (= LIBOR × $100 million)	$6,500,000	$7,000,000	$7,500,000

Notice that the total income on the overall position—bonds plus swap agreement—is now equal to the LIBOR rate in each scenario times $100 million. The manager has in effect converted a fixed-rate bond portfolio into a synthetic floating-rate portfolio.

You can see now that swaps can be immensely useful for firms in a variety of applications. For example, a corporation that has issued fixed-rate debt can convert it into synthetic floating-rate debt by entering a swap to receive a fixed interest rate (offsetting its fixed-rate coupon obligation) and pay a floating rate. Or, a bank that pays current market interest rates to its depositors might enter a swap to receive a floating rate and pay a fixed rate on some amount of notional principal. This swap position, added to its floating-rate deposit liability, would result in a net liability of a fixed stream of cash. The bank might then be able to invest in long-term fixed-rate loans without encountering interest rate risk.

What about the swap dealer? Why is the dealer, which is typically a financial intermediary such as a bank, willing to take on the opposite side of the swaps desired by these participants?

Consider a dealer who takes on one side of a swap, let's say paying LIBOR and receiving a fixed rate. The dealer will search for another trader in the swap market who wishes to receive a fixed rate and pay LIBOR. For example, company A may have issued a 7% coupon fixed-rate bond that it wishes to convert into synthetic floating-rate debt, while company B may have issued a floating-rate bond tied to LIBOR that it wishes to convert into synthetic fixed-rate debt. The dealer will enter a swap with company A in which it pays a fixed rate and receives LIBOR, and it will enter another swap with company B in which it pays LIBOR and receives a fixed rate. When the two swaps are combined, the dealer's position is effectively neutral on interest rates, paying LIBOR on one swap, and receiving it on another. Similarly, the dealer pays a fixed rate on one swap and receives it on another. The dealer is an intermediary, funneling payments from one party to the other.[5] The dealer finds this activity profitable because it will charge a bid–ask spread on the transaction.

This arrangement is illustrated in Figure 10.9. Company A has issued 7% fixed-rate debt (the leftmost arrow in the figure) but enters a swap to pay the dealer LIBOR and receive a 6.95% fixed rate. Therefore, the company's net payment is 7% + (LIBOR − 6.95%) = LIBOR + 0.05%. It has thus transformed its fixed-rate debt into synthetic floating-rate debt. Conversely, company B has issued floating-rate debt paying LIBOR (the rightmost arrow), but enters a swap to pay a 7.05% fixed rate in return for LIBOR. Therefore, its net payment is LIBOR + (7.05% − LIBOR) = 7.05%. It has thus transformed its floating-rate debt into synthetic fixed-rate debt. The bid–ask spread in the example illustrated in Figure 10.9 is 0.1% of notional principal each year.

[5]Actually, things are a bit more complicated. The dealer is more than just an intermediary because it bears the credit risk that one or the other of the parties to the swap might default on the obligation. Referring to Figure 10.9, if company A defaults on its obligation, for example, the swap dealer still must maintain its commitment to company B. In this sense, the dealer does more than simply pass through cash flows to the other swap participants.

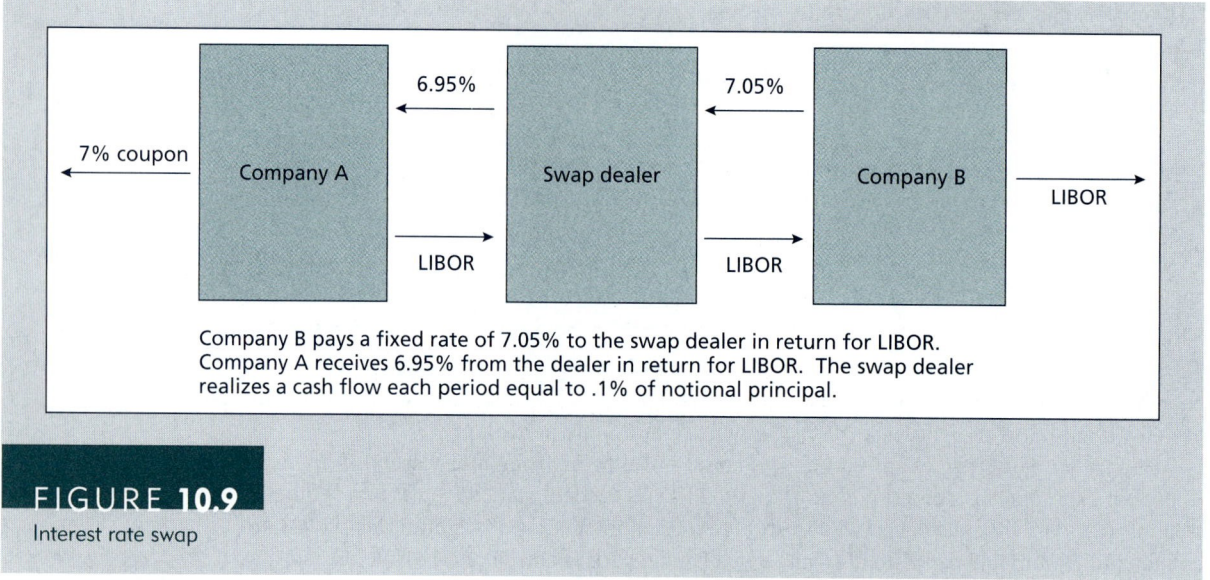

Company B pays a fixed rate of 7.05% to the swap dealer in return for LIBOR. Company A receives 6.95% from the dealer in return for LIBOR. The swap dealer realizes a cash flow each period equal to .1% of notional principal.

FIGURE 10.9
Interest rate swap

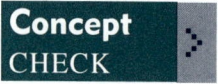

Concept CHECK

9. A pension fund holds a portfolio of money market securities that the manager believes are paying excellent yields compared to other comparable-risk short-term securities. However, the manager believes that interest rates are about to fall. What type of swap will allow the fund to continue to hold its portfolio of short-term securities while at the same time benefiting from a decline in rates?

SUMMARY

• Even default-free bonds such as Treasury issues are subject to interest rate risk. Longer term bonds generally are more sensitive to interest rate shifts than short-term bonds. A measure of the average life of a bond is Macaulay's duration, defined as the weighted average of the times until each payment made by the security, with weights proportional to the present value of the payment.

• Duration is a direct measure of the sensitivity of a bond's price to a change in its yield. The proportional change in a bond's price approximately equals the negative of duration times the proportional change in $1 + y$.

• Immunization strategies are characteristic of passive bond portfolio management. Such strategies attempt to render the individual or firm immune from movements in interest rates. This may take the form of immunizing net worth or, instead, immunizing the future accumulated value of a bond portfolio.

• Convexity refers to the curvature of a bond's price-yield relationship. Accounting for convexity can substantially improve on the accuracy of the duration approximation for bond-price sensitivity to changes in yields.

• Immunization of a fully funded plan is accomplished by matching the durations of assets and liabilities. To maintain an immunized position as time passes and interest rates change, the portfolio must be periodically rebalanced.

• A more direct form of immunization is dedication or cash flow matching. If a portfolio is perfectly matched in cash flow with projected liabilities, rebalancing will be unnecessary.

• Active bond management can be decomposed into interest rate forecasting techniques and intermarket spread analysis. One popular taxonomy classifies active strategies as substitution swaps, intermarket spread swaps, rate anticipation swaps, or pure yield pickup swaps.

- Interest rate swaps are important instruments in the fixed-income market. In these arrangements, parties trade the cash flows of different securities without actually exchanging any securities directly. This can be a useful tool to manage the duration of a portfolio.

cash flow matching, 358	interest rate swaps, 366	pure yield pickup swap, 362
contingent immuni- zation, 364	intermarket spread swap, 362	rate anticipation swap, 362
convexity, 359	Macaulay's duration, 342	rebalancing, 355
dedication strategy, 358	modified duration, 345	substitution swap, 362
horizon analysis, 363	notional principal, 366	tax swap, 363
immunization, 350		

1. A nine-year bond has a yield of 10% and a duration of 7.194 years. If the bond's yield changes by 50 basis points, what is the percentage change in the bond's price?

2. Find the duration of a 6% coupon bond making *annual* coupon payments if it has three years until maturity and a yield to maturity of 6%. What is the duration if the yield to maturity is 10%?

3. A pension plan is obligated to make disbursements of $1 million, $2 million, and $1 million at the end of each of the next three years, respectively. Find the duration of the plan's obligations if the interest rate is 10% annually.

4. If the plan in problem 3 wants to fully fund and immunize its position, how much of its portfolio should it allocate to one-year zero-coupon bonds and perpetuities, respectively, if these are the only two assets funding the plan?

5. You own a fixed-income asset with a duration of five years. If the level of interest rates, which is currently 8%, goes down by 10 basis points, how much do you expect the price of the asset to go up (in percentage terms)?

6. Rank the interest-rate sensitivity of the following pairs of bonds.
   a. Bond A is an 8% coupon bond, with 20-year time to maturity selling at par value. Bond B is an 8% coupon, 20-year maturity bond selling below par value.
   b. Bond A is a 20-year, noncallable coupon bond with a coupon rate of 8%, selling at par. Bond B is a 20-year, callable bond with a coupon rate of 9%, also selling at par.

7. Rank the following bonds in order of descending duration.

Bond	Coupon	Time to Maturity	Yield to Maturity
A	15%	20 years	10%
B	15	15	10
C	0	20	10
D	8	20	10
E	15	15	15

8. Philip Morris has issued bonds that pay annually with the following characteristics:

Coupon	Yield to Maturity	Maturity	Macaulay Duration
8%	8%	15 years	10 years

www.mhhe.com/bkm

   a. Calculate modified duration using the information above.

   b. Explain why modified duration is a better measure than maturity when calculating the bond's sensitivity to changes in interest rates.

   c. Identify the direction of change in modified duration if:

      i. The coupon of the bond were 4%, not 8%.

      ii. The maturity of the bond were 7 years, not 15 years.

9. You will be paying $10,000 a year in tuition expenses at the end of the next two years. Bonds currently yield 8%.

   a. What is the present value and duration of your obligation?

   b. What maturity zero-coupon bond would immunize your obligation?

   c. Suppose you buy a zero-coupon bond with value and duration equal to your obligation. Now suppose that rates immediately increase to 9%. What happens to your net position, that is, to the difference between the value of the bond and that of your tuition obligation? What if rates fall to 7%?

10. Pension funds pay lifetime annuities to recipients. If a firm remains in business indefinitely, the pension obligation will resemble a perpetuity. Suppose, therefore, that you are managing a pension fund with obligations to make perpetual payments of $2 million per year to beneficiaries. The yield to maturity on all bonds is 16%.

   a. If the duration of five-year maturity bonds with coupon rates of 12% (paid annually) is 4 years and the duration of 20-year maturity bonds with coupon rates of 6% (paid annually) is 11 years, how much of each of these coupon bonds (in market value) will you want to hold to both fully fund and immunize your obligation?

   b. What will be the *par value* of your holdings in the 20-year coupon bond?

11. You are managing a portfolio of $1 million. Your target duration is 10 years, and you can choose from two bonds: a zero-coupon bond with maturity 5 years, and a perpetuity, each currently yielding 5%.

   a. How much of each bond will you hold in your portfolio?

   b. How will these fractions change *next year* if target duration is now nine years?

12. You manage a pension fund that will provide retired workers with lifetime annuities. You determine that the payouts of the fund are essentially going to resemble level perpetuities of $1 million per year. The interest rate is 10%. You plan to fully fund the obligation using 5-year and 20-year maturity zero-coupon bonds.

   a. How much *market value* of each of the zeros will be necessary to fund the plan if you desire an immunized position?

   b. What must be the *face value* of the two zeros to fund the plan?

13. Your client is concerned about the apparent inconsistency between the following two statements.

   • Short-term interest rates are more volatile than long-term rates.

   • The rates of return of long-term bonds are more volatile than returns on short-term securities.

   Discuss why these two statements are not necessarily inconsistent.

14. As part of your analysis of debt issued by Monticello Corporation, you are asked to evaluate two specific bond issues, shown in the table on the next page.

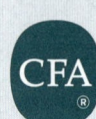

	Monticello Corporation Bond Information	
	Bond A (callable)	Bond B (noncallable)
Maturity	2013	2013
Coupon	11.50%	7.25%
Current price	125.75	100.00
Yield to maturity	7.70%	7.25%
Modified duration to maturity	6.20	6.80
Call date	2007	—
Call price	105	—
Yield to call	5.10%	—
Modified duration to call	3.10	—

a. Using the duration and yield information in the table, compare the price and yield behavior of the two bonds under each of the following two scenarios:
   i. Strong economic recovery with rising inflation expectations.
   ii. Economic recession with reduced inflation expectations.
b. Using the information in the table, calculate the projected price change for bond B if the yield-to-maturity for this bond falls by 75 basis points.
c. Describe the shortcoming of analyzing bond A strictly to call or to maturity.

15. A 30-year maturity bond making annual coupon payments with a coupon rate of 12% has duration of 11.54 years and convexity of 192.4. The bond currently sells at a yield to maturity of 8%. Use a financial calculator to find the price of the bond if its yield to maturity falls to 7% or rises to 9%. What prices for the bond at these new yields would be predicted by the duration rule and the duration-with-convexity rule? What is the percent error for each rule? What do you conclude about the accuracy of the two rules?

16. A 12.75-year maturity zero-coupon bond selling at a yield to maturity of 8% (effective annual yield) has convexity of 150.3 and modified duration of 11.81 years. A 30-year maturity 6% coupon bond making annual coupon payments also selling at a yield to maturity of 8% has nearly identical duration—11.79 years—but considerably higher convexity of 231.2.
a. Suppose the yield to maturity on both bonds increases to 9%. What will be the actual percentage capital loss on each bond? What percentage capital loss would be predicted by the duration-with-convexity rule?
b. Repeat part (a), but this time assume the yield to maturity decreases to 7%.
c. Compare the performance of the two bonds in the two scenarios, one involving an increase in rates, the other a decrease. Based on their comparative investment performance, explain the attraction of convexity.
d. In view of your answer to (c), do you think it would be possible for two bonds with equal duration, but different convexity, to be priced initially at the same yield to maturity if the yields on both bonds always increased or decreased by equal amounts, as in this example? Would anyone be willing to buy the bond with lower convexity under these circumstances?

17. One common goal among fixed-income portfolio managers is to earn high incremental returns on corporate bonds versus government bonds of comparable durations. The approach of some corporate-bond portfolio managers is to find and purchase those corporate bonds having the largest initial spreads over comparable-duration government

www.mhhe.com/bkm

bonds. John Ames, HFS's fixed-income manager, believes that a more rigorous approach is required if incremental returns are to be maximized.

The following table presents data relating to one set of corporate/government spread relationships (in basis points, b.p.) present in the market at a given date:

**CURRENT AND EXPECTED SPREADS AND DURATIONS
OF HIGH-GRADE CORPORATE BONDS (ONE-YEAR HORIZON)**

Bond Rating	Initial Spread over Governments	Expected Horizon Spread	Initial Duration	Expected Duration One Year from Now
Aaa	31 b.p.	31 b.p.	4 years	3.1 years
Aa	40 b.p.	50 b.p.	4 years	3.1 years

a. Recommend purchase of *either* Aaa *or* Aa bonds for a one-year investment horizon given a goal of maximizing incremental returns.

Ames chooses not to rely *solely* on initial spread relationships. His analytical framework considers a full range of other key variables likely to impact realized incremental returns including: call provisions, and potential changes in interest rates.

b. Describe variables, in addition to those identified above, that Ames should include in his analysis and explain how each of these could cause realized incremental returns to differ from those indicated by initial spread relationships.

18. The following questions appeared in past CFA examinations.

a. Which set of conditions will result in a bond with the greatest price volatility?
(1) A high coupon and a short maturity.
(2) A high coupon and a long maturity.
(3) A low coupon and a short maturity.
(4) A low coupon and a long maturity.

b. An investor who expects declining interest rates would be likely to purchase a bond that has a _____ coupon and a _____ term to maturity.
(1) Low, long
(2) High, short
(3) High, long
(4) Zero, long

c. With a zero-coupon bond:
(1) Duration equals the weighted average term to maturity.
(2) Term to maturity equals duration.
(3) Weighted average term to maturity equals the term to maturity.
(4) All of the above.

d. As compared with bonds selling at par, deep discount bonds will have:
(1) Greater reinvestment risk.
(2) Greater price volatility.
(3) Less call protection.
(4) None of the above.

19. The ability to *immunize* a bond portfolio is very desirable for bond portfolio managers in some instances.

a. Discuss the components of interest rate risk—that is, assuming a change in interest rates over time, explain the two risks faced by the holder of a bond.

b. Define immunization and discuss why a bond manager would immunize his or her portfolio.

c. Explain why a duration-matching strategy is a superior technique to a maturity-matching strategy for the minimization of interest rate risk.

d. Explain how contingent immunization, another bond portfolio management technique, differs from conventional immunization. Discuss why a bond portfolio manager would engage in contingent immunization.

20. You are the manager for the bond portfolio of a pension fund. The policies of the fund allow for the use of active strategies in managing the bond portfolio.

It appears that the economic cycle is beginning to mature, inflation is expected to accelerate, and, in an effort to contain the economic expansion, central bank policy is moving toward constraint. For each of the situations below, *state* which one of the two bonds you would prefer. *Briefly justify* your answer in each case.

a. Government of Canada (Canadian pay), 10% due in 2005, and priced at 98.75 to yield 10.50% to maturity;

or

Government of Canada (Canadian pay), 10% due in 2015, and priced at 91.75 to yield 11.19% to maturity.

b. Texas Power and Light Co., 7½% due in 2010, rated AAA, and priced at 85 to yield 10.1% to maturity;

or

Arizona Public Service Co., 7.45% due in 2010, rated A−, and priced at 75 to yield 12.1% to maturity.

c. Commonwealth Edison, 2¾% due in 2010, rated Baa, and priced at 61 to yield 12.2% to maturity;

or

Commonwealth Edison, 15⅜% due in 2010, rated Baa, and priced at 114 to yield 12.2% to maturity.

d. Shell Oil Co., 8¾% sinking fund debentures due in 2020, rated AAA (sinking fund begins in 2010 at par), and priced at 69 to yield 11.91% to maturity;

or

Warner-Lambert, 8⅞% sinking fund debentures due in 2020, rated AAA (sinking fund begins in 2014 at par), and priced at 75 to yield 11.31% to maturity.

e. Bank of Montreal (Canadian pay), 12% certificates of deposit due in 2004, rated AAA, and priced at 100 to yield 12% to maturity;

or

Bank of Montreal (Canadian pay), floating-rate notes due in 2010, rated AAA. Coupon currently set at 10.65% and priced at 100 (coupon adjusted semiannually to 0.5% above the three-month Government of Canada Treasury bill rate).

21. The following bond swaps could have been made in recent years as investors attempted to increase the total return on their portfolio.

From the information presented below, identify the reason(s) investors may have made each swap.

Action		Call	Price	YTM (%)
a. Sell	Baa1 Electric Pwr. 1st mtg. 10⅝% due 2009	108.24	95	11.71
Buy	Baa1 Electric Pwr. 1st mtg. 6⅜% due 2010	105.20	79	11.39
b. Sell	Aaa Phone Co. notes 8½% due 2010	101.50	90	10.02
Buy	U.S. Treasury notes 9½% due 2010	NC	97.15	9.78
c. Sell	Aa1 Apex Bank zero coupon due 2011	NC	35	10.51
Buy	Aa1 Apex Bank float rate notes due 2028	103.90	90	—
d. Sell	A1 Commonwealth Oil & Gas 1st mtg. 7½% due 2018	105.75	72	11.09
Buy	U.S. Treasury bond 7½% due 2024	NC	80.60	9.40
e. Sell	A1 Z mart convertible deb. 3% due 2018	103.90	62	6.92
Buy	A2 Lucky Ducks deb. 7¾% due 2024	109.86	65	12.43

22. A member of a firm's investment committee is very interested in learning about the management of fixed-income portfolios. He would like to know how fixed-income managers position portfolios to capitalize on their expectations concerning three factors which influence interest rates:

    a. Changes in the level of interest rates.
    b. Changes in yield spreads across/between sectors.
    c. Changes in yield spreads as to a particular instrument.

    Assuming that no investment policy limitations apply, formulate and describe a fixed-income portfolio management strategy for each of these factors that could be used to exploit a portfolio manager's expectations about that factor. (Note: Three strategies are required, one for each of the listed factors.)

23. Long-term Treasury bonds currently are selling at yields to maturity of nearly 8%. You expect interest rates to fall. The rest of the market thinks that they will remain unchanged over the coming year. In each question, choose the bond that will provide the higher capital gain if you are correct. *Briefly* explain your answer.

    a. (1) A Baa-rated bond with coupon rate 8% and time to maturity 20 years.
       (2) An Aaa-rated bond with coupon rate 8% and time to maturity 20 years.
    b. (1) An A-rated bond with coupon rate 4% and maturity 20 years, callable at 105.
       (2) An A-rated bond with coupon rate 8% and maturity 20 years, callable at 105.
    c. (1) A 6% coupon noncallable T-bond with maturity 20 years and YTM = 8%.
       (2) A 9% coupon noncallable T-bond with maturity 20 years and YTM = 8%.

24. Currently, the term structure is as follows: one-year bonds yield 7%, two-year bonds yield 8%, three-year bonds and greater maturity bonds all yield 9%. You are choosing between one-, two-, and three-year maturity bonds all paying *annual* coupons of 8%, once a year. Which bond should you buy if you strongly believe that at year-end the yield curve will be flat at 9%?

25. A fixed-income portfolio manager is unwilling to realize a rate of return of less than 3% annually over a five-year investment period on a portfolio currently valued at $1 million. Three years later, the interest rate is 8%. What is the trigger point of the portfolio at this time, that is, how low can the value of the portfolio fall before the manager will be forced to immunize to be assured of achieving the minimum acceptable return?

26. What type of interest rate swap would be appropriate for a corporation holding long-term assets that it funded with floating-rate bonds?

27. What type of interest rate swap would be appropriate for a speculator who believes interest rates soon will fall?

28. Several Investment Committee members have asked about interest rate swap agreements and how they are used in the management of domestic fixed-income portfolios.
    a. Define an interest rate swap and briefly describe the obligation of each party involved.
    b. Cite and explain two examples of how interest rate swaps could be used by a fixed-income portfolio manager to control risk or improve return.

29. A corporation has issued a $10 million issue of floating-rate bonds on which it pays an interest rate 1% over the LIBOR rate. The bonds are selling at par value. The firm is worried that rates are about to rise, and it would like to lock in a fixed interest rate on its borrowings. The firm sees that dealers in the swap market are offering swaps of LIBOR for 7%. What swap arrangement will convert the firm's borrowings to a synthetic fixed-rate loan? What interest rate will it pay on that synthetic fixed-rate loan?

30. A 30-year maturity bond has a 7% coupon rate, paid annually. It sells today for $867.42. A 20-year maturity bond has a 6.5% coupon rate, also paid annually. It sells today for $879.50. A bond market analyst forecasts that in five years, 25-year maturity bonds will sell at yields to maturity of 8% and that 15-year maturity bonds will sell at yields of 7.5%. Because the yield curve is upward sloping, the analyst believes that coupons will be invested in short-term securities at a rate of 6%. Which bond offers the higher expected rate of return over the five-year period?

31. *a.* Use a spreadsheet to calculate the durations of the two bonds in Spreadsheet 10.1 if the interest rate increases to 12%. Why does the duration of the coupon bond fall while that of the zero remains unchanged? [Hint: Examine what happens to the weights computed in column E.]
    b. Use the same spreadsheet to calculate the duration of the coupon bond if the coupon were 12% instead of 8%. Explain why the duration is lower. (Again, start by looking at column E.)

32. *a.* Footnote 2 presents the formula for the convexity of a bond. Build a spreadsheet to calculate the convexity of the 8% coupon bond in Spreadsheet 10.1 at the initial yield to maturity of 10%.
    b. What is the convexity of the zero-coupon bond?

WEBMASTER

Bonds

Many of the website for investors have a variety of bond calculators that are available. The calculators that are available on Yahoo's site are a good example of the type of calculators that are available. The calculators can be found at http://bonds.yahoo.com/calculator.html. The answers that you get with these calculators will vary slightly from values calculated on a financial calculator because of assumptions of receipt of the final coupon payment.

1. Use the "What Price Should I Pay Calculator", for the following conditions;

Yield to Maturity You Desire	6%
Face Value	1000
Coupon Rate	4.25%
Today's Market Rate	5.25%
Months to Maturity	60

What would be the market value?
What price would you need to pay to provide you 6%?

2. Use the "What is my current yield on coupon income received?" for the following conditions;

Bonds Price Today (% of Face)	102%
Face Value	1000
Coupon Rate	5.65%
Your Federal Tax Rate	36%
Your State Tax Rate	8%
Select corporate bond for type of bond	

What is your current yield before taxes?
What is your current yield after taxes?

SOLUTIONS TO 1. Interest rate: 0.09

	(B) Time until Payment (years)	(C) Payment	(D) Payment Discounted at 10%	(E) Weight	Column (B) times Column (E)
A. 8% coupon bond	1	80	73.394	0.0753	0.0753
	2	80	67.334	0.0691	0.1382
	3	1080	833.958	0.8556	2.5668
Sum:			974.687	1.0000	2.7803
B. Zero-coupon bond	1	0	0.000	0.0000	0.0000
	2	0	0.000	0.0000	0.0000
	3	1000	772.183	1.0000	3.0000
Sum:			772.183	1.0000	3.0000

The duration of the 8% coupon bond rises to 2.7803 years. Price increases to $974.687. The duration of the zero-coupon bond is unchanged at 3 years, although its price also increases when the interest rate falls.

2. *a.* If the interest rate increases from 9% to 9.05%, the bond price falls from $974.687 to $973.445. The percentage change in price is −0.127%.
   b. The duration formula would predict a price change of

   $$-\frac{2.7802}{1.09} \times .0005 = -.00127 = -.127\%$$

   which is the same answer that we obtained from direct computation in part (a).

3. The duration of a level perpetuity is $(1 + y)/y$ or $1 + 1/y$, which clearly falls as y increases. Tabulating duration as a function of y we get:

y	D
0.01 (i.e., 1%)	101 years
0.02	51
0.05	21
0.10	11
0.20	6
0.25	5
0.40	3.5

4. The perpetuity's duration now would be 1.08/0.08 = 13.5. We need to solve the following equation for w

   $$w \times 2 + (1 - w) \times 13.5 = 6$$

   Therefore, $w = 0.6522$.

5. *a.* The present value of the fund's obligation is $800,000/0.08 = $10 million. The duration is 13.5 years. Therefore, the fund should invest $10 million in zeros with a 13.5 year maturity. The face value of the zeros will be $10,000,000 \times 1.08^{13.5} = $28,263,159.
   b. When the interest rate increases to 8.1%, the present value of the fund's obligation drops to 800,000/0.081 = $9,876,543. The value of the zero-coupon bond falls by roughly the same amount, to $28,263,159/1.081^{13.5} = $9,875,835. The duration of the perpetual obligation falls to 1.081/0.081 = 13.346 years. The fund should sell the zero it currently holds and purchase $9,876,543 in zero-coupon bonds with maturity of 13.346 years.

6. Dedication would be more attractive. Cash flow matching eliminates the need for rebalancing and, thus, saves transaction costs.

7. Current price = $1,091.29
   Forecast price = $100 \times Annuity factor (10%, 18 years) + $1,000 \times PV factor (10%, 18 years)
   = $1,000
   The future value of reinvested coupons will be ($100 \times 1.08) + $100 = $208

   $$\text{The two-year return is } \frac{\$208 + (\$1,000 - \$1,091.29)}{\$1,091.29} = 0.107, \text{ or } 10.7\%$$

   The annualized rate of return over the two-year period would then be $(1.107)^{1/2} - 1 = .052$, or 5.2%.

8. The trigger point is the present value of the minimum acceptable terminal value:
   $10 million/$(1.08)^3$ = $7.94 million

9. The manager would like to hold on to the money market securities because of their attractive relative pricing compared to other short-term assets. However, there is an expectation that rates will fall. The manager can hold this *particular* portfolio of short-term assets and still benefit from the drop in interest rates by entering a swap to pay a short-term interest rate and receive a fixed interest rate. The resulting synthetic fixed-rate portfolio will increase in value if rates do fall.

www.mhhe.com/bkm

PART FOUR

SECURITY ANALYSIS

Tell your friends or relatives that you are studying investments and they will ask you, "What stocks should I buy?" This is the question at the heart of security analysis. How do analysts choose the stocks and other securities to hold in their portfolios?

Security analysis requires a wide mix of skills. You need to be a decent economist with a good grasp of both macroeconomics and microeconomics, the former to help you form forecasts of the general direction of the market and the latter to help you assess the relative position of particular industries or firms. You need a good sense of demographic and social trends to help identify industries with bright prospects. You need to be a quick study of the ins and outs of particular industries to choose the firms that will succeed within each industry. You need a good accounting background to analyze the financial statements that firms

provide to the public. You also need to have mastered corporate finance, since security analysis at its core is the ability to value a firm. In short, a good security analyst will be a generalist, with a grasp of the widest range of financial issues. This is where there is the biggest premium on "putting it all together."

The chapters in Part Four are an introduction to security analysis. We will provide you with a "top-down" approach to the subject, starting with an overview of international, macroeconomic, and industry issues, and only then progressing to the analysis of particular firms. Our treatment of firm valuation is primarily focused on fundamental analysis, but we also devote a chapter to technical analysis later in the text. After reading these chapters, you will have a good sense of the various techniques used to analyze stocks and the stock market.

11   Macroeconomic and Industry Analysis

12   Equity Valuation

13   Financial Statement Analysis

McGraw-Hill / Irwin presents
Investments online

www.mhhe.com/bkm

11

MACROECONOMIC AND INDUSTRY ANALYSIS

AFTER STUDYING THIS CHAPTER YOU SHOULD BE ABLE TO:

> Predict the effect of monetary and fiscal policies on key macroeconomic variables such as gross domestic product, interest rates, and the inflation rate.

> Use leading, coincident, and lagging economic indicators to describe and predict the economy's path through the business cycle.

> Predict which industries will be more or less sensitive to business cycle fluctuations.

> Analyze the effect of industry life cycles and structure on industry earnings prospects over time.

To determine a proper price for a firm's stock, the security analyst must forecast the dividends and earnings that can be expected from the firm. This is the heart of *fundamental analysis*, that is, the analysis of determinants of value such as earnings prospects. Ultimately, the business success of the firm determines the dividends it can pay to shareholders and the price it will command in the stock market. Because the prospects of the firm are tied to those of the broader economy, however, valuation analyses must consider the business environment in which the firm operates. For some firms, macroeconomic and industry circumstances might have a greater influence on profits than the firm's relative performance within its industry. In other words, investors need to keep the big economic picture in mind.

Therefore, in analyzing a firm's prospects it often makes sense to start with the broad economic environment, examining the state of the aggregate economy and even the international economy. From there, one considers the implications of the outside environment on the industry in which the firm operates. Finally, the firm's position within the industry is examined.

This chapter examines the broad-based aspects of fundamental analysis—macroeconomic and industry analysis. The following two chapters cover firm-specific analysis. We begin with a discussion of international factors relevant to firm performance and move on to an overview of the significance of the key variables usually used to summarize the state of the economy. We then discuss government macroeconomic policy and the determination of interest rates. We conclude the analysis of the macroeconomic environment with a discussion of business cycles. Next, we move to industry analysis, treating issues concerning the sensitivity of the firm to the business cycle, the typical life cycle of an industry, and strategic issues that affect industry performance.

**fundamental
analysis**

The analysis of
determinants of firm
value, such as
prospects for earnings
and dividends.

11.1 THE GLOBAL ECONOMY

A top-down analysis of a firm's prospects must start with the global economy. The international economy might affect a firm's export prospects, the price competition it faces from foreign competitors, or the profits it makes on investments abroad. Certainly, despite the fact that the economies of most countries are linked in a global macroeconomy, there is considerable variation in the economic performance across countries at any time. Consider, for example, Table 11.1, which presents data on several so-called emerging economies. The table documents striking variation in growth rates of economic output in 2001. For example, while the Indian economy grew by 5.3% in 2001, Turkish output fell by 7.1%. Similarly, there has been considerable variation in stock market returns in these countries in recent years.

These data illustrate that the national economic environment can be a crucial determinant of industry performance. It is far harder for businesses to succeed in a contracting economy than in an expanding one. This observation highlights the role of a big-picture macroeconomic analysis as a fundamental part of the investment process.

In addition, the global environment presents political risks of far greater magnitude than are typically encountered in U.S.-based investments. In the last decade, we have seen several instances where political developments had major impacts on economic prospects. For example, in 1992 and 1993, the Mexican stock market responded dramatically to changing assessments regarding the prospect of the passage of the North American Free Trade Agreement by the U.S. Congress. In 1997, the Hong Kong stock market was extremely sensitive to political developments leading up to the transfer of governance to China. The biggest international economic story in late 1997 and 1998 was the turmoil in several Asian economies, notably Thailand, Indonesia, and South Korea. These episodes also highlighted the close interplay between politics and economics, as both currency and stock values swung with enormous volatility in response to developments concerning the prospects for aid for these countries from the International Monetary Fund. In August 1998, the shock waves following Russia's devaluation of the ruble and default on some of its debt created havoc in world security markets, ultimately requiring a rescue of the giant hedge fund Long Term Capital Management to avoid further major disruptions. In the immediate future, the degree to which the European

TABLE **11.1** Economic performance in selected emerging markets	Country	Growth in Real GDP, 2001	Stock Market Return, 2001	
			Local Currency	$ Terms
	Brazil	0.3	−16.1	−31.5
	China	7.0	−29.8	−29.8
	Hong Kong	−0.3	−27.4	−27.4
	Hungary	3.7	−1.9	0.4
	India	5.3	−15.7	−18.4
	Indonesia	3.5	1.7	−5.2
	Israel	−2.7	−10.5	−20.2
	Mexico	−1.6	16.4	21.6
	Poland	0.8	−12.3	−12.0
	Russia	4.9	110.3	97.5
	Singapore	−7.0	−13.1	−17.8
	South Africa	0.1	28.0	−17.2
	South Korea	1.8	40.9	36.0
	Taiwan	−4.2	15.7	9.5
	Turkey	−7.1	35.2	−34.1

Source: *The Economist,* January 19, 2002.

Monetary Union is successful will again illustrate the important interaction between the political and economic arenas.

Of course, political developments can be positive, as well. For example, the end of apartheid in South Africa and the resultant end of the economic embargo seemed to portend great growth for that economy. These political developments (and the bumps along the way) offer significant opportunities to make or lose money.

Other political issues that are less sensational but still extremely important to economic growth and investment returns include issues of protectionism and trade policy, the free flow of capital, and the status of a nation's workforce.

One obvious factor that affects the international competitiveness of a country's industries is the exchange rate between that country's currency and other currencies. The **exchange rate** is the rate at which domestic currency can be converted into foreign currency. For example, in April 2002, it took about 130 Japanese yen to purchase one U.S. dollar. We would say that the exchange rate is ¥130 per dollar, or equivalently, $0.0077 per yen.

As exchange rates fluctuate, the dollar value of goods priced in foreign currency similarly fluctuates. For example, in 1980, the dollar–yen exchange rate was about $0.0045 per yen. Since the exchange rate in 2002 was $0.0077 per yen, a U.S. citizen would have needed about 1.7 times as many dollars in 2002 to buy a product selling for ¥10,000 as would have been required in 1980. If the Japanese producer were to maintain a fixed yen price for its product, the price expressed in U.S. dollars would have to increase by 70%. This would make Japanese products more expensive to U.S. consumers, however, and result in lost sales. Obviously, appreciation of the yen creates a problem for Japanese producers like automakers that must compete with U.S. producers.

Figure 11.1 shows the change in the purchasing power of the U.S. dollar relative to the purchasing power of the currencies of several major industrial countries in the period between 1986 and 2001. (The Italian, German, and French currencies have since been subsumed into the euro, the common currency of the 12 members of the European Union.) The ratio of purchasing powers is called the "real" or inflation-adjusted exchange rate. The change in the real exchange rate measures how much more or less expensive foreign goods have become to

exchange rate

The rate at which domestic currency can be converted into foreign currency.

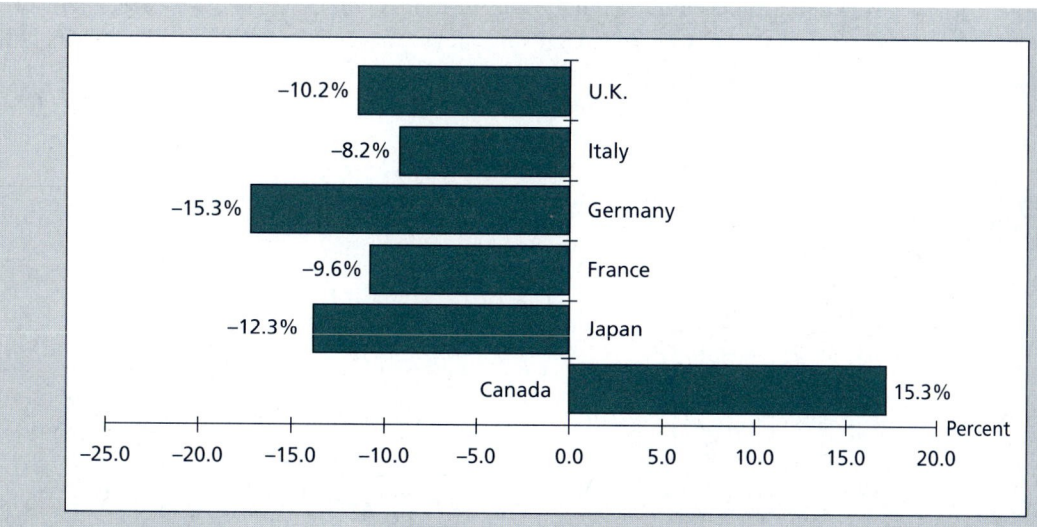

FIGURE 11.1

Change in real exchange rate: Dollar versus major currencies, 1986–2001

U.S. citizens, accounting for both exchange rate fluctuations and inflation differentials across countries. A positive value in Figure 11.1 means that the dollar has gained purchasing power relative to another currency; a negative number indicates a depreciating dollar. Therefore, the figure shows that goods priced in terms of the Japanese, U.K., and former German, Italian, or French currencies became more expensive to U.S. consumers in the last 15 years but that goods priced in Canadian dollars became cheaper. Conversely, goods priced in U.S. dollars became more affordable to Japanese consumers, but more expensive to Canadian consumers.

11.2 THE DOMESTIC MACROECONOMY

The macroeconomy is the environment in which all firms operate. The importance of the macroeconomy in determining investment performance is illustrated in Figure 11.2, which compares the level of the S&P 500 stock price index to estimates of earnings per share of the S&P 500 companies. The graph shows that stock prices tend to rise along with earnings. While the exact ratio of stock price to earnings per share varies with factors such as interest rates, risk, inflation rates, and other variables, the graph does illustrate that, as a general rule, the ratio has tended to be in the range of 10 to 20. Given "normal" price-to-earnings ratios, we would expect the S&P 500 Index to fall within these boundaries. While the earnings-multiplier rule clearly is not perfect—note the dramatic increase in the P/E multiple in the 1990s—it also seems clear that the level of the broad market and aggregate earnings do trend together. Thus, the first step in forecasting the performance of the broad market is to assess the status of the economy as a whole.

The ability to forecast the macroeconomy can translate into spectacular investment performance. But it is not enough to forecast the macroeconomy well. One must forecast it *better* than one's competitors to earn abnormal profits.

In this section, we will review some of the key economic statistics used to describe the state of the macroeconomy.

Gross Domestic Product

gross domestic product

The market value of goods and services produced over a period of time.

Gross domestic product, or GDP, is the measure of the economy's total production of goods and services. Rapidly growing GDP indicates an expanding economy with ample opportunity for a firm to increase sales. Another popular measure of the economy's output is *industrial production*. This statistic provides a measure of economic activity more narrowly focused on the manufacturing side of the economy.

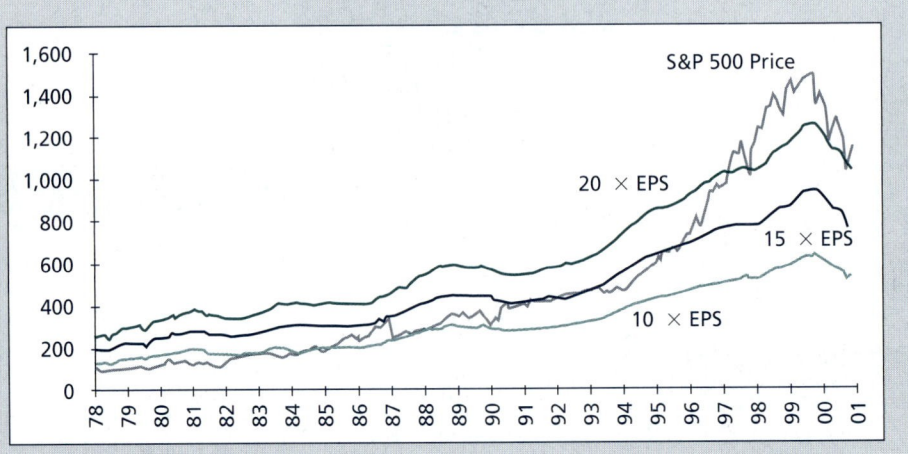

FIGURE **11.2**

S&P 500 Index versus earnings per share estimate

Source: Thomson Financial, *Global Comments*, December 3, 2001.

Employment

The **unemployment rate** is the percentage of the total labor force (i.e., those who are either working or actively seeking employment) yet to find work. The unemployment rate measures the extent to which the economy is operating at full capacity. The unemployment rate is a statistic related to workers only, but further insight into the strength of the economy can be gleaned from the employment rate of other factors of production. Analysts also look at the factory *capacity utilization rate,* which is the ratio of actual output from factories to potential output.

> **unemployment rate**
>
> The ratio of the number of people classified as unemployed to the total labor force.

Inflation

Inflation is the rate at which the general level of prices is rising. High rates of inflation often are associated with "overheated" economies, that is, economies where the demand for goods and services is outstripping productive capacity, which leads to upward pressure on prices. Most governments walk a fine line in their economic policies. They hope to stimulate their economies enough to maintain nearly full employment, but not so much as to bring on inflationary pressures. The perceived trade-off between inflation and unemployment is at the heart of many macroeconomic policy disputes. There is considerable room for disagreement as to the relative costs of these policies as well as the economy's relative vulnerability to these pressures at any particular time.

> **inflation**
>
> The rate at which the general level of prices for goods and services is rising.

Interest Rates

High interest rates reduce the present value of future cash flows, thereby reducing the attractiveness of investment opportunities. For this reason, real interest rates are key determinants of business investment expenditures. Demand for housing and high-priced consumer durables such as automobiles, which are commonly financed, also is highly sensitive to interest rates because interest rates affect interest payments. In Section 11.3 we will examine the determinants of real interest rates.

Budget Deficit

The **budget deficit** of the federal government is the difference between government spending and revenues. Any budgetary shortfall must be offset by government borrowing. Large amounts of government borrowing can force up interest rates by increasing the total demand for credit in the economy. Economists generally believe excessive government borrowing will "crowd out" private borrowing and investing by forcing up interest rates and choking off business investment.

> **budget deficit**
>
> The amount by which government spending exceeds government revenues.

Sentiment

Consumers' and producers' optimism or pessimism concerning the economy are important determinants of economic performance. If consumers have confidence in their future income levels, for example, they will be more willing to spend on big-ticket items. Similarly, businesses will increase production and inventory levels if they anticipate higher demand for their products. In this way, beliefs influence how much consumption and investment will be pursued and affect the aggregate demand for goods and services.

1. **Consider an economy where the dominant industry is automobile production for domestic consumption as well as export. Now suppose the auto market is hurt by an increase in the length of time people use their cars before replacing them. Describe the probable effects of this change on (*a*) GDP, (*b*) unemployment, (c) the government budget deficit, and (*d*) interest rates.**

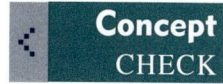

Concept
CHECK

11.3 | INTEREST RATES

The level of interest rates is perhaps the most important macroeconomic factor to consider in one's investment analysis. Forecasts of interest rates directly affect the forecast of returns in the fixed-income market. If your expectation is that rates will increase by more than the consensus view, you will want to shy away from longer term fixed-income securities. Similarly, increases in interest rates tend to be bad news for the stock market. Unanticipated increases in rates generally are associated with stock market declines. Thus, a superior technique to forecast rates would be of immense value to an investor attempting to determine the best asset allocation for his or her portfolio.

Unfortunately, forecasting interest rates is one of the most notoriously difficult parts of applied macroeconomics. Nonetheless, we do have a good understanding of the fundamental factors that determine the level of interest rates:

1. The supply of funds from savers, primarily households.
2. The demand for funds from businesses to be used to finance physical investments in plant, equipment, and inventories.
3. The government's net supply and/or demand for funds as modified by actions of the Federal Reserve Bank.
4. The expected rate of inflation.

Although there are many different interest rates economywide (as many as there are types of securities), these rates tend to move together, so economists frequently talk as though there were a single representative rate. We can use this abstraction to gain some insights into determining the real rate of interest if we consider the supply and demand curves for funds.

Figure 11.3 shows a downward-sloping demand curve and an upward-sloping supply curve. On the horizontal axis, we measure the quantity of funds, and on the vertical axis, we measure the real rate of interest.

The supply curve slopes up from left to right because the higher the real interest rate, the greater the supply of household savings. The assumption is that at higher real interest rates, households will choose to postpone some current consumption and set aside or invest more of their disposable income for future use.

The demand curve slopes down from left to right because the lower the real interest rate, the more businesses will want to invest in physical capital. Assuming that businesses rank projects by the expected real return on invested capital, firms will undertake more projects the lower the real interest rate on the funds needed to finance those projects.

FIGURE **11.3**

Determination of the equilibrium real rate of interest

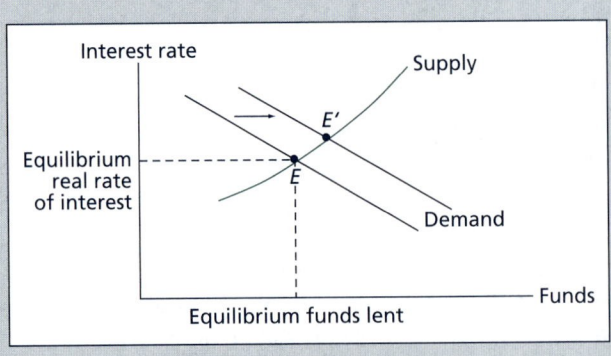

Equilibrium is at the point of intersection of the supply and demand curves, point E in Figure 11.3.

The government and the central bank (the Federal Reserve) can shift these supply and demand curves either to the right or to the left through fiscal and monetary policies. For example, consider an increase in the government's budget deficit. This increases the government's borrowing demand and shifts the demand curve to the right, which causes the equilibrium real interest rate to rise to point E'. That is, a forecast that indicates higher than previously expected government borrowing increases expectations of future interest rates. The Fed can offset such a rise through an increase in the money supply, which will increase the supply of loanable funds, and shift the supply curve to the right.

Thus, while the fundamental determinants of the real interest rate are the propensity of households to save and the expected productivity (or we could say profitability) of firms' investment in physical capital, the real rate can be affected as well by government fiscal and monetary policies.

The supply and demand framework illustrated in Figure 11.3 is a reasonable first approximation to the determination of the real interest rate. To obtain the *nominal* interest rate, one needs to add the expected inflation rate to the equilibrium real rate. As we discussed in Section 5.4, the inflation premium is necessary for investors to maintain a given real rate of return on their investments.

While monetary policy can clearly affect nominal interest rates, there is considerable controversy concerning its ability to affect real rates. There is widespread agreement that, in the long run, the ultimate impact of an increase in the money supply is an increase in prices with no permanent impact on real economic activity. A rapid rate of growth in the money supply, therefore, ultimately would result in a correspondingly high inflation rate and nominal interest rate, but it would have no sustained impact on the real interest rate. However, in the shorter run, changes in the money supply may well have an effect on the real interest rate.

11.4   DEMAND AND SUPPLY SHOCKS

A useful way to organize your analysis of the factors that might influence the macroeconomy is to classify any impact as a supply or demand shock. A **demand shock** is an event that affects the demand for goods and services in the economy. Examples of positive demand shocks are reductions in tax rates, increases in the money supply, increases in government spending, or increases in foreign export demand. A **supply shock** is an event that influences production capacity and costs. Examples of supply shocks are changes in the price of imported oil; freezes, floods, or droughts that might destroy large quantities of agricultural crops; changes in the educational level of an economy's workforce; or changes in the wage rates at which the labor force is willing to work.

Demand shocks usually are characterized by aggregate output moving in the same direction as interest rates and inflation. For example, a big increase in government spending will tend to stimulate the economy and increase GDP. It also might increase interest rates by increasing the demand for borrowed funds by the government as well as by businesses that might desire to borrow to finance new ventures. Finally, it could increase the inflation rate if the demand for goods and services is raised to a level at or beyond the total productive capacity of the economy.

Supply shocks usually are characterized by aggregate output moving in the opposite direction as inflation and interest rates. For example, a big increase in the price of imported oil will be inflationary because costs of production will rise, which eventually will lead to increases in prices of finished goods. The increase in inflation rates over the near term can lead to higher

demand shock

An event that affects the demand for goods and services in the economy.

supply shock

An event that influences production capacity and costs in the economy.

nominal interest rates. Against this background, aggregate output will be falling. With raw materials more expensive, the productive capacity of the economy is reduced, as is the ability of individuals to purchase goods at now-higher prices. GDP, therefore, tends to fall.

How can we relate this framework to investment analysis? You want to identify the industries that will be most helped or hurt in any macroeconomic scenario you envision. For example, if you forecast a tightening of the money supply, you might want to avoid industries such as automobile producers that might be hurt by the likely increase in interest rates. We caution you again that these forecasts are no easy task. Macroeconomic predictions are notoriously unreliable. And again, you must be aware that in all likelihood your forecast will be made using only publicly available information. Any investment advantage you have will be a result only of better analysis—not better information.

The nearby box gives an example of how investment advice is tied to macroeconomic forecasts. The article focuses on the different advice being given by two prominent analysts with differing views of the economy. The relatively bearish strategists believe the economy is about to slow down. As a result, they recommend asset allocation toward the fixed-income market, which will benefit if interest rates fall in a recession. Within the stock market, they recommend industries with below-average sensitivity to macroeconomic conditions. Two recession-resistant or "defensive" investments specifically cited are beverage and health care stocks, both of which are expected to outperform the rest of the market as investors become aware of the slowdown in growth. Conversely, the optimistic analysts recommend investments with greater sensitivity to the business cycle.

11.5 FEDERAL GOVERNMENT POLICY

As the previous section would suggest, the government has two broad classes of macroeconomic tools—those that affect the demand for goods and services and those that affect their supply. For much of postwar history, demand-side policy has been of primary interest. The focus has been on government spending, tax levels, and monetary policy. Since the 1980s, however, increasing attention has also been focused on supply-side economics. Broadly interpreted, supply-side concerns have to do with enhancing the productive capacity of the economy, rather than increasing the demand for the goods and services the economy can produce. In practice, supply-side economists have focused on the appropriateness of the incentives to work, innovate, and take risks that result from our system of taxation. However, issues such as national policies on education, infrastructure (such as communication and transportation systems), and research and development also are properly regarded as part of supply-side macroeconomic policy.

Fiscal Policy

fiscal policy

The use of government spending and taxing for the specific purpose of stabilizing the economy.

Fiscal policy refers to the government's spending and tax actions and is part of "demand-side management." Fiscal policy is probably the most direct way either to stimulate or to slow the economy. Decreases in government spending directly deflate the demand for goods and services. Similarly, increases in tax rates immediately siphon income from consumers and result in fairly rapid decreases in consumption.

Ironically, although fiscal policy has the most immediate impact on the economy, the formulation and implementation of such policy is usually painfully slow and involved. This is because fiscal policy requires enormous amounts of compromise between the executive and legislative branches. Tax and spending policy must be initiated and voted on by Congress, which requires considerable political negotiations, and any legislation passed must be signed by the president, requiring more negotiation. Thus, while the impact of fiscal policy is relatively

Conflicting Economic Signals

Despite last week's return to optimism in the stock market, nagging recession concerns continue to confound Wall Street.

With conflicting economic signals, investors find themselves in a quandary. Is the economy rapidly dropping into recession, or close to one? Or is it simply taking a modest breath before strengthening later this year?

The recession quandary has split Wall Street strategists. One camp, which includes Charles Clough, chief strategist at Merrill Lynch & Co., argues that the economy is slowing much faster than realized. He says rising corporate inventories and a spent consumer are contributing to a steepening slowdown. Moreover, the Federal Reserve is moving too slowly to stave off a period of extended sluggishness, and earnings will probably suffer more than anticipated this year.

The other camp, which includes Abby J. Cohen, market strategist at Goldman, Sachs & Co., believes that the economy will rebound later this year.

EMPHASIZING FINANCIAL STOCKS

The divergent views play a crucial role in near-term investing decisions. Mr. Clough has trimmed his exposure to the stock market in favor of bonds and emphasizes financial stocks, which would benefit in a low-rate environment.

Ms. Cohen, conversely, maintains a healthy exposure to the stock market and emphasizes not just financials, but also economically sensitive stocks such as autos and housing-related stocks. She further expects to emphasize later-cyclical commodity stocks as the year unfolds and the economic pace quickens.

James Weiss, deputy chief investment officer for growth equities at State Street in Boston, and David Shulman, chief strategist at Salomon Brothers, concur with much of Mr. Clough's analysis of the economy. Mr. Weiss says the recent uptick in cyclical stocks should be mostly ignored, and he favors steadier growth in defensive sectors like health care and beverages.

SOURCE: Dave Kansas, "Conflicting Economic Signals Are Dividing Strategist," *The Wall Street Journal*, February 26, 1996. Excerpted by permission of Dow Jones & Company, Inc. via Copyright Clearance Center, Inc. © 1996 Dow Jones & Company, Inc. All Rights Reserved Worldwide.

---

immediate, its formulation is so cumbersome that fiscal policy cannot in practice be used to fine-tune the economy.

Moreover, much of government spending, such as that for Medicare or Social Security, is nondiscretionary, meaning that it is determined by formula rather than policy and cannot be changed in response to economic conditions. This places even more rigidity into the formulation of fiscal policy.

A common way to summarize the net impact of government fiscal policy is to look at the government's budget deficit or surplus, which is simply the difference between revenues and expenditures. A large deficit means the government is spending considerably more than it is taking in by way of taxes. The net effect is to increase the demand for goods (via spending) by more than it reduces the demand for goods (via taxes), therefore, stimulating the economy.

Monetary Policy

Monetary policy refers to the manipulation of the money supply to affect the macroeconomy and is the other main leg of demand-side policy. Monetary policy works largely through its impact on interest rates. Increases in the money supply lower short-term interest rates, ultimately encouraging investment and consumption demand. Over longer periods, however, most economists believe a higher money supply leads only to a higher price level and does not have a permanent effect on economic activity. Thus, the monetary authorities face a difficult balancing act. Expansionary monetary policy probably will lower interest rates and thereby stimulate investment and some consumption demand in the short run, but these circumstances ultimately will lead only to higher prices. The stimulation/inflation trade-off is implicit in all debate over proper monetary policy.

monetary policy

Actions taken by the Board of Governors of the Federal Reserve System to influence the money supply or interest rates.

389

Fiscal policy is cumbersome to implement but has a fairly direct impact on the economy, while monetary policy is easily formulated and implemented but has a less immediate impact. Monetary policy is determined by the Board of Governors of the Federal Reserve System. Board members are appointed by the president for 14-year terms and are reasonably insulated from political pressure. The board is small enough and often sufficiently dominated by its chairperson that policy can be formulated and modulated relatively easily.

Implementation of monetary policy also is quite direct. The most widely used tool is the open market operation, in which the Fed buys or sells Treasury bonds for its own account. When the Fed buys securities, it simply writes a check, thereby increasing the money supply. (Unlike us, the Fed can pay for the securities without drawing down funds at a bank account.) Conversely, when the Fed sells a security, the money paid for it leaves the money supply. Open market operations occur daily, allowing the Fed to fine-tune its monetary policy.

Other tools at the Fed's disposal are the *discount rate,* which is the interest rate it charges banks on short-term loans, and the *reserve requirement,* which is the fraction of deposits that banks must hold as cash on hand or as deposits with the Fed. Reductions in the discount rate signal a more expansionary monetary policy. Lowering reserve requirements allows banks to make more loans with each dollar of deposits and stimulates the economy by increasing the effective money supply.

Monetary policy affects the economy in a more roundabout way than fiscal policy. While fiscal policy directly stimulates or dampens the economy, monetary policy works largely through its impact on interest rates. Increases in the money supply lower interest rates, which stimulate investment demand. As the quantity of money in the economy increases, investors will find that their portfolios of assets include too much money. They will rebalance their portfolios by buying securities such as bonds, forcing bond prices up and interest rates down. In the longer run, individuals may increase their holdings of stocks as well and ultimately buy real assets, which stimulates consumption demand directly. The ultimate effect of monetary policy on investment and consumption demand, however, is less immediate than that of fiscal policy.

2. **Suppose the government wants to stimulate the economy without increasing interest rates. What combination of fiscal and monetary policy might accomplish this goal?**

Supply-Side Policies

Fiscal and monetary policy are demand-oriented tools that affect the economy by stimulating the total demand for goods and services. The implicit belief is that the economy will not by itself arrive at a full employment equilibrium and that macroeconomic policy can push the economy toward this goal. In contrast, supply-side policies treat the issue of the productive capacity of the economy. The goal is to create an environment in which workers and owners of capital have the maximum incentive and ability to produce and develop goods.

Supply-side economists also pay considerable attention to tax policy. While demand-siders look at the effect of taxes on consumption demand, supply-siders focus on incentives and marginal tax rates. They argue that lowering tax rates will elicit more investment and improve incentives to work, thereby enhancing economic growth. Some go so far as to claim that reductions in tax rates can lead to increases in tax revenues because the lower tax rates will cause the economy and the revenue tax base to grow by more than the tax rate is reduced.

3. **Large tax cuts in the 1980s were followed by rapid growth in GDP. How would demand-side and supply-side economists differ in their interpretations of this phenomenon?**

11.6 ┊ BUSINESS CYCLES

We've looked at the tools the government uses to fine-tune the economy, attempting to maintain low unemployment and low inflation. Despite these efforts, economies repeatedly seem to pass through good and bad times. One determinant of the broad asset allocation decision of many analysts is a forecast of whether the macroeconomy is improving or deteriorating. A forecast that differs from the market consensus can have a major impact on investment strategy.

The Business Cycle

The economy recurrently experiences periods of expansion and contraction, although the length and depth of these cycles can be irregular. These recurring patterns of recession and recovery are called **business cycles.** Figure 11.4 presents graphs of several measures of production and output for the years 1967–2001. The production series all show clear variation around a generally rising trend. The bottom graph of capacity utilization also evidences a clear cyclical (although irregular) pattern.

    The transition points across cycles are called peaks and troughs, labeled P and T at the top of the graph. A **peak** is the transition from the end of an expansion to the start of a contraction. A **trough** occurs at the bottom of a recession just as the economy enters a recovery. The shaded areas in Figure 11.4 all represent periods of recession.

    As the economy passes through different stages of the business cycle, the relative profitability of different industry groups might be expected to vary. For example, at a trough, just before the economy begins to recover from a recession, one would expect that **cyclical industries,** those with above-average sensitivity to the state of the economy, would tend to outperform other industries. Examples of cyclical industries are producers of durable goods, such as automobiles or washing machines. Because purchases of these goods can be deferred during a recession, sales are particularly sensitive to macroeconomic conditions. Other cyclical industries are producers of capital goods, that is, goods used by other firms to produce their own products. When demand is slack, few companies will be expanding and purchasing capital goods. Therefore, the capital goods industry bears the brunt of a slowdown but does well in an expansion.

    In contrast to cyclical firms, **defensive industries** have little sensitivity to the business cycle. These are industries that produce goods for which sales and profits are least sensitive to the state of the economy. Defensive industries include food producers and processors, pharmaceutical firms, and public utilities. These industries will outperform others when the economy enters a recession.

    The cyclical/defensive classification corresponds well to the notion of systematic or market risk introduced in our discussion of portfolio theory. When perceptions about the health of the economy become more optimistic, for example, the prices of most stocks will increase as forecasts of profitability rise. Because the cyclical firms are most sensitive to such developments, their stock prices will rise the most. Thus, firms in cyclical industries will tend to have high-beta stocks. In general then, stocks of cyclical firms will show the best results when economic news is positive, but they will also show the worst results when that news is bad. Conversely, defensive firms will have low betas and performance that is relatively unaffected by overall market conditions.

    If your assessments of the state of the business cycle were reliably more accurate than those of other investors, choosing between cyclical and defensive industries would be easy. You would choose cyclical industries when you were relatively more optimistic about the economy, and you would choose defensive firms when you were relatively more pessimistic. As we know from our discussion of efficient markets, however, attractive investment choices will

business cycles

Repetitive cycles of recession and recovery.

peak

The transition from the end of an expansion to the start of a contraction.

trough

The transition point between recession and recovery.

cyclical industries

Industries with above-average sensitivity to the state of the economy.

defensive industries

Industries with below-average sensitivity to the state of the economy.

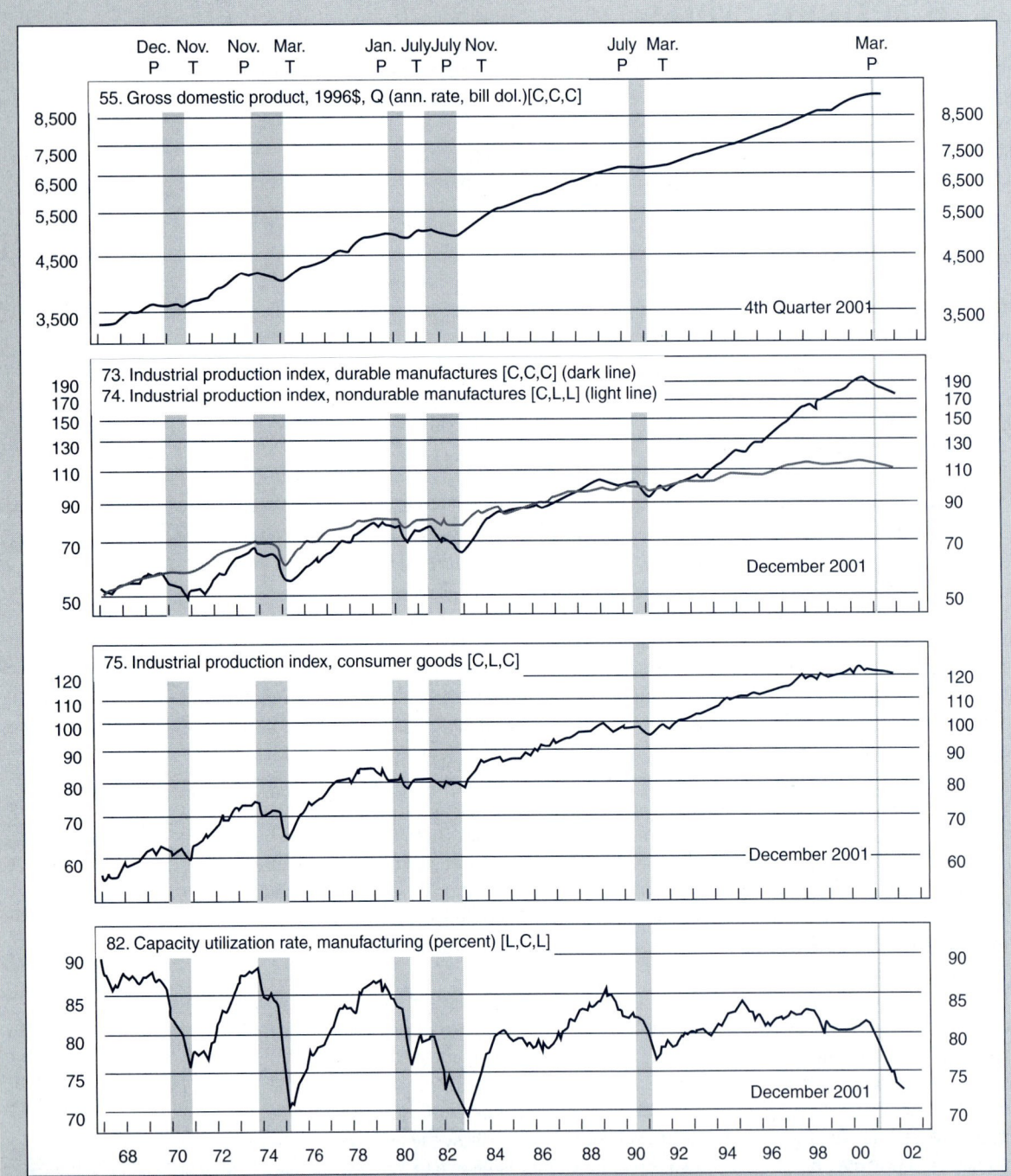

FIGURE **11.4**

Cyclical indicators, 1967–2001

Source: *Business Cycle Indicators*, The Conference Board, February 2002.

rarely be obvious. It usually is not apparent that a recession or expansion has started or ended until several months after the fact. With hindsight, the transitions from expansion to recession and back might be apparent, but it is often quite difficult to say whether the economy is heating up or slowing down at any moment.

Economic Indicators

Given the cyclical nature of the business cycle, it is not surprising that to some extent the cycle can be predicted. The Conference Board publishes a set of cyclical indicators to help forecast, measure, and interpret short-term fluctuations in economic activity. **Leading economic indicators** are those economic series that tend to rise or fall in advance of the rest of the economy. Coincident and lagging indicators, as their names suggest, move in tandem with or somewhat after the broad economy.

Ten series are grouped into a widely followed composite index of leading economic indicators. Similarly, four coincident and seven lagging indicators form separate indexes. The composition of these indexes appears in Table 11.2.

Figure 11.5 graphs these three series over the period 1958–2001. The numbers on the charts near the turning points of each series indicate the length of the lead time or lag time (in months) from the turning point to the designated peak or trough of the corresponding business cycle. While the index of leading indicators consistently turns before the rest of the economy, the lead time is somewhat erratic. Moreover, the lead time for peaks is consistently longer than that for troughs.

leading economic indicators

Economic series that tend to rise or fall in advance of the rest of the economy.

TABLE **11.2** Indexes of economic indicators	
	A. Leading indicators 1. Average weekly hours of production workers (manufacturing). 2. Initial claims for unemployment insurance. 3. Manufacturers' new orders (consumer goods and materials industries). 4. Vendor performance—slower deliveries diffusion index. 5. New orders for nondefense capital goods. 6. New private housing units authorized by local building permits. 7. Yield curve: spread between 10-year T-bond yield and federal funds rate. 8. Stock prices, 500 common stocks. 9. Money supply (M2). 10. Index of consumer expectations. **B. Coincident indicators** 1. Employees on nonagricultural payrolls. 2. Personal income less transfer payments. 3. Industrial production. 4. Manufacturing and trade sales. **C. Lagging indicators** 1. Average duration of unemployment. 2. Ratio of trade inventories to sales. 3. Change in index of labor cost per unit of output. 4. Average prime rate charged by banks. 5. Commercial and industrial loans outstanding. 6. Ratio of consumer installment credit outstanding to personal income. 7. Change in consumer price index for services.

Source: *Business Cycle Indicators,* The Conference Board, February 2002.

FIGURE **11.5**

Indexes of leading, coincident, and lagging indicators

Source: *Business Cycle Indicators,* The Conference Board, February 2002.

The stock market price index is a leading indicator. This is as it should be, as stock prices are forward-looking predictors of future profitability. Unfortunately, this makes the series of leading indicators much less useful for investment policy—by the time the series predicts an upturn, the market has already made its move. While the business cycle may be somewhat predictable, the stock market may not be. This is just one more manifestation of the efficient market hypothesis.

The money supply is another leading indicator. This makes sense in light of our earlier discussion concerning the lags surrounding the effects of monetary policy on the economy. An expansionary monetary policy can be observed fairly quickly, but it might not affect the economy for several months. Therefore, today's monetary policy might well predict future economic activity.

Other leading indicators focus directly on decisions made today that will affect production in the near future. For example, manufacturers' new orders for goods, contracts and orders for plant and equipment, and housing starts all signal a coming expansion in the economy.

A wide range of economic indicators are released to the public on a regular "economic calendar." Table 11.3 lists the public announcement dates and sources for about 20 statistics of

TABLE **11.3** Economic calendar	Statistic	Release Date*	Source
	Auto and truck sales	2nd of month	Commerce Department
	Business inventories	15th of month	Commerce Department
	Construction spending	1st business day of month	Commerce Department
	Consumer confidence	Last Tuesday of month	Conference Board
	Consumer credit	5th business day of month	Federal Reserve Board
	Consumer price index (CPI)	13th of month	Bureau of Labor Statistics
	Durable goods orders	26th of month	Commerce Department
	Employment cost index	End of first month of quarter	Bureau of Labor Statistics
	Employment record (unemployment, average workweek, nonfarm payrolls)	1st Friday of month	Bureau of Labor Statistics
	Existing home sales	25th of month	National Association of Realtors
	Factory orders	1st business day of month	Commerce Department
	Gross domestic product	3rd–4th week of month	Commerce Department
	Housing starts	16th of month	Commerce Department
	Industrial production	15th of month	Federal Reserve Board
	Initial claims for jobless benefits	Thursdays	Department of Labor
	International trade balance	20th of month	Commerce Department
	Index of leading economic indicators	Beginning of month	Conference Board
	Money supply	Thursdays	Federal Reserve Board
	New home sales	Last business day of month	Commerce Department
	Producer price index	11th of month	Bureau of Labor Statistics
	Productivity and costs	2nd month in quarter (approx. 7th day of month)	Bureau of Labor Statistics
	Retail sales	13th of month	Commerce Department
	Survey of purchasing managers	1st business day of month	National Association of Purchasing Managers

*Many of these release dates are approximate.

Source: Charter Media, Inc.

| Economic Calendar | | | | | | | | Jan. 22 - Jan. 25 |

Last Week   Next Week

Date	Time (ET)	Statistic	For	Actual	Briefing Forecast	Market Expects	Prior	Revised From
Jan 22	10:00 AM 2:00 AM	Leading Indicators Treasury Budget	Dec Dec	**1.2%** **$26.6B**	1.1% $24.0B	0.8% $24.0B	0.8% $32.7B	0.5% $32.7B
Jan 24	8:30 AM	Initial Jobless Claims	01/19	**376K**	380K	395K	391K	384K
Jan 25	10:00 AM	Existing Home Sales	Dec	**5.19M**	5.25M	5.18M	5.23M	5.21M

FIGURE 11.6

Economic calendar at Yahoo!

interest. These announcements are reported in the financial press, for example, *The Wall Street Journal,* as they are released. They also are available at many sites on the World Wide Web, for example, at Yahoo's website. Figure 11.6 is an excerpt from a recent Economic Calendar page at Yahoo!. The page gives a list of the announcements released during the week of January 22. Notice that recent forecasts of each variable are provided along with the actual value of each statistic. This is useful, because in an efficient market, security prices will already reflect market expectations. The *new* information in the announcement will determine the market response.

11.7   INDUSTRY ANALYSIS

Industry analysis is important for the same reason that macroeconomic analysis is: Just as it is difficult for an industry to perform well when the macroeconomy is ailing, it is unusual for a firm in a troubled industry to perform well. Similarly, just as we have seen that economic performance can vary widely across countries, performance also can vary widely across industries. Figure 11.7 illustrates the dispersion of industry earnings growth. It shows projected growth in earnings per share in 2001 and 2002 for several major industry groups. The forecasts for 2002, which come from a survey of industry analysts, range from −10.5% for natural resources to 69.6% for information technology.

Not surprisingly, industry groups exhibit considerable dispersion in their stock market performance. Figure 11.8 illustrates the stock price performance of 27 industries in 2001. The market as a whole was down dramatically in 2001, but the spread in annual returns was remarkable, ranging from a −50.3% return for the networking industry to a 25% return in the gold industry.

Even small investors can easily take positions in industry performance using mutual funds with an industry focus. For example, Fidelity offers over 30 Select funds, each of which is invested in a particular industry.

Defining an Industry

While we know what we mean by an industry, it can be difficult in practice to decide where to draw the line between one industry and another. Consider, for example, the finance industry. Figure 11.7 shows that the forecast for 2002 growth in industry earnings per share was 16.7%.

FIGURE 11.7

Estimates of earnings growth rates in several industries–2001 and 2002

But this "industry" contains firms with widely differing products and prospects. Figure 11.9 breaks down the industry into six subgroups. The forecast earnings growth of these more narrowly defined groups differs widely, from −0.9% to 60.5%, suggesting that they are not members of a homogeneous industry. Similarly, most of these subgroups in Figure 11.9 could be divided into even smaller and more homogeneous groups.

A useful way to define industry groups in practice is given by *Standard Industry Classification,* or **SIC, codes** or, more recently, North American Industry Classification System, or **NAICS codes.** These are codes assigned for the purpose of grouping firms for statistical analysis. The first two digits of the SIC codes denote very broad industry classifications. For example, the SIC codes assigned to any type of building contractor all start with 15. The third and fourth digits define the industry grouping more narrowly. For example, codes starting with 152 denote *residential* building contractors, and group 1521 contains *single family* building contractors. Firms with the same four-digit SIC code therefore are commonly taken to be in the same industry. Many statistics are computed for even more narrowly defined five-digit SIC groups. NAICS codes similarly group firms operating inside the NAFTA (North American Free Trade Agreement) region, which includes the U.S., Mexico, and Canada.

Neither NAICS nor SIC industry classifications are perfect. For example, both J.C. Penney and Neiman Marcus might be classified as department stores. Yet the former is a high-volume "value" store, while the latter is a high-margin elite retailer. Are they really in the same industry? Still, SIC classifications are a tremendous aid in conducting industry analysis since they provide a means of focusing on very broadly or fairly narrowly defined groups of firms.

Several other industry classifications are provided by other analysts, for example, Standard & Poor's reports on the performance of about 100 industry groups. S&P computes stock price indexes for each group, which is useful in assessing past investment performance. The *Value Line Investment Survey* reports on the conditions and prospects of about 1,700 firms, grouped into about 90 industries. Value Line's analysts prepare forecasts of the performance of industry groups as well as of each firm.

SIC and NAICS codes

Classification of firms into industry groups using numerical codes to identify industries.

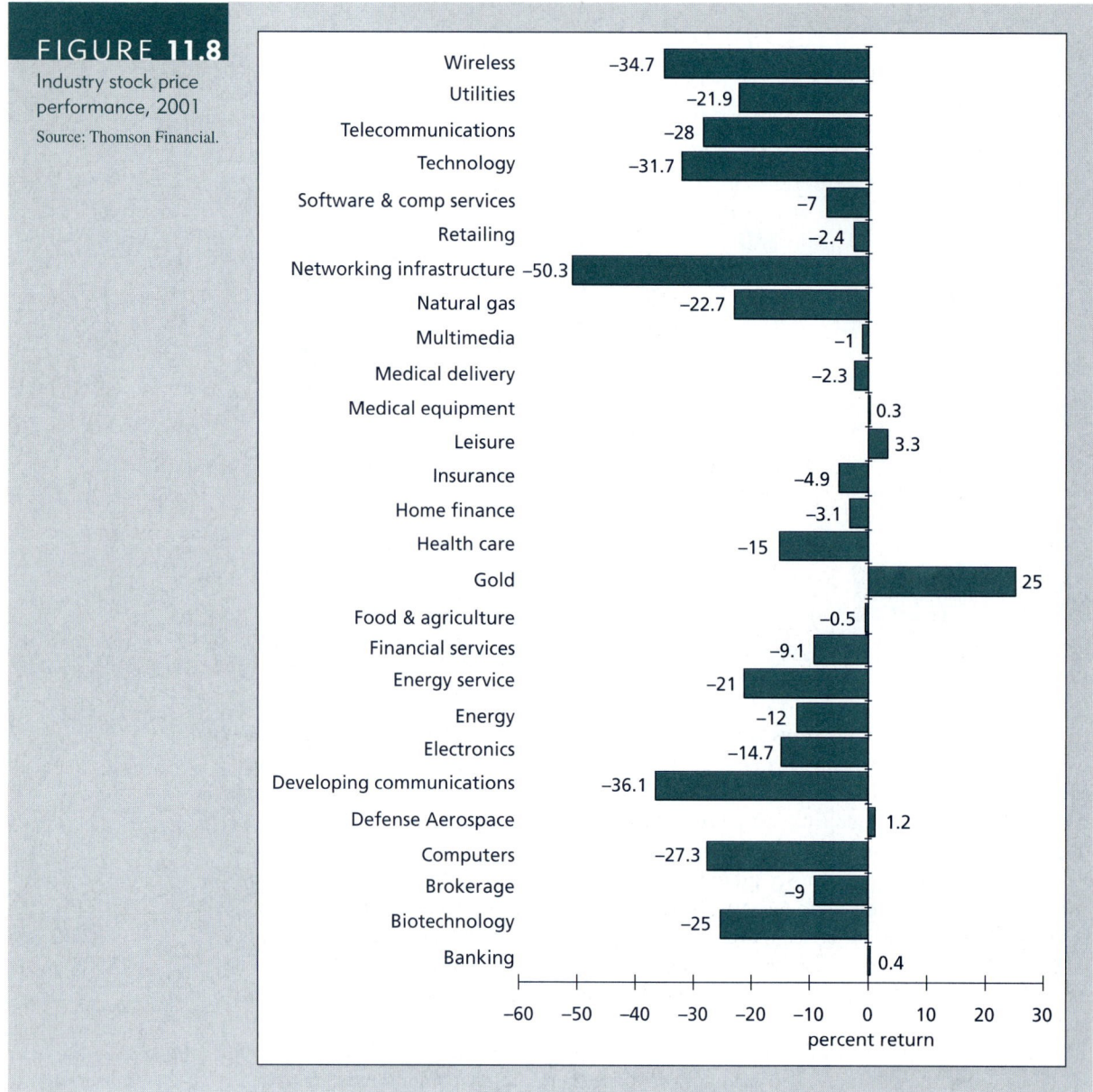

FIGURE 11.8

Industry stock price
performance, 2001

Source: Thomson Financial.

Sensitivity to the Business Cycle

Once the analyst forecasts the state of the macroeconomy, it is necessary to determine the implication of that forecast for specific industries. Not all industries are equally sensitive to the business cycle. For example, consider Figure 11.10, which is a graph of automobile production and shipments of tobacco products, both scaled so that 1963 has a value of 100.

Clearly, the tobacco industry is virtually independent of the business cycle. Demand for tobacco products does not seem to be affected by the state of the macroeconomy in any meaningful way: This is not surprising. Tobacco consumption is determined largely by habit and is a small enough part of most budgets that it will not be given up in hard times.

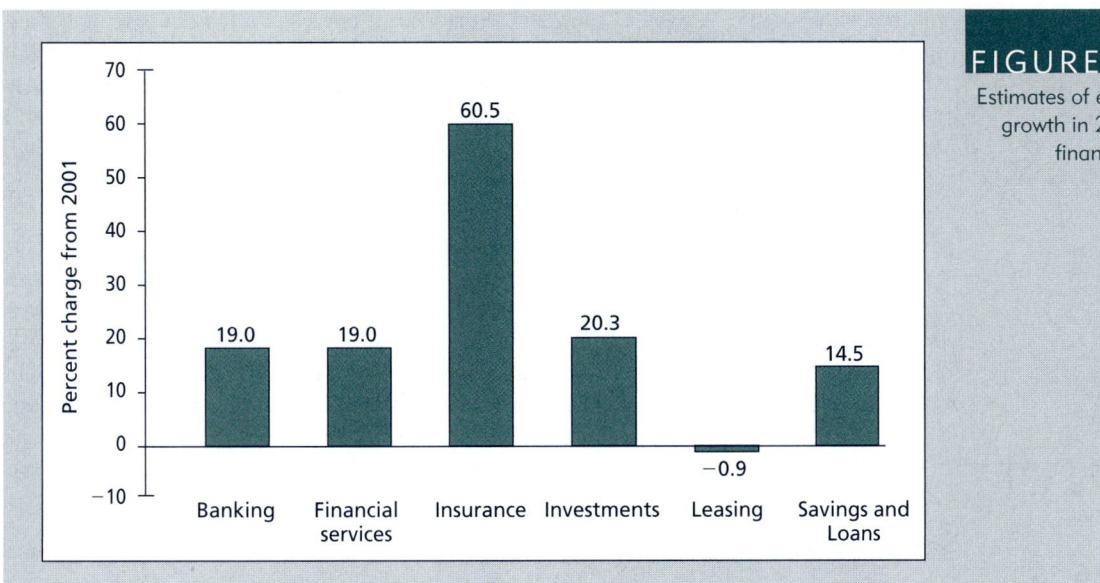

FIGURE **11.9**

Estimates of earnings growth in 2002 for finance firms

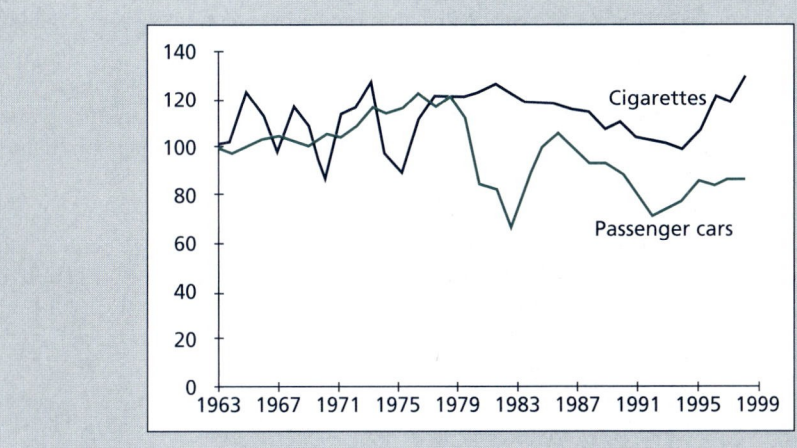

FIGURE **11.10**

Industry cyclicality. Industry sales, scaled so that sales in 1963 equal 100.

Sources: Passenger car sales: *Ward's Automobile Yearbook,* 1994 and www.nada.org. Cigarette sales: Department of Alcohol, Tobacco, and Firearms Statistical Releases and Statistical Abstract of the U.S.

Auto production by contrast is highly volatile. In recessions, consumers can try to prolong the lives of their cars until their income is higher. For example, the worst year for auto production, according to Figure 11.10, was 1982. This was also a year of deep recession, with the unemployment rate at 9.5%.

Three factors will determine the sensitivity of a firm's earnings to the business cycle. First is the sensitivity of sales. Necessities will show little sensitivity to business conditions. Examples of industries in this group are food, drugs, and medical services. Other industries with low sensitivity are those for which income is not a crucial determinant of demand. As we noted, tobacco products are examples of this type of industry. Another industry in this group is movies, because consumers tend to substitute movies for more expensive sources of entertainment when income levels are low. In contrast, firms in industries such as machine tools, steel, autos, and transportation are highly sensitive to the state of the economy.

The second factor determining business cycle sensitivity is operating leverage, which refers to the division between fixed and variable costs. (Fixed costs are those the firm incurs regardless of its production levels. Variable costs are those that rise or fall as the firm produces more or less product.) Firms with greater amounts of variable as opposed to fixed costs will be less sensitive to business conditions. This is because, in economic downturns, these firms can reduce costs as output falls in response to falling sales. Profits for firms with high fixed costs will swing more widely with sales because costs do not move to offset revenue variability. Firms with high fixed costs are said to have high operating leverage, as small swings in business conditions can have large impacts on profitability.

The third factor influencing business cycle sensitivity is financial leverage, which is the use of borrowing. Interest payments on debt must be paid regardless of sales. They are fixed costs that also increase the sensitivity of profits to business conditions. We will have more to say about financial leverage in Chapter 13.

Investors should not always prefer industries with lower sensitivity to the business cycle. Firms in sensitive industries will have high-beta stocks and are riskier. But while they swing lower in downturns, they also swing higher in upturns. As always, the issue you need to address is whether the expected return on the investment is fair compensation for the risks borne.

Sector Rotation

sector rotation

An investment strategy that entails shifting the portfolio into industry sectors that are expected to outperform others based on macroeconomic forecasts.

One way that many analysts think about the relationship between industry analysis and the business cycle is the notion of **sector rotation.** The idea is to shift the portfolio more heavily into industry or sector groups that are expected to outperform based on one's assessment of the state of the business cycle.

Figure 11.11 is a stylized depiction of the business cycle. Near the peak of the business cycle, the economy might be overheated with high inflation and interest rates, and price pressures on basic commodities. This might be a good time to invest in firms engaged in natural resource extraction and processing such as minerals or petroleum.

Following a peak, when the economy enters a contraction or recession, one would expect defensive industries that are less sensitive to economic conditions, for example, pharmaceuticals, food, and other necessities, to be the best performers. At the height of the contraction, financial firms will be hurt by shrinking loan volume and higher default rates. Toward the end

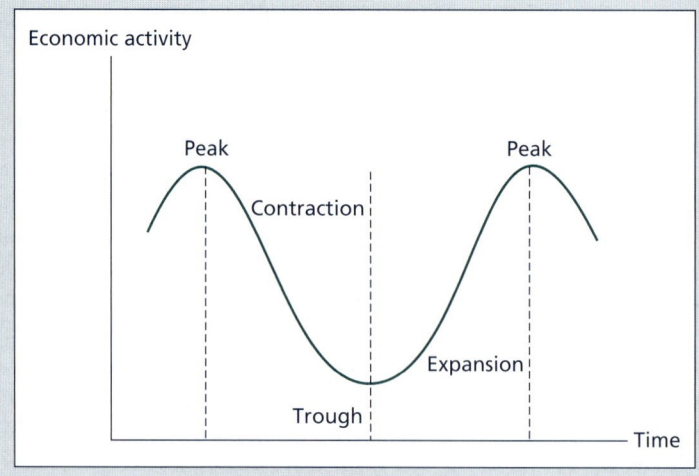

FIGURE 11.11

A stylized depiction of the business cycle

of the recession, however, contractions induce lower inflation and interest rates, which favor financial firms.

At the trough of a recession, the economy is posed for recovery and subsequent expansion. Firms might thus be spending on purchases of new equipment to meet anticipated increases in demand. This, then, would be a good time to invest in capital goods industries, such as equipment, transportation, or construction.

Finally, in an expansion, the economy is growing rapidly. Cyclical industries such as consumer durables and luxury items will be most profitable in this stage of the cycle. Banks might also do well in expansions, since loan volume will be high and default exposure low when the economy is growing rapidly.

Let us emphasize again that sector rotation, like any other form of market timing, will be successful only if one anticipates the next stage of the business cycle better than other investors. The business cycle depicted in Figure 11.11 is highly stylized. In real life, it is never as clear how long each phase of the cycle will last, nor how extreme it will be. These forecasts are where analysts need to earn their keep.

4. In which phase of the business cycle would you expect the following industries to enjoy their best performance?
   (a) Newspapers (b) Machine tools (c) Beverages (d) Timber.

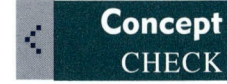

Concept
CHECK

Industry Life Cycles

Examine the biotechnology industry and you will find many firms with high rates of investment, high rates of return on investment, and very low dividends as a percentage of profits. Do the same for the electric utility industry and you will find lower rates of return, lower investment rates, and higher dividend payout rates. Why should this be?

The biotech industry is still new. Recently, available technologies have created opportunities for the highly profitable investment of resources. New products are protected by patents,

---

WEBMASTER

Analyzing Recent Economic Data and Trends

The Federal Reserve Bank of St. Louis publishes a monthly report on national economic trends. The report provides a wealth of information on trade data, employment data, inflation and levels of GDP. The current report can be found at the following location: http://research.stlouisfed.org/publications/net/netpub.pdf. After securing the most current report and examining its graphs and data answer the following questions.

1. What has been the trend in the consumer price index over the last three years?

2. What has been the trend in the producer price index for finished goods over the last three years?

3. Are there any significant trends in real disposable income and real consumption of the last three years?

4. What has been the trends in the housing markets over the last three years?

FIGURE 11.12
The industry life cycle

and profit margins are high. With such lucrative investment opportunities, firms find it advantageous to put all profits back into the firm. The companies grow rapidly on average.

Eventually, however, growth must slow. The high profit rates will induce new firms to enter the industry. Increasing competition will hold down prices and profit margins. New technologies become proven and more predictable, risk levels fall, and entry becomes even easier. As internal investment opportunities become less attractive, a lower fraction of profits are reinvested in the firm. Cash dividends increase.

Ultimately, in a mature industry, we observe "cash cows," firms with stable dividends and cash flows and little risk. Their growth rates might be similar to that of the overall economy. Industries in early stages of their life cycles offer high-risk/high-potential-return investments. Mature industries offer lower risk, lower return combinations.

industry life cycle

Stages through which firms typically pass as they mature.

This analysis suggests that a typical **industry life cycle** might be described by four stages: a start-up stage characterized by extremely rapid growth; a consolidation stage characterized by growth that is less rapid but still faster than that of the general economy; a maturity stage characterized by growth no faster than the general economy; and a stage of relative decline, in which the industry grows less rapidly than the rest of the economy, or actually shrinks. This industry life cycle is illustrated in Figure 11.12. Let us turn to an elaboration of each of these stages.

Start-up stage   The early stages of an industry often are characterized by a new technology or product, such as VCRs or personal computers in the 1980s, cell phones in the 1990s, or bioengineering today. At this stage, it is difficult to predict which firms will emerge as industry leaders. Some firms will turn out to be wildly successful, and others will fail altogether. Therefore, there is considerable risk in selecting one particular firm within the industry.

At the industry level, however, sales and earnings will grow at an extremely rapid rate since the new product has not yet saturated its market. For example, in 1990 very few households had cell phones. The potential market for the product therefore was huge. In contrast to this situation, consider the market for a mature product like refrigerators. Almost all households in the U.S. already have refrigerators, so the market for this good is primarily composed of households replacing old refrigerators. Obviously, the growth rate in this market will be far less than for cell phones.

Consolidation stage   After a product becomes established, industry leaders begin to emerge. The survivors from the start-up stage are more stable, and market share is easier to predict. Therefore, the performance of the surviving firms will more closely track the performance of the overall industry. The industry still grows faster than the rest of the economy as the product penetrates the marketplace and becomes more commonly used.

Maturity stage   At this point, the product has reached its full potential for use by consumers. Further growth might merely track growth in the general economy. The product has become far more standardized, and producers are forced to compete to a greater extent on the basis of price. This leads to narrower profit margins and further pressure on profits. Firms at this stage sometimes are characterized as "cash cows," firms with reasonably stable cash flow but offering little opportunity for profitable expansion. The cash flow is best "milked from" rather than reinvested in the company.

We pointed to VCRs as a start-up industry in the 1980s. By now, it is certainly a mature industry, with high market penetration, considerable price competition, low profit margins, and slowing or even declining sales. In September of 2001, monthly sales of DVD players, which seem to be the start-up product that will eventually replace VCRs, surpassed those of VCRs for the first time.

Relative decline   In this stage, the industry might grow at less than the rate of the overall economy, or it might even shrink. This could be due to obsolescence of the product, competition from new products, or competition from new low-cost suppliers.

At which stage in the life cycle are investments in an industry most attractive? Conventional wisdom is that investors should seek firms in high-growth industries. This recipe for success is simplistic, however. If the security prices already reflect the likelihood for high growth, then it is too late to make money from that knowledge. Moreover, high growth and fat profits encourage competition from other producers. The exploitation of profit opportunities brings about new sources of supply that eventually reduce prices, profits, investment returns, and finally, growth. This is the dynamic behind the progression from one stage of the industry life cycle to another. The famous portfolio manager Peter Lynch makes this point in *One Up on Wall Street.* He says:

> Many people prefer to invest in a high-growth industry, where there's a lot of sound and fury. Not me. I prefer to invest in a low-growth industry. . . . In a low-growth industry, especially one that's boring and upsets people [such as funeral homes or the oil-drum retrieval business], there's no problem with competition. You don't have to protect your flanks from potential rivals . . . and this gives you the leeway to continue to grow [page 131].

In fact, Lynch uses an industry classification system in a very similar spirit to the lifecycle approach we have described. He places firms in the following six groups:

1. *Slow Growers.* Large and aging companies that will grow only slightly faster than the broad economy. These firms have matured from their earlier fast-growth phase. They usually have steady cash flow and pay a generous dividend, indicating that the firm is generating more cash than can be profitably reinvested in the firm.
2. *Stalwarts.* Large, well-known firms like Coca-Cola or Colgate-Palmolive. They grow faster than the slow growers but are not in the very rapid growth start-up stage. They also tend to be in noncyclical industries that are relatively unaffected by recessions.
3. *Fast Growers.* Small and aggressive new firms with annual growth rates in the neighborhood of 20 to 25%. Company growth can be due to broad industry growth or to an increase in market share in a more mature industry.

4. *Cyclicals.* These are firms with sales and profits that regularly expand and contract along with the business cycle. Examples are auto companies (see Figure 11.10 again), steel companies, or the construction industry.

5. *Turnarounds.* These are firms that are in bankruptcy or soon might be. If they can recover from what might appear to be imminent disaster, they can offer tremendous investment returns. A good example of this type of firm would be Chrysler in 1982, when it required a government guarantee on its debt to avoid bankruptcy. The stock price rose fifteenfold in the next five years.

6. *Asset Plays.* These are firms that have valuable assets not currently reflected in the stock price. For example, a company may own or be located on valuable real estate that is worth as much or more than the company's business enterprises. Sometimes the hidden asset can be tax-loss carryforwards. Other times the assets may be intangible. For example, a cable company might have a valuable list of cable subscribers. These assets do not immediately generate cash flow and so may be more easily overlooked by other analysts attempting to value the firm.

Industry Structure and Performance

The maturation of an industry involves regular changes in the firm's competitive environment. As a final topic, we examine the relationship between industry structure, competitive strategy, and profitability. Michael Porter (1980, 1985) has highlighted these five determinants of competition: threat of entry from new competitors, rivalry between existing competitors, price pressure from substitute products, the bargaining power of suppliers, and the bargaining power of buyers.

Threat of entry   New entrants to an industry put pressure on price and profits. Even if a firm has not yet entered an industry, the potential for it to do so places pressure on prices, since high prices and profit margins will encourage entry by new competitors. Therefore, barriers to entry can be a key determinant of industry profitability. Barriers can take many forms. For example, existing firms may already have secure distribution channels for their products based on long-standing relationships with customers or suppliers that would be costly for a new entrant to duplicate. Brand loyalty also makes it difficult for new entrants to penetrate a market and gives firms more pricing discretion. Proprietary knowledge or patent protection also may give firms advantages in serving a market. Finally, an existing firm's experience in a market may give it cost advantages due to the learning that takes place over time.

Rivalry between existing competitors   When there are several competitors in an industry, there will generally be more price competition and lower profit margins as competitors seek to expand their share of the market. Slow industry growth contributes to this competition since expansion must come at the expense of a rival's market share. High fixed costs also create pressure to reduce prices since fixed costs put greater pressure on firms to operate near full capacity. Industries producing relatively homogeneous goods also are subject to considerable price pressure since firms cannot compete on the basis of product differentiation.

Pressure from substitute products   Substitute products means that the industry faces competition from firms in related industries. For example, sugar producers compete with corn syrup producers. Wool producers compete with synthetic fiber producers. The availability of substitutes limits the prices that can be charged to customers.

Bargaining power of buyers   If a buyer purchases a large fraction of an industry's output, it will have considerable bargaining power and can demand price concessions. For example, auto producers can put pressure on suppliers of auto parts. This reduces the profitability of the auto parts industry.

Bargaining power of suppliers   If a supplier of a key input has monopolistic control over the product, it can demand higher prices for the good and squeeze profits out of the industry. One special case of this issue pertains to organized labor as a supplier of a key input to the production process. Labor unions engage in collective bargaining to increase the wages paid to workers. When the labor market is highly unionized, a significant share of the potential profits in the industry can be captured by the workforce.

   The key factor determining the bargaining power of suppliers is the availability of substitute products. If substitutes are available, the supplier has little clout and cannot extract higher prices.

SUMMARY

- Macroeconomic policy aims to maintain the economy near full employment without aggravating inflationary pressures. The proper trade-off between these two goals is a source of ongoing debate.
- The traditional tools of macropolicy are government spending and tax collection, which comprise fiscal policy, and manipulation of the money supply via monetary policy. Expansionary fiscal policy can stimulate the economy and increase GDP but tends to increase interest rates. Expansionary monetary policy works by lowering interest rates.
- The business cycle is the economy's recurring pattern of expansions and recessions. Leading economic indicators can be used to anticipate the evolution of the business cycle because their values tend to change before those of other key economic variables.
- Industries differ in their sensitivity to the business cycle. More sensitive industries tend to be those producing high-priced durable goods for which the consumer has considerable discretion as to the timing of purchase. Examples are automobiles or consumer durables. Other sensitive industries are those that produce capital equipment for other firms. Operating leverage and financial leverage increase sensitivity to the business cycle.

KEY TERMS

budget deficit, 385	fundamental analysis, 382	peak, 391
business cycles, 391	gross domestic product, 384	sector rotation, 400
cyclical industries, 391	industry life cycle, 402	SIC codes, 397
defensive industries, 391	inflation, 385	NAICS codes, 397
demand shock, 387	leading economic	supply shock, 387
exchange rate, 383	indicators, 393	trough, 391
fiscal policy, 388	monetary policy, 389	unemployment rate, 385

PROBLEM SETS

1. What monetary and fiscal policies might be prescribed for an economy in a deep recession?

2. Unlike other investors, you believe the Fed is going to dramatically loosen monetary policy. What would be your recommendations about investments in the following industries?
   a. Gold mining
   b. Construction

3. If you believe the U.S. dollar is about to depreciate more dramatically than do other investors, what will be your stance on investments in U.S. auto producers?

www.mhhe.com/bkm

4. According to supply-side economists, what will be the long-run impact on prices of a reduction in income tax rates?

5. Consider two firms producing videocassette recorders. One uses a highly automated robotics process, while the other uses human workers on an assembly line and pays overtime when there is heavy production demand.
   a. Which firm will have higher profits in a recession? In a boom?
   b. Which firm's stock will have a higher beta?

6. Here are four industries and four forecasts for the macroeconomy. Choose the industry that you would expect to perform best in each scenario.
   Industries: Housing construction, health care, gold mining, steel production.
   Economic Forecasts:
   Deep recession: Falling inflation, falling interest rates, falling GDP.
   Superheated economy: Rapidly rising GDP, increasing inflation and interest rates.
   Healthy expansion: Rising GDP, mild inflation, low unemployment.
   Stagflation: Falling GDP, high inflation.

7. In which stage of the industry life cycle would you place the following industries? (Warning: There is often considerable room for disagreement concerning the "correct" answers to this question.)
   a. Oil well equipment.
   b. Computer hardware.
   c. Computer software.
   d. Genetic engineering.
   e. Railroads.

8. For each pair of firms, choose the one that you think would be more sensitive to the business cycle.
   a. General Autos or General Pharmaceuticals.
   b. Friendly Airlines or Happy Cinemas.

9. Choose an industry and identify the factors that will determine its performance in the next three years. What is your forecast for performance in that time period?

10. Why do you think the index of consumer expectations is a useful leading indicator of the macroeconomy? (See Table 11.2.)

11. Why do you think the change in the index of labor cost per unit of output is a useful lagging indicator of the macroeconomy? (See Table 11.2.)

11. You have $5,000 to invest for the next year and are considering three alternatives:
   a. A money market fund with an average maturity of 30 days offering a current yield of 6% per year.
   b. A one-year savings deposit at a bank offering an interest rate of 7.5%.
   c. A 20-year U.S. Treasury bond offering a yield to maturity of 9% per year.
   What role does your forecast of future interest rates play in your decisions?

13. As a securities analyst you have been asked to review a valuation of a closely held business, Wigwam Autoparts Heaven, Inc. (WAH), prepared by the Red Rocks Group (RRG). You are to give an opinion on the valuation and to support your opinion by analyzing each part of the valuation. WAH's sole business is automotive parts retailing. The RRG valuation includes a section called "Analysis of the Retail Auto Parts Industry," based completely on the data in Table 11.4 and the following additional information:

TABLE 11.4
Selected retail auto parts industry data

	1999	1998	1997	1996	1995	1994	1993	1992	1991	1990
Population 18–29 years old (percentage change)	−1.8%	−2.0%	−2.1%	−1.4%	−0.8%	−0.9%	−1.1%	−0.9%	−0.7%	−0.3%
Number of households with income more than $35,000 (percentage change)	6.0%	4.0%	8.0%	4.5%	2.7%	3.1%	1.6%	3.6%	4.2%	2.2%
Number of households with income less than $35,000 (percentage change)	3.0%	−1.0%	4.9%	2.3%	−1.4%	2.5%	1.4%	−1.3%	0.6%	0.1%
Number of cars 5–15 years old (percentage change)	0.9%	−1.3%	−6.0%	1.9%	3.3%	2.4%	−2.3%	−2.2%	−8.0%	1.6%
Automotive aftermarket industry retail sales (percentage change)	5.7%	1.9%	3.1%	3.7%	4.3%	2.6%	1.3%	0.2%	3.7%	2.4%
Consumer expenditures on automotive parts and accessories (percentage change)	2.4%	1.8%	2.1%	6.5%	3.6%	9.2%	1.3%	6.2%	6.7%	6.5%
Sales growth of retail auto parts companies with 100 or more stores	17.0%	16.0%	16.5%	14.0%	15.5%	16.8%	12.0%	15.7%	19.0%	16.0%
Market share of retail auto parts companies with 100 or more stores	19.0%	18.5%	18.3%	18.1%	17.0%	17.2%	17.0%	16.9%	15.0%	14.0%
Average operating margin of retail auto parts companies with 100 or more stores	12.0%	11.8%	11.2%	11.5%	10.6%	10.6%	10.0%	10.4%	9.8%	9.0%
Average operating margin of all retail auto parts companies	5.5%	5.7%	5.6%	5.8%	6.0%	6.5%	7.0%	7.2%	7.1%	7.2%

- WAH and its principal competitors each operated more than 150 stores at year-end 1999.
- The average number of stores operated per company engaged in the retail auto parts industry is 5.3.
- The major customer base for auto parts sold in retail stores consists of young owners of old vehicles. These owners do their own automotive maintenance out of economic necessity.

a. One of RRG's conclusions is that the retail auto parts industry as a whole is in the maturity stage of the industry life cycle. Discuss three relevant items of data from Table 11.4 that support this conclusion.

b. Another RRG conclusion is that WAH and its principal competitors are in the consolidation stage of their life cycle. Cite three items from Table 11.4 that suggest this conclusion. How can WAH be in a consolidation stage while its industry is in a maturity stage?

www.mhhe.com/bkm

14. Universal Auto is a large multinational corporation headquartered in the United States. For segment reporting purposes, the company is engaged in two businesses: production of motor vehicles and information processing services.

     The motor vehicle business is by far the larger of Universal's two segments. It consists mainly of domestic United States passenger car production, but it also includes small truck manufacturing operations in the United States and passenger car production in other countries. This segment of Universal has had weak operating results for the past several years, including a large loss in 1997. Although the company does not reveal the operating results of its domestic passenger car segments, that part of Universal's business is generally believed to be primarily responsible for the weak performance of its motor vehicle segment.

     Idata, the information processing services segment of Universal, was started by Universal about 15 years ago. This business has shown strong, steady growth that has been entirely internal: No acquisitions have been made.

     An excerpt from a research report on Universal prepared by Paul Adams, a CFA candidate, states: "Based on our assumption that Universal will be able to increase prices significantly on U.S. passenger cars in 1998, we project a multibillion dollar profit improvement . . ."

     a. Discuss the concept of an industrial life cycle by describing each of its four phases.
     b. Identify where each of Universal's two primary businesses—passenger cars and information processing—is in such a cycle.
     c. Discuss how product pricing should differ between Universal's two businesses, based on the location of each in the industrial life cycle.

15. Adams's research report (see problem 14) continued as follows: "With a business expansion already underway, the expected profit surge should lead to a much higher price for Universal Auto stock. We strongly recommend purchase."

     a. Discuss the business cycle approach to investment timing. (Your answer should describe actions to be taken on both stocks and bonds at different points over a typical business cycle.)
     b. Assuming Adams's assertion is correct (that a business expansion is already underway), evaluate the timeliness of his recommendation to purchase Universal Auto, a cyclical stock, based on the business cycle approach to investment timing.

16. Janet Ludlow is preparing a report on U.S.-based manufacturers in the electric toothbrush industry and has gathered the information shown in Tables 11.5 and 11.6. Ludlow's report concludes that the electric toothbrush industry is in the maturity (i.e. late) phase of its industry life cycle.

     a. Select and justify three factors from Table 11.5 that support Ludlow's conclusion.
     b. Select and justify three factors from Table 11.6 that refute Ludlow's conclusion.

17. General Weedkillers dominates the chemical weed control market with its patented product Weed-ex. The patent is about to expire, however. What are your forecasts for changes in the industry? Specifically, what will happen to industry prices, sales, the profit prospects of General Weedkillers, and the profit prospects of its competitors? What stage of the industry life cycle do you think is relevant for the analysis of this market?

18. The following questions have appeared on CFA examinations.

     a. Which one of the following statements *best* expresses the central idea of countercyclical fiscal policy?
        (1) Planned government deficits are appropriate during economic booms, and planned surpluses are appropriate during economic recessions.

TABLE **11.5** Ratios for Electric Toothbrush Industry Index and Broad Stock Market Index	Year	1992	1993	1994	1995	1996	1997
	Return on equity						
	Electric toothbrush industry index	12.5%	12.0%	15.4%	19.6%	21.6%	21.6%
	Market index	10.2	12.4	14.6	19.9	20.4	21.2
	Average P/E						
	Electric toothbrush industry index	28.5×	23.2×	19.6×	18.7×	18.5×	16.2×
	Market index	10.2	12.4	14.6	19.9	18.1	19.1
	Dividend payout ratio						
	Electric toothbrush industry index	8.8%	8.0%	12.1%	12.1%	14.3%	17.1%
	Market index	39.2	40.1	38.6	43.7	41.8	39.1
	Average dividend yield						
	Electric toothbrush industry index	0.3%	0.3%	0.6%	0.7%	0.8%	1.0%
	Market index	3.8	3.2	2.6	2.2	2.3	2.1

TABLE 11.6

Characterstics of the Electric Toothbrush Manufacturing Industry

- **Industry sales growth**—Industry sales have grown at 15–20% per year in recent years and are expected to grow at 10–15% per year over the next three years.
- **Non-U.S. markets**—Some U.S. manufacturers are attempting to enter fast-growing non-U.S. markets, which remain largely unexploited.
- **Mail order sales**—Some manufacturers have created a new niche in the industry by selling electric toothbrushes directly to customers through mail order. Sales for this industry segment are growing at 40% per year.
- **U.S. market penetration**—The current penetration rate in the United States is 60 percent of households and will be difficult to increase.
- **Price competition**—Manufacturers compete fiercely on the basis of price, and price wars within the industry are common.
- **Niche markets**—Some manufacturers are able to develop new, unexploited niche markets in the United States based on company reputation, quality, and service.
- **Industry consolidation**—Several manufacturers have recently merged, and it is expected that consolidation in the industry will increase.
- **New entrants**—New manufacturers continue to enter the market.

(2) The balanced budget approach is the proper criterion for determining annual budget policy.

(3) Actual deficits should equal actual surpluses during a period of deflation.

(4) Government deficits are planned during economic recessions, and surpluses are utilized to restrain inflationary booms.

b. The supply-side view stresses that:

(1) Aggregate demand is the major determinant of real output and aggregate employment.

(2) An increase in government expenditures and tax rates will cause real income to rise.

(3) Tax rates are a major determinant of real output and aggregate employment.

(4) Expansionary monetary policy will cause real output to expand without causing the rate of inflation to accelerate.

c. Based on historical data and assuming less-than-full employment, periods of sharp acceleration in the growth rate of the money supply tend to be associated *initially* with:
   (1) Periods of economic recession.
   (2) An increase in the velocity of money.
   (3) A rapid growth of gross domestic product.
   (4) Reductions in real gross domestic product.

d. Which *one* of the following propositions would a strong proponent of supply-side economics be *most* likely to stress?
   (1) Higher marginal tax rates will lead to a reduction in the size of the budget deficit and lower interest rates because they expand government revenues.
   (2) Higher marginal tax rates promote economic inefficiency and thereby retard aggregate output because they encourage investors to undertake low productivity projects with substantial tax-shelter benefits.
   (3) Income redistribution payments will exert little impact on real aggregate supply because they do not consume resources directly.
   (4) A tax reduction will increase the disposable income of households. Thus, the primary impact of a tax reduction on aggregate supply will stem from the influence of the tax change on the size of the budget deficit or surplus.

e. Which one of the following series is *not* included in the index of leading economic indicators?
   (1) New building permits; private housing units.
   (2) Net business formulation.
   (3) Stock prices.
   (4) Inventories on hand.

f. How would an economist who believes in crowding out complete the following sentence? "The increase in the budget deficit causes real interest rates to rise, and therefore, private spending and investment
   (1) Increase."
   (2) Stay the same."
   (3) Decrease."
   (4) Initially increase but eventually will decrease."

g. If the central monetary authorities want to reduce the supply of money to slow the rate of inflation, the central bank should:
   (1) Sell government bonds, which will reduce the money supply; this will cause interest rates to rise and aggregate demand to fall.
   (2) Buy government bonds, which will reduce the money supply; this will cause interest rates to rise and aggregate demand to fall.

1. Find the Industry Profile from Market Insight (**www.mhhe.com/edumarketinsight**) for the biotechnology and the water utility industries. Compare the price-to-book ratios for the two industries. (Price-to-book is price per share divided by book value per share.) Do the differences make sense to you in light of the different stages of these industries in terms of the typical industry life cycle?

2. Compare the price-to-earnings (P/E) ratios for these industries. Why might biotech have a negative P/E ratio in some periods? Why is its P/E ratio (when positive) so much higher than that of water utilities? Again, think in terms of where these industries stand in their life cycle.

STANDARD
&POOR'S

(3) Decrease the discount rate, which will lower the market rate of interest; this will cause both costs and prices to fall.

(4) Increase taxes, which will reduce costs and cause prices to fall.

WEBMASTER

Forecaster's Ability to Call Turns

There have been instances in recent times when forecasters actually missed predictions of a recession until it was over! A short article from the Federal Reserve Bank of San Francisco discusses the ability of forecasters in calling turning points in the economic cycle. It can be found at http://www.frbsf.org/publications/economics/letter/2002/el2002-07.pdf. After reading this article, discuss the following questions.

1.   What does the evidence show with respect to forecasters being able to forecast recessions?

2.   What factors were cited as being possible reasons for their performance in forecasting recessions?

3.   What is the experience with respect to forecasters' ability to forecast recoveries?

SOLUTIONS TO

Concept
CHECKS

1. The downturn in the auto industry will reduce the demand for the product in this economy. The economy will, at least in the short term, enter a recession. This would suggest that:
    a. GDP will fall.
    b. The unemployment rate will rise.
    c. The government deficit will increase. Income tax receipts will fall, and government expenditures on social welfare programs probably will increase.
    d. Interest rates should fall. The contraction in the economy will reduce the demand for credit. Moreover, the lower inflation rate will reduce nominal interest rates.

2. Expansionary fiscal policy coupled with expansionary monetary policy will stimulate the economy, with the loose monetary policy keeping down interest rates.

3. A traditional demand-side interpretation of the tax cuts is that the resulting increase in after-tax income increased consumption demand and stimulated the economy. A supply-side interpretation is that the reduction in marginal tax rates made it more attractive for businesses to invest and for individuals to work, thereby increasing economic output.

4. *a.* Newspapers will do best in an expansion when advertising volume is increasing.
    b. Machine tools are a good investment at the trough of a recession, just as the economy is about to enter an expansion and firms may need to increase capacity.
    c. Beverages are defensive investments, with demand that is relatively insensitive to the business cycle. Therefore, they are good investments if a recession is forecast.
    d. Timber is a good investment at a peak period, when natural resource prices are high and the economy is operating at full capacity.

www.mhhe.com/bkm

EQUITY VALUATION

> Calculate the intrinsic value of a firm using either a constant growth or multistage dividend discount model.

> Calculate the intrinsic value of a stock using a dividend discount model in conjunction with a price/earnings ratio.

> Assess the growth prospects of a firm from its P/E ratio.

You saw in our discussion of market efficiency that finding undervalued securities is hardly easy. At the same time, there are enough chinks in the armor of the efficient market hypothesis that the search for such securities should not be dismissed out of hand. Moreover, it is the ongoing search for mispriced securities that maintains a nearly efficient market. Even infrequent discoveries of minor mispricing justify the salary of a stock market analyst.

This chapter describes the ways stock market analysts try to uncover mispriced securities. The models presented are those used by *fundamental analysts*, those analysts who use information concerning the current and prospective profitability of a company to assess its fair market value. Fundamental analysts are different from *technical analysts*, who essentially use trend analysis to uncover trading opportunities. We discuss technical analysis in Chapter 19.

We start with a discussion of alternative measures of the value of a company. From there, we progress to quantitative tools called dividend discount models that security analysts commonly use to measure the value of a firm as an ongoing concern. Next, we turn to price–earnings, or P/E, ratios, explaining why they are of such interest to analysts but also highlighting some of their shortcomings. We explain how P/E ratios are tied to dividend valuation models and, more generally, to the growth prospects of the firm.

12.1 BALANCE SHEET VALUATION METHODS

book value

The net worth of common equity according to a firm's balance sheet.

A common valuation measure is **book value,** which is the net worth of a company as shown on the balance sheet. Table 12.1 gives the balance sheet totals for Intel to illustrate how to calculate book value per share.

Book value of Intel stock at the end of September 2001 was $5.35 per share ($35,902 million divided by 6,710 million shares). At the same time, Intel stock had a market price of $20.00. In light of this substantial difference between book and market values, would it be fair to say Intel stock was overpriced?

The book value is the result of applying a set of arbitrary accounting rules to spread the acquisition cost of assets over a specified number of years; in contrast, the market price of a stock takes account of the firm's value as a going concern. In other words, the price reflects the market consensus estimate of the present value of the firm's expected future cash flows. It would be unusual if the market price of Intel stock were exactly equal to its book value.

Can book value represent a "floor" for the stock's price, below which level the market price can never fall? Although Intel's book value per share was less than its market price, other evidence disproves this notion. While it is not common, there are always some firms selling at a market price below book value. Clearly, book value cannot always be a floor for the stock's price.

liquidation value

Net amount that can be realized by selling the assets of a firm and paying off the debt.

A better measure of a floor for the stock price is the firm's **liquidation value** per share. This represents the amount of money that could be realized by breaking up the firm, selling its assets, repaying its debt, and distributing the remainder to the shareholders. The reasoning behind this concept is that if the market price of equity drops below the liquidation value of the firm, the firm becomes attractive as a takeover target. A corporate raider would find it profitable to buy enough shares to gain control and then actually liquidate because the liquidation value exceeds the value of the business as a going concern.

replacement cost

Cost to replace a firm's assets.

Another balance sheet concept that is of interest in valuing a firm is the **replacement cost** of its assets less its liabilities. Some analysts believe the market value of the firm cannot get too far above its replacement cost because, if it did, competitors would try to replicate the firm. The competitive pressure of other similar firms entering the same industry would drive down the market value of all firms until they came into equality with replacement cost.

Tobin's q

Ratio of market value of the firm to replacement cost.

This idea is popular among economists, and the ratio of market price to replacement cost is known as **Tobin's q,** after the Nobel Prize–winning economist James Tobin. In the long run, according to this view, the ratio of market price to replacement cost will tend toward 1, but the evidence is that this ratio can differ significantly from 1 for very long periods of time.

Although focusing on the balance sheet can give some useful information about a firm's liquidation value or its replacement cost, the analyst usually must turn to the expected future cash flows for a better estimate of the firm's value as a going concern. We now examine the quantitative models that analysts use to value common stock in terms of the future earnings and dividends the firm will yield.

TABLE **12.1**	Assets	Liabilities and Owners' Equity	
Intel's balance sheet, Sept. 29, 2001 ($millions)	$44,231	Liabilities Common equity 6,710 million shares outstanding	$8,329 $35,902

12.2 INTRINSIC VALUE VERSUS MARKET PRICE

The most popular model for assessing the value of a firm as a going concern starts from the observation that the return on a stock investment comprises cash dividends and capital gains or losses. We begin by assuming a one-year holding period and supposing that ABC stock has an expected dividend per share, $E(D_1)$, of $4; that the current price of a share, P_0, is $48; and that the expected price at the end of a year, $E(P_1)$, is $52. For now, don't worry about how you derive your forecast of next year's price. At this point we ask only whether the stock seems attractively priced *today* given your forecast of *next year's* price.

The expected holding-period return is $E(D_1)$ plus the expected price appreciation, $E(P_1) - P_0$, all divided by the current price P_0.

$$\text{Expected HPR} = E(r) = \frac{E(D_1) + [E(P_1) - P_0]}{P_0}$$

$$= \frac{4 + (52 - 48)}{48} = 0.167 = 16.7\%$$

Note that $E(\ )$ denotes an expected future value. Thus, $E(P_1)$ represents the expectation today of the stock price one year from now. $E(r)$ is referred to as the stock's expected holding-period return. It is the sum of the expected dividend yield, $E(D_1)/P_0$, and the expected rate of price appreciation, the capital gains yield, $[E(P_1) - P_0]/P_0$.

But what is the required rate of return for ABC stock? We know from the capital asset pricing model (CAPM) that when stock market prices are at equilibrium levels, the rate of return that investors can expect to earn on a security is $r_f + \beta[E(r_M) - r_f]$. Thus, the CAPM may be viewed as providing the rate of return an investor can expect to earn on a security given its risk as measured by beta. This is the return that investors will require of any other investment with equivalent risk. We will denote this required rate of return as k. If a stock is priced "correctly," its *expected* return will equal the *required* return. Of course, the goal of a security analyst is to find stocks that are mispriced. For example, an underpriced stock will provide an expected return greater than the "fair" or required return.

Suppose that $r_f = 6\%$, $E(r_M) - r_f = 5\%$, and the beta of ABC is 1.2. Then the value of k is

$$k = 6\% + 1.2 \times 5\% = 12\%$$

The rate of return the investor expects exceeds the required rate based on ABC's risk by a margin of 4.7%. Naturally, the investor will want to include more of ABC stock in the portfolio than a passive strategy would dictate.

Another way to see this is to compare the intrinsic value of a share of stock to its market price. The **intrinsic value,** denoted V_0, of a share of stock is defined as the present value of all cash payments to the investor in the stock, including dividends as well as the proceeds from the ultimate sale of the stock, discounted at the appropriate risk-adjusted interest rate, k. Whenever the intrinsic value, or the investor's own estimate of what the stock is really worth, exceeds the market price, the stock is considered undervalued and a good investment. In the case of ABC, using a one-year investment horizon and a forecast that the stock can be sold at the end of the year at price $P_1 = \$52$, the intrinsic value is

> **intrinsic value**
>
> The present value of a firm's expected future net cash flows discounted by the required rate of return.

$$V_0 = \frac{E(D_1) + E(P_1)}{1 + k} = \frac{\$4 + \$52}{1.12} = \$50$$

Because intrinsic value, $50, exceeds current price, $48, we conclude that the stock is under-valued in the market. We again conclude investors will want to buy more ABC than they would following a passive strategy.

If the intrinsic value turns out to be lower than the current market price, investors should buy less of it than under the passive strategy. It might even pay to go short on ABC stock, as we discussed in Chapter 3.

In market equilibrium, the current market price will reflect the intrinsic value estimates of all market participants. This means the individual investor whose V_0 estimate differs from the market price, P_0, in effect must disagree with some or all of the market consensus estimates of $E(D_1)$, $E(P_1)$, or k. A common term for the market consensus value of the required rate of return, k, is the **market capitalization rate,** which we use often throughout this chapter.

market capitalization rate

The market-consensus estimate of the appropriate discount rate for a firm's cash flows.

1. You expect the price of IBX stock to be $59.77 per share a year from now. Its current market price is $50, and you expect it to pay a dividend one year from now of $2.15 per share.
   a. What is the stock's expected dividend yield, rate of price appreciation, and holding-period return?
   b. If the stock has a beta of 1.15, the risk-free rate is 6% per year, and the expected rate of return on the market portfolio is 14% per year, what is the required rate of return on IBX stock?
   c. What is the intrinsic value of IBX stock, and how does it compare to the current market price?

12.3 | DIVIDEND DISCOUNT MODELS

Consider an investor who buys a share of Steady State Electronics stock, planning to hold it for one year. The intrinsic value of the share is the present value of the dividend to be received at the end of the first year, D_1, and the expected sales price, P_1. We will henceforth use the simpler notation P_1 instead of $E(P_1)$ to avoid clutter. Keep in mind, though, that future prices and dividends are unknown, and we are dealing with expected values, not certain values. We've already established that

$$V_0 = \frac{D_1 + P_1}{1 + k} \qquad (12.1)$$

While this year's dividend is fairly predictable given a company's history, you might ask how we can estimate P_1, the year-end price. According to Equation 12.1, V_1 (the year-end value) will be

$$V_1 = \frac{D_2 + P_2}{1 + k}$$

If we assume the stock will be selling for its intrinsic value next year, then $V_1 = P_1$, and we can substitute this value for P_1 into Equation 12.1 to find

$$V_0 = \frac{D_1}{1 + k} + \frac{D_2 + P_2}{(1 + k)^2}$$

This equation may be interpreted as the present value of dividends plus sales price for a two-year holding period. Of course, now we need to come up with a forecast of P_2. Continuing in the same way, we can replace P_2 by $(D_3 + P_3)/(1 + k)$, which relates P_0 to the value of dividends plus the expected sales price for a three-year holding period.

More generally, for a holding period of H years, we can write the stock value as the present value of dividends over the H years, plus the ultimate sales price, P_H.

$$V_0 = \frac{D_1}{1+k} + \frac{D_2}{(1+k)^2} + \ldots + \frac{D_H + P_H}{(1+k)^H} \qquad \text{(12.2)}$$

Note the similarity between this formula and the bond valuation formula developed in Chapter 9. Each relates price to the present value of a stream of payments (coupons in the case of bonds, dividends in the case of stocks) and a final payment (the face value of the bond or the sales price of the stock). The key differences in the case of stocks are the uncertainty of dividends, the lack of a fixed maturity date, and the unknown sales price at the horizon date. Indeed, one can continue to substitute for price indefinitely to conclude

$$V_0 = \frac{D_1}{1+k} + \frac{D_2}{(1+k)^2} + \frac{D_3}{(1+k)^3} + \ldots \qquad \text{(12.3)}$$

Equation 12.3 states the stock price should equal the present value of all expected future dividends into perpetuity. This formula is called the **dividend discount model (DDM)** of stock prices.

It is tempting, but incorrect, to conclude from Equation 12.3 that the DDM focuses exclusively on dividends and ignores capital gains as a motive for investing in stock. Indeed, we assume explicitly in Equation 12.1 that capital gains (as reflected in the expected sales price, P_1) are part of the stock's value. At the same time, the price at which you can sell a stock in the future depends on dividend forecasts at that time.

The reason only dividends appear in Equation 12.3 is not that investors ignore capital gains. It is instead that those capital gains will be determined by dividend forecasts at the time the stock is sold. That is why in Equation 12.2 we can write the stock price as the present value of dividends plus sales price for *any* horizon date. P_H is the present value at time H of all dividends expected to be paid after the horizon date. That value is then discounted back to today, time 0. The DDM asserts that stock prices are determined ultimately by the cash flows accruing to stockholders, and those are dividends.

> **dividend discount model (DDM)**
>
> A formula for the intrinsic value of a firm equal to the present value of all expected future dividends.

The Constant Growth DDM

Equation 12.3 as it stands is still not very useful in valuing a stock because it requires dividend forecasts for every year into the indefinite future. To make the DDM practical, we need to introduce some simplifying assumptions. A useful and common first pass at the problem is to assume that dividends are trending upward at a stable growth rate that we will call g. Then if $g = 0.05$, and the most recently paid dividend was $D_0 = 3.81$, expected future dividends are

$$D_1 = D_0(1+g) = 3.81 \times 1.05 \quad = 4.00$$
$$D_2 = D_0(1+g)^2 = 3.81 \times (1.05)^2 = 4.20$$
$$D_3 = D_0(1+g)^3 = 3.81 \times (1.05)^3 = 4.41 \text{ etc.}$$

Using these dividend forecasts in Equation 12.3, we solve for intrinsic value as

$$V_0 = \frac{D_0(1+g)}{1+k} + \frac{D_0(1+g)^2}{(1+k)^2} + \frac{D_0(1+g)^3}{(1+k)^3} + \ldots$$

This equation can be simplified to

$$V_0 = \frac{D_0(1+g)}{k-g} = \frac{D_1}{k-g} \qquad \text{(12.4)}$$

Note in Equation 12.4 that we divide D_1 (not D_0) by $k - g$ to calculate intrinsic value. If the market capitalization rate for Steady State is 12%, we can use Equation 12.4 to show that the intrinsic value of a share of Steady State stock is

$$\frac{\$4.00}{0.12 - 0.05} = \$57.14$$

constant growth DDM

A form of the dividend discount model that assumes dividends will grow at a constant rate.

Equation 12.4 is called the **constant growth DDM** or the Gordon model, after Myron J. Gordon, who popularized the model. It should remind you of the formula for the present value of a perpetuity. If dividends were expected not to grow, then the dividend stream would be a simple perpetuity, and the valuation formula for such a nongrowth stock would be $P_0 = D_1/k$.[1] Equation 12.4 is a generalization of the perpetuity formula to cover the case of a _growing_ perpetuity. As g increases, the stock price also rises.

12.1 EXAMPLE

Preferred Stock and the DDM

Preferred stock that pays a fixed dividend can be valued using the constant growth dividend discount model. The constant growth rate of dividends is simply zero. For example, to value a preferred stock paying a fixed dividend of $2 per share when the discount rate is 8%, we compute

$$V_0 = \frac{\$2}{0.08 - 0} = \$25$$

12.2 EXAMPLE

The Constant Growth DDM

High Flyer Industries has just paid its annual dividend of $3 per share. The dividend is expected to grow at a constant rate of 8% indefinitely. The beta of High Flyer stock is 1.0, the risk-free rate is 6% and the market risk premium is 8%. What is the intrinsic value of the stock? What would be your estimate of intrinsic value if you believed that the stock was riskier, with a beta of 1.25?

Because a $3 dividend has just been paid and the growth rate of dividends is 8%, the forecast for the year-end dividend is $3 × 1.08 = $3.24. The market capitalization rate is 6% + 1.0 × 8% = 14%. Therefore, the value of the stock is

$$V_0 = \frac{D_1}{k - g} = \frac{\$3.24}{0.14 - 0.08} = \$54$$

If the stock is perceived to be riskier, its value must be lower. At the higher beta, the market capitalization rate is 6% + 1.25 × 8% = 16%, and the stock is worth only

$$\frac{\$3.24}{0.16 - 0.08} = \$40.50$$

The constant growth DDM is valid only when g is less than k. If dividends were expected to grow forever at a rate faster than k, the value of the stock would be infinite. If an analyst derives an estimate of g that is greater than k, that growth rate must be unsustainable in the long run. The appropriate valuation model to use in this case is a multistage DDM such as that discussed below.

The constant growth DDM is so widely used by stock market analysts that it is worth exploring some of its implications and limitations. The constant growth rate DDM implies that a stock's value will be greater:

[1]Recall from introductory finance that the present value of a $1 per year perpetuity is $1/k$. For example, if $k = 10\%$, the value of the perpetuity is $1/0.10 = $10. Notice that if $g = 0$ in Equation 12.4, the constant growth DDM formula is the same as the perpetuity formula.

1. The larger its expected dividend per share.
2. The lower the market capitalization rate, k.
3. The higher the expected growth rate of dividends.

Another implication of the constant growth model is that the stock price is expected to grow at the same rate as dividends. To see this, suppose Steady State stock is selling at its intrinsic value of \$57.14, so that $V_0 = P_0$. Then

$$P_0 = \frac{D_1}{k - g}$$

Note that price is proportional to dividends. Therefore, next year, when the dividends paid to Steady State stockholders are expected to be higher by $g = 5\%$, price also should increase by 5%. To confirm this, note

$$D_2 = \$4(1.05) = \$4.20$$

$$P_1 = D_2/(k - g) = \$4.20/(0.12 - 0.05) = \$60.00$$

which is 5% higher than the current price of \$57.14. To generalize

$$P_1 = \frac{D_2}{k - g} = \frac{D_1(1 + g)}{k - g} = \frac{D_1}{k - g}(1 + g)$$

$$= P_0(1 + g)$$

Therefore, the DDM implies that, in the case of constant expected growth of dividends, the expected rate of price appreciation in any year will equal that constant growth rate, g. Note that for a stock whose market price equals its intrinsic value ($V_0 = P_0$) the expected holding-period return will be

$$E(r) = \text{Dividend yield} + \text{Capital gains yield}$$

$$= \frac{D_1}{P_0} + \frac{P_1 - P_0}{P_0} = \frac{D_1}{P_0} + g \qquad \textbf{(12.5)}$$

This formula offers a means to infer the market capitalization rate of a stock, for if the stock is selling at its intrinsic value, then $E(r) = k$, implying that $k = D_1/P_0 + g$. By observing the dividend yield, D_1/P_0, and estimating the growth rate of dividends, we can compute k. This equation is known also as the *discounted cash flow (DCF) formula*.

This is an approach often used in rate hearings for regulated public utilities. The regulatory agency responsible for approving utility pricing decisions is mandated to allow the firms to charge just enough to cover costs plus a "fair" profit, that is, one that allows a competitive return on the investment the firm has made in its productive capacity. In turn, that return is taken to be the expected return investors require on the stock of the firm. The $D_1/P_0 + g$ formula provides a means to infer that required return.

Suppose that Steady State Electronics wins a major contract for its revolutionary computer chip. The very profitable contract will enable it to increase the growth rate of dividends from 5% to 6% without reducing the current dividend from the projected value of \$4.00 per share. What will happen to the stock price? What will happen to future expected rates of return on the stock?

EXAMPLE 12.3

The Constant Growth Model

(continued)

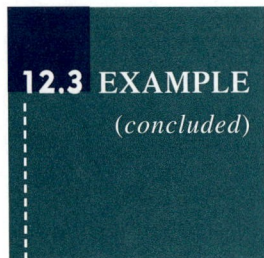

12.3 EXAMPLE
(concluded)

The stock price ought to increase in response to the good news about the contract, and indeed it does. The stock price rises from its original value of $57.14 to a postannouncement price of

$$\frac{D_1}{k-g} = \frac{\$4.00}{0.12 - 0.06} = \$66.67$$

Investors who are holding the stock when the good news about the contract is announced will receive a substantial windfall.

On the other hand, at the new price the expected rate of return on the stock is 12%, just as it was before the new contract was announced.

$$E(r) = \frac{D_1}{P_0} + g = \frac{\$4.00}{\$66.67} + 0.06 = 0.12, \text{ or } 12\%$$

This result makes sense, of course. Once the news about the contract is reflected in the stock price, the expected rate of return will be consistent with the risk of the stock. Since the risk of the stock has not changed, neither should the expected rate of return.

2. *a.* IBX's stock dividend at the end of this year is expected to be $2.15, and it is expected to grow at 11.2% per year forever. If the required rate of return on IBX stock is 15.2% per year, what is its intrinsic value?
   b. If IBX's current market price is equal to this intrinsic value, what is next year's expected price?
   c. If an investor were to buy IBX stock now and sell it after receiving the $2.15 dividend a year from now, what is the expected capital gain (i.e., price appreciation) in percentage terms? What is the dividend yield, and what would be the holding-period return?

Stock Prices and Investment Opportunities

Consider two companies, Cash Cow, Inc., and Growth Prospects, each with expected earnings in the coming year of $5 per share. Both companies could in principle pay out all of these earnings as dividends, maintaining a perpetual dividend flow of $5 per share. If the market capitalization rate were $k = 12.5\%$, both companies would then be valued at $D_1/k = \$5/0.125 = \$40$ per share. Neither firm would grow in value, because with all earnings paid out as dividends, and no earnings reinvested in the firm, both companies' capital stock and earnings capacity would remain unchanged over time; earnings[2] and dividends would not grow.

Now suppose one of the firms, Growth Prospects, engages in projects that generate a return on investment of 15%, which is greater than the required rate of return, $k = 12.5\%$. It would be foolish for such a company to pay out all of its earnings as dividends. If Growth Prospects retains or plows back some of its earnings into its highly profitable projects, it can earn a 15% rate of return for its shareholders, whereas if it pays out all earnings as dividends, it forgoes the projects, leaving shareholders to invest the dividends in other opportunities at a fair market rate of only 12.5%. Suppose, therefore, Growth Prospects chooses a lower **dividend payout ratio** (the fraction of earnings paid out as dividends), reducing payout from 100% to

dividend payout ratio

Percentage of earnings paid out as dividends.

[2]Actually, we are referring here to earnings net of the funds necessary to maintain the productivity of the firm's capital, that is, earnings net of "economic depreciation." In other words, the earnings figure should be interpreted as the maximum amount of money the firm could pay out each year in perpetuity without depleting its productive capacity. For this reason, the net earnings number may be quite different from the accounting earnings figure that the firm reports in its financial statements. We will explore this further in the next chapter.

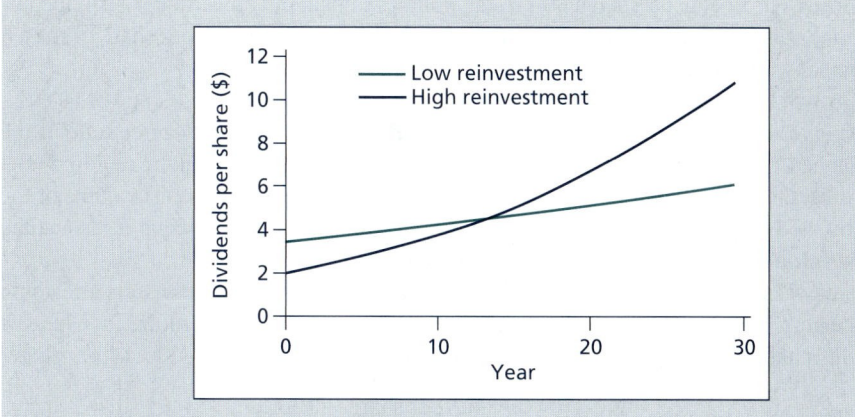

FIGURE **12.1**
Dividend growth for
two earnings
reinvestment policies

40%, and maintaining a **plowback ratio** (the fraction of earnings reinvested in the firm) of 60%. The plowback ratio also is referred to as the **earnings retention ratio.**

The dividend of the company, therefore, will be $2 (40% of $5 earnings) instead of $5. Will the share price fall? No, it will rise! Although dividends initially fall under the earnings reinvestment policy, subsequent growth in the assets of the firm because of reinvested profits will generate growth in future dividends, which will be reflected in today's share price.

Figure 12.1 illustrates the dividend streams generated by Growth Prospects under two dividend policies. A low reinvestment rate plan allows the firm to pay higher initial dividends but results in a lower dividend growth rate. Eventually, a high reinvestment rate plan will provide higher dividends. If the dividend growth generated by the reinvested earnings is high enough, the stock will be worth more under the high reinvestment strategy.

How much growth will be generated? Suppose Growth Prospects starts with plant and equipment of $100 million and is all-equity-financed. With a return on investment or equity (ROE) of 15%, total earnings are ROE × $100 million = 0.15 × $100 million = $15 million. There are 3 million shares of stock outstanding, so earnings per share are $5, as posited above. If 60% of the $15 million in this year's earnings is reinvested, then the value of the firm's capital stock will increase by 0.60 × $15 million = $9 million, or by 9%. The percentage increase in the capital stock is the rate at which income was generated (ROE) times the plowback ratio (the fraction of earnings reinvested in more capital), which we will denote as b.

Now endowed with 9% more capital, the company earns 9% more income and pays out 9% higher dividends. The growth rate of the dividends, therefore, is[3]

$$g = \text{ROE} \times b = 15\% \times 0.60 = 9\%$$

If the stock price equals its intrinsic value, and this growth rate can be sustained (i.e., if the ROE and payout ratios are consistent with the long-run capabilities of the firm), then the stock should sell at

$$P_0 = \frac{D_1}{k - g} = \frac{\$2}{0.125 - 0.09} = \$57.14$$

plowback ratio or earnings retention ratio

The proportion of the firm's earnings that is reinvested in the business (and not paid out as dividends).

---

[3]We can derive this relationship more generally by noting that with a fixed ROE, earnings (which equal ROE × Book value) will grow at the same rate as the book value of the firm. Abstracting from net new investment in the firm, the growth rate of book value equals reinvested earnings/book value. Therefore,

$$g = \frac{\text{Reinvested earnings}}{\text{Book value}} = \frac{\text{Reinvested earnings}}{\text{Total earnings}} \times \frac{\text{Total earnings}}{\text{Book value}} = b \times \text{ROE}$$

When Growth Prospects pursued a no-growth policy and paid out all earnings as dividends, the stock price was only $40. Therefore, you can think of $40 as the value per share of the assets the company already has in place.

When Growth Prospects decided to reduce current dividends and reinvest some of its earnings in new investments, its stock price increased. The increase in the stock price reflects the fact that planned investments provide an expected rate of return greater than the required rate. In other words, the investment opportunities have positive net present value. The value of the firm rises by the NPV of these investment opportunities. This net present value is also called the **present value of growth opportunities,** or **PVGO.**

present value of growth opportunities (PVGO)

Net present value of a firm's future investments.

Therefore, we can think of the value of the firm as the sum of the value of assets already in place, or the no-growth value of the firm, plus the net present value of the future investments the firm will make, which is the PVGO. For Growth Prospects, PVGO = $17.14 per share:

$$\text{Price} = \text{No-growth value per share} + \text{PVGO}$$

$$P_0 = \frac{E_1}{k} + \text{PVGO}$$

$$\$57.14 = \$40 + \$17.14 \tag{12.6}$$

We know that in reality, dividend cuts almost always are accompanied by steep drops in stock prices. Does this contradict our analysis? Not necessarily: Dividend cuts are usually taken as bad news about the future prospects of the firm, and it is the *new information* about the firm—not the reduced dividend yield per se—that is responsible for the stock price decline. The stock price history of Microsoft proves that investors do not demand generous dividends if they are convinced that the funds are better deployed to new investments in the firm.

In one well-known case, Florida Power & Light announced a cut in its dividend, not because of financial distress, but because it wanted to better position itself for a period of deregulation. At first, the stock market did not believe this rationale—the stock price dropped 14% on the day of the announcement. But within a month, the market became convinced that the firm had in fact made a strategic decision that would improve growth prospects, and the share price actually rose *above* its preannouncement value. Even including the initial price drop, the share price outperformed both the S&P 500 and the S&P utility index in the year following the dividend cut.

It is important to recognize that growth per se is not what investors desire. Growth enhances company value only if it is achieved by investment in projects with attractive profit opportunities (i.e., with ROE > k). To see why, let's now consider Growth Prospects' unfortunate sister company, Cash Cow. Cash Cow's ROE is only 12.5%, just equal to the required rate of return, k. Therefore, the NPV of its investment opportunities is zero. We've seen that following a zero-growth strategy with $b = 0$ and $g = 0$, the value of Cash Cow will be $E_1/k = \$5/0.125 = \$40$ per share. Now suppose Cash Cow chooses a plowback ratio of $b = 0.60$, the same as Growth Prospects' plowback. Then g would be

$$g = \text{ROE} \times b = 0.125 \times 0.60 = 0.075$$

but the stock price is still

$$P_0 = \frac{D_1}{k - g} = \frac{\$2}{0.125 - 0.075} = \$40$$

no different from the no-growth strategy.

In the case of Cash Cow, the dividend reduction that frees funds for reinvestment in the firm generates only enough growth to maintain the stock price at the current level. This is as it should be: If the firm's projects yield only what investors can earn on their own, shareholders cannot be made better off by a high reinvestment rate policy. This demonstrates that "growth" is not the same as growth opportunities. To justify reinvestment, the firm must engage in projects with better prospective returns than those shareholders can find elsewhere. Notice also that the PVGO of Cash Cow is zero: PVGO $= P_0 - E_1/k = 40 - 40 = 0$. With ROE $= k$, there is no advantage to plowing funds back into the firm; this shows up as PVGO of zero. In fact, this is why firms with considerable cash flow, but limited investment prospects, are called "cash cows." The cash these firms generate is best taken out of or "milked from" the firm.

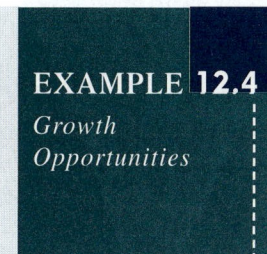

Takeover Target is run by entrenched management that insists on reinvesting 60% of its earnings in projects that provide an ROE of 10%, despite the fact that the firm's capitalization rate is $k = 15\%$. The firm's year-end dividend will be $2 per share, paid out of earnings of $5 per share. At what price will the stock sell? What is the present value of growth opportunities? Why would such a firm be a takeover target for another firm?

EXAMPLE 12.4
Growth Opportunities

Given current management's investment policy, the dividend growth rate will be

$$g = \text{ROE} \times b = 10\% \times 0.6 = 6\%$$

and the stock price should be

$$P_0 = \frac{\$2}{0.15 - 0.06} = \$22.22$$

The present value of growth opportunities is

$$\text{PVGO} = \text{Price per share} - \text{No-growth value per share}$$
$$= \$22.22 - E_1/k = \$22.22 - \$5/0.15 = -\$11.11$$

PVGO is *negative*. This is because the net present value of the firm's projects is negative: The rate of return on those assets is less than the opportunity cost of capital.

Such a firm would be subject to takeover, because another firm could buy the firm for the market price of $22.22 per share and increase the value of the firm by changing its investment policy. For example, if the new management simply paid out all earnings as dividends, the value of the firm would increase to its no-growth value, $E_1/k = \$5/0.15 = \$33.33$.

3. *a.* Calculate the price of a firm with a plowback ratio of 0.60 if its ROE is 20%. Current earnings, E_1, will be $5 per share, and $k = 12.5\%$.
   b. What if ROE is 10% less than the market capitalization rate? Compare the firm's price in this instance to that of a firm with the same ROE and E_1, but a plowback ratio of $b = 0$.

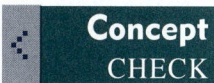
Concept CHECK

Life Cycles and Multistage Growth Models

As useful as the constant growth DDM formula is, you need to remember that it is based on a simplifying assumption, namely, that the dividend growth rate will be constant forever. In fact, firms typically pass through life cycles with very different dividend profiles in different phases. In early years, there are ample opportunities for profitable reinvestment in the company. Payout ratios are low, and growth is correspondingly rapid. In later years, the firm matures, production capacity is sufficient to meet market demand, competitors enter the market, and attractive opportunities for reinvestment may become harder to find. In this mature phase, the firm may choose to increase the dividend payout ratio, rather than retain earnings. The dividend level increases, but thereafter it grows at a slower rate because the company has fewer growth opportunities.

TABLE **12.2**		Return on Assets	Payout Ratio	Growth Rate* 2002–2005
Financial ratios in two industries	**Semiconductors**			
	Analog Devices	17.0%	0.0%	27.2%
	Cirrus Logic	12.0	0.0	34.6
	Intel	22.5	7.0	22.6
	LSI Logic Corp.	16.0	0.0	32.8
	Micron Technologies	21.5	0.0	22.5
	Motorola	10.5	17.0	41.7
	National Semiconductor	21.0	0.0	19.8
	Novellus	17.0	0.0	14.1
	Texas Instruments	10.0	9.0	25.9
	Average	16.4%	3.7%	26.8%
	Electric utilities			
	Alleghany Energy	10.0%	32.0%	9.8%
	Central Vermont	8.0	49.0	8.3
	Consolidated Edison	7.5	67.0	1.5
	Energy East	6.5	51.0	5.8
	G.P.U.	9.0	58.0	5.6
	Green Mountain Power	8.5	54.0	8.7
	Northeast Utilities	6.0	51.0	11.2
	Nstar	9.0	55.0	4.3
	United Illuminating	7.5	63.0	3.1
	Average	8.0%	53.3%	6.5%

*Year 2002 earnings for some semiconductor firms were negative, which would make growth rates meaningless. In these cases, we used an average of recent-year earnings, or longer term growth estimates from Value Line.

Source: From *Value Line Investment Survey,* 2001. Reprinted by permission of Value Line Investment Survey.

Table 12.2 illustrates this profile. It gives Value Line's forecasts of return on assets, dividend payout ratio, and three-year growth rate in earnings per share of a sample of the firms included in the semiconductor industry versus those of East Coast electric utilities. (We compare return on assets rather than return on equity because the latter is affected by leverage, which tends to be far greater in the electric utility industry than in the semiconductor industry. Return on assets measures operating income per dollar of total assets, regardless of whether the source of the capital supplied is debt or equity. We will return to this issue in the next chapter.)

Despite recent problems, the semiconductor firms as a group have attractive investment opportunities. The average return on assets of these firms is forecast to be 16.4%, and the firms have responded with quite high plowback ratios. Many of these firms pay no dividends at all. The high returns on assets and high plowback ratios result in rapid growth. The average growth rate of earnings per share in this group is projected at 26.8%.

In contrast, the electric utilities are more representative of mature firms. For this industry, return on assets is lower, 8.0%; dividend payout is higher, 53.3%; and average growth is lower, 6.5%.

two-stage DDM

Dividend discount model in which dividend growth is assumed to level off only at some future date.

To value companies with temporarily high growth, analysts use a multistage version of the dividend discount model. Dividends in the early high-growth period are forecast and their combined present value is calculated. Then, once the firm is projected to settle down to a steady growth phase, the constant growth DDM is applied to value the remaining stream of dividends.

We can illustrate this with a real-life example using a **two-stage DDM.** Figure 12.2 is a *Value Line Investment Survey* report on the defense contractor, Raytheon. Some of Raytheon's relevant information in late 2001 is highlighted.

Ⓑ

RAYTHEON NYSE-RTN | RECENT PRICE **32.50** | P/E RATIO **17.9** (Trailing: 21.0 Median: NMF) | RELATIVE P/E RATIO **1.14** | DIV'D YLD **2.5%** | VALUE LINE **566**

Ⓐ

| | | | | | High: | 57.0 | 59.6 | 75.4 | 33.3 | 36.2 | | Target Price Range 2004 2005 2006 |
| | | | | | Low: | 48.0 | 39.9 | 21.3 | 17.9 | 24.0 | | |

TIMELINESS **2** Raised 10/27/00
SAFETY **3** New 1/2/98
TECHNICAL **3** Raised 9/21/01
BETA .85 (1.00 = Market)

LEGENDS
.... Relative Price Strength
Options: Yes
Shaded area indicates recession

2004-06 PROJECTIONS
	Price	Gain	Ann'l Total Return
High	65	(+100%)	20%
Low	45	(+40%)	10%

Insider Decisions
	N	D	J	F	M	A	M	J	J
to Buy	0	0	0	0	0	0	0	0	0
Options	0	0	0	0	0	0	0	0	0
to Sell	0	0	0	0	0	0	0	0	0

Institutional Decisions
	4Q2000	1Q2001	2Q2001
to Buy	88	197	216
to Sell	82	191	178
Hld's(0)	63747	198165	232688

Percent 15.0
shares 10.0
traded 5.0

% TOT. RETURN 8/01
	THIS STOCK	VL ARITH. INDEX
1 yr.	—	1.6
3 yr.	—	56.0
5 yr.	—	87.6

(New) Raytheon Company was formed by the merger on December 18, 1997 of (old) Raytheon Company and the defense business of Hughes Electronics Corporation (a wholly owned subsidiary of General Motors). (Old) Raytheon stockholders received Class B common shares representing 70% of the equity of the new company. GM holders were given Class A shares, with the remaining 30% of the equity value. The A shares control the company through their 80.1% of the power to elect or remove directors.

CAPITAL STRUCTURE as of 7/1/01
Total Debt $8.9 bill. Due in 5 years $5.6 bill.
LT Debt $8.6 bill. LT Interest $600 mill.
(LT interest earned: 2.3x; total interest coverage: 2.1x) (45% of Cap'l E)
Leases, Uncapitalized Annual rentals $392 mill.
Pension Liability None

Pfd Stock None
Common Stock 359,377,000 shs. (55% of Cap'l E)

MARKET CAP: $11.7 billion (Large Cap)

CURRENT POSITION
($MILL.)	1999	2000	7/1/01
Cash Assets	230	871	529
Receivables	851	505	555
Inventory (LIFO)	7165	5969	6255
Other	685	643	775
Current Assets	8931	7988	8114
Accts Payable	1561	1099	1060
Debt Due	2472	877	255
Other	3853	2864	3237
Current Liab.	7886	4840	4552

ANNUAL RATES
of change (per sh)	Past 10 Yrs.	Past 5 Yrs.	Est'd '98-'00 to '04-'06
Sales	--	--	5.0%
"Cash Flow"	--	--	9.0%
Earnings	--	--	24.0%
Dividends	--	--	9.5%
Book Value	--	--	6.5%

QUARTERLY SALES ($ mill.)
Cal-endar	Mar.Per	Jun.Per	Sep.Per	Dec.Per	Full Year
1998	4574	5078	4746	5442	19840
1999	5025	5210	4776	4830	19841
2000	4231	4124	4160	4380	16895
2001	3968	4307	4450	4525	17250
2002	4225	4375	4525	4675	17800

EARNINGS PER SHARE A
Cal-endar	Mar.Per	Jun.Per	Sep.Per	Dec.Per	Full Year
1998	.63	.78	.85	1.08	3.34
1999	.77	.84	d.48	.21	1.34
2000	.24	.28	.39	.55	1.46
2001	.28	.33	.41	.58	1.60
2002	.50	.60	.75	1.00	2.85

QUARTERLY DIVIDENDS PAID B
Cal-endar	Mar.31	Jun.30	Sep.30	Dec.31	Full Year
1997	.20	.20	.20	.20	.80
1998	.20	.20	.20	.20	.80
1999	.20	.20	.20	.20	.80
2000	.20	.20	.20	.20	.80
2001	.20	.20	.20		

	1991	1992	1993	1994	1995	1996	1997	1998	1999	2000	2001	2002	© VALUE LINE PUB., INC. 04-06	
	--	--	--	--	--	60.51	63.09	58.91	58.57	49.60	47.90	49.50	Sales per sh	63.00
	--	--	--	--	--	5.45	5.65	3.49	3.50	3.65	3.90		"Cash Flow" per sh	5.40
	--	--	--	--	--	2.65	3.01	3.34	1.34	1.46	1.60	2.85	Earnings per sh A	4.25
	--	--	--	--	--	.80	.80	.80	.80	.80	.80	.80	Div'ds Decl'd per sh B ■	1.25
	--	--	--	--	--	--	1.36	1.51	1.57	1.27	1.10	1.25	Cap'l Spending per sh	1.65
	--	--	--	--	--	28.42	30.79	32.23	32.35	31.77	34.50	36.50	Book Value per sh C	44.25
	--	--	--	--	--	339.00	338.57	336.80	338.76	340.62	360.00	360.00	Common Shs Outst'g F	365.00
	--	--	--	--	--	--	16.0	16.0	40.3	16.7	Bold figures are		Avg Ann'l P/E Ratio	13.0
	--	--	--	--	--	--	.92	.83	2.30	1.09	Value Line		Relative P/E Ratio	.85
	--	--	--	--	--	--	1.7%	1.5%	1.5%	3.3%	estimates		Avg Ann'l Div'd Yield	2.3%
	--	--	--	--	--	20514	21359	19840	19841	16895	17250	17800	Sales ($mill) G	23000
	--	--	--	--	--	16.5%	16.7%	11.3%	13.7%	13.5%	13.5%	15.0%	Operating Margin	15.0%
	--	--	--	--	--	--	800	761.0	724.0	694.0	735	370	Depreciation ($mill) D	370
	--	--	--	--	--	901.0	1208.0	1141.0	457.0	498.0	570	1040	Net Profit ($mill)	1600
	--	--	--	--	--	35.6%	34.0%	42.6%	44.8%	43.2%	43.0%	39.0%	Income Tax Rate	39.0%
	--	--	--	--	--	4.4%	5.7%	5.8%	2.3%	2.9%	3.3%	5.8%	Net Profit Margin	7.0%
	--	--	--	--	--	--	d2653	1957.0	1045.0	3148.0	4500	4675	Working Cap'l ($mill)	5650
	--	--	--	--	--	--	4406.0	8163.0	7298.0	9054.0	8500	8000	Long-Term Debt ($mill)	6500
	--	--	--	--	--	9634.0	10425	10856	10959	10823	12400	13150	Shr. Equity ($mill)	16150
	--	--	--	--	--	9.4%	8.1%	7.2%	4.1%	4.2%	4.5%	6.0%	Return on Total Cap'l	8.0%
	--	--	--	--	--	9.4%	11.6%	10.5%	4.2%	4.6%	4.5%	7.5%	Return on Shr. Equity	10.0%
	--	--	--	--	--	9.4%	9.8%	8.0%	1.7%	2.1%	2.5%	5.0%	Retained to Com Eq	7.0%
	--	--	--	--	--	--	16%	24%	59%	55%	50%	30%	All Div'ds to Net Prof	29%

BUSINESS: (New) Raytheon Company represents the 12/97 merger of (old) Raytheon Co. and the defense electronics business of Hughes Electronics Corp. RC is a major provider of ground-based air defense systems, air intercept missiles, radars, communication and other military systems, and is a important producer of electronics-based aerospace and defense products & systems. Is a leading maker of general aviation aircraft. '00 depr. rate: 14.2% Officers & Directors control 1.8% of stock, Brandes Investment Partners, 5.0% (3/01 proxy). Has 87,500 employees, 283,000 shareholders. Chairman & CEO: Daniel P. Burnham. Incorporated: Delaware. Address: 141 Spring St., Lexington, Massachusetts 02421. Telephone: 781-862-6600. Internet: www.raytheon.com.

Raytheon Company's earnings are recovering as per our expectations this year. In fact, our per-share estimates were on the mark in the first two periods, with the bottom line heading, we believe, toward a 10% improvement from the prior-year figure. Weakness in the company's commercial units is being more than offset by the strengthening defense-related sectors, reflecting both internal improvements, as problems stemming from the integration of Raytheon's many components are gradually resolved, and increased sales in continuing units. **And the company's operations should continue to perform well in 2002.** Our estimates assume more of the same, with gains both internal and external. We are not counting any hard-to-measure gains from the likely surge in defense spending following the World Trade Center attack. In addition, **The absence of goodwill amortization will greatly bolster the bottom line.** Raytheon has not yet provided firm guidance on the favorable 2002 impact, but we note that in 2000, goodwill amortization amounted to $365 million pretax and $337 million aftertax. This year, the pretax figure seems to headed toward an 8% increase. Adjusting these trends forward to 2002 would furnish about a $1.00 increase to share earnings, which would bring the total to a hefty 78% gain over our 2001 estimate.

This corporation has an ongoing legal dispute about a divested unit, which was sold last year. But when the buyer declared bankruptcy, it triggered a Raytheon performance guarantee. So far, the company has taken charges in both the first and second quarters, which we have excluded, to cover the likely costs to complete. Management believes only small further charges are probable.

These shares look good for year-ahead relative price action. But they have below-average appreciation potential over the 3- to 5-year pull. It is impossible to foresee the magnitude of the impending surge in spending on attacking terrorists and defending the United States, but Raytheon's strength in electronics and missiles should give it a good share of the increase.

Morton L. Siegel September 28, 2001

(A) Prim. egs. for 1996, then diluted. Excl. nonrecur. chges.: '97, $1.35; '98, 81c; '99, 15c; '00, $1.05, '01, $1.16. Next egs. rpt. due late Oct. (B) Next div'd mtg. ab't Dec. 20. Next ex-
date ab't Oct. 5. Div'd pmnt. dts. ab't the 30th of Jan., Apr., Jul., Oct. ■ Div'd reinv. plan avail. (C) Incl. intang. In '00: $13.3 billion, $39.00/sh. (D) Accel. dep. (E) % of cap'l based on total
bold figures. (F) In millions. P&L data through 1997 are pro forma, with estimates in bold italics. (G) P&L data through 1997 are pro forma, with estimates in bold italics.

Company's Financial Strength	B+
Stock's Price Stability	25
Price Growth Persistence	25
Earnings Predictability	NMF

To subscribe call 1-800-833-0046.

Ⓒ Ⓓ Ⓔ

FIGURE 12.2

Value Line Investment Survey report on Raytheon

Source: From *Value Line Investment Survey*, 9/28/01. Reprinted by permission of Value Line Investment Survey.

Raytheon's beta appears at the circled A, its recent stock price at the B, the per-share dividend payments at the C, the ROE (referred to as "return on shareholder equity") at the D, and the dividend payout ratio (referred to as "all dividends to net profits") at the E. The rows ending at C, D, and E are historical time series. The boldfaced italicized entries under 2002 are estimates for that year. Similarly, the entries in the far right column (labeled 04–06) are forecasts for some time between 2004 and 2006, which we will take to be 2005.

Value Line projects rapid growth in the near term, with dividends rising from $.80 in 2002 to $1.25 in 2005. This rapid growth rate cannot be sustained indefinitely. We can obtain dividend inputs for this initial period by using the explicit forecasts for 2002 and 2005 and linear interpolation for the years between:

2002	$ .80
2003	$ .95
2004	$1.10
2005	$1.25

Now let us assume the dividend growth rate levels off in 2005. What is a good guess for that steady-state growth rate? Value Line forecasts a dividend payout ratio of 0.29 and an ROE of 10.0%, implying long-term growth will be

$$g = \text{ROE} \times b = 10.0\% \times (1 - 0.29) = 7.1\%$$

Our estimate of Raytheon's intrinsic value using an investment horizon of 2005 is therefore obtained from Equation 12.2, which we restate here

$$V_{2001} = \frac{D_{2002}}{(1+k)} + \frac{D_{2003}}{(1+k)^2} + \frac{D_{2004}}{(1+k)^3} + \frac{D_{2005} + P_{2005}}{(1+k)^4}$$

$$= \frac{.80}{1+k} + \frac{.95}{(1+k)^2} + \frac{1.10}{(1+k)^3} + \frac{1.25 + P_{2005}}{(1+k)^4}$$

Here, P_{2005} represents the forecast price at which we can sell our shares of Raytheon at the end of 2005, when dividends enter their constant growth phase. That price, according to the constant growth DDM, should be

$$P_{2005} = \frac{D_{2006}}{k-g} = \frac{D_{2005}(1+g)}{k-g} = \frac{1.25 \times 1.071}{k - .071}$$

The only variable remaining to be determined to calculate intrinsic value is the market capitalization rate, k.

One way to obtain k is from the CAPM. Observe from the Value Line data that Raytheon's beta is .85. The risk-free rate on longer term bonds in 2001 was about 5%. Suppose that the market risk premium were forecast at 8.0%. This would imply that the forecast for the market return was

$$\text{Risk-free rate} + \text{Market risk premium} = 5.0\% + 8.0\% = 13.0\%$$

Therefore, we can solve for the market capitalization rate for Raytheon as

$$k = r_f + \beta[E(r_M) - r_f]$$

$$= 5\% + .85 (13.0 - 5.0) = 11.8\%$$

Our forecast for the stock price in 2005 is thus

$$P_{2005} = \frac{\$1.25 \times 1.071}{.118 - .071} = \$28.48$$

and today's estimate of intrinsic value is

$$V_{2001} = \frac{.80}{1.118} + \frac{.95}{(1.118)^2} + \frac{1.10}{(1.118)^3} + \frac{1.25 + 28.48}{(1.118)^4} = \$21.29$$

We know from the Value Line report that Raytheon's actual price was $32.50 (at the circled B). Our intrinsic value analysis indicates Raytheon was overpriced. Should we sell our holdings of Raytheon or even sell Raytheon short?

Perhaps. But before betting the farm, stop to consider how firm our estimate is. We've had to guess at dividends in the near future, the ultimate growth rate of those dividends, and the appropriate discount rate. Moreover, we've assumed Raytheon will follow a relatively simple two-stage growth process. In practice, the growth of dividends can follow more complicated patterns. Even small errors in these approximations could upset a conclusion.

For example, suppose the market risk premium is lower than our estimate, 6% rather than 8%. While lower than the historical average, this value is consistent with some recent research.[4] This seemingly modest change will reduce the market capitalization rate to 10.1%. At this lower rate, the intrinsic value of the stock based on the two-stage growth model rises to $33.55, just about equal to the stock price at the time. Therefore, our conclusion regarding mispricing is reversed.

This exercise shows that finding bargains is not as easy as it seems. While the DDM is easy to apply, establishing its inputs is more of a challenge. This should not be surprising. In even a moderately efficient market, finding profit opportunities has to be more involved than sitting down with Value Line for a half-hour.

The exercise also highlights the importance of assessing the sensitivity of your analysis to changes in underlying assumptions when you attempt to value stocks. Your estimates of stock values are no better than your assumptions. Sensitivity analysis will highlight the inputs that need to be most carefully examined. For example, we just found that very small changes in the estimated risk premium of the stock result in big changes in intrinsic value. Similarly, small changes in the assumed growth rate change intrinsic value substantially. On the other hand, reasonable changes in the dividends forecast between 2002 and 2005 have a small impact on intrinsic value.

4. Confirm that the intrinsic value of Raytheon using $E(r_M) - r_f = 6.0\%$ is $33.55. (Hint: First calculate the discount rate and stock price in 2005. Then calculate the present value of all interim dividends plus the present value of the 2005 sales price.)

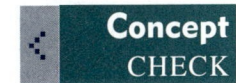

Concept
CHECK

Multistage Growth Models

The two-stage growth model that we just considered for Raytheon is a good start toward realism, but clearly we could do even better if our valuation model allowed for more flexible patterns of growth. Multistage growth models allow dividends per share to grow at several different rates as the firm matures. Many analysts use three-stage growth models. They may assume an initial period of high dividend growth (or instead make year-by-year forecasts of dividends for the short term), a final period of sustainable growth, and a transition period in

---

[4]Recent research suggests that in the last 50 years the average excess return of the market index portfolio was considerably better than market participants at the time were anticipating. Such a pattern could indicate that the economy performed better than initially expected during this period or that the discount rate declined. For evidence on this issue, see Ravi Jagannathan, Ellen R. McGrattan, and Anna Scherbina, "The Declining U.S. Equity Premium," *Federal Reserve Bank of Minneapolis Quarterly Review* 4 (Fall 2000) pp. 3–19, and Eugene F. Fama and Kenneth R. French, "The Equity Premium," *Journal of Finance* 57 (April 2002), pp. 637–660.

Three-Stage Growth Model: Raytheon Example

The spreadsheet in this box presents a three-stage dividend discount model. Rather than forecasting year-by-year dividends in the first stage, in this version of the model the analyst forecasts an initial high dividend growth rate. In the last stage, dividends are forecast to grow indefinitely at a constant rate. In the transition years, the analyst forecasts a dividend growth rate in between the initial high rate and the more moderate sustainable rate. This spreadsheet is available at www.mhhe.com.bkm.

	A	B
1	**Three Stage Growth Model**	
2		
3		
4	Initial Earnings	4.00
5	Initial Dividend	2.00
6	Stage 1 Growth	0.35
7	Duration of Growth 1	10
8	Stage 2 Growth	0.15
9	Duration of Growth 2	10
10	Estimated Constant Growth	0.08
11	Beta Coefficient	1.25
12	T-Bill Rate	0.05
13	Market Risk Premium	0.08
14		
15	Required Return	0.15
16	Ratio of (1+g1)/(1+k)	1.17391304
17	Ratio of (1+g2)/(1+k)	1
18	Closed End Ratio 1	26.80
19	Closed End Ratio 2	10.00
20		
21	PValue of the Stage 1 Dividends	53.60
22	PValue of the Stage 2 Dividends	99.40
23	PValue of the Constant Growth Dividends	153.36
24	Value of the Stock	306.36
25		
26	Analysis of Growth Opportunities	
27	Value of NoGrowth Firm	26.67
28	Present Value of Growth Opportunities	279.69
29		
30	Price to Earnings Ratios	
31	Price /Current Earnings	76.59
32	Price / Next Years Expected Earnings	56.73

between, during which dividend growth rates taper off from the initial rapid rate to the ultimate sustainable rate. These models are conceptually no harder to work with than a two-stage model, but they require many more calculations and can be tedious to do by hand. It is easy, however, to build an Excel spreadsheet for such a model. We refer you to the nearby Excel application for an example of such a spreadsheet.

12.4 PRICE–EARNINGS RATIOS

The Price–Earnings Ratio and Growth Opportunities

price–earnings multiple

The ratio of a stock's price to its earnings per share.

Much of the real-world discussion of stock market valuation concentrates on the firm's **price–earnings multiple,** the ratio of price per share to earnings per share, commonly called the P/E ratio. In fact, one common approach to valuing a firm is to use an earnings multiplier. The value of the stock is obtained by multiplying projected earnings per share by a forecast of the P/E ratio. This procedure seems simple, but its apparent simplicity is deceptive. First, forecasting earnings is challenging. As we saw in the previous chapter, earnings will depend on international, macroeconomic, and industry as well as firm-specific factors, many of which are highly unpredictable. Second, forecasting the P/E multiple is even more difficult. P/E ratios vary across industries and over time. Nevertheless, our discussion of stock valuation provides some insight into the factors that ought to determine a firm's P/E ratio.

Recall our discussion of growth opportunities, in which we compared two firms, Growth Prospects and Cash Cow, each of which had earnings per share of $5. Growth Prospects reinvested 60% of its earnings in prospects with an ROE of 15%, while Cash Cow paid out all of its earnings as dividends. Cash Cow had a price of $40, giving it a P/E multiple of 40/5 = 8.0, while Growth Prospects sold for $57.14, giving it a multiple of 57.14/5 = 11.4. This observation suggests the P/E ratio might serve as a useful indicator of expectations of growth opportunities. We can see this explicitly by rearranging Equation 12.6 to

$$\frac{P_0}{E_1} = \frac{1}{k}\left[1 + \frac{\text{PVGO}}{E_1/k}\right] \tag{12.7}$$

When PVGO = 0, Equation 12.7 shows that $P_0 = E_1/k$. The stock is valued like a nongrowing perpetuity of EPS$_1$. The P/E ratio is just $1/k$. However, as PVGO becomes an increasingly dominant contributor to price, the P/E ratio can rise dramatically. The ratio of PVGO to E/k has a simple interpretation. It is the ratio of the component of firm value reflecting growth opportunities to the component of value reflecting assets already in place (i.e., the no-growth value of the firm, E/k). When future growth opportunities dominate the estimate of total value, the firm will command a high price relative to current earnings. Thus, a high P/E multiple appears to indicate that a firm is endowed with ample growth opportunities.

Return again to Takeover Target, the firm we first encountered in Example 12.4. Earnings are $5 per share, and the capitalization rate is 15%, implying that the no-growth value of the firm is E_1/k = $5/0.15 = $33.33. The stock price actually is $22.22, implying that the present value of growth opportunities equals −$11.11. This implies that the P/E ratio should be

$$\frac{P_0}{E_1} = \frac{1}{k}\left[1 + \frac{\text{PVGO}}{E/k}\right] = \frac{1}{0.15}\left[1 + \frac{-\$11.11}{\$33.33}\right] = 4.44$$

In fact, the stock price is $22.22 and earnings are $5 per share, so the P/E ratio is $22.22/$5 = 4.44.

EXAMPLE 12.5
P/E Ratios and Growth Opportunities

Let's see if P/E multiples do vary with growth prospects. Between 1986 and 1999, Sun Microsystems' P/E ratio averaged about 19.4 while Consolidated Edison's average P/E was only 11.1. These numbers do not necessarily imply that Sun was overpriced compared to Con Ed. If investors believed Sun would grow faster than Con Ed, the higher price per dollar would be justified. That is, an investor might well pay a higher price per dollar of *current* earnings if he or she expected that earnings stream to grow more rapidly. In fact Sun's growth rate has been consistent with its higher P/E multiple. In the decade ending 1999, its earnings per share grew more than 14-fold, while Con Ed's earnings grew by only 26%. Figure 12.5 (on page 436) shows the EPS history of the two companies.

Clearly, it is differences in expected growth opportunities that justify particular differentials in P/E ratios across firms. The P/E ratio is in large part a reflection of the market's optimism concerning a firm's growth prospects. In their use of a P/E ratio, analysts must decide whether they are more or less optimistic than the market. If they are more optimistic, they will recommend buying the stock.

There is a way to make these insights more precise. Look again at the constant growth DDM formula, $P_0 = D_1/(k - g)$. Now recall that dividends equal the earnings that are *not* reinvested in the firm: $D_1 = E_1(1 - b)$. Recall also that $g = \text{ROE} \times b$. Hence, substituting for D_1 and g, we find that

$$P_0 = \frac{E_1(1 - b)}{k - (\text{ROE} \times b)}$$

TABLE **12.3**		Plowback Ratio (b)			
Effect of ROE and plowback on growth and the P/E ratio		0	0.25	0.50	0.75
		A. Growth Rate, g			
	ROE				
	10%	0%	2.5%	5.0%	7.5%
	12	0	3.0	6.0	9.0
	14	0	3.5	7.0	10.5
		B. P/E Ratio			
	ROE				
	10%	8.33	7.89	7.14	5.56
	12	8.33	8.33	8.33	8.33
	14	8.33	8.82	10.00	16.67

Note: Assumption: $k = 12\%$ per year.

implying that the P/E ratio for a firm growing at a long-run sustainable pace is

$$\frac{P_0}{E_1} = \frac{1 - b}{k - (\text{ROE} \times b)} \tag{12.8}$$

It is easy to verify that the P/E ratio increases with ROE. This makes sense, because high ROE projects give the firm good opportunities for growth.[5] We also can verify that the P/E ratio increases for higher plowback, b, as long as ROE exceeds k. This too makes sense. When a firm has good investment opportunities, the market will reward it with a higher P/E multiple if it exploits those opportunities more aggressively by plowing back more earnings into those opportunities.

Remember, however, that growth is not desirable for its own sake. Examine Table 12.3, where we use Equation 12.8 to compute both growth rates and P/E ratios for different combinations of ROE and b. While growth always increases with the plowback ratio (move across the rows in Panel A of Table 12.3), the P/E ratio does not (move across the rows in Panel B). In the top row of Table 12.3B, the P/E falls as the plowback rate increases. In the middle row, it is unaffected by plowback. In the third row, it increases.

This pattern has a simple interpretation. When the expected ROE is less than the required return, k, investors prefer that the firm pay out earnings as dividends rather than reinvest earnings in the firm at an inadequate rate of return. That is, for ROE lower than k, the value of the firm falls as plowback increases. Conversely, when ROE exceeds k, the firm offers superior investment opportunities, so the value of the firm is enhanced as those opportunities are more fully exploited by increasing the plowback ratio.

Finally, where ROE just equals k, the firm offers "break-even" investment opportunities with a fair rate of return. In this case, investors are indifferent between reinvestment of earnings in the firm or elsewhere at the market capitalization rate, because the rate of return in either case is 12%. Therefore, the stock price is unaffected by the plowback ratio.

One way to summarize these relationships is to say the higher the plowback ratio, the higher the growth rate, but a higher plowback ratio does not necessarily mean a higher P/E ratio. A higher plowback ratio increases P/E only if investments undertaken by the firm offer an expected rate of return higher than the market capitalization rate. Otherwise, higher

---

[5]Note that Equation 12.8 is a simple rearrangement of the DDM formula, with $\text{ROE} \times b = g$. Because that formula requires that $g < k$, Equation 12.8 is valid only when $\text{ROE} \times b < k$.

plowback hurts investors because it means more money is sunk into prospects with inadequate rates of return.

Notwithstanding these fine points, P/E ratios commonly are taken as proxies for the expected growth in dividends or earnings. In fact, a common Wall Street rule of thumb is that the growth rate ought to be roughly equal to the P/E ratio. In other words, the ratio of P/E to g, often called the *PEG ratio,* should be about 1.0. Peter Lynch, the famous portfolio manager, puts it this way in his book *One Up on Wall Street*:

> The P/E ratio of any company that's fairly priced will equal its growth rate. I'm talking here about growth rate of earnings. . . . If the P/E ratio of Coca-Cola is 15, you'd expect the company to be growing at about 15% per year, etc. But if the P/E ratio is less than the growth rate, you may have found yourself a bargain [page 198].

Let's try his rule of thumb.

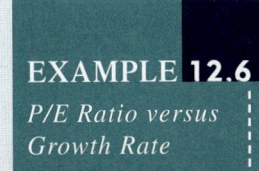

EXAMPLE 12.6

P/E Ratio versus Growth Rate

Assume:

$r_f = 8\%$ (about the value when Peter Lynch was writing)

$r_M - r_f = 8\%$ (about the historical average market risk premium)

$b = 0.4$ (a typical value for the plowback ratio in the U.S.)

Therefore, $r_M = r_f +$ Market risk premium $= 8\% + 8\% = 16\%$, and $k = 16\%$ for an average ($\beta = 1$) company. If we also accept as reasonable that ROE $= 16\%$ (the same value as the expected return on the stock) we conclude that

$$g = \text{ROE} \times b = 16\% \times 0.4 = 6.4\%$$

and

$$\text{P/E} = \frac{1 - 0.4}{0.16 - 0.064} = 6.26$$

Thus the P/E ratio and g are about equal using these assumptions, consistent with the rule of thumb. However, note that this rule of thumb, like almost all others, will not work in all circumstances. For example, the value of r_f today is more like 5%, so a comparable forecast of r_M today would be:

$$r_f + \text{Market risk premium} = 5\% + 8\% = 13\%$$

If we continue to focus on a firm with $\beta = 1$, and ROE still is about the same as k, then

$$g = 13\% \times 0.4 = 5.2\%$$

while

$$\text{P/E} = \frac{1 - 0.4}{0.13 - 0.052} = 7.69$$

The P/E ratio and g now diverge and the PEG ratio is now 1.5. Nevertheless, it still is the case that high P/E stocks are almost invariably expected to show rapid earnings growth, even if the expected growth rate does not precisely equal the P/E ratio.

Whatever its shortcomings, the PEG ratio is widely followed. Figure 12.3 is the PEG ratio for the S&P over the last 15 years. It typically has fluctuated within the range between 1.0 and 1.4.

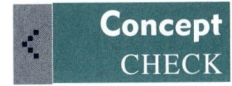

Concept CHECK

5. ABC stock has an expected ROE of 12% per year, expected earnings per share of $2, and expected dividends of $1.50 per share. Its market capitalization rate is 10% per year.
   a. What are its expected growth rate, its price, and its P/E ratio?
   b. If the plowback rate were 0.4, what would be the firm's expected dividend per share, growth rate, price, P/E, and PEG ratio?

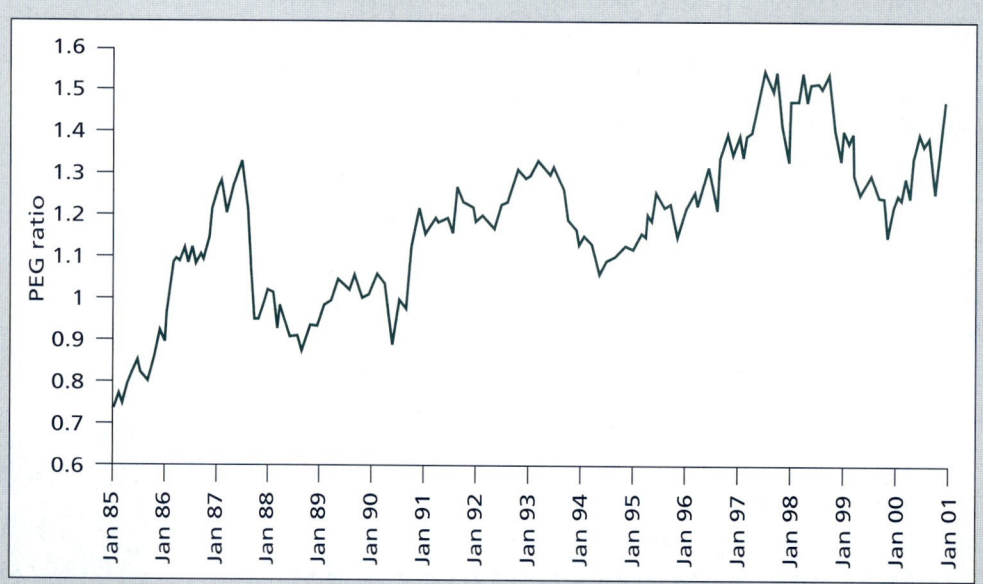

FIGURE 12.3

Historical PEG ratio for the S&P 500

Source: Thomson Financial Services, *Global Comments*, December 2001.

The importance of growth opportunities is nowhere more evident than in the Internet boom of the late 1990s. Many companies that had yet to turn a profit were valued by the market at billions of dollars. The value of these companies was *exclusively* growth opportunities. The box on page 433, written at the height of the boom, compares some of these "new-economy" firms to their "old-economy" cousins engaged in similar activities and points out that whether these tech firms were overvalued depended on one's assessment of future growth.

Of course, when company valuation is determined primarily by growth opportunities, those values can be very sensitive to reassessments of such prospects. For example, on September 27, 2000, Priceline.com announced that its third-quarter revenue would fall short of expectations by about 8% and that instead of breaking even for the quarter, it would have a loss of one cent per share. Its stock price fell 42% in one day. By the end of 2000, the stock price was about $2 per share, down from nearly $100 earlier that year. Priceline had plenty of company as the Internet bubble burst in 2000: The stock prices of most other Internet firms fell dramatically as the market became more skeptical of their business prospects, that is, as it revised the estimates of growth opportunities downward.

P/E Ratios and Stock Risk

One important implication of any stock valuation model is that (holding all else equal) riskier stocks will have lower P/E multiples. We can see this quite easily in the context of the constant growth model by examining the formula for the P/E ratio (Equation 12.8):

$$\frac{P}{E} = \frac{1 - b}{k - g}$$

The Great Divide: New vs. Old Economy

The stock market has divided the world into two camps: new-economy companies and old-economy companies. The gulf between them could not be wider.

New-economy companies do technology, including the Internet. Old-economy companies do everything else. The stocks of new-economy companies command [in 1999] tremendous price–earnings ratios, anywhere from 70 for Microsoft to 450 for America Online. Old-economy companies have ordinary multiples in the 10 to 25 range. A higher multiple reflects greater optimism about a company's future earnings.

On some level the gap reflects an underlying reality. The technology sector is growing much faster than the economy as a whole. Analysts expect technology giants like Dell, Cisco Systems, and Intel to increase earnings at a 20 to 25 percent pace; corporate earnings overall are expected to grow at about 6 percent annually.

But isn't it possible to accept the basic notion that technology is changing the world and still be skeptical about the levels certain technology stocks have reached? In a matter of months, some of the new-economy companies have achieved greater market valuations than some of their well-established old-economy competitors despite smaller or nonexistent earnings. (See table.)

Do these staggering valuations make sense? They don't if you think that the new economy is not quite as new as its advocates would like to believe. Consider competition, for example. Lucent Technologies and Cisco Systems are two of the hottest firms in technology. Both stocks sell at huge multiples to earnings. Yet the two companies are gearing up to go head-to-head in the market for telephone and data equipment. Won't the competition depress profit margins in the industry?

And what about those old-economy companies? Might not some of them jump into the Internet world and fight successfully to protect their market share? The world is more complex than the market currently suggests it is.

Market Values of Old-Economy versus New-Economy Firms

	Industry	Company	Market Cap	1998 Earnings
Old	Finance	Paine Webber	$6.2 billion	$473 million
New		E-Trade	10 billion	0
Old	Retail	Sears	17 billion	1 billion
New		Amazon.com	30 billion	−124 million
Old	Transportation	United Airlines	4.1 billion	821 million
New		Priceline.com	10 billion	−112 million
Old	Auction	Sotheby's	1.9 billion	45 million
New		eBay	22 billion	2.4 million

Riskier firms will have higher required rates of return (i.e., higher values of k). Therefore, their P/E multiples will be lower. This is true even outside the context of the constant growth model. For *any* expected earnings and dividend stream, the present value of those cash flows will be lower when the stream is perceived to be riskier. Hence the stock price and the ratio of price to earnings will be lower.

Of course, if you scan *The Wall Street Journal,* you will observe many small, risky, start-up companies with very high P/E multiples. This does not contradict our claim that P/E multiples should fall with risk: Instead, it is evidence of the market's expectations of high growth rates for those companies. This is why we said that high risk firms will have lower P/E ratios *holding all else equal.* Given a growth projection, the P/E multiple will be lower when risk is perceived to be higher.

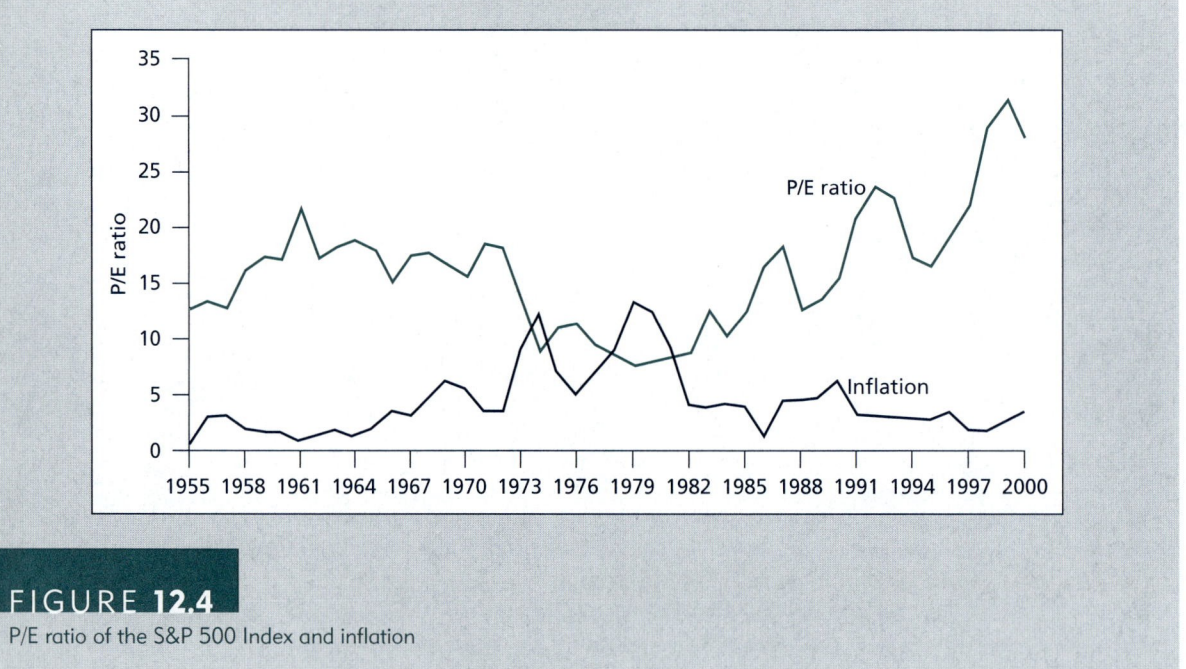

FIGURE 12.4

P/E ratio of the S&P 500 Index and inflation

Pitfalls in P/E Analysis

No description of P/E analysis is complete without mentioning some of its pitfalls. First, consider that the denominator in the P/E ratio is accounting earnings, which are influenced by somewhat arbitrary accounting rules such as the use of historical cost in depreciation and inventory valuation. In times of high inflation, historic cost depreciation and inventory costs will tend to underrepresent true economic values because the replacement cost of both goods and capital equipment will rise with the general level of prices. As Figure 12.4 demonstrates, P/E ratios have tended to be lower when inflation has been higher. This reflects the market's assessment that earnings in these periods are of "lower quality," artificially distorted by inflation, and warranting lower P/E ratios.

earnings management

The practice of using flexibility in accounting rules to improve the apparent profitability of the firm.

Earnings management is the practice of using flexibility in accounting rules to improve the apparent profitability of the firm. We will have much to say on this topic in the next chapter on interpreting financial statements. A version of earnings management that has become far more common in recent years is the reporting of "pro forma earnings" measures. These measures are sometimes called *operating earnings,* a term with no generally accepted definition.

Pro forma earnings are calculated ignoring certain expenses, for example, restructuring charges, stock-option expenses, or write-downs of assets from continuing operations. Firms argue that ignoring these expenses gives a clearer picture of the underlying profitability of the firm. For example, many companies incurred major expenses associated with the September 11 attacks, and rightly claim that it is useful to examine what their financial results would have been without those unusual expenses. Comparisons with earlier periods probably would make more sense if those costs were excluded.

But there is currently so much leeway for choosing what to exclude that it becomes hard for investors or analysts to interpret the numbers or to compare them across firms. The lack of standards gives firms considerable leeway to manage earnings. One analyst calculates that in the first three quarters of 2001, the companies that comprise the Nasdaq 100 index reported collective pro forma earnings of $82.3 billion, but GAAP losses of $19.1 billion, a difference of over $100 billion—for only these 100 firms.[6]

Even GAAP allows firms considerable discretion to manage earnings. For example, in the late 1990s, Kellogg took restructuring charges, which are supposed to be one-time events, nine quarters in a row. Were these really one-time events, or were they more appropriately treated as ordinary expenses? Given the available leeway in managing earnings, the justified P/E multiple becomes difficult to gauge.

In the wake of the accounting questions raised by the Enron, WorldCom, and Global Crossing bankruptcies, there seems to be a new focus on transparency in accounting statements. Firms with difficult-to-interpret statements suffered substantial stock market losses in the first months of 2002. The market clearly has established a new focus on quality of earnings.

Another confounding factor in the use of P/E ratios is related to the business cycle. We were careful in deriving the DDM to define earnings as being net of *economic* depreciation, that is, the maximum flow of income that the firm could pay out without depleting its productive capacity. And reported earnings, as we note above, are computed in accordance with generally accepted accounting principles and need not correspond to economic earnings. Beyond this, however, notions of a normal or justified P/E ratio, as in Equation 12.7 or 12.8, assume implicitly that earnings rise at a constant rate, or, put another way, on a smooth trend line. In contrast, reported earnings can fluctuate dramatically around a trend line over the course of the business cycle.

Another way to make this point is to note that the "normal" P/E ratio predicted by Equation 12.8 is the ratio of today's price to the trend value of future earnings, E_1. The P/E ratio reported in the financial pages of the newspaper, by contrast, is the ratio of price to the most recent *past* accounting earnings. Current accounting earnings can differ considerably from future economic earnings. Because ownership of stock conveys the right to future as well as current earnings, the ratio of price to most recent earnings can vary substantially over the business cycle, as accounting earnings and the trend value of economic earnings diverge by greater and lesser amounts.

As an example, Figure 12.5 graphs the earnings per share of Sun Microsystems and Consolidated Edison since 1986. Note that Sun's EPS fluctuate considerably. This reflects the company's relatively high degree of sensitivity to macroeconomic conditions. Value Line estimates its beta at 1.25. Con Ed, by contrast, shows much less variation in earnings per share around a smoother and flatter trend line. Its beta was only 0.75.

Because the market values the entire stream of future dividends generated by the company, when earnings are temporarily depressed, the P/E ratio should tend to be high—that is, the denominator of the ratio responds more sensitively to the business cycle than the numerator. This pattern is borne out well.

Figure 12.6 graphs the Sun and Con Ed P/E ratios. Sun, with the more volatile earnings profile, also has a more volatile P/E profile. For example, in 1989 and 1993, when its earnings were below the trend line (Figure 12.5), the P/E ratio correspondingly jumped (Figure 12.6). The market clearly recognized that earnings were depressed only temporarily.

This example shows why analysts must be careful in using P/E ratios. There is no way to say a P/E ratio is overly high or low without referring to the company's long-run growth prospects, as well as to current earnings per share relative to the long-run trend line.

Nevertheless, Figures 12.5 and 12.6 demonstrate a clear relationship between P/E ratios and growth. Despite considerable short-run fluctuations, Sun's EPS clearly trended upward over the period. Its compound rate of growth in the decade ending 1999 was 30%. Con Edison's earnings grew far less rapidly, with a 10-year compound growth rate of 2.3%. The growth prospects of Sun are reflected in its consistently higher P/E multiple.

This analysis suggests that P/E ratios should vary across industries and, in fact, they do. Figure 12.7 shows P/E ratios in late 2001 for a sample of industries. P/E ratios for each

[6]Reported in *The Economist,* February 23, 2002, p. 77.

FIGURE 12.5

Earnings growth for two companies

FIGURE 12.6

Price–earnings ratios

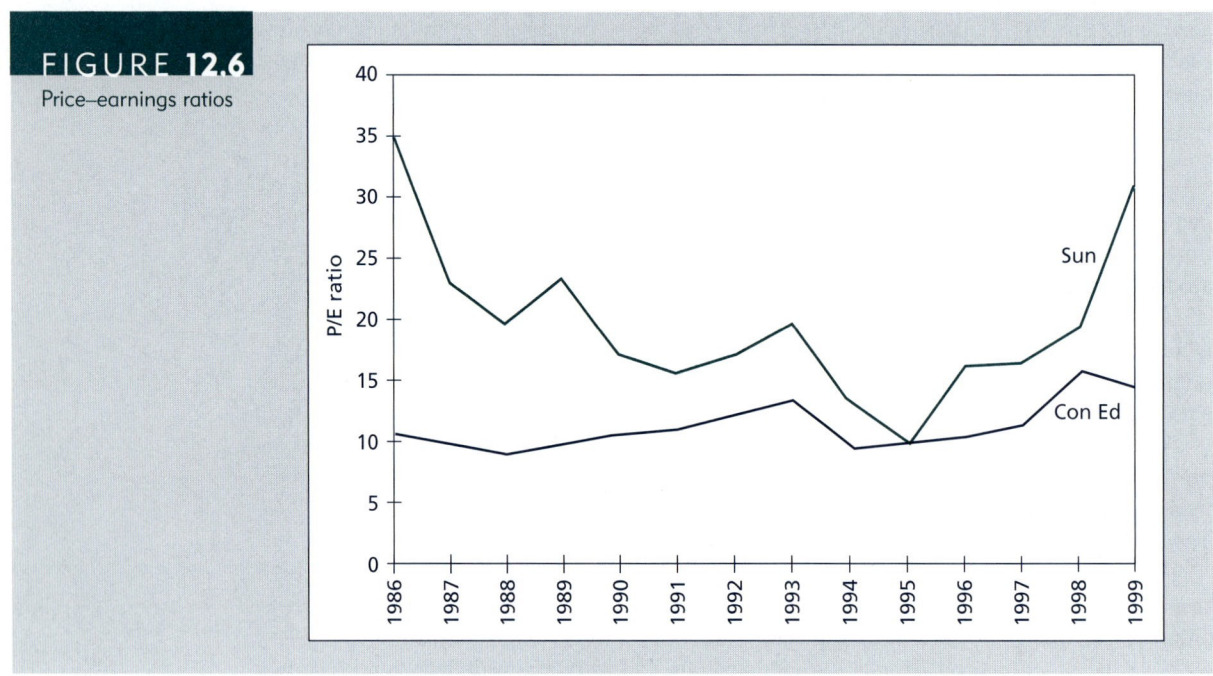

industry are computed in two ways: by taking the ratio of price to previous year earnings, and projected next-year earnings. Notice that while the P/E ratio for information technology firms based on 2001 earnings appear quite high, the ratio is far more moderate when prices are compared to projected 2002 earnings. This should not surprise you, since stock market prices are based on firms' future earnings prospects.

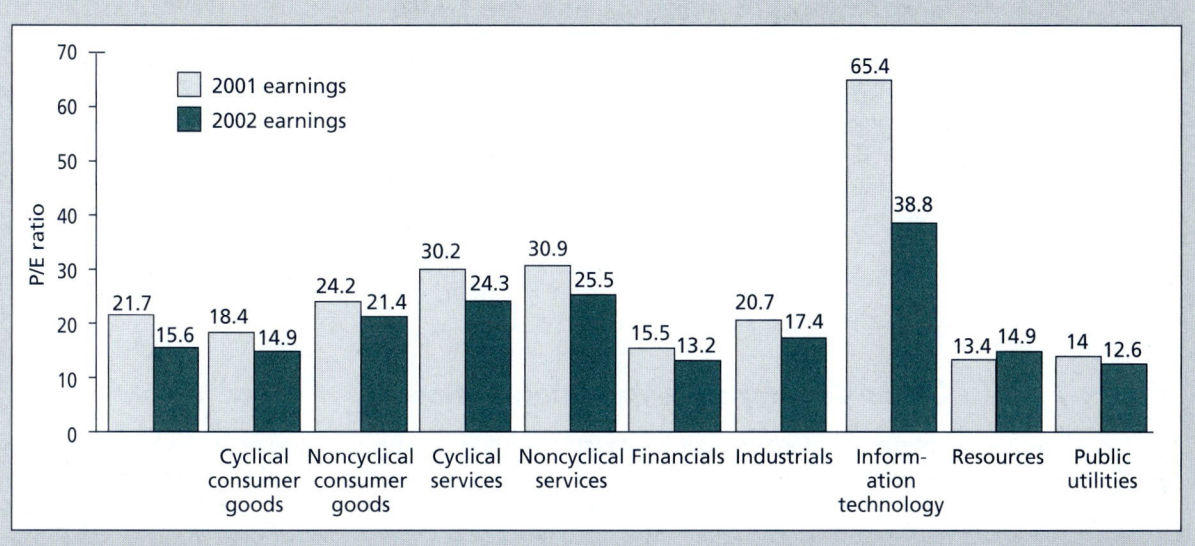

FIGURE 12.7

P/E ratios based on 2001 and 2002 EPS

Source: Thomson Financial Services, *Global Comments,* December 2001.

WEBMASTER

Equity Valuation

Go to the MoneyCentral Investor page at the address below. Use the Research Wizard function to obtain fundamentals, price history, price target, catalysts, and comparison for EMC Corporation (EMC). As comparison firms, use Network Appliance Inc. (NTAP) and Silicon Storage (SSTI).

1. What has been one-year sales and income growth for EMC?

2. What has been the company's five-year profit margin? How does that compare with the comparison firms?

3. What have been the percentage price changes for the last 3, 6, and 12 months? How do they compare with the comparison firms?

4. What is the estimated high and low price for EMC for the coming year using EMC's current P/E multiple?

5. Compare the price performance of EMC with NTAP and SSTI. Which of the companies appears to be the most expensive in terms of current earnings? Which of the companies is the least expensive in terms of current earnings?

http://moneycentral.msn.com/investor/home.asp

Combining P/E Analysis and the DDM

Some analysts use P/E ratios in conjunction with earnings forecasts to estimate the price of stock at an investor's horizon date. The Raytheon analysis in Figure 12.2 shows that Value Line forecasted a P/E ratio for 2005 of 13.0. EPS for 2005 were forecast at $4.25, implying a price in 2005 of 13.0 × $4.25 = $55.25. Given an estimate of $55.25 for the 2005 sales price, we would compute Raytheon's intrinsic value as

$$V_{2001} = \frac{\$0.80}{(1.118)} + \frac{\$0.95}{(1.118)^2} + \frac{\$1.10}{(1.118)^3} + \frac{\$1.25 + \$55.25}{(1.118)^4} = \$38.43$$

which is fairly close to the recent market price.

Other Comparative Valuation Ratios

The price–earnings ratio is an example of a comparative valuation ratio. Such ratios are used to assess the valuation of one firm versus another based on a fundamental indicator such as earnings. For example, an analyst might compare the P/E ratios of two firms in the same industry to test whether the market is valuing one firm "more aggressively" than the other. Other such comparative ratios are commonly used.

Price-to-book ratio   This is the ratio of price per share divided by book value per share. As we noted earlier in this chapter, some analysts view book as a useful measure of value and therefore treat the ratio of price-to-book value as an indicator of how aggressively the market values the firm.

Price-to-cash flow ratio   Earnings as reported on the income statement can be affected by the company's choice of accounting practices and thus are commonly viewed as subject to some imprecision and even manipulation. In contrast, cash flow—which tracks cash actually flowing into or out of the firm—is less affected by accounting decisions. As a result, some analysts prefer to use the ratio of price to cash flow per share rather than price to earnings per share. Some analysts use operating cash flow when calculating this ratio; others prefer free cash flow, that is, operating cash flow net of new investment.

Price-to-sales ratio   Many start-up firms have no earnings. As a result, the P/E ratio for these firms is meaningless. The price-to-sales ratio (the ratio of stock price to the annual sales per share) is sometimes taken as a valuation benchmark for these firms. Of course, price-to-sales ratios can vary markedly across industries, since profit margins vary widely.

Figure 12.8 presents the behavior of these valuation measures since 1955. While the levels of these ratios differ considerably, for the most part they track each other fairly closely, with upturns and downturns at the same times.

Be creative   Sometimes a standard valuation ratio will simply not be available, and you will have to devise your own. In the 1990s, some analysts valued retail Internet firms based on the number of Web hits their sites received. In retrospect, they valued these firms using too generous "price-to-hits" ratios. Nevertheless, in a new investment environment, these analysts used the information available to them to devise the best valuation tools they could.

Free Cash Flow Valuation Approaches

How might we value firms in the earliest stages of their life, for example, firms not currently paying dividends? In these cases, one approach is to discount the stream of *free cash flow* for

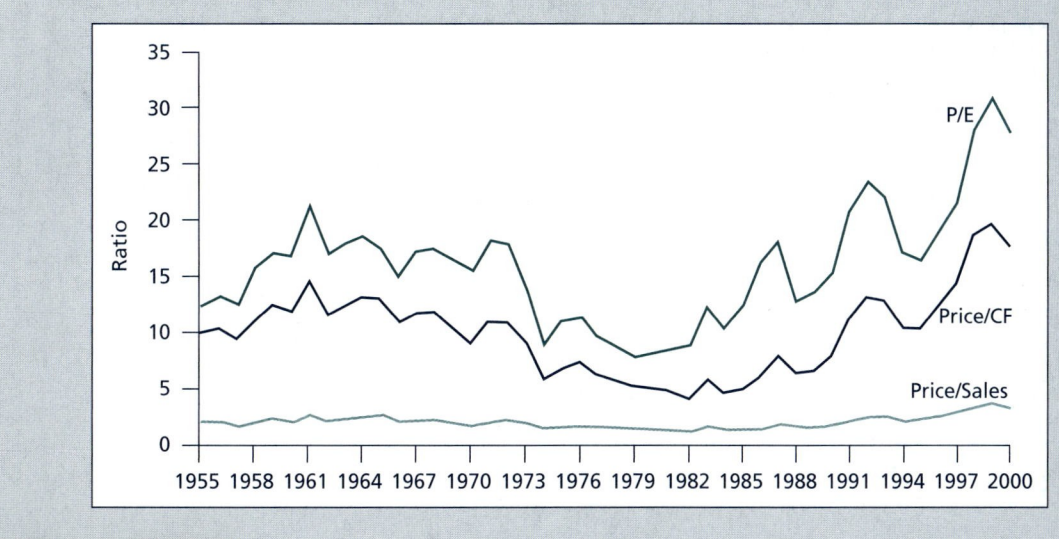

FIGURE 12.8
Market valuation statistics

the *firm* (FCFF) at the weighted-average cost of capital, and then subtract the value of debt to obtain the value of equity:

$$FCFF = EBIT\,(1 - Tax\ rate) + Depreciation - Capital\ expenditures - Increase\ in\ NWC$$

where

$EBIT$ = earnings before interest and tax,

NWC = net working capital.

We emphasize that this approach is fully consistent with the dividend discount model and ought to provide the same value estimate if one could extrapolate to a period in which the firm begins to pay dividends. However, for very young firms that do not pay dividends, this approach is more convenient.

We might also discount free cash flows to *equity* (FCFE) at the cost of *equity,* k_E:

$$FCFE = Net\ income + Depreciation - Capital\ expenditures - Increase\ in\ NWC -$$
$$Principal\ repayments + New\ debt\text{-}issue\ proceeds$$

$$P_0 = \sum_{t=1}^{n} \frac{FCFE_t}{(1 + k_E)^t} + \frac{P_n}{(1 + k_E)^n} \quad \text{where } P_n = \frac{FCFE_{n+1}}{k_E - g}$$

Notice that we need to compute a terminal value to avoid solving an infinite sum. That terminal value may simply be the present value of a constant growth perpetuity (as in the formula above) or it may be based on a multiple of EBIT, book value, earnings, or FCFF. As a general rule, these estimates of value depend critically on terminal value.

12.5 THE AGGREGATE STOCK MARKET

The most popular approach to forecasting the overall stock market is the earnings multiplier approach applied at the aggregate level. The first step is to forecast corporate profits for the coming period. Then we derive an estimate of the earnings multiplier, the aggregate P/E ratio,

FIGURE **12.9**

Earnings yield of S&P 500 versus 10-year Treasury bond yield

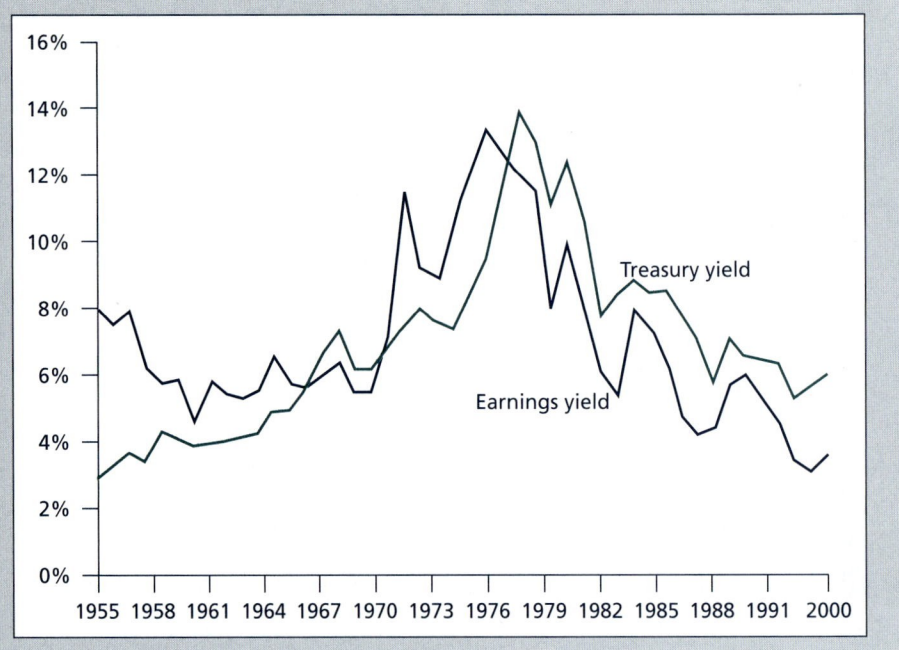

based on a forecast of long-term interest rates. The product of the two forecasts is the estimate of the end-of-period level of the market.

The forecast of the P/E ratio of the market is sometimes derived from a graph similar to that in Figure 12.9, which plots the *earnings yield* (earnings per share divided by price per share, the reciprocal of the P/E ratio) of the S&P 500 and the yield to maturity on 10-year Treasury bonds. The figure shows that both yields rose dramatically in the 1970s. In the case of Treasury bonds, this was because of an increase in the inflationary expectations built into interest rates. The earnings yield on the S&P 500, however, probably rose because of inflationary distortions that artificially increased reported earnings. We have already seen that P/E ratios tend to fall when inflation rates increase. When inflation moderated in the 1980s, both Treasury and earnings yields fell. For most of the last 15 years, the earnings yield ran about one percentage point below the T-bond rate.

One might use this relationship and the current yield on 10-year Treasury bonds to forecast the earnings yield on the S&P 500. Given that earnings yield, a forecast of earnings could be used to predict the level of the S&P in some future period. Let's consider a simple example of this procedure.

12.7 EXAMPLE

Forecasting the Aggregate Stock Market

The late 2001 forecast for 2002 earnings per share for the S&P 500 portfolio was about $53.[7] The 10-year Treasury bond yield at this time was about 5.2%. Since the earnings yield on the S&P 500 has been about one percentage point below the 10-year Treasury yield, a first guess for the earnings yield on the S&P 500 might be 4.2%. This would imply a P/E ratio of 1/.042 = 23.8. Our forecast for the level of the S&P 500 index would then be 23.8 × 53 = 1261.

Of course, there is uncertainty regarding all three inputs into this analysis: the actual earnings on the S&P 500 stocks, the level of Treasury yields at year-end, and the spread between

(continued)

[7]According to Thomson Financial, as of November 2001. Thomson surveys a large sample of stock analysts and reports several analyses of their forecasts for both the economy and individual stocks.

the Treasury yield and the earnings yield. One would wish to perform sensitivity or scenario analysis to examine the impact of changes in all of these variables. To illustrate, consider Table 12.4, which shows a simple scenario analysis treating possible effects of variation in the Treasury bond yield. The scenario analysis shows that the forecast level of the stock market varies inversely and with dramatic sensitivity to interest rate changes.

EXAMPLE 12.7
(concluded)

TABLE **12.4** S&P 500 price forecasts under various scenarios	Most Likely Scenario	Pessimistic Scenario	Optimistic Scenario
Treasury bond yield	5.2%	5.7%	4.7%
Earnings yield	4.2%	4.7%	3.7%
Resulting P/E ratio	23.8	21.3	27.0
EPS forecast	$53	$53	$53
Forecast for S&P 500	1,261	1,129	1,431

Note: The forecast for the earnings yield on the S&P 500 equals the Treasury bond yield minus 1%. The P/E ratio is the reciprocal of the forecasted earnings yield.

Some analysts use an aggregate version of the dividend discount model rather than an earnings multiplier approach. All of these models, however, rely heavily on forecasts of such macroeconomic variables as GDP, interest rates, and the rate of inflation, which are difficult to predict accurately.

Because stock prices reflect expectations of future dividends, which are tied to the economic fortunes of firms, it is not surprising that the performance of a broad-based stock index like the S&P 500 is taken as a leading economic indicator, that is, a predictor of the performance of the aggregate economy. Stock prices are viewed as embodying consensus forecasts of economic activity and are assumed to move up or down in anticipation of movements in the economy. The government's index of leading economic indicators, which is taken to predict the progress of the business cycle, is made up in part of recent stock market performance. However, the predictive value of the market is far from perfect. A well-known joke, often attributed to Paul Samuelson, is that the market has forecast eight of the last five recessions.

SUMMARY

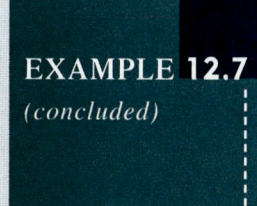

- One approach to firm valuation is to focus on the firm's book value, either as it appears on the balance sheet or adjusted to reflect the current replacement cost of assets or the liquidation value. Another approach is to focus on the present value of expected future dividends.
- The dividend discount model holds that the price of a share of stock should equal the present value of all future dividends per share, discounted at an interest rate commensurate with the risk of the stock.
- The constant growth version of the DDM asserts that, if dividends are expected to grow at a constant rate forever, then the intrinsic value of the stock is determined by the formula

$$V_0 = \frac{D_1}{k - g}$$

This version of the DDM is simplistic in its assumption of a constant value of g. There are more sophisticated multistage versions of the model for more complex environments.

When the constant growth assumption is reasonably satisfied, the formula can be inverted to infer the market capitalization rate for the stock

$$k = \frac{D_1}{P_0} + g$$

- Stock market analysts devote considerable attention to a company's price–earnings ratio. The P/E ratio is a useful measure of the market's assessment of the firm's growth opportunities. Firms with no growth opportunities should have a P/E ratio that is just the reciprocal of the capitalization rate, k. As growth opportunities become a progressively more important component of the total value of the firm, the P/E ratio will increase.
- The models presented in this chapter can be used to explain or to forecast the behavior of the aggregate stock market. The key macroeconomic variables that determine the level of stock prices in the aggregate are interest rates and corporate profits.

KEY TERMS

book value, 414	intrinsic value, 415	price–earnings
constant growth DDM, 418	liquidation value, 414	multiple, 428
dividend discount model	market capitalization	replacement cost, 414
(DDM), 417	rate, 416	Tobin's q, 414
dividend payout ratio, 420	plowback ratio, 421	two-stage DDM, 424
earnings management, 434	present value of growth	
earnings retention	opportunities	
ratio, 421	(PVGO), 422	

PROBLEM SETS

1. A common stock pays an annual dividend per share of $2.10. The risk-free rate is 7% and the risk premium for this stock is 4%. If the annual dividend is expected to remain at $2.10, what is the value of the stock?

2. Which of the following assumptions does the constant growth dividend discount model require?
   a. Dividends grow at a constant rate.
   b. The dividend growth rate continues indefinitely.
   c. The required rate of return is less than the dividend growth rate.

3. a. Computer stocks currently provide an expected rate of return of 16%. MBI, a large computer company, will pay a year-end dividend of $2 per share. If the stock is selling at $50 per share, what must be the market's expectation of the growth rate of MBI dividends?
   b. If dividend growth forecasts for MBI are revised downward to 5% per year, what will happen to the price of MBI stock? What (qualitatively) will happen to the company's price–earnings ratio?

4. Explain why the following statements are true/false/uncertain.
   a. Holding all else constant, a firm will have a higher P/E if its beta is higher.
   b. P/E will tend to be higher when ROE is higher (assuming plowback is positive).
   c. P/E will tend to be higher when the plowback rate is higher.

5. Even Better Products has come out with a new and improved product. As a result, the firm projects an ROE of 20%, and it will maintain a plowback ratio of 0.30. Its earnings this year will be $2 per share. Investors expect a 12% rate of return on the stock.
   a. At what price and P/E ratio would you expect the firm to sell?
   b. What is the present value of growth opportunities?
   c. What would be the P/E ratio and the present value of growth opportunities if the firm planned to reinvest only 20% of its earnings?

6. *a.* MF Corp. has an ROE of 16% and a plowback ratio of 50%. If the coming year's earnings are expected to be $2 per share, at what price will the stock sell? The market capitalization rate is 12%.

   b. What price do you expect MF shares to sell for in three years?

7. The constant growth dividend discount model can be used both for the valuation of companies and for the estimation of the long-term total return of a stock.

   Assume:

   $$\$20 = \text{Price of a stock today}$$
   $$8\% = \text{Expected growth rate of dividends}$$
   $$\$0.60 = \text{Annual dividend one year forward}$$

   a. Using *only* the above data, compute the expected long-term total return on the stock using the constant growth dividend discount model. Show calculations.

   b. Briefly discuss two disadvantages of the constant growth dividend discount model in its application to investment analysis.

   c. Identify two alternative methods to the dividend discount model for the valuation of companies.

8. At Litchfield Chemical Corp. (LCC), a director of the company said that the use of dividend discount models by investors is "proof" that the higher the dividend, the higher the stock price.

   a. Using a constant growth dividend discount model as a basis of reference, evaluate the director's statement.

   b. Explain how an increase in dividend payout would affect each of the following (holding all other factors constant):

     i. Sustainable growth rate.

     ii. Growth in book value.

9. The market consensus is that Analog Electronic Corporation has an ROE = 9% and a beta of 1.25. It plans to maintain indefinitely its traditional plowback ratio of 2/3. This year's earnings were $3 per share. The annual dividend was just paid. The consensus estimate of the coming year's market return is 14%, and T-bills currently offer a 6% return.

   a. Find the price at which Analog stock should sell.

   b. Calculate the P/E ratio.

   c. Calculate the present value of growth opportunities.

   d. Suppose your research convinces you Analog will announce momentarily that it will immediately reduce its plowback ratio to 1/3. Find the intrinsic value of the stock. The market is still unaware of this decision. Explain why V_0 no longer equals P_0 and why V_0 is greater or less than P_0.

10. If the expected rate of return of the market portfolio is 15% and a stock with a beta of 1.0 pays a dividend yield of 4%, what must the market believe is the expected rate of price appreciation on that stock?

11. The FI Corporation's dividends per share are expected to grow indefinitely by 5% per year.

    a. If this year's year-end dividend is $8 and the market capitalization rate is 10% per year, what must the current stock price be according to the DDM?

    b. If the expected earnings per share are $12, what is the implied value of the ROE on future investment opportunities?

    c. How much is the market paying per share for growth opportunities (that is, for an ROE on future investments that exceeds the market capitalization rate)?

12. Using the data provided, discuss whether the common stock of American Tobacco Company is attractively priced based on at least three different valuation approaches. (Hint: Use the asset value, DDM, and earnings multiplier approaches.)

	American Tobacco	S&P 500
Recent price	$54.00	$1160
Book value per share	$12.10	
Liquidation value per share	$ 9.10	
Replacement cost of assets per share	$19.50	
Anticipated next year's dividend	$ 2.10	$ 23
Estimated annual growth in dividends and earnings	10.0%	5.0%
Required return	13.0%	
Estimated next year's EPS	$ 4.80	$ 50
P/E ratio based on next year's earnings	11.3	23.2
Dividend yield	3.8%	2.0%

13. The risk-free rate of return is 10%, the required rate of return on the market is 15%, and High-Flyer stock has a beta coefficient of 1.5. If the dividend per share expected during the coming year, D_1, is $2.50 and $g = 5\%$, at what price should a share sell?

14. Imelda Emma, a financial analyst at Del Advisors, Inc. (DAI), has been asked to assess the impact that construction of a new Disney theme park might have on its stock. DAI uses a dividend discount valuation model that incorporates beta in the derivation of risk-adjusted required rates of return on stocks.

    Until now Emma has been using a five-year earnings and dividends per share growth rate of 15% and a beta estimate of 1.00 for Disney. Taking construction of the new theme park into account, however, she has raised her growth rate and beta estimates to 25% and 1.15, respectively. The complete set of Emma's current assumption is:

Current stock price	$37.75
Beta	1.15
Risk-free rate of return (T-bill)	4.0%
Required rate of return on the market	10.0%
Short-term growth rate (five years) for earnings and dividends	25.0%
Long-term growth rate (beyond five years) for earnings and dividends	9.3%
Dividend forecast for coming year (per share)	$ .287

   a. Calculate the risk-adjusted required rate of return on Disney stock using Emma's current beta assumption.
   b. Using the results of part (a), Emma's current assumptions, and DAI's dividend discount model, calculate the intrinsic value of Disney stock.
   c. After calculating the intrinsic value of Disney stock using her new assumptions and DAI's dividend discount model, Emma finds her recommendation for Disney should be changed from a "buy" to a "sell." Explain how the construction of the new theme park could have such a negative impact on the valuation of Disney stock, despite Emma's assumption of sharply higher growth rates (25%).

15. Phoebe Black's investment club wants to buy the stock of either NewSoft, Inc, or Capital Corp. In this connection, Black prepared the following table. You have been asked to help her interpret the data, based on your forecast for a healthy economy and a strong stock market over the next 12 months.

	NewSoft, Inc.	Capital Corp.	S&P 500 Index
Current price	$30	$32	
Industry	Computer Software	Capital Goods	
P/E ratio (current)	25	14	16
P/E ratio (5-year average)	27	16	16
Price/book ratio (current)	10	3	3
Price/book ratio (5-year average)	12	4	2
Beta	1.5	1.1	1.0
Dividend yield	.3%	2.7%	2.8%

a. Newsoft's shares have higher price–earnings (P/E) and price–book value (P/B) ratios than those of Capital Corp. (The price–book ratio is the ratio of market value to book value.) Briefly discuss why the disparity in ratios may not indicate that NewSoft's shares are overvalued relative to the shares of Capital Corp. Answer the question in terms of the two ratios, and assume that there have been no extraordinary events affecting either company.

b. Using a constant growth dividend discount model, Black estimated the value of NewSoft to be $28 per share and the value of Capital Corp. to be $34 per share. Briefly discuss weaknesses of this dividend discount model and explain why this model may be less suitable for valuing NewSoft than for valuing Capital Corp.

c. Recommend and justify a more appropriate dividend discount model for valuing NewSoft's common stock.

16. Your preliminary analysis of two stocks has yielded the information set forth below. The market capitalization rate for both stock A and stock B is 10% per year.

	Stock A	Stock B
Expected return on equity, ROE	14%	12%
Estimated earnings per share, E_1	$ 2.00	$ 1.65
Estimated dividends per share, D_1	$ 1.00	$ 1.00
Current market price per share, P_0	$27.00	$25.00

a. What are the expected dividend payout ratios for the two stocks?
b. What are the expected dividend growth rates of each?
c. What is the intrinsic value of each stock?
d. In which, if either, of the two stocks would you choose to invest?

17. Janet Ludlow's firm requires all its analysts to use a two-stage DDM and the CAPM to value stocks. Using these measures, Ludlow has valued QuickBrush Company at $63 per share. She now must value SmileWhite Corporation.

a. Calculate the required rate of return for SmileWhite using the information in the following table:

	December 1999	
	QuickBrush	SmileWhite
Beta	1.35	1.15
Market price	$45.00	$30.00
Intrinsic value	$63.00	?

Note: Risk-free rate = 4.50%; expected market return = 14.50%.

CFA

www.mhhe.com/bkm

b. Ludlow estimates the following EPS and dividend growth rates for SmileWhite:

First three years:	12% per year
Years thereafter:	9% per year

Estimate the intrinsic value of SmileWhite using the table above, and the two-stage DDM. Dividends per share in 1999 were $1.72.

c. Recommend QuickBrush or SmileWhite stock for purchase by comparing each company's intrinsic value with its current market price.

d. Describe *one* strength of the two-stage DDM in comparison with the constant growth DDM. Describe *one* weakness inherent in all DDMs.

18. The Tennant Company, founded in 1870, has evolved into the leading producer of large-sized floor sweepers and scrubbers, which are ridden by their operators. Some of the firm's financial data are presented in the following table:

TENNANT COMPANY
SELECTED HISTORIC OPERATING AND BALANCE SHEET DATA (000s OMITTED)
AS OF DECEMBER 31

	1990	1995	2000
Net sales	$47,909	$109,333	$166,924
Cost of goods sold	27,395	62,373	95,015
Gross profits	20,514	46,960	71,909
Selling, general, and administrative expenses	11,895	29,649	54,151
Earnings before interest and taxes	8,619	17,311	17,758
Interest on long-term debt	0	53	248
Pretax income	8,619	17,258	17,510
Income taxes	4,190	7,655	7,692
After-tax income	$ 4,429	$ 9,603	$ 9,818
Total assets	$33,848	$ 63,555	$106,098
Total common stockholders' equity	25,722	46,593	69,516
Long-term debt	6	532	2,480
Total common shares outstanding	5,654	5,402	5,320
Earnings per share	$ .78	$ 1.78	$ 1.85
Dividends per share	.28	.72	.96
Book value per share	4.55	8.63	13.07

a. Based on these data, calculate a value for Tennant common stock by applying the constant growth dividend discount model. Assume an investor's required rate of return is a five percentage point premium over the current risk-free rate of return of 7%.

b. To your disappointment, the calculation you completed in part (*a*) results in a value below the stock's current market price. Consequently, you apply the constant growth DDM using the same required rate of return as in your calculation for part (*a*), but using the company's stated goal of earning 20% per year on stockholders' equity and maintaining a 35% dividend payout ratio. However, you find you are unable to calculate a meaningful answer. Explain why you cannot calculate a meaningful answer, and identify an alternative DDM that may provide a meaningful answer.

19. You are a portfolio manager considering the purchase of Nucor common stock. Nucor is the preeminent "minimill" steel producer in the United States. Minimills use scrap steel

as their raw material and produce a limited number of products, primarily for the construction market. You are provided the following information:

NUCOR CORPORATION

Stock price (Dec. 30, 1997)	$53.00
1998 estimated earnings	$ 4.25
1998 estimated book value	$25.00
Indicated dividend	$ 0.40
Beta	1.10
Risk-free return	7.0%
High-grade corporate bond yield	9.0%
Risk premium—stocks over bonds	5.0%

a. Calculate the expected stock market return. Show your calculations.
b. Calculate the implied total return of Nucor stock.
c. Calculate the required return of Nucor stock using the CAPM.
d. Briefly discuss the attractiveness of Nucor based on these data.

20. The stock of Nogro Corporation is currently selling for $10 per share. Earnings per share in the coming year are expected to be $2. The company has a policy of paying out 50% of its earnings each year in dividends. The rest is retained and invested in projects that earn a 20% rate of return per year. This situation is expected to continue indefinitely.

a. Assuming the current market price of the stock reflects its intrinsic value as computed using the constant growth rate DDM, what rate of return do Nogro's investors require?
b. By how much does its value exceed what it would be if all earnings were paid as dividends and nothing were reinvested?
c. If Nogro were to cut its dividend payout ratio to 25%, what would happen to its stock price? What if Nogro eliminated the dividend?

21. The risk-free rate of return is 8%, the expected rate of return on the market portfolio is 15%, and the stock of Xyrong Corporation has a beta coefficient of 1.2. Xyrong pays out 40% of its earnings in dividends, and the latest earnings announced were $10 per share. Dividends were just paid and are expected to be paid annually. You expect that Xyrong will earn an ROE of 20% per year on all reinvested earnings forever.

a. What is the intrinsic value of a share of Xyrong stock?
b. If the market price of a share is currently $100, and you expect the market price to be equal to the intrinsic value one year from now, what is your expected one-year holding-period return on Xyrong stock?

1. Find ROE and calculate the plowback ratio for 20 of the firms included in the Market Insight Web page at **www.mhhe.com/edumarketinsight**. (Use the data in the financial highlights section.)
   a. Compute sustainable growth, $g = b \times ROE$.
   b. Compare the growth rates computed in (a) with the P/E ratio of the firms. (It would be useful to plot P/E against g in a scatter diagram. This is easy to do in Excel.) Is there a relationship between g and P/E?
   c. What is the average PEG ratio for the firms in your sample? How much variation is there across firms?

STANDARD &POOR'S

(continued)

(concluded)

  d. Find the price-to-book, price-to-sales, and price-to-cash flow ratios for your sample of firms. Plot a scatter diagram of P/E against these three ratios. What do you conclude?
  e. Calculate the historical growth rate of earnings per share, using the longest possible historical period. Is the actual rate of earnings growth correlated with the sustainable growth rate computed in part (a)?

2. a. Use the data from Market Insight to estimate the intrinsic value of a firm in the sample. You will need to calculate the beta from the historical return series, and you will need to make reasonable judgments about the market risk premium, long-term growth rates based on recent profitability, and plowback.
  b. How sensitive are our estimates to your assumptions? Which assumptions are most critical?
  c. Try using a three-stage growth model and comparing the values derived to a two-stage model. Which estimates seem more reasonable?

STANDARD
&POOR'S

WEBMASTER

Price, Risk and Growth

Go to **www.mhhe.com/edumarketinsight** to download the Excel reports entitled "Profitability" that appear in the Valuation section for two major drug firms, Johnson & Johnson (JNJ) and Merck & Co (MRK). Examine the reports for the last five years of reported data, then address the following questions:

1. What differences do you find with respect to the firms' use of financial leverage over the period? Briefly explain.

2. Which of the firms would you consider to be more expensive in terms of earnings? Briefly explain.

3. What factors would you examine to explain differences in price–earnings ratios? Briefly explain your logic.

SOLUTIONS TO

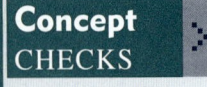
Concept
CHECKS

1. *a.* Dividend yield = $2.15/$50 = 4.3%
      Capital gains yield = (59.77 − 50)/50 = 19.54%
      Total return = 4.3% + 19.54% = 23.84%
  b. k = 6% + 1.15(14% − 6%) = 15.2%
  c. V_0 = ($2.15 + $59.77)/1.152 = $53.75, which exceeds the market price. This would indicate a "buy" opportunity.

2. *a.* $D_1/(k − g)$ = $2.15/(0.152 − 0.112) = $53.75
  b. $P_1 = P_0(1 + g)$ = $53.75(1.112) = $59.77
  c. The expected capital gain equals $59.77 − $53.75 = $6.02, for a percentage gain of 11.2%. The dividend yield is D_1/P_0 = 2.15/53.75 = 4%, for a holding-period return of 4% + 11.2% = 15.2%.

3. *a.* g = ROE × b = 0.20 × .60 = 0.12
      P_0 = 2/(0.125 − 0.12) = 400

    b. When the firm invests in projects with ROE less than *k,* its stock price falls.

       If $b = 0.60$, then $g = 10\% \times 0.60 = 6\%$ and $P_0 = \$2/(0.125 - 0.06) = \$30.77$. In contrast, if $b = 0$, then $P_0 = \$5/0.125 = \$40$

4. Because $\beta = .85, k = 5\% + .85 \times 6\% = 10.1\%$

$$V_{2001} = \frac{.80}{1.101} + \frac{.95}{(1.101)^2} + \frac{1.10}{(1.101)^3} + \frac{1.25 + P_{2005}}{(1.101)^4}$$

Now compute the sales price in 2005 using the constant growth dividend discount model.

$$P_{2005} = \frac{1.25 \times (1 + g)}{k - g} = \frac{1.25 \times 1.071}{.101 - .071} = \$44.62$$

Therefore, $V_{2001} = \$33.55$

5. *a.* ROE = 12%

    $b = \$0.50/\$2.00 = 0.25$
    $g = \text{ROE} \times b = 12\% \times 0.25 = 3\%$
    $P_0 = D_1/(k - g) = \$1.50/(0.10 - 0.03) = \$21.43$
    $P_0/E_1 = 21.43/\$2.00 = 10.71$

  b. If $b = 0.4$, then $0.4 \times \$2 = \$0.80$ would be reinvested and the remainder of earnings, or $1.20, would be paid as dividends

    $g = 12\% \times 0.4 = 4.8\%$
    $P_0 = D_1/(k - g) = \$1.20/(0.10 - 0.048) = \$23.08$
    $P_0/E_1 = \$23.08/\$2.00 = 11.54$
    $\text{PEG} = 11.54/4.8 = 2.4$

13

FINANCIAL STATEMENT ANALYSIS

AFTER STUDYING THIS CHAPTER YOU SHOULD BE ABLE TO:

> Use a firm's income statement, balance sheet, and statement of cash flows to calculate standard financial ratios.

> Calculate the impact of taxes and leverage on a firm's return on equity using ratio decomposition analysis.

> Measure a firm's operating efficiency by using various asset utilization ratios.

> Identify likely sources of biases in conventional accounting data.

In the previous chapter, we explored equity valuation techniques. These techniques take as inputs the firm's dividends and earnings prospects. While the valuation analyst is interested in economic earnings streams, only financial accounting data are readily available. What can we learn from a company's accounting data that can help us estimate the intrinsic value of its common stock?

In this chapter, we show how investors can use financial data as inputs into stock valuation analysis. We start by reviewing the basic sources of such data: the income statement, the balance sheet, and the statement of cash flows. We next discuss the difference between economic and accounting earnings. While economic earnings are more important for issues of valuation, whatever their shortcomings, accounting data still are useful in assessing the economic prospects of the firm. We show how analysts use financial ratios to explore the sources of a firm's profitability and evaluate the "quality" of its earnings in a systematic fashion. We also examine the impact of debt policy on various financial ratios. Finally, we conclude with a discussion of the limitations of financial statement analysis as a tool in uncovering mispriced securities. Some of these limitations are due to differences in firms' accounting procedures. Others arise from inflation-induced distortions in accounting numbers.

13.1 THE MAJOR FINANCIAL STATEMENTS

The Income Statement

income statement

A financial statement showing a firm's revenues and expenses during a specified period.

The **income statement** is a summary of the profitability of the firm over a period of time, such as a year. It presents revenues generated during the operating period, the expenses incurred during that same period, and the company's net earnings or profits, which are simply the difference between revenues and expenses.

It is useful to distinguish four broad classes of expenses: cost of goods sold, which is the direct cost attributable to producing the product sold by the firm; general and administrative expenses, which correspond to overhead expenses, salaries, advertising, and other costs of operating the firm that are not directly attributable to production; interest expense on the firm's debt; and taxes on earnings owed to federal and local governments.

Table 13.1 presents a 2000 income statement for PepsiCo, Inc. At the top are revenues from standard operations. Next come operating expenses, the costs incurred in the course of generating these revenues, including a depreciation allowance. The difference between operating revenues and operating costs is called operating income. Income from other, primarily nonrecurring, sources is then added to obtain earnings before interest and taxes (EBIT), which is what the firm would have earned if not for obligations to its creditors and the tax authorities. EBIT is a measure of the profitability of the firm's operations abstracting from any interest burden attributable to debt financing. The income statement then goes on to subtract net interest expense from EBIT to arrive at taxable income. Finally, the income tax due the government is subtracted to arrive at net income, the "bottom line" of the income statement.

The Balance Sheet

balance sheet

An accounting statement of a firm's financial position at a specified time.

While the income statement provides a measure of profitability over a period of time, the **balance sheet** provides a "snapshot" of the financial condition of the firm at a particular time. The balance sheet is a list of the firm's assets and liabilities at that moment. The difference in assets and liabilities is the net worth of the firm, also called *stockholders' equity* or,

TABLE **13.1** Consolidated statement of income for PepsiCo, Inc., for the year ended December 31, 2000 (figures in millions)		
Operating revenues		
Net sales		$20,438
Operating expenses		
Cost of sales		$ 7,943
Selling, general, and administrative expenses		8,172
Depreciation and amortization		960
Other expenses		138
Total operating expenses		$17,213
Operating income		$ 3,225
Nonoperating income		130
Earnings before interest and income taxes		$ 3,355
Net interest expense		145
Earnings before income taxes		$ 3,210
Income taxes		1,027
Net income		$ 2,183

Note: Column sums subject to rounding error.

Source: PepsiCo Annual Report, 2000.

equivalently, *shareholders' equity*. Like income statements, balance sheets are reasonably standardized in presentation. Table 13.2 is Pepsi's balance sheet for year-end 2000.

The first section of the balance sheet gives a listing of the assets of the firm. Current assets are presented first. These are cash and other items such as accounts receivable or inventories that will be converted into cash within one year. Next comes a listing of long-term assets, which generally corresponds to the company's property, plant, and equipment. The sum of current and long-term assets is total assets, the last line of the assets section of the balance sheet.

The liability and stockholders' equity section is arranged similarly. First are listed short-term or "current" liabilities, such as accounts payable, accrued taxes, and debts that are due within one year. Long-term debt and other liabilities due in more than a year follow. The difference between total assets and total liabilities is stockholders' equity. This is the net worth

TABLE **13.2** Consolidated balance sheet for PepsiCo, Inc., as of December 31, 2000	Dollars (millions)	Percent of Total Assets
Assets		
Current assets		
Cash and cash equivalents	$ 864	5%
Other short-term investments	466	3
Receivables	1,799	10
Inventories	905	5
Prepaid taxes and other expenses	570	3
Total current assets	$ 4,604	25%
Property, plant, and equipment (net of depreciation)	$ 5,438	30%
Net intangible assets	4,485	24
Other assets	3,812	21
Total assets	$18,339	100%
Liabilities and stockholders' equity		
Current liabilities		
Loans payable	$ 72	0%
Accounts payable and other current liabilities	3,815	21
Income taxes due	48	0
Total current liabilities	3,935	21
Long-term debt	2,346	13
Deferred income taxes	1,361	7
Other long-term liabilities	3,448	19
Total liabilities	$11,090	60%
Stockholders' equity		
Common stock, par value	$ 29	0%
Additional paid-in capital	955	5
Retained earnings	15,448	84
Cumulative foreign currency adjustments	(1,263)	(7)
Treasury stock (at cost)	(7,920)	(43)
Total stockholders' equity	$ 7,249	40%
Total liabilities and stockholders' equity	$18,339	100%

Note: Column sums subject to rounding error.

Source: PepsiCo Annual Report, 2000.

or book value of the firm. Stockholders' equity is divided into par value of stock, capital surplus (additional paid-in capital), and retained earnings, although this division is usually unimportant. Briefly, par value plus capital surplus represents the proceeds realized from the sale of stock to the public, while retained earnings represent the buildup of equity from profits plowed back into the firm. Even if the firm issues no new equity, book value will increase each year by reinvested earnings.

The first column of numbers in the balance sheet in Table 13.2 presents the dollar value of each asset. To make it easier to compare firms of different sizes, analysts sometimes present each item on the balance sheet as a percentage of total assets. This is called a *common-size balance sheet* and is presented in the last column of the table.

The Statement of Cash Flows

statement of cash flows

A financial statement showing a firm's cash receipts and cash payments during a specified period.

The **statement of cash flows** replaces what used to be called the statement of changes in financial position or flow of funds statement. It is a report of the cash flow generated by the firm's operations, investments, and financial activities. This statement was mandated by the Financial Accounting Standards Board in 1987 and is sometimes called the FASB Statement No. 95.

While the income statement and balance sheets are based on accrual methods of accounting, which means revenues and expenses are recognized when incurred even if no cash has yet been exchanged, the statement of cash flows recognizes only transactions in which cash changes hands. For example, if goods are sold now, with payment due in 60 days, the income statement will treat the revenue as generated when the sale occurs, and the balance sheet will be immediately augmented by accounts receivable, but the statement of cash flows will not recognize the transaction until the bill is paid and the cash is in hand.

Table 13.3 is the 2000 statement of cash flows for PepsiCo. The first entry listed under cash flows from operations is net income. The entries that follow modify that figure by components of income that have been recognized but for which cash has not yet changed hands. Increases in accounts receivable, for example, mean income has been claimed on the income statement, but cash has not yet been collected. Hence, increases in accounts receivable reduce the cash flows realized from operations in this period. Similarly, increases in accounts payable mean expenses have been incurred, but cash has not yet left the firm. Any payment delay increases the company's net cash flows in this period.

Another major difference between the income statement and the statement of cash flows involves depreciation, which accounts for a substantial addition in the adjustment section of the statement of cash flows in Table 13.3. The income statement attempts to "smooth" large capital expenditures over time to reflect a measure of profitability not distorted by large, infrequent expenditures. The depreciation expense on the income statement is a way of doing this by recognizing capital expenditures over a period of many years rather than at the specific time of those expenditures.

The statement of cash flows, however, recognizes the cash implication of a capital expenditure when it occurs. It will ignore the depreciation "expense" over time but will account for the full capital expenditure when it is paid.

Rather than smooth or allocate expenses over time, as in the income statement, the statement of cash flows reports cash flows separately for operations, investing, and financing activities. This way, any large cash flows such as those for big investments can be recognized explicitly as nonrecurring without affecting the measure of cash flow generated by operating activities.

TABLE **13.3**	Cash flows from operating activities	
Consolidated statement of cash flows for PepsiCo, Inc., for the year ended December 31, 2000 (figures in millions)	Net income	$ 2,183
	Adjustments to reconcile net income to net cash provided by operating activities:	
	Depreciation and amortization	$960
	Other	250
	Changes in operating assets and liabilities:	
	Decrease (increase) in accounts receivable	(15)
	Decrease (increase) in inventories	(26)
	Increase (decrease) in accounts payable	245
	Decrease (increase) in other current assets	0
	Increase (decrease) in taxes payable	314
	Total adjustments	$ 1,728
	Net cash provided by operating activities	$ 3,911
	Cash flows from investing activities	
	Cash provided (used) for additions to (disposal of) property, plant, and equipment	$(1,014)
	Acquisitions of businesses	(65)
	Short-term investments	(634)
	Net cash provided (used) in investing activities	$(1,713)
	Cash flow from financing activities	
	Proceeds from exercise of stock option and purchase plans	$559
	Proceeds from issuance of long-term debt	130
	Repayment of long-term debt	(795)
	Increase (decrease) in loans payable	0
	Dividends paid	(796)
	Share repurchases	(1,430)
	Other	34
	Net cash provided by (used in) financing activities	$(2,298)
	Effect of exchange rate changes	0
	Net increase (decrease) in cash and cash equivalents	$ (100)

Note: Column sums subject to rounding error.

Source: PepsiCo Annual Report, 2000.

The second section of the statement of cash flows is the accounting of cash flows from investing activities. These entries are investments in the capital stock necessary for the firm to maintain or enhance its productive capacity.

Finally, the last section of the statement lists the cash flows realized from financing activities. Issuance of securities will contribute positive cash flows, and redemption of outstanding securities will use up cash. For example, Pepsi repurchased $1,430 million of outstanding shares during 2000, which was a use of cash. However, it issued new long-term debt amounting to $130 million, which was a source of cash. The $796 million it paid in dividends reduced net cash flow. Notice that while dividends paid are included in the cash flows from financing, interest payments on debt are included with operating activities, presumably because, unlike dividends, interest payments are not discretionary.

The statement of cash flows provides evidence on the well-being of a firm. If a company cannot pay its dividends and maintain the productivity of its capital stock out of cash flow from operations, for example, and it must resort to borrowing to meet these demands, this is a serious warning that the firm cannot maintain payout at its current level in the long run. The statement of cash flows will reveal this developing problem when it shows that cash flow from operations is inadequate and that borrowing is being used to maintain dividend payments at unsustainable levels.

13.2 ACCOUNTING VERSUS ECONOMIC EARNINGS

accounting earnings

Earnings of a firm as reported on its income statement.

economic earnings

The real flow of cash that a firm could pay out forever in the absence of any change in the firm's productive capacity.

We've seen that stock valuation models require a measure of economic earnings or sustainable cash flow that can be paid out to stockholders without impairing the productive capacity of the firm. In contrast, **accounting earnings** are affected by several conventions regarding the valuation of assets such as inventories (e.g., LIFO versus FIFO treatment) and by the way some expenditures such as capital investments are recognized over time (as depreciation expenses). We will discuss problems with some of these accounting conventions in greater detail later in the chapter. In addition to these accounting issues, as the firm makes its way through the business cycle, its earnings will rise above or fall below the trend line that might more accurately reflect sustainable **economic earnings.** This introduces an added complication in interpreting net income figures. One might wonder how closely accounting earnings approximate economic earnings and, correspondingly, how useful accounting data might be to investors attempting to value the firm.

In fact, the net income figure on the firm's income statement does convey considerable information concerning a firm's products. We see this in the fact that stock prices tend to increase when firms announce earnings greater than market analysts or investors had anticipated. There are several studies to this effect. We showed you one such study in Chapter 8, Figure 8.5, which documented that firms that announced accounting earnings in excess of market expectations enjoyed increases in stock prices, while shares of firms that announced below-expected earnings fell in price.

13.3 RETURN ON EQUITY

Past versus Future ROE

return on equity (ROE)

The ratio of net profits to common equity.

We noted in Chapter 12 that **return on equity (ROE)** is one of the two basic factors in determining a firm's growth rate of earnings. Sometimes it is reasonable to assume that future ROE will approximate its past value, but a high ROE in the past does not necessarily imply a firm's future ROE will be high. A declining ROE, on the other hand, is evidence that the firm's new investments have offered a lower ROE than its past investments. The vital point for a security analyst is not to accept historical values as indicators of future values. Data from the recent past may provide information regarding future performance, but the analyst should always keep an eye on the future. Expectations of *future* dividends and earnings determine the intrinsic value of the company's stock.

Financial Leverage and ROE

An analyst interpreting the past behavior of a firm's ROE or forecasting its future value must pay careful attention to the firm's debt–equity mix and to the interest rate on its debt. An example will show why. Suppose Nodett is a firm that is all-equity financed and has total assets of $100 million. Assume it pays corporate taxes at the rate of 40% of taxable earnings.

Table 13.4 shows the behavior of sales, earnings before interest and taxes, and net profits under three scenarios representing phases of the business cycle. It also shows the behavior of

TABLE **13.4** Nodett's profitability over the business cycle	Scenario	Sales ($ millions)	EBIT ($ millions)	ROA (% per year)	Net Profit ($ millions)	ROE (% per year)
	Bad year	$ 80	$ 5	5%	$3	3%
	Normal year	100	10	10	6	6
	Good year	120	15	15	9	9

TABLE **13.5** Impact of financial leverage on ROE			Nodett		Somdett	
	Scenario	EBIT ($ millions)	Net Profits ($ millions)	ROE (%)	Net Profits* ($ millions)	ROE† (%)
	Bad year	$ 5	$3	3%	$1.08	1.8%
	Normal year	10	6	6	4.08	6.8
	Good year	15	9	9	7.08	11.8

*Somdett's after-tax profits are given by 0.6(EBIT − $3.2 million).

†Somdett's equity is only $60 million.

two of the most commonly used profitability measures: operating **return on assets (ROA),** which equals EBIT/total assets, and ROE, which equals net profits/equity.

Somdett is an otherwise identical firm to Nodett, but $40 million of its $100 million of assets are financed with debt bearing an interest rate of 8%. It pays annual interest expenses of $3.2 million. Table 13.5 shows how Somdett's ROE differs from Nodett's.

Note that annual sales, EBIT, and therefore ROA for both firms are the same in each of the three scenarios, that is, business risk for the two companies is identical. It is their financial risk that differs. Although Nodett and Somdett have the same ROA in each scenario, Somdett's ROE exceeds that of Nodett in normal and good years and is lower in bad years.

We can summarize the exact relationship among ROE, ROA, and leverage in the following equation[1]

$$ROE = (1 - \text{Tax rate})\left[ROA + (ROA - \text{Interest rate})\frac{\text{Debt}}{\text{Equity}}\right] \qquad \textbf{(13.1)}$$

return on assets (ROA)

Earnings before interest and taxes divided by total assets.

[1]The derivation of Equation 13.1 is as follows:

$$ROE = \frac{\text{Net profit}}{\text{Equity}}$$

$$= \frac{\text{EBIT} - \text{Interest} - \text{Taxes}}{\text{Equity}}$$

$$= \frac{(1 - \text{Tax rate})(\text{EBIT} - \text{Interest})}{\text{Equity}}$$

$$= (1 - \text{Tax rate})\frac{(\text{ROA} \times \text{Assets} - \text{Interest rate} \times \text{Debt})}{\text{Equity}}$$

$$= (1 - \text{Tax rate})\left[\text{ROA} \times \frac{(\text{Equity} + \text{Debt})}{\text{Equity}} - \text{Interest rate} \times \frac{\text{Debt}}{\text{Equity}}\right]$$

$$= (1 - \text{Tax rate})\left[\text{ROA} + (\text{ROA} - \text{Interest rate})\frac{\text{Debt}}{\text{Equity}}\right]$$

The relationship has the following implications. If there is no debt or if the firm's ROA equals the interest rate on its debt, its ROE will simply equal (1 minus the tax rate) times ROA. If its ROA exceeds the interest rate, then its ROE will exceed (1 minus the tax rate) times ROA by an amount that will be greater the higher the debt/equity ratio.

This result makes intuitive sense: If ROA exceeds the borrowing rate, the firm earns more on its money than it pays out to creditors. The surplus earnings are available to the firm's owners, the equityholders, which raises ROE. If, on the other hand, ROA is less than the interest rate, then ROE will decline by an amount that depends on the debt/equity ratio.

To illustrate the application of Equation 13.1, we can use the numerical example in Table 13.5. In a normal year, Nodett has an ROE of 6%, which is 0.6 (1 minus the tax rate) times its ROA of 10%. However, Somdett, which borrows at an interest rate of 8% and maintains a debt/equity ratio of 2/3, has an ROE of 6.8%. The calculation using Equation 13.1 is

$$ROE = 0.6[10\% + (10\% - 8\%)\tfrac{2}{3}]$$

$$= 0.6(10\% + \tfrac{4}{3}\%) = 6.8\%$$

The important point is that increased debt will make a positive contribution to a firm's ROE only if the firm's ROA exceeds the interest rate on the debt.

Note also that financial leverage increases the risk of the equityholder returns. Table 13.5 shows that ROE on Somdett is worse than that of Nodett in bad years. Conversely, in good years, Somdett outperforms Nodett because the excess of ROA over ROE provides additional funds for equityholders. The presence of debt makes Somdett more sensitive to the business cycle than Nodett. Even though the two companies have equal business risk (reflected in their identical EBIT in all three scenarios), Somdett carries greater financial risk than Nodett.

Even if financial leverage increases the expected ROE of Somdett relative to Nodett (as it seems to in Table 13.5), this does not imply the market value of Somdett's equity will be higher. Financial leverage increases the risk of the firm's equity as surely as it raises the expected ROE.

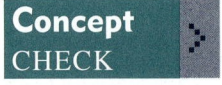

Concept CHECK

1. Mordett is a company with the same assets as Nodett and Somdett but a debt/equity ratio of 1.0 and an interest rate of 9%. What would its net profit and ROE be in a bad year, a normal year, and a good year?

13.4   RATIO ANALYSIS

Decomposition of ROE

To understand the factors affecting a firm's ROE, including its trend over time and its performance relative to competitors, analysts often "decompose" ROE into the product of a series of ratios. Each component ratio is in itself meaningful, and the process serves to focus the analyst's attention on the separate factors influencing performance. This kind of decomposition of ROE is often called the Du Pont system.

One useful decomposition of ROE is

$$ROE = \frac{\text{Net profit}}{\text{Pretax profit}} \times \frac{\text{Pretax profit}}{\text{EBIT}} \times \frac{\text{EBIT}}{\text{Sales}} \times \frac{\text{Sales}}{\text{Assets}} \times \frac{\text{Assets}}{\text{Equity}}$$

$$(1) \quad \times \quad (2) \quad \times (3) \times (4) \times (5)$$

Table 13.6 shows all these ratios for Nodett and Somdett under the three different economic scenarios. Let us first focus on factors 3 and 4. Notice that their product gives us the firm's ROA = EBIT/assets.

Factor 3 is known as the firm's operating **profit margin**, or **return on sales (ROS)**. ROS shows operating profit per dollar of sales. In an average year, Nodett's ROS is 0.10, or 10%; in a bad year, it is 0.0625, or 6.25%, and in a good year, 0.125, or 12.5%.

Factor 4, the ratio of sales to assets, is known as **asset turnover (ATO).** It indicates the efficiency of the firm's use of assets in the sense that it measures the annual sales generated by each dollar of assets. In a normal year, Nodett's ATO is 1.0 per year, meaning that sales of $1 per year were generated per dollar of assets. In a bad year, this ratio declines to 0.8 per year, and in a good year, it rises to 1.2 per year.

Comparing Nodett and Somdett, we see that factors 3 and 4 do not depend on a firm's financial leverage. The firms' ratios are equal to each other in all three scenarios.

Similarly, factor 1, the ratio of net income after taxes to pretax profit, is the same for both firms. We call this the tax-burden ratio. Its value reflects both the government's tax code and the policies pursued by the firm in trying to minimize its tax burden. In our example, it does not change over the business cycle, remaining a constant 0.6.

While factors 1, 3, and 4 are not affected by a firm's capital structure, factors 2 and 5 are. Factor 2 is the ratio of pretax profits to EBIT. The firm's pretax profits will be greatest when there are no interest payments to be made to debtholders. In fact, another way to express this ratio is

$$\frac{\text{Pretax profits}}{\text{EBIT}} = \frac{\text{EBIT} - \text{Interest expense}}{\text{EBIT}}$$

We will call this factor the *interest-burden (IB) ratio*. It takes on its highest possible value, 1, for Nodett, which has no financial leverage. The higher the degree of financial leverage, the lower the IB ratio. Nodett's IB ratio does not vary over the business cycle. It is fixed at 1.0, reflecting the total absence of interest payments. For Somdett, however, because interest expense is fixed in a dollar amount while EBIT varies, the IB ratio varies from a low of 0.36 in a bad year to a high of 0.787 in a good year.

> **profit margin or return on sales (ROS)**
>
> The ratio of operating profits per dollar of sales (EBIT divided by sales).
>
> **asset turnover (ATO)**
>
> The annual sales generated by each dollar of assets (sales/assets).

TABLE **13.6**
Ratio decomposition analysis for Nodett and Somdett

	ROE	(1) Net Profit Pretax Profit	(2) Pretax Profit EBIT	(3) EBIT Sales (ROS)	(4) Sales Assets (ATO)	(5) Assets Equity	(6) Compound Leverage Factor (2) × (5)
Bad year							
Nodett	0.030	0.6	1.000	0.0625	0.800	1.000	1.000
Somdett	0.018	0.6	0.360	0.0625	0.800	1.667	0.600
Normal year							
Nodett	0.060	0.6	1.000	0.100	1.000	1.000	1.000
Somdett	0.068	0.6	0.680	0.100	1.000	1.667	1.134
Good year							
Nodett	0.090	0.6	1.000	0.125	1.200	1.000	1.000
Somdett	0.118	0.6	0.787	0.125	1.200	1.667	1.311

TABLE **13.7**		**ROS**	×	**ATO**	=	**ROA**
Differences between ROS and ATO across industries	Supermarket chain	2%		5.0		10%
	Utility	20%		0.5		10%

leverage ratio

Measure of debt to
total capitalization
of a firm.

Factor 5, the ratio of assets to equity, is a measure of the firm's degree of financial leverage. It is called the **leverage ratio** and is equal to 1 plus the debt/equity ratio.[2] In our numerical example in Table 13.6, Nodett has a leverage ratio of 1, while Somdett's is 1.667.

From our discussion in Section 13.2, we know that financial leverage helps boost ROE only if ROA is greater than the interest rate on the firm's debt. How is this fact reflected in the ratios of Table 13.6?

The answer is that to measure the full impact of leverage in this framework, the analyst must take the product of the IB and leverage ratios (that is, factors 2 and 5, shown in Table 13.6 as column 6). For Nodett, factor 6, which we call the compound leverage factor, remains a constant 1.0 under all three scenarios. But for Somdett, we see that the compound leverage factor is greater than 1 in normal years (1.134) and in good years (1.311), indicating the positive contribution of financial leverage to ROE. It is less than 1 in bad years, reflecting the fact that when ROA falls below the interest rate, ROE falls with increased use of debt.

We can summarize all of these relationships as follows:

$$\text{ROE} = \text{Tax burden} \times \text{Interest burden} \times \text{Margin} \times \text{Turnover} \times \text{Leverage}$$

Because

$$\text{ROA} = \text{Margin} \times \text{Turnover}$$

and

$$\text{Compound leverage factor} = \text{Interest burden} \times \text{Leverage}$$

we can decompose ROE equivalently as follows:

$$\text{ROE} = \text{Tax burden} \times \text{ROA} \times \text{Compound leverage factor}$$

Table 13.6 compares firms with the same ROS and ATO but different degrees of financial leverage. Comparison of ROS and ATO usually is meaningful only in evaluating firms in the same industry. Cross-industry comparisons of these two ratios are often meaningless and can even be misleading.

For example, let us take two firms with the same ROA of 10% per year. The first is a supermarket chain and the second is a gas and electric utility.

As Table 13.7 shows, the supermarket chain has a "low" ROS of 2% and achieves a 10% ROA by "turning over" its assets five times per year. The capital-intensive utility, on the other hand, has a "low" ATO of only 0.5 times per year and achieves its 10% ROA by having an ROS of 20%. The point here is that a "low" ROS or ATO ratio need not indicate a troubled firm. Each ratio must be interpreted in light of industry norms.

Even within an industry, ROS and ATO sometimes can differ markedly among firms pursuing different marketing strategies. In the retailing industry, for example, Neiman-Marcus pursues a high-margin, low-ATO policy compared to Wal-Mart, which pursues a low-margin, high-ATO policy.

[2]$\dfrac{\text{Assets}}{\text{Equity}} = \dfrac{\text{Equity} + \text{Debt}}{\text{Equity}} = 1 + \dfrac{\text{Debt}}{\text{Equity}}$.

TABLE **13.8**				
Growth Industries financial statements, 2001–2003 ($thousands)				
	2000	**2001**	**2002**	**2003**
Income statements				
Sales revenue		$100,000	$120,000	$144,000
Cost of goods sold (including depreciation)		55,000	66,000	79,200
Depreciation		15,000	18,000	21,600
Selling and administrative expenses		15,000	18,000	21,600
Operating income		30,000	36,000	43,200
Interest expense		10,500	19,095	34,391
Taxable income		19,500	16,905	8,809
Income tax (40% rate)		7,800	6,762	3,524
Net income		11,700	10,143	5,285
Balance sheets (end of year)				
Cash and marketable securities	$ 50,000	$ 60,000	$ 72,000	$ 86,400
Accounts receivable	25,000	30,000	36,000	43,200
Inventories	75,000	90,000	108,000	129,600
Net plant and equipment	150,000	180,000	216,000	259,200
Total assets	$300,000	$360,000	$432,000	$518,400
Accounts payable	$ 30,000	$ 36,000	$ 43,200	$ 51,840
Short-term debt	45,000	87,300	141,957	214,432
Long-term debt (8% bonds maturing in 2007)	75,000	75,000	75,000	75,000
Total liabilities	$150,000	$198,300	$260,157	$341,272
Shareholders' equity (1 million shares outstanding)	$150,000	$161,700	$171,843	$177,128
Other data				
Market price per common share at year-end		$ 93.60	$ 61.00	$ 21.00

2. **Do a ratio decomposition analysis for the Mordett corporation of Question 1, preparing a table similar to Table 13.6.**

Concept
CHECK

Turnover and Other Asset Utilization Ratios

It is often helpful in understanding a firm's ratio of sales to assets to compute comparable efficiency-of-utilization, or turnover, ratios for subcategories of assets. For example, fixed-asset turnover would be

$$\frac{\text{Sales}}{\text{Fixed assets}}$$

This ratio measures sales per dollar of the firm's money tied up in fixed assets.

To illustrate how you can compute this and other ratios from a firm's financial statements, consider Growth Industries, Inc. (GI). GI's income statement and opening and closing balance sheets for the years 2001, 2002, and 2003 appear in Table 13.8.

GI's total asset turnover in 2003 was 0.303, which was below the industry average of 0.4. To understand better why GI underperformed, we compute asset utilization ratios separately for fixed assets, inventories, and accounts receivable.

GI's sales in 2003 were $144 million. Its only fixed assets were plant and equipment, which were $216 million at the beginning of the year and $259.2 million at year's end. Average fixed assets for the year were, therefore, $237.6 million [($216 million + $259.2 million)/2]. GI's fixed-asset turnover for 2003 was $144 million per year/$237.6 million = 0.606 per year. In other words, for every dollar of fixed assets, there was $0.606 in sales during the year 2003.

Comparable figures for the fixed-asset turnover ratio for 2001 and 2002 and the 2003 industry average are

2001	2002	2003	2003 Industry Average
0.606	0.606	0.606	0.700

GI's fixed-asset turnover has been stable over time and below the industry average.

Whenever a financial ratio includes one item from the income statement, which covers a period of time, and another from the balance sheet, which is a "snapshot" at a particular time, the practice is to take the average of the beginning and end-of-year balance sheet figures. Thus, in computing the fixed-asset turnover ratio you divide sales (from the income statement) by average fixed assets (from the balance sheet).

Another widely followed turnover ratio is the inventory turnover ratio, which is the ratio of cost of goods sold per dollar of inventory. It is usually expressed as cost of goods sold (instead of sales revenue) divided by average inventory. It measures the speed with which inventory is turned over.

In 2001, GI's cost of goods sold (less depreciation) was $40 million, and its average inventory was $82.5 million [($75 million + $90 million)/2]. Its inventory turnover was 0.485 per year ($40 million/$82.5 million). In 2002 and 2003, inventory turnover remained the same and continued below the industry average of 0.5 per year.

Another measure of efficiency is the ratio of accounts receivable to sales. The accounts receivable ratio usually is computed as average accounts receivable/sales × 365. The result is a number called the **average collection period**, or **days receivables**, which equals the total credit extended to customers per dollar of daily sales. It is the number of days' worth of sales tied up in accounts receivable. You can also think of it as the average lag between the date of sale and the date payment is received.

For GI in 2003, this number was 100.4 days:

$$\frac{(\$36 \text{ million} + \$43.2 \text{ million})/2}{\$144 \text{ million}} \times 365 = 100.4 \text{ days}$$

The industry average was 60 days.

In summary, use of these ratios lets us see that GI's poor total asset turnover relative to the industry is in part caused by lower than average fixed-asset turnover and inventory turnover, and higher than average days receivables. This suggests GI may be having problems with excess plant capacity along with poor inventory and receivables management procedures.

Liquidity and Coverage Ratios

Liquidity and interest coverage ratios are of great importance in evaluating the riskiness of a firm's securities. They aid in assessing the financial strength of the firm.

Liquidity ratios include the current ratio, quick ratio, and interest coverage ratio.

1. **Current ratio:** current assets/current liabilities. This ratio measures the ability of the firm to pay off its current liabilities by liquidating its current assets (that is, turning them into cash). It indicates the firm's ability to avoid insolvency in the short run. GI's current ratio in 2001, for example, was (60 + 30 + 90)/(36 + 87.3) = 1.46. In other years, it was

average collection period, or days receivables

The ratio of accounts receivable to daily sales, or the total amount of credit extended per dollar of daily sales.

current ratio

A ratio representing the ability of the firm to pay off its current liabilities by liquidating current assets (current assets/current liabilities).

2001	2002	2003	2003 Industry Average
1.46	1.17	0.97	2.0

This represents an unfavorable time trend and poor standing relative to the industry.

2. **Quick ratio:** (cash + receivables)/current liabilities. This ratio is also called the **acid test ratio.** It has the same denominator as the current ratio, but its numerator includes only cash, cash equivalents such as marketable securities, and receivables. The quick ratio is a better measure of liquidity than the current ratio for firms whose inventory is not readily convertible into cash. GI's quick ratio shows the same disturbing trends as its current ratio:

2001	2002	2003	2003 Industry Average
0.73	0.58	0.49	1.0

> **quick ratio, or acid test ratio**
>
> A measure of liquidity similar to the current ratio except for exclusion of inventories (cash plus receivables divided by current liabilities).

3. **Interest coverage ratio:** EBIT/interest expense. This ratio is often called **times interest earned.** It is closely related to the interest-burden ratio discussed in the previous section. A high coverage ratio tells the firm's shareholders and lenders that the likelihood of bankruptcy is low because annual earnings are significantly greater than annual interest obligations. It is widely used by both lenders and borrowers in determining the firm's debt capacity and is a major determinant of the firm's bond rating.

GI's interest coverage ratios are

2001	2002	2003	2003 Industry Average
2.86	1.89	1.26	5

> **interest coverage ratio, or times interest earned**
>
> A financial leverage measure arrived at by dividing earnings before interest and taxes by interest expense.

GI's interest coverage ratio has fallen dramatically over this three-year period, and by 2003 it is far below the industry average. Probably its credit rating has been declining as well, and no doubt GI is considered a relatively poor credit risk in 2003.

Market Price Ratios

There are two important market price ratios: the market-to-book-value ratio and the price–earnings ratio.

The **market-to-book-value ratio** (P/B) equals the market price of a share of the firm's common stock divided by its *book value,* that is, shareholders' equity per share. Analysts sometimes consider the stock of a firm with a low market-to-book value to be a "safer" investment, seeing the book value as a "floor" supporting the market price.

Analysts presumably view book value as the level below which market price will not fall because the firm always has the option to liquidate, or sell, its assets for their book values. However, this view is questionable. In fact, some firms do sometimes sell for less than book value. Nevertheless, a low market-to-book-value ratio is seen by some as providing a "margin of safety," and some analysts will screen out or reject high P/B firms in their stock selection process.

Proponents of the P/B screen would argue that, if all other relevant attributes are the same for two stocks, the one with the lower P/B ratio is safer. Nevertheless, book value does not necessarily represent liquidation value, which renders the margin of safety notion unreliable.

> **market-to-book-value ratio**
>
> Market price of a share divided by book value per share.

The theory of equity valuation offers some insight into the significance of the P/B ratio. A high P/B ratio is an indication that investors think a firm has opportunities of earning a rate of return on their investment in excess of the market capitalization rate, k.

To illustrate this point, we can return to the numerical example in Chapter 12, Section 12.4 (see Table 12.3). That example assumes the market capitalization rate is 12% per year. Now add the assumptions that the book value per share is $8.33 and that the coming year's expected EPS is $1, so that in the case for which the expected ROE on future investments also is 12%, the stock will sell at $1/0.12 = $8.33, and the P/B ratio will be 1.

Table 13.9 shows the P/B ratio for alternative assumptions about future ROE and plowback ratio. Reading down any column, you can see how the P/B ratio changes with ROE. The numbers reveal that, for a given plowback ratio, the P/B ratio is higher, the higher the expected ROE. This makes sense, because the greater the expected profitability of the firm's future investment opportunities, the greater its market value as an ongoing enterprise compared with the cost of acquiring its assets.

price–earnings ratio

The ratio of a stock's price to its earnings per share. Also referred to as the P/E multiple.

We've noted that the **price–earnings ratio** that is based on the firm's financial statements and reported in newspaper stock listings is not the same as the price–earnings multiple that emerges from a discounted dividend model. The numerator is the same (the market price of the stock), but the denominator is different. The P/E ratio uses the most recent past accounting earnings, while the P/E multiple predicted by valuation models uses expected future economic earnings.

Many security analysts pay careful attention to the accounting P/E ratio in the belief that among low P/E stocks they are more likely to find bargains than with high P/E stocks. The idea is that you can acquire a claim on a dollar of earnings more cheaply if the P/E ratio is low. For example, if the P/E ratio is 8, you pay $8 per share per $1 of *current* earnings, while if the P/E ratio is 12, you must pay $12 for a claim on $1 of current earnings.

Note, however, that current earnings may differ substantially from future earnings. The higher P/E stock still may be a bargain relative to the low P/E stock if its earnings and dividends are expected to grow at a faster rate. Our point is that ownership of the stock conveys the right to future earnings as well as to current earnings. An exclusive focus on the commonly reported accounting P/E ratio can be shortsighted because by its nature it ignores future growth in earnings.

An efficient markets adherent will be skeptical of the notion that a strategy of investing in low P/E stocks will result in an expected rate of return greater than that of investing in high or medium P/E stocks having the same risk. The empirical evidence on this question is mixed,

TABLE **13.9**		Plowback Ratio (b)			
Effect of ROE and plowback ratio on P/B	**ROE**	**0**	**25%**	**50%**	**75%**
	10%	1.00	0.95	0.86	0.67
	12	1.00	1.00	1.00	1.00
	14	1.00	1.06	1.20	2.00

Note: The assumptions and formulas underlying this table are: $E_1 = \$1$; book value per share $= \$8.33$; $k = 12\%$ per year.

$$g = b \times \text{ROE}$$

$$P_0 = \frac{(1 - b)E}{k - g}$$

$$\text{P/B} = P_0/\$8.33$$

but if the strategy has worked in the past, it surely should not work in the future because too many investors will be following it. This is the lesson of market efficiency.

Before leaving the P/B and P/E ratios, it is worth pointing out the relationship among these ratios and ROE.

$$\text{ROE} = \frac{\text{Earnings}}{\text{Book value}} = \frac{\text{Market price}}{\text{Book value}} \div \frac{\text{Market price}}{\text{Earnings}}$$

$$= \text{P/B ratio} \div \text{P/E ratio}$$

Rearranging terms, we find that a firm's **earnings yield,** the ratio of earnings to price, is equal to its ROE divided by the market-to-book-value ratio:

$$\frac{E}{P} = \frac{\text{ROE}}{\text{P/B}}$$

earnings yield

The ratio of earnings to price, E/P.

Thus, a company with a high ROE can have a relatively low earnings yield because its P/B ratio is high. This indicates that a high ROE does not in and of itself imply the stock is a good buy. The price of the stock already may be bid up to reflect an attractive ROE. If so, the P/B ratio will be above 1.0, and the earnings yield to stockholders will be below the ROE, as the equation demonstrates. The relationship shows that a strategy of investing in the stock of high ROE firms may produce a lower holding-period return than investing in the stock of firms with a low ROE.

For example, Clayman (1987) found that investing in the stocks of 29 "excellent" companies, with mean reported ROE of 19.05% during the period 1976 to 1980, produced results much inferior to investing in 39 "unexcellent" companies, those with a mean ROE of 7.09% during the period. An investor putting equal dollar amounts in the stock of the unexcellent companies would have earned a portfolio rate of return over the 1981 to 1985 period that was 11.3% higher per year than the rate of return on a comparable portfolio of excellent company stocks.

3. What were GI's ROE, P/E, and P/B ratios in the year 2003? How do they compare to the industry average ratios, which were:

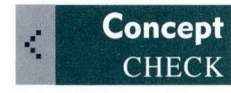

Concept
CHECK

$$\text{ROE} = 8.64\%$$
$$\text{P/E} = 8$$
$$\text{P/B} = 0.69$$

How does GI's earnings yield in 2003 compare to the industry average?

Choosing a Benchmark

We have discussed how to calculate the principal financial ratios. To evaluate the performance of a given firm, however, you need a benchmark to which you can compare its ratios. One obvious benchmark is the ratio for the same company in earlier years. For example, Figure 13.1 shows PepsiCo's return on assets, profit margin, and asset turnover ratio for the last few years. You can see there that ROA improved dramatically in 1999 and 2000. This was attributable largely to an improvement in profit margin, as asset turnover was relatively flat.

It is also helpful to compare financial ratios to those of other firms in the same industry. Financial ratios for industries are published by the U.S. Department of Commerce, Dun & Bradstreet, the Risk Management Association (formerly Robert Morris Associates), and others, and many ratios are available on the Web, for example on the Yahoo! site. Table 13.10

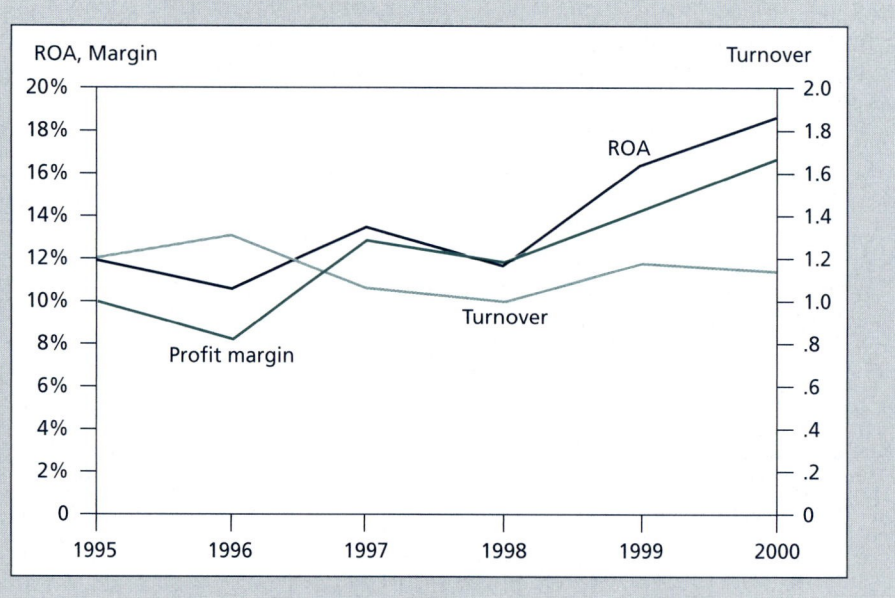

FIGURE 13.1

Pepsi's financial ratios over time. ROA improved largely due to increases in profit margin.

TABLE 13.10

Financial ratios for major industry groups

	LT Debt Assets	Interest Coverage	Current Ratio	Quick Ratio	Asset Turnover	Profit Margin (%)	Return on Assets (%)	Return on Equity (%)	Payout Ratio
All manufacturing	0.22	3.66	1.29	0.86	0.98	8.16	7.98	17.91	0.38
Food products	0.29	4.15	1.08	0.61	1.12	9.70	10.91	24.42	0.43
Clothing	0.27	3.19	1.89	1.01	1.62	6.73	10.91	18.89	0.25
Printing/publishing	0.29	3.70	1.22	1.01	0.90	10.48	9.42	22.48	0.38
Chemicals	0.24	2.94	1.11	0.77	0.71	10.46	7.43	20.86	0.53
Drugs	0.20	4.34	1.18	0.87	0.75	13.37	10.04	28.13	0.66
Machinery	0.17	3.55	1.45	1.03	1.00	5.93	5.94	6.26	0.23
Electrical/electronic	0.15	4.58	1.64	1.18	0.87	8.99	7.81	14.37	0.29
Motor vehicles	0.15	3.79	0.86	0.66	1.15	5.24	6.01	24.58	0.16

Source: U.S. Department of Commerce, *Quarterly Financial Report for Manufacturing, Mining and Trade Corporations,* first quarter 2000.

contains some of the principal ratios for a wide range of U.S. industries. These can be useful benchmarks. For example, if PepsiCo's turnover ratio is less than that of Coca-Cola or other firms in the soft-drink industry, one would want to know why.

13.5 ECONOMIC VALUE ADDED

One common use of financial ratios is to evaluate the performance of the firm. While it is common to use profitability to measure that performance, profitability is really not enough. A firm should be viewed as successful only if the return on its projects is better than the rate

TABLE **13.11** Economic value added, 1999	Economic Value Added ($ billions)	Capital ($ billions)	Return on Capital	Cost of Capital
A. Some EVA winners				
Microsoft	$7.85	$20.03	51.8%	12.6%
ExxonMobil	$6.32	$180.04	11.7%	8.2%
Intel	$5.48	$29.83	30.6%	12.2%
Merck	$3.66	$29.55	23.1%	10.7%
General Electric	$3.59	$75.83	17.2%	12.5%
B. Some EVA losers				
AT&T	−$8.54	$176.87	4.4%	9.2%
WorldCom	−$4.92	$94.02	5.6%	10.8%
Lucent	−$2.55	$65.59	9.8%	13.7%
Loews	−$2.38	$19.95	−2.4%	9.5%
Bank One Corp	−$1.60	$45.56	8.5%	12.0%

Source: Stern Stewart.

investors could expect to earn for themselves (on a risk-adjusted basis) in the capital market. Think back to Table 13.9, where we showed that plowing back funds into the firm increases share value only if the firm earns a higher rate of return on the reinvested funds than the opportunity cost of capital, that is, the market capitalization rate. To account for this opportunity cost, we might measure the success of the firm using the difference between the return on assets, ROA, and the opportunity cost of capital, k. **Economic value added** (EVA), or **residual income,** is the spread between ROA and k multiplied by the capital invested in the firm. It therefore measures the dollar value of the firm's return in excess of its opportunity cost.

> **economic value added, or residual income**
>
> A measure of the dollar value of a firm's return in excess of its opportunity cost.

Table 13.11 shows EVA for a small sample of firms drawn from a larger study of 1,000 firms by Stern Stewart, a consulting firm that has done much to develop and promote the concept of EVA. Microsoft had one of the highest returns on capital, at 51.8%. Since the cost of capital for Microsoft was only 12.6% percent, each dollar invested by Microsoft was earning about 39.2 cents more than the return that investors could have expected by investing in equivalent-risk stocks. Applying this 39.2% margin of superiority to Microsoft's capital base of $20.03 billion, we calculate annual economic value added as $7.85 billion.[3] Note that ExxonMobil's EVA was larger than Intel's, despite a far smaller margin between return on capital and cost of capital. This is because ExxonMobil applied this margin to a larger capital base. At the other extreme, AT&T earned less than its opportunity cost on a very large capital base, which resulted in a large negative EVA.

Notice that even the EVA "losers" in this study generally had positive profits. For example, AT&T's ROA was 4.4%. The problem is that AT&T's profits were not high enough to compensate for the opportunity cost of funds. EVA treats the opportunity cost of capital as a real cost that, like other costs, should be deducted from revenues to arrive at a more meaningful "bottom line." A firm that is earning profits but is not covering its opportunity cost might be able to redeploy its capital to better uses. Therefore, a growing number of firms now calculate EVA and tie managers' compensation to it.

---

[3]Actual EVA estimates reported by Stern Stewart differ somewhat from the values in Table 13.11 because of other adjustments to the accounting data involving issues such as treatment of research and development expenses, taxes, advertising expenses, and depreciation. The estimates in Table 13.11 are designed to show the logic behind EVA.

TABLE 13.12
Key financial ratios of Growth Industries, Inc.

Year	ROE	(1) Net Profit Pretax Profit	(2) Pretax Profit EBIT	(3) EBIT Sales (ROS)	(4) Sales Assets (ATO)	(5) Assets Equity	(6) Compound Leverage Factor (2) × (5)	(7) ROA (3) × (4)	P/E	P/B
2001	7.51%	0.6	0.650	30%	0.303	2.117	1.376	9.09%	8	0.58
2002	6.08	0.6	0.470	30	0.303	2.375	1.116	9.09	6	0.35
2003	3.03	0.6	0.204	30	0.303	2.723	0.556	9.09	4	0.12
Industry average	8.64	0.6	0.800	30	0.400	1.500	1.200	12.00	8	0.69

13.6 AN ILLUSTRATION OF FINANCIAL STATEMENT ANALYSIS

In her 2003 annual report to the shareholders of Growth Industries, Inc., the president wrote: "2003 was another successful year for Growth Industries. As in 2002, sales, assets, and operating income all continued to grow at a rate of 20%."

Is she right?

We can evaluate her statement by conducting a full-scale ratio analysis of Growth Industries. Our purpose is to assess GI's performance in the recent past, to evaluate its future prospects, and to determine whether its market price reflects its intrinsic value.

Table 13.12 shows some key financial ratios we can compute from GI's financial statements. The president is certainly right about the growth in sales, assets, and operating income. Inspection of GI's key financial ratios, however, contradicts her first sentence: 2003 was not another successful year for GI—it appears to have been another miserable one.

ROE has been declining steadily from 7.51% in 2001 to 3.03% in 2003. A comparison of GI's 2003 ROE to the 2003 industry average of 8.64% makes the deteriorating time trend especially alarming. The low and falling market-to-book-value ratio and the falling price–earnings ratio indicate that investors are less and less optimistic about the firm's future profitability.

The fact that ROA has not been declining, however, tells us that the source of the declining time trend in GI's ROE must be due to financial leverage. And we see that, while GI's leverage ratio climbed from 2.117 in 2001 to 2.723 in 2003, its interest-burden ratio fell from 0.650 to 0.204—with the net result that the compound leverage factor fell from 1.376 to 0.556.

The rapid increase in short-term debt from year to year and the concurrent increase in interest expense make it clear that, to finance its 20% growth rate in sales, GI has incurred sizable amounts of short-term debt at high interest rates. The firm is paying rates of interest greater than the ROA it is earning on the investment financed with the new borrowing. As the firm has expanded, its situation has become ever more precarious.

In 2003, for example, the average interest rate on short-term debt was 20% versus an ROA of 9.09%. (We compute the average interest rate on short-term debt by taking the total interest expense of $34,391,000, subtracting the $6 million in interest on the long-term bonds, and dividing by the beginning-of-year short-term debt of $141,957,000.)

GI's problems become clear when we examine its statement of cash flows in Table 13.13. The statement is derived from the income statement and balance sheet in Table 13.8. GI's cash flow from operations is falling steadily, from $12,700,000 in 2001 to $6,725,000 in 2003. The

TABLE **13.13**		**2001**	**2002**	**2003**
Growth Industries statement of cash flows ($thousands)	**Cash flow from operating activities**			
	Net income	$ 11,700	$ 10,143	$ 5,285
	+ Depreciation	15,000	18,000	21,600
	+ Decrease (increase) in accounts receivable	(5,000)	(6,000)	(7,200)
	+ Decrease (increase) in inventories	(15,000)	(18,000)	(21,600)
	+ Increase in accounts payable	6,000	7,200	8,640
		$ 12,700	$ 11,343	$ 6,725
	Cash flow from investing activities			
	Investment in plant and equipment*	$(45,000)	$(54,000)	$(64,800)
	Cash flow from financing activities			
	Dividends paid[†]	$ 0	$ 0	$ 0
	Short-term debt issued	42,300	54,657	72,475
	Change in cash and marketable securities[‡]	$ 10,000	$ 12,000	$ 14,400

*Gross investment equals increase in net plant and equipment plus depreciation.

[†]We can conclude that no dividends are paid because stockholders' equity increases each year by the full amount of net income, implying a plowback ratio of 1.0.

[‡]Equals cash flow from operations plus cash flow from investment activities plus cash flow from financing activities. Note that this equals the yearly change in cash and marketable securities on the balance sheet.

firm's investment in plant and equipment, by contrast, has increased greatly. Net plant and equipment (i.e., net of depreciation) rose from $150,000,000 in 2000 to $259,200,000 in 2003. This near doubling of the capital assets makes the decrease in cash flow from operations all the more troubling.

The source of the difficulty is GI's enormous amount of short-term borrowing. In a sense, the company is being run as a pyramid scheme. It borrows more and more each year to maintain its 20% growth rate in assets and income. However, the new assets are not generating enough cash flow to support the extra interest burden of the debt, as the falling cash flow from operations indicates. Eventually, when the firm loses its ability to borrow further, its growth will be at an end.

At this point, GI stock might be an attractive investment. Its market price is only 12% of its book value, and with a P/E ratio of 4, its earnings yield is 25% per year. GI is a likely candidate for a takeover by another firm that might replace GI's management and build shareholder value through a radical change in policy.

4. You have the following information for IBX Corporation for the years 2001 and 2004 (all figures are in $millions):

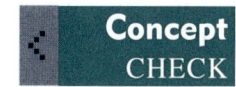

Concept
CHECK

	2004	2001
Net income	$ 253.7	$ 239.0
Pretax income	411.9	375.6
EBIT	517.6	403.1
Average assets	4,857.9	3,459.7
Sales	6,679.3	4,537.0
Shareholders' equity	2,233.3	2,347.3

What is the trend in IBX's ROE, and how can you account for it in terms of tax burden, margin, turnover, and financial leverage?

13.7 : COMPARABILITY PROBLEMS

Financial statement analysis gives us a good amount of ammunition for evaluating a company's performance and future prospects. But comparing financial results of different companies is not so simple. There is more than one acceptable way to represent various items of revenue and expense according to generally accepted accounting principles (GAAP). This means two firms may have exactly the same economic income yet very different accounting incomes.

Furthermore, interpreting a single firm's performance over time is complicated when inflation distorts the dollar measuring rod. Comparability problems are especially acute in this case because the impact of inflation on reported results often depends on the particular method the firm adopts to account for inventories and depreciation. The security analyst must adjust the earnings and the financial ratio figures to a uniform standard before attempting to compare financial results across firms and over time.

Comparability problems can arise out of the flexibility of GAAP guidelines in accounting for inventories and depreciation and in adjusting for the effects of inflation. Other important potential sources of noncomparability include the capitalization of leases and other expenses, the treatment of pension costs, and allowances for reserves, but they are beyond the scope of this book.

Inventory Valuation

LIFO

The last-in first-out accounting method of valuing inventories.

FIFO

The first-in first-out accounting method of valuing inventories.

There are two commonly used ways to value inventories: **LIFO** (last-in, first-out) and **FIFO** (first-in, first-out). We can explain the difference using a numerical example.

Suppose Generic Products, Inc. (GPI), has a constant inventory of 1 million units of generic goods. The inventory turns over once per year, meaning the ratio of cost of goods sold to inventory is 1.

The LIFO system calls for valuing the million units used up during the year at the current cost of production, so that the last goods produced are considered the first ones to be sold. They are valued at today's cost. The FIFO system assumes that the units used up or sold are the ones that were added to inventory first, and goods sold should be valued at original cost.

If the price of generic goods were constant, at the level of $1, say, the book value of inventory and the cost of goods sold would be the same, $1 million under both systems. But suppose the price of generic goods rises by 10 cents per unit during the year as a result of inflation.

LIFO accounting would result in a cost of goods sold of $1.1 million, while the end-of-year balance sheet value of the 1 million units in inventory remains $1 million. The balance sheet value of inventories is given as the cost of the goods still in inventory. Under LIFO, the last goods produced are assumed to be sold at the current cost of $1.10; the goods remaining are the previously produced goods, at a cost of only $1. You can see that, although LIFO accounting accurately measures the cost of goods sold today, it understates the current value of the remaining inventory in an inflationary environment.

In contrast, under FIFO accounting, the cost of goods sold would be $1 million, and the end-of-year balance sheet value of the inventory is $1.1 million. The result is that the LIFO firm has both a lower reported profit and a lower balance sheet value of inventories than the FIFO firm.

LIFO is preferred over FIFO in computing economics earnings (that is, real sustainable cash flow), because it uses up-to-date prices to evaluate the cost of goods sold. A disadvantage is that LIFO accounting induces balance sheet distortions when it values investment in inventories at original cost. This practice results in an upward bias in ROE because the investment base on which return is earned is undervalued.

In computing the gross national product, the U.S. Department of Commerce has to make an inventory valuation adjustment (IVA) to eliminate the effects of FIFO accounting on the cost of goods sold. In effect, it puts all firms in the aggregate onto a LIFO basis.

Depreciation

Another source of problems is the measurement of depreciation, which is a key factor in computing true earnings. The accounting and economic measures of depreciation can differ markedly. According to the *economic* definition, depreciation is the amount of a firm's operating cash flow that must be reinvested in the firm to sustain its real cash flow at the current level.

The *accounting* measurement is quite different. Accounting depreciation is the amount of the original acquisition cost of an asset that is allocated to each accounting period over an arbitrarily specified life of the asset. This is the figure reported in financial statements.

Assume, for example, that a firm buys machines with a useful economic life of 20 years at $100,000 apiece. In its financial statements, however, the firm can depreciate the machines over 10 years using the straight-line method, for $10,000 per year in depreciation. Thus, after 10 years, a machine will be fully depreciated on the books, even though it remains a productive asset that will not need replacement for another 10 years.

In computing accounting earnings, this firm will overestimate depreciation in the first 10 years of the machine's economic life and underestimate it in the last 10 years. This will cause reported earnings to be understated compared with economic earnings in the first 10 years and overstated in the last 10 years.

Depreciation comparability problems add one more wrinkle. A firm can use different depreciation methods for tax purposes than for other reporting purposes. Most firms use accelerated depreciation methods for tax purposes and straight-line depreciation in published financial statements. There also are differences across firms in their estimates of the depreciable life of plant, equipment, and other depreciable assets.

The major problem related to depreciation, however, is caused by inflation. Because conventional depreciation is based on historical costs rather than on the current replacement cost of assets, measured depreciation in periods of inflation is understated relative to replacement cost, and *real* economic income (sustainable cash flow) is correspondingly overstated.

The situation is similar to what happens in FIFO inventory accounting. Conventional depreciation and FIFO both result in an inflation-induced overstatement of real income because both use original cost instead of current cost to calculate net income.

For example, suppose Generic Products, Inc., has a machine with a three-year useful life that originally cost $3 million. Annual straight-line depreciation is $1 million, regardless of what happens to the replacement cost of the machine. Suppose inflation in the first year turns out to be 10%. Then the true annual depreciation expense is $1.1 million in current terms, while conventionally measured depreciation remains fixed at $1 million per year. Accounting income therefore overstates *real* economic income.

Inflation and Interest Expense

While inflation can cause distortions in the measurement of a firm's inventory and depreciation costs, it has perhaps an even greater effect on the calculation of *real* interest expense. Nominal interest rates include an inflation premium that compensates the lender for inflation-induced erosion in the real value of principal. From the perspective of both lender and borrower, therefore, part of what is conventionally measured as interest expense should be treated more properly as repayment of principal.

For example, suppose Generic Products has debt outstanding with a face value of $10 million at an interest rate of 10% per year. Interest expense as conventionally measured is $1 million per year. However, suppose inflation during the year is 6%, so that the real interest rate is 4%. Then $0.6 million of what appears as interest expense on the income statement is really an inflation premium, or compensation for the anticipated reduction in the real value of the $10 million principal; only $0.4 million is *real* interest expense. The $0.6 million reduction in the purchasing power of the outstanding principal may be thought of as repayment of principal, rather than as an interest expense. Real income of the firm is, therefore, understated by $0.6 million.

This mismeasurement of real interest means that inflation results in an underestimate of real income. The effects of inflation on the reported values of inventories and depreciation that we have discussed work in the opposite direction.

5. In a period of rapid inflation, companies ABC and XYZ have the same *reported* earnings. ABC uses LIFO inventory accounting, has relatively fewer depreciable assets, and has more debt than XYZ. XYZ uses FIFO inventory accounting. Which company has the higher *real* income and why?

Quality of Earnings and Accounting Practices

Many firms make accounting choices that present their financial statements in the best possible light. The different choices that firms can make give rise to the comparability problems we have discussed. As a result, earnings statements for different companies may be more or less rosy presentations of true "economic earnings"—sustainable cash flow that can be paid to shareholders without impairing the firm's productive capacity. Analysts commonly evaluate the **quality of earnings** reported by a firm. This concept refers to the realism and conservatism of the earnings number, in other words, the extent to which we might expect the reported level of earnings to be sustained.

Examples of the accounting choices that influence quality of earnings are:

quality of earnings

The realism and sustainability of reported earnings.

- *Allowance for bad debt.* Most firms sell goods using trade credit and must make an allowance for bad debt. An unrealistically low allowance reduces the quality of reported earnings. Look for a rising average collection period on accounts receivable as evidence of potential problems with future collections.

- *Nonrecurring items.* Some items that affect earnings should not be expected to recur regularly. These include asset sales, effects of accounting changes, effects of exchange rate movements, or unusual investment income. For example, in 1999, which was a banner year for equity returns, some firms enjoyed large investment returns on securities held. These contributed to that year's earnings, but should not be expected to repeat regularly. They would be considered a "low-quality" component of earnings. Similarly gains in corporate pension plans can generate large, but one-time, contributions to reported earnings. For example, IBM increased its year 2000 pretax income by nearly $200 million by changing the assumed rate of return on its pension fund assets by 0.5%.

- *Reserves management.* In the 1990s, W. R. Grace *reduced* its earnings by offsetting high earnings in one of its subsidiaries with extra reserves against unspecified future liabilities. Why would it do this? Because later, it could "release" those reserves if and when earnings were lower, thereby creating the appearance of steady earnings growth. Wall Street likes strong, steady earnings growth, but Grace planned to provide such growth through earnings management.

- *Stock options.* Many firms, particularly start-ups, compensate employees in large part with stock options. To the extent that these options replace cash salary that otherwise would need to be paid, the value of the options should be considered as one component of the firm's labor expense. But GAAP accounting rules do not require such treatment. Therefore, all else equal, earnings of firms with large employee stock option programs should be considered of lower quality.

- *Revenue recognition.* Under GAAP accounting, a firm is allowed to recognize a sale before it is paid. This is why firms have accounts receivable. But sometimes it can be hard to know when to recognize sales. For example, suppose a computer firm signs a contract to provide products and services over a five-year period. Should the revenue be booked immediately or spread out over five years? A more extreme version of this problem is called "channel stuffing," in which firms "sell" large quantities of goods to customers, but give them the right to later either refuse delivery or return the product. The revenue from the "sale" is booked now, but the likely returns are not recognized until they occur (in a future accounting period). According to the SEC, Sunbeam, which filed for bankruptcy in 2001, generated $60 million in fraudulent profits in 1999 using this technique. If you see accounts receivable increasing far faster than sales, or becoming a larger percentage of total assets, beware of these practices. Global Crossing, which filed for bankruptcy in 2002, illustrates a similar problem in revenue recognition. It swapped capacity on its network for capacity of other companies for periods of up to 20 years. But while it seems to have booked the *sale* of its capacity as immediate revenue, it treated the *acquired* capacity as capital assets that could be expensed over time. Given the wide latitude firms have to manipulate revenue, many analysts choose instead to concentrate on cash flow, which is far harder for a company to manipulate.

- *Off-balance-sheet assets and liabilities.* Suppose that one firm guarantees the outstanding debt of another firm, perhaps a firm in which it has an ownership stake. That obligation ought to be disclosed as a *contingent liability,* since it may require payments down the road. But these obligations may not be reported as part of the firm's outstanding debt. Similarly, leasing may be used to manage off-balance-sheet assets and liabilities. Airlines, for example, may show no aircraft on their balance sheets but have long-term leases that are virtually equivalent to debt-financed ownership. However, if the leases are treated as operating rather than capital leases, they may appear only as footnotes to the financial statements.

Enron Corporation, which filed for bankruptcy protection in December 2001, presents an extreme case of "management" of financial statements. The firm seems to have used several partnerships in which it was engaged to hide debt and overstate earnings. When disclosures about these partnerships came to light at the end of 2001, the company was forced to restate earnings amounting to almost $600 million dating back to 1997. Enron raises the question of where to draw the line that separates creative, but legal, interpretation of financial reporting rules from fraudulent reporting. It also raises questions about the proper relationship between a firm and its auditor, which is supposed to certify that the firm's financial statements are prepared properly. Enron's auditor, Arthur Andersen LLP, actually earned more money in 2000 doing nonauditing work for Enron than it did for its external audit. The dual role of the auditing firm creates a potential conflict of interest, since the auditor may be lenient in the audit to preserve its consulting business with the client. Andersen's dual role has become common in the auditing industry. However, in the wake of the Enron bankruptcy, many firms have voluntarily decided to no longer hire their auditors as consultants, and this practice may be banned by new legislation. Moreover, big auditors such as KMPG, Ernst & Young, Pricewaterhouse-Coopers, and Deloitte Touche Tohmatsu either have spun off their consulting practices as independent firms or have announced their intention to separate the audit and consulting businesses.

Unfortunately, Enron was hardly alone in preparing financial statements of questionable quality or utility. The nearby box points out that financial statements have increasingly become "black boxes," reporting data that are difficult to interpret or even to verify. As we noted in the previous chapter, however, the valuations of stocks with particularly hard-to-interpret financial statements have been adversely affected by the market's new focus on accounting uncertainty. The incentives for clearer disclosure induced by this sort of market discipline should foster greater transparency in accounting practice.

International Accounting Conventions

The examples cited above illustrate some of the problems that analysts can encounter when attempting to interpret financial data. Even greater problems arise in the interpretation of the financial statements of foreign firms. This is because these firms do not follow GAAP guidelines. Accounting practices in various countries differ to greater or lesser extents from U.S. standards. Here are some of the major issues that you should be aware of when using the financial statements of foreign firms.

Reserving practices Many countries allow firms considerably more discretion in setting aside reserves for future contingencies than is typical in the United States. Because additions to reserves result in a charge against income, reported earnings are far more subject to managerial discretion than in the United States.

(concluded)

"The boundaries of corporations are becoming increasingly blurred," says Mr. Lev. "It's very well defined legally what is inside the corporation but . . . we must restructure accounting so the primary entity will be the economic one, not the legal one."

Because of the leeway in current accounting rules, two companies in the same industry that perform identical transactions can report different numbers. Take the way companies can account for research-and-development costs. One company could spread the costs out over 10 years, while another might spread the same costs over five years.

Both methods would be allowable and defensible, but the longer time frame would tend to result in higher earnings because it reduces expenses allocated annually.

Another area that allows companies freedom to determine what results they report is in the accounting for intangible assets, such as the value placed on goodwill, or the amount paid for an asset above its book value. At best, the values placed on these items as recorded on company balance sheets are educated guesses. But they represent an increasing part of total assets.

Further complicating matters for investors, many companies have taken to providing pro forma earnings that, among other things, often show profits and losses without these changes in intangible values. The result

has been virtually a new accounting system without any set rules, in which companies have been free to show their performance any way they deem fit.

Finally, add to the equation the increasing importance of a rising stock price, and investors face an unprecedented incentive on the part of companies to obfuscate. No longer is a higher stock price simply desirable, it is often essential, because stocks have become a vital way for companies to run their businesses. The growing use of stock options as a way of compensating employees means managers need higher stock prices to retain talent. The use of stock to make acquisitions and to guarantee the debt of off-the-books partnerships means, as with Enron, that the entire partnership edifice can come crashing down with the fall of the underlying stock that props up the system.

And the growing use of the stock market as a place for companies to raise capital means a high stock price can be the difference between failure and success.

Hence, companies have an incentive to use aggressive—but, under the rules, acceptable—accounting to boost their reported earnings and prop up their stock price. In the worst-case scenario, that means some companies put out misleading financial accounts.

Source: Abridged version of the article of the same title by Steve Liesman for "Heard on the Street," *The Wall Street Journal,* January 21, 2002.

Germany is a country that allows particularly wide discretion in reserve practice. When Daimler-Benz AG (producer of the Mercedes Benz, now DaimlerChrysler) decided to issue shares on the New York Stock Exchange in 1993, it had to revise its accounting statements in accordance with U.S. standards. The revisions transformed a $370 million profit for 1993 using German accounting rules into a $1 million *loss* under more stringent U.S. rules.

Depreciation   As discussed above, in the United States firms typically maintain separate sets of accounts for tax and reporting purposes. For example, accelerated depreciation is used for tax purposes, while straight-line depreciation is used for reporting purposes. In contrast, most other countries do not allow dual sets of accounts, and most firms in foreign countries use accelerated depreciation to minimize taxes despite the fact that it results in lower reported earnings. This makes reported earnings of foreign firms lower than they would be if the firms were allowed to follow the U.S. practice.

Intangibles   Treatment of intangibles can vary widely. Are they amortized or expensed? If amortized, over what period? Such issues can have a large impact on reported profits.

Figure 13.2 summarizes some of the major differences in accounting rules in various countries. The effect of different accounting practices can be substantial.

A study by Speidell and Bavishi (1992) recalculated the financial statements of firms in several countries using common accounting rules. Figure 13.3, from their study, compares P/E ratios as reported and restated on a common basis. The variation is considerable.

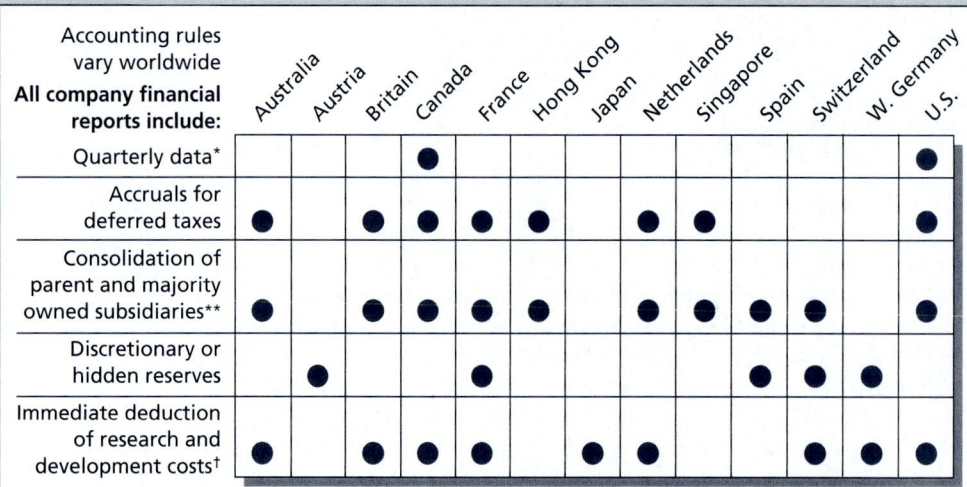

Accounting rules vary worldwide **All company financial reports include:**	Australia	Austria	Britain	Canada	France	Hong Kong	Japan	Netherlands	Singapore	Spain	Switzerland	W. Germany	U.S.
Quarterly data*				●									●
Accruals for deferred taxes	●		●	●	●	●		●	●				●
Consolidation of parent and majority owned subsidiaries**	●		●	●	●	●		●	●	●			●
Discretionary or hidden reserves		●			●				●	●	●		
Immediate deduction of research and development costs†	●		●	●	●		●	●			●	●	●

* In Austria companies issue only annual data. Other countries besides the U.S. and Canada issue semiannual data. In the Netherlands, companies issue quarterly or semiannual data.
** In Austria, Japan, Hong Kong, and West Germany, the minority of companies fully consolidate.
† In Austria, Hong Kong, Singapore, and Spain, the accounting treatment for R&D costs—whether they are immediately deducted or capitalized and deducted over later years—isn't disclosed in financial reports.

FIGURE 13.2

Comparative accounting rules

Source: Center for International Financial Analysis and Research, Princeton, NJ; and Frederick D. S. Choi and Gerhard G. Mueller, *International Accounting*, 2d. ed. (Englewood Cliffs, NJ: Prentice Hall, 1992).

FIGURE 13.3

Adjusted versus reported price–earnings ratios

Source: Lawrence S. Speidell and Vinod Bavishi, "GAAP Arbitrage: Valuation Opportunities in International Accounting Standards," *Financial Analysts Journal*, November–December 1992, pp. 58–66. Copyright 1992. Association for Investment Management and Research. Reproduced and republished from *Financial Analysts Journal* with permission from the Association for Investment Management and Research. All Rights Reserved.

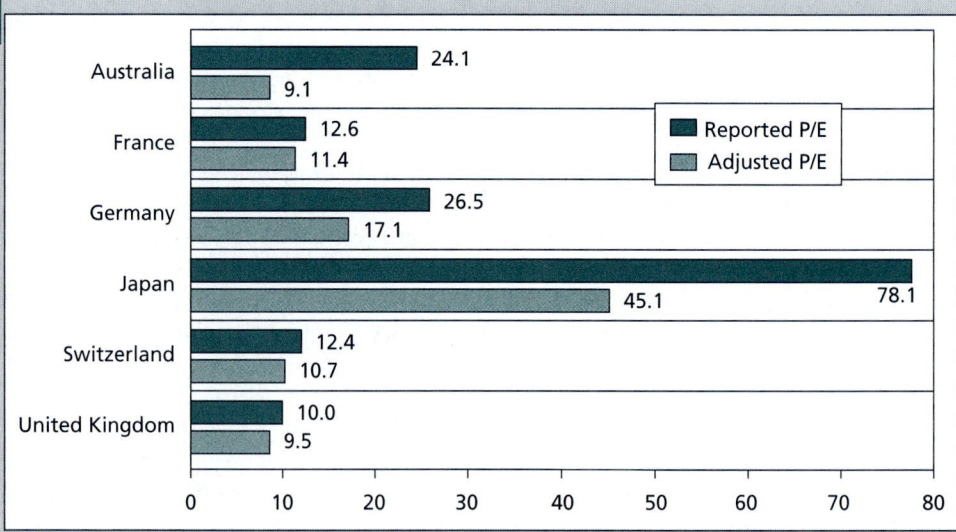

Such differences in international accounting standards have become more of a problem as the drive to globally integrate capital markets progresses. For example, many foreign firms would like to list their shares on the New York Stock Exchange in order to more easily tap the U.S. equity markets, and the NYSE would like to have those firms listed. But the Securities and Exchange Commission (SEC) will not allow such shares to be listed unless the firms prepare their financial statements in accordance with U.S. GAAP standards. This has limited the listing of non-U.S. companies dramatically.

In contrast to the U.S., most large non-U.S. national stock exchanges allow foreign firms to be listed if their financial statements conform to International Accounting Standards (IAS) rules. IAS disclosure requirements tend to be far more rigorous than those of most countries, and they impose greater uniformity in accounting practices. Its advocates argue that IAS rules are already fairly similar to GAAP rules and provide nearly the same quality financial information about the firm. While the SEC does not yet deem IAS standards acceptable for listing in U.S. markets, negotiations are currently underway to change that situation.

The Enron and other accounting debacles have given U.S. regulators a dose of humility concerning GAAP standards. While European IAS regulation tends to be principle-based, GAAP regulation tends to be rules-based. GAAP mandates lengthy, detailed, and specific rules about the widest range of allowed accounting practices. Critics argue that by doing so, it gives legal protection to firms that use clever accounting practice to misportray their true status while still satisfying a legalistic checklist approach to their financial statements. In the aftermath of Enron, Harvey Pitt, chairman of the SEC, stated his intention to move the U.S. more in the direction of principle-based standards and to require firms to explain both why they have chosen their accounting conventions and how their results would be affected by changes in those accounting assumptions.

13.8 | VALUE INVESTING: THE GRAHAM TECHNIQUE

No presentation of fundamental security analysis would be complete without a discussion of the ideas of Benjamin Graham, the greatest of the investment "gurus." Until the evolution of modern portfolio theory in the latter half of this century, Graham was the single most

---

WEBMASTER

Accounting in Crisis

The headlines in the last quarter of 2001 and the first half of 2002 were dominated by stories related to the meltdown and bankruptcy of the energy giant Enron. As the story unfolded, issues related to the accounting industry made the front pages of the financial press and stories related to Enron were featured on the evening news. The January issue of *BusinessWeek* contained a special report entitled "Accounting in Crisis," which can be found at http://www.businessweek.com/magazine/content/02_04/b3767712.htm.

After reading the article, identify and briefly describe the seven steps that the article discussed for reform of the accounting industry.

important thinker, writer, and teacher in the field of investment analysis. His influence on investment professionals remains very strong.

Graham's magnum opus is *Security Analysis,* written with Columbia Professor David Dodd in 1934. Its message is similar to the ideas presented in this chapter. Graham believed careful analysis of a firm's financial statements could turn up bargain stocks. Over the years, he developed many different rules for determining the most important financial ratios and the critical values for judging a stock to be undervalued. Through many editions, his book has had a profound influence on investment professionals. It has been so influential and successful, in fact, that widespread adoption of Graham's techniques has led to elimination of the very bargains they are designed to identify.

In a 1976 seminar Graham said[4]

> I am no longer an advocate of elaborate techniques of security analysis in order to find superior value opportunities. This was a rewarding activity, say, forty years ago, when our textbook "Graham and Dodd" was first published; but the situation has changed a good deal since then. In the old days any well-trained security analyst could do a good professional job of selecting undervalued issues through detailed studies; but in the light of the enormous amount of research now being carried on, I doubt whether in most cases such extensive efforts will generate sufficiently superior selections to justify their cost. To that very limited extent I'm on the side of the "efficient market" school of thought now generally accepted by the professors.

Nonetheless, in that same seminar, Graham suggested a simplified approach to identify bargain stocks:

> My first, more limited, technique confines itself to the purchase of common stocks at less than their working-capital value, or net current-asset value, giving no weight to the plant and other fixed assets, and deducting all liabilities in full from the current assets. We used this approach extensively in managing investment funds, and over a thirty-odd-year period we must have earned an average of some 20% per year from this source. For awhile, however, after the mid-1950s, this brand of buying opportunity became very scarce because of the pervasive bull market. But it has returned in quantity since the 1973–1974 decline. In January 1976 we counted over 100 such issues in the Standard & Poor's *Stock Guide*—about 10% of the total. I consider it a foolproof method of systematic investment—once again, not on the basis of individual results but in terms of the expectable group outcome.

There are two convenient sources of information for those interested in trying out the Graham technique. Both Standard & Poor's *Outlook* and *The Value Line Investment Survey* carry lists of stocks selling below net working capital value.

SUMMARY

- The primary focus of the security analyst should be the firm's real economic earnings rather than its reported earnings. Accounting earnings as reported in financial statements can be a biased estimate of real economic earnings, although empirical studies reveal that reported earnings convey considerable information concerning a firm's prospects.
- A firm's ROE is a key determinant of the growth rate of its earnings. ROE is affected profoundly by the firm's degree of financial leverage. An increase in a firm's debt/equity ratio will raise its ROE and hence its growth rate only if the interest rate on the debt is less than the firm's return on assets.

[4]As cited by John Train in *Money Masters* (New York: Harper & Row, Publishers, Inc., 1987).

- It is often helpful to the analyst to decompose a firm's ROE ratio into the product of several accounting ratios and to analyze their separate behavior over time and across companies within an industry. A useful breakdown is

$$\text{ROE} = \frac{\text{Net profits}}{\text{Pretax profits}} \times \frac{\text{Pretax profits}}{\text{EBIT}} \times \frac{\text{EBIT}}{\text{Sales}} \times \frac{\text{Sales}}{\text{Assets}} \times \frac{\text{Assets}}{\text{Equity}}$$

- Other accounting ratios that have a bearing on a firm's profitability and/or risk are fixed-asset turnover, inventory turnover, days receivable, and the current, quick, and interest coverage ratios.
- Two ratios that make use of the market price of the firm's common stock in addition to its financial statements are the ratios of market to book value and price to earnings. Analysts sometimes take low values for these ratios as a margin of safety or a sign that the stock is a bargain.
- A major problem in the use of data obtained from a firm's financial statements is comparability. Firms have a great deal of latitude in how they choose to compute various items of revenue and expense. It is, therefore, necessary for the security analyst to adjust accounting earnings and financial ratios to a uniform standard before attempting to compare financial results across firms.
- Comparability problems can be acute in a period of inflation. Inflation can create distortions in accounting for inventories, depreciation, and interest expense.

KEY TERMS

accounting earnings, 456
acid test ratio, 463
asset turnover, 459
average collection
    period, 462
balance sheet, 452
current ratio, 462
days receivables, 462
earnings yield, 465
economic
    earnings, 456
economic value
    added, 467
FIFO, 470
income statement, 452
interest coverage
    ratio, 463
leverage ratio, 460
LIFO, 470
market-to-book-value
    ratio, 463
price–earnings ratio, 464
profit margin, 459
quality of earnings, 472
quick ratio, 463
residual income, 467
return on assets, 457
return on equity, 456
return on sales, 459
statement of cash
    flows, 454
times interest earned, 463

PROBLEM SETS

1. The Crusty Pie Co., which specializes in apple turnovers, has a return on sales higher than the industry average, yet its ROA is the same as the industry average. How can you explain this?

2. The ABC Corporation has a profit margin on sales below the industry average, yet its ROA is above the industry average. What does this imply about its asset turnover?

3. Firm A and firm B have the same ROA, yet firm A's ROE is higher. How can you explain this?

4. Which of the following *best* explains a ratio of "net sales to average net fixed assets" that *exceeds* the industry average?
   a. The firm added to its plant and equipment in the past few years.
   b. The firm makes less efficient use of its assets than other firms.
   c. The firm has a lot of old plant and equipment.
   d. The firm uses straight-line depreciation.

5. A company's current ratio is 2.0. If the company uses cash to retire notes payable due within one year, would this transaction increase or decrease the current ratio and asset turnover ratio?

www.mhhe.com/bkm

6. The information in the following table comes from the 1997 financial statements of QuickBrush Company and SmileWhite Corporation:

NOTES TO THE 1997 FINANCIAL STATEMENTS

	QuickBrush	SmileWhite
Goodwill	The company amortizes goodwill over 20 years.	The company amortizes goodwill over 5 years.
Property, plant, and equipment	The company uses a straight-line depreciation method over the economic lives of the assets, which range from 5 to 20 years for buildings.	The company uses an accelerated depreciation method over the economic lives of the assets, which range from 5 to 20 years for buildings.
Accounts receivable	The company uses a bad debt allowance of 2% of accounts receivable.	The company uses a bad debt allowance of 5% of accounts receivable.

Determine which company has the higher quality of earnings by discussing *each* of the *three* notes.

7. An analyst applies the DuPont system of financial analysis to the following data for a company:
   - Leverage ratio   2.2
   - Total asset turnover   2.0
   - Net profit margin   5.5%
   - Dividend payout ratio   31.8%

   What is the company's return on equity?

8. An analyst gathers the following information about Meyer, Inc.:
   - Meyer has 1,000 shares of 8% cumulative preferred stock outstanding, with a par value of $100, and liquidation value of $110.
   - Meyer has 20,000 shares of common stock outstanding, with a par value of $20.
   - Meyer had retained earnings at the beginning of the year of $5,000,000.
   - Net income for the year was $70,000.
   - This year, for the first time in its history, Meyer paid no dividends on preferred or common stock.

   What is the book value per share of Meyer's common stock?

9. The cash flow data of Palomba Pizza Stores for the year ended December 31, 2001, are as follows:

Cash payment of dividends	$ 35,000
Purchase of land	14,000
Cash payments for interest	10,000
Cash payments for salaries	45,000
Sale of equipment	38,000
Retirement of common stock	25,000
Purchase of equipment	30,000
Cash payments to suppliers	85,000
Cash collections from customers	250,000
Cash at beginning of year	50,000

   a. Prepare a statement of cash flows for Palomba in accordance with FAS 95 showing:

- Net cash provided by operating activities.
- Net cash provided by or used in investing activities.
- Net cash provided by or used in financing activities.

b. Discuss, from an analyst's viewpoint, the purpose of classifying cash flows into the three categories listed above.

10. The financial statements for Chicago Refrigerator Inc. (see Tables 13.14 and 13.15) are to be used to compute the ratios *a* through *h* for 1999.

a. Quick ratio.
b. Return on assets.
c. Return on common shareholders' equity.
d. Earnings per share of common stock.
e. Profit margin.

TABLE **13.14**		1998	1999
Chicago Refrigerator Inc. balance sheet, as of December 31 ($ thousands)	**Assets**		
	Current assets		
	Cash	$ 683	$ 325
	Accounts receivable	1,490	3,599
	Inventories	1,415	2,423
	Prepaid expenses	15	13
	Total current assets	$3,603	$6,360
	Property, plant, equipment, net	1,066	1,541
	Other	123	157
	Total assets	$4,792	$8,058
	Liabilities		
	Current liabilities		
	Notes payable to bank	$ —	$ 875
	Current portion of long-term debt	38	115
	Accounts payable	485	933
	Estimated income tax	588	472
	Accrued expenses	576	586
	Customer advance payment	34	963
	Total current liabilities	$1,721	$3,945
	Long-term debt	122	179
	Other liabilities	81	131
	Total liabilities	$1,924	$4,255
	Shareholders' equity		
	Common stock, $1 par value 1,000,000 shares authorized; 550,000 and 829,000 outstanding, respectively	$ 550	$ 829
	Preferred stock, Series A 10%; $25.00 par value; 25,000 authorized; 20,000 and 18,000 outstanding, respectively	500	450
	Additional paid-in capital	450	575
	Retained earnings	1,368	1,949
	Total shareholders' equity	$2,868	$3,803
	Total liabilities and shareholders' equity	$4,792	$8,058

TABLE **13.15**		1998	1999
Chicago Refrigerator Inc. income statement, years ending December 31 ($ thousands)	Net sales	$7,570	$12,065
	Other income, net	261	345
	Total revenues	$7,831	$12,410
	Cost of goods sold	$4,850	$ 8,048
	General administrative and marketing expenses	1,531	2,025
	Interest expense	22	78
	Total costs and expenses	$6,403	$10,151
	Net income before tax	$1,428	$ 2,259
	Income tax	628	994
	Net income	$ 800	$ 1,265

    f. Times interest earned.
    g. Inventory turnover.
    h. Leverage ratio.
11. In an inflationary period, the use of FIFO will make which *one* of the following more realistic than the use of LIFO?
    a. Balance sheet
    b. Income statement
    c. Cash flow statement
    d. None of the above
12. A company acquires a machine with an estimated 10-year service life. If the company uses the Accelerated Cost Recovery System depreciation method instead of the straight-line method:
    a. Income will be higher in the 10th year.
    b. Total depreciation expense for the 10 years will be lower.
    c. Depreciation expense will be lower in the first year.
    d. Scrapping the machine after eight years will result in a larger loss.
13. Why might a firm's ratio of long-term debt to long-term capital be lower than the industry average, but its ratio of income-before-interest-and-taxes to debt-interest charges be lower than the industry average?
    a. The firm has higher profitability than average.
    b. The firm has more short-term debt than average.
    c. The firm has a high ratio of current assets to current liabilities.
    d. The firm has a high ratio of total cash flow to total long-term debt.
14. During a period of falling price levels, the financial statements of a company using FIFO instead of LIFO for inventory accounting would show:
    a. Lower total assets and lower net income.
    b. Lower total assets and higher net income.
    c. Higher total assets and lower net income.
    d. Higher total assets and higher net income.
15. Scott Kelly is reviewing MasterToy's financial statements in order to estimate its sustainable growth rate. Using the information presented in Table 13.16
    a. Identify and calculate the components of the DuPont formula.
    b. Calculate the ROE for 1999 using the components of the DuPont formula.
    c. Calculate the sustainable growth rate for 1999 from the firm's ROE and plowback ratios.

TABLE **13.16**		1998	1999
MasterToy, Inc.: Actual 1998 and Estimated 1999 financial statements for fiscal year ending December 31 ($ millions, except per-share data)	**Income Statement**		
	Revenue	$4,750	$5,140
	Cost of goods sold	2,400	2,540
	Selling, general, and administrative	1,400	1,550
	Depreciation	180	210
	Goodwill amortization	10	10
	Operating income	$ 760	$ 830
	Interest expense	20	25
	Income before taxes	$ 740	$ 805
	Income taxes	265	295
	Net income	$ 475	$ 510
	Earnings per share	$1.79	$1.96
	Average shares outstanding (millions)	265	260
	Balance Sheet		
	Cash	$ 400	$ 400
	Accounts receivable	680	700
	Inventories	570	600
	Net property, plant, and equipment	800	870
	Intangibles	500	530
	Total assets	$2,950	$3,100
	Current liabilities	$ 550	$ 600
	Long-term debt	300	300
	Total liabilities	$ 850	$ 900
	Stockholders' equity	2,100	2,200
	Total liabilities and equity	$2,950	$3,100
	Book value per share	$7.92	$8.46
	Annual dividend per share	0.55	0.60

16. In a cash flow statement prepared in accordance with FASB 95, cash flow from investing activities *excludes:*
    a. Cash paid for acquisitions.
    b. Cash received from the sale of fixed assets.
    c. Inventory increases due to a new (internally developed) product line.
    d. All of the above.

17. Cash flow from operating activities *includes:*
    a. Inventory increases resulting from acquisitions.
    b. Inventory changes due to changing exchange rates.
    c. Interest paid to bondholders.
    d. Dividends paid to stockholders.

18. Janet Ludlow is a recently hired analyst. After describing the electric toothbrush industry, her first report focuses on two companies, QuickBrush Company and SmileWhite Corporation, and concludes:

    QuickBrush is a more profitable company than SmileWhite, as indicated by the 40% sales growth and substantially higher margins it has produced over the last few years. Smile-White's sales and earnings are growing at a 10% rate and produce much lower margins. We

TABLE **13.17** QuickBrush Company financial statements: Yearly data ($000 except per share data)	Income Statement	December 1997	December 1998	December 1999
	Revenue	$3,480	$5,400	$7,760
	Cost of goods sold	2,700	4,270	6,050
	Selling, general, and admin. expense	500	690	1,000
	Depreciation and amortization	30	40	50
	Operating income (EBIT)	$250	$400	$660
	Interest expense	0	0	0
	Income before taxes	$250	$400	$660
	Income taxes	60	110	215
	Income after taxes	$190	$290	$445
	Diluted EPS	$0.60	$0.84	$1.18
	Average shares outstanding (000)	317	346	376

Financial Statistics	December 1997	December 1998	December 1999	3-Year Average
COGS as % of sales	77.59%	79.07%	77.96%	78.24%
General & admin. as % of sales	14.37	12.78	12.89	13.16
Operating margin (%)	7.18	7.41	8.51	
Pretax income/EBIT (%)	100.00	100.00	100.00	
Tax rate (%)	24.00	27.50	32.58	

Balance Sheet	December 1997	December 1998	December 1999
Cash and cash equivalents	$460	$50	$480
Accounts receivable	540	720	950
Inventories	300	430	590
Net property, plant, and equipment	760	1,830	3,450
Total assets	$2,060	$3,030	$5,470
Current liabilities	$860	$1,110	$1,750
Total liabilities	$860	$1,110	$1,750
Stockholders' equity	1,200	1,920	3,720
Total liabilities and equity	$2,060	$3,030	$5,470
Market price per share	$21.00	$30.00	$45.00
Book value per share	$3.79	$5.55	$9.89
Annual dividend per share	$0.00	$0.00	$0.00

do not think SmileWhite is capable of growing faster than its recent growth rate of 10% whereas QuickBrush can sustain a 30% long-term growth rate.

a. Criticize Ludlow's analysis and conclusion that QuickBrush is more profitable, as defined by return on equity (ROE), than SmileWhite and that it has a higher sustainable growth rate. Use only the information provided in Tables 13.17 and 13.18. Support your criticism by calculating and analyzing:
  • The five components that determine ROE.
  • The two ratios that determine sustainable growth: ROE and plowback.

TABLE **13.18** SmileWhite Corporation financial statements: Yearly data ($000 except per share data)	Income Statement	December 1997	December 1998	December 1999
	Revenue	$104,000	$110,400	$119,200
	Cost of goods sold	72,800	75,100	79,300
	Selling, general, and admin. expense	20,300	22,800	23,900
	Depreciation and amortization	4,200	5,600	8,300
	Operating income	$ 6,700	$ 6,900	$ 7,700
	Interest expense	600	350	350
	Income before taxes	$ 6,100	$ 6,550	$ 7,350
	Income taxes	2,100	2,200	2,500
	Income after taxes	$ 4,000	$ 4,350	$ 4,850
	Diluted EPS	$2.16	$2.35	$2.62
	Average shares outstanding (000)	1,850	1,850	1,850

Financial Statistics	December 1997	December 1998	December 1999	3-Year Average
COGS as % of sales	70.00%	68.00%	66.53%	68.10%
General & admin. as % of sales	19.52	20.64	20.05	20.08
Operating margin (%)	6.44	6.25	6.46	
Pretax income/EBIT (%)	91.04	94.93	95.45	
Tax rate (%)	34.43	33.59	34.01	

Balance Sheet	December 1997	December 1998	December 1999
Cash and cash equivalents	$ 7,900	$ 3,300	$ 1,700
Accounts receivable	7,500	8,000	9,000
Inventories	6,300	6,300	5,900
Net property, plant, and equipment	12,000	14,500	17,000
Total assets	$33,700	$32,100	$33,600
Current liabilities	$ 6,200	$ 7,800	$ 6,600
Long-term debt	9,000	4,300	4,300
Total liabilities	$15,200	$12,100	$10,900
Stockholders' equity	18,500	20,000	22,700
Total liabilities and equity	$33,700	$32,100	$33,600
Market price per share	$23.00	$26.00	$30.00
Book value per share	$10.00	$10.81	$12.27
Annual dividend per share	$1.42	$1.53	$1.72

b. Explain how QuickBrush has produced an average annual earnings per share (EPS) growth rate of 40% over the last two years with an ROE that has been declining. Use only the information provided in Table 13.17.

19. The DuPont formula defines the net return on shareholders' equity as a function of the following components:
   • Operating margin
   • Asset turnover
   • Interest burden

TABLE 13.19		1998	2002
Income statements and balance sheets	**Income statement data**		
	Revenues	$542	$979
	Operating income	38	76
	Depreciation and amortization	3	9
	Interest expense	3	0
	Pretax income	32	67
	Income taxes	13	37
	Net income after tax	$ 19	$ 30
	Balance sheet data		
	Fixed assets	$ 41	$ 70
	Total assets	245	291
	Working capital	123	157
	Total debt	16	0
	Total shareholders' equity	$159	$220

- Financial leverage
- Income tax rate

Using *only* the data in Table 13.19:

a. Calculate each of the five components listed above for 1998 and 2002, and calculate the return on equity (ROE) for 1998 and 2002, using all of the five components.

b. Briefly discuss the impact of the changes in asset turnover and financial leverage on the change in ROE from 1998 to 2002.

1. Use Market Insight (**www.mhhe.com/edumarketinsight**) to find the profit margin and asset turnover for firms in several industries. What seems to be the relationship between margin and turnover? Does this make sense to you?

2. Choose a few firms in similar lines of business, and compare their return on assets. Why does one firm do better or worse than others? Use the DuPont formula to guide your analysis. For example, compare debt ratios, asset turnover, and profit margins.

STANDARD
&POOR'S

SOLUTIONS TO

Concept CHECKS

1. A debt/equity ratio of 1 implies that Mordett will have $50 million of debt and $50 million of equity. Interest expense will be 0.09 × $50 million, or $4.5 million per year. Mordett's net profits and ROE over the business cycle will therefore be

		Nodett		Mordett	
Scenario	EBIT	Net Profits	ROE	Net Profits*	ROE†
Bad year	$5M	$3M	3%	$0.3M	0.6%
Normal year	10	6	6	3.3	6.6
Good year	15	9	9	6.3	12.6%

*Mordett's after-tax profits are given by: 0.6(EBIT − $4.5 million).

†Mordett's equity is only $50 million.

2. Ratio decomposition analysis for Mordett Corporation:

	ROE	(1) Net Profit Pretax Profit	(2) Pretax Profit EBIT	(3) EBIT Sales (ROS)	(4) Sales Assets (ATO)	(5) Assets Equity	(6) Compound Leverage Factor (2) × (5)
a. Bad year							
Nodett	0.030	0.6	1.000	0.0625	0.800	1.000	1.000
Somdett	0.018	0.6	0.360	0.0625	0.800	1.667	0.600
Mordett	0.006	0.6	0.100	0.0625	0.800	2.000	0.200
b. Normal year							
Nodett	0.060	0.6	1.000	0.100	1.000	1.000	1.000
Somdett	0.068	0.6	0.680	0.100	1.000	1.667	1.134
Mordett	0.066	0.6	0.550	0.100	1.000	2.000	1.100
c. Good year							
Nodett	0.090	0.6	1.000	0.125	1.200	1.000	1.000
Somdett	0.118	0.6	0.787	0.125	1.200	1.667	1.311
Mordett	0.126	0.6	0.700	0.125	1.200	2.000	1.400

3. GI's ROE in 2003 was 3.03%, computed as follows

$$\text{ROE} = \frac{\$5,285}{0.5(\$171,843 + \$177,128)} = 0.0303, \text{ or } 3.03\%$$

Its P/E ratio was $21/$5.285 = 4.0 and its P/B ratio was $21/$177 = .12. Its earnings yield was 25% compared with an industry average of 12.5%.

Note that in our calculations the earnings yield will not equal ROE/(P/B) because we have computed ROE with average shareholders' equity in the denominator and P/B with end-of-year shareholders' equity in the denominator.

4. IBX Ratio Analysis

Year	ROE	(1) Net Profit Pretax Profit	(2) Pretax Profit EBIT	(3) EBIT Sales (ROS)	(4) Sales Assets (ATO)	(5) Assets Equity	(6) Compound Leverage Factor (2) × (5)	(7) ROA (3) × (4)
2004	11.4%	0.616	0.796	7.75%	1.375	2.175	1.731	10.65%
2001	10.2	0.636	0.932	8.88	1.311	1.474	1.374	11.65

ROE went up despite a decline in operating margin and a decline in the tax burden ratio because of increased leverage and turnover. Note that ROA declined from 11.65% in 2001 to 10.65% in 2004.

5. LIFO accounting results in lower reported earnings than does FIFO. Fewer assets to depreciate result in lower reported earnings because there is less bias associated with the use of historic cost. More debt results in lower reported earnings because the inflation premium in the interest rate is treated as part of interest.

PART FIVE

DERIVATIVE MARKETS

Horror stories about large losses incurred by high-flying traders in derivatives markets such as those for futures and options periodically become a staple of the evening news. Indeed, there were some amazing losses to report in the last decade: several totaling hundreds of millions of dollars, and a few amounting to more than a billion dollars. In the wake of these debacles, some venerable institutions have gone under, notable among them, Barings Bank, which once helped the U.S. finance the Louisiana Purchase and the British Empire finance the Napoleonic Wars.

These stories, while important, fascinating, and even occasionally scandalous, often miss the point. Derivatives, when misused, can indeed provide a quick path to insolvency. Used properly, however, they are potent tools for risk management and control. In fact, you will discover in these chapters that one firm was sued for *failing* to use derivatives to hedge price risk. One headline in *The Wall Street Journal* on hedging applications using derivatives was entitled "Index Options Touted as Providing Peace of Mind." Hardly material for bankruptcy court or the *National Enquirer.*

Derivatives provide a means to control risk that is qualitatively different from the techniques traditionally considered in portfolio theory. In contrast to the mean-variance analysis we discussed in Parts Two and Three, derivatives allow investors to change the *shape* of the probability distribution of investment returns. An entirely new approach to risk management follows from this insight.

The following chapters will explore how derivatives can be used as parts of a well-designed portfolio strategy. We will examine some popular portfolio strategies utilizing these securities and take a look at how derivatives are valued.

14   Options Markets

15   Option Valuation

16   Futures Markets

McGraw-Hill / Irwin presents
Investments online

14

OPTIONS MARKETS

AFTER STUDYING THIS CHAPTER YOU SHOULD BE ABLE TO:

> Calculate the profit to various option positions as a function of ultimate security prices.

> Formulate option strategies to modify portfolio risk-return attributes.

> Identify embedded options in various securities and determine how option characteristics affect the prices of those securities.

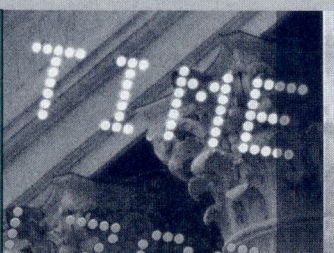

Derivative securities, or simply *derivatives*, play a large and increasingly important role in financial markets. These are securities whose prices are determined by, or "derive from," the prices of other securities. These assets also are called *contingent claims* because their payoffs are contingent on the prices of other securities.

Options and futures contracts are both derivative securities. We will see that their payoffs depend on the value of other securities. Swaps, which we discussed in Chapter 10, also are derivatives. Because the value of derivatives depends on the value of other securities, they can be powerful tools for both hedging and speculation. We will investigate these applications in the next three chapters, beginning in this chapter with options.

Trading of standardized options on a national exchange started in 1973 when the Chicago Board Options Exchange (CBOE) began listing call options. These contracts were almost immediately a great success, crowding out the previously existing over-the-counter trading in stock options.

Options contracts now are traded on several exchanges. They are written on common stock, stock indexes, foreign exchange, agricultural commodities, precious metals, and interest rate futures. In addition, the over-the-counter market also has enjoyed a tremendous resurgence in recent years as its trading in custom-tailored options has exploded. Popular and potent for modifying portfolio characteristics, options have become essential tools that every portfolio manager must understand.

This chapter is an introduction to options markets. It explains how puts and calls work and examines their investment characteristics. Popular option strategies are considered next. Finally, we will examine a range of securities with embedded options such as callable or convertible bonds.

14.1 THE OPTION CONTRACT

call option

The right to buy an asset at a specified exercise price on or before a specified expiration date.

A **call option** gives its holder the right to purchase an asset for a specified price, called the **exercise** or **strike price,** on or before some specified expiration date. For example, a July call option on Microsoft stock with exercise price $80 entitles its owner to purchase Microsoft stock for a price of $80 at any time up to and including the expiration date in July. The holder of the call is not required to exercise the option. The holder will choose to exercise only if the market value of the asset to be purchased exceeds the exercise price. When the market price does exceed the exercise price, the option holder may "call away" the asset for the exercise price. Otherwise, the option may be left unexercised. If it is not exercised before the expiration date of the contract, a call option simply expires and no longer has value. Therefore, if the stock price is greater than the exercise price on the expiration date, the value of the call option will equal the difference between the stock price and the exercise price; but if the stock price is less than the exercise price at expiration, the call will be worthless. The *net profit* on the call is the value of the option minus the price originally paid to purchase it.

exercise or strike price

Price set for calling (buying) an asset or putting (selling) an asset.

premium

Purchase price of an option.

The purchase price of the option is called the **premium.** It represents the compensation the purchaser of the call must pay for the ability to exercise the option if exercise becomes profitable. Sellers of call options, who are said to *write* calls, receive premium income now as payment against the possibility they will be required at some later date to deliver the asset in return for an exercise price lower than the market value of the asset. If the option is left to expire worthless because the market price of the asset remains below the exercise price, then the writer of the call clears a profit equal to the premium income derived from the sale of the option. But if the call is exercised, the profit to the option writer is the premium income derived when the option was initially sold *minus* the difference between the value of the stock that must be delivered and the exercise price that is paid for those shares. If that difference is larger than the initial premium, the writer will incur a loss.

14.1 EXAMPLE

Profit and Loss from a Call Option on Microsoft

To illustrate, consider an April 2002 maturity call option on a share of Microsoft stock with an exercise price of $70 per share selling on January 4, 2002, for $4.60. Exchange-traded options expire on the third Friday of the expiration month, which for this option is April 19. Until the expiration day, the purchaser of the calls is entitled to buy shares of Microsoft for $70. On January 4, Microsoft stock sells for $69.80, which is less than the exercise price. Because the stock price is currently less than $70 a share, it clearly would not make sense at the moment to exercise the option to buy at $70. Indeed, if Microsoft stock remains below $70 by the expiration date, the call will be left to expire worthless. If, on the other hand, Microsoft is selling above $70 at expiration, the call holder will find it optimal to exercise. For example, if Microsoft sells for $73 on April 19, the option will be exercised since it will give its holder the right to pay $70 for a stock worth $73. The value of the option on the expiration date will be

$$\text{Value at expiration} = \text{Stock price} - \text{Exercise price} = \$73 - \$70 = \$3$$

Despite the $3 payoff at maturity, the investor still realizes a loss of $1.60 on the investment in the call because the initial purchase price was $4.60:

$$\text{Profit} = \text{Final value} - \text{Original investment} = \$3 - \$4.60 = -\$1.60$$

Nevertheless, exercise of the call will be optimal at maturity if the stock price is above the exercise price because the exercise proceeds will offset at least part of the investment in the option. The investor in the call will clear a profit if Microsoft is selling above $74.60 at the maturity date. At that price, the proceeds from exercise will just cover the original cost of the call.

A **put option** gives its holder the right to *sell* an asset for a specified exercise or strike price on or before some expiration date. An April put on Microsoft with exercise price $70 entitles its owner to sell Microsoft stock to the put writer at a price of $70 at any time before expiration in April, even if the market price of Microsoft is less than $70. While profits on call options increase when the asset increases in value, profits on put options increase when the asset value falls. A put will be exercised only if the exercise price is greater than the price of the underlying asset, that is, only if its holder can deliver for the exercise price an asset with market value less than the exercise price. (One doesn't need to own the shares of Microsoft to exercise the Microsoft put option. Upon exercise, the investor's broker purchases the necessary shares of Microsoft at the market price and immediately delivers or "puts them" to an option writer for the exercise price. The owner of the put profits by the difference between the exercise price and market price.)

put option

The right to sell an asset at a specified exercise price on or before a specified expiration date.

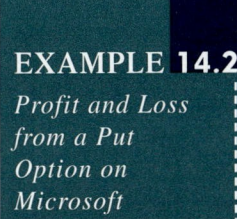

EXAMPLE 14.2

Profit and Loss from a Put Option on Microsoft

To illustrate, consider an April 2002 maturity put option on Microsoft with an exercise price of $70 selling on January 4, 2002, for $5.40. It entitles its owner to sell a share of Microsoft for $70 at any time until April 19. If the holder of the put option bought a share of Microsoft and immediately exercised the right to sell at $70, net proceeds would be $70 − $68.90 = $1.10. Obviously, an investor who pays $5.40 for the put has no intention of exercising it immediately. If, on the other hand, Microsoft is selling at $62 at expiration, the put will turn out to be a profitable investment. The value of the put on the expiration date would be

$$\text{Value at expiration} = \text{Exercise price} - \text{Stock price} = \$70 - \$62 = \$8$$

and profit would be $8.00 − $5.40 = $2.60. This is a holding-period return of $2.60/$5.40 = .481 or 48.1%—over only 105 days! Obviously, put option sellers (who are on the other side of the transaction) did not consider this outcome very likely.

An option is described as **in the money** when its exercise would produce a positive payoff for its holder. An option is **out of the money** when exercise would be unprofitable. Therefore, a call option is in the money when the exercise price is below the asset value. It is out of the money when the exercise price exceeds the asset value; no one would exercise the right to purchase for the exercise price an asset worth less than that price. Conversely, put options are in the money when the exercise price exceeds the asset's value, because delivery of the lower valued asset in exchange for the exercise price is profitable for the holder. Options are **at the money** when the exercise price and asset price are equal.

in the money

An option where exercise would be profitable.

out of the money

An option where exercise would not be profitable.

at the money

An option where the exercise price and asset price are equal.

Options Trading

Some options trade on over-the-counter (OTC) markets. The OTC market offers the advantage that the terms of the option contract—the exercise price, maturity date, and number of shares committed—can be tailored to the needs of the traders. The costs of establishing an OTC option contract, however, are relatively high. Today, most option trading occurs on organized exchanges.

Options contracts traded on exchanges are standardized by allowable maturity dates and exercise prices for each listed option. Each stock option contract provides for the right to buy or sell 100 shares of stock (except when stock splits occur after the contract is listed and the contract is adjusted for the terms of the split).

Standardization of the terms of listed option contracts means all market participants trade in a limited and uniform set of securities. This increases the depth of trading in any particular option, which lowers trading costs and results in a more competitive market. Exchanges, therefore, offer two important benefits: ease of trading, which flows from a central marketplace where buyers and sellers or their representatives congregate, and a liquid secondary market where buyers and sellers of options can transact quickly and cheaply.

FIGURE **14.1**

Listing of stock option
quotations

Source: From *The Wall Street
Journal*, February 7, 2002.
Reprinted by permission of
Dow Jones & Company, Inc.
via Copyright Clearance
Center, Inc. © 2002 Dow
Jones & Company, Inc. All
Rights Reserved Worldwide.

LISTED OPTIONS QUOTATIONS

OPTION/STRIKE		EXP.	-CALL- VOL.	LAST	-PUT- VOL.	LAST	OPTION/STRIKE		EXP.	-CALL- VOL.	LAST	-PUT- VOL.	LAST
MicronT	35	Jan	3279	2.25	1681	1.35	Peregrne	10	Jan	1597	0.50	169	1.05
Microsft	65	Jan	1452	4.50	3690	0.70	Pfizer	35	Mar	2	5.10	1985	0.70
68.90	65	Feb	497	5.60	10501	1.60	39.40	42.50	Mar	2579	0.70	...	...
68.90	65	Apr	51	7.70	10488	3.50	Pharmacia	40	Jan	2545	1.70	3	0.55
68.90	70	Jan	10783	1.35	6018	2.45	41.35	40	Feb	3250	2.70	83	1.35
68.90	70	Feb	2313	2.50	2499	3.60	41.35	45	Feb	2394	0.55	20	4.30
68.90	70	Apr	1408	4.60	2631	5.40	Ph Mor	45	Feb	15	2.20	1893	1
68.90	70	Jul	52	6.80	2502	7.20	ProcG	80	Apr	1586	3.30	1757	4.90
68.90	75	Jan	2882	0.30	620	6.30	Qualcom	50	Jan	1910	2.45	1030	1.95
68.90	75	Feb	2211	0.80	...	...	50.41	52.50	Jan	5739	1.20	555	3.30
MMM	105	Feb	...	...	4246	1.20	50.41	55	Jan	9436	0.55	1436	5.30
MSDiscov	50	Jan	109	10	1770	0.20	50.41	55	Feb	1820	1.95	61	6.40
59.64	60	Jan	3014	1.60	485	2.15	50.41	57.50	Jan	1703	0.25	33	7.10
Motorola	15	Jan	286	0.90	4058	0.35	QwestCom	15	Jan	4788	0.45	55	0.60

Figure 14.1 is a reproduction of listed stock option quotations from *The Wall Street Journal*. The highlighted options are for shares of Microsoft. The numbers in the column below the company name represent the last recorded price on the New York Stock Exchange for Microsoft stock, $68.90 per share.[1] The first column shows that options are traded on Microsoft at exercise prices of $65 through $75, in $5 increments. These values also are called the *strike prices*.

The exercise or strike prices bracket the stock price. While exercise prices generally are set at five-point intervals for stocks, larger intervals may be set for stocks selling above $100, and intervals of $2½ may be used for stocks selling below $30.[2] If the stock price moves outside the range of exercise prices of the existing set of options, new options with appropriate exercise prices may be offered. Therefore, at any time, both in-the-money and out-of-the-money options will be listed, as in the Microsoft example.

The next column in Figure 14.1 gives the maturity month of each contract, followed by two pairs of columns showing the number of contracts traded on that day and the closing price for the call and put, respectively.

When we compare the prices of call options with the same maturity date but different exercise prices in Figure 14.1, we see that the value of the call is lower when the exercise price is higher. This makes sense, for the right to purchase a share at a given exercise price is not as valuable when the purchase price is higher. Thus, the April maturity Microsoft call option with strike price $70 sells for $4.60, while the $65 exercise price April call sells for $7.70. Conversely, put options are worth *more* when the exercise price is higher: You would rather have the right to sell Microsoft shares for $70 than for $65, and this is reflected in the prices of the puts. The April maturity put option with strike price $70 sells for $5.40, while the $65 exercise price April put sells for only $3.50.

Throughout Figure 14.1, you will see that some options may go an entire day without trading. A lack of trading is denoted by three dots in the volume and price columns. Because trading is

---

[1]Occasionally, this price may not match the closing price listed for the stock on the stock market page. This is because some NYSE stocks also trade on the Pacific Stock Exchange, which closes after the NYSE, and the stock pages may reflect the more recent Pacific Exchange closing price. The options exchanges, however, close with the NYSE, so the closing NYSE stock price is appropriate for comparison with the closing option price.

[2]If a stock splits, the terms of the option—such as the exercise price—are adjusted to offset the impact of the split. Therefore, stock splits will also result in exercise prices that are not multiples of $5.

infrequent, it is not unusual to find option prices that appear out of line with other prices. You might see, for example, two calls with different exercise prices that seem to sell for the same price. This discrepancy arises because the last trades for these options may have occurred at different times during the day. At any moment, the call with the lower exercise price must be worth more, and the put less, than an otherwise-identical call or put with a higher exercise price.

Figure 14.1 illustrates that the maturities of most exchange-traded options tend to be fairly short, ranging up to only several months. For larger firms and several stock indexes, however, longer-term options are traded with maturities ranging up to three years. These options are called LEAPS (for Long-term Equity AnticiPation Securities).

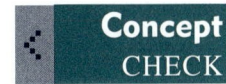

Concept
CHECK

1. *a.* **What will be the proceeds and net profits to an investor who purchases the April maturity Microsoft calls with exercise price $70 if the stock price at maturity is $60? What if the stock price at maturity is $80?**
   b. **Now answer part (*a*) for an investor who purchases an April maturity Microsoft put option with exercise price $70.**

American and European Options

An **American option** allows its holder to exercise the right to purchase (if a call) or sell (if a put) the underlying asset on *or before* the expiration date. **European options** allow for exercise of the option only on the expiration date. American options, because they allow more leeway than their European counterparts, generally will be more valuable. Most traded options in the U.S. are American-style. Foreign currency options and some stock index options are notable exceptions to this rule, however.

American option

Can be exercised on or before its expiration.

European option

Can be exercised only at expiration.

The Option Clearing Corporation

The Option Clearing Corporation (OCC), the clearinghouse for options trading, is jointly owned by the exchanges on which stock options are traded. The OCC places itself between options traders, becoming the effective buyer of the option from the writer and the effective writer of the option to the buyer. All individuals, therefore, deal only with the OCC, which effectively guarantees contract performance.

When an option holder exercises an option, the OCC arranges for a member firm with clients who have written that option to make good on the option obligation. The member firm selects from among its clients who have written that option to fulfill the contract. The selected client must deliver 100 shares of stock at a price equal to the exercise price for each call option contract written or must purchase 100 shares at the exercise price for each put option contract written.

Because the OCC guarantees contract performance, option writers are required to post margin to guarantee that they can fulfill their contract obligations. The margin required is determined in part by the amount by which the option is in the money, because that value is an indicator of the potential obligation of the option writer upon exercise of the option. When the required margin exceeds the posted margin, the writer will receive a margin call. The *holder* of the option need not post margin because the holder will exercise the option only if it is profitable to do so. After purchasing the option, no further money is at risk.

Margin requirements also depend on whether the underlying asset is held in portfolio. For example, a call option writer owning the stock against which the option is written can satisfy the margin requirement simply by allowing a broker to hold that stock in the brokerage account. The stock is then guaranteed to be available for delivery should the call option be exercised. If the underlying security is not owned, however, the margin requirement is determined by the value of the underlying security as well as by the amount by which the option is in or out of the money. Out-of-the-money options require less margin from the writer, for expected payouts are lower.

Other Listed Options

Options on assets other than stocks also are widely traded. These include options on market indexes and industry indexes, on foreign currency, and even on the futures prices of agricultural products, gold, silver, fixed-income securities, and stock indexes. We will discuss these in turn.

Index options   An index option is a call or put based on a stock market index such as the S&P 500 or the New York Stock Exchange index. Index options are traded on several broad-based indexes as well as on several industry-specific indexes. We discussed many of these indexes in Chapter 2.

The construction of the indexes can vary across contracts or exchanges. For example, the S&P 100 index is a value-weighted average of the 100 stocks in the Standard & Poor's 100 stock group. The weights are proportional to the market value of outstanding equity for each stock. The Dow Jones Industrial Average, by contrast, is a price-weighted average of 30 stocks.

Options contracts on many foreign stock indexes also trade. For example, options on the Nikkei Stock Index of Japanese stocks trade on the Chicago Mercantile Exchange and options on the Japan Index trade on the American Stock Exchange. Options on European indexes such as the Financial Times Share Exchange (FTSE 100) and the Eurotrak index also trade. The Chicago Board Options Exchange as well as the American exchange list options on industry indexes such as the high-tech, pharmaceutical, or banking industries.

In contrast to stock options, index options do not require that the call writer actually "deliver the index" upon exercise or that the put writer "purchase the index." Instead, a cash settlement procedure is used. The payoff that would accrue upon exercise of the option is calculated, and the option writer simply pays that amount to the option holder. The payoff is equal to the difference between the exercise price of the option and the value of the index. For example, if the S&P index is at 1,280 when a call option on the index with exercise price 1,270 is exercised, the holder of the call receives a cash payment equal to the difference, 1,280 − 1,270, times the contract multiplier of $100, or $1,000 per contract.

Figure 14.2 is a reproduction of listings for a few index options from *The Wall Street Journal.* The option listings are similar to those of stock options. However, instead of supplying separate columns for put and calls, the index options are all listed in one column, and the letters *p* or *c* are used to denote puts or calls. The index listings also report the "open interest" for each contract, which is the number of contracts currently outstanding. Options on the major indices, that is, the S&P 100 contract, often called the OEX after its ticker symbol, the S&P 500 index (the SPX), and the Dow Jones Industrials (the DJX) are by far the most actively traded contracts on the CBOE. Together, these contracts dominate CBOE volume.

Futures options   Futures options give their holders the right to buy or sell a specified futures contract, using as a futures price the exercise price of the option. Although the delivery process is slightly complicated, the terms of futures options contracts are designed in effect to allow the option to be written on the future price itself. The option holder receives upon exercise net proceeds equal to the difference between the current futures price on the specified asset and the exercise price of the option. Thus, if the futures price is, say, $37, and the call has an exercise price of $35, the holder who exercises the call option on the futures gets a payoff of $2.

INDEX OPTIONS TRADING

Monday, February 26, 2001

Volume, last, net change and open interest for all contracts. Volume figures are unofficial. Open interest reflects previous trading day. p-Put c-Call

CHICAGO

DJ INDUS AVG(DJX)

STRIKE	VOL.	LAST	NET CHG.	OPEN INT.
Mar 76 c	10	30^{10}	+ 1^{10}	10
Mar 88 p	350	0^{05}	− 0^{15}	2,207
Jun 90 p	1	1^{90}	+ 0^{70}	98
Mar 92 p	77	0^{10}	− 0^{20}	2,459
Apr 92 p	121	0^{40}	− 0^{20}	1,845
Mar 96 c	20	9^{90}	+ 0^{80}	91
Mar 96 p	105	0^{20}	− 0^{15}	11,296
Apr 96 p	34	1^{05}	+ 0^{15}	3,788
May 96 p	38	1^{85}	− 0^{10}	2,677
Jun 96 p	8	3^{30}	+ 0^{10}	678
Mar 98 p	145	0^{40}	− 0^{05}	1,529
Apr 112 p	50	6^{50}	+ 0^{50}	28
May 112 c	2	2^{65}	+ 0^{05}	1,566
Mar 116 c	40	0^{05}	...	5,939
Apr 116 c	10	0^{35}	− 0^{05}	2,283
Jun 116 c	5	1	− 1^{65}	387

Call Vol. 2,770   Open Int. 124,054
Put Vol. 9,764   Open Int. 189,107

DJ TRANP AVG(DTX)

STRIKE	VOL.	LAST	NET CHG.	OPEN INT.
Apr 310 c	15	4^{80}	...	...
Sep 360 p	3	59^{40}	− 5^{40}	...

Call Vol. 15   Open Int. 920
Put Vol. 3   Open Int. 98

DJ UTIL AVG(DUX)

STRIKE	VOL.	LAST	NET CHG.	OPEN INT.
Mar 380 p	1	4^{90}	− 2	1
Mar 390 p	1	9	+ 0^{88}	20

Call Vol. 0   Open Int. 45
Put Vol. 2   Open Int. 55

NASDAQ-MINI(MNX)

STRIKE	VOL.	LAST	NET CHG.	OPEN INT.
Apr 80 p	150	7^{70}	− 3^{30}	927
Mar 90 p	2,515	4^{20}	− 5^{70}	3,799
Apr 160 p	3	3^{80}	− 1^{20}	3,175

STRIKE	VOL.	LAST	NET CHG.	OPEN INT.
Mar 170 p	20	1^{50}	− 1^{50}	2,804
Mar 270 c	3,031	0^{40}	+ 0^{10}	10,122
May 300 c	200	1^{75}	...	

Call Vol. 33,843   Open Int. 235,268
Put Vol. 16,670   Open Int. 201,178

NASDAQ-100(NDX)

STRIKE	VOL.	LAST	NET CHG.	OPEN INT.
Mar 1400 p	9	2^{40}	− 0^{25}	297
Mar 1500 p	238	4^{80}	+ 0^{20}	272
Apr 1500 p	200	21	− 7	200
Mar 1600 p	39	8	− 11	368
Mar 1650 p	12	9	− 9	740
Mar 1700 p	7	12	− 16	1,123
Apr 1700 p	4	56	− 19	82
Mar 1750 p	7	20	− 23^{90}	729
Mar 1800 p	11	3^{30}	+ 27	20
Apr 3200 c	10	2^{45}	− 1^{55}	568
Jun 3300 c	1	13^{50}	+ 4	161
Apr 3400 c	280	1^{50}	− 3^{50}	1,622

Call Vol. 2,544   Open Int. 47,050
Put Vol. 1,772   Open Int. 39,457

RUSSELL 2000(RUT)

STRIKE	VOL.	LAST	NET CHG.	OPEN INT.
Mar 460 p	1	4^{80}	− 4^{30}	155
Mar 480 c	40	16^{70}	+ 2^{60}	821
Mar 490 c	10	10	+ 3^{80}	12
Apr 490 p	2	13^{10}	+ 3^{20}	18
Mar 500 c	133	7^{50}	+ 2^{40}	1,163
May 500 c	65	25^{40}	...	...
Jun 520 c	11	18^{90}	− 6^{70}	2
Mar 540 c	5	0^{90}	− 1^{60}	1,000

Call Vol. 264   Open Int. 5,721
Put Vol. 13   Open Int. 14,402

S & P 100(OEX)

STRIKE	VOL.	LAST	NET CHG.	OPEN INT.
Apr 540 c	38	2^{25}	...	
Mar 550 p	1,501	0^{60}	...	
Mar 560 c	829	0^{55}	− 1^{05}	6,362
Mar 560 p	685	3^{50}	− 2^{70}	1,173
May 560 p	1	7	− 1^{50}	91
Mar 570 p	401	0^{85}	...	2,647
Apr 570 p	21	4^{40}	...	10
Mar 580 p	364	1	− 2	5,962
Apr 580 p	217	5	− 5^{90}	732

STRIKE	VOL.	LAST	NET CHG.	OPEN INT.
May 580 p	3	9^{80}	− 0^{40}	114
Jun 580 p	18	10^{70}	− 4^{70}	86
Jun 1650 p	5	374^{10}	+ 87^{10}	2,629
Mar 1800 p	2	5^{25}	− 15	3,812
Jun 1800 p	1	5^{06}	+ 84	1,198
Mar 1995 p	80	7^{40}	− 15^{70}	11,012
Jun 1995 p	80	716^{50}	+ 54^{50}	193

Call Vol. 62,086   Open Int. 788,750
Put Vol. 25,533   Open Int. 777,239

AMERICAN

HONG KONG INDEX(HKO)

STRIKE	VOL.	LAST	NET CHG.	OPEN INT.
Mar 250 p	20	0^{75}	+ 0^{30}	110

Call Vol. 0   Open Int. 159
Put Vol. 20   Open Int. 162

INTERNET(IIX)

STRIKE	VOL.	LAST	NET CHG.	OPEN INT.
Mar 260 c	4	7	+ 1	10
Mar 260 p	4	27^{90}	− 4^{90}	10

Call Vol. 5   Open Int. 185
Put Vol. 4   Open Int. 469

JAPAN INDEX(JPN)

STRIKE	VOL.	LAST	NET CHG.	OPEN INT.
Mar 130 p	9	0^{65}	− 0^{30}	5
Jun 135 p	20	4^{60}	− ...	15
Mar 140 p	4	2^{45}	− 0^{65}	1,630
Jun 140 p	4	6^{30}	− 0^{60}	1,321

Call Vol. 0   Open Int. 5,226
Put Vol. 37   Open Int. 3,294

MAJOR MARKET(XMI)

STRIKE	VOL.	LAST	NET CHG.	OPEN INT.
Mar 970 p	1	3^{30}	+ 1^{90}	10
Mar 990 p	1	5^{70}	+ 1^{90}	5
Mar 1060 c	16	8^{50}	− 14^{50}	16
Mar 1080 p	6	39^{20}	− 10^{30}	1

Call Vol. 16   Open Int. 24,079
Put Vol. 8   Open Int. 24,161

MORGAN STANLEY(MOX)

STRIKE	VOL.	LAST	NET CHG.	OPEN INT.
Mar 30 p	16	4^{70}	− 2^{10}	1,791

Call Vol. 0   Open Int. 222
Put Vol. 16   Open Int. 1,889

FIGURE 14.2

Index options

Note: Prices are for February 26, 2001.

Source: *The Wall Street Journal*, February 27, 2001. Reprinted by permission of *The Wall Street Journal*, © 2001 Dow Jones & Company, Inc. All Rights Reserved Worldwide.

Foreign currency options   A currency option offers the right to buy or sell a quantity of foreign currency for a specified amount of domestic currency. Currency option contracts call for purchase or sale of the currency in exchange for a specified number of U.S. dollars. Contracts are quoted in cents or fractions of a cent per unit of foreign currency.

There is an important difference between currency options and currency *futures* options. The former provide payoffs that depend on the difference between the exercise price and the exchange rate at maturity. The latter are foreign exchange futures options that provide payoffs that depend on the difference between the exercise price and the exchange rate *futures price* at maturity. Because exchange rates and exchange rate futures prices generally are not equal, the options and futures-options contracts will have different values, even with identical expiration dates and exercise prices. Today, trading volume in currency futures options dominates by far trading in currency options.

Interest rate options   Options also are traded on Treasury notes and bonds, Treasury bills, certificates of deposit, GNMA pass-through certificates, and yields on Treasury securities of various maturities. Options on several interest rate futures also are traded. Among them are contracts on Treasury bond, Treasury note, municipal bond, LIBOR, Eurodollar, and British and euro-denominated interest rates.

14.2 VALUES OF OPTIONS AT EXPIRATION

Call Options

Recall that a call option gives the right to purchase a security at the exercise price. If you hold a call option on Microsoft stock with an exercise price of $60, and Microsoft is now selling at $70, you can exercise your option to purchase the stock at $60 and simultaneously sell the shares at the market price of $70, clearing $10 per share. Yet if the shares sell below $60, you can sit on the option and do nothing, realizing no further gain or loss. The value of the call option at expiration equals

$$\text{Payoff to call holder at expiration} = S_T - X \text{ if } S_T > X$$
$$0 \text{ if } S_T \leq X$$

where S_T is the value of the stock at the expiration date, and X is the exercise price. This formula emphasizes the option property because the payoff cannot be negative. That is, the option is exercised only if S_T exceeds X. If S_T is less than X, exercise does not occur, and the option expires with zero value. The loss to the option holder in this case equals the price originally paid. More generally, the *profit* to the option holder is the payoff to the option minus the original purchase price.

The value at expiration of the call on Microsoft with exercise price $60 is given by the following schedule.

Microsoft value	$50	$60	$70	$80	$90
Option value	0	0	10	20	30

For Microsoft prices at or below $60, the option expires worthless. Above $60, the option is worth the excess of Microsoft's price over $60. The option's value increases by one dollar for each dollar increase in the Microsoft stock price. This relationship can be depicted graphically, as in Figure 14.3.

The solid line in Figure 14.3 depicts the value of the call at expiration. The net *profit* to the holder of the call equals the gross payoff less the initial investment in the call. Suppose the call cost $14. Then the profit to the call holder would be as given in the dashed (bottom) line of Figure 14.3. At option expiration, the investor has suffered a loss of $14 if the stock price is less than or equal to $60.

Profits do not become positive unless the stock price at expiration exceeds $74. The break-even point is $74, because at that price the payoff to the call, $S_T - X = \$74 - \$60 = \$14$, equals the cost paid to acquire the call. Hence, the call holder shows a profit only if the stock price is higher.

Conversely, the writer of the call incurs losses if the stock price is high. In that scenario, the writer will receive a call and will be obligated to deliver a stock worth S_T for only X dollars.

$$\text{Payoff to call writer} = -(S_T - X) \text{ if } S_T > X$$
$$0 \text{ if } S_T \leq X$$

The call writer, who is exposed to losses if Microsoft increases in price, is willing to bear this risk in return for the option premium.

Figure 14.4 depicts the payoff and profit diagrams for the call writer. These are the mirror images of the corresponding diagrams for call holders. The break-even point for the option writer also is $74. The (negative) payoff at that point just offsets the premium originally received when the option was written.

Put Options

A put option conveys the right to sell an asset at the exercise price. In this case, the holder will not exercise the option unless the asset sells for *less* than the exercise price. For example, if Microsoft shares were to fall to $60, a put option with exercise price $70 could be exercised to give a $10 payoff to its holder. The holder would purchase a share of Microsoft for $60 and simultaneously deliver it to the put option writer for the exercise price of $70.

The value of a put option at expiration is

$$\text{Payoff to put holder} = 0 \qquad \text{if } S_T \geq X$$
$$X - S_T \text{ if } S_T < X$$

The solid line in Figure 14.5 illustrates the payoff at maturity to the holder of a put option on Microsoft stock with an exercise price of $60. If the stock price at option maturity is above

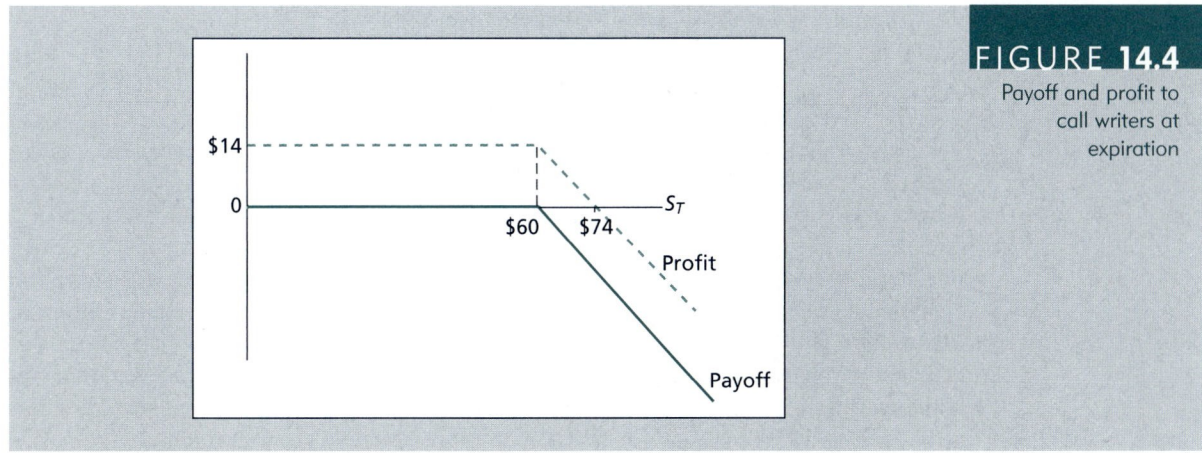

FIGURE 14.4

Payoff and profit to call writers at expiration

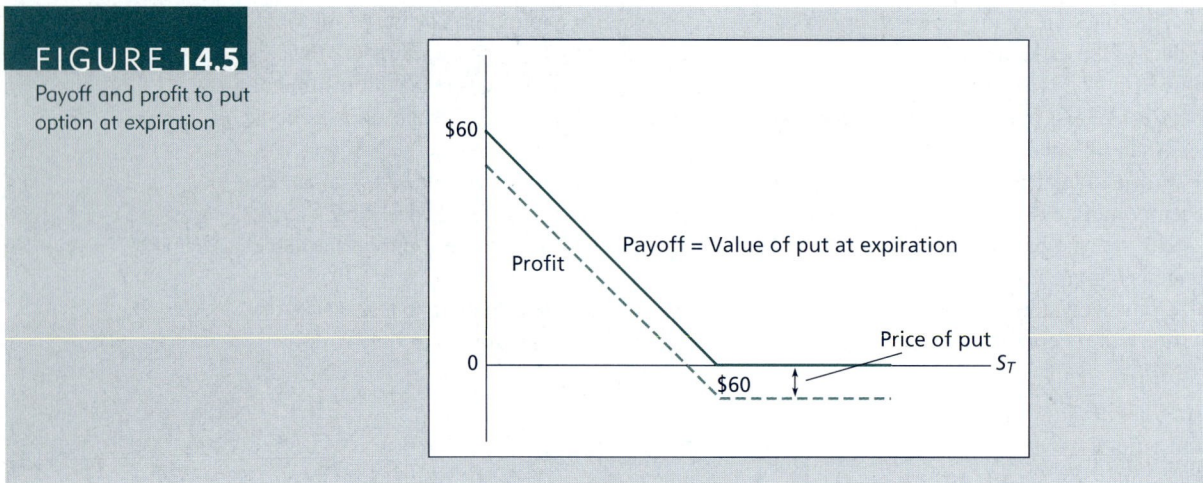

FIGURE **14.5**
Payoff and profit to put
option at expiration

$60, the put has no value, as the right to sell the shares at $60 would not be exercised. Below a price of $60, the put value at expiration increases by $1 for each dollar the stock price falls. The dashed line in Figure 14.5 is a graph of the put option owner's profit at expiration, net of the initial cost of the put.

Writing puts *naked* (i.e., writing a put without an offsetting short position in the stock for hedging purposes) exposes the writer to losses if the market falls. Writing naked out-of-the-money puts was once considered an attractive way to generate income, as it was believed that as long as the market did not fall sharply before the option expiration, the option premium could be collected without the put holder ever exercising the option against the writer. Because only sharp drops in the market could result in losses to the writer of the put, the strategy was not viewed as overly risky. However, the nearby box notes that in the wake of the market crash of October 1987, such put writers suffered huge losses. Participants now perceive much greater risk to this strategy.

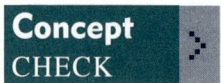

2. Consider these four option strategies: (*i*) buy a call; (*ii*) write a call; (*iii*) buy a put; (*iv*) write a put.
   a. For each strategy, plot both the payoff and profit diagrams as a function of the final stock price.
   b. Why might one characterize both buying calls and writing puts as "bullish" strategies? What is the difference between them?
   c. Why might one characterize both buying puts and writing calls as "bearish" strategies? What is the difference between them?

Options versus Stock Investments

Purchasing call options is a bullish strategy; that is, the calls provide profits when stock prices increase. Purchasing puts, in contrast, is a bearish strategy. Symmetrically, writing calls is bearish, while writing puts is bullish. Because option values depend on the price of the underlying stock, the purchase of options may be viewed as a substitute for direct purchase or sale of a stock. Why might an option strategy be preferable to direct stock transactions? We can begin to answer this question by comparing the values of option versus stock positions in Microsoft.

Suppose you believe Microsoft stock will increase in value from its current level, which we will round off to $70. You know your analysis could be incorrect, however, and that Microsoft

The Black Hole: Puts and the Market Crash

THEIR SALES OF "NAKED PUTS" QUICKLY COME TO GRIEF, DAMAGE SUITS ARE FILED

When Robert O'Connor got involved in stock-index options, he hoped his trading profits would help put his children through college. His broker, Mr. O'Connor explains, "said we would make about $1,000 a month, and if our losses got to $2,000 to $3,000, he would close out the account."

Instead, Mr. O'Connor, the 46-year-old owner of a small medical X-ray printing concern in Grand Rapids, Michigan, got caught in one of the worst investor blowouts in history. In a few minutes on October 19, he lost everything in his account plus an *additional* $91,000—a total loss of 175% of his original investment.

SCENE OF DISASTER

For Mr. O'Connor and hundreds of other investors, a little-known corner of the Chicago Board Options Exchange was the "black hole" of Black Monday's market crash. In a strategy marketed by brokers nationwide as a sure thing, these customers had sunk hundreds of millions of dollars into "naked puts"—unhedged, highly leveraged bets that the stock market was in no danger of plunging. Most of these naked puts seem to have been options on the Standard & Poor's 100 stock index, which are traded on the CBOE. When stocks crashed, many traders with unhedged positions got margin calls for several times their original investment.

THE 'PUT' STRATEGY

The losses were especially sharp in "naked, out-of-the-money puts." A seller of puts agrees to buy stock or stock-index contracts at a set price before the put expires. These contracts are usually sold "out of the money"—priced at a level below current market prices that makes it unprofitable to exercise the option so long as the market rises or stays flat. The seller pockets a small amount per contract.

But if the market plunges, as it did October 19, the option swings into the money. The seller, in effect, has to pay pre-plunge stock prices to make good on his contract—and he takes a big loss.

"You have to recognize that there is unlimited potential for disaster" in selling naked options, says Peter Thayer, executive vice president of Gateway Investment Advisors Inc., a Cincinnati-based investment firm that trades options to hedge its stock portfolios. Last September, Gateway bought out-of-the-money put options on the S&P 100 stock index on the CBOE at $2 to $3 a contract as "insurance" against a plunging market. By October 20, the day after the crash, the value of those contracts had soared to $130. Although Gateway profited handsomely, the parties on the other side of the trade were clobbered.

FIRM SUED

Brokers who were pushing naked options assumed that the stock market wouldn't plunge into uncharted territory. Frank VanderHoff, one of the two main brokers who put 50 to 70 H.B. Shaine clients into stock-index options, says he told clients that the strategy's risk was "moderate barring a nuclear attack or a crash like 1929." It wasn't speculative. The market could go up or down, but not *substantially* up or down. If the crash had only been as bad as '29, he adds, "we would have made it."

SOURCE: Abridged from *The Wall Street Journal*, December 2, 1987. Reprinted by permission of *The Wall Street Journal*, © 1987 Dow Jones & Company, Inc. All Rights Reserved Worldwide.

---

could fall in price. Suppose a six-month maturity call option with exercise price of $70 sells for $10, and the semiannual interest rate is 2%. Consider the following three strategies for investing a sum of $7,000. Remember that Microsoft does not pay any dividends.

Strategy *A:* Purchase 100 shares of Microsoft

Strategy *B:* Purchase 700 call options on Microsoft with exercise price $70. (This would require 7 contracts, each for 100 shares.)

Strategy *C:* Purchase 100 call options for $1,000. Invest the remaining $6,000 in six-month T-bills, to earn 2% interest.

Let us trace the possible values of these three portfolios when the options expire in six months as a function of Microsoft stock price at that time.

Portfolio	Microsoft Price					
	$65	**$70**	**$75**	**$80**	**$85**	**$90**
A: 100 shares stock	$6,500	$7,000	$7,500	$8,000	$ 8,500	$ 9,000
B: 700 call options	0	0	3,500	7,000	10,500	14,000
C: 100 calls plus						
$6,000 in T-bills	6,120	6,120	6,620	7,120	7,620	8,120

Portfolio *A* will be worth 100 times the share value of Microsoft. Portfolio *B* is worthless unless Microsoft sells for more than the exercise price of the call. Once that point is reached, the portfolio is worth 700 times the excess of the stock price over the exercise price. Finally, portfolio *C* is worth $6,120 from the investment in T-bills ($6,000 × 1.02 = $6,120) plus any profits from the 100 call options. Remember that each of these portfolios involves the same $7,000 initial investment. The rates of return on these three portfolios are as follows:

Portfolio	Microsoft Price					
	$65	**$70**	**$75**	**$80**	**$85**	**$90**
A: 100 shares stock	−7.1%	0.0%	7.1%	14.3%	21.4%	28.6%
B: 700 call options	−100.0	−100.0	−50.0	0.0	50.0	100.0
C: 100 calls plus						
$6,000 in T-bills	−12.6	−12.6	−5.4	1.7	8.9	16.0

These rates of return are graphed in Figure 14.6.

Comparing the returns of portfolios *B* and *C* to those of the simple investment in Microsoft stock represented by portfolio *A,* we see that options offer two interesting features. First, an option offers leverage. Compare the returns of portfolios *B* and *A*. When Microsoft stock fares poorly, ending anywhere below $70, the value of portfolio *B* falls precipitously to zero—a rate of return of negative 100%. Conversely, modest increases in the rate of return on the stock result in disproportionate increases in the option rate of return. For example, a 5.9% increase in the stock price from $85 to $90 would increase the rate of return on the call from 50% to

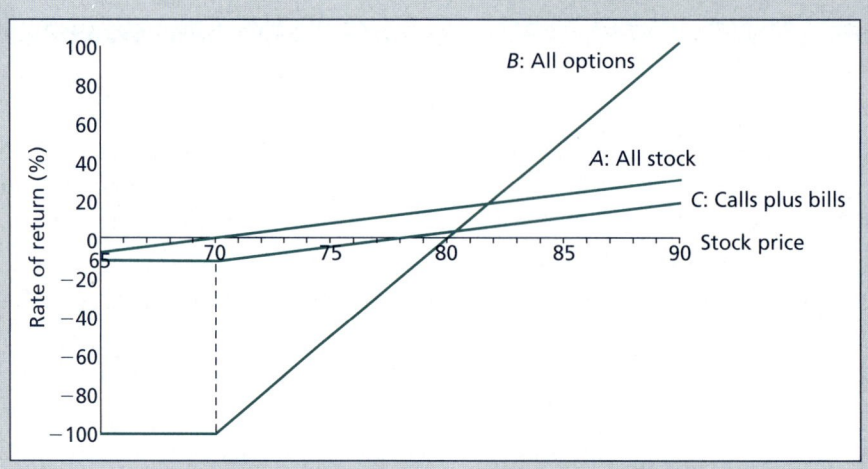

FIGURE 14.6

Rate of return to three strategies

EXCEL Applications

Options, Stock, and Lending

An Excel model based on the Microsoft example discussed in the text is shown below. The model allows you to use any variety of options, stock, and lending or borrowing with a set investment amount and demonstrates the investment flexibility of options.

You can learn more about this spreadsheet model by using the interactive version available on our website at www.mhhe.com/bkm.

	A	B	C	D	E	F	G	H	I	J	K
1	Chapter 14 Microsoft Example										
2	Comparison of Options, Equity and Combined Bills and Options										
3											
4	Basic Data for Spreadsheet										
5	Current Stock Price	$70									
6	Options Price	$10									
7	Exercise Price	$70						Ending Stock Price			
8	T-Bill Rate Annual	2%									
9	Ending Stock Price	$80									
10	Ending Value Per Option	$10		Option		65	70	75	80	85	90
11	Investment Amount	$7,000		Total Ending Value	$7,000	0	0	3500	7000	10500	14000
12											
13	Options Only Strategy										
14	Options Purchased	700									
15	Ending Value per Option	$10		Stock		65	70	75	80	85	90
16	Total Ending Value	$7,000		Total Ending Value	$8,000	6500	7000	7500	8000	8500	9000
17	Total Profit	$0									
18	Return on Investment	0.00%									
19											
20	Stock Only Strategy			Bills & Option		65	70	75	80	85	90
21	Shares Purchased	100		Total Ending Value	$7,120	6120	6120	6620	7120	7620	8120
22	Total Ending Value	$8,000									
23	Total Profit	$1,000									
24	Return on Investment	14.29%									
25				Addit. Combinations		65	70	75	80	85	90
26	Bills and Options Strategy			Total Ending Value	$7,424	3,824	4,024	5,724	7,424	9,124	10,824
27	Number of Options Purchased	100									
28	Investment in Options	$1,000									
29	Investment in Bills	$6,000									
30	Ending Value of the Options	$1,000		Option		65	70	75	80	85	90
31	Ending Value on the Bills	$6,120		Return	0.00%	-100.00%	-100.00%	-50.00%	0.00%	50.00%	100.00%
32	Total Ending Value	$7,120									
33	Total Profit	$120									
34	Return on Investment	1.71%									
35				Stock		65	70	75	80	85	90
36	Additional Combinations:			Return	14.29%	-7.14%	0.00%	7.14%	14.29%	21.43%	28.57%
37	Bills, Options and Stock										
38	Total Investment Amount	$7,000									
39	Options Purchased	300									
40	Options Investment	$3,000		Bill & Option		65	70	75	80	85	90
41	Stock Purchased	40		Return	1.71%	-12.57%	-12.57%	-5.43%	1.71%	8.86%	16.00%
42	Stock Investment	$2,800									
43	Bill Investment	$1,200									
44	Ending Value of the Options	$3,000									
45	Ending Value of the Stock	$3,200		Addit. Combinations		65	70	75	80	85	90
46	Ending Value of the Bills	1224		Return	6.06%	-45.37%	-42.51%	-18.23%	6.06%	30.34%	54.63%
47	Total Ending Value	$7,424									
48	Total Profit	$424									
49	Return on Investment	6.06%									
50											
51	Average Returns for Sample Returns										
52	Options	-16.67%									
53	Stock	10.71%									
54	Bill & Options	-0.67%									
55	Additional Combinations	-2.51%									
56											
57	St. Deviation for Sample Returns										
58	Options	81.65%									
59	Stock	13.36%									
60	Bill & Options	11.66%									
61	Additional Combinations	40.25%									

100%. In this sense, calls are a levered investment on the stock. Their values respond more than proportionately to changes in the stock value.

Figure 14.6 vividly illustrates this point. For stock prices above $70, the slope of the all-option portfolio is far steeper than that of the all-stock portfolio, reflecting its greater proportional sensitivity to the value of the underlying security. The leverage factor is the reason that investors (illegally) exploiting inside information commonly choose options as their investment vehicle.

The potential insurance value of options is the second interesting feature, as portfolio *C* shows. The T-bill plus option portfolio cannot be worth less than $6,120 after six months, as the option can always be left to expire worthless. The worst possible rate of return on portfolio *C* is −12.6%, compared to a (theoretically) worst possible rate of return of Microsoft stock of −100% if the company were to go bankrupt. Of course, this insurance comes at a price:

When Microsoft does well, portfolio C does not perform as well as portfolio A, the all-stock portfolio. For stock prices above $70, portfolio C underperforms portfolio A by about 12.6 percentage points.

This simple example makes an important point. While options can be used by speculators as effectively leveraged stock positions, as in portfolio B, they also can be used by investors who desire to tailor their risk exposures in creative ways, as in portfolio C. For example, the call plus T-bills strategy of portfolio C provides a rate of return profile quite unlike that of the stock alone. The absolute limitation on downside risk is a novel and attractive feature of this strategy. In the next section we will discuss several option strategies that provide other novel risk profiles that might be attractive to hedgers and other investors.

Option Strategies

An unlimited variety of payoff patterns can be achieved by combining puts and calls with various exercise prices. Below we explain the motivation and structure of some of the more popular ones.

Protective put   Imagine you would like to invest in a stock, but you are unwilling to bear potential losses beyond some given level. Investing in the stock alone seems risky to you because in principle you could lose all the money you invest. You might consider instead investing in stock and purchasing a put option on the stock.

Table 14.1 shows the total value of your portfolio at option expiration. Whatever happens to the stock price, you are guaranteed a payoff equal to the put option's exercise price because the put gives you the right to sell the share for the exercise price even if the stock price is below that value.

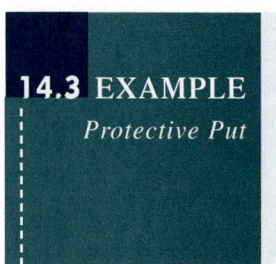

14.3 EXAMPLE

Protective Put

Suppose the strike price is $X = \$55$ and the stock is selling for $52 at option expiration. Then the value of your total portfolio is $55: The stock is worth $52 and the value of the expiring put option is

$$X - S_T = \$55 - \$52 = \$3$$

Another way to look at it is that you are holding the stock and a put contract giving you the right to sell the stock for $55. If $S < \$55$, you can still sell the stock for $55 by exercising the put. On the other hand, if the stock price is above $55, say $59, then the right to sell a share at $55 is worthless. You allow the put to expire unexercised, ending up with a share of stock worth $S_T = \$59$.

protective put

An asset combined with a put option that guarantees minimum proceeds equal to the put's exercise price.

Figure 14.7 illustrates the payoff and profit to this **protective put** strategy. The solid line in Figure 14.7C is the total payoff. The dashed line is displaced downward by the cost of establishing the position, $S_0 + P$. Notice that potential losses are limited.

It is instructive to compare the profit on the protective put strategy with that of the stock investment. For simplicity, consider an at-the-money protective put, so that $X = S_0$. Figure 14.8 compares the profits for the two strategies. The profit on the stock is zero if the stock price remains unchanged, and $S_T = S_0$. It rises or falls by $1 for every dollar swing in the ultimate stock price. The profit on the protective put is negative and equal to the cost of the put if S_T is below S_0. The profit on the protective put increases one for one with increases in the stock price once the stock price exceeds X.

TABLE **14.1**		$S_T \leq X$	$S_T > X$
Payoff to protective put strategy	Stock	S_T	S_T
	Put	$X - S_T$	0
	Total	X	S_T

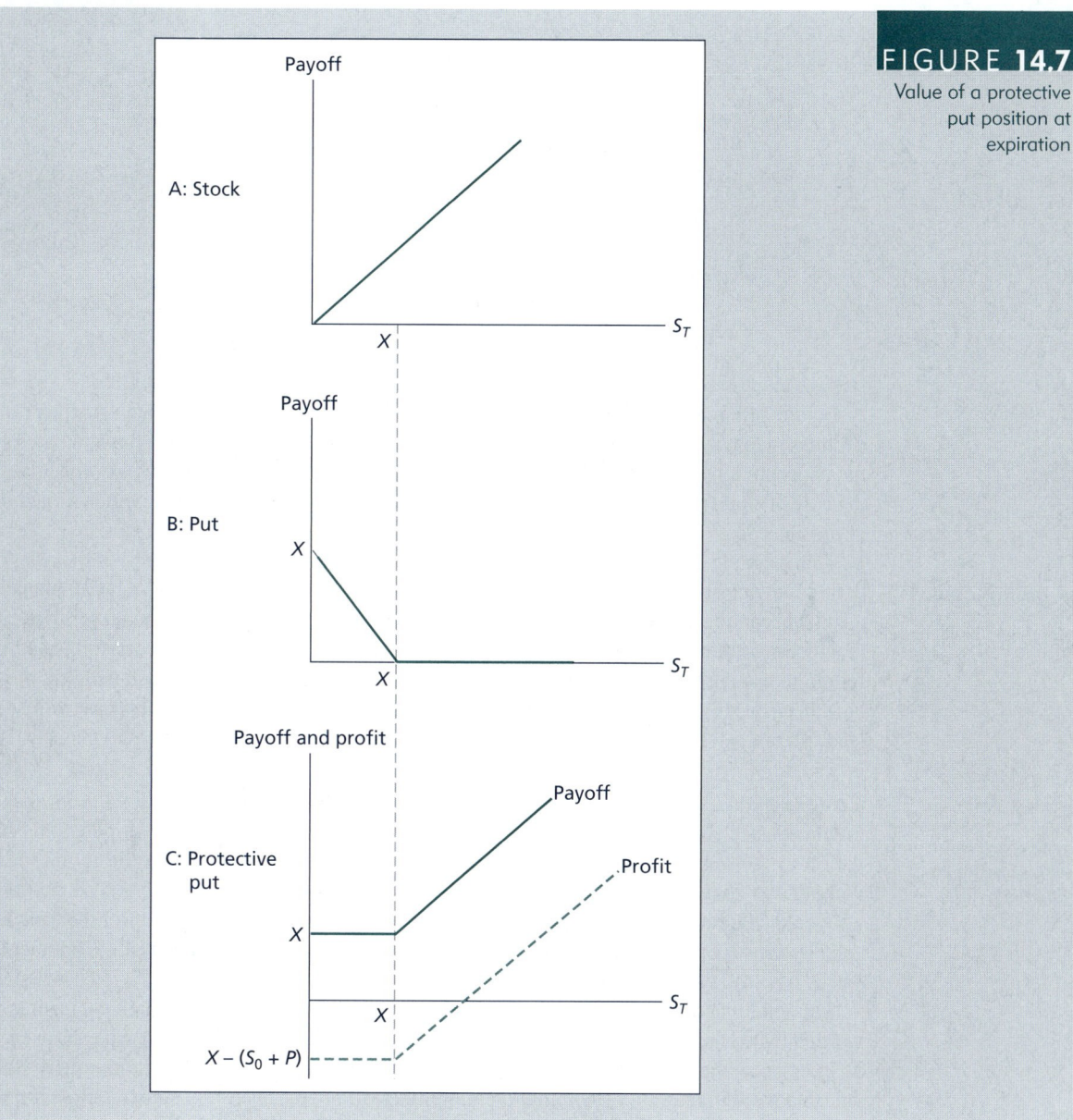

FIGURE **14.7**
Value of a protective put position at expiration

FIGURE 14.8
Protective put versus
stock investment

Figure 14.8 makes it clear that the protective put offers some insurance against stock price declines in that it limits losses. As we shall see in the next chapter, protective put strategies are the conceptual basis for the portfolio insurance industry. The cost of the protection is that, in the case of stock price increases, your profit is reduced by the cost of the put, which turned out to be unneeded.

This example also shows that despite the common perception that "derivatives mean risk," derivative securities can be used effectively for **risk management.** In fact, such risk management is becoming accepted as part of the fiduciary responsibility of financial managers. Indeed, in a recent court case, *Brane* v. *Roth,* a company's board of directors was successfully sued for failing to use derivatives to hedge the price risk of grain held in storage. Such hedging might have been accomplished using protective puts. Some observers believe that this case will soon lead to a broad legal obligation for firms to use derivatives and other techniques to manage risk.

risk management

Strategies to limit the
risk of a portfolio.

covered call

Writing a call on an
asset together with
buying the asset.

Covered calls   A **covered call** position is the purchase of a share of stock with the simultaneous sale of a call on that stock. The position is "covered" because the potential obligation to deliver the stock is covered by the stock held in the portfolio. Writing an option without an offsetting stock position is called by contrast *naked option writing.* The payoff to a covered call, presented in Table 14.2, equals the stock value minus the payoff of the call. The call payoff is subtracted because the covered call position involves issuing a call to another investor who can choose to exercise it to profit at your expense.

The solid line in Figure 14.9C illustrates the payoff pattern. You see that the total position is worth S_T when the stock price at time T is below X and rises to a maximum of X when S_T exceeds X. In essence, the sale of the call option means the call writer has sold the claim to any stock value above X in return for the initial premium (the call price). Therefore, at expiration, the position is worth at most X. The dashed line of Figure 14.9C is the net profit to the covered call.

Writing covered call options has been a popular investment strategy among institutional investors. Consider the managers of a fund invested largely in stocks. They might find it appealing to write calls on some or all of the stock in order to boost income by the premiums collected. Although they thereby forfeit potential capital gains should the stock price rise

TABLE **14.2**		$S_T \leq X$	$S_T > X$
Payoff to a covered call	Payoff of stock	S_T	S_T
	$-$Payoff of call	-0	$-(S_T - X)$
	Total	S_T	X

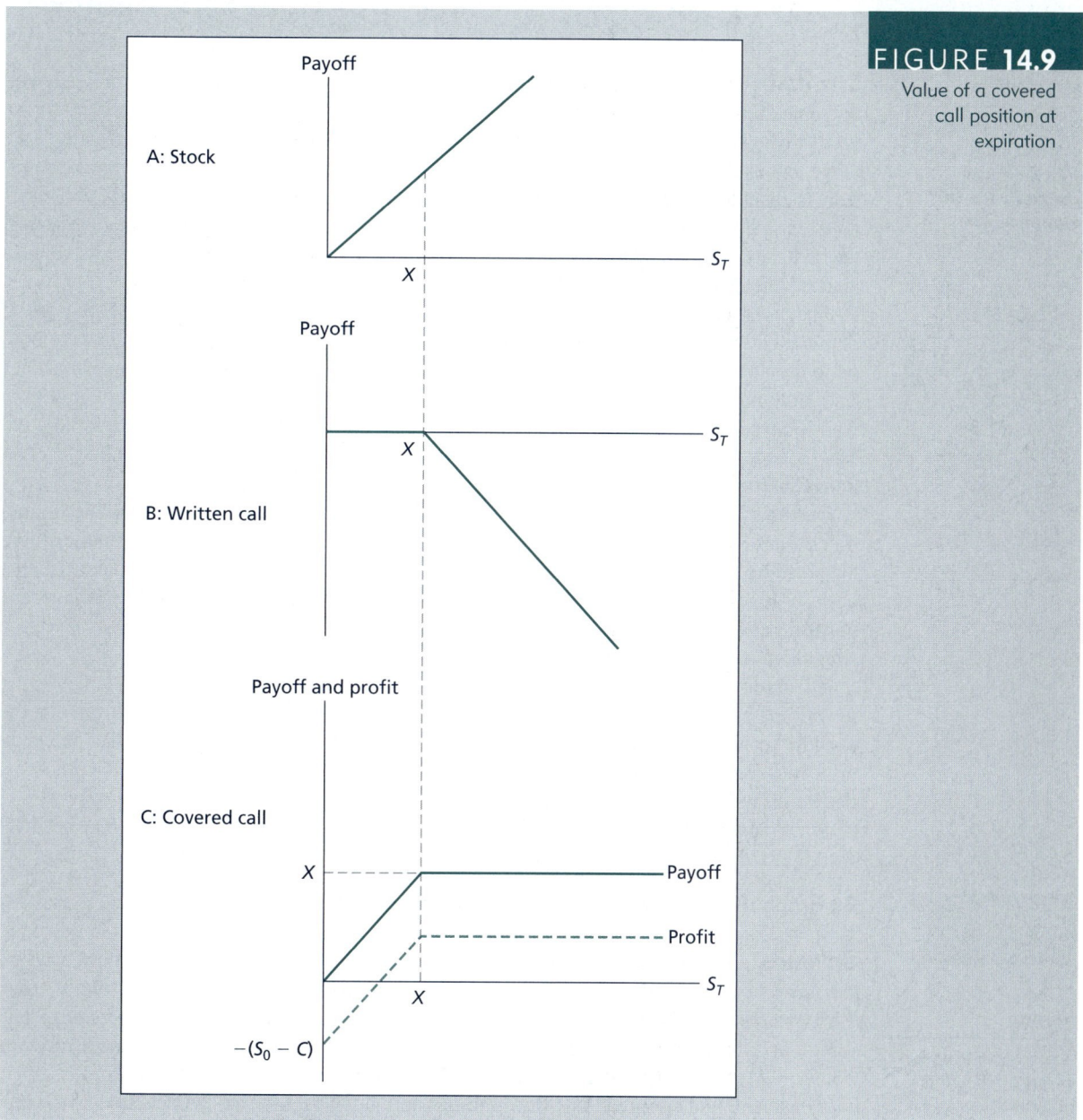

FIGURE 14.9

Value of a covered call position at expiration

above the exercise price, if they view X as the price at which they plan to sell the stock anyway, then the call may be viewed as enforcing a kind of "sell discipline." The written call guarantees the stock sale will occur as planned.

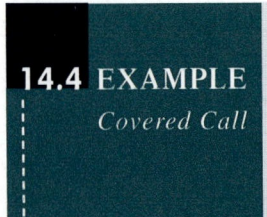

14.4 EXAMPLE

Covered Call

Assume a pension fund holds 1,000 shares of GXX stock, with a current price of $130 per share. Suppose management intends to sell all 1,000 shares if the share price hits $140, and a call expiring in 90 days with an exercise price of $140 currently sells for $5. By writing 10 GXX call contracts (100 shares each) the fund can pick up $5,000 in extra income. The fund would lose its share of profits from any movement of GXX stock above $140 per share, but given that it would have sold its shares at $140, it would not have realized those profits anyway.

straddle

A combination of a call and a put, each with the same exercise price and expiration date.

Straddle   A long **straddle** is established by buying both a call and a put on a stock, each with the same exercise price, X, and the same expiration date, T. Straddles are useful strategies for investors who believe a stock will move a lot in price but are uncertain about the direction of the move. For example, suppose you believe an important court case that will make or break a company is about to be settled, and the market is not yet aware of the situation. The stock will either double in value if the case is settled favorably or will drop by half if the settlement goes against the company. The straddle position will do well regardless of the outcome because its value is highest when the stock price makes extreme upward or downward moves from X.

The worst-case scenario for a straddle is no movement in the stock price. If S_T equals X, both the call and the put expire worthless, and the investor's outlay for the purchase of both options is lost. Straddle positions basically are bets on volatility. An investor who establishes a straddle must view the stock as more volatile than the market does. Conversely, investors who *write* straddles—selling both a call and a put—must believe the market is less volatile. They accept the option premiums now, hoping the stock price will not change much before option expiration.

The payoff to a straddle is presented in Table 14.3. The solid line of Figure 14.10C illustrates this payoff. Notice the portfolio payoff is always positive, except at the one point where the portfolio has zero value, $S_T = X$. You might wonder why all investors don't pursue such a no-lose strategy. The straddle requires that both the put and call be purchased. The value of the portfolio at expiration, while never negative, still must exceed the initial cash outlay for a straddle investor to clear a profit.

The dashed line of Figure 14.10C is the profit to the straddle. The profit line lies below the payoff line by the cost of purchasing the straddle, $P + C$. It is clear from the diagram that the straddle position generates a loss unless the stock price deviates substantially from X. The stock price must depart from X by the total amount expended to purchase the call *and* the put in order for the purchaser of the straddle to clear a profit.

Strips and *straps* are variations of straddles. A strip is two puts and one call on a security with the same exercise price and maturity date. A strap is two calls and one put.

Concept
CHECK

3. Graph the profit and payoff diagrams for strips and straps.

spread

A combination of two or more call options or put options on the same asset with differing exercise prices or times to expiration.

Spreads   A **spread** is a combination of two or more call options (or two or more puts) on the same stock with differing exercise prices or times to maturity. Some options are bought, while others are sold, or written. A *vertical* or *money spread* involves the purchase of one option and the simultaneous sale of another with a different exercise price. A *horizontal* or *time spread* refers to the sale and purchase of options with differing expiration dates.

Consider a money spread in which one call option is bought at an exercise price X_1, while another call with identical expiration date, but higher exercise price, X_2, is written. The payoff to this position will be the difference in the value of the call held and the value of the call written, as in Table 14.4.

There are now three instead of two outcomes to distinguish: the lowest-price region, where S_T is below both exercise prices; a middle region, where S_T is between the two exercise prices;

TABLE **14.3**		$S_T < X$	$S_T \geq X$
Payoff to a straddle	Payoff of call	0	$S_T - X$
	+Payoff of put	$+(X - S_T)$	$+0$
	Total	$X - S_T$	$S_T - X$

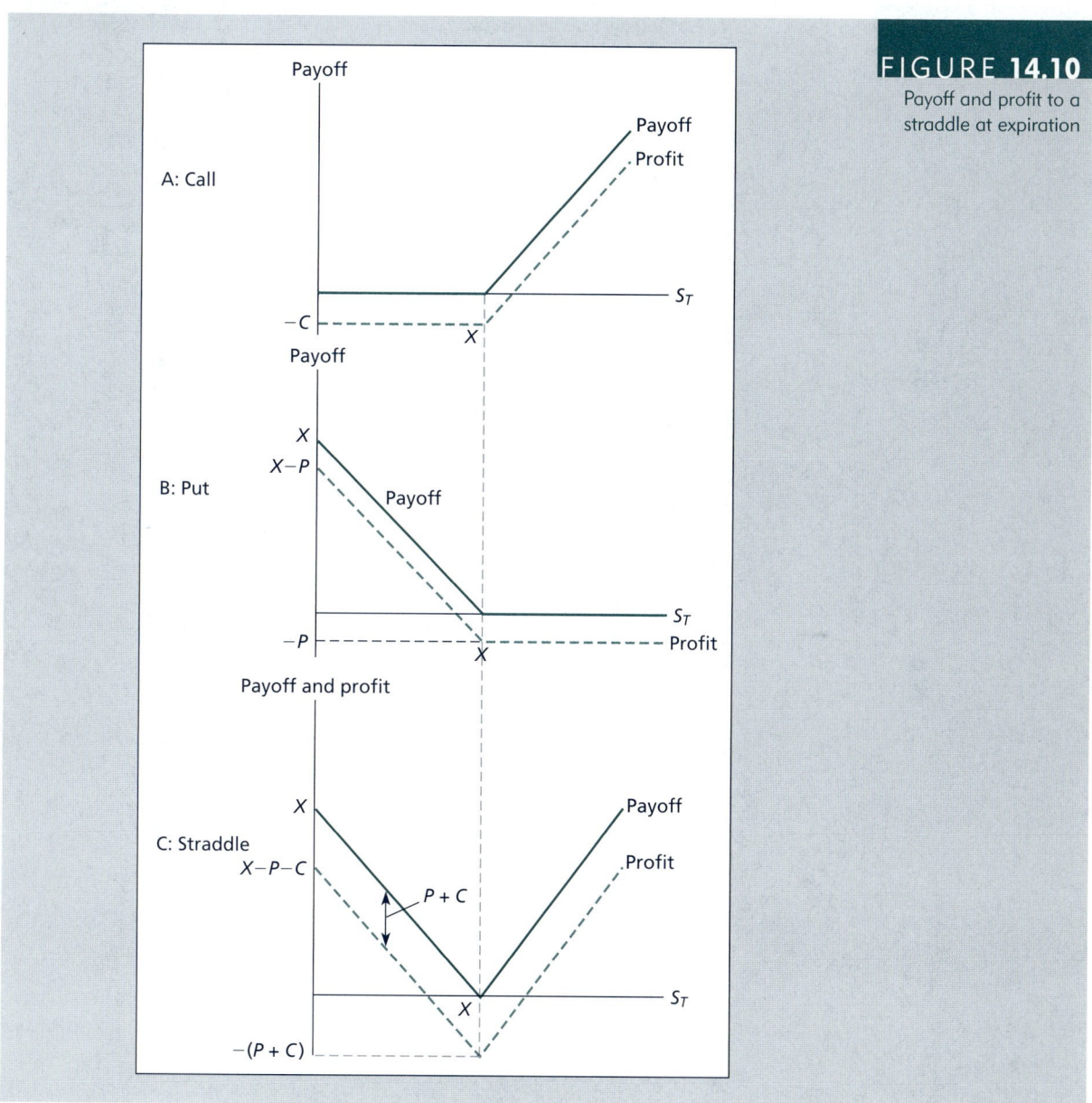

FIGURE **14.10**
Payoff and profit to a
straddle at expiration

and a high-price region, where S_T exceeds both exercise prices. Figure 14.11 illustrates the
payoff and profit to this strategy, which is called a *bullish spread* because the payoff either increases or is unaffected by stock price increases. Holders of bullish spreads benefit from stock
price increases.

TABLE **14.4**		$S_T \leq X_1$	$X_1 < S_T \leq X_2$	$S_T > X_2$
Payoff to a bullish spread	Payoff of first call, exercise price = X_1	0	$S_T - X_1$	$S_T - X_1$
	$-$Payoff of second call, exercise price = X_2	-0	-0	$-(S_T - X_2)$
	Total	0	$S_T - X_1$	$X_2 - X_1$

FIGURE **14.11**

Value of a bullish spread position at expiration

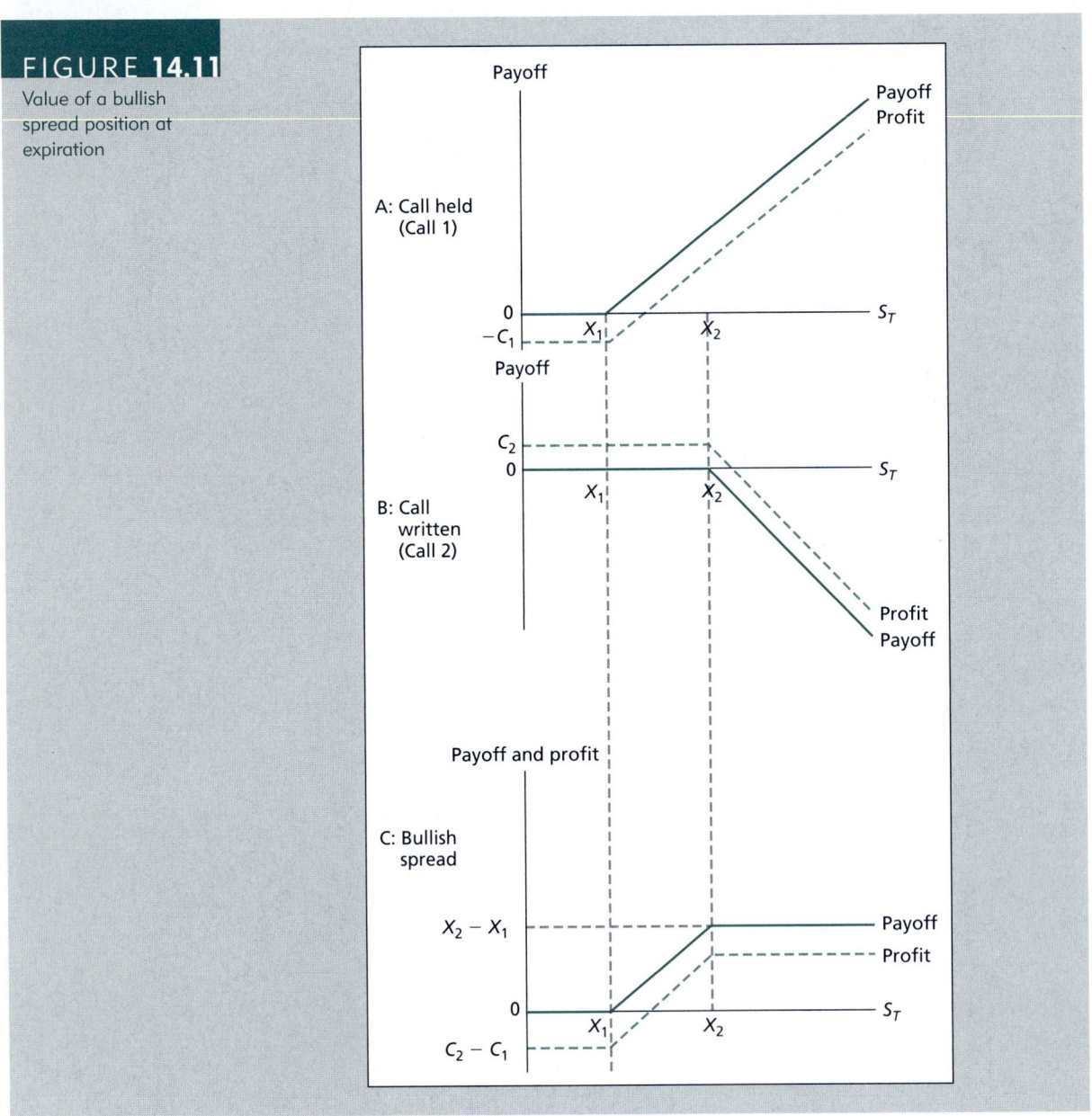

One motivation for a bullish spread might be that the investor thinks one option is over-priced relative to another. For example, an investor who believes an $X = \$50$ call is cheap compared to an $X = \$55$ call might establish the spread, even without a strong desire to take a bullish position in the stock.

Straddles and Spreads

Using spreadsheets to analyze combinations of options is very helpful. Once the basic models are built, it is easy to extend the analysis to different bundles of options. The Excel model "Spreads and Straddles" shown below can be used to evaluate the profitability of different strategies.

You can learn more about this spreadsheet model by using the interactive version available on our website at www.mhhe.com/bkm.

Spreads and Straddles

Stock Prices

Beginning Market Price	116.5
Ending Market Price	130

Buying Options:

Call Options Strike	Price	Payoff	Profit	Return %
110	22.80	20.00	-2.80	-12.28%
120	16.80	10.00	-6.80	-40.48%
130	13.60	0.00	-13.60	-100.00%
140	10.30	0.00	-10.30	-100.00%

Put Options Strike	Price	Payoff	Profit	Return %
110	12.60	0.00	-12.60	-100.00%
120	17.20	0.00	-17.20	-100.00%
130	23.60	0.00	-23.60	-100.00%
140	30.50	10.00	-20.50	-67.21%

Straddle	Price	Payoff	Profit	Return %
110	35.40	20.00	-15.40	-43.50%
120	34.00	10.00	-24.00	-70.59%
130	37.20	0.00	-37.20	-100.00%
140	40.80	10.00	-30.80	-75.49%

Selling Options:

Call Options Strike	Price	Payoff	Profit	Return %
110	22.80	-20	2.80	12.28%
120	16.80	-10	6.80	40.48%
130	13.60	0	13.60	100.00%
140	10.30	0	10.30	100.00%

Put Options Strike	Price	Payoff	Profit	Return %
110	12.60	0	12.60	100.00%
120	17.20	0	17.20	100.00%
130	23.60	0	23.60	100.00%
140	30.50	10	40.50	132.79%

Money Spread	Price	Payoff	Profit
Bullish Spread			
Purchase 110 Call	22.80	20.00	-2.80
Sell 140 Call	10.30	0	10.30
Combined Profit		20.00	7.50

X 110 Straddle

Ending Stock Price	Profit
Stock Price	-15.40
50	24.60
60	14.60
70	4.60
80	-5.40
90	-15.40
100	-25.40
110	-35.40
120	-25.40
130	-15.40
140	-5.40
150	4.60
160	14.60
170	24.60
180	34.60
190	44.60
200	54.60
210	64.60

X 120 Straddle

Ending Stock Price	Profit
Stock Price	-24.00
50	36.00
60	26.00
70	16.00
80	6.00
90	-4.00
100	-14.00
110	-24.00
120	-34.00
130	-24.00
140	-14.00
150	-4.00
160	6.00
170	16.00
180	26.00
190	36.00
200	46.00
210	56.00

Bullish Spread

Ending Stock Price	Spread
Stock Price	7.50
50	-12.5
60	-12.5
70	-12.5
80	-12.5
90	-12.5
100	-12.5
110	-12.5
120	-2.5
130	7.5
140	17.5
150	17.5
160	17.5
170	17.5
180	17.5
190	17.5
200	17.5
210	17.5

Collars

A **collar** is an options strategy that brackets the value of a portfolio between two bounds. Suppose that an investor currently is holding a large position in Microsoft, which is currently selling at $70 per share. A lower bound of $60 can be placed on the value of the portfolio by buying a protective put with exercise price $60. This protection, however, requires that the investor pay the put premium. To raise the money to pay for the put, the investor might write a call option, say with exercise price $80. The call might sell for roughly the same price as the put, meaning that the net outlay for the two options positions is approximately zero. Writing the call limits the portfolio's upside potential. Even if the stock price moves above $80, the investor will do no better than $80, because at a higher price the stock will be called away. Thus

> **collar**
>
> **An options strategy that brackets the value of a portfolio between two bounds.**

the investor obtains the downside protection represented by the exercise price of the put by selling her claim to any upside potential beyond the exercise price of the call.

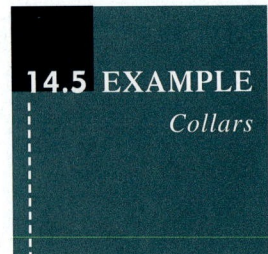

14.5 EXAMPLE
Collars

A collar would be appropriate for an investor who has a target wealth goal in mind but is unwilling to risk losses beyond a certain level. Suppose you are contemplating buying a house for $160,000, for example. You might set this figure as your goal. Your current wealth may be $140,000, and you are unwilling to risk losing more than $20,000. A collar established by (1) purchasing 2,000 shares of stock currently selling at $70 per share, (2) purchasing 2,000 put options (20 option contracts) with exercise price $60, and (3) writing 2,000 calls with exercise price $80 would give you a good chance to realize the $20,000 capital gain without risking a loss of more than $20,000.

The nearby box describes a newly designed bond with returns linked to the performance of Internet stocks. It should be clear from the description of the so-called "equity linked note" that the security is in fact a collar on an Internet stock index. Indeed, in the last paragraph of the article, one observer notes that the security would appeal only to retail investors since larger institutional investors can already engineer the bond for themselves using calls and puts.

Concept CHECK ➤

4. Graph the payoff diagram for the collar described in Example 14.5.

14.3 OPTIONLIKE SECURITIES

Suppose you never intend to trade an option directly. Why do you need to appreciate the properties of options in formulating an investment plan? Many financial instruments and agreements have features that convey implicit or explicit options to one or more parties. If you are to value and use these securities correctly, you must understand these embedded option attributes.

Callable Bonds

You know from Chapter 9 that many corporate bonds are issued with call provisions entitling the issuer to buy bonds back from bondholders at some time in the future at a specified call price. A call provision conveys a call option to the issuer, where the exercise price is equal to the price at which the bond can be repurchased. A callable bond arrangement is essentially a sale of a *straight bond* (a bond with no option features such as callability or convertibility) to the investor and the concurrent sale of a call option by the investor to the bond-issuing firm.

Bond Offers the Internet sans Anxiety

Want to invest in Internet stocks but don't have the stomach for the risk? Wall Street has concocted a product made just for you.

Proving that securities firms never miss an opportunity to jump on an investment craze, Salomon Smith Barney, a unit of Citigroup Inc., yesterday unveiled the first bond linked to a basket of Internet stocks.

Basically, it is an Internet play for wimps: The downside risk is limited to a loss of 10% of the original investment, no matter how much Internet stocks tumble during the seven-year life of the bonds. But if the index soars higher and the bonds are called, the upside would also be limited, to 25% a year.

Despite the Internet sector's weakness, $65 million of the newfangled securities were sold, mostly to individual investors.

Termed "callable equity linked notes," the securities' return is pegged to the performance of TheStreet.com Internet Index of 20 stocks.

At maturity, Salomon will repay the $10 principal per note plus or minus an amount linked to the increase or decrease in the value of the Internet index, with a minimum payout of $9 no matter how far the index drops. The maximum would be $25 per $10 note (the 25% maximum annual increase wouldn't be compounded), for a total return of 150% if the bonds are called after the sixth year, as they would likely be if

Internet stocks surge. The bonds, which provide no interest payments, are callable during a 30-day period each year after three years, but investors would get an annual premium of 25% of their original investment.

The obvious attraction of the securities: They allow investors to reap the rewards of the Internet without risking losing their shirt. The securities also provide some diversification within the volatile sector without forcing an investor to recreate the 20-stock index himself.

There are dangers in the bonds, however, despite their conservative nature. While investors can only lose 10% of their initial outlay, a $10 investment in a risk-free instrument such as Treasury securities, at today's rates, would return about $14.60 after seven years.

Investment bankers at other Wall Street firms said they are intrigued by the Salomon product and might pursue something similar aimed at individual investors. But some analysts doubt they will prove popular with larger investors. According to Steve Seefeld, president of ConvertBond.com, "An institution can just buy the stocks in index and recreate the securities using shares, puts and calls," Mr. Seefeld says.

SOURCE: Gregory Zuckerman, "Bond Offers the Internet sans Anxiety," *The Wall Street Journal*, May 26, 1999. Reprinted by permission of Dow Jones & Company, Inc. via Copyright Clearance Center, Inc. © 1999 Dow Jones & Company, Inc. All Rights Reserved Worldwide.

There must be some compensation for offering this implicit call option to the firm. If the callable bond were issued with the same coupon rate as a straight bond, we would expect it to sell at a discount to the straight bond equal to the value of the call. To sell callable bonds at par, firms must issue them with coupon rates higher than the coupons on straight debt. The higher coupons are the investor's compensation for the call option retained by the issuer. Coupon rates usually are selected so that the newly issued bond will sell at par value.

Figure 14.12 illustrates this optionlike property. The horizontal axis is the value of a straight bond with otherwise identical terms as the callable bond. The dashed 45-degree line represents the value of straight debt. The solid line is the value of the callable bond, and the dotted line is the value of the call option retained by the firm. A callable bond's potential for capital gains is limited by the firm's option to repurchase at the call price.

5. How is a callable bond similar to a covered call strategy on a straight bond?

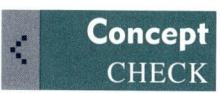

The option inherent in callable bonds actually is more complex than an ordinary call option because usually it may be exercised only after some initial period of call protection. The price at which the bond is callable may change over time also. Unlike exchange-listed options, these features are defined in the initial bond covenants and will depend on the needs of the issuing firm and its perception of the market's tastes.

6. Suppose the period of call protection is extended. How will this affect the coupon rate the company needs to offer to enable it to sell the bonds at par value?

FIGURE **14.12**

FIGURE **14.12**
Values of callable bonds compared with straight bonds

Convertible Securities

Convertible bonds and convertible preferred stock convey options to the holder of the security rather than to the issuing firm. A convertible security typically gives its holder the right to exchange each bond or share of preferred stock for a fixed number of shares of common stock, regardless of the market prices of the securities at the time.

Concept
CHECK

> 7. **Should a convertible bond issued at par value have a higher or lower coupon rate than a nonconvertible bond at par?**

For example, a bond with a conversion ratio of 10 allows its holder to convert one bond of par value $1,000 into 10 shares of common stock. Alternatively, we say the conversion price in this case is $100: To receive 10 shares of stock, the investor sacrifices bonds with face value $1,000 or $100 of face value per share. If the present value of the bond's scheduled payments is less than 10 times the value of one share of stock, it may pay to convert; that is, the conversion option is in the money. A bond worth $950 with a conversion ratio of 10 could be converted profitably if the stock were selling above $95, as the value of the 10 shares received for each bond surrendered would exceed $950. Most convertible bonds are issued "deep out of the money." That is, the issuer sets the conversion ratio so that conversion will not be profitable unless there is a substantial increase in stock prices and/or decrease in bond prices from the time of issue.

A bond's conversion value equals the value it would have if you converted it into stock immediately. Clearly, a bond must sell for at least its conversion value. If it did not, you could purchase the bond, convert it immediately, and clear a riskless profit. This condition could never persist, for all investors would pursue such a strategy and quickly bid up the price of the bond.

The straight bond value or "bond floor" is the value the bond would have if it were not convertible into stock. The bond must sell for more than its straight bond value because a convertible bond has more value; it is in fact a straight bond plus a valuable call option. Therefore, the convertible bond has two lower bounds on its market price: the conversion value and the straight bond value.

Figure 14.13 illustrates the optionlike properties of the convertible bond. Figure 14.13A shows the value of the straight debt as a function of the stock price of the issuing firm.

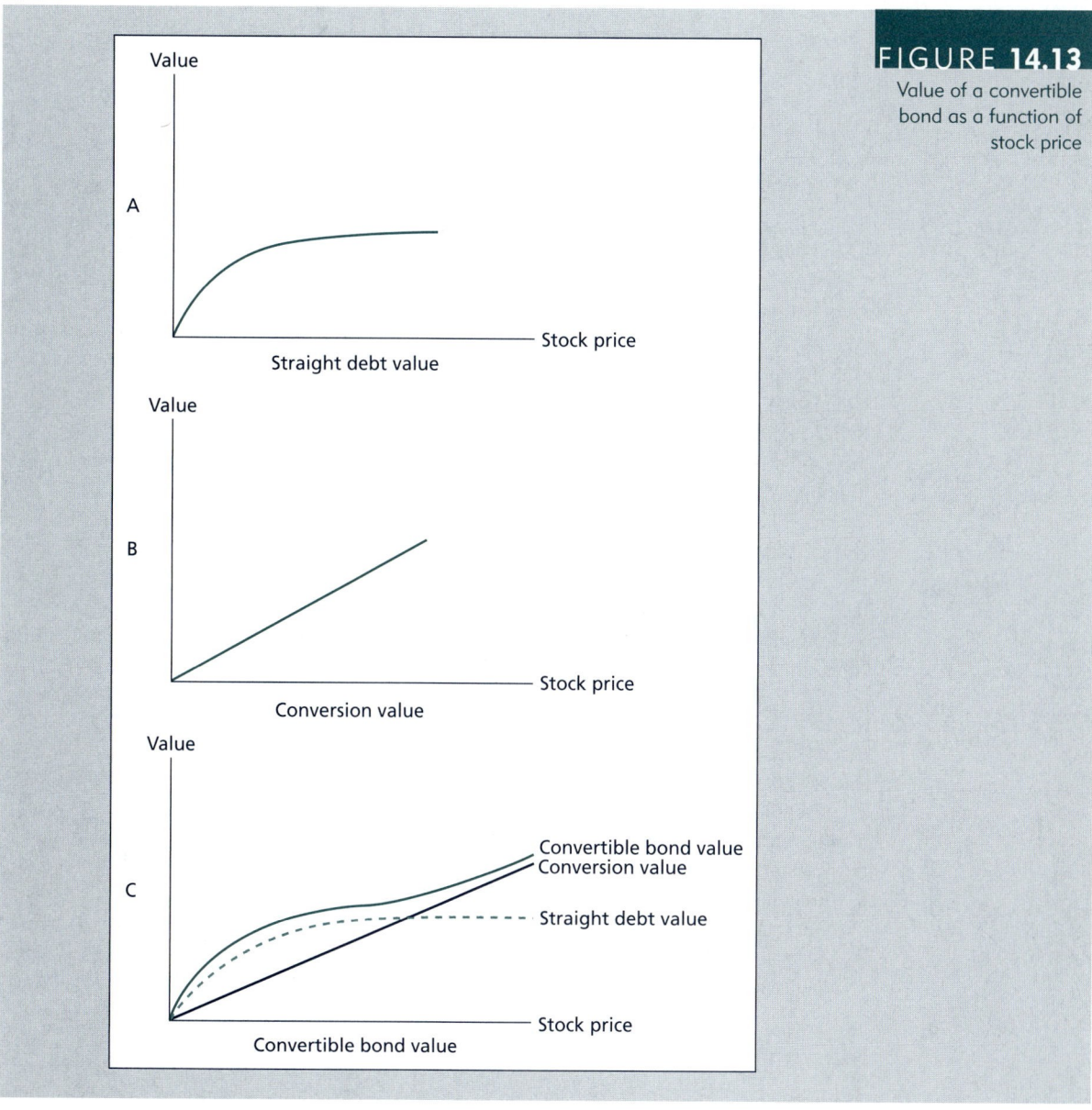

FIGURE **14.13**

Value of a convertible bond as a function of stock price

For healthy firms, the straight debt value is almost independent of the value of the stock because default risk is small. However, if the firm is close to bankruptcy (stock prices are low), default risk increases, and the straight bond value falls. Panel B shows the conversion value of the bond. Panel C compares the value of the convertible bond to these two lower bounds.

When stock prices are low, the straight bond value is the effective lower bound, and the conversion option is nearly irrelevant. The convertible will trade like straight debt. When stock prices are high, the bond's price is determined by its conversion value. With conversion all but guaranteed, the bond is essentially equity in disguise.

We can illustrate with two examples.

	Bond A	Bond B
Annual coupon	$80	$80
Maturity date	10 years	10 years
Quality rating	Baa	Baa
Conversion ratio	20	25
Stock price	$30	$50
Conversion value	$600	$1,250
Market yield on 10-year Baa-rated bonds	8.5%	8.5%
Value as straight debt	$967	$967
Actual bond price	$972	$1,255
Reported yield to maturity	8.42%	4.76%

Bond *A* has a conversion value of only $600. Its value as straight debt, in contrast, is $967. This is the present value of the coupon and principal payments at a market rate for straight debt of 8.5%. The bond's price is $972, so the premium over straight bond value is only $5, reflecting the low probability of conversion. Its reported yield to maturity based on scheduled coupon payments and the market price of $972 is 8.42%, close to that of straight debt.

The conversion option on bond *B* is in the money. Conversion value is $1,250, and the bond's price, $1,255, reflects its value as equity (plus $5 for the protection the bond offers against stock price declines). The bond's reported yield is 4.76%, far below the comparable yield on straight debt. The big yield sacrifice is attributable to the far greater value of the conversion option.

In theory, we could value convertible bonds by treating them as straight debt plus call options. In practice, however, this approach is often impractical for several reasons:

1. The conversion price frequently increases over time, which means the exercise price for the option changes.
2. Stocks may pay several dividends over the life of the bond, further complicating the option value analysis.
3. Most convertibles also are callable at the discretion of the firm. In essence, both the investor and the issuer hold options on each other. If the issuer exercises its call option to repurchase the bond, the bondholders typically have a month during which they still can convert. When issuers use a call option, knowing that bondholders will choose to convert, the issuer is said to have *forced a conversion*. These conditions together mean the actual maturity of the bond is indeterminate.

Warrants

warrant

An option issued by the firm to purchase shares of the firm's stock.

Warrants are essentially call options issued by a firm. One important difference between calls and warrants is that exercise of a warrant requires the firm to issue a new share of stock to satisfy its obligation—the total number of shares outstanding increases. Exercise of a call option requires only that the writer of the call deliver an already-issued share of stock to discharge the obligation. In this case, the number of shares outstanding remains fixed. Also unlike call options, warrants result in a cash flow to the firm when the warrant holder pays the exercise price. These differences mean warrant values will differ somewhat from the values of call options with identical terms.

Like convertible debt, warrant terms may be tailored to meet the needs of the firm. Also like convertible debt, warrants generally are protected against stock splits and dividends in that the exercise price and the number of warrants held are adjusted to offset the effects of the split.

Warrants often are issued in conjunction with another security. Bonds, for example, may be packaged together with a warrant "sweetener," frequently a warrant that may be sold separately. This is called a *detachable warrant*.

Issue of warrants and convertible securities creates the potential for an increase in out-standing shares of stock if exercise occurs. Exercise obviously would affect financial statistics that are computed on a per-share basis, so annual reports must provide earnings per share figures under the assumption that all convertible securities and warrants are exercised. These figures are called *fully diluted earnings per share.*[3]

Collateralized Loans

Many loan arrangements require that the borrower put up collateral to guarantee the loan will be paid back. In the event of default, the lender takes possession of the collateral. A nonre-course loan gives the lender no recourse beyond the right to the collateral. That is, the lender may not sue the borrower for further payment if the collateral turns out not to be valuable enough to repay the loan.[4]

This arrangement gives an implicit call option to the borrower. Assume the borrower is obligated to pay back L dollars at the maturity of the loan. The collateral will be worth S_T dollars at maturity. (Its value today is S_0.) The borrower has the option to wait until loan maturity and repay the loan only if the collateral is worth more than the L dollars necessary to satisfy the loan. If the collateral is worth less than L, the borrower can default on the loan, discharging the obligation by forfeiting the collateral, which is worth only S_T.

Another way of describing such a loan is to view the borrower as turning over collateral to the lender but retaining the right to reclaim it by paying off the loan. The transfer of the collateral with the right to reclaim it is equivalent to a payment of S_0 dollars, less a simultaneous recovery of a sum that resembles a call option with exercise price L. Basically, the borrower turns over collateral and keeps an option to "repurchase" it for L dollars at the maturity of the loan if L turns out to be less than S_T. This is a call option.

A third way to look at a collaterized loan is to assume the borrower will repay the L dollars with certainty but also retain the option to sell the collateral to the lender for L dollars, even if S_T is less than L. In this case, the sale of the collateral would generate the cash necessary to satisfy the loan. The ability to "sell" the collateral for a price of L dollars represents a put option, which guarantees the borrower can raise enough money to satisfy the loan simply by turning over the collateral.

Figure 14.14 illustrates these interpretations. Figure 14.14A is the value of the payment to be received by the lender, which equals the minimum of S_T or L. Panel B shows that this amount can be expressed as S_T minus the payoff of the call implicitly written by the lender and held by the borrower. Panel C shows it also can be viewed as a receipt of L dollars minus the proceeds of a put option.

Levered Equity and Risky Debt

Investors holding stock in incorporated firms are protected by limited liability, which means that if the firm cannot pay its debts, the firm's creditors may attach only the firm's assets and may not sue the corporation's equityholders for further payment. In effect, any time the corporation borrows money, the maximum possible collateral for the loan is the total of the firm's

---

[3] We should note that the exercise of a convertible bond need not reduce earnings per share (EPS). Diluted EPS will be less than undiluted EPS only if interest saved (per share) on the converted bonds is less than the prior EPS.

[4] In reality, of course, defaulting on a loan is not so simple. Losses of reputation are involved as well as considerations of ethical behavior. This is a description of a pure nonrecourse loan where both parties agree from the outset that only the collateral backs the loan and that default is not to be taken as a sign of bad faith if the collateral is insufficient to repay the loan.

FIGURE **14.14**

Collateralized loan

A. When S_T exceeds L, the loan is repaid and the collateral is reclaimed. Otherwise, the collateral is forfeited and the total loan repayment is worth only S_T.

assets. If the firm declares bankruptcy, we can interpret this as an admission that the assets of the firm are insufficient to satisfy the claims against it. The corporation may discharge its obligations by transferring ownership of the firm's assets to the creditors.

Just as is true for nonrecourse collateralized loans, the required payment to the creditors represents the exercise price of the implicit option, while the value of the firm is the underlying asset. The equityholders have a put option to transfer their ownership claims on the firm to the creditors in return for the face value of the firm's debt.

Alternatively, we may view the equityholders as retaining a call option. They have, in effect, already transferred their ownership claim to the firm to the creditors but have retained the right to reacquire the ownership claim by paying off the loan. Hence, the equityholders have the option to "buy back" the firm for a specified price, or they have a call option.

The significance of this observation is that analysts can value corporate bonds using option-pricing techniques. The default premium required of risky debt in principle can be estimated using option valuation models. We will consider some of these models in the next chapter.

14.4 EXOTIC OPTIONS

Investors clearly value the portfolio strategies made possible by trading options; this is reflected in the heavy trading volume in these markets and their tremendous success. Success breeds imitation, and in recent years we have witnessed tremendous innovation in the range of option instruments available to investors. Part of this innovation has occurred in the market for customized options, which now trade in active over-the-counter markets. Many of these options have terms that would have been highly unusual even a few years ago; they therefore are called "exotic options." In this section, we will survey some of the more interesting variants of these new instruments.

Asian Options

You already have been introduced to American and European options. *Asian options* are options with payoffs that depend on the average (rather than final) price of the underlying asset during at least some portion of the life of the option. For example, an Asian call option may have a payoff that is either equal to the average stock price over the last three months minus the strike price, if that value is positive, or zero. These options may be of interest to firms that wish to hedge a profit stream that depends on the average price of a commodity over some period of time.

Barrier Options

Barrier options have payoffs that depend not only on some asset price at option expiration but also on whether the underlying asset price has crossed through some "barrier." For example, a *down-and-out option* is one type of barrier option that automatically expires worthless if and when the stock price falls below some barrier price. Similarly, *down-and-in options* will not provide a payoff unless the stock price *does* fall below some barrier at least once during the life of the option. These options also are referred to as knock-out and knock-in options.

Lookback Options

Lookback options have payoffs that depend in part on the minimum or maximum price of the underlying asset during the life of the option. For example, a lookback call option might provide a payoff equal to the maximum stock price during the life of the option minus the exercise price, as opposed to the *closing* stock price minus the exercise price. Such an option provides (for a fee, of course) a form of perfect market timing, providing the call holder with a payoff equal to the one that would accrue if the asset were purchased for X dollars and later sold at what turns out to be its highest price.

Currency-Translated Options

Currency-translated options have either asset or exercise prices denominated in a foreign currency. A good example of such an option is the *quanto*, which allows an investor to fix in advance the exchange rate at which an investment in a foreign currency can be converted back into dollars. The right to translate a fixed amount of foreign currency into dollars at a given exchange rate is a simple foreign exchange option. Quantos are more interesting, however, because the amount of currency that will be translated into dollars depends on the investment performance of the foreign security. Therefore, a quanto in effect provides a *random number* of options.

Binary Options

Binary options (also called "bet" options) have fixed payoffs that depend on whether a condition is satisfied by the price of the underlying asset. For example, a binary call option might pay off a fixed amount of $100 if the stock price at maturity exceeds the exercise price.

SUMMARY

- A call option is the right to buy an asset at an agreed-upon exercise price. A put option is the right to sell an asset at a given exercise price.
- American options allow exercise on or before the exercise date. European options allow exercise only on the expiration date. Most traded options are American in nature.
- Options are traded on stocks, stock indexes, foreign currencies, fixed-income securities, and several futures contracts.
- Options can be used either to lever up an investor's exposure to an asset price or to provide insurance against volatility of asset prices. Popular option strategies include covered calls, protective puts, straddles, and spreads.
- Many commonly traded securities embody option characteristics. Examples of these securities are callable bonds, convertible bonds, and warrants. Other arrangements, such as collateralized loans and limited-liability borrowing, can be analyzed as conveying implicit options to one or more parties.

KEY TERMS

American option, 495	exercise price, 492	risk management, 506
at the money, 493	in the money, 493	spread, 508
call option, 492	out of the money, 493	straddle, 508
collar, 511	preminum, 492	strike price, 492
covered call, 506	protective put, 504	warrant, 516
European option, 495	put option, 493	

PROBLEM SETS

1. Which one of the following statements about the value of a call option at expiration is false?
   a. A short position in a call option will result in a loss if the stock price exceeds the exercise price.
   b. The value of a long position equals zero or the stock price minus the exercise price, whichever is higher.
   c. The value of a long position equals zero or the exercise price minus the stock price, whichever is higher.
   d. A short position in a call option has a zero value for all stock prices equal to or less than the exercise price.

2. The following diagram shows the value of a put option at expiration:

Ignoring transaction costs, which of the following statements about the value of the put option at expiration is *true*?
a. The value of the short position in the put is $4 if the stock price is $76.
b. The value of the long position in the put is −$4 if the stock price is $76.
c. The long put has value when the stock price is below the $80 exercise price.
d. The value of the short position in the put is zero for stock prices equaling or exceeding $76.

3. The following price quotations are for exchange-listed options on Primo Corporation common stock.

Company	Strike	Expiration	Call	Put
Primo 61.12	55	Feb	7.25	.48

Ignoring transaction costs, how much would a buyer have to pay for one call option contract?

4. Turn back to Figure 14.1, which lists the prices of various Microsoft options. Use the data in the figure to calculate the payoff and the profits for investments in each of the following January maturity options, assuming that the stock price on the maturity date is $70.
a. Call option, $X = 65$
b. Put option, $X = 65$
c. Call option, $X = 70$
d. Put option, $X = 70$
e. Call option, $X = 75$
f. Put option, $X = 75$

5. Suppose you think Wal-Mart stock is going to appreciate substantially in value in the next six months. Say the stock's current price, S_0, is $100, and the call option expiring in six months has an exercise price, X, of $100 and is selling at a price, C, of $10. With $10,000 to invest, you are considering three alternatives:
a. Invest all $10,000 in the stock, buying 100 shares.
b. Invest all $10,000 in 1,000 options (10 contracts).
c. Buy 100 options (one contract) for $1,000 and invest the remaining $9,000 in a money market fund paying 4% interest over six months.

What is your rate of return for each alternative for four stock prices six months from now? Summarize your results in the table and diagram below.

RATE OF RETURN ON INVESTMENT

	Price of Stock Six Months from Now			
	$80	$100	$110	$120
a. All stocks (100 shares)				
b. All options (1,000 shares)				
c. Bills + 100 options				

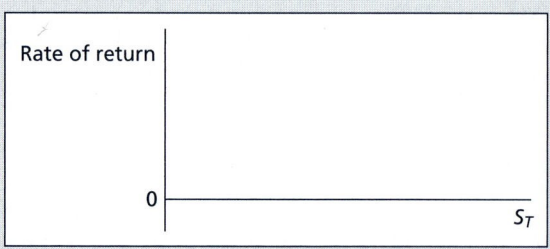

6. The common stock of the P.U.T.T. Corporation has been trading in a narrow price range for the past month, and you are convinced it is going to break far out of that range in the next three months. You do not know whether it will go up or down, however. The current price of the stock is $100 per share, the price of a three-month call option with an exercise price of $100 is $10, and a put with the same expiration date and exercise price costs $7.
   a. What would be a simple options strategy to exploit your conviction about the stock price's future movements?
   b. How far would the price have to move in either direction for you to make a profit on your initial investment?

7. The common stock of the C.A.L.L. Corporation has been trading in a narrow range around $50 per share for months, and you believe it is going to stay in that range for the next three months. The price of a three-month put option with an exercise price of $50 is $4, and a call with the same expiration date and exercise price sells for $7.
   a. What would be a simple options strategy using a put and a call to exploit your conviction about the stock price's future movement?
   b. What is the most money you can make on this position? How far can the stock price move in either direction before you lose money?
   c. How can you create a position involving a put, a call, and riskless lending that would have the same payoff structure as the stock at expiration? The stock will pay no dividends in the next three months. What is the net cost of establishing that position now?

8. Joseph Jones, a manager at Computer Science, Inc. (CSI), received 10,000 shares of company stock as part of his compensation package. The stock currently sells at $40 a share. Joseph would like to defer selling the stock until the next tax year. In January, however, he will need to sell all his holdings to provide for a down payment on his new house. Joseph is worried about the price risk involved in keeping his shares. At current prices, he would receive $40,000 for the stock. If the value of his stock holdings falls below $35,000, his ability to come up with the necessary down payment would be jeopardized. On the other hand, if the stock value rises to $45,000, he would be able to maintain a small cash reserve even after making the down payment. Joseph considers three investment strategies:

a. Strategy A is to write January call options on the CSI shares with strike price $45. These calls are currently selling for $3 each.

b. Strategy B is to buy January put options on CSI with strike price $35. These options also sell for $3 each.

c. Strategy C is to establish a zero-cost collar by writing the January calls and buying the January puts.

Evaluate each of these strategies with respect to Joseph's investment goals. What are the advantages and disadvantages of each? Which would you recommend?

9. a. A butterfly spread is the purchase of one call at exercise price X_1, the sale of two calls at exercise price X_2, and the purchase of one call at exercise price X_3. X_1 is less than X_2, and X_2 is less than X_3 by equal amounts, and all calls have the same expiration date. Graph the payoff diagram to this strategy.

b. A vertical combination is the purchase of a call with exercise price X_2 and a put with exercise price X_1, with X_2 greater than X_1. Graph the payoff to this strategy.

10. A bearish spread is the purchase of a call with exercise price X_2 and the sale of a call with exercise price X_1, with X_2 greater than X_1. Graph the payoff to this strategy and compare it to Figure 14.11.

11. You are attempting to formulate an investment strategy. On the one hand, you think there is great upward potential in the stock market and would like to participate in the upward move if it materializes. However, you are not able to afford substantial stock market losses and so cannot run the risk of a stock market collapse, which you also think is a possibility. Your investment adviser suggests a protective put position: Buy shares in a market index stock fund *and* put options on those shares with three-month maturity and exercise price of $1,040. The stock index is currently at $1,200. However, your uncle suggests you instead buy a three-month call option on the index fund with exercise price $1,120 and buy three-month T-bills with face value $1,120.

a. On the same graph, draw the *payoffs* to each of these strategies as a function of the stock fund value in three months. (Hint: Think of the options as being on one "share" of the stock index fund, with the current price of each share of the index equal to $1,200.)

b. Which portfolio must require a greater initial outlay to establish? (Hint: Does either portfolio provide a final payoff that is always at least as great as the payoff of the other portfolio?)

c. Suppose the market prices of the securities are as follows.

Stock fund	$1,200
T-bill (face value $1,120)	1,080
Call (exercise price $1,120)	160
Put (exercise price $1,040)	8

Make a table of profits realized for each portfolio for the following values of the stock price in three months: $S_T = \$0, \$1,040, \$1,120, \$1,200$, and $1,280. Graph the profits to each portfolio as a function of S_T on a single graph.

d. Which strategy is riskier? Which should have a higher beta?

12. The agricultural price support system guarantees farmers a minimum price for their output. Describe the program provisions as an option. What is the asset? The exercise price?

13. In what ways is owning a corporate bond similar to writing a put option? A call option?

14. An executive compensation scheme might provide a manager a bonus of $1,000 for every dollar by which the company's stock price exceeds some cutoff level. In what way is this arrangement equivalent to issuing the manager call options on the firm's stock?

15. Consider the following options portfolio. You write a January maturity call option on Microsoft with exercise price $75. You write a January maturity Microsoft put option with exercise price $70.
    a. Graph the payoff of this portfolio at option expiration as a function of Microsoft's stock price at that time.
    b. What will be the profit/loss on this position if Microsoft is selling at $72 on the option maturity date? What if Microsoft is selling at $80? Use *The Wall Street Journal* listing from Figure 14.1 to answer this question.
    c. At what two stock prices will you just break even on your investment?
    d. What kind of "bet" is this investor making; that is, what must this investor believe about Microsoft's stock price in order to justify this position?

16. A member of an investment committee, interested in learning more about fixed-income investment procedures, recalls that a fixed-income manager recently stated that derivative instruments could be used to control portfolio duration, saying "a futures-like position can be created in a portfolio by using put and call options on Treasury bonds."
    a. Identify the options market exposure or exposures that create a "futures-like position" similar to being long Treasury bond futures. Explain why the position you created is similar to being long Treasury bond futures.
    b. Explain in which direction and why the exposure(s) you identified in part (*a*) would affect portfolio duration.
    c. Assume that a pension plan's investment policy requires the fixed-income manager to hold portfolio duration within a narrow range. Identify and briefly explain circumstances or transactions in which the use of Treasury bond futures would be helpful in managing a fixed-income portfolio when duration is constrained.

17. Consider the following portfolio. You *write* a put option with exercise price $90 and *buy* a put with the same maturity date with exercise price $95.
    a. Plot the value of the portfolio at the maturity date of the options.
    b. On the same graph, plot the profit of the portfolio. Which option must cost more?

18. A Ford put option with strike price $60 trading on the Acme options exchange sells for $2. To your amazement, a Ford put with the same maturity selling on the Apex options exchange but with strike price $62 also sells for $2. If you plan to hold the options position to maturity, devise a zero-net-investment arbitrage strategy to exploit the pricing anomaly. Draw the profit diagram at maturity for your position.

19. You buy a share of stock, write a one-year call option with $X = \$10$, and buy a one-year put option with $X = \$10$. Your net outlay to establish the entire portfolio is $9.50. What must be the risk-free interest rate? The stock pays no dividends.

20. Joe Finance has just purchased a stock index fund, currently selling at $1,200 per share. To protect against losses, Joe also purchased an at-the-money European put option on the fund for $60, with exercise price $1,200, and three-month time to expiration. Sally Calm, Joe's financial adviser, points out that Joe is spending a lot of money on the put. She notes that three-month puts with strike prices of $1,170 cost only $45, and suggests that Joe use the cheaper put.
    a. Analyze Joe's and Sally's strategies by drawing the *profit* diagrams for the stock-plus-put positions for various values of the stock fund in three months.

b. When does Sally's strategy do better? When does it do worse?

c. Which strategy entails greater systematic risk?

21. You write a call option with $X = \$50$ and buy a call with $X = \$60$. The options are on the same stock and have the same maturity date. One of the calls sells for $3; the other sells for $9.

a. Draw the *payoff* graph for this strategy at the option maturity date.

b. Draw the *profit* graph for this strategy.

c. What is the break-even point for this strategy? Is the investor bullish or bearish on the stock?

22. Devise a portfolio using only call options and shares of stock with the following value (payoff) at the option maturity date. If the stock price is currently $53, what kind of bet is the investor making?

SOLUTIONS TO

Concept
CHECKS

1. *a.* Proceeds $= S_T - X = S_T - \$70$ if this value is positive; otherwise, the call expires worthless.
Profit = Proceeds − Price of call option = Proceeds − \$4.60.

	$S_T = \$60$	$S_T = \$80$
Proceeds	\$0	\$10
Profits	−4.60	5.40

b. Proceeds $= X - S_T = \$70 - S_T$ if this value is positive; otherwise, the put expires worthless.
Profit = Proceeds − Price of put option = Proceeds − \$5.40.

	$S_T = \$60$	$S_T = \$80$
Proceeds	\$10	\$0
Profits	4.60	−5.40

2. *a.*

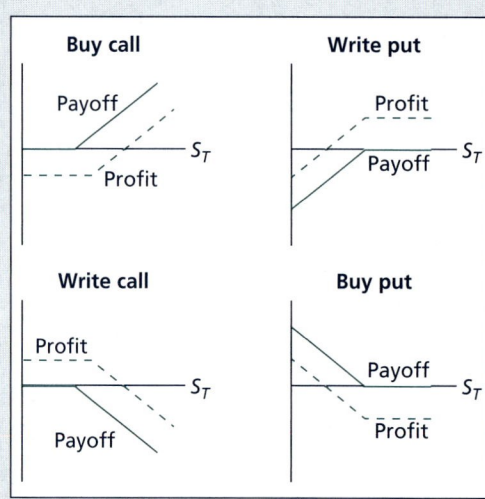

b. The payoffs and profits to both buying calls and writing puts generally are higher when the stock price is higher. In this sense, both positions are bullish. Both involve potentially taking delivery of the stock. However, the call holder will *choose* to take delivery when the stock price is high, while the put writer *is obligated* to take delivery when the stock price is low.

c. The payoffs and profits to both writing calls and buying puts generally are higher when the stock price is lower. In this sense, both positions are bearish. Both involve potentially making delivery of the stock. However, the put holder will *choose* to make delivery when the stock price is low, while the call writer *is obligated* to make delivery when the stock price is high.

3.

PAYOFF TO A STRIP

	$S_T \leq X$	$S_T > X$
2 Puts	$2(X - S_T)$	0
1 Call	0	$S_T - X$

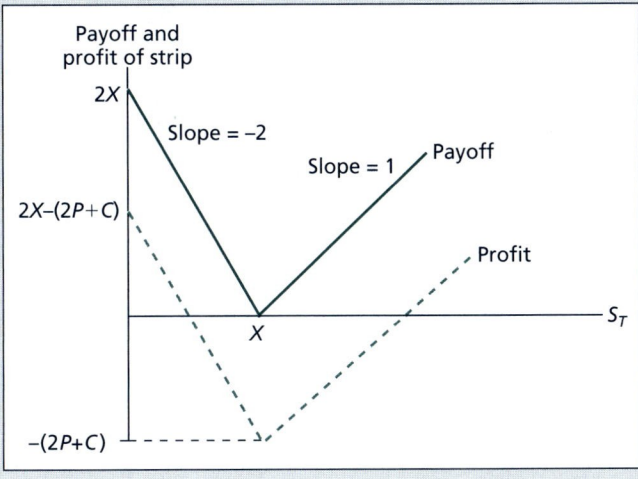

PAYOFF TO A STRAP

	$S_T \leq X$	$S_T > X$
1 Put	$X - S_T$	0
2 Calls	0	$2(S_T - X)$

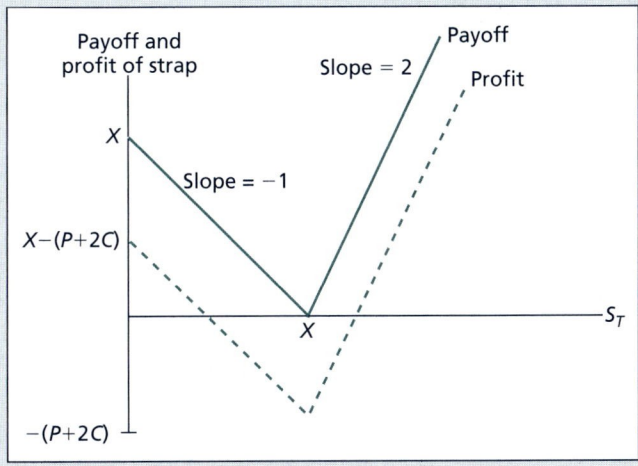

4. The payoff table on a per-share basis is as follows:

	$S_T < 60$	$60 < S_T < 80$	$S_T > 80$
Buy put ($X = 60$)	$60 - S_T$	0	0
Share	S_T	S_T	S_T
Write call ($X = 80$)	0	0	$-(S_T - 80)$
Total	60	S_T	80

The graph of the payoff follows. If you multiply the per-share values by 2,000, you will see that the collar provides a minimum payoff of $120,000 (representing a maximum loss of $20,000) and a maximum payoff of $160,000 (which is the cost of the house).

5. The covered call strategy would consist of a straight bond with a call written on the bond. The value of the covered call position at option expiration as a function of the value of the straight bond is given in the figure following, and is virtually identical to the value of the callable bond in Figure 14.12.

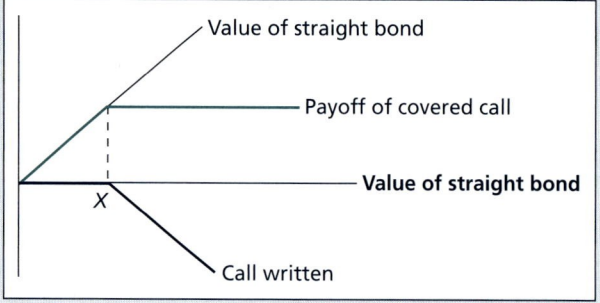

6. The call option is worth less as call protection is expanded. Therefore, the coupon rate need not be as high.

7. Lower. Investors will accept a lower coupon rate in return for the conversion option.

15

OPTION VALUATION

AFTER STUDYING THIS CHAPTER YOU SHOULD BE ABLE TO:

> Identify the features of an option that affect its market value.

> Compute an option value in a two-scenario model of the economy.

> Compute the Black-Scholes value of an option.

> Compute the proper relationship between call and put prices.

> Compute the hedge ratio of an option.

> Formulate a portfolio insurance plan using option hedge ratios.

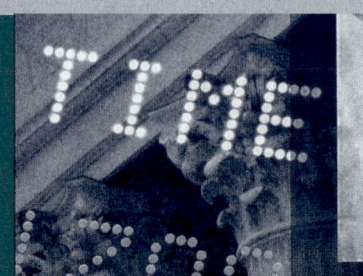

In the previous chapter, we examined option markets and strategies. We ended by noting that many securities contain embedded options that affect both their values and their risk-return characteristics. In this chapter, we turn our attention to option valuation issues. Understanding most option valuation models requires considerable mathematical and statistical background. Still, many of the ideas and insights of these models can be demonstrated in simple examples, and we will concentrate on these.

We start with a discussion of the factors that ought to affect option prices. After this qualitative discussion, we present a simple "two-state" quantitative option valuation model and show how we can generalize it into a useful and accurate pricing tool. Next, we move on to one particular valuation formula, the famous Black-Scholes model, one of the most significant breakthroughs in finance theory in the past three decades. Finally, we look at some of the more important applications of option pricing theory in portfolio management and control.

15.1 OPTION VALUATION: INTRODUCTION

Intrinsic and Time Values

Consider a call option that is out of the money at the moment, with the stock price below the exercise price. This does not mean the option is valueless. Even though immediate exercise today would be unprofitable, the call retains a positive value because there is always a chance the stock price will increase sufficiently by the expiration date to allow for profitable exercise. If not, the worst that can happen is that the option will expire with zero value.

intrinsic value

Stock price minus exercise price, or the profit that could be attained by immediate exercise of an in-the-money call option.

The value $S_0 - X$ is sometimes called the **intrinsic value** of an in-the-money call option because it gives the payoff that could be obtained by immediate exercise. Intrinsic value is set equal to zero for out-of-the-money or at-the-money options. The difference between the actual call price and the intrinsic value is commonly called the *time value* of the option.

Time value is an unfortunate choice of terminology because it may confuse the option's time value with the time value of money. Time value in the options context simply refers to the difference between the option's price and the value the option would have if it were expiring immediately. It is the part of the option's value that may be attributed to the fact that it still has positive time to expiration.

Most of an option's time value typically is a type of "volatility value." As long as the option holder can choose not to exercise, the payoff cannot be worse than zero. Even if a call option is out of the money now, it still will sell for a positive price because it offers the potential for a profit if the stock price increases, while imposing no risk of additional loss should the stock price fall. The volatility value lies in the right *not* to exercise the option if that action would be unprofitable. The option to exercise, as opposed to the obligation to exercise, provides insurance against poor stock price performance.

As the stock price increases substantially, it becomes more likely that the call option will be exercised by expiration. In this case, with exercise all but assured, the volatility value becomes minimal. As the stock price gets ever larger, the option value approaches the "adjusted" intrinsic value—the stock price minus the present value of the exercise price, $S_0 - PV(X)$.

Why should this be? If you *know* the option will be exercised and the stock purchased for X dollars, it is as though you own the stock already. The stock certificate might as well be sitting in your safe-deposit box now, as it will be there in only a few months. You just haven't paid for it yet. The present value of your obligation is the present value of X, so the present value of the net payoff of the call option is $S_0 - PV(X)$.[1]

Figure 15.1 illustrates the call option valuation function. The value curve shows that when the stock price is low, the option is nearly worthless because there is almost no chance that it will be exercised. When the stock price is very high, the option value approaches adjusted intrinsic value. In the midrange case, where the option is approximately at the money, the option curve diverges from the straight lines corresponding to adjusted intrinsic value. This is because, while exercise today would have a negligible (or negative) payoff, the volatility value of the option is quite high in this region. The option always increases in value with the stock price. The slope is greatest, however, when the option is deep in the money. In this case, exercise is all but assured, and the option increases in price one-for-one with the stock price.

---

[1]This discussion presumes the stock pays no dividends until after option expiration. If the stock does pay dividends before maturity, then there *is* a reason you would care about getting the stock now rather than at expiration—getting it now entitles you to the interim dividend payments. In this case, the adjusted intrinsic value of the option must subtract the value of the dividends the stock will pay out before the call is exercised. Adjusted intrinsic value would more generally be defined as $S_0 - PV(X) - PV(D)$, where D represents dividends to be paid before option expiration.

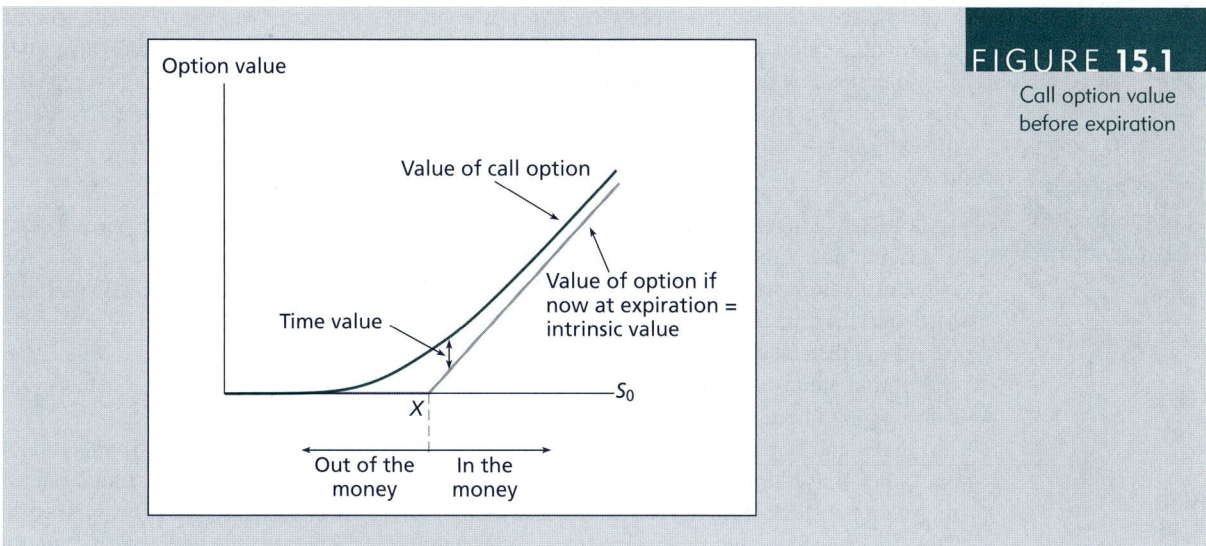

FIGURE 15.1
Call option value
before expiration

Determinants of Option Values

We can identify at least six factors that should affect the value of a call option: the stock price, the exercise price, the volatility of the stock price, the time to expiration, the interest rate, and the dividend rate of the stock. The call option should increase in value with the stock price and decrease in value with the exercise price because the payoff to a call, if exercised, equals $S_T - X$. The magnitude of the expected payoff from the call increases with the difference $S_0 - X$.

Call option value also increases with the volatility of the underlying stock price. To see why, consider circumstances where possible stock prices at expiration may range from $10 to $50 compared to a situation where stock prices may range only from $20 to $40. In both cases, the expected, or average, stock price will be $30. Suppose the exercise price on a call option is also $30. What are the option payoffs?

High-Volatility Scenario

Stock price	$10	$20	$30	$40	$50
Option payoff	0	0	0	10	20

Low-Volatility Scenario

Stock price	$20	$25	$30	$35	$40
Option payoff	0	0	0	5	10

If each outcome is equally likely, with probability 0.2, the expected payoff to the option under high-volatility conditions will be $6, but under the low-volatility conditions, the expected payoff to the call option is half as much, only $3.

Despite the fact that the average stock price in each scenario is $30, the average option payoff is greater in the high-volatility scenario. The source of this extra value is the limited loss an option holder can suffer, or the volatility value of the call. No matter how far below $30 the stock price drops, the option holder will get zero. Obviously, extremely poor stock price performance is no worse for the call option holder than moderately poor performance.

In the case of good stock performance, however, the call option will expire in the money, and it will be more profitable the higher the stock price. Thus, extremely good stock outcomes can improve the option payoff without limit, but extremely poor outcomes cannot worsen the payoff below zero. This asymmetry means volatility in the underlying stock price increases the expected payoff to the option, thereby enhancing its value.

1. Should a put option increase in value with the volatility of the stock?

Similarly, longer time to expiration increases the value of a call option. For more distant expiration dates, there is more time for unpredictable future events to affect prices, and the range of likely stock prices increases. This has an effect similar to that of increased volatility. Moreover, as time to expiration lengthens, the present value of the exercise price falls, thereby benefiting the call option holder and increasing the option value. As a corollary to this issue, call option values are higher when interest rates rise (holding the stock price constant), because higher interest rates also reduce the present value of the exercise price.

Finally, the dividend payout policy of the firm affects option values. A high dividend payout policy puts a drag on the rate of growth of the stock price. For any expected total rate of return on the stock, a higher dividend yield must imply a lower expected rate of capital gain. This drag on stock appreciation decreases the potential payoff from the call option, thereby lowering the call value. Table 15.1 summarizes these relationships.

2. Prepare a table like Table 15.1 for the determinants of put option values. How should put values respond to increases in S, X, T, σ, r_f, and dividend payout?

15.2   BINOMIAL OPTION PRICING

Two-State Option Pricing

A complete understanding of commonly used option valuation formulas is difficult without a substantial mathematics background. Nevertheless, we can develop valuable insight into option valuation by considering a simple special case. Assume a stock price can take only two possible values at option expiration: The stock will either increase to a given higher price or decrease to a given lower price. Although this may seem an extreme simplification, it allows us to come closer to understanding more complicated and realistic models. Moreover, we can extend this approach to describe far more reasonable specifications of stock price behavior. In fact, several major financial firms employ variants of this simple model to value options and securities with optionlike features.

Suppose the stock now sells at \$100, and the price will either double to \$200 or fall in half to \$50 by year-end. A call option on the stock might specify an exercise price of \$125 and a

TABLE **15.1**	If This Variable Increases	The Value of a Call Option
Determinants of call option values	Stock price, S	Increases
	Exercise price, X	Decreases
	Volatility, σ	Increases
	Time to expiration, T	Increases
	Interest rate, r_f	Increases
	Dividend payouts	Decreases

time to expiration of one year. The interest rate is 8%. At year-end, the payoff to the holder of the call option will be either zero, if the stock falls, or $75, if the stock price goes to $200. These possibilities are illustrated by the following "value trees."

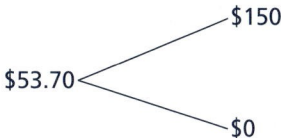

$$\text{Stock price} \qquad \text{Call option value}$$

Compare this payoff to that of a portfolio consisting of one share of the stock and borrowing of $46.30 at the interest rate of 8%. The payoff of this portfolio also depends on the stock price at year-end.

	$50	$200
Value of stock at year-end	$50	$200
− Repayment of loan with interest	−50	−50
Total	$ 0	$150

We know the cash outlay to establish the portfolio is $53.70: $100 for the stock, less the $46.30 proceeds from borrowing. Therefore, the portfolio's value tree is

$$\$53.70 \Big\langle\begin{array}{l}\$150\\ \\\$0\end{array}$$

The payoff of this portfolio is exactly twice that of the call option for either value of the stock price. In other words, two call options will exactly replicate the payoff to the portfolio; it follows that two call options should have the same price as the cost of establishing the portfolio. Hence, the two calls should sell for the same price as the "replicating portfolio." Therefore

$$2C = \$53.70$$

or each call should sell at $C = \$26.85$. Thus, given the stock price, exercise price, interest rate, and volatility of the stock price (as represented by the magnitude of the up or down movements), we can derive the fair value for the call option.

This valuation approach relies heavily on the notion of *replication*. With only two possible end-of-year values of the stock, the payoffs to the levered stock portfolio replicate the payoffs to two call options and so need to command the same market price. This notion of replication is behind most option-pricing formulas. For more complex price distributions for stocks, the replication technique is correspondingly more complex, but the principles remain the same.

One way to view the role of replication is to note that, using the numbers assumed for this example, a portfolio made up of one share of stock and two call options written is perfectly hedged. Its year-end value is independent of the ultimate stock price.

	$50	$200
Stock value	$50	$200
− Obligations from 2 calls written	−0	−150
Net payoff	$50	$ 50

The investor has formed a riskless portfolio with a payout of $50. Its value must be the present value of $50, or $50/1.08 = $46.30. The value of the portfolio, which equals $100 from the stock held long, minus $2C$ from the two calls written, should equal $46.30. Hence, $100 - 2C = $46.30, or $C = $26.85.

The ability to create a perfect hedge is the key to this argument. The hedge locks in the end-of-year payout, which can be discounted using the risk-free interest rate. To find the value of the option in terms of the value of the stock, we do not need to know either the option's or the stock's beta or expected rate of return. The perfect hedging, or replication, approach enables us to express the value of the option in terms of the current value of the stock without this information. With a hedged position, the final stock price does not affect the investor's payoff, so the stock's risk and return parameters have no bearing.

The hedge ratio of this example is one share of stock to two calls, or one-half. For every call option written, one-half share of stock must be held in the portfolio to hedge away risk. This ratio has an easy interpretation in this context: It is the ratio of the range of the values of the option to those of the stock across the two possible outcomes. The option is worth either zero or $75, for a range of $75. The stock is worth either $50 or $200, for a range of $150. The ratio of ranges, $75/$150, is one-half, which is the hedge ratio we have established.

The hedge ratio equals the ratio of ranges because the option and stock are perfectly correlated in this two-state example. When the returns of the option and stock are perfectly correlated, a perfect hedge requires that the option and stock be held in a fraction determined only by relative volatility.

We can generalize the hedge ratio for other two-state option problems as

$$H = \frac{C^+ - C^-}{S^+ - S^-}$$

where C^+ or C^- refers to the call option's value when the stock goes up or down, respectively, and S^+ and S^- are the stock prices in the two states. The hedge ratio, H, is the ratio of the swings in the possible end-of-period values of the option and the stock. If the investor writes one option and holds H shares of stock, the value of the portfolio will be unaffected by the stock price. In this case, option pricing is easy: Simply set the value of the hedged portfolio equal to the present value of the known payoff.

Using our example, the option-pricing technique would proceed as follows:

1. Given the possible end-of-year stock prices, $S^+ = $200 and $S^- = $50, and the exercise price of $125, calculate that $C^+ = $75 and $C^- = $0. The stock price range is $150, while the option price range is $75.
2. Find that the hedge ratio is $75/$150 = 0.5.
3. Find that a portfolio made up of 0.5 shares with one written option would have an end-of-year value of $25 with certainty.
4. Show that the present value of $25 with a one-year interest rate of 8% is $23.15.
5. Set the value of the hedged position equal to the present value of the certain payoff:

$$0.5S_0 - C_0 = \$23.15$$

$$\$50 - C_0 = \$23.15$$

6. Solve for the call's value, $C_0 = $26.85.

What if the option were overpriced, perhaps selling for $30? Then you can make arbitrage profits. Here is how.

	Initial Cash Flow	Cash Flow in 1 Year for Each Possible Stock Price	
		S = $50	S = $200
1. Write 2 options.	$ 60	$ 0	$-150
2. Purchase 1 share.	-100	50	200
3. Borrow $40 at 8% interest and repay in 1 year.	40	-43.20	-43.20
Total	$ 0	$ 6.80	$ 6.80

Although the net initial investment is zero, the payoff in one year is positive and riskless. If the option were underpriced, one would simply reverse this arbitrage strategy: Buy the option, and sell the stock short to eliminate price risk. Note, by the way, that the present value of the profit to the above arbitrage strategy equals twice the amount by which the option is overpriced. The present value of the risk-free profit of $6.80 at an 8% interest rate is $6.30. With two options written in the strategy above, this translates to a profit of $3.15 per option, exactly the amount by which the option was overpriced: $30 versus the "fair value" of $26.85.

3. Suppose the call option had been underpriced, selling at $24. Formulate the arbitrage strategy to exploit the mispricing, and show that it provides a riskless cash flow in one year of $3.08 per option purchased.

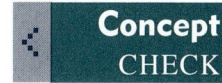 **Concept** CHECK

Generalizing the Two-State Approach

Although the two-state stock price model seems simplistic, we can generalize it to incorporate more realistic assumptions. To start, suppose we were to break up the year into two six-month segments and then assert that over each half-year segment the stock price could take on two values. Here we will say it can increase 10% or decrease 5%. A stock initially selling at $100 could follow the following possible paths over the course of the year:

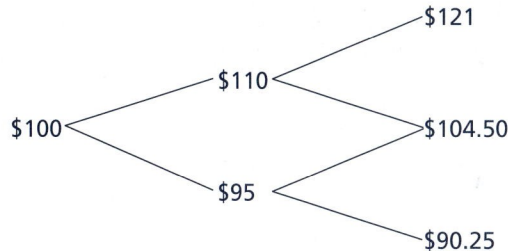

The midrange value of $104.50 can be attained by two paths: an increase of 10% followed by a decrease of 5%, or a decrease of 5% followed by an increase of 10%.

There are now three possible end-of-year values for the stock and three for the option:

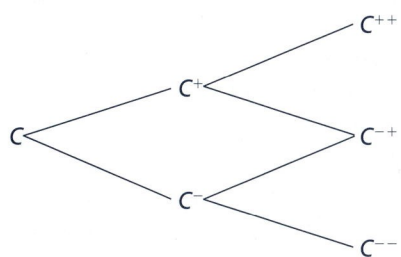

Using methods similar to those we followed above, we could value C^+ from knowledge of C^{++} and C^{+-}, then value C^- from knowledge of C^{-+} and C^{--}, and finally value C from knowledge of C^+ and C^-. And there is no reason to stop at six-month intervals. We could next break the year into 4 three-month units, or 12 one-month units, or 365 one-day units, each of which would be posited to have a two-state process. Although the calculations become quite numerous and correspondingly tedious, they are easy to program into a computer, and such computer programs are used widely by participants in the options market.

15.1 EXAMPLE

Binomial Option Pricing

Suppose that the risk-free interest rate is 5% per six-month period and we wish to value a call option with exercise price $110 on the stock described in the two-period price tree just above. We start by finding the value of C^+. From this point, the call can rise to an expiration-date value of $C^{++} = \$11$ (since at this point the stock price is $S^{++} = \$121$) or fall to a final value of $C^{+-} = 0$ (since at this point the stock price is $S^{+-} = \$104.50$, which is less than the $110 exercise price). Therefore, the hedge ratio at this point is

$$H = \frac{C^{++} - C^{+-}}{S^{++} - S^{+-}} = \frac{\$11 - 0}{\$121 - \$104.50} = \frac{2}{3}$$

Thus, the following portfolio will be worth $209 at option expiration regardless of the ultimate stock price:

	$S^{+-} = \$104.50$	$S^{++} = \$121$
Buy 2 shares at price $S^+ = \$110$	$209	$242
Write 3 calls at price C^+	0	− 33
Total	$209	$209

The portfolio must have a current market value equal to the present value of $209:

$$2 \times \$110 - 3C^+ = \$209/1.05 = \$199.047$$

Solve to find that $C^+ = \$6.984$.

Next we find the value of C^-. It is easy to see that this value must be zero. If we reach this point (corresponding to a stock price of $95), the stock price at option maturity will be either $104.50 or $90.25; in both cases, the option will expire out of the money. (More formally, we could note that with $C^{+-} = C^{--} = 0$, the hedge ratio is zero, and a portfolio of *zero* shares will replicate the payoff of the call!)

Finally, we solve for C by using the values of C^+ and C^-. Concept Check 4 leads you through the calculations that show the option value to be $4.434.

Concept CHECK

4. Show that the initial value of the call option in Example 15.1 is $4.434.
   a. Confirm that the spread in option values is $C^+ - C^- = \$6.984$.
   b. Confirm that the spread in stock values is $S^+ - S^- = \$15$.
   c. Confirm that the hedge ratio is .4656 shares purchased for each call written.
   d. Demonstrate that the value in one period of a portfolio comprising .4656 shares and one call written is riskless.
   e. Calculate the present value of this payoff.
   f. Solve for the option value.

As we break the year into progressively finer subintervals, the range of possible year-end stock prices expands and, in fact, will ultimately take on a familiar bell-shaped distribution. This can be seen from an analysis of the event tree for the stock for a period with three subintervals.

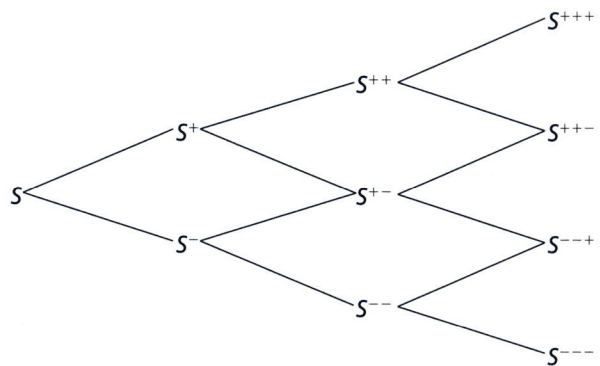

First, notice that as the number of subintervals increases, the number of possible stock prices also increases. Second, notice that extreme events such as S^{+++} or S^{---} are relatively rare, as they require either three consecutive increases or decreases in the three subintervals. More moderate, or midrange, results such as S^{++-} can be arrived at by more than one path; any combination of two price increases and one decrease will result in stock price S^{++-}. Thus, the midrange values will be more likely. The probability of each outcome is described by the binomial distribution, and this multiperiod approach to option pricing is called the **binomial model.**

For example, using our initial stock price of $100, equal probability of stock price increases or decreases, and three intervals for which the possible price increase is 5% and the decrease is 3%, we can obtain the probability distribution of stock prices from the following calculations. There are eight possible combinations for the stock price movement in the three periods: $+++, ++-, +-+, -++, +--, -+-, --+, ---$. Each has a probability of ⅛. Therefore, the probability distribution of stock prices at the end of the last interval would be as follows.

> **binomial model**
>
> An option valuation model predicated on the assumption that stock prices can move to only two values over any short time period.

Event	Probability	Stock Price	
3 up movements	⅛	$100 × 1.05³	= $115.76
2 up and 1 down	⅜	$100 × 1.05² × 0.97	= $106.94
1 up and 2 down	⅜	$100 × 1.05 × 0.97²	= $ 98.79
3 down movements	⅛	$100 × 0.97³	= $ 91.27

The midrange values are three times as likely to occur as the extreme values. Figure 15.2A is a graph of the frequency distribution for this example. The graph begins to exhibit the appearance of the familiar bell-shaped curve. In fact, as the number of intervals increases, as in Figure 15.2B, the frequency distribution progressively approaches the lognormal distribution rather than the normal distribution.[2]

Suppose we were to continue subdividing the interval in which stock prices are posited to move up or down. Eventually, each node of the event tree would correspond to an infinitesimally small time interval. The possible stock price movement within that time interval would be correspondingly small. As those many intervals passed, the end-of-period stock

---

[2]Actually, more complex considerations enter here. The limit of this process is lognormal only if we assume also that stock prices move continuously, by which we mean that over small time intervals only small price movements can occur. This rules out rare events such as sudden, extreme price moves in response to dramatic information (like a takeover attempt). For a treatment of this type of "jump process," see John C. Cox and Stephen A. Ross, "The Valuation of Options for Alternative Stochastic Processes," *Journal of Financial Economics* 3 (January–March 1976), pp. 145–66; or Robert C. Merton, "Option Pricing When Underlying Stock Returns Are Discontinuous," *Journal of Financial Economics* 3 (January–March 1976), pp. 125–44.

FIGURE 15.2
Probability distributions

A. Possible outcomes and associated probabilities for stock prices after three periods. The stock price starts at $100, and in each period it can increase by 5% or decrease by 3%.

B. Each period is subdivided into two smaller subperiods. Now there are six periods, and in each of these the stock price can increase by 2.5% or fall by 1.5%. As the number of periods increases, the stock price distribution approaches the familiar bell-shaped curve.

price would more and more closely resemble a lognormal distribution. Thus, the apparent oversimplification of the two-state model can be overcome by progressively subdividing any period into many subperiods.

At any node, one still could set up a portfolio that would be perfectly hedged over the next tiny time interval. Then, at the end of that interval, on reaching the next node, a new hedge ratio could be computed and the portfolio composition could be revised to remain hedged over the coming small interval. By continuously revising the hedge position, the portfolio would remain hedged and would earn a riskless rate of return over each interval. This is called *dynamic hedging,* the continued updating of the hedge ratio as time passes. As the dynamic hedge becomes ever finer, the resulting option valuation procedure becomes more precise.

Concept CHECK

5. **Would you expect the hedge ratio to be higher or lower when the call option is more in the money?**

15.3 BLACK-SCHOLES OPTION VALUATION

While the binomial model we have described is extremely flexible, it requires a computer to be useful in actual trading. An option-pricing *formula* would be far easier to use than the tedious algorithm involved in the binomial model. It turns out that such a formula can be derived if one is willing to make just two more assumptions: that both the risk-free interest rate and stock price volatility are constant over the life of the option.

Black-Scholes pricing formula

A formula to value an option that uses the stock price, the risk-free interest rate, the time to maturity, and the standard deviation of the stock return.

The Black-Scholes Formula

Financial economists searched for years for a workable option-pricing model before Black and Scholes (1973) and Merton (1973) derived a formula for the value of a call option. Now widely used by options market participants, the **Black-Scholes pricing formula** for a European-style call option is

$$C_0 = S_0 e^{-\delta T} N(d_1) - Xe^{-rT} N(d_2) \tag{15.1}$$

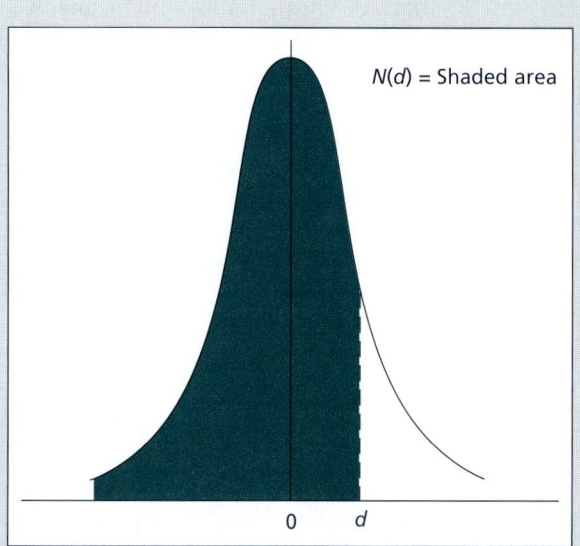

$N(d)$ = Shaded area

FIGURE **15.3**

A standard normal curve

where

$$d_1 = \frac{\ln(S_0/X) + (r - \delta + \sigma^2/2)T}{\sigma\sqrt{T}}$$

$$d_2 = d_1 - \sigma\sqrt{T}$$

and where

C_0 = Current call option value.

S_0 = Current stock price.

$N(d)$ = The probability that a random draw from a standard normal distribution will be less than d. This equals the area under the normal curve up to d, as in the shaded area of Figure 15.3.

X = Exercise price.

e = 2.71828, the base of the natural log function.

δ = Annual dividend yield of underlying stock. (We assume for simplicity that the stock pays a continuous income flow, rather than discrete periodic payments, such as quarterly dividends.)

r = Risk-free interest rate, expressed as a decimal (the annualized continuously compounded rate on a safe asset with the same maturity as the expiration date of the option, which is to be distinguished from r_f, the discrete period interest rate).

T = Time remaining until maturity of option (in years).

$\ln$ = Natural logarithm function.

σ = Standard deviation of the annualized continuously compounded rate of return of the stock, expressed as a decimal, not a percent.

The option value does not depend on the expected rate of return on the stock. In a sense, this information is already built into the formula with inclusion of the stock price, which itself depends on the stock's risk and return characteristics. This version of the Black-Scholes formula is predicated on the assumption that the underlying asset has a constant dividend (or income) yield.

Although you may find the Black-Scholes formula intimidating, we can explain it at a somewhat intuitive level. Consider a nondividend paying stock, for which $\delta = 0$. Then $S_0 e^{-\delta T} = S_0$.

The trick is to view the $N(d)$ terms (loosely) as risk-adjusted probabilities that the call option will expire in the money. First, look at Equation 15.1 assuming both $N(d)$ terms are close to 1.0; that is, when there is a very high probability that the option will be exercised. Then the call option value is equal to $S_0 - Xe^{-rT}$, which is what we called earlier the adjusted intrinsic value, $S_0 - PV(X)$. This makes sense; if exercise is certain, we have a claim on a stock with current value S_0 and an obligation with present value $PV(X)$, or with continuous compounding, Xe^{-rT}.

Now look at Equation 15.1, assuming the $N(d)$ terms are close to zero, meaning the option almost certainly will not be exercised. Then the equation confirms that the call is worth nothing. For middle-range values of $N(d)$ between 0 and 1, Equation 15.1 tells us that the call value can be viewed as the present value of the call's potential payoff adjusting for the probability of in-the-money expiration.

How do the $N(d)$ terms serve as risk-adjusted probabilities? This question quickly leads us into advanced statistics. Notice, however, that d_1 and d_2 both increase as the stock price increases. Therefore, $N(d_1)$ and $N(d_2)$ also increase with higher stock prices. This is the property we would desire of our "probabilities." For higher stock prices relative to exercise prices, future exercise is more likely.

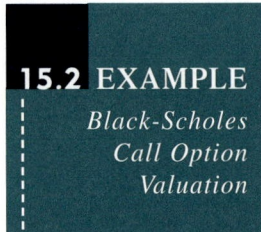

15.2 EXAMPLE

Black-Scholes
Call Option
Valuation

You can use the Black-Scholes formula fairly easily. Suppose you want to value a call option under the following circumstances:

Stock price	$S_0 = 100$
Exercise price	$X = 95$
Interest rate	$r = 0.10$
Dividend yield	$\delta = 0$
Time to expiration	$T = 0.25$ (one-quarter year)
Standard deviation	$\sigma = 0.50$

First calculate

$$d_1 = \frac{\ln(100/95) + (0.10 - 0 + 0.5^2/2)0.25}{0.5\sqrt{0.25}} = 0.43$$

$$d_2 = 0.43 - 0.5\sqrt{0.25} = 0.18$$

Next find $N(d_1)$ and $N(d_2)$. The normal distribution function is tabulated and may be found in many statistics textbooks. A table of $N(d)$ is provided on page 544 as Table 15.2. The normal distribution function $N(d)$, is also provided in any spreadsheet program. In Microsoft Excel, for example, the function name is NORMSDIST. Using either Excel or Table 15.2 (using interpolation for 0.43), we find that

$$N(0.43) = 0.6664$$

$$N(0.18) = 0.5714$$

Finally, remember that with $\delta = 0$, $S_0 e^{-\delta T} = S_0$. Thus, the value of the call option is

$$C = 100 \times 0.6664 - 95e^{-0.10 \times 0.25} \times 0.5714$$

$$= 66.64 - 52.94 = \$13.70$$

Concept
CHECK

6. Calculate the call option value if the standard deviation on the stock is 0.6 instead of 0.5. Confirm that the option is worth more using this higher volatility.

What if the option price in Example 15.2 were $15 rather than $13.70? Is the option mispriced? Maybe, but before betting your career on that, you may want to reconsider the valuation analysis. First, like all models, the Black-Scholes formula is based on some simplifying abstractions that make the formula only approximately valid.

Some of the important assumptions underlying the formula are the following:

1. The stock will pay a constant, continuous dividend yield until the option expiration date.

2. Both the interest rate, r, and variance rate, σ^2, of the stock are constant (or in slightly more general versions of the formula, both are *known* functions of time—any changes are perfectly predictable).

3. Stock prices are continuous, meaning that sudden extreme jumps, such as those in the aftermath of an announcement of a takeover attempt, are ruled out.

Variants of the Black-Scholes formula have been developed to deal with some of these limitations.

Second, even within the context of the Black-Scholes model, you must be sure of the accuracy of the parameters used in the formula. Four of these—S_0, X, T, and r—are straightforward. The stock price, exercise price, and time to maturity are readily determined. The interest rate used is the money market rate for a maturity equal to that of the option, and the dividend yield is usually reasonably stable, at least over short horizons.

The last input, though, the standard deviation of the stock return, is not directly observable. It must be estimated from historical data, from scenario analysis, or from the prices of other options, as we will describe momentarily. Because the standard deviation must be estimated, it is always possible that discrepancies between an option price and its Black-Scholes value are simply artifacts of error in the estimation of the stock's volatility.

In fact, market participants often give the option valuation problem a different twist. Rather than calculating a Black-Scholes option value for a given stock standard deviation, they ask instead: What standard deviation would be necessary for the option price that I can observe to be consistent with the Black-Scholes formula? This is called the **implied volatility** of the option, the volatility level for the stock that the option price implies. Investors can then judge

> **implied volatility**
>
> The standard deviation of stock returns that is consistent with an option's market value.

TABLE **15.2**	d	N(d)	d	N(d)	d	N(d)
Cumulative normal distribution	−3.00	0.0013	−1.58	0.0571	−0.76	0.2236
	−2.95	0.0016	−1.56	0.0594	−0.74	0.2297
	−2.90	0.0019	−1.54	0.0618	−0.72	0.2358
	−2.85	0.0022	−1.52	0.0643	−0.70	0.2420
	−2.80	0.0026	−1.50	0.0668	−0.68	0.2483
	−2.75	0.0030	−1.48	0.0694	−0.66	0.2546
	−2.70	0.0035	−1.46	0.0721	−0.64	0.2611
	−2.65	0.0040	−1.44	0.0749	−0.62	0.2676
	−2.60	0.0047	−1.42	0.0778	−0.60	0.2743
	−2.55	0.0054	−1.40	0.0808	−0.58	0.2810
	−2.50	0.0062	−1.38	0.0838	−0.56	0.2877
	−2.45	0.0071	−1.36	0.0869	−0.54	0.2946
	−2.40	0.0082	−1.34	0.0901	−0.52	0.3015
	−2.35	0.0094	−1.32	0.0934	−0.50	0.3085
	−2.30	0.0107	−1.30	0.0968	−0.48	0.3156
	−2.25	0.0122	−1.28	0.1003	−0.46	0.3228
	−2.20	0.0139	−1.26	0.1038	−0.44	0.3300
	−2.15	0.0158	−1.24	0.1075	−0.42	0.3373
	−2.10	0.0179	−1.22	0.1112	−0.40	0.3446
	−2.05	0.0202	−1.20	0.1151	−0.38	0.3520
	−2.00	0.0228	−1.18	0.1190	−0.36	0.3594
	−1.98	0.0239	−1.16	0.1230	−0.34	0.3669
	−1.96	0.0250	−1.14	0.1271	−0.32	0.3745
	−1.94	0.0262	−1.12	0.1314	−0.30	0.3821
	−1.92	0.0274	−1.10	0.1357	−0.28	0.3897
	−1.90	0.0287	−1.08	0.1401	−0.26	0.3974
	−1.88	0.0301	−1.06	0.1446	−0.24	0.4052
	−1.86	0.0314	−1.04	0.1492	−0.22	0.4129
	−1.84	0.0329	−1.02	0.1539	−0.20	0.4207
	−1.82	0.0344	−1.00	0.1587	−0.18	0.4286
	−1.80	0.0359	−0.98	0.1635	−0.16	0.4365
	−1.78	0.0375	−0.96	0.1685	−0.14	0.4443
	−1.76	0.0392	−0.94	0.1736	−0.12	0.4523
	−1.74	0.0409	−0.92	0.1788	−0.10	0.4602
	−1.72	0.0427	−0.90	0.1841	−0.08	0.4681
	−1.70	0.0446	−0.88	0.1894	−0.06	0.4761
	−1.68	0.0465	−0.86	0.1949	−0.04	0.4841
	−1.66	0.0485	−0.84	0.2005	−0.02	0.4920
	−1.64	0.0505	−0.82	0.2061	0.00	0.5000
	−1.62	0.0526	−0.80	0.2119	0.02	0.5080
	−1.60	0.0548	−0.78	0.2177	0.04	0.5160

whether they think the actual stock standard deviation exceeds the implied volatility. If it does, the option is considered a good buy; if actual volatility seems greater than the implied volatility, the option's fair price would exceed the observed price.

Another variation is to compare two options on the same stock with equal expiration dates but different exercise prices. The option with the higher implied volatility would be

TABLE **15.2** (concluded)	d	N(d)	d	N(d)	d	N(d)
	0.06	0.5239	0.86	0.8051	1.66	0.9515
	0.08	0.5319	0.88	0.8106	1.68	0.9535
	0.10	0.5398	0.90	0.8159	1.70	0.9554
	0.12	0.5478	0.92	0.8212	1.72	0.9573
	0.14	0.5557	0.94	0.8264	1.74	0.9591
	0.16	0.5636	0.96	0.8315	1.76	0.9608
	0.18	0.5714	0.98	0.8365	1.78	0.9625
	0.20	0.5793	1.00	0.8414	1.80	0.9641
	0.22	0.5871	1.02	0.8461	1.82	0.9656
	0.24	0.5948	1.04	0.8508	1.84	0.9671
	0.26	0.6026	1.06	0.8554	1.86	0.9686
	0.28	0.6103	1.08	0.8599	1.88	0.9699
	0.30	0.6179	1.10	0.8643	1.90	0.9713
	0.32	0.6255	1.12	0.8686	1.92	0.9726
	0.34	0.6331	1.14	0.8729	1.94	0.9738
	0.36	0.6406	1.16	0.8770	1.96	0.9750
	0.38	0.6480	1.18	0.8810	1.98	0.9761
	0.40	0.6554	1.20	0.8849	2.00	0.9772
	0.42	0.6628	1.22	0.8888	2.05	0.9798
	0.44	0.6700	1.24	0.8925	2.10	0.9821
	0.46	0.6773	1.26	0.8962	2.15	0.9842
	0.48	0.6844	1.28	0.8997	2.20	0.9861
	0.50	0.6915	1.30	0.9032	2.25	0.9878
	0.52	0.6985	1.32	0.9066	2.30	0.9893
	0.54	0.7054	1.34	0.9099	2.35	0.9906
	0.56	0.7123	1.36	0.9131	2.40	0.9918
	0.58	0.7191	1.38	0.9162	2.45	0.9929
	0.60	0.7258	1.40	0.9192	2.50	0.9938
	0.62	0.7324	1.42	0.9222	2.55	0.9946
	0.64	0.7389	1.44	0.9251	2.60	0.9953
	0.66	0.7454	1.46	0.9279	2.65	0.9960
	0.68	0.7518	1.48	0.9306	2.70	0.9965
	0.70	0.7580	1.50	0.9332	2.75	0.9970
	0.72	0.7642	1.52	0.9357	2.80	0.9974
	0.74	0.7704	1.54	0.9382	2.85	0.9978
	0.76	0.7764	1.56	0.9406	2.90	0.9981
	0.78	0.7823	1.58	0.9429	2.95	0.9984
	0.80	0.7882	1.60	0.9452	3.00	0.9986
	0.82	0.7939	1.62	0.9474	3.05	0.9989
	0.84	0.7996	1.64	0.9495		

considered relatively expensive because a higher standard deviation is required to justify its price. The analyst might consider buying the option with the lower implied volatility and writing the option with the higher implied volatility.

The Black-Scholes call-option valuation formula, as well as implied volatilities, are easily calculated using an Excel spreadsheet, as in Figure 15.4. The model inputs are listed in

Black-Scholes Option Pricing

Figure 15.4 captures a portion of the Excel model "B-S Option." The model is built to value puts and calls and extends the discussion to include analysis of intrinsic value and time value of options. The spreadsheet contains sensitivity analyses on several key variables in the Black-Scholes pricing model.

You can learn more about this spreadsheet model by using the interactive version available on our website at www.mhhe.com/bkm.

	A	B	C	D	E	F	G	H	I	J
1	INPUTS			OUTPUTS			FORMULA FOR OUTPUT IN COLUMN E			
2	Standard deviation (annual)	0.2783		d1	0.0029		LN(B5/B6)+(B4-B7+.5*B2^2)*B3)/(B2*SQRT(B3))			
3	Maturity (in years)	0.5		d2	-0.1939		E2-B2*SQRT(B3)			
4	Risk-free rate (annual)	0.06		N(d1)	0.5012		NORMSDIST(E2)			
5	Stock Price	100		N(d2)	0.4231		NORMSDIST(E3)			
6	Exercise price	105		B/S call value	7.0000		B5*EXP(-B7*B3)*E4 - B6*EXP(-B4*B3)*E5			
7	Dividend yield (annual)	0		B/S put value	8.8968		B6*EXP(-B4*B3)*(1-E5) - B5*EXP(-B7*B3)*(1-E4)			

FIGURE 15.4
Spreadsheet to calculate Black-Scholes call-option values

column B, and the outputs are given in column E. The formulas for d_1 and d_2 are provided in the spreadsheet, and the Excel formula NORMSDIST(d_1) is used to calculate $N(d_1)$. Cell E6 contains the Black-Scholes call option formula. To compute an implied volatility, we can use the Solver command from the Tools menu in Excel. Solver asks us to change the value of one cell to make the value of another cell (called the target cell) equal to a specific value. For example, if we observe a call option selling for $7 with other inputs as given in the spreadsheet, we can use Solver to find the value for cell B2 (the standard deviation of the stock) that will make the option value in cell E6 equal to $7. In this case, the target cell, E6, is the call price, and the spreadsheet manipulates cell B2. When you ask the spreadsheet to "Solve," it finds that a standard deviation equal to .2783 is consistent with a call price of $7; therefore, 27.83% would be the call's implied volatility if it were selling at $7.

Concept CHECK

7. Consider the call option in Example 15.2 If it sells for $15 rather than the value of $13.70 found in the example, is its implied volatility more or less than 0.5?

The Put-Call Parity Relationship

So far, we have focused on the pricing of call options. In many important cases, put prices can be derived simply from the prices of calls. This is because prices of European put and call

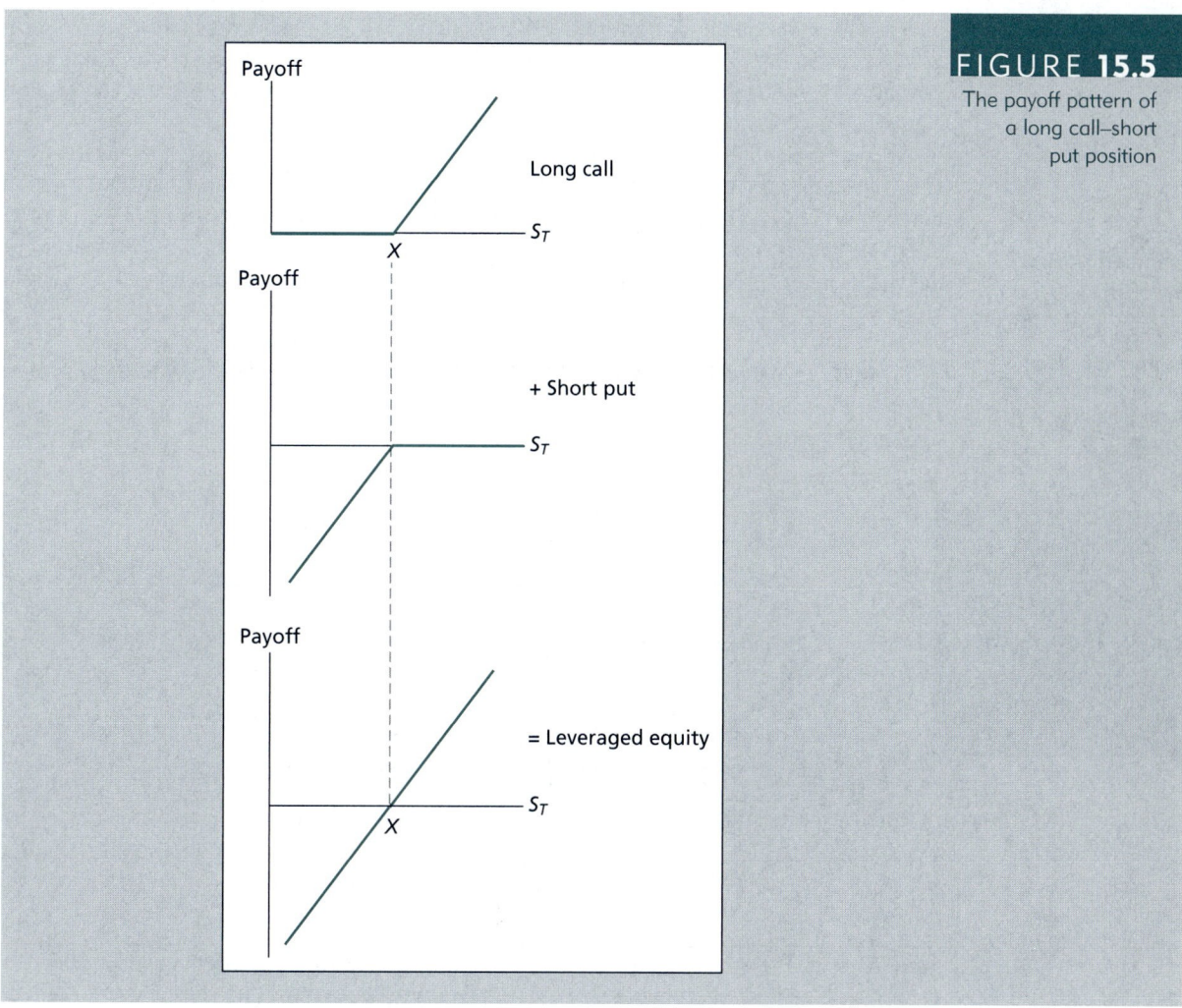

FIGURE **15.5**

The payoff pattern of
a long call–short
put position

options are linked together in an equation known as the put-call parity relationship. Therefore, once you know the value of a call, put pricing is easy.

To derive the parity relationship, suppose you buy a call option and write a put option, each with the same exercise price, X, and the same expiration date, T. At expiration, the payoff on your investment will equal the payoff to the call, minus the payoff that must be made on the put. The payoff for each option will depend on whether the ultimate stock price, S_T, exceeds the exercise price at contract expiration.

	$S_T \leq X$	$S_T > X$
Payoff of call held	0	$S_T - X$
−Payoff of put written	$-(X - S_T)$	0
Total	$S_T - X$	$S_T - X$

Figure 15.5 illustrates this payoff pattern. Compare the payoff to that of a portfolio made up of the stock plus a borrowing position, where the money to be paid back will grow, with interest, to X dollars at the maturity of the loan. Such a position is a *levered* equity position in

which $X/(1 + r_f)^T$ dollars is borrowed today (so that X will be repaid at maturity), and S_0 dollars is invested in the stock. The total payoff of the levered equity position is $S_T - X$, the same as that of the option strategy. Thus, the long call–short put position replicates the levered equity position. Again, we see that option trading provides leverage.

Because the option portfolio has a payoff identical to that of the levered equity position, the costs of establishing them must be equal. The net cash outlay necessary to establish the option position is $C - P$: The call is purchased for C, while the written put generates income of P. Likewise, the levered equity position requires a net cash outlay of $S_0 - X/(1 + r_f)^T$, the cost of the stock less the proceeds from borrowing. Equating these costs, we conclude

$$C - P = S_0 - X/(1 + r_f)^T \qquad (15.2)$$

put-call parity relationship

An equation representing the proper relationship between put and call prices.

Equation 15.2 is called the **put-call parity relationship** because it represents the proper relationship between put and call prices. If the parity relationship is ever violated, an arbitrage opportunity arises.

15.3 EXAMPLE

Put-Call Parity

Suppose you observe the following data for a certain stock.

Stock price	$110
Call price (six-month maturity, X = $105)	17
Put price (six-month maturity, X = $105)	5
Risk-free interest rate	10.25% effective annual yield (5% per 6 months)

We use these data in the put-call parity relationship to see if parity is violated.

$$C - P \overset{?}{=} S_0 - X/(1 + r_f)^T$$
$$17 - 5 \overset{?}{=} 110 - 105/1.05$$
$$12 \overset{?}{=} \qquad 10$$

This result, a violation of parity (12 does not equal 10) indicates mispricing and leads to an arbitrage opportunity. You can buy the relatively cheap portfolio (the stock plus borrowing position represented on the right-hand side of the equation) and sell the relatively expensive portfolio (the long call–short put position corresponding to the left-hand side, that is, write a call and buy a put).

Let's examine the payoff to this strategy. In six months, the stock will be worth S_T. The $100 borrowed will be paid back with interest, resulting in a cash outflow of $105. The written call will result in a cash outflow of $S_T - \$105$ if S_T exceeds $105. The purchased put pays off $\$105 - S_T$ if the stock price is below $105.

Table 15.3 summarizes the outcome. The immediate cash inflow is $2. In six months, the various positions provide exactly offsetting cash flows: The $2 inflow is realized risklessly without any offsetting outflows. This is an arbitrage opportunity that investors will pursue on a large scale until buying and selling pressure restores the parity condition expressed in Equation 15.2.

Equation 15.2 actually applies only to options on stocks that pay no dividends before the maturity date of the option. It also applies only to European options, as the cash flow streams from the two portfolios represented by the two sides of Equation 15.2 will match only if each position is held until maturity. If a call and a put may be optimally exercised at different times

TABLE **15.3**			Cash Flow in Six Months	
Arbitrage strategy	Position	Immediate Cash Flow	$S_T < 105$	$S_T \geq 105$
	Buy stock	-110	S_T	S_T
	Borrow $X/(1 + r_f)^T = \$100$	$+100$	-105	-105
	Sell call	$+17$	0	$-(S_T - 105)$
	Buy put	-5	$105 - S_T$	0
	Total	2	0	0

before their common expiration date, then the equality of payoffs cannot be assured, or even expected, and the portfolios will have different values.

The extension of the parity condition for European call options on dividend-paying stocks is, however, straightforward. Problem 22 at the end of the chapter leads you through the extension of the parity relationship. The more general formulation of the put-call parity condition is

$$P = C - S_0 + \text{PV}(X) + \text{PV(dividends)} \tag{15.3}$$

where PV(dividends) is the present value of the dividends that will be paid by the stock during the life of the option. If the stock does not pay dividends, Equation 15.3 becomes identical to Equation 15.2.

Notice that this generalization would apply as well to European options on assets other than stocks. Instead of using dividend income in Equation 15.3, we would let any income paid out by the underlying asset play the role of the stock dividends. For example, European put and call options on bonds would satisfy the same parity relationship, except that the bond's coupon income would replace the stock's dividend payments in the parity formula.

Let's see how well parity works using real data on the Microsoft options in Figure 14.1 from the previous chapter. The April maturity call with exercise price $70 and time to expiration of 105 days cost $4.60 while the corresponding put option cost $5.40. Microsoft was selling for $68.90, and the annualized 105-day interest rate on this date was 1.6%. Microsoft was paying no dividends at this time. According to parity, we should find that

$$P = C + \text{PV}(X) - S_0 + \text{PV(dividends)}$$

$$5.40 = 4.60 + \frac{70}{(1.016)^{105/365}} - 68.90 + 0$$

$$5.40 = 4.60 + 69.68 - 68.90$$

$$5.40 = 5.38$$

So, parity is violated by about $0.02 per share. Is this a big enough difference to exploit? Probably not. You have to weigh the potential profit against the trading costs of the call, put, and stock. More important, given the fact that options trade relatively infrequently, this deviation from parity might not be "real" but may instead be attributable to "stale" (i.e., out-of-date) price quotes at which you cannot actually trade.

Put Option Valuation

As we saw in Equation 15.3, we can use the put-call parity relationship to value put options once we know the call option value. Sometimes, however, it is easier to work with a put option valuation formula directly. The Black-Scholes formula for the value of a European put option is[3]

$$P = Xe^{-rT}[1 - N(d_2)] - S_0e^{-\delta T}[1 - N(d_1)] \qquad (15.4)$$

15.4 EXAMPLE

Black-Scholes Put Option Valuation

Using data from the Black-Scholes call option in Example 15.2 we find that a European put option on that stock with identical exercise price and time to maturity is worth

$$\$95e^{-.10 \times .25}(1 - .5714) - \$100(1 - .6664) = \$6.35$$

Notice that this value is consistent with put-call parity:

$$P = C + PV(X) - S_0 = 13.70 + 95e^{-.10 \times .25} - 100 = 6.35$$

As we noted traders can do, we might then compare this formula value to the actual put price as one step in formulating a trading strategy.

Equation 15.4 is valid for European puts. Listed put options are American options that offer the opportunity of early exercise, however. Because an American option allows its owner to exercise at any time before the expiration date, it must be worth at least as much as the corresponding European option. However, while Equation 15.4 describes only the lower bound on the true value of the American put, in many applications the approximation is very accurate.

15.4 USING THE BLACK-SCHOLES FORMULA

Hedge Ratios and the Black-Scholes Formula

In the last chapter, we considered two investments in Microsoft: 100 shares of Microsoft stock or 700 call options on Microsoft. We saw that the call option position was more sensitive to swings in Microsoft's stock price than the all-stock position. To analyze the overall exposure to a stock price more precisely, however, it is necessary to quantify these relative sensitivities. A tool that enables us to summarize the overall exposure of portfolios of options with various exercise prices and times to maturity is the hedge ratio. An option's **hedge ratio** is the change in the price of an option for a $1 increase in the stock price. A call option, therefore, has a positive hedge ratio, and a put option has a negative hedge ratio. The hedge ratio is commonly called the option's **delta.**

hedge ratio or delta

The number of shares of stock required to hedge the price risk of holding one option.

If you were to graph the option value as a function of the stock value as we have done for a call option in Figure 15.6, the hedge ratio is simply the slope of the value function evaluated at the current stock price. For example, suppose the slope of the curve at $S_0 = \$120$ equals 0.60. As the stock increases in value by $1, the option increases by approximately $0.60, as the figure shows.

For every call option written, 0.60 shares of stock would be needed to hedge the investor's portfolio. For example, if one writes 10 options and holds six shares of stock, according to the hedge ratio of 0.6, a $1 increase in stock price will result in a gain of $6 on the stock holdings,

---

[3]This formula is consistent with the put-call parity relationship, and in fact can be derived from it. If you want to try to do so, remember to take present values using continuous compounding, and note that when a stock pays a continuous flow of income in the form of a constant dividend yield, δ, the present value of that dividend flow is $S_0(1 - e^{-\delta T})$. (Notice that $e^{-\delta T}$ approximately equals $1 - \delta T$, so the value of the dividend flow is approximately $\delta T S_0$.)

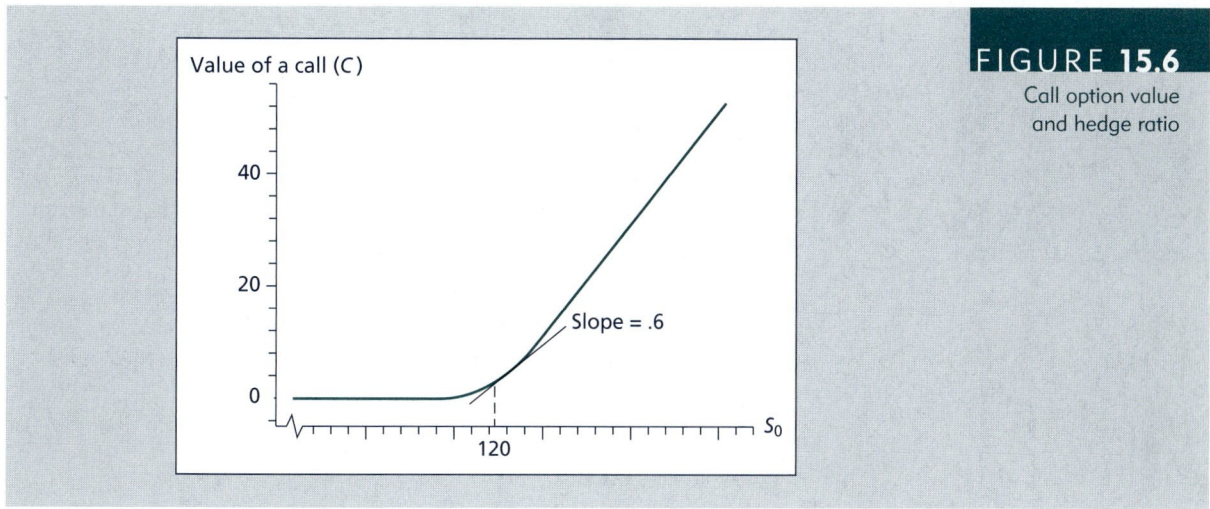

FIGURE **15.6**

Call option value
and hedge ratio

while the loss on the 10 options written will be 10 × $0.60, an equivalent $6. The stock price movement leaves total wealth unaltered, which is what a hedged position is intended to do. The investor holding both the stock and options in proportions dictated by their relative price movements hedges the portfolio.

Black-Scholes hedge ratios are particularly easy to compute. The hedge ratio for a call is $N(d_1)$, while the hedge ratio for a put is $N(d_1) - 1$. We defined $N(d_1)$ as part of the Black-Scholes formula in Equation 15.1. Recall that $N(d)$ stands for the area under the standard normal curve up to d. Therefore, the call option hedge ratio must be positive and less than 1.0, while the put option hedge ratio is negative and of smaller absolute value than 1.0.

Figure 15.6 verifies the insight that the slope of the call option valuation function is less than 1.0, approaching 1.0 only as the stock price becomes extremely large. This tells us that option values change less than one-for-one with changes in stock prices. Why should this be? Suppose an option is so far in the money that you are absolutely certain it will be exercised. In that case, every $1 increase in the stock price would increase the option value by $1. But if there is a reasonable chance the call option will expire out of the money, even after a moderate stock price gain, a $1 increase in the stock price will not necessarily increase the ultimate payoff to the call; therefore, the call price will not respond by a full $1.

The fact that hedge ratios are less than 1.0 does not contradict our earlier observation that options offer leverage and are sensitive to stock price movements. Although *dollar* movements in option prices are slighter than dollar movements in the stock price, the *rate of return* volatility of options remains greater than stock return volatility because options sell at lower prices. In our example, with the stock selling at $120, and a hedge ratio of 0.6, an option with exercise price $120 may sell for $5. If the stock price increases to $121, the call price would be expected to increase by only $0.60, to $5.60. The percentage increase in the option value is $0.60/$5.00 = 12%, however, while the stock price increase is only $1/$120 = 0.83%. The ratio of the percent changes is 12%/0.83% = 14.4. For every 1% increase in the stock price, the option price increases by 14.4%. This ratio, the percent change in option price per percent change in stock price, is called the **option elasticity.**

The hedge ratio is an essential tool in portfolio management and control. An example will show why.

option elasticity

The percentage
increase in an
option's value
given a 1% increase
in the value of the
underlying security.

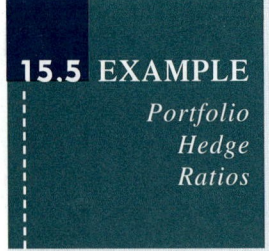

15.5 EXAMPLE

Portfolio
Hedge
Ratios

Consider two portfolios, one holding 750 IBM calls and 200 shares of IBM and the other holding 800 shares of IBM. Which portfolio has greater dollar exposure to IBM price movements? You can answer this question easily using the hedge ratio.

Each option changes in value by H dollars for each dollar change in stock price, where H stands for the hedge ratio. Thus, if H equals 0.6, the 750 options are equivalent to 450 ($= 0.6 \times 750$) shares in terms of the response of their market value to IBM stock price movements. The first portfolio has less dollar sensitivity to stock price change because the 450 share-equivalents of the options plus the 200 shares actually held are less than the 800 shares held in the second portfolio.

This is not to say, however, that the first portfolio is less sensitive to the stock's rate of return. As we noted in discussing option elasticities, the first portfolio may be of lower total value than the second, so despite its lower sensitivity in terms of total market value, it might have greater rate of return sensitivity. Because a call option has a lower market value than the stock, its price changes more than proportionally with stock price changes, even though its hedge ratio is less than 1.0.

Concept
CHECK

> 8. What is the elasticity of a put option currently selling for $4 with exercise price $120, and hedge ratio -0.4 if the stock price is currently $122?

Portfolio Insurance

In Chapter 14, we showed that protective put strategies offer a sort of insurance policy on an asset. The protective put has proven to be extremely popular with investors. Even if the asset price falls, the put conveys the right to sell the asset for the exercise price, which is a way to lock in a minimum portfolio value. With an at-the-money put ($X = S_0$), the maximum loss that can be realized is the cost of the put. The asset can be sold for X, which equals its original price, so even if the asset price falls, the investor's net loss over the period is just the cost of the put. If the asset value increases, however, upside potential is unlimited. Figure 15.7 graphs the profit or loss on a protective put position as a function of the change in the value of the underlying asset.

**portfolio
insurance**

**Portfolio
strategies that limit
investment losses
while maintaining
upside potential.**

While the protective put is a simple and convenient way to achieve **portfolio insurance,** that is, to limit the worst-case portfolio rate of return, there are practical difficulties in trying to insure a portfolio of stocks. First, unless the investor's portfolio corresponds to a standard market index for which puts are traded, a put option on the portfolio will not be available for purchase. And if index puts are used to protect a nonindexed portfolio, tracking error can result. For example, if the portfolio falls in value while the market index rises, the put will fail to provide the intended protection. Tracking error limits the investor's freedom to pursue active stock selection because such error will be greater as the managed portfolio departs more substantially from the market index.

Moreover, the desired horizon of the insurance program must match the maturity of a traded put option in order to establish the appropriate protective put position. Today, long-term index options called LEAPS (for Long-Term Equity AnticiPation Securities) trade on the Chicago Board Options Exchange with maturities of several years. However, in the mid-1980s, while most investors pursuing insurance programs had horizons of several years, actively traded puts were limited to maturities of less than a year. Rolling over a sequence of short-term puts, which might be viewed as a response to this problem, introduces new risks because the prices at which successive puts will be available in the future are not known today.

Providers of portfolio insurance with horizons of several years, therefore, cannot rely on the simple expedient of purchasing protective puts for their clients' portfolios. Instead, they follow trading strategies that replicate the payoffs to the protective put position.

FIGURE **15.7**

Profit on a
protective
put strategy

Here is the general idea. Even if a put option on the desired portfolio with the desired ex-piration date does not exist, a theoretical option-pricing model (such as the Black-Scholes model) can be used to determine how that option's price *would* respond to the portfolio's value if the option did trade. For example, if stock prices were to fall, the put option would increase in value. The option model could quantify this relationship. The net exposure of the (hypo-thetical) protective put portfolio to swings in stock prices is the sum of the exposures of the two components of the portfolio: the stock and the put. The net exposure of the portfolio equals the equity exposure less the (offsetting) put option exposure.

We can create "synthetic" protective put positions by holding a quantity of stocks with the same net exposure to market swings as the hypothetical protective put position. The key to this strategy is the option delta, or hedge ratio, that is, the change in the price of the protective put option per change in the value of the underlying stock portfolio.

Suppose a portfolio is currently valued at $100 million. An at-the-money put option on the portfolio might have a hedge ratio or delta of −0.6, meaning the option's value swings $0.60 for every dollar change in portfolio value, but in an opposite direction. Suppose the stock port-folio falls in value by 2%. The profit on a hypothetical protective put position (if the put existed) would be as follows (in millions of dollars):

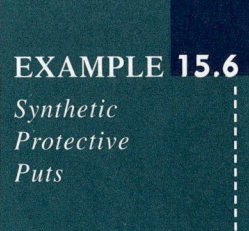

EXAMPLE **15.6**

*Synthetic
Protective
Puts*

Loss on stocks	2% of $100 =	$2.00
+Gain on put:	0.6 × $2.00 =	1.20
Net loss		$0.80

We create the synthetic option position by selling a proportion of shares equal to the put option's delta (i.e., selling 60% of the shares) and placing the proceeds in risk-free T-bills. The rationale is that the hypothetical put option would have offset 60% of any change in the stock portfolio's value, so one must reduce portfolio risk directly by selling 60% of the equity and putting the proceeds into a risk-free asset. Total return on a synthetic protective put position with $60 million in risk-free investments such as T-bills and $40 million in equity is

Loss on stocks:	2% of $40 =	$0.80
+Loss on bills:		0
Net loss		= $0.80

The synthetic and actual protective put positions have equal returns. We conclude that if you sell a proportion of shares equal to the put option's delta and place the proceeds in cash equivalents, your exposure to the stock market will equal that of the desired protective put position.

FIGURE 15.8

Hedge ratios change as the stock price fluctuates

The difficulty with synthetic positions is that deltas constantly change. Figure 15.8 shows that as the stock price falls, the absolute value of the appropriate hedge ratio increases. Therefore, market declines require extra hedging, that is, additional conversion of equity into cash. This constant updating of the hedge ratio is called **dynamic hedging,** as discussed in Section 15.2. Another term for such hedging is *delta hedging,* because the option delta is used to determine the number of shares that need to be bought or sold.

dynamic hedging

Constant updating of hedge positions as market conditions change.

Dynamic hedging is one reason portfolio insurance has been said to contribute to market volatility. Market declines trigger additional sales of stock as portfolio insurers strive to increase their hedging. These additional sales are seen as reinforcing or exaggerating market downturns.

In practice, portfolio insurers do not actually buy or sell stocks directly when they update their hedge positions. Instead, they minimize trading costs by buying or selling stock index futures as a substitute for sale of the stocks themselves. As you will see in the next chapter, stock prices and index future prices usually are very tightly linked by cross-market arbitrageurs so that futures transactions can be used as reliable proxies for stock transactions. Instead of

Delta-Hedging for Portfolio Insurance

Portfolio insurance, the high-tech hedging strategy that helped grease the slide in the 1987 stock market crash, is alive and well.

And just as in 1987, it doesn't always work out as planned, as some financial institutions found out in the recent European bond market turmoil.

Banks, securities firms, and other big traders rely heavily on portfolio insurance to contain their potential losses when they buy and sell options. But since portfolio insurance got a bad name after it backfired on investors in 1987, it goes by an alias these days—the sexier, Star Trek moniker of "delta-hedging."

Whatever you call it, the recent turmoil in European bond markets taught some practitioners—including banks and securities firms that were hedging options sales to hedge funds and other investors—the same painful lessons of earlier portfolio insurers: Delta-hedging can break down in volatile markets, just when it is needed most.

How you delta-hedge depends on the bets you're trying to hedge. For instance, delta-hedging would prompt options sellers to sell into falling markets and buy into rallies. It would give the opposite directions to options buyers, such as dealers who might hold big options inventories.

In theory, delta-hedging takes place with computer-timed precision, and there aren't any snags. But in real life, it doesn't always work so smoothly. "When volatility ends up being much greater than anticipated, you can't get your delta trades off at the right points," says an executive at one big derivatives dealer.

How does this happen? Take the relatively simple case of dealers who sell "call" options on long-term Treasury bonds. Such options give buyers the right to buy bonds at a fixed price over a specific time period. And compared with buying bonds outright, these options are much more sensitive to market moves.

Because selling the calls made those dealers vulnerable to a rally, they delta-hedged by buying bonds. As bond prices turned south [and option deltas fell], the dealers shed their hedges by selling bonds, adding to the selling orgy. The plunging markets forced them to sell at lower prices than expected, causing unexpected losses on their hedges.

Source: Abridged from Barbara Donnelly Granito, "Delta-Hedging: The New Name in Portfolio Insurance," *The Wall Street Journal*, March 17, 1994, p. C1. Reprinted by permission of Dow Jones & Company, Inc. via Copyright Clearance Center, Inc., © 1994 Dow Jones & Company, Inc. All Rights Reserved Worldwide.

---

selling equities based on the put option's delta, insurers will sell an equivalent number of futures contracts.[4]

Several portfolio insurers suffered great setbacks during the market "crash" of October 19, 1987, when the Dow Jones Industrial Average fell more than 20%. A description of what happened then should help you appreciate the complexities of applying a seemingly straightforward hedging concept.

1. Market volatility at the crash was much greater than ever encountered before. Put option deltas computed from historical experience were too low; insurers underhedged, held too much equity, and suffered excessive losses.

2. Prices moved so fast that insurers could not keep up with the necessary rebalancing. They were "chasing deltas" that kept getting away from them. The futures market saw a "gap" opening, where the opening price was nearly 10% below the previous day's close. The price dropped before insurers could update their hedge ratios.

3. Execution problems were severe. First, current market prices were unavailable, with trade execution and the price quotation system hours behind, which made computation of correct hedge ratios impossible. Moreover, trading in stocks and stock futures ceased during some periods. The continuous rebalancing capability that is essential for a viable insurance program vanished during the precipitous market collapse.

---

[4]Notice, however, that the use of index futures reintroduces the problem of tracking error between the portfolio and the market index.

4. Futures prices traded at steep discounts to their proper levels compared to reported stock prices, thereby making the sale of futures (as a proxy for equity sales) to increase hedging seem expensive. While you will see in the next chapter that stock index futures prices normally exceed the value of the stock index, Figure 15.9 shows that on October 19, futures sold far below the stock index level. When some insurers gambled that the futures price would recover to its usual premium over the stock index and chose to defer sales, they remained underhedged. As the market fell farther, their portfolios experienced substantial losses.

While most observers believe that the portfolio insurance industry will never recover from the market crash, the nearby box points out that delta hedging is still alive and well on Wall Street. Dynamic hedges are widely used by large firms to hedge potential losses from the options they write. The article also points out, however, that these traders are increasingly aware of the practical difficulties in implementing dynamic hedges in very volatile markets.

15.5 | EMPIRICAL EVIDENCE

There have been an enormous number of empirical tests of the Black-Scholes option-pricing model. For the most part, the results of the studies have been positive in that the Black-Scholes model generates option values quite close to the actual prices at which options trade. At the same time, some smaller, but regular empirical failures of the model have been noted. For example, Geske and Roll (1984) have argued that these empirical results can be attributed to the failure of the Black-Scholes model to account for the possible early exercise of American calls on stocks that pay dividends. They show that the theoretical bias induced by this failure corresponds closely to the actual "mispricing" observed empirically.

Whaley (1982) examines the performance of the Black-Scholes formula relative to that of more complicated option formulas that allow for early exercise. His findings indicate that formulas that allow for the possibility of early exercise do better at pricing than the Black-Scholes formula. The Black-Scholes formula seems to perform worst for options on stocks with high dividend payouts. The true American call option formula, on the other hand, seems to fare equally well in the prediction of option prices on stocks with high or low dividend payouts.

FIGURE 15.9

S&P 500 cash-to-futures spread in points at 15-minute intervals

Source: From *The Wall Street Journal.* Reprinted by permission of Dow Jones & Company, Inc. via Copyright Clearance Center, Inc. © 1987 Dow Jones & Company, Inc. All Rights Reserved Worldwide.

NOTE: Trading in futures contracts halted between 12:15 and 1:05.

Rubinstein (1994) points out that the performance of the Black-Scholes model has deteriorated in recent years in the sense that options on the same stock with the same expiration date, which *should* have the same implied volatility, actually exhibit progressively different implied volatilities as strike prices vary. He attributes this to an increasing fear of another market crash like that experienced in 1987, and he notes that, consistent with this hypothesis, out-of-the-money put options are priced higher (that is, with higher implied volatilities) than other puts.

SUMMARY

- Option values may be viewed as the sum of intrinsic value plus time or "volatility" value. The volatility value is the right to choose not to exercise if the stock price moves against the holder. Thus, option holders cannot lose more than the cost of the option regardless of stock price performance.
- Call options are more valuable when the exercise price is lower, when the stock price is higher, when the interest rate is higher, when the time to maturity is greater, when the stock's volatility is greater, and when dividends are lower.
- Options may be priced relative to the underlying stock price using a simple two-period, two-state pricing model. As the number of periods increases, the model can approximate more realistic stock price distributions. The Black-Scholes formula may be seen as a limiting case of the binomial option model, as the holding period is divided into progressively smaller subperiods.
- The put-call parity theorem relates the prices of put and call options. If the relationship is violated, arbitrage opportunities will result. Specifically, the relationship that must be satisfied is

$$P = C - S_0 + \text{PV}(X) + \text{PV(dividends)}$$

  where X is the exercise price of both the call and the put options, and $\text{PV}(X)$ is the present value of the claim to X dollars to be paid at the expiration date of the options.
- The hedge ratio is the number of shares of stock required to hedge the price risk involved in writing one option. Hedge ratios are near zero for deep out-of-the-money call options and approach 1.0 for deep in-the-money calls.
- Although hedge ratios are less than 1.0, call options have elasticities greater than 1.0. The rate of return on a call (as opposed to the dollar return) responds more than one-for-one with stock price movements.
- Portfolio insurance can be obtained by purchasing a protective put option on an equity position. When the appropriate put is not traded, portfolio insurance entails a dynamic hedge strategy where a fraction of the equity portfolio equal to the desired put option's delta is sold, with proceeds placed in risk-free securities.

KEY TERMS

binomial model, 539	dynamic hedging, 554	option elasticity, 551
Black-Scholes pricing	hedge ratio, 550	portfolio insurance, 552
formula, 540	implied volatility, 543	put-call parity
delta, 550	intrinsic value, 532	relationship, 548

www.mhhe.com/bkm

PROBLEM SETS

1. We showed in the text that the value of a call option increases with the volatility of the stock. Is this also true of put option values? Use the put-call parity relationship as well as a numerical example to prove your answer.

2. In each of the following questions, you are asked to compare two options with parameters as given. The risk-free interest rate for *all* cases should be assumed to be 6%. Assume the stocks on which these options are written pay no dividends.

a.

Put	T	X	σ	Price of Option
A	0.5	50	0.20	10
B	0.5	50	0.25	10

Which put option is written on the stock with the lower price?
(1) A
(2) B
(3) Not enough information

b.

Put	T	X	σ	Price of Option
A	0.5	50	0.2	10
B	0.5	50	0.2	12

Which put option must be written on the stock with the lower price?
(1) A
(2) B
(3) Not enough information

c.

Call	S	X	σ	Price of Option
A	50	50	0.20	12
B	55	50	0.20	10

Which call option must have the lower time to maturity?
(1) A
(2) B
(3) Not enough information

d.

Call	T	X	S	Price of Option
A	0.5	50	55	10
B	0.5	50	55	12

Which call option is written on the stock with higher volatility?
(1) A
(2) B
(3) Not enough information

e.

Call	T	X	S	Price of Option
A	0.5	50	55	10
B	0.5	55	55	7

Which call option is written on the stock with higher volatility?

(1) A

(2) B

(3) Not enough information

3. Reconsider the determination of the hedge ratio in the two-state model, where we showed that one-half share of stock would hedge one option. What is the hedge ratio at each of the following exercise prices: $115, $100, $75, $50, $25, and $10? What do you conclude about the hedge ratio as the option becomes progressively more in the money?

4. Show that Black-Scholes call option hedge ratios also increase as the stock price increases. Consider a one-year option with exercise price $50 on a stock with annual standard deviation 20%. The T-bill rate is 8% per year. Find $N(d_1)$ for stock prices $45, $50, and $55.

5. We will derive a two-state put option value in this problem. Data: $S_0 = 100$; $X = 110$; $1 + r = 1.1$. The two possibilities for S_T are 130 and 80.

a. Show that the range of S is 50 while that of P is 30 across the two states. What is the hedge ratio of the put?

b. Form a portfolio of three shares of stock and five puts. What is the (nonrandom) payoff to this portfolio? What is the present value of the portfolio?

c. Given that the stock currently is selling at 100, show that the value of the put must be 10.91.

6. Calculate the value of a *call* option on the stock in problem 5 with an exercise price of 110. Verify that the put-call parity relationship is satisfied by your answers to problems 5 and 6. (Do not use continuous compounding to calculate the present value of X in this example, because the interest rate is quoted as an effective annual yield.)

7. Use the Black-Scholes formula to find the value of a call option on the following stock:

Time to maturity   = 6 months

Standard deviation = 50% per year

Exercise price   = $50

Stock price   = $50

Interest rate   = 10%

8. Find the Black-Scholes value of a put option on the stock in the previous problem with the same exercise price and maturity as the call option.

9. What would be the Excel formula in Figure 15.4 for the Black-Scholes value of a straddle position?

10. Recalculate the value of the option in problem 7, successively substituting one of the changes below while keeping the other parameters as in problem 7:

a. Time to maturity = 3 months

b. Standard deviation = 25% per year

c. Exercise price = $55

d. Stock price = $55

e. Interest rate = 15%

www.mhhe.com/bkm

Consider each scenario independently. Confirm that the option value changes in accordance with the prediction of Table 15.1.

11. Would you expect a $1 increase in a call option's exercise price to lead to a decrease in the option's value of more or less than $1?

12. All else being equal, is a put option on a high beta stock worth more than one on a low beta stock? The firms have identical firm-specific risk.

13. All else being equal, is a call option on a stock with a lot of firm-specific risk worth more than one on a stock with little firm-specific risk? The betas of the stocks are equal.

14. All else being equal, will a call option with a high exercise price have a higher or lower hedge ratio than one with a low exercise price?

15. Should the rate of return of a call option on a long-term Treasury bond be more or less sensitive to changes in interest rates than the rate of return of the underlying bond?

16. If the stock price falls and the call price rises, then what has happened to the call option's implied volatility?

17. If the time to maturity falls and the put price rises, then what has happened to the put option's implied volatility?

18. According to the Black-Scholes formula, what will be the value of the hedge ratio of a call option as the stock price becomes infinitely large? Explain briefly.

19. According to the Black-Scholes formula, what will be the value of the hedge ratio of a put option for a very small exercise price?

20. The hedge ratio of an at-the-money call option on IBM is 0.4. The hedge ratio of an at-the-money put option is -0.6. What is the hedge ratio of an at-the-money straddle position on IBM?

21. These three put options all are written on the same stock. One has a delta of -0.9, one a delta of -0.5, and one a delta of -0.1. Assign deltas to the three puts by filling in the table below.

Put	X	Delta
A	10	
B	20	
C	30	

22. In this problem, we derive the put-call parity relationship for European options on stocks that pay dividends before option expiration. For simplicity, assume that the stock makes one dividend payment of $D per share at the expiration date of the option.
    a. What is the value of the stock-plus-put position on the expiration date of the option?
    b. Now consider a portfolio comprising a call option and a zero-coupon bond with the same maturity date as the option and with face value $(X + D)$. What is the value of this portfolio on the option expiration date? You should find that its value equals that of the stock-plus-put portfolio, regardless of the stock price.
    c. What is the cost of establishing the two portfolios in parts (a) and (b)? Equate the cost of these portfolios, and you will derive the put-call parity relationship, Equation 15.3.

23. A collar is established by buying a share of stock for $50, buying a six-month put option with exercise price $45, and writing a six-month call option with exercise price $55. Based on the volatility of the stock, you calculate that for an exercise price of $45 and maturity of six months, $N(d_1) = .60$, whereas for the exercise price of $55, $N(d_1) = .35$.

a. What will be the gain or loss on the collar if the stock price increases by $1?

b. What happens to the delta of the portfolio if the stock price becomes very large? Very small?

24. You are *very* bullish (optimistic) on stock EFG, much more so than the rest of the market. In each question, choose the portfolio strategy that will give you the biggest dollar profit if your bullish forecast turns out to be correct. Explain your answer.

  a. *Choice A:* $100,000 invested in calls with $X = 50$.

  Choice B: $100,000 invested in EFG stock.

  b. *Choice A:* 10 call options contracts (for 100 shares each), with $X = 50$.

  Choice B: 1,000 shares of EFG stock.

25. Imagine you are a provider of portfolio insurance. You are establishing a four-year program. The portfolio you manage is currently worth $100 million, and you promise to provide a minimum return of 0%. The equity portfolio has a standard deviation of 25% per year, and T-bills pay 5% per year. Assume for simplicity that the portfolio pays no dividends (or that all dividends are reinvested).

  a. What fraction of the portfolio should be placed in bills? What fraction in equity?

  b. What should the manager do if the stock portfolio falls by 3% on the first day of trading?

26. You would like to be holding a protective put position on the stock of XYZ Co. to lock in a guaranteed minimum value of $100 at year-end. XYZ currently sells for $100. Over the next year, the stock price will either increase by 10% or decrease by 10%. The T-bill rate is 5%. Unfortunately, no put options are traded on XYZ Co.

  a. Suppose the desired put option were traded. How much would it cost to purchase?

  b. What would have been the cost of the protective put portfolio?

  c. What portfolio position in stock and T-bills will ensure you a payoff equal to the payoff that would be provided by a protective put with $X = \$100$? Show that the payoff to this portfolio and the cost of establishing the portfolio matches that of the desired protective put.

27. You are attempting to value a call option with an exercise price of $100 and one year to expiration. The underlying stock pays no dividends, its current price is $100, and you believe it has a 50% chance of increasing to $120 and a 50% chance of decreasing to $80. The risk-free rate of interest is 10%. Calculate the call option's value using the two-state stock price model.

28. Consider an increase in the volatility of the stock in problem 27. Suppose that if the stock increases in price, it will increase to $130, and that if it falls, it will fall to $70. Show that the value of the call option is now higher than the value derived in problem 27.

29. Return to Example 15.1. Use the binomial model to value a one-year European put option with exercise price $110 on the stock in that example. Does your solution for the put price satisfy put-call parity?

WEBMASTER

Option Value and Greeks

Go to http://www.thegumpinvestor.com/options/home.asp. This site offers extensive information on options. From the quote tab, find the option quotes for both puts and calls for Dell Computer (DELL). Select the item that shows options within nine months to expiration with strike prices that are close to the underlying stock price (near the money). After examining the data, answer the following questions.

1. Does the Black-Scholes model predict the option prices perfectly?

2. What is the largest error noted in your screen?

3. What do the delta and theta of an option indicate?

4. Are the estimates of implied volatility similar for all of the options?

SOLUTIONS TO

1. Yes. Consider the same scenarios as for the call.

Stock price	$10	$20	$30	$40	$50
Put payoff	20	10	0	0	0
Stock price	20	25	30	35	40
Put payoff	10	5	0	0	0

The low volatility scenario yields a lower expected payoff.

2.

If This Variable Increases	. . .	The Value of a Put Option
S		Decreases
X		Increases
σ		Increases
T		Increases/Uncertain*
r_f		Decreases
Dividend payouts		Increases

*For American puts, increase in time to expiration must increase value. One can always choose to exercise early if this is optimal; the longer expiration date simply expands the range of alternatives open to the option holder, thereby making the option more valuable. For a European put, where early exercise is not allowed, longer time to expiration can have an indeterminate effect. Longer maturity increases volatility value since the final stock price is more uncertain, but it reduces the present value of the exercise price that will be received if the put is exercised. The net effect on put value is ambiguous.

3. Because the option now is underpriced, we want to reverse our previous strategy.

	Initial Cash Flow	Cash Flow in 1 Year for Each Possible Stock Price	
		S = $50	S = $200
Buy 2 options	$− 48	$ 0	$ 150
Short-sell 1 share	100	− 50	− 200
Lend $52 at 8% interest rate	− 52	56.16	56.16
Total	$ 0	$ 6.16	$ 6.16

4. *a.* $C^+ - C^- = \$6.984 - 0 = \$6.984$
  b. $S^+ - S^- = \$110 - \$95 = \$15$
  c. $6.984/15 = .4656$

d.

Action Today (time 0)	Value in Next Period as Function of Stock Price	
	$S^+ = \$95$	$S^- = \$110$
Buy .4656 shares at price $S = \$100$	$44.232	$51.216
Write 1 call at price C	0	−6.984
Total	$44.232	$44.232

The portfolio must have a market value equal to the present value of $44.232.
  e. $\$44.232/1.05 = \$42.126$
  f. $.4656 \times \$100 - C = \$42.126$
    $C = \$46.56 - \$42.126 = \$4.434$

5. Higher. For deep out-of-the-money options, an increase in the stock price still leaves the option unlikely to be exercised. Its value increases only fractionally. For deep in-the-money options, exercise is likely, and option holders benefit by a full dollar for each dollar increase in the stock, as though they already own the stock.

6. Because $\sigma = 0.6$, $\sigma^2 = 0.36$.

$$d_1 = \frac{\ln(100/95) + (0.10 + 0.36/2)0.25}{0.6\sqrt{0.25}} = 0.4043$$

$$d_2 = d_1 - 0.6\sqrt{0.25} = 0.1043$$

Using Table 15.2 and interpolation, or a spreadsheet function,

$$N(d_1) = 0.6570$$

$$N(d_2) = 0.5415$$

$$C = 100 \times 0.6570 - 95e^{-0.10 \times 0.25} \times 0.5415 = 15.53$$

7. Implied volatility exceeds 0.5. Given a standard deviation of 0.5, the option value is $13.70. A higher volatility is needed to justify the actual $15 price.

8. A $1 increase in stock price is a percentage increase of $1/122 = 0.82\%$. The put option will fall by $(0.4 \times \$1) = \$0.40$, a percentage decrease of $\$0.40/\$4 = 10\%$. Elasticity is $-10/0.82 = -12.2$.

16

FUTURES MARKETS

> ### AFTER STUDYING THIS CHAPTER YOU SHOULD BE ABLE TO:
>
> > Calculate the profit on futures positions as a function of current and eventual futures prices.
>
> > Formulate futures market strategies for hedging or speculative purposes.
>
> > Compute the futures price appropriate to a given price on the underlying asset.
>
> > Design arbitrage strategies to exploit futures market mispricing.

Futures and forward contracts are like options in that they specify the purchase or sale of some underlying security at some future date. The key difference is that the holder of an option to buy is not compelled to buy and will not do so if the trade is unprofitable. A futures or forward contract, however, carries the obligation to go through with the agreed-upon transaction.

A forward contract is not an investment in the strict sense that funds are paid for an asset. It is only a commitment today to transact in the future. Forward arrangements are part of our study of investments, however, because they offer a powerful means to hedge other investments and generally modify portfolio characteristics.

Forward markets for future delivery of various commodities go back at least to ancient Greece. Organized *futures markets*, though, are a relatively modern development, dating only to the 19th century. Futures markets replace informal forward contracts with highly standardized, exchange-traded securities.

Figure 16.1 documents the tremendous growth of trading activity in futures markets since 1976. The figure shows that trading in financial futures has grown particularly rapidly and that financial futures now dominate the entire futures market.

This chapter describes the workings of futures markets and the mechanics of trading in these markets. We show how futures contracts are useful investment vehicles for both hedgers and speculators and how the futures price relates to the spot price of an asset. Finally, we take a look at some specific financial futures contracts—those written on stock indexes, foreign exchange, and fixed-income securities.

16.1 THE FUTURES CONTRACT

To see how futures and forwards work and how they might be useful, consider the portfolio diversification problem facing a farmer growing a single crop, let us say wheat. The entire planting season's revenue depends critically on the highly volatile crop price. The farmer can't easily diversify his position because virtually his entire wealth is tied up in the crop.

The miller who must purchase wheat for processing faces a portfolio problem that is the mirror image of the farmer's. He is subject to profit uncertainty because of the unpredictable future cost of the wheat.

Both parties can reduce this source of risk if they enter into a **forward contract** requiring the farmer to deliver the wheat when harvested at a price agreed upon now, regardless of the market price at harvest time. No money need change hands at this time. A forward contract is simply a deferred-delivery sale of some asset with the sales price agreed upon now. All that is required is that each party be willing to lock in the ultimate price to be paid or received for delivery of the commodity. A forward contract protects each party from future price fluctuations.

forward contract

An arrangement calling for future delivery of an asset at an agreed-upon price.

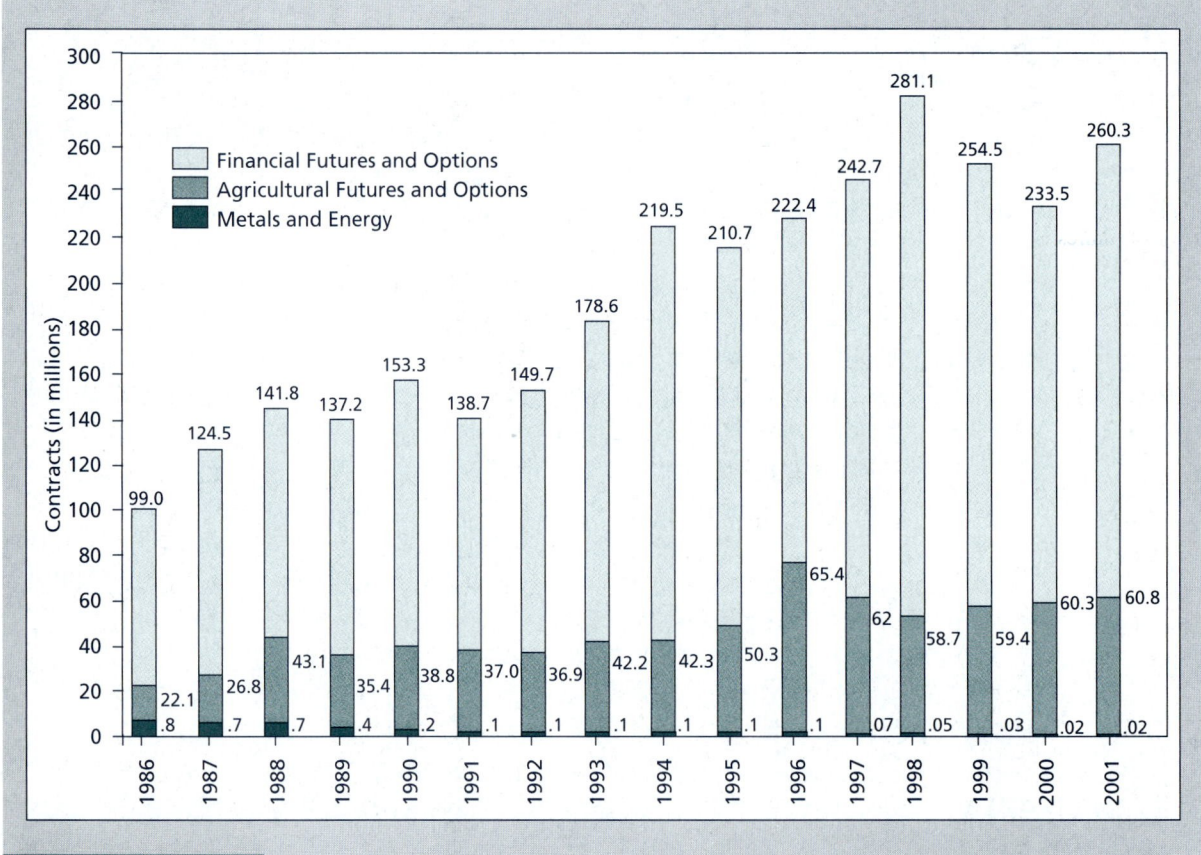

FIGURE 16.1
CBOT trading volume in futures contracts

Futures markets formalize and standardize forward contracting. Buyers and sellers do not have to rely on a chance matching of their interests; they can trade in a centralized futures market. The futures exchange also standardizes the types of contracts that may be traded: It establishes contract size, the acceptable grade of commodity, contract delivery dates, and so forth. While standardization eliminates much of the flexibility available in informal forward contracting, it has the offsetting advantage of liquidity because many traders will concentrate on the same small set of contracts. Futures contracts also differ from forward contracts in that they call for a daily settling up of any gains or losses on the contract. In contrast, in the case of forward contracts, no money changes hands until the delivery date.

In a centralized market, buyers and sellers can trade through brokers without personally searching for trading partners. The standardization of contracts and the depth of trading in each contract allows futures positions to be liquidated easily through a broker rather than personally renegotiated with the other party to the contract. Because the exchange guarantees the performance of each party to the contract, costly credit checks on other traders are not necessary. Instead, each trader simply posts a good faith deposit, called the *margin,* in order to guarantee contract performance.

The Basics of Futures Contracts

The futures contract calls for delivery of a commodity at a specified delivery or maturity date, for an agreed-upon price, called the **futures price,** to be paid at contract maturity. The contract specifies precise requirements for the commodity. For agricultural commodities, the exchange sets allowable grades (e.g., No. 2 hard winter wheat or No. 1 soft red wheat). The place or means of delivery of the commodity is specified as well. Delivery of agricultural commodities is made by transfer of warehouse receipts issued by approved warehouses. In the case of financial futures, delivery may be made by wire transfer; in the case of index futures, delivery may be accomplished by a cash settlement procedure such as those used for index options. (Although the futures contract technically calls for delivery of an asset, delivery rarely occurs. Instead, parties to the contract much more commonly close out their positions before contract maturity, taking gains or losses in cash.)[1]

Because the futures exchange specifies all the terms of the contract, the traders need bargain only over the futures price. The trader taking the **long position** commits to purchasing the commodity on the delivery date. The trader who takes the **short position** commits to delivering the commodity at contract maturity. The trader in the long position is said to "buy" a contract; the short-side trader "sells" a contract. The words *buy* and *sell* are figurative only, because a contract is not really bought or sold like a stock or bond; it is entered into by mutual agreement. At the time the contract is entered into, no money changes hands.

Figure 16.2 shows prices for futures contracts as they appear in *The Wall Street Journal.* The boldface heading lists in each case the commodity, the exchange where the futures contract is traded in parentheses, the contract size, and the pricing unit. For example, the first contract listed under "Grains and Oilseeds" is for corn, traded on the Chicago Board of Trade (CBT). Each contract calls for delivery of 5,000 bushels, and prices in the entry are quoted in cents per bushel.

The next several rows detail price data for contracts expiring on various dates. The March 2002 maturity corn contract, for example, opened during the day at a futures price of 211 cents per bushel. The highest futures price during the day was 214, the lowest was 210, and the

futures price

The agreed-upon price to be paid on a futures contract at maturity.

long position

The futures trader who commits to purchasing the asset.

short position

The futures trader who commits to delivering the asset.

---

[1]We will show you how this is done later in the chapter.

FUTURES PRICES

Tuesday, January 15, 2002

Open Interest Reflects Previous Trading Day.

GRAINS AND OILSEEDS

METALS AND PETROLEUM

LIVESTOCK AND MEAT

INDEX

FIGURE 16.2

Futures listings

FOOD AND FIBER

INTEREST RATE

CURRENCY

OTHER FUTURES

Settlement prices of selected contracts. Actual volume (from previous session) and open interest of all contract months.

EXCHANGE ABBREVIATIONS

(for commodity futures and futures options)

CANTOR–Cantor Exchange; CBT–Chicago Board of Trade; CME–Chicago Mercantile Exchange; CSCE–Coffee, Sugar & Cocoa Exchange, New York; CMX–COMEX (Div. of New York Mercantile Exchange; CTN–New York Cotton Exchange; EUREX–European Exchange; FINEX–Financial Exchange of New York Cotton Exchange; IPE–International Petroleum Exchange; KC–Kansas City Board of Trade; LIFFE–London International Financial Futures Exchange; MATIF–Marche a Terme International de France; ME–Montreal Exchange; MCE–MidAmerica Commodity Exchange; MPLS–Minneapolis Grain Exchange; NYFE–New York Futures Exchange (Sub. of New York Cotton Exchange); NYM–New York Mercantile Exchange; SFE–Sydney Futures Exchange; SGX–Singapore Exchange Ltd.; WPG–Winnipeg Commodity Exchange.

FIGURE 16.2

(Continued)

Source: From *The Wall Street Journal*, January 16, 2002, Reprinted by permission of Dow Jones & Company, Inc., via Copyright Clearance Center, Inc.

settlement price (a representative trading price during the last few minutes of trading) was 212¾. The settlement price increased by 1¾ cents from the previous trading day. The highest futures price over the contract's life to date was 270, the lowest 205 cents. Finally, open interest, or the number of outstanding contracts, was 255,712. Similar information is given for each maturity date.

The trader holding the long position, that is, the person who will purchase the good, profits from price increases. Suppose that when the contract matures in March, the price of corn turns out to be 217¾ cents per bushel. The long position trader who entered the contract at the futures price of 212¾ cents on January 15 (the date of the *Wall Street Journal* listing) earns a profit of 5 cents per bushel: The eventual price is 5 cents higher than the originally agreed-upon futures price. As each contract calls for delivery of 5,000 bushels (ignoring brokerage fees), the profit to the long position equals 5,000 × $0.05 = $250 per contract. Conversely, the short position loses 5 cents per bushel. The short position's loss equals the long position's gain.

To summarize, at maturity

$$\text{Profit to long} = \text{Spot price at maturity} - \text{Original futures price}$$

$$\text{Profit to short} = \text{Original futures price} - \text{Spot price at maturity}$$

where the spot price is the actual market price of the commodity at the time of the delivery.

The futures contract is, therefore, a zero sum game, with losses and gains to all positions netting out to zero. Every long position is offset by a short position. The aggregate profits to futures trading, summing over all investors, also must be zero, as is the net exposure to changes in the commodity price.

Figure 16.3, panel A, is a plot of the profits realized by an investor who enters the long side of a futures contract as a function of the price of the asset on the maturity date. Notice that profit is zero when the ultimate spot price, P_T, equals the initial futures price, F_0. Profit per unit of the underlying asset rises or falls one-for-one with changes in the final spot price. Unlike the payoff of a call option, the payoff of the long futures position can be negative: This will be the case if the spot price falls below the original futures price. Unlike the holder of a call, who has an *option* to buy, the long futures position trader cannot simply walk away from the contract. Also unlike options, in the case of futures there is no need to distinguish gross payoffs from net profits. This is because the futures contract is not purchased; it is simply a contract that is agreed to by two parties. The futures price adjusts to make the present value of either side of the contract equal to zero.

The distinction between futures and options is highlighted by comparing panel A of Figure 16.3 to the payoff and profit diagrams for an investor in a call option with exercise price, X, chosen equal to the futures price F_0 (see panel C). The futures investor is exposed to considerable losses if the asset price falls. In contrast, the investor in the call cannot lose more than the cost of the option.

Figure 16.3, panel B, is a plot of the profits realized by an investor who enters the short side of a futures contract. It is the mirror image of the profit diagram for the long position.

1. *a.* Compare the profit diagram in Figure 16.3B to the payoff diagram for a long position in a put option. Assume the exercise price of the option equals the initial futures price.

   b. Compare the profit diagram in Figure 16.3B to the payoff diagram for an investor who writes a call option.

Existing Contracts

Futures and forward contracts are traded on a wide variety of goods in four broad categories: agricultural commodities, metals and minerals (including energy commodities), foreign

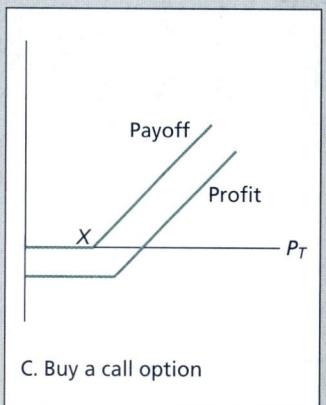

A. Long futures profit = $P_T - F_0$

B. Short futures profit = $F_0 - P_T$

C. Buy a call option

FIGURE 16.3

Profits to buyers and sellers of futures and options contracts

A: Long futures position (buyer)

B: Short futures position (seller)

C: Buy call option

currencies, and financial futures (fixed-income securities and stock market indexes). The financial futures contracts are a relatively recent innovation, for which trading was introduced in 1975. Innovation in financial futures has been rapid and is ongoing. Table 16.1 lists various contracts trading in the United States in 2002.

Contracts now trade on items that would not have been considered possible only a few years ago. For example, there are now electricity as well as weather futures and options contracts. Weather derivatives (which trade on the Chicago Mercantile Exchange), have payoffs that depend on the number of degree-days by which the temperature in a region exceeds or falls short of 65 degrees Fahrenheit. The potential use of these derivatives in managing the risk surrounding electricity or oil and natural gas use should be evident.

Outside the futures markets, a well-developed network of banks and brokers has established a forward market in foreign exchange. This forward market is not a formal exchange in the sense that the exchange specifies the terms of the traded contract. Instead, participants in a forward contract may negotiate for delivery of any quantity of goods at any time, whereas, in the formal futures markets, contract size and delivery dates are set by the exchange. In forward arrangements, banks and brokers simply negotiate contracts for clients (or themselves) as needed.

16.2 MECHANICS OF TRADING IN FUTURES MARKETS

The Clearinghouse and Open Interest

Trading in futures contracts is more complex than making ordinary stock transactions. If you want to make a stock purchase, your broker simply acts as an intermediary to enable you to buy shares from or sell shares to another individual through the stock exchange. In futures trading, however, the clearinghouse plays a more active role.

When an investor contacts a broker to establish a futures position, the brokerage firm wires the order to the firm's trader on the floor of the futures exchange. In contrast to stock trading,

TABLE 16.1
Sample of futures contracts

Foreign Currencies	Agricultural	Metals and Energy	Interest Rate Futures	Equity Indexes
British pound	Corn	Copper	Eurodollars	Dow Jones Industrials
Canadian dollar	Oats	Aluminum	Euroyen	S&P Midcap 400
Japanese yen	Soybeans	Gold	Euro-denominated	Nasdaq 100
Euro	Soybean meal	Platinum	bond	NYSE index
Swiss franc	Soybean oil	Palladium	Euroswiss	Russell 2000 index
Australian dollar	Wheat	Silver	Sterling	Nikkei 225 (Japanese)
Mexican peso	Barley	Crude oil	Gilt†	FTSE index (British)
Brazilian real	Flaxseed	Heating oil	German government	CAC index (French)
	Canola	Gas oil	bond	DAX index (German)
	Rye	Natural gas	Italian government	All ordinary (Australian)
	Cattle	Gasoline	bond	Toronto 35 (Canadian)
	Milk	Propane	Canadian	Dow Jones Euro STOXX 50
	Hogs	CRB index*	government bond	
	Pork bellies	Electricity	Treasury bonds	
	Cocoa	Weather	Treasury notes	
	Coffee		Treasury bills	
	Cotton		LIBOR	
	Orange juice		EURIBOR	
	Sugar		Municipal bond index	
	Lumber		Federal funds rate	
	Rice		Bankers' acceptance	
			S&P 500 index	

*The Commodity Research Bureau's index of futures prices of agricultural as well as metal and energy prices.

†Gilts are British government bonds.

which involves specialists or market makers in each security, most futures trades in the United States occur among floor traders in the "trading pit" for each contract. Traders use voice or hand signals to signify their desire to buy or sell. Once a trader willing to accept the opposite side of a trade is located, the trade is recorded and the investor is notified.

At this point, just as is true for options contracts, the **clearinghouse** enters the picture. Rather than having the long and short traders hold contracts with each other, the clearinghouse becomes the seller of the contract for the long position and the buyer of the contract for the short position. The clearinghouse is obligated to deliver the commodity to the long position and to pay for delivery from the short; consequently, the clearinghouse's position nets to zero. This arrangement makes the clearinghouse the trading partner of each trader, both long and short. The clearinghouse, bound to perform on its side of each contract, is the only party that can be hurt by the failure of any trader to observe the obligations of the futures contract. This arrangement is necessary because a futures contract calls for future performance, which cannot be as easily guaranteed as an immediate stock transaction.

Figure 16.4 illustrates the role of the clearinghouse. Panel A shows what would happen in the absence of the clearinghouse. The trader in the long position would be obligated to pay the futures price to the short position trader, and the trader in the short position would be obligated to deliver the commodity. Panel B shows how the clearinghouse becomes an intermediary, acting as the trading partner for each side of the contract. The clearinghouse's position is neutral, as it takes a long and a short position for each transaction.

clearinghouse

Established by exchanges to facilitate trading. The clearinghouse may interpose itself as an intermediary between two traders.

FIGURE 16.4

A. Trading without the clearinghouse
B. Trading with a clearinghouse

The clearinghouse makes it possible for traders to liquidate positions easily. If you are currently long in a contract and want to undo your position, you simply instruct your broker to enter the short side of a contract to close out your position. This is called a *reversing trade*. The exchange nets out your long and short positions, reducing your net position to zero. Your zero net position with the clearinghouse eliminates the need to fulfill at maturity either the original long or reversing short position.

The *open interest* on the contract is the number of contracts outstanding. (Long and short positions are not counted separately, meaning that open interest can be defined as either the number of long or short contracts outstanding.) The clearinghouse's position nets out to zero, and so it is not counted in the computation of open interest. When contracts begin trading, open interest is zero. As time passes, open interest increases as progressively more contracts are entered. Almost all traders, however, liquidate their positions before the contract maturity date.

Instead of actually taking or making delivery of the commodity, virtually all market participants enter reversing trades to cancel their original positions, thereby realizing the profits or losses on the contract. The fraction of contracts that result in actual delivery is estimated to range from less than 1% to 3%, depending on the commodity and the activity in the contract. The image of a trader awakening one delivery date with a mountain of wheat in the front yard is amusing, but unlikely.

You can see the typical pattern of open interest in Figure 16.2. In the silver contract, for example, the January delivery contracts are close to maturity, and open interest is relatively small; most contracts have been reversed already. The next few maturities have significantly greater open interest. Finally, the most distant maturity contracts have little open interest, as they have been available only recently, and few participants have yet traded.

Marking to Market and the Margin Account

Anyone who saw the film "Trading Places" knows that Eddie Murphy as a trader in orange juice futures had no intention of purchasing or delivering orange juice. Traders simply bet on the futures price of juice. The total profit or loss realized by the long trader who buys a contract at time 0 and closes, or reverses, it at time t is just the change in the futures price over the period, $F_t - F_0$. Symmetrically, the short trader earns $F_0 - F_t$.

marking to market

The daily settlement of obligations on futures positions.

The process by which profits or losses accrue to traders is called **marking to market.** At initial execution of a trade, each trader establishes a margin account. The margin is a security account consisting of cash or near-cash securities, such as Treasury bills, that ensures the trader will be able to satisfy the obligations of the futures contract. Because both parties to the futures contract are exposed to losses, both must post margin. If the initial margin on corn, for example, is 10%, the trader must post $1063.75 per contract for the margin account. This is 10% of the value of the contract ($2.1275 per bushel $\times$ 5,000 bushels per contract).

Because the initial margin may be satisfied by posting interest-earning securities, the requirement does not impose a significant opportunity cost of funds on the trader. The initial margin is usually set between 5% and 15% of the total value of the contract. Contracts written on assets with more volatile prices require higher margins.

On any day that futures contracts trade, futures prices may rise or fall. Instead of waiting until the maturity date for traders to realize all gains and losses, the clearinghouse requires all positions to recognize profits as they accrue daily. If the futures price of corn rises from 212¾ to 214¾ cents per bushel, for example, the clearinghouse credits the margin account of the long position for 5,000 bushels times 2 cents per bushel, or $100 per contract. Conversely, for the short position, the clearinghouse takes this amount from the margin account for each contract held. Therefore, as futures prices change, proceeds accrue to the trader's account immediately.

Although the price of corn has changed by only 0.94% (i.e., 2/212.75), the percentage return on the long corn position on that day is 10 times greater: The $100 gain on the position is 9.4% of the $1,063.75 posted as margin. The 10-to-1 ratio of percentage changes reflects the leverage inherent in the futures position, since the corn contract was established with an initial margin of 1/10th the value of the underlying asset.

2. What must be the net inflow or outlay from marking to market for the clearinghouse?

maintenance margin

An established value below which a trader's margin may not fall. Reaching the maintenance margin triggers a margin call.

If a trader accrues sustained losses from daily marking to market, the margin account may fall below a critical value called the **maintenance margin.** Once the value of the account falls below this value, the trader receives a margin call. For example, if the maintenance margin on corn is 5%, then the margin call will go out when the 10% margin initially posted has fallen about in half, to $532 per contract. (This requires that the futures price fall only about 11 cents, as each 1 cent drop in the futures price results in a loss of $50 to the long position.) Either new funds must be transferred into the margin account or the broker will close out enough of the trader's position to meet the required margin for that position. This procedure safeguards the position of the clearinghouse. Positions are closed out before the margin account is exhausted—the trader's losses are covered, and the clearinghouse is not put at risk.

Marking to market is the major way in which futures and forward contracts differ, besides contract standardization. Futures follow this pay- (or receive-) as-you-go method. Forward contracts are simply held until maturity, and no funds are transferred until that date, although the contracts may be traded.

It is important to note that the futures price on the delivery date will equal the spot price of the commodity on that date. As a maturing contract calls for immediately delivery, the futures price on that day must equal the spot price—the cost of the commodity from the two competing sources is equalized in a competitive market.[2] You may obtain delivery of the

---

[2]Small differences between the spot and futures prices at maturity may persist because of transportation costs, but this is a minor factor.

commodity either by purchasing it directly in the spot market or by entering the long side of a futures contract.

A commodity available from two sources (the spot and futures markets) must be priced identically, or else investors will rush to purchase it from the cheap source in order to sell it in the high-priced market. Such arbitrage activity could not persist without prices adjusting to eliminate the arbitrage opportunity. Therefore, the futures price and the spot price must converge at maturity. This is called the **convergence property.**

For an investor who establishes a long position in a contract now (time 0) and holds that position until maturity (time T), the sum of all daily settlements will equal $F_T - F_0$, where F_T stands for the futures price at contract maturity. Because of convergence, however, the futures price at maturity, F_T, equals the spot price, P_T, so total futures profits also may be expressed as $P_T - F_0$. Thus, we see that profits on a futures contract held to maturity perfectly track changes in the value of the underlying asset.

convergence property

The convergence of futures prices and spot prices at the maturity of the futures contract.

Assume the current futures price for silver for delivery five days from today is $5.10 per ounce. Suppose that over the next five days, the futures price evolves as follows:

Day	Futures Price
0 (today)	$5.10
1	5.20
2	5.25
3	5.18
4	5.18
5 (delivery)	5.21

EXAMPLE 16.1

Marking to Market and Futures Contract Profits

The spot price of silver on the delivery date is $5.21: The convergence property implies that the price of silver in the spot market must equal the futures price on the delivery day.

The daily mark-to-market settlements for each contract held by the long positions will be as follows:

Day	Profit (loss) per Ounce × 5,000 Ounces/Contract	= Daily Proceeds
1	$5.20 − $5.10 = $ 0.10	$ 500
2	5.25 − 5.20 = 0.05	250
3	5.18 − 5.25 = −0.07	−350
4	5.18 − 5.18 = 0	0
5	5.21 − 5.18 = 0.03	150
		Sum = $ 550

The profit on day 1 is the increase in the futures price from the previous day, or ($5.20 − $5.10) per ounce. Because each silver contract on the Commodity Exchange calls for purchase and delivery of 5,000 ounces, the total profit per contract is 5,000 times $0.10, or $500. On day 3, when the futures price falls, the long position's margin account will be debited by $350. By day 5, the sum of all daily proceeds is $550. This is exactly equal to 5,000 times the difference between the final futures price of $5.21 and the original futures price of $5.10. Thus, the sum of all the daily proceeds (per ounce of silver held long) equals $P_T - F_0$.

Cash versus Actual Delivery

Most futures markets call for delivery of an actual commodity, such as a particular grade of wheat or a specified amount of foreign currency, if the contract is not reversed before maturity. For agricultural commodities, where quality of the delivered good may vary, the exchange sets quality standards as part of the futures contract. In some cases, contracts may be settled with higher or lower grade commodities. In these cases, a premium or discount is applied to the delivered commodity to adjust for the quality differences.

cash delivery

The cash value of the underlying asset (rather than the asset itself) is delivered to satisfy the contract.

Some futures contracts call for **cash delivery.** An example is a stock index futures contract where the underlying asset is an index such as the Standard & Poor's 500 index. Delivery of every stock in the index clearly would be impractical. Hence, the contract calls for "delivery" of a cash amount equal to the value that the index attains on the maturity date of the contract. The sum of all the daily settlements from marking to market results in the long position realizing total profits or losses of $S_T - F_0$, where S_T is the value of the stock index on the maturity date T, and F_0 is the original futures price. Cash settlement closely mimics actual delivery, except the cash value of the asset rather than the asset itself is delivered by the short position in exchange for the futures price.

More concretely, the S&P 500 index contract calls for delivery of $250 times the value of the index. At maturity, the index might list at 1,200, a market value-weighted index of the prices of all 500 stocks in the index. The cash settlement contract calls for delivery of $250 × 1,200, or $300,000 cash in return for 250 times the futures price. This yields exactly the same profit as would result from directly purchasing 250 units of the index for $300,000 and then delivering it for 250 times the original futures price.

Regulations

Futures markets are regulated by the Commodities Futures Trading Commission (CFTC), a federal agency. The CFTC sets capital requirements for member firms of the futures exchanges, authorizes trading in new contracts, and oversees maintenance of daily trading records.

The futures exchange may set limits on the amount by which futures prices may change from one day to the next. For example, if the price limit on silver contracts is $1, and silver futures close today at $5.10 per ounce, trades in silver tomorrow may vary only between $6.10 and $4.10 per ounce. The exchange may increase or reduce these price limits in response to perceived changes in the price volatility of the contract. Price limits often are eliminated as contracts approach maturity, usually in the last month of trading.

Price limits traditionally are viewed as a means to limit violent price fluctuations. This reasoning seems dubious. Suppose an international monetary crisis overnight drives up the spot price of silver to $8.00. No one would sell silver futures at prices for future delivery as low as $5.10. Instead, the futures price would rise each day by the $1 limit, although the quoted price would represent only an unfilled bid order—no contracts would trade at the low quoted price. After several days of limit moves of $1 per day, the futures price would finally reach its equilibrium level, and trading would occur again. This process means no one could unload a position until the price reached its equilibrium level. This example shows that price limits offer no real protection against fluctuations in equilibrium prices.

Taxation

Because of the mark-to-market procedure, investors do not have control over the tax year in which they realize gains or losses. Instead, price changes are realized gradually, with each daily settlement. Therefore, taxes are paid at year-end on cumulated profits or losses regardless of whether the position has been closed out.

16.3 FUTURES MARKET STRATEGIES

Hedging and Speculation

Hedging and speculating are two polar uses of futures markets. A speculator uses a futures contract to profit from movements in futures prices, a hedger to protect against price movements.

If speculators believe prices will increase, they will take a long position for expected profits. Conversely, they exploit expected price declines by taking a short position.

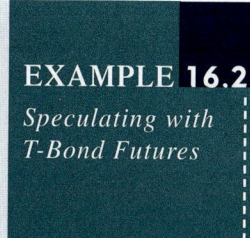

EXAMPLE 16.2
Speculating with T-Bond Futures

Let's consider the use of the T-bond futures contract, the listings for which appear in Figure 16.2. Each T-bond contract on the Chicago Board of Trade (CBT) calls for delivery of $100,000 par value of bonds. The listed futures price of 103-29 (that is, $103\frac{29}{32}$) means the market price of the underlying bonds is 103.90625% of par, or $103,906.25. Therefore, for every increase of one point in the T-bond futures price (e.g., to 104-29), the long position gains $1,000, and the short loses that amount. Therefore, if you are bullish on bond prices, you might speculate by buying T-bond futures contracts.

If the T-bond futures price increases by one point to 104-29, you profit by your speculation by $1,000 per contract. If the forecast is incorrect, and T-bond futures prices decline, you lose $1,000 times the decrease in the futures price for each contract purchased. Speculators bet on the direction of futures price movements.

Why would a speculator buy a T-bond futures contract? Why not buy T-bonds directly? One reason lies in transaction costs, which are far smaller in futures markets.

Another reason is the leverage futures trading provides. Recall that each T-bond contract calls for delivery of $100,000 par value, worth about $103,906 in our example. The initial margin required for this account might be only $15,000. The $1,000 per contract gain translates into a 6.67% ($1,000/$15,000) return on the money put up, despite the fact that the T-bond futures price increases only 0.96% (1/103.906). Futures margins, therefore, allow speculators to achieve much greater leverage than is available from direct trading in a commodity.

Hedgers, by contrast, use futures markets to insulate themselves against price movements. An investor holding a T-bond portfolio, for example, might anticipate a period of interest rate volatility and want to protect the value of the portfolio against price fluctuations. In this case, the investor has no desire to bet on price movements in either direction. To achieve such protection, a hedger takes a short position in T-bond futures, which obligates the hedger to deliver T-bonds at the contract maturity date for the current futures price. This locks in the sales price for the bonds and guarantees that the total value of the bond-plus-futures position at the maturity date is the futures price.[3]

---

[3]To keep things simple, we will assume that the T-bond futures contract calls for delivery of a bond with the same coupon and maturity as that in the investor's portfolio. In practice, a variety of bonds may be delivered to satisfy the contract, and a "conversion factor" is used to adjust for the relative values of the eligible delivery bonds. We will ignore this complication.

16.3 EXAMPLE

Hedging with T-Bond Futures

Suppose as in Figure 16.2 that the T-bond futures price for March 2002 delivery is $103.90625 (per $100 par value), which we will round off to $103.91, and that the only three possible T-bond prices in March are $102.91, $103.91, and $104.91. If investors currently hold 200 bonds, each with par value $1,000, they would take short positions in two contracts, each for $100,000 value. Protecting the value of a portfolio with short futures positions is called **short hedging**.

The profits in March from each of the two short futures contracts will be 1,000 times any decrease in the futures price. At maturity, the convergence property ensures that the final futures price will equal the spot price of the T-bonds. Hence, the futures profit will be 2,000 times $(F_0 - P_T)$, where P_T is the price of the bonds on the delivery date, and F_0 is the original futures price, $103.91.

Now consider the hedged portfolio consisting of the bonds and the short futures positions. The portfolio value as a function of the bond price in March can be computed as follows:

	T-Bond Price in March 2002		
	$102.91	**$103.91**	**$104.91**
Bond holdings (value = 2,000 P_T)	$205,820	$207,820	$209,820
Futures profits or losses	+2,000	0	−2,000
Total	$207,820	$207,820	$207,820

The total portfolio value is unaffected by the eventual bond price, which is what the hedger wants. The gains or losses on the bond holdings are exactly offset by those on the two contracts held short.

For example, if bond prices fall to $102.91, the losses on the bond portfolio are offset by the $2,000 gain on the futures contracts. That profit equals the difference between the futures price on the maturity date (which equals the spot price on that date, $102.91) and the originally contracted futures price of $103.91. For short contracts, a profit of $1 per $100 par value is realized from the fall in the spot price. Because two contracts call for delivery of $200,000 par value, this results in a $2,000 gain that offsets the decline in the value of the bonds held in the portfolio. In contrast to a speculator, a hedger is indifferent to the ultimate price of the asset. The short hedger, who has in essence arranged to sell the asset for an agreed-upon price, need not be concerned about further developments in the market price.

To generalize the example, note that the bond will be worth P_T at the maturity of the futures contract, while the profit on the futures contract is $F_0 - P_T$. The sum of the two positions is F_0 dollars, which is independent of the eventual bond price.

A *long hedge* is the analogue to a short hedge for a purchaser of an asset. Consider, for example, a pension fund manager who anticipates a cash inflow in two months that will be invested in fixed-income securities. The manager views T-bonds as very attractively priced now and would like to lock in current prices and yields until the investment actually can be made two months hence. The manager can lock in the effective cost of the purchase by entering the long side of a contract, which commits her to purchasing at the current futures price.

Concept
CHECK

3. **Suppose that T-bonds will be selling in March at $102.91, $103.91, or $104.91. Show that the cost in March of purchasing $200,000 par value of T-bonds net of the profit/loss on two long T-bond contracts will be $207,820 regardless of the eventual bond price.**

Exact futures hedging may be impossible for some goods because the necessary futures contract is not traded. For example, a portfolio manager might want to hedge the value of a diversified, actively managed portfolio for a period of time. However, futures contracts are listed only on indexed portfolios. Nevertheless, because returns on the manager's diversified portfolio will have a high correlation with returns on broad-based indexed portfolios, an effective hedge may be established by selling index futures contracts. Hedging a position using futures on another asset is called *cross-hedging*.

4. **What are the sources of risk to an investor who uses stock index futures to hedge an actively managed stock portfolio?**

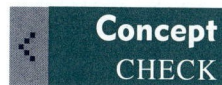
Concept CHECK

Basis Risk and Hedging

The **basis** is the difference between the futures price and the spot price.[4] As we have noted, on the maturity date of a contract, the basis must be zero: The convergence property implies that $F_T - P_T = 0$. Before maturity, however, the futures price for later delivery may differ substantially from the current spot price.

We discussed the case of a short hedger who holds an asset (T-bonds, in our example) and a short position to deliver that asset in the future. If the asset and futures contract are held until maturity, the hedger bears no risk, as the ultimate value of the portfolio on the delivery date is determined by the current futures price. Risk is eliminated because the futures price and spot price at contract maturity must be equal: Gains and losses on the futures and the commodity position will exactly cancel. If the contract and asset are to be liquidated early, before contract maturity, however, the hedger bears **basis risk,** because the futures price and spot price need not move in perfect lockstep at all times before the delivery date. In this case, gains and losses on the contract and the asset need not exactly offset each other.

Some speculators try to profit from movements in the basis. Rather than betting on the direction of the futures or spot prices per se, they bet on the changes in the difference between the two. A long spot–short futures position will profit when the basis narrows.

> **basis**
>
> The difference between the futures price and the spot price.

> **basis risk**
>
> Risk attributable to uncertain movements in the spread between a futures price and a spot price.

Consider an investor holding 100 ounces of gold, who is short one gold futures contract. Suppose that gold today sells for $291 an ounce, and the futures price for June delivery is $296 an ounce. Therefore, the basis is currently $5. Tomorrow, the spot price might increase to $294, while the futures price increases to $298.50, so the basis narrows to $4.50. The investor's gains and losses are as follows:

Gain on holdings of gold (per ounce): $294 − $291 = $3.00

Loss on gold futures position (per ounce): $298.50 − $296 = $2.50

The investor gains $3 per ounce on the gold holdings, but loses $2.50 an ounce on the short futures position. The net gain is the decrease in the basis, or $0.50 an ounce.

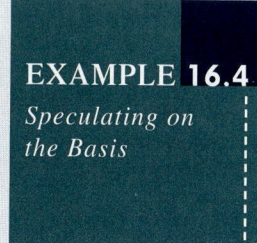
EXAMPLE 16.4
Speculating on the Basis

A related strategy is a **spread** position, where the investor takes a long position in a futures contract of one maturity and a short position in a contract on the same commodity, but with a different maturity. Profits accrue if the difference in futures prices between the two contracts changes in the hoped-for direction; that is, if the futures price on the contract held long increases by more (or decreases by less) than the futures price on the contract held short. Like basis strategies, spread positions aim to exploit movements in relative price structures rather than to profit from movements in the general level of prices.

> **spread (futures)**
>
> Taking a long position in a futures contract of one maturity and a short position in a contract of a different maturity, both on the same commodity.

[4]Usage of the word *basis* is somewhat loose. It sometimes is used to refer to the futures-spot difference, $F - P$, and other times it is used to refer to the spot-futures difference, $P - F$. We will consistently call the basis $F - P$.

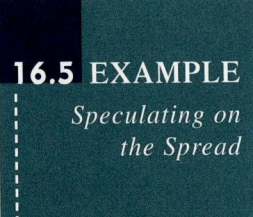

16.5 EXAMPLE

*Speculating on
the Spread*

Consider an investor who holds a September maturity contract long and a June contract short. If the September futures price increases by 5 cents while the June futures price increases by 4 cents, the net gain will be 5 cents − 4 cents, or 1 cent.

16.4 THE DETERMINATION OF FUTURES PRICES

Spot-Futures Parity

There are at least two ways to obtain an asset at some date in the future. One way is to purchase the asset now and store it until the targeted date. The other way is to take a long futures position that calls for purchase of the asset on the date in question. As each strategy leads to an equivalent result, namely, the ultimate acquisition of the asset, you would expect the market-determined cost of pursuing these strategies to be equal. There should be a predictable relationship between the current price of the asset, including the costs of holding and storing it, and the futures price.

To make the discussion more concrete, consider a futures contract on gold. This is a particularly simple case: Explicit storage costs for gold are minimal, gold provides no income flow for its owners (in contrast to stocks or bonds that make dividend or coupon payments), and gold is not subject to the seasonal price patterns that characterize most agricultural commodities. Instead, in market equilibrium, the price of gold will be at a level such that the expected rate of capital gains will equal the fair expected rate of return given gold's investment risk. Two strategies that will assure possession of the gold at some future date T are:

Strategy A: Buy the gold now, paying the current or "spot" price, S_0, and hold it until time T, when its spot price will be S_T.

Strategy B: Initiate a long futures position, and invest enough money now in order to pay the futures price when the contract matures.

Strategy B will require an immediate investment of the *present value* of the futures price in a riskless security such as Treasury bills, that is, an investment of $F_0/(1 + r_f)^T$ dollars, where r_f is the rate paid on T-bills. Examine the cash flow streams of the following two strategies.[5]

	Action	Initial Cash Flow	Cash Flow at Time T
Strategy A:	Buy gold	$-S_0$	S_T
Strategy B:	Enter long position	0	$S_T - F_0$
	Invest $F_0/(1 + r_f)^T$ in bills	$-F_0/(1 + r_f)^T$	F_0
	Total for strategy B	$-F_0/(1 + r_f)^T$	S_T

---

[5]We ignore the margin requirement on the futures contract and treat the cash flow involved in establishing the futures position as zero for the two reasons mentioned above: First, the margin is small relative to the amount of gold controlled by one contract; and second, and more importantly, the margin requirement may be satisfied with interest-bearing securities. For example, the investor merely needs to transfer Treasury bills already owned into the brokerage account. There is no time-value-of-money cost.

The initial cash flow of strategy A is negative, reflecting the cash outflow necessary to purchase the gold at the current spot price, S_0. At time T, the gold will be worth S_T.

Strategy B involves an initial investment equal to the present value of the futures price that will be paid at the maturity of the futures contract. By time T, the investment will grow to F_0. In addition, the profits to the long position at time T will be $S_T - F_0$. The sum of the two components of strategy B will be S_T dollars, exactly enough to purchase the gold at time T regardless of its price at that time.

Each strategy results in an identical value of S_T dollars at T. Therefore, the cost, or initial cash outflow, required by these strategies also must be equal; it follows that

$$F_0/(1 + r_f)^T = S_0$$

or

$$F_0 = S_0(1 + r_f)^T \tag{16.1}$$

This gives us a relationship between the current price and the futures price of the gold. The interest rate in this case may be viewed as the "cost of carrying" the gold from the present to time T. The cost in this case represents the time-value-of-money opportunity cost—instead of investing in the gold, you could have invested risklessly in Treasury bills to earn interest income.

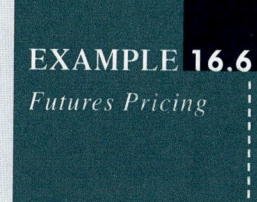

Suppose that gold currently sells for $280 an ounce. If the risk-free interest rate is 0.5% per month, a six-month maturity futures contract should have a futures price of

$$F_0 = S_0(1 + r_f)^T = \$280(1.005)^6 = \$288.51$$

If the contract has a 12-month maturity, the futures price should be

$$F_0 = \$280(1.005)^{12} = \$297.27$$

EXAMPLE 16.6

Futures Pricing

If Equation 16.1 does not hold, investors can earn arbitrage profits. For example, suppose the six-month maturity futures price in Example 16.6 were $289 rather than the "appropriate" value of $288.51 that we just derived. An investor could realize arbitrage profits by pursuing a strategy involving a long position in strategy A (buy the gold) and a short position in strategy B (sell the futures contract and borrow enough to pay for the gold purchase).

Action	Initial Cash Flow	Cash Flow at Time T (6 months)
Borrow $280, repay with interest at time T	+$280	$-\$280(1.005)^6 = -\$288.51$
Buy gold for $280	−280	S_T
Enter short futures position ($F_0 = \$289$)	0	$289 - S_T$
Total	$0	$0.49

The net initial investment of this strategy is zero. Moreover, its cash flow at time T is positive and riskless: The total payoff at time T will be $0.49 regardless of the price of gold. (The profit is equal to the mispricing of the futures contract, $289 rather than $288.51.) Risk has been eliminated because profits and losses on the futures and gold positions exactly offset each other. The portfolio is perfectly hedged.

Such a strategy produces an arbitrage profit—a riskless profit requiring no initial net investment. If such an opportunity existed, all market participants would rush to take advantage of it. The results? The price of gold would be bid up, and/or the futures price offered down, until Equation 16.1 is satisfied. A similar analysis applies to the possibility that F_0 is less than \$288.51. In this case, you simply reverse the above strategy to earn riskless profits. We conclude, therefore, that in a well-functioning market in which arbitrage opportunities are competed away, $F_0 = S_0(1 + r_f)^T$.

Concept CHECK

5. Return to the arbitrage strategy just laid out. What would be the three steps of the strategy if F_0 were too low, say \$288? Work out the cash flows of the strategy now and at time T in a table like the one on the previous page.

The arbitrage strategy can be represented more generally as follows:

Action	Initial Cash Flow	Cash Flow at Time T
1. Borrow S_0	$-S_0$	$-S_0(1 + r_f)^T$
2. Buy gold for S_0	$-S_0$	S_T
3. Enter short futures position	0	$F_0 - S_T$
Total	0	$F_0 - S_0(1 + r_f)^T$

The initial cash flow is zero by construction: The money necessary to purchase the stock in step 2 is borrowed in step 1, and the futures position in step 3, which is used to hedge the value of the stock position, does not require an initial outlay. Moreover, the total cash flow to the strategy at time T is riskless because it involves only terms that are already known when the contract is entered. This situation could not persist, as all investors would try to cash in on the arbitrage opportunity. Ultimately prices would change until the time T cash flow was reduced to zero, at which point F_0 would equal $S_0(1 + r_f)^T$. This result is called the **spot-futures parity theorem** or **cost-of-carry relationship**; it gives the normal or theoretically correct relationship between spot and futures prices.

We can easily extend the parity theorem to the case where the underlying asset provides a flow of income to its owner. For example, consider a futures contract on a stock index such as the S&P 500. In this case, the underlying asset (i.e., the stock portfolio indexed to the S&P 500 index), pays a dividend yield to the investor. If we denote the dividend yield as d, then the net cost of carry is only $r_f - d$; the foregone interest earnings on the wealth tied up in the stock is offset by the flow of dividends from the stock. The net opportunity cost of holding the stock is the foregone interest less the dividends received. Therefore, in the dividend-paying case, the spot-futures parity relationship is[6]

$$F_0 = S_0(1 + r_f - d)^T \qquad (16.2)$$

where d is the dividend yield on the stock. Problem 8 at the end of the chapter leads you through a derivation of this result.

The arbitrage strategy just described should convince you that these parity relationships are more than just theoretical results. Any violations of the parity relationship give rise to arbitrage opportunities that can provide large profits to traders. We will see shortly that index arbitrage in the stock market is a tool used to exploit violations of the parity relationship for stock index futures contracts.

spot-futures parity theorem, or cost-of-carry relationship

Describes the theoretically correct relationship between spot and futures prices. Violation of the parity relationship gives rise to arbitrage opportunities.

---

[6]This relationship is only approximate in that it assumes the dividend is paid just before the maturity of the contract.

Suppose that the risk-free interest rate is 0.5% per month, the dividend yield on the stock index is 0.1% per month, and the stock index is currently at 1,200. The net cost of carry is therefore 0.5% − 0.1% = 0.4% per month. Given this, a three-month contract should have a futures price of $1,200(1.004)^3 = 1,214.46$, while a six-month contract should have a futures price of $1,200(1.004)^6 = 1,229.09$. If the index rises to 1,210, both futures prices will rise commensurately: The three-month futures price will rise to $1,210(1.004)^3 = 1,224.58$, while the six-month futures price will rise to $1,210(1.004)^6 = 1,239.33$.

Spreads

Just as we can predict the relationship between spot and futures prices, there are similar ways to determine the proper relationships among futures prices for contracts of different maturity dates. Equation 16.2 shows that the futures price is in part determined by time to maturity. If $r_f > d$, as is usually the case for stock index futures, then the futures price will be higher on longer-maturity contracts. You can easily verify this by examining Figure 16.2, which includes *Wall Street Journal* listings of several stock index futures contracts. (A warning to avoid confusion. You will notice that for some stock index contracts in Figure 16.2, such as the S&P 500 contract, the financial pages omit decimal points to save space. Thus, the settlement price for the March maturity contract should be interpreted as 1,149.00.) For futures on assets like gold, which pay no "dividend yield," we can set $d = 0$ and conclude that F must increase as time to maturity increases.

Equation 16.2 shows that futures prices should all move together. It is not surprising that futures prices for different maturity dates move in unison, for all are linked to the same spot price through the parity relationship. Figure 16.5 plots futures prices on gold for three maturity dates. It is apparent that the prices move in virtual lockstep and that the more distant delivery dates require higher futures prices, as Equation 16.2 predicts.

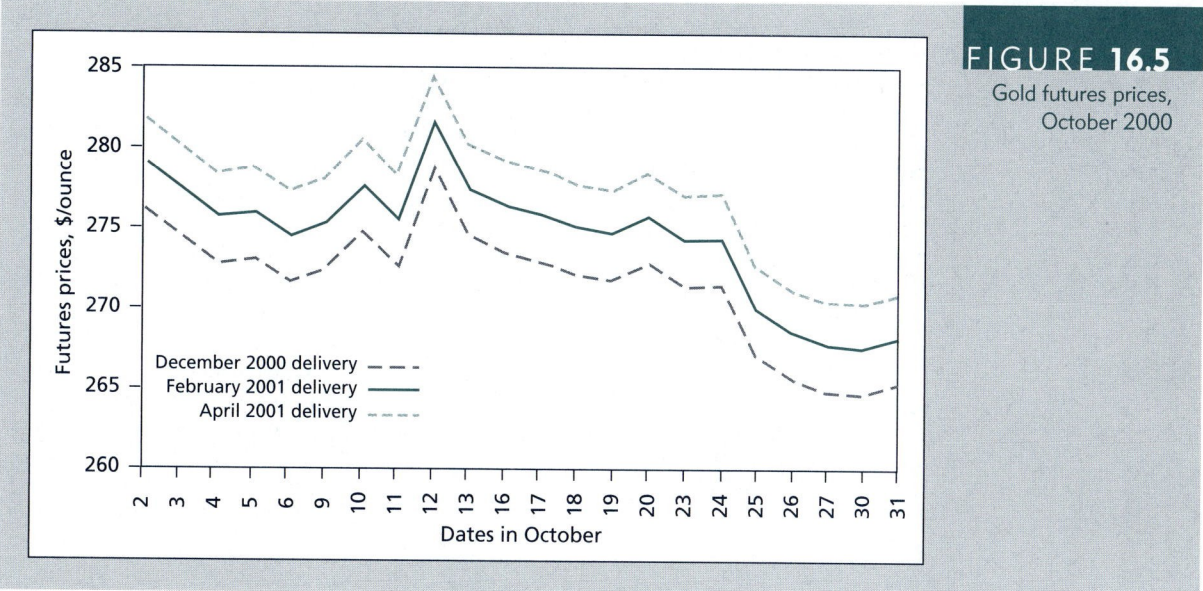

FIGURE **16.5**
Gold futures prices, October 2000

16.5 | FINANCIAL FUTURES

Although futures markets have their origins in agricultural commodities, today's market is dominated by contracts on financial assets, as we saw in Figure 16.1.

Stock Index Futures

Currently, there are no stock futures on individual shares; futures trade instead on stock market indexes such as the Standard & Poor's 500. In contrast to most futures contracts, which call for delivery of a specified commodity, these contracts are settled by a cash amount equal to the value of the stock index in question on the contract maturity date times a multiplier that scales the size of the contract. This cash settlement duplicates the profits that would arise with actual delivery.

There are several stock index futures contracts currently traded. Table 16.2 lists some contracts on major indexes, showing under contract size the multiplier used to calculate contract settlements. An S&P 500 contract with an initial futures price of 1,200 and a final index value

TABLE 16.2
Stock index futures

Contract	Underlying Market Index	Contract Size	Exchange
S&P 500	Standard & Poor's 500 index. A value-weighted arithmetic average of 500 stocks.	$250 times the S&P 500 index.	Chicago Mercantile Exchange
Dow Jones Industrials (DJIA)	Price-weighted arithmetic average of 30 blue-chip stocks.	$10 times the Dow Jones Industrial Average.	Chicago Board of Trade
S&P Midcap	Index of 400 firms of mid-range market value.	$500 times index.	Chicago Mercantile Exchange
Nasdaq 100	Value-weighted arithmetic average of 100 of the largest over-the-counter stocks.	$100 times the OTC index.	Chicago Mercantile Exchange
Russell 2000	Index of 2,000 smaller firms.	$500 times the index.	Chicago Mercantile Exchange
Nikkei	Nikkei 225 stock average.	$5 times the Nikkei index.	Chicago Mercantile Exchange
FT-SE 100	Financial Times-Share Exchange Index of 100 U.K. firms.	£10 times the FT-SE Index.	London International Financial Futures Exchange
CAC 40	Index of 40 of the largest French firms.	10 euros times the index.	MATIF (Marché à Terme International de France)
DAX 30	Index of 30 of the largest German firms.	25 euros times the index.	DTB (Deutsche Terminboerse)
DJ Euro STOXX 50	Value-weighted index of 50 large stocks in Eurozone.	10 euros times the index.	Eurex

TABLE 16.3		S&P	NYSE	Nasdaq	DJIA
Correlations among major U.S. stock market indexes	S&P	1	0.988	0.980	0.992
	NYSE		1	0.944	0.994
	Nasdaq			1	0.960
	DJIA				1

Note: Correlations were computed from monthly percentage rates of price appreciation between 1992 and 1999.

of 1,210, for example, would result in a profit for the long side of $250 \times (1,210 - 1,200) = $2,500. The S&P contract by far dominates the market in stock index futures.

The broad-based U.S. stock market indexes are all highly correlated. Table 16.3 presents a correlation matrix for four U.S. indexes. Even the DJIA, with only 30 stocks, exhibits a correlation above 0.96 with the S&P, Nasdaq, and NYSE indexes. This is testament to the power of even moderate diversification.

Creating Synthetic Stock Positions

One reason stock index futures are so popular is that they substitute for holdings in the underlying stocks themselves. Index futures let investors participate in broad market movements without actually buying or selling large numbers of stocks.

Because of this, we say futures represent "synthetic" holdings of the market position. Instead of holding the market directly, the investor takes a long futures position in the index. Such a strategy is attractive because the transaction costs involved in establishing and liquidating futures positions are much lower than what would be required to take actual spot positions. Investors who wish to buy and sell market positions frequently find it much cheaper and easier to play the futures market. Market timers who speculate on broad market moves rather than individual securities are large players in stock index futures for this reason.

One way to market time is to shift between Treasury bills and broad-based stock market holdings. Timers attempt to shift from bills into the market before market upturns and to shift back into bills to avoid market downturns, thereby profiting from broad market movements. Market timing of this sort, however, can result in huge trading costs with the frequent purchase and sale of many stocks. An attractive alternative is to invest in Treasury bills and hold varying amounts of market index futures contracts.

The strategy works like this. When timers are bullish, they will establish many long futures positions that they can liquidate quickly and cheaply when expectations turn bearish. Rather than shifting back and forth between T-bills and stocks, traders buy and hold T-bills and adjust only the futures position. (Recall strategies A and B of the preceding section where we showed that a T-bill plus futures position resulted in a payoff equal to the stock price.) This strategy minimizes transaction costs. An advantage of this technique for timing is that investors can implicitly buy or sell the market index in its entirety, whereas market timing in the spot market would require the simultaneous purchase or sale of all the stocks in the index. This is technically difficult to coordinate and can lead to slippage in the execution of a timing strategy.

The nearby box illustrates that it is now commonplace for money managers to use futures contracts to create synthetic equity positions in stock markets. The article notes that futures positions can be particularly helpful in establishing synthetic positions in foreign equities, where trading costs tend to be greater and markets tend to be less liquid.

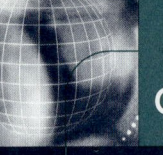

Got a Bundle to Invest Fast? Think Index Futures

As investors go increasingly global and market turbulence grows, stock-index futures are emerging as the favorite way for nimble money managers to deploy their funds.

What's the big appeal? Speed, ease, and cheapness. For most major markets, stock futures not only boast greater liquidity but also offer lower transaction costs than traditional trading methods.

Portfolio managers stress that in today's fast-moving markets, it's critical to implement decisions quickly. For giant mutual and pension funds eager to keep assets fully invested, shifting billions around through stock-index futures is much easier than trying to identify individual stocks to buy and sell.

"When I decide it's time to move into France, Germany, or Britain, I don't necessarily want to wait around until I find exactly the right stocks," says Fabrizio Pierallini, manager of New York-based Vontobel Ltd.'s Euro Pacific Fund.

Mr. Pierallini, who has $120 million invested in stocks in Europe, Asia, and Latin America, says he later finetunes his market picks by gradually shifting out of futures into favorite stocks. To the extent Mr. Pierallini's stocks outperform the market, futures provide a means to preserve those gains, even while hedging against market declines.

For instance, by selling futures equal to the value of the underlying portfolio, a manager can almost completely insulate a portfolio from market moves. Say a manager succeeds in outperforming the market, but still loses 3% while the market as a whole falls 10%. Hedging with futures would capture that margin of outperformance, transforming the loss into a profit of roughly 7%. Demand for such protection helped account for stock futures' surging popularity in last year's difficult markets, Goldman said in its report.

"You can get all the value your managers are going to add" relative to the market, "and you don't need to worry about the costs of trading" actual securities, said David Leinweber, director of research at First Quadrant Corp., a Pasadena, Calif., investment firm that traded some $59 billion of futures in 1994.

Among First Quadrant's futures-intensive strategies is "global tactical asset allocation," which involves trading whole markets worldwide as traditional managers might trade stocks. The growing popularity of such asset-allocation strategies has given futures a big boost in recent years.

When it comes to investing overseas, futures are often the only vehicle that makes sense from a cost standpoint. Abroad, transaction taxes and sky-high commissions can wipe out more than 1% of the money deployed on each trade. By contrast, a comparable trade in futures costs as little as 0.05%.

SOURCE: Suzanne McGee, *The Wall Street Journal*, February 21, 1995. Reprinted by permission of *The Wall Street Journal*, © 1995 Dow Jones & Company, Inc. All Rights Reserved Worldwide.

WEBMASTER

Hedging by Using Index Futures

The Chicago Mercantile Exchange, along with most of the organized exchanges, offers significant educational material online. A good introduction to hedging and the use of futures can be found at the following website: http://www.cme.com/allaire/spectra/system/securemediastore/G96_Hedge_Portfolio 2002.pdf

After reviewing this short pamphlet, address the following questions:

1. Which index futures contracts trade on the Chicago Mercantile Exchange?

2. What ranges of correlation were reported in this publication between the S&P 500 Index and the returns on selected mutual funds?

3. Review the results and basic plan in strategy A for hedging a long position. If the market index had risen, what type of results would you have expected? Briefly explain.

Index Arbitrage and the Triple-Witching Hour

Whenever the actual futures price differs from its parity value, there is an opportunity for profit. This is why the parity relationships are so important. One of the most notable developments in trading activity has been the advent of **index arbitrage,** an investment strategy that exploits divergences between the actual futures price on a stock market index and its theoretically correct parity value.

In principle, index arbitrage is simple. If the futures price is too high, short the futures contract and buy the stocks in the index. If it is too low, go long in futures and short the stocks. You can perfectly hedge your position and should earn arbitrage profits equal to the mispricing of the contract.

In practice, however, index arbitrage can be difficult to implement. The problem lies in buying the stocks in the index. Selling or purchasing shares in all 500 stocks in the S&P 500 is difficult for two reasons. The first is transaction costs, which may outweigh any profits to be made from the arbitrage. Second, it is extremely difficult to buy or sell the stock of 500 different firms simultaneously—and any lags in the execution of such a strategy can destroy the effectiveness of a plan to exploit short-lived price discrepancies.

Arbitrageurs need to trade an entire portfolio of stocks quickly and simultaneously if they hope to exploit temporary disparities between the futures price and its corresponding stock index. For this they need a coordinated trading program; hence the term **program trading,** which refers to coordinated purchases or sales of entire portfolios of stocks. Such strategies can be executed using the NYSE SuperDot (designated order turnaround) system, which enables traders to send coordinated buy or sell programs to the floor of the stock exchange over computer lines. (We discussed the SuperDot system in Chapter 3.)

In each year, there are four maturing S&P 500 futures contracts. On these four Fridays, which occur simultaneously with the expiration of S&P index options and options on some individual stocks, the market has tended to exhibit above-average volatility. These dates have been dubbed the **triple-witching hour** because of the occasional volatility associated with the expirations in the three types of contracts.

The program trading associated with index arbitrage commonly accounts for 10–20% of NYSE daily volume. *The Wall Street Journal* regularly reports on program trading, both in aggregate and for the largest traders.

Foreign Exchange Futures

Exchange rates between currencies vary continually and often substantially. This variability can be a source of concern for anyone involved in international business. A U.S. exporter who sells goods in England, for example, will be paid in British pounds, and the dollar value of those pounds depends on the exchange rate at the time payment is made. Until that date, the U.S. exporter is exposed to foreign exchange rate risk. This risk can be hedged through currency futures or forward markets. For example, if you know you will receive £100,000 in 60 days, you can sell those pounds forward today in the forward market and lock in an exchange rate equal to today's forward price.

The forward market in foreign exchange is relatively informal. It is simply a network of banks and brokers that allows customers to enter forward contracts to purchase or sell currency in the future at a currently agreed-upon rate of exchange. The bank market in currencies is among the largest in the world, and most large traders with sufficient creditworthiness execute their trades here rather than in futures markets. Contracts in these markets are not standardized in a formal market setting. Instead, each is negotiated separately. Moreover, there is

index arbitrage

Strategy that exploits divergences between actual futures prices and their theoretically correct parity values to make a riskless profit.

program trading

Coordinated buy orders and sell orders of entire portfolios, usually with the aid of computers, often to achieve index arbitrage objectives.

triple-witching hour

The four times a year that the S&P 500 futures contract expires at the same time as the S&P 100 index option contract and option contracts on individual stocks.

no marking to market as would occur in futures markets. Forward contracts call for execution only at the maturity date.

For currency futures, however, there are formal markets established by the Chicago Mercantile Exchange (International Monetary Market), the London International Financial Futures Exchange, and other exchanges. Here, contracts are standardized by size, and daily marking to market is observed. Moreover, there are standard clearing arrangements that allow traders to enter or reverse positions easily.

Figure 16.6 reproduces a *Wall Street Journal* listing of foreign exchange spot and forward rates. The listing gives the number of U.S. dollars required to purchase a unit of foreign currency and then the amount of foreign currency needed to purchase $1.

The forward quotations in Figure 16.6 always apply to rolling delivery in 30, 90, or 180 days. Thus, tomorrow's forward listings will apply to a maturity date one day later than today's listing. In contrast, foreign exchange futures contracts mature at specified dates in March, June, September, and December (see Figure 16.2); these four maturity days are the only dates each year when futures contracts settle.

FIGURE **16.6**

Spot and forward prices in foreign exchange

Source: From *The Wall Street Journal*, January 16, 2002. Reprinted by permission of Dow Jones & Company, Inc., via Copyright Clearance Center, Inc. © Dow Jones & Company, Inc. All Rights Reserved Worldwide.

CURRENCY TRADING

Tuesday, January 15, 2002
EXCHANGE RATES

The New York foreign exchange mid-range rates below apply to trading among banks in amounts of $1 million and more, as quoted at 4 p.m. Eastern time by Reuters and other sources. Retail transactions provide fewer units of foreign currency per dollar. Rates for the 12 Euro currency countries are derived from the latest dollar-euro rate using the exchange ratios set 1/1/99.

Country	U.S. $ EQUIV. Tue	U.S. $ EQUIV. Mon	CURRENCY PER U.S. $ Tue	CURRENCY PER U.S. $ Mon
Argentina (Peso)-y	.5405	.5882	1.8500	1.7000
Australia (Dollar)	.5174	.5188	1.9326	1.9277
Austria (Schilling)	.06414	.06500	15.592	15.385
Bahrain (Dinar)	2.6525	2.6525	.3770	.3770
Belgium (Franc)	.0219	.0222	45.7083	45.1028
Brazil (Real)	.4211	.4175	2.3750	2.3950
Britain (Pound)	1.4399	1.4498	.6945	.6898
1-month forward	1.4369	1.4467	.6959	.6912
3-months forward	1.4317	1.4416	.6985	.6937
6-months forward	1.4235	1.4332	.7025	.6977
Canada (Dollar)	.6292	.6270	1.5893	1.5949
1-month forward	.6290	.6269	1.5898	1.5951
3-months forward	.6287	.6268	1.5905	1.5955
6-months forward	.6286	.6268	1.5909	1.5954
Chile (Peso)	.001498	.001496	667.65	668.65
China (Renminbi)	.1208	.1208	8.2768	8.2767
Colombia (Peso)	.0004391	.0004356	2277.50	2295.50
Czech. Rep. (Koruna)				
Commercial rate	.02741	.02777	36.487	36.016
Denmark (Krone)	.1187	.1203	8.4225	8.3114
Ecuador (US Dollar)-e	1.0000	1.0000	1.0000	1.0000
Finland (Markka)	.1484	.1504	6.7370	6.6477
France (Franc)	.1345	.1364	7.4325	7.3340
Germany (Mark)	.4512	.4573	2.2161	2.1868
Greece (Drachma)	.002590	.002625	386.08	381.03
Hong Kong (Dollar)	.1282	.1282	7.7987	7.7986
Hungary (Forint)	.003618	.003663	276.43	272.98
India (Rupee)	.02072	.02070	48.260	48.310
Indonesia (Rupiah)	.0000963	.0000961	10388	10405
Ireland (Punt)	1.1206	1.1356	.8924	.8806
Israel (Shekel)	.2207	.2225	4.5320	4.4950
Italy (Lira)	.0004558	.0004619	2193.95	2164.88
Japan (Yen)	.007625	.007573	131.14	132.04
1-month forward	.007637	.007585	130.94	131.84
3-months forward	.007656	.007604	130.61	131.51

Country	U.S. $ EQUIV. Tue	U.S. $ EQUIV. Mon	CURRENCY PER U.S. $ Tue	CURRENCY PER U.S. $ Mon
6-months forward	.007691	.007637	130.03	130.93
Jordan (Dinar)	1.4108	1.4108	.7088	.7088
Kuwait (Dinar)	3.2541	3.2573	.3073	.3070
Lebanon (Pound)	.0006606	.0006606	1513.88	1513.75
Malaysia (Ringgit)-b	.2632	.2632	3.8000	3.8000
Malta (Lira)	2.2109	2.2292	.4523	.4486
Mexico (Peso)				
Floating rate	.1089	.1084	9.1788	9.2242
Netherlands (Guilder)	.4005	.4059	2.4970	2.4639
New Zealand (Dollar)	.4230	.4231	2.3641	2.3635
Norway (Krone)	.1116	.1124	8.9625	8.8958
Pakistan (Rupee)	.01665	.01667	60.050	60.000
Peru (new Sol)	.2895	.2886	3.4545	3.4655
Philippines (Peso)	.01951	.01948	51.250	51.325
Poland (Zloty)-d	.2449	.2466	4.0838	4.0545
Portugal (Escudo)	.004402	.004461	227.16	224.15
Russia (Ruble)-a	.03274	.03281	30.545	30.475
Saudi Arabia (Riyal)	.2666	.2666	3.7504	3.7506
Singapore (Dollar)	.5474	.5451	1.8267	1.8345
Slovak Rep. (Koruna)	.02072	.02102	48.264	47.570
South Africa (Rand)	.0854	.0864	11.7045	11.5700
South Korea (Won)	.0007623	.0007649	1311.90	1307.30
Spain (Peseta)	.005304	.005375	188.53	186.03
Sweden (Krona)	.0959	.0967	10.4301	10.3423
Switzerland (Franc)	.5979	.6040	1.6726	1.6557
1-month forward	.5979	.6040	1.6725	1.6556
3-months forward	.5979	.6039	1.6726	1.6558
6-months forward	.5980	.6040	1.6723	1.6555
Taiwan (Dollar)	.02861	.02859	34.950	34.980
Thailand (Baht)	.02281	.02277	43.840	43.910
Turkey (Lira)-f	.00000073	.00000073	1366000	1370000
United Arab (Dirham)	.2722	.2723	3.6731	3.6730
Uruguay (New Peso)				
Financial	.07080	.07042	14.125	14.200
Venezuela (Bolivar)	.001311	.001315	762.75	760.50
SDR	1.2594	1.2594	.7940	.7940
Euro	.8826	.8944	1.1330	1.1181

Special Drawing Rights (SDR) are based on exchange rates for the U.S., German, British, French , and Japanese currencies. Source: International Monetary Fund.
a-Russian Central Bank rate. b-Government rate. d-Floating rate; trading band suspended on 4/11/00. e-Adopted U.S. dollar as of 9/11/00. f-Floating rate, eff. Feb. 22. y-Floating rate.

Interest Rate Futures

The late 1970s and 1980s saw a dramatic increase in the volatility of interest rates, leading to investor desire to hedge returns on fixed-income securities against changes in interest rates. As one example, thrift institutions that had loaned money on home mortgages before 1975 suffered substantial capital losses on those loans when interest rates later increased. An interest rate futures contract could have protected banks against such large swings in yields. The significance of these losses has spurred trading in interest rate futures.

The major U.S. interest rate contracts currently traded are on Eurodollars, Treasury bills, Treasury notes, and Treasury bonds. The range of these securities provides an opportunity to hedge against a wide spectrum of maturities from very short (T-bills) to long term (T-bonds). In addition, futures contracts tied to interest rates in Europe (euro-denominated), Japan, the United Kingdom, and several other countries trade and are listed in *The Wall Street Journal*. Figure 16.2 shows listings of some of these contracts in *The Wall Street Journal*.

The Treasury contracts call for delivery of a Treasury bond, bill, or note. Should interest rates rise, the market value of the security at delivery will be less than the original futures price, and the deliverer will profit. Hence, the short position in the interest rate futures contract gains when interest rates rise and bond prices fall.

Similarly, Treasury bond futures can be useful hedging vehicles for bond dealers or underwriters. We saw earlier, for example, how the T-bond contract could be used by an investor to hedge the value of a T-bond portfolio or by a pension fund manager who anticipates the purchase of a Treasury bond.

An episode that occurred in October 1979 illustrates the potential hedging value offered by T-bond contracts. Salomon Brothers, Merrill Lynch, and other underwriters brought out a $1 billion issue of IBM bonds. As is typical, the underwriting syndicate quoted an interest rate at which it guaranteed the bonds could be sold. This underwriting arrangement is called a "firm commitment," and is discussed in more detail in Chapter 3. (In essence, the syndicate buys the company's bonds at an agreed-upon price and then takes the responsibility of reselling them in the open market. If interest rates increase before the bonds can be sold to the public, the syndicate, not the issuer, bears the capital loss from the fall in the value of the bonds.)

In this case, the syndicate led by Salomon Brothers and Merrill Lynch brought out the IBM debt to sell at yields of 9.62% for $500 million of 7-year notes and 9.41% for $500 million of 25-year bonds. These yields were only about four basis points above comparable maturity U.S. government bond yields, reflecting IBM's excellent credit rating. The debt issue was brought to market on Thursday, October 4, when the underwriters began placing the bonds with customers. Interest rates, however, rose slightly that Thursday, making the IBM yields less attractive, and only about 70% of the issue had been placed by Friday afternoon, leaving the syndicate still holding between $250 million and $300 million of bonds.

Then on Saturday, October 6, the Federal Reserve Board announced a major credit-tightening policy. Interest rates jumped by almost a full percentage point. The underwriting syndicate realized the balance of the IBM bonds could not be placed to its regular customers at the original offering price and decided to sell them in the open bond market. By that time, the bonds had fallen nearly 5% in value, so that the underwriter's loss was about $12 million on the unsold bonds. The net loss on the underwriting operation came to about $7 million, after the profit of $5 million that had been realized on the bonds that were placed.

As the major underwriter with the lion's share of the bonds, Salomon lost about $3.5 million on the bond issue. Yet, while most of the other underwriters were vulnerable to the interest rate movement, Salomon had hedged its bond holdings by shorting about $100 million in Government National Mortgage Association (GNMA) and Treasury bond futures. Holding a short position, Salomon Brothers realized profits on the contract when interest rates increased.

The profits on the short futures position resulted because the value of the bonds required to be delivered to satisfy the contract decreased when interest rates rose. Salomon Brothers probably about broke even on the entire transaction, making estimated gains on the futures position of about $3.5 million, which largely offset the capital loss on the bonds it was holding.

How could Salomon Brothers have constructed the proper hedge ratio, that is, the proper number of futures contracts per bond held in its inventory? The T-bond futures contract nominally called for delivery of an 8% coupon, 20-year maturity government bond in return for the futures price. (In practice, other bonds may be substituted for this standard bond to settle the contract, but we will use the 8% bond for illustration.) Suppose the market interest rate is 10% and Salomon is holding $100 million worth of bonds, with a coupon rate of 10% and 20 years to maturity. The bonds currently sell at 100% of par value. If the interest rate were to jump to 11%, the bonds would fall in value to a market value of $91.98 per $100 of par value, a loss of $8.02 million. (We use semiannual compounding in this calculation.)

To hedge this risk, Salomon would need to short enough futures so that the profits on the futures position would offset the loss on the bonds. The 8%, 20-year bond of the futures contract would sell for $82.84 at an interest rate of 10%. If the interest rate were to jump to 11%, the bond price would fall to $75.93, and the fall in the price of the 8% bond, $6.91, would approximately equal the profit on the short futures position per $100 par value.[7] Because each contract calls for delivery of $100,000 par value of bonds, the gain on each short position would equal $6,910. Thus, to offset the $8.02 million loss on the value of the bonds, Salomon theoretically would need to hold $8.02 million/$6,910 = 1,161 contracts short. The total gain on the contracts would offset the loss on the bonds and leave Salomon unaffected by interest rate swings.

The actual hedging problem is more difficult for several reasons, most of which are due to the fact that this is really a cross-hedge: Salomon is hedging its IBM bonds by selling contracts on Treasury bonds and, to a lesser extent, GNMA bonds. Some of the complications in this hedging strategy are: (1) Salomon probably would hold more than one issue of bonds in its inventory; (2) interest rates on government and corporate bonds will not be equal and need not move in lockstep; (3) the T-bond contract may be settled with any of several bonds instead of the 8% benchmark bond; and (4) taxes could complicate the picture. Nevertheless, the principles illustrated here underlie all hedging activity.

www.mhhe.com/bkm

SUMMARY

- Forward contracts are arrangements that call for the future delivery of an asset at a currently agreed-upon price. The long trader is obligated to purchase the good, and the short trader is obligated to deliver it. If the price at the maturity of the contract exceeds the forward price, the long side benefits by virtue of acquiring the good at the contract price.
- A futures contract is similar to a forward contract, differing most importantly in the aspects of standardization and marking to market, which is the process by which gains and losses on futures contract positions are settled daily. In contrast, forward contracts call for no cash transfers until contract maturity.
- Futures contracts are traded on organized exchanges that standardize the size of the contract, the grade of the deliverable asset, the delivery date, and the delivery location. Traders negotiate only the contract price. This standardization creates increased liquidity

[7]We say approximately because the exact figure depends on the time to maturity of the contract. We assume here that the maturity date is less than a month away so that the futures price and the bond price move in virtual lockstep.

in the marketplace and means buyers and sellers can easily find many traders for a desired purchase or sale.

- The clearinghouse acts as an intermediary between each pair of traders, acting as the short position for each long, and as the long position for each short, so traders need not be concerned about the performance of the trader on the opposite side of the contract. Traders are required to post margins in order to guarantee their own performance on the contracts.

- The gain or loss to the long side for a futures contract held between time 0 and t is $F_t - F_0$. Because $F_T = P_T$ at maturity, the long's profit if the contract is held until maturity is $P_T - F_0$, where P_T is the spot price at time T and F_0 is the original futures price. The gain or loss to the short position is $F_0 - P_T$.

- Futures contracts may be used for hedging or speculating. Speculators use the contracts to take a stand on the ultimate price of an asset. Short hedgers take short positions in contracts to offset any gains or losses on the value of an asset already held in inventory. Long hedgers take long positions in futures contracts to offset gains or losses in the purchase price of a good.

- The spot-futures parity relationship states that the equilibrium futures price on an asset providing no service or payments (such as dividends) is $F_0 = P_0(1 + r_f)^T$. If the futures price deviates from this value, then market participants can earn arbitrage profits.

- If the asset provides services or payments with yield d, the parity relationship becomes $F_0 = P_0(1 + r_f - d)^T$. This model is also called the cost-of-carry model, because it states that the futures price must exceed the spot price by the net cost of carrying the asset until maturity date T.

- Futures contracts calling for cash settlement are traded on various stock market indexes. The contracts may be mixed with Treasury bills to construct artificial equity positions, which makes them potentially valuable tools for market timers. Market index contracts also are used by arbitrageurs who attempt to profit from violations of the parity relationship.

- Interest rate futures allow for hedging against interest rate fluctuations in several different markets. The most actively traded contract is for Treasury bonds.

KEY TERMS

basis, 579
basis risk, 579
cash delivery, 576
clearinghouse, 572
convergence property, 575
cost-of-carry
  relationship, 582

forward contract, 566
futures price, 567
index arbitrage, 587
long position, 567
maintenance margin, 574
marking to market, 574
program trading, 587

short position, 567
spot-futures parity
  theorem, 582
spread, 579
triple-witching hour, 587

PROBLEM SETS

1. The open interest on a futures contract at any given time is the total number of outstanding:
   a. Contracts.
   b. Unhedged positions.
   c. Clearinghouse positions.
   d. Long and short positions.

2. In futures trading, the minimum level to which an equity position may fall before requiring additional margin is *most accurately* termed the:
   a. Initial margin.
   b. Variation margin.
   c. Cash flow margin.
   d. Maintenance margin.

www.mhhe.com/bkm

3. A silver futures contract requires the seller to deliver 5,000 Troy ounces of silver. Jerry Harris sells one July silver futures contract at a price of $8 per ounce, posting a $2,025 initial margin. If the required maintenance margin is $1,500, what is the *first* price per ounce at which Harris would receive a maintenance margin call?

4. *a.* Using Figure 16.2, compute the dollar value of the stocks traded on one contract on the Standard & Poor's 500 index. The closing spot price of the S&P index is given in the last line of the figure. If the margin requirement is 10% of the futures price times the multiplier of $250, how much must you deposit with your broker to trade the March contract?

   b. If the March futures price were to increase to $1,200, what rate of return would you earn on your net investment if you entered the long side of the contract at the price shown in the figure?

   c. If the March futures price falls by 1%, what is the percentage gain or loss on your net investment?

5. Why is there no futures market in cement?

6. Why might individuals purchase futures contracts rather than the underlying asset?

7. What is the difference in cash flow between short-selling an asset and entering a short futures position?

8. Consider a stock that will pay a dividend of D dollars in one year, which is when a futures contract matures. Consider the following strategy: Buy the stock, short a futures contract on the stock, and borrow S_0 dollars, where S_0 is the current price of the stock.

   a. What are the cash flows now and in one year? (Remember the dividend the stock will pay.)

   b. Show that the equilibrium futures price must be $F_0 = S_0(1 + r) - D$ to avoid arbitrage.

   c. Call the dividend yield $d = D/S_0$, and conclude that $F_0 = S_0(1 + r - d)$.

9. *a.* A hypothetical futures contract on a nondividend-paying stock with current price $150 has a maturity of one year. If the T-bill rate is 6%, what should the futures price be?

   b. What should the futures price be if the maturity of the contract is three years?

   c. What if the interest rate is 8% and the maturity of the contract is three years?

10. Your analysis leads you to believe the stock market is about to rise substantially. The market is unaware of this situation. What should you do?

11. In each of the following cases, discuss how you, as a portfolio manager, could use financial futures to protect a portfolio.

   a. You own a large position in a relatively illiquid bond that you want to sell.

   b. You have a large gain on one of your long Treasuries and want to sell it, but you would like to defer the gain until the next accounting period, which begins in four weeks.

   c. You will receive a large contribution next month that you hope to invest in long-term corporate bonds on a yield basis as favorable as is now available.

12. Suppose the value of the S&P 500 stock index is currently $1,300. If the one-year T-bill rate is 5% and the expected dividend yield on the S&P 500 is 2%, what should the one-year maturity futures price be?

13. It is now January. The current interest rate is 5%. The June futures price for gold is $346.30, while the December futures price is $360.00. Is there an arbitrage opportunity here? If so, how would you exploit it?

14. The Chicago Board of Trade has just introduced a new futures contract on the stock of Brandex, a company that currently pays no dividends. Each contract calls for delivery of 1,000 shares of stock in one year. The T-bill rate is 6% per year.
   a. If Brandex stock now sells at $120 per share, what should the futures price be?
   b. If the Brandex stock price drops by 3%, what will be the change in the futures price and the change in the investor's margin account?
   c. If the margin on the contract is $12,000, what is the percentage return on the investor's position?

15. The multiplier for a futures contract on the stock market index is $250. The maturity of the contract is one year, the current level of the index is 1,200, and the risk-free interest rate is .5% per month. The dividend yield on the index is .2% per month. Suppose that after one month, the stock index is at 1,210.
   a. Find the cash flow from the mark-to-market proceeds on the contract. Assume that the parity condition always holds exactly.
   b. Find the one-month holding-period return if the initial margin on the contract is $15,000.

16. Futures contracts and options contracts can be used to modify risk. Identify the fundamental distinction between a futures contract and an option contract, and briefly explain the difference in the manner that futures and options modify portfolio risk.

17. Suppose an S&P index portfolio pays a dividend yield of 2% annually. The index currently is 1,200. The T-bill rate is 5%, and the S&P futures price for delivery in one year is $1,243. Construct an arbitrage strategy to exploit the mispricing and show that your profits one year hence will equal the mispricing in the futures market.

18. a. How should the parity condition (Equation 16.2) for stocks be modified for futures contracts on Treasury bonds? What should play the role of the dividend yield in that equation?
   b. In an environment with an upward-sloping yield curve, should T-bond futures prices on more distant contracts be higher or lower than those on near-term contracts?
   c. Confirm your intuition by examining Figure 16.2.

19. The one-year futures price on a particular stock-index portfolio is 406, the stock index currently is 400, the one-year risk-free interest rate is 3%, and the year-end dividend that will be paid on a $400 investment in the index portfolio is $5.
   a. By how much is the contract mispriced?
   b. Formulate a zero-net-investment arbitrage portfolio and show that you can lock in riskless profits equal to the futures mispricing.
   c. Now assume (as is true for small investors) that if you short sell the stocks in the market index, the proceeds of the short sale are kept with the broker, and you do not receive any interest income on the funds. Is there still an arbitrage opportunity (assuming you don't already own the shares in the index)? Explain.
   d. Given the short-sale rules, what is the no-arbitrage *band* for the stock-futures price relationship? That is, given a stock index of 400, how high and how low can the futures price be without giving rise to arbitrage opportunities?

20. The S&P 500 index is currently at 1,400. You manage a $7 million indexed equity portfolio. The S&P 500 futures contract has a multiplier of $250.
   a. If you are temporarily bearish on the stock market, how many contracts should you sell to fully eliminate your exposure over the next six months?
   b. If T-bills pay 2% per six months and the semiannual dividend yield is 1%, what is the parity value of the futures price? Show that if the contract is fairly priced, the

total risk-free proceeds on the hedged strategy in part (*a*) provide a return equal to the T-bill rate.

c. How would your hedging strategy change if, instead of holding an indexed portfolio, you hold a portfolio of only one stock with a beta of 0.6? How many contracts would you now choose to sell? Would your hedged position be riskless? What would be the beta of the hedged position?

21. The margin requirement on the S&P 500 futures contract is 10%, and the stock index is currently 1,200. Each contract has a multiplier of $250. How much margin must be put up for each contract sold? If the futures price falls by 1% to 1,188, what will happen to the margin account of an investor who holds one contract? What will be the investor's percentage return based on the amount put up as margin?

22. The multiplier for a futures contract on a certain stock market index is $500. The maturity of the contract is one year, the current level of the index is 400, and the risk-free interest rate is 0.5% per *month*. The dividend yield on the index is 0.2% per month. Suppose that *after one month,* the stock index is at 410.
    a. Find the cash flow from the mark-to-market proceeds on the contract. Assume that the parity condition always holds exactly.
    b. Find the holding-period return if the initial margin on the contract is $15,000.

23. You are a corporate treasurer who will purchase $1 million of bonds for the sinking fund in three months. You believe rates soon will fall and would like to repurchase the company's sinking fund bonds, which currently are selling below par, in advance of requirements. Unfortunately, you must obtain approval from the board of directors for such a purchase, and this can take up to two months. What action can you take in the futures market to hedge any adverse movements in bond yields and prices until you actually can buy the bonds? Will you be long or short? Why?

WEBMASTER

Contract Specifications for Financial Futures and Options

Go to the Chicago Board of Trade site at http://www.cbot.com. Under the Knowledge Center item find the contract specifications for the Dow Jones Industrial Average Futures and the Dow Jones Industrial Average Options. Then, answer the following questions:

1. What contract months are available for both the futures and the options?

2. What is the trading unit on the futures contract?

3. What is the trading unit on the option contract?

Obtain current prices on the Dow Jones Industrial Average Futures Contract. This can be found under Equity Futures quotes.

4. What is the futures price for the two delivery months that are closest to the current month? (Use the last trade for price.)

5. How does that compare to the current price of the Dow Jones Industrial Average?

6. What are the prices for the put and call options that are deliverable in the same months as the futures contracts? Choose exercise prices as close as possible to the futures price.

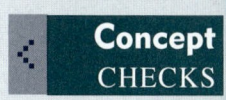

1. *a.* The payoff on the put looks like that on the short futures contract when the asset price falls below X or F_0, but when the asset price rises above F_0, the futures payoff turns negative whereas the value of the put cannot fall below zero. The put (which must be purchased) gives you upside potential if the asset price falls but limits downside risk, whereas the futures gives you both upside and downside exposure.

   b. The payoff on the written call looks like that on the short futures contract when the asset price rises above F_0, but when the asset price falls, the futures payoff is positive, whereas the payoff on the written call is never positive. The written call gives you downside exposure, but your upside potential is limited to the premium you received for the option.

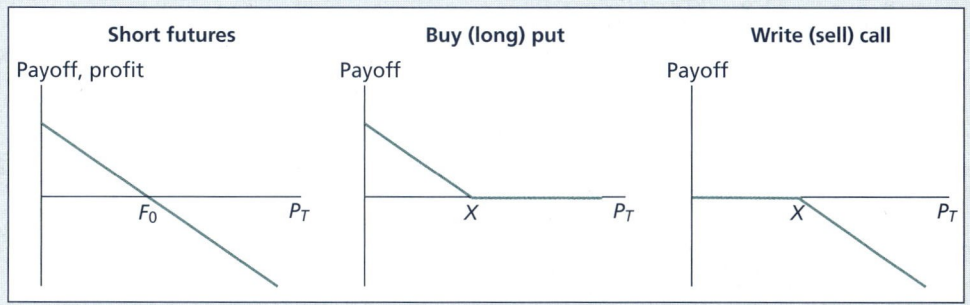

2. The clearinghouse has a zero net position in all contracts. Its long and short positions are offsetting, so that net cash flow from marking to market must be zero.

3.

	T-Bond Price in March		
	$102.91	**$103.91**	**$104.91**
Cash flow to purchase bonds ($= -2{,}000\, P_T$)	$-$205,820	$-$207,820	$-$209,820
Profits on long futures position	$-$2,000	$0	2,000
Total cash flow	$-$207,820	$-$207,820	$-$207,820

4. The risk would be that the index and the portfolio do not move perfectly together. Thus, risk involving the spread between the futures price and the portfolio value could persist even if the index futures price were set perfectly relative to index itself.

5.

Action	Initial Cash Flow	Time-T Cash Flow
Lend $280	$-$280	$280(1.005)^6 = \$288.51$
Sell gold short	$+280$	$-S_T$
Long futures	0	$S_T - \$288$
Total	$0	$0.51 risklessly

PART SIX

ACTIVE INVESTMENT MANAGEMENT

Passive investment, or indexing, is the preferred strategy for those who believe markets are efficient. While administration of passive portfolios requires an efficient organizational structure, there is comparatively less need for knowledge of investments in managing index portfolios. In contrast, active management takes it on faith that markets are not always efficient and that, at least occasionally, bargains are to be found in security markets. Active managers must apply asset valuation and portfolio theory to client portfolios.

Professional management of active investments begins with a contractual relationship between client and portfolio manager. The economic needs of clients must be articulated and their objectives translated into an operational financial plan. For this purpose, the Association of Investment Management and Research (AIMR) designed a framework for financial planning that can be understood by lay clients. Chapter 17 familiarizes you with this framework.

Investments originate with a savings plan that diverts funds from consumption to investment. How much should an individual household save? Taxes and inflation complicate the relationship between how much you save and what you will be able to achieve with your accumulating investment fund. Chapter 18 formulates a comprehensive household savings/investment plan.

Active management attempts to exploit market inefficiency that potentially could arise from market frictions or less-than-fully rational investor behavior. Chapter 19 explores the emerging field of behavioral finance and lays down the fundamentals of behavior that may affect security prices. We also catalogue and explain certain techniques known as technical analysis aimed at uncovering deviations from market efficiency in order to improve investment performance.

Regardless of why prices may not reflect all relevant information, efficient exploitation of security mispricing calls for balancing investment in underpriced securities with diversification. How should this balance be struck? The answer is inseparable from the quandary of how to assess the performance of an active portfolio. Accordingly, Chapter 20 begins with the theory of performance evaluation and proceeds to suggest portfolio management techniques to achieve the goal of superior performance.

Investing across borders is conceptually a simple expansion of portfolio diversification. Yet this pursuit confronts the effects of political risk and uncertain exchange rates on future performance. These issues, unique to international investment, are addressed in Chapter 21.

17 Investors and the Investment Process

18 Taxes, Inflation, and Investment Strategy

19 Behavioral Finance and Technical Analysis

20 Performance Evaluation and Active Portfolio Management

21 International Investing

McGraw-Hill / Irwin presents
Investments online

www.mhhe.com/bkm

17

INVESTORS AND THE INVESTMENT PROCESS

**AFTER STUDYING THIS CHAPTER
YOU SHOULD BE ABLE TO:**

> Specify investment objectives of individual and institutional investors.

> Identify constraints on individual and institutional investors.

> Compare and contrast major types of investment policies.

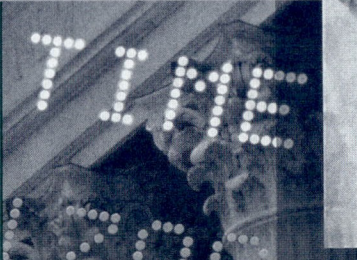

Translating the aspirations and circumstances of diverse households into appropriate investment decisions is a daunting task. The task is equally difficult for institutions, most of which have many stakeholders and often are regulated by various authorities. The investment process is not easily reduced to a simple or mechanical algorithm.

While many principles of investments are quite general and apply to virtually all investors, some issues are peculiar to the specific investor. For example, tax bracket, age, risk tolerance, wealth, job prospects, and uncertainties make each investor's circumstances somewhat unique. In this chapter we focus on the process by which investors systematically review their particular objectives, constraints, and circumstances. Along the way, we survey some of the major classes of institutional investors and examine the special issues they must confront.

There is of course no unique "correct" investment process. However, some approaches are better than others, and it can be helpful to take one high-quality approach as a useful case study. For this reason, we will examine the systematic approach suggested by the Association for Investment Management and Research (AIMR). Among other things, the AIMR administers examinations to certify investment professionals as Chartered Financial Analysts. Therefore, the approach we outline is also one that a highly respected professional group endorses through the curriculum that it requires investment practitioners to master. The nearby box describes how to become a Chartered Financial Analyst.

The basic framework involves dividing the investment process into four stages: specifying objectives, specifying constraints, formulating policy, and monitoring and updating the portfolio as needed. We will treat each of these activities in turn. We start with a description of the major types of investors, both individual and institutional, as well as their special objectives. We turn next to the constraints or circumstances peculiar to each investor class, and we consider some of the investment policies that each can choose.

17.1 INVESTORS AND OBJECTIVES

Most investors would agree with the notion that they want to earn as much money on their investments as possible. But while the concept "earn money" is simple enough *after the fact,* since you simply count the profits on your investments, it is vague when applied to an investment *before the fact,* since you rarely will know for sure what your earnings will be. Almost all investments entail uncertainty. Thus, while investors all wish to earn the highest rate of return possible, they also seek to avoid risk. It is not surprising that ultimately, then, investments that offer higher expected returns will impose greater risk. This is the risk-return trade-off.

Investors will differ in their choice of investments because they differ in their willingness to trade off expected return against risk. We describe the willingness to accept higher risk to attain higher expected returns the investor's **risk tolerance;** equivalently, we can describe attitudes toward risk using the concept of the investor's **risk aversion,** or reluctance to accept risk. The nearby box explores these concepts and shows that while they seem straightforward, real-life behavior can be difficult to characterize so neatly.

These terms describe behavior: If we could observe an investor making many choices among assets whose return and risk were well understood, we could measure an investor's risk aversion (or risk tolerance) by observing his or her willingness to invest in various portfolios with differing risk and return attributes. With no access to such data, and without perfect insight into the risk-return characteristics of investments, we can only surmise an investor's risk aversion. Note that, explicitly or implicitly, many professional investors do exactly that (although, obviously they do more than just that); by choosing investments on behalf of their clients, they make the risk-return choice for their clients.

risk tolerance

The investor's willingness to accept higher risk to attain higher expected returns.

risk aversion

The investor's reluctance to accept risk.

TABLE **17.1**		Under 25	35–54	55 and Over
Amount of risk investors said they were willing to take by age	No risk	54%	55%	71%
	A little risk	30	28	21
	Some risk	14	16	8
	A lot of risk	2	1	1

Source: From Market Facts, Inc., Chicago, IL. Reprinted by permission of Market Facts, Inc.

A natural place to begin a study of the investment process, therefore, is to specify the investor's objectives with two indicators: *return requirement* and *risk tolerance.* The investor then must reconcile these objectives with what is feasible, since any investor faces several constraints. This means that the objective cannot be set as a hard number, but rather as a set of guidelines as to the choice of assets.

Investor objectives arise from a number of factors. Understanding these factors helps investors determine appropriate objectives. It also makes it easier for professional investors to derive appropriate policies for their clients.

Individual Investors

The basic factors affecting an individual investor usually arise from that investor's stage in the life cycle. The first significant investment decision for most individuals concerns education, which is an investment in "human capital." The major asset most people have during their early working years is the earning power derived from their skills. For these people, the financial risk due to illness or injury is far greater than that associated with the rate of return on their portfolios of financial assets. At this point in the life cycle, the most important financial decisions concern insurance against the possibility of disability or death.

The first major economic asset many people acquire is their own house. One can view the purchase of a house as a hedge[1] against two types of risk. The first is the risk of increases in rental rates. If you "pay rent to yourself," you do not need to be concerned with increases in the cost of housing. The second kind of risk is that the particular house or apartment where you live may not always be available to you. By buying, you guarantee its availability.

As one ages and accumulates savings to provide for consumption during retirement, the composition of wealth shifts from human capital toward financial capital. At this point, portfolio choices become progressively more important. In middle age, most investors will be willing to take on a meaningful amount of portfolio risk in order to increase their expected rates of return. As retirement draws near, however, risk tolerance seems to diminish.

The evidence in Table 17.1 supports the life-cycle view of investment behavior. Questionnaire results suggest that attitudes shift away from risk tolerance and toward risk aversion as investors near retirement age. With age, individuals lose the potential to recover from a disastrous investment performance. When they are young, investors can respond to a loss by working harder and saving more of their income. But as retirement approaches, investors realize there will be less time to recover, hence, the shift to safe assets.

---

[1]To hedge means to mitigate a financial risk, a possible loss from a decline in the value of an asset. The return on a hedging asset will be higher when losses from the risk in question are greater. In other words, the return on the hedge asset offsets the risk in question—its returns are inversely related to the exposure from that risk. The greater the negative correlation between the returns on the hedge asset and the risk, the better the hedge. For example, an insurance policy against a specified risk is a perfect hedge, since it is designed precisely to cover a potential loss; its correlation is perfectly negative, -1.

Time for Investing's Four-Letter Word

What four-letter word should pop into mind when the stock market takes a harrowing nose dive?

No, not those. R-I-S-K.

Risk is the potential for realizing low returns or even losing money, possibly preventing you from meeting important objectives, like sending your kids to the college of their choice or having the retirement lifestyle you crave.

Assessing your risk tolerance, however, can be tricky. You must consider not only how much risk you can *afford* to take but also how much risk you can *stand* to take. Determining how much risk you can stand—your temperamental tolerance for risk—is more difficult. It isn't quantifiable.

To that end, many financial advisers, brokerage firms, and mutual-fund companies have created risk quizzes to help people determine whether they are conservative, moderate or aggressive investors. Some firms that offer such quizzes include Merrill Lynch, T. Rowe Price Associates Inc., Baltimore, Zurich Group Inc.'s Scudder Kemper Investments Inc., New York, and Vanguard Group in Malvern, Pa.

Typically, risk questionnaires include 7 to 10 questions about a person's investing experience, financial security and tendency to make risky or conservative choices.

The benefit of the questionnaires is that they are an objective resource people can use to get at least a rough idea of their risk tolerance. "It's impossible for someone to assess their risk tolerance alone," says Mr. Bernstein. "I may say I don't like risk, yet will take more risk than the average person."

Many experts warn, however, that the questionnaires should be used simply as a first step to assessing

risk tolerance. The second step, many experts agree, is to ask yourself some difficult questions, such as: How much can you stand to lose over the long term?

"Most people can stand to lose a heck of a lot temporarily," says Mr. Schatsky. The real acid test, he says, is how much of your portfolio's value you can stand to lose over months or years.

As it turns out, most people rank as middle-of-the-road risk-takers, say several advisers. "Only about 10% to 15% of my clients are aggressive," says Mr. Roge.

What's Your Risk Tolerance?

Circle the letter that corresponds to your answer.

1. Just 60 days after you put money into an investment, its price falls 20 percent. Assuming none of the fundamentals have changed, what would you do?
   a. Sell to avoid further worry and try something else
   b. Do nothing and wait for the investment to come back
   c. Buy more. It was a good investment before; now it's a cheap investment, too.

2. Now look at the previous question another way. Your investment fell 20 percent, but it's part of a portfolio being used to meet investment goals with three different time horizons.

2A. What would you do if the goal were five years away?
   a. Sell
   b. Do nothing
   c. Buy more

The task of life-cycle financial planning is a formidable one for most people. It is not surprising that a whole industry has sprung up to provide personal financial advice.

Professional Investors

Professional investors provide investment management services for a fee. Some are employed directly by wealthy individual investors. Most professional investors, however, either pool many individual investor funds and manage them or serve institutional investors.

personal trust

An interest in an asset held by a trustee for the benefit of another person.

Personal trusts   A **personal trust** is established when an individual confers legal title to property to another person or institution, who then manages that property for one or more beneficiaries. The holder of the title is called the *trustee*. The trustee is usually a bank, a lawyer, or an investment professional. Investment of a trust is subject to state trust laws and *prudent investor rules* that limit the types of allowable trust investment.

2B. What would you do if the goal were 15 years away?
a. Sell
b. Do nothing
c. Buy more

2C. What would you do if the goal were 30 years away?
a. Sell
b. Do nothing
c. Buy more

3. The price of your retirement investment jumps 25% a month after you buy it. Again, the fundamentals haven't changed. After you finish gloating, what do you do?
a. Sell it and lock in your gains
b. Stay put and hope for more gain
c. Buy more: It could go higher

4. You're investing for retirement, which is 15 years away. Which would you rather do?
a. Invest in a money-market fund or guaranteed investment contract, giving up the possibility of major gains, but virtually assuring the safety of your principal
b. Invest in a 50-50 mix of bond funds and stock funds, in hopes of getting some growth, but also giving yourself some protection in the form of steady income
c. Invest in aggressive growth mutual funds whose value will probably fluctuate significantly during the year, but have the potential for impressive gains over five or 10 years

5. You just won a big prize! But which one? It's up to you.
a. $2,000 in cash
b. A 50% chance to win $5,000
c. A 20% chance to win $15,000

6. A good investment opportunity just came along. But you have to borrow money to get in. Would you take out a loan?
a. Definitely not
b. Perhaps
c. Yes

7. Your company is selling stock to its employees. In three years, management plans to take the company public. Until then, you won't be able to sell your shares and you will get no dividends. But your investment could multiply as much as 10 times when the company goes public. How much money would you invest?
a. None
b. Two months' salary
c. Four months' salary

Scoring Your Risk Tolerance

To score the quiz, add up the number of answers you gave in each category a–c, then multiply as shown to find your score:

(a) answers _____ × 1 = _____ points
(b) answers _____ × 2 = _____ points
(c) answers _____ × 3 = _____ points

YOUR SCORE _____ points

If you scored. . .	You may be a:
9–14 points	Conservative investor
15–21 points	Moderate investor
22–27 points	Aggressive investor

SOURCE: Reprinted with permission from Dow Jones & Company, Inc. via Copyright Clearance Center, Inc. © 1998 Dow Jones & Company. All Rights Reserved Worldwide.

The objectives of personal trusts normally are more limited in scope than those of the individual investor. Because of their fiduciary responsibility, personal trust managers typically are expected to invest with more risk aversion than individual investors. Certain asset classes, such as options and futures contracts for example, and strategies, such as short-selling (betting the price of a security will fall) or buying on margin (borrowing up to 50% of the purchase price), are ruled out. Short sales and margin purchases were discussed in Chapter 3.

Mutual funds **Mutual funds** are firms that manage pools of individual investor money. They invest in accordance with their objectives and issue shares that entitle investors to a pro rata portion of the income generated by the funds.

A mutual fund's objectives are spelled out in its prospectus. We discussed mutual funds in detail in Chapter 4.

mutual fund

A firm pooling and managing funds of investors.

Pension Funds   There are two basic types of pension plans: *defined contribution* and *defined benefit.* Defined contribution plans are in effect savings accounts established by the firm for its employees. The employer contributes funds to the plan, but the employee bears all the risk of the fund's investment performance. These plans are called defined contribution because the firm's only obligation is to make the stipulated contributions to the employee's retirement account. The employee is responsible for directing the management of the assets, usually by selecting among several investment funds in which the assets can be placed. Investment earnings in these retirement plans are not taxed until the funds are withdrawn, usually after retirement.

In defined benefit plans, by contrast, the employer has an obligation to provide a specified annual retirement benefit. That benefit is defined by a formula that typically takes into account years of service and the level of salary or wages. For example, the employer may pay the retired employee a yearly amount equal to 2% of the employee's final annual salary for each year of service. A 30-year employee would then receive an annual benefit equal to 60% of his or her final salary. The payments are an obligation of the employer, and the assets in the pension fund provide collateral for the promised benefits. If the investment performance of the assets is poor, the firm is obligated to make up the shortfall by contributing additional assets to the fund. In contrast to defined contribution plans, the risk surrounding investment performance in defined benefit plans is borne by the firm.

A pension actuary makes an assumption about the rate of return that will be earned on the plan's assets and uses this assumed rate to compute the amount the firm must contribute regularly to fund the plan's liabilities. For example, if the actuary assumes a rate of return of 10%, then the firm must contribute $385.54 now to fund $1,000 of pension liabilities that will arise in 10 years, because $385.54 \times 1.10^{10} = \$1,000$.

If a pension fund's *actual* rate of return exceeds the actuarial *assumed* rate, then the firm's shareholders reap an unanticipated gain, because the excess return can be used to reduce future contributions. If the plan's actual rate of return falls short of the assumed rate, however, the firm will have to increase future contributions. Because the sponsoring firm's shareholders bear the risk in a defined benefit pension plan, the objective of the plan will be consistent with the objective of the firm's shareholders.

Many pension plans view their assumed actuarial rate of return as their target rate of return and have little tolerance for earning less than that. Hence, they will take only as much risk as necessary to earn the actuarial rate.

Life Insurance Companies

Life insurance companies generally invest so as to hedge their liabilities, which are defined by the policies they write. The company can reduce its risk by investing in assets that will return more in the event the insurance policy coverage becomes more expensive.

For example, if the company writes a policy that pays a death benefit linked to the consumer price index, then the company is subject to inflation risk. It might search for assets expected to return more when the rate of inflation rises, thus hedging the price-index linkage of the policy.

There are as many objectives as there are distinct types of insurance policies. Until the 1970s, only two types of life insurance policies were available for individuals: whole-life and term.

A *whole-life insurance policy* combines a death benefit with a kind of savings plan that provides for a gradual buildup of cash value that the policyholder can withdraw later in life, usually at age 65. *Term insurance,* on the other hand, provides death benefits only, with no buildup of cash value.

The interest rate imbedded in the schedule of cash value accumulation promised under the whole-life policy is a fixed rate. One way life insurance companies try to hedge this liability is by investing in long-term bonds. Often the insured individual has the right to borrow at a prespecified fixed interest rate against the cash value of the policy.

During the high-interest-rate years of the 1970s and early 1980s, many older whole-life policies allowed policyholders to borrow at rates as low as 4 or 5% per year; some holders borrowed heavily against the cash value to invest in assets paying double-digit yields. Other actual and potential policyholders abandoned whole-life policies and took out term insurance, which accounted for more than half the volume of new sales of individual life policies.

In response to these developments, the insurance industry came up with two new policy types: variable life and universal life. A *variable life policy* entitles the insured to a fixed death benefit plus a cash value that can be invested in the policyholder's choice of mutual funds. A universal life policy allows policyholders to increase or reduce either the insurance premium (the annual fee paid on the policy) or the death benefit (the cash amount paid to beneficiaries in the event of death) according to their changing needs. Furthermore, the interest rate on the cash value component changes with market interest rates.

The great advantage of variable and universal life insurance policies is that earnings on the cash value are not taxed until the money is withdrawn.

Non-Life-Insurance Companies

Non-life-insurance companies such as property and casualty insurers have investable funds primarily because they pay claims *after* they collect policy premiums. Typically, they are conservative in their attitude toward risk.

A common thread in the objectives of pension plans and insurance companies is the need to hedge predictable long-term liabilities. Investment strategies typically call for hedging these liabilities with bonds of various maturities.

Banks

Most bank investments are loans to businesses and consumers, and most of their liabilities are accounts of depositors. As investors, banks try to match the risk of assets to liabilities while earning a profitable spread between the lending and borrowing rates. The difference between the interest charged to a borrower and the interest rate that banks pay on their liabilities is called the bank interest rate spread.

Most liabilities of banks and thrift institutions are checking accounts, time or savings deposits, and certificates of deposit (CDs). Checking account funds may be withdrawn at any time, so they are of the shortest maturity. Time or savings deposits are of various maturities. Some time deposits may extend as long as seven years, but, on average, they are of fairly short maturity. CDs are bonds of various maturities that the bank issues to investors. While the range of maturities is from 90 days to 10 years, the average is about one year.

Traditionally, a large part of the loan portfolio of savings and loan (S&L) institutions was in collateralized real estate loans, better known as mortgages. Typically, mortgages are of 15 to 30 years, significantly longer than the maturity of the average liability. Thus, profits were exposed to interest rate risk. When rates rose, thrifts had to pay higher rates to depositors, while the income from their longer-term investments was relatively fixed. This problem probably was a contributing factor in the S&L debacle of the 1980s. When interest rates rose throughout the 1970s, the financial condition of many banks and thrift institutions deteriorated, making them more willing to assume greater risk in order to achieve higher returns. The greater risk of the loan portfolios was of little concern to depositors because deposits were insured by the Federal Deposit Insurance Corporation (FDIC) or the now-defunct Federal Savings and Loan Insurance Corporation (FSLIC).

As we noted in Chapter 2, most long-term fixed-rate mortgages today are securitized into pass-through certificates and held as securities in the portfolios of mutual funds, pension funds, and other institutional investors. Mortgage originators typically sell the mortgages they originate to pass-through agencies like Fannie Mae or Freddie Mac rather than holding them in a portfolio. They earn their profits on mortgage origination and servicing fees. The trend away from maintaining portfolio holdings of long-term mortgages also has reduced interest rate risk.

Endowment Funds

endowment funds

Portfolios operated for the benefit of a nonprofit entity.

Endowment funds are held by organizations chartered to use their money for specific nonprofit purposes. They are financed by gifts from one or more sponsors and are typically managed by educational, cultural, and charitable organizations or by independent foundations established solely to carry out the fund's specific purposes. Generally, the investment objectives of an endowment fund are to produce a steady flow of income subject to only a moderate degree of risk. Trustees of an endowment fund, however, can specify other objectives as circumstances dictate.

Concept CHECK

1. Describe several distinguishing characteristics of endowment funds that differentiate them from pension funds.

17.2 INVESTOR CONSTRAINTS

Even with identical attitudes toward risk, different households and institutions might choose different investment portfolios because of their differing circumstances. These circumstances include tax status, requirements for liquidity or a flow of income from the portfolio, or various regulatory restrictions. These circumstances impose *constraints* on investor choice. Together, objectives and constraints determine appropriate investment policy.

As noted, constraints usually have to do with investor circumstances. For example, if a family has children about to enter college, there will be a high demand for liquidity since cash will be needed to pay tuition bills. Other times, however, constraints are imposed externally. For example, banks and trusts are subject to legal limitations on the types of assets they may hold in their portfolios. Finally, some constraints are self-imposed. For example, "social investing" means that investors will not hold shares of firms involved in ethically objectionable activities. Some criteria that have been used to judge firms as ineligible for a portfolio are: involvement in nuclear power generation; production of tobacco or alcohol; participation in polluting activities.

Five common types of constraints are described below.

liquidity

Liquidity refers to the speed and ease with which an asset can be converted to cash.

Liquidity

Liquidity is the speed and ease with which an asset can be sold and still fetch a fair price. It is a relationship between the time dimension (how long it will take to sell) and the price dimension (the discount from fair market price) of an investment asset.

When an actual concrete measure of liquidity is necessary, one thinks of the discount when an immediate sale is unavoidable.[2] Cash and money market instruments such as Treasury bills and commercial paper, where the bid–ask spread is a fraction of 1%, are the most liquid assets, and real estate is among the least liquid. Office buildings and manufacturing structures in extreme cases can suffer a 50% liquidity discount.

Both individual and institutional investors must consider how likely they are to require cash at short notice. From this likelihood, they establish the minimum level of liquid assets they need in the investment portfolio.

Investment Horizon

This is the *planned* liquidation date of the investment. Examples of an individual's **investment horizon** could be the time to fund a college education or the retirement date for a wage earner. For a university or hospital endowment, an investment horizon could relate to the time to fund a major construction project. Horizon dates must be considered when investors choose between assets of various maturities. For example, the maturity date of a bond might make it a more attractive investment if it coincides with a date on which cash is needed.

> **investment horizon**
>
> The planned liquidation date.

Regulations

Only professional and institutional investors are constrained by regulations. First and foremost is the **prudent investor rule.** That is, professional investors who manage other people's money have a fiduciary responsibility to restrict investment to assets that would have been approved by a prudent investor. The law is purposefully nonspecific. Every professional investor must stand ready to defend an investment policy in a court of law, and interpretation may differ according to the standards of the times.

> **prudent investor rule**
>
> The fiduciary responsibility of a professional investor.

Also, specific regulations apply to various institutional investors. For instance, U.S. mutual funds may not hold more than 5% of the shares of any publicly traded corporation.

Sometimes, "self-imposed" regulations also affect the investment choice. We have noted several times, for example, that mutual funds describe their investment policies in a prospectus. These policy guidelines amount to constraints on the ability to choose portfolios freely.

Tax Considerations

Tax consequences are central to investment decisions. The performance of any investment strategy should be measured by its rate of return *after* taxes. For household and institutional investors who face significant tax rates, tax sheltering and deferral of tax obligations may be pivotal in their investment strategy.

Unique Needs

Virtually every investor faces special circumstances. Imagine husband-and-wife aeronautical engineers holding high-paying jobs in the same aerospace corporation. The entire human capital of that household is tied to a single player in a rather cyclical industry. This couple would need to hedge the risk of a deterioration in the economic well-being of the aerospace industry.

---

[2]In many cases, it is impossible to know the liquidity of an asset with certainty until it is put up for sale. In dealer markets (described in Chapter 3), however, the liquidity of the traded assets can be observed from the bid–ask spread that is quoted by the dealers, that is, the difference between the "bid" quote (the lower price the dealer will pay the owner) and the "ask" quote (the higher price a buyer would have to pay the dealer).

Looking to Lower Your Risk? Just Add More

If you're like a lot of investors these days, you're looking to make your portfolio "less risky."

The way to do that is by adding more risk, or at least more types of risk.

That strange twist—adding more to get less—is why risk is one of the hardest elements of investing to understand.

The first rule in risk is the hardest for many investors to accept: There is no such thing as a "risk-free investment."

Avoiding one form of risk means embracing another; the safest of investments generally come with the lowest returns, while the biggest potential gainers bring larger potential losses.

The primary risks in fund investing include the following.

Market risk: This is the big one, also known as principal risk, and it's the chance that downturn chews up your money.

Purchasing power risk: Sometimes called "inflation risk," this is the "risk of avoiding risk," and it's at the opposite end of the spectrum from market risk. In a nutshell, this is the possibility that you are too conservative and your money can't grow fast enough to keep pace with inflation.

Interest-rate risk: This is a key factor in the current environment of declining rates, where you face potential income declines when a bond or certificate of deposit matures and you need to reinvest the money.

Goosing returns using higher-yielding, longer-term securities creates the potential to get stuck losing ground to inflation if the rate trend changes again.

Timing risk: This is another highly individual factor, revolving around your personal time horizon. Simply put, the chance of stock mutual funds making money over the next 20 years is high; the prospects for the next 18 months are murky.

If you need money at a certain time, this risk must be factored into your asset allocation.

Liquidity risk: Another risk heightened by current tensions, it affects everything from junk bonds to foreign stocks. If world events were to alter the flow of money in credit markets or to close some foreign stock exchanges for an extended period, your holdings in those areas could be severely hurt.

Political risk: This is the prospect that government decisions will affect the value of your investments. Given the current environment, it is probably a factor in all forms of investing, whether you are looking at stocks or bonds.

Societal risk: Call this "world-event risk." It was evident when the first anthrax scares sent markets reeling briefly. Some businesses are more susceptible (airlines, for example), though virtually all types of investing have some concerns here.

Even after all of those risks, some investments face currency risk, credit risk, and more. Every type of risk deserves some consideration as you build your holdings.

Ultimately, by making sure that your portfolio addresses all types of risk—heavier on the ones you prefer and lighter on those that make you queasy—you ensure that no one type of risk can wipe you out.

That's something that a "less risky" portfolio may not be able to achieve.

SOURCE: Abridged from Charles A. Jaffee's article of the same title, *Boston Sunday Globe*, October 21, 2001. BOSTON SUNDAY GLOBE ("GLOBE STAFF"/"CONTRIBUTING REPORTER" PRODUCED COPY ONLY) by CHARLES A. JAFFE. Copyright 2001 by GLOBE NEWSPAPER CO (MA). Reproduced with permission of GLOBE NEWSPAPER CO (MA) in the format Textbook via Copyright Clearance Center.

Similar issues would confront an executive on Wall Street who owns an apartment near work. Because the value of the home in that part of Manhattan probably depends on the vitality of the securities industry, the individual is doubly exposed to the vagaries of the stock market. Because both job and home already depend on the fortunes of Wall Street, the purchase of a typical diversified stock portfolio would actually increase the exposure to the stock market.

These examples illustrate that the job is often the primary "investment" of an individual, and the unique risk profile that results from employment can play a big role in determining a suitable investment portfolio.

Other unique needs of individuals often center around their stage in the life cycle, as discussed above. Retirement, housing, and children's education constitute three major demands for funds, and investment policy will depend in part on the proximity of these expenditures.

Institutional investors also face unique needs. For example, pension funds will differ in their investment policy, depending on the average age of plan participants. Another example of a unique need for an institutional investor would be a university whose trustees allow the administration to use only cash income from the endowment fund. This constraint would translate into a preference for high-dividend-paying assets.

Table 17.2 summarizes the types of objectives and constraints that investors must face as they form their investment portfolios. The nearby box also explores some of the issues that interact with an investor's particular situation. We turn next to an examination of the specific objectives and constraints of the major investor types.

17.3 OBJECTIVES AND CONSTRAINTS OF VARIOUS INVESTORS

We are now in a position to compare investors on the basis of their objectives and constraints. The next two tables will show how we can apply the objective/constraint approach to the formation of policies.

Objectives

Table 17.3 presents a matrix of objectives for various investors. For mutual funds, the return requirement and risk tolerance are said to be variable because mutual funds segment the

TABLE **17.2** Determination of portfolio policies	Objectives	Constraints
	Return requirements	Liquidity
	Risk tolerance	Horizon
		Regulations
		Taxes
		Unique needs, such as:
		Ethical concerns
		Specific hedging needs
		Age
		Wealth

TABLE **17.3** Matrix of objectives	Type of Investor	Return Requirement	Risk Tolerance
	Individual and personal trusts	Life cycle (education, children, retirement)	Life cycle (younger are more risk tolerant)
	Mutual funds	Variable	Variable
	Pension funds	Assumed actuarial rate	Depends on proximity of payouts
	Endowment funds	Determined by current income needs and need for asset growth to maintain real value	Generally conservative
	Life insurance companies	Should exceed new money rate by sufficient margin to meet expenses and profit objectives; also actuarial rates important	Conservative
	Non-life-insurance companies	No minimum	Conservative
	Banks	Interest spread	Variable

investor market. Various funds appeal to distinct investor groups and will adopt a return requirement and risk tolerance that fit an entire spectrum of market niches. For example, "high-income" funds cater to the conservative investor, while "high-growth" funds seek out the more risk-tolerant ones. Tax-free bond funds segment the market by tax obligation.

Pension funds must meet the actuarial rate; otherwise, the corporation sponsoring the plan will need to make additional contributions. Once a pension fund's actuarial rate is set, it establishes the fund return requirement, and additional risk tolerance becomes very low.

Endowment funds are classified as having "conservative" risk tolerance on the basis of observation, although individual institutions can differ in investment policy.

Life insurance companies have obligations to whole-life policyholders that are similar to those of pension funds. These obligations require them to earn a minimum rate (analogous to the pension fund's actuarial rate), if the company is to meet its liabilities.

Banks earn profit from the interest rate spread between loans extended (the bank's assets) and deposits and CDs (the bank's liabilities), as well as from fees for services. Managing bank assets calls for balancing the loan portfolio with the portfolio of deposits and CDs. A bank can increase the interest rate spread by lending to riskier borrowers and by increasing the proportion of longer-term loans. Both policies threaten bank solvency though, so their deployment must match the risk tolerance of the bank shareholders. In addition, bank capital regulations now are risk-based, so higher-risk strategies will elicit higher capital requirements as well as the possibility of greater regulatory interference in the bank's affairs.

Constraints

Table 17.4 presents a matrix of constraints for various investors. As you would expect, liquidity and tax constraints for individuals are variable because of wealth and age differentials.

A particular constraint for mutual funds arises from investor response to the fund performance. When a mutual fund earns an unsatisfactory rate of return, investors often redeem their shares—they withdraw money from the fund. The mutual fund then contracts. The reverse happens when a mutual fund earns an unusually high return: It can become popular with investors overnight, and its asset base will grow dramatically.

Pension funds are heavily regulated by the Employee Retirement Income Security Act of 1974 (ERISA). This law revolutionized savings for retirement in the United States and remains a major piece of social legislation. Thus, for pension funds, regulatory constraints are relatively important. Also, mature pension funds are required to pay out more than young funds and hence need more liquidity.

TABLE 17.4 Matrix of constraints	Type of Investor	Liquidity	Horizon	Regulatory	Taxes
	Individuals and personal trusts	Variable	Life cycle	Prudent investor laws (for trusts)	Variable
	Mutual funds	Low	Short	Little	None
	Pension funds	Young, low; mature, high	Long	ERISA	None
	Endowment funds	Little	Long	Little	None
	Life insurance companies	Low	Long	Complex	Yes
	Non–life insurance companies	High	Short	Little	Yes
	Banks	Low	Short	Changing	Yes

Endowment funds, on the other hand, usually do not need to liquidate assets, or even use dividend income, to finance payouts. Contributions are expected to exceed payouts and increase the real value of the endowment fund, so liquidity is not an overriding concern.

Life insurance companies are subject to complex regulation. The corporate tax rate, which today is 35% for large firms, also applies to insurance company investment income, so taxes are an important concern.

Property and casualty insurance, like term life insurance, is written on a short-term basis. Most policies must be renewed annually, which means property and casualty insurance companies are subject to short-term horizon constraints.

The short horizon constraint for banks comes from the interest rate risk component of the interest rate spread (i.e., the risk of interest rate increases that banks face when financing long-term assets with short-term liabilities).

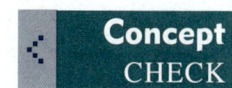

2. *a.* **Think about the financial circumstances of your closest relative in your parents' generation (for example, your parents' household if you are fortunate enough to have them around). Write down the objectives and constraints for their investment decisions.**

   b. **Now consider the financial situation of your closest friend or relative who is in his or her 30s. Write down the objectives and constraints that would fit his or her investment decision.**

   c. **How much of the difference between the two statements is due to the age of the investors?**

17.4   INVESTMENT POLICIES

Once objectives and constraints are determined, an investment policy that suits the investor can be formulated. That policy must reflect an appropriate risk-return profile as well as needs for liquidity, income generation, and tax positioning. For example, the most important portfolio decision an investor makes is the proportion of the total investment fund allocated to risky as opposed to safe assets such as money market securities, usually called cash equivalents or simply cash. This choice is the most fundamental means of controlling investment risk.

It follows that the first decision an investor must make is the asset allocation decision. Asset allocation refers to the allocation of the portfolio across major asset categories such as:

1. Money market assets (cash equivalents).
2. Fixed-income securities (primarily bonds).
3. Stocks.
4. Non-U.S. stocks and bonds.
5. Real estate.
6. Precious metals and other commodities.

Only after the broad asset classes to be held in the portfolio are determined can one sensibly choose the specific securities to purchase.

Investors who have relatively high degrees of risk tolerance will choose asset allocations more concentrated in higher-risk investment classes, such as equity, to obtain higher expected rates of return. More conservative investors will choose asset allocations with a greater weight in bonds and cash equivalents. The nearby box about Vanguard's asset allocation recommendations illustrates this principle.

Asset Allocation for Strength and Balance

There is one decision about your investments that will have more impact on your returns than any other: the allocation of your assets among stocks, bonds, and cash reserves.

Far more than any particular mutual funds you may select, your portfolio's asset allocation will govern not only the long-term returns you may receive, but the level of short-term risk you will assume, too. A portfolio of stock funds should provide a higher total return over time than one that concentrates on bond or money market funds. However, the latter portfolio offers a higher degree of stability plus the comfort of regular income. A balanced approach has characteristics of both portfolios, plus the benefit of diversification across asset classes. Drawing on these strengths, a balanced portfolio is well suited to withstand the financial markets' ups and downs.

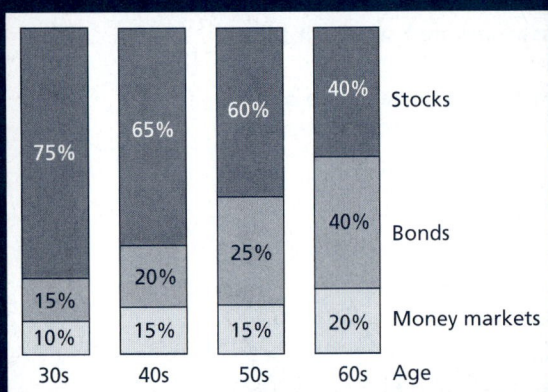

THE LIFE CYCLE APPROACH

In your early years, your goal is to accumulate capital for retirement. Later, conserving and spending capital take precedence. Logically, your investment strategy should be tailored to these life stages.

When you are in your 20s, 30s, and 40s, emphasize stocks for their potentially higher long-term returns. You have the time to recover from spasmodic short-term declines that grip equity markets with varying degrees of severity. A portfolio mix of 65–75% stocks and 25–35% bonds and money market investments would seem reasonable. As you move into your 50s, reduce risk and increase income by trimming stocks (perhaps to 50%) and raising bond and money market investments.

Once you retire, your emphasis shifts to receiving income. The majority (some 60%) of your portfolio should be allocated to bonds and money market funds. As an inflation hedge, maintain a significant stock position (40% is a good starting point), particularly early in your retirement years.

REBALANCING YOUR PORTFOLIO

Whichever approach you choose will require fortitude to make necessary rebalancing decisions. Moving assets from high-performing funds to those that may be lagging (on a relative basis) is not easy—but it is at the heart of a balanced investment strategy.

SOURCE: Abridged from "Asset Allocation for Strength and Balance," *In the Vanguard*, Summer 1993. The Vanguard Group, Inc. Reprinted with permission.

Top-Down Policies for Institutional Investors

Individual investors need not concern themselves with organizational efficiency. But professional investors with large amounts to invest must structure asset allocation activities to decentralize some of the decision making.

A common feature of large organizations is the investment committee and the asset universe. The investment committee includes top management officers, senior portfolio managers, and senior security analysts. The committee determines investment policies and verifies that portfolio managers and security analysts are operating within the bounds of specified policies. A major responsibility of the investment committee is to translate the objectives and constraints of the company into an **asset universe,** an approved list of assets for each of the company's portfolios.

Thus, the investment committee has responsibility for broad asset allocation. While the investment manager might have some leeway to tilt the portfolio toward or away from one or another asset class, the investment committee establishes the benchmark allocation that largely determines the risk characteristics of the portfolio. The task of choosing specific securities from the approved universe is more fully delegated to the investment manager.

asset universe

Approved list of assets in which a portfolio manager may invest.

Figure 17.1 illustrates the stages of the portfolio choice process for Palatial Investments, a hypothetical firm that invests internationally. The first two stages are asset allocation choices. The broadest choice is in the weighting of the portfolio between U.S. and Japanese securities. Palatial has chosen a weight of 75% in the United States and 25% in Japan. The allocation of the portfolio across asset classes may now be determined. For example, 15% of the U.S. portfolio is invested in cash equivalents, 40% in fixed income, and 45% in equity. The asset-class weights are, in general, a policy decision of the investment committee, although the investment manager might have some authority to alter the asset allocation to limited degrees based

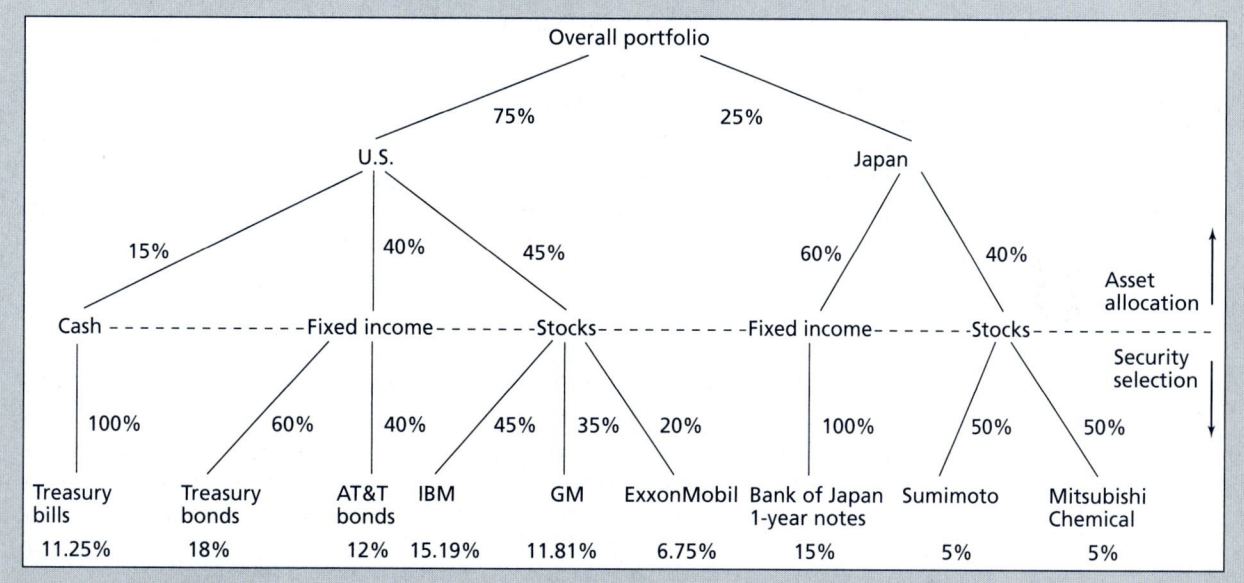

FIGURE 17.1

Asset allocation and security selection for Palatial Investments

⋮ **WEBMASTER**

Asset Allocation

The EfficientFrontier.com website contains access to an online journal that features the entertaining writing of William J. Bernstein. His article "The Online Asset Allocator: What the Investment Industry Doesn't Want You to Know" discusses some important ideas related to investment success. Go to http://www.efficientfrontier.com/aa/index.shtml to read the article. Then, answer the following questions:

1. What is it that the investment industry doesn't want you to know?
2. What is the central conclusion of the article?
3. What type of investment (active or passive) policy does it suggest?

on her expectations concerning the investment performance of various asset classes. Finally, security selection within each country is determined by the portfolio manager from the approved universe. For example, 45% of funds held in the U.S. equity market will be placed in IBM, 35% in GM, and 20% in ExxonMobil. (We show only three securities in the figure because of space limitations. Obviously a $1 billion fund will hold securities of many more firms.)

These ever-finer decisions determine the proportion of each individual security in the overall portfolio. As an example, consider the determination of the proportion of Palatial's portfolio invested in ExxonMobil, 6.75%. This fraction results from the following decisions. First, the United States receives a weight of 75% of the overall portfolio, and equities comprise 45% of the U.S. component of the portfolio. These are asset allocation choices. ExxonMobil comprises 20% of the U.S. equity component of the portfolio. This is a security selection choice. Therefore, ExxonMobil's weight in the overall portfolio is $0.75 \times 0.45 \times 0.20 = .0675$, or 6.75%. If the entire portfolio is $1 billion, $67,500,000 will be invested in ExxonMobil. If ExxonMobil is selling for $60 a share, 1,125,000 shares must be purchased. The bottom line in Figure 17.1 shows the percentage of the overall portfolio held in each asset.

This example illustrates a top-down approach that is consistent with the needs of large organizations. The top managers set the overall policy of the portfolio by specifying asset allocation guidelines. Lower-level portfolio managers fill in the details with their security selection decisions.

Active versus Passive Policies

One choice that must be confronted by all investors, individual as well as institutional, is the degree to which the portfolio will be actively versus passively managed. Recall that passive management is based on the belief that security prices usually are at close to "fair" levels. Instead of spending time and other resources attempting to "beat the market," that is, to find mispriced securities with unusually attractive risk-return characteristics, the investor simply assumes that she will be fairly compensated for the risk she is willing to take on and selects a portfolio consistent with her risk tolerance.[3]

Passive management styles can be applied to both the security selection and the asset allocation decisions. With regard to asset allocation, passive management simply means that the manager does not depart from his or her "normal" asset-class weightings in response to changing expectations about the performance of different markets. Those "normal" weights are based on the investor's risk and return objectives, as discussed earlier. For example, we saw in an earlier box that Vanguard's asset allocation recommendation for a 45-year-old investor was 65% equity, 20% bonds, and 15% cash equivalents. A purely passive manager would not depart from these weights in response to forecasts of market performances. The weighting scheme would be adjusted only in response to changes in risk tolerance as age and wealth change over time.

Next consider passive security selection. Imagine that you must choose a portfolio of stocks without access to any special information about security values. This would be the case if you believed that anything you know about a stock is already known by the rest of the investors in the market and therefore is already reflected in the stock price. If you cannot predict which stocks will be winners, you should broadly diversify your portfolio to avoid putting all your eggs in one basket. A natural course of action for such an investor would be to choose a portfolio with "a little bit of everything."

This reasoning leads one to look for a portfolio that is invested across the entire security market. We saw in Chapter 2 that some mutual fund operators have established index funds

---

[3]We discussed arguments for passive management in previous chapters. Here, we simply present an overview of the issues.

that follow just such a strategy. These funds hold each stock or bond in proportion to its representation in a particular index, such as the Standard & Poor's 500 stock price index or the Lehman Brothers bond index. Holding an indexed portfolio represents purely passive security selection since the investor's return simply duplicates the return of the overall market without making a bet on one or another stock or sector of the market.

In contrast to passive strategies, active management assumes an ability to outguess the other investors in the market and to identify either securities or asset classes that will shine in the near future. Active security selection for institutional investors typically requires two layers: security analysis and portfolio choice. Security analysts specialize in particular industries and companies and prepare assessments of their particular market niches. The portfolio managers then sift through the reports of many analysts. They use forecasts of market conditions to make asset allocation decisions and use the security analysts' recommendations to choose the particular securities to include within each asset class.

The choice between active and passive strategies need not be all-or-nothing. One can pursue both active security selection and passive asset allocation, for example. In this case, the manager would maintain fixed asset allocation targets but would actively choose the securities within each asset class. Or one could pursue active asset allocation and passive security selection. In this case, the manager might actively shift the allocation between equity and bond components of the portfolio but hold indexed portfolios within each sector. Another mixed approach is called a *passive core* strategy. In this case, the manager indexes *part* of the portfolio, the passive core, and actively manages the rest of the portfolio.

Is active or passive management the better approach? It might seem at first blush that active managers have the edge because active management is necessary to achieve outstanding performance. But remember that active managers start out with some disadvantages as well. They incur significant costs when preparing their analyses of markets and securities and incur heavier trading costs from the more rapid turnover of their portfolios. If they don't uncover information or insights currently unavailable to other investors (not a trivial task in a nearly efficient market), then all of this costly activity will be wasted, and they will underperform a passive strategy. In fact, low-cost passive strategies have performed surprisingly well in the last few decades, as we saw in Chapters 4 and 8.

3. Identify the following conditions according to where each fits in the objective-constraints-policies framework.
   a. Invest 5% in bonds and 95% in stocks.
   b. Do not invest more than 10% of the budget in any one security.
   c. Shoot for an average rate of return of 11%.
   d. Make sure there is $95,000 in cash in the account on December 31, 2015.
   e. If the market is bearish, reduce the investment in stocks to 80%.
   f. As of next year, we will be in a higher tax bracket.
   g. Our new president believes pension plans should take no risk whatsoever with the pension fund.
   h. Our acquisition plan will require large sums of cash to be available at any time.

Concept
CHECK

17.5 MONITORING AND REVISING INVESTMENT PORTFOLIOS

Choosing the investment portfolio requires the investor to set objectives, acknowledge constraints, determine asset-class proportions, and perform security analysis. Is the process ever finished and behind us? By the time we have completed all of these steps, many of the inputs we have used will be out of date. Moreover, our circumstances as well as our objectives change over time. Therefore, the investment process requires that we continually monitor and update our portfolios.

Moreover, even if our circumstances do not change, our portfolios necessarily will. For example, suppose you currently hold 1,000 shares of ExxonMobil, selling at $65 a share, and 1,000 shares of Microsoft, selling at $80 a share. If the price of ExxonMobil falls to $50 a share, while that of Microsoft rises to $90 a share, the fractions of your portfolio allocated to each security change without your taking any direct action. The value of your investment in ExxonMobil is now lower, and the value of the Microsoft investment is higher. Unless you are happy with this reallocation of investment proportions, you will need to take some action to restore the portfolio weights to desired levels.

Asset allocation also will change over time, as the investment performance of different asset classes diverges. If the stock market outperforms the bond market, the proportion of your portfolio invested in stocks will increase, while the proportion invested in bonds will decrease. If you are uncomfortable with this shift in the asset mix, you must rebalance the portfolio by selling some of the stocks and purchasing bonds.

Therefore, investing is a *dynamic process,* meaning that you must continually update and reevaluate your decisions over time.

SUMMARY

- The Association for Investment Management and Research developed a systematic framework for the translation of investor goals to investment strategy. Its three main parts are: objectives, constraints, and policy. Investor objectives include the return requirement and risk tolerance, reflecting the overriding concern of investment with the risk-return trade-off. Investor constraints include liquidity requirements, investment horizon, regulatory concerns, tax obligations, and the unique needs of various investors. Investment policies specify the degree of involvement in market timing, asset allocation, and security selection decisions.

- Major institutional investors include pension funds, mutual funds, life insurance companies, nonlife insurance companies, banks, and endowment funds. For individual investors, life-cycle concerns are the most important factor in setting objectives, constraints, and policies.

- Major asset classes include: cash (money market assets), fixed-income securities (bonds), stocks, real estate, precious metals, and collectibles. Asset allocation refers to the decision made as to the investment proportion to be allocated to each asset class. An active asset allocation strategy calls for the production of frequent market forecasts and the adjustment of asset allocation according to these forecasts.

- Active security selection requires security analysis and portfolio choice. Analysis of individual securities is required to choose securities that will make up a coherent portfolio and outperform a passive benchmark.

- Perhaps the most important feature of the investment process is that it is dynamic. Portfolios must be continually monitored and updated. The frequency and timing of various decisions are in themselves important decisions. Successful investment management requires management of these dynamic aspects.

KEY TERMS

asset universe, 612	liquidity, 606	prudent investor rule, 607
endowment funds, 606	mutual funds, 603	risk aversion, 600
investment horizon, 607	personal trust, 602	risk tolerance, 600

1. Your client says, "With the unrealized gains in my portfolio, I have almost saved enough money for my daughter to go to college in eight years, but educational costs keep going up." Based on this statement alone, which one of the following appears to be least important to your client's investment policy?
   a. Time horizon.
   b. Purchasing power risk.
   c. Liquidity.
   d. Taxes.

2. The aspect least likely to be included in the portfolio management process is
   a. Identifying an investor's objectives, constraints, and preferences.
   b. Organizing the management process itself.
   c. Implementing strategies regarding the choice of assets to be used.
   d. Monitoring market conditions, relative values, and investor circumstances.

3. A clearly written investment policy statement is critical for
   a. Mutual funds
   b. Individuals
   c. Pension funds
   d. All investors

4. The investment policy statement of an institution must be concerned with all of the following *except*:
   a. Its obligations to its clients.
   b. The level of the market.
   c. Legal regulations.
   d. Taxation.

5. Under the provisions of a typical corporate defined-benefit pension plan, the employer is responsible for:
   a. paying benefits to retired employees.
   b. investing in conservative fixed-income assets.
   c. counseling employees in the selection of asset classes.
   d. maintaining an actuarially determined, fully funded pension plan.

6. Which of the following statements reflects the importance of the asset allocation decision to the investment process? The asset allocation decision:
   a. helps the investor decide on realistic investment goals.
   b. identifies the specific securities to include in a portfolio.
   c. determines most of the portfolio's returns and volatility over time.
   d. creates a standard by which to establish an appropriate investment time horizon.

7. You are a portfolio manager and senior executive vice president of Advisory Securities Selection, Inc. Your firm has been invited to meet with the trustees of the Wood Museum Endowment Funds. Wood Museum is a privately endowed charitable institution that is dependent on the investment return from a $25 million endowment fund to balance the budget. The treasurer of the museum has recently completed the budget that indicates a need for cash flow of $3 million in 2005, $3.2 million in 2006, and $3.5 million in 2007 from the endowment fund to balance the budget in those years. Currently, the entire endowment portfolio is invested in Treasury bills and money market funds because the trustees fear a financial crisis. The trustees do not anticipate any further capital contributions to the fund.

   The trustees are all successful businesspeople, and they have been critical of the fund's previous investment advisers because they did not follow a logical decision-making process. In fact, several previous managers have been dismissed because of their inability to communicate with the trustees and their preoccupation with the fund's relative performance rather than the cash flow needs.

Advisory Securities Selection, Inc., has been contacted by the trustees because of its reputation for understanding and relating to the client's needs. The trustees have asked you, as a prospective portfolio manager for the Wood Museum Endowment Fund, to prepare a written report in response to the following questions. Your report will be circulated to the trustees before the initial interview on June 15, 2005.

Explain in detail how each of the following relates to the determination of either investor objectives or investor constraints that can be used to determine the portfolio policies for this three-year period for the Wood Museum Endowment Fund.

a. Liquidity requirements.
b. Return requirements.
c. Risk tolerance.
d. Time horizon.
e. Tax considerations.
f. Regulatory and legal considerations.
g. Unique needs and circumstances.

8. Mrs. Mary Atkins, age 66, has been your firm's client for five years, since the death of her husband, Dr. Charles Atkins. Dr. Atkins had built a successful newspaper business that he sold two years before his death to Merit Enterprises, a publishing and broadcasting conglomerate, in exchange for Merit common stock. The Atkinses have no children, and their wills provide that upon their deaths the remaining assets shall be used to create a fund for the benefit of Good Samaritan Hospital, to be called the Atkins Endowment Fund.

Good Samaritan is a 180-bed, not-for-profit hospital with an annual operating budget of $12.5 million. In the past, the hospital's operating revenues have often been sufficient to meet operating expenses and occasionally even generate a small surplus. In recent years, however, rising costs and declining occupancy rates have caused Good Samaritan to run a deficit. The operating deficit has averaged $300,000 to $400,000 annually over the last several years. Existing endowment assets (that is, excluding the Atkins's estate) of $7.5 million currently generate approximately $375,000 of annual income, up from less than $200,000 five years ago. This increased income has been the result of somewhat higher interest rates, as well as a shift in asset mix toward more bonds. To offset operating deficits, the Good Samaritan Board of Governors has determined that the endowment's current income should be increased to approximately 6% of total assets (up from 5% currently). The hospital has not received any significant additions to its endowment assets in the past five years.

Identify and describe an appropriate set of investment objectives and constraints for the Atkins Endowment Fund to be created after Mrs. Atkins's death.

9. Several discussion meetings have provided the following information about one of your firm's new advisory clients, a charitable endowment fund recently created by means of a one-time $10 million gift:

Objectives
Return requirement. Planning is based on a minimum total return of 8% per year, including an initial current income component of $500,000 (5% on beginning capital). Realizing this current income target is the endowment fund's primary return goal. (See "unique needs" below.)

Constraints
Time horizon. Perpetuity, except for requirement to make an $8,500,000 cash distribution on June 30, 2006. (See "unique needs.")

Liquidity needs. None of a day-to-day nature until 2006. Income is distributed annually after year-end. (See "unique needs.")

Tax considerations. None; this endowment fund is exempt from taxes.

Legal and regulatory considerations. Minimal, but the prudent investor rule applies to all investment actions.

Unique needs, circumstances, and preferences. The endowment fund must pay out to another tax-exempt entity the sum of $8,500,000 in cash on June 30, 2006. The assets remaining after this distribution will be retained by the fund in perpetuity. The endowment fund has adopted a "spending rule" requiring a first-year current income payout of $500,000; thereafter, the annual payout is to rise by 3% in real terms. Until 2006, annual income in excess of that required by the spending rule is to be reinvested. After 2006, the spending rate will be reset at 5% of the then-existing capital.

With this information and information found in this chapter, do the following:
a. Formulate an appropriate investment policy statement for the endowment fund.
b. Identify and briefly explain three major ways in which your firm's initial asset allocation decisions for the endowment fund will be affected by the circumstances of the account.

10. You have been named as investment adviser to a foundation established by Dr. Walter Jones with an original contribution consisting entirely of the common stock of Jomedco, Inc. Founded by Dr. Jones, Jomedco manufactures and markets medical devices invented by the doctor and collects royalties on other patented innovations.

   All of the shares that made up the initial contribution to the foundation were sold at a public offering of Jomedco common stock, and the $5 million proceeds will be delivered to the foundation within the next week. At the same time, Mrs. Jones will receive $5 million in proceeds from the sale of her stock in Jomedco.

   Dr. Jones's purpose in establishing the Jones Foundation was to "offset the effect of inflation on medical school tuition for the maximum number of worthy students."

   You are preparing for a meeting with the foundation trustees to discuss investment policy and asset allocation.
a. Define and give examples that show the differences between an investment objective, an investment constraint, and investment policy.
b. Identify and describe an appropriate set of investment objectives and investment constraints for the Jones Foundation.
c. Based on the investment objectives and investment constraints identified in part *b*, prepare a comprehensive investment policy statement for the Jones Foundation to be recommended for adoption by the trustees.

11. You are P. J. Walter, CFA, a managing partner of a prestigious investment counseling firm that specializes in individual rather than institutional accounts. The firm has developed a national reputation for its ability to blend modern portfolio theory and traditional portfolio methods. You have written a number of articles on portfolio management. You are an authority on the subject of establishing investment policies and programs for individual clients, tailored to their particular circumstances and needs.

   Dr. and Mrs. A. J. Mason have been referred to your firm and to you in particular. At your first meeting on June 2, 2001, Dr. Mason explained that he is an electrical engineer and long-time professor at the Essex Institute. He is also an inventor and, after 30 years of teaching, the rights to one of his patented inventions, the "inverse thermothrocle valve," has just been acquired by a new electronics company, ACS, Inc.

   In anticipation of the potential value of his invention, Dr. Mason had followed his accountant's advice and established a private corporation, wholly owned by the Masons, to hold the title to the inverse thermothrocle valve patent. It was this corporation that

ACS acquired from the Masons for $1 million in cash, payable at the closing on June 7, 2001. In addition, ACS has agreed to pay royalties to Dr. Mason or his heirs, based on its sales of systems that utilize the inverse thermothrocle valve.

Since ACS has no operating record, it is difficult for either the company or Dr. Mason to forecast future sales and royalties. While all parties are optimistic about prospects for success, they are also mindful of the risks associated with any new firm, especially those exposed to the technological obsolescence of the electronics industry. The management of ACS has indicated to Dr. Mason that he might expect royalties of as much as $100,000 in the first year of production and maximum royalties of as much as $500,000 annually thereafter.

During your counseling meeting, Mrs. Mason expressed concern for the proper investment of the $1,000,000 initial payment. She pointed out that Dr. Mason has invested all of their savings in his inventions. Thus, they will have only their Social Security retirement benefits and a small pension from the Essex Institute to provide for their retirement. Dr. Mason will be 65 in 2005. His salary from the Essex Institute is $55,000 per year. Additionally, he expects to continue earning $10,000–$25,000 annually from consulting and speaking engagements.

The Masons have two daughters and a son, all of whom are married and have families of their own. Dr. and Mrs. Mason are interested in helping with the education of their grandchildren and have provided in their wills for their estate to be divided among their children and grandchildren.

In the event that the royalty payments from ACS meet the projections cited above, Mrs. Mason is interested in providing a scholarship fund in the name of Dr. Mason for the benefit of enterprising young engineers attending the Essex Institute. The scholarship fund ranks third behind the provision for the Masons' retirement and for the education of their grandchildren.

In your discussions with Dr. and Mrs. Mason, you have stressed the importance of identifying investment objectives and constraints and having an appropriate investment policy. Identify and describe an appropriate set of investment objectives and investment constraints for Dr. and Mrs. Mason, and prepare a comprehensive investment policy statement based on these investment objectives and constraints.

12. You are being interviewed for a job as a portfolio manager at an investment counseling partnership. As part of the interview, you are asked to demonstrate your ability to develop investment portfolio policy statements for the clients listed below:
    a. A pension fund that is described as a mature defined-benefit plan; with the workforce having an average age of 54; no unfunded pension liabilities; and wage cost increases forecast at 9% annually.
    b. A university endowment fund that is described as conservative; with investment returns being utilized along with gifts and donations received to meet current expenses, the spending rate is 5% per year; and inflation in costs is expected at 8% annually.
    c. A life insurance company that is described as specializing in annuities; policy premium rates are based on a minimum annual accumulation rate of 14% in the first year of the policy and a 10% minimum annual accumulation rate in the next five years.

List and discuss separately for *each* client described above the objectives and constraints that will determine the portfolio policy you would recommend for that client.

WEBMASTER

Personal Diversification

Go to http://www.money.com/money/depts/retirement and find the calculator for diversifying your portfolio. When you work in a given industry, other industries may be more effective in diversifying your overall economic well-being. This calculator shows good and bad choices for diversification for different employment industries.

Select the following industries and obtain the listing of the 10 best and 10 worst industries for diversification: oil and gas (drilling and equipment); homebuilding; electronics (semiconductor). Then, answer the following questions:

1. Are the industries identified as best and worst considerably different for these three employment industries?

2. Contrast the differences present in the categories for these industries.

---

1. A convenient and effective way to organize the answer to this question is to cast it in the context of the investment policy statement framework.

SOLUTIONS TO

Concept
CHECKS

Risk: Endowment funds have no "safety nets" such as pension funds enjoy in the event of difficulty, either in the form of corporate assets to fall back on or a call on public assistance, such as from the Pension Benefit Guaranty Corporation. Moreover, endowment fund cash flows may be highly erratic due to the uncertain timing of income from gifts and/or bequests, while pension fund cash flows tend to be very predictable and steady. These differences suggest the typical endowment fund will adopt a more conservative risk-bearing posture than will the typical pension fund, both as to asset-class exposures and to the type of security content of such exposures.

Return: Because investment-related spending usually is limited to "income yield," endowment funds often focus their return goals on the matter of current spendable income; pension funds, on the other hand, tend to adopt total return approaches, at least until a plan matures. Although inflation protection is of great importance to both types of funds, endowment funds appear to be less concerned with real return production than are pension funds, perhaps because of their common emphasis on "income now" in setting return goals.

Time horizon: Theoretically, an endowment fund is a perpetuity while a pension fund may well have a finite life span. Therefore, an endowment fund should operate with a very long-term view of investment. However, such funds in practice tend to adopt shorter horizons than are typical of pension funds (just as they typically assume less risk). Their tendency to emphasize income production in the near term is the probable reason for this common occurrence.

Liquidity: Endowment funds, particularly those that use gifts and bequests to supplement their investment income, often have fairly large liquidity reserves—both to protect against fluctuations in their cash flows and reflecting their generally conservative outlooks—while, except for very mature plans, pension funds tend to require minimum liquidity reserves. Endowment funds also frequently maintain substantial liquid holdings to provide for known future cash payout requirements, such as for new buildings.

Taxes: Here, although differing in detail, the situation of the two forms of institutions are very much the same. In the United States, tax considerations are normally of minimal importance in both cases.

Regulatory/Legal: Endowment fund investment is carried out under state governance, while pension fund investment, in the United States, is carried out under federal law, specifically under ERISA. The difference is significant. Endowment funds operate under the prudent investor rule, where each investment must be judged on its own merits apart from any other portfolio holdings, while pension plans operate under a broader context for investment—each security being judged in terms of the portfolio as a whole—and an ERISA-mandated diversification requirement that often leads to wider asset-class exposures.

Unique circumstances: Endowment funds often are faced with unique situations that infrequently affect pension fund management, including the scrutiny of such special-interest groups as trustees, alumni, faculty, student organizations, local community pressure groups, etc., each with separate and often incompatible constraints and goals that may need to be accommodated in policy setting and/or in investment content. Similarly, endowment funds often are subjected to severe "social pressures" that, as in the case of tobacco firm divestment, can have an important investment impact by restricting the available universe of investment securities, mandating participation or nonparticipation in certain industries, sectors, or countries, or otherwise changing investment action from what it would otherwise have been. In pension fund investment, ERISA requires that no other interests be put ahead of the interests of the beneficiaries in determining investment actions.

2. Identify the elements that are life-cycle driven in the two schemes of objectives and constraints.

3. *a.* Policy, asset allocation.
    b. Constraint, regulation.
    c. Objective, return requirement.
    d. Constraint, horizon.
    e. Policy, market timing.
    f. Constraint, taxes.
    g. Objectives, risk tolerance.
    h. Constraint, liquidity.

18

TAXES, INFLATION, AND INVESTMENT STRATEGY

**AFTER STUDYING THIS CHAPTER
YOU SHOULD BE ABLE TO:**

> Analyze lifetime savings plans.

> Account for inflation in formulating savings and investment plans.

> Account for taxes in formulating savings and investment plans.

> Understand tax shelters.

> Design your own savings plan.

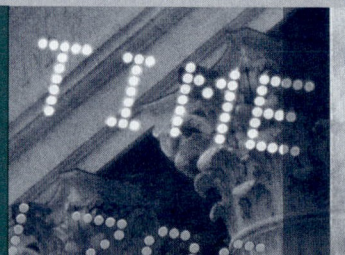

Related Websites

http://www.tamasset.com

This site contains information on asset class returns and studies on portfolio management.

http://www3.troweprice.com/retincome/RIC

The above site has a simulation retirement planner that can be used to assess the ability to meet goals under different allocation strategies.

http://flagship.vanguard.com/VGApp/hnw/PlanningAndAdvice

Here you will find general educational information on financial planning.

http://www.ssa.gov

Visit the above site to find information on Social Security.

http://www.bloomberg.com

http://www.morningstar.com

http://www.quicken.com

The sites listed above contain information on personal financial planning.

In previous chapters we concentrated mostly on the role of professional management of investments. In this chapter we are concerned with individual investors' management of their overall lifetime savings plans. Our major objective is to introduce you to the *principles* of managing personal savings in a complex environment in which taxes and inflation interact, rather than to provide a detailed analysis of the (ever-changing) tax code.

Retirement, purchase of a home, and financing the education of children are the major objectives of saving in most households. Inflation and taxes make the task of gearing investment to accomplish these objectives complex. The long-term nature of savings intertwines the power of compounding with inflation and tax effects. Only the most experienced investors tend to fully integrate these issues into their investment strategies. Appropriate investment strategy also includes adequate insurance coverage for contingencies such as death, disability, and property damage.

We introduce some of these issues by focusing on one of the long-term goals: formulating a retirement plan. We investigate the effect of inflation on the savings plan and examine how tax shelters may be integrated into one's strategy.[1] Next we incorporate Social Security and show how to generalize the savings plan to meet other objectives such as owning a home and financing children's education. Finally, we discuss uncertainty about longevity and other contingencies. Understanding the spreadsheets we develop along the way will enable you to devise savings/investment plans for yourself and other households and adapt them to an ever-changing environment.

---

[1] Readers in other countries will find it easy to adapt the analysis to the tax code of their own country.

18.1 | SAVING FOR THE LONG RUN

In Chapter 17 we described the framework that the Association of Investment Management and Research (AIMR) has established to help financial advisers communicate with and involve client households in structuring their savings/investment plans.[2] Our objective here is to quantify the essentials of savings/investment plans and adapt them to environments in which investors confront both inflation and taxes. As a first step in the process, we set up a spreadsheet for a simple retirement plan, ignoring for the moment saving for other objectives.

Before diving in, a brief word on what we mean by saving. Economists think of saving as a way to smooth out the lifetime consumption stream; you save when you have high earnings in order to support consumption in low-income years. In a "global" sense, the concept implies that you save for retirement so that consumption during the retirement years will not be too low relative to consumption during the saving years. In a "local" sense, smoothing consumption implies that you would finance a large purchase such as a car, rather than buy it for cash. Clearly, local consumption smoothing is of second-order importance, that is, how you purchase durable goods has little effect on the overall savings plan, except, perhaps, for very large expenditures such as buying a home or sending children to college. We begin therefore with a savings plan that ignores even large expenditures and later discuss how to augment the plan to account for these needs.

A Hypothetical Household

Imagine you are now 30 years old and have already completed your formal education, accumulated some work experience, and settled down to plan the rest of your economic life. Your plan is to retire at age 65 with a remaining life expectancy of an additional 25 years. Later on, we will further assume that you have two small children and plan to finance their college education.

For starters, we assume you intend to obtain a (level) annuity for your 25-year retirement period; we postpone discussion of planning for the uncertain time of death. (You may well live to over 100 years; what then?) Suppose your gross income this year was $50,000, and you expect annual income to increase at a rate of 7% per year. In this section, we assume that you ignore the impact of inflation and taxes. You intend to steadily save 15% of income and invest in safe government bonds that will yield 6% over the entire period. Proceeds from your investments will be automatically reinvested at the same 6% until retirement. Upon retirement, your funds in the retirement account will be used to purchase a 25-year annuity (using the same 6% interest rate) to finance a steady consumption annuity. Let's examine the consequences of this framework.

The Retirement Annuity

retirement annuity

Stream of cash flows available for consumption during one's retirement years.

We can easily obtain your **retirement annuity** from Spreadsheet 18.1, where we have hidden the lines for ages 32–34, 36–44, 46–54, and 56–64. You can obtain all the spreadsheets in this chapter from the Web page for the text: http://www.mhhe.com/bkm.

Let's first see how this spreadsheet was constructed. To view the formulas of all cells in an Excel spreadsheet, choose "Preferences" under the "Tools" menu, and select the box "Formulas" in the "View" tab. The formula view of Spreadsheet 18.1 is also shown on the next page (numbers are user inputs).

---

[2]If you skipped Chapter 17, you may want to skim through it to get an idea of how financial planners articulate a saver's objectives, constraints, and investment policy.

SPREADSHEET **18.1**
The savings plan

	A	B	C	D	E
1	Retirement Years	Income Growth	Savings Rate	ROR	
2	25	0.07	0.15	0.06	
3	Age	Income	Savings	Cumulative Savings	Consumption
4	30	50,000	7,500	7,500	42,500
5	31	53,500	8,025	15,975	45,475
6	32	57,245	8,587	25,520	48,658
9	35	70,128	10,519	61,658	59,608
19	45	137,952	20,693	308,859	117,259
29	55	271,372	40,706	943,477	230,666
39	65	533,829	80,074	2,457,518	453,755
40	Total	7,445,673	1,116,851	Retirement Annuity	192,244

	A	B	C	D	E
1	Retirement Years	Income Growth	Savings Rate	ROR	
2	25	0.07	0.15	0.06	
3	Age	Income	Savings	Cumulative Savings	Consumption
4	30	50000	=B4*$C$2	=C4	=B4-C4
5	31	=B4*(1+$B$2)	=B5*$C$2	=D4*(1+$D$2)+C5	=B5-C5
39	65	=B38*(1+$B$2)	=B39*$C$2	=D38*(1+$D$2)+C39	=B39-C39
40	Total	=SUM(B4:B39)	=SUM(C4:C39)	Retirement Annuity	=PMT($D$2,$A$2,-$D$39,0,0)

Inputs in row 2 include: retirement years (cell A2 = 25); income growth (cell B2 = .07); Age (column A); and income at age 30 (B4 = 50,000). Column B computes income in future years using the growth rate in cell B2; column C computes annual savings by applying the savings rate (cell C2) to income; and column E computes consumption as the difference between income and savings: column B − column C. Cumulative savings appear in column D. To obtain the value in D6, for example, multiply cell D5 by 1 plus the assumed rate of return in cell D2 (the ROR) and then add current savings from column C. Finally, C40 shows the sum of dollars saved over the lifetime, and E40 converts cumulative savings (including interest) at age 65 to a 25-year annuity using the financial function PMT from Excel's function menu. Excel provides a function to solve for annuity levels given the values of the interest rate, the number of periods, the present value of the savings account, and the future value of the account: PMT(rate, nper, PV, FV).

We observe that your retirement fund will accumulate approximately $2.5 million (cell D39) by age 65. This hefty sum shows the power of compounding, since your contributions to the savings account were only $1.1 million (C40). This fund will yield an annuity of $192,244 per year (E40) for your 25-year retirement, which seems quite attractive, except that the standard of living you'll have to get accustomed to in your retirement years is much lower than your consumption at age 65 (E39). In fact, if you unhide the hidden lines, you'll see that upon retirement, you'll have to make do with what you used to consume at age 51.[3] This may not worry you much since, with your children having flown the coop and the mortgage paid up, you may be able to maintain the luxury to which you recently became accustomed. But your projected well being is deceptive: get ready to account for inflation and taxes.

1. **If you project an ROR of only 5%, what savings rate would you need to maintain the same retirement annuity?**

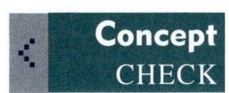

Concept
CHECK

---

[3]It would make sense (and would be easy) to rig the retirement fund to provide an annuity with a choice growth rate to allow your standard of living to grow with that of your social circle. We will abstract from this detail here.

18.2 ACCOUNTING FOR INFLATION

Inflation puts a damper on your plans in two ways: First, it erodes the purchasing power of the cumulative dollars you have so far saved. Second, the *real* dollars you earn on your portfolio each year depend on the *real* interest rate, which, as Chapter 5 showed, is approximately equal to the nominal rate minus inflation. Since an appropriate savings plan must generate a decent *real* annuity, we must recast the entire plan in real dollars. We will assume your income still is forecast to grow at a 7% rate, but now you recognize that part of income growth is due to inflation, which is running at 3% per year.

A Real Savings Plan

To convert nominal dollars to real dollars we need to calculate the price level in future years relative to today's prices. The "deflator" (or relative price level) for a given year is that year's price level divided by today's. It equals the dollars needed at that future date which provide the same purchasing power as $1 today (at age 30). For an inflation rate of $i = 3\%$, the deflator for age 35 is $(1 + i)^5$, or in Excel notation, $(1 + i)\wedge5 = 1.03\wedge5 = 1.16$. By age 65, the deflator is 2.81. Thus, even with a moderate rate of inflation (3% is below the historical average, as you can see from Figure 5.4), nominal dollars will lose a lot of purchasing power over long horizons. We also can compute the *real* rate of return (rROR) from the nominal ROR of 6%: $rROR = (ROR - i)/(1 + i) = 3/1.03 = 2.91\%$.

Spreadsheet 18.2, with the formula view below it, is the reworked Spreadsheet 18.1 adjusted for inflation. In addition to the rate of inflation (cell C2) and the real rate of return (F2), the major addition to this sheet is the price level deflator (column C). Instead of nominal **real consumption** consumption, we present **real consumption** (column F), calculated by dividing nominal consumption (column B − column D) by the price deflator, column C.

real consumption

Nominal consumption divided by the price deflator.

The numbers have changed considerably. Gone is the luxurious retirement we anticipated earlier. At age 65 and beyond, with a real annuity of $49,668, you will have to revert to a standard of living equal to that you attained at age 34; this is less than a third of your real consumption in your last working year, at age 65. The reason is that the retirement fund of $2.5 million (E39) is worth only $873,631 in today's purchasing power (E39/C39). Such is the effect of inflation. If you wish to do better than that, you must save more.

SPREADSHEET 18.2

A real retirement plan

	A	B	C	D	E	F
1	Retirement Years	Income growth	Rate of Inflation	Savings rate	ROR	rROR
2	25	0.07	0.03	0.15	0.06	0.0291
3	Age	Income	Deflator	Saving	Cumulative Savings	rConsumption
4	30	50,000	1.00	7,500	7,500	42,500
5	31	53,500	1.03	8,025	15,975	44,150
9	35	70,128	1.16	10,519	61,658	51,419
19	45	137,952	1.56	20,693	308,859	75,264
29	55	271,372	2.09	40,706	943,477	110,167
39	65	533,829	2.81	80,074	2,457,518	161,257
40	Total	7,445,673		1,116,851	Real Annuity	49,668

	A	B	C	D	E	F
1	Retirement Years	Income Growth	Rate of Inflation	Savings Rate	ROR	rROR
2	25	0.07	0.03	0.15	0.06	=(E2-C2)/(1+C2)
3	Age	Income	Deflator	Savings	Cumulative Savings	rConsumption
4	30	50000	1	=B4*$D$2	=D4	=(B4-D4)/C4
5	31	=B4*(1+$B$2)	=C4*(1+$C$2)	=B5*$D$2	=E4*(1+$E$2)+D5	=(B5-D5)/C5
39	65	=B38*(1+$B$2)	=C38*(1+$C$2)	=B39*$D$2	=E38*(1+$E$2)+D39	=(B39-D39)/C39
40	Total	=SUM(B4:B39)		=SUM(D4:D39)	Real Annuity	=PMT($F$2,$A$2,-$E$39/$C$39,0,0)

In our initial plan (Spreadsheet 18.1), we envisioned consuming a level, nominal annuity for the retirement years. This is an inappropriate goal once we account for inflation, since it would imply a declining standard of living starting at age 65. Its purchasing power at age 65 in terms of current dollars would be $64,542 (i.e., $181,362/2.81), and at age 90 only $30,792. (Check this!)

It is tempting to contemplate solving the problem of an inadequate retirement annuity by increasing the assumed rate of return on investments. However, this can only be accomplished by putting your savings at risk. Much of this text elaborates on how to do so efficiently; yet it also emphasizes that while taking on risk will give you an *expectation* for a better retirement, it implies as well a nonzero probability of doing a lot worse. At the age of 30, you should be able to tolerate some risk to the retirement annuity for the simple reason that if things go wrong, you can change course, increase your savings rate, and work harder. As you get older, this option progressively fades, and increasing risk becomes less of a viable option. If you do choose to increase risk, you can set a "safety-first target" (i.e., a minimum acceptable goal) for the retirement annuity and continuously monitor your risky portfolio. If the portfolio does poorly and approaches the safety-first target, you progressively shift into risk-free bonds—you may recognize this strategy as a version of dynamic hedging.

The difficulty with this strategy is twofold: First it requires monitoring, which is time-consuming and may be nerve-racking as well. Second, when decision time comes, it may be psychologically hard to withdraw. By shifting out of the risky portfolio if and when your portfolio is hammered, you give up any hope of recovery. This is hard to do and many investors fail the test. For these investors, therefore, the right approach is to stick with the safe, lower ROR and make the effort to balance standard of living before and after retirement. Avoiding sleepless nights is ample reward.

Therefore, the only variable we leave under your control in this spreadsheet is the rate of saving. To improve retirement life style relative to the preretirement years, without jeopardizing its safety, you will have to lower consumption during the saving years—there is no free lunch.

2. **If you project a rate of inflation of 4%, what nominal ROR on investments would you need to maintain the same real retirement annuity as in Spreadsheet 18.2?**

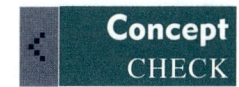

Concept
CHECK

An Alternative Savings Plan

In Spreadsheet 18.2, we saved a constant fraction of income. But since real income grows over time (nominal income grows at 7% while inflation is only 3%), we might consider deferring our savings toward future years when our real income is higher. By applying a higher savings rate to our future (higher) real income, we can afford to reduce the current savings rate. In Spreadsheet 18.3, we use a base savings rate of 10% (lower than the savings rate in the previous spreadsheet), but we increase the savings target by 3% per year. Saving in each year therefore equals a fixed savings rate times annual income (column B), times 1.03^t. By saving a larger fraction of income in later years, when real income is larger, you create a smoother profile of real consumption.

Spreadsheet 18.3 shows that with an *initial* savings rate of 10%, compared with the unchanging 15% rate in the previous spreadsheet, you can achieve a retirement annuity of $59,918, larger than the $49,668 annuity in the previous plan.

Notice that real consumption in the early years is greater than with the previous plan. What you have done is to postpone saving until your income is much higher. At first blush, this plan is preferable: It allows for a more comfortable consumption of 90% of income at the outset, a consistent increase in standard of living during your earning years, all without significantly affecting the retirement annuity. But this program has one serious downside: By postponing the

SPREADSHEET 18.3
Saving from real income

	A	B	C	D	E	F
1	Retirement Years	Income Growth	Rate of Inflation	Savings Rate	ROR	rROR
2	25	0.07	0.03	0.1	0.06	0.0291
3	Age	Income	Deflator	Savings	Cumulative Savings	rConsumption
4	30	50,000	1.00	5,000	5,000	45,000
5	31	53,500	1.03	5,511	10,811	46,592
9	35	70,128	1.16	8,130	44,351	53,480
19	45	137,952	1.56	21,492	260,927	74,751
29	55	271,372	2.09	56,819	947,114	102,471
39	65	533,829	2.81	150,212	2,964,669	136,331
40	Total	7,445,673		1,572,466	Real Annuity	59,918

	A	B	C	D	E	F
1	Retirement Years	Income Growth	Rate of Inflation	Savings Rate	ROR	rROR
2	25	0.07	0.03	0.1	0.06	=(E2-C2)/(1+C2)
3	Age	Income	Deflator	Savings	Cumulative Savings	rConsumption
4	30	50000	1	=B4*C4*$D$2	=D4	=(B4-D4)/C4
5	31	=B4*(1+$B$2)	=C4*(1+$C$2)	=B5*C5*$D$2	=E4*(1+$E$2)+D5	=(B5-D5)/C5
39	65	=B38*(1+$B$2)	=C38*(1+$C$2)	=B39*C39*$D$2	=E38*(1+$E$2)+D39	=(B39-D39)/C39
40	Total	=SUM(B4:B39)		=SUM(D4:D39)	Real Annuity	=PMT($F$2,$A$2,-$E$39/$C$39,0,0)

bulk of your savings to a later age, you come to depend on your health, longevity, and, more ominously (and without possibility of insurance), on a successful future career. Put differently, this plan achieves comfort by increasing risk, making this choice a matter of risk tolerance.

3. Suppose you like the plan of tilting savings toward later years, but worry about the increased risk of postponing the bulk of your savings to later years. Is there anything you can do to mitigate the risk?

18.3 ACCOUNTING FOR TAXES

flat tax

A tax code that taxes all income above some exemption at a fixed rate.

To initiate a discussion of taxes, let's assume that you are subject to a **flat tax** rate of 25% on taxable income less one exemption of $15,000. This is similar to several proposals for a simplified U.S. tax code that have been floated by one presidential candidate or another prior to elections—at least when you add state taxes to the proposed flat rate. An important feature of this (and the existing) tax code is that the tax rate is levied on nominal income and applies as well to investment income. (This is the concept of double taxation—you pay taxes when you earn income and then you pay taxes again when your savings earn interest). Some relief from the effect of taxing nominal dollars both in this proposal and the current U.S. code is provided by raising the exemption, annually, by the rate of inflation. To adapt our spreadsheet to this simple tax code, we must add columns for taxes and after-tax income. The tax-adjusted plan is shown in Spreadsheet 18.4. It adapts the savings plan of Spreadsheet 18.2.

The top panel of the sheet deals with the earning years. Column D adjusts the exemption (D2) by the price level (column C). Column E applies the tax rate (cell E2) to taxable income (column B − column D). The savings rate (F2) is applied to after-tax income (column B − column E), allowing us to calculate cumulative savings (column G) and real consumption (column H). The formula view shows the detailed construction.

As you might have expected, real consumption is lower in the presence of taxes, as are savings and the retirement fund. The retirement fund provides for a real, before-tax annuity of only $37,882, compared with $49,668 absent taxes in Spreadsheet 18.2.

The bottom panel of the sheet shows the further reduction in real consumption due to taxes paid during the retirement years. While you do not pay taxes on the cumulative savings in the retirement plan (you did that already as the savings accrued interest), you do pay taxes on interest earned by the fund while you are drawing it down. These taxes are quite significant and further deplete the fund and its net-of-tax earning power. For this reason, your

SPREADSHEET 18.4
Saving with a simple tax code

	A	B	C	D	E	F	G	H
1	Retirement Years	Income Growth	Rate of Inflation	Exemption Now	Tax Rate	Savings Rate	ROR	rROR
2	25	0.07	0.03	15000	0.25	0.15	0.06	0.0291
3	Age	Income	Deflator	Exemption	Taxes	Savings	Cumulative Savings	rConsumption
4	30	50,000	1.00	15,000	8,750	6,188	6,188	35,063
5	31	53,500	1.03	15,450	9,605	6,584	13,143	36,224
9	35	70,128	1.16	17,389	13,775	8,453	50,188	41,319
19	45	137,952	1.56	23,370	31,892	15,909	245,334	57,864
29	55	271,372	2.09	31,407	69,943	30,214	733,467	81,773
39	65	533,829	2.81	42,208	148,611	57,783	1,874,346	116,365
40	Total				1,884,163	834,226	Real Annuity=	37,882
41	**RETIREMENT**							
42	Age	Nom Withdraw	Deflator	Exemption	Taxes		Funds Left	rConsumption
43	66	109,792	2.90	43,474	17,247		1,877,014	31,931
47	70	123,572	3.26	48,931	15,743		1,853,382	33,056
52	75	143,254	3.78	56,724	12,200		1,721,015	34,656
57	80	166,071	4.38	65,759	6,047		1,422,954	36,503
62	85	192,521	5.08	76,232	0		883,895	37,882
67	90	223,185	5.89	88,374	0		0	37,882
68	Total	4,002,944			203,199			

	A	B	C	D	E	F	G	H
1	Retirement Years	Income Growth	Rate of Inflation	Exemption Now	Tax Rate	Savings Rate	ROR	rROR
2	25	0.07	0.03	15000	0.25	0.15	0.06	=(G2-C2)/(1+C2)
3	Age	Income	Deflator	Exemption	Taxes	Savings	Cumulative Savings	rConsumption
4	30	50000	1	=$D$2*C4	=(B4-D4)*$E$2	=(B4-E4)*$F$2	=F4	=(B4-E4-F4)/C4
5	31	=B4*(1+$B$2)	=C4*(1+$C$2)	=$D$2*C5	=(B5-D5+G4*$G$2)*$E$2	=(B5-E5)*$F$2	=G4*(1+$G$2)+F5	=(B5-E5-F5)/C5
39	65	=B38*(1+$B$2)	=C38*(1+$C$2)	=$D$2*C39	=(B39-D39+G38*$G$2)*$E$2	=(B39-E39)*$F$2	=G38*(1+$G$2)+F39	=(B39-E39-F39)/C39
40	Total				=SUM(E4:E39)	=SUM(F4:F39)	Real Annuity	=PMT($H$2,$A$2,-$G$39/$C$39,0,0)
41	**RETIREMENT**							
42	Age	Nom Withdraw	Deflator	Exemption	Taxes		Funds Left	rConsumption
43	66	=$H$40*C43	=C39*(1+$C$2)	=$D$2*C43	=MAX(0,(G39*$G$2-D43)*$E$2)		=G39*(1+$G$2)-B43	=(B43-E43)/C43
44	67	=$H$40*C44	=C43*(1+$C$2)	=$D$2*C44	=MAX(0,(G43*$G$2-D44)*$E$2)		=G43*(1+$G$2)-B44	=(B44-E44)/C44
67	90	=$H$40*C67	=C66*(1+$C$2)	=$D$2*C67	=MAX(0,(G66*$G$2-D67)*$E$2)		=G66*(1+$G$2)-B67	=(B67-E67)/C67
68	Total	=SUM(B43:B67)			=SUM(E43:E67)			

consumption annuity is lower in the early years when your fund has not yet been depleted and earns quite a bit.

In the end, despite a handsome income that grows at a real rate of almost 4%, an aggressive savings rate of 15%, a modest rate of inflation, and a modest tax, you will only be able to achieve a modest (but at least low-risk) real retirement income. This is a reality with which most people must struggle. Whether to sacrifice more of today's standard of living through an increased rate of saving, or take some risk in the form of saving a real annuity and/or invest in a risky portfolio with a higher expected return, is a question of preference and risk tolerance.

One often hears complaints about the double taxation resulting from taxing income earned on savings from dollars on which taxes were already paid. It is interesting to see what effective tax rate is imposed on your lifetime earnings by double taxation. To do so, we use Spreadsheet 18.4 to set up your lifetime earnings, exemptions, and taxes:

Income

Labor income		$7,445,673
Total exemptions during working years	949,139	
(i) Lifetime taxable income		$6,496,534

Taxes

During labor years	1,884,163	
During retirement	203,199	
(ii) Lifetime taxes		$2,087,362
Lifetime tax rate (ii)/(i)		**32.13%**

Thus, double taxation is equivalent to raising the effective tax rate on long-term savers from the statutory rate of 25% to an effective rate of over 32%.

4. Would a 1% increase in the exemption compensate you for a 1% increase in the tax rate?

Concept
CHECK

18.4   THE ECONOMICS OF TAX SHELTERS

tax shelters

Means by which to postpone payment of tax liabilities for as long as possible.

Tax shelters range from the simple to the mind-bogglingly complex, yet they all have one common objective: to postpone payment of tax liabilities for as long as possible. We know already that this isn't small fry. Postponement implies a smaller present value of tax payment, and a tax paid with a long delay can have present value near zero. However, delay is necessarily beneficial only when the tax rate doesn't increase over time. If the tax rate on retirement income is higher than during earning years, the value of a tax deferral may be questionable; if the tax rate will decline, deferral is even more preferable.

A Benchmark Tax Shelter

Postponing tax payments is the only attainable (legal) objective since, whenever you have taxable income, a tax liability is created that can (almost) never be erased.[4] For this reason, a benchmark tax shelter *postpones all* taxes on savings and the income on those savings. In this case, your entire savings account is liable to taxation and will be paid upon retirement, as you draw down the retirement fund. This sort of shelter is actually equivalent to the tax treatment of Individual Retirement Accounts (IRAs) which we discuss later, so we will describe this structure as having an "IRA style."

To examine the impact of an IRA-style structure (assuming you could shelter all your savings) in a situation comparable to the nonsheltered flat-tax case, we maintain the same consumption level as in Spreadsheet 18.4 (flat tax with no shelter), but now input the new, sheltered savings plan in Spreadsheet 18.5. This focuses the entire effect of the tax shelter onto retirement consumption.

In this sheet, we input desired real consumption (column H, copied from Spreadsheet 18.4). Taxes (column E) are then calculated by applying the tax rate (E2) to nominal consumption less the exemption (H $\times$ C − D). The retirement panel shows that you pay taxes on all withdrawals—all funds in the retirement account are subject to tax.

The results are quite surprising. The tax protection means faster accumulation of the retirement fund, which grows to $3.7 million (column G), compared with only $1.9 million without the shelter, but you also owe taxes on the entire amount. You pay taxes as you draw income from the retirement funds, and this tax load results in an effective tax rate of about 20% on your withdrawals (E68/B68). Still, your real retirement annuity ($60,789) is far greater than the average $35,531 absent the shelter, a result of the earning power of the savings on which you postponed taxes. Note that the source of effectiveness of the shelter is twofold: postponing taxes on both savings and the investment earnings on those savings.

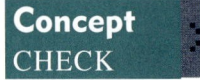

5. With the IRA-style tax shelter, all your taxes are due during retirement. Is the trade-off between exemption and tax rate different from the circumstance where you have no shelter?

The Effect of the Progressive Nature of the Tax Code

Because of the exemption, the flat tax is somewhat progressive: taxes are an increasing fraction of income as income rises. For very high incomes, the marginal tax rate (25%) is only slightly higher than the average rate. For example, with income of $50,000 at the outset, the average tax rate is 17.5% (.25 $\times$ 35,000/50,000), and grows steadily over time. In general, with a flat tax, the ratio of the average to marginal rate equals the ratio of taxable to gross

---

[4]Bankruptcy or death can erase some tax liabilities, though. We will avoid dealing with these unhappy outcomes.

SPREADSHEET 18.5

Saving with a flat tax and an IRA-style tax shelter

	A	B	C	D	E	F	G	H
1	Retirement Years	Income Growth	Rate of Inflation	Exemption Now	Tax Rate	Savings Rate	ROR	rROR
2	25	0.07	0.03	15000	0.25	0.15	0.06	0.0291
3	Age	Income	Deflator	Exemption	Taxes	Savings	Cumulative Savings	rConsumption
4	30	50,000	1.00	15,000	5,016	9,922	9,922	35,063
5	31	53,500	1.03	15,450	5,465	10,724	21,242	36,224
9	35	70,128	1.16	17,389	7,628	14,600	83,620	41,319
19	45	137,952	1.56	23,370	16,695	31,106	438,234	57,864
29	55	271,372	2.09	31,407	34,952	65,205	1,393,559	81,773
39	65	533,829	2.81	42,208	71,307	135,087	3,762,956	116,365
40	Total				944,536	1,773,854	Real Annuity	76,052
41	**RETIREMENT**							
42	Age	Nom Withdraw	Deflator	Exemption	Taxes		Funds Left	rConsumption
43	66	220,420	2.90	43,474	44,236		3,768,313	60,789
47	70	248,085	3.26	48,931	49,789		3,720,867	60,789
52	75	287,598	3.78	56,724	57,719		3,455,127	60,789
57	80	333,405	4.38	65,759	66,912		2,856,737	60,789
62	85	386,508	5.08	76,232	77,569		1,774,517	60,789
67	90	448,068	5.89	88,374	89,924		0	60,789
68	Total	8,036,350			1,612,828			

	A	B	C	D	E	F	G	H
1	Retirement Years	Income Growth	Rate of Inflation	Exemption Now	Tax Rate	Savings Rate	ROR	rROR
2	25	0.07	0.03	15000	0.25	0.15	0.06	=(G2-C2)/(1+C2)
3	Age	Income	Deflator	Exemption	Taxes	Savings	Cumulative Savings	rConsumption
4	30	50000	1	=$D$2*C4	=(H4*C4-D4)*$E$2	=B4-E4-H4*C4	=F4	35062.5
5	31	=B4*(1+$B$2)	=C4*(1+$C$2)	=$D$2*C5	=(H5*C5-D5)*$E$2	=B5-E5-H5*C5	=G4*(1+$G$2)+F5	36223.7712378641
39	65	=B38*(1+$B$2)	=C38*(1+$C$2)	=$D$2*C39	=(H39*C39-D39)*$E$2	=B39-E39-H39*C39	=G38*(1+$G$2)+F39	116364.980523664
40	Total				=SUM(E4:E39)	=SUM(F4:F39)	Real Annuity	=PMT($H$2,$A$2,-$G$39/$C$39,0,0)
41	**RETIREMENT**							
42	Age	Nom Withdraw	Deflator	Exemption	Taxes		Funds Left	rConsumption
43	66	=$H$40*C43	=C39*(1+$C$2)	=$D$2*C43	=MAX(0,(B43-D43)*$E$2)		=G39*(1+$G$2)-B43	=(B43-E43)/C43
44	67	=$H$40*C44	=C43*(1+$C$2)	=$D$2*C44	=MAX(0,(B44-D44)*$E$2)		=G43*(1+$G$2)-B44	=(B44-E44)/C44
67	90	=$H$40*C67	=C66*(1+$C$2)	=$D$2*C67	=MAX(0,(B67-D67)*$E$2)		=G66*(1+$G$2)-B67	=(B67-E67)/C67
68	Total	=SUM(B43:B67)			=SUM(E43:E67)			

income. This ratio becomes .89 at age 45 (check this) at which point the average tax rate is above 22%. The current U.S. tax code, with multiple income brackets, is much more progressive than our assumed structure.

In Spreadsheet 18.6 we work with a more **progressive tax** structure that is closer to the U.S. Federal tax code augmented with an average state tax. Our hypothetical tax schedule is described in Table 18.1.

Spreadsheet 18.6 is identical to Spreadsheet 18.4, the only difference being the tax built into column E according to the schedule in Table 18.1.

Despite the more progressive schedule of this tax code, at the income level we assume, you would end up with a similar standard of living. This is due to the large lower-rate bracket. Although the lifetime tax rate is higher, 34.66% compared with 32.13% for the flat tax, you actually pay lower taxes until you reach the age of 41. The early increased savings offset some of the bite of the overall higher tax rate. Another important result of the nature of this code is the lower marginal tax rate upon retirement when taxable income is lower. This is the environment in which a tax shelter is most effective, as we shall soon see.

Spreadsheet 18.7 augments the progressive tax code with our benchmark (IRA-style) tax shelter that allows you to pay taxes on consumption (minus an exemption) and accumulate tax liability to be paid during your retirement years. The construction of this spreadsheet is identical to Spreadsheet 18.5, with the only difference being the tax structure built into column E. We copied the real pre-retirement consumption stream from Spreadsheet 18.6 to focus the

progressive tax

Taxes are an increasing fraction of income as income rises.

SPREADSHEET 18.6
Saving with a progressive tax

	A	B	C	D	E	F	G	H
1	Retirement Years	Income Growth	Rate of Inflation	Exemption Now	Tax rates in	Savings Rate	ROR	rROR
2	25	0.07	0.03	10000	Table 18.1	0.15	0.06	0.0291
3	Age	Income	Deflator	Exemption	Taxes	Savings	Cumulative Savings	rConsumption
4	30	50,000	1.00	10,000	8,000	6,300	6,300	35,700
5	31	53,500	1.03	10,300	8,716	6,718	13,396	36,958
9	35	70,128	1.16	11,593	12,489	8,646	51,310	42,262
19	45	137,952	1.56	15,580	32,866	15,763	248,018	57,333
29	55	271,372	2.09	20,938	76,587	29,218	731,514	79,076
39	65	533,829	2.81	28,139	186,335	52,124	1,833,644	104,970
40	**Total**		Total	**632,759**	**2,116,533**	**799,371**	**Real Annuity**	**37,059**
41	**RETIREMENT**							
42	Age	Nom Withdraw	Deflator	Exemption	Taxes		Fund Left	rConsumption
43	66	107,408	2.90	28,983	16,207		1,836,254	31,467
47	70	120,889	3.26	32,620	15,371		1,813,134	32,347
52	75	140,143	3.78	37,816	13,083		1,683,643	33,599
57	80	162,464	4.38	43,839	8,831		1,392,054	35,045
62	85	188,341	5.08	50,821	1,757		864,701	36,714
67	90	218,338	5.89	58,916	0		0	37,059
68	**Total**	**3,916,018**			**227,675**			

TABLE 18.1
Income tax schedule used for the progressive tax*

Taxable Income** Over	But Not Over	The Tax Is	of the Amount Over
$ 0	$ 50,000	$ 0 + 20%	$ 0
50,000	150,000	10,000 + 30	50,000
150,000	. . .	40,000 + 40	150,000

*The capital gains tax rate is assumed to be 8% when income is in the low two brackets and 28% for the highest bracket.

**Current exemption with this code is assumed to be $10,000. The exemption and tax brackets are adjusted for future inflation.

effect of the tax shelter on the standard of living during the retirement years. Spreadsheet 18.7 shows that the lower tax bracket during the retirement years allows you to pay lower taxes over the life of the plan and significantly increases retirement consumption. The use of the IRA-style tax shelter increases the retirement annuity by an average of $34,000 a year, a better improvement than we obtained from the shelter with the flat tax.

The effectiveness of the shelter also has a sort of hedge quality. If you become fortunate and strike it rich, the tax shelter will be less effective, since your tax bracket will be higher at retirement. However, mediocre or worse outcomes will result in low marginal rates upon retirement, making the shelter more effective and the tax bite lower.

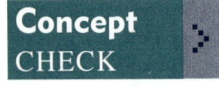

Concept CHECK

6. Are you indifferent between an increase in the low-income bracket tax rate versus an equal increase in the high bracket tax rates?

18.5 A MENU OF TAX SHELTERS

Individual Retirement Accounts

Individual Retirement Accounts (IRAs) were set up by Congress to increase the incentives to save for retirement. The limited scope of these accounts is an important feature. Currently, annual contributions are limited to $3,000 with a scheduled increase to $4,000 in tax years 2005–2007 and then to $5,000 afterward. Workers 50 years of age and up can increase annual

SPREADSHEET **18.7**

The benchmark (IRA) tax shelter with a progressive tax code

	A	B	C	D	E	F	G	H
1	Retirement Years	Income Growth	Rate of Inflation	Exemption Now	Tax rates in	Savings Rate	ROR	rROR
2	25	0.07	0.03	10000	Table 18.1	0.15	0.06	0.0291
3	Age	Income	Deflator	Exemption	Taxes	Savings	Cumulative Savings	rConsumption
4	30	50,000	1.00	10,000	5,140	9,160	9,160	35,700
5	31	53,500	1.03	10,300	5,553	9,880	19,590	36,958
9	35	70,128	1.16	11,593	7,480	13,654	77,112	42,262
19	45	137,952	1.56	15,580	14,749	33,880	434,916	57,333
29	55	271,372	2.09	20,938	32,920	72,885	1,455,451	79,076
39	65	533,829	2.81	28,139	66,100	172,359	4,125,524	104,970
40	Total			632,759	879,430	2,036,474	Real Annuity	83,380
41	**RETIREMENT**							
42	Age	Nom Withdraw	Deflator	Exemption	Taxes		Funds Left	rConsumption
43	66	241,658	2.90	28,983	49,311		4,131,398	66,366
47	70	271,988	3.26	32,620	55,500		4,079,381	66,366
52	75	315,309	3.78	37,816	64,340		3,788,036	66,366
57	80	365,529	4.38	43,839	74,588		3,131,989	66,366
62	85	423,749	5.08	50,821	86,467		1,945,496	66,366
67	90	491,241	5.89	58,916	100,239		0	66,366
68	Total	8,810,670	Total		1,797,848			

contributions by another $1,000. IRAs are somewhat illiquid (as are most shelters), in that there is a 10% penalty on withdrawals prior to age 59½. However, allowances for early withdrawal with no penalty for qualified reasons such as (one-time) purchase of a home or higher education expenses substantially mitigate the problem.

There are two types of IRAs to choose from; the better alternative is not easy to determine.

Traditional IRA   Contributions to **traditional IRA** accounts are tax deductible, as are the earnings until retirement. In principle, if you were able to contribute all your savings to a traditional IRA, your savings plan would be identical to our benchmark tax shelter (Spreadsheets 18.5 and 18.7), with the effectiveness of tax mitigation depending on your marginal tax rate upon retirement.

Roth IRA   A **Roth IRA** is a variation on the traditional IRA tax shelter, with both a drawback and an advantage. Contributions to Roth IRAs are *not* tax deductible. However, earnings on the accumulating funds in the Roth account are tax-free, and unlike a traditional IRA, no taxes are paid upon withdrawals of savings during retirement. The trade-off is not easy to evaluate. To gain insight and illustrate how to analyze the trade-off, we contrast Roth with traditional IRAs under our two alternative tax codes.

Roth IRA with the Progressive Tax Code

As we have noted, a traditional IRA is identical to the benchmark tax shelter set up under two alternative tax codes in Spreadsheets 18.5 and 18.7. We saw that, as a general rule, the effectiveness of a tax shelter depends on the progressivity of the tax code: lower tax rates during retirement favor the postponement of tax obligations until one's retirement years. However, with a Roth IRA, you pay no taxes at all on withdrawals during the retirement phase. In this case, therefore, the effectiveness of the shelter does not depend on the tax rates during the retirement years. The question for any investor is whether this advantage is sufficient to compensate for the nondeductibility of contributions, which is the primary advantage of the traditional IRA.

traditional IRA

Contributions to the account and investment earnings are tax sheltered until retirement.

Roth IRA

Contributions are not tax sheltered, but investment earnings are tax free.

To evaluate the trade-off, Spreadsheet 18.8 modifies Spreadsheet 18.7 (progressive tax) to conform to the features of a Roth IRA, that is, we eliminate deductibility of contributions and taxes during the retirement phase. We keep consumption during the earning years the same as they were in the benchmark (traditional IRA) tax shelter to compare the standard of living in retirement afforded by a Roth IRA tax shelter.

Table 18.2 demonstrates the difference between the two types of shelters. The first line shows the advantage of the traditional IRA in sheltering contributions. Taxes paid during the working years are lower, yet taxes during the retirement years are significant and, later in life, you pay less tax with Roth IRAs (line 2). For the middle-class income we examine here, this is not sufficient to make Roth IRA more attractive, as the after-tax annuities demonstrate. The reason is that early tax payments weigh more heavily than later payments. However, one can find situations in which a Roth IRA will be more advantageous. This is why it is important for investors to check their unique circumstances. Those who are not able to do so themselves can log on to one of the many websites that provide tools to do so (e.g., http://www.quicken.com).

Notice in Table 18.2 that the lifetime tax rate for saving with traditional IRAs is 39.37%. This is a result of large accumulation of earnings on savings that are taxed on retirement and shows the importance of early accumulation. Despite the higher lifetime taxes, this tax shelter ends up with larger after-tax real consumption during retirement.

SPREADSHEET 18.8
Roth IRA with a progressive tax

	A	B	C	D	E	F	G	H
1	Retirement Years	Income Growth	Rate of Inflation	Exemption Now	Tax Rates in	Savings Rate	ROR	rROR
2	25	0.07	0.03	10000	Table 18.1	0.15	0.06	0.0291
3	Age	Income	Deflator	Exemption	Taxes	Savings	Cumulative Savings	rConsumption
4	30	50,000	1.00	10,000	8,000	6,300	6,300	35,700
5	31	53,500	1.03	10,300	8,640	6,793	13,471	36,958
9	35	70,128	1.16	11,593	11,764	9,370	52,995	42,262
19	45	137,952	1.56	15,580	28,922	19,707	278,528	57,333
29	55	271,372	2.09	20,938	64,661	41,143	883,393	79,076
39	65	533,829	2.81	28,139	145,999	92,460	2,432,049	104,970
40	**Total**		Total	632,759	1,752,425	1,163,478	**Real Annuity**	49,153
41	**RETIREMENT**		Tax factors					
42	Age	Nom Withdraw	Deflator	Interest	Exemption	Taxes	Funds Left	rConsumption
43	66	142,460	2.90	137,375	28,983	0	2,435,512	49,153
47	70	160,340	3.26	135,579	32,620	0	2,404,847	49,153
52	75	185,879	3.78	125,770	37,816	0	2,233,096	49,153
57	80	215,484	4.38	103,778	43,839	0	1,846,348	49,153
62	85	249,805	5.08	64,070	50,821	0	1,146,895	49,153
67	90	289,593	5.89	-984	58,916	0	0	49,153
68	**Total**			2,450,313		0		

TABLE 18.2
Traditional vs. Roth IRA tax shelters under a progressive tax code

	Traditional IRA	Roth IRA
Taxes:		
Earning years	$ 879,430	$1,752,425
Retirement years	1,797,848	0
Total paid over lifetime	2,677,278	1,752,425
Retirement annuity:		
Before-tax	$83,380	$49,153
After-tax	66,366	49,153
Lifetime tax rate	39.37%	29.19%

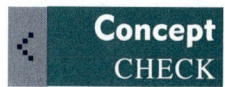

7. Suppose all taxpayers were like you, and the IRS wished to raise a fixed tax revenue. Would it be wise to offer the Roth IRA option?

401k and 403b Plans

These days the majority of employees receive retirement benefits in the form of a defined contribution plan (see Chapter 17). These are named after the relevant sections of the U.S. tax code: 401k in the corporate sector and 403b in the public and tax-exempt sectors. These are quite similar and the discussion of 401k plans applies to 403b plans as well.

401k plans have two distinct features. First and foremost, your employer may match your contribution to various degrees, up to a certain level. This means that if you elect not to participate in the plan, you forego part of your potential employment compensation. Needless to say, regardless of tax considerations, any employee should contribute to the plan at least as much as the employer will match, except for extreme circumstances of cash needs. While some employees may face cash constraints and think they would be better off skipping contributions, in many circumstances, they would be better off borrowing to bridge the liquidity shortfall while continuing to contribute up to the level matched by the employer.

The second feature of the plan is akin to a traditional IRA in tax treatment and similar in other restrictions. Contributions to 401k plans are restricted (details can be found on many websites, e.g., http://www.Morningstar.com), but the limits on contributions generally exceed the level matched by the employer. Hence you must decide how much of your salary to contribute beyond the level matched by your employer. You can incorporate 401k plans, like the traditional IRA, in your savings-plan spreadsheet, review the trade-off, and make an informed decision on how much to save.

401k plans

Defined employee contribution plans wherein the employer matches the employee's contribution up to a set percentage.

Risky Investments and Capital Gains as Tax Shelters

So far we limited our discussion to safe investments that yield a sure 6%. This number, coupled with the inflation assumption (3%), determined the results of various savings rules under the appropriate tax configuration. You must recognize, however, that the 6% return and 3% inflation are not hard numbers and consider the implications of other possible scenarios over the life of the savings plan. The spreadsheets we developed make scenario analysis quite easy. Once you set up a spreadsheet with a contemplated savings plan, you simply vary the inputs for ROR (the nominal rate of return) and inflation and record the implications for each scenario. The probabilities of possible deviations from the expected numbers and your risk tolerance will dictate which savings plan provides you with sufficient security of obtaining your goals. This sensitivity analysis will be even more important when you consider risky investments.

The tax shelters we have described allow you to invest in a broad array of securities and mutual funds and you can invest your nonsheltered savings in anything you please. Which portfolio to choose is a matter of risk versus return. That said, taxes lend importance to the otherwise largely irrelevant aspect of dividends versus capital gains.

According to current U.S. tax law, there are two applicable capital gains rates for most investments: 20% if your marginal tax rate is higher than 27.5%, and 8%[5] if you are in a lower tax bracket. More importantly, you pay the applicable rate only when you sell the security. Thus, investing in non-dividend-paying securities is an automatic partial tax shelter with no restrictions on contributions or withdrawals. Because this investment is not tax deductible, it

[5]The rate goes up to 10% if you hold the security for less than five years.

SPREADSHEET 18.9
Saving with no-dividend stocks under a progressive tax

	A	B	C	D	E	F	G	H
1	Retirement Years	Income Growth	Rate of Inflation	Exemption Now	Tax rates in	Savings Rate	ROR	rROR
2	25	0.07	0.03	10000	Table 18.1	0.15	0.06	0.0291
3	Age	Income	Deflator	Exemption	Taxes	Savings	Cumulative Savings	rConsumption
4	30	50,000	1.00	10,000	8,000	6,300	6,300	35,700
5	31	53,500	1.03	10,300	8,640	6,793	13,471	36,958
9	35	70,128	1.16	11,593	11,764	9,370	52,995	42,262
19	45	137,952	1.56	15,580	28,922	19,707	278,528	57,333
29	55	271,372	2.09	20,938	64,661	41,143	883,393	79,076
39	65	533,829	2.81	28,139	145,999	92,460	2,432,049	104,970
40	Total				1,752,425	1,163,478	Real Annuity	49,153
41	RETIREMENT				Tax rate on	capital gain	0.08	0.2
42	Age	Nom Withdraw	Deflator	Cum cap gains	Exemption	Taxes	Funds Left	rConsumption
43	66	142,460	2.90	1,340,186	28,983	0	2,435,512	49,153
47	70	160,340	3.26	1,561,124	32,620	5,504	2,404,847	47,466
52	75	185,879	3.78	1,660,844	37,816	7,874	2,233,096	47,071
57	80	215,484	4.38	1,503,386	43,839	10,416	1,846,348	46,778
62	85	249,805	5.08	995,489	50,821	13,204	1,146,895	46,555
67	90	289,593	5.89	1,500	58,916	16,471	0	46,358
68	Total				1,056,691	236,555		

is similar to a Roth IRA, but somewhat inferior in that you do pay a tax on withdrawal, however low. Still, such investments can be more effective than traditional IRA and 401k plans, as we discussed earlier. Since annual contributions to all IRAs and 401k plans are quite limited, investment in a low- or no-dividend portfolio may be the efficient shelter for many investors who wish to exceed the contribution limit. Another advantage of such portfolios is that you can sell those securities that have lost value to realize capital losses and thereby reduce your tax bill in any given year. This virtue of risky securities is called the *tax-timing option.* Managing a portfolio with efficient utilization of the tax-timing option requires expert attention, however, and may not be appropriate for many savers.

The average dividend yield on the S&P 500 stocks is less than 2%, and other indexes (such as Nasdaq) bear an even lower yield. This means that you can easily construct a well-diversified portfolio with a very low dividend yield. Such a portfolio allows you to utilize the tax advantage of capital gains versus dividends. Spreadsheet 18.9 adapts Spreadsheet 18.6 (progressive tax with no shelter) to a no-dividend portfolio of stocks, maintaining the same preretirement consumption stream and holding the ROR at 6%. Real retirement consumption, averaging $47,756, is almost identical to that supported by a Roth IRA (Spreadsheet 18.7).[6]

Sheltered versus Unsheltered Savings

Suppose your desired level of savings is double the amount allowed in IRAs and 401k (or 403b) plans. At the same time you wish to invest equal amounts in stocks and bonds. Where should you keep the stocks and where the bonds? You will be surprised to know how many investors make the costly mistake of holding the stocks in a tax-protected account and the bonds in an unsheltered account. This is a mistake because most of the return from bonds is in the form of taxable interest payments, while stocks by their nature already provide some tax shelter.

---

[6]In Spreadsheet 18.9 we did not take full advantage of the tax code. You can defer capital gains longer by accounting for the shares you sell so that you sell first new shares with little capital gains and old shares last.

TABLE **18.3** Investing Roth IRA contributions in stocks and bonds	Phase	Asset	Stocks Inside; Bonds Outside	Stocks Outside; Bonds Inside
	Savings	Bonds	Taxed upon accrual	No taxes
		Stocks	No taxes	Taxes deferred
	Withdrawal	Bonds	No taxes	No taxes
		Stocks	No taxes	Taxed at capital gains rate

TABLE **18.4** Investing traditional IRA or 401k contributions in stocks and bonds	Phase	Asset	Stocks Inside; Bonds Outside	Stocks Outside; Bonds Inside
	Savings	Bonds	Taxed on accrual	Taxes deferred
		Stocks	Tax deferred	Taxes deferred
	Withdrawal	Bonds	No taxes	Taxed at marginal rate
		Stocks	Taxed at marginal rate	Taxed at capital gains rate

Recall that tax shelters enhance the retirement annuity with two elements: (1) tax deferral on contributions and (2) tax deferral on income earned on savings. The effectiveness of each element depends on the tax rate on withdrawals. Of the two types of tax shelters we analyzed, traditional IRA and 401k (or 403b) plans contain both elements, while a Roth IRA provides only the second, but with the advantage that the tax rate on withdrawals is zero. Therefore, we need to analyze the stock–bond shelter question separately for each type of retirement plan. Table 18.3 shows the hierarchy of this analysis when a Roth IRA is used. The difference is apparent by comparing the taxes in each column. With stocks inside and bonds outside the shelter you pay taxes early and at the ordinary income rate. When you remove stocks from and move bonds into the shelter you pay taxes later at the lower capital gains rate.

When you use either a traditional IRA or 401k plan, contributions are tax deferred regardless of whether you purchase stocks or bonds, so we need to compare only taxes on income from savings and withdrawal. Table 18.4 shows the trade-off for a traditional IRA or 401k plan.

The advantage ends up being the same as with the Roth IRA. By removing stocks from and moving bonds into the shelter you gain the deferral on the bond interest during the savings phase. During the retirement phase you gain the difference between the ordinary income and the capital gains rate on the gains from the stocks.

8. Does the rationale of sheltering bonds rather than stocks apply to preferred stocks?

> **Concept**
> CHECK

18.6 SOCIAL SECURITY

Social Security (SS) is a cross between a pension and insurance plan. It is quite regressive in the way it is financed, in that employees pay a proportional (currently 7.65%) tax on gross wages, with no exemption but with an income cap (currently $89,400). Employers match employees' contributions and pay SS directly.[7]

> **Social Security**
>
> Federally mandated pension plan established to provide minimum retirement benefits to all workers.

---

[7]Absent the SS tax, it is reasonable to assume that the amount contributed by employers would be added to your pretax income, hence your actual contribution is really 15.3%. For this reason, self-employed individuals are required to contribute 15.3% to SS.

On the other hand, SS is progressive in the way it allocates benefits; low-income individuals receive a relatively larger share of preretirement income upon retirement. Of the SS tax of 7.65%, 6.2% goes toward the retirement benefit and 1.45% toward retirement healthcare services provided by Medicare. Thus, combining your payments with your employer's, the real retirement annuity is financed by $2 \times 6.2 = 12.4\%$ of your income (up to the aforementioned cap); we do not examine the Medicare component of SS in this chapter.

SS payments are made throughout one's entire working life; however, only 35 years of contributions count for the determination of benefits. Benefits are in the form of a lifetime real annuity based on a retirement age of 65, although you can retire earlier (as of age 62) or later (up to age 70) and draw a smaller or larger annuity, respectively. One reason SS is projected to face fiscal difficulties in future years is the increased longevity of the population. The current plan to mitigate this problem is to gradually increase the retirement age.

Calculation of benefits for individuals retiring in a given year is done in four steps:

1. The series of your taxed annual earnings (using the cap) is compiled. The status of this series is shown in your annual SS statement.
2. An indexing factor series is compiled for all past years. This series is used to account for the time value of your lifetime contributions.
3. The indexing factors are applied to your recorded earnings to arrive at the Average Indexed Monthly Earnings (AIME).
4. Your AIME is used to determine the Primary Insurance Amount (PIA), which is your monthly retirement annuity.

All this sounds more difficult than it really is, so let's describe steps 2 through 4 in detail.

The Indexing Factor Series

Suppose your first wage on which you paid the SS tax was earned 40 years ago. To arrive at today's value of this wage, we must calculate its future value over the 40 years, that is, $FV = \text{wage} \times (1 + g)^{40}$. The SS administration refers to this as the indexed earnings for that year, and the FV factor, $(1 + g)^{40}$, is the index for that year. This calculation is made for each year, resulting in a series of indexed earnings which, when summed, is the value today of the entire stream of lifetime taxed earnings.

A major issue is what rate, g, to use in producing the index for each year. SS uses for each year the growth in the average wage of the U.S. working population in that year. Arbitrarily, the index for the most recent two years is set to 1.0 (a growth rate of zero) and then increased each year, going backward, by the growth rate of wages in that year. For example, in the year 2001 the index for 1967 (35 years earlier) was 6.16768. Thus the 1967 wage is assumed to have been invested for 35 years at 5.34% ($1.0534^{35} = 6.16768$). The actual average growth rate of wages in the U.S. over the years 1967–2001 was 5.48%[8]; the index is slightly lower because the growth rate in the two most recent years prior to retirement has been set to zero.

Wage growth was not constant over these years. For example, it was as high as 10.07% in 1980–1981, and as low as 0.86% in 1992–1993. At the same time, the (geometric) average T-bill rate over the years 1967–2001 was 6.53% and the rate of inflation 4.92%, implying a real interest rate of 1.53%. For retirees of 2002, the average *real* growth rate applied to their SS contributions is about 0.40% (depending on how much they contributed in each year), significantly lower than the real interest rate over their working years, but closer to the longer-term (1926–2001) real rate of 0.72%. (See Table 5.2).

---

[8]We use a wage growth rate of 7% in our exercises, assuming our readers are well educated and can expect a higher than average growth. Special attention must be given to this input (and the others) if you advise other people.

TABLE **18.5**
Calculation of the retirement annuity of representative retirees of 2002

	Low	Average	High	Maximum
AIME rank:				
% of Average Wage	45	100	160	Max*
AIME ($ month)	1,207	2,683	4,145	5,489
PIA formula:				
90% of the first $592	532.80	532.80	532.80	532.80
32% of AIME over $592 through $3,567	196.80	669.12	952.00	952.00
15% of AIME over $3,567	0	0	86.70	289.80
Total = PIA ($/month)	729.60	1201.92	1571.50	1774.60
Real retirement annuity = PIA × 12	8,755	14,423	18,858	21,295
Income replacement (%)	60.45	44.80	37.91	NA*
IRR** assuming longevity = 81; inflation = 3%	7.44	6.20	5.49	4.72
IRR** assuming longevity = 84; inflation = 3%	7.76	6.56	5.89	5.18
Longevity implied by SS (years) for IRR = 6%	11	15	18	23

*Income is above the maximum taxable and income replacement cannot be calculated.

**Internal Rate of Return.

The Average Indexed Monthly Income

The series of a retiree's lifetime indexed contributions (there may be zeros in the series for periods when the retiree was unemployed) is used to determine the base for the retirement annuity. The 35 highest indexed contributions are identified, summed, and then divided by $35 \times 12 = 420$ to achieve your Average Indexed Monthly Income (AIME). If you worked less than 35 years, all your indexed earnings will be summed, but your AIME might be low since you still divide the sum by 420. If you worked more than 35 years, your reward is that only the 35 highest indexed wages will be used to compute the average.

The Primary Insurance Amount

In this stage of the calculation of monthly SS benefits, low-income workers (with a low AIME) are favored in order to increase income equality. The exact formula may change from one year to the next, but the example of four representative individuals who retired in 2002 demonstrates the principle. The AIME of these individuals relative to the average in the population and their Primary Insurance Amount (PIA) are calculated in Table 18.5.

Table 18.5 presents the value of SS to U.S. employees who retired in 2002. The first part of the table shows how SS calculates the real annuity to be paid to retirees.[9] The results differ for the four representative individuals. One measure of this differential is the *income replacement rate* (i.e., retirement income as a percent of working income) provided to the four income brackets in Table 18.5. Low-income retirees have a replacement rate of 60.45%, more than 1.5 times that of the high-wage employees (37.91%).

The net after-tax benefits may be reduced if the individual has other sources of income, because a portion of the retirement annuity is subject to income tax. Currently, retired households with combined taxable income over $32,000 pay taxes on a portion of the SS benefits. At income of $44,000, 50% of the SS annuity is subject to tax and the proportion reaches 85%

[9]The annuity of special-circumstance low-income retirees is supplemented.

at higher income. You can find the current numbers and replicate the calculations in Table 18.5 by logging on to http://www.ssa.gov/OACT/ProgData/nominalEarn.html. This website also allows you to project Social Security benefits at various levels of sophistication.

When evaluating the attractiveness of SS as an investment for current retirees (the bottom part of Table 18.5), we must consider current **longevity** figures. For a male, current remaining life expectancy at age 65 is an additional 15.6 years, and for a female 19.2 years. Using these figures, the current PIA provides male retirees an internal rate of return on SS contributions in the range of 7.44–4.72%, and female retirees 7.76–5.18%.[10] These IRRs are obtained by taking 12.4% (the combined SS tax) of the series of 35 annual earnings of the four employees as cash outflows. The series of annuity payments (16 years for males and 19 for females), assuming inflation at 3%, is used to compute cash inflows.

To examine SS performance another way, the last line in the table shows the longevity (number of payments) required to achieve an IRR of 6%. Except for the highest income bracket, all have life expectancy greater than this threshold. Why are these numbers so attractive, when SS is so often criticized for poor investment performance? The reason benefits are so generous is that the PIA formula sets a high replacement rate relative to the SS tax rate, the proportion of income taxed. Taking history as a guide, to achieve an IRR equal to the rate of inflation plus the historical average rate on a safe investment such as T-bills (with a historical real rate of 0.7%), the formula would need to incorporate a lower replacement rate. With a future rate of inflation of 3%, this would imply a nominal IRR of 3.7%. Is the ROR assumed in our spreadsheets (6%) the right one to use, or is the expected IRR based on past real rates the correct one to use? In short, we simply don't know. But averaging across the population, SS may well be a fair pension plan, taking into consideration its role in promoting equality of income.

The solvency of SS is threatened by two factors: population longevity and a below-replacement growth of the U.S. population. Over the next 35 years, longevity is expected to increase by almost two years, increasing steady-state expenditures by more than 10%. To keep a level population (ignoring immigration) requires an average of 2.1 children per female, yet the current average of 1.9 is expected to decline further.[11] The projected large deficit, beginning in 2016, requires reform of SS. Increasing the retirement age to account for increased longevity does not constitute a reduction in the plan's IRR and therefore seems a reasonable solution to deficits arising from this factor. Eliminating the deficit resulting from population decline is more difficult. It is projected that doing so by increasing the SS tax may require an increase in the combined SS tax of as much as 10% within your working years. Such a simple solution is considered politically unacceptable, so you must expect changes in benefits.

The question of privatizing a portion of SS so that investors will be able to choose portfolios with risk levels according to their personal risk tolerance has become a hot public policy issue. Clearly, the current format that provides a guaranteed real rate is tailored to individuals with low risk tolerance. Although we advocate that at least a portion of SS be considered as a safety-first proposition (with a very low-risk profile), investors who are willing to monitor and rebalance risky portfolios cannot be faulted for investing in stocks. The main point with respect to this option is that the media and even some finance experts claim that a long-term investment in stocks is not all that risky. We cannot disagree more. We project that with

longevity

Remaining life expectancy.

---

[10]However, income is correlated with longevity and with durability of marriage. This means that wealthy retirees and their spouses draw longer annuities than the poor do. It is suggested that this difference may as much as completely offset the progressivity built into the PIA schedule.

[11]Fertility rates in Europe, Japan, and (until recently) in China are even lower, exacerbating the problems of their Social Security systems.

appropriate risk adjustment, future retirees will find it difficult to beat the SS plan and should be made fully aware of this fact.[12]

9. Should you consider a dollar of future Social Security benefits as valuable as a dollar of your projected retirement annuity? For example, suppose your target is a real annuity of $100,000 and you project your SS annuity at $20,000. Should you save to produce a real annuity of $80,000?

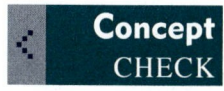

Concept
CHECK

18.7   CHILDREN'S EDUCATION AND LARGE PURCHASES

Sending a child to a private college can cost a family in excess of $40,000 a year, in current dollars, for four years. Even a state college can cost in excess of $25,000 a year. Many families will send two or more children to college within a few years, creating a need to finance large expenditures within a few years. Other large expenditures such as a second home (we deal with the primary residence in the next section) or an expensive vehicle present similar problems on a smaller scale.

The question is whether planned, large outflows during the working years require a major innovation to our planning tools. The answer is no. All you need to do is add a column to your spreadsheet for extra-consumption expenditures that come out of savings. As long as cumulative savings do not turn negative as the outflows take place, the only effect to consider is the reduction in the retirement annuity that results from these expenditures. To respond to a lower-than-desired retirement annuity you have four options: (1) increase the savings rate, (2) live with a smaller retirement annuity, (3) do away with or reduce the magnitude of the expenditure item, or (4) increase expected ROR by taking on more risk. Recall though, that in Section 18.2, we suggested option 4 isn't viable for many investors.

The situation is a little more complicated when the extra-consumption expenditures create negative savings in the retirement plan. In principle, one can simply borrow to finance these expenditures with debt (as is common for large purchases such as automobiles). Again, the primary variable of interest is the retirement annuity. The problem, however, is that if you arrive at a negative savings level quite late in your savings plan, you will be betting the farm on the success of the plan in later years. Recalling, again, the discussion of Section 18.2, the risk in later years, other things being equal, is more ominous since you will have little time to recover from any setbacks.

An illuminating example requires adding only one column to Spreadsheet 18.2, as shown in Spreadsheet 18.10. Column G adds the extra-consumption expenditures. We use as input (cell G2) the current cost of one college year per child—$40,000. We assume your first child will be collegebound when you are 48 years old and the second when you are 50. The expenditures in column G are inflated by the price level in column C and subtracted from cumulative savings in column E.

The real retirement annuity prior to this extra-consumption expenditure was $48,262, but "after-children" only $22,048, less than half. The expenditure of $320,000 in today's dollars cost you total lifetime real consumption of 25 × ($48,262 − $21,424) = $6,710,950 because

---

[12]Here, again, we collide with those who consider stocks low-risk investments in the long run (some of them esteemed colleagues). One cannot overestimate the misleading nature of this assessment (see the Appendix to Chapter 6). The difference between the 35-year average real rate over 1967–2001 (1.53%) and 1932–1966 (−1.05%), was 2.58%! Over long horizons, such a difference has staggering effects on retirement income. Check your spreadsheets to see the impact of a 1% change in ROR.

SPREADSHEET **18.10**
Financing children's education

	A	B	C	D	E	F	G
1	Retirement Years	Income Growth	Rate of Inflation	Savings Rate	ROR	rROR	Extra-Cons
2	25	0.07	0.03	0.15	0.06	0.0291	40,000
3	Age	Income	Deflator	Savings	Cumulative Savings	rConsumption	Expenditures
4	30	50,000	1.00	7,500	7,500	42,500	0
5	31	53,500	1.03	8,025	15,975	44,150	0
9	35	70,128	1.16	10,519	61,658	51,419	0
19	45	137,952	1.56	20,693	308,859	75,264	0
22	48	168,997	1.70	25,349	375,099	84,378	68,097
23	49	180,826	1.75	27,124	354,588	87,654	70,140
24	50	193,484	1.81	29,023	260,397	91,058	144,489
25	51	207,028	1.86	31,054	158,252	94,595	148,824
26	52	221,520	1.92	33,228	124,331	98,268	76,644
27	53	237,026	1.97	35,554	88,401	102,084	78,943
28	54	253,618	2.03	38,043	131,748	106,049	0
29	55	271,372	2.09	40,706	180,359	110,167	0
39	65	533,829	2.81	80,074	1,090,888	161,257	0
40	Total			1,116,851	Real Annuity	22,048	

of the loss of interest on the funds that would have been saved. If you change the input in G2 to $25,000 (reflecting the cost of a public college), the retirement annuity falls to $32,405, a loss of "only" 35% in the standard of living.

Concept CHECK

10. **What if anything should you do about the risk of rapid increase in college tuition?**

18.8 HOME OWNERSHIP: THE RENT-VERSUS-BUY DECISION

Most people dream of owning a home and for good reason. In addition to the natural desire for roots that goes with owning your home, this investment is an important hedge for most families. Dwelling is the largest long-term consumption item for most people and fluctuations in the cost of dwelling are responsible for the largest consumption risk they face. Dwelling costs, in turn, are subject to general price inflation, as well as to significant fluctuations specific to geographic location. This combination makes it difficult to hedge the risk with investments in securities. In addition, the law favors home ownership in a number of ways, chief of which is tax deductibility of mortgage interest.

Common (though not necessarily correct) belief is that the mortgage tax break is the major reason for investing in rather than renting a home. In competitive markets, though, rents will reflect the mortgage tax-deduction that applies to rental residence as well. Moreover, homes are illiquid assets and transaction costs in buying/selling a house are high. Therefore, purchasing a home that isn't expected to be a long-term residence for the owner may well be a speculative investment with inferior expected returns. The right time for investing in your home is when you are ready to settle someplace for the long haul. Speculative investments in real estate ought to be made in a portfolio context through instruments such as Real Estate Investment Trusts (REITs).

With all this in mind, it is evident that investment in a home enters the savings plan in two ways. First, during the working years the cash down payment should be treated just like any other large extra-consumption expenditure as discussed earlier. Second, home ownership affects your retirement plan because if you own your home free and clear by the time you retire, you will need a smaller annuity to get by; moreover, the value of the house is part of retirement wealth.

11. Should you have any preference for fixed versus variable rate mortgages?

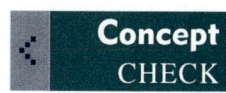

18.9 UNCERTAIN LONGEVITY AND OTHER CONTINGENCIES

Perhaps the most daunting uncertainty in our life is the time it will end. Most people consider this uncertainty a blessing, yet, blessing or curse, this uncertainty has economic implications. Old age is hard enough without worrying about expenses. Yet the amount of money you may need is at least linear in longevity, if not exponential. Not knowing how much you will need, plus a healthy degree of risk aversion, would require us to save a lot more than necessary just to insure against the fortune of longevity.

One solution to this problem is to invest in a life annuity to supplement Social Security benefits, your base life annuity. When you own a **life annuity** (an annuity that pays you income until you die), the provider takes on the risk of the time of death. To survive, the provider must be sure to earn a rate of return commensurate with the risk. Except for wars and natural disasters, however, an individual's time of death is a unique, nonsystematic risk.[13] It would appear, then, that the cost of a life annuity should be a simple calculation of interest rates applied to life expectancy from mortality tables. Unfortunately, adverse selection comes in the way.

Adverse selection is the tendency for any proposed contract (deal) to attract the type of party who would make the contract (deal) a losing proposition to the offering party. A good example of adverse selection arises in health care. Suppose that Blue Cross offers health coverage where you choose your doctor and Blue Cross pays 80% of the costs. Suppose another HMO covers 100% of the cost and charges only a nominal fee per treatment. If HMOs were to price the services on the basis of a survey of the average health care needs in the population at large, they would be in for an unpleasant surprise. People who need frequent and expensive care would prefer the HMO over Blue Cross. The adverse selection in this case is that high-need individuals will choose the plan that provides more complete coverage. The individuals that the HMO most wants *not* to insure are most likely to sign up for coverage. Hence, to stay in business HMOs must expect their patients to have greater than average needs, and price the policy on this basis.

Providers of life annuities can expect a good dose of adverse selection as well, as people with the longest life expectancies will be their most enthusiastic customers. Therefore, it is advantageous to acquire these annuities at a younger age, before individuals are likely to know much about their personal life expectancies. The SS trust does not face adverse selection since virtually the entire population is forced into the purchase, allowing it to be a fair deal on both sides.

Unfortunately we also must consider untimely death or disability during the working years. These require an appropriate amount of life and disability insurance, particularly in the early stage of the savings plan. The appropriate coverage should be thought of in the context of a retirement annuity. Coverage should replace at least the most essential part of the retirement annuity.

Finally, there is the need to hedge labor income. Since you cannot insure wages, the least you can do is maintain a portfolio that is uncorrelated with your labor income. As the Enron case has taught us, too many are unaware of the perils of having their pension income tied to their career, employment, and compensation. Investing a significant fraction of your portfolio in the industry you work in is akin to a "Texas hedge," betting on the horse you own.

life annuity

An annuity that pays you income until you die.

adverse selection

The tendency for any proposed deal to attract the type of party who would make the deal a losing proposition to the offering party.

---

[13]For this reason, life insurance policies include fine print excluding payment in case of events such as wars, epidemics, and famine.

12. **Insurance companies offer life insurance on your children. Is this a good idea?**

18.10 : MATRIMONY, BEQUEST, AND INTERGENERATIONAL TRANSFERS

In the context of a retirement plan we think of risk in terms of safety first, where mean-variance analysis is inadequate. We have already touched on this issue earlier, in the context of (1) raising the ROR with risky investments, (2) avoiding savings plans that rely too heavily on savings in later years, and (3) acquiring life insurance and including life annuities in the savings portfolio.

One sort of insurance the market cannot supply is wage insurance. If we could obtain wage insurance, a savings plan would be a lot easier to formulate. **Moral hazard** is the reason for this void in the marketplace. Moral hazard is the phenomenon whereby a party to a contract (deal) has an incentive to change behavior in a way that makes the deal less attractive to the other party.[14] For example, a person who buys wage insurance would then have an incentive to consume leisure at the expense of work effort. Moral hazard is also why insuring items for more than their market or intrinsic value is prohibited. If your warehouse were insured for lots more than its value, you might have less incentive to prevent fires, an obvious moral hazard.

In contrast, marriage provides a form of co-insurance that extends also to the issue of longevity. A married couple has a greater probability that at least one will survive to an older age, giving greater incentive to save for a longer life. Put differently, saving for a longer life has a smaller probability of going to waste. A study by Spivak and Kotlikoff (1981)[15] simulated reasonable individual preferences to show that a marriage contract increases the dollar value of lifetime savings by as much as 25%. Old sages who have been preaching the virtue of matrimony for millennia must have known more about economics than we give them credit for.

Bequest is another motive for saving. There is something special about bequest that differentiates it from other "expense" items. When you save for members of the next generation (and beyond), you double the planning horizon, and by considering later generations as well, you can make it effectively infinite. This has implications for the composition of the savings portfolio. For example, the conventional wisdom that as you grow older you should gradually shift out of stocks and into bonds is not as true when bequest is an important factor in the savings plan.

Having discussed marriage co-insurance and bequest, we cannot fail to mention that despite the virtues of saving for the longest term, many individuals overshoot the mark. When a person saves for old age and passes on before taking full advantage of the nest egg, the estate is called an "involuntary, intergenerational transfer." Data shows that such transfers are widespread. Kotlikoff and Summers (1981)[16] estimate that about 75% of wealth left behind is actually involuntary transfer. This suggests that people make too little use of the market for life annuities. Hopefully you will not be one of them, both because you will live to a healthy old age and because you'll have a ball spending your never-expiring annuity.

13. **If matrimony is such a good deal, but you haven't yet found a soul mate, should you rush to surf the Web for a potential spouse?**

---

[14]Moral hazard and adverse selection can reinforce each other. Restaurants that offer an all-you-can-eat meal attract big eaters (adverse selection) and induce "normal" eaters to overeat (moral hazard).

[15]Laurence J. Kotlikoff and Avia Spivak, "The Family as an Incomplete Annuities Market," *Journal of Political Economy*, 89, no. 2 (April 1981), pp. 372–91.

[16]Laurence J. Kotlikoff and Lawrence H. Summers, "The Role of Intergenerational Transfers in Aggregate Capital Accumulation," *The Journal of Political Economy*, 89, no. 4. (August, 1981), pp. 706–32.

moral hazard

The phenomenon whereby a party to a contract has an incentive to change behavior in a way that makes the contract less attractive to the other party.

- The major objective of a savings plan is to provide for adequate retirement income.
- Even moderate inflation will affect the purchasing power of the retirement annuity. Therefore, the plan must be cast in terms of real consumption and retirement income.
- From a standpoint of smoothing consumption it is advantageous to save a fixed or rising fraction of real income. However, postponement of savings to later years increases the risk of the retirement fund.
- The IRA-style tax shelter, akin to a consumption tax, defers taxes on both contributions and earnings on savings.
- The progressive tax code sharpens the importance of taxes during the retirement years. High tax rates during retirement reduce the effectiveness of the tax shelter.
- A Roth IRA tax shelter does not shield contributions but eliminates taxes during retirement. Savers who anticipate high retirement income (and taxes) must examine whether this shelter is more beneficial than a traditional IRA account.
- 401k plans are similar to traditional IRAs and allow matched contributions by employers. This benefit should not be foregone.
- Capital gains can be postponed and later taxed at a lower rate. Therefore, investment in low-dividend stocks is a natural tax shelter. Investments in interest-bearing securities should be sheltered first.
- Social Security benefits are an important component of retirement income.
- Savings plans should be augmented for large expenditures such as children's education.
- Home ownership should be viewed as a hedge against rental cost.
- Uncertain longevity and other contingencies should be handled via life annuities and appropriate insurance coverage.

401k plans, 637	moral hazard, 646	Social Security, 639
adverse selection, 645	progressive tax, 633	tax shelters, 632
flat tax, 630	real consumption, 628	traditional IRA, 635
life annuity, 645	retirement annuity, 626	
longevity, 642	Roth IRA, 635	

1. With no taxes or inflation (Spreadsheet 18.1), what would be your retirement annuity if you increase the savings rate by 1%?

2. With a 3% inflation (Spreadsheet 18.2), by how much would your retirement annuity grow if you increase the savings rate by 1%? Is the benefit greater in the face of inflation?

3. What savings rate from real income (Spreadsheet 18.3) will produce the same retirement annuity as a 15% savings rate from nominal income?

4. Under the flat tax (Spreadsheet 18.4), will a 1% increase in ROR offset a 1% increase in the tax rate?

5. With an IRA tax shelter (Spreadsheet 18.5), compare the effect on real consumption during retirement of a 1% increase in the rate of inflation to a 1% increase in the tax rate.

6. With a progressive tax (Spreadsheet 18.6), compare an increase of 1% in the lower tax bracket to an increase of 1% in the highest tax bracket.

7. Verify that the IRA tax shelter with a progressive tax (Spreadsheet 18.7) acts as a hedge. Compare the effect of a decline of 2% in the ROR to an increase of 2% in ROR.

8. What is the trade-off between ROR and the rate of inflation with a Roth IRA under a progressive tax (Spreadsheet 18.8)?

9. Suppose you could defer capital gains income tax to the last year of your retirement (Spreadsheet 18.9). Would it be worthwhile given the progressivity of the tax code?

10. Project your Social Security benefits with the parameters of Section 18.6.

11. Using Spreadsheet 18.10, assess the present value of a 1% increase in college tuition as a fraction of the present value of labor income.

12. Give another example of adverse selection.

13. In addition to expected longevity, what traits might affect an individual's demand for a life annuity?

14. Give another example of a moral hazard problem.

WEBMASTER

Retirement Calculator

As was discussed in Chapters 17 and 18 one of the major factors that affects investment performance is asset allocation. A retirement calculator that allows you to specify different allocations and different levels of desired income to test the ability to meet your retirement goals is available at http://www3.troweprice.com/ric/RIC. Use the calculator to answer the following questions:

1. What level of retirement assets will you need to support a retirement income level of $7,000 per month with 90% certainty? Assume that you will retire when you are 60, you expect to live for 30 years after you retire, and your portfolio allocation is 60% stock, 30% bonds, and 10% cash. Work in increments of $100,000 in retirement assets.

2. How much would you need to have in retirement assets to meet the same goal with a 99% certainty?

3. If you return to the original 90% certainty level, how much would you need in retirement assets to meet your original goal with a 40% stock, 40% bond, and 20% cash allocation?

SOLUTIONS TO

Concept
CHECKS

1. When ROR falls by 1% to 5%, the retirement annuity falls to from $192,244 to $149,855 (i.e., by 22.45%). To restore this annuity, the savings rate must rise by 4.24 percentage points to 19.24%. With this savings rate, the entire loss of 1% in ROR falls on consumption during the earning years.

2. Intuition suggests you need to keep the real rate (2.91%) constant, that is, increase the nominal rate to 7.03 (confirm this). However, this will not be sufficient because the nominal income growth of 7% has a lower real growth when inflation is higher. Result: You must increase the real ROR to compensate for a lower growth in real income, ending with a nominal rate of 7.67%.

3. There are two components to the risk of relying on future labor income: disability/death and career failure/unemployment. You can insure the first component, but not the second.

4. Holding before-tax income constant, your after-tax income will remain unchanged if your average tax rate, and hence total tax liability, is unchanged:

$$\text{Total tax} = (\text{Income} - \text{Exemption}) \times \text{Tax rate, or } T = (I - E) \times t$$

A 1% increase in the tax rate will increase T by $.01(I - E)$. A 1% increase in the exemption will decrease T by $.01 \times E \times t$. Realistically, $I - E$ will be greater than $E \times t$ and hence you will be worse off with the increase in exemption and tax rate.

5. The qualitative result is the same. However, with no shelter you are worse off early and hence lose also the earning power of the additional tax bills.

6. No, an increase in the low-bracket tax rate applies to your entire taxable income, while an increase in the high-bracket tax rate applies only to a fraction of your taxable income.

7. No, in your hypothetical case, the Roth IRA tax shelter produces less taxes yet a smaller real retirement annuity. The reason is the timing of the taxes. The timing issue does not affect the stream of tax revenues to the IRS because at any point in time, taxpayers are distributed over all ages. In this case, the IRS can replace all Roth IRAs with traditional IRAs and lower the tax rates. The IRS will collect similar revenue each year, and retirees will enjoy higher real retirement annuities.

8. No, in terms of cash income, preferred stocks are more similar to bonds.

9. Your projected retirement fund is risky because of uncertainty about future labor income and future real returns on savings. The projected Social Security real annuity is risky because of political uncertainty about future benefits. It's hard to judge which risk is greater.

10. You can invest in savings accounts that yield a floating rate tied to an index of college tuition.

11. A fixed-rate mortgage is the lower risk, higher expected cost option. Homeowners with greater risk tolerance might opt for a variable-rate mortgage which is expected to average a lower rate over the life of the mortgage.

12. In the old days, children were more than a bundle of joy; they also provided a hedge for old-age income. Under such circumstance, insuring children would make economic sense. These days, children may well be a financial net expenditure, ruling out insurance on economic grounds. Other nonfinancial considerations are a matter of individual preference.

13. Rushing into marriage for economic reasons is a very risky proposition. A bad marriage can be a financial, as well as an emotional, calamity.

19

BEHAVIORAL FINANCE AND TECHNICAL ANALYSIS

**AFTER STUDYING THIS CHAPTER
YOU SHOULD BE ABLE TO:**

> Understand the principles of behavioral finance.

> Identify reasons why technical analysis may be profitable.

> Use the Dow theory to identify situations that technicians would characterize as buy or sell opportunities.

> Use indicators such as volume, put/call ratios, breadth, short interest, or confidence indexes to measure the "technical conditions" of the market.

The Capital Asset Pricing Model (CAPM) explains security prices by assuming rational behavior on the part of investors. Components of this behavior, like mean-variance optimization, suggest investors must be able to solve complicated equations to construct optimal portfolios. Obviously, this assumption is unrealistic. The standard response to this criticism is that a large number of investors intuitively behave in a reasonable way which, on average, is similar to mean-variance optimization. Yet observations cannot confirm that this is the case either. The Arbitrage Pricing Theory (APT) provides another line of defense for the idea that rational behavior will dominate capital asset price formation. This theory proposes that it will take few professionals deploying large investment funds to dominate price formation in security markets. The evidence of persistent anomalies in asset prices, as catalogued in Chapter 8, leaves us with a conundrum: Are these anomalies just sampling phenomena, are they driven by institutional trade friction, or are they a result of persistent, widespread behavior that is inconsistent with the assumption of economic theory? Behavioral finance is a growing specialization in pursuit of a coherent theory that explains market anomalies. We describe some of the major tenets of this emerging theory at the top of the chapter.

Regardless of origin, as long as anomalies in asset pricing persist, technical analysis may be considered a defensible tool to exploit observed, inefficient prices. As such, technical analysis is part of the study of active portfolio management. Its test is in its ability to generate abnormal profits in this pursuit. Technical analysis focuses more on past price movements of a company or an index than on the underlying fundamental determinants of future profitability. Technicians believe that past price and volume data signal future price movements. As we lay out the basics of technical analysis in the second part of this chapter, we point out the contradictions between the assumptions on which these strategies are based and the notion of well-functioning capital markets with rational and informed investors.

19.1 WHAT IS BEHAVIORAL FINANCE?

The premise of behavioral finance is that conventional financial theory ignores people, and that people make a difference. Supporters suggest one reason for this failure is that data on prices and returns are easy to come by but studying behavior is more difficult. The objective of behavioral finance is to consider *all* explanations in the search for understanding security returns.

The search for explanations of price series that stand in contradiction to conventional models is difficult. As in any science, new theories come up short on occasion and often remain controversial for some time. We point out such examples in the field of behavioral finance. Yet a field of science should never be judged a failure as long as its reason for being—explaining puzzling data—is still valid. Behavioral finance is an infant science, yet it is important for anyone interested in finance to be knowledgeable about its essential developments.

19.2 INDIVIDUAL BEHAVIOR

One of the major tenets of rational behavior is selfishness. This is to say that the individual attempts to maximize his or her own welfare, with little attention paid to others' welfare. Yet even casual observations confirm that this is not the case. The summary provided here draws heavily on Thaler (1992, 1993).

Cooperation and Altruism

We begin our analysis of cooperation with the famous "prisoner's dilemma." Two felons are caught and separated from each other. If both refuse to confess, they can be convicted on only minor charges and will each receive a one-year sentence. If both confess, each will receive a sentence of five years. If only one confesses and gives evidence against the other, he goes free and the other receives a 10-year sentence. Examination of the possible outcomes shows that the dominant strategy, that is, the best strategy, not knowing what the other felon will do, is to confess. Thus, the rational strategy leads to a worse outcome than cooperation would have.

Another example of suboptimal results due to lack of cooperation is called the tragedy of the commons. A community of fishermen lives off a fertile strip of (common) fishing grounds. A fisherman's daily catch depends on investment in equipment. The aggregate investment determines whether the fishing grounds will be depleted over time. If each fisherman maximizes the net present value (NPV) of investment, they will deplete the grounds in a hurry. No fisherman takes into account the fact that his take reduces the stock of fish available to other fishermen. As a result, the grounds are over-fished. It is the common "ownership" of fishing grounds that induces a prisoner's dilemma. The declining state of the world's fishing grounds is testimony to the force of this dynamic.

It turns out, however, that under a variety of conditions, individuals do cooperate and will defy predictions of economic theory. A manifestation of such behavior is shown in various forms of the ultimatum game. Here, individual *A* is given $100 to divide with another individual *B*. *A* makes an offer to *B*, say $10. *B* has a choice of taking the offer, in which case *A* takes home $90 and *B*, $10. If *B* refuses the offer, both players get nothing. Conventional rational behavior would induce *B* to accept any offer, since the alternative is zero. Knowing this, *A*'s rational offer is very small. But experiments clearly show that many deviate from this rational dictum. You can explain this either by *A*'s anticipation that *B* will be insulted and hence reject a small offer, or by an altruistic motive of *A* to induce a reasonably fair allocation. The degree to which people deviate from rational behavior varies greatly and is materially affected by circumstances. But the fact remains that investor decision making is often perturbed by various motives extraneous to conventional rationality.

Bidding and the Winner's Curse

How much should you bid on an auctioned item whose value, *you believe,* is equally likely to be anywhere in the range of $6 to $10? Should your bid depend on who else is bidding? Intuition calls for bidding the expected value of $8, regardless of how many participate in the auction. The logic of this solution, however, misses this important question: What is the value of the item, *conditional* on your winning the bid? Assuming all participants bid their expected values, this question is really: What is the expected value of the item given that you win the auction, i.e., that the *maximum* of N independent bids is your bid of $8? Surely, this expected value depends on the number of estimates. The larger the number of estimates, the lower is the expected value given that you win the auction with a bid of $8. Thus, if you hold your bid at your expected value while the number of bidders grows, the probability that if you win, you have overbid grows and so does your expected loss. This is the winner's curse: if you win the auction, everyone else must think the asset is worth less than you do, so you likely have overpaid.

Armed with this insight, you must bid less than your estimate of the expected value; in game-theory parlance you must "shave your bid." The optimal bid depends on the distribution of the true value, the number of bidders, and the degree of independence of their estimates. If everyone bids optimally, the winner can expect to pay a fair value and, more generally, assets traded in auctions would fetch a fair price. Can we assume this to be the case? Economic theorists would answer in the affirmative. Faced with the observation that most bidders do not have the knowledge required to derive the optimal bid, they would argue that rules of thumb derived from experience eventually lead traders to avoid the winner's curse.

Experiments appear to contradict this assertion, however. Findings suggest that the learning curve of participants in auctions is flat. Moreover, even managers in the construction industry, where bidding is the normal way of lending contracts, did not show savvy in avoiding the winner's curse. This leaves open the question of whether assets priced in auctions fetch a fair value.

The Endowment Effect, the Status Quo Bias, and Loss Aversion

What is the value of an item, say a Harley Davidson, to an individual? Economic theory takes this value to be unambiguous given the individual's tastes and resources. It turns out this isn't so. When asked to bid on the item, an individual may bid $5,000. Once in possession of an item, however, that same individual may not be willing to sell it for less than $6,000. This ambiguous preference is called the *endowment effect,* whereby an individual's preference for a good increases by virtue of ownership. This ambiguity is part of a broader phenomenon called the *status quo bias.* Individuals appear to prefer the status quo over a new position even if, a priori, the new position would have been preferred to the current position.

Researchers explain the endowment effect and the status quo bias by a type of preference called *loss aversion,* shown in Figure 19.1. In any given position, potential losses are given more weight than gains as conventional utility theory would predict. But the slope and origin of the preference function will abruptly change with a change in wealth, that is, preferences continuously vary as fortunes change, leading to decisions that are inconsistent with predictions from economic theory. One result is that opportunity costs are not equal to out-of-pocket costs. That is, forgone opportunities are valued less than perceived losses and investors will not update portfolios to account for changes in security values in the manner predicted from mean-variance considerations.

Observed inconsistent behavior also manifests itself in intertemporal choices, producing ambiguity in the time value of money. For example, it has been estimated that individuals consistently assign excessive discount rates (from 25% to as high as 300%) to savings on energy

FIGURE **19.1**

Loss aversion
preference function

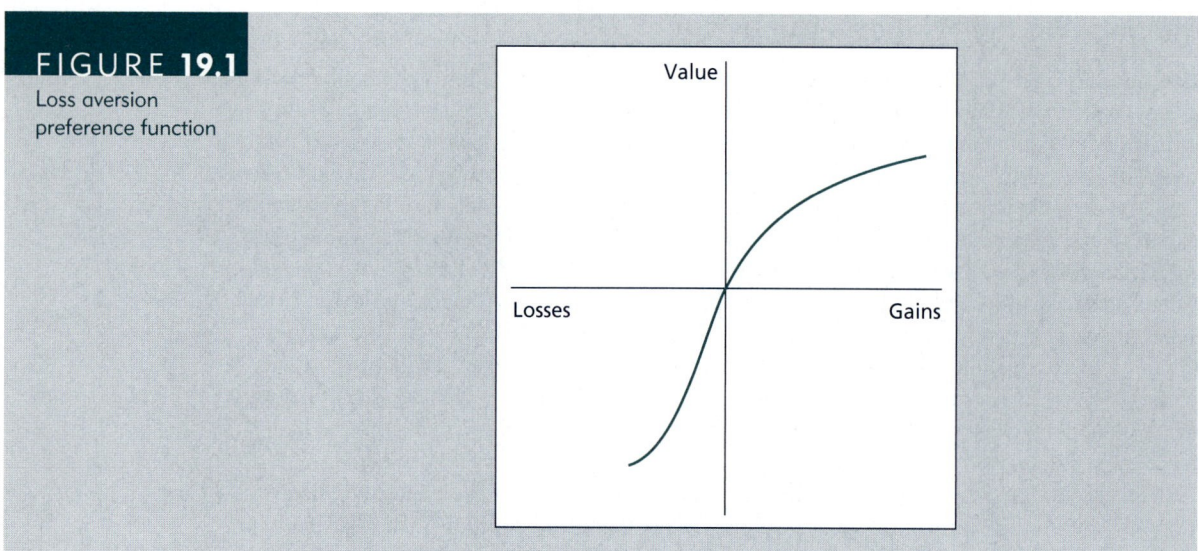

cost when they can invest in items such as insulation or energy-efficient appliances. But, researchers also find that individuals implicitly assign too low, even negative, time value when they choose the timing of a lottery prize. Studies of individual choices show significant inconsistency in assigning discount rates for consumption that changes with the timing and magnitude of future cash flows. More generally, refuting the theory of life-cycle consumption, it appears that young and old people consume too little and middle-aged people consume too much relative to predictions of conventional theory. Moreover, consumption appears to be too highly correlated with income and too little correlated with various forms of wealth such as home equity and pension accumulation.

Mental Accounts

The behaviorists' explanation of various inconsistencies in consumption and investment behavior is based on a system of "mental accounts" in which individuals mentally segregate assets into independent accounts rather than viewing them as part of a unified portfolio. One such set of accounts is equity in assets, current income, and future income. With this breakdown, the marginal propensity to consume (MPC) out of wealth, that is, the amount consumed from an increase of $1 in wealth depends on the "account" where the extra dollar appears. MPC from current income is close to 1.0, MPC from future income is close to zero, and MPC from equity is in-between. As discussed in the nearby box, this separation of mental accounts serves to impose discipline on consumption behavior despite impatience to consume—future income and equity in assets accounts are preserved while consumption binges are limited to current income.

The "disposition effect," another outcome of mental accounts and loss aversion, refers to the tendency to sell winners too early in order to increase cash accounts and to hang on to losers for too long to avoid realizing losses. The fact that the demand of "disposition investors" for a stock depends too heavily on the price history of the stock means that prices may close in on fundamentals only over time, imparting momentum to price evolution. Grinblatt and Han (2001) show that disposition effects can lead to momentum in stock prices even if fundamentals follow a random walk.

We All Make Irrational Decisions, But That May Not Be a Bad Thing

The perfect is the enemy of the good.

I write a lot about rational investing. But none of us is completely rational. We trade too much. We chase hot funds. We take a flier on dubious stocks. And, more often than not, we end up hurting our performance.

But I am unwilling to dismiss this behavior as mere foolishness. Why not? Seemingly foolish behavior can help us with our struggle.

Saving Ourselves

When saving for financial goals, we are supposed to figure out how much each goal will cost, make a reasonable estimate of what return we are likely to earn and then diligently save the appropriate sum every month.

Sound like the way you go about saving money? Me neither. Saving is a messy business, because of the constant temptation to spend.

To compensate for our lack of self-control, we often fall back on mental games. For instance, we might have a chunk of cash sitting in a money-market fund earning 1%, which we have earmarked for our toddler's college education. But right now, we need a new car.

Financially, it would make sense to "borrow" from the college fund and then pay the money back. But instead, we take out a car loan, even though the loan will likely cost us far more than we are earning on the money-market fund.

Why do we go this route? Mentally, we have earmarked the money-market fund for the kid's college education, and we don't trust ourselves to replenish the account if we dip into it.

"Lots of us know that we won't make those payments to ourselves," says John Nofsinger, author of "Investment Madness" and a finance professor at Washington State University in Pullman, Wash. "Mental accounting helps us stay disciplined."

Winning by Losing

The evidence is undeniable: Market-tracking index funds outperform actively managed stock funds. Despite this lackluster performance, actively managed funds still account for 91% of all stock-fund assets. Why do we continue to bank so heavily on a losing proposition?

It seems we like having the chance, however slim, to beat the market. In fact, it makes us more inclined to invest in stocks. We also find it comforting when professional stock pickers watch over our money. Their oversight gives us added confidence in our strategy and makes us more tenacious during rough markets.

To be sure, all this is likely to cost us, with the price paid in market-lagging performance. But when we suffer this performance penalty, maybe we are getting our money's worth.

Seeking Solace

Studies suggest you won't beat the market by following the advice of newsletter writers and stock analysts.

Yet, as we try to summon the nerve necessary to buy individual stocks, we often latch onto the recommendations of these experts.

Are we misguided? Maybe not. "Even if the stocks don't turn out to be better than other stocks, at least it gives us the courage to get started," Prof. Nofsinger notes.

Injecting Fun

While many investors struggle to find the courage to buy stocks, some folks have too much confidence. These investment junkies buy and sell stocks like crazy, thereby incurring exorbitant trading costs and taking unnecessary risks.

Still, such enthusiasm isn't all bad. After all, if we are enthused about investing, we are probably more keenly aware of how much money we need for retirement and thus we are more likely to save enough.

The trick is to make sure our enthusiasm for trading doesn't do too much damage.

"If you must trade and invest in foolish stocks, allocate $10,000 or 5% of your money, whichever is smaller, to a fun-money account," suggests Meir Statman, a finance professor at Santa Clara University in California. "And then, very much like in Vegas, try to make the money last as long as possible."

Playing the Percentages

We should all decide what portion of our portfolio we want in stocks and then stick with this percentage through thick and thin. But as many folks have discovered, this advice can be tough to follow.

Inevitably, some investors get skittish, and start dancing in and out of the stock market. This isn't a smart strategy. But it will probably lead to better results than simply leaving everything in a money-market fund.

SOURCE: Jonathan Clements, "We All Make Irrational Decisions, But That May Not Be a Bad Thing." Abridged from *The Wall Street Journal* online, March 26, 2002.

In sum, while economic theory relies on rational expectations and rational behavior, behaviorists have documented evidence and explanations of fundamentals of behavior that are inconsistent with this theory. However, the test of success of the efforts of the behaviorists is in explaining deviations of assets prices from predictions of classic theory. In the next section we provide an assessment of these efforts.

19.3 ASSET RETURNS AND BEHAVIORAL EXPLANATIONS

It is natural for behaviorists to concentrate on documented anomalies in asset prices and attempt to explain them by behavior that is excluded by economic theory. Here are the mainstream of these anomalies and offered explanations.

Calendar Effects

Calendar effects are prominent among the anomalies documented in Chapter 8 on market efficiency. An extraordinary pattern of abnormal returns occurs around the turn of the year and turn of months. Behaviorists point to the following explanations:

1. The timing of the flow of funds into the market is derived, at least in part, by the flow of funds to individual and institutional investors. These tend to be concentrated around calendar turns.
2. "Window dressing" by institutional investors refers to trades timed to load quarterly balance sheets with stocks of recently successful firms and rid them of stocks that have recently stumbled.
3. The publication of good and bad news under the control of the proprietors is mostly issued around calendar turns.

Cash Dividends

Dividend irrelevance in the absence of taxes and transaction costs is a fundamental tenet of financial theory. Tax-code discrimination against dividend income should, if anything, punish high-yield stocks. Finally, the clientele effect predicts that, if investors exhibited preference for dividends over capital gains, supply of dividends by corporations would materialize so as to eliminate risk-adjusted differentials in expected returns. Nevertheless, high dividends seem to endow stocks with a price premium.

Preference for cash dividends can be justified by mental accounts, since dividends increase current income at the expense of the "higher self control" equity account. As evidence for such bias in the population, Lease, Lewellen, and Schlarbaum (1976) compiled Table 19.1, which shows that older and retired investors, those with the most funds to invest, value dividends more highly and concentrate their (better diversified!) portfolios in high income securities.

Overraction and Mean Reversion

Perhaps the most notable influence of behavioral finance in explaining as set returns can be found in the literature of overreaction and mean reversion. Investors assign a probability distribution to future asset returns based on a relevant history of previous returns. Appropriate reaction to an unexpected event (return) is to update one's prior probability distribution by assigning a weight to the most recent event. Overreaction results when investors assign too

TABLE **19.1**		(1) Highly Educated Young Professional Men	(2) Young Unmarried Professionals & Managers	(3) Older Males, Still at Work	(4) Females, Mostly Retired	(5) Retired Males
Importance of alternative investment goals to various demographic groups as measured by average rating (4 = very important goal, 1 = low-priority goal) and percent of portfolio in income securities	Investment Goal Rating:					
	Short term capital gains	2.19	2.00	1.86	1.50	1.53
	Long-term capital gains	3.61	3.54	3.63	3.46	3.45
	Dividend income	2.04	2.30	2.46	3.36	3.39
	Percent of portfolio in income securities	27%	34%	39%	57%	56%
	Average number of securities in portfolio	9.4	10.4	11.6	12.1	12.1

Source: *R. Lease, W. Lewellen, and G. Schlarbaum,* "Market Segmentation: Evidence on the Individual Investor," *Financial Analysts Journal* (1976), 53–60.

large a weight on the most recent event. Thus, if investors overreact, a negative event would drive a stock price too low until additional developments lead investors to revalue the price in line with fundamentals.

In the presence of regular overreaction to changes in fundamentals, prices would tend to reverse themselves as investors correct for the overreaction. This tendency is called *mean reversion* and can be detected by negative serial correlation in asset returns. Numerous studies have uncovered negative correlation measured from weekly to five-year holding-period returns. Moreover, while anomalies such as calendar and dividend effects do not appear strong enough to allow abnormal profits, the degree of serial correlation in stock returns is such that profit opportunities appear plausible. Using return histories, portfolios constructed by buying losers and selling winners would have returned significant positive returns. Thus, overreaction suggested by mean reversion in stock returns appears to lend credibility to behavioral finance; using predictions from behavioral analysis apparently can lead to profitable portfolio strategies.

19.4 CONTROVERSIAL EXPLANATIONS FROM BEHAVIORAL FINANCE

Empirical explanations from new fields of science often engender controversy and resistance before they become conventional wisdom. Behavioral explanations of asset returns are no exception, and we provide two examples.

Closed-End Funds

The average closed-end fund sells at a discount of about 10% from its net asset value and discounts of individual funds are quite volatile. Such significant discounts have long been considered a puzzle. It is no wonder that closed-end fund discounts have attracted explanations from behavioral finance.

Stephen A. Ross (2002) illustrates that observed discounts of closed-end fund values can easily be explained by the funds' expenses. As a simple example, suppose a closed-end fund invests its net asset value, NAV, in the market index (and hence adds no value from superior management). The index has an expected return of r and pays out an annual dividend yield of δ. Using the constant growth dividend discount model, the value of the fund is given by $P = \delta \, \text{NAV}/(r - g)$, where δ NAV is the next dollar dividend and g is the growth rate of the fund's assets. The growth rate of the fund will be $g = r - \delta$ because the portfolio earns a rate r and pays out δ. Thus, $P = \delta \, \text{NAV}/(r - r + \delta) = \text{NAV}$ as expected from a fund that provides no added value. Now suppose the fund charges the portfolio an annual fee at a rate of ε. In this case, the growth rate of the fund's portfolio is reduced to $g = r - (\delta + \epsilon)$, and the value of the fund is reduced to: $P = \text{NAV} \, \delta/(r - r + \delta + \epsilon) = \text{NAV}\delta/(\delta + \epsilon)$. Thus, the discount of price from the net asset value of the portfolio will be $(\text{NAV} - P)/\text{NAV} = \epsilon/(\delta + \epsilon)$. With an annual dividend yield of 2% and expense ratio of .5%, the discount will be 20% $(.5/(2 + .5) = .2)$. By this calculation, observed discounts are not extraordinary.

Obviously, closed-end funds are initiated and successfully sold when investors expect the fund management to do better than the market. For example, if the portfolio's expected return is $r + u$ and its risk is similar to that of the market index, then the required rate of return is r and the growth rate of assets will be $g = r + u - (\delta + \epsilon)$. If the expected abnormal return, u, is greater than the expense ratio, ε, the fund will sell at a premium.[1] This explains why IPOs (initial public offerings) of closed-end funds are at a premium; if investors do not expect u to exceed ε, they won't purchase the fund shares. The fact that in most cases the premium turns into a discount indicates how difficult it is for management to fulfill these expectations in a nearly efficient market.

We can expect the abnormal expected return, u, to vary quite a bit as investors ingest the volatile actual returns of the fund, and hence the discount itself will be volatile. Also, it is not surprising that u (hence the discount) is correlated across closed-end funds, as well as with market returns and investor sentiment variables.

An interesting question is why the same logic does not apply to open-end funds, since they charge similar expense ratios. The reason is that investors can always redeem open-end fund shares at the NAV. Thus, the expense ratio is a period cost that accumulates to those who hold on to their shares, but the stream of future expenses is not capitalized in the price of the fund shares. Investors in closed-end funds do not have this option so the stream of future expenses must be capitalized in the NAV, resulting in a discount from the portfolio value.

When a discount of a closed-end fund becomes large, indicating that investors expect u to be negative, the question arises: Why don't investors purchase the fund and liquidate the portfolio at net asset value to instantly gain the discount? Investors can reasonably expect that management will not readily consent to the liquidation of the fund and hence such an event will not be likely (or inexpensive). Therefore, the possibility that the fund will be liquidated may not severely limit the size of potential discounts.

Excessive Volatility of Stock Market Prices

Robert J. Shiller (1981) rocked the world of economists and financial practitioners when he produced evidence suggesting that the stock market is excessively volatile. If true, this finding would be an outright refutation of the efficient market hypothesis (EMH) and must result from irrational investment behavior. Excessive volatility would be a natural outcome of overreaction and lead to mean reversion. It is consistent with predictions from behavioral finance as explained earlier.

To demonstrate that stock prices are excessively volatile Shiller used a long time series of value and annual dividends on the S&P (the market) portfolio over the period 1871–1979,

---

[1]When u is too large, that is, $g = r + u - (\delta + \epsilon) > r$, then the dividend growth model is not valid. In other words, it is not plausible that u can be sustained in the long run. In that case, we can recast the model as $P = \text{NAV}\delta/(\delta + \epsilon) + M$, where M is the present value of future abnormal returns, with the same results.

denoted by $P_1, P_2, \ldots, P_T$, and $D_1, D_2, \ldots D_T$, respectively. For each year, starting in 1871, Shiller used a reasonable estimate of a discount factor to compute the present value of all future dividends plus the present value of the terminal price and arrived at a rational price for the market portfolio for that year. This method of generating rational prices assumes that investor expectations for future dividends and terminal price were in fact equal to the actual values. Having calculated rational stock prices, P_t^*, for all periods, Shiller compared the volatility of the series of actual prices, P, to that of the rational prices, P^*. The standard deviation of actual prices was more than five times that of rational prices. Shiller argued that the excess volatility of actual over rational prices could not be explained by data problems or by model assumptions, and several subsequent studies came to similar conclusions, even when allowing for a time-varying discount rate.

Shiller's model assumes that volatility of dividends represents the volatility of stock fundamentals. It is true that expected future dividends (knowing the appropriate discount rate) are sufficient to compute a rational stock value, and it is plausible to take actual dividends to represent expected dividends. It is not obvious, however, that the *volatility* of actual dividends represents the volatility of stock fundamentals and, therefore, it is not obvious that the variance of the series of computed rational prices represents the variance we should expect from actual prices.

Consider an alternative model that derives the rational price from discounted future earnings. If it turned out that firms actually paid out a fixed proportion of earnings, then the discounted earnings model would yield the same dividends as in Shiller's model and identical rational prices. But in this case, the volatility of earnings will be the same as the volatility of dividends and we would all agree that the volatility of the computed rational prices captures the volatility of fundamentals.

Of course, in reality firms do not pay out a fixed proportion of earnings, and thus the two models will not yield the same results. In fact, since earnings are far more volatile than dividends, the volatility of rational prices will be much larger in the discounted earnings model and will indicate that actual prices do not exhibit excess volatility. While it may appear that the discounted dividends model is the right one because it captures the actual payout ratios, we should ask: Why then do firms vary payout ratios? The answer is that firms tend to smooth dividends, and herein lies the problem with Shiller's model. The use of actual dividends to compute rational prices and their volatility would be justified only if the dividend smoothing were a response to *transitory* changes in earnings. In that case, but only in that case, the volatility of dividends would capture the volatility of fundamentals and the resultant volatility of the computed rational prices would still be a valid benchmark for the volatility of actual prices. This, however, is the less likely situation. Research suggests that managers do not quickly adjust dividends to changes in fundamentals, particularly to worsening fundamentals (explaining why reaction of stock prices to dividend cuts is so violent). Hence, the dividend series is likely too smooth for tests of excessive volatility. It appears, therefore, that explanations from behavioral finance for "excess volatility" may have jumped the gun.

As of now, then, behavioral theories successfully demonstrate that individual behavior is not well approximated by standard utility analysis of economic theory. But with the possible exception of overreaction of stock prices, behavioral finance has yet to make its mark in explaining asset returns.

19.5   TECHNICAL ANALYSIS

Technical analysis is in most instances an attempt to exploit recurring and predictable patterns in stock prices to generate abnormal trading profits. In the words of one of its leading practitioners, the technical approach to investment is essentially a reflection of the idea that the stock market moves in trends which are determined by the changing attitudes of investors to a variety of economic, monetary, political, and psychological forces. The art of technical analysis, for it is an art, is to identify changes in such trends at an early stage and to maintain an investment posture until a reversal of that trend is indicated.[2]

Technicians do not necessarily deny the value of fundamental information, such as we have discussed in the three past chapters. Many technical analysts believe stock prices eventually "close in on" their fundamental values. Technicians believe, nevertheless, that shifts in market fundamentals can be discerned before the impact of those shifts is fully reflected in prices. As the market adjusts to a new equilibrium, astute traders can exploit these price trends.

Technicians also believe that market fundamentals can be perturbed by irrational or behavioral factors. More or less random fluctuations in price will accompany any underlying trend. If these fluctuations dissipate slowly, they can be taken advantage of for abnormal profits.

These presumptions, of course, clash head-on with those of the EMH and with the logic of well-functioning capital markets. According to the EMH, a shift in market fundamentals should be reflected in prices immediately. According to technicians, though, that shift will lead to a gradual price change that can be recognized as a trend. Such exploitable trends in stock market prices would be damning evidence against the EMH, as they would indicate profit opportunities that market participants had left unexploited.

A more subtle version of technical analysis holds that there are patterns in stock prices that can be explained, but that once investors identify and attempt to profit from these patterns, their trading activity affects prices, thereby altering price patterns. This means the patterns that characterize market prices will be constantly evolving, and only the best analysts who can identify new patterns earliest will be rewarded. We call this phenomenon *self-destructing* patterns and explore it in some depth in the chapter.

The notion of evolving patterns is consistent with almost but not-quite efficient markets. It allows for the possibility of temporarily unexploited profit opportunities, but it also views market participants as aggressively exploiting those opportunities once they are uncovered. The market is continually groping toward full efficiency, but it is never quite there.

This is in some ways an appealing middle position in the ongoing debate between technicians and proponents of the EMH. Ultimately, however, it is an untestable hypothesis. Technicians will always be able to identify trading rules that would have worked in the past but need not work any longer. Is this evidence of a once viable trading rule that has now been eliminated by competition? Perhaps. But it is far more likely the trading rule could have been identified only after the fact.

Until technicians can offer rigorous evidence that their trading rules provide *consistent* trading profits, we must doubt the viability of those rules. As you saw in the chapter on the efficient market hypothesis, the evidence on the performance of professionally managed funds generally does not support the efficacy of technical analysis.

19.6 CHARTING

Technical analysts are sometimes called *chartists* because they study records or charts of past stock prices and trading volume, hoping to find patterns they can exploit to make a profit. In this section, we examine several specific charting strategies.

---

[2]Martin J. Pring, *Technical Analysis Explained,* 2nd ed. (New York: McGraw-Hill Book Company, 1985), p. 2.

The Dow Theory

The **Dow theory,** named after its creator Charles Dow (who established *The Wall Street Journal*), is the grandfather of most technical analysis. While most technicians today would view the theory as dated, the approach of many more statistically sophisticated methods are essentially variants of Dow's approach. The aim of the Dow theory is to identify long-term trends in stock market prices. The two indicators used are the Dow Jones Industrial Average (DJIA) and the Dow Jones Transportation Average (DJTA). The DJIA is the key indicator of underlying trends, while the DJTA usually serves as a check to confirm or reject that signal.

The Dow theory posits three forces simultaneously affecting stock prices:

1. The *primary trend* is the long-term movement of prices, lasting from several months to several years.

2. *Secondary* or *intermediate trends* are caused by short-term deviations of prices from the underlying trend line. These deviations are eliminated via *corrections* when prices revert back to trend values.

3. *Tertiary* or *minor trends* are daily fluctuations of little importance.

Figure 19.2 represents these three components of stock price movements. In this figure, the primary trend is upward, but intermediate trends result in short-lived market declines lasting a few weeks. The intraday minor trends have no long-run impact on price.

Figure 19.3 depicts the course of the DJIA during 1988. The primary trend is upward, as evidenced by the fact that each market peak is higher than the previous peak (point F versus D versus B). Similarly, each low is higher than the previous low (E versus C versus A). This pattern of upward-moving "tops" and "bottoms" is one of the key ways to identify the underlying primary trend. Notice in Figure 19.3 that, despite the upward primary trend, intermediate trends still can lead to short periods of declining prices (points B through C, or D through E).

The Dow theory incorporates notions of support and resistance levels in stock prices. A **support level** is a value below which the market is relatively unlikely to fall. A **resistance level** is a level above which it is difficult to rise. Support and resistance levels are determined by the recent history of prices. In Figure 19.3, the price at point D would be viewed as a

---

Dow theory

A technique that attempts to discern long- and short-term trends in stock market prices.

---

support level

A price level below which it is supposedly unlikely for a stock or stock index to fall.

---

resistance level

A price level above which it is supposedly unlikely for a stock or stock index to rise.

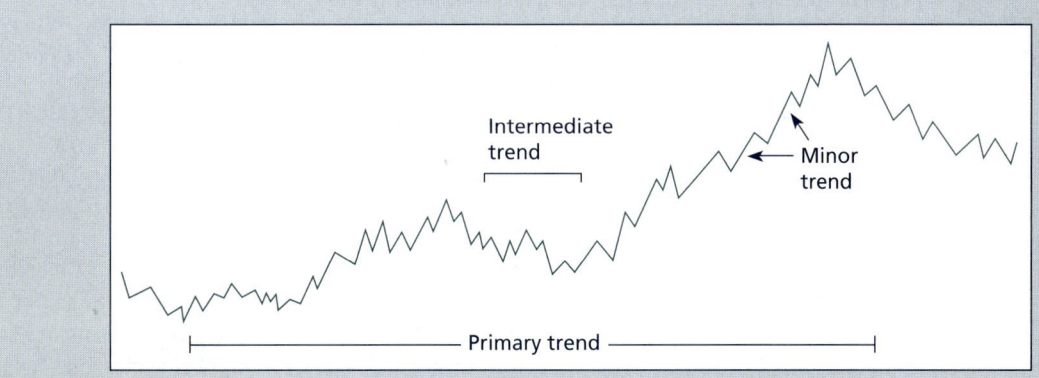

FIGURE **19.2**
Dow theory trends

Source: From Melanie F. Bowman and Thom Hartle, "Dow Theory," *Technical Analysis of Stocks and Commodities,* September 1990, p. 690.

FIGURE 19.3

Dow Jones Industrial Average in 1988

Source: From Melanie F. Bowman and Thom Hartle, "Dow Theory," *Technical Analysis of Stocks and Commodities,* September 1990, p. 690.

resistance level because the recent intermediate-trend high price was unable to rise above C. Hence, piercing the resistance point is a bullish signal.

Technicians see resistance and support levels as resulting from common psychological investor traits. Consider, for example, stock XYZ, which traded for several months at a price of $72 and then declined to $65. If the stock eventually begins to increase in price, $72 will be a natural resistance level because the many investors who originally bought at $72 will be eager to sell their shares as soon as they can break even on their investment. Therefore, whenever prices near $72, a wave of selling pressure will develop. Such activity imparts to the market a type of "memory" that allows past price history to influence current stock prospects.

Concept
CHECK

1. **Describe how technicians might explain support levels.**

In evaluating the Dow theory, don't forget the lessons of the efficient market hypothesis. The Dow theory is based on a notion of predictably recurring price patterns. Yet the EMH holds that if any pattern is exploitable, many investors would attempt to profit from such predictability, which would ultimately move stock prices and cause the trading strategy to self-destruct. While Figure 19.3 certainly appears to describe a classic upward primary trend, one always must wonder whether we can see that trend only *after* the fact. Recognizing patterns as they emerge is far more difficult.

Recent variations on the Dow theory are the Elliott wave theory and the theory of Kondratieff waves. Like the Dow theory, the idea behind Elliott waves is that stock prices can be described by a set of wave patterns. Long-term and short-term wave cycles are superimposed and result in a complicated pattern of price movements, but by interpreting the cycles, one can, according to the theory, predict broad movements. Similarly, Kondratieff waves are named after a Russian economist who asserted that the macroeconomy (and therefore the stock market) moves in broad waves lasting between 48 and 60 years. The Kondratieff waves are therefore analogous to Dow's primary trend, although they are of far longer duration. Kondratieff's assertion is hard to evaluate empirically, however, because cycles that last about 50 years provide only two full data points per century, which is hardly enough data to test the predictive power of the theory.

Other Charting Techniques

The Dow theory posits a particular, and fairly simple, type of pattern in stock market prices: long-lasting trends with short-run deviations around those trends. Not surprisingly, several more involved patterns have been identified in stock market prices. If stock prices were to actually follow any of these patterns, profit opportunities would result. The patterns are reasonably straightforward to discern, meaning future prices can be extrapolated from current prices.

A variant on pure trend analysis is the *point and figure chart* depicted in Figure 19.4. This figure has no time dimension. It simply traces significant upward or downward movements in stock prices without regard to their timing. The data for Figure 19.4 come from Table 19.2.

Suppose, as in Table 19.2, that a stock's price is currently $40. If the price rises by at least $2, you put an X in the first column at $42 in Figure 19.4. Another increase of at least $2 calls for placement of another X in the first column, this time at the $44 level. If the stock then falls by at least $2, you start a new column and put an O next to $42. Each subsequent $2 price fall results in another O in the second column. When prices reverse yet again and head upward, you begin the third column with an X denoting each consecutive $2 price increase.

The single asterisks in Table 19.2 mark an event resulting in the placement of a new X or O in the chart. The daggers denote price movements that result in the start of a new column of Xs or Os.

Sell signals are generated when the stock price *penetrates* previous lows, and buy signals occur when previous high prices are penetrated. A *congestion area* is a horizontal band of Xs and Os created by several price reversals. These regions correspond to support and resistance levels and are indicated in Figure 19.5, which is an actual chart for Atlantic Richfield.

One can devise point and figure charts using price increments other than $2, but it is customary in setting up a chart to require reasonably substantial price changes before marking pluses or minuses.

2. Draw a point and figure chart using the history in Table 19.2 with price increments of $3.

Another graphical technique used to summarize price data and aid in the identification of trends is the so-called *candlestick chart,* illustrated in Figure 19.6. The box with the vertical line drawn through it allows the chartist to ascertain the open and close price for the day, as

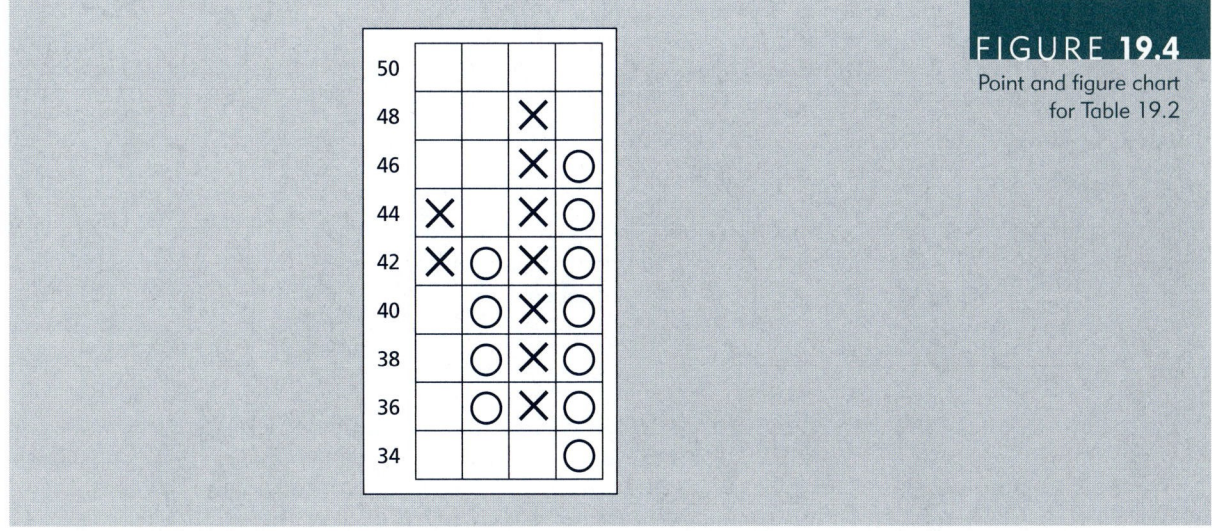

FIGURE 19.4
Point and figure chart for Table 19.2

TABLE **19.2**	Date	Price	Date	Price
Stock price history	January 2	$40	February 1	$40*
	January 3	40.50	February 2	41
	January 4	41	February 5	40.50
	January 5	42*	February 6	42*
	January 8	41.50	February 7	45*
	January 9	42.50	February 8	44.50
	January 10	43	February 9	46*
	January 11	43.75	February 12	47
	January 12	44*	February 13	48*
	January 15	45	February 14	47.50
	January 16	44	February 15	46†
	January 17	41.50†	February 16	45
	January 18	41	February 19	44*
	January 19	40*	February 20	42*
	January 22	39	February 21	41
	January 23	39.50	February 22	40*
	January 24	39.75	February 23	41
	January 25	38*	February 26	40.50
	January 26	35*	February 27	38*
	January 29	36†	February 28	39
	January 30	37	March 1	36*
	January 31	39*	March 2	34*

*Indicates an event that has resulted in a stock price increase or decrease of at least $2.

†Denotes a price movement that has resulted in either an upward or downward reversal in the stock price.

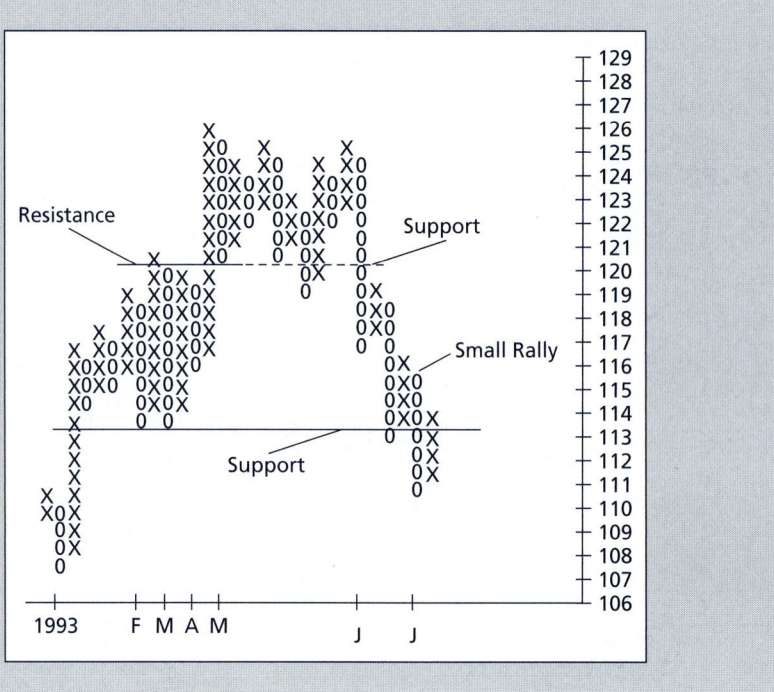

FIGURE **19.5**

Point and figure chart for Atlantic Richfield

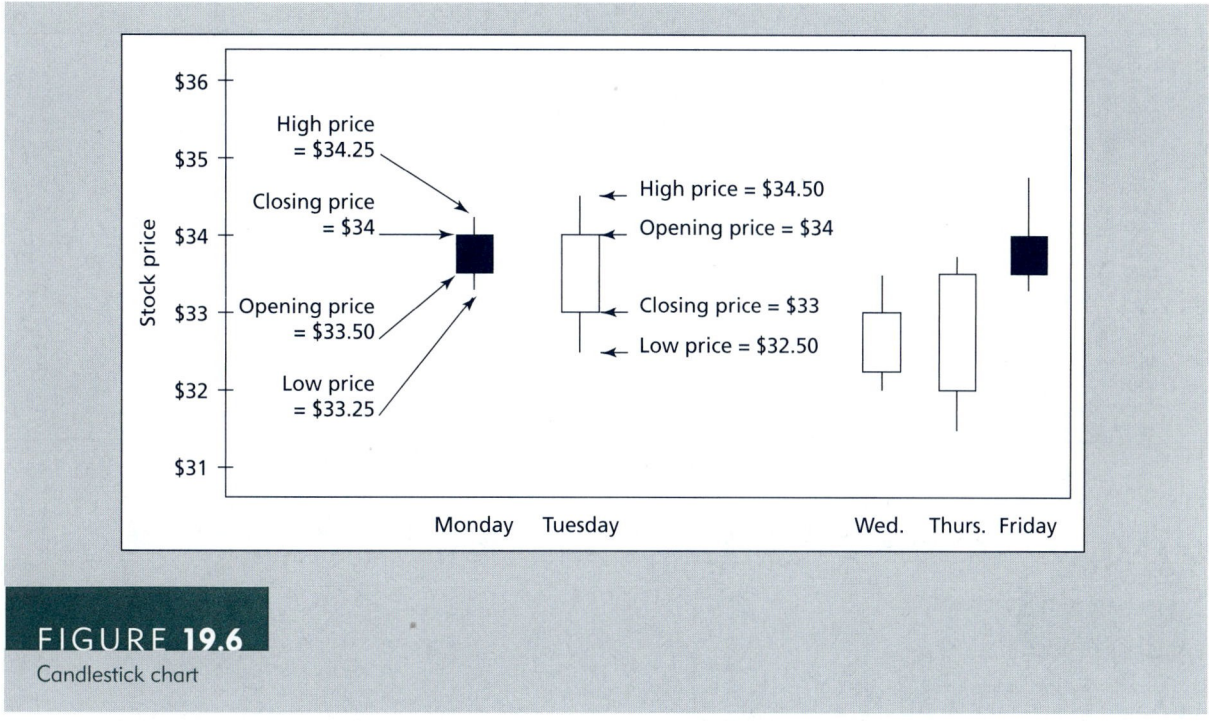

FIGURE 19.6
Candlestick chart

well as the high and low price. The top and bottom of each vertical line represent the high and low price, respectively. If the price increases during the day (e.g., Monday in Figure 19.6), the box is shaded, so the analyst knows that the closing price is at the top of the box and the opening price is at the bottom. If the box is left unshaded (e.g., Tuesday), the stock price is understood to have fallen, and the closing price is at the bottom of the box. The vertical lines extend from the daily high to the daily low price. The chart thus conveys a considerable amount of information about recent stock price history. Obviously, candlestick charts can be drawn using either shorter or longer time periods than one-day returns, for example, using intraday or weekly prices.

A Warning

The search for patterns in stock market prices is nearly irresistible, and the ability of the human eye to discern apparent patterns is remarkable. Unfortunately, it is possible to perceive patterns that really don't exist. Consider Figure 19.7, which presents simulated and actual values of the Dow Jones Industrial Average during 1956 taken from a famous study by Harry Roberts (1959). In Figure 19.7B, it appears as though the market presents a classic head-and-shoulders pattern where the middle hump (the head) is flanked by two shoulders. When the price index "pierces the right shoulder"—a technical trigger point—it is believed to be heading lower, and it is time to sell your stocks. Figure 19.7A also looks like a "typical" stock market pattern.

Can you tell which of the two graphs is constructed from the real value of the Dow and which from the simulated data? Figure 19.7A is based on the real data. The graph in B was generated using "returns" created by a random number generator. These returns *by construction* were patternless, but the simulated price path that is plotted appears to follow a pattern much like that of A.

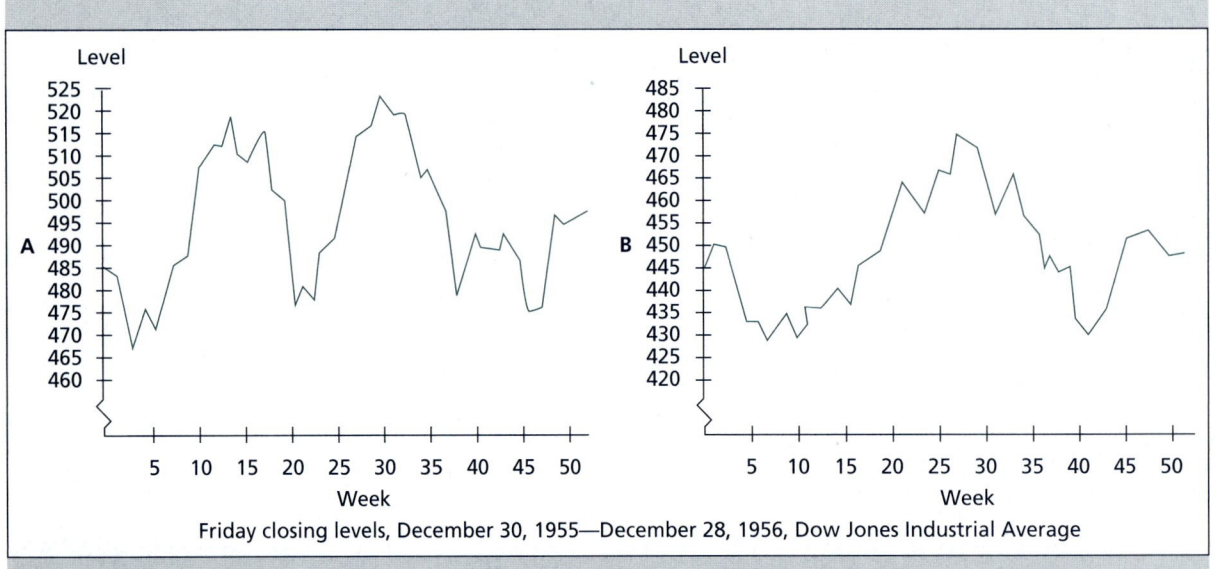

FIGURE 19.7

Actual and simulated levels for stock market prices of 52 weeks

Note: Friday closing levels, December 30, 1955–December 28, 1956, Dow Jones Industrial Average.
Source: From Harry Roberts, "Stock Market Patterns and Financial Analysis: Methodological Suggestions," *Journal of Finance*, March 1959, pp. 5–6.

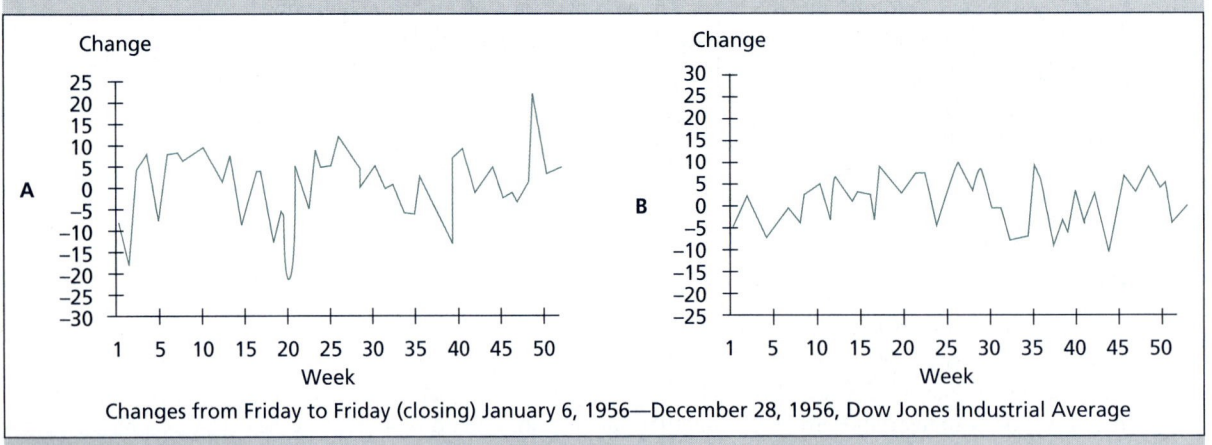

FIGURE 19.8

Actual and simulated changes in weekly stock prices for 52 weeks

Note: Changes from Friday to Friday (closing) January 6, 1956–December 28, 1956, Dow Jones Industrial Average.
Source: From Harry Roberts, "Stock Market Patterns and Financial Analysis: Methodological Suggestions," *Journal of Finance*, March 1959, pp. 5–6.

Figure 19.8 shows the weekly price *changes* behind the two panels in Figure 19.7. Here the randomness in both series—the stock price as well as the simulated sequence—is obvious.

A problem related to the tendency to perceive patterns where they don't exist is data mining. After the fact, you can always find patterns and trading rules that would have generated

TABLE 19.3
The Superbowl as a predictor of stock market returns

Year	Winning Conference	S&P 500 Return	Year	Winning Conference	S&P 500 Return	Year	Winning Conference	S&P 500 Return
1967	N	+	1979	A	+	1991	N	+
1968	N	+	1980	A	+	1992	N	+
1969	A	−	1981	A	−	1993	N	+
1970	A	+	1982	N	+	1994	N	+
1971	A	+	1983	N	+	1995	N	+
1972	N	+	1984	A	+	1996	N	+
1973	A	−	1985	N	+	1997	N	+
1974	A	−	1986	N	+	1998	A	+
1975	A	+	1987	N	−	1999	A	+
1976	A	+	1988	N	+	2000	N	−
1977	A	−	1989	N	+	2001	A	−
1978	N	+	1990	N	+	2002	A	?

Note: N = National Football League or Conference

A = American Football League or Conference

"+" means the S&P 500 return (including dividends) in the 12 months (February through February) following the Superbowl was positive.

"−" means the S&P 500 return was negative.

enormous profits. If you test enough rules, some will have worked in the past. Unfortunately, picking a theory that would have worked after the fact carries no guarantee of future success.

In this regard, consider an investment rule that worked with uncanny precision between 1967 and 1997. Suppose that in years when an original National Football League team won the Superbowl (played in mid-to-late January) you had bet on the S&P 500 rising in the following 12 months, and in years when a team from the American Football Conference won, you bet on a market decline. You would have won this bet in 23 out of 31 of those years.

Given the impressive success rate of this strategy, would you have used it to invest your money? We hope not. If you had, Table 19.3 shows that you would have lost this bet in three of the four years ending in 2001.

In evaluating trading rules, you should always ask whether the rule would have seemed reasonable *before* you looked at the data. If not, you might be buying into the one arbitrary rule among many that happened to have worked in the recent past. The hard but crucial question is whether there is reason to believe that what worked in the past should continue to work in the future.

19.7 TECHNICAL INDICATORS

Technical analysts use technical indicators besides charts to assess prospects for market declines or advances. There are three types of technical indicators: sentiment indicators, flow of funds indicators, and market structure indicators. *Sentiment indicators* are intended to measure the expectations of various groups of investors, for example, mutual fund investors, corporate insiders, or NYSE specialists. *Flow of funds indicators* are intended to measure the potential for various investor groups to buy or sell stocks in order to predict the price pressure from those actions. Finally, *market structure indicators* monitor price trends and cycles. The charting techniques described in the last section are examples of market structure indicators. We will examine a few more market structure indicators in this section.

Sentiment Indicators

Trin statistic   Market volume is sometimes used to measure the strength of a market rise or fall. Increased investor participation in a market advance or retreat is viewed as a measure of the significance of the movement. Technicians consider market advances to be a more favorable omen of continued price increases when they are associated with increased trading volume. Similarly, market reversals are considered more bearish when associated with higher volume. The *trin statistic* is the ratio of the number of advancing to declining issues divided by the ratio of volume in advancing versus declining issues.

$$\text{Trin} = \frac{\text{Number advancing/Number declining}}{\text{Volume advancing/Volume declining}}$$

This expression can be rearranged as

$$\text{Trin} = \frac{\text{Volume declining/Number declining}}{\text{Volume advancing/Number advancing}}$$

Therefore, trin is the ratio of average volume in declining issues to average volume in advancing issues. Ratios above 1.0 are considered bearish because the falling stocks would then have higher average volume than the advancing stocks, indicating net selling pressure. *The Wall Street Journal* reports trin every day in the market diary section, as in Figure 19.9.

Note, however, that for every buyer, there must be a seller of stock. Rising volume in a rising market should not necessarily indicate a larger imbalance of buyers versus sellers. For example, a trin statistic above 1.0, which is considered bearish, could equally well be interpreted as indicating that there is more *buying* activity in declining issues.

Odd-lot trading   Just as short-sellers tend to be larger institutional traders, odd-lot traders are almost always small individual traders. (An odd lot is a transaction of fewer than 100 shares; 100 shares is one round lot.) The **odd-lot theory** holds that these small investors tend to miss key market turning points, typically buying stock after a bull market has already run its course and selling too late into a bear market. Therefore, the theory suggests that when odd-lot traders are widely buying, you should sell, and vice versa.

The Wall Street Journal publishes odd-lot trading data every day. You can construct an index of odd-lot trading by computing the ratio of odd-lot purchases to sales. A ratio substantially above 1.0 is bearish because it implies small traders are net buyers.

odd-lot theory

The theory that net buying of small investors is a bearish signal for a stock.

FIGURE 19.9

Market diary

DIARIES

NYSE	FRI	THU	WK 1/25
Issues traded	3,314	3,348	3,467
Advances	1,606	1,736	1,817
Declines	1,488	1,394	1,522
Unchanged	220	218	128
New highs	112	114	255
New lows	25	15	87
zAdv vol (000)	712,318	903,130	3,093,261
zDecl vol (000)	582,866	578,597	2,399,354
zTotal vol (000)	1,338,009	1,501,576	5,592.453
Closing tick[1]	+626	+137	....
Closing Arms[2] (trin)	.88	.80	....
zBlock trades	25,661	29,593	y107,442

Confidence index *Barron's* computes a confidence index using data from the bond market. The presumption is that actions of bond traders reveal trends that will emerge soon in the stock market.

The **confidence index** is the ratio of the average yield on 10 top-rated corporate bonds divided by the average yield on 10 intermediate-grade corporate bonds. The ratio will always be below 100% because higher rated bonds will offer lower promised yields to maturity. When bond traders are optimistic about the economy, however, they might require smaller default premiums on lower rated debt. Hence, the yield spread will narrow, and the confidence index will approach 100%. Therefore, higher values of the confidence index are bullish signals.

confidence index

Ratio of the yield of top-rated corporate bonds to the yield on intermediate-grade bonds.

3. Yields on lower rated debt will rise after fears of recession have spread through the economy. This will reduce the confidence index. Should the stock market now be expected to fall or will it already have fallen?

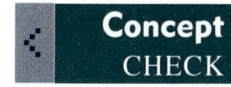

Concept
CHECK

Put/call ratio Call options give investors the right to buy a stock at a fixed "exercise" price and therefore are a way of betting on stock price increases. Put options give the right to sell a stock at a fixed price and therefore are a way of betting on stock price decreases.[3] The ratio of outstanding put options to outstanding call options is called the **put/call ratio.** Typically, the put/call ratio hovers around 65%. Because put options do well in falling markets while call options do well in rising markets, deviations of the ratio from historical norms are considered to be a signal of market sentiment and therefore predictive of market movements.

put/call ratio

Ratio of put options to call options outstanding on a stock.

Interestingly, however, a change in the ratio can be given a bullish or a bearish interpretation. Many technicians see an increase in the ratio as bearish, as it indicates growing interest in put options as a hedge against market declines. Thus, a rising ratio is taken as a sign of broad investor pessimism and a coming market decline. Contrarian investors, however, believe that a good time to buy is when the rest of the market is bearish because stock prices are then unduly depressed. Therefore, they would take an increase in the put/call ratio as a signal of a buy opportunity.

Mutual fund cash positions Technical traders view mutual fund investors as being poor market timers. Specifically, the belief is that mutual fund investors become more bullish after a market advance has already run its course. In this view, investor optimism peaks as the market is nearing its peak. Given the belief that the consensus opinion is incorrect at market turning points, a technical trader will use an indicator of market sentiment to form a contrary trading strategy. The percentage of cash held in mutual fund portfolios is one common measure of sentiment. This percentage is viewed as moving in the opposite direction of the stock market, since funds will tend to hold high cash positions when they are concerned about a falling market and the threat that investors will redeem shares.

Flow of Funds

Short interest **Short interest** is the total number of shares of stock currently sold short in the market. Some technicians interpret high levels of short interest as bullish, some as bearish. The bullish perspective is that, because all short sales must be covered (i.e., short-sellers eventually must purchase shares to return the ones they have borrowed), short interest represents latent future demand for the stocks. As short sales are covered, the demand created by the share purchase will force prices up.

short interest

The total number of shares currently sold short in the market.

[3]Puts and calls were defined in Chapter 2, Section 2.5.

The bearish interpretation of short interest is based on the fact that short-sellers tend to be larger, more sophisticated investors. Accordingly, increased short interest reflects bearish sentiment by those investors "in the know," which would be a negative signal of the market's prospects.

Credit balances in brokerage accounts   Investors with brokerage accounts will often leave credit balances in those accounts when they plan to invest in the near future. Thus, credit balances may be viewed as measuring the potential for new stock purchases. As a result, a buildup of balances is viewed as a bullish indicator for the market.

Market Structure

Moving averages   The moving average of a stock index is the average level of the index over a given interval of time. For example, a 52-week moving average tracks the average index value over the most recent 52 weeks. Each week, the moving average is recomputed by dropping the oldest observation and adding the latest. Figure 19.10 is a moving average chart for Microsoft. Notice that the moving average plots (the colored curves) are "smoothed" versions of the original data series (dark blue curve) and that the longer moving average (the 200-day average) smooths the data more than the shorter (50-day) average.

After a period in which prices have generally been falling, the moving average will be above the current price (because the moving average "averages in" the older and higher prices). When prices have been rising, the moving average will be below the current price.

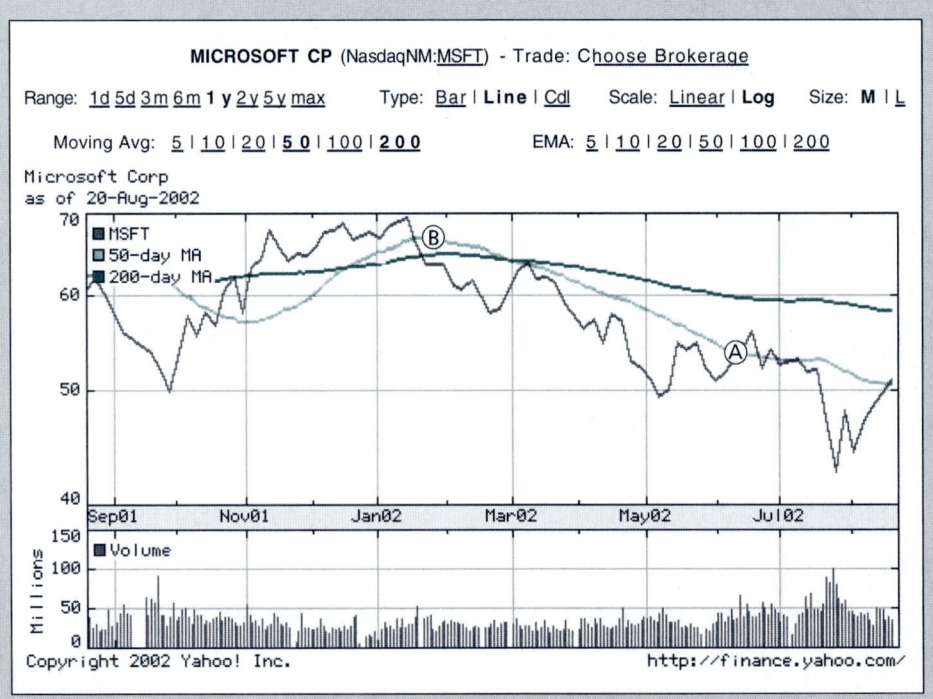

FIGURE 19.10

Moving average for Microsoft

Source: Yahoo!, February 5, 2002.

When the market price breaks through the moving average line from below, as at point A in Figure 19.10, it is taken as a bullish signal because it signifies a shift from a falling trend (with prices below the moving average) to a rising trend (with prices above the moving average). Conversely, when prices fall below the moving average as at point B, it's considered time to sell. (In this instance, however, the buy sell signal turned out to be faulty.)

There is some variation in the length of the moving average considered most predictive of market movements. Two popular measures are 200-day and 53-week moving averages.

A study by Brock, Lakonishok, and LeBaron (1992) actually supports the efficacy of moving average strategies. They find that stock returns following buy signals from the moving average rule are higher and less volatile than those after sell signals. However, a more recent paper by Ready (1997), which uses intraday price data, finds that the moving average rule would not be able to provide profits in practice because of trading costs and the fact that stock prices would already have moved adversely by the time the trader could act on the signal.

Consider the following price data. Each observation represents the closing level of the Dow Jones Industrial Average (DJIA) on the last trading day of the week. The five-week moving average for each week is the average of the DJIA over the previous five weeks. For example, the first entry, for week 5, is the average of the index value between weeks 1 and 5: 9,290, 9,380, 9,399, 9,379, and 9,450. The next entry is the average of the index values between weeks 2 and 6, and so on.

EXAMPLE 19.1
Moving Averages

Week	DJIA	5-Week Moving Average	Week	DJIA	5-Week Moving Average
1	9,290		11	9,590	9,555
2	9,380		12	9,652	9,586
3	9,399		13	9,625	9,598
4	9,379		14	9,657	9,624
5	9,450	9,380	15	9,699	9,645
6	9,513	9,424	16	9,647	9,656
7	9,500	9,448	17	9,610	9,648
8	9,565	9,481	18	9,595	9,642
9	9,524	9,510	19	9,499	9,610
10	9,597	9,540	20	9,466	9,563

Figure 19.11 plots the level of the index and the five-week moving average. Notice that while the index itself moves up and down rather abruptly, the moving average is a relatively smooth series, since the impact of each week's price movement is averaged with that of the previous weeks. Week 16 is a bearish point according to the moving average rule. The price series crosses from above the moving average to below it, signifying the beginning of a downward trend in stock prices.

Breadth The **breadth** of the market is a measure of the extent to which movement in a market index is reflected widely in the price movements of all the stocks in the market. The most common measure of breadth is the spread between the number of stocks that advance and decline in price. If advances outnumber declines by a wide margin, then the market is viewed as being stronger because the rally is widespread. These breadth numbers also are reported daily in *The Wall Street Journal* (see Figure 19.9).

breadth

The extent to which movements in broad market indexes are reflected widely in movements of individual stock prices.

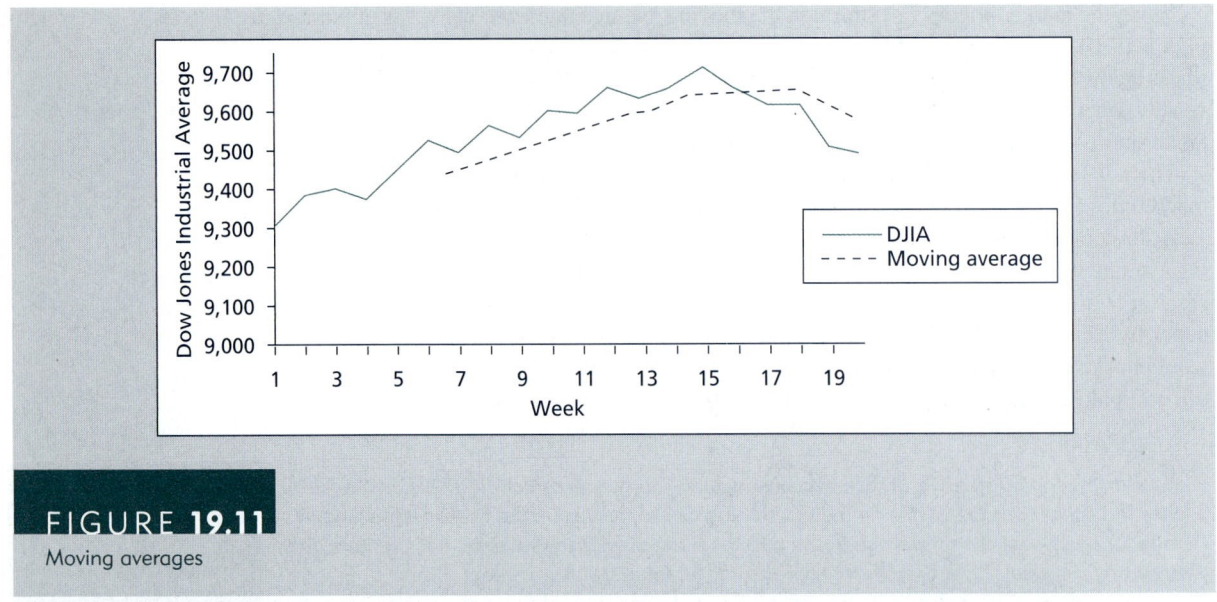

FIGURE 19.11
Moving averages

TABLE **19.4** Breadth	Day	Advances	Declines	Net Advances	Cumulative Breadth
	1	802	748	54	54
	2	917	640	277	331
	3	703	772	−69	262
	4	512	1122	−610	−348
	5	633	1004	−371	−719

Note: The sum of advances plus declines varies across days because some stock prices are unchanged.

Some analysts cumulate breadth data each day as in Table 19.4. The cumulative breadth for each day is obtained by adding that day's net advances (or declines) to the previous day's total. The direction of the cumulated series is then used to discern broad market trends. Analysts might use a moving average of cumulative breadth to gauge broad trends.

relative strength

Recent performance of a given stock or industry compared to that of a broader market index.

Relative strength   **Relative strength** measures the extent to which a security has outperformed or underperformed either the market as a whole or its particular industry. Relative strength is computed by calculating the ratio of the price of the security to a price index for the industry. For example, the relative strength of Ford versus the auto industry would be measured by movements in the ratio of the price of Ford divided by the level of an auto industry index. A rising ratio implies Ford has been outperforming the rest of the industry. If relative strength can be assumed to persist over time, then this would be a signal to buy Ford.

Similarly, the relative strength of an industry relative to the whole market can be computed by tracking the ratio of the industry price index to the market price index.

Some evidence in support of the relative strength strategy is provided in a study by Jegadeesh and Titman (1993). They ranked firms according to stock market performance in a six-month base period and then examined returns in various follow-up periods ranging from 1 to 36 months. They found that the best performers in the base period continued to outperform other stocks for several months. This pattern is consistent with the notion of persistent relative strength. Ultimately, however, the pattern reverses, with the best base-period performers giving up their initial superior returns. Figure 19.12 illustrates this pattern. The graph shows the

Cumulative difference in returns of previously best-performing and worst-performing stocks in subsequent months

Source: Jegadeesh and Titman (1993).

cumulative difference in return between the 10% of the sample of stocks with the best base-period returns and the 10% with the worst base-period returns. Initially, the curve trends upward, indicating that the best performers continue to outperform the initial laggards. After about a year, however, the curve turns down, suggesting that abnormal returns on stocks with momentum are ultimately reversed.

The middle two columns of the following table present data on the levels of an auto industry index and a broad market index. Does the auto industry exhibit relative strength? That can be determined by examining the last column, which presents the ratio of the two indexes. Despite the fact that the auto industry as a whole has exhibited positive returns, reflected in the rising level of the industry index, the industry has *not* shown relative strength. The falling ratio of the auto industry index to the market index shows that the auto industry has underperformed the broad market.

EXAMPLE 19.2
Relative Strength

Week	Auto Industry	Market Index	Ratio
1	165.6	447.0	0.370
2	166.7	450.1	0.370
3	168.0	455.0	0.369
4	166.9	459.9	0.363
5	170.2	459.1	0.371
6	169.2	463.0	0.365
7	171.0	469.0	0.365
8	174.1	473.2	0.368
9	173.9	478.8	0.363
10	174.2	481.0	0.362

19.8 | THE VALUE LINE SYSTEM

Value Line is the largest investment advisory service in the world. Besides publishing the *Value Line Investment Survey,* which provides information on investment fundamentals for approximately 1,700 publicly traded companies, Value Line also ranks each of these stocks according to their anticipated price appreciation over the next 12 months. Stocks ranked in group 1 are expected to perform the best, while those in group 5 are expected to perform the worst. Value Line calls this "ranking for timeliness."

Figure 19.13 shows the performance of the Value Line ranking system over the 25 years from 1965 to March 1990. Over the total period, the different groups performed just as the rankings predicted, and the differences were quite large. The total 25-year price appreciation for the group 1 stocks was 3,083% (or 14.8% per year) compared to 15% (or 0.5% per year) for group 5.

How does the Value Line ranking system work? As Bernhard (1979) explains it, the ranking procedure has three components: (1) relative earnings momentum, (2) earnings surprise, and (3) a value index. Most (though not all) of the Value Line criteria are technically oriented, relying on either price momentum or relative strength. Points assigned for each factor determine the stock's overall ranking.

The relative earnings momentum factor is calculated as each company's year-to-year change in quarterly earnings divided by the average change for all stocks.

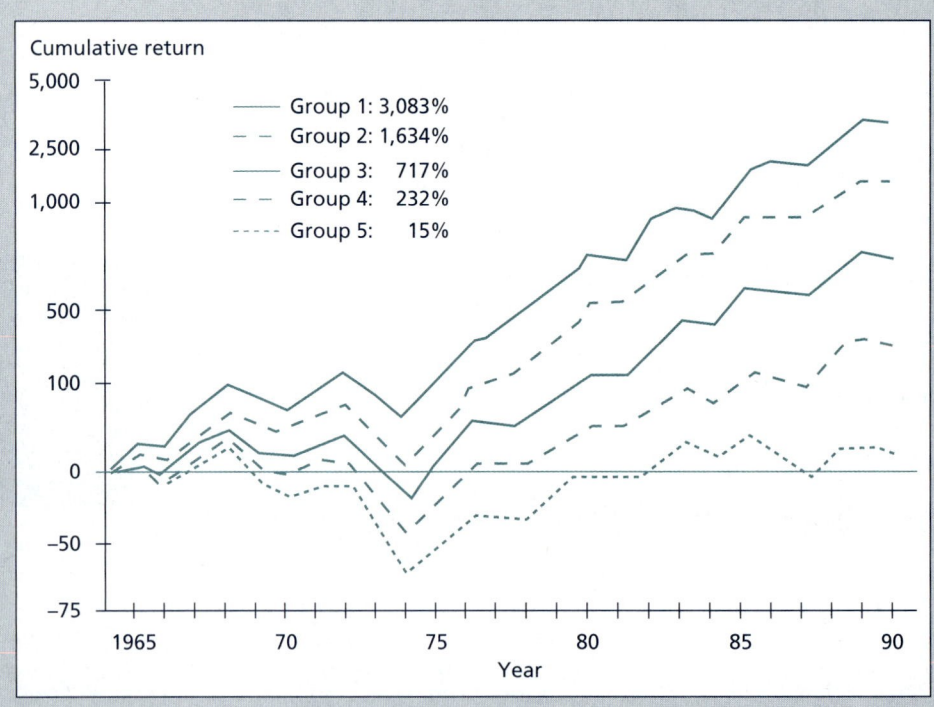

FIGURE 19.13

Record of Value Line ranking for timeliness (without allowing for changes in rank, 1965–1990)

The earnings surprise factor has to do with the difference between actual reported quarterly earnings and Value Line's estimate. The points assigned to each stock increase with the percentage difference between reported and estimated earnings.

The value index is calculated from the following regression equation

$$V = a + b_1x_1 + b_2x_2 + b_3x_3$$

where

x_1 = A score from 1 to 10 depending on the relative earnings momentum ranking, compared with the company's rank for the last 10 years;

x_2 = A score from 1 to 10 based on the stock's relative price, with ratios calculated in a similar way to the earnings ratio;

x_3 = The ratio of the stock's latest 10-week average relative price (stock price divided by the average price for all stocks) to its 52-week average relative price; and a, b_1, b_2, and b_3 are the coefficients from the regression estimated on 12 years of data.

Finally, the points for each of the three factors are added, and the stocks are classified into five groups according to the total score.

Investing according to this system does seem to produce superior results on paper, as Figure 19.13 shows. Yet, as the nearby box points out, in practice, things are not so simple—Value Line's own mutual funds have not kept up even with the broad market averages. The box illustrates that even apparently successful trading rules can be difficult to implement in the market.

19.9   CAN TECHNICAL ANALYSIS WORK IN EFFICIENT MARKETS?

Self-Destructing Patterns

It should be abundantly clear from our presentations that most of technical analysis is based on ideas totally at odds with the foundations of the efficient market hypothesis. The EMH follows from the idea that rational profit-seeking investors will act on new information so quickly that prices will nearly always reflect all publicly available information. Technical analysis, on the other hand, posits the existence of long-lived trends that play out slowly and predictably. Such patterns, if they exist, would violate the EMH notion of essentially unpredictable stock price changes.

An interesting question is whether a technical rule that seems to work will continue to work in the future once it becomes widely recognized. A clever analyst may occasionally uncover a profitable trading rule, but the real test of efficient markets is whether the rule itself becomes reflected in stock prices once its value is discovered.

Suppose, for example, the Dow theory predicts an upward primary trend. If the theory is widely accepted, it follows that many investors will attempt to buy stocks immediately in anticipation of the price increase; the effect would be to bid up prices sharply and immediately rather than at the gradual, long-lived pace initially expected. The Dow theory's predicted trend would be replaced by a sharp jump in prices. It is in this sense that price patterns ought to be *self-destructing*. When a useful technical rule (or price pattern) is discovered, it ought to be invalidated once the mass of traders attempts to exploit it, thereby forcing prices to their "correct" levels.

Thus, the market dynamic is one of a continual search for profitable trading rules, followed by destruction by overuse of those rules found to be successful, followed by yet another search for yet-undiscovered rules.

ON PAPER, VALUE LINE'S PERFORMANCE IN PICKING STOCKS IS NOTHING SHORT OF DAZZLING . . . FOR AN INVESTOR TO CAPITALIZE ON THAT PERFORMANCE IS A DIFFERENT MATTER

Value Line, Inc., publishes the *Value Line Investment Survey*, that handy review of 1,652 companies. Each week the survey rates stocks from I (best buys) to V (worst). Can you beat the market following these rankings? Value Line tracks the performance of group I from April 1965, when a new ranking formula went into effect. If you bought group I then and updated your list every week, you would have a gain of 15,391% by June 30. That means $10,000 would have grown to about $1.5 million, dividends excluded. The market is up only 245% since 1965, dividends excluded.

Quite an impressive record. There is only one flaw: It ignores transaction costs. Do transaction costs much matter against a performance like that? What does the investor lose in transaction costs? A percentage point a year? Two percent?

None other than Value Line provides an answer to this question, and the answer is almost as startling as the paper performance. Since late 1983, Value Line has run a mutual fund that attempts to track group I precisely. Its return has averaged a dismal 11 percentage points a year worse than the hypothetical results in group I. The fund hasn't even kept up with the market (*see chart*).

What went wrong? "Inefficiencies and costs of implementation," says Mark Tavel, manager of the fund, Value Line Centurion.

SUMMARY

- Behavioral finance seeks to identify behavior patterns that are inconsistent with standard economic theory and can explain observed anomalies in asset prices.
- So far, a rich set of "irrational" behavior has been documented. But with the possible exception of overreaction, none has been shown to clearly explain asset returns.
- Technical analysis is the search for recurring patterns in stock market prices. It is based essentially on the notion that market prices adjust slowly to new information and, thus, is at odds with the efficient market hypothesis.
- The Dow theory is the earliest chart-based version of technical analysis. The theory posits the existence of primary, intermediate, and minor trends that can be identified on a chart and acted on by an analyst before the trends fully dissipate. Other trend-based theories are based on relative strength, the point and figures chart, and the candlestick diagram.
- Technicians believe high volume and market breadth accompanying market trends add weight to the significance of a trend.
- Odd-lot traders are viewed as uninformed, which suggests informed traders should pursue trading strategies in opposition to their activity. In contrast, short-sellers are viewed as informed traders, lending credence to their activity.
- Value Line's ranking system uses technically based data and has shown great ability to discriminate between stocks with good and poor prospects, but the Value Line mutual fund

year. That's quite a bit of turnover—although by no means the highest in the business. The turnover is high because in a typical week, 4 of the 100 group I stocks drop down in rank and have to be replaced with new group I stocks. It's not impossible for traders like Centurion to beat the market, but they start out with a handicap.

What are these inefficiencies and costs? And what do they tell investors about the perils of in-and-out trading?

Fund overhead is not a big item. At the $244 million Centurion, which is available only through variable life and annuity policies sold by Guardian Life, the annual expense ratio averages 0.6%. Nor are brokerage commissions large. Funneled at about 5 cents a share mostly to a captive Value Line broker, commissions eat up 0.4% of Centurion's assets per year.

So far we have 1%. Where's the other 10% of the shortfall? Bid–ask spreads, for one. A stock quoted at 39 to sellers might cost a buyer 39½—or even 41 or 42 if the buyer wants a lot of it. With about 95 of the 100 group I stocks at any given time in the Centurion portfolio, Tavel needs to amass an average $2.5 million position in each. Some of these companies have $150 million or less in outstanding shares. The very smallest Tavel doesn't even try to buy.

Timing explains some of the gulf between hypothetical and actual results. The hypothetical performance assumes a purchase at the Wednesday close before publication of the new rankings. Most subscribers get their surveys on Friday morning, however, and buy at the Friday opening—if they are lucky. An internal Value Line rule forbids the funds to act on rank changes before Friday morning.

A day makes all the difference. A 1985 study by Scott Stickel showed that almost all of the excess return on a group I stock is concentrated on three days, almost evenly divided: the Friday when subscribers read about the stock's being promoted into group I, the Thursday before, and the Monday following. Wait until Tuesday to buy and you might as well not subscribe.

Why are prices moving up on Thursday, the day before publication? Eisenstadt suspects the Postal Service of acting with uncharacteristic efficiency in some parts of the country, giving a few subscribers an early start. Another reason for an uptick: Enough is known about the Value Line formula for smart investors to anticipate a rank change by a few days. The trick is to watch group II (near-top) stocks closely. If a quarterly earnings report comes in far better than the forecast published in *Value Line*, grab the stock. "What happens if you're wrong? You're stuck with a group II stock with terrific earnings," says Eisenstadt.

SOURCE: Reprinted by permission from *Forbes* magazine, October 19, 1987. © Forbes, Inc. 1987.

that uses this system most closely has been only a mediocre performer, suggesting that implementation of the Value Line timing system is difficult.

• New theories of information dissemination in the market suggest there may be a role for the examination of past prices in formulating investment strategies. They do not, however, support the specific charting patterns currently relied on by technical analysts.

KEY TERMS

breadth, 671	odd-lot theory, 668	resistance level, 661
confidence index, 669	put/call ratio, 669	short interest, 669
Dow theory, 661	relative strength, 672	support level, 661

PROBLEM SETS

1. Consider the graph of stock prices over a two-year period in Figure 19.14. Identify likely support and resistance levels.

2. Use the data from *The Wall Street Journal* in Figure 19.9 to construct the trin ratio for the market. Is the trin ratio bullish or bearish?

3. Calculate market breadth using the data in Figure 19.9. Is the signal bullish or bearish?

4. Collect data on the DJIA for a period covering a few months. Try to identify primary trends. Can you tell whether the market currently is in an upward or downward trend?

5. Baa-rated bonds currently yield 9%, while Aa-rated bonds yield 8%. Suppose that due to an increase in the expected inflation rate, the yields on both bonds increases by 1%. What would happen to the confidence index? Would this be interpreted as bullish or bearish by a technical analyst? Does this make sense to you?

www.mhhe.com/bkm

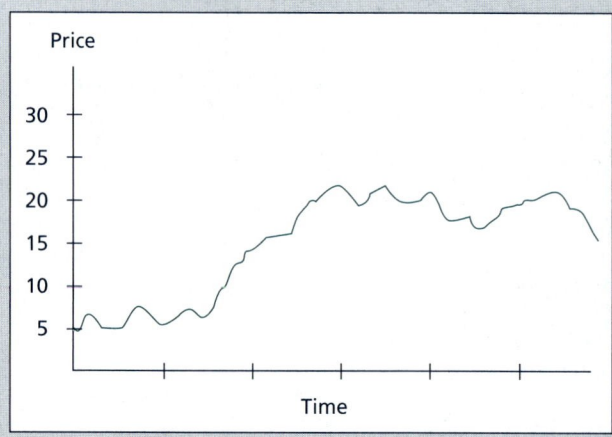

FIGURE **19.14**

Simulated stock price over time

6. Using Figure 19.15 from *The Wall Street Journal,* determine whether market price movements and volume patterns were bullish or bearish around the following dates: September 17, November 5, and January 5. In each instance, compare your prediction to the subsequent behavior of the DJIA in the following few weeks.

7. Table 19.5 presents price data for Computers, Inc., and a computer industry index. Does Computers, Inc., show relative strength over this period?

8. Use the data in Table 19.5 to compute a five-day moving average for Computers, Inc. Can you identify any buy or sell signals?

1. Find the weekly price for the most recent two years for a firm from the Market Insight database (**www.mhhe.com/edumarketinsight**). Also, collect the level of the S&P 500 Index for the same period.

   a. Calculate the eight-week moving average of both the stock and the S&P 500 over time. For each series, use Excel to plot the moving average against the actual level of the stock price or index. Examine the instances where the moving average and price series cross. Is the stock more or less likely to increase when the price crosses through the moving average? Does it matter whether the price crosses the moving average from above or below? How reliable would an investment rule based on moving averages be? Perform your analysis for both the stock price and the S&P 500.

   b. Calculate and plot the relative strength of the stock compared to the S&P 500 over your sample period. Find all instances in which relative strength of the stock increases by more than 10 percentage points (e.g., an increase in the relative strength index from .93 to 1.03) and all those instances in which relative strength of the stock decreases by more than 10 percentage points. Is the stock more or less likely to outperform the S&P in the following two weeks when relative strength has increased or to underperform when relative strength has decreased? In other words, does relative strength continue? How reliable would an investment rule based on relative strength be?

2. Obtain weekly price data for a one-year period for a stock from the Market Insight database (**www.mhhe.com/edumarketinsight**). Use the price data to construct a point and figure chart with price intervals of $2. Do you observe any buy or sell signals? If so, what percentage of times do these signals turn out to be correct?

STANDARD &POOR'S

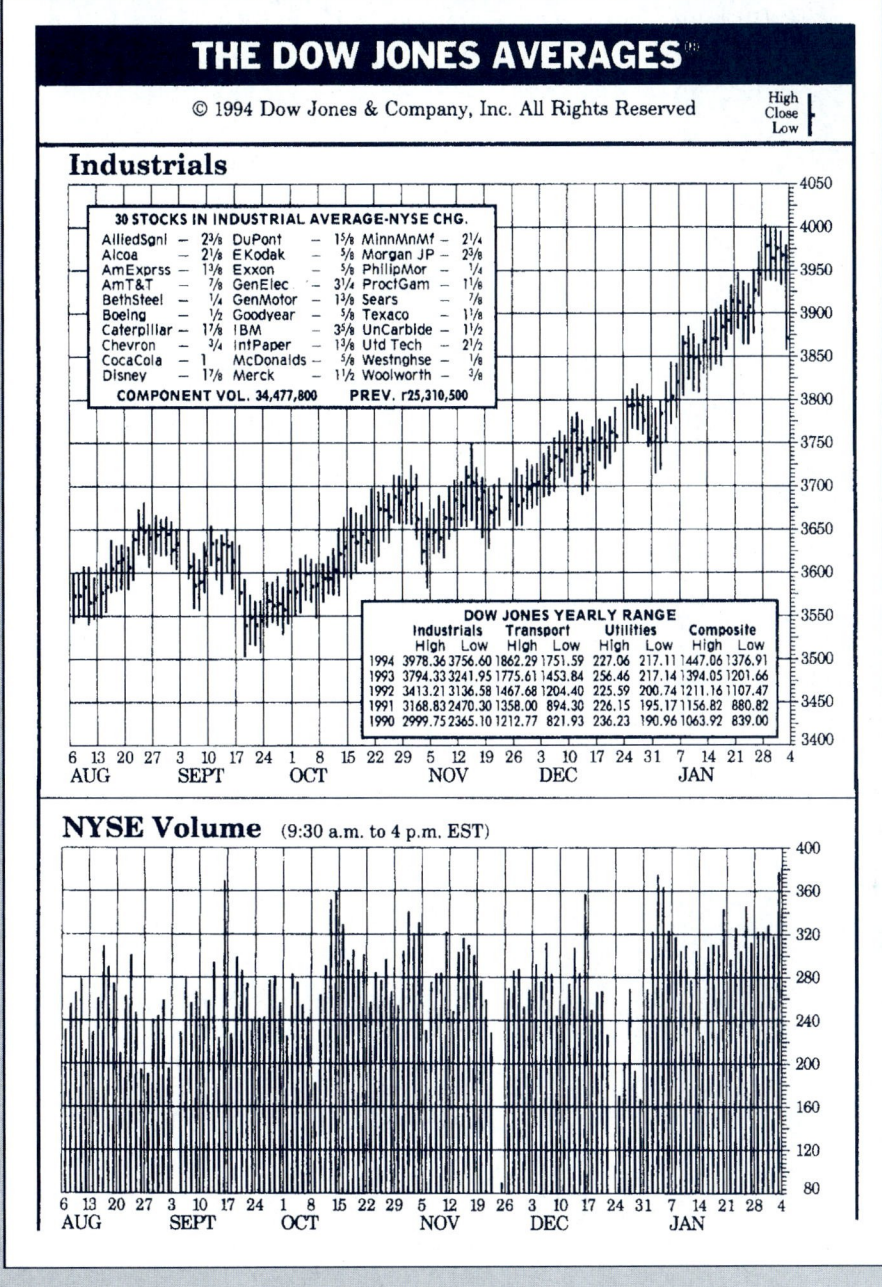

FIGURE **19.15**

Dow Jones Industrial Average and market volume

Source: From *The Wall Street Journal,* February 7, 1994, p. C3. Reprinted by permission of Dow Jones & Company, Inc. via Copyright Clearance Center, Inc. © 1994 Dow Jones & Company, Inc. All Rights Reserved Worldwide.

9. Construct a point and figure chart for Computers, Inc., using the data in Table 19.5. Use $2 increments for your chart. Do the buy or sell signals derived from your chart correspond to those derived from the moving average rule (see problem 8)?

10. Yesterday, the Dow Jones industrials gained 54 points. However, 1,704 issues declined in price while 1,367 advanced. Why might a technical analyst be concerned even though the market index rose on this day?

11. Table 19.6 contains data on market advances and declines. Calculate cumulative breadth and decide whether this technical signal is bullish or bearish.

TABLE **19.5** Computers, Inc., stock price history	Trading Day	Computers, Inc.	Industry Index
	1	19.63	50.0
	2	20	50.1
	3	20.50	50.5
	4	22	50.4
	5	21.13	51.0
	6	22	50.7
	7	21.88	50.5
	8	22.50	51.1
	9	23.13	51.5
	10	23.88	51.7
	11	24.50	51.4
	12	23.25	51.7
	13	22.13	52.2
	14	22	52.0
	15	20.63	53.1
	16	20.25	53.5
	17	19.75	53.9
	18	18.75	53.6
	19	17.50	52.9
	20	19	53.4
	21	19.63	54.1
	22	21.50	54.0
	23	22	53.9
	24	23.13	53.7
	25	24	54.8
	26	25.25	54.5
	27	26.25	54.6
	28	27	54.1
	29	27.50	54.2
	30	28	54.8
	31	28.50	54.2
	32	28	54.8
	33	27.50	54.9
	34	29	55.2
	35	29.25	55.7
	36	29.50	56.1
	37	30	56.7
	38	28.50	56.7
	39	27.75	56.5
	40	28	56.1

12. If the trading volume in advancing shares on day 1 in the previous problem was 330 million shares, while the volume in declining issues was 240 million shares, what was the trin statistic for that day? Was trin bullish or bearish?

13. Is the confidence index rising or falling?

	This Year	Last Year
Yield on top-rated corporate bonds	8%	9%
Yield on intermediate-grade corporate bonds	9	10

TABLE **19.6**	Day	Advances	Declines
Market advances and declines	1	906	704
	2	653	986
	3	721	789
	4	503	968
	5	497	1095
	6	970	702
	7	1002	609
	8	903	722
	9	850	748
	10	766	766

WEBMASTER

Charting and Technical Analysis

Go to http://finance.yahoo.com. Compare the charts and short interest ratios for GE and SWY. For each of the companies, compare a one-year chart to the 50- and 200-day average as well as the S&P 500 Index. Under the charting function, you can specify comparisons by choosing the technical analysis tab. Short interest ratios are found under the company profile report.

After you have secured the reports, discuss the following questions:

1. Which if either of the companies is priced above its 50- and 200-day averages?

2. Would you consider its chart as bullish or bearish? Explain.

3. What are the short ratios for the two companies?

4. Has the short interest displayed any significant trend?

1. Suppose a stock had been selling in a narrow trading range around $50 for a substantial period and later increased in price. Now the stock falls back to a price near $50. Potential buyers might recall the price history of the stock and remember that the last time the stock fell so low, they missed an opportunity for large gains when it later advanced. They might then view $50 as a good opportunity to buy. Therefore, buying pressure will materialize as the stock price falls to $50, which will create a support level.

SOLUTIONS TO

Concept
CHECKS

2.

```
      |   |   |   |   |   |
49 ___|___|___|___|___|___|
      |   | X |   |   |   |
46 ___|___|___|___|___|___|
    X |   | X | O |   |   |
43 ___|___|___|___|___|___|
      |   | O | X | O |   |
40 ___|___|___|___|___|___|
      |   | O |   | O |   |
37 ___|___|___|___|___|___|
      |   |   |   | O |   |
34 ___|___|___|___|___|___|
```

3. By the time the news of recession affects bond yields, it also ought to affect stock prices. The market should fall *before* the confidence index signals that the time is ripe to sell.

20

PERFORMANCE EVALUATION AND ACTIVE PORTFOLIO MANAGEMENT

AFTER STUDYING THIS CHAPTER YOU SHOULD BE ABLE TO:

> Compute risk-adjusted rates of return, and use these rates to evaluate investment performance.

> Decompose excess returns into components attributable to asset allocation choices versus security selection choices.

> Assess the performance of portfolio managers.

> Assess the value of market timing ability.

> Use the Treynor-Black model of efficient security analysis.

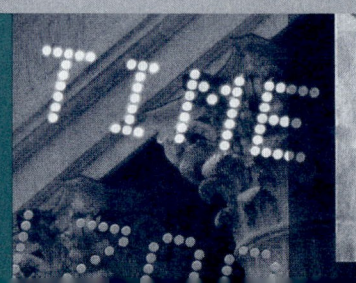

In previous chapters, we derived predictions for expected return as a function of risk. In this chapter, we ask how we can evaluate the performance of a portfolio manager given the risk of his or her portfolio. Even measuring average portfolio returns is not as straightforward as it might seem. Difficulties in adjusting average returns for risk present a host of other problems.

We begin with conventional approaches to risk adjustment. These use the risk measures developed in Part Two of the text to compare investment results. We show the problems with these approaches when you apply them in a real and complex world. Finally, we examine evaluation procedures used in the field. We show how overall investment results can be decomposed and attributed to the underlying asset allocation and security selection decisions of the portfolio manager.

Even if you largely accept the efficient market hypothesis, we will see that there are reasons to consider active portfolio management. We consider the objective of active management and analyze two forms: market timing based solely on macroeconomic factors, and security selection that includes microeconomic forecasting.

20.1 RISK-ADJUSTED RETURNS

Comparison Groups

The major difficulty in portfolio performance evaluation is that average portfolio returns must be adjusted for risk before we can compare them meaningfully.

The fact that common stocks have offered higher average returns than Treasury bonds (as demonstrated in Table 20.1) does not prove that stocks are superior investment vehicles. One must consider the fact that stocks also have been more volatile investments. For the same reason, the fact that a mutual fund outperforms the S&P 500 over a long period is not necessarily evidence of superior stock selection ability. If the mutual fund has a higher beta than the index, it *should* outperform the index (on average) to compensate investors in the fund for the higher nondiversifiable risk they bear. Thus, performance evaluation must involve risk as well as return comparisons.

The simplest and most popular way to adjust returns for portfolio risk is to compare rates of return with those of other investment funds with similar risk characteristics. For example, high-yield bond portfolios are grouped into one "universe," growth stock equity funds are grouped into another universe, and so on. Then the average returns of each fund within the universe are ordered, and each portfolio manager receives a percentile ranking depending on relative performance within the **comparison universe,** the collection of funds to which performance is compared. For example, the manager with the ninth-best performance in a universe of 100 funds would be the 90th percentile manager: Her performance was better than 90% of all competing funds over the evaluation period.

These relative rankings usually are displayed in a chart like that shown in Figure 20.1. The chart summarizes performance rankings over four periods: one quarter, one year, three years, and five years. The top and bottom lines of each box are drawn at the rate of return of the 95th and 5th percentile managers. The three dotted lines correspond to the rates of return of the 75th, 50th (median), and 25th percentile managers. The diamond is drawn at the average return of a particular fund, the Markowill Group, and the square is drawn at the average return of a benchmark index such as the S&P 500. This format provides an easy-to-read representation of the performance of the fund relative to the comparison universe.

This comparison with other managers of similar investment groups is a useful first step in evaluating performance. Even so, such rankings can be misleading. Consider that within a particular universe some managers may concentrate on particular subgroups, so that portfolio characteristics are not truly comparable. For example, within the equity universe, one manager may concentrate on high-beta stocks. Similarly, within fixed-income universes, interest rate risk can vary across managers. These considerations show that we need a more precise means for risk adjustment.

comparison universe

The set of portfolio managers with similar investment styles that is used in assessing the relative performance of an individual portfolio manager.

TABLE **20.1** Average annual returns by investment class, 1926–2001	Arithmetic Average	Geometric Average	Standard Deviation
Common stocks of small firms*	18.3	12.2	39.3
Common stocks of large firms	12.5	10.5	20.3
Long-term Treasury bonds	5.5	5.3	8.2
U.S. Treasury bills	3.9	3.9	3.3

Source: Prepared from data in Table 5.2

*These are firms with relatively low market values of equity. Market capitalization is computed as price per share times shares outstanding.

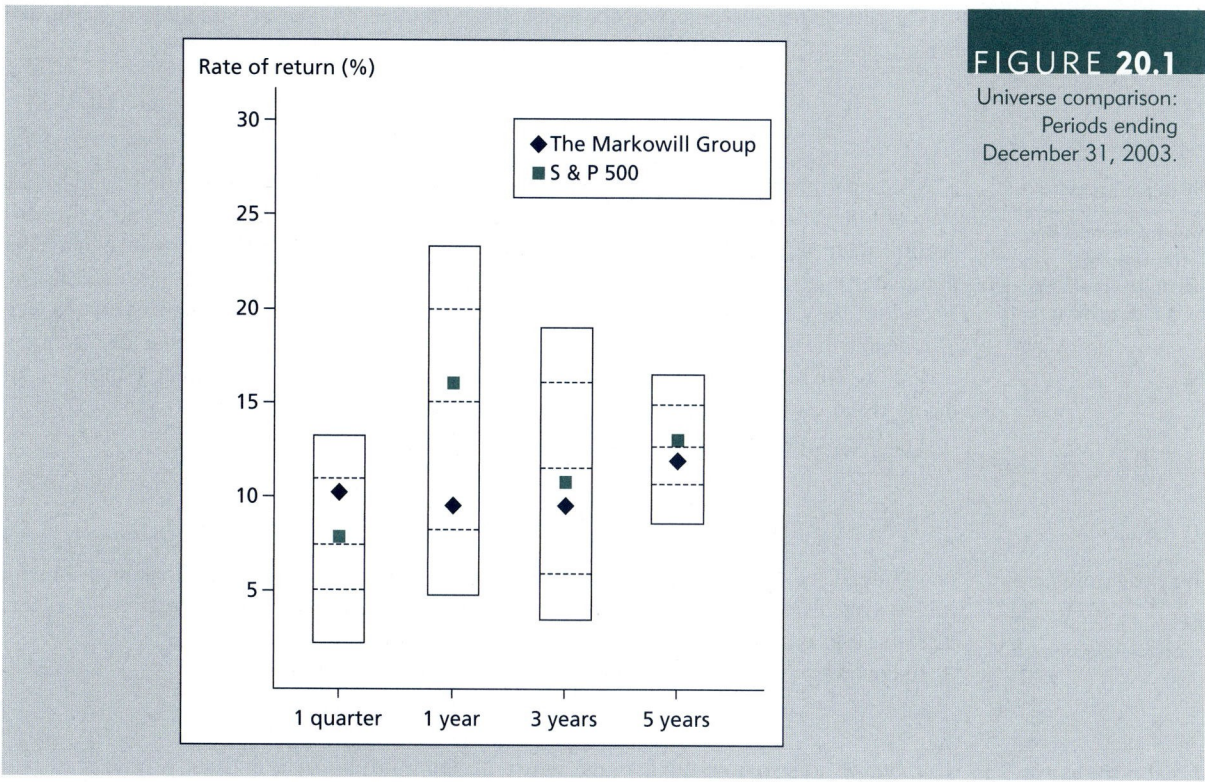

Rate of return (%)

◆ The Markowill Group
■ S & P 500

1 quarter   1 year   3 years   5 years

FIGURE **20.1**
Universe comparison:
Periods ending
December 31, 2003.

Risk Adjustments

Methods of risk-adjusted performance using mean-variance criteria developed simultaneously with the capital asset pricing model (CAPM). Jack Treynor (1966), William Sharpe (1966), and Michael Jensen (1969) were quick to recognize the implications of the CAPM for rating the performance of managers. Within a short time, academicians were in command of a battery of performance measures, and a bounty of scholarly investigation of mutual fund performance was pouring from the ivory tower. Soon after, agents emerged who were willing to supply rating services to portfolio managers eager for regular feedback. These days, risk-adjusted performance measures are accessible to all investors on the Internet. We will use these statistics in our analysis here.

We begin with a catalogue of the major risk-adjusted performance measures and examine the circumstances in which each measure might be most relevant. To illustrate these measures, we will use a hypothetical portfolio for which monthly returns in the past five years resulted in the following statistics. We also present comparable data for the market portfolio for the same period.

	Portfolio	Market
Average return	16%	14%
Standard deviation	20%	24%
Beta	0.8	1.0

Finally, suppose the average return on risk-free assets during the five-year period was 6%.

The Sharpe measure, the Treynor measure, and the Jensen measure are three risk-adjusted performance statistics. The Sharpe measure is calculated as follows:

$$\frac{\bar{r}_p - \bar{r}_f}{\sigma_p}$$

Sharpe measure

Reward-to-volatility ratio; ratio of portfolio excess return to standard deviation.

The **Sharpe measure** divides average portfolio excess return over the sample period by the standard deviation of returns over that period. The numerator is the incremental return the portfolio earned in comparison with an alternative investment in the risk-free asset, and the denominator is the increment in portfolio volatility compared with the risk-free alternative. Therefore, the ratio measures the reward to (total) volatility trade-off. (The bars over r_p as well as r_f denote the fact that, because the risk-free rate may not be constant over the measurement period, we are taking a sample average of both.) Using our numbers, the Sharpe measure for the portfolio is $(16 - 6)/20 = 0.5$, while for the market it is $(14 - 6)/24 = 0.33$.

In contrast, the Treynor measure is given as follows:

$$\frac{\bar{r}_p - \bar{r}_f}{\beta_p}$$

Treynor measure

Ratio of portfolio excess return to beta.

Like Sharpe's, the **Treynor measure** gives average excess return per unit of risk incurred, but it uses systematic risk instead of total risk. The Treynor measure for the portfolio over this period is $(16 - 6)/0.8 = 12.5$, while for the market portfolio it is $(14 - 6)/1.0 = 8$.

In contrast to these two methods, the Jensen measure is as follows:

$$\alpha_p = \bar{r}_p - [\bar{r}_f + \beta_p(\bar{r}_M - \bar{r}_f)]$$

Jensen measure

The alpha of an investment.

The **Jensen measure** is the average return on the portfolio over and above that predicted by the CAPM, given the portfolio's beta and the average market return. The Jensen measure is the portfolio's alpha value. Using our numbers, the Jensen measure is $16 - [6 + 0.8(14 - 6)] = 3.6\%$.

Each measure has its own appeal. In this instance, all three measures are consistent in revealing that the portfolio outperformed the market benchmark on a risk-adjusted basis. However, this need not be the case. As the following Concept Check illustrates, the three measures do not necessarily provide consistent assessments of relative performance, as the approach used to adjust returns for risk differ substantially.

Concept CHECK

1. Consider the following data for a particular sample period:

	Portfolio P	Market M
Average return	35%	28%
Beta	1.2	1.0
Standard deviation	42%	30%

Calculate the following performance measures for portfolio P and the market: Sharpe, Jensen (alpha), and Treynor. The T-bill rate during the period was 6%. By which measures did portfolio P outperform the market?

The M² Measure of Performance

While the Sharpe ratio can be used to rank portfolio performance, its numerical value is not easy to interpret. Comparing the ratios for portfolios M and P in Concept Check 1, you should have found that $S_P = .69$ and $S_M = .73$. This suggests that portfolio P underperformed the

FIGURE **20.2**
The M^2 of portfolio P

market index. But is a difference of .04 in the Sharpe ratio economically meaningful? We are used to comparing rates of return, but these ratios are difficult to interpret.

A variant of Sharpe's measure was introduced by Graham and Harvey and by Leah Modigliani of Morgan Stanley and her grandfather Franco Modigliani, past winner of the Nobel Prize for economics.[1] Their approach has been dubbed the M^2 measure (for Modigliani-squared). Like the Sharpe ratio, the M^2 measure focuses on total volatility as a measure of risk, but its risk-adjusted measure of performance has the easy interpretation of a differential return relative to the benchmark index.

To compute the M^2 measure, we imagine that a managed portfolio, P, is mixed with a position in T-bills so that the complete, or "adjusted," portfolio matches the volatility of a market index such as the S&P 500. For example, if the managed portfolio has 1.5 times the standard deviation of the index, the adjusted portfolio would be two-thirds invested in the managed portfolio and one-third invested in bills. The adjusted portfolio, which we call P^*, would then have the same standard deviation as the index. (If the managed portfolio had *lower* standard deviation than the index, it would be leveraged by borrowing money and investing the proceeds in the portfolio.) Because the market index and portfolio P^* have the same standard deviation, we may compare their performance simply by comparing returns. This is the M^2 measure:

$$M^2 = r_{P*} - r_M$$

In the example of Concept Check 1, P has a standard deviation of 42% versus a market standard deviation of 30%. Therefore, the adjusted portfolio P^* would be formed by mixing bills and portfolio P with weights 30/42 = .714 in P and $1 - .714 = .286$ in bills. The expected return on this portfolio would be $(.286 \times 6\%) + (.714 \times 35\%) = 26.7\%$, which is 1.3% less than the market return. Thus portfolio P has an M^2 measure of -1.3%.

A graphical representation of the M^2 measure appears in Figure 20.2. We move down the capital allocation line corresponding to portfolio P (by mixing P with T-bills) until we reduce

[1]John R. Graham and Campbell R. Harvey, "Grading the performance of market timing newsletter," *Financial Analysts Journal* 53 (November/December 1997), pp. 54–66; and Franco Modigliani and Leah Modigliani, "Risk-Adjusted Performance," *Journal of Portfolio Management,* Winter 1997, pp. 45–54.

the standard deviation of the adjusted portfolio to match that of the market index. The M^2 measure is then the vertical distance (i.e., the difference in expected returns) between portfolios P^* and M. You can see from Figure 20.2 that P will have an M^2 measure below that of the market when its capital allocation line is less steep than the capital market line, that is, when its Sharpe ratio is less than that of the market index.

The nearby box reports on the growing popularity of the M^2 measure in the investment community.

Choosing the Right Measure of Risk

Because different risk adjustment procedures can yield different implications for performance evaluation, it is essential that you choose the appropriate measure for the task. For example, suppose you are a pension fund manager who is selecting potential portfolio managers to oversee investment of the fund's assets. If you envision hiring one investment manager to manage all the fund's assets, then you must be concerned with the total variability of investment performance. Both the systematic and firm-specific risk remaining in the portfolio will affect total risk because the pension fund is not diversified across managers. The manager's portfolio will investment style or its portfolio manager or grown a lot in size. While you can look at an attractive historical number for a particular fund, Ms. Modigliani says, "you are not sure to get that return going forward."

Stock Funds: Risk-Adjusted Winners

Among stock funds with a 10-year history, these scored highest on the Modigliani-Modigliani (M-squared) measure of risk-adjusted performance.

Fund Name	Returns 1988–1997 Average Annual	M-Squared Risk-Adjusted*	% Cash Needed to Adjust**
Fidelity Select Food & Agriculture	21.5%	20.5%	6%
Putnam Fund for Gr. & Inc. (A shares)	16.7	20.1	−30
Mutual Beacon (Z shares)	17.2	20.0	−24
Gateway Index Plus	11.8	20.0	−129
Fidelity Contrafund	23.0	19.4	21
Hancock Regional Bank (B shares)	26.1	19.3	33
Mutual Qualified (Z shares)	17.4	19.1	−15
Benchmark: S&P 500	17.9	17.9	0

*The return an investor would have earned by combining fund shares with cash—or alternatively, borrowing money—to create a hypothetical portfolio with the same volatility as the benchmark S&P 500.

**Percent of the hypothetical portfolio needed to be invested in cash equivalents to match the benchmark's volatility—or, if a negative figure, amount of borrowing.

Source: Morgan Stanley Dean Witter, using quarterly returns from Morningstar.

be the entire portfolio, with no further opportunities for diversification. In this case, the Sharpe measure (and M^2) is the appropriate basis on which to evaluate the portfolio manager. Because that manager is in charge of the entire portfolio, she must be attentive to diversification of firm-specific risk and should be judged on her achievement of excess return to *total* portfolio volatility.

In contrast, suppose your pension fund is large, and you envision hiring many managers, giving each a fraction of the total assets of the plan. You hope that hiring a set of managers, each with an investment specialty, will enhance returns. This means the pension plan effectively ends up with a portfolio of portfolio managers. Each manager can pursue his or her specialty without paying much attention to issues of diversification because the plan as a whole will have diversified returns across the several managed portfolios. With assets spread across many portfolio managers, the residual firm-specific risks of each portfolio become irrelevant because of diversification across portfolios. In this case, only nondiversifiable risk should matter. Such circumstances call for the use of a beta-based risk adjustment, and the Treynor measure would be appropriate.

We can use a variant of the Treynor measure to express the difference in portfolio performance in terms of rates of return. Consider a portfolio P, with the characteristics summarized in Table 20.2. To convert the difference between the Treynor measure of P and that of the market to an easier-to-interpret percentage return basis, we will consider a measure

TABLE **20.2**		Portfolio P	Portfolio Q	Market
Portfolio performance	Excess return, $r - r_f$	13%	20%	10%
	Beta	0.80	1.80	1.0
	Alpha*	5%	2%	0
	Treynor measure	16.25	11.11	10

*Alpha = Excess return $\times$ (Beta 3 Market excess return)

$\qquad = (r - r_f) - \beta(r_M - r_f)$

$\qquad = r - [r_f + \beta(r_M - r_f)]$

analogous to M^2 that we call Treynor-Square (T^2). To start, we will create a portfolio P^* by mixing P and T-bills to match the beta of the market, 1.0. (In contrast, to obtain the M^2 measure we mixed bills and P to match the *standard deviation* of the market.)

Recall that both the beta and the excess return of T-bills are zero. Therefore, if we construct portfolio P^* by investing w in portfolio P and $1 - w$ in T-bills, the excess return and beta of P^* will be:

$$R_{P*} = wR_P, \qquad \beta_{P*} = w\beta_P$$

We can construct P^* from portfolio P and T-bills with any desired beta. If you desire a beta equal to β_{P*}, simply set: $w = \beta_{P*}/\beta_P$; hence, $R_{P*} = wR_P = R_P \times \beta_{P*}/\beta_P$. Because the market beta is 1.0, P^* can be constructed to match the market beta by setting

$$w = \beta_M/\beta_P = 1/\beta_P = 1/0.8$$

Therefore, $R_{P*} = wR_P = (1/\beta_P) \times R_P = 13\%/0.8 = 16.25\%$. Notice that $w > 1$ implies that P^* is a leveraged version of P. Leverage is necessary to match the market beta since the beta of P is less than that of the market. Notice also that R_{P*} is in fact the Treynor measure of portfolio P—it equals the excess return of P divided by beta.

Portfolio P^* is constructed to have the same beta as the market, so the difference between the return of P^* and the market is a valid measure of relative performance when systematic risk is of concern to investors. Therefore, as an analogy to the M^2 measure of performance, we define the Treynor-square measure as

$$T_P^2 = R_{P*} - R_M = R_P/\beta_P - R_M = 13/0.8 - 10 = 6.25\%.$$

Figure 20.3A shows a graphical representation of the T^2 measure for portfolio P. Portfolio P^* is a leveraged version of portfolio P with the same beta as the market, 1.0. The T^2 measure is simply the difference in expected returns at this common beta.

To compare the T^2 measure for the two portfolios, P and Q, described in Table 20.2, we compute for portfolio Q

$$T_Q^2 = 20/1.8 - 10 = 1.11\%$$

which is smaller than the T^2 measure of P by 5.14%. Figure 20.3B shows the positions of P and Q. Portfolios on a given line from the origin (notice that the vertical axis measures *excess* returns), all have the same Treynor measure. P is located on a steeper line because it has a higher Treynor measure. As a result, P^* is farther above the SML than Q^*, and the difference between the T^2 measures, the line segment P^*Q^*, measures the difference in the systematic risk-adjusted percent return.

It is clear that we must adjust portfolio returns for risk before evaluating performance. The nearby box shows how important such adjustments can be. It reports on the results of a series of investment "contests" between investment professionals and randomly chosen stocks (the

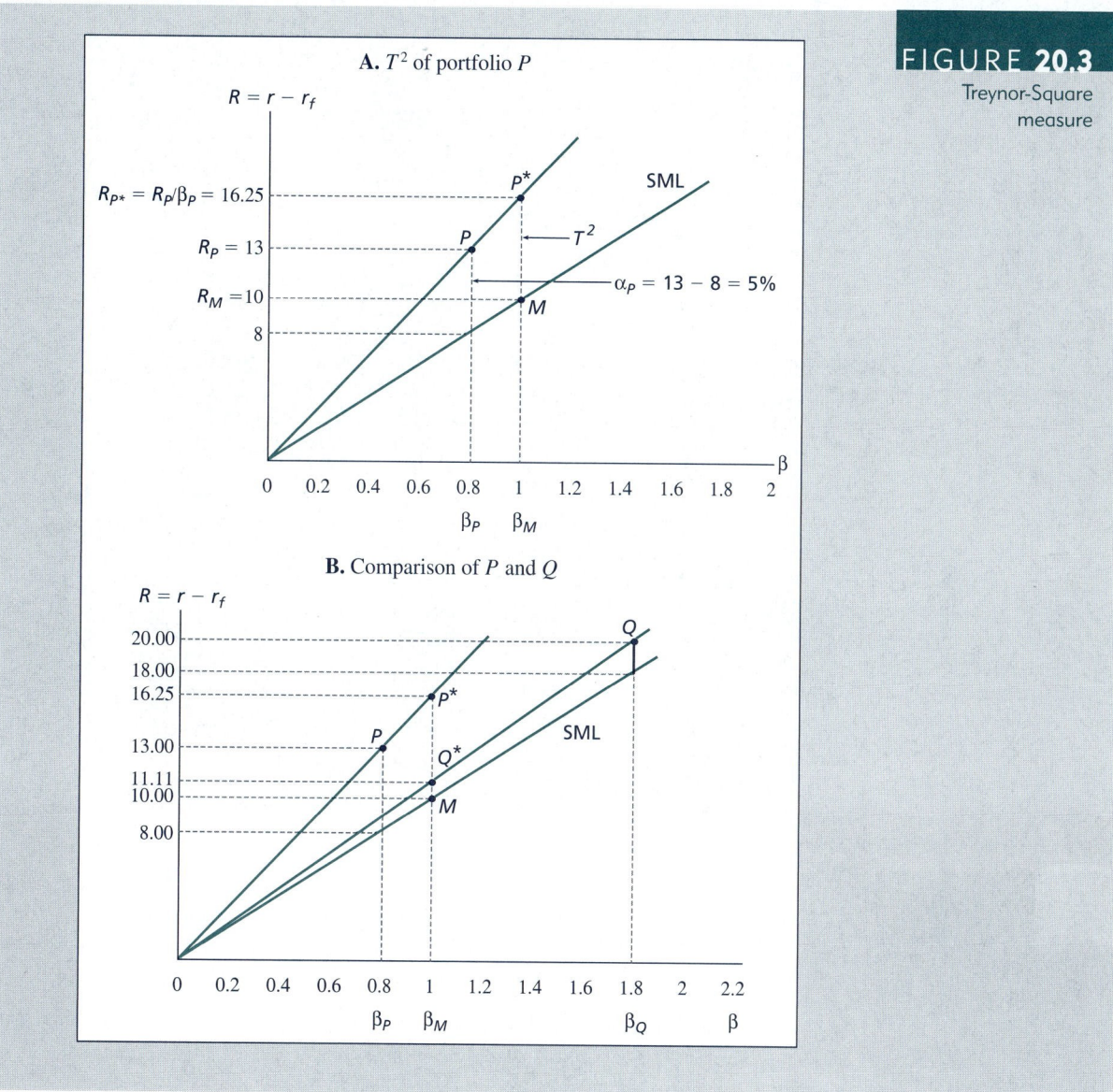

FIGURE 20.3
Treynor-Square measure

dartboard portfolio) sponsored by *The Wall Street Journal*. While the professionals have tended to win the contest, the box shows that risk-adjustment nearly wipes out the differential.

Risk Adjustments with Changing Portfolio Composition

One potential problem with risk-adjustment techniques is that they all assume that portfolio risk, whether it is measured by standard deviation or beta, is constant over the relevant time period. This isn't necessarily so. If a manager attempts to increase portfolio beta when she thinks the market is about to go up and to decrease beta when she is pessimistic, both the standard deviation and the beta of the portfolio will change over time. This can wreak havoc with our performance measures.

20.1 EXAMPLE

Risk Measurement with Changing Portfolio Composition

Suppose the Sharpe measure of the passive strategy (investing in a market index fund) is 0.4. A portfolio manager is in search of a better, active strategy. Over an initial period of, say, four quarters, he executes a low-risk or defensive strategy with an annualized mean excess return of 1% and a standard deviation of 2%. This makes for a Sharpe measure of 0.5, which beats the passive strategy.

Over the next period of another four quarters, this manager finds that a high-risk strategy is optimal, with an annual mean excess return of 9% and standard deviation of 18%. Here again the Sharpe measure is 0.5. Over the two years, our manager maintains a better-than-passive Sharpe measure.

Figure 20.4 shows a pattern of (annualized) quarterly returns that is consistent with our description of the manager's strategy over two years. In the first four quarters, the excess returns are −1%, 3%, −1%, and 3%, making for an average of 1% and standard deviation of 2%. In the next four quarters, the returns are −9%, 27%, −9%, and 27%, making for an average of 9% and standard deviation of 18%. Thus, *each* year undoubtedly exhibits a Sharpe measure of 0.5.

But if we take the eight-quarter sequence as a single measurement period, instead of two independent periods, and measure the portfolio's mean and standard deviation over that full period, we get an average excess return of 5% and standard deviation of 13.42%, resulting in a Sharpe measure of only 0.37, apparently inferior to the passive strategy!

What happened? Sharpe's measure does not recognize the shift in the mean from the first four quarters to the next as a result of a strategy change. Instead, the difference in mean returns

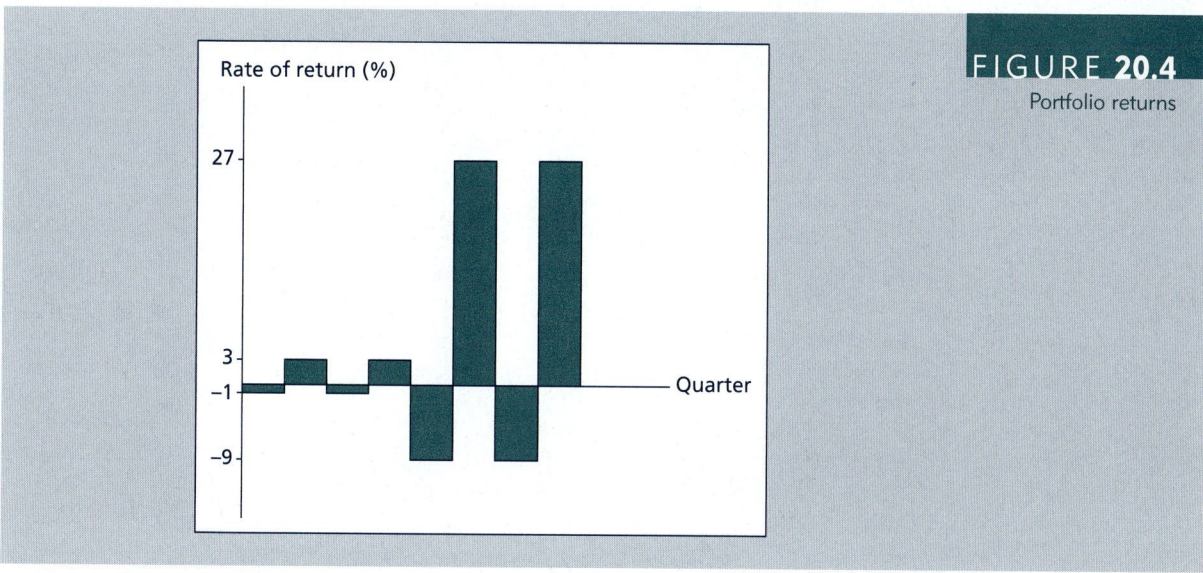

FIGURE **20.4**
Portfolio returns

in the two years adds to the *appearance* of volatility in portfolio returns. The change in mean returns across time periods contributed to the variability of returns over the same period. But in this case, variability per se should not be interpreted as volatility or riskiness in returns. Part of the variability in returns is due to intentional choices that shift the expected or mean return. This part should not be ascribed to uncertainty in returns. Unfortunately, an outside observer might not realize that policy changes within the sample period are the source of some of the return variability. Therefore, the active strategy with shifting means appears riskier than it really is, which biases the estimate of the Sharpe measure downward.

For actively managed portfolios, therefore, it is crucial to keep track of portfolio composition and changes in portfolio mean return and risk. We will see another example of this problem when we talk about market timing.

Finally, we must be careful in assigning value to the performance of the most successful mutual fund over a given period. In assessing the significance of such performance we must account for the fact that even if all mutual funds were equally well managed, a winner would emerge by sheer chance every period. When thousands of funds compete for investor savings, we should expect spectacular performance by the winner. This principle is explained in the nearby box.

20.2 PERFORMANCE ATTRIBUTION PROCEDURES

Rather than focus on risk-adjusted returns, practitioners often want simply to ascertain which decisions resulted in superior or inferior performance. Superior investment performance depends on an ability to be in the "right" securities at the right time. Such timing and selection ability may be considered broadly, such as being in equities as opposed to fixed-income securities when the stock market is performing well. Or it may be defined at a more detailed level, such as choosing the relatively better-performing stocks within a particular industry.

Portfolio managers constantly make both broad-brush asset market allocation decisions as well as more detailed sector and security allocation decisions within markets. Performance attribution studies attempt to decompose overall performance into discrete components that may be identified with a particular level of the portfolio selection process.

Attribution analysis starts from the broadest asset allocation choices and progressively focuses on ever-finer details of portfolio choice. The difference between a managed portfolio's performance and that of a benchmark portfolio then may be expressed as the sum of the contributions to performance of a series of decisions made at the various levels of the portfolio construction process. For example, one common attribution system decomposes performance into three components: (1) broad asset market allocation choices *across* equity, fixed-income, and money markets; (2) industry (sector) choice *within* each market; and (3) security choice within each sector.

To illustrate this method, consider the attribution results for a hypothetical portfolio. The portfolio invests in stocks, bonds, and money market securities. An attribution analysis appears in Tables 20.3 through 20.6. The portfolio return over the month is 5.34%.

The first step is to establish a benchmark level of performance against which performance ought to be compared. This benchmark is called the **bogey.** It is designed to measure the returns the portfolio manager would earn if she were to follow a completely passive strategy. "Passive" in this context has two attributes. First, it means the allocation of funds across broad asset classes is set in accord with a notion of "usual" or neutral allocation across sectors. This would be considered a passive asset market allocation. Second, it means that, within each asset class, the portfolio manager holds an indexed portfolio, for example, the S&P 500 index for the equity sector. The passive strategy used as a performance benchmark rules out both asset allocation and security selection decisions. Any departure of the manager's return from

bogey

The return an investment manager is compared to for performance evaluation.

compute the frequency distribution of the winning number of heads over the 10,000 trials.

Table 1 (column 1) presents the results of such an experiment simulated on a computer. The table shows that in 9.2% of the contests, the winning number of heads was nine; in 47.4% of the trials ten heads would be enough to emerge as the best manager. Interestingly, in 43.3% of the trials, the winning number of heads was eleven or better out of thirteen.

Viewed in this context, the performance of Magellan is still impressive but somewhat less surprising. The simulation shows that out of a large sample of managers, chance alone would provide a 43.3% probability that *someone* would beat the market at least eleven out of thirteen years. Averaging over all 10,000 trials, the mean number of winning years necessary to emerge as most reliable manager over the thirteen-year contest was 10.43.

Therefore, once we recognize that Magellan is not a fund chosen at random, but a fund that came to our attention precisely because it turned out to perform so well in competition with more than fifty managers, the frequency with which it beat the market is no longer high enough to constitute a contradiction of market efficiency. Indeed, using the conventional 5% confidence level, we could not reject the hypothesis that the consistency of its performance was due to chance.

The other columns in Table 1 present the frequency distributions of the winning number of successful coin flips (analogously, the number of years in which the

TABLE 1

Probability Distribution of Number of Successful Years out of Thirteen for the Best-Performing Money Manager

Winning Years	Managers in Contest			
	50	100	250	500
8	0.1%	0	0	0
9	9.2	0.9	0	0
10	47.4	31.9	5.7	0.2
11	34.8	51.3	59.7	42.3
12	7.7	14.6	31.8	51.5
13	0.8	1.2	2.8	5.9
Mean winning years of best performer	10.43	10.83	11.32	11.63

best-performing manager beats an efficient market) for other possible sample sizes. Not surprisingly, as the pool of managers increases, the predicted best performance steadily gets better. . . . By providing as a benchmark the probability distribution of the best performance, rather than the average performance, the table tells us how many grains of salt to add to reports of the latest investment guru.

SOURCE: Alan J. Marcus, "The Magellan Fund and Market Efficiency." *The Journal of Portfolio Management,* Fall 1990.

the passive benchmark must be due to either asset allocation bets (departures from the neutral allocation across markets) or security selection bets (departures from the passive index within asset classes).

While we've already discussed in earlier chapters the justification for indexing within sectors, it is worth briefly explaining the determination of the neutral allocation of funds across the broad asset classes. Weights that are designated as "neutral" will depend on the risk tolerance of the investor and must be determined in consultation with the client. For example, risk-tolerant clients may place a large fraction of their portfolio in the equity market, perhaps directing the fund manager to set neutral weights of 75% equity, 15% bonds, and 10% cash equivalents. Any deviation from these weights must be justified by a belief that one or another market will either over- or underperform its usual risk-return profile. In contrast, more risk-averse clients may set neutral weights of 45%/35%/20% for the three markets. Therefore, their portfolios in normal circumstances will be exposed to less risk than that of the risk-tolerant clients. Only intentional bets on market performance will result in departures from this profile.

In Table 20.3, the neutral weights have been set at 60% equity, 30% fixed-income, and 10% cash equivalents (money market securities). The bogey portfolio, comprising investments in each index with the 60/30/10 weights, returned 3.97%. The managed portfolio's measure of performance is positive and equal to its actual return less the return of the bogey: $5.34 - 3.97 = 1.37\%$. The next step is to allocate the 1.37% excess return to the separate decisions that contributed to it.

EXCEL Applications   www.mhhe.com/bkm

Performance Measures

The Excel model "Performance Measures" calculates all of the performance measures discussed in this chapter. The model that is available on the book website is built to allow you to compare eight different portfolios and to rank them on all measures discussed in this chapter.

You can learn more about this spreadsheet model by using the interactive version available on our website at www.mhhe.com/bkm.

	A	B	C	D	E	F	G	H	I	J	K
1	Performance Measurement										
2											
3											
4											
5		Average	Standard	Beta	Unsystematic	Sharpe	Treynor	Jensen	M²	T²	Appraisal
6	Fund	Return	Deviation	Coefficient	Risk	Ratio	Measure	Alpha	Measure	Measure	Ratio
7	Alpha	0.2800	0.2700	1.7000	0.0500	0.8148	0.1294	-0.0180	-0.0015	-0.0106	-0.3600
8	Omega	0.3100	0.2600	1.6200	0.0600	0.9615	0.1543	0.0232	0.0235	0.0143	0.3867
9	Omicron	0.2200	0.2100	0.8500	0.0200	0.7619	0.1882	0.0410	-0.0105	0.0482	2.0500
10	Millennium	0.4000	0.3300	2.5000	0.2700	1.0303	0.1360	-0.0100	0.0352	-0.0040	-0.0370
11	Big Value	0.1500	0.1300	0.9000	0.0300	0.6923	0.1000	-0.0360	-0.0223	-0.0400	-1.2000
12	Momentum Watcher	0.2900	0.2400	1.4000	0.1600	0.9583	0.1643	0.0340	0.0229	0.0243	0.2125
13	Big Potential	0.1500	0.1100	0.5500	0.0150	0.8182	0.1636	0.0130	-0.0009	0.0236	0.8667
14	S & P Index Return	0.2000	0.1700	1.0000	0.0000	0.8235	0.1400	0.0000	0.0000	0.0000	0.0000
15	T-Bill Return	0.06		0							
16											
17	Ranking By Sharpe										
18		Return	S.D.	Beta	Unsy. Risk	Sharpe	Treynor	Jensen	M²	T²	Appraisal
19	Millennium	0.4000	0.3300	2.5000	0.2700	1.0303	0.1360	-0.0100	0.0352	-0.0040	-0.0370
20	Omega	0.3100	0.2600	1.6200	0.0600	0.9615	0.1543	0.0232	0.0235	0.0143	0.3867
21	Momentum Watcher	0.2900	0.2400	1.4000	0.1600	0.9583	0.1643	0.0340	0.0229	0.0243	0.2125
22	S & P Index Return	0.2000	0.1700	1.0000	0.0000	0.8235	0.1400	0.0000	0.0000	0.0000	0.0000
23	Big Potential	0.1500	0.1100	0.5500	0.0150	0.8182	0.1636	0.0130	-0.0009	0.0236	0.8667
24	Alpha	0.2800	0.2700	1.7000	0.0500	0.8148	0.1294	-0.0180	-0.0015	-0.0106	-0.3600
25	Omicron	0.2200	0.2100	0.8500	0.0200	0.7619	0.1882	0.0410	-0.0105	0.0482	2.0500
26	Big Value	0.1500	0.1300	0.9000	0.0300	0.6923	0.1000	-0.0360	-0.0223	-0.0400	-1.2000
27											
28	Ranking by Treynor										
29		Return	S.D.	Beta	Unsy. Risk	Sharpe	Treynor	Jensen	M²	T²	Appraisal
30	Omicron	0.2200	0.2100	0.8500	0.0200	0.7619	0.1882	0.0410	-0.0105	0.0482	2.0500
31	Momentum Watcher	0.2900	0.2400	1.4000	0.1600	0.9583	0.1643	0.0340	0.0229	0.0243	0.2125
32	Big Potential	0.1500	0.1100	0.5500	0.0150	0.8182	0.1636	0.0130	-0.0009	0.0236	0.8667
33	Omega	0.3100	0.2600	1.6200	0.0600	0.9615	0.1543	0.0232	0.0235	0.0143	0.3867
34	S & P Index Return	0.2000	0.1700	1.0000	0.0000	0.8235	0.1400	0.0000	0.0000	0.0000	0.0000
35	Millennium	0.4000	0.3300	2.5000	0.2700	1.0303	0.1360	-0.0100	0.0352	-0.0040	-0.0370
36	Alpha	0.2800	0.2700	1.7000	0.0500	0.8148	0.1294	-0.0180	-0.0015	-0.0106	-0.3600
37	Big Value	0.1500	0.1300	0.9000	0.0300	0.6923	0.1000	-0.0360	-0.0223	-0.0400	-1.2000
38											

TABLE 20.3
Performance of the managed portfolio

	Bogey Performance and Excess Return	
Component	Benchmark Weight	Return of Index during Month (%)
Equity (S&P 500)	0.60	5.81
Bonds (Lehman Bros. Index)	0.30	1.45
Cash (money market)	0.10	0.48

Bogey = $(0.60 \times 5.81) + (0.30 \times 1.45) + (0.10 \times 0.48) = 3.97\%$

Return of managed portfolio	5.34%
− Return of bogey portfolio	3.97
Excess return of managed portfolio	1.37%

Asset Allocation Decisions

The managed portfolio is actually invested in the equity, fixed-income, and money markets with weights of 70%, 7%, and 23%, respectively. The portfolio's performance could be due to the departure of this weighting scheme from the benchmark 60/30/10 weights and/or to superior or inferior results *within* each of the three broad markets.

To isolate the effect of the manager's asset allocation choice, we measure the performance of a hypothetical portfolio that would have been invested in the *indexes* for each market with weights 70/7/23. This return measures the effect of the shift away from the benchmark 60/30/10 weights without allowing for any effects attributable to active management of the securities selected within each market.

Superior performance relative to the bogey is achieved by overweighting investments in markets that turn out to perform better than the bogey and by underweighting those in poorly performing markets. The contribution of asset allocation to superior performance equals the sum over all markets of the excess weight in each market times the return of the market index.

Table 20.4A demonstrates that asset allocation contributed 31 basis points to the portfolio's overall excess return of 137 basis points. The major factor contributing to superior performance in this month is the heavy weighting of the equity market in a month when the equity market has an excellent return of 5.81%.

Sector and Security Selection Decisions

If 0.31% of the excess performance can be attributed to advantageous asset allocation across markets, the remaining 1.06% then must be attributable to sector selection and security selection within each market. Table 20.4B details the contribution of the managed portfolio's sector and security selection to total performance.

TABLE 20.4

Performance attribution

A. Contribution of Asset Allocation to Performance

Market	(1) Actual Weight in Market	(2) Benchmark Weight in Market	(3) Excess Weight	(4) Index Return (%)	(5) = (3) × (4) Contribution to Performance (%)
Equity	0.70	0.60	0.10	5.81	.5810
Fixed-income	0.07	0.30	−0.23	1.45	−.3335
Cash	0.23	0.10	0.13	0.48	.0624
Contribution of asset allocation					0.3099

B. Contribution of Selection to Total Performance

Market	(1) Portfolio Performance (%)	(2) Index Performance (%)	(3) Excess Performance (%)	(4) Portfolio Weight	(5) = (3) × (4) Contribution (%)
Equity	7.28	5.81	1.47	0.70	1.03
Fixed-income	1.89	1.45	0.44	0.07	0.03
Contribution of selection within markets					1.06

TABLE **20.5**
Sector selection within the equity market

Sector	Beginning of Month Weights (%)		(3) Difference in Weights	(4) Sector Return	(5) Sector Over/Under- Performance*	(6) = (3) × (5) Sector Allocation Contribution (basis points)
	(1) Portfolio	(2) S&P 500				
Basic materials	1.96	8.3	−6.34	6.4	0.9	−5.7
Business services	7.84	4.1	3.74	6.5	1.0	3.7
Capital goods	1.87	7.8	−5.93	3.7	−1.8	10.7
Consumer cyclical	8.47	12.5	−4.03	8.4	2.9	−11.7
Consumer noncyclical	40.37	20.4	19.97	9.4	3.9	77.9
Credit sensitive	24.01	21.8	2.21	4.6	0.9	2.0
Energy	13.53	14.2	−0.67	2.1	−3.4	2.3
Technology	1.95	10.9	−8.95	−0.1	−5.6	50.1
Total						129.3

*S&P 500 performance net of dividends was 5.344%. Returns were compared net of dividends.

Panel B shows that the equity component of the managed portfolio has a return of 7.28% versus a return of 5.81% for the S&P 500. The fixed-income return is 1.89% versus 1.45% for the Lehman Brothers Index. The superior performance in both equity and fixed-income markets weighted by the portfolio proportions invested in each market sums to the 1.06% contribution to performance attributable to sector and security selection.

Table 20.5 documents the sources of the equity market performance by each sector within the market. The first three columns detail the allocation of funds within the equity market compared to their representation in the S&P 500. Column (4) shows the rate of return of each sector, and column (5) documents the performance of each sector relative to the return of the S&P 500. The contribution of each sector's allocation presented in column (6) equals the product of the difference in the sector weight and the sector's relative performance.

Note that good performance (a positive contribution) derives from overweighting well-performing sectors such as consumer nondurables, as well as underweighting poorly performing sectors such as capital goods. The excess return of the equity component of the portfolio attributable to sector allocation alone is 129 basis points, or 1.29%. As the equity component of the portfolio outperformed the S&P 500 by 1.47%, we conclude that the effect of security selection within sectors must have contributed an additional 1.47 − 1.29, or 0.18%, to the performance of the equity component of the portfolio.

A similar sector analysis can be applied to the fixed-income portion of the portfolio, but we do not show those results here.

Summing Up Component Contributions

In this particular month, all facets of the portfolio selection process were successful. Table 20.6 details the contribution of each aspect of performance. Asset allocation across the major security markets contributes 31 basis points. Sector and security allocation within those markets contributes 106 basis points, for total excess portfolio performance of 137 basis points.

The sector and security allocation of 106 basis points can be partitioned further. Sector allocation within the equity market results in excess performance of 129.3 basis points, and security selection within sectors contributes 18 basis points. (The total equity excess performance

TABLE **20.6** Portfolio attribution: summary			Contribution (basis points)
	1. Asset allocation		31.0
	2. Selection		
	a. Equity excess return		
	i. Sector allocation	129	
	ii. Security allocation	18	
		147 × 0.70 (portfolio weight) =	102.9
	b. Fixed-income excess return	44 × 0.07 (portfolio weight) =	3.1
	Total excess return of portfolio		137.0

of 147 basis points is multiplied by the 70% weight in equity to obtain contribution to portfolio performance.) Similar partitioning could be done for the fixed-income sector.

2. *a.* Suppose the benchmark weights had been set at 70% equity, 25% fixed-income, and 5% cash equivalents. What then would be the contributions of the manager's asset allocation choices?
   b. Suppose the S&P 500 return had been 5%. Recompute the contribution of the manager's security selection choices.

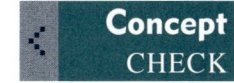

Concept
CHECK

20.3 | THE LURE OF ACTIVE MANAGEMENT

Now that we know how to measure the success of active portfolio managers, we reconsider the rationale for active management. How can a theory of active portfolio management make sense if we accept the notion that markets are in equilibrium? Chapter 8 on market efficiency gives a thorough analysis of efficient market theory; here we summarize how the theory fits with active management strategy.

Market efficiency prevails when many investors are willing to depart from a passive strategy of efficient diversification, so that they can add mispriced securities to their portfolios. Their objective is to realize "abnormal" returns.

The competition for such returns ensures that prices will be near their "fair" values. This means most managers will not beat the passive strategy *if we take risk into account with reward.* Exceptional managers, however, might beat the average forecasts that are built into market prices and consequently construct portfolios that will earn abnormal returns.

How can this happen? There is economic logic behind the result, as well as some empirical evidence indicating that exceptional portfolio managers can beat the average forecast. First the economic logic. If no analyst can beat the passive strategy, investors eventually will not be willing to pay for expensive analysis; they will adopt less-expensive, passive strategies. In that case, funds under active management will dry up, and prices will no longer reflect sophisticated forecasts. The resulting profit opportunities will lure back active managers who once again will become successful.[2] The critical assumption here is that investors make wise decisions on how to manage their money. Direct evidence on that has yet to be produced.

As for empirical evidence, consider the following: (1) some portfolio managers experience streaks of abnormal returns that are hard to label as lucky outcomes; (2) the "noise" in realized rates of return is enough that we cannot reject outright the hypothesis that some investment managers can beat the passive strategy by a statistically small, yet economically significant,

---

[2]This point is worked out fully in Sanford J. Grossman and Joseph E. Stiglitz, "On the Impossibility of Informationally Efficient Markets," *American Economic Review* 70 (June 1980), pp. 393–408.

Performance Attribution

The Excel model "Performance Attribution" that is available on the book's website is built on the example that appears in section 20.2. The model allows you to specify different allocations and to analyze the contribution sectors and weightings for different performances.

You can learn more about this spreadsheet model by using the interactive version available on our website at www.mhhe.com/bkm.

	A	B	C	D	E	F
1	Chapter 20 Performance Attribution					
2	Solution to Question					
3	**Bogey Portfolio**		**Weight**	**Return on**	**Portfolio**	
4	**Component**	**Index**	**Benchmark**	**Index**	**Return**	
5	Equity	S&P500	0.6	5.8100%	3.4860%	
6	Bonds	Lehman Index	0.3	1.4500%	0.4350%	
7	Cash	Money Market	0.1	0.4800%	0.0480%	
8						
9	Return on Bogey				3.9690%	
10						
11	**Managed Portfolio**		**Portfolio**	**Actual**	**Portfolio**	
12	**Component**		**Weight**	**Return**	**Return**	
13	Equity		0.75	6.5000%	4.8750%	
14	Bonds		0.12	1.2500%	0.1500%	
15	Cash		0.13	0.4800%	0.0624%	
16						
17	Return on Managed				5.0874%	
18						
19	Excess Return				1.1184%	
20						
21						
22			**Contribution of Asset Allocation**			
23		**Actual Weight**	**Benchmark**	**Excess**	**Market**	**Performance**
24	**Market**	**in Portfolio**	**Weight**	**Weight**	**Return**	**Contribution**
25						
26	Equity	0.75	0.6	0.15	5.8100%	0.8715%
27	Fixed Income	0.12	0.3	-0.18	1.4500%	-0.2610%
28	Cash	0.13	0.1	0.03	0.4800%	0.0144%
29	Contribution of					
30	Asset Allocation					0.6249%

margin; and (3) some anomalies in realized returns—such as the turn-of-the-year effects—have been sufficiently persistent to suggest that managers who identified them, and acted on them in a timely fashion, could have beaten the passive strategy over prolonged periods.

These observations are enough to convince us that there is a role for active portfolio management. Active management offers an inevitable lure, even if investors agree that security markets are *nearly* efficient.

At the extreme, suppose capital markets are perfectly efficient, an easily accessible market index portfolio is available, and this portfolio is the efficient risky portfolio. In this case, security selection would be futile. You would do best following a passive strategy of allocating funds to a money market fund (the safe asset) and the market index portfolio. Under these simplifying assumptions, the optimal investment strategy seems to require no effort or know-how.

But this is too hasty a conclusion. To allocate investment funds to the risk-free and risky portfolios requires some analysis. You need to decide the fraction, y, to be invested in the risky market portfolio, M, so you must know the reward-to-variability ratio

$$S_M = \frac{E(r_M) - r_f}{\sigma_M}$$

where $E(r_M) - r_f$ is the risk premium on M, and σ_M is the standard deviation of M. To make a rational allocation of funds requires an estimate of σ_M and $E(r_M)$, so even a passive investor needs to do some forecasting.

Forecasting $E(r_M)$ and σ_M is complicated further because security classes are affected by different environment factors. Long-term bond returns, for example, are driven largely by changes in the term structure of interest rates, while returns on equity depend also on changes in the broader economic environment, including macroeconomic factors besides interest rates. Once you begin considering how economic conditions influence separate sorts of investments, you might as well use a sophisticated asset allocation program to determine the proper mix for the portfolio. It is easy to see how investors get lured away from a purely passive strategy.

Even the definition of a "pure" passive strategy is not very clear-cut, as simple strategies involving only the market index portfolio and risk-free assets now seem to call for market analysis. Our strict definition of a pure passive strategy is one that invests only in index funds and weights those funds by fixed proportions that do not change in response to market conditions: a portfolio strategy that always places 60% in a stock market index fund, 30% in a bond index fund, and 10% in a money market fund, regardless of expectations.

Active management is attractive because the potential profit is enormous, even though competition among managers is bound to drive market prices to near-efficient levels. For prices to remain efficient to some degree, decent profits to diligent analysts must be the rule rather than the exception, although large profits may be difficult to earn. Absence of profits would drive people out of the investment management industry, resulting in prices moving away from informationally efficient levels.

Objectives of Active Portfolios

What does an investor expect from a professional portfolio manager, and how do these expectations affect the manager's response? If all clients were risk neutral (indifferent to risk), the answer would be straightforward: The investment manager should construct a portfolio with the highest possible expected rate of return, and the manager should then be judged by the realized *average* rate of return.

When the client is risk averse, the answer is more difficult. Lacking standards to proceed by, the manager would have to consult with each client before making any portfolio decision in order to ascertain that the prospective reward (average return) matched the client's attitude toward risk. Massive, continuous client input would be needed, and the economic value of professional management would be questionable.

Fortunately, the theory of mean-variance efficiency allows us to separate the "product decision," which is how to construct a mean-variance efficient risky portfolio, from the "consumption decision," which describes the investor's allocation of funds between the efficient risky portfolio and the safe asset. You have learned already that construction of the optimal risky portfolio is purely a technical problem and that there is a single optimal risky portfolio appropriate for all investors. Investors differ only in how they apportion investment between that risky portfolio and the safe asset.

The mean-variance theory also speaks to performance in offering a criterion for judging managers on their choice of risky portfolios. In Chapter 6, we established that the optimal risky portfolio is the one that maximizes the reward-to-variability ratio, that is, the expected excess return divided by the standard deviation. A manager who maximizes this ratio will satisfy all clients regardless of risk aversion.

Clients can evaluate managers using statistical methods to draw inferences from realized rates of return about prospective, or ex ante, reward-to-variability ratios. The Sharpe measure, or the equivalent M^2, is now a widely accepted way to track performance of professionally managed portfolios:

$$S_P = \frac{E(r_P) - r_f}{\sigma_P}$$

The most able manager will be the one who consistently obtains the highest Sharpe measure, implying that the manager has real forecasting ability. A client's judgment of a manager's ability will affect the fraction of investment funds allocated to this manager; the client can invest the remainder with competing managers and in a safe fund.

If managers' Sharpe measures were reasonably constant over time, and clients could reliably estimate them, allocating funds to managers would be an easy decision.

Actually, the use of the Sharpe measure as the prime measure of a manager's ability requires some qualification. We know from the discussion of performance evaluation earlier in this chapter that the Sharpe ratio is the appropriate measure of performance only when the client's entire wealth is managed by the professional investor. Moreover, clients may impose additional restrictions on portfolio choice that further complicate the performance evaluation problem.

20.4 | MARKET TIMING

Consider the results of three different investment strategies, as gleaned from Table 5.3:

1. Investor *X*, who put $1 in 30 day T-bills (or their predecessors) on January 1, 1926, and always rolled over all proceeds into 30-day T-bills, would have ended on December 31, 2001, 76 years later, with $16.98.

2. Investor *Y*, who put $1 in large stocks (the S&P 500 portfolio) on January 1, 1926, and reinvested all dividends in that portfolio, would have ended on December 31, 2001, with $1,987.01.

market timing

Asset allocation in which the investment in the market is increased if one forecasts that the market will outperform bills.

3. Suppose we define perfect **market timing** as the ability to tell with certainty at the beginning of each year whether stocks will outperform bills. Investor *Z*, the perfect timer, shifts all funds at the beginning of each year into either bills or stocks, whichever is going to do better. Beginning at the same date, how much would Investor *Z* have ended up with 76 years later? Answer: $115,233.89!

Concept
CHECK

3. **What are the annually compounded rates of return for the *X*, *Y*, and perfect-timing strategies over the period 1926–2001?**

These results have some lessons for us. The first has to do with the power of compounding. Its effect is particularly important as more and more of the funds under management represent pension savings. The horizons of pension investments may not be as long as 76 years, but they are measured in decades, making compounding a significant factor.

The second is a huge difference between the end value of the all-safe asset strategy ($16.98) and of the all-equity strategy ($1,987.01). Why would anyone invest in safe assets given this historical record? If you have absorbed all the lessons of this book, you know the reason: risk. The averages of the annual rates of return and the standard deviations on the all-bills and all-equity strategies were

	Arithmetic Mean	Standard Deviation
Bills	3.85%	3.25%
Equities	12.49	20.30

The significantly higher standard deviation of the rate of return on the equity portfolio is commensurate with its significantly higher average return. The higher average return reflects the risk premium.

Is the return premium on the perfect-timing strategy a risk premium? Because the perfect timer never does worse than either bills or the market, the extra return cannot be compensation for the possibility of poor returns; instead it is attributable to superior analysis. The value of superior information is reflected in the tremendous ending value of the portfolio. This value does not reflect compensation for risk.

To see why, consider how you might choose between two hypothetical strategies. Strategy 1 offers a sure rate of return of 5%; strategy 2 offers an uncertain return that is given by 5% *plus* a random number that is zero with a probability of 0.5 and 5% with a probability of 0.5. The results for each strategy are

	Strategy 1 (%)	Strategy 2 (%)
Expected return	5	7.5
Standard deviation	0	2.5
Highest return	5	10
Lowest return	5	5

Clearly, strategy 2 dominates strategy 1, as its rate of return is *at least* equal to that of strategy 1 and sometimes greater. No matter how risk averse you are, you will always prefer strategy 2 to strategy 1, even though strategy 2 has a significant standard deviation. Compared to strategy 1, strategy 2 provides only good surprises, so the standard deviation in this case cannot be a measure of risk.

You can look at these strategies as analogous to the case of the perfect timer compared with either an all-equity or all-bills strategy. In every period, the perfect timer obtains at least as good a return, in some cases better. Therefore, the timer's standard deviation is a misleading measure of risk when you compare perfect timing to an all-equity or all-bills strategy.

Valuing Market Timing as an Option

Merton (1981) shows that the key to analyzing the pattern of returns of a perfect market timer is to compare the returns of a perfect foresight investor with those of another investor who holds a call option on the equity portfolio. Investing 100% in bills plus holding a call option on the equity portfolio will yield returns identical to those of the portfolio of the perfect timer who invests 100% in either the safe asset or the equity portfolio, whichever will yield the higher return. The perfect timer's return is shown in Figure 20.5. The rate of return is bounded from below by the risk-free rate, r_f.

To see how the value of information can be treated as an option, suppose the market index currently is at S_0 and a call option on the index has exercise price of $X = S_0(1 + r_f)$. If the market outperforms bills over the coming period, S_T will exceed X; it will be less than X otherwise. Now look at the payoff to a portfolio consisting of this option and S_0 dollars invested in bills.

	Payoff to Portfolio	
Outcome:	$S_T \leq X$	$S_T > X$
Bills	$S_0(1 + r_f)$	$S_0(1 + r_f)$
Option	0	$S_T - X$
Total	$S_0(1 + r_f)$	S_T

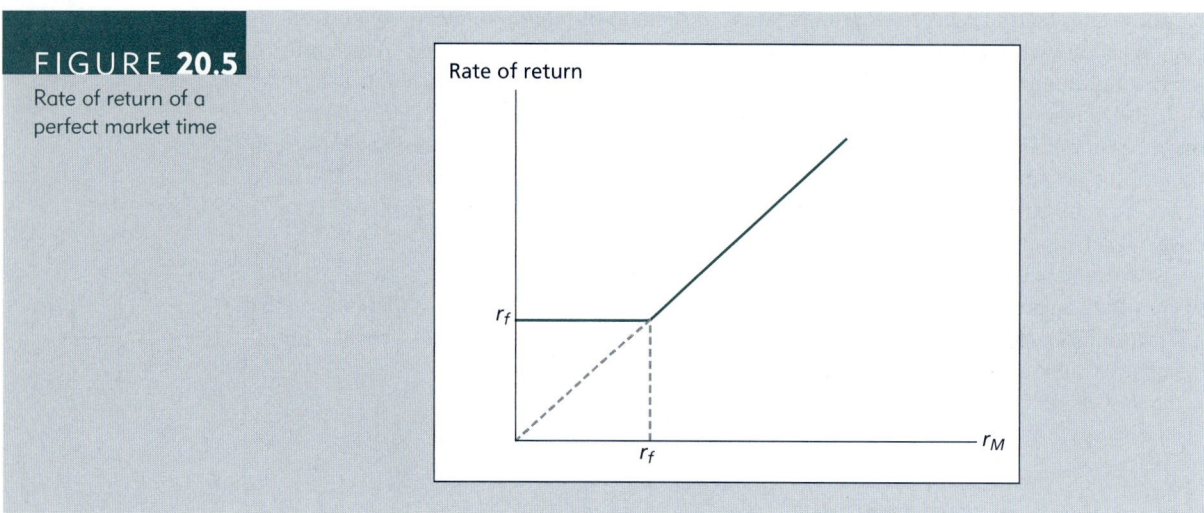

FIGURE 20.5

Rate of return of a perfect market time

The portfolio returns the risk-free rate when the market is bearish (that is, when the market return is less than the risk-free rate) and pays the market return when the market is bullish and beats bills. This represents perfect market timing. Consequently, the value of perfect timing ability is equivalent to the value of the call option, for a call enables the investor to earn the market return only when it exceeds r_f.

Valuation of the call option embedded in market timing is relatively straightforward using the Black-Scholes formula. Set $S = \$1$ (to find the value of the call per dollar invested in the market), use an exercise price of $X = (1 + r_f)$ (the current risk-free rate is about 3%), and a volatility of $\sigma = .203$ (the historical volatility of the S&P 500). For a once-a-year timer, $T = 1$ year. According to the Black-Scholes formula, the call option conveyed by market timing ability is worth about 8.1% of assets, and this is the annual fee one could presumably charge for such services. More frequent timing would be worth more. If one could time the market on a monthly basis, then $T = \frac{1}{12}$ and the value of perfect timing would be 2.3% *per month*.

The Value of Imperfect Forecasting

But managers are not perfect forecasters. While managers who are right most of the time presumably do very well, "right most of the time" does not mean merely the *percentage* of the time a manager is right. For example, a Tucson, Arizona, weather forecaster who *always* predicts "no rain" may be right 90% of the time, but this "stopped clock" strategy does not require any forecasting ability.

Neither is the overall proportion of correct forecasts an appropriate measure of market forecasting ability. If the market is up two days out of three, and a forecaster always predicts a market advance, the two-thirds success rate is not a measure of forecasting ability. We need to examine the proportion of bull markets ($r_M > r_f$) correctly forecast *and* the proportion of bear markets ($r_M < r_f$) correctly forecast.

If we call P_1 the proportion of the correct forecasts of bull markets and P_2 the proportion for bear markets, then $P_1 + P_2 - 1$ is the correct measure of timing ability. For example, a forecaster who always guesses correctly will have $P_1 = P_2 = 1$ and will show ability of 1 (100%). An analyst who always bets on a bear market will mispredict all bull markets ($P_1 = 0$), will correctly "predict" all bear markets ($P_2 = 1$), and will end up with timing ability of $P_1 + P_2 - 1 = 0$. If C denotes the (call option) value of a perfect market timer, then $(P_1 + P_2 - 1)C$ measures the value of imperfect forecasting ability.

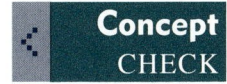

FIGURE **20.6**
Characteristic lines
A: No market timing,
beta is constant
B: Market timing,
beta increases with
expected market
excess return

The incredible potential payoff to accurate timing versus the relative scarcity of billionaires should suggest to you that market timing is far from a trivial exercise and that very imperfect timing is the most that we can hope for.

4. **What is the market timing score of someone who flips a fair coin to predict the market?**

Concept
CHECK

Measurement of Market Timing Performance

In its pure form, market timing involves shifting funds between a market index portfolio and a safe asset, such as T-bills or a money market fund, depending on whether the market as a whole is expected to outperform the safe asset. In practice, most managers do not shift fully between bills and the market. How might we measure partial shifts into the market when it is expected to perform well?

To simplify, suppose the investor holds only the market index portfolio and T-bills. If the weight on the market were constant, say 0.6, then the portfolio beta would also be constant, and the portfolio characteristic line would plot as a straight line with a slope 0.6, as in Figure 20.6A. If, however, the investor could correctly time the market and shift funds into it in periods when the market does well, the characteristic line would plot as in Figure 20.6B. The idea is that if the timer can predict bull and bear markets, more will be shifted into the market when the market is about to go up. The portfolio beta and the slope of the characteristic line will be higher when r_M is higher, resulting in the curved line that appears in 20.6B.

Treynor and Mazuy (1966) tested to see whether portfolio betas did in fact increase prior to market advances, but they found little evidence of timing ability. A similar test was implemented by Henriksson (1984). His examination of market timing ability for 116 funds in

TABLE **20.7** Sharpe's style portfolios for the Magellan fund	Regression Coefficient*
Bills	0
Intermediate bonds	0
Long-term bonds	0
Corporate bonds	0
Mortgages	0
Value stocks	0
Growth stocks	47
Medium-cap stocks	31
Small stocks	18
Foreign stocks	0
European stocks	4
Japanese stocks	0
Total	100.00
R-squared	97.3

*Regressions are constrained to have nonnegative coefficients and to have coefficients that sum to 100%.

Source: William F. Sharpe, "Asset Allocation: Management Style and Performance Evaluation," *Journal of Portfolio Management,* Winter 1992, pp. 7–19.

1968–1980 found that, on average, portfolio betas actually *fell* slightly during the market advances, although in most cases the response of portfolio betas to the market was not statistically significant. Eleven funds had statistically positive values of market timing, while eight had significantly negative values. Overall, 62% of the funds had negative point estimates of timing ability.

In sum, empirical tests to date show little evidence of market timing ability. Perhaps this should be expected; given the tremendous values to be reaped by a successful market timer, it would be surprising to uncover clear-cut evidence of such skills in nearly efficient markets.

20.5 STYLE ANALYSIS

Style analysis was introduced by Nobel laureate William Sharpe.[3] The popularity of the concept was aided by a well-known study[4] concluding that 91.5% of the variation in returns of 82 mutual funds could be explained by the funds' asset allocation to bills, bonds, and stocks. Later studies that considered asset allocation across a broader range of asset classes found that as much as 97% of fund returns can be explained by asset allocation alone.

Sharpe considered 12 asset class (style) portfolios. His idea was to regress fund returns on indexes representing a range of asset classes. The regression coefficient on each index would then measure the implicit allocation to that "style." Because funds are barred from short positions, the regression coefficients are constrained to be either zero or positive and to sum to 100%, so as to represent a complete asset allocation. The *R*-square of the regression would then measure the percentage of return variability attributed to the effects of security selection.

To illustrate the approach, consider Sharpe's study of the monthly returns on Fidelity's Magellan Fund over the period January 1985 through December 1989, shown in Table 20.7.

---

[3]William F. Sharpe, "Asset Allocation: Management Style and Performance Evaluation," *Journal of Portfolio Management,* Winter 1992, pp. 7–19.

[4]Gary Brinson, Brian Singer, and Gilbert Beebower, "Determinants of Portfolio Performance," *Financial Analysts Journal,* May/June 1991.

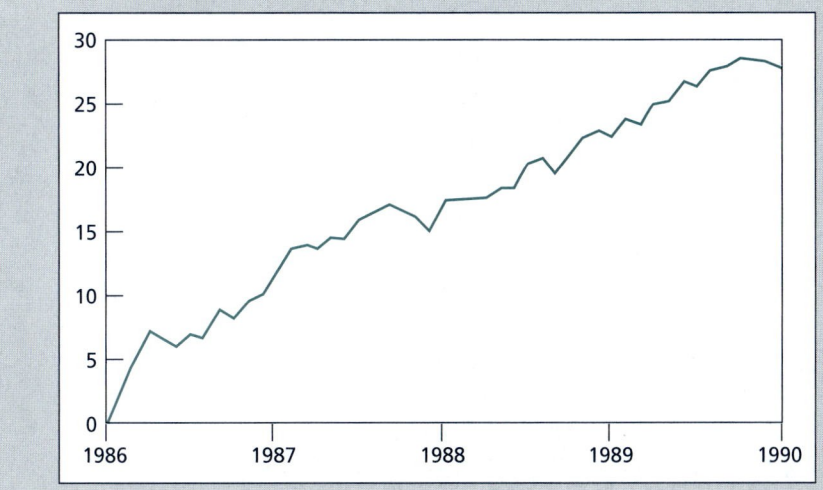

FIGURE 20.7

Fidelity Magellan Fund cumulative return difference: fund versus style benchmark

Source: William F. Sharpe, "Asset Allocation: Management Style and Performance Evaluation," *Journal of Portfolio Management*, Winter 1992, pp. 7–19.

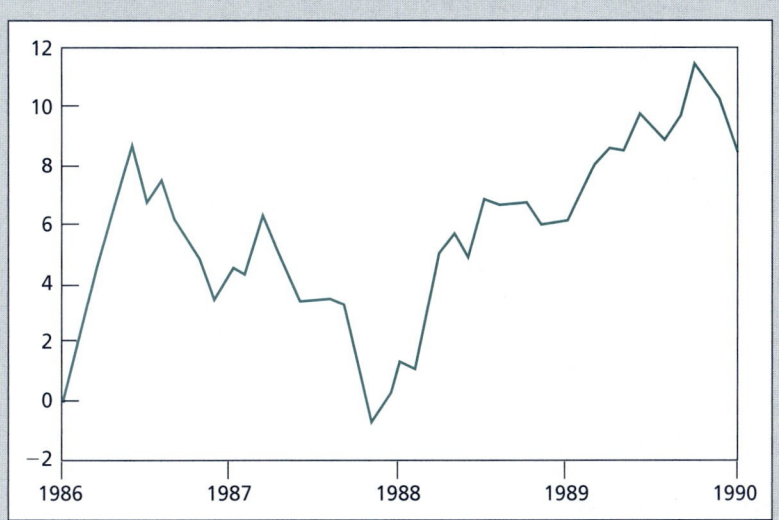

FIGURE 20.8

Fidelity Magellan Fund cumulative return difference: fund versus S&P 500

Source: William F. Sharpe, "Asset Allocation: Management Style and Performance Evaluation," *Journal of Portfolio Management*, Winter 1992, pp. 7–19.

While there are 12 asset classes, each one represented by a stock index, the regression coefficients are positive for only 4 of them. We can conclude that the fund returns are well explained by only four style portfolios. Moreover, these three style portfolios alone explain 97.3% of returns.

The proportion of return variability *not* explained by asset allocation can be attributed to security selection within asset classes. For Magellan, this was $100 - 97.3 = 2.7\%$. To evaluate the average contribution of stock selection to fund performance we track the residuals from the regression, displayed in Figure 20.7. The figure plots the cumulative effect of these residuals; the steady upward trend confirms Magellan's success at stock selection in this period. Notice that the plot in Figure 20.7 is far smoother than the plot in Figure 20.8, which shows Magellan's performance compared to a standard benchmark, the S&P 500. This reflects the fact that the regression-weighted index portfolio tracks Magellan's overall style much better than the S&P 500. The performance spread is much noisier using the S&P as the benchmark.

Of course, Magellan's consistently positive residual returns (reflected in the steadily increasing plot of cumulative return difference) is hardly common. Figure 20.9 shows the

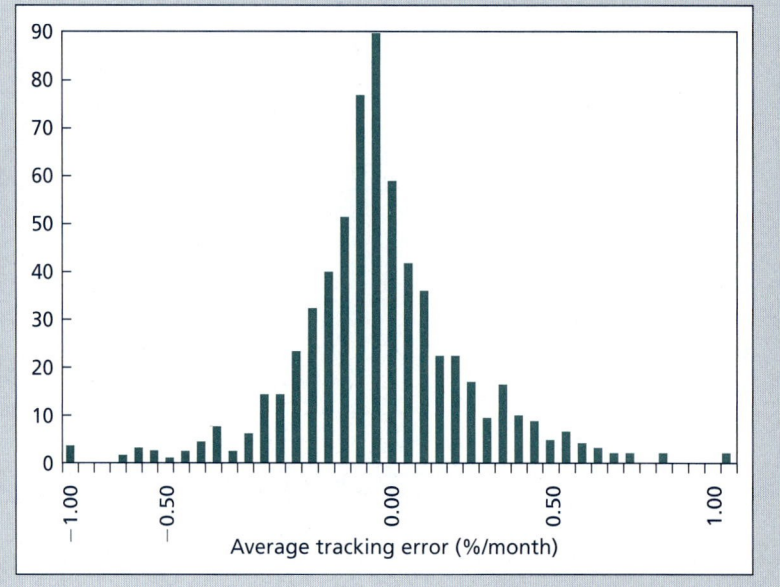

FIGURE 20.9

Average tracking error, 636 mutual funds, 1985–1989

Source: William F. Sharpe, "Asset Allocation: Management Style and Performance Evaluation," *Journal of Portfolio Management,* Winter 1992, pp. 7–19.

frequency distribution of average residuals across 636 mutual funds. The distribution has the familiar bell shape with a slightly negative mean of −.074% per month.

Style analysis has become very popular in the investment management industry and has spawned quite a few variations on Sharpe's methodology. Many portfolio managers utilize websites that help investors identify their style and stock selection performance.

20.6 MORNINGSTAR'S RISK-ADJUSTED RATING

The commercial success of Morningstar, Inc., the premier source of information on mutual funds, has made its *Risk Adjusted Rating* (RAR) among the most widely used performance measures. The Morningstar five-star rating is coveted by the managers of the thousands of funds covered by the service.

Morningstar calculates a number of RAR performance measures that are similar, although not identical, to the standard mean-variance measures. The most distinct measure, the Morningstar Star Rating, is based on comparison of each fund to a peer group. The peer group for each fund is selected on the basis of the fund's investment universe (e.g., international, growth versus value, fixed-income, and so on) as well as portfolio characteristics such as average price-to-book value, price-earnings ratio, and market capitalization.

Morningstar computes fund returns (adjusted for loads) as well as a risk measure based on fund performance in its worst years. The risk-adjusted performance is ranked across funds in a style group and stars are awarded based on the following table:

Percentile	Stars
0–10	1
10–32.5	2
32.5–67.5	3
67.5–90	4
90–100	5

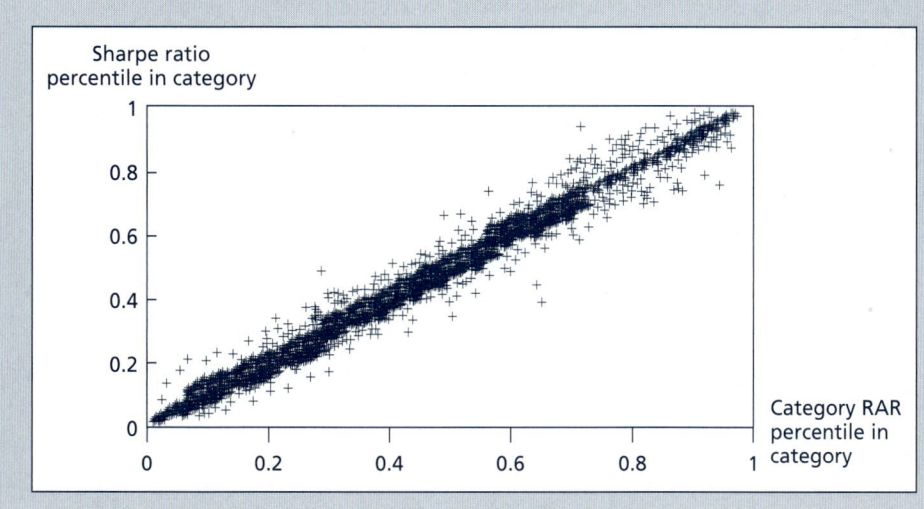

FIGURE 20.10

Rankings based on Morningstar's category RARs and excess return Sharpe ratios

Source: William F. Sharpe, "Morningstar Performance Measures," www.wsharpe.com.

The Morningstar RAR method produces results that are similar but not identical to that of the mean/variance-based Sharpe ratios. Figure 20.10 demonstrates the fit between ranking by RAR and by Sharpe ratios from the performance of 1,286 diversified equity funds over the period 1994–1996. Sharpe notes that this period is characterized by high returns that contribute to a good fit.

20.7 SECURITY SELECTION: THE TREYNOR-BLACK MODEL

Overview of the Treynor-Black Model

Security analysis is the other dimension of active investment besides timing the overall market and asset allocation. Suppose you are an analyst studying individual securities. Quite likely, you will turn up several securities that appear to be mispriced and offer positive alphas. But how do you exploit your analysis? Concentrating a portfolio on these securities entails a cost, namely, the firm-specific risk you could shed by more fully diversifying. As an active manager, you must strike a balance between aggressive exploitation of security mispricing and diversification considerations that dictate against concentrating a portfolio in a few stocks.

Jack Treynor and Fischer Black (1973) developed a portfolio construction model for managers who use security analysis. It assumes security markets are nearly efficient. The essence of the model is this:

1. Security analysts in an active investment management organization can analyze in depth only a relatively small number of stocks out of the entire universe of securities. The securities not analyzed are assumed to be fairly priced.

2. For the purpose of efficient diversification, the market index portfolio is the baseline portfolio, which is treated as the passive portfolio.

3. The macro forecasting unit of the investment management firm provides forecasts of the expected rate of return and variance of the passive (market index) portfolio.

4. The objective of security analysis is to form an active portfolio of a necessarily limited number of securities. Perceived mispricing of the analyzed securities is what determines the composition of this active portfolio.

5. Analysts follow several steps to make up the active portfolio and forecast its performance:

   a. Estimate the characteristic line of each analyzed security and obtain its beta and residual variance. From the beta and the macro forecast, $E(r_M) - r_f$, determine the *required* rate of return of the security.

   b. Determine the expected return. Subtracting the required return yields the expected *abnormal* return (alpha) of the security.

   c. Use the estimates for the values of alpha, beta, and residual risk to determine the optimal weight of each security in the active portfolio.

   d. Estimate the alpha, beta, and residual variance for the active portfolio according to the weights of the securities in the portfolio.

6. The macroeconomic forecasts for the passive index portfolio and the composite forecast for the active portfolio are used to determine the optimal risky portfolio, which will be a combination of the passive and active portfolios.

Treynor-Black model

An optimizing model for portfolio managers who use security analysis in a nearly efficient market.

Although some sophisticated investment managers use the **Treynor-Black model,** it has not taken the industry by storm. This is unfortunate for several reasons:

1. Just as even imperfect market-timing ability has enormous value, security analysis of the sort Treynor and Black propose has similar potential value. Even with far-from-perfect security analysis, active management can add value.

2. The Treynor-Black model is easy to implement. Moreover, it is useful even relaxing some of its simplifying assumptions.

3. The model lends itself to use with decentralized decision making, which is essential to efficiency in complex organizations.

Portfolio Construction

Assuming all securities are fairly priced and using the index model as a guideline for the rate of return on securities, the rate of return on security i is given by

$$r_i = r_f + \beta_i(r_M - r_f) + e_i \qquad (20.1)$$

where e_i is the zero mean, firm-specific (nonsystematic) component.

Absent security analysis, Treynor and Black take Equation 20.1 to represent the rate of return on all securities and assume the index portfolio (M) is efficient. For simplicity, they also assume the nonsystematic components of returns, e_i, are independent across securities. Market timing is incorporated in the terms r_M and σ_M, representing index portfolio forecasts. The overall investment in the risky portfolio will be affected by the optimism or pessimism reflected in these numbers.

Assume a team of security analysts investigates a subset of the universe of available securities, with the objective of forming an active portfolio. That portfolio will then be mixed with the index portfolio to improve diversification. For each security, k, that is researched, we write the rate of return as

$$r_k = r_f + \beta_k(r_M - r_f) + e_k + \alpha_k \qquad (20.2)$$

where α_k represents the extra (abnormal) expected return attributable to the mispricing of the security. Thus, for each security analyzed, the research team estimates the parameters

$$\alpha_k, \beta_k, \sigma^2(e_k)$$

If all the α_k turn out to be zero, there would be no reason to depart from the passive strategy, and the index portfolio would remain the manager's choice. But this is a remote

FIGURE **20.11**
The optimization process with active and passive portfolios

possibility. In general, there will be a significant number of nonzero α values, some positive and some negative.

Consider first how you would use the active portfolio once you found it. Suppose the **active portfolio** (A) has been constructed and has the parameters

$$\alpha_A, \beta_A, \sigma^2(e_A)$$

The total variance of the active portfolio is the sum of its systematic variance, $\beta_A^2\sigma_M^2$, plus the nonsystematic variance, $\sigma^2(e_A)$. These three parameters, plus the mean and variance of the index portfolio, are sufficient to identify the opportunity set generated by the active and passive portfolios.

Figure 20.11 shows the optimization process with active and passive portfolios. The dashed efficient frontier line represents the universe of all securities, assuming they are all fairly priced, that is, that all alphas are zero. By definition, the market index (M) is on this efficient frontier and is tangent to the (dashed) capital market line (CML). In practice, our analysts do not need to (indeed cannot) know this frontier, but they need to forecast the index portfolio and construct the optimal risky portfolio using the index and active (A) portfolios. The optimal portfolio (P) will lie on the capital allocation line (CAL) that lies above the CML.

From the viewpoint of an investor with superior analysis, the index portfolio will be inefficient; that is, the active portfolio (A) constructed from mispriced securities will lie above the CML.

The optimal combination of the active portfolio with the passive portfolio takes off from the construction of an optimal risky portfolio from two risky assets that we first encountered in Chapter 6. As the active portfolio is not perfectly correlated with the index, further diversification—that is, mixing it with the index—is likely to be beneficial.

We can judge the success of active management, and the contribution of the active portfolio (A), by the Sharpe measure (ratio of reward to variability) of the resultant risky portfolio (P), compared with that of the index portfolio (M).

active portfolio

In the context of the Treynor-Black model, the portfolio formed by mixing analyzed stocks with perceived nonzero alpha values. This portfolio is ultimately mixed with the passive market index portfolio.

The mathematics of the efficient frontier reveal that the Sharpe measure of the risky portfolio is

$$S(P) = [S^2(M) + \alpha_A^2/\sigma^2(e_A)]^{1/2} \qquad (20.3)$$

Thus, the critical variable in determining the success of the active portfolio is its ratio of alpha to nonsystematic risk, $\alpha_A/\sigma(e_A)$.

The intuition here is straightforward. You mix the active portfolio with the index for the benefit of diversification. The position to take in the active portfolio relative to the market portfolio depends on the ratio of the active portfolio's abnormal return, α_A, relative to its weakness given by its diversifiable risk, $\sigma(e_A)$. This ratio is sometimes referred to as the *appraisal ratio*.

The contribution of individual securities (say, k) to the active portfolio (A) is analogous to that of the active portfolio to the risky portfolio (P). It is measured by the appraisal ratio, $\alpha_k/\sigma(e_k)$.

SUMMARY

- The appropriate performance measure depends on the investment context. The Sharpe measure is most appropriate when the portfolio represents the entire investment fund. The Treynor measure or Jensen measure is appropriate when the portfolio is to be mixed with several other assets, allowing for diversification of firm-specific risk outside of each portfolio.

- The shifting mean and variance of actively managed portfolios make it harder to assess performance. A typical example is the attempt of portfolio managers to time the market, resulting in ever-changing portfolio betas and standard deviations.

- Common attribution procedures partition performance improvements to asset allocation, sector selection, and security selection. Performance is assessed by calculating departures of portfolio composition from a benchmark or neutral portfolio.

- Active portfolio managers attempt to construct a risky portfolio that improves on the reward-to-variability (Sharpe) ratio of a passive strategy.

- Active management has two components: market timing (or, more generally, asset allocation) and security analysis.

- The value of perfect market-timing ability is enormous. The rate of return to a perfect market timer will be uncertain, but the risk cannot be measured by standard deviation, because perfect timing dominates a passive strategy, providing only "good" surprises.

- Perfect-timing ability is equivalent to having a call option on the market portfolio. The value of that option can be determined using valuation techniques such as the Black-Scholes formula.

- The value of *imperfect* market timing depends on the sum of the probabilities of the true outcome conditional on the forecast: $P_1 + P_2 - 1$. If perfect timing is equivalent to call option C, then imperfect timing can be valued by: $(P_1 + P_2 - 1)C$.

- The Treynor-Black model is based on an index model that takes market-timing forecasts as given. The investment manager uses security analysis to construct an active portfolio. The active portfolio is mixed with the index portfolio to maximize the Sharpe measure of the optimal risky portfolio.

- In the Treynor-Black model, the weight of each analyzed security is proportional to the ratio of its alpha to its residual variance.

active portfolio, 711
bogey, 694
comparison universe, 684

Jensen measure, 686
market timing, 702
Sharpe measure, 686

Treynor-Black model, 710
Treynor measure, 686

Questions 1–3 appeared in past CFA examinations.

1. A plan sponsor with a portfolio manager who invests in small-capitalization, high-growth stocks should have the plan sponsor's performance measured against which *one* of the following?
   a. S&P 500 index.
   b. Wilshire 5000 index.
   c. Dow Jones Industrial Average.
   d. Russell 2000 index.

2. Assume you purchased a rental property for $50,000 and sold it one year later for $55,000 (there was no mortgage on the property). At the time of the sale, you paid $2,000 in commissions and $600 in taxes. If you received $6,000 in rental income (all of it received at the end of the year), what annual rate of return did you earn?
   a. 15.3%
   b. 15.9%
   c. 16.8%
   d. 17.1%

3. A two-year investment of $2,000 results in a return of $150 at the end of the first year and a return of $150 at the end of the second year, in addition to the return of the original investment. The internal rate of return on the investment is:
   a. 6.4%
   b. 7.5%
   c. 15.0%
   d. None of the above

4. Based on current dividend yields and expected capital gains, the expected rates of return on portfolios A and B are 11% and 14%, respectively. The beta of A is 0.8 while that of B is 1.5. The T-bill rate is currently 6%, while the expected rate of return of the S&P 500 index is 12%. The standard deviation of portfolio A is 10% annually, while that of B is 31%, and that of the index is 20%.
   a. If you currently hold a market index portfolio, would you choose to add either of these portfolios to your holdings? Explain.
   b. If instead you could invest *only* in bills and *one* of these portfolios, which would you choose?

5. Evaluate the timing and selection abilities of four managers whose performances are plotted in the following four scatter diagrams.

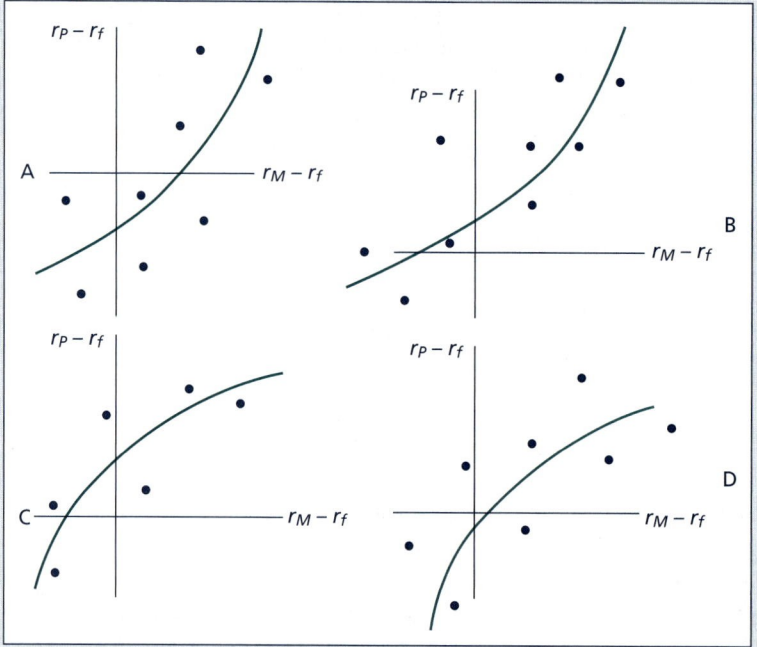

6. Consider the following information regarding the performance of a money manager in a recent month. The table presents the actual return of each sector of the manager's portfolio in column (1), the fraction of the portfolio allocated to each sector in column (2), the benchmark or neutral sector allocations in column (3), and the returns of sector indexes in column (4).

	(1) Actual Return	(2) Actual Weight	(3) Benchmark Weight	(4) Index Return
Equity	2.0%	0.70	0.60	2.5% (S&P 500)
Bonds	1.0	0.20	0.30	1.2 (Aggregate Bond index)
Cash	0.5	0.10	0.10	0.5

a. What was the manager's return in the month? What was her over- or underperformance?

b. What was the contribution of security selection to relative performance?

c. What was the contribution of asset allocation to relative performance? Confirm that the sum of selection and allocation contributions equals her total "excess" return relative to the bogey.

7. Conventional wisdom says one should measure a manager's investment performance over an entire market cycle. What arguments support this contention? What arguments contradict it?

8. Does the use of universes of managers with similar investment styles to evaluate relative investment performance overcome the statistical problems associated with instability of beta or total variability?

9. During a particular year, the T-bill rate was 6%, the market return was 14%, and a portfolio manager with beta of 0.5 realized a return of 10%. Evaluate the manager based on the portfolio alpha.

10. The chairman provides you with the following data, covering one year, concerning the portfolios of two of the fund's equity managers (manager *A* and manager *B*). Although the portfolios consist primarily of common stocks, cash reserves are included in the calculation of both portfolio betas and performance. By way of perspective, selected data for the financial markets are included in the following table.

	Total Return	Beta
Manager A	24.0%	1.0
Manager B	30.0	1.5
S&P 500	21.0	
Lehman Bond Index	31.0	
91-day Treasury bills	12.0	

   a. Calculate and compare the risk-adjusted performance of the two managers relative to each other and to the S&P 500.

   b. Explain *two* reasons the conclusions drawn from this calculation may be misleading.

11. Carl Karl, a portfolio manager for the Alpine Trust Company, has been responsible since 1990 for the City of Alpine's Employee Retirement Plan, a municipal pension fund. Alpine is a growing community, and city services and employee payrolls have expanded in each of the past 10 years. Contributions to the plan in fiscal 1995 exceeded benefit payments by a three-to-one ratio.

   The plan's Board of Trustees directed Karl five years ago to invest for total return over the long term. However, as trustees of this highly visible public fund, they cautioned him that volatile or erratic results could cause them embarrassment. They also noted a state statute that mandated that not more than 25% of the plan's assets (at cost) be invested in common stocks.

   At the annual meeting of the trustees in November 1995, Karl presented the following portfolio and performance report to the Board.

ALPINE EMPLOYEE RETIREMENT PLAN

Asset Mix as of 9/30/95	At Cost (millions)		At Market (millions)	
Fixed-income assets:				
Short-term securities	$ 4.5	11.0%	$ 4.5	11.4%
Long-term bonds and mortgages	26.5	64.7	23.5	59.5
Common stocks	10.0	24.3	11.5	29.1
	$41.0	100.0%	$39.5	100.0%

INVESTMENT PERFORMANCE

	Annual Rates of Return for Periods Ending 9/30/95	
	5 Years	1 Year
Total Alpine Fund:		
Time-weighted	8.2%	5.2%
Dollar-weighted (Internal)	7.7%	4.8%
Assumed actuarial return	6.0%	6.0%

U.S. Treasury bills	7.5%	11.3%
Large sample of pension funds (average 60% equities, 40% fixed income)	10.1%	14.3%
Common stocks—Alpine Fund	13.3%	14.3%
Average portfolio beta coefficient	0.90	0.89
Standard & Poor's 500 stock index	13.8%	21.1%
Fixed-income securities—Alpine Fund	6.7%	1.0%
Salomon Brothers' bond index	4.0%	−11.4%

Karl was proud of his performance and was chagrined when a trustee made the following critical observations:

a. "Our one-year results were terrible, and it's what you've done for us lately that counts most."

b. "Our total fund performance was clearly inferior compared to the large sample of other pension funds for the last five years. What else could this reflect except poor management judgment?"

c. "Our common stock performance was especially poor for the five-year period."

d. "Why bother to compare your returns to the return from Treasury bills and the actuarial assumption rate? What your competition could have earned for us or how we would have fared if invested in a passive index (which doesn't charge a fee) are the only relevant measures of performance."

e. "Who cares about time-weighted return? If it can't pay pensions, what good is it!"

Appraise the merits of each of these statements and give counterarguments that Mr. Karl can use.

12. Historical data suggest the standard deviation of an all-equity strategy is about 5.5% per month. Suppose the risk-free rate is now 1% per month and market volatility is at its historical level. What would be a fair monthly fee to a perfect market timer, according to the Black-Scholes formula?

13. A fund manager scrutinizing the record of two market timers comes up with this information:

Number of months that $r_M > r_f$	135
Correctly predicted by timer A	78
Correctly predicted by timer B	86
Number of months that $r_M < r_f$	92
Correctly predicted by timer A	57
Correctly predicted by timer B	50

a. What are the conditional probabilities, P_1 and P_2, and the total ability parameters for timers A and B?

b. Using the historical data of problem 12, what is a fair monthly fee for the two timers?

14. A portfolio manager summarizes the input from the macro and micro forecasts in the following table:

Micro Forecasts			
Asset	Expected Return (%)	Beta	Residual Standard Deviation (%)
Stock A	20	1.3	58
Stock B	18	1.8	71
Stock C	17	0.7	60
Stock D	12	1.0	55

Macro Forecasts		
Asset	Expected Return (%)	Standard Deviation (%)
T-bills	8	0
Passive equity portfolio	16	23

a. Calculate expected excess returns, alpha values, and residual variances for these stocks.

b. Construct the optimal risky portfolio.

c. What is Sharpe's measure for the optimal portfolio and how much of it is contributed by the active portfolio? What is the M^2?

WEBMASTER

Analyzing Performance

Go to http://www.morningstar.com/Cover/Funds.html to access the Morningstar Fund Quick Rank program.

Using this screening program, get a listing of funds that are ranked the highest in both 5- and 10-year returns. From those lists, select the highest-ranking fund that appears on both lists. Once you have identified the fund, click on its ticker to get a Morningstar Quicktake report. Using that report, answer the following questions:

1. What is the fund's Sharpe ratio?

2. What are the beta and alpha coefficients for both the S&P 500 and the Russell 2000 Index?

3. What are the top three investment sectors in the fund?

---

1. Sharpe: $(\bar{r} - \bar{r}_f)/\sigma$

$S_P = (35 - 6)/42 = 0.69$

$S_M = (28 - 6)/30 = 0.733$

Jensen: $\bar{r} - [\bar{r}_f + \beta(\bar{r}_M - \bar{r}_f)]$

$\alpha_P = 35 - [6 + 1.2(28 - 6)] = 2.6\%$

$\alpha_M = 0$

Treynor: $(\bar{r} - \bar{r}_f)/\beta$

$T_P = (35 - 6)/1.2 = 24.2$

$T_M = (28 - 6)/1.0 = 22$

SOLUTIONS TO

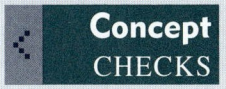

Concept CHECKS

www.mhhe.com/bkm

2. Performance attribution
   First compute the new bogey performance as
   $(0.70 \times 5.81) + (0.25 \times 1.45) + (0.05 \times 0.48) = 4.45\%$
   a. Contribution of asset allocation to performance

Market	(1) Actual Weight in Market	(2) Benchmark Weight in Market	(3) Excess Weight	(4) Index Return (%)	(5) = (3) × (4) Contribution to Performance (%)
Equity	0.70	0.70	0.00	5.81	0.000
Fixed-income	0.07	0.25	−0.18	1.45	−.261
Cash	0.23	0.05	0.18	0.48	.086
Contribution of asset allocation					−.175

   b. Contribution of selection to total performance

Market	(1) Portfolio Performance (%)	(2) Index Performance (%)	(3) Excess Performance (%)	(4) Portfolio Weight	(5) = (3) × (4) Contribution (%)
Equity	7.28	5.00	2.28	0.70	1.60
Fixed-income	1.89	1.45	0.44	0.07	0.03
Contribution of selection within markets					1.63

3. Beginning-of-period fund: $F_0 = \$1$
   End-of-period fund for each strategy:

$$F_1 = \begin{cases} 16.98 & \text{Strategy} = \text{Bills only} \\ 1,987.01 & \text{Strategy} = \text{Market only} \\ 115,233.89 & \text{Strategy} = \text{Perfect timing} \end{cases}$$

Number of periods: $N = 76$ years
Annual compounded rate:

$$(1 + r_A)^N = \frac{F_1}{F_0}$$

$$r_A = \left(\frac{F_1}{F_0}\right)^{1/N} - 1$$

$$r_A = \begin{cases} 3.80\% & \text{Strategy} = \text{Bills only} \\ 10.51\% & \text{Strategy} = \text{Market only} \\ 16.57\% & \text{Strategy} = \text{Perfect timing} \end{cases}$$

4. The timer will guess bear or bull markets randomly. One-half of all bull markets will be preceded by a correct forecast, and similarly, one-half of all bear markets will be preceded by a correct forecast. Hence, $P_1 + P_2 - 1 = 1/2 + 1/2 - 1 = 0$.

21

INTERNATIONAL INVESTING

AFTER STUDYING THIS CHAPTER YOU SHOULD BE ABLE TO:

> Demonstrate the advantages of international diversification.

> Formulate hedge strategies to offset the currency risk involved in international investments.

> Understand international investment strategies.

> Decompose investment returns into contributing factors such as country, currency, and stock selection.

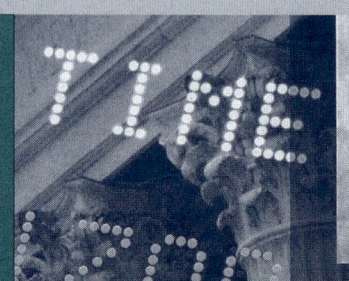

Although we in the United States customarily treat the S&P 500 as the market index portfolio, this practice is increasingly inappropriate. Equities represent less than 25% of total U.S. wealth and a much smaller proportion than that of world wealth. In this chapter, we look beyond domestic markets to survey issues of extended diversification.

In one sense, international investing may be viewed as no more than a straight-forward generalization of our earlier treatment of portfolio selection with a larger menu of assets from which to construct a portfolio. One faces similar issues of diversification, security analysis, security selection, and asset allocation. On the other hand, international investments pose some problems not encountered in domestic markets. Among these are the presence of exchange rate risk, restrictions on capital flows across national boundaries, an added dimension of political risk and country-specific regulations, and differing accounting practices in different countries.

We begin by looking at market capitalization of stock exchanges around the world and its relation to the home country GDP. Next, we examine exchange rate risk and how such risk can be mitigated by using foreign exchange futures and forward contracts. We also introduce political and country-specific risk that must be considered in the overall risk assessment of international investments. We then examine correlation across country portfolios with and without hedging foreign exchange risk. Based on these insights, we assess the efficacy of investing globally in the context of equilibrium in international capital markets. Finally, we show how performance attribution procedures can be adapted to an international setting.

21.1 GLOBAL MARKETS FOR EQUITIES

Developed Countries

To appreciate the myopia of an exclusive investment focus on U.S. stocks and bonds, consider the data in Table 21.1. Developed (high-income) countries are defined as those with per capita income exceeding $9,300 (in 2000), and their broad stock indexes are generally less risky than those of emerging markets. The World Bank listed 52 developed countries in 2000, many of them with very small exchanges. Our list includes 25 countries with the largest equity capitalization, the smallest of which is New Zealand with a capitalization of $19 billion in 2001. These countries made up 79% of the World gross domestic product in 2001.

The first five columns of Table 21.1 show market capitalization over the years 1996–2001. The first line shows capitalization for all world exchanges, showing total capitalization of corporate equity in 2001 as $25.7 trillion, of which U.S. stock exchanges made up $13.2 trillion (49%). The figures in these columns demonstrate the volatility of these markets; indeed, world capitalization in 2001 was less than it was two years earlier and in the entire Pacific Basin it was less than it was in 1996!

The next three columns of Table 21.1 show country equity capitalization as a percentage of the world's in 2001 and 1996 and the growth in capitalization over the five years 1996–2001. The large volatility of country stock indexes resulted in significant changes in relative size. For example, U.S. weight in the world equity portfolio increased from 37% in 1996 to 49% in 2001, while that of Japan decreased from 24% to 11%. The weights of the five largest countries behind the U.S. (Japan, U.K., France, Germany, and Switzerland) added up to 39.2% in 2001, so that in the universe of these six countries alone, the weight of the U.S. was only 62% [49/(49 + 39.2)]. Clearly, U.S. stocks may not comprise an adequately diversified portfolio of equities.

Unlike the 1980s and early 1990s, the period 1996–2001 saw a decline in the value of equities of the Pacific Basin (growth of −4%), but a resurgence in North America (growth of 136%) and Europe (104%). These numbers show that economic position of countries is just as precarious as the stock prices that capitalize the future value of the particular corporate sectors of these economies.

The last tree columns of Table 21.1 show GDP, per capita GDP, and the equity capitalization as a percentage of GDP for the year 2001. As we would expect, per capital GDP in developed countries is not as variable across countries as total GDP, which is determined in part by total population. But market capitalization as a percentage of GDP is quite variable, suggesting widespread differences in economic structure even across developed countries. We return to this issue in the next section.

Emerging Markets

For a passive strategy one could argue that a portfolio of equities of just the six countries with the largest capitalization would make up 79.2% (in 2001) of the world portfolio and may be sufficiently diversified. This argument will not hold for active portfolios that seek to tilt investments toward promising assets. Active portfolios will naturally include many stocks or even indexes of emerging markets.

Table 21.2 makes the point. Surely, active portfolio managers must prudently scour stocks in markets such as China, Brazil, or Korea. Table 21.2 shows data from the 20 largest emerging markets, the most notable of which is China with equity capitalization of $170 billion (0.66% of world capitalization) in 2001, and growth of 651% over the five years 1966–2001. But managers also would not want to have missed a market like Poland (0.09% of world capitalization) with a growth of 287% over the same years.

TABLE 21.1

Market capitalization of stock exchanges in developed countries

	Market Capitalization U.S. Dollars (billions)						Percent of World		Growth	GDP	GDP per Capita	Capitalization as % of GDP
	2001	2000	1999	1998	1997	1996	2001	1996	1996–2001	2001	2001	2001
World	$25,711	$31,668	$26,198	$20,703	$17,966	$14,494	100%	100%	77%	30,960	5,450	83
North America	13,169	15,601	13,166	10,008	7,685	5,590	51.2	38.6	135.6			
United States	12,597	14,882	12,623	9,528	7,271	5,294	49.0	36.5	137.9	10,208	35,900	123
Canada	572	719	543	479	413	295	2.2	2.0	94.0	700	22,525	82
Europe	7,305	9,185	7,657	6,948	4,878	3,585	28	25	104			
United Kingdom	2,256	2,639	2,475	2,179	1,635	1,206	8.8	8.3	87	1,424	23,750	158
France	1,119	1,356	937	843	518	427	4.4	2.9	162	1,307	21,910	86
Germany	896	1,204	1,062	992	709	481	3.5	3.3	86	1,848	22,500	48
Switzerland	633	712	662	596	447	303	2.5	2.1	109	247	34,019	256
Netherlands	559	723	634	607	479	339	2.2	2.3	65	381	23,810	147
Italy	556	736	526	464	247	214	2.2	1.5	160	1,090	18,950	51
Spain	336	337	310	311	212	150	1.3	1.0	124	582	14,590	58
Sweden	212	375	253	247	188	139	0.8	1.0	52	210	23,580	101
Finland	164	379	173	93	60	42	0.6	0.3	295	121	23,260	136
Belgium	130	158	152	173	105	82	0.5	0.6	58	230	22,420	56
Denmark	90	101	75	88	61	44	0.3	0.3	103	163	30,450	55
Ireland	76	75	58	59	36	27	0.3	0.2	185	103	27,140	73
Norway	69	54	52	56	47	35	0.2	0.2	100	165	36,600	42
Greece	55	88	83	51	27	17	0.2	0.1	224	116	11,000	47
Portugal	49	74	59	75	47	23	0.2	0.2	111	110	10,940	45
Israel	39	47	35	29	24	18	0.2	0.1	120	110	17,159	35
Austria	24	28	31	35	27	26	0.1	02	−8	189	23,078	13
New Zealand	19	23	26	26	36	29	0.1	0.2	−34	49	12,763	39
Pacific Basin	4,642	6,184	4,764	3,201	4,729	4,830	18	33	−4			
Japan	2,947	4,246	3,092	2,188	3,138	3,509	11	24	−16	4,148	32,720	71
Hong Kong	532	553	404	254	452	289	2.1	2.0	84	162	10,940	329
Australia	363	384	378	249	276	219	1.4	1.5	65	357	18,459	102
Taiwan	205	331	260	173	232	152	0.8	1.0	35	282	12,620	73
Singapore	113	143	133	72	116	138	0.4	0.9	−18	86	20,880	132

Source: Datastream, July 2002.

TABLE 21.2

Market capitalization of stock exchanges in emerging markets

	Market Capitalization U.S. Dollars (billions)						Percent of World		Growth	GDP	GDP per Capita	Capitalization as % of GDP
	2001	2000	1999	1998	1997	1996	2001	1996	1996–2001	2001	2001	2001
China	$170	$ 94	$ 78	$ 67	$ 48	$ 23	0.66%	0.16%	651%	1,180	928	14%
Brazil	169	220	155	135	175	86	0.66	0.59	97	503	2,810	34
Korea	151	218	181	35	95	104	0.59	0.72	45	423	8,870	36
Mexico	140	128	115	96	97	74	0.55	0.51	89	621	6,190	23
South Africa	101	123	126	121	148	124	0.39	0.86	−19	112	2,520	90
India	88	139	93	72	113	88	0.34	0.61	−1	485	470	18
Malaysia	76	98	90	50	170	167	0.30	1.15	−54	89	3,720	86
Russia	66	49	35	44	93	37	0.26	0.25	80	310	2,144	21
Chile	53	49	47	45	61	48	0.20	0.33	10	64	4,170	82
Turkey	36	75	39	54	36	24	0.14	0.16	50	148	2,230	24
Argentina	29	37	51	48	56	43	0.11	0.30	−31	267	7,120	11
Thailand	26	30	46	17	46	89	0.10	0.61	−71	115	1,820	23
Poland	22	29	25	14	7	6	0.09	0.04	287	176	4,566	13
Philippines	20	23	41	26	55	62	0.08	0.42	−68	71	862	28
Indonesia	19	32	39	12	76	60	0.07	0.41	−68	145	688	13
Czech Republic	10	13	12	13	11	13	0.04	0.09	−26	52	5,137	19
Hungary	9	14	14	15	8	4	0.04	0.03	128	56	5,482	16
Peru	6	8	7	8	11	10	0.02	0.07	−36	54	2,070	11
Colombia	6	5	7	10	22	17	0.02	0.12	−65	83	1,940	7
Venezuela	4	4	4	4	10	4	0.02	0.03	2	130	5,280	3

Source: Datastream, July 2002.

These 20 emerging markets make up 16% of the world GDP and, together with the 25 developed markets in Table 21.1, make up 95% of the world GDP. Per capita GDP in these countries in 2001 was quite variable, ranging from $470 (India) to $8,870 (Korea); still, no active manager would want to ignore India in an international portfolio. Market capitalization as a percent of GDP, which ranges from 3% (Venezuela) to 90% (South Africa), suggests that these markets are expected to show significant growth over the coming years, even absent spectacular growth in GDP.

The growth of capitalization in emerging markets over 1966–2001 was much more volatile than growth in developed countries (as disastrous as −71% for Thailand), suggesting that both risk and rewards in this segment of the globe may be substantial.

Market Capitalization and GDP

The contemporary view of economic development (rigorously stated in deSoto 2000) holds that a major requirement for economic advancement is a developed code of business laws, institutions, and regulation that allows citizens to legally own, capitalize, and trade capital assets. As a corollary, we expect that development of equity markets will serve as catalysts for enrichment of the population, that is, that countries with larger relative capitalization of equities will tend to be richer.

Figure 21.1 is a simple (perhaps simplistic since other relevant explanatory variables are omitted) rendition of the argument that a developed market for corporate equity contributes to the enrichment of the population. The R-square of the regression line shown in Figure 21.1 is 35% and the regression coefficient is .73, suggesting that an increase of 1% in the ratio of market capitalization to GDP is associated with an increase in per capita GDP of 0.73%. It is remarkable that not one of the 25 developed countries is below the regression line; only low-income emerging markets lie below the line. Countries like Venezuela and Norway that lie above the line, that is, exhibit higher per capita GDP than predicted by the regression, enjoy oil wealth that contributes to population income. Countries below the line, such as Indonesia, South Africa, Philippines, and India, suffered from deterioration of the business environment due to political strife and/or government policies that restricted

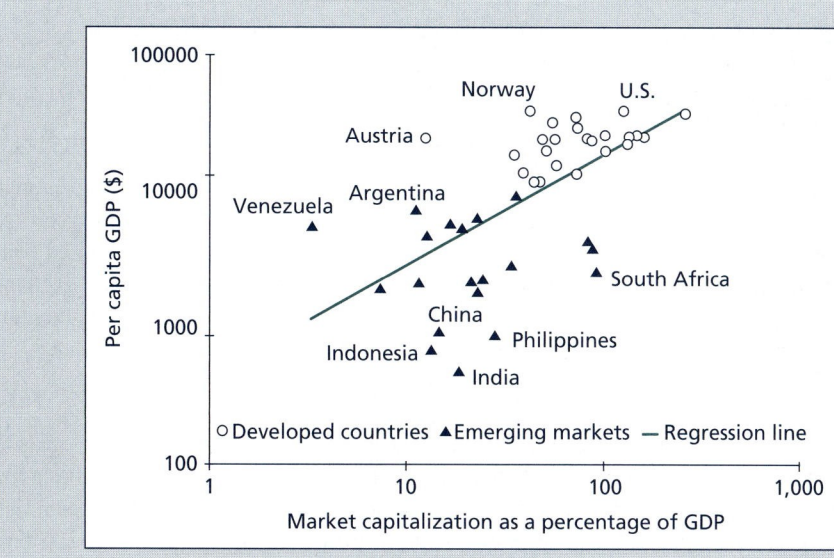

FIGURE 21.1

Per capita GDP tends to be higher when market capitalization as a percentage of GDP is higher. (log scale)

the private sector. China's policies of freeing up economic activities contributed to the remarkable growth in market capitalization over 1996–2001. The expected continuation of this process will likely move China toward the predicted relationship in coming years.

Home-Country Bias

One would expect that most investors, particularly institutional and professional investors, would be aware of the opportunities offered by international investing. Yet in practice, investor portfolios notoriously overweight home-country stocks compared to a neutral indexing strategy and underweight, or even completely ignore, foreign equities. This has come to be known as the *home-country bias.* Despite a continuous increase in cross-border investing, home-country bias still dominates investor portfolios.

21.2 RISK FACTORS IN INTERNATIONAL INVESTING

Opportunities in international investments do not come free of risk or of the cost of specialized analysis. The risk factors that are unique to international investments are exchange rate risk and country-specific risk, discussed in the next two sections.

Exchange Rate Risk

It is best to begin with a simple example.

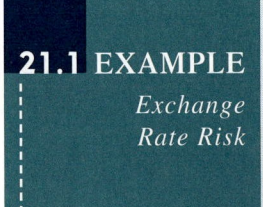

21.1 EXAMPLE

Exchange Rate Risk

Consider an investment in risk-free British government bills paying 10% annual interest in British pounds. While these U.K. bills would be the risk-free asset to a British investor, this is not the case for a U.S. investor. Suppose, for example, the current exchange rate is $2 per pound, and the U.S. investor starts with $20,000. That amount can be exchanged for £10,000 and invested at a riskless 10% rate in the United Kingdom to provide £11,000 in one year.

What happens if the dollar–pound exchange rate varies over the year? Say that during the year, the pound depreciates relative to the dollar, so that by year-end only $1.80 is required to purchase £1. The £11,000 can be exchanged at the year-end exchange rate for only $19,800 (= £11,000 × $1.80/£), resulting in a loss of $200 relative to the initial $20,000 investment. Despite the positive 10% pound-denominated return, the dollar-denominated return is a negative 1%.

We can generalize from Example 21.1. The $20,000 is exchanged for $20,000/$E_0$ pounds, where E_0 denotes the original exchange rate ($2/£). The U.K. investment grows to $(20,000/E_0)[1 + r_f(UK)]$ British pounds, where $r_f(UK)$ is the risk-free rate in the United Kingdom. The pound proceeds ultimately are converted back to dollars at the subsequent exchange rate E_1, for total dollar proceeds of $20,000(E_1/E_0)[1 + r_f(UK)]$. The dollar-denominated return on the investment in British bills, therefore, is

$$1 + r(US) = [1 + r_f(UK)]E_1/E_0 \qquad \text{(21.1)}$$

We see in Equation 21.1 that the dollar-denominated return for a U.S. investor equals the pound-denominated return times the exchange rate "return." For a U.S. investor, the investment in British bills is a combination of a safe investment in the United Kingdom and a risky investment in the performance of the pound relative to the dollar. Here, the pound fared poorly, falling from a value of $2.00 to only $1.80. The loss on the pound more than offsets the earnings on the British bill.

FIGURE 21.2

Stock market returns in dollars and local currencies for 2001

Source: Datastream.

Country	Return (in local currency)	Return (in $)
New Zealand	8.7	15.5
Taiwan	10.7	17
Spain	−9.6	−4.7
Denmark	−16.6	−12.4
Ireland	−2.2	3.1
Canada	−15.6	−10.3
Singapore	−17.7	−12.4
Japan	−30.0	−19.6
Hong Kong	−19.5	−19.6
Australia	0.5	9.1
United Kingdom	−15.0	−12.7
Switzerland	−22.3	−20.4
Netherlands	−21.2	−16.9
Italy	−27.5	−23.5
Germany	−21.6	−17.4
France	−21.9	−17.7

Figure 21.2 illustrates this point. It presents rates of returns on stock market indexes in several countries for 2001. The dark boxes depict returns in local currencies, while the light boxes depict returns in dollars, adjusted for exchange rate movements. It's clear that exchange rate fluctuations over this period had large effects on dollar-denominated returns in several countries.

1. **Using the data in Example 21.1, calculate the rate of return in dollars to a U.S. investor holding the British bill if the year-end exchange rate is: (a) $E_1 = \$2.00/\pounds$; (b) $E_1 = \$2.20/\pounds$.**

Concept CHECK

exchange rate risk

The uncertainty in asset returns due to movements in the exchange rates between the U.S. dollar and foreign currency.

Pure **exchange rate risk** is the risk borne by investments in foreign safe assets. The investor in U.K. bills of Example 21.1 bears only the risk of the U.K./U.S. exchange rate. We can assess the magnitude of exchange rate risk by examination of historical rates of change in various exchange rates and their correlations.

Table 21.3A shows historical exchange rate risk measured from monthly percent changes in the exchange rates of major currencies over the period 1997–2001. The data shows that currency risk is quite high. The annualized standard deviation of the percent changes in the exchange rate ranged from 5.01% (Canadian dollar) to 14.18% (Japanese yen). The standard deviation of monthly returns on U.S. large stocks for the same period was 18.81%. Hence, major currency exchange risk alone would amount to between 27% (5.01/18.81) and 75% (14.18/18.81) of the risk on stocks. Clearly, an active investor who believes that Japanese stocks are underpriced, but has no information about any mispricing of the Japanese yen,

TABLE 21.3

Rates of change in the value of the U.S. dollar against major world currencies, 1997–2001 (monthly data)

A. Standard Deviation (annualized)

Country Currency	Euro (E)	U.K. (£)	Japan (¥)	Australia ($A)	Canada ($C)
Standard dev.	9.61	6.61	14.18	11.44	5.01

B. Correlation Matrix

	Euro	U.K.	Japan	Australia	Canada
Euro	1.00				
U.K.	0.64	1.00			
Japan	0.29	0.21	1.00		
Australia	0.29	0.22	0.35	1.00	
Canada	−0.02	0.02	0.13	0.53	1.00

C. Average Increases

	Average Annualized Dollar Return on Cash Investments		Average Annualized % Increase in the Value of the U.S. Dollar
U.S.	5.67		
France	−2.64	Euro	7.28
Germany	−2.82	Euro	7.28
Italy	−1.81	Euro	7.28
Netherlands	−2.88	Euro	7.28
Switzerland	−1.48	Euro	7.28
U.K.	3.34	U.K.	3.47
Australia	−2.74	Australia	9.46
Japan	−0.97	Japan	3.44
Canada	1.90	Canada	3.17

would be advised to hedge the yen risk exposure when tilting the portfolio toward Japanese stocks. Exchange rate risk of the major currencies is quite stable over time. For example, a study by Solnik (1999) for the period 1971–1998 finds similar standard deviations, ranging from 4.8% (Canadian dollar) to 12.0% (Japanese yen).

In the context of international portfolios, exchange rate risk may be mostly diversifiable. This is evident from the low correlation coefficients in Table 21.3B. (This observation will be reinforced when we compare the risk of hedged and unhedged country portfolios in a later section.) Thus, passive investors with well-diversified international portfolios need not be concerned with hedging exposure to foreign currencies.

The annualized average monthly increase in the value of the U.S. dollar against the major currencies over the five-year period and dollar returns on foreign bills (cash investments) appear in Table 21.3C. The table shows that the value of the U.S. dollar consistently increased in this particular period. For example, the total increase against the Japanese yen over the five years was 18% and against the Australian dollar, 57%. This currency appreciation of the U.S.

dollar was not offset by higher interest rates available in other countries. Had an investor been able to forecast the large exchange rate movements, it would have been a source of great profit. The currency market thus provided attractive opportunities for investors with superior information or analytical ability.

The investor in Example 21.1 could have hedged the exchange rate risk using a forward or futures contract in foreign exchange. Recall that a forward or futures contract on foreign exchange calls for delivery or acceptance of one currency for another at a stipulated exchange rate. Here, the U.S. investor would agree to deliver pounds for dollars at a fixed exchange rate, thereby eliminating the future risk involved with conversion of the pound investment back into dollars.

If the futures exchange rate had been $F_0 = \$1.93/£$ when the investment was made, the U.S. investor could have assured a riskless dollar-denominated return by locking in the year-end exchange rate at $\$1.93/£$. In this case, the riskless U.S. return would have been 6.15%:

$$[1 + r_f(\text{UK})]F_0/E_0$$
$$= (1.10)1.93/2.00$$
$$= 1.0615$$

> **EXAMPLE 21.2**
>
> *Hedging Exchange Rate Risk*

Here are the steps to lock in the dollar-denominated returns. The futures contract entered in the second step exactly offsets the exchange rate risk incurred in step 1.

Initial Transaction	End-of-Year Proceeds in Dollars
Exchange $20,000 for £10,000 and invest at 10% in the United Kingdom.	£11,000 × E_1
Enter a contract to deliver £11,000 for dollars at the (forward) exchange rate $1.93/£.	£11,000(1.93 − E_1)
Total	£11,000 × $1.93/£ = $21,230

You may recall that the futures hedge in Example 21.2 is the same type of hedging strategy at the heart of the spot-futures parity relationship discussed in Chapter 16. In both instances, futures markets are used to eliminate the risk of holding another asset. The U.S. investor can lock in a riskless dollar-denominated return either by investing in the United Kingdom and hedging exchange rate risk or by investing in riskless U.S. assets. Because the returns on two riskless strategies must provide equal returns, we conclude

$$\frac{F_0}{E_0} = \frac{1 + r_f(\text{US})}{1 + r_f(\text{UK})} \qquad (21.2)$$

This relationship is called the **interest rate parity relationship** or **covered interest arbitrage relationship**.

Consider the intuition behind this result. If $r_f(\text{US})$ is greater than $r_f(\text{UK})$, money invested in the United States will grow at a faster rate than money invested in the United Kingdom. If this is so, why wouldn't all investors decide to invest their money in the United States? One important reason is that the dollar may be depreciating relative to the pound. Although dollar investments in the United States grow faster than pound investments in the United Kingdom, each dollar is worth progressively fewer pounds as time passes. Such an effect will exactly offset the advantage of the higher U.S. interest rate.

interest rate parity relationship, or covered interest arbitrage relationship

The spot-futures exchange rate relationship that precludes arbitrage opportunities.

To complete the argument, we need only determine how a depreciating dollar will affect Equation 21.2. If the dollar is depreciating, meaning that progressively more dollars are required to purchase each pound, then the forward exchange rate, F_0 (which equals the dollars required to purchase one pound for delivery in the future), must exceed E_0, the current exchange rate.

That is exactly what Equation 21.2 tells us: When $r_f(\text{US})$ exceeds $r_f(\text{UK})$, F_0 must exceed E_0. The depreciation of the dollar embodied in the ratio of F_0 to E_0 exactly compensates for the difference in interest rates available in the two countries. Of course, the argument also works in reverse: If $r_f(\text{US})$ is less than $r_f(\text{UK})$, then F_0 will be less than E_0.

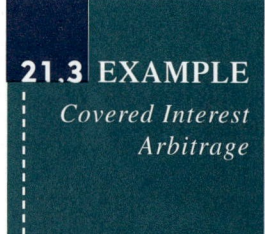

21.3 EXAMPLE

Covered Interest Arbitrage

What if the interest rate parity relationship were violated? Suppose $r_f(\text{US})$ is 6.15%, but the futures price is \$1.90/£ instead of \$1.93/£. You could adopt a strategy to reap arbitrage profits. In this example, let E_1 denote the exchange rate that will prevail in one year. E_1 is, of course, a random variable from the perspective of today's investors.

Action	Initial Cash Flow (in \$)	Cash Flow in One Year (in \$)
1. Borrow 1 UK pound in London. Repay in one year.	\$ 2.00	$-E_1(1.10)$
2. Convert the pound to \$2 and lend in the United States.	\$−2.00	$2.00(1.0615)$
3. Enter a contract to purchase 1.10 pounds at a (futures) price of $F_0 = \$1.90/£$	0	$1.10(E_1 - 1.90)$
Total	\$ 0	\$0.033

In step 1, you borrow one pound in the United Kingdom (worth \$2 at the current exchange rate) and, after one year, repay the pound borrowed with interest. Because the loan is made in the United Kingdom at the U.K. interest rate, you would repay 1.10 pounds, which would be worth $E_1(1.10)$ dollars. The U.S. loan in step 2 is made at the U.S. interest rate of 6.15%. The futures position in step 3 results in receipt of 1.10 pounds, for which you would first pay F_0 (i.e., 1.90) dollars each and then convert into dollars at exchange rate E_1.

The exchange rate risk here is exactly offset between the pound obligation in step 1 and the futures position in step 3. The profit from the strategy is, therefore, riskless and requires no net investment. This is an arbitrage opportunity.

Concept
CHECK

2. **What are the arbitrage strategy and associated profits if the initial future price is** $F_0 = \$1.95/\text{pound}$?

Ample empirical evidence bears out this theoretical relationship. For example, on January 25, 2000, the interest rate on U.S. Treasury securities with maturity of one-half year was 5.84%, while the comparable rate in the United Kingdom was 5.88%. The spot exchange rate was \$1.6450/£. Substituting these values into Equation 21.2, we find that interest rate parity implies that the forward exchange rate for delivery in one-half year should have been $1.6450 \times (1.0584/1.0588)^{1/2} = \$1.6447/£$. The actual forward rate was \$1.644/£, which was so close to the parity value that transaction costs would have prevented arbitrageurs from profiting from the discrepancy.

Unfortunately, such perfect exchange rate hedging usually is not so easy. In our example, we knew exactly how many pounds to sell in the forward or futures market because the pound-denominated proceeds in the United Kingdom were riskless. If the U.K. investment had not been in bills, but instead had been in risky U.K. equity, we would know neither the ultimate value in pounds of our U.K. investment nor how many pounds to sell forward. That is, the hedging opportunity offered by foreign exchange forward contracts would be imperfect.

To summarize, the generalization of Equation 21.1 is that

$$1 + r(US) = [1 + r(foreign)]E_1/E_0 \qquad \textbf{(21.3)}$$

where $r(foreign)$ is the possibly risky return earned in the currency of the foreign investment. You can set up a perfect hedge only in the special case that $r(foreign)$ is itself a known number. In that case, you know you must sell in the forward or futures market an amount of foreign currency equal to $[1 + r(foreign)]$ for each unit of that currency you purchase today.

3. **How many pounds would the investor in Example 21.2 need to sell forward to hedge exchange rate risk if: (a) $r(UK) = 20\%$; and (b) $r(UK) = 30\%$?**

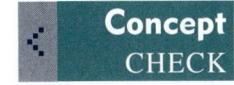
Concept
CHECK

Country-Specific Risk

In principle, security analysis at the macroeconomic, industry, and firm-specific level is similar in all countries. Such analysis aims to provide estimates of expected returns and risk of individual assets and portfolios. To achieve the same quality of information about assets in a foreign country is by nature more difficult and hence more expensive. Moreover, the risk of coming by false or misleading information is greater.

Consider two investors: an American wishing to invest in Indonesian stocks and an Indonesian wishing to invest in U.S. stocks. While each would have to consider macroeconomic analysis of the foreign country, the task would be much more difficult for the American investor. The reason is not that investment in Indonesia is necessarily riskier than investment in the U.S. You can easily find many U.S. stocks that are, in the final analysis, riskier than a number of Indonesian stocks. The difference lies in the fact that the U.S. investment environment is more predictable than that of Indonesia.

In the past, when international investing was novel, the added risk was referred to as **political risk** and its assessment was an art. As cross-border investment has increased and more resources have been utilized, the quality of related analysis has improved. A leading organization in the field (which is quite competitive) is the PRS Group (Political Risk Services) and the presentation here follows the PRS methodology.[1]

PRS's country risk analysis results in a country composite risk rating on a scale of 0 (most risky) to 100 (least risky). Countries are then ranked by composite risk measure and divided into five categories: very low risk (100–80), low risk (79.9–70), moderate risk (69.9–60), high risk (59.9–50), and very high risk (less than 50). To illustrate, Table 21.4 shows the placement of five countries in the September 2001 issue of the PRS *International Country Risk Guide*. The countries shown are the two largest capitalization countries (U.S. and Japan) and the three most populous emerging markets (China, India, and Indonesia). Surprisingly, Table 21.4 shows that the U.S. ranked only 20th in September of 2001, having deteriorated from the 11th rank in the previous year. Japan actually ranked higher at 13. Both these developed countries placed in the "very low risk" category. Of the three emerging markets, it is not surprising to see Indonesia ranked 115th of 140 countries, placing it in the "high risk" category, while China ranked 60th, in the "low risk" category, and India ranked 92nd, in the "moderate risk" category.

The composite risk rating is an average of three measures: political risk, financial risk, and economic risk. Political risk is measured on a scale of 100–0, while financial and economic risk are measured on a scale of 50–0. The three measures are added and divided by

political risk

Possibility of expropriation of assets, changes in tax policy, restrictions on the exchange of foreign currency for domestic currency, or other changes in the business climate of a country.

[1]You can find more information on the website: http://www.prsgroup.com.

TABLE **21.4**					
Composite risk ratings for October 2000 and September 2001					
Rank, Sept. 2001	Country	Composite Risk Rating, Sept. 2001	Composite Risk Rating, Oct. 2000	Sept. 2001 Rating Minus Oct. 2000 Rating	Rank, Oct. 2000
	Very low risk				
13	Japan	86.5	83.5	3	12
20	United States	83.3	83.8	−0.5	11
	Low risk				
60	China	72.5	73.5	−1	47
	Moderate risk				
92	India	64.8	63.3	1.5	89
	High risk				
115	Indonesia	59.8	56.5	3.3	118

Source: *International Country Risk Guide,* September 2001, Table 1.

TABLE **21.5**	Political Risk Variables	Financial Risk Variables	Economic Risk Variables
Variables used in PRS's political risk score	Government stability	Foreign debt (% of GDP)	GDP per capita
	Socioeconomic conditions	Foreign debt service (% of GDP)	Real annual GDP growth
	Investment profile	Current account (% of exports)	Annual inflation rate
	Internal conflicts		Budget balance (% of GDP)
	External conflicts	Net liquidity in months of imports	Current account balance (% GDP)
	Corruption	Exchange rate stability	
	Military in politics		
	Religious tensions		
	Law and order		
	Ethnic tensions		
	Democratic accountability		
	Bureaucracy quality		

two to obtain the composite rating. This amounts to a weighted average of the three measures with a weight of .5 on political risk and .25 each on financial and economic risk. The variables used by PRS to determine the composite risk rating of the three measured are shown in Table 21.5.

Table 21.6 shows the three risk measures for the five countries in Table 21.4, in order of the September 2001 ranking of the composite risk ratings. The table shows that by political risk, the five countries ranked in the same order. But in the financial risk measure, the U.S. ranked below China and India (!), and by the economic risk measure, the U.S. ranked above Japan, and India ranked below Indonesia. More interesting are the ratings forecasts for one and five years. These forecasts are quite pessimistic about the U.S., whose composite rating is expected to continue to deteriorate over the years 2002–2006. (This may have been prescient, since it appears this report was prepared prior to the September 11, 2001, attacks.) At the same time, the ratings of three of the other four countries were expected to improve over the next five years.

The country risk is captured in greater depth by scenario analysis for the composite measure and each of its components. Table 21.7 (A and B) shows one- and five-year worst case and best case scenarios for the composite ratings and for the political risk measure. Risk stability is defined as the difference in the rating between the best and worst case scenarios and is quite large in most cases. The worst case scenario is in some cases sufficient to move a

TABLE **21.6**

Current risk ratings and composite risk forecasts

	Current Ratings			Composite Ratings			
Country	Political Risk, Sept. 2001	Financial Risk, Sept. 2001	Economic Risk, Sept. 2001	Year Ago, Oct. 2000	Current, Sept. 2001	One-Year Forecast	Five-Year Forecast
Japan	90	45.5	37.5	83.5	**86.5**	84.5	85.5
United States	89.5	37.5	39.5	83.8	**83.3**	82.5	80.5
China	62	45	38	73.5	**72.5**	72.5	76.5
India	56	40.5	33	63.3	**64.8**	64	68
Indonesia	49.5	35	35	56.5	**59.8**	52.5	64.5

Source: *International Country Risk Guide,* September 2001, Table 2B.

TABLE **21.7**

Composite and political risk forecasts

A. Composite Risk Forecasts

		One Year Ahead				Five Years Ahead			
	Current Rating	Worst Case	Most Probable	Best Case	Risk Stability	Worst Case	Most Probable	Best Case	Risk Stability
Japan	**86.5**	79.5	84.5	88	8.5	78.5	85.5	91	12.5
United States	**83.3**	75	82.5	85.5	10.5	73	80.5	84	11
China	**72.5**	68	72.5	74.5	6.5	67	76.5	81	14
India	**64.8**	58	64	66.5	8.5	60	68	70.5	10.5
Indonesia	**59.8**	45	52.5	55	10	46.5	64.5	68.5	22

B. Political Risk Forecasts

		One Year Ahead				Five Years Ahead			
	Current Rating	Worst Case	Most Probable	Best Case	Risk Stability	Worst Case	Most Probable	Best Case	Risk Stability
Japan	**90**	76	83	88	12	76	85	94	18
United States	**89.5**	78	90	93	15	80	85	88	8
China	**62**	58	63	65	7	60	70	74	14
India	**56**	50	60	63	13	58	65	67	9
Indonesia	**49.5**	40	48	50	10	40	60	64	24

Sources: A: *International Country Risk Guide,* September 2001, Table 2C; B: *International Country Risk Guide,* September 2001, Table 3C.

country to a higher risk category. Table 21.7B shows that U.S. political risk was forecast to deteriorate in five years (2006) to the level of Japan.

Finally, Table 21.8 shows ratings of political risk by each of its 12 components. Corruption (variable F) in China is rated worse than in India and equal to that of Indonesia. In democratic accountability (variable K), China ranked worst and India best, while Indonesia ranked better than both in external conflict (variable E).

TABLE 21.8

Political risk points by component, September 2001

This table lists the total points for each of the following political risk components out of the maximum points indicated. The symbol ↑ indicates a rise in the points awarded to that specific risk component from the previous month (an improving risk), while the symbol ↓ indicates a decrease (deteriorating risk). The final columns in the table show the overall political risk rating (the sum of the points awarded to each component) and the change from the preceding month.

A	Government stability	12	E	External conflict	12	J	Ethnic tensions	6
B	Socioeconomic conditions	12	F	Corruption	6	K	Democratic accountability	6
C	Investment profile	12	H	Religious tensions	6	L	Bureaucracy quality	4
D	Internal conflict	12	I	Law and order	6			

Country	A	B	C	D	E	F	G	H	I	J	K	L	Political Risk Rating	
United States	10	10.5	11	12	10.5	4	5.5	6	6	5	5	4	**89.5**	0
Japan	10.5	8.5	↑12.0	12	↓11.0	3	6	5	5	6	5	4	**88**	−0.5
China	10	7	↓7.5	10	9.5	1	2	4	4	4	1	2	**62**	−0.5
India	↑7.5	3.5	↓8.0	↓7.0	↓8.0	2	3	2	4	2	6	3	**56**	−1.5
Indonesia	↑9.5	2	↑7.0	6.5	10	1	2.5	1	2	2	4	2	**49.5**	2

Each monthly issue of the *International Country Risk Guide* of the PRS Group includes great detail and holds some 250 pages. Other organizations compete in supplying such evaluations. The result is that today's investor can become well equipped to properly assess the risk involved in international investing.

21.3 INTERNATIONAL INVESTING: RISK, RETURN, AND BENEFITS FROM DIVERSIFICATION

U.S. investors have several avenues through which they can invest internationally. The most obvious method, which is available in practice primarily to larger institutional investors, is to purchase securities directly in the capital markets of other countries. However, even small investors now can take advantage of several investment vehicles with an international focus.

Shares of several foreign firms are traded in U.S. markets in the form of American depository receipts, or ADRs. A U.S. financial institution such as a bank will purchase shares of a foreign firm in that firm's country, then issue claims to those shares in the United States. Each ADR is then a claim on a given number of the shares of stock held by the bank. In this way, the stock of foreign companies can be traded on U.S. stock exchanges. Trading foreign stocks with ADRs has become increasingly easy.

There is also a wide array of mutual funds with an international focus. Single-country funds are mutual funds that invest in the shares of only one country. These tend to be closed-end funds, as the listing of these funds in Table 21.9 indicates. In addition to single-country funds, there are several open-end mutual funds with an international focus. For example, Fidelity offers funds with investments concentrated overseas, generally in Europe, in the Pacific Basin, and in developing economies in an emerging opportunities fund. Vanguard, consistent with its indexing philosophy, offers separate index funds for Europe, the Pacific Basin, and emerging markets. The nearby box discusses a wide range of single-country index funds.

TABLE **21.9**	Closed-End Funds		Closed-End Funds	
Sampling of emerging country funds	**Fund Name**	**Symbol**	**Fund Name**	**Symbol**
	Europe/Middle East		**Pacific/Asia**	
	First Israel	ISL	India Fund	IFN
	Turkish Inv.	TKF	Jardine Fleming China	JFC
	Latin America		Korea	KF
	Brazil	BZF	Malaysia	MF
	Chile	CH	Scudder New Asia	SAF
	Latin Amer. Eqty.	LAQ	Taiwan	TWN
	Mexico	MXF	Thai	TTF
	Pacific/Asia		**Global**	
	Asia Pacific	APB	Emerging Markets Tele.	ETF
	China	CHN	Morgan Stanley EmMkFd	MSF
	First Philippine	FPF	Templeton Emerging	EMF

Open-End Funds	
Fund Name	**Assets (millions)**
Fidelity Emerging Markets	$ 333
Merrill Developing Cap. Market	87
Merrill Latin Amer. Developing Cap.	130
Montgomery Emerging Mkt.	151
Morgan Stanley Dean Witter EM	785
Scudder Emerging Market Income	127
Templeton Dev. Mkts.	1,400
Vanguard Int'l Index: Emerging	985

Source: *The Wall Street Journal,* July 5, 2002.

U.S. investors also can trade derivative securities based on prices in foreign security markets. For example, they can trade options and futures on the Nikkei stock index of 225 stocks traded on the Tokyo stock exchange, or on FTSE (Financial Times Share Exchange) indexes of U.K. and European stocks.

Risk and Return: Summary Statistics

Table 21.10 presents annualized average returns and standard deviations in U.S. dollars and in local currency from monthly returns over the period 1997–2001. Developed countries appear in panel A and emerging markets in panel B. We use this table to develop insights into the risk and reward in international investing. The equity markets in both panels of Table 21.10 are ordered by standard deviation.

Are Investments in Emerging Markets Riskier?

In Figure 21.3, developed countries and emerging markets are ordered from low to high standard deviation. The standard deviations of investments in emerging markets are charted over those in developed countries. The graphs clearly show that investment in emerging markets is largely riskier than in developed countries, at least as measured by total volatility of returns. Still, you can find emerging markets that appear safer than some developed countries.

TABLE **21.10** Risk and return across the globe, 1997–2001		% Per Annum in U.S. Dollars		% Per Annum in Local Currency	
Country		**Average**	**Standard Dev.**	**Average**	**Standard Dev.**
A. Developed countries					
U.K.		5.97	15.24	9.39	16.23
Belgium		5.36	17.98	12.42	17.58
Austria		−3.09	18.41	4.00	18.32
U.S.		11.98	18.78	11.98	18.78
Denmark		8.30	19.38	15.62	21.04
Netherlands		6.84	19.55	14.34	20.87
Switzerland		8.74	19.86	13.31	21.05
Ireland		10.73	20.16	19.21	21.73
Germany		5.55	20.43	13.13	22.49
Australia		4.86	20.74	12.42	13.01
France		11.45	21.36	18.84	22.81
Canada		10.08	22.41	12.51	19.37
Spain		8.38	24.20	15.94	25.20
Italy		12.30	24.50	20.02	26.47
New Zealand		−3.17	24.51	5.99	17.65
Norway		1.57	25.61	7.80	23.34
Portugal		6.51	25.63	14.12	26.10
Japan		−3.96	25.96	−2.84	19.68
Israel		15.37	28.13	20.98	26.04
Sweden		9.25	29.10	17.45	27.61
Singapore		−2.47	32.86	1.98	29.26
Hong Kong		3.01	33.34	3.17	33.32
Taiwan		2.89	38.28	6.67	35.41
Greece		20.50	39.70	28.83	40.64
Finland		29.99	42.09	38.10	43.33
B. Emerging markets					
Peru		−5.61	23.15	−0.36	21.74
Chile		0.39	23.85	8.64	20.89
China		8.23	25.37	8.17	25.37
Colombia		−15.96	29.67	−0.66	27.81
Czech Rep.		0.54	32.66	4.60	28.71
Mexico		13.44	33.65	14.76	28.49
India		4.36	33.78	9.93	32.75
South Africa		−0.33	34.06	16.77	28.22
Argentina		−0.47	34.08	−0.41	34.29
Poland		2.78	40.83	7.17	35.88
Hungary		10.45	41.29	20.76	40.73
Venezuela		−9.81	41.90	−1.10	41.14
Philippines		−20.63	41.91	−9.81	34.76
Brazil		6.09	42.40	19.38	34.91
Malaysia		−4.25	51.37	0.49	43.70
Korea		18.56	56.85	22.84	49.30
Thailand		−11.92	57.27	−3.08	54.66
Russia		29.23	61.25	29.23	61.25
Turkey		29.43	73.54	81.40	73.56
Indonesia		−1.67	86.11	−2.41	47.37

New Funds that Track Foreign Markets

LOW-COST FOREIGN INDEX FUNDS CALLED WEBS ELIMINATE SOME OF THE GUESSWORK AND COSTS OF INVESTING ABROAD

With foreign markets generally stronger this year, a new way to invest abroad has appeared at a good time. WEBS, an acronym for World Equity Benchmark Shares, represents an investment in a portfolio of publicly traded foreign stocks in a selected country. Each WEBS Index Series seeks to generate investment results that generally correspond to the price and yield performance of a specific Morgan Stanley Capital International (MSCI) index.

You sell these shares rather than redeeming them, but there the similarity to closed-end country funds ends. WEBS are equity securities, not mutual funds. WEBS shares trade continuously on a secondary market, the Amex, during regular Amex trading hours, like any other publicly traded U.S. stock listed on the exchange. In contrast, mutual fund shares do not trade in the secondary market, and are normally bought and sold from the issuing mutual fund at prices determined only at the end of the day. The new funds create and redeem shares in large blocks as needed, thus preventing the big premiums or discounts to net asset value typical of closed-end country funds. As index portfolios, WEBS are passively managed, so their expenses run much lower than for current open- or closed-end country funds.

WEBS shares offer U.S. investors portfolio exposure to country-specific equity markets, in a single, listed security you can easily buy, sell, or short on the Amex. Unlike American Depository Receipts (ADRs) that give you an investment in just one company, WEBS shares enable you to gain exposure to a broad portfolio of a desired foreign country's stocks. You gain broad exposure in the country or countries of your choice without the complications usually associated with buying, owning, or monitoring direct investments in foreign countries. You also have the conveniences of trading on a major U.S. exchange and dealing in U.S. dollars.

Some investors may prefer the active management, diversity, and flexibility of open-end international equity index funds as a way to limit currency and political risks of investing in foreign markets. As conventional open-end funds, however, the international funds are sometimes forced by net redemptions to sell stocks at inopportune times, which can be a particular problem in foreign markets with highly volatile stocks.

You pay brokerage commissions on the purchase and sale of WEBS, but since their portfolios are passively managed, their management and administrative fees are relatively low and they eliminate most of the transaction charges typical of managed funds.

Foreign Index Baskets

WEBS	Ticker Symbol	WEBS	Ticker Symbol
Australia	EWA	Malaysia	EWM
Austria	EWO	Mexico	EWW
Belgium	EWK	Netherlands	EWN
Canada	EWC	Singapore	EWS
France	EWQ	Spain	EWP
Germany	EWG	Sweden	EWD
Hong Kong	EWH	Switzerland	EWL
Italy	EWI	U.K.	EWU
Japan	EWJ		

SOURCES: Modified from *The Outlook*, May 22, 1996, and Amex website, www.amex.com/indexshares/index_shares_webs.stm, February 2000.

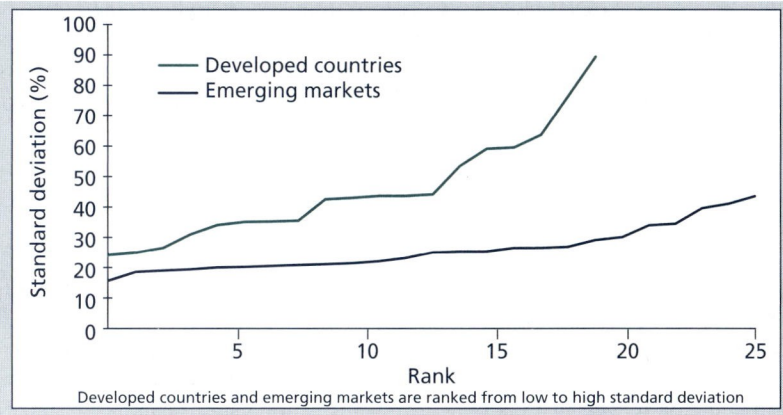

FIGURE 21.3

Annualized standard deviation of investments across the globe, 1997–2001.

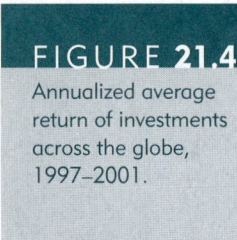

FIGURE **21.4**

Annualized average return of investments across the globe, 1997–2001.

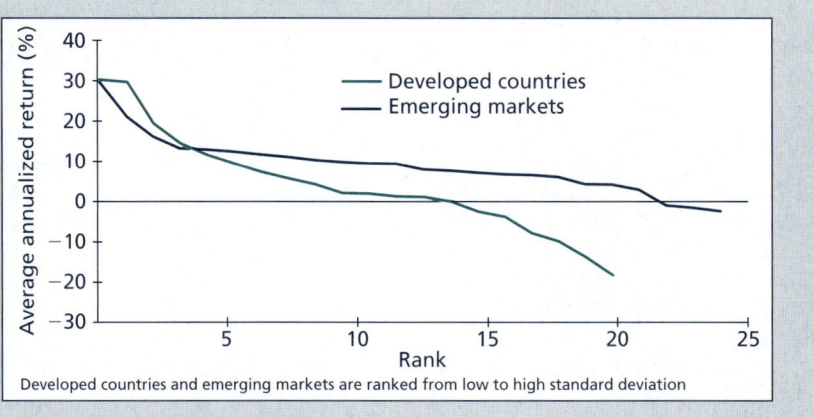

Are Average Returns in Emerging Markets Greater?

Figure 21.4 repeats the previous exercise for average returns. The graphs show that investing in emerging markets generally provided lower returns than investing in developed countries. Of course these data are far from conclusive since five-year averages are still subject to considerable imprecision. The fact that a number of markets averaged a negative rate of return is proof positive that expectations were not realized over the period and hence these data are inadequate for risk-return analysis. But regardless of these qualifications, we should not even expect any clear relationship since the higher standard deviation of emerging market equities is not an adequate measure of risk. In the context of a diversified international portfolio, the risk of any single market is measured by its covariance with the overall portfolio. Assessment of the proportion of systematic risk in country portfolios can be gleaned from the correlation matrix that we will examine shortly. First, we inquire about the role of exchange rate risk in overall country risk.

Is Exchange Rate Risk Important in International Portfolios?

Table 21.3 revealed that changes in exchange rates are not highly correlated across countries. This feature suggests that when international portfolios are well diversified, the exchange rate component of overall risk will be effectively diminished. Another feature that would render exchange rate risk diversifiable is low correlation between changes in exchange rates and country stock returns in local currencies.

In Figure 21.5, all 45 stock markets are ordered from low to high standard deviation of returns in U.S. dollars. The figure contrasts the graph of standard deviation of returns in local currency with that of returns in U.S. dollars. The graphs are quite close in most cases, reinforcing the notion that hedging exchange rate risk is not crucial in well-diversified international portfolios.

Benefits from International Diversification

Table 21.11 presents correlations between returns on stock and long-term bond portfolios in various countries. Panel A shows correlation of returns in U.S. dollars, that is, returns to a U.S. investor when currency risk is not hedged. Panel B shows correlation of returns in local currencies, that is, returns to a U.S. investor when the exchange risk is hedged. As noted earlier, the correlation coefficients of the hedged (local currency) and unhedged (U.S. dollars) returns are very similar, confirming that hedging currencies is not a significant issue in diversifying internationally.

The correlation coefficients between a stock index of one country and bond portfolios of another are very low, suggesting that income portfolios that are balanced between stocks and bonds would greatly benefit from international diversification. The correlation among unhedged stock portfolios of the countries in Table 21.11A is much larger, in the range of .45 (Japan–Germany) to .89 (France–Germany). These correlation coefficients are much larger than conventional wisdom; they suggest that cross-border correlation of stock indexes has been increasing. For another, independent example, Table 21.12 shows the correlation of various country indexes with U.S. stocks using monthly excess returns over the period 1970–1989, next to the same coefficients estimated over 1996–2001. The marked increase in correlation with 17 stock indexes and the world portfolio is uniform.

These results raise the question of whether the increase in correlation is an artifact of the sample period or a result of globalization and increased capital market integration that would be expected to increase cross-border correlation. While there is no question that a five-year sample period is quite short and limits precision, the fact that we find the increase in correlation across the board suggests that globalization and market integration are the more plausible cause, as discussed in the nearby box.

The observed high correlation across markets brings into question the conventional wisdom of large diversification benefits from international investing. This conventional wisdom is depicted in Figure 21.6, which is based on data for the period 1961–1975. Figure 21.6 suggests that international diversification can reduce the standard deviation of a domestic portfolio by as much as half (from about 27% to about 12%). This improvement may well be exaggerated if correlation across markets has markedly increased as data from recent years suggest. Still, benefits from international diversification are significant, as we will show shortly. But first it is well to dispose of a misleading, yet widespread, representation of benefits from diversification.

Misleading Representation of Diversification Benefits

The baseline technique for constructing efficient portfolios is the efficient frontier. A useful efficient frontier is constructed from *expected* returns and an estimate of the covariance matrix of returns. This frontier, combined with cash assets generates the capital allocation line, the set of efficient complete portfolios, as elaborated in Chapter 6 and the first section of Chapter 7. The benefit from this efficient diversification is reflected in the curvature of the efficient frontier. Other things equal, the lower the covariance across stocks, the greater the curvature of the efficient frontier and the greater the risk reduction for any desired *expected* return. So far, so good.

TABLE 21.11
Correlations for asset returns: unhedged and hedged currencies

A. Correlation of month's asset return 1997–2001 in $U.S. (unhedged currencies)

Asset/Country	Stocks							Bonds						
	U.S.	Germany	U.K.	Japan	Australia	Canada	France	U.S.	Germany	U.K.	Japan	Australia	Canada	France
Stocks														
U.S.	1.00													
Germany	0.75	1.00												
U.K.	0.83	0.80	1.00											
Japan	0.58	0.45	0.57	1.00										
Australia	0.71	0.62	0.73	0.60	1.00									
Canada	0.82	0.74	0.73	0.52	0.67	1.00								
France	0.70	0.89	0.82	0.49	0.57	0.70	1.00							
Bonds														
U.S. Treas.	0.09	0.17	0.08	0.00	−0.11	0.11	0.08	1.00						
Germany	0.00	0.06	−0.03	−0.25	−0.19	−0.01	−0.02	0.77	1.00					
U.K.	0.11	0.17	0.13	−0.07	−0.08	0.00	0.06	0.83	0.76	1.00				
Japan	0.02	0.09	0.12	−0.04	−0.06	0.04	0.02	0.80	0.57	0.72	1.00			
Australia	0.00	0.12	0.04	−0.01	−0.08	0.15	−0.01	0.88	0.70	0.71	0.71	1.00		
Canada	0.00	0.08	0.00	−0.03	−0.05	0.12	−0.03	0.88	0.75	0.65	0.64	0.90	1.00	
France	−0.06	0.03	−0.07	−0.24	−0.18	−0.04	−0.05	0.69	0.98	0.66	0.46	0.63	0.72	1.00

B. Correlation of monthly asset return 1997–2001 in local currency (hedged currencies)

Asset/Country	Stocks							Bonds						
	U.S.	Germany	U.K.	Japan	Australia	Canada	France	U.S.	Germany	U.K.	Japan	Australia	Canada	France
Stocks														
U.S.	1.00													
Germany	0.78	1.00												
U.K.	0.83	0.78	1.00											
Japan	0.55	0.51	0.46	1.00										
Australia	0.72	0.60	0.73	0.47	1.00									
Canada	0.80	0.75	0.77	0.47	0.66	1.00								
France	0.75	0.90	0.82	0.51	0.56	0.74	1.00							
Bonds														
U.S.	0.09	0.22	0.06	0.05	−0.03	0.12	0.13	1.00						
Germany	−0.02	0.11	−0.01	−0.19	−0.08	0.01	0.03	0.82	1.00					
U.K.	0.13	0.18	0.12	−0.07	0.02	0.05	0.10	0.85	0.79	1.00				
Japan	0.06	0.18	0.12	−0.01	−0.02	0.06	0.11	0.82	0.66	0.78	1.00			
Australia	0.05	0.19	0.06	−0.01	0.04	0.16	0.10	0.92	0.81	0.77	0.77	1.00		
Canada	0.02	0.12	0.01	−0.03	0.01	0.11	0.04	0.89	0.85	0.71	0.67	0.95	1.00	
France	−0.05	0.08	−0.05	−0.20	−0.09	0.00	0.00	0.76	0.98	0.70	0.57	0.76	0.83	1.00

TABLE **21.12**	Sample Period (monthly excess returns in $U.S.)	
Correlation of U.S. equity returns with country equity returns	1967–2001*	1970–1989**
World	0.95	0.86
United Kingdom	0.83	0.49
Canada	0.82	0.72
Germany	0.75	0.33
Sweden	0.73	0.38
Netherlands	0.71	0.56
Australia	0.71	0.47
France	0.70	0.42
Denmark	0.67	0.33
Hong Kong	0.67	0.29
Spain	0.65	0.25
Switzerland	0.65	0.49
Norway	0.63	0.44
Japan	0.58	0.27
Italy	0.55	0.22
Austria	0.46	0.12
Belgium	0.46	0.41

*Source: Datastream.

**Source: Campbell R. Harvey, "The World Price of Covariance Risk," *Journal of Finance,* March 1991.

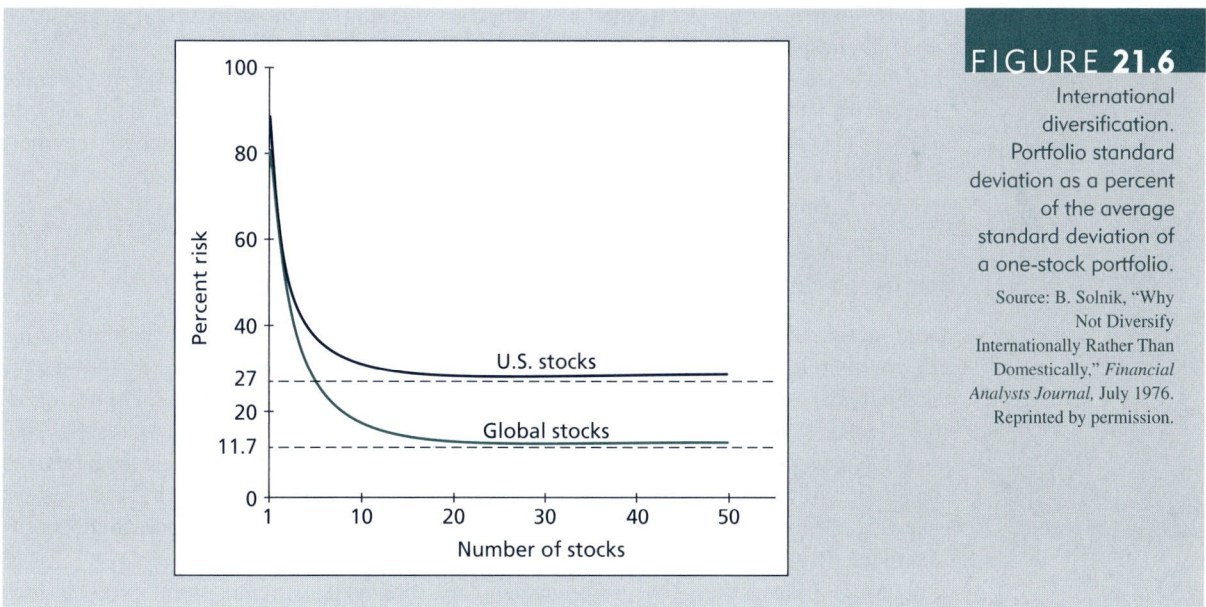

FIGURE **21.6**

International diversification. Portfolio standard deviation as a percent of the average standard deviation of a one-stock portfolio.

Source: B. Solnik, "Why Not Diversify Internationally Rather Than Domestically," *Financial Analysts Journal,* July 1976. Reprinted by permission.

But suppose we replace *expected* returns with *realized* average returns from a sample period to construct an efficient frontier; what is the possible use of this graph?

The ex post efficient frontier (derived from realized returns) describes the portfolio of only one investor—the clairvoyant who actually expected the precise averages of realized returns on all assets and estimated a covariance matrix that materialized, precisely, in the actual realizations of the sample period returns on all assets. Obviously, we are talking about a slim to

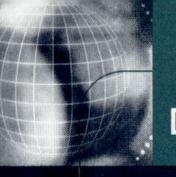

Dancing in Step

Individual stock markets are increasingly being driven by global rather than local factors. But why do national markets not have minds of their own? They did have once.

Traditionally, one way that investors sought to reduce risk was by diversifying overseas: when American shares slumped, the loss there would be offset by a gain in, say, European shares. That, at any rate, was the theory. In recent years, however, stock markets seem to have moved more closely in step with one another. The correlation between changes in American and European share prices has risen from 0.4 in the mid-1990s to 0.8 last year.

The health of a market's home economy may matter less than it used to for a number of reasons. First, the scrapping of controls on capital (combined with more efficient trading systems) has increased cross-border trading of shares, creating something closer to a global equity market. Second, it has become increasingly common for big companies to be listed on more than one market. Third, as a result of the wave of cross-border mergers and acquisitions, overseas profits account for a bigger slice of many companies' overall profits—high-tech firms are especially global in their reach. And finally, the Internet has made it easier for investors to get information on foreign firms. So firms in the same industry, but in different economies, are valued on a similar basis.

By breaking down movements in share prices into global effects, country-specific effects, and firm-specific effects, a new study by economists at the IMF tries to find out what percentage of a stock's performance is due to global rather than country factors. The model distinguishes between two kinds of global factors: the global business cycle and global-industry effects, which similarly influence firms in the same sector but in different countries.

The study finds that there has indeed been a big increase in the importance of global factors—of both kinds—in explaining movements in share prices since the mid-1990s.

SOURCE: Abridged from *The Economist*, March 22, 2001. Copyright © 2001 The Economist Newspaper Ltd. All rights reserved. Reprinted with permission. Further reproduction prohibited. www.economist.com.

empty set of investors. For all other, less than clairvoyant investors, such a frontier may have value only for purposes of performance evaluation.

In the world of volatile stocks, some stocks are bound to realize large, *unexpected* average returns. This will be reflected in ex post efficient frontiers of enormous "potential." They will, however, suggest exaggerated diversification benefits. Such (elusive) potential was enumerated in Chapter 20 on performance evaluation. It has no meaning as a tool to discuss the potential for future investments for real-life investors.

Realistic Benefits from International Diversification

While recent realized returns can be highly misleading estimates of expected future returns, they are more useful for measuring prospective risk. There are two compelling reasons for this. First, market efficiency (or even near efficiency) implies that stock prices will be impossible to predict with any accuracy, but no such implication applies to risk measures. Second, it is a statistical fact that errors in estimates of standard deviation and correlation from realized data are of a lower order of magnitude than estimates of expected returns. For these reasons, using risk estimates from realized returns does not exaggerate as much the potential benefits from diversification.

Figure 21.7 shows the efficient frontier using realized average monthly returns on the stock indexes of the 25 developed countries, with and without short sales. Even when the (ex post) efficient frontier is constrained to preclude short sales, it greatly exaggerates the benefits from diversification. Unfortunately, such misleading efficient frontiers are presented in many articles and texts on the benefits of diversification.

A more reasonable description of diversification is achievable only when we input reasonable equilibrium expected returns. Absent superior information, such expected returns are best based on appropriate risk measures of the assets. The capital asset pricing model (CAPM)

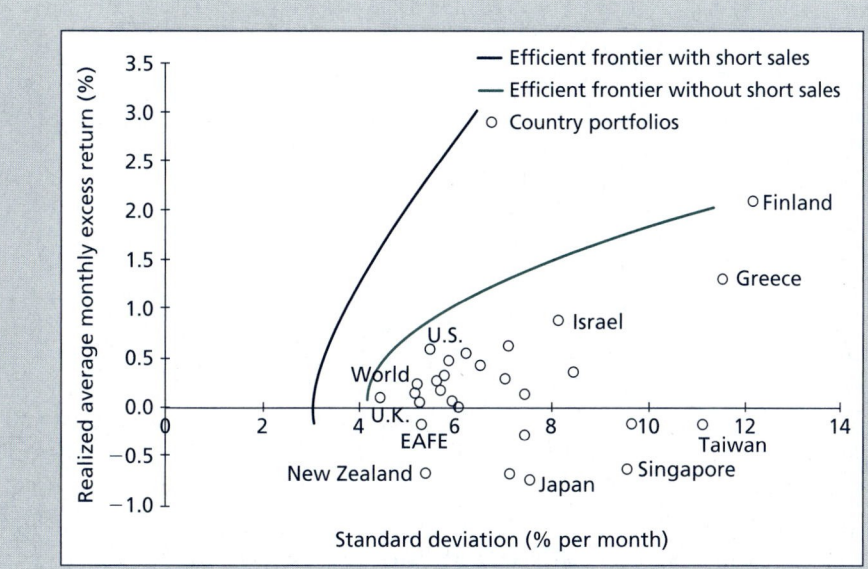

FIGURE **21.7**

Ex-post-efficient frontier of country portfolios, 1997–2001.

suggests using the beta of the stock against the world portfolio. To generate expected excess returns (over the risk-free rate) for all assets, we specify the expected excess return on the world portfolio. We obtain the expected excess return on each asset by multiplying the beta of the asset by the world portfolio expected excess return. This procedure presupposes that the world portfolio will lie on the efficient frontier, at the point of tangency with the world capital market line. The curvature of the efficient frontier will not be affected by the estimate of the world portfolio excess return. A higher estimate will shift the curve upward. The capital market line will have a steeper slope.

We perform this procedure with risk measures estimated from actual returns and further impose the likely applicable constraint on short sales. We use the betas to compute the expected return on individual markets, assuming the expected excess return on the world portfolio is .6% per month. This is a larger excess return than the average realized over the period 1996–2001, but is in line with the average return over the previous 50 years. Varying this estimate would not qualitatively affect the results shown in Figure 21.8 (which is drawn on the same scale as Figure 21.7). The figure shows a realistic assessment that reveals modest but significant benefits from international diversification using only developed markets. Incorporating emerging markets would slightly increase these benefits.

Are Benefits from International Diversification Preserved in Bear Markets?

Some studies (e.g., Longin and Solnik, 1995, or Jacquier and Marcus, 2001) suggest that correlation in country portfolio returns increase during periods of turbulence in capital markets. If so, benefits from diversification would be lost exactly when they are needed the most. For example, a study by Roll (1988) of the crash of October 1987 shows that all 23 country indexes studied declined over the crash period of October 12–26. This correlation is reflected in the movements of regional indexes depicted in Figure 21.9. Roll found that the beta of a country index on the world index (estimated prior to the crash) was the best predictor of that index's response to the October crash of the U.S. stock market. This suggests a common factor underlying the movement of stocks around the world. This model predicts that a

FIGURE 21.8

Efficient frontier of country portfolios (world expected excess return = .6% per month)

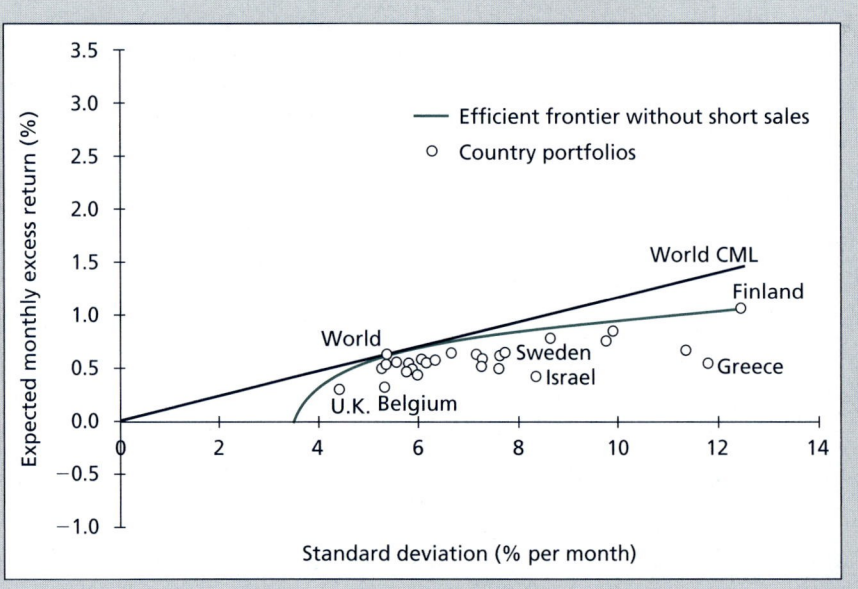

FIGURE 21.9

Regional indexes around the crash, October 14–October 26, 1987

Source: From Richard Roll, "The International Crash of October 1987," *Financial Analysts Journal*, September–October 1988. Copyright 1998, Association for Investment Management and Research. Reproduced and republished from *Financial Analysts Journal* with permission from the Association for Investment Management and Research. All Rights Reserved.

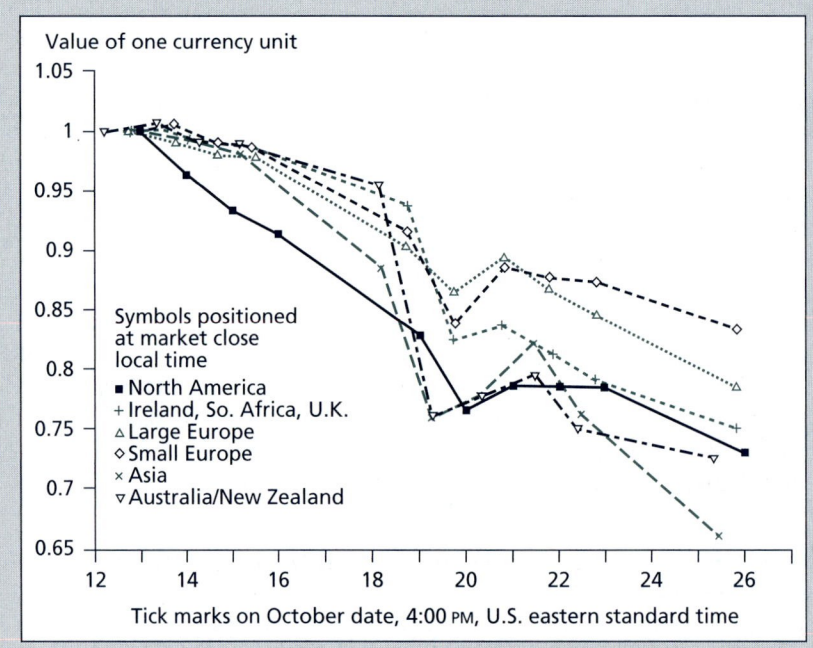

macroeconomic shock would affect all countries and that diversification can only mitigate country-specific events. Our best guess is that the diversification benefits shown by the world CAPM model are realistic.

21.4 INTERNATIONAL INVESTING AND PERFORMANCE ATTRIBUTION

The benefits from international diversification may be modest for passive investors but for active managers international investing offers greater opportunities. International investing calls for specialization in additional fields of analysis: currency, country and worldwide industry, as well as a greater universe for stock selection.

Constructing a Benchmark Portfolio of Foreign Assets

Active international investing, as well as passive, requires a benchmark portfolio (the bogey). One widely used index of non-U.S. stocks is the **European, Australian, Far East (EAFE) index** computed by Morgan Stanley. Additional indexes of world equity performance are published by Capital International Indices, Salomon Brothers, Credit Suisse First Boston, and Goldman Sachs. Portfolios designed to mirror or even replicate the country, currency, and company representation of these indexes would be the obvious generalization of the purely domestic passive equity strategy.

> **European, Australian, Far East (EAFE) index**
>
> A widely used index of non-U.S. stocks computed by Morgan Stanley.

An issue that sometimes arises in the international context is the appropriateness of market-capitalization weighting schemes in the construction of international indexes. Capitalization weighting is far and away the most common approach. However, some argue that it might not be the best weighting scheme in an international context. This is in part because different countries have differing proportions of their corporate sector organized as publicly traded firms.

Table 21.13 shows 1996 and 2001 data for market capitalization weights versus the GDP for countries in the EAFE index. As in Table 21.13, these data reveal substantial disparities between the relative sizes of market capitalization and GDP. Since market capitalization is a stock figure (the value of equity at one point in time), while GDP is a flow figure (production of goods and services during the entire year), we expect capitalization to be more volatile and the relative shares to be more variable over time. Some discrepancies are persistent, however. For example, the U.K.'s share of capitalization is about double its share of GDP, while Germany's share of capitalization is much less than its share of GDP. These disparities indicate that a greater proportion of economic activity is conducted by incorporated business in the U.K. than in Germany. Table 21.13 also illustrates the influence of stock market volatility on market-capitalization weighting schemes. For example, as its stock market swooned in the 1990s, Japan's share of EAFE capitalization declined from 44%, more than its share of GDP in 1996 to 26%, below its share of GDP in 2001.

Some argue that it would be more appropriate to weight international indexes by GDP rather than market capitalization. The justification for this view is that an internationally diversified portfolio should purchase shares in proportion to the broad asset base of each country, and GDP might be a better measure of the importance of a country in the international economy than the value of its outstanding stocks. Others have even suggested weights proportional to the import share of various countries. The argument is that investors who wish to hedge the price of imported goods might choose to hold securities in foreign firms in proportion to the goods imported from those countries. The nearby box considers the question of global asset allocation for investors seeking effective international diversification.

TABLE 21.13
Weighting schemes for EAFE countries

Country	2001		1996	
	% of EAFE Market Capitalization	% of EAFE GDP	% of EAFE Market Capitalization	% of EAFE GDP
Japan	25.8	31.0	43.5	31.5
United Kingdom	19.6	10.6	15.5	8.0
Germany	7.9	13.8	6.3	16.0
France	9.8	9.8	5.6	10.4
Netherlands	5.0	2.8	4.4	2.8
Switzerland	5.5	1.8	3.9	2.0
Hong Kong	4.7	1.2	3.8	1.0
Australia	3.2	2.7	2.8	2.7
Italy	5.0	8.1	2.7	8.3
Taiwan	1.7	2.1	2.0	1.9
Spain	2.9	4.3	1.9	4.1
Sweden	1.9	1.6	1.8	1.8
Singapore	1.0	0.6	1.7	0.6
Belgium	1.2	1.7	1.1	1.8
Denmark	0.8	1.2	0.6	1.2
Finland	1.4	0.9	0.5	0.9
Norway	0.6	1.2	0.4	1.1
New Zealand	0.2	0.4	0.4	0.4
Ireland	0.7	0.8	0.3	0.5
Austria	0.2	1.4	0.3	1.5
Portugal	0.4	0.8	0.3	0.8
Greece	0.5	0.9	0.2	0.8
Luxemburg	0.2	0.1	0.1	0.1

Source: Datastream.

Performance Attribution

We can measure the contribution of each of these factors following a manner similar to the performance attribution techniques introduced in Chapter 20.

currency selection

Asset allocation in which the investor chooses among investments denominated in different currencies.

1. **Currency selection** measures the contribution to total portfolio performance attributable to exchange rate fluctuations relative to the investor's benchmark currency, which we will take to be the U.S. dollar. We might use a benchmark like the EAFE index to compare a portfolio's currency selection for a particular period to a passive benchmark. EAFE currency selection would be computed as the weighted average of the currency appreciation of the currencies represented in the EAFE portfolio using as weights the fraction of the EAFE portfolio invested in each currency.

country selection

Asset allocation in which the investor chooses among investments in different countries.

2. **Country selection** measures the contribution to performance attributable to investing in the better-performing stock markets of the world. It can be measured as the weighted average of the equity *index* returns of each country using as weights the share of the manager's portfolio in each country. We use index returns to abstract from the effect of security selection within countries. To measure a manager's contribution relative to a passive strategy, we might compare country selection to the weighted average across

International Investing Raises Questions

As Yogi Berra might say, the problem with international investing is that it's so darn foreign.

Currency swings? Hedging? International diversification? What's that?

Here are answers to five questions that I'm often asked:

- Foreign stocks account for some 60% of world stock market value, so shouldn't you have 60% of your stock market money overseas?

The main reason to invest abroad isn't to replicate the global market or to boost returns. Instead, "what we're trying to do by adding foreign stocks is to reduce volatility," explains Robert Ludwig, chief investment officer at money manager SEI Investments.

Foreign stocks don't move in sync with U.S. shares and, thus, they may provide offsetting gains when the U.S. market is falling. But to get the resulting risk reduction, you don't need anything like 60% of your money abroad.

- So, how much foreign exposure do you need to get decent diversification?

"Based on the volatility of foreign markets and the correlation between markets, we think an optimal portfolio is 70% in the U.S., 20% in developed foreign markets, and 10% in emerging markets," Mr. Ludwig says.

Even with a third of your stock market money in foreign issues, you may find that the risk-reduction benefits aren't all that reliable. Unfortunately, when U.S. stocks get really pounded, it seems foreign shares also tend to tumble.

- Can U.S. companies with global operations give you international diversification?

"When you look at these multinationals, the factor that drives their performance is their home market," says Mark Riepe, a vice president with Ibbotson Associates, a Chicago research firm.

How come? U.S. multinationals tend to be owned by U.S. investors, who will be swayed by the ups and downs of the U.S. market. In addition, Mr. Riepe notes that while multinationals may derive substantial profits and revenue abroad, most of their costs—especially labor costs—will be incurred in the U.S.

- Does international diversification come from the foreign stocks or the foreign currency?

"It comes from both in roughly equal pieces," Mr. Riepe says. "Those who choose to hedge their foreign currency raise the correlation with U.S. stocks, and so the diversification benefit won't be nearly as great."

Indeed, you may want to think twice before investing in a foreign-stock fund that frequently hedges its currency exposure in an effort to mute the impact of—and make money from—changes in foreign-exchange rates.

"The studies that we've done show that stock managers have hurt themselves more than they've helped themselves by actively managing currencies," Mr. Ludwig says.

- Should you divvy up your money among foreign countries depending on the size of each national stock market?

At issue is the nagging question of how much to put in Japan. If you replicated the market weightings of Morgan Stanley Capital International's Europe, Australasia and Far East index, you would currently have around a third of your overseas money in Japan.

That's the sort of weighting you find in international funds, which seek to track the performance of the EAFE or similar international indexes. Actively managed foreign-stock funds, by contrast, pay less attention to market weights and on average, these days have just 14% in Japan.

If your focus is risk reduction rather than performance, the index—and the funds that track it—are the clear winners. Japan performs quite unlike the U.S. market, so it provides good diversification for U.S. investors, says Tricia Rothschild, international editor at Morningstar Mutual Funds, a Chicago newsletter.

"But correlations aren't static," she adds. "There's always a problem with taking what happened over the past 20 years and projecting it out over the next 20 years."

SOURCE: Jonathan Clements, "International Investing Raises Questions on Allocation, Diversification, Hedging," *The Wall Street Journal*, July 29, 1997. Excerpted by permission of *The Wall Street Journal*. © 1997 Dow Jones & Company, Inc. All Rights Reserved Worldwide.

countries of equity index returns using as weights the share of the EAFE portfolio in each country.

3. **Stock selection** ability may, as in Chapter 20, be measured as the weighted average of equity returns *in excess of the equity index* in each country. Here, we would use local currency returns and use as weights the investments in each country.

stock selection

Choice of specific stocks within a country's equity market.

TABLE **21.14** Example of performance attribution: international	EAFE Weight	Return on Equity Index	Currency Appreciation $E_1/E_0 - 1$	Manager's Weight	Manager's Return
Europe	0.30	10%	10%	0.35	8%
Australia	0.10	5	−10	0.10	7
Far East	0.60	15	30	0.55	18

Overall performance (dollar return = return on index + currency appreciation)
EAFE: .30(10 + 10) + .10(5 − 10) + .60(15 + 30) = 32.5%
Manager: .35(8 + 10) + .10(7 − 10) + .55(18 + 30) = 32.4%
Loss of .10% relative to EAFE

Currency selection
EAFE: (0.30 × 10%) + (0.10 × (−10%)) + (0.60 × 30%) = 20% appreciation
Manager: (0.35 × 10%) + (0.10 × (−10%)) + (0.55 × 30%) = 19% appreciation
Loss of 1% relative to EAFE

Country selection
EAFE: (0.30 × 10%) + (0.10 × 5%) + (0.60 × 15%) = 12.5%
Manager: (0.35 × 10%) + (0.10 × 5%) + (0.55 × 15%) = 12.25%
Loss of 0.25% relative to EAFE

Stock selection
            (8% − 10%)0.35 + (7% − 5%)0.10 + (18% − 15%)0.55 = 1.15%
Contribution of 1.15% relative to EAFE

Sum of attributions (equal to overall performance)
Currency (−1%) + country (−.25%) + selection (1.15%) = −.10%

---

cash/bond selection

Choice between money market versus longer-term bonds.

4. **Cash/bond selection** may be measured as the excess return derived from weighting bonds and bills differently from some benchmark weights.

Table 21.14 gives an example of how to measure the contribution of the decisions an international portfolio manager might make.

Concept CHECK

4. Using the data in Table 21.14, compute the manager's country and currency selection if portfolio weights had been 40% in Europe, 20% in Australia, and 40% in the Far East.

International Portfolios

This Excel model provides an efficient frontier analysis similar to that in Chapter 6. In Chapter 6 the frontier was based on individual securities, whereas this model examines the returns on international exchange traded funds. Using the model with return data enables us to analyze the benefits of international diversification.

	A	B	C	D	E	F	G	H	I	J
58			Bordered Covariance Matrix for Target Return Portfolio							
59			EWD	EWH	EWI	EWJ	EWL	EWP	EWW	SP 500	
60	Weights		0.00	0.00	0.08	0.38	0.02	0.00	0.00	0.52	
61		0.0000	0.00	0.00	0.00	0.00	0.00	0.00	0.00	0.00	
62		0.0000	0.00	0.00	0.00	0.00	0.00	0.00	0.00	0.00	
63		0.0826	0.00	0.00	4.63	3.21	0.55	0.00	0.00	7.69	
64		0.3805	0.00	0.00	3.21	98.41	1.82	0.00	0.00	53.79	
65		0.0171	0.00	0.00	0.55	1.82	0.14	0.00	0.00	2.09	
66		0.0000	0.00	0.00	0.00	0.00	0.00	0.00	0.00	0.00	
67		0.0000	0.00	0.00	0.00	0.00	0.00	0.00	0.00	0.00	
68		0.5198	0.00	0.00	7.69	53.79	2.09	0.00	0.00	79.90	
69		1.0000	0.00	0.00	16.07	157.23	4.59	0.00	0.00	143.47	
70											
71	Port Via	321.36									
72	Port S.D.	17.93									
73	Port Mean	12.00									
74											
75											
76					Weights						
77	Mean	St. Dev	EWD	EWH	EWI	EWJ	EWL	EWP	EWW	SP 500
78	6	21.89	0.02	0.00	0.00	0.71	0.00	0.02	0.00	0.26
79	9	19.66	0.02	0.00	0.02	0.53	0.02	0.00	0.00	0.41
80	12	17.93	0.00	0.00	0.08	0.38	0.02	0.00	0.00	0.52
81	15	16.81	0.00	0.00	0.14	0.22	0.02	0.00	0.00	0.62
82	18	16.46	0.00	0.00	0.19	0.07	0.02	0.00	0.00	0.73
83	21	17.37	0.00	0.00	0.40	0.00	0.00	0.00	0.00	0.60
84	24	21.19	0.00	0.00	0.72	0.00	0.00	0.00	0.00	0.28
85	27	26.05	0.00	0.00	1.00	0.00	0.00	0.00	0.00	0.00
86											
87											

SUMMARY

- U.S. assets are only a part of the world portfolio. International capital markets offer important opportunities for portfolio diversification with enhanced risk-return characteristics.
- Exchange rate risk imparts an extra source of uncertainty to investments denominated in foreign currencies. Much of that risk can be hedged in foreign exchange futures or forward markets, but a perfect hedge is not feasible unless the foreign currency rate of return is known.
- Several world market indexes can form a basis for passive international investing. Active international management can be partitioned into currency selection, country selection, stock selection, and cash/bond selection.

www.mhhe.com/bkm

KEY TERMS

cash/bond selection, 748
country selection, 746
covered interest arbitrage
   relationship, 729

currency selection, 746
European, Australian, Far
   East (EAFE) index, 745
exchange rate risk, 727

interest rate parity
   relationship, 729
political risk, 731
stock selection, 747

PROBLEM SETS

1. Suppose a U.S. investor wishes to invest in a British firm currently selling for £40 per share. The investor has $10,000 to invest, and the current exchange rate is $2/£.

   a. How many shares can the investor purchase?

   b. Fill in the table below for rates of return after one year in each of the nine scenarios (three possible prices per share in pounds times three possible exchange rates).

Price per Share (£)	Pound-Denominated Return (%)	Dollar-Denominated Return for Year-End Exchange Rate		
		$1.80/£	$2/£	$2.20/£
£35				
£40				
£45				

   c. When is the dollar-denominated return equal to the pound-denominated return?

2. If each of the nine outcomes in problem 1 is equally likely, find the standard deviation of both the pound- and dollar-denominated rates of return.

3. Now suppose the investor in problem 1 also sells forward £5,000 at a forward exchange rate of $2.10/£.

   a. Recalculate the dollar-denominated returns for each scenario.

   b. What happens to the standard deviation of the dollar-denominated return? Compare it to both its old value and the standard deviation of the pound-denominated return.

4. Calculate the contribution to total performance from currency, country, and stock selection for the manager in the example below. All exchange rates are expressed as units of foreign currency that can be purchased with one U.S. dollar.

	EAFE Weight	Return on Equity Index	E_1/E_0	Manager's Weight	Manager's Return
Europe	0.30	20%	0.9	0.35	18%
Australia	0.10	15	1.0	0.15	20
Far East	0.60	25	1.1	0.50	20

5. If the current exchange rate is $1.75/£, the one-year forward exchange rate is $1.85/£, and the interest rate on British government bills is 8% per year, what risk-free dollar-denominated return can be locked in by investing in the British bills?

6. If you were to invest $10,000 in the British bills of problem 5, how would you lock in the dollar-denominated return?

7. Renée Michaels, CFA, plans to invest $1 million in U.S. government cash equivalents for the next 90 days. Michaels's client has authorized her to use non-U.S. government cash equivalents, but only if the currency risk is hedged to U.S. dollars by using forward currency contracts.

   a. Calculate the U.S. dollar value of the hedged investment at the end of 90 days for each of the two cash equivalents in the table below. Show all calculations.

   b. Briefly explain the theory that best accounts for your results.

c. Based upon this theory, estimate the implied interest rate for a 90-day U.S. government cash equivalent.

Interest Rates 90-Day Cash Equivalents	
Japanese government	7.6%
Swiss government	8.6

Exchange Rates Currency Units per U.S. Dollar		
	Spot	90-Day Forward
Japanese yen	133.05	133.47
Swiss franc	1.5260	1.5348

8. Suppose that the spot price of the Euro is currently 90 cents. The 1-year futures price is 95 cents. Is the U.S. interest rate higher than the Euro rate?

9. *a.* The spot price of the British pound is currently $1.50. If the risk-free interest rate on one-year government bonds is 4% in the United States and 3% in the United Kingdom, what must the forward price of the pound be for delivery one year from now?

   b. How could an investor make risk-free arbitrage profits if the forward price were higher than the price you gave in answer to (*a*)? Give a numerical example.

10. Consider the following information:

    $r_{US} = 5\%$
    $r_{UK} = 7\%$
    $E_0 = 2.0$ dollars per pound
    $F_0 = \$1.97/\pounds$ (one-year delivery)

    where the interest rates are annual yields on U.S. or U.K. bills. Given this information:
    a. Where would you lend?
    b. Where would you borrow?
    c. How could you arbitrage?

11. John Irish, CFA, is an independent investment adviser who is assisting Alfred Darwin, the head of the Investment Committee of General Technology Corporation, to establish a new pension fund. Darwin asks Irish about international equities and whether the Investment Committee should consider them as an additional asset for the pension fund.
    a. Explain the rationale for including international equities in General's equity portfolio. Identify and describe three relevant considerations in formulating your answer.
    b. List three possible arguments against international equity investment and briefly discuss the significance of each.
    c. To illustrate several aspects of the performance of international securities over time, Irish shows Darwin the accompanying graph of investment results experienced by a U.S. pension fund in the recent past. Compare the performance of the U.S. dollar and non-U.S. dollar equity and fixed-income asset categories, and explain the significance of the result of the account performance index relative to the results of the four individual asset class indexes.

WEBMASTER

International Diversification

Should U.S. Investors Hold Foreign Stocks? This question has been debated by investment advisers and investors alike. In theory, an investor should be able to reduce risk as long as the investments aren't perfectly correlated. In a recent article that was published by the Federal Reserve Bank of New York, Asani Sarkar and Kai Li investigated the benefits of international diversification. The article can be found on the bank's website at http://www.newyorkfed.org/rmaghome/curr_iss/ci8-3.html

After reading this article, address the following questions:

1. What two measures did the authors use to examine the potential benefits of international diversification?

2. Compare the deletions of stock returns for G7 countries with emerging market countries. What should that imply about benefits of diversification? Were the benefits associated with diversification solely due to the ability to short sell? What is the potential impact of global market integration on diversification benefits?

3. How did the authors investigate the impact of global market integration?

SOLUTIONS TO

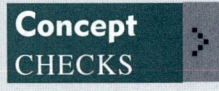

Concept
CHECKS

1. $1 + r(US) = [(1 + r_f(UK)] \times (E_1/E_0)$
    a. $1 + r(US) = 1.1 \times 1.0 = 1.10$. Therefore, $r(US) = 10\%$.
    b. $1 + r(US) = 1.1 \times 1.1 = 1.21$. Therefore, $r(US) = 21\%$.

2. According to interest rate parity, F_0 should be $1.93. As the futures price is too high, we should reverse the arbitrage strategy just considered.

Action	Cash Flow Now ($)	Cash Flow in One Year ($)
Borrow $2 in the United States.	$ 2.00	$-2.00(1.0615)
Convert the borrowed dollars to pounds, and lend in the United Kingdom at a 10% interest rate.	-2.00	$1.10E_1$
Enter a contract to sell 1.10 pounds at a futures price of $1.95/£.	0.00	$1.10(1.95 - E_1)$
Total	$ 0.00	$0.022

3. You must sell forward the number of pounds you will end up with at the end of the year. This value cannot be known with certainty, however, unless the rate of return of the pound-denominated investment is known.

   a. $10,000 \times 1.20 = 12,000$ pounds

   b. $10,000 \times 1.30 = 13,000$ pounds

4. *Country selection:*

$$(0.40 \times 10\%) + (0.20 \times 5\%) + (0.40 \times 15\%) = 11\%$$

This is a loss of 1.5% (11% versus 12.5%) relative to the EAFE passive benchmark.

Currency selection:

$$(0.40 \times 10\%) + (0.20 \times (-10\%)) + (0.40 \times 30\%) = 14\%$$

This is a loss of 6% (14% versus 20%) relative to the EAFE benchmark.

APPENDIXES

A References

B References to CFA Questions

Appendix A

REFERENCES

Affleck-Graves, John, and Richard R. Mendenhall. "The Relation between the Value Line Enigma and Post-Earnings-Announcement Drift." *Journal of Financial Economics* 31 (February 1992), pp. 75–96.

Alexander, Sidney. "Price Movements in Speculative Markets: Trends or Random Walks, No. 2." In *The Random Character of Stock Market Prices,* ed. Paul Cootner. Cambridge, MA: MIT Press, 1964.

Amihud, Yakov, and Haim Mendelson. "Asset Pricing and the Bid-Ask Spread." *Journal of Financial Economics* 17 (December 1986), pp. 223–50.

――― . "Liquidity, Asset Prices, and Financial Policy." *Financial Analysts Journal* 47 (November/December 1991), pp. 56–66.

Arbel, Avner. "Generic Stocks: An Old Product in a New Package." *Journal of Portfolio Management*, Summer 1985, pp. 4–13.

Arbel, Avner, and Paul J. Strebel. "Pay Attention to Neglected Firms." *Journal of Portfolio Management*, Winter 1983, pp. 37–42.

Banz, Rolf. "The Relationship between Return and Market Value of Common Stocks." *Journal of Financial Economics* 9 (March 1981), pp. 3–18.

Barber, Brad, and Terrance Odean. "Trading Is Hazardous to Your Wealth: The Common Stock Investment Performance of Individual Investors." *Journal of Finance* 55 (2000), pp. 773–806.

――― . "Boys Will Be Boys: Gender, Overconfidence, and Common Stock Investment." *Quarterly Journal of Economics* 16 (2001), pp. 262–92.

Basu, Sanjoy. "The Investment Performance of Common Stocks in Relation to Their Price-Earnings Ratios: A Test of the Efficient Market Hypothesis." *Journal of Finance* 32 (June 1977), pp. 663–82.

――― . "The Relationship between Earnings Yield, Market Value, and Return for NYSE Common Stocks: Further Evidence." *Journal of Financial Economics* 12 (June 1983), pp. 129–56.

Bernhard, Arnold. *Value Line Methods of Evaluating Common Stocks.* New York: Arnold Bernhard and Co., 1979.

756

Bernard, Victor L., and Jacob K. Thomas. "Post-Earnings-Announcement Drift: Delayed Price Response or Risk Premium?" *Journal of Accounting Research* 27 (1989), pp. 1–36.

Black, Fischer. "Yes, Virginia, There Is Hope: Tests of the Value Line Ranking System." Graduate School of Business, University of Chicago, 1971.

Black, Fischer; Michael C. Jensen; and Myron Scholes. "The Capital Asset Pricing Model: Some Empirical Tests." *Studies in the Theory of Capital Markets,* ed. Michael C. Jensen. Praeger, 1972.

Black, Fischer, and Myron Scholes. "The Pricing of Options and Corporate Liabilities." *Journal of Political Economy* 81 (May–June 1973), pp. 637–59.

From Black-Scholes to Black Holes: New Frontiers in Options. London: *RISK Magazine,* 1992.

Blume, Marshall E., and Robert F. Stambaugh. "Biases in Computed Returns: An Application to the Size Effect." *Journal of Finance Economics,* 1983, pp. 387–404.

Bogle, John C. "Investing in the 1990s: Remembrance of Things Past, and Things Yet to Come." *Journal of Portfolio Management,* Spring 1991, pp. 5–14.

————— . *Bogle on Mutual Funds.* Burr Ridge, IL: Irwin Professional Publishing, 1994.

Brennan, Michael. "Taxes, Market Valuation and Corporate Financial Policy." *National Tax Journal,* 1970.

Brinson, G.; C. R. Hood; and G. Beebower. "Determinants of Portfolio Performance." *Financial Analysts Journal,* July–August 1986.

Brock, William; Josef Lakonishok; and Blake LeBaron. "Simple Technical Trading Rules and the Stochastic Properties of Stock Returns." *Journal of Finance* 47 (December 1992), pp. 1731–64.

Brown, David, and Robert H. Jennings. "On Technical Analysis." *Review of Financial Studies* 2 (1989), pp. 527–52.

Brown, Lawrence D., and Michael Rozeff. "The Superiority of Analysts' Forecasts as Measures of Expectations: Evidence from Earnings." *Journal of Finance,* March 1978.

Campbell, John Y., and Robert Shiller. "Stock Prices, Earnings and Expected Dividends." *Journal of Finance* 43 (July 1988), pp. 661–76.

Carhart, Mark. "On Persistence in Mutual Fund Performance." *Journal of Finance* 52 (1997), pp. 57–82.

Chopra, Navin; Josef Lakonishok; and Jay R. Ritter. "Measuring Abnormal Performance: Do Stocks Overreact?" *Journal of Financial Economics* 31 (1992), pp. 235–68.

Clarke, Roger, and Mark P. Kritzman, *Currency Management: Concepts and Practices.* Charlottesville: Research Foundation of the Institute of Chartered Financial Analysts, 1996.

Clayman, Michelle. "In Search of Excellence: The Investor's Viewpoint." *Financial Analysts Journal,* May–June 1987.

Connolly, Robert. "An Examination of the Robustness of the Weekend Effect." *Journal of Financial and Quantitative Analysis* 24 (June 1989), pp. 133–69.

Conrad, Jennifer, and Gautam Kaul. "Time-Variation in Expected Returns." *Journal of Business* 61 (October 1988), pp. 409–25.

Copeland, Thomas E., and David Mayers. "The Value Line Enigma (1965–1978): A Case Study of Performance Evaluation Issues." *Journal of Financial Economics,* November 1982.

De Bondt, W. F. M., and R. H. Thaler. "Further Evidence on Investor Overreaction and Stock Market Seasonality." *Journal of Finance* 42 (1987), pp. 557–81.

———— . "Do Security Analysts Overreact?" *American Economic Review* 80 (1990), pp. 52–57.

———— . "Financial Decision Making in Markets and Firms." In *Handbooks in Operations Research and Management Science, Volume 9: Finance,* eds. R. A. Jarrow, V. Maksimovic, and W. T. Ziemba. Amsterdam: Elsevier, 1995.

———— . "Does the Stock Market Overreact.?" *Journal of Finance* 40 (1985), pp. 793–805.

Dimson, E.; P. R. Marsh; and M. Staunton. *Millenium Book II: 101 Years of Investment Returns,* ABN-Amro and London Business School, London, 2001.

Douglas, George W. "Risk in Equity Markets: An Empirical Appraisal of Market Efficiency." *Yale Economic Essays* IX (Spring 1969).

Dunn, Patricia, and Rolf D. Theisen. "How Consistently Do Active Managers Win?" *Journal of Portfolio Management* 9 (Summer 1983), pp. 47–53.

Elton, E. J.; M. J. Gruber; S. Das; and M. Hlavka. "Efficiency with Costly Information: A Reinterpretation of Evidence from Managed Portfolios." *Review of Financial Studies* 6 (1993), pp. 1–22.

Errunza, Vihang, and Etienne Losq. "International Asset Pricing under Mild Segmentation: Theory and Test." *Journal of Finance* 40 (March 1985), pp. 105–24.

Fama, Eugene. "The Behavior of Stock Market Prices." *Journal of Business* 38 (January 1965), pp. 34–105.

Fama, Eugene, and Marshall Blume. "Filter Rules and Stock Market Trading Profits." *Journal of Business* 39 (Supplement, January 1966), pp. 226–41.

Fama, Eugene F., and Kenneth R. French. "Permanent and Temporary Components of Stock Prices." *Journal of Political Economy* 96 (1987), pp. 246–73.

———— . "Dividend Yields and Expected Stock Returns." *Journal of Financial Economics* 22 (October 1988), pp. 3–25.

———— . "Business Conditions and Expected Returns on Stocks and Bonds." *Journal of Financial Economics* 25 (November 1989), pp. 3–22.

———— . "The Cross Section of Expected Stock Returns." *Journal of Finance* 47 (June 1992), pp. 427–465.

———— . "Common Risk Factors in the Returns on Stocks and Bonds." *Journal of Financial Economics* 33 (1993), pp. 3–56.

———— . "The Equity Premium." *Journal of Finance* 57 (April 2002), 637–60.

Fama, Eugene, and James MacBeth. "Risk, Return and Equilibrium: Empirical Tests." *Journal of Political Economy* 81 (March 1973).

Fisher, Irving. *The Theory of Interest: As Determined by Impatience to Spend Income and Opportunity to Invest It.* New York: Augustus M. Kelley, Publishers, 1965, originally published in 1930.

Flannery, Mark J., and Christopher M. James. "The Effect of Interest Rate Changes on the Common Stock Returns of Financial Institutions." *Journal of Finance* 39 (September 1984), pp. 1141–54.

Foster, George; Chris Olsen; and Terry Shevlin. "Earnings Releases, Anomalies, and the Behavior of Security Returns." *The Accounting Review* 59 (October 1984).

French, Kenneth. "Stock Returns and the Weekend Effect." *Journal of Financial Economics* 8 (March 1980), pp. 55–69.

Gervais, S., and T. Odean. "Learning to be Overconfident." *Review of Financial Studies* 14 (2001), pp. 1–27.

Geske, Robert, and Richard Roll. "On Valuing American Call Options with the Black-Scholes European Formula." *Journal of Finance* 39 (June 1984), pp. 443–56.

Gibbons, Michael, and Patrick Hess. "Day of the Week Effects and Asset Returns." *Journal of Business* 54 (October 1981), pp. 579–98.

Givoly, Dan, and Dan Palmon. "Insider Trading and Exploitation of Inside Information: Some Empirical Evidence." *Journal of Business* 58 (1985), pp. 69–87.

Goetzmann, William N., and Roger G. Ibbotson. "Do Winners Repeat?" *Journal of Portfolio Management*, Winter 1994, pp. 9–18.

Graham, J. R., and C. R. Harvey. "Expectations of Equity Risk Premia, Volatility and Asymmetry from a Corporate Finance Perspective." Working Paper, Duke University, Fuqua School of Business, November 2001.

Graham, J. R., and C. R. Harvey. "Grading the Performance of Market Timing Newletters." *Financial Analysts Journal* 53 (November/December 1997), pp. 54–66.

Grieves, Robin, and Alan J. Marcus. "Riding the Yield Curve: Reprise." *Journal of Portfolio Management,* Winter 1992.

Grinblatt, Mark, and Bing Han. "The Disposition Effect and Momentum." Working Paper, UCLA, 2001.

Grinblatt, Mark, and Sheridan Titman. "Mutual Fund Performance: An Analysis of Quarterly Portfolio Holdings." *Journal of Business* 62 (1989), pp. 393–416.

Grossman, Sanford J., and Joseph E. Stiglitz. "On the Impossibility of Informationally Efficient Markets." *American Economic Review* 70 (June 1980), pp. 393–408.

Haugen, Robert A. *The New Finance: The Case Against Efficient Markets.* Englewood Cliffs, NJ: Prentice Hall, 1995.

Henriksson, Roy D. "Market Timing and Mutual Fund Performance: An Empirical Investigation." *Journal of Business* 57 (January 1984).

Hirshleifer, David. "Investor Psychology and Asset Pricing." *Journal of Finance* 56 (August 2001), pp. 1533–97.

Homer, Sidney, and Martin L. Leibowitz. *Inside the Yield Book: New Tools for Bond Market Strategy.* Englewood Cliffs, NJ: Prentice Hall, 1972.

Ibbotson, Roger G. "Price Performance of Common Stock New Issues." *Journal of Financial Economics* 2 (September 1975).

Ibbotson, Roger; Richard C. Carr; and Anthony W. Robinson. "International Equity and Bond Returns." *Financial Analysts Journal*, July–August 1982.

Ibbotson, R. C., and L. B. Siegel. "The World Market Wealth Portfolio." *Journal of Portfolio Management,* Winter 1983.

Ibbotson, R. C.; L. B. Siegel; and K. Love. "World Wealth: Market Values and Returns." *Journal of Portfolio Management*, Fall 1985.

Jacquier, Eric, and Alan Marcus. "Asset Allocation Models and Market Volatility," *Financial Analysts Journal* 57 (March/April 2001), pp. 16–30.

Jaffe, Jeffrey F. "Special Information and Insider Trading." *Journal of Business* 47 (July 1974), pp. 410–28.

———— . "Gold and Gold Stocks as Investments for Institutional Portfolios." *Financial Analysts Journal* 45 (March–April 1989), pp. 53–59.

Jagannathan, R., E. R. McGrattan; and A. Scherbina. "The Declining U.S. Equity Premium." *Federal Reserve Bank of Minneapolis Quarterly Review* 24 (Fall 2000), pp. 3–19.

Jagannathan, Ravi, and Zhenyu Wang. "The Conditional CAPM and the Cross-Section of Expected Returns." *Staff Report 208, Federal Reserve Bank of Minneapolis*, 1996.

Jegadeesh, Narasimhan. "Evidence of Predictable Behavior of Security Returns." *Journal of Finance* 45 (September 1990), pp. 881–98.

Jegadeesh, Narasimhan, and Sheridan Titman. "Returns to Buying Winners and Selling Losers: Implications for Stock Market Efficiency." *Journal of Finance* 48 (March 1993), pp. 65–91.

Jensen, Michael C. "The Performance of Mutual Funds in the Period 1945–1964." *Journal of Finance,* May 1968.

—— . "Risk, the Pricing of Capital Assets, and the Evaluation of Investment Portfolios." *Journal of Business* 42 (April 1969), pp. 167–247.

Kahneman, D., and A. Tversky. "Subjective Probability: A Judgment of Representativeness." *Cognitive Psychology* 3 (1972), pp. 430–54.

—— . "On the Psychology of Prediction." *Psychology Review* 80 (1973), pp. 237–51.

Keim, Donald B. "Size Related Anomalies and Stock Return Seasonality: Further Empirical Evidence." *Journal of Financial Economics* 12 (June 1983), pp. 13–32.

Keim, Donald B., and Robert F. Stambaugh. "Predicting Returns in the Stock and Bond Markets." *Journal of Financial Economics* 17 (1986), pp. 357–90.

Kendall, Maurice. "The Analysis of Economic Time Series, Part I: Prices." *Journal of the Royal Statistical Society* 96 (1953), pp. 11–25.

Kopcke, Richard W., and Geoffrey R. H. Woglom. "Regulation Q and Savings Bank Solvency—The Connecticut Experience." In *The Regulation of Financial Institutions*, Federal Reserve Bank of Boston Conference Series, No. 21, 1979.

Lakonishok, Josef; Andrei Shleifer; and Robert W. Vishney. "Contrarian Investment, Extrapolation, and Risk." *Journal of Finance* 50 (1995), pp. 1541–78.

La Porta, Raphael. "Expectations and the Cross-Section of Stock Returns." *Journal of Finance* 51 (December 1996), pp. 1715–42.

Latane, H. A., and C. P. Jones. "Standardized Unexpected Earnings—1971–1977." *Journal of Finance,* June 1979.

Lease, R.; W. Lewellen; and G. Schlarbaum. "Market Segmentation: Evidence on the Individual Investor," *Financial Analysts Journal* 32 (1976), pp. 53–60.

Lehmann, Bruce. "Fads, Martingales and Market Efficiency." *Quarterly Journal of Economics* 105 (February 1990), pp. 1–28.

Levy, Robert A. "The Predictive Significance of Five-Point Chart Patterns." *Journal of Business* 44 (July 1971). pp. 316–23.

Lo, Andrew W., and Craig MacKinlay. "Stock Market Prices Do Not Follow Random Walks: Evidence from a Simple Specification Test." *Review of Financial Studies* 1 (Spring 1988), pp. 41–66.

Loeb, T. F. "Trading Cost: The Critical Link between Investment Information and Results." *Financial Analysts Journal*, May–June 1983.

Longin, F., and B. Solnik. "Is the Correlation in International Equity Returns Constant: 1960–1990?" *Journal of International Money and Finance* 14 (1995), pp. 3–26.

Lynch, Peter, with John Rothchild. *One Up on Wall Street.* New York: Penguin Books, 1989.

Macaulay, Frederick. *Some Theoretical Problems Suggested by the Movements of Interest Rates, Bond Yields, and Stock Prices in the United States Since 1856.* New York: National Bureau of Economic Research, 1938.

Malkiel, Burton G. "Expectations, Bond Prices, and the Term Structure of Interest Rates." *Quarterly Journal of Economics* 76 (May 1962), pp. 197–218.

――――― . "Returns from Investing in Equity Mutual Funds: 1971–1991." *Journal of Finance* 50 (June 1995), pp. 549–72.

Marcus, Alan J. "The Magellan Fund and Market Efficiency." *Journal of Portfolio Management* 17 (Fall 1990), pp. 85–88.

Mayers, David. "Nonmarketable Assets and Capital Market Equilibrium under Uncertainty." In *Studies in the Theory of Capital Markets,* ed. M. C. Jensen. New York: Praeger, 1972.

Merton, Robert C. "Theory of Rational Option Pricing." *Bell Journal of Economics and Management Science* 4 (Spring 1973), pp. 141–83.

――――― . "On Market Timing and Investment Performance: An Equilibrium Theory of Value for Market Forecasts." *Journal of Business* 54 (July 1981).

Merton, Robert C. "A Simple Model of Capital Market Equilibrium with Incomplete Information." *Journal of Finance* 42 (1987), pp. 483–510.

Miller, Merton H., and Myron Scholes. "Rate of Return in Relation to Risk: A Re-examination of Some Recent Findings." In *Studies in the Theory of Capital Markets*, ed. Michael C. Jensen. Praeger, 1972.

Morrell, John A. "Introduction to International Equity Diversification." In *International Investing for U.S. Pension Funds*, Institute for Fiduciary Education, London/Venice, May 6–13. 1989.

Niederhoffer, Victor, and Patrick Regan. "Earnings Changes, Analysts' Forecasts, and Stock Prices." *Financial Analysts Journal*, May–June 1972.

Norby, W. C. "Applications of Inflation-Adjusted Accounting Data." *Financial Analysts Journal*, March–April 1983.

Perry, Kevin, and Robert A. Taggart. "The Growing Role of Junk Bonds in Corporate Finance." *Continental Bank Journal of Applied Corporate Finance* 1 (Spring 1988).

Porter, Michael E. *Competitive Advantage: Creating and Sustaining Superior Performance.* New York: The Free Press, a Division of Macmillan, Inc., 1985.

――――― . *Competitive Strategy: Techniques for Analyzing Industries and Competitors.* New York: The Free Press, a Division of Macmillan, Inc., 1980.

Poterba, James M., and Lawrence Summers. "Mean Reversion in Stock Market Prices: Evidence and Implications." *Journal of Financial Economics* 22 (1987), pp. 27–59.

Ready, Mark J. "Profits from Technical Trading Rules." *Financial Management,* forthcoming.

Redington, F. M. "Review of the Principle of Life-Office Valuations." *Journal of the Institute of Actuaries* 78 (1952), pp. 286–340.

Reinganum, Marc R. "The Anatomy of a Stock Market Winner." *Financial Analysts Journal*, March–April 1988, pp. 272–84.

――――― . "The Anomalous Stock Market Behavior of Small Firms in January: Empirical Tests for Tax-Loss Effects." *Journal of Financial Economics* 12 (June 1983), pp. 89–104.

Ritter, Jay R. "The Buying and Selling Behavior of Individual Investors at the Turn of the Year." *Journal of Finance* 43 (July 1988), pp. 701–17.

Roberts, Harry. "Stock Market 'Patterns' and Financial Analysis: Methodological Suggestions." *Journal of Finance* 14 (March 1959), pp. 11–25.

Roll, Richard. "A Critique of the Capital Asset Theory Tests: Part I: On Past and Potential Testability of the Theory." *Journal of Financial Economics* 4 (1977).

_____ . "The International Crash of October 1987." *Financial Analysts Journal*, September–October 1988.

Ross, Stephen A. "Return, Risk and Arbitrage." In *Risk and Return in Finance*, eds. I. Friend and J. Bicksler. Cambridge, MA: Ballinger, 1976.

Rubinstein, Mark. "Implied Binomial Trees." *Journal of Finance* 49 (July 1994), pp. 771–818.

Samuelson, Paul. "The Judgment of Economic Science on Rational Portfolio Management." *Journal of Portfolio Management* 16 (Fall 1989), pp. 4–12.

Seyhun, H. Nejat. "Insiders' Profits, Costs of Trading and Market Efficiency." *Journal of Financial Economics* 16 (1986), pp. 189–212.

Sharpe, William F. "Mutual Fund Performance." *Journal of Business* 39 (January 1966).

Sharpe, William S. "A Simplified Model for Portfolio Analysis." *Management Science* IX (January 1963), pp. 277–93.

Shiller, Robert. "Do Stock Prices Move Too Much to Be Justified by Subsequent Changes in Dividends?" *American Economic Review* 71 (June 1981).

Solnik, B. *International Investing*, 4th ed. Addison Wesley, 1999.

Solnik, Bruno, and A. De Freitas. "International Factors of Stock Price Behavior." CESA Working Paper, February 1986 (cited in Bruno Solnik. *International Investments*. Reading, MA: Addison Wesley Publishing Co., 1988).

de Soto, Hernando. *The Mystery of Capital.* Basic Books, 2000.

Speidell, Lawrence S., and Vinod Bavishi. "GAAP Arbitrage: Valuation Opportunities in International Accounting Standards." *Financial Analysts Journal*, November–December 1992, pp. 58–66.

Statman, Meir. "Behavioral Finance." *Contemporary Finance Digest* 1 (Winter 1997), pp. 5–22.

Stickel, Scott E. "The Effect of Value Line Investment Survey Rank Changes on Common Stock Prices." *Journal of Financial Economics* 14 (1986), pp. 121–44.

Tobin, James. "Liquidity Preference as Behavior toward Risk." *Review of Economic Studies* XXVI (February 1958), pp. 65–86.

Treynor, Jack L. "How to Rate Management Investment Funds." *Harvard Business Review* 43 (January–February 1966).

Treynor, Jack L., and Kay Mazuy. "Can Mutual Funds Outguess the Market?" *Harvard Business Review* 43 (July–August 1966).

Treynor, Jack, and Fischer Black. "How to Use Security Analysis to Improve Portfolio Selection." *Journal of Business* 46 (January 1973).

Trippi, Robert R., and Duane Desieno. "Trading Equity Index Futures with Neural Networks." *Journal of Portfolio Management* 19 (Fall 1992).

Trippi, Robert R.; Duane Desieno; and Efraim Turban, eds. *Neural Networks in Finance and Investing*. Chicago: Probus Publishing Co., 1993.

Wallace, A. "Is Beta Dead?" *Institutional Investor* 14 (July 1980), pp. 22–30.

Whaley, Robert E. "Valuation of American Call Options on Dividend-Paying Stocks: Empirical Tests." *Journal of Financial Economics* 10 (1982), pp. 29–58.

REFERENCES TO CFA QUESTIONS

Each end-of-Chapter CFA question is reprinted with permission from the Association for Investment Management and Research (AIMR), Charlottesville, Virginia.[1] Following is a list of the CFA questions in the end-of-Chapter material and the exams/study guides from which they were taken and updated.

Chapter 2

1. 1986 Level II CFA Study Guide, © 1986.
2. 1986 Level II CFA Study Guide, © 1986.

Chapter 3

19. 1986 Level I CFA Study Guide, © 1986.
20. 1986 Level I CFA Study Guide, © 1986.
21. 1986 Level I CFA Study Guide, © 1986.

Chapter 5

1. 1998 Level I CFA Study Guide, © 1998.
2. 1998 Level I CFA Study Guide, © 1998.
3. 1998 Level I CFA Study Guide, © 1998.

Chapter 6

1. 1998 Level I CFA Study Guide, © 1998.
2. 1998 Level I CFA Study Guide, © 1998.
3. 1998 Level I CFA Study Guide, © 1998.
20. 1982 Level III CFA Study Guide, © 1982.
21. 1982 Level III CFA Study Guide, © 1982.
22. 1982 Level III CFA Study Guide, © 1982.

Chapter 7

1. 1998 Level I CFA Study Guide, © 1998.
2. 1998 Level I CFA Study Guide, © 1998.

[1]The Association for Investment Management and Research[SM] does not endorse, promote, review, or warrant the accuracy of the product or services offered by The McGraw-Hill Companies.

Chapter 8

1.   1998 Level I CFA Study Guide, © 1998.
6.   1998 Level I CFA Study Guide, © 1998.
15.   1981 Level I CFA Study Guide, © 1981.
16.   1989 Level III CFA Study Guide, © 1989.
20.   1985 Level III CFA Study Guide, © 1985.
21.   1985 Level III CFA Study Guide, © 1985.
22.   1985 Level III CFA Study Guide, © 1985.

Chapter 9

6.   1998 Level I CFA Study Guide, © 1998.
28.   1986 Level I CFA Study Guide, © 1986.
29.   1986 Level I CFA Study Guide, © 1986.
32.   From various CFA exams.

Chapter 10

7.   1985 Level I CFA Study Guide, © 1985.
8.   1985 Level I CFA Study Guide, © 1985.
13.   From various CFA exams.
14.   From various CFA exams.
17.   1983 Level III CFA Study Guide, © 1983.
18.   1981 Level I CFA Study Guide, © 1981.
19.   1983 Level III CFA Study Guide, © 1983.
20.   1983 Level III CFA Study Guide, © 1983.
21.   1983 Level III CFA Study Guide, © 1983.
27.   1983 Level III CFA Study Guide, © 1983.

Chapter 11

13.   From various CFA exams.
14.   1993 Level II CFA Study Guide, © 1993.
15.   1993 Level II CFA Study Guide, © 1993.
18.   From various CFA exams.

Chapter 12

1.   1998 Level I CFA Study Guide, © 1998.
2.   1998 Level I CFA Study Guide, © 1998.
7.   1987 Level I CFA Study Guide, © 1987.
8.   1987 Level I CFA Study Guide, © 1987.
12.   1987 Level I CFA Study Guide, © 1987.
14.   1987 Level I CFA Study Guide, © 1987.
15.   1987 Level I CFA Study Guide, © 1987.
17.   1988 Level I CFA Study Guide, © 1988.
18.   1986 Level I CFA Study Guide, © 1986.

Chapter 13

4.   1988 Level I CFA Study Guide, © 1988.
5.–8.   From various CFA exams.
9.   1988 Level I CFA Study Guide, © 1988.
10.   1987 Level I CFA Study Guide, © 1987.
11.   1986 Level I CFA Study Guide, © 1986.
12.   1985 Level I CFA Study Guide, © 1985.
13.–21.   From various CFA exams.

Chapter 14

5.   1984 Level III CFA Study Guide, © 1984.

16. 1984 Level III CFA Study Guide, © 1984.

Chapter 16

1.–3. 1998 Level I CFA Study Guide, © 1998.

11. 1982 Level III CFA Study Guide, © 1982.

16. 1986 Level III CFA Study Guide, © 1986.

Chapter 17

1. 1988 Level I CFA Study Guide, © 1988.

2. 1988 Level I CFA Study Guide, © 1988.

3. From various CFA exams.

4. From various CFA exams.

5. 1981 Level II CFA Study Guide, © 1981.

6. 1985 Level III CFA Study Guide, © 1985.

7. 1988 Level I CFA Study Guide, © 1988.

8. 1982 Level III CFA Study Guide, © 1982.

9. From various CFA exams.

10. From various CFA exams.

Chapter 20

1.–3. From various CFA exams.

10. 1983 Level III Study Guide, © 1983.

11. 1981 Level III Study Guide, © 1981.

Chapter 21

7. 1986 Level III Study Guide, © 1986.

11. 1986 Level III Study Guide, © 1986.

A

Accounting earnings, 434, 456
Accounting fraud, 435, 473, 474–475
Accounting income, 470
Accounting measure of
    depreciation, 471
Accounting practices
    and accounting fraud, 435, 473,
        474–475
    international conventions,
        474–477
    national comparisons, 476
    pro forma earnings, 475
    and quality of earnings, 472–474
Accounts payable, 454
Accounts receivable, 454
Accounts-receivable-to-sales
    ratio, 462
Accrual methods of accounting, 454
Accrued interest, and bond prices, 298
Acid-test ratio, 463
Active bond management, 339
    contingent immunization, 364
    example of, 364–366
    horizon analysis, 363
    interest rate forecasting, 361–362
    sources of potential profit,
        361–363
    taxonomy of, 362–363
Active investment management
    and behavioral finance, 652–659
    savings plan, 626–631
    and tax shelters, 632–639
    technical analysis, 659–676
Active investment policy, 614–615
Active portfolio, 701–702, 711–712
Active portfolio management, 10
    client-manager relationship, 597
    and EMH, 267–268
    lure of, 699–702
    and market inefficiency, 597
    with Treynor-Black model,
        709–712
Adams, Paul, 408
Adjustable preferred stock, 300–301
Adjustable-rate mortgages, 37
Adjusted betas, 238
ADRs; see American
    Depository Receipts
Adverse selection, 645
After-tax rate of return, 607
After-tax returns, 315–316
After-tax yields, 35
Agency bonds, 301
Agency debt, 32–33
Agency problem, 8, 39
Aggregate stock market valuation,
    439–441

AIMR; *see* Association for
    Investment Management
    and Research
Alexander, Sidney, 271
Allowance for bad debt, 472
Alpha, 227, 234, 246, 282–283
Altruism, 652
American Depository Receipts, 15,
    734, 737
American options, 495, 550, 556
American Stock Exchange, 15–16, 46,
    65, 77, 496
    annual returns, 146
America Online, 433
Ameritrade, 80
Amihud, Yakov, 241, 275–276
Animal spirits, 261
Annual percentage rate, 32,
    134–135, 307
Annuity factor, 303–304
Apple Computer, 67, 205, 258
Appraisal ratio, 712
Arbel, Avner, 275
Arbitrage, 215, 242
    and capital asset pricing
        model, 244
    in futures markets, 575
Arbitrage opportunity, 587
Arbitrage portfolio, 244
Arbitrage pricing theory, 216,
    241–250, **244–245**
    and CAPM, 247
    criticisms of, 240
    multifactor generalization,
        247–250
    opportunities and profits,
        242–244
    rational behavior assumption, 651
    well-diversified portfolio,
        244–247
Arbitrage profit, 582
Arbitrage strategy, 549
Arbitrageurs, 244n
ARCH models, 239
Arithmetic average, 133
Arithmetic mean, 143
Arizona Public Service Company, 373
Arthur Andersen, 473
Asian financial crisis, 382
Asian options, 519
Ask price, 14, 31–32, **67,** 74,
    296–297
Asset allocation, 8, 129, **148**
    across broad asset classes, 695
    across risky/risk-free portfolios,
        148–155
    asset categories, 611
    changes over time, 616
    decisions, 171, 697

Asset allocation—*Cont.*
    and EMH, 268–269
    life-cycle approach, 612
    and portfolio performance, 173
    with risk-free asset, 184–187
    and risk tolerance, 154–155
    style analysis, 706–708
    with two risky assets, 171–184
        covariance and correlation,
          171–175
        mean-variance criterion,
          178–184
        risk-return trade-off,
          177–178
        three rules for, 177
        using historical data,
          175–176
Asset allocation funds, 105
Asset-backed bonds, 302
Asset-backed securities, 16–17
Asset classes, 697
    optimal combination, 129
Asset plays, 404
Asset-pricing anomalies, 651
Asset risk, 227
Assets
    on balance sheet, 452–453
    of individual investors, 601–602
    investment, 8
    liquidity, 606–607
    off-balance sheet, 473
    real *vs.* financial, 4–5
Asset turnover, 459
Asset universe, 612
Asset utilization ratio, 461–462
Association for Investment
    Management and Research,
    597, 599, 626
    Code of Ethics, 600
    standards of professional
        conduct, 90
AT&T, 36, 298, 467
At-the-money options, 493
At-the-tail bid, 27
Auction market, 15
    Treasury bill purchase, 27
Automated Bond System, 70
Auto parts industry data, 407
Autoregressive conditional
    heteroscedasticity, 239n
Average annual return, 9
Average collection period, 462
Average excess returns, 157–158
Average first-day returns, 63, 64
Average Indexed Monthly Income,
    640, 641
Average rate of return, 212
Average returns, 142
Average security, 196

B

Back-end load, 108
Bad debt allowance, 472
Balanced funds, 105
Balance sheet, 452–454
    financial institutions, 11–12
    nonfinancial companies, 11–12
    of U. S. households, 4–5
Balance sheet valuation methods, 414
Bankers' acceptances, 28
Bank of Montreal, 373
Bank One Corporation, 467
Banks, 11
    capital guidelines, 350
    constraints and objectives,
        610, 611
    forward market, 571
    and immunization, 350
    investment objectives, 605–606
    and securitization, 17
    time deposits, 27–28
Banz, Rolf, 274
Barber, Brad, 280
Barclays Global Investors, 113
Bargaining power
    of buyers, 404–405
    of suppliers, 405
Barings Bank, 489
Barrier options, 519
Barriers to entry, 404
Barron's, 669
Basis, 579
Basis risk, 579–580
Basu, Sanjoy, 274
Bavishi, Vinod, 476
Bearer bonds, 299
Bear markets, 743–744
Beebower, Gilbert, 706n
Behavioral finance, 651
    aspects of individual behavior,
        652–656
    asset returns
        calendar effects, 656
        cash dividends, 656
        mean reversion, 656–657
        overreaction, 656–657
    controversial explanations
        closed-end funds, 657–658
        stock price volatility,
          658–659
    definition, 652
Benchmark, 283
Benchmark level of performance,
    694–695
Benchmark rate of return, 215
Benchmark tax shelters, 632
Benveniste, Lawrence, 63n
Bequests, 646

Berkshire Hathaway, 284
Bernard, Victor L., 278
Bernard Madoff, 69
Bernstein, William J., 114
Berra, Yogi, 747
Berton, Lee, 50
Best customer limit orders, 77
Best-efforts agreement, 60
Beta, 193, 199, 226, 241
  average, 196n
  criticism of, 240
  and market timing, 691–693
  negative, 196
  predicting, 238–239
  ratio of risk premium to, 224–226
Beta coefficient, 222
Bet options, 520
Bid
  at-the-tail, 27
  competitive, 27
  noncompetitive, 27
Bid-ask spread, 67, 74–75, **80**
Bidding, 653
Bid price, 14, 31–32, **67,** 74, 296–297
Bid yields, 309–310
Binary options, 520
Binomial model, 539
Binomial option pricing, 534–540
Biotechnology industry, 401–402
Black, Fischer, 240, 241, 709
Black-Scholes pricing formula, 540–546, 550, 704
Black-Scholes pricing model
  empirical evidence, 556–557
  formula, 540–546
  hedge ratio, 550–552
  performance determination, 557
  portfolio insurance, 552–556
  put-call party relationship, 546–549
  put option valuation, 549–550
  simplifying assumptions, 453
Block houses, 14
Block transactions, 75
Blue Cross, 645
Blue-sky laws, 89
Blume, Marshall E., 271, 275
Bogey benchmark, **694**–695, 696, 745
Bogle, John C., 116, 148, 149
Boise Cascade Corporation, 18
Bond duration; *see* Duration
Bond equivalent yield, 32, 307
Bond floor, 54
Bond funds, 105
Bond indenture, 296, **318**–320
Bond market
  amount of trading in, 293
  components, 25
  corporate bonds, 35–37
  federal agency debt, 32–33
  indexes, 49
  innovation in, 301–303
  international bonds, 33
  liquidity risk, 70
  mortgage-backed securities, 37–39
  municipal bonds, 33–35
  trading in, 70, 298–299
  Treasury notes and bonds, 31–32
Bond market indicators, 47
Bond price risk, 306

Bond pricing, 303–306
  and accrued interest, 298
  convexity, 305, 358–361
  corporate bonds, 306
  and default risk, 316–322
  and interest rate risk, 340–349
  interest rate sensitivity, 339, 340–342
  invoice price, 298
  over time, 312–316
    after-tax returns, 315–316
    yield to maturity versus holding-period return, 313–314
    zero-coupon bonds, 314–315
  and passive management, 350–357
  present value formula, 303–304, 312–313
  Treasury bonds, 31–32
  versus yield, 306
Bond ratings, 316–317
  key ratios, 318
Bonds, 296
  asset-backed, 302
  as assets, 4
  bearer, 299
  Brady bonds, 17
  bulldog bonds, 301
  callable, 296, 512–514
  catastrophe, 302
  characteristics, 301
  collateral trust, 320
  compared to preferred stock, 41, 300–301
  convertible, 36, 299–300, 514–516
  and convexity, 358–361
  corporate, 298–300
  current yield, 36–37, 298
  default-free, 150
  default premium, 322
  discount, 309
  duration, 342–349
  equipment obligations, 320
  versus equities, 157
  Eurobonds, 301
  as fixed-income securities, 6, 295
  floating-rate, 300
  foreign, 301
  historical record, 139–146
  indexed, 302–303
  international, 33, 301
  investment grade, 316–317
  mortgage, 320
  municipal, 33–35
  original issue discount, 314–316
  pay-in-kind, 302
  premium, 308
  price indexed, 150
  primary market issues, 60
  put, 300
  registered, 298–299
  reverse floaters, 302
  Samurai, 301
  secured, 36
  serial issue, 319–320
  speculative grade, 316–317
  state and federal agency bonds, 301
  Treasury bonds and notes, 296–298

Bonds—*Cont.*
  unsecured, 36, 320
  Yankee, 301
  yield curve, 322–327
    expectations theory, 323–325
    liquidity preference theory, 325–326
    synthesis of theories, 327
    zero-coupon, 296, 314–315, 342, 347–348
Bond safety
  collateral, 318
  determinants, 318
  dividend restrictions, 318
  protective covenants, 318–320
  sinking funds, 319–320
  subordination clauses, 318
Bond swaps
  intermarket spread swap, 362
  pure yield pickup swap, 362–363
  rate anticipation swap, 362
  substitution swap, 362
  tax swap, 363
Bond yields
  current, 298, 308–309
  expected *vs.* promised, 318–320
  horizon analysis, 312
  yield to maturity, 298, 306–309
    and bond price change, 340–341
    calculating, 307–308
    and default risk, 320–322
    versus holding-period return, 313–314
    and interest rate risk, 340–342
    versus realized compound yield, 310–312
Book, 62
Bookbuilding, 62
Book-to-market effect, 276
Book value, 414, **463**–464
Borrowing, 13–14
Boston Stock Exchange, 65, 70
Bottom-up portfolio construction, 9
Bowman, Melanie F., 661
Bradaran, Mehrdad, 84
Brady, Nicholas, 17
Brady bonds, 17
Brand loyalty, 404
Brane v. Roth, 506
Breadth of the market, **671**–672
Break-even investment opportunities, 430
Brennan, Michael, 225
Brinson, Gary, 706n
Brock, William, 671
Brokerage houses, 81
Brokered markets, 14
Brokers
  churning accounts, 80
  forward market, 571
  in over-the-counter market, 67–68
  specialists, 74
Broker's call loans, 84
Brokers' calls, 29
Budget deficit, 385
Buffet, Warren, 284
Built-to-order fund, 113–114
Bulldog bonds, 301
Bullish spread, 509–510
Bundling, 18–19

Bureau of Labor Statistics, 147
Business cycles, 261, **391**
  cyclical/defensive classification, 391–393
  cyclical indicators, 392
  depiction of, 400–401
  industry sensitivity to, 398–400
  leading economic indicators, 393–396
  and P/E ratios, 435
  terminology for, 391
Buyers' bargaining power, 404–405

C

Calendar effect, 656
Callable bonds, 31, **296,** 299, 309–310, 512–514
Callable equity linked notes, 513
Callable stock, 41
Call options, 48–49, 51, 53, **492,** 669
  Black-Scholes pricing formula, 545–546
  compared to warrants, 516–517
  determinants of value, 534
  hedge ratio, 550
  straddle, 508
  strategies, 506–508
  valuation, 532–534
  value at expiration, 498–499
Call option valuation function, 532, 533, 550
Call price, 299
Call protection, 299, 310
Call provision, 299
Campbell, John Y., 273
Candlestick chart, 663–665
Capacity utilization rate, 385, 392
Capital allocation line, 152–153, 154, 191–192, 221, 711
  optimal risky portfolio, 184–186
  in passive strategy, 223
Capital asset pricing model, 221–241, 426, 651
  to adjust for risk, 273
  applications, 227–228
  and arbitrage, 244
  and arbitrage pricing theory, 247
  assumptions, 221
  attack on, 240–241
  and equilibrium prices, 220
  expected return-beta relationship, 225
  expected returns, 224–226
  functions, 215
  historical record, 241
  and index models, 228–229
  for international investments, 742–743
  limitations of, 228
  market portfolio of investors, 222–223
  modified versions, 225
  multifactor generalization, 247–250
  mutual fund theorem, 223
  passive strategy, 223
  for performance rating, 685
  rate of return, 233–234, 415
  and real world, 239–240
  risk premium of market portfolio, 223–224

Capital asset pricing model—*Cont.*
security market line, 226–227,
231–232
Capital budgeting decision, 228
Capital gains, 111, 312, 417
Capitalization weighting, 745–746
Capital market line, 156, 221,
222–223, 235–237, 711
historical evidence, 156–158
and passive strategies, 155–158
and security market line,
226–227
Capital markets, 6, **26**
fixed-income, 30–31
segments, 26
Capital market theory, 215
CAPM; see Capital asset
pricing model
Carhart, Mark M., 284, 285
Cash, 26
Cash/bond selection, 748
Cash cows, 402, 403
Cash delivery, 576
Cash dividends, 656
Cash equivalents, 26
Cash flow matching, 357–**358**
Cash flows
from financing activities,
454–456
and interest rates, 385
from investing activities,
454–456
in Macaulay's duration,
342–344
from operations, 454–456
promised *vs.* expected, 318–320
Cash flow-to-debt ratio, 318
Cash settlement, 496
Catastrophe bonds, 302
Central order-flow system, 81
Certificates of deposit, 6, **27–28**
in Eurodollars, 29
yields on, 30
Channel surfing, 473
Charles Schwab, 80, 107
Chartered Financial Analysts,
599, 600
Charting, 660–667
candlestick chart, 663–65
congestion area, 663
Dow theory, 661–662
Elliott wave theory, 662
Kondratieff wave theory, 662
point and figure chart, 663
warning on, 665–667
Chartists, 266, 660
Chevron, 43
Chicago Board of Trade, 51, 566, 567,
577, 584
Chicago Board Options Exchange,
491, 496, 501, 512, 552
Chicago Mercantile Exchange, 496,
571, 584, 586, 588
Chicago Refrigerator Inc., 481–482
Choi, Frederick D. S., 476
Chopra, Navin, 272
Chrysler Corporation, 404
Churning, 80
Circuit breakers, 89–91
Cisco Systems, 433
Clayman, Michelle, 465
Clearinghouse, 571–573, **572**

Clements, Jonathan, 155, 173, 282,
655, 747
Closed-end funds, 101–103
in behavioral finance, 657–658
international investments,
734–735
Closely held corporation, 39
Clough, Charles, 389
Coca-Cola Company, 403–404, 431
Cohen, Abby Joseph, 389
Colgate-Palmolive, 403–404
Collars, 90, **511**–512
Collateral, 320
Collateralized loans, 517
Collateral trust bond, 320
College costs, 543
Commercial paper, 28
Commingled funds, 103
Commission brokers, 71
Commission broker seats, 65
Commission schedule, 80
Commodities; *see* Futures contracts;
Futures market
Commodity Futures Trading
Commission, 89, 576
Common-size balance sheet, 454
Common stock, 39
average annual return, 9
characteristics, 40
as ownership shares, 39
primary market issues, 60
Commonwealth Edison, 373
Comparability problems
in financial statement analysis,
470–477
and GAAP, 470
Comparison universe, 684
Competition, source of efficiency,
263–265
Competitive bid, 27
Competitors, rivalry between, 404
Complete portfolio, 149, 186
asset allocation, 151
and separation property, 192
Compound yield, 310–312
Computer networks, 19–20
Conference Board, 393
Confidence index, 669
Congestion area, 663
Conrad, Jennifer, 270
Consolidated Edison, 226, 435–436
Consolidated Quotations Service,
69–70
Consolidated Tape, 69–70
Consolidation stage, 403
**Constant growth dividend discount
model,** 417–420, **418**
Consumer Price Index, 146–147
Consumer sentiment, 385
Consumption basket, 146–147
Consumption timing, 7
Contingent claims, 48, 489
Contingent deferred sales
charges, 108
Contingent immunization, 364
Contingent liability, 473
Contrarian investment strategy, 272
Convergence bets, 104
Convergence parity, 579
Conversion premium, 300
Conversion ratio, 54, 299–300
ConvertBond.com, 513

Convertible bonds, 36, **299**–300
Convertible securities, 514–516
Convertible stock, 41
Convexity, 305, 358–261, **359**
Cooperation, 652
Copernicus, N., 240, 241
Corporate bonds, 6, **35–37,** 298–300
and bond safety covenants,
318–320
call provisions, 299
convertible, 299–300
default premium, 322
default risk, 316–322
floating-rate, 300
investment grade, 316–317
pricing of, 306
put bonds, 300
speculative grade, 316–317
Corporations, 39
Corrections, 661
Correlation, 171–175
perfect negative, 181–182
perfect positive, 180
Correlation coefficient, 175, 176, 177,
196, 739, 740, 741
Cost-of carry relationship, 582
Cost of goods sold, 452
Country selection, 746–747
Country-specific risk, 721, 731–734
Coupon bond, 296
Coupon payments, 31
Coupon rate, 296, 299, 300, 302,
306, 312
and interest rate risk, 341
Covariance, 171–175, 176, 239
Coverage ratio, 318, 462–463
Covered call, 506–508
**Covered interest arbitrage
relationship, 729**
Covering the short position, 86
Cox, John C., 539n
Credit balances in brokerage
accounts, 670
Credit Suisse First Boston, 745
Credit unions, 11
"Critique of Capital Asset Pricing
Tests" (Roll), 241
Cross-hedging, 579, 590
Crowding-out effect, 385
Cubes, 112
Cumulative dividends, 41
Cumulative normal distribution,
544–545
Currency selection, 746
Currency-translated options, 519–520
Current assets, 453
Current earnings, 464
Current liabilities, 453
Current ratio, 318, **462**–463
Current yield, 36–37, 298, **308**–309
CUSIP number, 315
Cutoff tax bracket, 35
Cyclical industries, 391
Cyclicals, 404

D

Daimler-Benz, 475
DaimlerChrysler, 475
Damato, Karen, 689
Dartboard games, 692
Das, S., 283–284
Data mining, 279

David Bowie bonds, 302
DAX (German stock exchange), 46
Days' receivables, 462
Dealer market, 14–15, 81
over-the-counter market, 76–77
Debenture bonds, 320
Debentures, 36
DeBondt, Werner F. M., 272, 280, 281
Debt, risky, 517–519
Debt financing; *see* Bond *entries;*
Money market
Debt market, 26
Debt securities, 295; *see also* Bonds
Debt-to-equity ratio, 318
Decimal pricing, 72
Decomposition of ROE, 458–460
Dedication strategy, 357–**358**
Default, 517n
on commercial paper, 28
Default-free bonds, 150
Default premium, 322
Default risk, 6, 153
bond indentures, 318–320
and bond pricing, 316–322
corporate bonds, 36
determinants of bond safety, 318
junk bonds, 317–318
and yield to maturity, 320–325
Defensive industries, 391
Deferred callable bonds, 299
Defined benefit plans, 604
Defined contribution plans, 604
Dell Computer, 170, 193, 195–196,
225, 433, 562
Deloitte Touche Tohmatsu, 473
Delta Air Lines, 223
Delta hedging, 554, 555
Delta of an option, **550,** 553, 554
Demand curve
horizontal aggregation, 220
and interest rate, 386–387
Demand for stocks
and equilibrium prices, 216–220
index funds, 219–220
Demand shock, 387–388
Department of Commerce, 465, 471
Depreciation
accounting *vs.* economic, 435
economic *vs.* accounting
measures, 471
international accounting
conventions, 475
Depreciation expense, 452, 454
Derivative assets, 48
Derivative markets, 25, 47–53
futures contracts, 51–53
options, 48–51
Derivative securities, 6; *see also*
Futures contracts; Options
characteristics, 491
explanation of, 50
losses on, 489
property used, 489
for risk management, 506
De Soto, Hernando, 725
Detachable warrant, 516
Deutsche Terminboerse, 584
Developed countries
equity market, 722
GDP, 722, 723
Diamonds, 112
Diluted earnings per share, 517n

Dimson, Elroy, 157, 158
Direct-marketed funds, 107
Directory of Mutual Funds, 118
Direct search markets, 14
Disaster bonds, 302
Disclosure requirements, 477
Discount bonds, 309, 319
Discount brokers, 80
Discounted cash flow formula, 419
Discount rate, 303, 307, 390
Discounts, closed-end funds, 657–658
Discretionary account, 80
Discretionary closed-end funds,
    102–103
Display Book, 71, 75, 76
Disposition effect, 654
Diversifiable risk, 171
Diversification, 10, 169
    elimination of risk, 268
    with futures or forward contracts,
        566–567
    in international investments,
        738–744
    with many risky assets, 187–192
    mean-variance criterion, 178–182
    naive strategy, 170
    neutral approach, 156
    and portfolio risk, 170–171
    return of, in 2002, 172
    risk eliminated by, 171
    in single-factor market, 199
    time, 211–212
Dividend discount models,
    416–428, **417**
    combined with P/E ratios, 438
    constant growth, 417–420
    life cycles model, 423–427
    multistage growth model,
        423–428
    stock prices and investment
        opportunities, 420–423
    two stage, 424–427
Dividend payout ratio, 420–421
Dividend restrictions, 320
Dividends
    cumulative, 41
    preferred stock, 300–301
    volatility of, 659
Dividend yields, 41
Dodd, David, 478
Dollar
    average monthly increase,
        728–729
    depreciation of, 730
    nominal *vs.* real, 628–629
    purchasing power, 383–384
Dollar-weighted return, 134
Domestic macroeconomy, 384–385
Double taxation, 630
Doubling option, 319
Dow, Charles, 661
Dow Jones Composite Average, 44
Dow Jones Industrial Average, 112,
    496, 555, 585, 661, 665
    changes since 1928, 44
    fall in 1987, 89
    functions, 42–45
Dow Jones Public Utility Average, 44
Dow Jones Transportation
    Average, 44
Down-and-in options, 519
Down-and-out options, 519

Downside risk, 122
Dow theory, 661–662, 675
Drexel Burnham Lambert, 318
Dreyfus, 104
Duff and Phelps, 316
Dun and Bradstreet, 465
Du Pont system, 458
Duration of bonds, 339, 342–346
    and convexity, 358–361
    determinants, 346–349
    Macaulay's formula, 342–344
    modified, 345–346
    perpetuity, 348
    of a portfolio, 351–353
    reasons for importance of, 344
    variations in, 348–349
Dutch auction, 65
Dynamic hedge, 540, **554,** 556

E

Earnings
    accounting *vs.* economic,
        434–435, 456
    current *vs.* future, 464–465
Earnings announcements, 276–278
Earnings before interest and taxes,
    439, 452, 459
Earnings growth, 399
Earnings growth rates, 396, 397
Earnings management, 434–435
Earnings multiplier, 439–440
Earnings per share, 384
Earnings retention ratio, 421
Earnings yield, 440–441, **465**
E-baskets, 113–114
EBIT; *see* Earnings before
    interest and taxes
ECN; *see* Electronic
    communication network
Economic calendar, 395–396
Economic depreciation, 420n, 435
Economic development,
    prerequisites, 725
Economic earnings, 435, **456**
Economic forecasts, 384–385; *see
    also* Forecasting
Economic income, 470
Economic measure of
    depreciation, 471
Economic time series, 261
Economic value added, 466–467
Economies of scale, 13
Economist, 241
Economy; *see also* Macroeconomy
    financial assets in, 4–5
    financial markets in, 7–8
    new *vs.* old, 433
    possible scenarios for, 172
Effective annual rate, 134–135
Effective annual yield, 307
Efficient diversification
    and demand for stocks, 216
    with many risky assets, 187–192
    mean-variance criterion, 178–182
    with two risky assets, 171–182
Efficient frontier, 189, 235–237,
    739–742, 743, 744
    market portfolio, 221
    of risky assets, 188–191
    for various stocks, 191
Efficient market hypothesis, 10,
    261–286, **262**

Efficient market hypothesis—*Cont.*
    and dartboard games, 692
    debate over, 269–270
    implications
        active *vs.* passive
            management, 267–268
        for fundamental analysis,
            266–267
        for resource allocation,
            268–269
        role of portfolio
            management, 268
        for technical analysis,
            265–266
    interpreting evidence on,
        278–281
    and random walks, 262–265
    refutation of, 658–659
    semistrong form, 265
    semistrong-form tests, 273–278
    strong form, 265
    strong-form tests, 278
    technical analysis, 660, 675
    weak form, 265
    weak-form tests, 270–273
Efficient markets
    belief in, 285
    issues
        lucky-event, 270
        magnitude, 269
        selection bias, 269–270
    mutual fund performance,
        281–286
    and passive management, 597
    predictors of broad
        movements, 273
    reversals, 272–273
    semistrong-form tests, 273–278
    strong-form tests, 278
    and technical analysis, 675
    weak-form tests
        returns over long horizons,
            271–272
        returns over short horizons,
            270–271
Efficient portfolio, 226
Efficient pricing, 4
Eisenstadt, Samuel, 676–677
Electrolux, 302
Electronic communication network,
    20, **68**–69, 81
    and market fragmentation, 70
    registered, 69
Elliott wave theory, 662
Elton, E. J., 171, 283–284
Emerging markets
    average returns, 738
    economic performance, 392
    equity securities in, 722–725
    investment risks, 735
    political risk, 732–733
EMH; *see* Efficient market
    hypothesis
Employee Retirement Income
    Security Act, 610
Employment, 385
Endowment effect, 653–654
Endowment funds, 606
    constraints and objectives,
        610, 611
    lack of safety nets, 621
    liquidity, 621

Endowment funds—*Cont.*
    regulation, 621–622
    return on, 621
    and taxes, 621
    time horizon, 621
    unique situations, 622
Enron collapse, 172, 318–320, 435,
    473, 474–475, 477, 645
Equally weighted indexes, 46
Equilibrium nominal rate of interest,
    147–148
Equilibrium price
    and arbitrage, 215, 244
    and CAPM, 220
    and demand for stocks, 216–220
Equilibrium real interest rate, 386
Equilibrium risk premium, 224
Equipment obligation bonds, 320
Equity, 6
    levered, 517–519
Equity funds, 104–105, 284
Equity markets, 25
Equity risk premium, 157
Equity securities
    versus bonds, 157
    common stock, 39–40
    dollar volume in 2000, 78
    global market for
        developed countries, 722
        emerging markets, 722–725
    home country bias, 726
    percentage of U. S. wealth, 721
    preferred stock, 40
    stock market listings, 40
Equity trusts, 103
Equity valuation, 413–442
    with accounting data, 451
    aggregate stock market,
        439–441
    balance sheet methods, 413
    dividend discount models,
        416–428
    and earnings management, 434
    free cash flow approaches,
        438–439
    intrinsic value *vs.* market
        price, 415–416
    and market-to-book-value
        ratio, 464
    new/old economy, 433
    P/E ratio
        combined with dividend
            discount models, 438
        and growth opportunities,
            428–432
        pitfalls in analysis, 434–436
        and stock risk, 432–433
    price-to-book ratio, 438
    price-to-cash flow ratio, 438
    price-to-sales ratio, 438
Equivalent taxable yield, 34–35
Ernst and Young, 473
E*Trade, 80
Eurex, 584
Euro, 15–16
Eurobond, 33, 301
Eurodollars, 28–29
Euronext, 78, 79
Euro Pacific Fund, 586
**European, Australian, Far East
    Index, 745**–748
European Monetary Union, 382–383

European options, 495, 540, 546–547, 549
Eurosterling bonds, 301
Euroyen bonds, 301
Excess rates of return, 234
Excess return, 138, 193, 194, 195, 229, 233–234, 245
instability of, 157–158
Exchange rate, 382–383, 587
Exchange rate risk, 587, 721, **727**
hedging, 728–731
historical record, 727–729
in international investment, 726–731
in international portfolio, 738
Exchange-traded funds, 112–114
Executive compensation, 8, 39
Exercise price, 48–49, **492**
Expansionary monetary policy, 389
Expectations hypothesis, 323–325, **324**
Expected bond yield, 320–322
Expected rate of return
versus rate of return, 128
two risky assets, 172–173
Expected return, 9–10, **136,** 229, 415
and CAPM, 215, 224–226
determination of, 216–220
international investments, 739–742
and risk, 151–152
with two risky assets, 172
Expected return-beta relationship, 225–227
and APT, 247
index model, 229–230
Expense recognition, 454
Expenses, 452
Ex post efficient frontier, 741–742
ExxonMobil, 170, 467, 614, 616

F

Face value, 296
Factor models, 193
Factor portfolio, 248
Fads hypothesis, 272
Fair and orderly market, 74
Fama, Eugene F., 158, 240, 241, 271, 273, 276, 279, 427n
Farm Credit agencies, 301
Fast growers, 403
Federal agency debt, 32–33
Federal Deposit Insurance Corporation, 28, 89, 606
Federal funds, 29
Federal government policies
budget deficit, 385
fiscal policy, 388–389
futures markets, 576
for inflation, 385
for interest rates, 387
monetary policy, 389–390
regulation of markets, 89–92
supply-side policies, 388, 390
Federal Home Loan Bank Board, 32–33, 301
Federal Home Loan Mortgage Corporation, 17, 32–33, 39
Federal National Mortgage Association, 17, 32–33, 39

Federal Reserve Bank of New York, 280
Federal Reserve Bank of St. Louis, 165
Federal Reserve System, 28, 29, 89, 589
Board of Governors, 82
and interest rates, 390
tools of, 390
Federal Savings and Loan Insurance Corporation, 606
Fee structure
and mutual fund returns, 109–111
mutual funds, 107–109
Fidelity Investment Grade Bond Fund, 149–150
Fidelity Investments, 80, 104, 105, 107, 734
Fidelity Magellan Fund, 118–122, 270, 284, 286, 706–708
Fidelity Management Research Corporation, 101
Fidelity Select funds, 396
FIFO; *see* First-in, first-out system
Filter rule, 271
Finance industry, 396–397
Financial Accounting Standards Board Statement No. 95, 454
Financial Analysts Federation, 600
Financial assets, 4–5
versus real assets, 4
taxonomy of, 506
Financial engineering, 18–**19**
Financial futures
creating synthetic stock positions, 585
foreign exchange, 587–588
index arbitrage, 587
interest rate futures, 589–590
program trading, 587
stock index futures, 584–585, 586
triple-witching hour, 587
Financial instruments, 24–53
bond market, 30–39
corporate bonds, 35–37
federal agency debt, 32–33
international bonds, 33
mortgage-backed securities, 37–39
municipal bonds, 33–35
Treasury notes and bonds, 31–32
derivative markets, 47–53
futures contracts, 51–53
options, 48–51
equity securities, 39–41
money market, 26–30
bankers' acceptances, 28
brokers' calls, 29
certificates of deposit, 27–28
commercial paper, 28
Eurodollars, 28–29
federal funds, 29
London Interbank Offer Rate, 29
repos and reverses, 29
Treasury bills, 27
yields, 30
Websites for, 25
Financial intermediaries, 11–13
investment companies, 100–104
mutual funds, 104–107

Financial leverage, 400
and interest-burden ratio, 459
and ROE, 456–458
Financial markets
anomalies
calendar effect, 656
mean reversion, 657
overreaction, 656–657
in pricing, 651
bond market, 30–39
bond market indicators, 47
competitiveness, 1, 9–10
decimal system, 72
in economy
consumption timing, 7
ownership-management separation, 7–8
risk allocation, 7
efficient markets, 10
for equity securities, 39–41
national comparisons, 77–79
national market system, 69–70
online trading, 2
over-the-counter market, 76–77
players in
financial intermediaries, 11–13
investment bankers, 13–14
major kinds, 11
primary market, 60
recent trends
computer networks, 19–20
financial engineering, 18
globalization, 15–16
securitization, 16–18
regulation of, 89–92
risk-return trade-off, 9–10
secondary market, 60
stock market indexes
Dow Jones Averages, 42–45
equally weighted indexes, 46
foreign and international, 46–47
market value indexes, 46
Standard and Poor's indexes, 45–46
structure and types, 25
structure of
auction markets, 15
brokered markets, 14
dealer markets, 14–15
direct search markets, 14
primary market, 14
secondary market, 15
Financial ratios, 424; *see also* Ratio analysis
for major industry groups, 466
Financial statement analysis, 451–478
comparability problems
accounting practices, 472–474
depreciation, 471
inflation, 471–472
interest expense, 471–472
international accounting conventions, 474–477
inventory valuation, 470–471
quality of earnings, 472–474
economic value added, 466–467
Graham technique, 477–478
illustration of, 468–469

Financial statement analysis—*Cont.*
and return on assets, 457–458
return on equity, 456–458
Financial statements
balance sheet, 452–454
income statement, 452
statement of cash flows, 454–456
Financial stocks, 389
Financial Times, 46
Financial Times Share Exchange, 496, 735
Firm commitment, 60, 589
Firms
agency problems, 8
borrowing by, 13–14
commercial paper, 28
earnings management, 434
owners-manager separation, 7–8
takeover threat, 8
Firm-specific risk, 170, **171,** 192–193, 194, 196, 199, 230
First-in, first-out system, 470
First Quadrant Corporation, 586
Fiscal policy, 388–389
Fisher, Irving, 147
Fisher equation, 147
Fitch Investor Services, 316
Fixed-asset turnover, 461–462
Fixed-charge coverage ratio, 318
Fixed costs, 399–400
Fixed-income capital market, 6, 30–31
mispricing in, 361
Fixed-income funds, 105
Fixed-income investment strategy, 364–366
Fixed-income securities, 5–**6**
advantages, 295
bond characteristics, 296–303
preferred stock, 300–301
yield *vs.* price, 306
Fixed-rate mortgages, 37, 606
Flat tax, 630
Floating-rate bonds, 6, 300
Floating-rate preferred stock, 300–301
Floating securities, 60
Floor brokers, 71
Florida Power and Light, 422
Flow of funds indicators, 667
credit balances in brokerage accounts, 670
short interest, 669–670
Folios, 113–114
Ford Motor Company, 672
Forecasting
domestic economy, 384–385
earnings growth, 397
imperfect, 704–705
interest rates, 386–387
merits of stock prices, 441
P/E ratio, 428, 440
unreliable predictions, 388–389
Forecasting errors, 280
Foreign bonds, 301
Foreign currency options, 497
Foreign exchange forward market, 571
Foreign exchange futures, 587–588
Foreign index funds, 737

Foreign stock market indexes, 46–47, 48
Fortune, 280
44 Wall Street Fund, 286
Forward contracts, 50, **566**–567
  compared to options, 565
  types of existing contracts, 570–571
Forward market, 565, 570–571
  in foreign exchange, 587–588
Forward rate, 325–326
Foster, George, 277
401K plans, 111, 637, 639
  effect of Enron collapse, 172
403B plans, **637,** 639
Fourth market, 68–69
Framing, 280
Francis, Theo, 172
Free cash flow of the firm, 438–439
Free cash flows to equity, 439
Free cash flow valuation approaches, 438–439
French, Kenneth R., 158, 240, 241, 271n, 273, 276, 279, 427n
Frequency distributions, 539–540
Front-end load, 108
FTSE, 735
FTSE index, 46
Full-service brokers, 80–81
Fully diluted earnings per share, 517
Fundamental analysis, 266–267, 273, 381, **382**
  and business cycles, 391–396
  demand and supply shocks, 387–388
  domestic macroeconomy, 384–385
  federal government policies, 388–390
  and global economy, 382–384
  Graham technique, 477–478
  industry analysis, 396–405
  interest rates, 386–387
Fundamental analysts, 266, 413
Future earnings, 464
Futures contracts, 6, **51**–53, 491, 566–571
  basics of, 567–570
  compared to options, 565, 570, 571
  kinds of, 572
  margin accounts, 567
  price determinants, 580–583
  types of existing contracts, 571–572
  volume of trading in, 566
  zero sum game, 570
Futures market, 565
  financial futures
    creating synthetic stock positions, 585
    foreign exchange, 587–588
    index arbitrage, 587
    interest rate futures, 589–590
    program trading, 587
    stock index futures, 584–585
    triple witching, 587
  functions, 567
  mechanics of trading
    cash *vs.* actual delivery, 576
    clearinghouse, 571–573
    convergence property, 575

Futures market—*Cont.*
  mechanics of trading—*Cont.*
    kinds of contracts, 570–571
    long *vs.* short positions, 567
    maintenance margin, 574
    margin account, 573–575
    marking to market, 573–575
    open interest, 571–573
    reversing trade, 573
  price determinants, 580–583
  regulation of, 89, 576
  strategies
    basis risk and hedging, 579–580
    hedging, 577–579
    speculation, 577–579
    spread position, 579–580
  and taxation, 576–577
  volume of trading, 566
Futures options, 496
Futures prices, 51, 497, **567**–570, 574–575
  arbitrage opportunity, 587
  movement in unison, 583
  price determinants
    spot-futures parity, 580–583
    spreads, 583
    traded at discounts, 556
Future value of index earnings, 6440

G

Gateway Investment Advisers, 501
General and administrative expenses, 452
General Electric, 7, 40–41, 467
Generalized two-state approach, 537–540
Generally accepted accounting principles
  earnings management, 434–435
  economic *vs.* accounting income, 470
  and international accounting practices, 477
  revenue recognition, 473
  and stock options, 473
General Motors, 4, 7, 156, 222, 230–232, 268, 299, 351, 362, 614
General obligation bonds, 33
Geometric average, 133
Geometric mean, 143
Geske, Robert, 556
GIC; *see* Guaranteed investment contract
Global Crossing collapse, 435, 473
Global economy, 382–384
  international accounting conventions, 474–477
  stock index futures, 586
Globalization, 15–16, 79
Goetzmann, William N., 116
Goldman, Sachs and Company, 13, 18, 69, 70, 389, 745
Goodwill, 475
Goodyear Tire and Rubber, 43
Gordon, Myron J, 418
Government National Mortgage Association, 16–17, 32–33, 38–39, 589–590
Government of Canada bonds, 373
Govoly, Dan, 278

Graham, Benjamin, 477–478
Graham, John R., 158, 687
Granito, Barbara Donnelly, 555
Greenspan, Alan, 50
Grinblatt, Mark, 654
Gross Domestic Product, 384, 392
  emerging markets, 725
  versus market capitalization weights, 745
  and market capitalization, 725–726
Grossman, Sanford J., 264n, 699n
Growth funds, 105
Growth opportunities, 428–432
Growth stocks, 122
Growth-value continuum, 122
Gruber, M. J., 171, 283–284
Guaranteed investment contract, 350, 352–353

H

Han, Bing, 654
Hartle, Thomas, 661
Harvey, Campbell R., 158, 687
Haugen, Robert A., 273
Health care insurance, 645
Health maintenance organizations, 645
Hedge funds, 103–104
Hedge ratio, 536, **550,** 553–554, 590
  and Black-Scholes model, 550–552
Hedging, 6, 491, 506
  and basis risk, 579–580
  cross, 579, 590
  delta, 554, 555
  dynamic, 540, 554
  exchange rate risk, 587–588, 728–731
  in futures markets, 577–579
  interest rate futures, 589–590
  labor income, 645
  by life insurance companies, 605
  long hedge, 578
  perfect, 536
Hendricksson, Roy D., 705–706
High-yield bonds, 317–318
Historical rates of return
  and inflation, 146–148
  record of, 139–146
Historical record
  bond prices, 312–316
  on CAPM, 241
  capital market line, 156–158
  exchange rate risk, 727–729
  price-share performance, 157
  two risky assets, 175–176
Historical variance, 142
Hlavka, M., 283–284
Holding-period return, 132, 229
  and expectations hypothesis, 324
  expected excess, 193
  expected return and, 136
  historical record, 140–141
  interpretation of, 314
  probability distribution, 136
  and risk-free rate, 137
  scenario analysis, 135–137
  variability, 146
  versus yield to maturity, 313–314
Holding time to maturity, 347
Home country bias, 726

Home Depot, 43
Home ownership, 601, 644
Homer, Sydney, 341, 362, 366
Horizon analysis, 312, 363
Horizon date, 351–352
Horizontal aggregation, 220
Horizontal spread, 508
Households
  balance sheet, 4–5
  and financial intermediaries, 11–13
  savings by, 626
HPR; *see* Holding-period return
Hurdle rate, 228
Hybrid securities, 18

I

Ibbotson, Roger G., 116
Ibbotson Associates, 155, 747
IBM, 48, 51, 60, 72, 84–86, 472, 552, 589–590
Immunization, 350–357
  cash flow matching, 358
  contingent, 364
  and convexity, 361
Implied volatility, 543–544
Income allocation, 4
Income funds, 105
Income replacement rate, 641
Income statement, 452
Indentures, 318–320
Index arbitrage, 587
Index arbitrage orders, 90
Indexed bonds, 302–303
Index funds, 46, 105, **267**–268, 655
  demand for stocks, 219–220
  foreign, 737
Indexing, 156, 267, 695
  Social Security, 640
Index model, 194
  and CAPM, 228–229
  estimating, 230–232
  expected-return-beta relationship, 229–230
  predicting betas, 238–239
  and security market line, 231–232
Index options, 496
Index 500 Portfolio, 267
Index portfolios, 597
Index puts, 552
Individual asset risk, 227
Individual behavior
  bidding, 653
  cooperation and altruism, 652
  endowment effect, 653–654
  irrational decisions, 655
  loss aversion, 653–654
  mental accounts, 654, 656
  status quo bias, 653–654
  winner's curse, 653
Individual investors, objectives, 601–602
Individual Retirement Accounts, 111, 632, 634–635
Industrial development bonds, 33
Industrial long-term debt, 319
Industrial production, 384
Industrial production index, 392
Industry analysis, 396–405
  capacity utilization rate, 385
  cyclical industries, 391
  defensive industries, 391

Industry analysis—*Cont.*
defining an industry, 396–397
financial ratios, 424
industry life cycle, 401–404
sector rotation, 400–401
sensitivity to business cycles, 398–400
structure and performance, 404–405
Industry classification systems, 397
Industry cyclicality, 399
Industry earnings growth, 396, 397
Industry life cycle, 401–402
consolidation stage, 403
Lynch's groupings, 403–404
maturity stage, 403
relative decline stage, 403–404
start-up stage, 402
Industry sales growth, 409
Industry stock price performance, 398
Industry structure and performance
buyer bargaining power, 404–405
competitor rivalry, 404
substitute products, 404
supplier bargaining power, 405
threat of entry, 404
Inefficient markets, 278–279, 279
Inflation, 385
and earnings, 434
historical record, 139–146
and real interest expense, 471–472
and real rates of return, 146–148
and savings plans, 628–629
Inflation-adjusted exchange rate, 383–384
Inflation assumption, 637
Inflation-indexed bonds, 302
Inflation rate, 146–147
effect of demand/supply shocks, 387–388
Inflation-unemployment trade-off, 385
Initial public offerings, 60, 61–65
allocated across investors, 63
average first-day returns, 63, 64
Dutch auction, 65
poor long-term performance, 63–64
road shows, 62
underpriced, 63
Web-based, 63–64
Inside information, 91, 278
Inside quotes, 68, 72
Insider trading, 91–92, 265, 278
Instinet, 69
Institute of Chartered Financial Analysts, 600
Code of Ethics, 89
Institutional investors
block transactions, 75
objectives, 602–606
top-down policy, 612–614
Insurance companies, 11, 13, 350–351
Insurance principle, 170
Intangible assets, 475
international accounting conventions, 475–477
Intel Corporation, 6, 43, 72, 414, 467
Interest
equivalent taxable yield, 34–35

Interest—*Cont.*
floating-rate bonds, 300
on mortgages, 37
time deposits, 27–28
Interest-burden ratio, 459
Interest coverage ratio, 463
Interest expense, 471–472
Interest rate forecasting, 361
Interest rate futures, 589–590
Interest rate options, 50, 498
Interest rate parity relationship, 729
Interest rate risk
banks and pension funds, 350
and bond coupon rate, 341
duration, 342–349
interest rate sensitivity, 340–342
and interest rate swaps, 366–368
and investment strategy, 339
shed by immunization, 350–357
Interest rates, 385
annual percentage rate, 32, 134–135, 307
and bond pricing, 303–306
callable bonds, 309–310
determining level of, 386–387
effective annual rate, 134–135
effect of demand/supply shocks, 387–388
equilibrium nominal rate, 147–148
forward rate, 325
and inflation, 146–148
insurance policies, 605
and monetary policy, 389–390
on mortgages, 37
nominal, 147
real, 147
realized compound yield, 310–312
risk structure, 322
term structure of, 322–323
volatility, 293, 589
and yield to maturity, 307–309
Interest rate sensitivity, 339, 340–342
Interest rate swaps, 366
Intergenerational transfers, 646
Intermarket spread swap, 362
Intermarket Trading System, 70
Intermediate trend, 661
Internal rate of return, 134, 228, 307
on Social Security benefits, 642
Internal Revenue Service, 315–316
International accounting conventions
depreciation, 475
intangibles, 475–477
reserving practices, 474–475
International Accounting Standards, 477
International bonds, 33, 301
International Country Risk Guide, 73, 721, 732, 734
International diversification
and bear market, 743–744
benefits, 738–739
misleading representation of benefits, 739–742
realistic benefits from, 742–743
International investments
benefits of diversification, 738–744

International investments—*Cont.*
correlation coefficient, 739, 740, 741
global market for equities, 722–726
home country bias, 726
performance attribution, 746–748
portfolio construction, 746–748
questions about, 747
risk and return, 734–738
risk factors
country-specific risk, 731–734
exchange rate risk, 726–731
political risk, 731–732
riskless strategies, 729
special problems, 721
International Monetary Fund, 742
International stock market indexes, 46–47, 48
Internet, 19–20
Internet boom, 432
Internet Index, 513
Interval closed-end funds, 102–103
In-the-money options, 493, 532–534
Intrinsic value, 532
versus market price, 415–416
of shares, 216
Inventory turnover ratio, 462
Inventory valuation, 470–471
Inventory valuation adjustment, 471
Inverted yield curve, 322
Investment assets, 8
Investment bankers, 13–14
best-efforts agreement, 60
initial public offerings, 61–65
issuance of securities, 60–61
road shows, 62
Investment committee, 612–614
Investment companies, 11, 13, 99, 100, 101
commingled funds, 103
functions for investors, 100
hedge funds, 103–104
managed, 101–103
real estate investment trusts, 103
types of, 100–104
unit investment trusts, 100
Investment Companies, 118
Investment Company Act of 1940, 100–101
Investment Company Institute, 118
Investment decisions, 3–4
Investment environment, 1
derivative securities, 6
recent trends
computer networks, 19–20
financial engineering, 18–19
globalization, 15–16
securitization, 16–18
Investment grade bonds, 316–317
Investment horizon, 607
Investment opportunities, 420–423, 430
Investment opportunity set, 178, 179
Investment policies, 611–615
active *vs.* passive, 267–268, 614–615
asset allocation, 611–612
life-cycle approach, 621

Investment policies—*Cont.*
monitoring and revision portfolios, 615–616
for mutual funds, 104–106
rational, 268
resource allocation, 268–269
social investing, 606
and taxes, 268
top-down, 612–614
Investment portfolio; *see* Portfolio
Investment process, 8–9
stages of, 599
Investment risk, 135; *see also* Portfolio risk; Risk
Investments, 2, 3; *see also* International investments; Savings plans
asset allocation, 148–155
bonds *vs.* stocks, 157
historical record, 139–146
impact of expenses, 109–111
and interest rates, 385
and macroeconomic forecasting, 388, 389
options *vs.* stocks, 500–504
passive *vs.* active management, 10
performance of mutual funds, 114–118
in real assets, 6
in real estate, 644
right mix, 155
risk in, 6–7, 9–10
risks and risk premium, 135–139
risky, 637–638
uncertainty surrounding, 136
underperforming IPOs, 63, 64
websites for, 2
Investment strategies
active, 339
contrarian, 272
fixed-income, 364–366
and industry life cycle, 403
market timing, 702–706
passive, 339, 350–358
passive core, 613
with Treynor-Black model, 709–712
using tax shelters, 632–639
Investors
age differences, 268
anticipated return, 9
asset allocation choice, 151–152
bookbuilding, 62
buying on margin, 82–86
and Capital asset pricing model, 221
constraints on
investment horizon, 607
liquidity, 606–607
regulations, 607
short-sale restrictions, 190
tax considerations, 607
unique needs, 607–609
and convexity, 361
and financial intermediaries, 11–13
forecasting errors, 280
foreign investment opportunities, 15–16
framing, 281
and investment brokers, 62–63

Investors—*Cont.*
  investment company
    functions, 100
  irrational decisions, 655
  life-cycle view of, 601
  limit orders, 72–73
  losses on debt securities, 293
  and market anomalies, 656–657
  market orders, 72
  and market portfolio, 221
  matrix of constraints, 610–611
  mental accounting, 281
  objectives, 600–606
    banks, 605–606
    endowment funds, 606
    individual investors, 601–602
    life insurance companies,
     604–605
    monitoring and revising,
     615–616
    professional investors,
     602–604
    unique needs compared to
     constraints, 608–609
  overconfidence, 280–281
  in over-the-counter market, 76–77
  passive strategies, 155–158
  portfolio choice, 192
  primary kinds of risk, 608
  prudent investor rule, 607
  rational behavior assumption, 651
  regret avoidance, 281
  risk aversion, 138, 600
  risk-return trade-off, 9–10
  risk tolerance, 600, 601
  short sales, 86–88
  social investing, 606
  trade-offs, 131
  value investing, 477–478
Invoice prices, 298
IPO; *see* Initial public offerings
Irrationalities, 280–281
"Is Beta Dead?", 241

J

Jacquier, Eric, 743
Jaffe, Jeffrey A., 91, 278, 317
Jaffee, Charles A., 608
Jagannathan, Ravi, 158, 427n
January effect, 275
Japan Index, 496
Jarrow, R. A., 280n
Jasen, Georgette, 692
JC Penney, 397
Jegadeesh, Narasimhan, 271,
  272–273, 672, 673
Jensen, Michael C., 241, 685
Jensen measure, 686
Johnson & Johnson, 448
Joint tests, 274
Journal of Finance, 241
Junior debtholders, 320
Junk bonds, 6, 105, 317
  default risk, 317–318
  yields since 1954, 322
Justice Department, 77

K

Kahneman, Daniel, 280
Kansas, Dave, 389
Kao, G. Wenchi, 49

Kaul, Gautam, 270
Keim, Donald B., 273, 275
Kellogg, 434–435
Kendall, Maurice, 261, 262, 270
Keown, Arthur, 263
KMPG, 473
Kondratieff wave theory, 662
Kotlikoff, Laurence J., 646

L

Labor unions, 405
Lakonishok, Josef, 272, 279, 671
Large company stocks, 143
Last-in, first-out system, 470, 471
Law of one price, violation of, 242
Leading economic indicators,
  393–396
  economic calendar, 395, 396
  key economic statistics, 384–385
LEAPS, 495, 552
Lease, R., 656, 657
Le Baron, Blake, 671
Lehman Brothers, 47, 49, 139, 613
Lehman Brothers Aggregate Bond
  Index, 267
Lehman Brothers Index, 364, 698
Lehmann, Bruce, 272–273
Leinweber, David, 586
Lev, Baruch, 474–475
Leverage, 50
  futures contracts, 577
Leverage ratio, 318, 460
Levered equity, 517–519
Levered equity position, 547–548
Lewellen, W., 656, 657
Li, Kai, 752
Liabilities
  on balance sheet, 453–454
  off-balance sheet, 473
Liebowitz, Martin L., 341, 362,
  364, 366
Liesman, Steve, 475
Life annuity, **645**
Life cycles dividend discount model,
  423–427
Life-cycle view of investors, 601
Life insurance companies
  constraints and objectives,
   610, 611
  investment objectives, 604–605
LIFO; *see* Last-in, first-out system
Limited liability, 40
Limit order book, 70, 79
Limit orders, 72–73, 75–76, 77
Linear regression equation, 230–231
Lipper General Equity Fund
  Average, 115
Liquidation date, 607
Liquidation value, 134, 414
Liquidity, 241, 606–607
  endowment funds, 621
  of Treasury bills, 27
  uncertain, 645
Liquidity effect, 275–276
Liquidity preference theory,
  323–**326**
Liquidity premium, 326
Liquidity ratios, 318, 462–463
Liquidity risk, 70, 608
Lloyd's of London, 14
Lo, Andrew W., 270
Load, 103

Loan arrangements, 517
Loan portfolio, 605–606
Loews, 467
London Financial Futures
  Exchange, 588
London Interbank Offer Rate, 29,
  366–368
London International Financial
  Futures and Options Exchange,
  78, 584
London Stock Exchange, 46, 67, 78
Longevity, 642
Long hedge, 578
Longin, F., 743
Long position, 52–53, 567–570, 580
Long-term assets, 453
Long-term Capital Management, 30,
  104, 293, 382–383
Long-term debt, 453
Long-term Equity AnticiPation
  Securities, 495, 552
Long-term government bonds, 143
Lookback options, 519
Loss aversion, 653–654
Loughran, T., 64
Lowenstein, Roger, 351
Low-load funds, 108
Luccheth, Aaron, 172
Lucent Technologies, 433, 467
Lucky-event issue, 270
Ludwig, Robert, 747
Lynch, Peter, 270, 284, 286, 403, 431

M

Macaulay, Frederick, 342
Macaulay's duration, 342–344
MacBeth, James, 241
MacKinley, Craig, 270
Macroeconomic factors, 170, 193
Macroeconomy
  business cycles, 391–396
  demand and supply shocks,
   387–388
  domestic, 384–385
  effect of interest rates, 386–387
  federal government policies,
   388–390
  global, 382–384
  industry analysis, 396–405
  key economic statistics, 384–385
  leading economic indicators,
   393–396
  unreliable forecasting, 388, 389
Magnitude issue, 269
Maintenance margin, 83, 574
Maksimivic, V., 280n
Malkiel, Burton G., 117, 282, 283,
  341, 346–347, 358, 692
Managed investment companies,
  101–103
Management
  agency problem, 8
  separate from ownership, 7–8
Marcus, Alan, 743
Margin, 82–86
  futures contracts, 567
  requirements on options, 495–496
Margin account, 153
Marginal propensity to consume, 654
Margin calls, 83
Market anomalies, 273–278
  book-to-market effect, 276

Market anomalies—*Cont.*
  insider trading, 278
  interpreting evidence on
   behavioral interpretation,
   278–281
   data mining, 279
   risk premiums *vs.*
    inefficiencies, 278–279
   irrationalities, 280–281
   January effect, 275
   liquidity effect, 275–276
   neglected-firm effect, 275
   post-earnings price drift, 276–278
   small-firm effect, 274–275
Market capitalization
  in developed countries, 722–723
  in emerging markets, 723–725
  and GDP, 725–726
  stock exchanges, 721
Market capitalization rate, 416,
  426–427
Market capitalization weights,
  745–746
Market conversion, 300
Market demand, 220
Market efficiency, 699
Market equilibrium, 216
Market index, 232–233
Market inefficiency, 597
Market makers, 68
Market making, 74
Market orders, 72
Market portfolio, 221–222, 229
  mutual fund theorem, 223
  reasons for holding, 222–223
  risk premium, 223–224
Market price ratios, 463–465
Market price vs. intrinsic value,
  415–416
Market risk, 170, 194, 199,
  230–232, 608
Market structure indicators, 667
  breadth of the market, 671–672
  moving averages, 670–671
  relative strength, 672–673
Market timing, 691–693, **702**
  and beta, 691–693
  measuring performance, 705–706
  value of imperfect forecasting,
   704–705
  valuing as an option, 703–704
Market-to-book-value ratio,
  463–464
Market-tracking index funds, 655
Market value-weighted indexes,
  45–46
Market value-weighted portfolio, 139
Marking to market, 573–575, **574**
Markowill Group, 684
Markowitz, Harry, 10, 169, 189
Markowitz algorithm, 235–237
Marriage, 646
Marsh, Paul, 157, 158
Marshall, Larry, 84
MasterToy Inc., 483
MATIF, 584
Maturities
  on commercial paper, 28
  municipal bonds, 33
  put options, 552
  Treasury securities, 31,
   296–297, 315

Maturity date, 342
Maturity stage, 403
May Day commissions, 68
Mayers, David, 225
Mazuy, Kay, 705
McGee, Suzanne, 586
McGrattan, Ellen R., 158, 427n
Mean return, 136, 142
Mean reversion, 657
Mean-variance criterion, 178–182
Mean-variance efficiency, 701–702
Me-first rule, 320
Mendelson, Haim, 241, 275–276
Mental accounts, 280, 654–655
Merck and Company, 9, 448, 467
Merrill Lynch, 13, 47, 49, 69, 70, 84,
   109, 293, 389, 589, 602–603
Merton, Robert C., 539n, 540, 703
Metcalf, Gilbert, 692
Mexico, 302
Microsoft Corporation, 43, 67,
   112, 226, 422, 433, 467,
   492–493, 494, 498–503,
   511, 549, 550, 670
Milken, Michael, 318
Miller, Merton H., 215
Minor trends, 661
Mispricing, identification of, 361
Mobil, 320, 321
Modern portfolio theory, 10
Modified duration, 345–346
Modigliani, Franco, 215, 687, 688
Modigliani, Leah, 687, 688
Monetary policy, 389–390
   Effect on interest rates, 387
Monetary Trends, 165
Money market, 6, 26, 26–30
   bankers' acceptances, 28
   brokers' calls, 29
   certificates of deposit, 27–28
   commercial paper, 28
   components, 25, 27
   Eurodollars, 28–29
   federal funds, 29
   London Interbank Offer Rate
      market, 29
   rates on securities, 26
   repurchase agreements, 29
   Treasury bills, 27
   yields, 30
Money market funds, 104
Money market mutual fund,
   150–151
Money spread, 508
Money supply, 389–390
   economic indicator, 395
Moody's Industrial Manual,
   320, 321
Moody's Investor Services,
   316–317
Moral hazard, 646
Morgan Stanley, 69, 745
Morgan Stanley Capital
   International, 747
   stock indexes, 46–47, 48
Morgan Stanley Capital Investment
   index, 737
Morgan Stanley Dean Witter, 688
Morningstar, Inc., 108, 118,
   122–123, 172
   Risk Adjusted rating, 708–709
Morningstar Mutual Funds, 747

Mortgage-backed securities, 32–33,
   37–39, 301
   market in, 293
Mortgage bond, 320
Mortgage pools, 16–17, 37
Mortgages, 37–39
Mortgage tax deduction, 644
Mortgage trusts, 103
Morton, Robert C., 275
Moving averages, 670–671
M^2 measure, 686–688
Mueller, Gerhard G., 476
Multifactor generalization, 247–250
Multifactor security market line, 249
Multinational corporations, 747
Multiple periods, 132–134
Multistage growth dividend discount
   model, 423–428
Municipal bonds, 33–35
Murphy, Eddie, 573
Mutual fund cash positions, 669
Mutual fund managers, 284–285, 286
Mutual funds, 13, 99, 103, 603,
   688–689
   classes, 108–109
   closed-end, 101–103
   constraints on, 610
   costs of investing in, 107–111
   disclosure documents, 120–121
   and economic downturn, 172
   and exchange-traded funds,
      112–114
   fees and returns, 109–111
   fee structure, 107–109
   indexed portfolios, 267–268
   information sources, 118–123
   international focus, 734
   investment performance, 114–118
   investment policies, 104–106
   kinds of, 104–106
   low-load, 108
   management companies, 104
   no-load, 108
   open-end, 101–103
   performance of, 281–286
   prospectus, 118
   risk-adjusted rating, 708–709
   selling of, 107
   taxation of income, 111–112
   time-weighted average, 118
Mutual Fund Sourcebook, 108, 118
Mutual fund theorem, 223

N

NAICS codes, 397
Naive diversification strategy, 170
Naked option writing, 500, 506
Naked put options, 501
NASDAQ, 1, 67, 585
   annual returns, 146
   competition for New York Stock
      Exchange, 66–67
   indexes, 46
   investigation of, 77
   margin calls, 83
   operation of, 67–68
   self-regulation, 89–91
   Small Order Execution
      System, 76–77
   subscribers, 68
   trading in, 76–77
   trading through on, 77

NASDAQ Canada, 79
NASDAQ Composite Index
   fall in, 84
NASDAQ Europe, 79
NASDAQ Japan, 79
NASDAQ National Market
   System, 67
NASDAQ 100 Index, 112, 434–435
NASDAQ SmallCap Market, 67
NASDAQ Stock Market, 67
National Association of Securities
   Dealers, 67, 69; *see also*
   NASDAQ
   Securities and Exchange
      Commission settlement, 77
National market system, 81
National securities market, 69–70
NAV; *see* Net asset value
Negative beta, 196
Negative correlation, 181–182
Negative serial correlation, 270–271
Negative systematic risk, 196
Neglected-firm effect, 275
Neiman Marcus, 397, 460
Net asset value, 100, 101–102, 106,
   109–110, 112–113, 657–658
Net cash flows, 134
Net profit on call option, 492
New Quotation System, 78
New *vs.* old economy, 432, 433
New York Stock Exchange, 1, 15,
   40–41, 171, 274, 306, 320, 475,
   477, 585
   alliances, 79
   annual returns, 146
   block transactions, 75
   bond exchange, 70
   bond trading, 298–299
   and electronic communication
      network, 69
   going public, 69
   indexes, 46
   initial listing requirements, 66
   and Intermarket Trading
      System, 70
   market making, 72
   operation of, 64–67
   price priority, 77
   Rule 80A, 90
   seat prices, 66
   self-regulation, 89–91
   and specialist firms, 74–75
   SuperDot System, 59, 76, 587
   and third market, 68
   and trading costs, 81–82
New York Stock Exchange index, 496
New York Times, 241
Nicoliasen, Donald, 50
Nikkei Index, 46, 496, 735
No-arbitrage restriction, 215
No-free-lunch rule, 9–10
Nofsinger, John, 655
No-load funds, 108
Nominal interest rate, 147, 387, 471
   equilibrium, 147–148
Nominal rate of return, 302–303
Nominal risk-free interest rate, 303
Noncompetitive bid, 27
Nondiversifiable risk, 171, 247
Nonrecurring items, 472
Nonsystematic risk, 171,
   199, 224

Nordic Countries Alliance, 79
Normal distribution, 145
North American Free Trade
   Agreement, 382, 397
North American Industry
   Classification System, 397
Northwestern-most portfolio, 178,
   189–190
Notional principle, 366

O

Obligation to purchase, 53
O'Connell, Vanessa, 121
O'Connor, Robert, 501
Odd-lot trading, 668–669
Odean, Terrance, 280
Off-balance sheet assets and
   liabilities, 473
*Official Summary of Insider
   Trading,* 278
*Official Summary of Securities
   Transactions and Holdings,* 91
Old economy, 433
Olsen, Chris, 277
One Up on Wall Street (Lynch),
   403, 431
Online brokers, 69
Online trading, 1, 19–20, 63–64, 80
Open-end funds, 101–103
Open interest, 52
OpenIPO, 65
Open market operation, 390
Operating earnings, 434
Operating expenses, 108
Operating leverage, 399–400
Optimal risky portfolio, 185, 226
   asset allocation, 151–152
   choosing, 191–192
   with risk-free asset, 184–187
Option Clearing Corporation,
   495–496
Option contract, 492–498
Option elasticity, 551
Optionlike securities
   callable bonds, 512–514
   collateralized loans, 517
   convertible securities, 514–516
   levered equity and risky debt,
      517–519
   warrants, 516–517
Options, 6, 491
   and agency problem, 8
   American, 495, 550, 556
   at-the-money, 493
   call options, 48–51, 492
   delta, 550
   European, 495, 540,
      546–547, 549
   exotic types, 519–520
   foreign currency, 497
   futures options, 496
   hedge ratio, 550–552
   index options, 496
   interest rate, 498
   in-the-money, 493
   LEAPS, 495, 552
   margin requirements, 495–496
   out-of-the-money, 493
   purchase price, 492–493
   put options, 48–48, 492
   versus stocks, 500–504
   value at expiration

Options—Cont.
  call options, 498–499
  compared to stocks, 500–504
  put options, 499–500
Options market/trading
  Chicago Board Options
      Exchange, 491
  foreign currency options, 497
  futures options, 496
  index options, 496
  interest rate options, 498
  naked option writing, 506
  Option Clearing Corporation,
      495–496
  over-the-counter market, 493
  strategies
    collars, 511–512
    covered calls, 506–508
    protective put, 504–506
    spreads, 508–510
    straddle, 508
    trading mechanisms, 493–495
Option valuation
  binomial pricing
    generalized two-state
        approach, 537–540
    two-state pricing, 534–537
  Black-Scholes formula, 540–546
  Black-Scholes model
    empirical evidence, 556–557
    hedge ratios, 550–552
    portfolio insurance, 552–556
    put-call parity relationship,
        546–549
    put option valuation,
        549–550
    simplifying assumptions, 543
  determinants, 533–534
  implied volatility, 543–544
  intrinsic and time values, 532
  and replication, 535–536
Organization of Petroleum Exporting
    Countries, 30
Original issue discount bonds,
    314–316
Outlook (S&P), 478
Out-of-the-money options, 493,
    496, 501
Overconfidence, 280–281
Overreaction, 656–657
Over-the-counter market, 14–15,
    67–68
  bond trading, 70, 298–299
  options trading, 493
  self-regulation, 89–91
  trading on, 76–77

P

Pacific Stock Exchange, 65
Palmon, Dan, 278
Par value, 296, 312
Passive bond management, 339
  cash flow matching, 357–358
  dedication strategy, 357–358
  immunization, 350–357
  rebalancing portfolio, 355, 356
Passive core strategy, 613
Passive investment policy, 614–615
Passive investment strategy, 267
Passive portfolio management, 10
  and efficient markets, 597
  and EMH, 267–268

Passive strategies, 155
  and capital market line, 155–158
  costs and benefits, 158
  efficiency of, 223
Pass-through securities, 16–17,
    32–33, 38–39
Pass-through status, 111
Patell, James M., 264
Paying for order flow, 82
Pay-in-kind bonds, 302
Peak, 391
P/E effect, 274, 280
PEG ratio, 431–432
P/E multiple, 384
Penn Central bankruptcy, 28, 30
Penn Square Bank, 30
Pension actuary, 604
Pension Benefit Guaranty
    Corporation, 621
Pension funds
  constraints and objectives,
      610, 611
  and immunization, 350
  interest rate risk, 350
  investment objectives, 604
  losses during market boom, 351
PepsiCo, Inc., 452, 453, 454, 455,
    465–466
Percentage margin, 82–83
Perfect hedge, 536
Perfect negative correlation, 181–182
Perfect positive correlation, 180
Performance evaluation
  bonds vs. stocks, 157
  for efficient markets, 270–275
  in industry analysis, 404–405
  industry stock prices, 398
  market timing, 691–693,
      705–706
  of money managers, 694–695
  Morningstar's risk-adjusted
      rating, 708–709
  mutual funds, 114–118, 281–286
  performance attribution
      procedures, 693–699
    asset allocation
        decisions, 697
    bogey benchmark, 694–695,
        696, 745
    cash/bond selection, 748
    country selection, 746–747
    currency selection, 746
    international investments,
        746–747
    sector/security selection,
        697–698
    stock selection, 747
    summing up component
        contributions, 698–699
  rates of return, 139–146
  risk-adjusted returns
    with changing portfolio
        composition, 691–693
    choosing right measure,
        688–691
    comparison universe, 694
    M^2 measure, 686–688
    risk adjustments, 685–686
  style analysis, 706–708
  Treynor-Black model, 710
Perpetuity, 348
Personal funds, 113–114

Personal trust, 602–603
Pfizer, 9
Pierallini, Fabrizio, 586
Pinkerton, John, 263
Pink sheets, 67
Pitt, Harvey, 477
Plowback ratio, 421, 464–465
  effect on growth and
      P/E ratio, 430
Plus tick, 90
Point and figure chart, 663
Political risk, 731–732
Porter, Michael E., 404
Portfolio, 8; see also Complete
    portfolio; Market portfolio
  apart from labor income, 645
  arbitrage, 244
  diversified, 10
  efficient, 226
  in efficient frontier, 190
  expected return and risk, 151–152
  of foreign stocks, 15–16
  historical record, 139–146
  home-country bias, 726
  of households, 13
  mean-variance criterion, 178–182
  modern theory of, 10
  optimal risky, 184–187
  passive, 158
  perfectly hedged, 540
  rebalancing, 612
  satisfactory, 131
  standard deviation, 178, 180
  turnover rate, 111–112
  with two risky assets, 171–184
  zero-investment, 242
Portfolio choice, 192
Portfolio composition, 691–693
Portfolio construction, 131
  asset allocation, 695
  bottom-up, 9
  diversification with many risky
      assets, 187–192
  with foreign assets, 745–746
  immunized portfolio, 356
  mean-variance criterion, 178–182
  optimization technique, 192
  top-down, 9
  with Treynor-Black model,
      709–712
  with two risky assets, 171–182
Portfolio dividend yield, 190
Portfolio duration, 351–353
Portfolio insurance, 552–556
Portfolio management
  active, 361–366
  active vs. passive, 267–268
  asset allocation, 148–155
  bond portfolios, 339–368
  and convexity, 358–361
  duration concept, 344
  hedge ratio tool, 551–552
  interest rate swaps, 366–368
  investment companies, 100–101
  investment policies, 104–107
  life-cycle approach, 621
  lure of active management,
      699–702
  monitoring and revising, 615–616
  mutual fund performance,
      114–118, 281–286
  mutual funds, 13

Portfolio management—Cont.
  passive, 155–158, 350–357
  performance attribution
      procedures, 693–699
  performance evaluation, 684–699
  rebalancing, 355
  right mix, 155
  risk reduction, 608
  role in efficient market, 268
  soft-dollar credits, 110–112
  stock market futures, 586
  tax-timing option, 638
  three rules for two risky
      assets, 177
Portfolio managers, 701–702
Portfolio risk, 122
  adjusting for, 273
  and diversification, 10, 170–171
  key determinants, 171–172
  mutual funds, 114
  and risk premium, 224
  single-factor asset market,
      192–199
Posit, 69
Positive correlation, 180
Positive serial correlation, 270–271
Post-earnings announcements price
    drift, 276–278
Poterba, James, 271n
Preferred stock, 41
  convertible, 514–516
  as fixed-income security,
      300–301
Premium bonds, 308, 310, 319
Premium of options, 53, 492
Present value, 216, 343, 580–581
  of annuity, 303–304
  of bonds, 303–304
Present value formula, 312–313
Present value of growth
    opportunities, 422, 423, 429
Price appreciation/depreciation
  built-in, 315
  and company stock, 300
  corporate bonds, 298
Price continuity, 75
Price discovery, 77
Price-earnings multiple, 429–430
Price-earnings ratio, 41, 274,
    464–465
  and business cycles, 435
  combined with dividend discount
      models, 438
  forecast of, 440
  and growth opportunities,
      429–432
  pitfalls in analysis, 434–436
  and stock risk, 432–433
Price-earnings ratio equation, 432
Price-fixing agreements, 50
Price improvements, 72
Price-indexed government bond, 150
Price level deflator, 628–629
Priceline.com, 432
Price priority, 77
Price quotation system, 68, 76
Price risk, 351–352
Prices
  and inflation, 146–147
  versus net asset value, 102
  open-end funds, 103
Price-to-book ratio, 438

Price-to-cash flow ratio, 438
Price-to-sales ratio, 438
PricewaterhouseCoopers, 473
Price-weighted average, 42–43
Primary Insurance Amount, 640,
    641–643
Primary market, 14, 60
Primary trend, 661
Primex, 69
Pring, Michael J., 660n
Prisoner's dilemma game, 652
Private placement, 60, 61
Probability distribution, 135–137,
    539–540
Probability-weighted average, 175
Procter and Gamble, 50, 293
Producer sentiment, 385
Product life cycle; *see*
    Industry life cycle
Professional investors
    mutual funds, 603
    objectives of, 602–603
    pension funds, 604
    personal trusts, 602–603
Profitability, and earnings
    management, 434
Profitability ratios, 318
Profit margin, 459
Pro forma earnings, 434–435, 475
Program trade, 76, 587
Progressive tax, 633–635, 634
Progressive tax code, 632–634
    and Roth IRAs, 635–636
Proprietary knowledge, 404
Prospectus, 60, 118
Protective covenants, 318–320
Protective put, 504–506, 552–554
Proxy contest, 8, 39
PRS Group, 731, 734
Prudent investor rule, 602, 607
Public offerings, 60
    versus private placement, 61
Purchasing power, 146, 383–384
Purchasing power risk, 608
Pure yield pickup swap, 362–363
Put bonds, 300
Put-call parity relationship,
    546–549, **548**
Put/call ratio, 669
Putnam, 104
Put options, 49, 53, 492–493
    and crash of 1987, 501
    valuation, 549–550
    value at expiration, 499–500
PV factor, 304
PVGO; *see* Present value of growth
    opportunities

Q

Quality of earnings, 472–474
Quanto, 519–520
Quantum Funds, 285
Quick ratio, 318, 463
Quoted bond prices, 298

R

Random walks, 262–265
Rate anticipation swap, 362
Rates of return
    actual *vs.* expected, 151

Rates of return—*Cont.*
    after-tax, 607
    alpha, 227
    annualized, 31–32
    average, 157–158, 212
    benchmark, 215
    bonds *vs.* equity securities, 157
    in capital asset pricing model,
        225, 233–234
    comparisons, 684
    conventions for quoting,
        134–135
    definition, 132
    versus expected rate of
        return, 129
    historical record, 139–146
    holding-period return, 132
    measured over multiple periods,
        132–134
        arithmetic average, 133
        dollar-weighted return, 134
        geometric average, 133
        time-weighted average, 133
    mutual funds, 109–111
    nominal, 302–303
    pension funds, 604
    probability distribution, 135–137
    real, 146–148
    required, 415
    risk and risk premium, 135–137
    scenario analysis, 135–137
    single index model, 193–194
    subperiod data, 156–158
    total variability, 194
    with two risky assets, 177
    volatility of an option, 551
Ratio analysis
    appraisal ratio, 712
    asset turnover, 459
    asset utilization ratio, 461–462
    book-to-market ratio, 276
    cash flow-to-debt ratio, 318
    choosing a benchmark, 465–466
    comparative valuation
        ratios, 438
    conversion ratio, 299–300
    coverage ratio, 318, 462–463
    decomposition of ROE, 458–460
    interest-burden, 459
    leverage ratio, 318, 460
    liquidity ratios, 318, 462–463
    market price ratios, 463–465
    price-earnings ratio, 274,
        428–438, 464–465
    profitability ratios, 318
    profit margin, 459
    put/call ratio, 669
    by rating class, 319
    return on sales, 459
    Trin statistic, 668
    turnover, 461–462
Rational behavior assumption, 651
Raytheon, 427–428, 438
Ready, Mark J., 671
Real assets, 4–5, 269
    versus financial assets, 4
    investment in, 6
Real consumption, 628
Real Estate Investment Trusts,
    103, 644
Real estate market, 14
Real exchange rate, 383–384

Real interest rate, 147, 472
    determinants, 386–387
Realized compound yield, 310–312
Realized rate of return index
    model, 194
Realized return index model, 229
Real rates of return, 628–629
    and inflation, 146–148
Rebalancing, 355, 356
Recession, 389, 400–401
Redeemable stock, 41
Redeemable trust certificates, 101
Red herring, 60
Redington, F. M., 350
Refunding, 299
Regional exchanges, 66
Registered bonds, 298–299
Registration statement, 60
Regression analysis, 195, 234–235
Regression equation, 194–195
Regression toward the mean, 238
Regressive tax, 639
Regret avoidance, 280
Regulation; *see* Federal government
    policy; Securities and Exchange
    Commission
Reilly, Frank B., 49
Reinganum, Mark R., 275, 276
Reinvestment rate, 310–312
Reinvestment rate risk, 351–352
REITs; *see* Real estate
    investment trusts
Rekenthaler, John, 172
Relative decline stage, 403–404
Relative strength, 672–673
Rent *vs.* buy decision, 644
Replacement cost, 414
Replication, 535–536
Repurchase agreements, 29
Required return, 415
Reserve requirement, 390
Reserves management, 472
    international accounting
        conventions, 474–475
Residual claim, 40
Residual income, 467
Residuals, 231, 233
Residual variance, 196
Resistance level, 661–662
Retchenstein, William, 282
Retirement annuity, 626–627
    alternate savings plan, 629
    calculation of, 641
    enhanced by tax shelters, 639
    real savings plan, 628–629
Retirement plan, 625
    accounting for inflation, 628–629
    accounting for taxation, 630–631
    bequests, 646
    intergenerational transfers, 646
    and marriage, 646
    and Social Security, 639–643
    and tax shelters, 632–639
    and uncertain liquidity, 645
Return-beta relationships, 245
Return on assets, 318, 457–458,
    460, 467
Return on equity, 421–423,
    429–431, **456**, 464–465
    decomposition of, 458–460
    effect on growth and
        P/E ratio, 430

Return on equity—*Cont.*
    financial leverage, 456
    past *vs.* future, 456
Return on sales, 459
Return requirement, 601
Returns; *see also* Expected return;
        Rates of return
    behavioral explanations, 656–659
    calendar effect, 656
    cash dividends, 656
    endowment funds, 621
    mean reversion, 656–657
    over long horizons, 271–272
    overreaction to, 656–657
    over short horizons, 270–271
    risk-adjusted, 274, 282
Revenue bonds, 33
Revenue recognition, 454, 473
Reversal effect, 272–273
Reverse floaters, 302
Reverse repo, 29
Reversing trade, 573
Reward-to-variability ratio,
    152–153, 185–186, 700–701
    common stocks 1926–2001, 156
Riepe, Mark, 747
Right to purchase, 53
Risk, 602–603
    allocation of, 7
    in bond markets, 293
    bond price, 306
    of derivatives, 50
    in floating-rate bonds, 300
    in global environment, 392
    hedge funds, 104
    historical record, 139–146
    insurance principle, 170
    in international investments,
        726–731
    kinds of, 171, 608
    measures
        standard deviation, 136–137
        variance, 136–137
    passive management, 350
    probability distributions,
        135–137
    to retirement annuity, 629
    and risk premium, 135–137
    scenario analysis, 135–137
    and speculation, 138
    three-factor model, 279
    and time diversification, 212
Risk Adjusted rating, 708–709
Risk-adjusted returns, 274, 282
    choosing right measure, 688–691
    comparison universe, 684
    Jensen measure, 686
    M^2 measure, 686–688
    risk adjustments, 685–686
    Sharpe measure, 686
    Treynor measure, 686
    with changing portfolio
        composition, 691–693
Risk adjustments, 683, 685–686
    with changing portfolio
        composition, 691–693
Risk and return, 131–159
    asset allocation choice, 148–155
    capital allocation line, 152–153
    capital market line, 155–158
    expected return, 151–152
    historical data for, 175–176

Risk and return—*Cont.*
 international investments,
  734–738
 national comparisons, 736
 passive strategies, 155–158
 risk tolerance and asset
  allocation, 154–155
 with two risky assets, 172–173
Risk aversion, 137–139, **138,** 154,
 226, **600**
Risk-based capital guidelines, 350
Risk control, 131
Risk-free assets, 150–151, 191–192
 optimal risky portfolio, 184–187
Risk-free interest rate, 303
Risk-free portfolio, 148–155
Risk-free rate, 137, 153,
 232–233, 704
Riskless arbitrage, 247
Riskless arbitrage opportunity,
 242, 246
Risk management, 506
 with derivatives, 6
Risk Management Association, 465
Risk pooling, 211
Risk premium, 137
 anomalies as expressions of, 279
 common stocks 1926–2001, 156
 of complete portfolio, 152
 debate about, 157–158
 versus inefficiencies, 278–279
 of market portfolio, 223–224
 on market portfolio, 222
 ratio of beta to, 224–226
 and risk aversion, 137–139
 worldwide, 157
Risk reduction, 608
Risk-return opportunity set, 189–190
Risk-return trade-off, 4, 9–**10,** 138
 mix of investments, 155
 risk-free asset, 150–151
 risky assets, 149–150
 with two risky-asset portfolio,
  177–178
Risk sharing, 211
Risk stability, 732–733
Risk structure of interest rates, 322
Risk tolerance, 600
 assessing, 602–603
 and asset allocation, 154–155
Risky assets, 149–150
 diversification with many,
  187–192
 diversification with two, 171–184
 efficient frontier, 188–191
Risky debt, 517–519
Risky portfolio, 148–155
 reasons for holding, 222
 Sharpe measure, 712
 sources of uncertainty, 170
 and tax shelters, 637–638
 with two risky assets, 171–184
Ritter, Jay R., 64, 272, 275
Road shows, 62
Robert Morris Associates, 465
Roberts, Harry, 270, 665, 666
Roll, Richard, 241, 556, 743, 744
Rollover strategy, 324–325
Ross, Stephen A., 216, 241–242, 317,
 539n, 657–658
Roth IRAs, 635
 tax deferred, 639

Rothschild, Tricia, 747
Rubinstein, Mark, 557
Rule 415; *see* Securities and
  Exchange Commission
Rule 144A; *see* Securities and
  Exchange Commission
Russell 2000 Index, 46, 106, 139,
 267–267
Rydqvist, K., 64

S

Saitori, 79
Sales sensitivity, 399
Salomon Brothers, 589–590, 745
Salomon Smith Barney, 13, 47, 49,
 69, 70, 513
Samuelson, Paul A., 285, 441
Samurai bonds, 33, 301
Sanford Bernstein and Company,
 364–366
Sarkar, Asani, 752
Saving, 601
 by households, 626
 irrational decisions, 655
 for long run, 626–627
 objectives, 625
 reasons for, 626
 retirement annuity, 626–627
 sheltered *vs.* unsheltered,
  638–639
Savings and loan associations,
 605–606
Savings plan
 accounting for inflation, 628–629
 accounting for taxation, 630–631
 accounting for taxes, 630–631
 bequests, 646
 for college costs, 643–644
 contingencies, 645
 and home ownership, 644
 intergenerational transfers, 646
 for large purchases, 643–644
 marriage, 646
 real and alternative, 628–629
 uncertain liquidity, 645
 using tax shelters, 632–639
SBC Communications, 43
Scatter diagram, 195
Scenario analysis, 135–137, **136**
Scherbina, Anna, 158, 427n
Schiller, Robert J., 658–659
Schlarbaum, G., 565, 657
Scholes, Myron, 241, 540
Scudder Kemper Investments, 602
Sears, Roebuck, 43
Seats on exchanges, 65
Secondary market, 15, 60
 bond sales, 306
 over-the-counter market, 67–68
 stock exchanges, 65–67
 Treasury bill purchase, 27
Secondary trend, 661
Sector rotation, 400–401
Sector selection, 697–698
Secured bonds, 36
Securities; *see also* Bonds; Equity
  securities; Financial
  Instruments; Stocks
 asset-backed, 16–17
 convertible, 514–516
 creation of, 18–19

Securities—*Cont.*
 financial assets as, 4
 issuance of
  initial public offering, 60–65
  by investment bankers, 60–61
  private placement, 60, 61
  public offering, 60
  seasoned issues, 60
  shelf-registration, 61
  underpricing, 63
 mispriced, 413
 optionlike, 512–517
Securities Act Amendments of
 1975, 69
Securities Act of 1933, 89
Securities and Exchange Commission,
 28, 301, 473, 477
 establishment of, 89
 and fourth market, 69
 and globalization, 81
 on inside information, 278
 and insider trading, 91
 mutual fund prospectus, 118
 mutual fund rules, 112
 NASD settlement, 77
 national securities market, 69–70
 *Official Summary of Insider
  Trading,* 278
 *Official Summary of
  Securities Transactions
  and Holdings,* 91
 registration statement, 60
 regulation of markets, 89–92
 Rule 415, 61
 Rule 144A, 61
 Rule 10b-5, 265
 12b-1 fees, 108–109
Securities Exchange Act of 1934, 89
Securities Investor Protection
 Act, 89
Securities trading
 and ADRs, 734
 bid-ask spread, 67
 block sales, 75–76
 bond trading, 70
 buying on margin, 82–86
 dollar volume in 2000, 78
 on exchanges, 71–76
 exchange traded funds, 112–114
 execution of trades, 74–75
 financial market structure, 11–15
 foreign index funds, 737
 in foreign securities, 15–16
 fourth market, 68–69
 futures markets, 571–577
 globalization and SEC, 81
 national comparisons, 77–79
 national securities market,
  69–70
 odd-lot trading, 668–669
 online, 1, 19–20
 over-the-counter market, 67–68,
  76–77
 program trade, 76
 in secondary markets, 65–67
 settlement, 76
 short sales, 86–88
 in stock exchanges, 65–67
 SuperDot System, 76
 third market, 68
 trading costs, 80–82
 transaction costs, 676–677

Securities trading—*Cont.*
 Treasury bills, 27
 volume of, 67
 Websites for, 2, 59
Securitization, 16–**17**
Security analysis, 9; *see also* Equity
  valuation; Fundamental
  analysis; Technical analysis
 and country-specific risk,
  731–734
 federal government policies,
  388–390
 fundamental analysis, 381
 Graham technique, 477–478
 industry life cycle, 401–405
 skills needed for, 379
 with Treynor-Black model,
  709–712
Security Analysis (Graham &
  Dodd), 478
**Security characteristic line, 195,
 231**–232
Security Exchange Act of 1934, 265
Security market line, 226–227,
 235–237, 247, 249
Security prices
 anomalies, 651
 and efficient markets, 10
 and market demand, 220
 no-arbitrage restrictions, 215
Security selection, 8–9, 697–698
 Treynor-Black model, **710**
Seefeld, Steve, 513
Selection bias issue, 269–270
Self-destructing patterns, 660, 675
Self-regulation, 89–91
Sell-at-market order, 72
Semistrong-form EMH, 265
Semistrong-form tests, 273–278
Sentiment indicators, 667
 confidence index, 669
 mutual fund cash position, 669
 odd-lot theory, 668
 put/call ratio, 669
 Trin statistic, 668
Separate Trading of Registered
 Interest and Principal
 Securities, 315
Separation of ownership and
 management, 7–8
Separation property, 192
Serial bond issue, 319–320
Serial correlation, 270–271
Settlement, 76
Seyhun, H. Nejat, 278
Shareholders
 of common stock, 39–40
 limited liability, 40
 proxy contests, 8
 residual claim, 40
Shareholders' equity, 452–454
Sharpe, William F., 10, 193, 215, 221,
 240, 241, 685, 706–709
Sharpe measure, 686, 687, 688, 692,
 693, 701–702, 709, 711–172
Shelf registration, 61
Shevlin, Terry, 277
Shiller, Robert J., 272n, 273
Shliefer, Andrei, 279
Short interest, 669–670
Short position, 52, 53, **567**–570

Short-sale restrictions, 190
Short sales, 73, **86**–88
Short-term CDs, 28
SIC Codes, 397
Siegel, Jeremy J., 81
Simple interest technique, 32
Singer, Brian, 706n
Single-country mutual funds, 734
Single-factor asset market, 192–199
    in APT, 245
    diversification in, 199
Single-index model
    security characteristic line,
        231–232
    specification of, 193–194
    statistical graphical
        representation, 194–197
Sinking funds, **319**–322
Slow growers, 403
Small company stocks, 143
Small-firm effect, 274–275
Small Order Execution System, 76–77
Smith, Ruth, 84
Social investing, 606
Social Security, 639–643, **639**
    Average Indexed Monthly
        Income, 640, 641
    benefits allocation, 640
    calculating benefits, 640
    indexing factor series, 640
    Primary Insurance Amount, 640,
        641–643
    privatization proposal, 642–643
    threat to solvency of, 642
Societal risk, 608
Soft dollars, 110–111
Solnik, Bruno, 743
Soros, George, 285
Specialists, 71, **74**–75
Specialized sector funds, 105–106
Speculation, 6, 50, 138, 491, 577–579
Speculative grade bonds, 316–317
Speidell, Lawrence S., 476
Spider (SPDR), 112
Spillane, Rick, 688
Spivaj, Avia, 646
Spot-futures parity theorem,
    580–**582**
Spread, 508–510
Spread position, **579**, 583
Spring Street Brewing Company,
    63–64
Squared deviation, 136
Stalwarts, 403
Stambaugh, Robert F., 273, 275
Standard & Poor's Corporation, 28,
    316–317, 318, 397
    market value-weighted
        portfolio, 139
Standard & Poor's Depository
    Receipt, 112
Standard & Poor's Financial Index, 46
Standard & Poor's Index, 267
Standard & Poor's 500 Index, 46,
    105, 139, 144, 155, 156, 193,
    205, 228–229, 266, 282–283,
    286, 496, 576, 584–585, 587,
    613, 638, 684, 688, 694, 698,
    704, 707, 721
    earnings yield vs. T-bond yield,
        440–441
    versus earnings per share, 384

Standard & Poor's 500 Index—Cont.
    functions, 45–46
    price forecasts, 441
Standard & Poor's Transportation
    Index, 46
Standard & Poor's Utility Index, 46
Standard deviation, 136–137, 142,
    144, 146, 178, 180,
    543–544, 690
Standard Industry Classification, 397
Start-up stage, 402
Statement of cash flows, 454–456
Statman, Meir, 281–282, 655
Status quo bias, 653–654
Staunton, Michael, 157, 158
Stein, Charles, 433
Stern Stewart and Company, 139, 467
Stickell, Scott, 676–677
Stiglitz, Joseph E., 264n, 699n
Stock, alpha, 227
Stock Exchange Automated
    Quotations System, 78
Stock Exchange Electronic Trading
    Service, 78
Stock exchanges, 15, **65**–67; see also
        Financial markets;
        Stock market
    dollar volume in 2000, 78
    foreign, 46
    fourth market, 68–69
    market capitalization, 721
    national comparisons, 77–79
    over-the-counter market, 76–77
    participants, 71–72
    price continuity, 75
    regulation of, 89–92
        circuit breakers, 89–91
        insider trading, 91
        self-regulation, 89–91
    specialists in, 74–75
    third market, 68
    trading costs, 80–82
    types of orders
        limit orders, 72–73
        market orders, 72
        stop-buy orders, 73
        stop-loss orders, 73
Stock funds, 105, 688–689
Stock Guide (S&P), 478
Stockholders' equity, 452–454
Stock index futures, 586
    listing of, 584–585
Stock listings
    NASDAQ, 68
    New York Stock Exchange, 65
    and SEC, 477
Stock market; see also Efficient
        market hypothesis
    best and worst years, 9
    broad movements, 273
    crash of 1987, 76, 89, 501, 555,
        743, 744
    decline since 2000, 172
    driven by global factors, 742
    forecasting ability, 441
    foreign, 382
    globalization, 79
    historical record, 139–146
    market anomalies, 273–278
    new/old economy, 433
    reaction to earnings
        announcements, 276–278

Stock market—Cont.
    reaction to takeover attempts,
        262–263
    response to economic signals, 389
    successful times of, 271
    tech bubble, 172
Stock market fads, 272
Stock market indexes, 25, 42–47
    comparison of national
        returns, 727
    equally weighted, 46
    market value-weighted, 45–46
    price-weighted averages, 42–45
Stock market listings, 40–41
Stock market price, 395–396
Stock options, 8, 50, 472–473
Stock prices, 420–423
    and accounting fraud, 475
    and book value, 414
    continuity, 75
    decimal system, 72
    in Dow theory, 661
    and earnings, 384
    economic indicator, 395–396
    excessive volatility, 658–659
    forecasts of economic
        activity, 441
    history of, 664
    industry performance, 398
    and liquidation value, 414
    and option valuation, 532–534
    price-weighted average, 42–43
    random walk, 262
    resistance level, 661–662
    search for patterns, 665–667
    and straddles, 508
    and Super Bowl, 665
    support level, 661–662
    time series analysis, 262
Stock risk, 432–433
Stocks; see also Equity valuation
    average annual return, 9
    equilibrium prices and demand
        for, 216–220
    financial, 389
    historical record, 139–146
    indexing, 156
    versus options, 500–504
    price-share performance, 157
Stock selection, 747
Stock splits, 43
Stop-buy orders, 73
Stop-loss orders, 73
Straddle, 508
Straight bond, 512–514
Straps, 508
Street.com Internet Index, 513
Street name, 76
Streibel, Paul J., 275
Strike price, 48–49, **492**
Strips, 315, 508
Strong-form EMH, 265
Style analysis, 706–708
Style choice, 283
Subordinated debentures, 36
Subordination clause, 320
Subordination of further debt, 320
Substitute products, 404
Substitution swap, 362
Summers, Lawrence H., 271n, 646
Sunbeam Corporation, 473
Sun Microsystems, 67, 435–436

Super Bowl theory, 665
SuperDot System, 59, 76
Suppliers' bargaining power, 405
Supply and demand analysis
    demand/supply shocks, 387–388
    of interest rates, 386–387
Supply curve, and interest rate,
    386–387
Supply shock, 387–388
Supply-side policies, 388, 390
Support level, 661–662
Swap dealer, 367
Swaps, 491; see also Bond swaps;
        Interest rate swaps
Symmetric return, 137
Synthetic protective put, 553–554
Synthetic stock positions, 586
Systematic market risk, 170–171
Systematic risk, 192–193, 194, 199,
    224, 238
    negative, 196
Systematic variance, 196

T

T. Rowe Price, 121, 602–603
Takeover attempts, 262–263
Takeover threat, 8, 39
Tavel. Mark, 676–677
Tax code, 632–634
Tax deferral, 639
Taxes
    endowment funds, 621
    exchange-traded funds, 112
    flat tax, 630
    and futures market, 576–577
    and investment decisions, 607
    and investment policy, 268
    and January effect, 275
    on mutual fund income, 111–112
    preferred stock dividends,
        300–301
    and REITs, 103
    and savings plan, 630–631
    on Social Security benefits,
        641–642
Tax-exempt bonds, 33–35
Tax-inefficient portfolio, 111–112
Tax policy, 388–389, 390
Tax Reform Act of 1986, 34
Tax shelters, 632
    benchmark, 632
    capital gains, 637–638
    economics of, 632–634
    enhancing retirement annuity, 639
    401K plans, 637
    403B plans, 637
    IRAs, 634–635
    risky investments, 637–638
    and tax code, 632
    versus unsheltered savings,
        638–639
Tax swap, 363
Tax timing option, 638
TD Waterhouse Group, 84
Tech bubble, 172
Technical analysis, 265–266,
    273, 651
    charting, 660–667
    in efficient markets, 675
    nature and purpose, 659–660
    self-destructing patterns, 660, 675

Technical analysis—*Cont.*
　technical indicators, 667–674
　Value Line system, 674–675
Technical analysts, 266, 413
Technical indicators
　flow of funds, 669–670
　market structure indicators,
　　670–673
　Sentiment indicators, 668–669
　types of, 667
Templeton, John, 284
Templeton Funds, 285
Term insurance, 605
Term repo, 29
**Term structure of interest rates,
　322**–323
　expectations theory, 323–325
　liquidity preference rates,
　　325–326
Tertiary trends, 661
Texas hedge, 645
Texas Power and Light Company, 373
Thaler, Richard H., 272, 280, 281,
　282, 652
Thayer, Peter, 501
Theglobe.com, 63
Third market, 68
Thomas, Jeffrey H., 278
Threat of entry, 404
Three-factor model, 279
Three-stage growth models, 427–428
Tick test, 90
Time deposits, 27–28
Time diversification, 211–212
Time horizon, endowment funds, 621
Times interest earned ratio,
　318, **463**
Time spread, 508
Time to maturity, 347, 348
Time values, 532
Time-weighted average, 133
TIPS; *see* Treasury Inflation
　Protected Securities
Titman, Sheridan, 271, 272–273,
　672, 673
Tobin, James, 192, 414
Tobin's q, 414
Tokyo Stock Exchange, 46, 79
Tombstone advertisements, 60–61
Top-down investment policies,
　612–614
Top-down portfolio construction, 9
Total assets, 453
Total return, 41
Total variance, 196
Toyota Motors, 4
Tracking error, 552
Trading costs, 80–82
Trading halts, 89–90
Trading Places, 573
Trading through, 77
**Traditional Individual Retirement
　Accounts, 635**
Tragedy of the commons, 652
Train, John, 478n
Trainer, Francis, 346–365
Transaction costs, 676–677

Treasury bills, 6, **27**
　historical record, 139–146
　prices, 314
　rate of return, 138
　risk-free asset, 150
　yields on, 30
Treasury bond futures contract,
　577–578, 589–590
Treasury bonds, 31–32
　characteristics, 296–298
　earnings yield, 440–441
　maturities, 315
Treasury Inflation Protected
　Securities, 302–303
Treasury notes, 31–32, 296–298
Treasury strips, 315
Treasury yield curve, 323
Trend analysis
　filter rule, 271
　predictability in stock returns,
　　270–273
Treynor, Jack L., 221, 685, 705, 709
Treynor-Black model, 709–712, **710**
Treynor measure, 686, 689–690
Trin statistic, 668
Triple witching hour, 587
Trough, 391
Trustee, 602
T+3 settlement, 76
Turnarounds, 404
Turnover, 111–112
Turnover ratios, 461–462
Tversky, Amos, 280
12b-1 fees, 108–109
Two-factor model, 248
Two-risky-asset portfolio
　asset allocation, 171–184
　risk-return trade-off, 177–178
　three rules of, 177
**Two-stage dividend discount
　models, 424**–427
Two-state option pricing, 534–537

U

Unbundling, 18–19
Underpricing, 63
Underwriters, 60–61
　best-efforts agreement, 60
　of bond issue, 306
　firm commitment, 60, 589
　initial public offerings, 61–65
Underwriting syndicate, 60
Unemployment rate, 384
Uniform Securities Act of 1956, 89
Union Carbide, 43
Unique risk, 171, 199
United States industrial long-term
　debt, 319
United States Supreme Court, 91
Unit investment trust, 101, 101
Universal life policy, 605
Unmanaged portfolios, 100
Unmanaged trusts, 101
Unsecured bonds, 36, 320
USX-Marathon, 75
Utility rate-making, 228

V

VA Linux, 63
Valuation; *see also* Equity valuation;
　　Financial statement analysis;
　　Fundamental analysis; Option
　　valuation
　conversion of bonds, 54
　of inventories, 470–471
　of options at expiration, 498–504
Value investing, 477–478
Value Line, Inc., 435, 438, 676–677
Value Line Centurion Fund, 677
Value Line Investment Survey, 263,
　397, 478, 674, 676, 424–427
Value Line system, 674–675
Value stocks, 122
VanderHoff, Frank, 501
Vanguard 500 Index Fund, 105,
　149–150
Vanguard GNMA Fund, 106
Vanguard Group, 46, 101, 104, 106,
　113, 115, 148, 267, 602, 611,
　612, 734
Variable costs, 400
Variable life policy, 605
Variance, 136–137, 176, 177, 194
　historical, 142–144
Vertical spread, 508
Vishney, Robert W., 279
Volatility, 239, 293
　of dividends, 659
　of stock prices, 658–659
Volatility value, 532
Vontobel Ltd., 586

W

W. R. Grace and Company, 472
W. R. Hambrecht and Company, 65
Wage insurance, 646
Wallace, A., 241n
Wall Street Journal, 1, 26, 31, 32, 36,
　40–41, 46, 49, 51, 101–102,
　105, 268, 269, 270, 296, 298,
　322, 396, 433, 489, 494, 496,
　567–570, 583, 587, 589, 661,
　668, 671, 692
Wal-Mart, 460
Walt Disney Company, 302
Wang, Zhenyu, 241
Warner-Lambert, 373
Warrants, 516–517
Weak-form EMH, 265
Wealth, national, 4–5
WEBS; *see* World Equity Benchmark
　　Shares
Weighted average of betas, 196n
Weighted average time until
　payments, 342–344, 347
Weighting schemes, 745–746
Weiss, James, 389
Well-diversified portfolio, 245
　and APT, 247
　and arbitrage pricing theory,
　　244–247
Wellington Fund, 106

Wellington Management, 101
Westerfield, Randolph W., 317
Whaley, Robert E., 556
Whole-life insurance policy, 605
Wiesenberger Investment Companies
　　Services, 105, 108, 118
Wilhelm, William, 63n
Wilshire 5000 Index, 46, 106,
　115–116, 120, 267, 281
Windsor Fund, 106
Winner's curse, 653
Winterthur, 302
Wit Capital, 64, 65
Wolfson, Mark A., 264
World Bank, 722–723
WorldCom, 467
World Equity Benchmark Shares,
　15–16, 112, 737
World-event risk, 608
Wright, David J., 49
Writing calls, 492

Y

Yahoo!, 396, 465
Yankee bonds, 33, 301
Yield
　versus bond price, 306
　money market instruments, 30
　on preferred stock, 41
　S&P 500 *vs.* T-bonds, 440–441
Yield curve, 322–327
　expectations theory, 323–325
　inverted, 322
　liquidity preference theory,
　　325–326
　synthesis of theories, 327
Yield premium, 300
Yield ratio, 35
Yield to call, 309–310
Yield to maturity, 31–32, 297,
　306–307
　and bond price changes, 340–341
　and bond prices, 306–309
　calculation of, 307–308
　compared to current yield,
　　308–309
　and default risk, 320–325
　versus holding-period return,
　　313–314
　interpretation of, 314
　versus realized compound yield,
　　310–312

Z

Zero correlation coefficient, 178n
Zero-coupon bonds, 296, 342,
　347–348
　prices of, 314–315
Zero-investment portfolio, 242
Zero-plus tick, 90
Zero sum game, 570
Ziemba, W. T., 280n
Zuckerman, Gregory, 513
Zurich Group Inc., 602

Useful Formulas

Measures of Risk

Variance of returns: $\sigma^2 = \sum_s p(s)[r(s) - E(r)]^2$

Standard deviation: $\sigma = \sqrt{\sigma^2}$

Covariance between returns: $\text{Cov}(r_i, r_j) = \sum_s p(s)[r_i(s) - E(r_i)]\,[r_j(s) - E(r_j)]$

Beta of security i: $\beta_i = \dfrac{\text{Cov}(r_i, r_M)}{\text{Var}(r_M)}$

Portfolio Theory

Expected rate of return on a portfolio with weights w_i in each security: $E(r_p) = \sum_{i=1}^{n} w_i E(r_i)$

Variance of portfolio rate or return: $\sigma_p^2 = \sum_{j=1}^{n} \sum_{i=1}^{n} w_j w_i \, \text{Cov}(r_i, r_j)$

Market Equilibrium

The security market line: $E(r_i) = r_f + \beta_i[E(r_M) - r_f]$

Fixed-Income Analysis

Present value of $1:

Discrete period compounding: $\text{PV} = 1/(1 + r)^T$

Continuous compounding: $\text{PV} = e^{-rT}$

Forward rate of interest for period T: $f_T = \dfrac{(1 + y_T)^T}{(1 + y_{T-1})^{T-1}} - 1$

Real interest rate: $r = \dfrac{1 + R}{1 + i} - 1$

where R is the nominal interest rate and i is the inflation rate

Duration of a security: $D = \sum_{t=1}^{T} t \times \dfrac{CF_t}{(1 + y)^t} \Big/ \text{Price}$